OXFORD READER'S COMPANION TO CONRAD

OXFORD READER'S COMPANION TO

Conrad

Owen Knowles and Gene M. Moore

OXFORD
UNIVERSITY PRESS

OXFORD
UNIVERSITY PRESS

Great Clarendon Street, Oxford OX2 6DP

Oxford University Press is a department of the University of Oxford.
It furthers the University's objective of excellence in research, scholarship,
and education by publishing worldwide in

Oxford New York

Athens Auckland Bangkok Bogotá Buenos Aires Cape Town
Chennai Dar es Salaam Delhi Florence Hong Kong Istanbul Karachi
Kolkata Kuala Lumpur Madrid Melbourne Mexico City Mumbai Nairobi
Paris São Paulo Shanghai Singapore Taipei Tokyo Toronto Warsaw

and associated companies in Berlin Ibadan

Published in the United States
by Oxford University Press Inc., New York

First published 2000

First issued without illustrations as an
Oxford University Press paperback 2001

British Library Cataloguing in Publication Data

Data available

Library of Congress Cataloging in Publication Data

Data available

ISBN 0–19–860421–1

1 3 5 7 9 10 8 6 4 2

Typeset in Minion
by Alliance Phototypesetters, Pondicherry, India
Printed in Great Britain by
Mackays of Chatham plc
Chatham, Kent

ACKNOWLEDGEMENTS

As a digest of existing criticism and factual research, this volume incorporates the findings of a large community of past and present Conrad scholars, to whom we owe an enormous debt of gratitude. Institutions have also played an important part, and we would like to thank the library staffs at: the Beinecke Rare Book and Manuscript Library, Yale University; the Berg Collection, New York Public Library; the British Library; the Brynmor Jones Library, University of Hull; the Firestone Library, Princeton University; the Harry Ransom Humanities Research Center, University of Texas at Austin; and the Lilly Library, Indiana University, Bloomington, Indiana.

A number of individuals have kindly responded to our calls for help and advice. Robert Hampson, Zdzisław Najder, Allan H. Simmons, and J. H. Stape generously agreed to undertake a number of entries. We are grateful for other forms of assistance to Keith Carabine, Philip Conrad, Gena Maresch, Ray Stevens, Donald W. Rude, Andrea White, and Rowland Wymer. Frederick R. Karl and Laurence Davies, editors of *The Collected Letters of Joseph Conrad*, kindly granted us permission to use extracts from Conrad's unpublished letters. The staff at Oxford University Press has been unfailingly patient and supportive; we are indebted in particular to Pam Coote, Michael Cox, Alison Jones, Rebecca Collins, and Jackie Pritchard. Owen Knowles would also like to thank Kim Wilson for her unstinting help with the preparation and typing of portions of the manuscript.

Our chief debt is to J. H. Stape and especially to the late Hans van Marle. Their supportive friendship was as important to us as their practical help in overseeing the project from its inception, assiduously reading the typescript, and offering advice at every stage.

PREFACE

JOSEPH CONRAD's sense of himself as a 5-year-old boy in 1863 was typically multiple: in his earliest known writing, an inscription on the back of a photograph, he described himself as a 'Pole, Catholic, and nobleman'. In 1874, orphaned and restless, the adolescent Conrad escaped from a partitioned and oppressed Poland to a freer and more romantic life as a Mediterranean seaman based in France. By 1878 he had joined the British Merchant Service, although he was still officially a Russian subject and as yet unable to speak English. His wide-ranging travels and multicultural encounters would ultimately find expression in fictions spanning the globe, from the Netherlands East Indies to the Congo Free State and the Caribbean, and bring to English literature a liberating sense of irony and a refreshing awareness of cultural differences. By 1904, nine years after publishing his first work, he produced the most radically experimental English novel of the early Modernist period, the monumental *Nostromo*. By the time of his death in Kent on 3 August 1924, he was an internationally renowned writer.

The *Oxford Reader's Companion to Conrad* offers a clear, accurate, and comprehensive guide to a man and writer whose multiple allegiances make special demands on his readers. Conrad's life develops through three interconnected phases, beginning with what he described as a 'standing jump' out of his original surroundings and thereafter involving a complex passage across linguistic and cultural boundaries. His first sixteen years (1857–74) call for a number of entries designed to familiarize the reader with the unusual circumstances of Conrad's Poland: a brief history of the country, the symbolic significance of his Polish names (Józef Teodor Konrad Nałęcz), and the familial, political, and social traditions that he inherited and was sometimes thought to have betrayed in abandoning his country.

Conrad's twenty-year career as a seaman (1874–94) finds him in constant global transit, discovering in the British Merchant Service a travelling home and sense of family to replace those he had lost, while at the same time encountering an extraordinarily diverse range of countries, cultures, and languages. The entries and chronologies in this Companion enable the reader to follow the ships he sailed in, the progress of his voyages, and the places he visited. Upon reading Conrad's maritime reminiscences in 1906, Henry James responded: 'No one has *known*—for intellectual use—the things you know, & you have, as the artist of the whole matter, an authority that no one has approached.' Conrad embodied the Jamesian ideal of a writer as someone upon whom nothing is lost, and the 'authority' he derived from his pre-literary years informs his writing in unusual ways that merit attention and amply justify the encyclopedic approach taken in the present volume.

The majority of our entries are devoted to the three decades of Conrad's writing life (1895–1924), and explore his unique position in the English literary culture of the time. It is astonishing to realize that up to the age of 21, Conrad seems not to have known English, and yet, within fifteen years and while still a seaman, he began the narrative in English that would turn out to be his first published novel. His linguistic situation anticipates a literary position also in many respects marginal to the traditions of 'national' British literature. As can be seen from a quick survey of our list of contents, his sources and influences reflect the geographical breadth and historical depth of his Western legacy, including his kinship with European writers ranging from Cervantes and Gustave Flaubert to Adam Mickiewicz and Ivan Turgenev.

A cosmopolitan life such as Conrad's emerges out of an unusual number and variety of influences, practical as well as artistic. The history of his development can never be divorced from a complex of related factors, including the history of his illnesses, financial difficulties, collaborations, dependencies, the books he read, and the marketing of his fiction. A more unusual consideration in Conrad's case is that when he first committed himself to a writer's career in England, he was a virtual stranger to its literary establishment. The process by which he became a professional author often required the help of others, with the result that many of his novels were, in a sense, collaborative occasions. An account of his unfolding career would be unthinkable without detailed reference to a group of intimates and staunch supporters such as Edward Garnett, Ford Madox Ford, his agent J. B. Pinker, R. B. Cunninghame Graham, and John Galsworthy, whose own careers and relations with Conrad are explored in this volume.

By coincidence, the very first entry, on the so-called 'achievement-and-decline' thesis, is a fitting place for the reader to begin. Proponents of this thesis have sought to distinguish the 'achievements' of Conrad's middle period from his early and late work, disparaging the early novels as exotic romances while dismissing the later works as the products of an exhausted artist in a state of 'decline'. This attitude has dissuaded students and scholars from serious study of the early and late works. We wish rather to convey a sense of Conrad's achievement in its entirety and in the full range of its sources and implications.

Conrad's increasing reputation among the general public and in schools and universities suggests that the time is ripe to take stock of his position in modern literature, and to gain a fresh overview of his achievements. This Companion provides a means of access to the history and diversity of his works, and an introduction to the many ways in which they have been understood. It should be read not as if it contained the answers to all questions about Conrad, but rather as a guide and encouragement to pursue the many questions that have yet to be answered satisfactorily. In this spirit, for example, we have indicated the locations of important surviving documents relevant to Conrad's works. Now that his reputation extends beyond literature to include films, comic books, operas, and other modes of transmission, the need for a full account of his life and works is all the greater. We hope that the more than 400 entries in this Companion, the most comprehensive of its kind ever to be undertaken in Conrad studies, will assist readers to find even more enjoyment in the work of a writer whose unique voice, while speaking from his own world and time, also helps us to understand our own.

Owen Knowles
Gene M. Moore

Note to Paperback Edition

In this paperback edition, we have taken the opportunity to update a number of entries, correct a small number of errors, and remedy minor omissions in the account of pre-publication documents relevant to Conrad's works.

Owen Knowles
Gene M. Moore

CONTENTS

MAPS

AUTHORS AND CONTRIBUTORS

Authors

OWEN KNOWLES, Senior Lecturer at the University of Hull, is the author of *A Conrad Chronology* (1989) and *An Annotated Critical Bibliography of Joseph Conrad* (1992). A former editor of *The Conradian*, he has also edited Conrad's *Almayer's Folly* in the Everyman's Library and is co-editor of *A Portrait in Letters: Correspondence to and about Conrad* (1996) and the Cambridge Edition of *The Collected Letters of Joseph Conrad*, vi: *1917–1919*.

GENE M. MOORE teaches English and American literature at the Universiteit van Amsterdam. His publications include *Conrad's Cities: Essays for Hans van Marle* (1992), *Conrad on Film* (1997), and numerous Conradian essays and reviews. He is a co-editor of the Cambridge Edition of Conrad's *Suspense* and of *The Collected Letters of Joseph Conrad*, viii: *1923–1924*.

Advisers

HANS VAN MARLE, a Conrad scholar of international reputation, was Consulting Editor for *The Collected Letters of Joseph Conrad* and the Cambridge Edition of the Works of Joseph Conrad. He wrote numerous essays on Conrad and was a co-editor of the Cambridge Edition of *Suspense*.

J. H. STAPE has written widely on Joseph Conrad, E. M. Forster, and Virginia Woolf. He is the editor of *The Cambridge Companion to Joseph Conrad* (1996) and co-editor of the World's Classics editions of *An Outcast of the Islands* and *The Rover*, and of *A Portrait in Letters: Correspondence to and about Conrad* (1996). He is also editor of the Cambridge Edition of Conrad's *Notes on Life and Letters*.

Contributors

RH ROBERT HAMPSON, Reader in English at Royal Holloway and Bedford New College, University of London, is the author of *Joseph Conrad: Betrayal and Identity* (1991) and numerous essays on Conrad. A former editor of *The Conradian*, he has also edited many Conrad texts, including 'Heart of Darkness', *Lord Jim*, *Victory*, and *The Arrow of Gold*.

AHS ALLAN H. SIMMONS is Senior Lecturer in English at St Mary's University College, University of Surrey. The present General Editor of *The Conradian*, he has written extensively on Conrad and edited *The Nigger of the 'Narcissus'* (1997) for Everyman's Library.

JHS J. H. STAPE. See above.

ZN ZDZISŁAW NAJDER, the celebrated Polish Conrad scholar, has written and edited many volumes relating to Conrad, including *Conrad's Polish Background: Letters to and from Polish Friends* (1964), *Congo Diary and Other Uncollected Pieces* (1978), *Joseph Conrad: A Chronicle* (1983), *Conrad under Familial Eyes* (1983), and *Conrad in Perspective: Essays on Art and Fidelity* (1997).

CLASSIFIED CONTENTS LIST

[entries are arranged alphabetically by headword]

ABBREVIATIONS

CCH Norman Sherry (ed.), *Conrad: The Critical Heritage*. Routledge & Kegan Paul, 1973.

CDOUP Zdzisław Najder (ed.), *Congo Diary and Other Uncollected Pieces*. New York: Doubleday, 1978.

CEW Norman Sherry, *Conrad's Eastern World*. CUP, 1966.

CL Frederick R. Karl and Laurence Davies (eds.), *The Collected Letters of Joseph Conrad*. CUP, 1983– .

CPB Zdzisław Najder (ed.), *Conrad's Polish Background: Letters to and from Polish Friends*. OUP, 1964.

CTF Richard Curle (ed.), *Conrad to a Friend: 150 Selected Letters from Joseph Conrad to Richard Curle*. Sampson, Low, Marston, 1928.

CUFE Zdzisław Najder (ed.), *Conrad under Familial Eyes*. CUP, 1983.

CWW Norman Sherry, *Conrad's Western World*. CUP, 1971.

JCC Zdzisław Najder, *Joseph Conrad: A Chronicle*. CUP, 1983.

JCHC Jessie Conrad, *Joseph Conrad and his Circle*. Jarrolds, 1935.

JCIR Martin Ray (ed.), *Joseph Conrad: Interviews and Recollections*. Macmillan, 1990.

JCKH Jessie Conrad, *Joseph Conrad as I Knew Him*. Heinemann, 1926.

JCPR Ford Madox Ford, *Joseph Conrad: A Personal Remembrance*. Duckworth, 1924.

JCTL Frederick R. Karl, *Joseph Conrad: The Three Lives. A Biography*. Faber, 1979.

JCTR John Conrad, *Joseph Conrad: Times Remembered*. CUP, 1981.

LCG C. T. Watts (ed.), *Joseph Conrad's Letters to Cunninghame Graham*. CUP, 1969.

LFC Edward Garnett (ed.), *Letters from Conrad, 1895 to 1924*. Nonesuch, 1928.

LL G. Jean-Aubry (ed.), *Joseph Conrad: Life and Letters*. 2 volumes. Heinemann, 1927.

LTY Richard Curle, *The Last Twelve Years of Joseph Conrad*. Sampson, Low, Marston, 1928.

MFJC Borys Conrad, *My Father: Joseph Conrad*. Calder & Boyars, 1970.

PL J. H. Stape and Owen Knowles (eds.), *A Portrait in Letters: Correspondence to and about Conrad*. Amsterdam: Rodopi, 1996.

A NOTE TO THE READER

THE *Oxford Reader's Companion to Conrad* is organized around alphabetically listed entries, each one carrying an identifying headword. As the 'Classified Contents List' indicates, the entries are drawn from seven broad areas: Conrad's personal life; the places associated with his life and writings; the written works themselves; sources and influences; his working literary career; historical and cultural contexts; and his reputation. The entries naturally vary in size and scope. Some of the longer ones aspire to a synoptic overview—for example, of large topics such as Conrad's 'languages', 'finances', and 'Polish inheritance': their aim is to survey and assimilate widely dispersed evidence and often to highlight significant patterns of development in the life or work. Substantial entries are also reserved for Conrad's novels, volumes of reminiscences, and collaborative works. Each of these entries offers a narrative outline before moving on to survey textual and publishing history, sources and influences, themes and techniques, initial reception and subsequent reputation. The reader will also find shorter entries on significant particulars, whether devoted to an important moment in the writer's personal life (such as 'suicide'), a feature of his working life ('dictation' and 'typewriters'), or perhaps a recurring aspect of technique ('delayed decoding').

Throughout the volume, cross-references are indicated by the use of an asterisk before the headword or by an explicit invitation to 'see' a further relevant entry. Since the reader can expect to find entries on all of the items in the Conrad canon, these are not cross-referenced. Similarly, the four members of the Conrad family—the author himself, his wife Jessie, and sons Borys and John— do not receive asterisks. Cross-references are given only when they enrich and extend the substance of the entry in which they appear, and are not employed in every case where a headword appears. A concluding 'Index of References to Conrad's Works' enables the reader to locate all significant references to a specific work in addition to the cross-references provided in the headwords.

References to Conrad's works are normally to Dent's Collected Edition (1946–55), which shares its pagination not only with most earlier collected editions but also with most of the volumes in the World's Classics paperback series published by OUP. This edition is supplemented by Zdzisław Najder's *Congo Diary and Other Uncollected Pieces* (1978), which makes available a number of Conrad items not included in the Dent volumes. The reader seeking additional information on a given topic will find bibliographical advice presented, we trust, with a minimum of pedantic detail. Cited works having no direct bearing on Conrad are identified by author, title, and date. Volumes directly relevant to the author and his works are identified by publisher, and also by place of publication for works not published in London. Articles in periodicals are identified by volume number and year of publication, and issue numbers have been added when volumes are not paginated continuously.

A small number of letter-collections and important biographies are identified by abbreviations, such as *CL* for *The Collected Letters of Joseph Conrad* (1983–   ) or *JCC* for Zdzisław Najder's *Joseph Conrad: A Chronicle* (1983). To avoid a proliferation of acronyms, we have not shortened the titles of Conrad's novels and collections. There are, however, three exceptions: where appropriate, the Dent's Collected title *Youth, Heart of Darkness, The End of the Tether: Three Stories* is shortened to *Youth*; *Typhoon and Other Stories* to *Typhoon*; and *Notes on Life and Letters* to *Notes*. Frequently cited works are identified by the author's surname or, in cases where more than one work belongs to the same author, by surname and date. Full details of these works can be found in the bibliography of 'Frequently Cited Texts' at the end of the volume.

Three other features are intended to supplement its value as a useful reference work. A 'Conrad Family Tree' and a 'Chronology' of significant events in Conrad's life precede the main body of entries, while the last entry is followed by a collection of maps relevant to Conrad's life and travels.

CONRAD FAMILY TREE

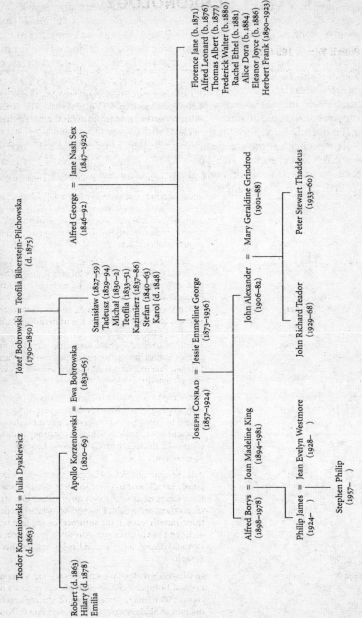

Teodor Korzeniowski = Julia Dyakiewicz
(d. 1863)

Józef Bobrowski = Teofila Biberstejn-Pilchowska
(1790–1850)   (d. 1875)

Robert (d. 1863)
Hilary (d. 1878)
Emilia

Apollo Korzeniowski = Ewa Bobrowska
(1820–69)   (1832–65)

Stanisław (1827–59)
Tadeusz (1829–94)
Michał (1830–2)
Teofila (1833–51)
Kazimierz (1837–86)
Stefan (1840–65)
Karol (d. 1848)

Alfred George = Jane Nash Sex
(1846–92)   (1847–1925)

Florence Jane (b. 1871)
Alfred Leonard (b. 1876)
Thomas Albert (b. 1877)
Frederick Walter (b. 1880)
Rachel Ethel (b. 1881)
Alice Dora (b. 1884)
Eleanor Joyce (b. 1886)
Herbert Frank (1890–1923)

JOSEPH CONRAD = Jessie Emmeline George
(1857–1924)   (1873–1936)

John Alexander = Mary Geraldine Grindrod
(1906–82)   (1901–88)

John Richard Teador   Peter Stewart Thaddeus
(1929–68)   (1933–60)

Alfred Borys = Joan Madeline King
(1898–1978)   (1894–1981)

Philip James = Jean Evelyn Westmore
(1924–)   (1928–)

Stephen Philip
(1957–)

CHRONOLOGY

Polish Years: 1857–73

1857	3 December	Józef Teodor Konrad Nałęcz Korzeniowski is born in Berdyczów in Ukraine, a part of Poland annexed by Russia since 1793. He is the only child of Ewa (née Bobrowska) and Apollo Korzeniowski. His varied inheritances come together in his three given names, the first two derived from his grandfathers and the third (Konrad) from the name of the hero and romantic patriot in Adam Mickiewicz's poem *Dziady* (1832). He is also a Nałęcz Korzeniowski, 'Nałęcz' being 'the heraldic name of the family coat-of-arms' (Baines, 1).
1859		After Apollo Korzeniowski's financial failure as an estate manager in Derebczynka, the family moves at the beginning of the year to Żytomierz, where Apollo can devote himself to his literary ambitions and underground political activities.
1861	*May*	By this month, Conrad's father has moved to Warsaw ostensibly to establish a new literary journal, *Dwutygodnik*, but mainly to devote himself to clandestine political activity.
	October	When Ewa and her son join Apollo in Warsaw, their home is already a centre for the underground Committee of the Movement.
	20 October	Apollo is arrested for anti-Russian conspiracy and spends almost seven months imprisoned in Warsaw's Citadel. Ewa too is later accused of unlawful revolutionary activity.
1862	*9 May*	After trial by a military tribunal, Conrad's parents are sentenced to exile and, with their 4-year-old son, escorted to Vologda, 300 miles north-east of Moscow. Ewa and her son fall ill before the journey ends in mid-June—she through physical collapse, he with pneumonia.
1863	*January*	After several months in Vologda, the Korzeniowski family are allowed to move south to Chernikhov, near Kiev, where news of the 1863 insurrection and its failure meets them on arrival. Ewa and her son are permitted a three-month leave in the summer for medical treatment and to visit relatives. Already a 'great reader' (*A Personal Record*, 70), Conrad has his first lessons in French.
1864–5		In Chernikhov, Apollo completes several of his translations of European classics, and his son makes a first contact with imaginative literature, through an introduction to Shakespeare, Dickens, and Polish Romantic poetry.

	18 April 1865	Conrad's mother dies, leaving Apollo and his son in lonely companionship, with the father overseeing the education of his 'poor little orphan' as best he can and kept afloat by an allowance from his brother-in-law Tadeusz Bobrowski.
1866	*Summer*	Conrad's long stay with his maternal grandmother Teofila Bobrowska at Nowochwastów is marred by his frequent illnesses.
	Autumn	Accompanied by his grandmother, Conrad returns to Chernikhov but, still suffering from migraine, nervous fits, and epileptic symptoms, requires stays in Kiev for medical treatment.
1867	*Early spring*	Conrad falls ill with German measles and requires medical treatment in Żytomierz. In the company of Tadeusz Bobrowski, has his first sight of the sea at Odessa.
	December	The now-ailing Apollo Korzeniowski is granted a permit to leave Chernikhov for Madeira or Algiers.
1868	*February*	The seriously ill Apollo and his son settle in Lwów in Austrian Poland. Now able to write fluently, Conrad is remembered as having produced some literary pieces on the theme of the insurgents engaged in 'battles with the Muscovites' (*CUFE*, 139). By the end of the year responsibility for Conrad's education passes from Apollo to a young private tutor.
1869		Apollo Korzeniowski and his son move to Cracow.
	23 May	Apollo dies; his funeral turns into a patriotic demonstration, with the 11-year-old Conrad at the head of a procession of several thousand people. Temporarily placed in a boarding school, the orphan is looked after by his father's close friend Stefan Buszczyński and his maternal grandmother.
1870–1	*2 August 1870*	Official guardianship of the young Conrad is granted to his grandmother Teofila Bobrowska, assisted by Count Władysław Mniszek. From late 1870 to May 1873, Conrad goes to live with his grandmother in her Cracow flat. Little is known about Conrad's formal education during this period, although his persistent illnesses suggest that it is probably spasmodic and placed in the hands of private tutors, one of whom, medical student Adam Pulman, accompanies him on summer travels.
1872		Repeated attempts by Conrad's relatives to secure Austrian nationality for him are unsuccessful. He surprises his family circle by expressing the desire to go to sea, a romantic aspiration fired by his reading of explorers' lives and sea literature, and one apparently viewed by his uncle Tadeusz Bobrowski as a scandalous 'betrayal of patriotic duties' (*CUFE*, 141). Bobrowski becomes increasingly influential in overseeing Conrad's education and upbringing.

1873	*May*	Adam Pulman accompanies Conrad on a trip to Switzerland and attempts to dissuade him, 'an incorrigible, hopeless Don Quixote' (*A Personal Record*, 44), from his steadily growing desire to go to sea.
	August	On their return, Conrad goes to live in Lwów with Antoni Syroczyński, who runs a boarding house for boys orphaned by the 1863 insurrection.

Sea Years: 1874–93

1874	*September*	Conrad returns from Lwów to Cracow, and preparations are made for his departure from his homeland.
	13 October	Leaves for Marseilles and makes what he will later describe as 'a, so to speak, standing jump out of his racial surroundings and associations' (*A Personal Record*, 121).
	15 December	Conrad's sea life begins when he sails as a passenger in the *Mont-Blanc* from Marseilles to Martinique.
1875	*6 February*	Arrives in Saint-Pierre, Martinique.
	31 March	Departs from Saint-Pierre.
	23 May	Arrives back in France.
	25 June	Again leaves in the *Mont-Blanc* as a 'novice' or ship's boy for Martinique and other Caribbean ports, arriving in Saint-Pierre on 31 July.
	1 November	Leaves Haïti on the return voyage.
	23 December	Arrives back in France.
1876		The first six months find Conrad enjoying the social, cultural, and bohemian excitements of Marseilles.
	10 July	Sails as a steward in the *Saint-Antoine*, bound for Martinique and other Caribbean ports, arriving in Saint-Pierre on 18 August.
	23 December	Leaves Haïti on the return voyage.
1877	*15 February*	Arrives back in Marseilles. The following period (until March 1878) constitutes one of the most mysterious periods in Conrad's life. The main sources for one version of his activities, his own highly coloured accounts in *The Mirror of the Sea* and *The Arrow of Gold*, suggest that as one of a syndicate of four, and in the company of Dominique and César Cervoni, he is engaged in an ill-fated expedition running guns in the *Tremolino* to Spain for the Carlist cause, ending when she is deliberately sunk to avoid capture. The smuggling venture is organized by 'Rita de Lastaola', with whom Conrad supposedly falls in love and for whose sake he is wounded in a duel in March 1878. Some of this account is patently disqualified by known facts, and corroboration for many of the events is, at best, slight.
1878		Another, more prosaic account of events by Conrad's uncle Tadeusz Bobrowski suggests that after a variety of personal and professional difficulties, including some indiscreet gambling in Monte Carlo, Conrad returns to

		Marseilles virtually penniless and attempts suicide by shooting himself in the chest, although without suffering serious injury.
	Early March	Bobrowski learns that Conrad is 'wounded' and leaves Kiev (8 March) for Marseilles, arriving to find Conrad out of bed and mobile. Bobrowski settles his nephew's debts, and it is decided that Conrad will join the British Merchant Service.
	24 April	He sails as unofficial apprentice in the *Mavis*, a British steamer bound for the Sea of Azov via Constantinople.
	10 June	Arriving in Lowestoft, Conrad first sets foot in England.
	11 July	Sails in the *Skimmer of the Sea* as an ordinary seaman, making three voyages from Lowestoft to Newcastle and back, before signing off on 23 September.
	15 October	Departs from London as an ordinary seaman in the *Duke of Sutherland*, bound for Australia.
	3 December	Celebrates his 21st birthday on the outward passage.
1879	*31 January*	The *Duke of Sutherland* arrives in Sydney, with Conrad remaining on board as watchman during her five-month stay.
	5 July	Leaves Sydney.
	19 October	Arrives back in London.
	12 December	Sails as an ordinary seaman in the *Europa*, bound for the Mediterranean, with ports-of-call in Italy and Greece.
1880	*30 January*	Arrives back in the *Europa*, lodging at Tollington Park, near Finsbury Park, London N4, and soon meets G. F. W. Hope.
	May	Moves to new lodgings at 6 Dynevor Road, Stoke Newington, London N16 (his base until 1889), where he meets Adolf P. Krieger, a fellow lodger.
	28 May	After attending a tutorial course, passes his second-mate's examination.
	22 August	Sails as third mate—his first berth as an officer—in the *Loch Etive*, bound for Australia.
	24 November	Arrives in Sydney.
1881	*11 January*	Leaves Sydney.
	25 April	Arrives back in London.
	10 August	In a desperate letter to his uncle Tadeusz Bobrowski requesting money, Conrad claims that after sustaining an injury on a June voyage in the *Annie Frost* he has been in hospital. No documentary evidence exists to support this alleged 'disaster'.
	19 September	Signs on as second mate in the *Palestine*, whose erratic progress to Bangkok forms the basis of 'Youth'.
	21 September	The *Palestine* departs, stopping at Gravesend, and then taking almost three weeks to reach Newcastle (18 October).
	29 November	The ship leaves Newcastle and, some days later, loses her sails and springs a leak in the English Channel.
	24 December	With the crew refusing to continue, the *Palestine* puts back for Falmouth.

1882		The *Palestine* remains in Falmouth for eight months undergoing repairs, Conrad deciding to stay with the ship as a way of accumulating service in preparation for his first-mate's examination.
	17 September	The *Palestine* leaves Falmouth for Bangkok with a new crew.
1883	12 March	Spontaneous combustion leads to the *Palestine*'s catching fire and (14 March) causes a coal-gas explosion. The crew, forced to abandon ship in Bangka Strait, off Sumatra, take to boats and row the short distance to Bangka Island.
	2 April	In Singapore, a marine court of inquiry exonerates the master, officers, and crew from all blame.
	3 April	The crew is discharged, with Conrad staying in Singapore until mid-April, before sailing home as a passenger via the Suez Canal and arriving in London at the end of May.
	Late July	Travels to Marienbad to meet his uncle Tadeusz Bobrowski.
	13 September	Conrad sails as second mate in the *Riversdale*, bound for Madras, stopping at Port Elizabeth, South Africa (7 December–9 February 1884).
1884	6 April	The *Riversdale* arrives in Madras, where, following a dispute with the captain, Conrad is relieved of his position and discharged. He immediately travels across India to Bombay.
	28 April	In Bombay, signs on as second mate in the *Narcissus*.
	16 October	Arrives back in Dunkirk.
	17 November	Fails his first attempt at the first-mate's examination.
	3 December	On his 27th birthday, successfully retakes the first-mate's examination.
1885	27 April	Sails as second mate in the *Tilkhurst* from Hull to Singapore and Calcutta, stopping over for a month at Penarth (13 May–10 June), where he meets Joseph Kliszczewski and his family.
	22 September	Arrives in Singapore.
	19 October	The *Tilkhurst* begins her return voyage.
	19 November	Arrives in Calcutta for a seven-week stay.
1886	12 January	The *Tilkhurst* sails from Calcutta.
	16 June	Arriving in Dundee, Conrad signs off the same day and travels to London.
	Early summer	May have written his first exercise in fiction, 'The Black Mate', for a literary competition in *Tit-Bits*.
	28 July	Fails his first attempt at the master's examination.
	19 August	Becomes a naturalized British subject.
	10 November	Successfully retakes the master's examination.
	28 December	Signs on as second mate in the *Falconhurst*, leaving London for Penarth.
1887	2 January	Signs off the *Falconhurst* in Penarth.
	18 February	Sails from Amsterdam as first mate in the *Highland Forest*, bound for Java.

	1 July	After sustaining a back injury on the voyage, Conrad signs off during the ship's stay in the Semarang roads and leaves for medical treatment in Singapore.
	20 August	On or about this date signs on as first mate in the *Vidar*, making four trading trips between Singapore and small Netherlands East Indies ports on Borneo and Celebes. One port of call, the Malay settlement of Berau on the Berau River in east Borneo where he meets William Charles Olmeijer, later provides the basis for Conrad's fictional Sambir in his first two novels.
1888	4 January	Signs off the *Vidar* in Singapore.
	19 January	Receives notice of appointment as master of the *Otago*, his only command, and joins the ship in Bangkok (24 January) for a voyage to Australia.
	9 February	Departs from Bangkok, taking three weeks to reach Singapore.
	2 March	Leaves Singapore.
	7 May	Arrives in Sydney.
	22 May	The ship leaves for a round trip to Melbourne (6 June–7 July), arriving back on 11 July.
	7 August	Takes the *Otago* to Port Louis, Mauritius, via the Torres Strait.
	30 September	Arrives in Mauritius for a seven-week stay.
	21 November	Leaves Mauritius.
1889	4 January	Arrives back in Melbourne.
	13 February	Sails with the *Otago* to Minlacowie, South Australia, where she remains for a month.
	Late March	After the *Otago*'s return to Port Adelaide (26 March), Conrad resigns his command and on 3 April returns via the Suez Canal to Europe in the SS *Nürnberg*.
	14 May	Arrives in Southampton. In London, Conrad soon takes rented rooms at 6 Bessborough Gardens, Pimlico, London SW1.
	2 July	Conrad's release from the status of Russian subject is officially gazetted.
	Autumn	During a long shore-leave begins a story that over the next five years evolves into *Almayer's Folly*.
	24 October	Takes steps to obtain a visa for a visit to Poland.
	November	Through the agency of Adolf P. Krieger, goes to Brussels to be interviewed by Albert Thys of the Société Anonyme Belge pour le Commerce du Haut-Congo, with a view to captaining one of the company's ships on the Congo River.
1890	February–April	Returns to Poland for the first time in sixteen years to visit his uncle Tadeusz Bobrowski. On the way, he stops in Brussels to visit Marguerite Poradowska and her terminally ill husband.
	29 April	Arrives back there to find that his three-year appointment to the Congo is confirmed.
	10 May	From Bordeaux, leaves for Africa, arriving at Boma on 12 June.

	13 June	Makes the short river journey to Matadi where he remains a fortnight and meets Roger Casement.
	28 June	Begins a gruelling overland trek to Kinshasa.
	2 August	Arrives in Kinshasa, disillusioned and under stress.
	3 August	Departs for Stanley Falls in the *Roi des Belges* under Captain Koch.
	1 September	Arrives in Stanley Falls, where he is ill with dysentery.
	6 September	Takes charge of the *Roi des Belges* for part of her return voyage, arriving back at Kinshasa on 24 September.
	26 September	A change in the company's plans sends Conrad to Bamou, where, falling seriously ill, he decides to return home.
	October–December	Makes a slow six-week journey back to the coast, reaching Matadi on 4 December and sailing from Boma back to Europe.
1891	January	Still severely ill, arrives back in London by the end of the month.
	March	In the German Hospital, Dalston, London N16, suffering from malaria, rheumatism, and neuralgia.
	21 May–14 June	Stays three weeks in Champel-les-Bains, Switzerland, for medical treatment.
	Summer	Takes a temporary job at the Barr, Moering & Company warehouse in London; some time before September, he moves to new lodgings at 17 Gillingham Street, near Victoria Station, London SW1.
	21 November	Sails from London for Australia as first mate in the *Torrens*, one of the fastest sailing ships of her day.
1892	28 February	Arrives in Adelaide.
	10 April	Leaves Adelaide.
	2 September	Arrives back in London.
	25 October	Again sails as first mate in the *Torrens*, bound for Australia, and meets W. H. Jacques, a passenger and the first reader of *Almayer's Folly* in manuscript.
	3 December	Conrad's 35th birthday.
1893	30 January	Arrives in Adelaide.
	24 March	Leaves Adelaide and meets two passengers, John Galsworthy and E. L. Sanderson, on the voyage home.
	August–September	Spends several weeks in Ukraine visiting his uncle Tadeusz Bobrowski.
	27 November	As second mate, joins the *Adowa*, a steamer chartered by the Franco-Canadian Transport Company to carry French emigrants from France to Canada.
	4 December	Arrives in Rouen, where the *Adowa* remains idle when the company's plans fail to materialize.

Conrad the Writer: 1894–1924

1894	17 January	Signs off the *Adowa*, marking the end of his professional sea career at the age of 36.
	10 February	Tadeusz Bobrowski dies.
	24 April	Finishes a draft of *Almayer's Folly*, followed by revision during the next month.

	4 July	Sends the typescript of *Almayer's Folly* to T. Fisher Unwin's office.
	8 August	Lonely and in poor health, Conrad is again in Champel-les-Bains, Switzerland, for hydrotherapy.
	Mid-August	Begins *An Outcast of the Islands*.
	6 September	Leaves Champel for London.
	4 October	Learns that *Almayer's Folly* has been accepted by Unwin.
	8 October	Meets Unwin at his office and agrees to contractual terms. The novel's first professional reader, W. H. Chesson, is also present. On this occasion (or soon after) Conrad meets Edward Garnett, senior reader at Unwin's, who will become his early mentor and enduring friend.
	November	About this time, first meets Jessie George, his future wife.
1895	*8 March*	Visits Marguerite Poradowska in Brussels.
	29 April	*Almayer's Folly* published by T. Fisher Unwin (3 May by Macmillan in America).
	May	Spends the month in Champel-les-Bains, Switzerland, undergoing medical treatment and there meets Émilie Briquel with whom he forms a romantic attachment.
	16 September	Finishes *An Outcast of the Islands*, delivered to Unwin two days later.
1896	*Early February*	According to Jessie Conrad (*JCC*, 12–15), Conrad proposes marriage.
	4 March	*An Outcast of the Islands* published by T. Fisher Unwin (15 August by Appleton in America).
	23 March	*The Sisters*, a novel started in the previous year, is abandoned in favour of 'The Rescuer' (later *The Rescue*).
	24 March	Marries Jessie George in a London registry office, the couple leaving the next day for a five-month stay in Brittany.
	April	Begins *The Rescue*.
	May	Writes 'The Idiots' and makes a first contact by letter with H. G. Wells.
	July	Writes 'An Outpost of Progress'.
	9 August	Completes 'The Lagoon'.
	2 September	The Conrads return from Brittany, preparing to set up their first home in Stanford-le-Hope, Essex. Having temporarily abandoned *The Rescue*, Conrad returns in earnest to the composition of *The Nigger of the 'Narcissus'* (begun in June).
	22 December	The Conrads leave to spend Christmas with Joseph Kliszczewski and his family in Cardiff.
1897	*17 January*	Completes a draft of *The Nigger of the 'Narcissus'*.
	25 February	First meets Henry James.
	February–April	Writes 'Karain: A Memory', William Blackwood's acceptance of the story marking the beginning of an important five-year publishing connection.
	13 March	Moves to a new home at Ivy Walls, in Stanford-le-Hope, Essex.

	Late April	Begins 'The Return', with its composition occupying all the summer months.
	15 October	First meets Stephen Crane.
	26 November	First meets R. B. Cunninghame Graham.
	30 November	*The Nigger of the 'Narcissus'* published by Dodd Mead in America under the title *The Children of the Sea: A Tale of the Forecastle* (2 December by Heinemann).
	3 December	Conrad's 40th birthday.
1898	*15 January*	Borys Conrad born.
	26 March	*Tales of Unrest* published by Scribner's in America (4 April by T. Fisher Unwin).
	May	Writes 'Youth'. A 28-page precursor to *Lord Jim*, 'Jim: A Sketch', may also have been written this month, although an earlier date is possible.
	7 June	Lays aside the 'Jim' story to grapple again with *The Rescue*, which occupies him until December.
	September	First meets Ford Madox Ford.
	26 October	The Conrads move to a new home at Pent Farm in Postling, Kent, sublet to them by Ford.
	28 October	After consulting Edward Garnett and W. E. Henley, Conrad finalizes plans to collaborate with Ford.
	Mid-December	Sets aside *The Rescue* to begin 'The Heart of Darkness'.
1899	*14 January*	The *Academy* 'crowns' *Tales of Unrest* as one of the outstanding books of the previous year, awarding Conrad a 50-guinea prize.
	6 February	Finishes 'The Heart of Darkness', followed by a four-month break.
	6 July	Has by this date sent off 31 manuscript leaves of *Lord Jim*, as yet conceived as a 40,000-word story to be finished in July, but which turns out to occupy him for a whole year.
	August	First meets Hugh Clifford.
	6 October	Collaboration with Ford Madox Ford begins when Ford visits Conrad to read out the first chapters of *The Inheritors* (although Conrad plays a minor part in the writing).
1900	*17 February*	Has submitted manuscript of *The Inheritors* to Heinemann.
	5 June	Stephen Crane dies.
	14 July	Finishes a draft of *Lord Jim*, with revision and correction to follow.
	20 July–18 August	The Conrads holiday with Ford Madox Ford and his wife in Bruges and Knokke-Heist, Belgium.
	Late September	Begins 'Typhoon'.
	3 October	Meets the literary agent J. B. Pinker in London and begins an association with him lasting over twenty years.
	9 October	*Lord Jim* published by Blackwood (31 October by Doubleday, McClure in America).
1901	*10 January*	Finishes 'Typhoon'.
	January–April	Illness slows up the composition of 'Falk'.

	May	Spends two weeks with Ford Madox Ford at Winchelsea where he finishes 'Falk' and begins 'Amy Foster', completed by mid-June.
	1 June	*The Inheritors* published by McClure, Phillips in America (26 June by Heinemann).
	November–December	Ford and Conrad work on *Romance*.
1902	16 January	Finishes 'To-morrow'.
	January–March	Works on *Romance*, finishing in early March.
	17 March	Begins 'The End of the Tether', with its troublesome composition occupying the next several months.
	23 June	A batch of 'The End of the Tether' manuscript and typescript is destroyed by fire when a lamp overturns.
	11 July	Receives an award of £300 from the Royal Literary Fund.
	4 September	*Typhoon* published as a separate volume by Putnam in America.
	13 November	The *Youth* volume published by Blackwood (8 February 1903 by McClure, Phillips in America).
	3 December	Conrad's 45th birthday. Later in the month, meditates on a short story which will turn out to be *Nostromo*, his largest canvas.
1903	January	Begins work on *Nostromo*, which dominates the next eighteen months.
	22 April	*Typhoon and Other Stories* published by Heinemann (in October by McClure, Phillips in America under the title *Falk, Amy Foster, To-morrow: Three Stories*).
	28 August	First meets William Rothenstein when the artist comes to make drawings for a portrait.
	16 October	*Romance* published by Smith, Elder (2 May 1904 by McClure, Phillips in America).
1904	17 January	The Conrads take a flat in London for the next two months. During this period, Conrad, in close contact with Ford Madox Ford, juggles with several competing projects—the writing of *Nostromo*, a new venture involving semi-autobiographical essays (*The Mirror of the Sea*), and a one-act adaptation of his short story 'To-morrow' entitled *One Day More*.
	Late January	Jessie Conrad injures both legs in a serious fall, the beginning of a permanent disability.
	6 February	Conrad's bankers fail.
	5 April	By this date secures the secretarial services of Lilian Hallowes, who will remain with him for twenty years.
	June	Receives a Royal Literary Fund award of £200.
	30 August	Finishes a draft of *Nostromo*.
	14 October	*Nostromo* published by Harper (23 November by the same publisher in America).
	Mid-November	The Conrads spend the rest of the year in London, where Jessie undergoes an operation on her leg.
1905	13 January	The Conrads depart for a four-month stay on Capri, where Conrad works on *Chance*, writes 'Autocracy and War', and first meets Norman Douglas.

	Late March	Learns that he has been awarded a grant of £500 from the Royal Bounty Fund.
	25–7 June	*One Day More* given three performances by the Stage Society at the Royalty Theatre, London.
	Mid-October	Finishes 'Gaspar Ruiz'.
	Mid-November	The Conrads spend the rest of the year in London, where Borys is hospitalized with scarlet fever.
	29 December	Finishes 'An Anarchist' by this date.
1906	*11 January*	Completes 'The Informer' by this date.
	11 February	The Conrads depart for a two-month stay in Montpellier, where 'Verloc' (later retitled *The Secret Agent*) is begun.
	21 February	Completes 'The Brute' by this date.
	May	Visits Ford Madox Ford in Winchelsea and probably first meets Arthur Marwood; collaborates with Ford on *The Nature of a Crime*.
	10 July–early September	The Conrads move to London for several weeks.
	2 August	John Conrad born.
	4 October	*The Mirror of the Sea* published by Methuen (on the same date by Harper in America).
	4 December	Finishes 'Il Conde'.
	16 December	The Conrads again leave for Montpellier.
1907	*11 April*	In Montpellier, finishes 'The Duel'.
	15 May	The children having fallen ill, the Conrads travel to Geneva and take up residence at Champel-les-Bains.
	May–June	Expands *The Secret Agent* for book publication.
	10 August	The Conrads return home to confront their severe financial crisis.
	12 September	*The Secret Agent* published by Methuen (on the same date by Harper in America). During this month the Conrads move from Pent Farm to their new home Someries, in Luton Hoo, Bedfordshire.
	3 December	Conrad's 50th birthday.
	Early December	Begins 'Razumov' (later retitled *Under Western Eyes*).
1908	*Late January*	Dashes off (or refurbishes) 'The Black Mate' for quick magazine publication and then returns to his main project, *Under Western Eyes*.
	April	Receives a grant of £200 from the Royal Literary Fund.
	6 August	*A Set of Six* published by Methuen (15 January 1915 by Doubleday, Page in America).
	29 August	The Conrads begin a three-week stay with Ford Madox Ford and his wife in Aldington.
	September	Tensions with his agent J. B. Pinker intensify when Conrad informs him of his new plans to write a serial, 'Some Reminiscences', for Ford's *English Review*; interrupting his work on *Under Western Eyes*, completes the first four papers by early December.
1909	*14 February*	The Conrads move from Someries into rented rooms in Aldington, near Hythe, Kent.
	11 April	Conrad quarrels with Ford Madox Ford and later in the month becomes embroiled in Ford's domestic crisis.

	Mid-July	Conrad's debt to his agent J. B. Pinker now totals £2,250.
	31 July	Deteriorating relations with Ford culminate in a decisive break, when they quarrel over Conrad's contributions to the *English Review*.
	September	At the end of the month, a visit from Captain Carlos Marris, a trader from the Eastern archipelago, revives old memories and prompts Conrad to return to Eastern material for stories in his later *'Twixt Land and Sea*.
	Early December	Breaks off from *Under Western Eyes* to write 'The Secret Sharer'.
	Mid-December	Tensions between Conrad and Pinker reach a crisis, when the latter demands more regular copy; Conrad threatens to throw the manuscript of *Under Western Eyes* into the fire.
1910	*26 January*	Finishes *Under Western Eyes* and, upon delivery of the manuscript the next day in London, has an explosive row with his agent, which leads to a two-year estrangement. After completion of the novel, Conrad suffers a physical and mental breakdown that renders him an invalid for three months.
	18 May	Begins 'A Smile of Fortune', finished by September.
	28 May	First meets F. Warrington Dawson.
	24 June	The Conrads move from Aldington to a new home, Capel House, in Orlestone, Kent.
	July	Writes four book reviews for the *Daily Mail*.
	9 August	Granted a Civil List Pension of £100 annually.
	September	Finishes 'Prince Roman' and, later in the year, 'The Partner'.
1911	*January–February*	Writes 'Freya of the Seven Isles'.
	17 July	André Gide and Valery Larbaud make a visit to Capel House.
	Late August	The American collector John Quinn buys the first of many manuscripts.
	10 September	About this time makes a fresh start on *Chance*, which occupies him until March 1912.
	22 September	Borys Conrad joins HMS *Worcester*, a nautical training ship.
	5 October	*Under Western Eyes* published by Methuen (19 October by Harper in America).
1912	*19 January*	*A Personal Record* published by Harper in America (at the end of the month by Eveleigh Nash under the title *Some Reminiscences*).
	25 March	Finishes a draft of *Chance*.
	15 April	The *Titanic* disaster occurs, prompting Conrad to write two essays. The 'Karain' manuscript, bound for John Quinn, the American collector, goes down with the *Titanic*.
	Late April	Begins composing *Victory*, which occupies the next two years.
	14 October	*'Twixt Land and Sea* published by J. M. Dent (3 December by Hodder and Stoughton, Doran in America).

	November	First-meets Richard Curle and Józef H. Retinger.
	3 December	Conrad's 55th birthday.
	23 December	Completes 'The Inn of the Two Witches' by this date.
1913	*26 March*	J. B. Pinker takes Conrad to lunch with F. N. Doubleday, who suggests a collected edition of his work.
	September	Evolving with painful slowness, *Victory* is half completed; publication of *Chance* is delayed by a bookbinders' strike.
	10 September	First meets Bertrand Russell.
	November–December	During a break from *Victory*, writes 'The Planter of Malata'.
1914	*8 January*	Finishes 'Because of the Dollars' by this date.
	15 January	Publication of *Chance* by Methuen (26 March by Doubleday, Page in America).
	27 June	Finishes a draft of *Victory*.
	25 July	Accompanied by Otolia and Józef H. Retinger, the Conrads leave for Poland, travelling via Hamburg and Berlin to Cracow.
	31 July	With the general mobilization of Austria, the party seeks refuge in unmilitarized territory and (2 August) moves to Zakopane in the Tatra Mountains, taking up residence at Aniela Zagórska's *pension*, where Conrad meets Stefan Żeromski.
	6 October	The Conrads receive permission to leave Poland and (8 October) begin the journey home via Austria and Italy.
	2 November	Arrive back in England at Tilbury.
	December	Despite illness and depression, possibly begins 'Poland Revisited', an evocation of the recent visit to Poland.
1915	*24 February*	*Within the Tides* published by J. M. Dent (15 January 1916 by Doubleday, Page in America); begins *The Shadow-Line* by this date.
	27 March	*Victory* published by Doubleday, Page in America (24 September by Methuen).
	20 September	Borys Conrad reports for basic training in the Army Service Corps.
	15 December	Finishes a draft of *The Shadow-Line*.
1916	*28 February*	Henry James dies.
	10 March	Sits for a bust by the sculptor Jo Davidson.
	30 March	Finishes 'The Warrior's Soul' by this date and is ready to revise texts and compose 'Author's Notes' for the collected edition of his works.
	19 April	Jane Anderson visits Capel House.
	13 May	Arthur Marwood dies.
	19 May	Responds positively to André Gide's offer to translate 'Youth' and 'Heart of Darkness'.
	21 July	Accepts B. Macdonald Hastings's offer to dramatize *Victory*.
	Mid-August	With Józef H. Retinger, visits the Foreign Office in connection with a memorandum Conrad has written, 'A Note on the Polish Problem'.

	5 September	Visits the Admiralty to discuss propaganda articles on the Royal Naval Reserve, prelude to a series of tours of naval bases later in the year.
	October	Writes 'The Tale'.
	6 November	Departs from Granton harbour in Scotland on a ten-day mission in the North Sea in the 'Q-boat' HMS *Ready*.
1917	19 March	*The Shadow-Line* published by J. M. Dent (27 April by Doubleday, Page in America).
	2 June	Relinquishes his annual Civil List Pension.
	July	Begins working on *The Arrow of Gold*, the first of his novels to be largely dictated.
	25 November	The Conrads leave for a three-month stay in London, where Jessie undergoes major surgery on her leg.
	3 December	Conrad's 60th birthday.
1918	21 January	First meets Hugh Walpole.
	January–June	Despite illness and wartime gloom, continues work on *The Arrow of Gold*, finishing it in early June.
	May	First meets G. Jean-Aubry.
	24 June	The Conrads begin a seven-week stay in London, where Jessie's leg is operated on by Sir Robert Jones.
	July	Reads the unfinished manuscript of *The Rescue*, preparing for a decisive return to it in the autumn.
	10 October	Suffering from shell-shock, Borys Conrad enters hospital in Rouen.
	11 November	Armistice Day.
1919	25 March	The Conrads leave Capel House to take up temporary residence at Spring Grove, in Wye, near Ashford, Kent.
	26 March	The stage version of *Victory* opens at the Globe Theatre, London, running until 14 June.
	12 April	*The Arrow of Gold* published by Doubleday, Page in America (6 August by T. Fisher Unwin).
	23 May	Sells the film rights to four of his novels, receiving $20,000.
	25 May	Finishes a draft of *The Rescue*, 23 years after its inception.
	2 October	The Conrads move to their last home, Oswalds, in Bishopsbourne, near Canterbury, Kent.
	15 October	Has begun a stage version of *The Secret Agent*, finishing the first draft in late November.
	30 November	The Conrads leave for a month's stay in Liverpool where Sir Robert Jones operates on Jessie Conrad.
1920	27 February	Karola Zagórska arrives for a six-month stay with the Conrads.
	21 May	*The Rescue* published by Doubleday, Page in America (24 June by J. M. Dent).
	June	Visits the British Museum and begins work on *Suspense*.
	1 September	Begins a three-week stay in Deal, Kent, where he revises the essays collected in *Notes on Life and Letters* and collaborates with J. B. Pinker on *Gaspar the Strong Man*, a film scenario of 'Gaspar Ruiz' (*A Set of Six*).

	10 December	Finishes a draft of *Laughing Anne*, a two-act adaptation of 'Because of the Dollars' (*Within the Tides*), which he revises over the following week.
1921	*23 January*	With Jessie, Conrad leaves for a nine-week visit to Corsica for research on *Suspense*, staying in Ajaccio where he is joined by J. B. Pinker and family, and by Miss Hallowes. Collected editions begin to appear in Britain and America.
	25 February	*Notes on Life and Letters* published by J. M. Dent (22 April by Doubleday, Page in America).
	12 June	Receives Bruno Winawer's Polish play *Księga Hioba*, which he proceeds to translate into English.
	September	Begins a short story later to become *The Rover* by this date, interrupting work on *Suspense*.
1922	*8 February*	J. B. Pinker dies suddenly in New York, his son Eric now taking over as Conrad's literary agent.
	27 June	Finishes a draft of *The Rover*, revising and expanding until 16 July.
	8 August	Draws up his will, with Richard Curle and Ralph Wedgwood as executors.
	2 November	Stage version of *The Secret Agent* opens at the Ambassadors Theatre, London, running for only ten performances.
	3 December	Conrad's 65th birthday.
1923	*15 March*	Declines an honorary degree from Cambridge University, having already refused such offers from several other universities.
	21 April	Leaves Glasgow in the *Tuscania* for a promotional tour in America, arriving in New York on 1 May and staying with F. N. Doubleday on Long Island.
	10 May	Gives a public reading from *Victory*.
	15–24 May	Tours New England with the Doubledays, visiting Yale and Harvard.
	9 June	Arrives home, to be informed that Borys Conrad has been secretly married since September 1922.
	1 December	*The Rover* published by Doubleday, Page in America (3 December by T. Fisher Unwin).
1924	*11 January*	Conrad's first grandson, Philip James, is born.
	March	Sits for the sculptor Jacob Epstein.
	27 May	Declines Prime Minister Ramsay MacDonald's offer of a knighthood.
	13 June–24 July	Following knee surgery, Jessie Conrad recuperates in a Canterbury nursing home.
	3 August	Dies of a heart attack at 8.30 a.m., aged 66, and is buried four days later in Canterbury Cemetery.
	26 September	*The Nature of a Crime* published by Duckworth (on the same date by Doubleday, Page in America).
	5 October	Ford Madox Ford completes *Joseph Conrad: A Personal Remembrance* (published in November).
	21 October	*Laughing Anne & One Day More: Two Plays by Joseph Conrad* published by Castle (8 May 1925 by Doubleday, Page in America).

A

achievement-and-decline thesis. This thesis is commonly associated with Thomas C. Moser's influential study *Joseph Conrad: Achievement and Decline* (1957), although he was by no means the first to put forward the case that Conrad's later fiction, in the aftermath of his breakdown in 1910, is subject to a marked decline. This case receives some support from Conrad's own *letters after 1910, in which he repeatedly complains of a weariness and depletion manifested inwardly by constant 'nervous exasperation' with his faltering progress (*CL*, iv. 487) and outwardly by long fallow periods alternating with spells of wearily dogged composition. John *Galsworthy was only one of several early commentators to assert a version of the achievement-and-decline view: 'It does disservice to Conrad's memory to be indiscriminate in praise of his work. . . . He was very tired towards the end; he wore himself clean out. To judge him by tired work is absurd' (81). Moser's monograph was also the recognizable product of a period (1940–60) associated with the arrival of Conrad's works in academe, when the common impulse was to assert his stature as a major writer by establishing a canon of his best work. Prior to Moser, F. R. Leavis (1948) offered the first memorably argued construction of a Conrad canon (in this case excluding 'Heart of Darkness' and *Lord Jim* and including post-1911 works such as *Chance* and *Victory*), to be quickly followed by Douglas Hewitt (1952), who more closely anticipated Moser by asserting a major period of Conradian achievement (1898–1909) followed by a sharp decline.

More systematically than previous critics, Moser employs a form of psycho-criticism to diagnose what in his view are fundamental weaknesses and eccentricities in the author's later creative responses. According to this position, Conrad's major works, all concerned with the 'anatomy of moral failure', belong to the period 1897–1911, after which his fiction suffers from a debilitating enervation. Moser identifies two stages in this decline. The first results from Conrad's disabling involvement with the 'uncongenial subject' of love and sexually charged relationships, a problem present in the early fiction, but disturbingly central in a novel such as *Victory* (1914). Its manifestations—a 'preposterous' melodramatic code, sexually inadequate villains, strains of voyeurism and misogyny, and obscure failures of male passion—all suggest a 'creative imagination [that] is not co-operating with the intended theme' (111). According to Moser, the second stage arrives in Conrad's post-*First World War works, in which an exhausted weariness prevails and manifests itself in a progressively facile and sentimentalized 'affirmation'. Generous in its admiration but forthright in dissent, Moser's study has reverberated widely and persistently in later criticism: it underpins Albert J. Guerard's important early study (1958), Bernard C. Meyer's psychoanalytic biography (1967), and many full-length treatments of Conrad's 'major period'.

The first significant challenge to Moser's view came in John A. Palmer's study of Conrad's literary growth (1968), which includes a helpful appendix on the formation of the achievement-and-decline paradigm. Palmer's quarrel is ultimately less with Moser's 'moral' terms than with his application of them. Nevertheless, Palmer attempts to retrace the lines of growth in Conrad's work, arguing for underlying moral imperatives present from the very beginning, but which evolve in three stages, each marked by a period of trial and error which then yields a major achievement. He prompts a rethinking of Conrad's development on several fronts, not least in his downgrading of *Nostromo* and his championing of *Victory* as the high point of Conrad's third period.

A newer generation of critics has mounted a more strenuous challenge to Moser's thesis and its influence, either by questioning the sometimes reductive *psychoanalytic assumptions underpinning it, or by pointing to ways in which Conrad's later fiction may demand altered critical perspectives, or, more radically, by challenging the basis of canon-formation itself. In two full-length studies of Conrad's later fiction, Gary Geddes (1980) and Daniel R. Schwarz (1982) reopened the achievement-and-decline question, the first arguing that Conrad's later works represent a new phase of artistic consolidation and experimentation in a mode of ironic romance, and the second that they form 'an evolution and development of his prior methods' (p. xi). Following upon their studies, Daphna Erdinast-Vulcan (1991) and Robert Hampson (1992) give lengthy and serious readings of the late novels, their views growing out of a marked dissatisfaction with the achievement-and-decline paradigm, which, in Hampson's words, 'reveals not so much Conrad's imaginative exhaustion as the exhaustion of its own critical assumptions' (251). In 'The Decline of the Decline: Notes on Conrad's Reputation', Ian Watt examines the later novels for signs of artistic falling-off and concludes that 'Conrad is a writer to whom the decline theory does not really apply' (in Edward J. Brown *et al.* (eds.), *Literature, Culture and Society in the Modern Age: In Honour of Joseph Frank*, Stanford Slavic Sudies 4 (1991), 168). While many critics still embrace a version of the achievement-and-decline view of Conrad's development, there is clearly some evidence of a growing challenge to this consensus.

Aïssa is the *femme fatale* in *An Outcast of the Islands* whose passionate love affair with Peter *Willems leads to the betrayal of Tom *Lingard's secret river to the Arabs and ultimately to Willems's death. She is one of Conrad's most intensely sensual creations, to such an extent that the first American publishers of the novel, D. Appleton and Company, censored a number of passages describing her encounters with Willems before including the novel in their family series, the 'Town and Country Library'.

In the popular tradition of adventure fiction, Aïssa epitomizes the dangerous beauty of the exotic East; her name (after one of the wives of the prophet Muhammad) echoes that of Ayesha, the heroine of Rider Haggard's *She* (1887). Aïssa is actually of mixed racial origin, the daughter of Omar el Badavi, once the dreaded chief of the Brunei pirates, and a 'Baghdadi' woman 'from the west'. Like Willems, she is an outcast in *Sambir, shunned and disparaged by Malays like Lakamba as 'a she-dog with white teeth, like a woman of the Orang Putih [white men]' (47). Too pale for Lakamba, she is not white enough for Willems, who describes her as 'a damned mongrel, half-Arab, half-Malay' (271). Her importance in Conrad's fiction is discussed by Krenn and Nadelhaft.

Almayer family. Kaspar Almayer, his wife, and daughter Nina appear in Conrad's first two novels, *Almayer's Folly* and *An Outcast of the Islands*, which dramatize the family's history in reverse order, the first novel being set about 1887, and the second around 1872. A main source for Almayer was a *Java-born Dutch Eurasian, William Charles *Olmeijer, whom Conrad met during four trips to east *Borneo in 1887 and to whom, in *A Personal Record*, he flatteringly attributed his birth as a writer: 'if I had not got to know Almayer pretty well it is almost certain there would never have been a line of mine in print' (87). From Olmeijer, Conrad seems to have borrowed the outline of a personal history for his first major figure: Olmeijer was related by marriage to Captain William *Lingard (who figures in the novels as Tom *Lingard), went to east Borneo around 1869 to manage Lingard's trading agency, built himself a large house which he neglected, and was obsessed by thoughts of discovering gold.

Berthoud observes that Almayer is to a marked degree the product of a specific time and place, belonging to 'a class of petty-bourgeois colonials who hold power over a native population for purely contingent reasons, and who therefore exhibit all the symptoms of unearned self-esteem' (1992: pp. xxx–xxxi). A representative type who is fired by the prevailing fantasy of the colony-as-Eldorado, Almayer makes an alliance with the presiding mercantile 'King', Tom Lingard, and risks an enforced marriage in *Sambir. A country-born colonial who feels himself to be an outcast from Europe, Almayer is also partly driven by the class ideals of his Dutch parents as well as the dictates of the European caste system from which he inherits his sense of racial superiority.

In bringing together a Caucasian of Dutch parentage (Almayer), a Malay of Sulu origin (Mrs Almayer), and their Eurasian daughter (Nina), the Almayer family functions as a representative test-case and microcosm for conflicting racial needs and expectations. As a character naïvely acting out the rituals of his presumed superiority as the only white man in Sambir, Almayer reveals much of the inflexible egotism underlying European caste assumptions. Although he himself suffers from having violated these unspoken laws, he myopically and selfishly believes that he can expiate his own racial shame by giving Nina a 'white' education in *Singapore in preparation for the re-entry of father and daughter into European life. One significant challenge to Almayer arrives through his wife's betrayal, a form of cultural revenge against the Dutch colonial whom she increasingly despises. Another comes through Nina who, in the first part of the novel a hapless victim of her father's racial phobias, begins the quest for more authentic social and cultural traditions. As Almayer sees it, her relationship with Dain Maroola, a Balinese prince, constitutes a further shameful betrayal of his European racial heritage. By the end of the novel, the disintegration of the Almayer family is complete, with Mrs Almayer having returned to her Malay community and Nina, Dain, and their child forming a new family in independent Bali.

This fragmentation of the Almayer family also leads to the first appearance of a structural feature that will become central in many of Conrad's later novels: that of a sustained counterpointing of two very different value-based worlds which implicitly question and enter into debate with each other. In *Almayer's Folly*, the paradise available to Nina's youthfully hopeful sense of the world is framed and complicated by the more sombre intimations of imprisoning exile and lost paradise thrust upon the ageing and declining Almayer. Twin stories are thus juxtaposed with an ambiguity reminiscent of John Keats's 'The Eve of St Agnes' (1819), where two youthful lovers escape to a fairy-tale realm, leaving the reader to participate in the final ruinous stages of what, it is implied, is *our* world, the world of the aged, disillusioned, and wrinkled.

The dramatization in *Almayer's Folly* of Almayer's later state of mind constitutes the first of Conrad's portraits of a kind of hysteria that results when shocking knowledge of 'wreck, ruin, and waste' (200) is forced upon one of life's short-sighted pilgrims. With Nina's departure, Almayer can no longer remain comfortably blind to the fact that he is a superfluous derelict in a world remorselessly *Darwinian and therefore essentially impersonal and alien. Shocked into awareness of his abandonment, he undergoes an 'infernal' cycle of narcissistic indulgence in his victim-position, morbid imaginings of impending collapse, a Sisyphean sense of absurdity, culminating in the self-destructive urge not to live. The final stages of this cycle involve Almayer in the fruitless quest to forget what experience has painfully made known, a state only achieved by the embrace of a zombie-like mindlessness that represents his abdication of the right to exist in the world at all. At his death, the broken Almayer is linked with a despoiled wooden Mr Punch figure, a 'man-doll broken and flung there out of the way' (204). On Conrad's use of Mrs Almayer and Nina to pose active female alternatives to male European colonial assumptions, see Nadelhaft, 13–27. See also Peter D.

O'Connor, 'The Function of Nina in *Almayer's Folly*', *Conradiana*, 7 (1975), 225–32.

Almayer's Folly: A Story of an Eastern River.

Conrad's first novel was written intermittently during a five-year period (1889–94) at the end of his career at *sea and made him increasingly feel, as he later described it, 'as if already the story-teller were being born into the body of a seaman' (*A Personal Record*, 17). Published in 1895 when Conrad was 37 years old, *Almayer's Folly* also marks the beginning of a wonderfully rich and productive career that spanned almost three decades.

The novel opens with an introduction to Kaspar *Almayer on the verandah of his half-built but already decaying house, 'Almayer's Folly', in Bornean *Sambir. Almayer dreams obsessively of large amounts of gold that will bring escape to Europe for himself and his Eurasian daughter Nina, and looks forward to the arrival of a Balinese prince, Dain Maroola, who is to be employed in a plan to find it. Almayer retrospectively reviews 'twenty-five years of heart-breaking struggle' (4) in Sambir where, as the protégé and agent of Tom *Lingard, a seaman-adventurer, he has managed Lingard's trading company. The racially proud, white Almayer is especially offended by his long-standing marriage to Lingard's 'adopted daughter' (10), a woman of Sulu origin, whom he would like now to abandon. Almayer's reverie is broken by the sudden arrival of Dain Maroola who, however, disappoints him by first visiting Lakamba, the Rajah of Sambir. Almayer returns to his 'old' home, where his daughter reacts with unusual expectancy to news of Dain's arrival.

Chapters 2 to 5 provide an extended retrospective survey of Almayer's failed hopes during his past life in Sambir, failures brought about by Lingard's bankruptcy and disappearance to Europe, inter-tribal rivalry in Sambir, and the steady deterioration of Almayer's commercial hopes. During these years, the young Nina is sent to *Singapore for ten years to receive a European education, but returns to Sambir disillusioned with colonial society and becomes increasingly responsive to her Malay heritage. Almost simultaneously, Mrs Almayer begins actively to scheme against her husband by working with Lakamba. The account of Almayer's more recent past in chapters 4 and 5 reveals that, ironically, while he dreams of a future for himself and Nina in Europe, she—with her mother's encouragement—has been planning an escape to Bali with her lover Dain. At the end of chapter 5, the action returns to Almayer's 'present' of chapter 1 and to Dain's sudden arrival back in Sambir.

From chapter 6 to the first part of chapter 12, the action covers 24 eventful hours. A plan devised by Lakamba to hide Dain from the Dutch authorities involves the pretence that Dain has been drowned. Deceived by this subterfuge, Almayer succumbs to 'the utter abandonment of despair' (99) at the loss of his dream of wealth. In chapter 10, a drunken Almayer awakens to the full measure of his blindness when he learns from a slave-girl, Taminah, that Mrs Almayer and Nina have deserted him and that the latter is about to flee with Dain. Confronting the two lovers, Almayer threatens, pleads, and finally tries to blackmail Nina into deserting Dain, but, when he is rejected by her, insists upon helping them to escape, claiming that it would be a disgrace if the island's community were to know of his daughter's marriage to a 'native'.

On the day after the lovers' departure, Almayer returns to his wrecked home and, in an effort to erase all evidence of his past, burns down the remains of Lingard's trading company. Retiring to 'Almayer's Folly', he vainly seeks oblivion and escape. On periodic visits to Sambir over the next few months, the European Captain Ford is shocked by evidence of Almayer's steadily worsening plight: Almayer's possessions are stolen, he is locked away in a dark room, and has become an opium addict. The happy news that Nina has given birth to a son in Bali finally provides a stark contrast to Almayer's miserable end in Sambir: he dies alone and in squalor, his epitaph delivered by his greatest enemy, the Arab Abdulla.

Looking back on the origin of his first novel in *A Personal Record*, Conrad asserted that the coming into existence of his first book in the autumn of 1889 was an 'inexplicable event' (90). It was begun, he explained, during an extended period of shore-leave in his Pimlico lodgings in *London as a light holiday task with no thought of publication. The impulse to write may have been obscure, but the story's subsequent evolution, as described in the same memoir, soon draws upon the language of compulsion: the beginning writer enjoyed 'the idleness of a haunted man' (8), was spell-bound by the 'hallucination of the Eastern Archipelago' (5), and responded to its 'silent and irresistible appeal' (9). During the five years of its composition the battered manuscript of the novel accompanied Conrad to many parts of the world on his sea voyages and other travels—*Poland, the *Congo, *Australia (on which journey it had its first reader, W. H. *Jacques), and *France. He finished the first draft of the novel on 24 April 1894 and, after a period for revision, submitted the typescript under the pseudonym of 'Kamudi' (approximate Malay for 'rudder') to T. Fisher *Unwin on 4 July. A few days after its acceptance on 4 October, Conrad was invited to meet Unwin at his office, where the author accepted a fee of £20 plus French rights. On that occasion (or soon after) Conrad also made a first contact with the two Unwin readers, W. H. *Chesson and Edward *Garnett, who had recommended the novel for publication. At the very end of 1894, Conrad wrote a preface to accompany the novel, although it was not published in the first edition and did not make an appearance in print until the Doubleday, Page 'Sun-Dial' edition of 1921. Not serialized before book publication, *Almayer's Folly* was first issued by Unwin on 29 April 1895 and by Macmillan in America on 3 May 1895. For useful histories of the chronology of the novel's composition and the genesis of its text, see Gordan (1940), and Berthoud, 1992: pp. xxxix–xlii. Advanced students should note that a scholarly edition of *Almayer's Folly* (CUP, 1994), with history of composition,

revision, publication, and reception, and full textual apparatus, has appeared in the Cambridge Edition of the Works of Joseph Conrad, edited by Floyd Eugene Eddleman and David Leon Higdon, with an introduction by Ian Watt.

Almayer's Folly, like most of Conrad's fiction, rests upon an act of retrospective memory, in this case his memories of four trips he had made to east Borneo in 1887, when he had come into contact with William Charles *Olmeijer, a Dutch Eurasian living and working on the remote Berau River, the basis of the fictional Sambir. In *A Personal Record* Conrad typically stresses the actual meeting with Olmeijer as the inspiring force behind his first work, but it seems equally clear that the novel draws indirectly upon the history of his own youthful experience. In particular, Nina's dilemma as an individual with roots in two cultures but who belongs to neither provides a resonant echo of Conrad's own quest to forge an Anglo-Polish identity out of conflicting national claims. The possibility of any strong umbilical link between Almayer and his creator seems less likely, although even Almayer may function as a mockingly distorted mirror image, reflecting both upon the quixotic strains of the youthful Conrad and the obsessive 'hallucination' to which the beginning writer was devoting himself.

Watt's admirable survey (1980: 41–55) of the formative literary influences upon the novel tends to suggest the picture of a writer richly poised on the borderlines between varying national literary traditions as well as genres. Two major French novelists, Gustave *Flaubert and Guy de *Maupassant, figure centrally in Watt's account of early influences, leading him to speak of Almayer as 'a Borneo Bovary' (51) and of Conrad as subject to the powerful technical influence of Maupassant. But along with these, other important models and inheritances can be detected in Conrad's reworking of the conventions of French exotic literature (as found in the fiction of Pierre Loti) and the tradition of Stevensonian romance. In addition, Watt's analogies between Conrad and Thomas Hardy suggest a literary kinship that has not been sufficiently explored. More mundanely, *Almayer's Folly* resonates with the kind of detail that Conrad was in the habit of picking up from his prodigious leisure *reading—travel journals, popular magazine stories, newspapers, and semi-scientific accounts of natural life and customs in the Malay Archipelago. With his astonishingly retentive memory, he was already in 1889 becoming a writer upon whom no experience was lost.

On its publication in 1895, reviews were generally as favourable as any beginning writer could hope for and must have left Conrad with the feeling that he could find a commercial niche in the English literary market. Flatteringly, some early reviewers chose to stress the measure of his difference from English writers and invoked a range of French authors—Victor Hugo, Pierre Loti, and Émile *Zola among others. But a majority of reviewers categorized *Almayer's Folly* as a 'romance' or novel of 'local colour' by virtue of its Eastern location, exotic atmosphere, and love interest, linking it with the work of Robert Louis *Stevenson and Rudyard *Kipling. Interestingly, a small group of reviewers also rightly realized that this was a 'romance' with marked differences from its kind: it had no happy ending, was not overcoloured, and had 'no place in the prevalent fiction of the hour' (*CCH*, 60). Impressionistic though their judgements are, the more perceptive of these first reviews offered later critics a basis upon which to build a more systematic account of the novel's teasingly oblique relation to earlier semi-popular fictional traditions as well as its more modern character as a novel of predicament.

The traditional equation of romance with youth and the fulfilment of youthful dream is, in *Almayer's Folly*, severely complicated by Conrad's inclusion of what the traditional form can rarely accommodate—a foolish, middle-aged dreamer who is about to experience the utter ruination of a lifetime's wishful fantasy. Indeed, in Almayer's dream at the very beginning of the narrative one of the main motivating

urges of the exotic novel—the flight from metropolitan Europe to the liberating freshness of the mysterious East—is immediately reversed. His is an exhausted yearning for the opposite, a release from the prison-like Bornean jungle to *Amsterdam. Moreover, the spectacle of the middle-aged Almayer's absorption in his 'dream' immediately raises questions rarely asked in late Victorian romances: notably, questions about the neurotic origins of the fantasy habit and the persistent use of dreams as a compensatory drug-like fiction by which to obliterate the unwelcome present. The ways in which *Almayer's Folly* demystifies and reverses the ends of traditional exotic romance and develops into a novel *about* the dangerously ambiguous marriage of adventure, commercial adventurism, and invasive Western empire-building has preoccupied a number of critics. Hunter's chapter on 'Conrad and Adventure' (1982), 124–52, offers a stimulating study of how, in Conrad's novels, the conventions of popular adventure are contaminated by evidence of 'deformed imperialism' (130) and of imperialism as 'institutionalized adventurism' (133). His work is complemented by White's full-length study both of the romance writers whom Conrad is likely to have read and his subversive treatment of their assumptions in his fiction from *Almayer's Folly* to 'Heart of Darkness'.

However insular in its assumptions, Victorian exotic and adventure fiction had served to introduce metropolitan British readers to remote countries and different races. During the period's last two decades, however, these popular kinds inevitably became involved with the imperial adventure and yielded a thriving body of 'naïve' colonial literature (as represented by the works of G. A. Henty, H. Rider Haggard, and Captain Mayne Reid), in which the mission of the British Empire itself furnished patriotic adventure, heroic possibilities, and recurring tests upon manhood. By contrast, Conrad's early Malay fiction belongs to a period when the imperial mission fell increasingly under suspicion and when the very term 'imperialism' was to acquire its present pejorative meanings. As many of Conrad's critics have attempted to show, even his earliest fiction, written at a time when he was probably not so nervously sensitive to the susceptibilities of English readers, seems crucial in forging a passage from the 'naïve' tradition of British Empire fiction to a new kind of sceptical and interrogative colonial novel. Significantly, too, on its publication in 1895, *Almayer's Folly* found a newly inaugurated publishing venture suited to its more serious aims: T. Fisher Unwin's 'Colonial Library' (later the Overseas Library), whose prospectus envisaged a series with 'no pretence at Imperial drum beating' and promised a more sceptical measuring of the debits and credits of European colonialism through a depiction of 'the actual life of the English immigrants, travellers, traders, officers, overseas away among foreign and native races, black or white' (quoted in Jefferson, 46).

The preface Conrad wrote immediately after finishing the novel is an important indicator of the fledgling writer's sense of high mission. In it, he begins by tilting ironically at the popular conventions shaping both 'naïve' colonial literature and exotic romance. But Conrad's more positive purpose is to position his own attitudes in the novel well apart from the prevailing Eurocentric responses to the supposed 'inferiority' of non-European peoples. As David Leon Higdon explains in 'The Text and Context of Conrad's First Critical Essay', *Polish Review*, 20 (1975), 97–105, the anonymous 'lady'-critic upbraided by Conrad in the preface was Alice Meynell, a well-known poet and critic of the 1890s, who, in an essay called 'Decivilised' (1891; reprinted in Knowles 1995: 190–2), had scornfully dismissed colonial literature and other forms of 'decivilised' art for their connection with degraded and outlandish subjects that departed from a civilized English norm. Echoing Matthew Arnold's concern for cultural continuity and giving voice to topical fears of degeneration, Meynell represented herself as speaking for the 'well-born' assailed by the vulgar, the metropolitan endangered by the provin-

cial, and for the ethnocentric view that regards all non-Europeans as permanently trapped at a lower stage in the history of human development. In his response, Conrad attacks all those who believe that in non-European countries 'all joy is a yell and a war dance, all pathos is a howl and a ghastly grin of filed teeth'. Teasingly paralleling life in London and Borneo, he goes on to assert the essential unity between Europeans and 'that humanity so far away': 'I am content to sympathize with common mortals, no matter where they live; in houses or in tents, in the streets under a fog, or in the forests behind the dark line of dismal mangroves' ('Author's Note', pp. vii, viii).

As several critics have shown, *Almayer's Folly* is in practice more mobile, wavering, and self-challenging in its attitudes to non-European peoples than its preface might imply. If, in his preface, Conrad draws a number of cross-cultural similitudes between 'here' (Europe) and 'there' (Borneo), the novel often reverses that pattern and offers Malay characters the opportunity to speak of 'here' (Borneo) in contrast to 'there' (Europe). In doing so, the novel admits a wide field of conflicting cultural, religious, and linguistic codes that increasingly vie with each other as alternative ways of seeing and feeling. These alternatives and cross-cultural mobilities are discussed in Lloyd Fernando's 'Conrad's Eastern Expatriates: A New Version of his Outcasts' *PMLA*, 91 (1976), 78–90; Todd G. Willy's '*Almayer's Folly* and the Imperatives of Conradian Atavism', *Conradiana*, 24 (1992), 3–20; and Allan H. Simmons's '"Conflicting Impulses": Focalization and the Presentation of Culture in *Almayer's Folly*', *Conradiana*, 29 (1997), 163–72, which argues that 'the narrating voice, which commences by underscoring the voice of the Occidental coloniser, is gradually infiltrated by the voices of the colonised' and becomes 'culturally polyphonic' (170).

Almayer's Folly is not, however, a novel whose sense of the problematic is shaped by racial determinants alone, important though these are. Indeed, its strenuous global sense of breakdown and predicament is the very thing that most characterizes it as a novel of the 1890s. The novel's general landscape is a characteristically epochal one: it registers a sense of the Bornean natural world as remorselessly Darwinian and therefore essentially impersonal and alien to merely human hopes; on the other hand, the nearer scene as associated with Almayer appears to resemble a shrinking prison-house or a wasteland characterized by squalid neglect, premature ageing, and impotence. Its pervading mood is, in other words, that of the *fin de siècle*, a mood prompted by the late Victorian sense of itself as 'Between two worlds | One dead, the other powerless to be born' (Matthew Arnold). Paul Wiley's early, but still lively study sees Almayer as belonging to a group of hermit-figures who, following upon the example of Flaubert's *La Tentation de Saint Antoine* (1874), people late 19th-century literature (*Conrad's Measure of Man* (Madison: University of Wisconsin Press, 1954), 28–34); while Johnson also regards Almayer's predicament as a characteristically epochal one, 'the *mal du siècle*: paralysis of will' (9). In delineating the philosophical postulates that shape Almayer's predicament and world, several later critics have drawn upon the more modern terms of Sartrean existentialism as being the most appropriate to the central figure's confrontation with *le néant*.

There are several helpful studies of the novel's narrative aspects, techniques, and styles, of which Watt's is the most wide-ranging (1980: 55–67). Others cover more specific areas such as free indirect speech (Hawthorn 1990: 2–9), the presence of a 'covert plot' (Watts 1984: 47–53), *delayed decoding and the effects of an enforced 'backward' reading of events (Knowles 1995: pp. xxxvi–xli), and perspective and relativism (Berthoud 1992: pp. xxiv–xxx). To these may also be added Allan H. Simmons's 'Ambiguity as Meaning: The Subversion of Suspense in *Almayer's Folly*', *The Conradian*, 14 (1989), 1–18, and Claude Maisonnat's 'Discursive Deception and the Quest for Meaning in *Almayer's Folly*', in Carabine *et al.* (eds.) 1992: 3–20. The manuscript of the novel is held at the Rosenbach Museum and Library, Philadelphia, and its final corrected typescript at the Harry Ransom Humanities Research Center, University of Texas at Austin.

'Alphonse Daudet'. Begun on 18 January 1898 and finished the next day, this obituary tribute to the French novelist who had died the previous month was, according to G. *Jean-Aubry, written in response to a derogatory article about *Daudet that had appeared in a London journal. Conrad's first exercise in literary appreciation, the essay, initially sent to the *New Review* which apparently rejected it, was published in *Outlook*, 1 (9 April 1898), 294–5. It was collected in revised form in *Notes on Life and Letters*. Revealing an affectionate familiarity with a wide range of Daudet's works, Conrad pays generous tribute to qualities of spontaneity, tolerance, honesty, and freedom from narrow theories that had made the French writer one of his early enthusiasms and led him to contemplate sending a copy of his first novel, *Almayer's Folly*, to Daudet. At the same time, the essay implicitly explains why that early enthusiasm was tempered: however appealing Daudet's humanity may have been, he was 'not an artist', and 'it is sometimes very hard to forgive him the dotted i's, the pointing finger, this making plain of obvious mysteries' (24). The manuscript and a corrected typescript are held at the Beinecke Rare Book and Manuscript Library, Yale University.

America. Although Conrad spent little time in the New World, American settings and characters figure importantly in his works, and American *publishers played a major role in establishing his international reputation. His first deep-water voyages in 1874 and 1875 were to Martinique and Haiti in the *Caribbean, and he may possibly have paid a brief visit to the coast of South America. He was an avid reader of Latin American histories and memoirs, and echoes of his transatlantic experiences and *readings can be found in many of his works: *Romance* is largely set in Jamaica; *Costaguana, the imaginary setting of

Nostromo, is based loosely on Colombia; 'Gaspar Ruiz' is set in the mountains of Chile; and the villains of *Victory* are based on characters he encountered in the Caribbean. An American soldier-of-fortune named Blunt was a member of the *Tremolino* 'syndicate' described in *A Personal Record* and dramatized in *The Arrow of Gold*; Conrad would later allege, to escape the shame of a failed *suicide attempt, that he had fought and lost a romantic duel with him. Conrad's sailing career never took him to North America, but among the various money-making schemes that he proposed to his uncle and guardian Tadeusz *Bobrowski was one in June 1880 which apparently involved a plan to emigrate to the United States and enter the service of an American politician (*CPB*, 65). In his letters to R. B. Cunninghame *Graham, Conrad was critical of American involvement in the *Spanish-American War, writing 'By all means Viva l'España!!!!' (*CL*, ii. 60) and 'If one could set the States & Germany by the ears! That would be *real fine*' (*CL*, ii. 81). At the same time, he praised the skill of the American navy to Cora Crane, whose husband *Stephen was covering the war in the Caribbean, and congratulated her 'on the success of American arms' (*CL*, ii. 73). Watts (*LCG*, 39) suggests that Conrad's anti-American sentiments may have been among the motives that led him to write *Nostromo*. Conrad praised Cunninghame Graham's study of *Hernando de Soto* (1903), and expressed his desire to 'forget all about our modern Conquistadores', including 'the Yankee Conquistadores in Panama' (*CL*, iii. 101–2).

As Richard *Curle noted, 'Conrad's work, once it was discovered in America, was discovered much more enthusiastically than in England' (*LTY*, 203). After years of near-penury and humiliating requests for loans and advances, Conrad was first brought to the attention of a wider American public by a campaign to promote the serialization of *Chance* in the *New York Herald*. Thanks to his American readers, he was at last able to pay off his substantial debts and achieve financial security. The sale of *film rights to an American company in 1919 made it possible for him to move to Oswalds, the last and grandest of his *homes. The *letters of his later years frequently contain patronizing and supercilious remarks about American cultural *naïveté*, mixed with wry comments about the dazzling immensity of American wealth. The first collector of Conrad's *manuscripts was a prosperous New York lawyer, John *Quinn, and most of Conrad's literary manuscripts are held in American university libraries and archival collections.

Not until the end of his career, in May 1923, did Conrad visit the United States at the invitation of his American publisher, F. N. *Doubleday. Conrad addressed Doubleday employees in Garden City, New York, and delivered a rare public lecture at the Manhattan home of Mrs Curtiss James. He briefly toured New England, visiting the campuses of both Yale and Harvard Universities. By that time, he was at the height of his popularity, was frequently *interviewed, and his visit was widely reported in the American press. For a brief account of this trip, see William V. Costanzo, 'Conrad's American Visit', *Conradiana*, 13 (1981), 7–18; for an anthology of Conrad's American interviews, see *JCIR*, 175–201.

Americans figure frequently in Conrad's works, often as villainous stereotypes, like the racist Yankee trader in *The Rescue* who sells Tom *Lingard arms and ammunition for his expedition to Wajo, or the lanky Yankee deserter in Gentleman *Brown's gang in *Lord Jim*. Holroyd, the San Francisco financier who provides Charles *Gould with capital for his silver mine, is a memorable caricature of the American capitalist: 'Time itself has got to wait on the greatest country in the whole of God's Universe . . . We shall run the world's business whether the world likes it or not. The world can't help it—and neither can we, I guess!' (*Nostromo*, 77). At the other end of the social scale, the *Professor in *The Secret Agent* may also be an American, as Berthoud (1978: 134) has assumed. The nihilistic bomb-maker's comments to Tom Ossipon do indicate some experience of American attitudes: 'They have more character over there, and their character is essentially anarchistic. Fertile ground for us, the States—very good ground. The great Republic has the root of the destructive matter in her. The collective temperament is lawless. Excellent' (72).

Conrad's feelings about America and Americans are surveyed by Richard Curle in 'Conrad's Fame in America' (*LTY*, 202–15). A compendious account of Conrad's influence on American culture is provided by Robert Secor and Debra Moddelmog in *Joseph Conrad and American Writers: A Bibliographical Study of Affinities, Influences, and Relations* (Westport, Conn.: Greenwood, 1985).

Amsterdam, the capital and largest city of the Netherlands, had a population of some 379,000 in January 1887, when Conrad arrived from *London to serve as chief mate of the barque *Highland Forest*. He found the ship moored on the Oostelijke Handelskade, a quay in the eastern harbour, waiting to load a mixed but otherwise unknown cargo bound for Semarang and Surabaya in the *Netherlands East Indies. As chief mate, Conrad was responsible for the loading of the ship, but the arrival of the cargo was delayed because some inland waterways were frozen over. In the absence of the captain (who had retired and gone home) and the crew (who had been paid and dismissed), Conrad was thus forced to endure the icy cold of his iron-hulled ship for weeks and to load the cargo piecemeal as it arrived. A typescript memoir by G. F. W. *Hope recounts that Conrad sent regular and detailed reports to the owners in London, who were very pleased with his diligence.

Conrad's impressions of Amsterdam are recorded in 'The Weight of the Burden', a section of *The Mirror of the Sea* which Ford Madox *Ford took down from Conrad's dictation in 1904. Conrad chiefly recalled his own discomfort in the bitter cold, although in fact the average temperature during Conrad's time in the city was slightly above freezing and not unusually

cold for Amsterdam in winter. He described his trips into the centre of town by horse-drawn tram to drink coffee and warm himself in the spacious, brightly lit café of the Wintertuin (Winter Garden) of the Grand Hotel Krasnapolsky on Dam Square. There he wrote letters to the ship's owners in Glasgow, who urged him to visit the charterers and insist that the cargo be delivered promptly. Accordingly, he called on a Mr Hudig, who was probably Jan Hudig (1840–1927), a robust member of a well-known Rotterdam shipping family, who had returned from the Netherlands East Indies to become director of the Koloniale Bank, with offices at Nieuwe Doelenstraat 4 (on the present site of the Hôtel de l'Europe).

In due course, the cargo was loaded, the ship's new captain, John McWhir, arrived, and the *Highland Forest* left Amsterdam on 18 February 1887. It soon became evident that Conrad's careful loading had brought the ship's centre of gravity down too low, so that it pitched and rolled severely during the entire four-month voyage out to *Java. Two crew members died on the voyage, and Conrad was injured by a falling spar and forced to leave the ship in Semarang to enter a hospital in *Singapore, an incident reflected in chapter 2 of *Lord Jim*. In the 1965 film version of the novel, *Stein receives a letter from Amsterdam denying Jim a commission as Stein's representative in *Patusan.

Amsterdam, where the idea of joint shares was first developed and the first stock market established, was the commercial and administrative base for colonial exploitation of the Netherlands East Indies, and in Conrad's novels the city symbolizes Dutch power in the Far East. The opening chapter of *Victory* mentions the liquidation of the Tropical Belt Coal Company 'in London and Amsterdam' (5). The city is also the home of *Almayer's mother, who 'from the depths of her long easy-chair bewailed the lost glories of Amsterdam, where she had been brought up, and of her position as the daughter of a cigar dealer there' (5). The city that Conrad remembered as an 'arctic wasteland' becomes for Almayer the 'earthly paradise of his dreams, where . . . he would pass the evening of his days in inexpressible splendour' (10).

For more detailed information, see G. J. Resink, 'Conrads Hudigs', *Bijdragen tot de Taal-, Land- en Volkenkunde,* 128 (1972), 358–63, and Gene M. Moore's illustrated article 'Conrad in Amsterdam' reprinted in Moore (ed.) 1992: 97–124. A typescript copy of the memoirs of the 'real' Mr Hudig, *Herinneringen door Jan Hudig Dzn.* (Hilversum, 1918), is held in the Manuscript Collection of the Royal Institute of Linguistics and Anthropology in Leiden.

'Amy Foster'. This 12,500-word story was composed in a three-week break during the final stages of Conrad's joint work with Ford Madox *Ford on *Romance* in 1901. The only one of Conrad's stories 'written entirely out of doors' (*CL*, v. 89) during an especially fine period of weather in late May–early June, the tale had working titles of 'The Castaway' and 'The Husband' (the title on its manuscript). It was first published in the *Illustrated London News* (December 1901) and later collected in the *Typhoon* volume.

The story's events are narrated by Dr Kennedy, the village doctor in Colebrook, *Kent, who tells a visiting friend of a 'simply tragic' episode in the village's history which began when Yanko *Goorall, a Pole from the Eastern Carpathians, left his homeland in Austrian *Poland to emigrate to America. During the stormy sea passage from Hamburg, the vessel capsized and sank, leaving Yanko, the sole survivor, to be washed ashore on a remote part of the Kent coast. During his first days in Colebrook, he is treated with universal suspicion by the provincial community who label him 'a hairy sort of gipsy fellow' (118), an 'escaped lunatic' (120), or a 'dangerous maniac' (121). The only person to make him welcome is a simple village girl, Amy Foster, whom he eventually marries. But ethnic and linguistic differences reappear in their domestic life when Amy responds negatively to her husband's foreignness and objects to his teaching their baby boy to speak Polish. Yanko's tragic death turns upon a linguistic misunderstanding when, seriously ill and feverish, he makes a plea for water in his native Polish tongue. His wife, believing him to be a serious threat, flees their home and leaves him to die alone.

Conrad's only tale about *England with a Pole as its central character, 'Amy Foster' has often been regarded, especially by Polish readers, as the Anglo-Polish Conrad's most directly autobiographical work, embodying his own residual feelings of insecurity and alienation in the country of his adoption. However, such interpretations should be treated with caution. In her study of 'Conrad's Revisions to "Amy Foster"', *Conradiana,* 20 (1988), 181–93, Gail Fraser draws upon manuscript evidence to show that while Conrad may have originally identified with Yanko's plight, he subsequently took pains to expunge obvious signs of identification in order to secure greater personal detachment and aesthetic distance in a work that is—to use Watt's fine formulation—'characteristically personal without being autobiographical' (1980: 93). Additionally, many of the sources for 'Amy Foster' belong as much to Conrad's reading as to his personal experiences. The primary germinating hint for the tale was an anecdote in Ford Madox Ford's *The Cinque Ports: A Historical and Descriptive Record* (Blackwood, 1900), concerning the 'tragic' story of a German castaway who arrives destitute in Romney Marshes, a remote coastal region in southwest Kent: 'He had nothing, no clothes, no food; he came ashore on a winter's night. . . . He knocked at doors, tried to make himself understood. The Marsh people thought him either a lunatic or a supernatural visitor. . . . He got the name of Mad Jack. Knowing nothing of the country, nothing of the language, he could neither ask his way nor read the names on signposts, and even if he read them, they meant nothing to him' (163). Other sources have been detected in Victor Hugo's *Les Travailleurs de la mer* (1866), Gustave *Flaubert's 'Un cœur simple' (1877), and Stephen *Crane's 'The Monster' (1899).

The central idea of 'Amy Foster' was, according to Conrad, 'the essential difference of the races' (*CL*, ii. 402). A vivid preoccupation with cultural and racial differences from his early Malay fiction is thus replayed, but with the significant difference that England itself, as seen through the experiences of the castaway and mediated by Dr Kennedy, becomes 'an undiscovered country' (112). Many of the most valuable studies of the story have addressed the ways in which Conrad's position as a social and cultural outsider in the country of his adoption allowed him a distinctively off-centre position as a writer. One version of that position can be detected in the status of Dr Kennedy who, though an Englishman, is both an insider and an outsider in the Colebrook community: combining many of the qualities of *Marlow and *Stein, he has spent many years abroad 'in the days when there were continents with unexplored interiors' (106) and so brings to events in Colebrook a sympathetically democratic vision. But a more dramatic version of the outsider's position is, of course, developed through Yanko, 'the lost stranger' (113), and his apprehension of England as both alien and otherworldly. The tale is remarkable for the effects of defamiliarization created through Yanko's sense of the commonplace as frighteningly unfamiliar, with the result that provincial Kent emerges in the form of a Kafkaesque nightmare: 'He could talk to no one, and had no hope of ever understanding anybody. It was as if these had been the faces of people from the other world—dead people.' Yanko's life, adds the narrator, was 'over-shadowed, oppressed, by the everyday material appearances, as if by the visions of nightmare' (129). Richard Ruppel points to a related source of defamiliarization in his suggestion that 'Amy Foster' may be seen as a parodic inversion of the usual late Victorian colonial story in which the Englishman travels abroad to confront unfamiliar peoples. In Conrad's tale, there is a dramatic upturning of these familiar conventions, since in this instance the isolated castaway arrives in Kent to be confronted by strange and threatening 'natives'

who pursue and hunt him like a wild animal and collectively contribute to his death (see 'Yanko Goorall in the Heart of Darkness: "Amy Foster" as Colonialist Text', *Conradiana*, 28 (1996), 126–32). The manuscript, dated 18 June 1901, is held at the Beinecke Rare Book and Manuscript Library, Yale University.

anarchism. In *Lord Jim*, *Stein famously advocates that *Jim 'immerse' himself in 'the destructive element' (214). Conrad's evident fascination with the forces that simultaneously define and destroy his individual characters made it inevitable that, at some stage, he would find subject matter in the social and political expression of these forces, anarchism. *The Secret Agent* (1907) is the result of this fascination, a novel whose concern is 'a mankind always so tragically eager for self-destruction' ('Author's Note', p. ix). Conrad's source, an actual event, took place on 15 February 1894, when a French anarchist named Martial Bourdin was killed by his own bomb while apparently attempting to blow up the *Greenwich Royal Observatory. The closing decades of the 19th century saw a spate of such bombings in *London and other major cities. For instance, in London in 1884, terrorist plots were foiled by the discovery of bombs at Charing Cross, Paddington, and Ludgate Hill Stations, and in Trafalgar Square, but there were explosions at Victoria Station, the Junior Carlton Club, Scotland Yard, and London Bridge. Some of these were the work of Fenians, while others belonged to the growing movement for international anarchism, dedicated to ushering in a new world order by destroying the old through 'creative' violence. In 1840, in his book *What is Property?* (which contained the celebrated claim: 'Property is theft'), Pierre-Joseph Proudhon proudly proclaimed: 'I am an anarchist!' He went on to reject authority in the creation of social order: 'Anarchy—the absence of a master, of a sovereign—such is the form of government to which we are every day approximating.' This idea links Proudhon with later anarchists like Mikhail Bakunin and Prince Peter

Kropotkin. According to Sherry, Michaelis in *The Secret Agent* resembles the former in physique and the latter in ideas (*CWW*, 269–73).

In his 'Author's Note' to *The Secret Agent*, Conrad commented that 'a visitor from America informed me that all sorts of revolutionary refugees in New York would have it that the book was written by somebody who knew a lot about them. This seemed to me a very high compliment, considering that, as a matter of hard fact, I had seen even less of their kind than the omniscient friend who gave me the first suggestion for the novel.' Such humility needs to be tempered with Conrad's professionalism as a writer, for, as he says in the same passage: 'I was simply attending to my business. In the matter of all my books I have always attended to my business' (p. xiv). Despite his protestations of ignorance, Conrad chose anarchism as his subject for 'The Informer', 'An Anarchist', and *The Secret Agent*. The main source for Conrad's information on this subject was his friend and collaborator Ford Madox *Ford, who is the 'omniscient friend' of the 'Author's Note' and who elsewhere claimed to know 'a great many anarchists of the Goodge Street group, as well as a great many of the police who watched them' (*JCPR*, 231).

Subtle points of connection between the three anarchist tales suggest that their sources can all be traced back to Ford. For instance, in 'The Informer', anarchist propaganda is said to be produced in the basement of a house in Hermione Street. In actuality, Ford's precocious teenage cousins Olive, Helen, and Arthur Rossetti started an anarchist magazine called *The Torch*, which they sold in Hyde Park, using a printing press in the basement of their home. Sherry suggests that the character of the *Professor in 'The Informer'—a precursor of his namesake in *The Secret Agent*—is modelled upon Arthur Rossetti (*CWW*, 215). In 'An Anarchist', Paul's escape from the penal settlement on St Joseph's Island in French Guyana is based upon an actual mutiny on the island on 21 October 1894, which was widely reported

in anarchist literature, including *The Torch*, which Conrad identifies by name as one of the 'obscure newspapers, badly printed, with . . . rousing titles' in Adolf *Verloc's shop on the opening page of *The Secret Agent*. In 'The Informer' and 'An Anarchist', Conrad experimented with ideas that he would later elaborate in *The Secret Agent*. 'The Informer' attacks what Mr X calls 'an idle and selfish class' that 'loves to see mischief being made, even if it is made at its own expense' (*A Set of Six*, 78). This class thus includes not only the young Lady Amateur, who 'had acquired all the appropriate gestures of revolutionary convictions' (81), but also the narrator's Parisian friend, the collector of acquaintances. Aptly subtitled 'An Ironic Tale', 'The Informer' exposes the destructive contradiction at the heart of anarchism: when the anarchists are raided, it is by other anarchists, and when Severin is described as a 'genius amongst betrayers' (93), he *is* so, but in relation to the anarchists themselves. (This deceit will find an echo in Verloc's role as informer in *The Secret Agent*.) By contrast, 'An Anarchist', subtitled 'A Desperate Tale', offers a portrait of the anarchist as humanist. But while Conrad's presentation of Paul as the victim of society neatly inverts the usual image of society as victim of the anarchist, sympathy is then shifted away from Paul as he recounts his cold-blooded killing of Simon and Mafile. The image of society anarchically willing its own ruin in these tales finds its perfect expression in *The Secret Agent* where the Professor wanders around London with a bomb in his pocket.

In 'A Familiar Preface', Conrad writes: 'The revolutionary spirit is mighty convenient in this, that it frees one from all scruples as regards ideas. Its hard, absolute optimism is repulsive to my mind by the menace of fanaticism and intolerance it contains' (*A Personal Record*, pp. xix–xxi). Conrad's boyhood in *Poland had left him with a distrust of revolution and revolutionary ideology that can at times make him seem very conservative indeed. For instance, commenting upon the 1885 election in which the Conservatives had suffered setbacks, he says: 'the International

Socialist Association are triumphant, and every disreputable ragamuffin in Europe feels that the day of universal brotherhood, despoliation and disorder is coming apace, and nurses day-dreams of well-plenished pockets amongst the ruin of all that is respectable, venerable and holy. . . . England was the only barrier to the pressure of infernal doctrines born in continental backslums. Now, there is nothing!' (*CL*, i. 16). But, as Watts points out, this attitude was by no means unusual: the memory of the French Revolution lingered over the 19th century and 'numerous British writers . . . feared that democratic pressures might result in "mobocracy" and violent chaos' (1993: 56). Against this, one needs to set Conrad's close friendship with the pioneer socialist R. B. Cunninghame *Graham, who, from 1888 onwards, helped to found Britain's first Labour Party. Writing to Graham in February 1899, Conrad's cynical view is that society serves to restrain the *naturally* anarchic tendencies of mankind which, in their extreme form, are 'justifiable': 'Man is a vicious animal. His viciousness must be organised. Crime is a necessary condition of organised existence. Society is fundamentally criminal—or it would not exist. Selfishness preserves everything—absolutely everything—everything we hate and everything we love. And everything holds together. That is why I respect the extreme anarchists.—"I hope for general extermination". Very well. It's justifiable and, moreover, it is plain' (*CL*, ii. 160).

In *The Secret Agent*, Conrad presents the anarchists as grotesques, parasitic, and physically or temperamentally unfitted for decent work. Their apparent desire to destroy society coexists with their dependence upon the charity and support of the women in their lives: Michaelis depends upon his 'Lady Patroness', Yundt on an 'indomitable snarling old witch', and Ossipon on each young woman he seduces (104, 52). Hardly surprisingly, Conrad says of his anarchists in a letter to Graham: 'All these people are not revolutionaries—they are shams' (*CL*, iii. 491). Numerous critics have demonstrated that Conrad's an-

archists exhibit traits identified by the 19th-century criminologist Cesare *Lombroso, who classified anarchists as degenerates. Conrad, however, goes on to make a different claim for the Professor: 'And as regards the Professor I did not intend to make him despicable. He is incorruptible at any rate. . . . At the worst he is a megalomaniac of an extreme type. And every extremist is respectable' (*CL*, iii. 491). The rest of the anarchists talk about political action, but the Professor facilitates it by providing the explosive. He is referred to as the 'perfect anarchist' (95). As Hawthorn says: 'It is a measure of the society with which Conrad is concerned that the two most completely sincere characters in the novel are the Professor and Stevie—a megalomaniac and a half-wit' (1979: 83). The novel provides a blanket attack on English society, examining it from top to bottom, from Sir Ethelred to the cabman, and stressing the parallels between the different social groups to a degree that the anarchists 'are treated as *symptomatic* of the society in which they are resident, rather than as worrying *exceptions* to its norms' (ibid. 82). While Conrad's decision to base the novel on a *failed* terrorist plot to blow up the Greenwich Observatory (and the sense of scientific order it represents) serves to ridicule the anarchists, this sphere of public anarchism is also extended into the private world of the Verlocs' marriage. As the Assistant Commissioner says: 'From a certain point of view we are here in the presence of a domestic drama' (222). Thus, in his most extended treatment of the subject, anarchism served Conrad as a metaphor for the 'destructive element' within which our social existence immerses us. See also Carol Vanderveer Hamilton, 'Revolution from Within: Conrad's Natural Anarchists', *The Conradian*, 18: 2 (1994), 31–48, and Jacques Berthoud's '*The Secret Agent*', in Stape (ed.) 1996: 100–21.   AHS

'Anarchist, An'. This story of a life ruined by a misunderstanding was completed in December 1905, immediately before 'The Informer'. As Conrad told John *Galsworthy, 'I write these stories because they bring more money than the sea papers' (*CL*, iii. 300). Some 8,000 words in length, 'An Anarchist' was *serialized in *Harper's Magazine* in August 1906 (illustrated by Thornton Oakley) and was included as the fourth of the six stories in *A Set of Six* (1908), with the added subtitle of 'A Desperate Tale'.

The story of the 'anarchist' is told by an itinerant lepidopterist who is visiting the Marañon Estancia, a remote cattle estate on an island in the estuary of a South American river. The narrator first hears of the 'anarchist' from Mr Harry Gee, the boorish and overbearing manager of the BOS Company Ltd., manufacturers of meat-extract products, who boasts of how he found an escaped convict (whom he nicknames 'Crocodile') on the beach and employs him to operate the company's derelict steam-launch. Harry Gee ruthlessly exploits the man he calls a 'citizen anarchist from Barcelona' (139), and spreads the rumour of his anarchism so that he will be unable to leave the island to find work elsewhere. Then, in a double narrative frame typical of the manner of Guy de *Maupassant, the narrator learns at first hand the 'true' story of Paul, the engineer. An honest Parisian workman, one of many with 'warm hearts and weak heads' (158), Paul was celebrating his 25th birthday with friends when anarchists at an adjoining table fuelled his drunken indignation at the world's injustice and led him to shout anarchist slogans. The revellers were arrested, and on his release from jail, Paul found that his reputation as an anarchist made it impossible for him to return to work. He again fell in with anarchists, took part in an attempted bank robbery, and was sentenced to prison on St Joseph's Island (French Guyana). During a prison revolt he found a loaded revolver and a small row-boat, and was joined by two anarchist companions, who were unaware that he was armed. He forced them to row out into the shipping lanes, and when a rescue vessel came into view, he shot them and threw their bodies overboard. 'I deny nothing!' is Paul's motto, although no one suspects that he is guilty of taking such dire vengeance on those who had wrecked his life.

Conrad's first reference to 'An Anarchist' occurs in a letter to John Galsworthy of 29 December 1905, while he was writing 'The Informer' (*CL*, iii. 300). In subsequent letters Conrad often mentioned the stories together, and both were serialized in *Harper's Magazine*.

Reviewing *A Set of Six*, W. L. Courtney praised 'An Anarchist' as one of three 'fine achievements' in the volume, and Edward *Garnett called it 'a gem of Conrad's art . . . simply and ironically profound' (*CCH*, 217, 222). Sherry traces the historical background of the story to an actual convict mutiny on St Joseph's Island on 21 October 1894, in which a number of convicts, including one named Simon and another called Biscuit, went to their deaths shouting 'Vive l'anarchie!' The incident was reported briefly in anarchist journals like *The Torch*, which was published by Ford Madox *Ford's young Rossetti cousins and could be purchased in *Verloc's shop in *The Secret Agent* (*CWW*, 219–27). Hervouet (95–7) describes the similarities between 'An Anarchist' and Anatole *France's story 'Crainquebille', which Conrad had praised in a review written in July 1904 and later included in *Notes on Life and Letters*. In 'The Lepidopterist's Revenge: Theme and Structure in Conrad's "An Anarchist"', *Studies in Short Fiction*, 8 (1971), 330–4, Daniel R. Schwarz argues that the narrator, frustrated by the abuse he receives from Harry Gee, tells the story of Paul as a way of taking revenge. The story is also a bitter satire of capitalism and advertising, and the use of language in this political context is examined by Jennifer Shaddock in 'Hanging a Dog: The Politics of Naming in "An Anarchist"', *Conradiana*, 26 (1994), 56–69. In 'Revolution from Within: Conrad's Natural Anarchists', *The Conradian*, 18: 2 (1994), 31–48, Carol Vanderveer Hamilton discusses the story in the context of Conrad's attitude towards *anarchism in general, and notes similarities between the moral attitudes of Paul and *Stevie in *The Secret Agent*. A stylometric analysis of the various voices in the story provides the basis of

Michael A. Lucas's 'Stylistic Variation in "An Anarchist"', *Conradiana*, 28 (1996), 86–95.

Conrad sold the first part of the manuscript of 'An Anarchist' to John *Quinn in 1913 (*CL*, v. 230, 255), but could not locate the remainder until 1920 (letter to Quinn, 2 March 1920). Both portions, together nearly complete, are at the Huntington Library, San Marino, California.

'Anatole France I. *Crainquebille*'. Written at Edward *Garnett's request at a time when Conrad was finishing *Nostromo*, this brief paper was composed intermittently over three days and completed on 6 July 1904. It was published in the *Speaker*, 10 (16 July 1904), 359–61, and later revised for *Notes on Life and Letters*. Although Conrad had read some of *France's work in the 1890s, his more tenacious admiration for the 'Prince of Prose' dates from the period 1903–4, and this review of France's 1904 collection of stories was the first public expression of his respect. By this time, he had come to admire the intellectual quality of France's work—'the proceedings of his thought compel our . . . admiration' (39–40)—along with its mixture of humane compassion, acerbic scepticism, and philosophic Pyrrhonism. Conrad's equanimity falters only at the point where he confronts the force of France's committed socialism, although he avers that even here France's large-heartedness leads him to triumph over 'the stupidity of the dogma and the unlovely form of the ideal' (38). A heavily rewritten and corrected typescript of the essay is held at the Beinecke Rare Book and Manuscript Library, Yale University.

'Anatole France II. *L'Île des Pingouins*'. Conrad's second review of *France's work—in this case of his celebrated fable of modern French history (1908)—was written in November 1908 in response to Ford Madox *Ford's last-minute appeal for copy to fill the first number of a journal he was in the process of launching. It appeared in the *English Review*, 1 (December 1908), 188–90, and was later revised for *Notes on Life and Letters*.

Conrad's quickly written *causerie* celebrates 'a mind marvellously incisive in its scepticism, and a heart that, of all contemporary hearts gifted with a voice, contains the greatest treasure of charitable irony'. He also expresses his admiration for the four-volume *La Vie littéraire* (1888–92), a collection of France's occasional essays 'describing the adventures of a choice soul amongst masterpieces' (41), and a work often echoed by Conrad in his own writings. No pre-publication documents are known.

Anderson, Jane Foster (*c.*1888–?), journalist and socialite, was introduced to the Conrads in April 1916. Born in Atlanta, Georgia, Jane Anderson spent much of her early life in remote desert towns in Arizona, from where she emerged as a vivaciously handsome 'Southern belle who defied convention and was determined to make a striking impression' in the world (Meyers, 295). Shortly after marrying the American composer Deems Taylor in 1910, she began writing stories for such American magazines as *Harper's Weekly* and *Collier's* (see the 'Bibliography of Jane Anderson', Meyers, 413–16).

In 1915, Jane Anderson came to *London, working there and on the Western Front as a war correspondent for *The Times* and the *Daily Mail*. Numerous connections in high places allowed her access to submarine bases, war-plane exercises, and munition factories, and also led to sexual liaisons with such powerful figures as the newspaper magnate Lord *Northcliffe and Sir Leo Money, the politician and private secretary to Lloyd George. In April 1916, she wrote to Deems Taylor describing her first visit to Capel House to meet Conrad, 'the greatest writer in the world' (quoted in John Halverson and Ian Watt, 'Notes on Jane Anderson: 1955–1990', *Conradiana*, 23 (1991), 61). Her subsequent animated contacts with the family during that year produced contrasting reactions. When she spent a month convalescing at the Conrads' home in the summer, Conrad relished her presence with a mixture of parental interest and sexual excitement: 'She comes from Arizona and . . . has a European mind. She is seeking to get herself adopted as our big daughter and is succeeding fairly. To put it shortly she's quite yum-yum' (*CL*, v. 637). On the other hand, Jessie Conrad, having initially warmed to Jane and welcomed her into the household, came to feel that 'our fair American friend had been amusing herself at my expense' (*JCHC*, 207), probably suspecting that her husband's attention to Jane was more than merely platonic or professional. Although Meyers asserts that the 58-year-old Conrad had a sexual affair with the woman he referred to as the 'dear Chestnut filly' (*CL*, v. 666), there is no way of knowing in what direction and how far their relationship developed. Rebecca West remarked that Conrad thought Jane to be 'marvelous' (quoted in Halverson and Watt, 76), and his intimate friend Richard *Curle reported that Conrad 'always had an eye for a pretty face and a pretty ankle', and believed that 'there may have been a *tendresse* with the American journalist' (quoted in Meyers, 306). In addition, Jane's impact can also be measured by the strong possibility that she served as a partial model for *Arlette in *The Rover* and the seductive *Doña Rita in *The Arrow of Gold*, 'a woman formed in mind and body, mistress of herself, free in her choice, independent in her thoughts' (210). Conrad seems to have kept in touch with Jane's love affairs in Paris the following year. These probably involved Conrad's son Borys (whom Jane had imagined—even before she met him—as 'of extraordinary caste, with the strength of his mother and the fire of Conrad himself' (Halverson and Watt, 63)) and his friend Józef H. *Retinger, whose liaison with her resulted in the break-up of his first marriage and seems to have caused a breach in his friendship with Conrad.

After the war, Jane Anderson tried unsuccessfully to become a Hollywood actress, mixed in Paris bohemian circles from where she was rescued from drug and alcohol addiction by Catholic nuns, married a Spanish nobleman, and sided with the Fascists in Spain where she was later imprisoned by the loyalists on a charge of espionage. During the Second World War, she surfaced in Berlin as a broadcaster for Nazi propaganda, and in 1943 was charged with treason in an American indictment that also named Ezra Pound. She was arrested by the American military authorities in Austria in 1947, but the case against her was dropped through lack of evidence. Halverson and Watt conclude their study of her as follows: 'Jane knew only the here and now. Like a child she needed endless attention, and became very skilled at getting it. She could wholly become a coquette, a writer, a charmer, a woman of the world, an international correspondent, a contessa, a martyr, a Catholic, a Hitlerite. We do not know all the fantasies that came to dominate her. But there was no prudence, no sense of personal reciprocities, no looking back at her past life' (81). When and where she died remains a mystery.

Anthony, Roderick, the captain of the *Ferndale* in *Chance*, who ran away to sea as a young man to escape from the tyranny of his father Carleon Anthony, whom *Marlow describes as 'a delicate erotic poet of a markedly refined and autocratic temperament' (309). When he elopes with Flora *de Barral, Anthony finds himself subjected to another kind of paternal tyranny, since the enmity of Flora's father on board the *Ferndale* poisons the ship's atmosphere and isolates him from his crew. Called Harold Roderick in the serial version, Anthony was apparently based on Milnes Patmore, the rebellious son of the poet Coventry Patmore (1823–96), who was best known as the author of *The Angel in the House* (1854–63), a sentimental poetic tribute to Victorian womanhood (see E. E. Duncan-Jones, 'Some Sources of *Chance*', *Review of English Studies*, 20 (1969), 468–71). Like Roderick Anthony, Milnes Patmore rebelled against the tyranny of his father and eventually became a captain in the merchant navy.

anti-Semitism. The cultural milieu of English literature at the turn of the century included a repertoire of anti-Semitic attitudes that finds expression variously in

Conrad's works and *letters. Often this expression is passive, as when Conrad praised Marguerite *Poradowska's novel *Yaga* (1887) without having taken offence at her outrageously stereotypical descriptions of noisy Jews who smell of garlic (see Gene M. Moore, 'The Colonial Context of Anti-Semitism: Poradowska's *Yaga* and the Thys Libel Case', *The Conradian*, 18: 1 (1993), 25–36); or when he added his name to Ford Madox *Ford's *The Inheritors* despite its narrator's persistent and offensive references to a Jewish journalist in Paris who typifies his 'kind' (102 ff.). Anti-Semitic remarks appear especially in Conrad's correspondence with Edward *Garnett, to whom Conrad could speak of his publisher William *Heinemann as 'That Israelite' (*CL*, i. 395), or of the tight-fisted T. Fisher *Unwin—who was not Jewish—as 'The Patron Jew' (*CL*, i. 406). Following the peculiar logic of this tradition, Karl has erroneously claimed that Conrad's agent J. B. *Pinker was Jewish (*JCTL*, 867); it was in letters to Pinker that Conrad twice described American sculptor Jo Davidson as Jewish (*CL*, v. 565).

Conrad's biographers, in acknowledging his anti-Semitism, have often attributed the prejudice to his origins as a Polish Catholic and member of the landed gentry, as if all Poles were somehow 'naturally' anti-Semitic. Baines, for example, noted that Conrad 'sometimes showed signs of the anti-Jewish prejudice so widespread among Eastern Europeans' (374). Bernard C. Meyer, the most prominent of Conrad's *psychoanalytic biographers, adapts the theory of Conrad's 'betrayal' of his Polish homeland as grounds for suggesting that his anti-Semitism had nothing necessarily to do with Jews, but that it, 'like much racial prejudice, was in large measure a manifestation of projection, the displaced hatred of one's own kind, and of one's own self' (353). Against this tradition of displacing and explaining Conrad's anti-Semitism in terms of his Polish origins, Jeffrey Meyers contends that 'Conrad, for a man of his time and place, was astonishingly free of anti-Semitic prejudice' and 'essentially sympathetic to the Jews' ('Conrad and the Jews', *Conradiana*, 24 (1992), 33).

Anti-Semitic remarks or stereotypes occur infrequently in Conrad's works. In *Under Western Eyes*, *Razumov, the Russian protagonist, calls Julius Laspara a 'Cursed Jew!' (287); and a stereotypical Jewish innkeeper makes a brief appearance in an incident described by Dr Martel in *Suspense* (179). There are only two important characters in Conrad's fiction who are explicitly Jewish: Yankel, the 'portly, dignified' (39) innkeeper in the story 'Prince Roman' (*Tales of Hearsay*), and the merchant *Hirsch in *Nostromo*. Yankel is essentially Jewish by virtue of his profession, since (as in Dr Martel's anecdote, and as Poradowska's novels make clear) selling alcohol was one of the few trades not prohibited to Jews in eastern Europe; he is described literally as 'a Polish patriot' (39). The case of Hirsch is more ambiguous: a caricature based on the standard fictional repertoire of Jewish stereotypical attributes, with his 'cringing jargon' and his 'hooked beak' of a nose (201–2), the hide merchant ultimately musters astonishing courage under torture and spits in his tormentor's face. For a more detailed discussion of Hirsch, see 'The Jews in Conrad's Fiction', in Gillon 1994: 163–82.

According to Richard *Curle, 'many people . . . could not get out of their heads the idea that Conrad, just because he came from *Poland, must be a Jew—and this, of course, annoyed him intensely' (*LTY*, 199). When one reviewer of *Under Western Eyes* suggested that the English *teacher of languages who narrates the novel 'must have been a Jew, holding the balance between the West and the East', Conrad reacted angrily in a letter to John *Galsworthy, noting that 'that preposterous Papist Belloc has been connecting me with Father Abraham, whether to hurt me or to serve me, or simply because he's an idiot—I don't know. . . . It's an absurd position to be in for I trust I have no contemptible prejudices against any kind of human beings— and yet it isn't pleasant to be taken out of one's own skin, as it were, by an irresponsible chatterer' (*CL*, iv. 486). The rumour that Conrad was Jewish may have been encouraged by Ford Madox Ford's satiric portrayal of him in *The Simple Life Limited* (1911) as the émigré novelist Simon Brandson, né Simeon Brandetski, whose ethnic origins are uncertain but possibly Jewish. Again in 1918, when Frank Harris, the editor of the *Saturday Review*, attempted to insult Conrad by calling him a Jew, Conrad responded with an open letter in the *New Republic* under the title 'Mr. Conrad Is Not a Jew' (24 August 1918), in which he documented his non-Jewish origins but concluded: 'Had I been an Israelite I would never have denied being a member of a race occupying such a unique place in the religious history of mankind.'

These charges, and the vehemence of Conrad's reponses to them, remind us that his 'time and place' were not the eastern Europe of tsars and pogroms, but Victorian and post-Victorian England. Those tempted to explain or excuse Conrad's alleged anti-Semitism with reference to his 'eastern' origins would do well to remember that Anglo-Saxon attitudes have often been anti-Semitic as well.

archetypal approaches. This form of critical practice, which flourished during the period 1950–75, values the literary work as an expression or embodiment of recurrent mythic patterns and 'timeless' archetypes (from the Greek words *arkhe*, a beginning or first instance, and *tupos*, a stamp or impression). At its most characteristic, the practice is based upon the assumption that a work's specific narrative structure and symbolism are important in so far as they invoke patterns that derive from ancient religions, myths, and folklore and are so recurrent in human history and past literature as to be considered 'universal'. Such archetypes commonly involve a family of narrative rituals (for example, the quest theme, seasonal change, sacrificial death and rebirth, and the passage from innocence to experience), repeated character types (the Earth Mother, the dying god, the blood brother, and the scapegoat), and a variety of recurrent symbolic motifs. The founding fathers of modern archetypal

criticism are generally taken to be Sir James Frazer and his anthropological study of magic and ancient ritual in *The Golden Bough* (1890–1915) and Carl Gustav Jung, whose influential concept of the archetype as originating in the 'collective unconscious' and finding its most common manifestation in dreams provided a rationale for many critics during the period 1950–70, including Leslie Fiedler, Northrop Frye, and Robert Graves.

An important strand in Conrad studies during this period, archetypal criticism was given an early impetus by Albert J. Guerard, whose influential study (1958) included among its many interests a preoccupation with the Jungian 'night journey'. Subsequent criticism of this kind was more theorized and systematic in method; it was also more explicit in its rejection of what were perceived as the narrow orthodoxies of New Criticism and in its impatience with repeated studies of Conrad's existential philosophy. Representative archetypal studies during the 1960s include Elliott B. Gose Jr's 'Pure Exercise of Imagination: Archetypal Symbolism in *Lord Jim*', *PMLA*, 79 (1964), 137–47; Ted E. Boyle's *Symbol and Meaning in the Fiction of Joseph Conrad* (The Hague: Mouton, 1965); and Claire Rosenfield's *Paradise of Snakes: An Archetypal Analysis of Conrad's Political Novels* (University of Chicago Press, 1967). In many ways the most rewarding of its kind, Rosenfield's study effects an insistent universalization of Conrad's interests into a despairingly ironic lament for the 'loss of eternal values' (176). If, on the one hand, the proliferation of underworlds, lost Edens, and night journeys in her subsequent analyses may finally be purchased at too high a cost to the very defining qualities of the 'political' novel, there is nevertheless a careful attempt to situate Conrad historically in a way that emphasizes the co-presence of archetype, existential anxiety, and pervasive *irony in his work: 'In Conrad's novels, the tone of which is so consonant with our contemporary despair and insecurity, the recurrence of past motifs, their effect upon design, intensify the irony; belief, after all, no longer accompanies the stories that now echo exploits in godless worlds by unheroic mediocrities' (9).

Although no longer enjoying its earlier vogue, archetypal practice still exerts an influence in Conrad studies, albeit in a form much modified by newer theoretical preoccupations. Generally, critical interest has moved away from the content of myth and its claimed basis in 'universals' to its status as one perceptual mode or 'discourse' among many in Conrad's fiction, coexisting and competing with others. Thus, Janet Burstein, in 'On Ways of Knowing in *Lord Jim*', *Nineteenth-Century Fiction*, 26 (1972), 456–68, attempts to characterize two contrasting ways of seeing in the novel—the mythic mode and a more discursive mode of cognition and abstraction—neither of which alone is fully adequate to *Jim's case, and both of which are found to combine in *Marlow, who performs the poet's function. More ambitiously, Daphna Erdinast-Vulcan's 1991 study *Joseph Conrad and the Modern Temper* discovers evidence for Conrad's complex modernity in the sharp conflict between mythical and historicist modes of perception in his fiction as a whole: employing a *Bakhtinian approach, she regards 'mythicity' as 'a *mode of discourse* rather than a repertoire of recycled or displaced mythical motifs' and 'as a voice which operates dialogically against the voice of modernity in the text' (28). Conrad's own sophisticated interest in the transformation of fact into legend, and legend into myth, figures in Robert Hampson's resourceful study of 'Conrad and the Formation of Legends', in Carabine *et al.* (eds.) 1993: 167–85, which dwells on *Lord Jim*, *Nostromo*, and 'The Planter of Malata' (*Within the Tides*). See also Carol Schreier Rupprecht's helpful entry on 'Archetypal Theory and Criticism', in Michael Groden and Martin Kreiswirth (eds.), *The Johns Hopkins Guide to Literary Theory and Criticism* (Baltimore: Johns Hopkins UP, 1994), 36–40.

archives. See MANUSCRIPT AND ARCHIVAL COLLECTIONS.

Arlette, the main female in *The Rover*, repeats a character type Conrad had already essayed in Flora of *Chance* and *Lena of Victory*. Like them, she undergoes a transformation from a girl in distress into a fully mature woman capable of committing herself to life and love. Psychically wounded by the brutal execution of her parents during the French Revolution, Arlette suffers a spiritual malaise that prevents her from realizing herself. Although guarded jealously by her aunt Catherine, she lives under sexual threat from the brutal and feeble-minded Jacobin Scevola Bron. The arrival of *Peyrol at Escampobar alters this psychological configuration, and he comes to play various roles in the young woman's drama: as mentor-into-life, as father-figure, and, in a fashion, as platonic lover. Through Peyrol's affectionate concern, Arlette finds the fortitude to re-establish ties to the human community. Taken from the southern French town of Arles, her name indicates her emblematic function, while her gradual restoration to psychological health, her awakening to love, her marriage to Lieutenant Eugène Réal, and her release from Scevola's attempted domination symbolize the victory of humane values over the chaotic and antisocial forces of the Revolution.

Modelled distantly on the suffering heroines of classical tragedy, and perhaps as much on the Miranda as the Ophelia of *Shakespeare, Arlette also has Victorian predecessors, particularly the psychologically orphaned young women of *Dickens (Nell and Little Dorrit, for instance). Real-life sources for her can perhaps be found in the American journalist Jane *Anderson, for whom Conrad appears to have harboured a sexual attraction, and Karola *Zagórska, a Polish relative, who stayed with the Conrads for nearly six months in 1920, the year before Conrad began writing *The Rover*. Aspects of Conrad himself may also be glimpsed in Peyrol's self-sacrificing relationship with Arlette.   JHS

Arrow of Gold, The. This novel of 1919 was the first of Conrad's works to be *dictated and the first of his novels to be

published after the *First World War. Set in
*Marseilles in the 1870s, *The Arrow of Gold*
is narrated by a young sailor known as
'M. *George', who recounts his involvement in gun-running for the *Carlists during the Second Carlist War. M. George's
narration highlights his initiation into the
life of passion through his relationship
with the enigmatic *Doña Rita, while Rita
herself gradually emerges as another of
Conrad's late-novel studies of damaged
women.

The Arrow of Gold was originally
planned to take the form of 'Selected Passages from Letters' written by the protagonist to a woman whom he had known
35 years earlier. As it developed, however,
the novel became 'a tale between two notes'.
An unidentified editor provides an introductory and concluding note to a narrative which is presented as edited from
M. George's much longer memoir of his
youth in Marseilles. Thus the novel presents three virtual levels: the sequence of
events over twelve months in Marseilles;
the narrative of these events by the mature
M. George; and the editor's later abridged
version of M. George's text.

In the First Note, the editor introduces
the manuscript from which the text to follow has been extracted. He explains how it
was produced in response to an exchange
of letters between the author and a childhood friend not seen for many years since
the author's departure from his native
land. Part I begins at carnival time in Marseilles. M. George has just returned from
his second voyage to the *Caribbean and,
sitting in a café, he is joined by Mr Mills
and Captain Blunt, active supporters of
Carlism. The three men go to Blunt's
rooms, where Mills and Blunt discuss
Doña Rita, her relationship with the
painter and collector Henry Allègre, and
her involvement with Don Carlos. In Part
II, M. George is taken by Mills to meet
Doña Rita. His journal records how he involves his friend Dominic in the gun-
running enterprise he has undertaken,
purchases a *balancelle*, a 'fast sailing craft'
(90), and continues to see Doña Rita. In
Part III, M. George returns from his first

gun-running trip and visits Doña Rita,
who describes her Basque childhood, and
her relationships with her cousin Ortega
and with her sister Therese. M. George tells
Rita about his first visit to Blunt's rooms
and how he listened to Blunt and Mills discussing her. He also realizes that he has
fallen in love with Rita. After his return
from his third gun-running expedition, he
again visits Rita at her villa and witnesses a
'mysterious quarrel' (148) between Rita
and Blunt, in which Blunt accuses her of
leading him on and she accuses him of
pride and lack of feeling. In Part IV,
M. George continues to suffer from sleep-
lessness and torment as a result of his love
for Doña Rita. Blunt's mother arrives in
Marseilles and meets with Therese and
M. George. Mrs Blunt reveals to M. George
her plan for her son to marry Rita, despite
his resistance on moral and class grounds.
She tries to warn M. George against becoming involved with Doña Rita. When
M. George visits Rita at her villa, she gives
an account of her first meeting with Allègre, and he declares his love. In Part V,
M. George learns that Rita has left Marseilles for Paris and, for three months, he
throws himself into the work of gun-
running. But the Carlist position in Spain
is deteriorating, and the gun-running
episode ends with the shipwreck of the *balancelle* after a close scrape with the Carabi-
neers. M. George makes his way back to
Marseilles, arriving during the carnival. He
reports the failed mission to the Carlist
agent, and is sent to the railway station to
meet another agent who is arriving from
Paris. Unknown to M. George, the agent is
Ortega, the man Rita fears. Questioned by
Ortega about her, M. George realizes the
identity of his companion and contem-
plates murdering him in order to protect
Doña Rita. M. George takes Ortega back to
the house in 'the street of Consuls' to stay
the night and then discovers that Rita is
also in residence there. A long conversation
between M. George and Rita is interrupted
by Ortega, who shouts abuse at Doña Rita,
but accidentally wounds himself before he
can harm her. M. George and Rita are reconciled and spend the night together. In

the Second Note, the editor offers a summary of the events of the next six months, during which Doña Rita and M. George withdraw from Marseilles into what appears to be a love idyll. On a short visit to Marseilles, M. George hears that the Carlist enterprise has collapsed but also that Blunt has been describing him as an adventurer exploiting Doña Rita. This provocation leads to a duel in which M. George is wounded. Upon his recovery, he discovers that Doña Rita has disappeared. The novel ends with M. George discussing Rita with Mills.

On 3 February 1915, Conrad wrote to his agent J. B. *Pinker that he intended to write a 'military tale' deriving from an episode of his youth. It was to be an 'early personal experience thing' (*CL*, v. 441), drawing on his memories of the time he had spent in and around Marseilles, from October 1874 to April 1878. Towards the end of July 1917, Conrad began the short story which turned into *The Arrow of Gold*. He worked on it throughout the summer, and again during the first half of 1918, finishing on 4 June 1918 and then writing the First and Second Notes. The novel was *serialized in *Lloyd's Magazine* from December 1918 to February 1920. It was published on 12 April 1919 by Doubleday, Page in America, and by T. Fisher *Unwin on 6 August 1919.

Conrad had tried to make fictional use of this material earlier. In a letter to his American publisher F. N. *Doubleday, Conrad observed that he had had the subject in his mind 'for some eighteen years' (*LL*, ii. 213). He refers here to his unfinished novel, *The Sisters*, which he began in late 1895 but soon abandoned on the advice of his friend Edward *Garnett. There are numerous points of resemblance between the earlier fragment and *The Arrow of Gold*: both involve two sisters, Rita and Theresa, and their uncle, the Basque priest, who has brought them up; and the transplanting of Rita, 'the wild girl of Basque mountains' (*CDOUP*, 79), to an orange-merchant's house in Passy is also common to both, as is the background of Carlist politics. There are also connections between *The Arrow of Gold* and Conrad's autobiographical writings, *The Mirror of the Sea* (1906) and *A Personal Record* (1911), in which Conrad describes his initiation into the craft of the sea during his Marseilles years. In *The Mirror of the Sea* he recalled his involvement in a Carlist smuggling syndicate whose members included 'a North Carolinian gentleman, J. M. K. B.' (157). The syndicate used information supplied by Doña Rita, 'a Carlist . . . of Basque blood' (160), and owned a *balancelle*, the *Tremolino*, whose *padrone* was based on the Corsican sailor Dominique *Cervoni. All of these elements—as well as 'a certain Madame Leonore who kept a small cafe for sailors in one of the narrowest streets of the old town' (159)—reappear in *The Arrow of Gold*. The novel thus reflects Conrad's memories of his youth in Marseilles (as well as, for the First Note, his memories of earlier experiences as an adolescent in *Poland), but these memories had already been subjected to repeated fictionalization and would be considerably elaborated.

Contemporary reviewers found the novel disappointing. An anonymous reviewer in the *New Statesman* complained about the lack of gun-running incidents (*CCH*, 332). More seriously, Walter de la Mare's anonymous review in the *Times Literary Supplement* described it as 'fragmentarily and insecurely told' and thought the conclusion was a 'douche' to the story's 'romance' (ibid. 320). Later, the *'achievement-and-decline' school of Conrad critics used *The Arrow of Gold* in particular as evidence of Conrad's decline. Douglas Hewitt, for example, described it as 'a work which his admirers do well to overlook' (2). Moser similarly saw it as 'virtually without a redeeming feature', and dated the moment of Conrad's 'decline' precisely as immediately following *The Shadow-Line*, that is, just preceding *The Arrow of Gold* (4).

Conrad himself thought the disappointing reviews were 'the penalty for having produced something unexpected' (*LL*, ii. 227). Paul Wiley, in a sympathetic and insightful account in *Conrad's Measure of Man* (Madison: University of Wisconsin Press, 1954), found merit in the pictorial aspects of the novel, discussing the artistry of

Conrad's portrait of Rita (66), the chiaroscuro of Therese (138–9), and the presentation of Mrs Blunt in *grisaille* (180). Conrad produces similar vignettes for almost all the characters, and, in each case, achieves not just a painterly effect in prose, but one that explicitly draws upon the conventions and methods of the visual arts. The narrative is thus characterized not, as Wiley suggests, by the objective transcription of sense impressions, but rather by the presentation of these impressions in heightened aesthetic terms. As in *Victory*, the narrative rests on the juxtaposition of various perspectives, each of which embodies a different mode of interpreting what is seen.

A second, related element of this new method of presentation involves M. George's role as narrator. While his perspective governs the main narrative, he is not a privileged interpreter, but, like the *Marlow of *Chance*, an unreliable and even obtuse witness. Recent critics have paid more attention to the nature of M. George's narration than to the events he narrates. In his own words, he is 'beautifully unthinking—infinitely receptive' (8). He suggests that, if he represents anything, 'it was a perfect freshness of sensations and a refreshing ignorance' (31). However, as Andrew Michael Roberts has argued, this quality of 'freshness' can be misleading (see 'The Gaze and the Dummy: Sexual Politics in *The Arrow of Gold*', in Keith Carabine (ed.), *Joseph Conrad: Critical Assessments* (Robertsbridge: Helm International, 1992), iii. 528–50). When M. George at last meets Rita, his response is one of immediate identification with her. His conclusion that 'there was nothing more for us to know about each other' (70) means, as Roberts has argued, that he feels no need to listen to what she says about herself. Her words are not allowed to disturb his narcissistic involvement. His concept of love as an identification with the beloved leads him to disregard Rita's individuality and to address her not with 'freshness' but in romantic clichés, seeing her in terms of 'that something secret and obscure which is in all women' (146). From this perspective, the romantic rhetoric of *The Arrow of Gold*, which some have taken as evidence of Conrad's declining powers, may be seen as part of Conrad's critique of M. George.

Following the efforts of Wiley and Gary Geddes (1980) to reclaim *The Arrow of Gold* for serious critical attention, later critics have brought out other aspects of the novel. Erdinast-Vulcan, for example, focuses on its 'unresolved generic ambiguity'. She notes how the novel 'proclaims itself as a romance' (186) through the deployment of various generic signals, but then undermines romance expectations through 'a series of striking and blatant transgressions of the generic code' (188). Thus, while the plot of M. George's rivalry with Captain Blunt and his 'rescue' of Rita can be 'summarized as a version of classical knight-errantry' (186), M. George's presentation of himself in his own narrative as an experienced mariner is undermined by the editor's comment, in the First Note, that he 'pretended rather absurdly to be a seaman' (5). In the same way, M. George's role as a chivalrous knight is undermined by the editor's revelation that Blunt and Mills have manipulated him into taking part in 'the affair' (5). The Second Note also violates conventional romantic expectations, since its very existence—which removes the reader from the moment of resolution with which M. George's narrative ends—'goes beyond the sanctioned boundaries of the genre' (Erdinast-Vulcan, 189). Moreover, the Note is marked by a strain of scepticism and the recurrent suggestion that Rita might merely have been acting a part during the six-month idyll to make M. George happy (337–9). Furthermore, as Erdinast-Vulcan points out, M. George's romance narrative is also subverted from within by oscillations between 'a passionate affirmation of the code of romance' and sceptical deflations of 'the rhetoric of passion' (191). These oscillations may also be understood as the mature M. George reflecting on his younger self, so that the youthful M. George's romance of love and adventure is doubly challenged by the perspective of his disillusioned older self and by the scepticism of the editor.

Hampson (1992) argues that the primary focus is not M. George but Rita: that Rita is 'the enigma which the narrative is designed to solve' (254). In particular, the narrative is directed towards disclosing the nature and the origins of her 'fear', which can be found in the trauma of her childhood sexual relations with Ortega. Rita's initial account in Part III offers an explanation of her fear, but subsequent events make clear that this version of events is incomplete. Her memory of being trapped in a shelter by Ortega is re-enacted in the narrative climax, when she and M. George are trapped by him in a locked room, and Hampson argues that this re-enactment finally liberates Rita from these traumatic memories. Hampson contextualizes the novel by reference to studies of hysteria, and compares M. George's role in this climactic scene to that of an analyst. However, this positive reading of Rita's experience ignores the dissonant notes in the later parts of the novel. For example, after the crisis, M. George describes himself as yelling 'in a sort of frenzy' as though he 'had been a second Ortega' (328), and the next morning, when Rita (as before) recoils from him, he describes how a 'grown man's bitterness, informed, suspicious, resembling hatred, welled out of my heart' (334). The particular 'grown man' he seems to have in mind is suggested when he goes on to say that he 'won't throw stones' as Ortega used to do (334). Rather than freeing Rita from her traumatic memories, the episode seems to have released in M. George emotions similar to Ortega's; and, if M. George's experiences represent a process of maturation, at this point Ortega seems to be his role model. Indeed, Ortega can be said to represent the novel's extreme case of the male tendency to project needs and expectations onto women. Ortega's tormented love–hate relation to Rita subverts the novel's male discourse, and the moments when Blunt and Ortega appear as doubles of M. George problematize his own 'love' for Rita and prevent it from emerging as a norm or ideal.

Roberts (1992) offers a reading of *The Arrow of Gold* turning upon sexual politics

and the male psychic economy, focusing particularly on male projections and the circulation of male discourse about women. The discussion of Doña Rita by Mills and Blunt introduces her through a series of images and impressions. In some cases the images are visual images, paintings, produced by Allègre. These visual images serve to emphasize the reification of Rita by Allègre and also by Mills and Blunt. Rita first appears in the novel in their dialogue as an object for consumption or exchange: as the aesthetic object of the male gaze or the sexual object of male desire. Subsequently, this objectification of Rita is confirmed by her 'double', the dummy that stood in for her during Allègre's painting sessions, which continues to function as her surrogate for both M. George and the reader. This 'mutilated dummy' (122), Roberts argues, suggests both the implicit sadism of the male gaze and Rita's function as the body upon which male spectators project various roles and identities.

Nadelhaft has also focused on sexual politics in *The Arrow of Gold*, arguing that for M. George, as 'a young man raised on sexual stereotypes and romance', Rita 'can only be an "exotic" creature, or a magnificent statue, not a particular idiosyncratic woman' (125). She notes how he 'tends always to turn Rita into a metaphor or a symbol' (124) rather than accept her for what she is, and how he shares this tendency with the other men in the novel. Where Roberts draws attention to the omnipresence of male discourse, Nadelhaft emphasizes the role of women's speech: Rita, Mme Leonore, and Rose all struggle to make their voices heard 'over, under and around' male discourse (110). However, so coercive is M. George's narration that it is almost possible to miss this submerged narrative of Rita's relations with women.

These interpretations notwithstanding, the novel's canonical status is still in dispute. Erdinast-Vulcan makes clear that her purpose was not 'to redeem the novel from literary disrepute', but rather 'to diagnose its failure' (186). Her analysis reaffirms the importance of genre and implicitly challenges the negative reactions expressed by contemporary reviewers. While acceding to the earlier charge of the novel's 'inflated rhetoric', she also suggests ways in which this rhetoric is revelatory of the characters who produce it rather than symptomatic of Conrad. Hampson, Roberts, and Nadelhaft seek, explicitly or implicitly, to rescue *The Arrow of Gold* from critical neglect: Hampson and Nadelhaft by attending to Rita, and Roberts and Nadelhaft by emphasizing the importance of gender and sexual politics, and all three pay close attention to the rhetorical strategies through which sexual power becomes manifest.

An incomplete manuscript ('The Laugh'), an incomplete typescript ('Rita de Lastaola'), and a complete typescript are held at the Beinecke Rare Book and Manuscript Library, Yale University, and a carbon copy of the typescript is at Colgate University. An incomplete typescript of the Second Note is at the Lilly Library, Indiana University. Two typescripts of the 'Author's Note' survive: one at Yale, and another in the Berg Collection, New York Public Library. A proof copy of *The Arrow of Gold* is held at Hofstra University, and two ink drawings of Rita by Conrad are also at Yale.
                                                                    RH

'Ascending Effort, The'. This review of *The Ascending Effort* (1910) by George Bourne (pen-name of George Sturt) was one of four written in July 1910 at the invitation of Lindsay Bashford, literary editor of the *Daily Mail*, who towards the end of June had offered Conrad a regular Saturday review-column. It appeared in the *Daily Mail* (30 July 1910), 8, under the title 'Can Poetry Flourish in a Scientific Age?' and was later revised and retitled for collection in *Notes on Life and Letters*. Conrad soon found the task of reviewing popular books uncongenial and sustained the column for only three issues. In response to Bourne's wish to see a marriage between science and the arts to promote the cause of national 'progress', Conrad offers a more pungent version of the argument advanced in his 'Preface' to *The Nigger of the 'Narcissus'* several years earlier: 'Life and the arts follow dark courses, and will not turn aside

to the brilliant arc-lights of science' (74). In 1921, on its reprinting in *Notes and Life and Letters*, this review occasioned a difference of opinion with Edward *Garnett, prompting Conrad to clarify his position: 'The thesis of his book is vitiated by the fact that poetry and religion having their source in an emotional state may act and react on each other worthily—whereas "Science" at its amplest (and profoundest) is only the exercise of a certain kind of imagination springing either from facts eminently prosaic or from tentative assumptions of the commonest kind of common-sense' (*LFC*, 305). A typed transcript made for Conrad's revision for *Notes on Life and Letters* is held at Colgate University.

auctions and sales. For most of his writing career, Conrad had no idea that the physical by-products of his life as a writer (*letters, *manuscript drafts, typescripts, corrected proofs, inscribed or association copies) had any market value as collectable items or research materials. The first offer to buy his working papers came in 1911 from New York lawyer and art collector John *Quinn, who eventually acquired almost all of Conrad's surviving pre-1917 literary manuscripts. Conrad had made a gentleman's agreement with Quinn, who paid whatever price the writer would ask; but in 1919 Quinn learned that Conrad was also selling documents to the London bibliophile Thomas J. *Wise. By 1923, Quinn's relations with Conrad had deteriorated, and he included his entire Conrad collection in a massive sale of his personal library held over a period of five months, from November 1923 to March 1924, at the Anderson Galleries in New York. The Conrad items sold in November 1923 were only a small part of the Quinn sale, representing 228 lots from a total of more than 12,000; but they were the most lucrative and newsworthy items in the sale, and laid the foundations for the major Conrad collections at the Rosenbach Museum and Library, Philadelphia, and at Colgate University (which also holds Henry Colgate's priced copy of the Quinn catalogue). Quinn's timing was impeccable: Conrad's visit to New

York and Boston the previous May had been highly publicized, and at the time of the Quinn sale, Conrad's popularity in *America had soared to unprecedented heights. Quinn had paid a total of some $10,000 for his Conrad items, and sold them for nearly eleven times as much, thus realizing a profit of 1,000 per cent. The sum of $8,100 paid by Dr A. S. W. Rosenbach for the original manuscript of *Victory* was at that time the highest price ever paid for a manuscript by a living author. The items purchased by songwriter Jerome Kern, including the manuscripts of 'Youth' and *Under Western Eyes*, were again auctioned by the Anderson Galleries on 7–10 January 1929.

Selling inscribed presentation copies during Conrad's lifetime (as Quinn had done) would have appeared rude, but Conrad's death in August 1924 meant that holders of inscribed copies or other Conrad materials felt free to bring them to the market. Conrad's literary agent J. B. *Pinker had died suddenly in February 1922. His Conrad collection, consisting chiefly of inscribed copies of Conrad's works but also including the (currently unlocated) marked copies of *Almayer's Folly* and *An Outcast of the Islands* bearing Conrad's revisions for the *collected edition, were auctioned by Sotheby in London on 15–17 December 1924. Three months later, on 13 March 1925, the books, manuscripts, and typescripts left in the possession of Conrad's widow Jessie were auctioned by Messrs Hodgson & Co. in London. This sale is of particular interest to scholars because the catalogue is a partial list of the volumes in Conrad's personal library. Nearly fifty of these books were bought at auction and resold later the same year by the Cambridge firm of W. Heffer & Sons, Ltd. (Heffer catalogue no. 251).

Many of Conrad's close friends sold their Conrad manuscripts and letters in the late 1920s, often in American auction houses for the sake of the higher prices to be found there. Thus Richard *Curle auctioned his extensive Conrad collection (including the typescript fragments or 'scraps' of Conrad's last novel, *Suspense*) at the American Art Association in New York on 28 April 1927. A year later, on 24–5 April 1928, the same auction house sold *The Edward Garnett Collection of Inscribed Books and Autograph Material by Joseph Conrad and W. H. Hudson*, with 254 lots devoted to Conrad, including many letters from Conrad to Edward *Garnett. Later the same year, on 21–3 November 1928, the same house also sold the Conrad collection of Ford Madox *Ford's estranged wife Elsie Hueffer.

The market value of Conrad's letters was also rising during this period. More than 100 letters from Conrad to Sidney *Colvin were auctioned by the Anderson Galleries on 7 May 1928 (a priced copy of the catalogue—*Letters to the Colvins, Mainly about Stevenson & Keats, Sold by Order of E. V. Lucas, Esq., London*—is held at the Grolier Club, New York). Some twenty letters from Conrad to his first publisher, T. Fisher *Unwin, were auctioned by Hodgson on 6–8 June 1928.

The Great Depression of the 1930s witnessed a fall in the market value of Conrad items. A typewritten draft of Part IV of *Suspense* (currently unlocated) that sold for $170 at the Curle sale in 1927 fetched only $30 at the American Art Association ten years later. By the end of the Second World War, most of Conrad's manuscripts and letters had found their way into university libraries or other library collections in the United States, and relatively few remained on the market. Nevertheless, a number of important private collections have been offered for sale in recent years. Of these, the largest is the collection of Raymond M. Sutton Jr., comprising nearly 1,000 items described in two catalogues (numbers 9 and 10, January and March 1985) of David J. Holmes Autographs, Philadelphia. In addition to the original manuscripts of 'The Secret Sharer' and 'The Tale' (both now in the Berg Collection, New York Public Library), the Sutton Collection contained not only letters and first editions, but also miscellaneous items including *bibliographies, *films and filmscripts and posters, and hundreds of auction catalogues relating to Conrad's works.

The descriptions provided in the Sutton catalogues contain rare and often important information.

In 1993 the Robert C. Findlay Collection of Conrad materials was sold by Randall House of Santa Barbara, California. The Findlay Collection was soon purchased by a single buyer and thus kept intact, with the exception of the manuscript of Conrad's essay on 'Certain Aspects of the Admirable Inquiry into the Loss of the *Titanic*', which was acquired by the Lilly Library, Indiana University. The lavish catalogue prepared for the sale (Randall House catalogue 27) contains reproductions of the dust-jackets of many Conrad first editions.

In the summer of 1995, Richard Curle's archive appeared on the market in York with items that Curle chose not to sell in 1927, including a number of unpublished letters tucked into inscribed copies of Conrad's works. The entire Curle archive is now at the Lilly Library. In October 1996 some 27 letters from Conrad to Ford, Violet Hunt, and Elsie Hueffer turned up at auction in Detroit, Michigan, and were sold to a private buyer.

Given the scarcity of Conrad items on the market and the ongoing critical esteem in which his works are held, the market value of Conrad manuscripts has risen by the end of the 20th century to roughly $1,000 per handwritten page. Scholars working on projects such as the critical edition of Conrad's works or the collected edition of his letters have come to appreciate auction catalogues as a neglected but useful source of detailed information about the composition and disposition of Conrad's texts.

Australia. During his sea years, Conrad undertook five voyages to Australia and spent about seventeen months ashore there, a longer period than in the Far East which provided him with so much source material. His working life as a mariner in Australia kept him mainly in Sydney, Adelaide, Melbourne, and ports in South Australia. Whether he made any excursions into the interior remains unknown. Conrad's later affectionate memories of the country seem to have rested upon his liking for the 'youthfulness' of the colonies (in contrast perhaps to the tortured history of his Polish homeland), and the association of the country with his only official command: 'Like all the sailors of the old wool fleet I have the warmest regard for Australians generally[,] for New South Wales in particular and for charming Sydney especially. Moreover I am a fellow citizen. Haven't I commanded an Australian ship for over two years?' (*CL*, v. 50).

Conrad's first voyage to Australia was as ordinary seaman in the wool clipper *Duke of Sutherland*, which arrived in Sydney on 31 January 1879 and departed on 5 July. He remained on board as night-watchman during her five-month stay in port, an experience vividly evoked in *The Mirror of the Sea* and 'Well Done!' (*Notes*). There, he recalls nights spent on board ship alongside the Circular Quay, from where he could see and hear the busy life of George Street. In a letter written from Sydney to his uncle Tadeusz *Bobrowski, Conrad communicated that he had met 'some captain [possibly William Henry Eldred, a founding member of the Geographical Society of Australasia] famous for his knowledge of the trade' in the Malay Archipelago, who had offered him a job which Conrad was obliged to refuse because of his agreement to make the return voyage in the *Duke of Sutherland*. Nevertheless, excited by possible prospects open to him in the Antipodes, he hoped to make a quick return, 'but this time in order to stay there several years—or at least two' (*CPB*, 180).

Although Conrad did make a quick return to Australia, his plan to base himself there did not materialize. Ten months after arriving back in *London, he enlisted as third mate—his first berth as an officer—in the iron clipper *Loch Etive*, which arrived in Sydney on 24 November 1880, remaining there until 11 January 1881. Two months after Conrad's return to England in April, his uncle warmly encouraged him to 'collect some reminiscences from the voyage to Australia' and send them to a *Warsaw weekly journal (*CPB*, 72).

Seven years later, Conrad made his third voyage, this time as master of the *Otago*, an Australian-owned barque whose captaincy he had taken over in *Bangkok. Leaving on 9 February 1888, the *Otago* suffered an arduous voyage through the Gulf of Siam, arriving in Sydney on 7 May. A fortnight later the *Otago* made a round voyage to Melbourne with a portion of her original freight, arriving back in Sydney on 11 July. The *Otago* left Sydney for *Mauritius on 7 August during a tense shipping crisis, when, negotiations having broken down between the Seamen's Federated Union and the Steamship Owners' Association, there was considerable disruption and a general strike of seamen threatened. The *Otago* arrived back in Melbourne on 4 January 1889. Five weeks later, on what had evidently been planned as the first stage of a longer voyage to Port Elizabeth in South Africa, Conrad took the *Otago* to Minlacowie, South Australia, where over the next month she loaded a cargo of wheat. Here, he had a chance to mix with the local community: 'The farmers around were very nice to me, and I gave their wives (on a never-to-be-forgotten day) a tea-party on board the dear old "Otago" then lying alongside the God-forsaken jetty there' (to A. T. Saunders, 14 June 1917). The shipowners' change of plan brought the *Otago* back to Adelaide, where she docked on 26 March. At the end of the month Conrad resigned his command and sailed in the *Nürnberg* for Europe on 3 April.

Two more voyages to Australia followed towards the end of Conrad's sea career, both in the celebrated *Torrens*, one of the fastest sailing ships of her day. On the first, he arrived in Adelaide on 28 February 1892 and spent six weeks there, leaving on 10 April. Seven weeks after arriving back in London he rejoined the *Torrens*, again as first mate, for another Australian voyage. During the last two weeks of the outward passage, Conrad was ill and, soon after the ship's arrival in Adelaide on 28 January 1893, took a week's sick-leave. On the outward passage he had become friendly with a passenger, W. H. *Jacques, who read *Almayer's Folly* in manuscript; and on the

homeward voyage (beginning on 23 March) he met two more passengers, John *Galsworthy and E. L. *Sanderson, who, attracted by Conrad's fascinating talk and wide *reading, were destined to become his lifelong friends.

'The Planter of Malata' ('*Twixt Land and Sea*) and 'The Brute' (*A Set of Six*) are Conrad's only stories to have an Australian location, both of them including scenes set in Sydney. Nevertheless, indirect allusions to the Antipodes invariably figure in the depiction of the social and economic realities of the Far East, embracing a number of characters who have left Australia to live and work there. Some, like Laughing Anne and Mrs Davidson in 'Because of the Dollars' ('*Twixt Land and Sea*), associate Australia with a happier past in contrast to their present lives as unwilling exiles. But through the collective presence of other Australians in his work, Conrad acknowledges a further reality, the growing importance of Australia as a base for commercial adventurism into countries to the north. In *Almayer's Folly*, the Celebes port of Macassar is represented as a thrusting commercial centre 'where tended all those bold spirits who, fitting out schooners on the Australian coast, invaded the Malay Archipelago in search of money and adventure' (6). His two notable Australian characters, Chester in *Lord Jim* and Bamtz in 'Because of the Dollars', clearly belong to this 'invasion'. Chester has been 'pearler, wrecker, trader, whaler, too . . . in his own words—anything and everything a man may be at sea, but a pirate', whose 'hunting-ground' was in the north and south Pacific (161); the armless villain Bamtz (based upon a similarly disabled tobacco-seller whose shop in Sydney's George Street Conrad had frequented) belongs to the same movement of colonial rowdyism that Conrad seems to associate with expanding Australian involvement in Eastern commerce. For further details, see Lech Paszkowski, 'Joseph Conrad', in *Poles in Australia and Oceania 1790–1940* (Australian National UP, 1986), 268–81. Stape and van Marle (1995) offer a detailed record of Conrad's *Torrens* connection. See also SHIPS AND VOYAGES.

Austria, one of the triad of powers involved in the late 18th-century partition of *Poland, took control of an area of the country known as Red Ruthenia in addition to Małopolska, a province south of the Vistula River subsequently renamed Galicia. In 1868, Conrad and his father were granted permission by the Russian authorities to move to Austrian Poland, but even in their less repressive new home in *Lwów, Apollo *Korzeniowski disliked both the prevailing Germanization of Polish culture and the passivity of the Galicians. After his father's death in *Cracow, Conrad continued to live in Austrian Poland, where in 1872 moves were made to obtain Austrian *naturalization for him, although this did not materialize. Later, after Conrad's *suicide attempt in *Marseilles in 1878, the possibility of his securing Austrian citizenship again arose, when his uncle attempted, without success, to persuade him to 'return to Galicia, get naturalized, and look for a career there' (*CPB*, 177). Conrad's later political essays are somewhat less antagonistic to Austria as a partitioning power than to the main perpetrators of the historical 'crime', *Russia and Prussia. The former is seen as 'traditionally unaggressive whenever her hand is not forced' (*Notes*, 104) and as participating unwillingly 'in the destruction of a State which she would have preferred to preserve as a possible ally against Prussian and Russian ambitions' (ibid. 117).

Author's Notes. All of Conrad's introductory 'Author's Notes', with the exception of those written for *Almayer's Folly* and *The Nigger of the 'Narcissus'*, were composed between 1917 and 1920, most of them in readiness for the *collected editions of his work being prepared simultaneously by Doubleday, Page in America and *Heinemann in Britain for publication in 1921. The enterprise thus involved him in following the process undertaken by Henry *James in preparing the famous 1908 New York Edition of his novels and stories. Like James, Conrad took a personal and professional interest in the developing project: he prepared publicity, carefully

meditated the physical appearance of the volumes, and penned an 'Author's Note' for each volume.

It is important to see Conrad's prefaces within the wider context of his collaboration with his publishers in the plan to crown his career with a fittingly prepared monument. They belong to a stage in his later life when he was engaged in what Michael Millgate, in his study of literary career closure, calls 'testamentary acts' or the end-games of writers who, aware of approaching death, prepare their work for future readers and, consciously or unconsciously, fashion an image of themselves for posterity. According to G. *Jean-Aubry, Conrad was in 1918 'haunted by the idea of his approaching end and wanted to set himself straight with the future' (1957: 274). Written many years after the stress and passion of composition, his 'Author's Notes' are part of this process of undertaking acts of valediction and settlement with the future. In such an endeavour, Conrad may be found to emulate many ageing writers who, as Millgate puts it, attempt to 'impose upon posterity versions of their works and selves specifically reflective of the aesthetic perceptions, moral discriminations, and creative choices they have arrived at late in life—however profoundly these may differ from those which prevailed earlier in their careers' (*Testamentary Acts: Browning, Tennyson, James, Hardy* (Clarendon, 1992), 4).

In 1917, at an early stage in the writing of his 'Author's Notes', Conrad was clear that he would not emulate the kind of highly technical prefaces that James had supplied for his New York Edition: 'I can't rivalise with poor dear HJ and I don't know that it would be wise even to try. Besides I don't feel the need somehow. And then I have formed for myself a conception of my public that would accept graciously a few intimate words but would not care for long disquisitions about art. And, lately, I have no "aims" to explain' (to J. B. *Pinker, 14 July? 1917). Typically Conradian reserve combines with a certain weary diffidence in the 'eminent' writer's decision to aim for brevity and intimacy of address—what he had earlier in his career described as a 'chat, an appreciation, something light and interesting' (*CL*, ii. 139)—as a way of embracing the widest possible audience. The rules of polite conversation prevail throughout his 'Author's Notes', with the implication that excessive engagement with wider literary issues, technical matters, or open controversy would be bad form. Hence Conrad often gives the impression of cautiously paddling in shallow waters and creating few ripples. Each preface touches upon the origin and sources of the work, with a recurring emphasis on 'real-life' models, considers one or two specific objections from past reviews, and disclaims any offence to the audience's decent expectations; each one also maintains a seemingly effortless cordiality, broken only occasionally by hints of Conrad's slightly tired sense that all of his novels must be given the same treatment 'lest a false impression of indifference or weariness should be created' ('Author's Note', *The Mirror of the Sea*, p. vii).

Given their often hasty composition, the 'Author's Notes' are inevitably variable in range and quality. In the more extended and revealing—for example, the introductions to *Nostromo*, *A Personal Record*, *The Secret Agent*, and *Under Western Eyes*—Conrad appears to warm to his task and imaginatively re-engage with issues from his past work. But others, like the introductions to *An Outcast of the Islands*, *Lord Jim*, and *Victory*—bear signs of hasty production and are frankly disappointing in a way described by Karl: 'It is not so much that the Author's Notes are trivial as that they are misleading. They were written to catch the eye and mind of those he would have once disdained, and they are part of a relaxation of effort, not an expenditure of it' (*JCTL*, 822). During the period 1919–20, when Conrad wrote many of the prefaces, he harboured the ambition of winning the Nobel Prize for Literature. Whether accidentally or not, many of his 'Author's Notes' employ an elevated rhetoric and invoke values that might certainly catch the eye of a Nobel committee.

In Conrad's defence, the whole project may have exposed him to conflicting pressures against which he could hardly defend himself. The enterprise brought an unwelcome reminder of his mortality and imposed upon him the awkward and unenviable role of playing curator in the formation of his own museum. Other pressures from a post-*First World War world that desired retrenchment, moderate moods, and a return to the normative can clearly be felt in Conrad's tendency in the 'Author's Notes' to dilute the pessimistic content of his work, temper its extremes, and link it with time-hallowed 'ideal' values. An anxious Conrad is repeatedly drawn to defend his fiction against immoderate pessimism, offence to good taste, or 'evil intention' in order to assert 'higher' motives: 'I have never sinned against the basic feelings and elementary convictions which make life possible to the mass of mankind and, by establishing a standard of judgment, set their idealism free to look for plainer ways, for higher feelings, for deeper purposes' ('Author's Note', *Chance*, p. x). The 1920 introduction to *Victory* again finds Conrad hoping that his own 'bit of imagined drama' has not aggravated a war-torn world 'already full of doubts and fears' and solemnly addressing the 'unchanging Man of history' (p. ix).

One happy result is that Conrad, whether by intention or default, rarely attempts to coerce the reader into specific interpretations of particular works or adopts any crude version of the intentionalist fallacy. The meanings in his fiction are, he implies, plural and inconclusive, depending upon the reader's active participation for their full realization: 'Each of them has more than one intention. With each the question is what the writer has done with his opportunity; and each answers the question for itself in words which, if I may say so without undue solemnity, were written with a conscientious regard for the truth of my own sensations. And each of those stories, to mean something, must justify itself in its own way to the conscience of each successive reader' ('Author's Note', *Typhoon*, p. vii). See also Vivienne

Rundle, 'Defining Frames: The Prefaces of Henry James and Joseph Conrad', *Henry James Review*, 16 (1995), 66–92.

'Autocracy and War'. On 12 January 1905, Conrad wrote to H.-D. *Davray, one of his French translators, that he intended to write three articles on the Russian Empire, and began the first of these in mid-January during a journey to Capri. By late February, developments in *Russia had caused him to alter tack; and he was then dictating to his wife Jessie an article entitled 'The Concord of Europe'. By his own account, he sent a typescript of the essay to his agent J. B. *Pinker in early April, but it was lost in the post and a replacement was forwarded on 23 April. Conrad's report to H. G. *Wells on the 25th that he had been 'trying to get something off to Pinker for dear life' (*CL*, iii. 234) raises the suspicion that he may, in fact, have completed the piece only towards the end of that month. Arriving home in mid-May to learn of the essay's acceptance, he made some revisions at the request of the editor of the *Fortnightly Review*. It appeared there on 1 July 1905, 1–21, was published in the July issue of the *North American Review*, 33–55, and was printed as a pamphlet by Thomas J. *Wise in 1919. The essay was collected in *Notes on Life and Letters*.

Occasioned by the Russo-Japanese War and the social and political upheavals it had spawned in Russia, the essay surveys a range of historical and political issues of a kind dealt with under a displaced and fictional guise in *Nostromo*. Although marred by some rhetorical excesses—on its reprinting in *Notes on Life and Letters* the *Weekly Review*'s notice characterized it as 'condemnation in the form of rhapsody' (3 September 1921, 217)—and an awkward organizational structure, the essay presents its theses forcefully; but it does so as much through imagery and impassioned rhythm as through sustained argument. Conrad contends that the inherent irrationality of autocracy, whose Russian incarnation he alternately images as a 'monster' or 'ghoul', necessitates its eventual demise and a consequent crisis in the European balance of power. Urgently warning against the emergence of an aggressively expansionist *Germany in the wake of Russia's collapse and as a result of its own economic strength, Conrad pessimistically foresees a divided Europe engaged in competition for 'material interests' and, in the absence of any ideological cohesiveness, doomed to war. His scepticism about the innate inability of democratic governments, 'without other ancestry but the sudden shout of a multitude' (105), to combat these problems forms a significant sub-theme.

Andrzej Busza's 'The Rhetoric of Conrad's Non-fictional Political Discourse', *Annales de la Faculté des Lettres et Sciences Humaines de Nice*, 34 (1978), 159–70, offers a nuanced analysis of the essay as a cross-generic form, demonstrating how Conrad drew upon a battery of fictional strategies to present his thematic concerns. A carbon-copy typescript, altered by an editor but untouched by Conrad himself, is held at Syracuse University, and a set of pamphlet proofs with Conrad's revisions for the essay's reprinting in *Notes on Life and Letters* is held at the Beinecke Rare Book and Manuscript Library, Yale University.   JHS

awards. See GRANTS AND AWARDS; HONOURS AND PRIZES.

B

Bakhtinian approaches. Although his work remained untranslated and virtually unknown during his lifetime, the Russian thinker and teacher Mikhail Mikhailovich Bakhtin (1895–1975) has had a major influence on Western literary criticism in recent decades. The reissue in 1963 of his 1929 study of Fyodor *Dostoevsky, *Problems in Dostoevsky's Poetics*, led to the rediscovery of his writings and their dissemination in France and the United States. As translations became available in English, French, and other languages, Bakhtin's reputation spread rapidly from university departments of Slavic languages and comparative literature into other fields, including linguistics, anthropology, and philosophy. Given the adversities of Bakhtin's life, the quality and even the very survival of his work appear almost miraculous. He was imprisoned and exiled to Kazakhstan in 1929, his right leg was amputated in 1938, and most of his teaching was done at an obscure pedagogical institute in Saransk. In spite of these difficulties, the vocabulary he developed, introducing concepts such as 'dialogism', 'polyphony', 'carnivalization', 'heteroglossia', and 'chronotope', offers liberating alternatives to the systemic excesses of structuralism and *Marxism, and provides a refreshing counterpart to the bitter wisdom of post-structuralism and deconstructionism.

There is no record that Bakhtin ever mentioned Conrad in his writings or conversations, although *The Secret Agent* was available in Russian as early as 1908, and Russian *translations of most of the major novels and stories were in print by 1928, including a five-volume edition of *Selected Works*. These volumes were occasionally reprinted or newly translated, but no further works were translated into Russian between 1928 and 1958. Conrad's multilingual patrimony and multicultural experience, which found expression in various forms of narrative *irony, 'double-voicing', and translinguistic *'borrowings', make him an ideal subject for Bakhtinian criticism, which celebrates polyphony and the creation of meaning as a social bond often shared across boundaries of class, culture, or language.

It is curious, therefore, to note that the first extended study linking Bakhtin with Conrad should emphasize not the freedom of language but its use as a coercive instrument of power. Aaron Fogel's *Coercion to Speak: Conrad's Poetics of Dialogue* (1985) is a wide-ranging and assertive interpretation of Conrad's dialogues, and dialogue more generally, in terms of *anakrisis* or 'examination' understood as a form of Oedipal inquisition or forced speech. Fogel is convinced that 'forced dialogue—the fact that someone must make someone else talk—is the forgotten essence or ground of all dialogue' (136). In his famous 'Preface' to *The Nigger of the 'Narcissus'* Conrad stated that his task as an artist was 'to make you hear, to make you feel . . . before all, to make you *see*' (p. x). Fogel in effect shifts the emphasis of Conrad's credo from the verbs of perception to the modal verb *make*: to *make* you hear, to *make* you feel, to *make* you see. He derives a critical vocabulary from a general sense of coercion in which dialogue is never a free exchange of ideas or search for meaning, but always an uneven inquisition in which speech is forced. According to Fogel, 'Conrad's dialogical bias or signature is the scene in which one person tries to force another to speak, and finally provokes a "detonation"' (202). Hearing is also forced, and even overhearing is in this account essentially 'involuntary' or 'coercive'.

This obsessive concern with duress seems quite alien both to the reverberating ironies of Conrad's prose and to the refreshing generosity of Bakhtin's understanding of language as a social celebration of 'answer-ability'. In particular, Fogel's definition of dialogue as 'forced' discourse runs directly counter to Bakhtin's valorization of 'dialogic' over 'monologic' speech. Fogel recognizes this, but argues that Conrad's language is far more coercive than that of Bakhtin. According to Fogel, 'Conrad imagined a more forced and negative "polyglossia," not exactly Babel, but a world in which the plurality of languages and ideas does not amount to a new plenitude. It only exists, marked by ironies, emptinesses, contractions, and contractualities of its own, rather than by glorious worldliness and freedom. That is, Conrad created, from his Polish-English contractual standpoint, a deliberately hollow and coercive international polyphony' (109). Fogel illustrates his claim by examining important scenes of inquisition in Conrad's works, like *Marlow's 'forced' lie to *Kurtz's *Intended in 'Heart of Darkness', or *Razumov's confession in *Under Western Eyes*. The torture of *Hirsch in *Nostromo* is emblematic for Fogel, who regards the 'South American inquisitions' as 'a vivid formal example, suspended between force and farce, of what most dialogue *is*' (138). This focus on dialogue (so defined) excludes from consideration many other important aspects of Conrad's work that could readily be addressed in terms of Bakhtinian theory, like Conrad's sense of humour and the carnivalesque, his multi-voiced narrative irony, his 'borrowings' from French and other sources, and his use of specific chronotopes.

In *Nomadic Voices: Conrad and the Subject of Narrative* (Urbana: University of Illinois Press, 1992), Bruce Henricksen concedes that Fogel's study is 'provocative', but rejects the argument that Conradian dialogue is always forced, and concludes with the claim that Conrad's texts point 'beyond oppression and coercion toward the open and always unfinished project of justice' (169). Basing his approach on Bakhtin and Jean-François Lyotard, Henricksen traces a line of development in Conrad's career that moves away from the relatively 'monologic' master-narratives of *The Nigger of the 'Narcissus'* and the early Marlow stor-

ies, and towards the more elaborate and polyphonic orchestrations in *Nostromo* and *Under Western Eyes*.

In 'Chronotopes and Voices in *Under Western Eyes*', *Conradiana*, 18 (1986), 9–25, Gene M. Moore examines the novel's problematic 'double authority' in terms of Bakhtin's concept of the 'chronotope', which defines the conditions of time and space in which specific forms of discourse are possible. This novel is narrated by an English *teacher of languages who competes with the protagonist Razumov not only for the attentions of Natalia *Haldin but also for control of the text. The teacher is ostensibly translating and presenting Razumov's diary to his Western readers, but he paraphrases this document in ways that clearly diverge from Razumov's perspective, and both he and Razumov appear as characters in each other's narratives. Moore's narratological approach contrasts Razumov's 'Petersburg' chronotope of anguished, 'Dostoevskian' time and space with the English teacher's more leisurely 'Genevan' chronotope, and examines the ways in which the two chronotopes interact.

Paul Kirschner has applied Bakhtin's notion of 'dialogism' to the topography of *Geneva in a series of essays, especially 'Topodialogic Narrative in *Under Western Eyes* and the Rasoumoffs of "La Petite Russie"' (in Moore (ed.) 1992: 223–54). In a similar spirit of neologism, Daphna Erdinast-Vulcan's essay 'On the Edge of the Subject: The Heterobiography of Joseph K. Conrad' (*Genre*, 28 (1995), 303–22) adapts Bakhtin's notion of 'heteroglossia' in discussing *Under Western Eyes* in connection with Dostoevsky and the theoretical work of Jacques Derrida. In 'The Dialogism of *Lord Jim*', *The Conradian*, 22 (1997), 58–74, Gail Fincham uses Bakhtin's concept to examine Marlow's account of *Jim in the context of British *colonialism. The Bakhtin Centre at the University of Sheffield provides many research services, including an electronic bibliography of materials by and about Bakhtin.

In his fascination with the interplay of voices in various languages and the indeterminacies through which we attempt to create meaning, Conrad was clearly Bakhtinian *avant la lettre*. As Marlow says in *Lord Jim*: 'the last word is not said,—probably shall never be said. Are not our lives too short for that full utterance which through all our stammerings is of course our only and abiding intention?' (225).

Bangkok. Of Conrad's one stay in this city, the capital of Siam (present-day Thailand), Sherry writes that although 'extremely short [24 January–9 February 1888] . . . it was to be almost as fruitful a source for his fiction as was Berau' (*CEW*, 32). The reason for his journey there was significant: he travelled from *Singapore to assume his only command at sea, the *Otago* (see SHIPS AND VOYAGES), whose departure was delayed due to severe dysentery and cholera among the crew, but probably also by problems connected with charterers and towage. Conrad later commented: 'In Bangkok when I took command, I hardly ever left the ship except to go to my charterers . . . I was really too busy ever to *hear* much about shore people' (to W. G. St Clair, 31 March 1917).

Given the association of Bangkok with Conrad's own first initiation into the role of ship master, it is hardly surprising that his memories of the city, its quays, and waterway should come into play in his three stories about first command, 'Falk' (*Typhoon*), 'The Secret Sharer' ('*Twixt Land and Sea*), and *The Shadow-Line*, all belonging to what Conrad later called his 'Otago Cycle' (to A. T. Saunders, 14 June 1917). Centred upon the episode of a ship's delay in Bangkok, the first story stresses the towage difficulties standing in the way of her departure and may draw upon problems similar to those Conrad had to confront as master of the *Otago*. It also features a narrator who makes some contact with the city's bustling life, especially when he takes a gharry-ride to a native compound in search of a potential pilot and explores 'an infinity of infamous grog shops, gambling dens, opium dens' (190). Additionally, as Lester points out (63–5), there is

some attempt to build into the story a Buddhist presence through several references to Bangkok's temples 'where shaven priests cherish the thoughts of that Annihilation which is the worthy reward of us all' (210). The death of a crew member mentioned in 'Falk' (155) and *The Shadow-Line* (67) did not form part of Conrad's actual experience in Bangkok, but was based upon an event that had occurred eight days before he arrived: the death from cholera of the *Otago*'s Swedish cook and steward John Carlson. *The Shadow-Line*'s 'excellent doctor' who oversees the crew's sickness is based upon William Willis (1837–94), a Scottish physician who had taken up a Foreign Office posting in Bangkok between 1885 and 1892. For a detailed account of these and other sources pertaining to Christian *Falk and *Schomberg, see Sherry's chapter on 'The Delay in Bangkok' in *CEW*, 228–45. On Conrad's stay in the city more generally, see Yasuko Shidara, 'Conrad and Bangkok: Another Excursion to his "Eastern World"', in Karin Hansson (ed.), *Journeys, Myths and the Age of Travel: Joseph Conrad's Era* (University of Ronneby, 1998), 76–96.

Both 'The Secret Sharer' and *The Shadow-Line* incorporate features of the ship's passage along the Chao Phraya River and across its 'bar' to memorable emblematic effect. In 'The Secret Sharer', the opening description of the ship's departure from Bangkok, her approach to the bar, with two clumps of trees 'one on each side of the only fault in the impeccable joint' (91), and her passage into the Gulf of Siam prefigures a story of initiation marked by unknown boundaries, dualities, and thresholds: 'In this breathless pause at the threshold of a long passage we seemed to be measuring our fitness for a long and arduous enterprise . . . to be carried out, far from all human eyes, with only sky and sea for spectators and for judges' (92). In the latter story, the young man's first arrival in Bangkok coincides with the height of his youthful romantic expectation; but when, after a harrowing delay, he and his ship depart, throw off 'the mortal coil of shore affairs', and cross the bar (a phrase that can also be applied to the act of dying), they pass into a still, unknown, and isolated world: 'My command might have been a planet flying vertiginously on its appointed path in a space of infinite silence' (73, 74). If a special resonance attaches to these depictions of departure and initiation, it may also be because, in autobiographical terms, Conrad's own voyage in the *Otago* from Bangkok to *Australia marked the end of a significant phase in his own life: that is, his final break with the East and, at the age of 30, the entry into a new phase of his maritime life.

Barral. See DE BARRALS, THE.

Barrie, J[ames] M[atthew] (1860–1937; knighted 1913), Scottish novelist and dramatist. J. M. Barrie seems to have been an early admirer of Conrad's work. He entered Conrad's sphere in 1903 with moral and considerable financial support (a sum of £150), although their subsequent relationship was not close. In 1904, Conrad sent his first dramatic adaptation, *One Day More*, to be read by the dramatist who had in that same year enjoyed a popular success with *Peter Pan* and had useful theatre connections. In 1908, Barrie also supported Conrad's application for a Royal Literary Fund award. See also GRANTS AND AWARDS.

'Because of the Dollars' was anticipated in a letter of Conrad's to his agent J. B. *Pinker in early December 1913 when he announced that 'next week I shall begin another story' (*CL*, v. 311). Written during a break in the composition of *Victory*, it was finished in early January 1914. In the course of trying to secure *serialization for the tale, Pinker approached *Pall Mall Magazine*, whose editor recommended that the title be changed to 'Davidson of Saigon'. In response, Conrad suggested simply 'The Dollars' and, as an alternative, 'The Spoiled Smile'. Critics have noted that the story's final title echoes that of a play by Conrad's father Apollo *Korzeniowski, *Because of the Money* (1859). When the tale was first published in *Metropolitan Magazine*, in September 1914, it was under the title

'Laughing Anne', a title Conrad revived when he adapted it as a two-act play in 1920. The story was included as the fourth and final tale in *Within the Tides*.

'Because of the Dollars' is the story of Captain Davidson, 'a really *good* man' (169), and, in particular, of the incident 'that spoiled Davidson's smile for him' (210–11). Told to an anonymous narrator by Hollis and occasioned by their brief meeting with Davidson in 'a great Eastern port' (169), the tale reveals how Davidson foiled a combined murder and robbery attempt against him with the help of 'Laughing Anne', a reformed 'painted woman' (184) he had known in his youth. After a life of being deserted by men, Anne has been reduced to living up 'some God-forsaken creek' in the Mirrah Settlement, a 'wild place that you couldn't find on a map, and more squalid than the most poverty-stricken Malay settlement had a right to be' (177, 181), with Bamtz, a reformed loafer turned rattan-trader. With characteristic 'goodness' (and in order to ensure an income for Anne and her young son Tony), Davidson has included Bamtz on his regular trading voyages so that when, in response to a government order that old currency be exchanged for new, he visits the isolated outposts of his traders to collect their old dollars, he also stops to collect Bamtz's rattans. Lying in wait for him there are a trio of villains led by a murderous Frenchman without hands but with an iron weight tied to his right stump. With Bamtz, they sneak onto Davidson's steamer under cover of darkness but he surprises them, having learned of their intentions from Anne. Guessing that it was she who betrayed them, the Frenchman bludgeons Anne to death and is, in turn, killed by Davidson. The others escape empty-handed. Davidson returns to port with the dollars and with Tony, for whom he intends to provide a home. His wife's heart, though, is 'about the size of a parched pea' (207), and, once she learns about Laughing Anne's reputation, she assumes that the boy is Davidson's child and has Tony sent away, before taking her 'pure, sensitive, mean little soul' (210) back to her parents.

The sequel to the story, according to Hollis, is that Tony has grown up with the desire to be a missionary.

'Because of the Dollars' prefigures the novel *Victory* in various ways. For instance, Captain Davidson of the *Sissie* reappears in the novel. In addition, there are a number of structural and thematic connections between short story and novel: thus, the texts share a trio of villains in search of easy riches and the spectacle of the heroine's self-sacrifice; see Schwarz 1982: 23–9. The manuscript is held at the Rosenbach Museum and Library, Philadelphia, and the typescript at the Lilly Library, Indiana University.   AHS

Beerbohm, [Henry] Max[imilian] (1872–1956; knighted 1939), writer and caricaturist. Max Beerbohm met Conrad rarely, although he greatly admired his works. On the occasion of the writer's death, he wrote to Jessie Conrad about the 'illustrious and wondrous Joseph Conrad . . . a man of great genius whom the world had for many years neglected, whom the world (in its stupid but decent way) had at last made much of' (*PL*, 247). Beerbohm's affectionate parody of Conrad's early work in 'The Feast' in *A Christmas Garland* (1912) signalled Conrad's arrival as a major literary personality and offered a clever criticism of the overwrought style, impalpable atmosphere, and world-weariness of his early stories. Conrad later wrote: 'I have lived long enough to see it ["The Lagoon"] most agreeably guyed by Mr. Max Beerbohm in a volume of parodies . . . where I found myself in very good company. I was immensely gratified. I began to believe in my public existence' ('Author's Note', *Tales of Unrest*, p. vi). Beerbohm also drew caricatures of Conrad, notably in a series called 'The Young Self and the Older Self' (1924) in which he artfully telescopes an entire lifetime by showing the monocled and goateed older Conrad confronting his younger self, for whom Beerbohm invents a gibberish representing Polish. See also Addison C. Bross, 'Beerbohm's "The Feast" and Conrad's Early Fiction', *Nineteenth-Century Fiction*, 26 (1971), 329–36, and Ed-

mund A. Bojarski, 'Beerbohm and Conrad', *Conradiana*, 4: 1 (1972), 60–2.

Bennett, [Enoch] Arnold (1867–1931), the chronicler of turn-of-the-century urban experience in the 'Five Towns' area that makes up the city of Stoke-on-Trent in such novels as *The Old Wives' Tale* (1908) and *The Clayhanger Trilogy* (1910–16). Arnold Bennett was, with H. G. *Wells and Edward *Garnett, amongst the earliest champions of Conrad's fiction. As assistant editor of the *Academy* in the late 1890s, he created a policy of having Conrad's works regularly reviewed and actually undertook some of the reviews himself. Probably the author of the *Academy*'s tribute to *Tales of Unrest* as one of its 'crowned' books of the year 1898 (*CCH*, 109–10), Bennett may also have been the journal's 'anonymous' reviewer of *Lord Jim* (ibid. 115–17), whose criticism of the length of this 'after-dinner story' provoked a rebuttal in Conrad's 1917 'Author's Note' to the novel. In a series of more general *Academy* articles in 1901–2, Bennett set Conrad among a very distinguished European literary company, including Tolstoy, *Flaubert, and Henry *James.

Introduced to each other by Wells in 1899, their paths crossed only infrequently. Conrad, however, read many of Bennett's novels, including *A Man from the North* (1898), *Anna of the Five Towns* (1902), and *Leonora* (1903), and corresponded with him on the limits of his naturalistic methods: 'You just stop short of being absolutely real because you are faithful to your dogmas of realism. Now realism in art will never approach reality. And your art, your gift should be put to the service of a larger and freer faith' (*CL*, ii. 390). As his journals and letters testify, Bennett remained an appreciative and discriminating reader of Conrad's work (for example, in 1912 he judged *Nostromo* to be 'the finest novel of this generation (bar none)' (*CCH*, 161)). A moving exchange of letters took place between the two writers in the last months of Conrad's life, when the latter thanked Bennett for a presentation copy of *Riceyman's Steps* (1923), which had been inscribed,

'Joseph Conrad from his faithful admirer, Arnold Bennett, Xmas 1923'. See also Owen Knowles, 'Arnold Bennett as an "Anonymous" Reviewer of Conrad's Early Fiction', *The Conradian*, 10 (1985), 26–36.

Berdyczów, or Berdichev, now in *Ukraine, Conrad's putative birthplace, lies some 30 miles (50 km) south of Żytomierz in eastern Volhynia, which had been Lithuanian and Polish territory before it was annexed by *Russia in the second partition of *Poland in 1793. In 1857 Conrad's father Apollo *Korzeniowski was the leaseholder of an estate called Derebczynka, in Podolia, but he and his wife Ewa apparently went to stay with his wife's mother in Terechowa, near Berdyczów, as the pregnancy neared term. Berdyczów is cited as Conrad's birthplace in the 'Document' written for him by his uncle Tadeusz *Bobrowski (*CPB*, 201). A poem written by Conrad's father to celebrate his christening 'in the 85th year of Muscovite oppression' is dated 23 November (5 December new style) 1857 at Berdyczów (*CUFE*, 32–3). The baby was christened 'with water only' by a member of the Carmelite order from the Berdyczów Monastery. No baptismal certificate was issued until five years later, when the christening was 'confirmed with oil' in Żytomierz, apparently in the family's absence; and this curious duplication has been among the factors contributing to confusion about Conrad's actual birthplace.

Conrad himself always gave Żytomierz and not Berdyczów as his place of birth. He did not visit the area between 1868, when he and his father were allowed to leave Russian territory, and 1890, when he returned to visit his uncle Tadeusz Bobrowski. In the meantime, he named 'Gitomir' as his birthplace on the crew lists of the French *ships in which he served, on his *examination applications in 1880 and 1886, and also when joining the *Palestine* in 1881. On his application for *naturalization and in all the other British ships in which he served, his birthplace was given simply as 'Poland' even though Poland did not exist as a sovereign state from 1795 to 1918. An auto-

biographical sketch sent to a Polish scholar from Capri in 1905 begins: 'I was born on the 3rd December 1857 at Żytomierz' (*CL*, iii. 233).

A further complication was caused by a photograph that Conrad described to his family as a picture of the house in which he was born (reproduced as the frontispiece to the *Victory* volume in the 1925 Medallion Edition, and also in *JCHC*). This strikingly decorated structure was later identified as a pavilion located in two different places, neither Berdyczów nor Żytomierz. In an article published in Russian in 1972, Dmitri Urnov cited a local taxi-driver who claimed that the house was still standing in Iwańkowce, about five miles from Berdyczów. Najder, on the other hand, has identified it as a neo-Gothic pavilion that once stood in Nowochwastów, too far to the east to have been the place of Conrad's birth (see Ugo Mursia's exchanges with Najder recorded in 'The True Birthplace of Joseph Conrad', in Sherry (ed.) 1976: 202–4, and in Najder, *JCC*, 10 n.). Najder has also been instrumental in promoting efforts to create a Conrad *museum in a part of the monastery at Berdyczów.

bibliographies. There is, as yet, no single comprehensive and systematic primary bibliography of Conrad's entire *œuvre* for advanced scholars. The catalogues of what were originally two major private Conrad collections remain helpful: Thomas J. *Wise's *A Bibliography of Joseph Conrad*, 2nd edn. (Richard Clay, 1921), lists Wise's collection of manuscripts, typescripts, limited-edition *pamphlets, and signed first editions, most now in the British Library's Ashley Collection; secondly, George T. Keating's *A Conrad Memorial Library: The Collection of George T. Keating* (Garden City, NY: Doubleday, Doran, 1929) describes the largest single collection of original materials and miscellaneous Conradiana, now housed at the Beinecke Rare Book and Manuscript Library, Yale University. More systematic, if still preliminary research was undertaken by Gordon Lindstrand in his listing of Conrad manuscripts in 'A Bibliographical Survey of the Literary

Manuscripts of Joseph Conrad', *Conradiana*, 2: 1 (1969), 23–32; 2: 2 (1969–70), 105–14; and 2: 3 (1969–70), 153–62; and by Walter E. Smith in *Joseph Conrad: A Bibliographical Catalogue of his Major First Editions, with Facsimiles of Several Title Pages* (privately printed, 1979). William R. Cagle's scholarly bibliography of Conrad's *œuvre*, begun in the 1960s, remains incomplete and unpublished. (Photocopies of it may be obtained at cost from: The Curator, The Lilly Library, Indiana University, Bloomington, IN 47405–3301, USA.) In a number of essays and articles, Donald W. Rude has also made an important contribution to the discovery and description of items in the Conrad canon.

Two early pioneering bibliographies of Conrad criticism, Kenneth A. Lohf and Eugene P. Sheehy's *Joseph Conrad at Mid-Century: Essays and Studies, 1895–1955* (Minneapolis: University of Minnesota Press, 1957) and Theodore G. Ehrsam's *A Bibliography of Joseph Conrad* (Metuchen, NJ: Scarecrow Press, 1969), are now inevitably outdated, although the latter is still useful for its listing of editions of Conrad's work, *translations, and contemporary reviews. As regards secondary sources and scholarship, both have been overtaken by Bruce E. Teets and Helmut E. Gerber's *Joseph Conrad: An Annotated Bibliography of Writings about Him* (De Kalb: Northern Illinois UP, 1971), a comprehensive scholarly guide to criticism from 1895 to 1966, with items arranged chronologically. It supersedes all previous bibliographies in its scope (almost 2,000 entries, including reviews and dissertations), width of coverage (abstracts of items in fourteen languages), and detailed annotation (mainly expository but with occasional brief evaluations). A single main deficiency is the absence of a systematic subject-index. Teets continues this project in *Joseph Conrad: An Annotated Bibliography* (New York: Garland, 1990), a valuable sequel that includes over 700 items missed in the first volume and a further 1,400 entries extending coverage from 1967 to 1975. On the debit side, the volume is marred by many small slips and errors, including a missing portion of

text where items 2075–97 should appear. Owen Knowles's *An Annotated Critical Bibliography of Joseph Conrad* (Hemel Hempstead: Harvester Wheatsheaf, 1992) provides a helpfully selective and thematically organized guide to the important critical items, with a primary emphasis on post-1975 criticism and its underlying trends. Conrad criticism during the period 1968–89 is helpfully listed in a series of bibliographies published in *Conradiana*. Students and scholars can also keep abreast of recent scholarship by searching for Conrad items in the *MLA International Bibliography*, which is also available on CD-ROM and on-line.

More specialized bibliographies include Robert D. Hamner's 'Joseph Conrad and the Colonial World: A Selected Bibliography', *Conradiana*, 14 (1982), 217–29, a valuable listing of books, articles, and theses, including many unfamiliar items by African, Indian, and Malaysian critics. Robert Secor and Debra Moddelmog's *Joseph Conrad and American Writers: A Bibliographical Study of Affinities, Influences, and Relations* (Westport, Conn. Greenwood Press, 1985) seems immoderately partisan in claiming a powerful American 'influence' upon Conrad, an impression confirmed by a sometimes inflated number of entries. Nevertheless, the volume is helpfully organized and valuable for its listing of comparative studies of Conrad and such major American writers as Herman Melville, Henry *James, T. S. Eliot, and F. Scott Fitzgerald. In *Joseph Conrad and his Contemporaries: An Annotated Bibliography of Interviews and Recollections* (Joseph Conrad Society, UK, 1988), Martin Ray usefully compiles and annotates almost 300 items of literary or biographical interest, with well-known reminiscences excluded in favour of those relatively unfamiliar or inaccessible. David W. Tutein's *Joseph Conrad's Reading: An Annotated Bibliography* (West Cornwall, Conn.: Locust Hill Press, 1990) attempts a comprehensive listing of Conrad's reading matter and books owned by him, but it lacks a sophisticated methodology and overlooks many references. Hans van

Marle's review-article 'A Novelist's Dukedom: From Joseph Conrad's Library', *The Conradian*, 16: 1 (1991), 55–78, lists 181 items missing from Tutein's volume and outlines a more systematic methodology for dealing with the topic. Wanda Perczak's *Polska Bibliografia Conradowska, 1896–1992* (Toruń: Wydawnictwo Uniwersytetu Mikołaja Kopernika, 1993) offers a comprehensive listing of Polish translations of Conrad's works; books, articles, and theses in Polish about his work; and studies in English about Conrad's Polish background, influence, and reception.

biographies. Several early attempts to grapple with Conrad's elusive individuality, life, and cultural traditions were made by his family and friends in memoirs published after his death in 1924. Often factually unreliable and over-indulgently worshipful, they nevertheless convey a quality of excited first-hand testimony. Among the most important are Ford Madox *Ford's Joseph Conrad: A Personal Remembrance* (Duckworth, 1924); John *Galsworthy's brief portrait of 1924 for a French audience, later translated as 'Reminiscences of Conrad: 1924', in *Castles in Spain & Other Screeds* (Heinemann, 1927); Richard *Curle's *The Last Twelve Years of Joseph Conrad* (Sampson Low, Marston, 1928); Edward *Garnett's introductory portrait in *Letters from Conrad, 1895 to 1924* (Nonesuch, 1928); Jessie Conrad's two memoirs, *Joseph Conrad as I Knew Him* (Heinemann, 1926) and *Joseph Conrad and his Circle* (Jarrolds, 1935); and J. H. *Retinger's *Conrad and his Contemporaries: Souvenirs* (Minerva, 1941). These and other reminiscences of Conrad at various stages of his life are usefully excerpted and collected in Ray's *JCIR* and in Najder's *CUFE*.

G. *Jean-Aubry, selected by Conrad to be his first biographer, completed his two-volume *Joseph Conrad: Life & Letters* (Heinemann, 1927) within three years of the novelist's death. His biographical interchapters on Conrad's early years still retain some interest for what they record of Jean-Aubry's first-hand contact with the writer,

but in the second volume the account dwindles into a perfunctory survey of the years after 1905. Jean-Aubry's *The Sea Dreamer: A Definitive Biography of Joseph Conrad* (Allen & Unwin, 1957), a translation of a work first published in France in 1947, largely reworks the material of *Life & Letters* and suffers from the same imbalances. The first properly researched and comprehensive factual biography was Jocelyn Baines's *Joseph Conrad: A Critical Biography* (Weidenfeld & Nicolson, 1960), which incorporates much unpublished material and is structured around fourteen phases of Conrad's life. It is distinguished by a careful attempt to sift fact from fiction (particularly relating to Conrad's *suicide attempt) and a shrewdly pragmatic approach to Conrad's habit of self-mythologizing. Only serviceable in the quality of its literary judgements, Baines's study has nevertheless proved very durable and still needs to be consulted for its clear and independent views.

As early as 1930, a *psychoanalytic tradition of Conrad biography was established with Gustav Morf's *The Polish Heritage of Joseph Conrad* (Sampson Low, Marston). This tenacious pursuit of Conrad's 'alien complex' by a Swiss critic postulates that his life unfolded in the shadow of his distant past by virtue of a persistent guilt complex at having deserted his homeland and so betrayed the Polish national cause. Employing methods based upon Freudian mechanisms of repression and sublimation, Morf explores the novels—*Lord Jim* and *Nostromo* in particular—as Conrad's 'confessionals', efforts by symbolic indirection to justify or expiate his desertion; he also regards Conrad's central characters as 'all more or less his doubles, . . . their fate . . . modelled on his own or on *what he feared his own fate might be*' (96). Despite the reductiveness of some of Morf's assumptions and the far-fetchedness of some of his conclusions (for example, Jim's jump from the *Patna* matches 'exactly what happened to Joseph Conrad. *The sinking ship is Poland.* . . . And finally, Jim yielded and jumped, i.e. Conrad became a British subject' (163, 164)), his core idea has commended itself to some later critics as a way of approaching Conrad as *homo duplex*, 'tortured' by an Anglo-Polish dualism. Morf's *The Polish Shades and Ghosts of Joseph Conrad* (New York: Astra Books, 1976) essentially restates this thesis. Bernard C. Meyer's *Joseph Conrad: A Psychoanalytic Biography* (Princeton UP, 1967) goes well beyond Morf in applying psychoanalytic methods to Conrad's life and fiction-making, tracing in both a complex of ruling psychic and neurotic manifestations. Fetishizations, oedipalism, incest motifs, and an insecure sense of masculinity form a standard part of Meyer's lexicon, helping him to explain the psychogenesis of the novels, their recurrent symbolizations, and their therapeutic status as symptomatic 'confessionals' in which Conrad effects a compensatory revision of a painful reality. Always controversial, and now partly out of favour with a younger generation of critics, Meyer's work at its best still offers a valuable and unsensational account by a practising psychiatrist of the inner sources of Conrad's art (especially in the more minor works) and its changed quality after his breakdown in 1910.

During the period 1955–75, the biographical endeavour received a new charge with the appearance of a number of more specialized forays into areas of Conrad's life and traditions, notably his Polish background and *sea years. Czesław Miłosz's 'Joseph Conrad in Polish Eyes', *Atlantic Monthly*, 200 (1957), 219–28, Zdzisław Najder's introduction to *Conrad's Polish Background: Letters to and from Polish Friends* (OUP, 1964), Andrzej Busza's 'Conrad's Polish Literary Background and Some Illustrations of the Influence of Polish Literature on his Work', *Antemurale*, 10 (1966), 109–255, and Robert R. Hodges's *The Dual Heritage of Joseph Conrad* (The Hague: Mouton, 1966) all offer indispensable perspectives upon Conrad's Polish background and its influence upon the man and writer. This period also witnessed the beginnings of a modern tradition of Conrad biography in Poland itself, although works by such critics as Andrzej Braun, Barbara Koc, and Stefan Zabierowski remain unavailable in English. A number of other studies, while not strictly biographical, nevertheless present new kinds of factual information about Conrad's sea years. Norman Sherry's *Conrad's Eastern World* (CUP, 1966) and *Conrad's Western World* (CUP, 1971), and Jerry Allen's *The Sea Years of Joseph Conrad* (Methuen, 1967), rest upon intrepid detective work that involves the researcher in following Conrad's footsteps and, through a process combining on-site interviews, archival research, and other forms of historical archaeology, in an attempt to recreate the 'original' complex of events and observations that became sources for the future novelist. If these works provide rich evidence of Conrad as an author upon whom nothing was lost, they are often less satisfactory in accounting for the eclectic fullness of the creative process: for one thing, too many sources (for example, from Conrad's vast *reading of literature) are missing; and for another, the equation of 'real-life' models and fictional counterparts can be severely limiting.

Undoubtedly the most ambitious of the major modern biographies, Frederick R. Karl's *Joseph Conrad: The Three Lives. A Biography* (Faber, 1979), is devoted to showing Conrad as 'representative modern man and artist' who 'found in marginality itself a way of life' (p. xiv) and essays an inclusive psychological portrait. Expansive in its conception of the biographer's art and drawing upon many unpublished letters, Karl's study is also inordinately bulky, and the sheer gigantism of its 1,000 pages tends to render the conception of Conrad's 'three lives'—as Pole, seaman, and writer—clumsy and diffuse. Some of Karl's factual unreliability also has serious implications for the larger biographical narrative. Nevertheless, he can often be more rewardingly speculative and contextually inclusive than Zdzisław Najder, Conrad's other major biographer. Karl has also written several rewarding essays on problems of Conrad biography, including 'Three Problematical Areas in Conrad Biography' (Murfin (ed.) 1985: 13–30) and 'Letters into Biography', *Conradiana*, 23 (1991), 11–18.

The central purposes of Zdzisław Najder's indispensable *Joseph Conrad: A Chronicle* (CUP, 1983; also available in Polish and French) are spelled out in its introduction. Najder begins by describing his purpose in largely negative terms: he declines the possibilities offered by psychoanalysis, does not believe that the writer's works inevitably shed light on the man, and eschews speculation in favour of 'concrete scholarly demand'. Severely circumscribed though these aims may seem, Najder's study derives from a twofold belief. First, he argues that Conrad's *Polish inheritance is best understood neither through his personal reactions to it nor through the individual's guilt complex, but in cultural and collective terms that embrace his family links, 'the cultural traditions of his environment, its typical moral and political problems, its collective concerns, its whole ethos'. Hence, he concludes, 'in the case of Joseph Conrad, the proper study of the biographist is a study of culture' ('Conrad's Polish Background, or, From Biography to a Study of Culture', *Conradiana*, 18 (1986), 6, 8). Second, and as a consequence, Najder presents himself as an interpretative 'lexicographer' whose function is to explain 'certain cultural and intellectual categories to the English-speaking reader who, while understanding the language, is not always able to decipher the implicit meanings; and to Poles who are apt to see in Conrad a Polish writer and forget about his later life . . . and his complex attitude towards his Polish background' (*JCC*, p. vii). Not always as studiously unpartisan as it claims, Najder's detailed portrait is nevertheless invaluable for its assimilation of Polish materials and approaches definitiveness as a narrative 'chronicle'; it is also tonic in its shrewd questioning of some of Conrad's self-myths and commitment to clear outline and unvarnished fact.

Several biographies have attempted to balance scholarship and popular needs. Norman Sherry's *Conrad and his World* (Thames & Hudson, 1972) offers the best brief factual biography, with over 100 striking photographs. Cedric Watts's *Joseph Conrad: A Literary Life* (Macmillan, 1989) begins conventionally with chapters on biographical and cultural background, but then gives an animated and much-needed, if severely foreshortened, account of the part played by economic and material circumstances in the formation, development, and later 'popular' flowering of Conrad's literary career. Its emphases fall upon the writer's awkwardly tense relation to the forces of the burgeoning Edwardian and transatlantic publishing industry and its serial markets, the exigencies of financial need and the deadlines that often led Conrad the writer to make painful compromises, and the part played in his life by supportive friends, *publishers, and his literary agent J. B. *Pinker. Conrad's personal and professional relationship with his agent requires a much fuller study than Watts gives it and is an important area awaiting future research. Owen Knowles's *A Conrad Chronology* (Macmillan, 1989) supplies a biographical reference work with a detailed month-by-month summary, with special emphasis on Conrad's working career from 1894 to 1924: it embraces the compositional and publishing history of his writings, his reading of other authors, *finances, *health problems, and significant friendships. Of the three more popular introductory biographies to have appeared since 1980—Roger Tennant's *Joseph Conrad: A Biography* (Sheldon Press, 1981), Jeffrey Meyers's *Joseph Conrad: A Biography* (Murray, 1991), and John Batchelor's *The Life of Joseph Conrad* (Oxford: Blackwell, 1994)—the third can be especially recommended for its comprehensive and balanced coverage of the life and works, lively sense of issue, and readability.

'Black Mate, The'. This 10,500-word story, first published in the *London Magazine* in April 1908 and uncollected until its appearance in the posthumous volume *Tales of Hearsay*, is something of a curiosity in the canon because it occasioned a disagreement between Conrad and his wife about its origins. Conrad was clearly embarrassed by the tale when in 1922 he informed his agent J. B. *Pinker: 'I wrote that thing in '86 for a prize competition, started, I think, by *Tit-Bits*. It is an extraneous phenomenon. . . . However, the history of the "Black Mate," its origin etc., etc., need not be proclaimed on housetops, and *Almayer's Folly* may keep its place as my first serious work' (*LL*, ii. 264). He further indicated in Richard *Curle's copy of the privately printed 1922 edition of the story that 'I have a notion that it was first written some time in the late eighties and retouched later.' On the other hand, Jessie Conrad repeatedly claimed that she provided her husband with the material for the tale at a much later date. Given that an earlier version of the tale has not survived, it is virtually impossible to unravel the mystery at the heart of this marital disagreement about what may be Conrad's very first attempt at fiction. For a fuller account of the controversy about the tale's origins, see *JCTL*, 234–6, and *JCC*, 328–9.

Keith Carabine, in '"The Black Mate": June–July 1886; January 1908', *The Conradian*, 13 (1988), 128–48, carefully weighs the circumstantial evidence and argues for the strong possibility that Conrad did write a version of the tale in June–July 1886 for *Tit-Bits*, an immensely popular paper founded by George Newnes in 1881. Carabine points out that in 1886 the paper offered two kinds of prize—the weekly 'Prize Tit-Bit', which paid one guinea for small contributions, and a more ambitious 'Special Prize', which invited different people to write about their work experiences. Conrad could appropriately have competed for the 'Special Prize for Sailors' first advertised on 1 May 1886, which offered 20 guineas for a maximum length of about 5,400 words. With a closing date of 31 July 1886, this particular prize attracted some 740 entries.

The biographical evidence canvassed by Carabine is also suggestive. Briefly, Conrad spent the summer of 1886 on extended shore-leave in *London studying for his master's certificate (an *examination he failed on 28 July). During his previous berth as second mate in the *Tilkhurst*, which landed at Dundee on 16 June, he clearly felt himself to be at a watershed in his professional life. He wanted to 'make a

fresh start in the world.—In what direction to shape my course? That is the question!—' (*CL*, i. 13). Among the options he considered during this Hamlet-like crisis in 1885–6 were a whaling project, a business partnership with Adolf P. *Krieger, and an importing venture. A significantly different option could well have emerged through his decision to submit an entry for the 'Special Prize for Sailors' competition and thereby to explore the possibility of writing as a career.

It is feasible, then, that in the last few days of January 1908 Conrad amplified an earlier version of 'The Black Mate' when Pinker, misled by Conrad's promise that *Under Western Eyes* would make a story of 9,000 words in all, offered to place the latter with the *London Magazine*, a popular monthly. In order to save *Under Western Eyes* from being 'mangled by fools' (*CL*, iv. 39) and to buy himself time for the proper development of his Russian novel, he pacified Pinker with something appropriate for the *London Magazine* in the form of 'The Black Mate'. Carabine's analysis of the internal textual evidence sheds further interesting light on its mixed provenance. He detects in the tale a vestigial *ur*-narrative of jaunty 'tricks' characteristic of the 1880s competition story—in this case, a sailor (Bunter) dyes his prematurely white hair in order to get a job, and then, having lost his hair-dye during a storm at sea, further tricks his gullible captain by claiming that he fell on the stairs after being frightened by a ghost, an encounter that suddenly turned his hair white. Carabine also analyses the several ways in which Conrad probably reworked and complicated the story in 1908 with his addition of a more expansive and self-reflexive *frame-narrative. Interestingly, Ford Madox *Ford used the same hair-dye 'trick' in the middle episode of an obscure trilogy of detective stories entitled 'Fathead' published in *The Tramp* (March–June 1910), but possibly written also in January 1908. See also Dale Kramer, 'The Maturity of Conrad's First Tale', *Studies in Short Fiction*, 20 (1983), 45–9. The manuscript is held at the British Library.

Blackwood, William (1836–1912), grandson of the original publisher and founder of *Blackwood's Magazine*. William Blackwood brought out several of Conrad's works in magazine and book form between 1897 and 1902. 'Karain' (*Tales of Unrest*), 'Youth', 'Heart of Darkness', 'The End of the Tether' (*Youth*), and *Lord Jim* belong to what Conrad would later regard as the happiest period of his career, 'associated in my grateful memory with the late Mr. William Blackwood's encouraging and helpful kindness' ('Author's Note', *Youth*, p. v). In Blackwood, Conrad found not only a publisher and mentor, but a sustaining father-figure who, rather like a benevolent ship's captain, presided over a largely male family or club of authors. This family included Blackwood's two nephews, George William (1876–1942) and James Hugh (1878–1951), and David S. *Meldrum, who became a friend of Conrad's. Many of the values cherished by Conrad in his sea life—solidarity, male camaraderie, loyalty, and pride in time-honoured traditions—were also embodied in the Blackwood house's venerable Tory dynasty. Although Conrad's association with the firm did not bring him financial security, it nevertheless provided welcome relief from the pressures of the market-place and gave him a new professional stability and continuity: 'I had much rather work for *Maga* and the House than for the "market": were the "market" stuffed with solid gold throughout' (*CL*, ii. 376).

'It was, I think, the ambition of all young writers in my day to find themselves in *Blackwood* and old Mr. William Blackwood . . . prided himself on trying to pick out good work by unknown authors and "to give it a show,"' remarked Conrad's friend Hugh *Clifford (quoted in Blackburn (ed.), p. xv). Giving Conrad a 'show' involved Blackwood in drawing upon his considerable fund of patience, since during the period of their association Conrad's writing life and financial state were in extreme disarray. The publisher also quietly suffered the eccentricities and accidents of the Conradian working method, which, for example, saw *Lord Jim* mushroom from a planned short story to a free and wander-ing tale of some 130,000 words, and part of the manuscript of 'The End of the Tether' destroyed by fire. To Conrad's burgeoning problems of financial hardship, Blackwood also responded with generous advances. These and many other services made up what Conrad gratefully acknowledged in July 1900 as 'conditions which you have created for me to work in by your friendly and unwearied indulgence' (*CL*, ii. 281). For its part, the Blackwood house, although it may not have fully appreciated the magnitude of Conrad's talent, could take pride in having nurtured the author of the *Youth* volume—according to Meldrum 'the most notable book we have published since George Eliot' (Blackburn (ed.), 172).

The causes for the estrangement between Conrad and Blackwood were twofold. The long-suffering publisher, increasingly embroiled in Conrad's financial difficulties, finally baulked when asked for a large loan against future copyrights and, at a meeting in a *London hotel in May 1902, bluntly told the writer that the firm could not continue to carry him at a loss. The sharpness of the break left Conrad feeling disappointed, humiliated, and deserted, but also proudly defiant, as is evident in the magnificent letter of defence he wrote to Blackwood on the same day: 'I am *modern*, and I would rather recall Wagner the musician and Rodin the Sculptor who both had to starve a little in their day' (*CL*, ii. 418). The other reason for the break involved the fact that by 1902 Conrad had become firmly attached to the literary agent J. B. *Pinker who, although initially barred by the author from interfering with his personal relationship with Blackwood, was increasingly seen by the publisher as an intrusively unwelcome middleman. See also 'Conrad and William Blackwood', in Blackburn (ed.), pp. xiii–xxxiii.

Blackwood's Magazine, known as *Blackwood's Edinburgh Magazine* before 1906, was a monthly magazine begun in July 1817 by the Edinburgh publisher William Blackwood as a Tory alternative to the *Edinburgh Review*. It was at the time of Conrad's association with it run by the original founder's grandson, also named William *Blackwood. What Conrad called his 'Blackwood period' extended from 1897 to 1902 during which 'Karain', 'Youth', 'Heart of Darkness', 'The End of the Tether', and *Lord Jim* appeared in the famous journal known familiarly as 'Maga'. The journal dropped the 'Edinburgh' from its title in 1906 and survived, although in much diminished form, until 1980.

The works of Conrad's Blackwood period represent an important stage in his struggle to negotiate with his English cultural identity and discover an audience. His connection with the magazine coincides not only with the emergence of his English narrator Charles *Marlow but also with a more direct contact with an English middle-class audience, 'decent company ... a good sort of public' (*CL*, iv. 506), whose characteristic outlook or 'horizon of expectation' Conrad may have tried to capture in his portrait of the 'privileged man' in chapter 36 of *Lord Jim* and which Ivo Vidan summarizes as follows: '*Blackwood's Magazine* was conservative and imperialist, an old British magazine with a long reputation and a steady readership in the Establishment: the army, the administration, the landed gentry, the upper middle class, the clergy, and the teaching profession, people who liked seriously intoned reading on royalty and the aristocracy, on the problems of the army and the navy ... and about other countries in the world. ... Above all, it focused on the colonial world: India, in the first place, was for a while dealt with in every issue, then—very often—Africa, British and . . . other colonial powers, mainly France' (in Curreli (ed.), 405). And, it may be added, *Blackwood's* liked stories of a bracingly masculine and action-based sort. That Conrad was intent upon exploring the journal's informing ethos is suggested by his conscious effort in late 1897 to read the many issues of *Blackwood's* sent to him by William Blackwood and even to familiarize himself with Margaret Oliphant's *Annals of a Publishing House: William Blackwood and his Sons* (1897). He later helped to celebrate a significant occasion in the journal's history when Blackwood chose 'Heart of Darkness' for inclusion in its thousandth number.

The impress of *Blackwood's* conventions is most evident in 'Youth', the first of Conrad's stories to be consciously composed for the magazine (the earlier 'Karain' had been written for the open market). Its opening pages stress the Englishness of the storytelling occasion ('This could have occurred nowhere but in England . . .') but also the potentially exotic quality of the forthcoming yarn of 'the Eastern seas' (*Youth*, 3), so establishing a combination of the familiar and foreign congenial to *Blackwood's* readers. Conrad also devises for Marlow a group of auditors—including a company director, an accountant, and a lawyer ('a fine crusted Tory, High Churchman, the best of old fellows, the soul of honour' (3))—who make up a clubbish gathering around the claret bottle and may be seen to reproduce a typical cross-section of a *Blackwood's* audience. All of them are middle-aged males, bonded together by their past careers in the *British Merchant Service, with a nostalgic preference for the good old days of their youth, and all are likely to lean instinctively towards Marlow's taste for reading Frederick Burnaby's *Ride to Khiva* (1876) rather than Thomas *Carlyle's *Sartor Resartus* (1836). Delighted by Conrad's effort to adapt himself to the needs of the journal, Blackwood confidently predicted that 'Youth' would 'be a favourite item for Maga's readers' (Blackburn (ed.), 28).

Although Conrad later flattered Blackwood by claiming to be '"plus royaliste que le roi"—more conservative than Maga' (*CL*, ii. 162), his works for *Blackwood's* after 'Youth' suggest a new ambition to build his own off-centre position as *homo duplex* into his fiction and exploit a growingly sophisticated sense of how a concept of Englishness can be used to complicate the contract between writer and English audience. Figuratively speaking, it proves to be a contract with much fine print and many hidden codicils. Thus, if Marlow partly grows out of his creator's need to find an English identity and voice appropriate to *Blackwood's*, it may also be true, as John

*Galsworthy long ago remarked, that 'though English in name', Marlow is 'not so in nature' (78). Galsworthy's description here allows for the possibility that in 'Heart of Darkness' and *Lord Jim* Marlow unites within his apparently single identity the position of both welcoming English host *and* disconcerting stranger. Conrad's developing relations with the implied audience of *Blackwood's* are surveyed in Graver's study of the shorter fiction (20–4). Todd G. Willy, in 'The Call to Imperialism in Conrad's "Youth": A Historical Reconstruction', *Journal of Modern Literature*, 8 (1980), 39–50, treats 'Youth' as the Conrad work most responsive to the magazine's prevailing ethos. In 'Conrad in his *Blackwood's* Context: An Essay in Applied Reception Theory' (in Curreli (ed.), 399–422), Ivo Vidan provides a highly resourceful study of 'Heart of Darkness' as a historically specific transmission and follows the combination of outward mutuality and provocative challenge in Conrad's complexly fashioned address to *Blackwood's* audiences. 'Heart of Darkness' also figures centrally in 'Conrad and the Idea of Empire', *L'Époque conradienne* (1989), 9–22, in which Robert Hampson gives welcome attention to the idea of empire prevailing in *Blackwood's* and shows how Conrad's African story, while overtly employing the dominant imperialist discourse, complicates its effect through rhetorical traps and ultimately subverts its potency. Finally, readers may find amusement and food for thought in Edgar Allan Poe's satiric spoof in 'How to Write a Blackwood's Article', where, under the name of Signora Psyche Zenobia, Poe instructs the budding writer in a style 'elevated, diffusive, and interjectional', in which the 'words must be all in a whirl, like a humming top . . . which answers remarkably well instead of meaning' (*The Complete Tales and Poems of Edgar Allan Poe*, Modern Library (New York: Random House, 1938), 341).

Bobrowska, Teofila (d. 1875), wife of Józef Bobrowski (1790–1850) and Conrad's maternal grandmother. Teofila Bobrowska frequently looked after her beloved 'Kon-radek' during his youthful years, nursing him through several illnesses. She moved to *Cracow shortly after the death of Conrad's father in May 1869 and that summer took Conrad to Bavaria for a water cure in Wartenberg. Appointed the young boy's guardian in August 1870, she arranged for him to live with her in Cracow at 9 Szpitalna Street, his *home until May 1873. Her son Tadeusz *Bobrowski described her as 'truly religious and ready to accept without a murmur the painful decrees of Providence, she had a warm heart and a brave soul—she unfailingly knew how to suffer and how to love!' (*CUFE*, 5). Her photograph is reproduced in *JCC*. One of her daughters, the younger sister of Conrad's mother, was also named Teofila (1833–51).

Bobrowski, Tadeusz (1829–94), Conrad's maternal uncle and unofficial guardian from 1869 until his death. Tadeusz Bobrowski abandoned a promising career in jurisprudence to manage the family estate in *Kazimierówka (in the *guberniya* of Kiev) upon the death of his father in 1850. His father had opposed the marriage of Tadeusz's favourite sister Ewa to Apollo *Korzeniowski (who was his elder by nine years) on the grounds that the Korzeniowskis were irresponsible dreamers and political fanatics. Tadeusz Bobrowski agreed with his father, who eventually relented and allowed the couple to marry.

When Conrad was orphaned in 1869 at the age of 11, Bobrowski, who had lost his own wife in childbirth, assumed responsibility for his nephew and became in effect a surrogate father for Conrad throughout the years of his career at *sea, providing him with regular financial support and avuncular advice. His letters represent the most extensive written record of Conrad's life and thoughts during this period, although the correspondence is one-sided: some 70 of Bobrowski's letters are held in the Biblioteka Narodowa, Warsaw (*CPB*, 35–172), but Conrad's letters to his uncle were destroyed when the Bobrowski estate was burnt down in 1917.

Bobrowski never approved of the political extremism of Conrad's father, for which his own beloved sister had paid so heavy a price; and this disapproval found frequent expression in his letters to Conrad and in a 'Document' written for Conrad giving an account of the contrasting traditions of the Bobrowski and Korzeniowski families (reprinted in *CPB*, 183–202). Conrad's *biographers have generally regarded Bobrowski as a tendentious and moralizing Polonius, dismissing him as an ineffectual moderate, pointing out the many inconsistencies in his statements, and denying him credit for his accomplishments. Najder, for example, declares that Bobrowski's efforts to promote the liberation of the serfs were undertaken 'not because he was particularly compassionate, but because such a position accorded with his principles' (*CUFE*, p. xvii). Apparently Bobrowski never acknowledged to Conrad the degree to which his mother was also involved in preparing the 1863 insurrection, which leads Najder to conclude that Bobrowski 'was ready to sacrifice truth for the sake of a family mythology' (*CPB*, 18). Such mythologies have made it all but impossible to stake any claim to historical objectivity in trying to understand the origins of the January rising and the reasons why it failed. Addison Bross has compared Apollo Korzeniowski's account of an 1855 uprising with other historical accounts and argued that Bobrowski's understanding of Ukrainian peasants was more realistic than his brother-in-law's romantic expectation that they would rise up against the Russian tsar on behalf of Polish landlords who were not willing to share ownership of the land; see 'Apollo Korzeniowski's Mythic Vision: *Poland and Muscovy*, "Note A"', *The Conradian*, 20 (1995), 77–102. Bross prefers to call Bobrowski a 'reformer', as against Korzeniowski the 'insurrectionist'. Najder usefully surveys Bobrowski's life and relations with Conrad in 'Joseph Conrad and Tadeusz Bobrowski' (1997: 44–67).

There can be no doubt about the strong bond of affection between Bobrowski and his nephew. When news of Conrad's attempted *suicide reached Bobrowski in 1878, he rushed to *Marseilles and stayed a fortnight settling Conrad's accounts. Conrad travelled to Marienbad (now Mariánské Lázně, Czech Republic) to spend a month with his uncle in the summer of 1883, and after his release from Russian nationality he returned to visit Bobrowski in Kazimierówka in 1890 and 1893; in *A Personal Record*, the latter two visits are described as a single event. Conrad dedicated his first novel, *Almayer's Folly*, 'To the memory of T. B.'

Bobrowski spent years working on his memoirs, which were finally published posthumously in 1900, totalling more than 900 pages in two volumes. Their publication provoked an outcry because of the anecdotal gossip they contained, which gave offence to members of the families concerned. They provided Conrad with source material for *A Personal Record* and also for his story 'Prince Roman' (*Tales of Hearsay*); see Ludwik Krzyżanowski, 'Joseph Conrad's "Prince Roman": Fact and Fiction', in Krzyżanowski (ed.), *Joseph Conrad: Centennial Essays* (New York: Polish Institute, 1960), 27–69. Conrad's own copy of Bobrowski's memoirs is now in the POSK Library, London.

Bone, David William (1874–1959; knighted 1946), one of three talented sons of a Clydeside family. David Bone was a seaman-writer who, on sending his first novel *The Brassbounder* to Conrad in 1910, was advised by him not to give up the sea for a full-time writing career. Their first meeting took place in December 1919 when both men addressed the University Club of Liverpool at an occasion in honour of the *British Merchant Service. In 1923 Bone, then a senior commander with the Anchor Line, was captain of the *Tuscania*, in which Conrad sailed to *America, a voyage recalled in Bone's *Landfall at Sunset: The Life of a Contented Sailor* (1955). His brother Muirhead (1876–1953; knighted 1937), a talented artist, also made the trip, undertook *portraits of Conrad, and became the novelist's close friend during the last year of his life. The third brother, James (1872–1962), also known to Conrad, was London editor of the *Manchester Guardian*. See also Owen

Knowles, 'Conrad and David Bone: Some Unpublished Letters', *The Conradian*, 11 (1986), 98–115.

Book of Job, The. Originally written in Polish under the title *Księga Hioba* and staged at *Warsaw's Little Theatre in May 1921, this play was the work of Polish author and journalist Bruno Winawer (1883–1944). Winawer sent the newly published Polish original to Conrad in early June 1921, asking him about the possibility of having it translated into English. Partly attracted by its subject—a satiric version of the biblical story set in fashionable contemporary Warsaw society—and partly by the prospect of creating a saleable manuscript for purchase by Thomas J. *Wise, Conrad interrupted work on *Suspense* and unexpectedly undertook the translation himself during July. He suggested to Winawer that the play might be stageworthy and reported that his agent J. B. *Pinker would explore possibilities in London and New York (*CPB*, 269), although, in the end, the play was never performed outside Poland.

One of the few literary translations undertaken by Conrad as a professional writer, *The Book of Job* belongs to a period in his later career when he was often preoccupied with the practice of stage and *film adaptation. In this case, he made Winawer's play less specifically Polish (and Jewish) in its social references and adapted it for non-Polish audiences. He and Winawer continued to correspond, with Conrad taking an interest in Winawer's writings and the latter reciprocating by joining Otylia *Retinger in a translation of the stage version of *The Secret Agent* and finding a theatre for its performance in Warsaw, where it opened on 23 March 1923. He also offered to undertake a stage adaptation of *The Rover*. Privately printed during Conrad's lifetime, *The Book of Job: A Satirical Comedy* was published in the Warsaw monthly *Pologne littéraire* (1931) and in the same year brought out in book form by J. M. *Dent. The dictated typescript with corrections in holograph is held at the British Library. A typescript was auctioned in New York in 1939, but its present location is unknown.

'Books'. No details are known about the writing of this brief essay. It may have been composed in early January 1905 when Conrad was contemplating a hybrid volume of literary essays and sea papers, but it seems more likely that he wrote it after his return from Capri on 18 May. It was published in the *Speaker*, 12 (15 July 1905), 369–70, and collected in *Notes on Life and Letters*. Although Edward *Garnett praised the essay as expressing all of the Conradian 'philosophy of life' (*CL*, iii. 276), Conrad rightly demurred. Lacking the pioneering verve of the earlier 'Preface' to *The Nigger of the 'Narcissus'*, 'Books' is a more relaxed and generalized *causerie* on the relationship between art and life, on the freedoms and restraints of the novelist, and on the exemplary standards set by Stendhal, Balzac, and Henry *James. Its predominant tone is that of the eminent artist engaged in a masterclass. Although there are some memorable individual formulations ('To be hopeful in an artistic sense it is not necessary to think that the world is good. It is enough to believe that there is no impossibility of its being made so' (9)), Conrad's advocacy of the artistic middle way does not reveal much about the dangerous tensions of his own art. As Sylvère Monod comments: 'The essay as a whole suffers from its lack of firm coherence . . . and does not say much that has not been said before, more forcibly, by George Eliot' (*The Conradian*, 14 (1989), 146–7). No pre-publication documents are known.

'Books of my Childhood, The'. Conrad's brief response for a regular series run by *T. P.'s Weekly* appeared on 9 January 1903. In it, he mentions only one of the works important to him as a child, Victor Hugo's sea epic *Les Travailleurs de la mer* (1866), preferring to list the authors he has enjoyed with his son Borys—the brothers Grimm, Hans Christian Andersen, and Edward Lear. The note is reprinted in *CDOUP*, 77.

Borneo, which straddles the equator as the world's third largest island, was a fertile source of inspiration for Conrad, providing locations, details, and characters for many of his novels and stories. Conrad first met William Charles *Olmeijer, the historical prototype of *Almayer, on the east coast of Borneo, and he later claimed that 'if I had not got to know Almayer pretty well it is almost certain there would never have been a line of mine in print' (*A Personal Record*, 87). The legendary Sir James *Brooke, who ruled as the 'White Rajah' of Sarawak along the island's north-west coast, provided a model for *Jim's conquest of *Patusan in the second half of *Lord Jim*, while *The Rescue* opens with an anonymous tribute to Brooke as a 'disinterested adventurer' (4). Along the east coast, the English trader William *Lingard, known as the 'Rajah Laut' or 'King of the Sea', was the primary model for Conrad's Tom *Lingard, whose biography links together the three novels of the so-called 'Malay trilogy' (which, following the chronology of Lingard's life, begins with *The Rescue*, followed by *An Outcast of the Islands* and *Almayer's Folly*). Lingard found a secret passage into the Pantai River, and the trading post he subsequently established at Berau (Tanjung Redeb) was the prototype for the fictional *Sambir, the primary setting of *Almayer's Folly* and *An Outcast of the Islands* (the main events of *The Rescue* take place years earlier, off the south-west coast of the island).

'Discovered' by Portuguese seafarers early in the 16th century, Borneo was also visited by Spanish and Muslim ('Arab') traders, but in the course of time the Dutch East India Company (the VOC, or Verenigde Oost-Indische Compagnie) and the British East India Company emerged as the most powerful trading rivals in the Malay Archipelago. Following the deaths of English traders at Amboina in 1628, the English concentrated more on trade with India and left Borneo nominally to the Dutch, whose headquarters were in Batavia (now Jakarta) on the island of *Java. The relative balance of power between the English and the Dutch depended on local conditions, but also on circumstances in Europe. While the French ruled the Netherlands, Sir Stamford Raffles, the founder of *Singapore, took over the Dutch strongholds in the East (1811–16). In 1841, the English adventurer James Brooke helped Rajah Muda Hassim, uncle and heir to the Sultan of Brunei, to put down an uprising by rebellious Dyaks. In return, Brooke, a British subject, was made Rajah of Sarawak, thus securing British control of most of the north-west coast of Borneo with a dynasty that lasted for 100 years, until shortly after the Second World War. Rivalry between the Dutch and the English for the remaining territories continued well into Conrad's time: in *An Outcast of the Islands*, Almayer tries to invoke protection from his enemies by hoisting the Union Jack in Dutch territory, and *Willems declares his new regime by running up a home-made Dutch flag and forcing everyone to salute it (176, 179). The final borders between the Dutch and English colonial territories in Borneo were not defined until late in the 19th century, and their long commercial rivalry is reflected in the division of the island between Indonesia and Malaysia: Kalimantan (the former Dutch Borneo) has been part of the Republic of Indonesia since 1945, while the states of Sabah and Sarawak (former British colonies) have since 1963 been member states of the Federation of Malaysia.

As Conrad shows in his novels, political and economic life in Borneo was complicated by the local mix of cultures and interests among the Malay, Arab, Chinese, and Bugis traders who lived along the coasts and traded with the Dyaks further inland for exotic raw materials like gutta-percha, rattans, gum-dammar, beeswax, and bird's nests, or used this innocent trade as a pretext for gun-running or prospecting for gold, while Sea Dyaks and Sulu pirates threatened shipping.

As second mate of the small steamer *Vidar*, Conrad made four trips along the east coast of Borneo between August 1887 and January 1888 (see SHIPS AND VOYAGES). Based in Singapore, the *Vidar* followed a regular circuit taking about one month, passing around the south of Borneo with brief stops at Banjarmasin and again at

Pulau Laut to take on coal before crossing the Macassar Strait to Donggala (on Celebes, or present-day Sulawesi), and then returning to the east coast of Borneo to stop at Samarinda, Berau, and Bulungan before returning to Singapore. The owner of Conrad's ship, the Arab merchant Syed Mohsin bin Salleh Al Jooffree, had branch houses at Berau and Bulungan, and so perhaps the *Vidar* lingered there longer than at the other ports. Even so, it is not likely that Conrad spent more than a month or two actually in Borneo, yet the island and the people he met there left an indelible mark on his creative imagination. As he told Lady Margaret *Brooke, Dowager Ranee of Sarawak, in 1920, 'my time in the Archipelago was short though it left most vivid impressions and some highly valued memories' (*LCG*, 210). Watts has suggested that Margaret Brooke's 1913 memoir, *My Life in Sarawak*, may have encouraged Conrad to resume work on the long-abandoned *The Rescue* in 1918 (*LCG*, 209). Although Conrad's memories of Borneo remained vivid, the monotony of a regular sailing run is also reflected in the route of the *Sofala* in 'The End of the Tether,' even though Captain *Whalley's route takes him up the Strait of Malacca (between Malaya and Sumatra) and not up the Macassar Strait. Conrad also found information about Borneo in Alfred Russel *Wallace's *The Malay Archipelago* (1869), which was one of his favourite books; but Wallace explored the area around Kuching (Sarawak) and not the east coast of the island, while Conrad never visited Sarawak.

Conrad confessed to Marguerite *Poradowska that the characters he had found on Borneo were so 'true' that they almost constrained his freedom to write about them; but he also warned W. H. *Chesson against seeking a close identification of his creations with real persons and places: 'After all, river and people have nothing true about them—in the vulgar sense—but the names. Any criticism that would look for real description of places and events would be disastrous to that particle of the universe, which is nobody and nothing in the world but myself' (*CL*, i. 186).

This caveat notwithstanding, Conrad's contacts with people and places in Borneo have been described in detail by Sherry (*CEW*), who has also taken Berau as the primary geographical model for Patusan in *Lord Jim*. This assumption is opposed by Hans van Marle and Pierre Lefranc (1988), who cite textual evidence to show that Patusan must be located inland from the western coast of Sumatra, which Conrad never visited.

A number of intrepid scholars have followed Conrad's trail to Borneo, among them John Dozier Gordan, who visited Bulungan in 1939 in search of information about Olmeijer, only to learn that his source (G. *Jean-Aubry, apparently using information from Captain Craig) was mistaken, and that the original of Almayer had lived not at Bulungan but in Berau (see Gordan, 39–54). Andrzej Braun's *Śladami Conrada* (In Conrad's Footsteps; Warsaw: Czytelnik, 1972) is a scholarly record of information collected on Borneo and elsewhere, but the book is unavailable in English, as is also the case with *Zwischen den Flüssen: Reisen zu Joseph Conrad* (Between the Rivers: Journeys to Joseph Conrad; Frankfurt: Syndikat, 1982), by German dramatist Horst Laube. Gavin Young's *In Search of Conrad* (Hutchinson, 1991) gives a lively account of a visit to Tanjung Redeb, as does Ron Visser's article 'An Out-of-the-Way Place Called Berau', *The Conradian*, 18: 1 (1993), 37–47. A French video documentary entitled *Bérau, sur les traces de Conrad* (Berau: On the Trail of Conrad, 1993) also includes film footage of the Pantai area.

borrowing. Conrad's use and remodelling of the ideas, effects, and even the exact words of other writers in his fiction and occasional prose is nothing short of remarkable in its extent, and the related terms 'influence' or 'allusiveness' inadequately define his practice. His borrowing from literary as well as non-literary sources was systematic, copious, and, by necessity, unacknowledged. In addition to the verbatim translation of sentences and entire paragraphs, a catalogue of such borrowings includes appropriations for local colour, the reshaping of scenes, and the refashioning of thematic materials. In his writings up to 1910, his principal quarry for these appropriations was French fiction. While borrowing was an especially strong feature of the early and mid-period writings, it noticeably tapered off in Conrad's later work, possibly because of his own greater self-confidence as a writer and possibly because he was a less avid reader than he had once been. Borrowing may be flexibly interpreted to include the appropriation of non-verbal artefacts such as settings: thus, for example, the cityscape of *London is 'borrowed' for *The Secret Agent* and the South of *France 'borrowed' for *The Rover*.

Ford Madox *Ford's recollection (*JCPR*, 36) that Conrad knew and could recite by heart passages from certain French writers, especially Gustave *Flaubert and Guy de *Maupassant, has been cited to explain the appearance of exact translations in his work; and claims for his having a 'remarkable but erratic memory' have been based on it (Watt 1980: 50). While Conrad's memory was keenly alert to the cadences of French prose, the sheer quantity of evidence that has accumulated overturns earlier assessments of this habit as mainly a feat of memory. Borrowings for both his journalistic writings and fiction (in particular, *Nostromo*) from such journeyman-work as the newspaper columns of Anatole *France, collected under the title *La Vie littéraire* (1888–92), foreclose this line of argument. While Conrad's response to France's writings was sympathetic, this is a functional, competent prose lacking preponderating aesthetic interest and in itself unmemorable. Conrad's translations from it were almost certainly deliberate.

Conrad borrowed from a wide variety of sources. He relied, for example, on Maupassant's *Bel-Ami* (1885) for James *Wait's death scene in *The Nigger of the 'Narcissus'*, and on Stefan *Żeromski's *Dzieje grzechu* (The History of a Sin, 1909) for *Lena's triumphant death in *Victory*; he called on a number of 'dull, wise books' (*CL*, ii. 130) of history, topography, and travel to construct what Henry *James called 'the solidity of specification' for the Malay and South American worlds of his early fiction and *Nostromo*; he lifted directly from the memoirs of Lady Margaret *Brooke the shipboard 'cage' in *The Rescue*; and he relied heavily on the *Memoirs of the Comtesse de Boigne* (1907) for parts of *Suspense*.

The word 'plagiarism' is not only inaccurate but also too crude and lacking in historical perspective to serve as a frame for analysing and evaluating Conrad's complex interactions with the writings of his literary predecessors and contemporaries. As Hervouet (1990) has argued, borrowing was no less than a method of composition, integral to Conrad's fictional practice, and derived in part from his special linguistic situation as a writer using his third language and thereby inevitably experiencing some degree of insecurity. Placed in perspective, Conrad's habit can be seen as analogous to the labours of a bricoleur assembling from disparate materials a coherent, new, and independent work, rooted in an established artistic tradition. In this respect, his affinities (despite his ardent admiration for a Flaubertian detachment of narrative method) were with an earlier, more social paradigm of artistic production, one that postmodernist thought has attempted to reinvigorate in its efforts to democratize the artist-figure. The medieval or Renaissance artist, who held imitation as essential to the creative act, apprenticed himself to a master, conscientiously copying his work in an effort to assimilate its techniques and values. Emphasizing collaboration, this mode of artistic production was often appropriately anonymous. By contrast, the Romantic and post-Romantic conceptions of the inspired artist privilege the solitary individual with exclusive 'property rights' over a unique and signed production.

In addition to its practical or functional implications, Conrad's borrowing has psychological dimensions. His habitual recourse to the work of other writers, with whom he shared his primary professional identity, to a certain extent mitigated a sense of isolation. Fated to fill up the blank page for an audience ever hungry for novelty, he shared the common condition of the writer of fiction pressured by economic necessity; and the exigencies of his social role collaborated with inner compulsion to make him a borrower. As the long history of a wide variety of art forms suggests, borrowing, transformation, and appropriation lend authenticity and even authority to methods and ideas that are radically novel. They also help to confirm the status of a work (and of a self) that one might question or at least be uncertain of. Conrad's creative interactions with other writers and prior texts are thus, at least partly, the expression of a need to situate himself in the ranks of a community of tellers of tales of broadly similar aim and method. Such an act of identification affords at least an illusion of security that is not present in the anonymous and impersonal relationship of an author with his readership. In this sense, for Conrad, borrowing served as a means of establishing an identity and affirming connectedness. Partly an assertion of fraternity, it also laid claims to a literary heritage.

Busza (1966) explores significant influences from Polish literature on Conrad's works. The questions raised by Kirschner's pioneering study of Conrad's borrowings from French literature (1968) are taken up exhaustively by Hervouet (1990). See also Moore *et al.* (eds.) 1997, for a collection of essays focusing on a variety of specific borrowings as well as larger theoretical issues. The various annotated editions of Conrad currently available usually draw attention to individual debts.   JHS

Briquel, Émilie (*c.*1875–1961). Émilie Briquel met Conrad in May 1895 at *Champel-les-Bains, in *Geneva, Switzerland, when she, her mother, and her brother Paul were staying at the same hotel as the fledgling author. A romantic attachment seems to have formed between him and the 20-year-old Frenchwoman, the daughter of a rich, cultured bourgeois family from Lunéville in Lorraine. Émilie and he spent much time together during that month, playing billiards and croquet, taking boat-trips on Lake Leman, and discuss-

ing music and literature (in her journal Émilie mentions Conrad's animated talk about Victor Hugo, Alphonse *Daudet, and Pierre Loti). On 20 May, Conrad presented her with a copy of *Almayer's Folly* inscribed to one 'whose charming musical gift and everbright presence has cheered for him the dull life of Champel'. The gift prompted Émilie to think of translating the novel into French.

So attentive was Conrad to Émilie, whom he hoped to visit in Lunéville in the autumn of 1895, that the Briquel family appears to have anticipated a proposal of marriage from a suitor who, oddly enough, had given them the impression that he was English. He corresponded with members of the Briquel family during the remainder of 1895, although, Najder suggests, Conrad had by this time 'apparently been made to understand that, because of the age gap [of some eighteen years] between them and his nomadic life-style, he could not hope to win the girl's hand' (*JCC*, 189). In February 1896, Émilie's mother wrote to Conrad, telling him of her daughter's engagement to a local doctor, to which he responded with the news that he himself was soon to be married: 'No one can be more surprised at it than myself. However, I am not frightened at all, for as you know, I am accustomed to an adventurous life and to facing terrible dangers' (*CL*, i. 265). The extent to which his relationship with Émilie influenced the course of Conrad's other romantic attachments at the time is impossible to gauge. The episode in Champel was soon followed by a mysterious five-year gap in his surviving correspondence with Marguerite *Poradowska, leading Baines to conjecture that in 1895 Conrad unsuccessfully proposed marriage to her and may well have turned to Jessie 'on the rebound' (171) Whether the news of Émilie's engagement precipitated Conrad's proposal to Jessie is also impossible to gauge, although, as Najder suggests, 'the impression of some connection between both events is difficult to dispel' (*JCC*, 191).

British Merchant Service. In *A Personal Record*, Conrad recounts how he touched his first British ship, the *James Westoll*, in *Marseilles harbour and 'felt it already throbbing under my open palm' (137). The memory of this sensuous communion culminates in the image of the Red Ensign, the flag of the merchant navy under which Conrad sailed as a British sailor for fifteen years, from 1878 to 1893, 'a Polish nobleman cased in British tar' by his own definition (*CL*, i. 52). Barred from working in French ships by new regulations requiring crew members to have completed national service in their own country, Conrad first served in a British vessel in 1878, at a time when the British Merchant Service was entering its apogee, with the expansion of its fleet far outstripping the nation's supply of sailors. This historical fact is reflected in the multiracial crew in *The Nigger of the 'Narcissus'*. In the mid-19th century, the British Merchant Service benefited, first, from decisions of the British government in 1849 to repeal its old Navigation Laws and to establish marine boards dedicated to raising standards in the service, and, second, from the fact that the cost of the Civil War left the American government little capital to sustain the naval supremacy it had developed in the first half of the century. As Berthoud comments: 'The span of Conrad's life coincided almost exactly with an historical phase in which the trade of the world multiplied several times in volume, complexity and interdependence, and in which British ships [carried] about half this trade and over a third of all trade between foreign countries' (1984: p. xii). It is not surprising that Conrad should remember this period as a golden age in the merchant service. As he wrote in 1920: 'The sailing ship, as evolved by the needs and enterprise of shipowners, the imagination of shipbuilders and the requirements of seamen, reached its perfection of design in the years between '50 and '80. . . . After 1880 there was strictly speaking no evolution, there was only growth in a literal sense, in the mere size of ships, implying a loss in other directions' (*LL*, ii. 246).

After payment of a considerable deposit, Conrad began his career in the British Merchant Service on 24 April 1878, sailing as an unofficial apprentice in the *Mavis*, a steamer bound from Marseilles for the Sea of Azov. During this voyage he made his first sustained contact with both the traditions of the merchant marine and the English language. While Conrad rarely stayed with a ship for long, his career provides a fitting testament to the health of the merchant service at the time: he rose through the ranks and passed the successive Board of Trade *examinations, obtaining his master's certificate by the age of 30; he made many deep-water voyages to *Australia and the Far East; and he acquired his evident pride in the traditions of the Red Ensign. Significantly, Conrad's first formal public *speech, at the University Club in Liverpool in December 1919, was on the traditions of the merchant marine. As he says in *A Personal Record*, 'The sea is strong medicine. Behold what the quarter-deck training even in a merchant ship will do' (100). Having set foot on English soil for the first time at Lowestoft in June 1878, he soon obtained a berth as an ordinary seaman in the humble *Skimmer of the Seas*, shipping coal from Newcastle to Lowestoft, during which he earned the nickname 'Polish Joe'. He later recalled of this experience: 'it is on board a Lowestoft coaster that I began my life under the merchant flag', and of the sailors with whom he served: 'They may have been amused at me but they taught many of a seaman's duties and the very terms of our sea-speech' (*CDOUP*, 110–11). In October 1878, Conrad sailed again as an ordinary seaman, in the *Duke of Sutherland*, a wool clipper bound for Australia on a one-year round voyage. Having passed his second-mate's examination in May 1880, Conrad secured his first berth as an officer later that year, as third mate in the *Loch Etive*, on his second voyage to Australia.

The experiences in Eastern waters which would provide such a fertile source of inspiration in Conrad's fiction began when he signed on as second mate in the *Palestine* in September 1881. The *Palestine* was an old barque, bound for *Bangkok, but after a series of mishaps, Conrad arrived in the East at Bangka Island, off Sumatra, in March 1883. This ill-fated voyage was the basis for 'Youth' (where the *Palestine* is renamed the *Judea*). Conrad was officially discharged from his next position, as second mate in the *Riversdale*, in which he had sailed from London to Madras, following a dispute with the captain. He returned to Europe from Bangkok in late 1884 as second mate in the *Narcissus*, a ship he would later immortalize in *The Nigger of the 'Narcissus'*. Having successfully appealed against a bad-conduct record from Captain McDonald of the *Riversdale*, he was allowed by the London Marine Board to sit for his first-mate's examination, which he passed at the second attempt. By the time he signed off from his next ship in mid-1886, after another long voyage to the East as second mate in the *Tilkhurst*, Conrad had become dissatisfied with *sea life in the merchant marine and was exploring the possibilities of a job ashore. His appetite for the service quickly revived later that year, however, following his *naturalization as a British subject (in August) and after successfully passing his master's examination (in November), when he became 'a British master mariner beyond a doubt' (*A Personal Record*, 120). Serving as first mate in the *Vidar* between 1887 and 1888, he made four voyages from *Singapore to small *Netherlands East Indies ports on *Borneo and Celebes, voyages that would later provide the basis for his fiction set in the Malay Archipelago. Following this, Conrad obtained his only command at sea, in the *Otago*, an Australian-owned barque, a fourteen-month connection that would provide material for *The Shadow-Line* and 'A Smile of Fortune'. Conrad's last sustained connection with the merchant marine was also his least taxing: between 1891 and 1893 he served as first mate in the *Torrens*, one of the fastest ships of her day, memorialized much later in Conrad's essay 'The *Torrens*: A Personal Tribute', where, in sentiments that reflect his sense of seamanship as a duty, he writes that she 'attracted the right kind of sailor' and 'all her life, was so worthy of men's loyal service' (*Last Essays*, 22, 28).

Conrad served in the British merchant marine in the last great age of sailing ships. By this time, British steamships were seizing the maritime trading initiative from American clippers, sounding the obsolescence of full-rigged iron sailing ships such as the *Tilkhurst* and romantic clippers like the *Torrens*. When Conrad was born, the annual construction of steamships in Britain equalled that of sailing ships, but, by the time he started writing his first novel in 1889, three times as many steamers as sailing ships were being built. Conrad expressed his feelings about this transition in December 1903: 'As a work of fiction *The Nigger of the 'Narcissus'* puts a seal on that epoch of the greatest possible perfection which was at the same time the end of the sailing fleet' (*CL*, iii. 89). Thus, Conrad's sea fiction is often thought of as a romantic elegy to the world of sail which had, historically, already been superseded by the age of steamers. At times, he goes out of his way to underscore this impression: 'A passage under sail brings out in the course of days whatever there may be of sea love and sea sense in any individual whose soul is not indissolubly wedded to the pedestrian shore' (*Last Essays*, 23). Conrad's fiction is underpinned by the gritty realism of the merchant marine: his ships sail in service of trade, and their sailors are bound by codes of duty and the *work ethic. The intimate bond between a captain and a sailing ship is dramatized in tales such as 'The Secret Sharer' and *The Shadow-Line*; but as 'Typhoon' demonstrates, the steamship is also capable of inspiring romance.

When Conrad left the merchant marine to take up a career as a writer, he took with him a knowledge of exotic locales, sailing ships, and seamanship, causing Henry *James to remark on 'the prodigy' of Conrad's experiences: 'No one has *known*—for intellectual use—the things you know' (*PL*, 58). More than this, though, he brought a sense of sea life as a life of service. The portrait he paints of life in the merchant marine is of a community bound by an unshakeable code of professional duty, solidarity, and a keen sense of the value of work. Thus, Conrad invokes such concepts as 'the bond of the sea' in 'Heart of Darkness' (45) and 'the honour of the craft' in *Lord Jim* (46). He commented on the ideals of the merchant marine even more explicitly when asked for advice about the running of a prospective training ship for officers of the merchant service. His 'Memorandum' (*Last Essays*) provides a revealing summary of his opinions. Having stated that he is 'drawing on my own experience as a seaman trained to his duties under the British flag' (67), Conrad makes such declarations as 'it may be laid down as an axiom that no labour done on board ship in the way of duty is either too hard or in any way unworthy of the best effort and attention or, so to speak, beneath the dignity of any youngster wishing to fit himself to be a good officer' (70), and 'the comfort of the boys should be cared for strictly within the limits of due regard for their health, physical development and opportunity for study, and no more. . . . no boy properly constituted and wishing to be a seaman will resent such a system' (74).

Both Conrad's idealization of the service and such absolute principles as those expressed above have led some critics to claim that his view of the merchant marine is over-idealized. Najder, for instance, argues that Conrad's presentation of the service is a necessary myth, constructed in order to invest his first career with a significance and purpose it lacked: 'A myth of the beauty, dignity, and noble solidarity of his life at sea, not unfounded but exaggerated as all myths are, was the only way to counterbalance the disappointments' (*JCC*, 163). In fairness, however, the fictions tend with unremitting honesty to reveal human failures to meet this ideal standard. As *Marlow claims in *Lord Jim*: 'In no other kind of life is the illusion more wide of reality—in no other is the beginning *all* illusion—the disenchantment more swift —the subjugation more complete. Hadn't we all commenced with the same desire, ended with the same knowledge, carried the memory of the same cherished glamour through the sordid days of imprecation?' (129). See also SHIPS AND VOYAGES,

and the following essays: Robert Foulke's 'Life in the Dying World of Sail, 1879–1910', *Journal of British Studies*, 3 (1963), 105–36, and William E. Messenger's 'Conrad and his "Sea Stuff"', *Conradiana*, 6 (1974), 3–18.

AHS

Brooke, James (1803–68; knighted 1848). One of Conrad's 'boyish admirations' to whom he later paid homage for 'the greatness of his character and the unstained rectitude of his purpose' (*LCG*, 210), James Brooke was an English explorer-adventurer during the second expansive and consolidating phase of European incursion into South-East Asia. Born in Benares in India, Brooke attended grammar school in Norwich, running away at 16 to join the British infantry in Bengal. Arriving in *Borneo in 1839, he became involved in suppressing a rebellion, and, in 1841, was named the first Rajah of Sarawak. He spent the last five years of his life in England.

Not having been to Sarawak during his sojourns in the Far East, Conrad could nonetheless recollect a passing encounter with the world of 'the Great Rajah' in sighting 'the old steamer "Royalist"' in 1887 in *Singapore harbour (ibid.). (The ship must have been Brooke's *Rainbow*, since the *Royalist* was a schooner.) His knowledge of Brooke's personality and activities came from wide-ranging *reading in the history of exploration. He had read Captain Rodney Mundy's *Narrative of Events in Borneo and Celebes down to the Occupation of Labuan, from the Journals of James Brooke* (1848), and was also familiar with Captain Henry Keppel's *The Expedition to Borneo and Celebes of HMS Dido for the Suppression of Piracy; with Extracts from the Journals of James Brooke, Esq.* (1846) and *A Visit to the Indian Archipelago in H.M. Ship Maeander with Portions of the Private Journal of Sir James Brooke, K.C.B* (1853). The journals vividly record Brooke's encounters with native rulers and peoples, and trace his successful *mission civilisatrice* in areas where piracy, slavery, the disruption of civic life, and arbitrary, sometimes brutal, rule were endemic before he established his personal *imperium*.

While Brooke's journals served mainly as a source for general atmosphere and local colour in *Almayer's Folly* and *An Outcast of the Islands*, their greater influence is on *The Rescue* and *Lord Jim*, where they provided names, characters, and incidents. In *The Rescue*, the name Jaffir was borrowed directly from the faithful follower Jaffer, an individual who also provided the basis for *Jim's servant Tamb' Itam. The motif of the talismanic ring and the strong mutual friendship and respect between a Malay dignitary and an Englishman is used in both novels, with Conrad relying upon the description of Brooke's friendship with Pangeran Budrudeen, the basis for Hassim in *The Rescue* and for Dain Waris in *Lord Jim*.

Brooke himself, who is specifically alluded to in *Almayer's Folly* as 'an English Rajah' ruling in Kuching (206), supplied hints for both the personality and actions of Jim in the *Patusan chapters of *Lord Jim*. Of equal or even greater importance to Conrad than Brooke's own journals in developing Jim's character was the idealized portrait of Brooke given in *The Malay Archipelago: The Land of the Orang-Utan and the Bird of Paradise* (1869) by Alfred Russel *Wallace. During his travels in the region, Wallace had encountered legends of Brooke as a mythologized figure of magical powers and supernatural abilities, the historical basis for the 'Jim-myth' that, to *Marlow's wonderment, flourishes in Patusan. Commenting on Brooke's determination to establish order and justice, Wallace counts among Brooke's achievements his assurance of security of person and property from the raiding pirates who had regularly preyed upon the Dyaks, his success in winning the gratitude and affection of both the Dyak and Malay populations, and his disinterested and benevolent motives in the pursuit of his goals. Conrad's transformations of Wallace's description of Brooke as a self-sacrificing idealist engaged in a fierce combat with predatory greed and self-seeking are complex. In addition to obvious echoes in the character of Jim, Wallace's tribute to Brooke may influence the portrayal of Marlow as Jim's

apologist. It also possibly colours the presentation of Gentleman *Brown as Jim's determined antagonist and Cornelius as his detractor, and it offers a model for the stance of the final chapters, which summarize and defend Jim's achievement for the sceptical 'privileged man'. The elegiac note in Wallace's comment possibly echoes in the novel's closing pages.

Gordan's pioneering study (1940: 64–73) and his 'The Rajah Brooke and Joseph Conrad', *Studies in Philology*, 35 (1938), 613–34, explore Brooke's influence on *The Rescue* and *Lord Jim*, and were useful to Sherry for his further pursuit of this topic in *CEW*. C. T. Watts's 'Joseph Conrad and the Ranee of Sarawak', *Review of English Studies*, NS 15 (1964), 404–7 (reprinted in *LCG*), offers documentary support for Gordan's work in Conrad's own comments on Brooke. Robert Payne's *The White Rajahs of Sarawak* (1960) gives a portrait of Brooke and his life's work, and also traces the gradual decline and eventual disappearance of the dynasty he founded. See also BROOKE, LADY MARGARET.   JHS

Brooke, Lady Margaret [Alice Lily],

Dowager Ranee of Sarawak (née de Windt, 1849–1936), after 1917 the widow of Sir Charles Brooke, the second Rajah of Sarawak. Lady Margaret Brooke returned to Britain in later life and mingled in London literary circles. A copy of her *My Life in Sarawak* (1913) reached Conrad through R. B. Cunninghame *Graham and evoked the comment in January 1914 that in addition to its 'delightfully ladylike' quality, it offered an 'obviously genuine' response to the land and its people (*CL*, v. 336). Repeated readings seem to have left a more abiding mark since, as Conrad confessed in a letter to the Ranee of July 1920, *My Life in Sarawak* was one of the items of Brookeiana from which he borrowed details for *The Rescue*. For an account of this influence and a transcription of Conrad's 1920 letter, see Watts's appendix in *LCG*, 209–11. In 'The Ranee of Sarawak and Conrad's *Victory*', *Conradiana*, 18 (1986), 41–4, Jeffrey Meyers has suggested that one of the Ranee's ingenious matchmaking schemes may also have inspired the ladies' orchestra in *Victory*. See also BROOKE, JAMES.

Brown, Gentleman, a malevolent buccaneer and instigator of the final crisis in *Jim's career in *Lord Jim*. Gentleman Brown first appears in chapter 37 when *Marlow meets him on his deathbed in a hovel in *Bangkok. The gloating pirate tells him how he has been instrumental in bringing about the entire collapse of what Jim had succeeded in making in *Patusan. Chapters 38 and 39 deal with Brown's past and his arrival in a stolen ship in Patusan when Jim is absent but when his reputation of 'invincible, supernatural power' (361) is at its height; chapters 40 to 42 dramatize the confrontation between Jim and Brown over a threatening chasm and the subsequent disaster that occurs when Brown and his henchmen are allowed by Jim to depart from Patusan but not before they kill some of the community upon whose safety Jim has pledged his life.

Like other Mephistophelean visitants in Conrad's fiction—plain Mr *Jones, for instance, in *Victory*—Brown is a resonantly symbolic emissary of evil and agent of nemesis. In this particular case, his presence in Patusan serves to recapitulate some of the terms of Jim's earlier crisis aboard the *Patna*, reopen the question of 'How to be' (213), and provide the novel with its open-ended coda. As Andrea White argues, the damage inflicted by Brown also involves the laying waste of Patusan, since if Jim has represented the benevolent face of colonial involvement, Brown 'is the unforeseen but inevitable consequence of modern imperialistic ideology in its commercial ruthlessness' ('Conrad and Imperialism', in Stape (ed.) 1996: 193). Described as 'a blind accomplice of Dark Powers' with 'a satanic gift of finding out the best and the weakest spot in his victims' (385), Brown also provides readers with an extreme interpretative crux, challenging us to determine how and in what measure this malign Iago-like figure draws on the 'best' and 'weakest' spots in Jim. His satanic aspect has encouraged a view that Jim is more sinned against than sinning and

therefore dies as an essentially Christ-like figure (Verleun 1979) or is redeemed by his commitment to an ideal of honour (Watt 1980). As an emissary 'with whom the world he had renounced was pursuing him in his retreat' (385), Brown also completes a process by which Jim, a character with butterfly-like aspirations, is consistently and meanly betrayed by the world's beetle-like creatures and so may figure in what can be regarded as an elegiac romance. A further critical problem has been to come to terms with all of the circumstances that make the confrontation between Jim and Brown, two apparently polarized types, into a mysteriously potent 'recognition' scene. Brown's ability to render Jim indecisive by insinuating 'a vein of subtle reference to their common blood, a sickening suggestion of common guilt, of secret knowledge that was like a bond of their minds and of their hearts' (387) has exercised many critics, leading some to conclude that the mirror he holds up to Jim reveals not so much a flawed romantic aspirant as a perversely self-defeating narcissist, for whom death is finally an escape and easy way out.

Brussels, the capital of Belgium and the administrative centre of the *Congo Free State, is most famous in Conrad's work as the 'sepulchral city' described in 'Heart of Darkness'. Before it became Belgian state property in 1908, the Congo was recognized by international powers as the private property of Belgian King Leopold II, and its administration was in the hands of a network of trading companies based in Brussels. Conrad first visited the city in November 1889 for an interview with Leopold's managing director, Albert *Thys, and a comparable interview is described in 'Heart of Darkness'. In February 1890, on his first trip to the *Ukraine since he left for *Marseilles, he stopped in Brussels to see his ailing cousin Aleksander Poradowski. The morbidity of Conrad's descriptions of Brussels evokes the evil of *colonialism, but probably also owes something to Poradowski's death only two days after Conrad arrived. Poradowski's widow, Marguerite *Poradowska, was the author of novels and stories published in the prestigious Parisian *Revue des Deux Mondes*. She was well known in Brussels society for her wit and beauty, and counted Charles Buls, the mayor, among her suitors. Conrad wrote her more than 100 letters in French and visited her briefly in Brussels in 1894 and 1895. Once she established herself in Paris, Conrad ceased to have any reason to revisit a city of which he was never fond. Brussels is also described as the 'centre' of revolutionary activity in 'The Informer' (*A Set of Six*, 84).

'Brute, The'. Composed quickly in early 1906, this 8,200-word horror story was declined by Willam *Blackwood in April 1906 on the grounds that its central idea was too close to Edward *Noble's novel *The Edge of Circumstance: A Story of the Sea*, which he had published in 1904. It appeared in the *Daily Chronicle* (5 December 1906), subtitled a 'tale of a bloodthirsty brig', and in America in *McClure's Magazine* (November 1907), subtitled 'A Piece of Invective'. Later collected in *A Set of Six*, it bears yet another subtitle—'An Indignant Tale'. In his 'Author's Note' to the volume, Conrad explained that the story combines material from two separate anecdotes to have come his way. The first—about a rogue ship that by some malignant accident had turned into a monster and killed at least one human being on each of her voyages—was communicated to him by Captain Edwin John Blake, under whom he had served in the *Tilkhurst* in 1885–6. The other anecdote—involving a ship that ran aground on the rocks because the officer of the watch was romantically preoccupied with a woman-passenger—provides the story with its sensational climax when the 'brute' ship, the *Apse Family*, is finally destroyed.

This tale of uncanny malevolence exploits Conrad's favourite formula of the *frame-narrative, in which an unnamed sailor and ex-crew member of the *Apse Family* reminisces to a group of fellow sailors, one of whom introduces the proceedings and can interject his more detached comments. Commentary, however, takes second place to a swift, eventful narrative of the ship's successive crimes, culminating in the startling scene when a young woman is dragged to her death by the 'great, rough iron arm' of an anchor (124). Although some of the narrator's bluff assumptions are occasionally challenged, one of them appears not only to remain unquestioned but to be perversely indulged—that is, the sentiment that the story's women characters can be associated with the fickle but fundamentally criminal vessel and share in the larger destructive force embodied in the ship. Such a link appears at the story's outset, where allusions to a 'she' (105) appear to refer to a woman but actually designate the rogue ship. And at the climax, the account of the destruction of the *Apse Family*, now conceived as a vicious she-devil, 'rotten at heart' (131), borrows the language of violent rape in depicting how she is ripped apart, 'stripped', and violated by the rocks (130). Schwarz concludes not unfairly that 'the entire effort to place sexual innuendoes in socially permissible contexts demonstrates Conrad's own leering enjoyment of adolescent sexual humour, perhaps a vestige of the bachelor ethos of maritime life' (1980: 182). The manuscript of the story is held at Dartmouth College.

C

Capes, Harriet Mary (1849–1936), writer of uplifting literature for children, and sister of the novelist Bernard Capes. Harriet Capes was a friend of the Conrads from 1895. When, in 1907, the Conrads were looking for a new house, this 'charming old lady in Winchester' (*CL*, ii. 416) explored possibilities for them in Winchester itself, an act of kindness that possibly prompted Conrad to dedicate *A Set of Six* to her in 1908. Her compilation, *Wisdom and Beauty from Conrad: An Anthology* (Melrose, 1915), although undertaken with Conrad's approval, was withdrawn soon after its publication because it had infringed copyright and was not reissued until 1922. Described by Conrad in 1912 as 'an old girl but as intelligent as they make them' (*CL*, v. 119), she remained a lifelong friend of the Conrad family.

Caribbean, the. At the beginning of his career as a seaman, Conrad's first three voyages were to the Caribbean between 1874 and 1877, the first two in the *Mont-Blanc* and the third in the *Saint-Antoine*, his stays in the area spanning close to 40 weeks (see SHIPS AND VOYAGES). Martinique's Saint-Pierre was a main port-of-call on all these voyages, but the last two included stays in Haiti and Saint-Thomas (now part of the Virgin Islands). A number of unresolved questions attend the voyage in the *Saint-Antoine*, when Conrad had Dominique and César *Cervoni as fellow crew members. Did Conrad, as he vaguely hinted in later life, actually visit various ports in Central and South America with Dominique in late 1876 and, if so, when, how, and for what purpose? These questions are taken up by Hans van Marle, who, after carefully sifting the available evidence, cautiously concludes that 'we cannot reject out of hand his repeated statements that he was involved in un-lawful activities together with the exemplary sailor Cervoni' (1991: 110).

Entries in the ship's records indicate beyond doubt that on arriving in Martinique on 18 August 1876 the *Saint-Antoine* stayed in the Saint-Pierre roads and did not visit ports in Colombia and Venezuela. It remains possible that Conrad and Cervoni absented themselves temporarily and unofficially from their ship, and if they did, then—van Marle suggests—the most likely time period would be during the two months separating her arrival in Saint-Thomas and her departure from Haiti (September–December 1876). Van Marle further conjectures that, given the short period of time at their disposal and the distances to be covered, their itinerary would only be possible in regular mail steamers, not under sail, in order to enable them to be back in time for the ship's departure for *France. As for the motives of their possible 'unlawful' activities, G. *Jean-Aubry explains that they were 'bound on the ticklish and illegal mission of carrying arms and munitions for a political party in one of the Central American republics. We do not know at what point in the Gulf of Mexico a landing was made, but several passages in Conrad's work showed traces of this contraband adventure and of a visit to the North Coast of South America' (*LL*, i. 37). The area of operations and the destination of the contraband remain a mystery. As van Marle points out, gun-running frequently occurred in both Central America and the Caribbean coast of South America at this time, but whereas Jean-Aubry specified a Central American destination, later critics have preferred a Colombian landing and connected Conrad's 'unlawful' activities with that country's 1876 civil war.

The question of whether and how widely the author of *Nostromo* had previously made contact with South American coastal ports must, therefore, remain open. According to Conrad, other fleeting contacts during his Caribbean landfalls provided hints that were incorporated into *Romance*, and suggestions for such later characters as Axel *Heyst, Mr *Jones, Ricardo, and Pedro in *Victory*. While in this area, he also recalled hearing an anecdote about 'some man who was supposed to have stolen single-handed a whole lighter-full of silver, somewhere on the Tierra Firme seaboard during the troubles of a revolution' ('Author's Note', *Nostromo*, pp. xv–xvi). Through a later reading of Frederick Benton Williams's *On Many Seas: The Life and Exploits of a Yankee Sailor* (1897) Conrad learned the identity of the thief, a piratical seaman named Nicolo, whose audacious exploit furnished details for *Nostromo's later career.

Carlism, the movement that motivated the Second Carlist War (1872–6), provides the context for Conrad's novel *The Arrow of Gold* (1919), whose protagonist, a young sailor known as 'M. *George', becomes involved in running guns from the South of *France to Carlists in northern Spain. The main narrative follows his movements for a year, and his life in *Marseilles is plotted against the conflict between Carlists and Alfonsists in Spain, and the disintegration of the Carlist forces in the final year of the war. The political events in the novel apparently take place in 1875–6, while the personal events are a fictional elaboration of Conrad's own life in Marseilles in 1876–7.

Carlism began with the death of Ferdinand VII of Spain in September 1833. His three marriages had produced no heir, and his brother Carlos was expected (and expecting) to succeed him. Ferdinand's third wife died in May 1829; had he not remarried, Don Carlos would have succeeded to the Spanish throne without dispute. But Ferdinand did remarry, and when his fourth wife became pregnant, he set aside the Bourbons' Salic Law (stipulating male succession) to enable the child (whether male or female) to succeed him. In October 1830, the future Queen Isabel was born, the elder of two daughters born to Ferdinand

and his final wife. The immediate basis of Carlism was the reassertion of the Salic Law and the refusal to recognize Isabel's right to the throne. There were Carlist plots and a Carlist uprising in Catalonia even before Ferdinand's death. However, Don Carlos (Carlos V) did not issue a call to arms until November 1833 after he had been outlawed. The First Carlist War ended in July 1840 with the defeat of the Carlists. In May 1845, Carlos abdicated in favour of his son Carlos Luis (Carlos VI), who revived the Carlist claim. In autumn 1846 Carlist bands began a guerrilla campaign in Catalonia; in 1848, Carlist forces fought one or two small battles in Catalonia; and, in 1849, Don Carlos Luis attempted to cross from France into Spain but was stopped at the border. Between 1849 and 1860, the Carlist claim was virtually in abeyance. There were sporadic risings after the death of Carlos V in 1855; and, in 1860, Carlos VI made a second attempt to enter Spain. He was captured and made to renounce his claim to the throne.

In 1867, his nephew Carlos VII took up the Carlist claim. Isabel was overthrown in a *coup d'état* in 1868, resulting in an Interregnum (1868–70) during which Spain was governed by the constituent Cortes. Amedeo ruled as elected king from 1871–3, followed by a republic (1873–5). During this period there was a Carlist revival, when in April 1870 Carlos VII formally took the leadership of the party into his own hands. In the same year, Isabel formally abdicated and named her son Alfonso as her legitimate successor. In April 1872, Carlos called for a general uprising, but his few volunteers were soon routed. In July 1873, Carlos came back to Spain and the Basque provinces rose in support. The main principles of Carlist doctrine, 'God, Country, and King', were asserted against the new republic and attracted considerable support. The Basque provinces supported Don Carlos because of his pledge to defend the *fueros* and their traditions of independence. However, in November 1874, Don Alfonso came of age, and the Carlists were now confronted by another monarchist party, the Alfonsists. Most of the middle and

upper classes in Spain were either Alfonsists or Carlists. Alfonso's accession to the
throne at the start of 1875 was the death
blow to the Carlist cause. During the summer the government armies continued to
regain territory from the Carlists, and in
February 1876, Don Carlos crossed the
frontier into France, never to return.
Carlism remained a force in Spain after
Don Carlos's departure, but its proponents
turned to legal and parliamentary political
means.   RH

Carlyle, Thomas (1795–1881), Victorian
writer and sage. Thomas Carlyle is alluded
to only once in Conrad's fiction, in 'Youth'
(*Youth*, 7), where *Marlow refers with little
apparent enthusiasm to *Sartor Resartus*
(1836). However, the presence of several
Carlylean echoes, particularly in the turn-
of-the-century Marlow stories, suggest that
Conrad's *reading soon came to include
Signs of the Times (1829), *The French Revolution: A History* (1837), *On Heroes, Hero-
Worship, and the Heroic in History* (1841),
and *Past and Present* (1843). Carlylean
echoes in Conrad's work suggest that he
was familiar with, and partially responsive
to the appeal of the Victorian sage's
preachments about the spiritual value of
duty, renunciation, and the *work ethic.
The boldest claim to date for a Carlylean
legacy appears in Fleishman's 1967 study
of Conrad's politics, which views the latter
as essentially the inheritor of a 19th-cen-
tury conservative-organicist tradition of
thought associated with Carlyle and Edmund Burke, although Fleishman adds the
proviso that 'Conrad's politics stand in the
Arnoldian rather than the Carlylean
branch of the tradition' (64).

Later studies include more emphatic
reservations and tend to find in Conrad's
response to Carlyle an example of his characteristic ability 'to use ideas in a paradoxical mode of partial endorsement and
partial criticism' (Watts 1989: 48). In 'Carlyle and Conrad: *Past and Present* and
Heart of Darkness', *Review of English Studies*, NS 23 (1972), 162–72, Alison L. Hopwood
maintains that while Conrad's story may
be indebted to Carlyle's *Past and Present* on

questions of the cash nexus and the work
ethic, it also demonstrates a 'complex and
critical response' (163) in the form of a
largely ironic revision of Carlylean views.
Indeed, she suggests, 'as a journalist with a
turn for the exalted and rhetorical, a
prophetic voice of civilization and empire,
Kurtz looks rather like a sardonic sketch of
Carlyle himself' (168). Another view of the
'largely negative' influence of Carlyle informs V. J. Emmett Jr's 'Carlyle, Conrad,
and the Politics of Charisma: Another Perspective on *Heart of Darkness*', *Conradiana*,
7 (1975), 145–53, where the story is regarded
as 'a critique of the widespread nineteenth-
century phenomenon of hero worship'
(146), with internal evidence to indicate
that Conrad had in mind Carlyle's *On
Heroes, Hero-Worship, and the Heroic in
History*. In '*Nostromo*: Conrad's Organicist
Philosophy of History', *Mosaic*, 15 (1982),
27–41, T. McAlindon meditates on the
influence of Carlyle (and secondarily, of
the 19th-century historian of South America, W. H. Prescott) in fostering Conrad's
interest in true and false heroism, the organic nature of the historical process, and
the part played by worship and belief in the
world's history. He concurs with other
critics in finding 'an imaginative critique as
well as an exploration of the ideas which
Carlyle had stereotyped' (38).

Casement, Roger [David] (1864–1916;
knighted 1911, de-knighted 1916), a Protestant Irish patriot and a passionate and
strikingly handsome crusader for human
rights, whether they be those of Congolese
Africans, Putumayo Indians, or his fellow
Irishmen. When they first met in the
*Congo in June 1890, Conrad found Roger
Casement 'most intelligent and very
sympathetic' (*CDOUP*, 7). Casement approached Conrad in 1903 to enlist his support in calling international attention to
the atrocities committed in King Leopold's
private police state. Conrad declined to become actively involved, but recommended
Casement warmly to the ever reform-
minded R. B. Cunninghame *Graham.
Casement's arrest and trial in 1916 for supporting an armed Irish rebellion during

the *First World War led Conrad to change his mind about Casement, and in his later comments Conrad portrayed his erstwhile room-mate and fellow veteran of the heart of darkness as a much more troubled and sinister figure.

Like Conrad, Casement was orphaned by the age of 12; but unlike Conrad, he had no guardian to provide moral and financial support and so followed the example of his elder brothers and set out for the colonies. By the time of his meeting with Conrad, Casement had been roaming in Africa for six years, assisting various expeditions and working for organizations including King Leopold's International Association for the Congo and the Baptist Missionary Society. An accomplished hiker and swimmer, Casement recalled years later that he was perhaps the only white man living who had swum the crocodile-infested Nkisi River. When Conrad first met him, Casement, who 'knew the coast languages well' (*CL*, v. 596), was recruiting native labour for caravans along the route of a planned narrow-gauge railway designed to provide access to the interior of the Congo by linking Matadi with Stanley Pool 230 miles upriver. As Conrad recalled, 'I went with him several times on short expeditions to hold "palavers" with neighbouring village-chiefs' (*CL*, v. 597). Conrad told Lady Ottoline *Morrell that already at that time Casement had been looked upon as having 'a rather enigmatical personality' (*CL*, v. 630).

In 1916 Conrad remembered meeting Casement in *London twenty years earlier at a dinner of the Johnson Society, from which they adjourned to the Sports Club and talked until 3 a.m. (*CL*, v. 597). This meeting could not have occurred in 1896, as Conrad claimed, since Casement spent all of that year in Africa. It could have taken place during Casement's brief return to England in 1897, or during a longer stay in 1898, the year in which Conrad began writing 'Heart of Darkness'.

Casement entered the British consular service in 1892 and served for over twenty years in a variety of posts on both coasts of Africa and in South America. His African experience culminated in 1903 with a report to the British government based on a journey into the interior of the Congo to find evidence of what would now be called human rights violations. He had covered much of the same route on a previous expedition in 1887, and was well placed to observe the depopulation and misery caused by fifteen years of ruthless exploitation. His report was instrumental in calling attention to the horrors of King Leopold's colonial rule. When Casement urged Conrad to support what would soon become the Congo Reform Association, Conrad forwarded Casement's appeal to Cunninghame Graham with an introduction in which he described Casement as a 'protestant Irishman, pious too', a 'limpid personality' with 'a touch of the Conquistador in him': 'I've seen him start off into an unspeakable wilderness swinging a crookhandled stick for all weapons, with two bull-dogs: Paddy (white) and Biddy (brindle) at his heels and a Loanda boy carrying a bundle for all company. A few months afterwards it so happened that I saw him come out again, a little leaner a little browner, with his stick, dogs, and Loanda boy, and quietly serene as though he had been for a stroll in a park' (*CL*, iii. 101–2).

On 3 January 1904, Casement accepted Conrad's invitation to visit Pent Farm. Jessie Conrad remembered him as 'a fanatical Irish Protestant' and 'a very handsome man with a thick dark beard and piercing, restless eyes' (*JCHC*, 103). Conrad maintained that he had never heard of 'the alleged custom of cutting off hands amongst the natives' and did not believe the custom ever existed along the Congo River; but he described the Congo situation as 'in every aspect an enormous and atrocious lie in action' (*CL*, iii. 95). Ford Madox *Ford, who was never in Africa, claimed to have seen Casement's evidence: 'I have myself seen in the hands of Sir Roger Casement who had smuggled them out of the country, the hands and feet of Congolese children which had been struck off by Free State officials, the parents having failed to bring in their quota of rubber or ivory'

(Ford, *A History of our Own Times*, ed. Solon Beinfeld and Sondra J. Stang (Bloomington: Indiana UP, 1988), 126 n.). In a report submitted to the United States Congress in 1890, George Washington Williams, who had just preceded Conrad into the interior of the Congo, had noted that 'Human hands and feet and limbs, smoked and dried, are offered and exposed for sale in many of the native village markets.' Williams blamed the severed limbs not on King Leopold's police but on the 'barbarous religious and funeral rites' of the Congolese themselves (quoted in *Heart of Darkness*, ed. Robert Kimbrough, Norton Critical Edition, 3rd edn. (New York: Norton, 1988), 91).

Posted as consul to Brazil in 1908, Casement took up the cause of the Putumayo Indians and stirred public opinion with another report in 1912 before retiring from government service in 1913. Ford claims that Casement saw the German invasion of Belgium in 1914 as a form of divine retribution. Travelling to Germany after the outbreak of war, Casement visited a prisoner-of-war camp in Limburg on the Lahn to recruit men for an Irish Brigade to fight for Irish independence. Arrested shortly after he was put ashore on the coast of Ireland by a German submarine in 1916, Casement was brought back to London and charged with high treason. Conrad told John *Quinn that he remembered meeting Casement for the last time by chance in London in 1911, when Conrad noticed 'a strange austerity in his aspect'. Conrad saw Casement no longer as a 'limpid personality' but as 'A creature of sheer temperament —a truly tragic personality: all but the greatness of which he had not a trace. Only vanity' (*CL*, v. 597–8).

From 26 to 29 June 1916 Casement was tried in the Court of King's Bench, London. The defence argued that the crime of treason as defined in 25 Edward III (dating from the year 1351) could be applied only to acts committed in England, and that Casement had committed no treason on English soil. For his part, Casement steadfastly refused to recognize the jurisdiction of an English court, and spoke of his own 'judicial assassination'. His statement to the court upon hearing the verdict was an eloquent and moving plea for human liberty: 'If there be no right of rebellion against a state of things that no savage tribe need endure without resistance, then I am sure that it is better for men to fight and die without right than to live in such a state of right as this' (George H. Knott (ed.), *Trial of Sir Roger Casement* (Edinburgh: William Hodge, 1917), 204). Casement thanked the jurors for their verdict and assured them that he did not wish to impugn their personal honour.

A number of petitions for clemency were circulated. Sir Arthur Conan Doyle gathered the signatures of Arnold *Bennett, Muirhead *Bone, G. K. Chesterton, John *Galsworthy, Clement K. *Shorter, and Israel Zangwill. During this campaign, excerpts purporting to be from Casement's private diaries were circulated and leaked to the press in a deliberate campaign to discredit him as homosexual. Conrad, whose elder son Borys was at that time on the western front, refused to sign the petition; he described the Irish rebellion as a 'stab in the back' (*CL*, v. 620). Casement was hanged in Pentonville prison (London) on 3 August 1916.

During his American visit in 1923 Conrad again had occasion to remember Casement, but the impression had become more ominous and suggestive of *Kurtz: 'Conrad was running his boat down the sluggish river when a tall, gaunt figure rose against the perpendicular face of a dark bluff. Crouching behind him, in an attitude suggesting a perverted sort of worship, was his servant and at his heels were two black bull-dogs' (John Powell, 'Conrad and Casement Hut Mates in Africa', *New York Evening Post*, 11 May 1923, 15).

Serious biographies include Brian Inglis, *Roger Casement* (1973), B. L. Reid, *The Lives of Roger Casement* (1976), and Roger Sawyer, *Casement: The Flawed Hero* (1984). On the Conrad connection see also Jeffrey Meyers, 'Conrad and Roger Casement', *Conradiana*, 5: 3 (1973), 64–9; Hunt Hawkins, 'Joseph Conrad, Roger Casement, and the Congo Reform Movement',

Journal of Modern Literature, 9 (1981–2), 65–80; and Jane Ford, 'An African Encounter: A British Traitor and *Heart of Darkness*', *Conradiana*, 27 (1995), 123–34. Details of Casement's trial are given in George H. Knott (ed.), *Trial of Roger Casement* (1917).

Catholicism. Conrad's description of himself to his grandmother, at the tender age of 5 years old, as 'grandson, Pole, Catholic, and nobleman' makes the connection between nationalism and religion that lies at the heart of Polish identity. As he wrote to Marguerite *Poradowska over thirty years later: 'Don't forget that with us religion and patriotism go hand in hand' (*CL*, i. 174). This linking of Catholicism and Polish nationalism has its roots in the fact that the Polish Catholic Church, the state religion of Poland, was restricted under the occupying Russians, who placed a Russian Orthodox representative at its head and censored the contents of sermons. Inevitably, Catholicism became inseparable from politics. In the poem written to commemorate Conrad's baptism, his father, Apollo *Korzeniowski, wrote: 'You are without land, without love, I without country, without people, I while *Poland— your Mother* is in her grave. I For your only *Mother* is dead—and yet I She is your faith, your palm of martyrdom' (*CUFE*, 33). This mixture of religious fervour and patriotism was further fuelled by the mystical writings of *Poland's Romantic poets, like Adam *Mickiewicz and Zygmunt Krasiński, who envisaged a Messianic role for Poland in the world. For his part, Korzeniowski claimed after his wife's death, 'I am a monk and moreover a simple *frater* in the Polish Order. I have hitherto confined my thoughts in a small cell of patriotism' (*CUFE*, 117). To Edward *Garnett, Conrad described his father's 'strong religious feeling degenerating after the loss of his wife into mysticism and despair' (*CL*, ii. 247). The young Conrad's Catholic inheritance was thus suffused with Polish nationalism and the morbid pietism of his father's final years, during which, as he later described it, he experienced 'mo-

ments of revolt which stripped off me some of my simple trust in the government of the universe' (*Notes*, 168).

The adult Conrad's attitude to Catholicism is often seen as typical of the general loss of faith of the late Victorian period, as a result of *Darwin's discoveries and the popularization of such scientific theories as Lord Kelvin's second law of thermodynamics (the law of entropy). Friedrich *Nietzsche's claim in the 'Introductory Discourse' to *Thus Spake Zarathustra* (1883–91) that 'God is dead' signals the degree to which scepticism about religion had taken root among the intelligentsia by the time Conrad began his writing career. But, in keeping with Conrad's definition of himself as *homo duplex* (*CL*, iii. 89), his attitude to the religion of his youth, and to Christianity in general, is more complex. On the one hand, the Conrads preferred a civil marriage in a registry office, and he refused to allow his younger son, John, to learn any religion until he was 6 years old—whereupon, Jessie reports, Conrad was amused by his son's observation that the crucifixion was 'disgusting, it ought to be forgotten, it's not a thing to be proud of' (*JCHC*, 151). But, on the other hand, John Conrad recalled his father's caution: 'Don't assume that because I do not go to church that I do not believe, I do; all true seamen do in their hearts' (*JCTR*, 152). Similarly, refusing the invitation to join a London club that stipulated the Protestant religion as one of its conditions, Conrad wrote: 'I was born a R. C. and though dogma sits lightly on me I have never renounced that form of Christian religion' (quoted in Lester, 19).

More usually, though, Conrad's comments about religion, particularly those contained in his letters to R. B. Cunninghame *Graham and Garnett, attack Christianity for duping man into believing that life is meaningful. For instance, to Graham he writes that 'Faith is a myth and beliefs shift like mists on the shore' (*CL*, ii. 17) and 'I don't care a damn for the best heaven ever invented by Jew or Gentile' (*CL*, ii. 238), while he complains to Garnett of 'the idiotic mystery of Heaven' (*CL*, i. 268).

Even when talking of his past, Conrad's comments are directed not at Catholicism in particular but rather at Christianity generally: 'I always, from the age of fourteen, disliked the Christian religion, its doctrines, ceremonies and festivals.... And the most galling feature is that nobody—not a single Bishop of them—believes in it' (*CL*, ii. 468–9). Moreover, Conrad, who also claimed that 'Everyone must walk in the light of his own heart's gospel. No man's light is good to any of his fellows' (*CL*, i. 253), does not offer a total disavowal of Christianity, but rather a debunking of its dogma and extremism. For instance, when criticizing Leo Tolstoy, he says: 'the base from which he starts—Christianity—is distasteful to me. I am not blind to its services but the absurd oriental fable from which it starts irritates me. Great, improving, softening, compassionate it may be but it has lent itself with amazing facility to cruel distortion and is the only religion which, with its impossible standards, has brought an infinity of anguish to innumerable souls—on this earth' (*CL*, v. 358).

That Conrad's critique of Catholicism might itself be more *duplex* than is commonly thought is noted by Lester, who points out that Conrad's comments on religion are very often tailored to suit his addressee. Thus, the religious scepticism in the letters to Graham is extenuated by the suggestion of Christian succour in correspondence with Marguerite Poradowska: 'For charity is eternal and universal love, the divine virtue, the only manifestation of the Almighty which can in some way justify the act of creation' (*CL*, i. 107). This letter is intended as a rebuke to Poradowska for carrying her self-sacrifice too far (Conrad asks rhetorically, 'Have you found the peace which is the reward of these sacrifices accepted by the master of our souls?' (107–8)), but it simultaneously—and contradictorily—acknowledges the existence of such aspects of Christian doctrine as 'the Almighty' and 'master of our souls'. This is no impasse, but rather a reasoned middle path that eschews the excesses of Christian dogma. Conrad is equally wary of the claims of science,

whose advances in the 19th century, more than anything else, rendered traditional religious belief untenable.

While Conrad's Catholic heritage contributes very little to his fiction (beyond the fact that the Slavic castaway Yanko *Goorall in 'Amy Foster' is Catholic), his general scepticism of Christianity is pervasive. It extends explicitly to the presentation of hypocritical religious zealots, like Podmore in *The Nigger of the 'Narcissus'*, Therese in *The Arrow of Gold*, and the French (Catholic) clergy living off peasant villagers in 'The Idiots' (*Tales of Unrest*), and implicitly to the influence of priest-fathers, upon the *Professor in *The Secret Agent*, and *Jim in *Lord Jim*. (Actually, the narrative's presentation of his father's advice immediately before the disaster that befalls Jim on *Patusan dramatically signals the ineffectuality of Christianity.) Added to this, the despair his characters experience is often the metaphysical anguish born of a faithless age. Taminah 'knew of no heaven to send her prayer to' (*Almayer's Folly*, 118–19) while *Heyst 'regretted that he had no Heaven to which he could recommend' *Lena (*Victory*, 354). Inevitably, in its quest for mythical patterns, *archetypal criticism of Conrad's fiction has yielded readings that identify certain novels as religious allegories. So, for instance, Edwin Mosely interprets the two-part structure of *Lord Jim* as replicating the development from the Old Testament to the New Testament, in which Jim is transformed from 'the archetypal Adam . . . Everyman' in the first half of the novel to 'the archetypal Christ . . . the sacrificial scapegoat for Everyman' in the second (*Pseudonyms of Christ in the Modern Novel* (University of Pittsburgh Press, 1962), 29–30). Such conclusions do not imply that a residual religious heritage persisted in Conrad; but by showing the degree of indebtedness of Conradian fiction to the King James Version of the Bible, Dwight H. Purdy, in *Joseph Conrad's Bible* (Norman: University of Oklahoma Press, 1984), argues that Conrad, who was not a practising Catholic in adulthood, must nonetheless have read the Bible in English during this time. The task of verifying this claim is complicated by the fact that the Bible, like the works of Shakespeare, constitutes an unavoidable repository of English mythology. Conrad himself noted the symbiotic nature of the relationship: 'Art has served Religion; artists have found the most exalted inspiration in Christianity' (*Notes*, 75). Conrad's final resting place is at St Thomas's Church in Canterbury, where he lies, in the words of the parish register, 'in that part reserved for Catholics'. See also C. F. Burgess, 'Conrad's Catholicism', *Conradiana*, 15 (1983), 111–26.   AHS

'Censor of Plays: An Appreciation, The'. This essay was written at Edward *Garnett's request following upon the Lord Chamberlain's refusal to grant a licence for his play *The Breaking Point* (1907). On 4 October 1907, Conrad responded with relish: 'You say: *The Censor should be a policeman etc.* But my conviction is that the Censor should *not be at all*' (*CL*, iii. 489). On 8 October, Conrad sent Garnett the completed essay, which was printed as a letter to the editor of the *Daily Mail* (12 October), 4. In it, he responded with a more aggressive attack than Garnett anticipated, and the latter cut some of its more belligerent passages, with the *Daily Mail* making further cuts in the interests of space. It was collected in *Notes on Life and Letters* in a fuller but nonetheless truncated form, since the *Notes on Life and Letters* copy-text still incorporated Garnett's excisions. Presenting the office of the Censor as a form of disguised tyranny and absurd anachronism—and hence an offence to the self-respect of the public and the artist alike—the essay deploys a mixture of colourful invective, acerbic sarcasm, and Dickensian lampoon: 'This Chinese monstrosity, disguised in the trousers of the Western Barbarian and provided by the State with the immortal Mr. Stiggins's plug hat and umbrella, is with us' (78). Garnett rightly considered it 'a masterpiece of rhetoric, and its spirit of ironical raillery plays around its unhappy subject in a manner most fascinating to watch' (*LFC*, 216 n.). Later that month, at John

*Galsworthy's request, Conrad joined over seventy signatories in a letter to *The Times* continuing the protest against theatre censorship. The manuscript is held at the Beinecke Rare Book and Manuscript Library, Yale University.

'Certain Aspects of the Admirable Inquiry into the Loss of the *Titanic*'. Written partly in response to criticisms by John *Quinn of Conrad's prior essay, 'Some Reflections on the Loss of the *Titanic*', and partly to review the findings of a Board of Trade inquiry into the *Titanic* disaster held during May–June 1912, this sequel was completed in mid-June and published in the *English Review*, 11 (July 1912), 581–95. It was later revised for *Notes on Life and Letters*. More stridently critical in tone than its predecessor, the essay again measures the 'Drury Lane aspects' of the public reaction against the awfulness of the human loss: 'But I, who am not a sentimentalist think it would have been finer if the band of the *Titanic* had been quietly saved, instead of being drowned while playing . . . the poor devils' (248). It also asserts a vision of 'right feeling and right conduct' in order to attack shipowners who treat men and women as 'cattle of the Western-ocean trade' (242). Conrad again dwells satirically on the massive liner's supposed 'unsinkability', focusing upon the *Titanic*'s paucity of safety measures as compared with its spurious 'seaside hotel luxury': 'It is inconceivable to think that there are people who can't spend five days of their life without a suite of apartments, *cafés*, bands, and such-like refined delights' (234–5). For a view of the essay's rhetorical structures, see Stape 1988. The manuscript is held at the Lilly Library, Indiana University.

Cervoni, Dominique-André (1834–90), born in Luri, *Corsica, and **César** (1858–1936), also Luri-born and possibly very distantly related to Dominique. Dominique and César Cervoni were Conrad's fellow crew members on his third *Caribbean voyage in the *Saint-Antoine* in 1876. Aged 42 at that time and with over twenty years' experience as a seaman, Dominique may have been a partner with the youthful Conrad in an illegal contraband venture during their Caribbean stay. If Conrad's highly coloured accounts in *The Mirror of the Sea* and *The Arrow of Gold* are credible, then sometime in late 1877 he joined both Dominique and César in an expedition in the *balancelle Tremolino*, illegally running guns along the Mediterranean coast to Spanish Carlists. In an ill-fated outcome, the ship was deliberately sunk to avoid capture, with César being ignominiously drowned. Factual corroboration for this colourful reminiscence is, however, extremely slight and some of its events are patently disqualified by known facts (for example, César outlived Conrad by more than a decade).

The colourful portrait in *The Mirror* of Dominique the virile male and Corsican bandit-adventurer is itself significant in suggesting the strength of the youthful Conrad's ardent hero-worship. Cervoni emerges with the combined force of a Ulysses, Robin Hood, d'Artagnan, and Byronic hero: 'On board the *Tremolino*, wrapped up in a black *caban*, the picturesque cloak of Mediterranean seamen, with those massive moustaches and his remorseless eyes set off by the shadow of the deep hood, he looked piratical and monkish and darkly initiated into the most awful mysteries of the sea' (164). Here was a father figure and role model who, in contrast to Conrad's prudent guardian Tadeusz *Bobrowski, acted as 'a mentor of a rather unusual kind, with a contempt for law, an ardent, romantic scepticism and a love of adventure which found an echo in the restless heart of his pupil' (*LL*, i. 36). Dominique also seems to find an echo in several of the later writer's fictional creations, such as Tom *Lingard in the Malay trilogy, *Peyrol in *The Rover*, Dominic in *The Arrow of Gold*, and Attilio in *Suspense*, although these characters often attract a tonic authorial scepticism absent from *The Mirror*. Of all of Conrad's creations, however, it is *Nostromo who most strongly bears the imprint of the audacious Dominique. In his 'Author's Note' to *Nos-*

tromo, Conrad points out that 'Dominic . . . might under given circumstances have been a Nostromo' (p. xx); and from the former, Nostromo would seem to inherit his imposing stature and charisma as 'much of a man' (15), his love of risk-taking, desire for popular fame, and attractiveness to women. As Sherry points out (*CWW*, 165), it is when Nostromo is at sea with the lighter of silver that he most closely resembles Dominique 'the fearful and feared leader'. Sherry might have added that *Nostromo*, one of Conrad's most sceptical novels, also revalues through the title-character and his romantic self-image the entire mystique of the proud and lawless hero.

Whether César Cervoni exerted a similarly persistent influence upon Conrad the writer is more difficult to ascertain, although this snake-like 'monster' whose 'depraved nature was expressed in physical terms' and who would 'writhe on the deck, gnashing his teeth in impotent rage' (*The Mirror of the Sea*, 166) may be partly echoed in characters as disparate as *Donkin in *The Nigger of the 'Narcissus'* and Ricardo in *Victory*.

Champel-les-Bains. Conrad made four visits—in 1891, 1894, 1895, and 1907—to this *Genevan suburb for a period of some 170 days, almost all of them spent at the Hôtel-Pension de la Roseraie. Seeking relief for his post-*Congo ailments, he undertook the first three visits in order to attend the nearby hydropathy centre in the Hôtel Beau-Séjour and undergo a water cure, a form of treatment involving high-pressure showers that employed the healing water both internally and externally (see HEALTH). On his third visit in May 1895, during the composition of *An Outcast of the Islands*, Conrad met the Briquels, a French family who were staying at the same hotel, and seems to have formed a romantic attachment to Émilie *Briquel. His fourth visit in 1907 unexpectedly grew out of a family holiday in *Montpellier when Borys Conrad fell seriously ill and was taken to Champel for treatment. During this three-month stay, Conrad corrected and revised *The Secret Agent* for book publication, adding some 28,000 words to it; he also deepened his acquaintance with Geneva, a city that would figure as a main setting in his next novel, *Under Western Eyes*. For further details, see Kirschner 1988, and Kirschner's sequel in Moore (ed.) 1992: 223–54.

Chance: A Tale in Two Parts. This novel (1913–14) marked a watershed in Conrad's literary career and holds a unique place among his works. Thanks largely to 'the unexpected power of successful advertising' (264) it was Conrad's first popular success, although there is no agreement among critics as to its proper place in his canon. It has been variously described as the most Jamesian, the most Fordian, and the most 'English' of Conrad's novels. Some 134,000 words long, the narrative is complex even by Conradian standards, and marks the final appearance of *Marlow, who has become more sardonic and pontifical since his appearance in *Lord Jim* thirteen years earlier. Marlow is forever sounding the note of chance and happenstance, but the novel he helps to narrate is based on a number of conventional generic models, including a melodramatic plot in which a knight in the form of a sea captain rescues a damsel in distress from the clutches of her villainous father. In keeping with this fairy-tale mode, *Chance* has arguably the happiest ending of all of Conrad's novels. *Feminist critics have shown interest in *Chance* as a work written with female readers in mind, and as the only one of Conrad's works to deal explicitly with the *women's movement. Thanks to F. N. *Doubleday's pre-publication advertising campaign, the novel was a huge success in *America, where some 10,000 copies were sold in the first week of publication. Since that time, it has been translated into eleven languages, but remains unique among Conrad's major works in never having been adapted for the stage or *film.

Part I of *Chance*, entitled 'The Damsel', begins at a riverside inn on the *Thames estuary, where Marlow and the unnamed narrator dine with a recent acquaintance named Charles Powell, who entertains his companions with the story of how he obtained his first command as second mate in the *Ferndale*, under Captain *Anthony. Later, Marlow explains to the narrator how he came to know of Captain Anthony through the *Fynes, Marlow's neighbours during three successive holidays in the country. Mr Fyne and Marlow would meet occasionally for a game of chess. One day while he was walking, Marlow came upon a young girl walking with the Fynes' dog dangerously close to the edge of a precipice above a quarry, and escorted her home. On his next visit, Marlow arrives late in the evening to find that the girl, one of the 'girl-friends' collected by the feminist Mrs Fyne, is missing. Fearing that she may have committed suicide, Marlow and Fyne return to inspect the quarry in the dark. The next day, Mrs Fyne receives a letter from the girl announcing that she has eloped with Captain Anthony to *London. Marlow learns at this point that the girl, whom he had known as 'Miss Smith', is really Flora *de Barral, whose once immensely wealthy father has been imprisoned for fraud after a notorious bankruptcy trial.

In the course of a lengthy conversation over tea at Marlow's cottage, during most of which Fyne is occupied with his boisterous dog, Mrs Fyne insists that her reluctant husband follow Flora to London to stop her from marrying Captain Anthony. Not convinced by Mrs Fyne's arguments, Marlow nevertheless accompanies Fyne to London. While Fyne is 'wrangling' (248) upstairs with Captain Anthony in the Eastern Hotel, Marlow encounters Flora on the busy pavement outside. She admits to having been suicidal, and tells Marlow the story of her involvement with Captain Anthony. Fyne reappears without seeing Flora, revealing to Marlow his worry that Flora is marrying Anthony only in order to provide for her father, who is soon to be released from prison.

At this point Marlow's relations with the Fynes are interrupted by his long voyage. In Part II, 'The Knight', Marlow tells of how he later found Powell's boat in a creek flowing into the Thames estuary and heard from Powell the further story of his joining the *Ferndale* some seven months after Flora's marriage to Captain Anthony on the eve of her father's release from prison. As the ship sails off to the southern tip of Africa with a cargo of 40 tons of dynamite, Powell gradually becomes aware of the strange and ominous situation created by the presence of two 'shore people' (306) on board. To the great dismay of shipmates like his apoplectic first mate Mr Franklin and his morose steward, Captain Anthony has given up his quarters to Flora and her father (known only as 'Mr Smith') and re-treated into stoic and miserable isolation. Combining Powell's account with what he knows of the Fynes, Marlow realizes that Anthony is convinced that Flora does not love him, while she remains convinced that no one could possibly love her. The 'Great de Barral' feels that he has merely traded one form of incarceration for another, and convinces himself that Flora wants to get away from Captain Anthony. The tension culminates when Powell, keeping watch by night on the poop, notices by chance that he can see into the Captain's cabin through a pane of clear glass in the skylight. Shocked to observe a hand emerge from behind a curtain to tamper with the Captain's brandy-and-water, he goes below to warn Captain Anthony. There follows a confrontation, at the end of which de Barral dies by drinking his own poison. Powell then tells Marlow of Captain Anthony's accidental death six years later as the result of a collision. Powell frequents the Thames estuary in order to visit the widowed Flora, at which point Marlow's story ends, with a reversal of the damage done by the Fynes and a happy ending that reunites Flora with Powell.

In a letter to Edward *Garnett written in the late spring of 1898, Conrad spoke of including a story about 'Dynamite' in a volume of tales to be narrated by Marlow (*CL*, ii. 62). Nine months later, writing to David *Meldrum, Conrad mentioned a story 'about a Captains wife' (*CL*, ii. 169). The idea was then set aside until 1904, when Conrad apparently began work on a short story about a shipload of explosives bound

for the Malay Archipelago. By May 1905 'Explosives' was declared 'ready' (*CL*, iii. 243); by September, the title had been changed to *Chance*, and Conrad was hoping to finish the story by the end of the year (*CL*, iii. 280). In the event, *Chance* suffered many interruptions for the sake of other projects, and was not completed until March 1912, two months after *serialization had begun in the Sunday magazine section of the *New York Herald* (21 January to 30 June 1912). The differences between the serial and book versions of the novel are discussed by Robert Siegle in 'The Two Texts of *Chance*', *Conradiana*, 16 (1984), 83–101, and by Susan Jones in 'The Three Texts of *Chance*', *The Conradian*, 21: 1 (1996), 57–78, the latter giving particular attention to the earliest manuscript pages of 'Dynamite'.

Conrad was under contract to publish the book version with *Methuen, but by 1913 his relations with the publisher had reached a low ebb. The American edition was published by Doubleday, Page in October 1913, but a bookbinders' strike delayed the appearance of the English edition from September 1913 until January 1914, and the consequent redating of the Methuen title-pages has generated a good deal of bibliographical confusion, leaving *Chance* with the most notorious publishing history of all Conrad's works, and making copies of the first English edition with uncancelled 1913 title-pages the rarest of Conrad volumes. In his bibliographies Thomas J. *Wise warned that forgeries of the first printing were in circulation, and indicated how the fraudulent copies could be distinguished from genuine ones. This charge gains interest from the fact that, after Conrad's death, Wise was himself unmasked as a forger of more than 100 early printed editions (but not of Conrad's works). The complex bibliographical history of *Chance* has been traced in detail by William R. Cagle, who concludes that Wise's alleged 'forgeries' are probably genuine publisher's volumes with cancel titles on which the date had not been changed (see 'The Publication of Joseph Conrad's *Chance*', *Book Collector*, 16 (1967), 305–22).

The most famous study of *Chance* is Henry *James's review-essay of 'The Younger Generation' first published in the *Times Literary Supplement* (19 March and 2 April 1914) and then revised and expanded into 'The New Novel' in *Notes on Novelists* (excerpted in *CCH*, 263–70). Deploring a lack of 'method' in the works of Arnold *Bennett and H. G. *Wells, James offers the contrasting example of *Chance*, which he considers 'an extraordinary exhibition of method' (265). James memorably describes Marlow's narrative as a 'prolonged hovering flight of the subjective over the outstretched ground of the case exposed', and seems to praise its author for standing 'absolutely alone as a votary of the way to do a thing that shall make it undergo most doing' (267, 265), but he also implied that the story of Flora de Barral hardly warranted such an elaborate display of technical virtuosity. Conrad, who was fourteen years younger and considered James his artistic *maître*, later told John *Quinn that this was 'the *only time* a criticism affected me painfully' (*CL*, v. 595). In a letter to Edith *Wharton, James, offended at not having been invited to participate in a *Festschrift* for Conrad, had been even more dismissive of the major novels, speaking of 'the last three or four impossibilities, wastes of desolation, that succeeded the two or three final good things of his earlier time' (*PL*, 97). Another early reviewer, Robert Lynd, asserted that many readers would find the novel 'tedious', but conceded that its 'atmosphere of puzzlement' made the characters 'mysteriously interesting' (*CCH*, 271–2). Other reviewers like C. E. Montague enjoyed the novel's 'system of interpenetrative lights, or interplaying mirrors, where nothing comes to you as a fact directly and impersonally stated'; this technique, for Montague, had the result that 'the whole atmosphere in which the narrative moves acquires a strange and exciting luminousness' (ibid. 275).

Most critics have agreed with James's judgement that the novel's narrative complexity seems out of proportion to the interest of its subject. Does such an appar-

ently melodramatic and highly contrived romantic situation deserve to be treated with so much effort and attention, or is the novel merely an exercise in technique for its own sake? Despite Marlow's efforts to identify the sources of his information, the reconstruction of Flora's story often requires him to invoke a kind of 'conjectural omniscience' in order to relate things that no one could have told him, such as the private conversations between Flora's governess and the dubious 'nephew', or the inner feelings of Captain Anthony (whom Marlow never meets) about Flora. Like the narrator, the reader may want to ask Marlow: 'How do you know all this?' (264). This potential implausibility is stretched even further in the final scenes, where the reader learns that Flora's elopement took place only ten years earlier, and that Marlow met Flora for the third time only the previous day.

After the Second World War, the problem of *Chance* was taken as evidence to support the notion, increasingly popular among *psychoanalytic critics, that Conrad was unable to create convincing female characters or deal with themes involving sexuality. In his influential study, Moser (1957) saw *Chance* as symptomatic of Conrad's 'almost belligerent lack of genuine, dramatic interest in sexual problems' (128) and called it 'a long novel on a subject that he did not understand' (130). However, in 'Conrad, James and *Chance*' (in Mack and Gregor (eds.) 1968: 301–22), Ian Watt surveyed the friendship of the two authors and attempted to refute James and other critics of the novel by showing that the narrative indirections of *Chance* are purposeful and necessary. The novel can in this sense be understood as the culmination of Conrad's lifelong predilection for scenes of intimate misunderstanding (as between *Almayer and Nina, or Winnie and Adolf *Verloc, or *Razumov and Natalia *Haldin). The elaborate mediations of *Chance* make it possible for Marlow and his interlocutor to share with the reader a privileged perspective from which the misunderstandings generated by the relatively limited experience of the other narrators

(Powell, the Fynes, Mr Franklin, and Flora herself) come into view. In 'Textuality and Surrogacy in Conrad's *Chance*', *L'Époque Conradienne* (1989), 51–65, Daphna Erdinast-Vulcan discusses the ways in which the various narrators in the novel serve as surrogate 'knights' in the effort to rescue Flora.

Conrad's plots are commonly based on generic models of the kind found in popular adventure stories or melodramas, but rarely with the degree of self-consciousness manifest in *Chance*. As Marlow tells Powell, 'We are the creatures of our light literature much more than is generally suspected' (288), thus suggesting that the difficulties encountered by Flora and Captain Anthony are largely caused (like those of Lord *Jim) by their faith in images of proper behaviour drawn from popular fiction. Captain Anthony's elopement is also described by Marlow as the 'affair of the purloined brother' (148), recalling the detective stories of Edgar Allan Poe. Elsewhere, Marlow's interlocutor alludes to James Fenimore *Cooper by comparing Marlow's narrative to 'one of those Redskin stories where the noble savages carry off a girl and the honest backwoodsman with his incomparable knowledge follows the track and reads the signs of her fate in a footprint here, a broken twig there, a trinket dropped by the way' (311). Conrad's use of the conventions of detective fiction is discussed by Robert Hampson in '*Chance*: The Affair of the Purloined Brother', *The Conradian*, 6: 2 (1980), 5–15.

Conrad's portrait of Mrs Fyne as a self-styled 'feminist' has attracted the attention of feminist literary critics, who have discovered new interest in Conrad's female characters. Four essays devoted to various aspects of *Chance* are included in *The Conradian*, 17: 2 (1993): Susan Jones traces the influence in *Chance* of Marguerite *Poradowska's works; Laurence Davies describes the way in which *Chance* was marketed for a specifically female audience; Andrew Michael Roberts discusses the feminine 'passivity' of male representations of women in the novel; and Robert Hampson traces additional literary influences and correspondences in '*Chance* and the Secret Life: Conrad, Thackeray, Stevenson'.

The manuscript of *Chance* is in the Berg Collection, New York Public Library. Major typescripts and other fragments are held at the Beinecke Rare Book and Manuscript Library, Yale University; at Colgate University; and at the Harry Ransom Humanities Research Center at the University of Texas at Austin. The original typescript of the 'Author's Note', dated May 1920, is at the Philadelphia Free Library.

Chesson, Wilfrid Hugh (1870–1952), an employee of the publisher T. Fisher *Unwin. Wilfrid Chesson was the first professional reader to see the manuscript of Conrad's first novel *Almayer's Folly*, soon after it arrived at Unwin's office on 4 July 1894. Immediately recognizing its promise, he drew it to the attention of Unwin's senior reader, Edward *Garnett. Chesson seems also to have edited the manuscript, collated proofs, and prepared advertisements for it. An auction catalogue of Chesson materials (1970) further indicates that Chesson had 'a disastrous quarrel with Unwin over the question of writing a preface for the new edition of *Almayer's Folly*', presumably referring to the preface Conrad completed in early 1895, but not included in the first edition. According to Chesson, Conrad in turn became his first reader when he perused the manuscript of *Name This Child: A Story of Two* (1894), and in 1897 he received a presentation copy of Chesson's next novel *A Great Lie* (1897). The two men maintained contact in later life, and Chesson went on to write several perceptive reviews of Conrad's fiction. Looking back in 1919 on his first contact with *Almayer's Folly*, he commented that 'the purely stylistic and academic merits of Mr. Conrad's work were even in 1894 too obvious to make the "discovery" of him by a literary critic much more than an evidence of reasonable attention to his business' (quoted in Ugo Mursia, 'The True "Discoverer" of Joseph Conrad's Literary Talent and Other Notes on Conradian Biography, with Three Unpublished Letters', *Conradiana*, 4: 2 (1972), 8).

'Christmas Day at Sea'. Sent to his agent J. B. *Pinker on 3 July 1923, this article about the practice of celebrating Christmas at sea was published in the Christmas number of the *Daily Mail* (24 December), 4, and collected in *Last Essays*. As often occurs in his essays, Conrad's reminiscence contains a factual inaccuracy. The throwing into the sea of a Christmas gift for the crew of a passing American whaler, the *Alaska*, in the Southern Ocean south-west of New Zealand in latitude 51, is said to have taken place at Christmas 1879. At this date, however, Conrad was in the Mediterranean. If the event actually took place, it almost certainly happened in late January 1881 on Conrad's return voyage from *Australia in the *Loch Etive*. The manuscript, dated 1 July 1923, two revised typescripts, and the corrected galley proofs are held at the Harry Ransom Humanities Research Center, University of Texas at Austin; the corrected carbon copy of the third typescript and the second corrected galley proofs are held at Texas Tech University, Lubbock.

Clifford, Hugh [Charles] (1866–1941; knighted 1909). Hugh Clifford, a lifelong friend of Conrad's, combined a distinguished career as a colonial administrator and governor in Malaya, north Borneo, Trinidad and Tobago, Nigeria, and Ceylon (present-day Sri Lanka) with that of man of letters. In April 1898, Conrad wrote 'An Observer in Malaya' (*Notes*), a review of Clifford's *Studies in Brown Humanity* (1898), the first of many books by a man who prided himself on his intimate knowledge of Malay culture and language. Later that year, a pseudonymous review from the weekly edition of the *Singapore Free Press* (1 September), 142, reached Conrad. Entitled 'Mr Conrad at Home and Abroad', it was—unbeknown to him at the time—by Clifford. One of the first general surveys of Conrad's work, this article warmly applauds his early fiction, but complains that their creator's knowledge of Malay customs and society was superficial and that he ought to write on subjects familiar to him. On reading this review, Conrad de-

fended himself to his publisher: 'Well I never did set up as an authority on Malaysia. I looked for a medium in which to express myself' (*CL*, ii. 130). A first meeting with Clifford took place in August 1899, when both were fellow contributors to *Blackwood's Magazine*. Thereafter they corresponded, exchanged volumes, and entered into detailed discussions of each other's work and style, Conrad believing that while Clifford possessed unusual knowledge, he made indifferent artistic use of it, and Clifford holding that although Conrad was an exemplary craftsman and stylist, his knowledge was defective. Their correspondence also prompted Conrad's memorable distinction: 'you are favoured by the subject while I have always to struggle with a moral horror of some sort' (*CL*, ii. 227). Clifford went on to write a further general appreciation in 'The Art of Mr. Joseph Conrad', *Spectator*, 89 (29 November 1902), 827–8. He continued to champion his friend's reputation, although his assertion, in a *North American Review* article of June 1904, that at the beginning of his writing career Conrad wavered between French and English as a literary language always irritated Conrad and led him to refute it publicly: 'English was for me neither a matter of choice nor adoption . . . if I had not written in English I would not have written at all' ('Author's Note', *A Personal Record*, pp. v, vi). Conrad dedicated *Chance* (1914) to Clifford in acknowledgement of his help in securing American serial publication for it in the *New York Herald*. Although Clifford continued to serve abroad, he maintained contact with Conrad and regularly saw him on his visits to England. See also Asako Nakai, 'A Kurtz in Malaya: Hugh Clifford's "Unreasoning" Text', *Conradiana*, 29 (1997), 173–92, and Linda Dryden, 'Conrad and Hugh Clifford: An "Irreproachable Player on the Flute" and "A Ruler of Men"', *The Conradian*, 23: 1 (1998), 51–73.

collaborations. Literary collaborations were a common occurrence in the period 1880–1920, with many leading authors, Rudyard *Kipling and Robert Louis

*Stevenson among them, working with lesser-known partners. As Watts comments, such collaborations were a feature of the expanding literary market place and invariably represented 'a victory of expediency over artistic integrity' (1989: 91). It is perhaps strange that Conrad, who in his 1897 'Preface' to *The Nigger of the 'Narcissus'* described the artist as essentially a lonely and single-minded Promethean quester, should within a few months commit himself to a long-term collaboration with Ford Madox *Ford. Some of his friends and associates—Edward *Garnett, H. G. *Wells, and Henry *James—were not only surprised, but also strongly disapproved of the plan. Yet it is important to remember that at the time of his first meeting with Ford, Conrad was embroiled in a painfully protracted and unavailing struggle to finish *The Rescue*, a creative ordeal introducing him to the full horror of writer's block, broken deadlines, and 'suicidal' self-recrimination. On his side, therefore, a variety of personal and professional needs may have commended the idea of collaboration: the urge for friendship and support as well as the pressing necessity to produce marketable fiction more speedily.

Before meeting Ford, Conrad was already alive to the possibility of one kind of collaboration. In July 1894, while impatiently waiting for T. Fisher *Unwin to make a decision about the manuscript of his first novel, *Almayer's Folly*, he proposed to his 'aunt' Marguerite *Poradowska, a published author in France, that she might translate the novel into French and publish it 'not as a translation but as a collaboration' (*CL*, i. 165), with her name attached as a way of winning literary attention and with Conrad represented pseudonymously as 'Kamudi' (approximate Malay for 'rudder'), the name he had used when submitting the novel to Unwin. When Unwin accepted the novel soon after, the plan became redundant.

Conrad first met Ford in late 1898, and from their meeting, described by Baines as 'the most important event in Conrad's literary career' (214–15), there quickly de-

veloped a plan to collaborate on a long-term basis. The subsequent friendship and working association between the two extended over ten years and, according to Conrad, made Ford 'a sort of life-long habit' (*CL*, iii. 287). Instigated by Conrad, this collaboration was conceived as an open one, a 'partnership in prose'. While it brought together two writers with an obvious liking for each other and—as Ford's *Joseph Conrad: A Personal Remembrance* (Duckworth, 1924) makes clear—an excited commitment to the exacting standards of French literature and an openness to experimental writing, it was always designed to be flexible enough to leave each free to take an independent direction. Ford, the younger partner by sixteen years, had published only one novel when he first met Conrad and so might be helped towards publication; Conrad anticipated that the collaboration would bring material benefits and help him to 'keep under the particular devil that spoils my work for me as quick as I turn it out' (*CL*, ii. 107). In the event, the published fruits of their formal collaboration—*The Inheritors* (largely written by Ford), *Romance*, and *The Nature of a Crime*—failed to bring the material reward and recognition aimed at by the two writers.

The main value of the collaboration lay elsewhere, in its indirect benefits for both writers. During their ten-year association, significantly coinciding with Conrad's major period, 'there was, beneath Conrad's fierce pride, a real dependence on Ford. It was never a dependence for a knowledge of his craft or for imaginative insight. . . . It was psychological support—assurance that these gifts were really his—that Conrad needed, and for it he expressed extravagant gratitude' (Mizener, 46). Additionally, there are good grounds for endorsing Ford's claim that at the height of their association he was heavily involved in Conrad's 'literary dustings and sweepings, correcting his proofs, writing from his dictation, suggesting words when he was at a loss, or bringing to his memory incidents that he had forgotten' (1932: 187). Directly or indirectly, Ford contributed to a number of Conrad's works—'The End of the Tether', 'Amy Foster', 'To-morrow', parts of *Nostromo*, *The Mirror of the Sea*, *The Secret Agent*, and *A Personal Record*. The high point of Conrad's dependency occurred in early 1904 at a time when financial pressures required him to produce quick saleable copy and growing despondency prevented him from doing so. Ford selflessly stepped in to help his friend with the production of semi-autobiographical papers (later collected in *The Mirror of the Sea*) and may also have composed—or perhaps merely acted as scribe for—a section of *Nostromo* (manuscript leaves 588–603—a fragment of Part II, chapter 5). On his side, Ford benefited from his association with a writer whose name carried increasing prestige, and during the period 1905–9 he was as prolific an independent writer as was Conrad. He, too, relied on his collaborator's personal and professional support, particularly during his severe nervous breakdown in 1904 and at the time in 1908 when he was launching the *English Review*.

The value of the Conrad–Ford collaboration needs also to be measured by its productive and generative effect upon the independent careers of the two writers. For Ford, the younger writer, the partnership is likely to have involved a technical apprenticeship and initiation into methods of indirect narration, the full significance of which was only realized some years after the collaboration had ended, in works like *The Good Soldier* (1915) and *Parade's End* (1924–8). In Conrad's case, the collaborative novel *Romance* appears to have opened up significant new territory in its foreshadowing of the South American setting and treatment of political themes in his next novel, *Nostromo*. Frederick R. Karl makes the boldest claim to date for the importance of their collaboration: he argues that, as in the association between T. S. Eliot and Ezra Pound, they 'were on to what would be the entire modern movement in prose fiction and poetry' and assigns to their turn-of-the-century debate a central place in the emergence of new and experimental Modernist writing ('Conrad, Ford, and the

Novel', *Midway*, 10 (1969), 17). Max Saunders's magisterial biography *Ford Madox Ford: A Dual Life*, 2 vols. (OUP, 1996) sheds new light on Ford's involvement in the collaboration. John A. Meixner's 'Ford and Conrad', *Conradiana*, 6 (1974), 157–69, offers one of the best short assessments of Ford's importance to Conrad's development as a writer, while in 'Ford's Interpretation of Conrad's Technique', in Sherry (ed.) 1976: 183–93, Ivo Vidan discusses the value and appropriateness of the guiding concepts put forward in Ford's *Joseph Conrad: A Personal Remembrance*— *impressionism, new form, justification, rendering, and *progression d'effet. For a more specialized account of their working collaboration, see Raymond Brebach, *Joseph Conrad, Ford Madox Ford, and the Making of 'Romance'* (Ann Arbor: UMI Research Press, 1985).

Conrad's diverse friendships, contacts, and ventures also brought with them the possibility of short-term collaborations, although most of these did not materialize. Friendship with Stephen *Crane raised the prospect of their collaborating on a play in 1898, but the project was probably never very serious—it was, said Conrad, 'merely the expression of our affection for each other' (*Last Essays*, 116). Their animated discussions concerned a play to be called *The Predecessor*, the subject of which 'consisted in a man personating his "predecessor" (who had died) in the hope of winning a girl's heart. The scenes were to include a ranch at the foot of the Rocky Mountains' (ibid. 115). This scenario seems, however, to have lingered in Conrad's memory, since he later used certain of its features in 'The Planter of Malata' (*Within the Tides*). A further proposal by S. S. *Pawling in May 1904 that Conrad and R. B. Cunninghame *Graham might collaborate on a joint article was initially 'fascinating' (*CL*, iii. 140), but turned out to be impracticable. Three later desultory attempts at collaboration similarly came to nothing. The first involved Conrad in discussions in early 1913 with his good friend Perceval *Gibbon about a play to be based upon the former's African stories, and the other two—about which little is known—with Norman *Douglas and, later, Józef H. *Retinger on a play with a South American subject that temporarily attracted both men as a way of making 'heaps of money' (Józef H. Retinger, *Conrad and his Contemporaries: Souvenirs* (Minerva, 1941), 120).

Later, the possible dramatization of *Victory* again involved the question of collaboration. An approach from an unidentified actor in January 1916 to adapt the novel yielded the response from Conrad that if it 'were *collaborated* (not merely adapted) it would have a better chance of being accepted. My name is worth something in that way' (*CL*, v. 551). When nothing came of this plan, the field was left open for an approach by B. Macdonald *Hastings, the play's eventual adaptor. Conrad approved Hastings's first scenario, but in this case insisted that there could be 'no question of collaboration' since that would entail 'a close daily intercourse for six weeks or so' and involve him in having a decisive say 'in the construction and in the very words of the play' (*CL*, v. 635). His preferred formula was that the stage *Victory* should be advertised as a play adapted by Hastings from a novel by Joseph Conrad. Subsequently, however, Conrad was as committed to the novel's adaptation as any active collaborator could be, offering advice on its dialogue, staging, and casting. The experience must have been a happy one, since Conrad and Hastings made further plans (which did not materialize) to work together on an original play set in Italy with English characters, about a faked painting by an old master. Two further collaborations occupied Conrad for short periods in his later years. In autumn 1920, he and his agent J. B. *Pinker worked together on a silent 'filmplay' of 'Gaspar Ruiz' entitled *Gaspar the Strong Man*, although the screenplay was never filmed. A final variant of collaboration found Conrad in 1921 translating a Polish play, *Księga Hioba*, which had been sent to him by Bruno Winawer and which he thought had theatrical possibilities. The resulting English version, *The Book of Job*, was published in 1931 but never performed.

collected editions. Conrad proves no exception to the generalization that the appearance of a collected edition marks a major stage in the consolidation of a writer's reputation as regards both his contemporaries and posterity. While such an undertaking offered the promise of handsome and immediate financial rewards, Conrad was not immune to the venture's symbolic character. In 'Henry James: An Appreciation', he describes a collected edition as a testamentary act 'putting forth a hasty claim to completeness, and conveying to my mind a hint of finality' (*Notes*, 11). In the event, he took a considerable and typically professional interest in the preparation of his own collected edition: he wrote prefaces for the volumes, supervised their proof-reading, fussed over their appearance, and signed sheets for the first volume of each set. He was also interested in the edition's critical reception, and proudly presented inscribed sets to his family and friends. Heinemann Collected sets went to Borys and John Conrad, to John *Galsworthy, Edward *Garnett, André *Gide, G. *Jean-Aubry, and Sir Robert *Jones. Doubleday Sun-Dial sets were presented to Desmond Bevan, Hugh *Clifford, Richard *Curle, Conrad Hope, Dr R. D. Mackintosh, the Ridgeways, the *Sandersons, and Aniela *Zagórska. No doubt as a sign of gratitude for his agent's years of devoted service, J. B. *Pinker alone received both the American and English sets.

The history of the collected editions began as early as March 1913, when F. N. *Doubleday broached the idea with Conrad and Pinker over lunch in *London. At this stage, preparations were stalled by the outbreak of the *First World War, which occasioned disruptions in transatlantic communications and a shortage of paper. Plans resurfaced in the spring of 1916, with Doubleday, who then wished to call his printing the 'Otago Edition', urging Conrad to write *'Author's Notes' for volumes soon to be reprinted. At this point, it was agreed that Heinemann and Doubleday would each issue 1,000 sets. Conrad himself had 'settled the format, the bindings, the fount and the paper' and intended the text to be 'freed from misprints and with, perhaps, a few (very few) verbal alterations' (to R. H. Leon, 22 February 1917).

In December 1918, plans for the edition seriously advanced when Doubleday, in London on business, expressed an eagerness to close with William *Heinemann for co-publication in England. Doubleday, who met with Conrad about his plans, convinced him to begin writing prefaces for each volume, and even before the conclusion of formal arrangements Conrad began this task. Conrad consciously aimed in these 'Notes'—a deliberately suggestive word—to refrain from offering his public 'long disquisitions about art' as had Henry *James in the prefaces to his New York Edition, preferring to offer his readers 'a few intimate words' (to Pinker, 14 July? 1917).

Over the next year, protracted negotiations were carried on between Pinker, Doubleday, Heinemann, and the author himself, some by correspondence, others in personal discussion. Although from the outset the editions had been planned as 'de luxe' limited editions for collectors, some major and minor issues needed to be resolved. The exact number of sets to be printed proved a point of intense deliberation. A smaller number of sets was more valuable from the book collector's point of view, and the advice of John *Quinn was called upon. After protracted haggling between Pinker and Conrad and his publishers, it was decided that 735 sets would be printed by Doubleday and 780 sets by Heinemann, with 750 for sale and 30 for presentation. Heinemann and Doubleday raised questions about the discrepancy in the size of volumes, a topic vexing to Conrad but finally settled by the binding of items together in certain volumes. Some time during the planning stage, Doubleday received Conrad's permission to call his edition the Sun-Dial, after the sundial at Doubleday's works in Garden City on Long Island, New York. The Heinemann Collected Edition, by agreement, was to be unnamed, although at an earlier point the name 'Orlestone Edition' had been mooted. Doubleday's set eventually grew

to include 24 volumes, and Heinemann's twenty, with the addition of the posthumous *Suspense.*

A particular sticking point in arrangements was that, having with varying success acted as his own agent during the early years of his career, Conrad had made *ad hoc* deals with a number of *publishers, as the result of which his copyrights both in England and America were variously assigned. While Doubleday had as early as 1913 begun purchasing rights in America with an eye to an eventual collected edition, seemingly intractable problems remained. Prolonged and somewhat acrimonious bargaining was required with T. Fisher *Unwin, who, only upon winning the sweetener of a contract for two new Conrad novels and a volume of short stories, reluctantly ceded rights to *Almayer's Folly,* which he owned outright. The inclusion of *Romance* and *The Inheritors,* the *collaborations with Ford Madox *Ford, also required separate negotiation. These hurdles cleared, Conrad could finally sign contracts with Doubleday and with Heinemann in late February 1920; his active involvement extended to at least October 1920 when he completed the last 'Author's Note', that for *Notes on Life and Letters.*

The original production plan was cumbersome, and, in the event, rapidly abandoned. Doubleday was to set up a volume and then send proofs to Conrad for revision and correction. After receiving these back, Doubleday was to effect changes and then forward corrected proofs to Heinemann to set up the English edition. As it turned out, this scheme, which required multiple transatlantic exchanges, proved impractical; and in the end each publishing house based its edition on different copy. Moreover, despite his contractual obligations, Conrad himself appears to have read proofs in only one or two instances, making only a few trifling changes, the proofreading being delegated to his secretary, Lilian M. *Hallowes.

At Heinemann's, the task of overseeing the edition fell to S. S. *Pawling, an early champion of Conrad, with day-to-day matters falling to C. S. Evans particularly as

Pawling's health declined. It is possible that Evans, who wrote to Conrad about the varying pronunciation of cockney English in *The Nigger of the 'Narcissus'* in September 1920, was the person responsible for tidying Conrad's texts for their appearance in Heinemann's Collected Edition. But whether by him or someone else, the Heinemann texts, in addition to being liberally house-styled, suffered various unauthorized changes: punctuation was regularized; grammar was corrected; spellings were altered; and Conrad's phrasing and wording were modified in an effort to gentrify his prose.

Doubleday and Heinemann issued the volumes of the collected edition more or less in the order of their original publication, with the first five volumes of their respective editions appearing in January 1921, the next five following in April, and the remaining volumes in the autumn. After publication, type for the Heinemann Collected Edition was distributed; it was thus genuinely a limited edition, and no later printings derive from it.

As a counterbalance to the expensive, de luxe editions issued by Doubleday and Heinemann, a collected edition of Conrad in a more popularly priced and unlimited printing formed a topic of discussion, with Doubleday's initial interest in producing such an edition for the English market eventually taken over by J. M. *Dent. In October 1922, Dent rented the plates made for Doubleday's Sun-Dial printing, issuing his Uniform Edition from these in 1924. The same plates, leased from Dent, were used to produce the so-called Medallion Edition published by Grant of Edinburgh in 1925. Dent used these plates to reissue its Uniform Edition, which it renamed Dent's Collected Edition, during the late 1940s and early 1950s. Despite the English publisher and place of publication, these so-called 'editions' were in fact issues of Doubleday's American texts, and they have come to serve, *faute de mieux*, as the standard text of reference in most Conrad studies. The major works in this edition have had a long afterlife; some volumes were reprinted in Dent's Everyman series, and

many have been revived for the World's Classics series published by Oxford University Press (1983–92), where the Dent texts (albeit with some corrections and changes in pagination) are equipped with paratexts consisting of introductions, chronologies, notes on the text, explanatory notes, and glossaries.

In America, Doubleday marketed Conrad throughout the 1920s in variously named collected 'editions' derived from the plates made for its Sun-Dial printing: the Concord Edition of 1923; the Complete and Canterbury Editions of 1924; the Kent, Memorial, Personal, and Inclusive Editions of 1925; and the Deep Sea, Malay, and Special Editions of 1928. Although Conrad himself was consulted about bindings for the 1923 and 1924 'editions' and supplied photographs for the frontispieces of the Concord Edition of 1923, he made no alterations to his texts for these. Some readings from the Heinemann Collected Edition were, however, incorporated into the Concord Edition and thus appear in subsequent American issues. The work of a Doubleday editor, these alterations perpetuated the interventions of Heinemann's fastidious gentleman-grammarian.

The Heinemann Collected Edition had for many years an unexamined and unmerited prestige as an authoritative text, and was the copy-text of choice for scholarly editions of the 1960s, when textual work on Conrad was in its infancy. Like F. N. Doubleday, who declared that proofs 'had been read by Mr. Conrad and passed by him, and [are] spelled in the English tongue and just the way he wants [them]' (to Dent, 25 September 1922), scholars did not look beyond the surface. Despite a considerably more sophisticated understanding of the extreme complexity of Conrad's texts, following upon the labours for the Cambridge Edition of the Works of Joseph Conrad, the Heinemann Edition as late as the 1990s was selected for reprinting as an 'authoritative text' on the baseless ground that it benefited from a special authorial imprimatur.

Virtually complete collected editions of Conrad, with the plays and *collaborations usually omitted, have appeared in *translation in French, Italian, and Polish. The French edition, first under the care of André Gide and then of G. Jean-Aubry, benefited from Conrad's advice. That edition has now been superseded by the new or refurbished translations of the five-volume Pléiade edition of Conrad's *Œuvres* (Paris: Gallimard, 1982–92), by a team of translators under the direction of Sylvère Monod. The translations are accompanied by an apparatus that includes an introductory essay to each volume by Monod, essays on each work by its translator or another critic, and explanatory notes that are particularly useful on Gallicisms, *borrowings from French writers, and French literary influences. The Italian translation entitled *Opere*, edited by Ugo Mursia in five thematically arranged volumes (Mursia, 1967–82), offers erudite notes. The first Polish edition, a selected one of six volumes, appeared from 1923 to 1926. An effort by Conrad's distant family relation Aniela Zagórska, it featured an introduction by the novelist Stefan *Żeromski. A second, more complete, pre-war edition, comprising 22 volumes, was published from 1928 to 1939. In a 23-volume Polish edition that appeared from 1956 to 1970, Soviet influence mandated the omission of *The Secret Agent* and *Under Western Eyes*, *Notes on Life and Letters*, and *Last Essays*. A full 27-volume edition, but lacking notes or a critical apparatus, was published during 1972–4 under the direction of Zdzisław Najder. Censorship forbade the inclusion of ideologically sensitive pieces, but 'Autocracy and War', 'The Censor of Plays', the 'Author's Note' to *Under Western Eyes*, 'The Crime of Partition', and 'Note on the Polish Problem' were published in London as volume xxviii: *Szkice polityczne* (Polonia Book Fund, 1975).

The Cambridge Edition, based on modern textual scholarship and involving the computer collation of pre-printing and printed forms, began publication with *The Secret Agent* in 1990. It aims to produce an authoritative collected edition that will replace all previous texts. The ongoing work of the edition is supported by an archive of Conrad materials in original, photocopied, and digital forms at the Institute for Bibliography and Editing, Kent State University, Ohio.

Although the volumes of the Cambridge Edition extensively discuss textual matters, no full study of the collected editions as such has been published. Proof volumes of Heinemann's Collected Edition, some marked for printing, are held at Hofstra University, New York, and at the Rosenbach Museum and Library, Philadelphia. No pre-publication materials are known for Doubleday's Sun-Dial Edition.   JHS

colonialism. Conrad's early life as a Pole in Russian-dominated *Ukraine gave him first-hand experience of imperial subjugation. Later Conrad's sea life took him to various outposts of empire; and, subsequently settling in an *England then at the peak of its imperialism, he could witness some of the intoxicated jingoism accompanying the 'adventure' of empire. According to Edward Said, '"imperialism" means the practice, the theory, and the attitudes of a dominating metropolitan centre ruling a distant territory; "colonialism", which is almost always a consequence of imperialism, is the implanting of settlements on distant territory' (*Culture and Imperialism* (Chatto & Windus, 1993), 8). In the second half of the 19th century, the crude application of Social Darwinism strengthened European attitudes to the colonized as not simply outside history and civilization, but genetically inferior. As a result of such ahistoric formulations, late 19th-century colonization could be represented as a necessary 'civilizing' task, with colonizers urged to 'Take up the White Man's Burden' in Rudyard *Kipling's phrase (1899). As an Anglophile, Conrad's attitude to colonialism was janiform: his national and familial experiences at the hands of Russian imperialism meant that he questioned the basis of European colonialism, while his fervent Anglophilia meant that he shared some of the imperial enthusiasms sustaining the British Empire. Thus, in 'Heart of Darkness', he could write of colonialism, the same colonialism upon which the glory of the British Empire rested, that 'The conquest of the earth, which mostly means the taking it away from those who have a different complexion or slightly flatter noses than ourselves, is not a pretty thing when you look into it too much' (*Youth*, 50–1).

Conrad saw through the philanthropic pretence to the commercial interest behind colonialism, noting sarcastically, in 'Autocracy and War' (1905), how European powers had divided Africa into 'territorial spheres of influence . . . to keep the competitors for the privilege of improving the nigger (as a buying machine) from flying prematurely at each other's throats' (*Notes*, 107). Watts observes: 'His use of the term "nigger" may make present readers flinch; but his sardonically reductive view of imperialism is a reminder that Conrad had seen at first hand the exploitative system in the Belgian Congo' (1993: 58). If Conrad's works are generally critical of late Victorian colonialism, they nevertheless portray some nations as behaving worse than others in their colonial practices. For their treatment of *Poland, *Russia and Prussia are deemed the most criminal. For example, in 'Autocracy and War' Conrad says of Russia that it 'has not the right to give her voice on a single question touching the future of humanity, because from the very inception of her being the brutal destruction of dignity, of truth, of rectitude, of all that is faithful in human nature has been made the imperative condition of her existence' (*Notes*, 99).

As 'Heart of Darkness', 'An Outpost of Progress', and the essay 'Geography and Some Explorers' (*Last Essays*) make clear, Conrad's experiences in the *Congo Free State imbued him with a lifelong loathing of Belgian colonialism. This revulsion is also expressed in his well-known letter of 21 December 1903 to Roger *Casement, who would later be knighted for his efforts to expose the atrocities in King Leopold's Congo: 'It is an extraordinary thing that the conscience of Europe which seventy years ago has put down the slave trade on humanitarian grounds tolerates the Congo State to day. It is as if the moral clock had been put back many hours. . . . in 1903,

seventy five years or so after the abolition of the slave trade (because it was cruel) there exists in Africa a Congo State, created by the act of European Powers where ruthless systematic cruelty towards the blacks is the basis of administration, and bad faith towards all the other states the basis of commercial policy.' In the same letter, Conrad claims that 'the Belgians are worse than the seven plagues of Egypt' (*CL*, iii. 96, 97). In 1923 Conrad described African colonialism as 'the vilest scramble for loot that ever disfigured the history of human conscience and geographical exploration' (*Last Essays*, 17). Although responsibility for the cruelties and scramble for wealth represented in 'Heart of Darkness' can be laid at the door of Belgian colonialism—*Marlow is employed by a 'Continental concern' whose offices are in *Brussels, the 'sepulchral city' (*Youth*, 53, 152)—Conrad is careful to identify *Kurtz with European colonialism generally, emphasizing that 'All Europe contributed to the making of Kurtz' (117). Marlow's arrival at the Outer Station (63–5) quickly demonstrates the attitude towards colonialism in the novella: the wastefulness and the 'objectless blasting' provide instances of the futility of the venture, and the chain-gang illustrates its human price.

'An Outpost of Progress' was also part of the 'spoil' with which Conrad returned from Africa (*Youth*, p. vii). As in *Almayer's Folly*, the setting for the tale is a trading station in the jungle. Although Conrad has exchanged the jungles of *Borneo for those of Africa, the European presence in the area is generated by the same avaricious impulse. However much Kayerts and Carlier try to view their presence in Africa as bearers of civilization—'In a hundred years, there will be perhaps a town here. Quays, and warehouses, and barracks, and—and—billiard-rooms. Civilization, my boy, and virtue—and all' (*Tales of Unrest*, 95)—the quest for easy wealth is their real motivation, a desire revealed to be morally debasing as they connive in the slave trade. 'An Outpost of Progress' was published in the year of Queen Victoria's Diamond Jubilee in 1897. Conrad's critique of colonialism in the tale is thrown into stark relief by the other essays in *Cosmopolis*, the magazine in which it first appeared. For instance, its July issue includes an essay on the Jubilee celebrations: 'Britain is Imperialistic now. . . . The political party which should talk of reducing the navy or snubbing the Colonies would have a short shrift. We are Imperialists first, and Liberals or Tories afterwards' (quoted in Watts 1993: 61).

One feature of Conrad's colonial fictions which distinguishes his 'romances' from those of most of his contemporaries is that they repeatedly strip the imperial adventure of its claims to anything finer than crude commercialism. They reveal that imperial interests were to be found wherever there was trade, and that the adage 'trade follows the flag' is invariably the opposite of the truth. So, for instance, his first novel, *Almayer's Folly*, set in the village of *Sambir, the fictional counterpart of Tanjung Redeb on the Berau River in north-east Borneo, charts the declining fortunes of the resident Dutch colonial, Kaspar *Almayer, a failed trader who is outmanœuvred by his native counterparts. Almayer's defeat at the hands of his trading rivals provides an ironic comment upon Dutch imperialism in the islands since economic interests drive the events, whether providing the basis for aspirations and alliances, or particularizing the larger forces of history and nationality. Closely linked to the commercial greed that motivates Almayer are the racist attitudes that blind him to the truth of his predicament, and implicit in this connection is the fact that colonialism is often sustained by *racism (and vice versa). Thus, from the outset, Conrad's imperial fiction portrays the immorality of colonialism and its disturbing implications for the Western self-image.

The idea that 'colonialism' may be simply another word for 'material interests' is underscored in *Nostromo* where, predominant among the welter of forces combining to bring the Occidental Republic into being, is the financial colonization of *Costaguana, with the silver from the San Tomé mine as the prize. Conrad's concern with the emergence of the imaginary South American republic reveals how inextricably linked to its history are the material interests of the Europeans and of the American financier Holroyd. Nor should Conrad's equating of colonialism with commercialism in his fiction surprise us, for the very ships in which he served and sailed the world in the final phase of British expansionism were themselves engaged in the pursuit of material interests.

Perhaps offering a further instance of his much-discussed 'immigrant complex', Conrad's attitude to British colonialism was very different. Prepared to be censorious to varying degrees about the imperialism of other nations, he generally regarded Britain's overseas rule as benevolent and paternal. For example, in 'An Observer in Malaya' (1898), he writes: 'And of all the nations conquering distant territories in the name of the most excellent intentions, England alone sends out men who, with such a transparent sincerity of feeling, can speak, as Mr. Clifford does, of the place of toil and exile as "the land which is very dear to me, where the best years of my life have been spent"—and where (I would stake my right hand on it) his name is pronounced with respect and affection by those brown men about whom he writes' (*Notes*, 58–9). Thus, not only did the Anglophile Conrad extend the libertarian values he associated with England to its colonialism, but, as Watts argues, some of his sea tales 'are clearly inflected so as to flatter a British readership' (1993: 59). The qualities Marlow praises in the crew of the *Judea* in 'Youth' are those that, to his mind, render them unmistakably English: 'it was something in them, something inborn and subtle and everlasting. I don't say positively that the crew of a French or German merchantman wouldn't have done it, but I doubt whether it would have been done in the same way. There was a completeness in it, something solid like a principle, and masterful like an instinct—a disclosure of something secret—of that hidden something, that gift of good or evil that makes racial difference, that shapes the fate of nations' (*Youth*, 28–9).

By contrast, the eulogistic description of England at the end of *The Nigger of the 'Narcissus'*, which celebrates the country as 'A ship mother of fleets and nations! The great flagship of the race' (163), becomes progressively more sombre as the *Narcissus* enters and is towed up the River *Thames towards *London. This recalls the darkness that seems to emanate from London, the heart of the British Empire, at the beginning of 'Heart of Darkness' where, as early as the second paragraph, the air 'seemed condensed into a mournful gloom, brooding motionless over the biggest, and the greatest, town on earth' (*Youth*, 45). In this context it is also significant that, in Conrad's early fiction, both Almayer and Willems are protégés of the one-man English imperialist Captain Tom *Lingard, and that Almayer's dream of riches is a second-hand dream, deriving from Lingard's dream of riches. To these criticisms, however subtle, of British colonialism in Conrad's fiction can be added the failure of Captain Lingard in *The Rescue* to safeguard the lives of his Malay friends Hassim and Immada, who, despite his pledge to them, are betrayed because of his infatuation for Mrs *Travers. In *Lord Jim*, too, European involvement ends in disaster as *Jim's attempt to establish order on *Patusan leads, ultimately, to the massacre of Dain Waris and his men by Gentleman *Brown and his desperadoes, whose revenge is exacted largely because Jim's very presence there offends Brown.

In 'Conrad and the Psychology of Colonialism', in Murfin (ed.) 1985: 71–87, Hunt Hawkins argues that Conrad, in his presentation of the colonial encounter, demonstrates that the European desire to dominate others is born of a deep sense of inadequacy. For an essay arguing that Western criticism of 'Heart of Darkness' ultimately colludes to exonerate Conrad from the charge of colonial bias, see Frances B. Singh, 'The Colonialist Bias of *Heart of Darkness*', *Conradiana*, 10 (1978), 41–54. AHS

Colvin, Sidney (1845–1927; knighted 1911), a cultured critic of the fine arts and literature. Sidney Colvin was a loyal friend and admirer of Robert Louis *Stevenson (whose letters he edited) and Conrad. After a period as Slade Professor of Fine Arts at Cambridge, he was Keeper in the Department of Prints and Drawings at the British Museum from 1884 to 1912. Introduced to Conrad by H. G. *Wells in early 1904, Colvin promptly encouraged the writer to adapt his short story 'To-morrow' for the stage and helped to produce that adaptation, *One Day More*, for its performance by the Stage Society in June 1905. From 1913 onwards, Colvin was one of Conrad's closest friends: they met and corresponded regularly, discussed reviews that Colvin was writing of Conrad's fiction, and commiserated with each other during periods of illness. E. V. *Lucas's description of Colvin as a man of patricianly instincts who was 'all for the traditions, perfect courtesy, an unflinching code of honour, decent manners and a certain avoidance of the crudities of modern life' (*The Colvins and their Friends* (Methuen, 1928), 350–1) also points to the quality of elegant *politesse* at the basis of Conrad's friendship with Colvin and his wife Frances.

comic books. Conrad's works have inspired adaptations of many kinds, including also comic books or 'graphic novels'. The first and most widely distributed comic-book adaptation of Conrad was an edition of *Lord Jim* issued in January 1957 as no. 136 in the Classics Illustrated series, with drawings by George Evans, at a price of 15 cents. The complicated plot of the novel was treated with respect, and Evans's drawings advanced the story effectively. According to Dan Malan, the author of *The Complete Guide to Classics Illustrated* (1992), this edition was reprinted in English at least five times between 1957 and 1975, and by 1960 foreign-language editions had been published in ten other countries, including four editions in Greece.

The elaborate publicity attending Richard Brooks's *film adaptation of *Lord Jim* included not only a cover story in *Life* magazine and a phonograph recording of the film music but also a comic-book version of the movie published in September 1965. This crude adaptation is even more melodramatic than the movie: Jim (Peter O'Toole) says things like 'Thanks, O chief', and the ending is changed to show him captured by Gentleman *Brown but managing nevertheless to 'wipe out' the pirates even though his hands are tied behind his back. The following month, *MAD* magazine cleverly spoofed the pretensions of the film with a cartoon entitled 'Lord Jump', drawn by Mort Drucker and written by Larry Siegel.

When the Classics Illustrated series was revived in the early 1990s, it included a comic-book adaptation of *The Secret Agent* designed by John K. Snyder III (New York: Berkley/First Publishing, 1991). Snyder's style departs radically from the narrative conventions of traditional comics, replacing Conrad's narrative with a confusing and seemingly arbitrary collage of images and bits of dialogue, and this adaptation conveys almost no idea of the plot or the point of Conrad's novel.

The graphic novel has an especially strong tradition in francophone countries, where comic books relevant to Conrad include not only *Tintin au Congo* but also *Corto Maltese—mémoires* (Tournai: Casterman, 1988), with text by Michel Pierre and artwork by Hugo Pratt. Although not a comic book in the strict sense, the 'Futuropolis' edition of *L'Agent secret* (Paris: Gallimard, 1991) contains an abundance of illustrations by Miles Hyman.

concordances. A series of computer-generated concordances for most of Conrad's full-length works has been underaken under the general editorship of Todd K. Bender at the University of Wisconsin at Madison, published by New York's Garland Press in their Reference Library in the Humanities series. Each volume offers an alphabetical listing of all words appearing in the chosen text, with a field of reference for each keyed item indicating the contexts in which it appears, and a helpful word-frequency table.

Begun in 1970 and described as embodying interim research in the progress towards a master-lexicon of Conrad's vocabulary, the project's aims are outlined and discussed in Todd K. Bender's 'Computer Analysis of Conrad', *Polish Review*, 20 (1975), 123–32. In practice, however, the developing edition has varied considerably in the quality of its authority, format, and user-friendliness. In the absence of a standard scholarly edition of Conrad's novels, the problem of establishing a copy-text from a variety of available published forms is obviously of foremost importance. Yet many of the compilers seem unaware of the need to set out a rationale for the credentials of their chosen texts, and volumes in the edition can be found to opt for texts as widely different as the English first edition and the 1921 American Doubleday, Page edition. Similarly, the volumes have varied considerably in format. In some, the extensive verbal index takes the form of a 'key word in context' format, which places the keyed item of vocabulary within the complete sentence(s) in which it appears in any one work; other volumes employ a 'key word out of context' format and so involve the user in consulting a 'Field of Reference' section where the chosen text is reproduced in miniature. A standard feature in all volumes, the word-frequency table, has also appeared in varying formats, sometimes listing words alphabetically, and sometimes in order of frequency.

The texts established in the evolving Cambridge Edition of the Works of Joseph Conrad, with their obvious scholarly credentials, will clearly be essential to the authority of any future master-lexicon of Conrad's vocabulary, although such a project is likely to be rivalled by the possibility of searching texts electronically. In the meantime, the published concordances provide a basic, if sometimes fallible guide to Conrad's characteristic word-usages, range of vocabulary, and types of imagery and metaphor. Students can, for example, consult the concordance to 'Heart of Darkness' and quickly gain access to occurrences of the word 'heart' (22 in number) and 'darkness' (25).

'Confidence'. The *Daily Mail* commissioned this essay for its Golden Peace number celebrating the signing of the Treaty of Versailles in June 1919. Composed over the period of a week, it was finished by 16 April and appeared in the *Daily Mail* (30 June 1919), 3. It was collected in revised form in *Notes on Life and Letters*. Taking issue with American proposals for reducing the size of the British Navy and displacing the *British Merchant Service from its leading international position, Conrad's meditation expresses 'unshaken confidence' in the worth and persistency of the values symbolized by the Red Ensign. Sent to the Paul R. Revere Company of New York to be placed in *America, 'Confidence' was later withdrawn by Conrad on the grounds that it might hurt public feelings there. Commenting on the essay in a letter, he confessed that its public sentiments did not match his private sense of the post-war world: 'As to my own confidence in the future I don't mind telling you privately that it isn't the confidence that dwells in one and runs like soothing balsam in one's veins. It is the sort of confidence one holds on to with teeth and claws for dear life. However I don't say that in my article' (to L. R. Macleod, 16 April 1919). A corrected typescript of the essay is held at the British Library, and the pamphlet page proofs are at Colgate University.

Congo. Conrad spent only six months in the Congo, from June to December 1890, but the experience changed his life. Two of his closest friends, Edward *Garnett and G. *Jean-Aubry, agreed that 'Conrad's Congo experiences were the turning-point in his mental life and . . . determined his transformation from a sailor to a writer' (*LFC*, p. xii). Conrad told Garnett that in his early years at sea, he had 'not a thought in his head' and 'was a perfect animal'; it was apparently in the Congo that Conrad began to think. His single journey up the Congo River also ruined his *health, leaving him with a legacy of physical ailments, the lingering after-effects of near-fatal dysentery and malaria, on which he later blamed a variety of chronic or recurrent

forms of paralysis, nervous disorders, and gout.

In circumstances which he was later to dramatize in 'Heart of Darkness', Conrad was hired in *Brussels in 1890 by Albert *Thys, the managing director of the Société Anonyme Belge pour le Commerce du Haut-Congo, to replace a riverboat captain named Johannes Freiesleben who had recently been killed, and to take command of a small paddle-wheel steamer on the 1,000 miles (1,600 km) of swift and treacherous water between Stanley Pool (Kinshasa) and Stanleyville (now Kisangani). Arriving at Kinshasa after three weeks of trekking uphill, Conrad found that the steamer meant for his use was damaged, so he continued upriver with the Danish master of the *Roi des Belges*, Captain Ludvig Rasmus Koch. In the event, Conrad was never to serve as master of a fresh-water steamship except for ten days on the return downriver, when he replaced Captain Koch, who had become too ill to command. Conrad himself became so ill on the return voyage that he was unable to walk, and had to be carried most of the 200 miles from Kinshasa back down to Matadi. His immediate impressions were recorded in the two notebooks of his *Congo Diary*, and later reworked in fictional form in 'An Outpost of Progress' (*Tales of Unrest*) and most notably in 'Heart of Darkness'. In 'Geography and Some Explorers' (*Last Essays*) he described Congolese exploitation as 'the vilest scramble for loot that ever disfigured the history of human conscience and geographical exploration' (17).

Conrad's Congo was the Congo Free State, a vast and varied land that by 1890 was anything but free. The mouth of the Congo River was 'discovered' by Portuguese sailors in 1482, but access to the interior was blocked by hundreds of miles of impassable rapids that served for centuries as a barrier against European exploitation. The Anglo-American adventurer Sir Henry Morton Stanley, who had achieved fame by 'finding' the missionary explorer Dr David Livingstone in 1871, descended most of the Congo River in 1874–7 on an expedition of which he was the only white survivor.

Stanley failed to interest the British in its commercial potential, but found support from Belgian King Leopold II, who sent him back to establish stations along the river and make 'treaties' with local village chiefs appropriating their land and labour in the name of Leopold's newly founded International Association of the Congo. The United States government recognized Leopold's claim to the Congo in 1884, and the following year the European powers gathered for the Conference of Berlin recognized the Congo Free State as Leopold's private property in return for guarantees of neutrality, free trade, and opposition to slavery. Under the guise of a humanitarian mission to bring civilization to the 'dark' continent and oppose Afro-Arab slavery, Leopold's trading stations along the Congo River and its tributaries were chiefly concerned with grabbing ivory. With the coming of the 'rubber boom' in the mid-1890s, the stations became prisons and collecting points for the wild rubber that natives were forced to seek in the jungle while their wives and families were held as hostages.

Leopold's skill in controlling public relations was so great that at the time of Conrad's journey, no information about Congolese abuses had yet been leaked to the wider world. The very first public outcry was raised by the Afro-American historian George Washington Williams (1849–91), who travelled inland with the caravan just ahead of Conrad. By 1903, reports of atrocities (collected by Roger *Casement and others, and widely publicized by Edmund Dene Morel, the founder of the Congo Reform Association) provoked a scandal that Leopold hoped to calm by ordering a second opinion in the form of a second, 'independent' report. Although meant to serve as whitewash, this second report also proved negative, and Leopold finally sold the Congo Free State to the Belgian government in 1908. The state archives were burned on Leopold's orders, but a variety of materials have been preserved in the Royal Museum of Central Africa in Tervuren, east of Brussels. Adam Hochschild provides a vivid and appalling

account of the Congo Free State in *King Leopold's Ghost* (New York: Houghton Mifflin, 1998), which contains a useful bibliography.

The Congolese context of Conrad's fictions was first examined in detail by Jean-Aubry in *Conrad in the Congo* (Boston: Little, Brown, 1926), now superseded by *CWW*, which remains the most detailed account of the historical prototypes of *Kurtz and other characters in Conrad's two African stories. Hunt Hawkins has also written numerous articles on the subject of Conrad and the Congo, among them 'Conrad's Critique of Imperialism in *Heart of Darkness*', *PMLA*, 94 (1979), 286–99; 'Conrad and Congolese Exploitation', *Conradiana*, 13 (1981), 94–9; and 'Joseph Conrad, Roger Casement, and the Congo Reform Movement', *Journal of Modern Literature*, 9 (1981/2), 65–80. The Norton Critical Edition of *Heart of Darkness*, ed. Robert Kimbrough, 3rd edn. (New York: W. W. Norton, 1988) includes a useful supplement (77–194) of historical materials on Conrad and the Congo.

Congo Diary, The. This title is given to one or both of the small black leather-bound notebooks in which Conrad kept notes about his journey to the *Congo in 1890. Together with a half-dozen letters in French to Marguerite *Poradowska and one letter in Polish to Maria Tyszkowa, they provide the only first-hand information about the events on which 'Heart of Darkness' is based. They are also among the earliest examples of Conrad's written English, along with the first seven manuscript chapters of *Almayer's Folly*, which he carried with him in the Congo. The first of the two notebooks is properly a diary in which Conrad recorded his impressions and movements from 13 June to 1 August 1890, together with notes on the weather, the nature of the terrain, and the meanings of certain native terms. On 28 June, Conrad left Matadi, the station at the foot of the Congo River rapids, with the agent Prosper Harou and 31 men in a caravan bound for Kinshasa, where the river again becomes navigable. On 8 July the caravan arrived at Manyanga, roughly the halfway point of the 200-mile (320-km) journey, where it was necessary to hire new carriers. After more than a fortnight at Manyanga (about which the diary is silent), they resumed their journey on 25 July, arriving at Stanley Pool on 1 August. The diary records Conrad's immediate disappointment in the mentality of the Western traders and his initiation into the desolation and misery of African *colonialism. The country was largely depopulated—'Villages quite invisible' (*CDOUP*, 8)—but he encountered two dead bodies along the trail, saw an albino woman whose skin was a 'Horrid chalky white with pink blotches' (9), passed a human skeleton tied to a post, and was asked to administer medical aid to a 13-year-old boy with a bullet wound to the head. The progress of the caravan was also slowed by the illness of Harou, who had to be carried much of the way in a hammock.

The second notebook, which Conrad labelled his 'Up-river book', begins on 3 August and records in detail the features and obstacles in the river noted by Conrad during the first sixteen days (roughly the first half, as far as Bangala) of his thousand-mile (1,600-km) journey upriver in the steamer *Roi des Belges*, under the command of a young Dane, Captain Ludvig Rasmus Koch. It includes maps and sketches, and was clearly meant as a practical guide for navigation. Najder (ibid. 5) speculates that Conrad probably stopped taking notes either because he fell ill or because he became convinced that he would never command a Congo steamer.

A transcription of the first notebook (but not the 'Up-river book') was included in Richard *Curle's edition of Conrad's *Last Essays*. The full texts of both notebooks (minus maps and sketches) were first printed by Najder in *CDOUP*. A transcription of the first notebook reproducing Conrad's spelling and punctuation is included in the Penguin edition of 'Heart of Darkness', ed. Robert Hampson (Harmondsworth, 1995). The original notebooks are now at the Houghton Library, Harvard University.

Conrad, [Alfred] Borys (1898–1978), Conrad's elder son. Borys Conrad received two given names that were intended to signify his parents' respect for 'the rights of the two nations': Jessie selected the Saxon name Alfred, and the name Borys was chosen by Conrad, who 'wanted to have a purely Slavonic name, but one which could not be distorted either in speech or in writing—and at the same time one which was not too difficult for foreigners (non-Slavonic)' (*CL*, ii. 24). Borys was baptized in a Catholic church in Hythe, *Kent, in January 1899. After a period of conventional schooling, the 13-year-old boy began a two-year course at the Thames Nautical Training College aboard HMS *Worcester*, a merchant navy training ship moored at Greenhithe, Kent. It was planned that his course in the *Worcester* would be the prelude to a career in civil engineering, and in mid-1915, on his second try at the entrance examinations, he was accepted by the Engineering Faculty at Sheffield University.

Borys's educational plans were cut short by his enlistment for active war service. In September 1915, he was granted a commission in the Army Service Corps, and by March 1916 was attached to the heavy artillery of the 34th brigade near Armentières. Borys's wartime experiences included an amorous episode in 1917 with Jane *Anderson, 'the glamorous lady from Arizona' (*MFJC*, 117), who had previously bedazzled some of the males in the Conrad circle and who was then also involved with a good friend of the Conrad family, Józef H. *Retinger. Upon hearing of Borys's five-day stay in Jane Anderson's circle in Paris, Conrad responded with a mixture of worldly-wise understanding and parental alarm. According to Borys, when he returned to his military unit, his father 'expressed the hope that the enemy would keep me sufficiently pre-occupied to enable me to "get Jane out of my system"' (ibid. 122). In that same year, Conrad dedicated *The Shadow-Line* 'To Borys and all others who like himself have crossed in early youth the shadow-line of their generation'. Gassed and severely shell-shocked during the Second Army's advance into Flanders in mid-October 1918, he was in hospital in Le Havre when the Armistice was signed.

According to Richard *Curle, Borys 're-turned from the war morose and silent and obviously a changed man mentally' (*New York Times* (23 July 1927), 2), with the result that his reintegration into civilian life was both troubled and uncertain. Moving through a succession of jobs in the motor industry, he also suffered chronic financial problems. Deep in debt in 1922, he falsely assured his creditors that his father had invested £1,000 for him in America, and left Conrad to settle his debts. Another family crisis occurred just before Conrad's visit to *America in May 1923, when Jessie Conrad learned that Borys had been secretly married on the previous 2 September to Joan Madeline King (1894–1981), whom he had met during the war in France. Borys's 'secret' was kept from his father until he returned to Britain in June 1923. Although initially furious at hearing the news, Conrad seems gradually to have reconciled himself to the marriage, and, in an effort to avoid a break with his son, soon arranged a wedding present in the form of a regular allowance. Borys and his wife had one child, Philip James, born in January 1924, the year of Conrad's death.

Severe financial problems again plagued Borys after his father's death. In 1927, he was brought to court and charged with ob-taining £1,100 from a Mrs Dorothy Bevan under the false pretence that the sum would be added to £2,900 already in his possession in order to purchase Conrad manuscripts that might be resold for a considerable profit. In fact, as a *New York Times* report of 31 July 1927 ('Joseph Con-rad's Son Gets Year in Prison for Swindling a Friend out of £1,100') makes clear, he had paid off his urgent debts with Mrs Bevan's money, was found guilty of embezzlement, and sentenced to prison. In later life, Borys wrote an affectionate reminiscence in *My Father: Joseph Conrad* (Calder & Boyars, 1970), played an active ambassadorial role at Conrad conferences in Britain and Poland, and served as the first president of the Joseph Conrad Society, UK.

Conrad, Jessie [Emmeline] (née George, 1873–1936), Conrad's wife. Jessie Conrad was the second-born of nine chil-dren in a lower middle-class Peckham fam-ily that had been left in straitened circumstances in 1892 by the death of the father, identified in the 1891 census as a 'bookseller's assistant'. According to Con-rad, he and Jessie (sixteen years his junior) first met in 1894, when she was working as a typist for the Calligraph Company in *London and living with her widowed mother. In late 1895 or early 1896, a sudden proposal of marriage seems to have been made on the steps of London's National Gallery. It was finalized a few days later when Conrad pressed for a speedy wed-ding, urging that 'he hadn't very long to live and further that there would be no family' (*JCHC*, 15). Although both were of Catholic upbringing, on 24 March 1896 they preferred a civil marriage ceremony at a registry office in Hanover Square, Lon-don W1, with Jessie's mother acting as one of the witnesses. In a letter of the time, Conrad described his prospective bride as 'a small, not at all striking-looking per-son (to tell the truth alas—rather plain!) who nevertheless is very dear to me' (*CL*, i. 265).

Jessie and her husband had two chil-dren, Borys, born in 1898, and John, in 1906. She also brought Conrad a large fam-ily of in-laws, to whom—according to Borys—his father's attitude was decidedly mixed. Conrad and his mother-in-law, 'a grim-featured old lady ... detested one an-other' (*MFJC*, 13, 25). Of Jessie's siblings, Conrad preferred Ethel, sixth in order of age, who, Borys explained, 'acted from time to time as voluntary, unpaid, governess to her youngest brother my Uncle Frank, her young sister Nellie, and myself'. Conrad nevertheless met the costs of sending Jessie's two youngest sisters, Dolly and Nel-lie, to a convent school. His chief favourite among the George circle was, however, Jessie's aunt Miss Alice Sex, 'a handsome old lady of imposing presence ... highly intelligent and a brilliant conversationalist' (ibid. 13).

Throughout their married life, Jessie took her duties as a writer's wife very seriously, acting as Conrad's full-time typist in their early years, evidently keeping a close eye on his completed manuscripts, and being generally content to act as devoted home-maker and cook to her 'boy', whose volatile moods, hypochondria, and extreme nervous anxiety often required her to take the role of protective mother. Their marriage, comments Watt, followed 'a special version of a deeply bourgeois model; the author's wife, allotted a subordinate role, accepts it and survives through a sturdy, amused, and even sometimes faintly contemptuous, toleration of the husband's vagaries' (1980: 72). A knee dislocated during childhood left Jessie prone to leg trouble and, after a serious fall in 1904, she was almost permanently disabled and had to undergo a series of major operations during the period 1917–24. As the result of her troubled health, she grew increasingly stout and immobile. In later life, she had a private companion-nurse and presided over an increasingly large household staff.

Impressions of Jessie by members of Conrad's circle are varied, many of them being unflattering and some unfairly antagonistic. Edward *Garnett, believing that Conrad's 'ultra-nervous organization appeared to make matrimony extremely hazardous' (*LFC*, p. xxii), had deep misgivings about their marriage; Lady Ottoline *Morrell described Jessie as 'a good and reposeful mattress for this hypersensitive, nerve-racked man, who did not ask from his wife high intelligence, but only an assuagement of life's vibrations' (quoted in Watt 1980: 72); and the historian Dame Veronica Wedgwood commented that her parents 'found her a bore but Conrad treated her with tremendous and rather formal protective courtesy and expected everyone who came to see him to do the same' (quoted in Meyers, 144). Even Borys Conrad, while regarding his mother as the 'ideal wife' for his hypersensitive father, suggested that her 'unassailable

placidity' could be 'almost frightening at times' (*MFJC*, 12, 18). Something of Jessie's widely acknowledged impassivity and stolidity may also be reflected in two of Conrad's characters: the unresponsive Amy in 'Amy Foster' (*Typhoon*), and Winnie *Verloc in *The Secret Agent* (whose phlegmatic indifference provokes her husband into the exasperated comment, 'Oh, yes! I know your deaf-and-dumb trick' (256)).

Jessie Conrad's involvement in events after Conrad's death in 1924 has inevitably coloured the biographical record. During these years, Jessie found herself alone, neglected by all but a few of her husband's admirers, and seems to have felt that her contribution to his achievement had been ignored. Relishing the role of the literary man's widow, she wrote several articles on Conrad, stoutly defended his reputation against what she felt were demeaning views, and created family discord both by selling Conrad manuscripts to support her gambling habit and by leaving instructions in her will for a lavish memorial to herself to be placed on Conrad's gravestone. In response to a virulent attack upon her second Conrad memoir (*JCHC*) by Edward Garnett, charging that she had belittled the great writer and betrayed her husband's trust, Jessie responded frostily: 'I can claim to have been a complete success as *his* wife, a task that many other more intelligent and better educated wives have been unable to accomplish in their married life. . . . I may not be capable—as you say—of appreciating or even understanding his genius, but you may remember one point I make . . . which is to live in this world one talented partner is enough, the other must be more commonplace and ordinary. I have claimed that distinction for myself' (*PL*, 257).

Conrad dedicated the *Youth* volume and *Romance* (with Elsie Hueffer as co-dedicatee) to her. She ventured into print with *A Handbook of Cookery for a Small House* (completed in 1907, published by *Heinemann in 1923, with a preface by Conrad) and after her husband's death wrote two intimate, but unreliable memoirs, *Joseph*

Conrad as I Knew Him (Heinemann, 1926) and *Joseph Conrad and his Circle* (Jarrolds, 1935).

Conrad, John [Alexander] (1906–82), Conrad's younger son. John Conrad, named after John *Galsworthy, was affectionately known by the family as Jack or Jackolo. He was educated at boarding schools at Ripley Court in Surrey and Tonbridge, and, aged 17, spent some months in Le Havre to improve his French. He later practised as an architect and married Mary Geraldine Grindrod in 1928, with whom he had two sons, John Richard Teador and Peter Stewart Thaddeus. John took an active interest in preserving Conrad's literary reputation: he became his father's literary executor in 1944, gave a BBC radio address in 1957 on the centenary of Conrad's birth, and was anxious that Jocelyn Baines, the author of the first properly researched Conrad *biography in 1960, suppress the information that his father had attempted *suicide as a young man in *Marseilles. John's reminiscences, *Joseph Conrad: Times Remembered* (CUP, 1981), dedicated to the memory of Richard *Curle, present an engaging portrait of Conrad as a writer, family man, and father who told his son that he should try to 'justify . . . [his] existence on this earth, be honest with . . . [himself] and with all men, be confident but not conceited' (p. xiii). His recollections also betray a degree of resentment about his mother's sale in 1925 to the American collector George T. *Keating of a number of signed first editions that Conrad had apparently intended for his sons: 'it never occurred to me that my father's wishes would be ignored and that so few personal things of JC's should be retained. My mother was, relatively, well provided for but she never discussed with me the sale of any object; in fact it was all done without my knowledge so I was presented with a *fait accompli* about which nothing could be done' (168). Items of Conradiana from the writer's last *home at Oswalds that had been inherited by John Conrad were, after his death, donated by his widow Mary to the Canterbury Heritage Museum.

Conrad, Joseph. See 'Chronology' (pp. xxiii–xxxviii) for an account of Conrad's life.

contracts. In the earliest part of his writing career (up to 1906), Conrad did not enjoy the security of long-term publishing contracts. His first eleven volumes in Britain were brought out by five different *publishers, and the first eight in America by seven different firms. During this period Conrad did, of course, have close and sustained working relationships with individual publishers, such as William *Heinemann and William *Blackwood, but these were based upon unspoken gentlemanly agreements and still involved Conrad or his agent J. B. *Pinker in negotiating terms for each volume. Such informal arrangements allowed Conrad the freedom to transfer his allegiance if a publisher's offer no longer suited him (as when he broke with T. Fisher *Unwin and offered *The Nigger of the 'Narcissus'* to Heinemann), but, on the other hand, they offered the struggling writer no prospect of continuous financial security. Thus, when Conrad's close association with Blackwood was coming to an end in 1902, he commented wistfully: 'I wish M^r B'wood could be induced to—so to speak—hire me permanently[,] take all my stuff as it comes—lock it up—in a desk if he likes—publish when he likes, never publish! Anything! That would be an ideal state of affairs for me' (*CL*, ii. 368).

A new pattern emerged in Conrad's professional life at the point where, as an author with a reputation, he became a sought-after acquisition. In 1906, he entered into his first long-term contractual agreement with Algernon *Methuen for three volumes, which brought him a signing-on fee of £50 and a fixed sum per novel over the next few years. Relations with Methuen were, however, never very good, and by late 1911 Conrad was describing the company as a 'modern manufactory of books' and mere 'shop', and determined to sever connections at the soonest possible moment. 'I am an individual writer and I prefer to go to a publisher who will think it worth his while to treat me accordingly. . . . Three novels they must have and they shall have them but not a line more if I can help it' (*CL*, iv. 502, 503). By March 1913, this simmering dissatisfaction developed into an acrimonious contractual wrangle, with an obdurate Conrad claiming that the publication of *Chance* had fulfilled his contract for three books; Methuen, however, insisted that the earlier *The Secret Agent* was not covered by the original contract and expected another Conrad novel. Rumbling on for many months, the argument deteriorated to a point where the company only communicated with the author through Pinker, who finally reconciled Conrad to the prospect that *Victory* would have to be a Methuen volume.

Part of Conrad's frustration with Methuen arose from the fact that he was already in the process of negotiating a new three-novel contract with J. M. *Dent and wanted 'to be off with the old love(?) before taking on another' (*CL*, v. 177). On freeing himself from Methuen in 1915, Conrad's contractual position became altogether more regular and uncomplicated: in Britain, he was now contracted to Dent, and in America solely to the Doubleday, Page Company, both of which also engaged to bring out future *collected editions of his works. By 1913, Conrad and Pinker were a formidable negotiating team, as is evident in their discussions with F. N. *Doubleday about an American collected edition: the two men made careful plans before meeting Doubleday, Pinker conquered various trade jealousies with 'perseverance and diplomacy', and the whole agreement was hammered out—reported Conrad with relish—'*without it costing me a penny*' (*CL*, v. 632).

In the last ten years of his career, Conrad was thus a heavily contracted author, fulfilling agreements that covered both his work-in-progress and collected editions. In its final phase, his career was to turn a curious circle. When his first publisher, Unwin, was approached with a view to his ceding copyright to Conrad's earliest fiction for the purpose of the collected edition, he did so on condition that Conrad

return to the Unwin fold. Hence in 1919, Conrad signed a long-term contract with that firm, which brought out some of the author's last volumes—*The Arrow of Gold*, *The Rover*, and the posthumous *Tales of Hearsay*. Few of Conrad's contracts have survived, but the notebook kept by his secretary Miss Lilian *Hallowes (*The Conradian*, 25: 2 (2000), 205–44) records the contents of some of the later ones.

'Cookery'. Conrad composed this piece quickly in January 1907 as a preface to a cookbook originally compiled by Jessie Conrad for the publisher Alston Rivers, but which did not appear until 1923, when it was brought out by Heinemann under the title *A Handbook of Cookery for a Small House*. Conrad's preface first appeared as a privately printed *pamphlet in 1921, and was collected in *Last Essays*. Its tone of light whimsy—which Conrad described as 'a mock serious thing into which I dragged Red Indians and other incongruities' (*CL*, iii. 410)—may partly serve to disguise his embarrassment at being associated with a project so frankly designed to make money and without literary merit. No pre-publication documents are known.

Cooper, James Fenimore (1789–1851), American novelist. James Fenimore Cooper figured with Frederick *Marryat as one of the main authors in Conrad's youthful reading. As he repeatedly testified, their colourful adventure fictions—augmented by accounts of explorers' lives—had a vivid and awakening effect in his adolescent years, partly inspiring his urge to leave *Poland for what he felt to be his share of the world's opportunities. Years later, in 1902, he sent three of Cooper's novels to Edward *Garnett's 10-year-old son David, with the advice: 'I would recommend you to begin with the *Last of the Mohicans* [1826]—then go on with the *Deerslayer* [1841] and end with the *Prairie* [1827]. I read them at your age in that order; and I trust that you, of a much later generation, shall find in these pages some at least of the charm which delighted me then and has not evaporated even to this day' (*CL*, ii. 467). Cooper's sea fiction no doubt exerted a similar 'charm' for the young Conrad as well as the later author whose character Singleton in *The Nigger of the 'Narcissus'* bears a marked resemblance to Long Tom Coffin in *The Pilot* (1824).

That Cooper was a lasting literary enthusiasm for Conrad is also indicated in his 1898 essay on 'Tales of the Sea', in which he regards both Cooper and Marryat as having 'shaped' his life and exerted an appeal that has 'withstood the brutal shock of facts and the wear of laborious years'. Of Cooper, he remarks: 'His sympathy is large, and his humour is as genuine—and as perfectly unaffected—as is his art' (*Notes*, 56, 57). This essay coincides with Conrad's early work on *Lord Jim* and suggests that Cooper's fiction, in his mind at this time, may well have had a general influence upon the novel, connecting with that body of 'light holiday literature' (5) in which Jim seeks an image of himself and supplying some of the generic romance motifs—the heroic endeavour of sea life, the bond of male camaraderie, and the flight from society to a withdrawn island or forest—that the novel incorporates but also questions and complicates. Batchelor argues that the 'relationship between *Lord Jim* and Cooper's romances is similar to (though obviously less direct than) the relationship between William Golding's *Lord of the Flies* and Ballantyne's *Coral Island*: in each, a simple adventure story provides the dramatic structure for a profound moral inquiry' (1988: 33). To Arthur *Symons in August 1908, Conrad reaffirmed his belief that Cooper was 'a rare artist' and one of his 'masters' (*CL*, iv. 101); he also recalls Cooper's Leatherstocking Tales in the later *Chance*, another novel that both inherits and subverts chivalric and adventure motifs. Here the narrator describes *Marlow as 'the expert in the psychological wilderness' and playfully goes on: 'This is like one of those Redskin stories where the noble savages carry off a girl and the honest backwoodsman with his incomparable knowledge follows the track and reads the signs of her fate in a footprint here, a broken twig there, a trinket dropped by the way. I

have always liked such stories' (311). See also Allen F. Stein, 'Conrad's Debt to Cooper: *The Sea Lions* and "The Secret Sharer"', *Conradiana*, 8 (1976), 247–52.

Corsica. In a letter to J. B. *Pinker of 6 December 1918, Conrad looked forward to a future visit to Corsica as a way of preparing for his Napoleonic novel, *Suspense*: '[It] may take 18 months in writing. I would like too to have a look at Elba and Corsica before I get too deep into the tale—say next winter.' By the time the journey got under way in early 1921, there were other strong reasons for the three-month visit: Jessie Conrad would be able to convalesce after a recent operation, the Conrads could celebrate their silver wedding anniversary abroad, and the trip would provide the ageing Conrad, then feeling world-weary and 'beastly invalidish' (*LFC*, 299), with his last sentimental return to the Mediterranean of his youth and to an island inescapably connected with Dominique *Cervoni.

Leaving on 23 January, they travelled by car through *France in easy stages, with Borys Conrad driving them via the battlefields at Armentières as far as Rouen, from whence they proceeded via Orléans and Lyons to *Marseilles, and from there by boat to Corsica. During the first week of February they settled at the Grand-Hôtel d'Ajaccio & Continental, soon joined by Pinker and his wife, and Conrad's secretary, Miss *Hallowes. Through Sir Maurice and Lady Cameron, whom they knew through Hugh *Clifford, they made a new friend in Alice S. Kinkead, an Irish artist. Conrad also met H.-R. Lenormand, a French playwright, who found Conrad a writer haunted by 'the spectres of fatigue and of creative inertia' who repeatedly cried out that he could '"no longer work!"' (Stallman (ed.), 5). Apart from composing a brief foreword for *A Hugh Walpole Anthology* (1921), Conrad by his own account felt unable either to work or to relax: 'I am neither the better nor the worse for being here—in health, that is. I would perhaps [have] done some work if I had stayed at home. . . . Head empty. Feelings as of dead' (*LFC*, 306–7). More positively, however, he did 'breathe the right atmosphere for his novel about Napoleon' (*LL*, ii. 166): he immersed himself in Ajaccio's port-life, visited *Napoleon's birthplace, and borrowed books on Napoleon from the town library, including Stendhal's *Vie de Napoléon* (1876), Gaspard Gourgaud's *Sainte-Hélène* (1889), General Jean Rapp's *Mémoires écrits par lui-même* (1823), and L. Lanzac de Laborie's *Paris sous Napoléon* (1905–13). After a few days at the end of March in Bastia, on the island's north-east coast, the Conrads returned to *England via Toulon, Avignon, and Lyons, arriving home in early April.

Costaguana, the imaginary South American republic created in *Nostromo*, has a name which may be translated as 'Land of the Palm Tree Coast' from the Spanish *costa* ('coast') and *guana* ('palm tree'), its national flag being 'diagonal red and yellow, with green palm trees in the middle' (217). The novel's events take place in one of the republic's provinces, the Occidental Province of *Sulaco, which is separated from the rest of the country—and its capital, Santa Marta—by a high mountain range.

Various attempts have been made to identify Costaguana with one or other of the South American republics. In 'Where is Costaguana?', *Conradiana*, 23 (1991), 203–15, M. Claudia Benassi summarizes previous enquiries and argues that fictional Costaguana corresponds most closely to Colombia, which borders on two oceans, features a large mountain range, and has a city called Santa Marta. Conrad himself avoided such specificity and, some years after the novel's publication, stressed the synthetic and representative quality of his created country: 'The geographical basis is . . . mainly Venezuela; but there are bits of Mexico in it, and the aspect presented by the mountains appertains in character more to the Chilian seaboard than to any other. . . . The rest of the meteorology belongs to the Gulf of Panama and, generally, to the Western Coast of Mexico as far as Mazatlan. The historical part is an achievement in mosaic too, though, personally, it

seems to me much more true than any history I ever learned. In the last instance I may say that Sulaco is intended for *all* South America in the seventh decade of the nineteenth century' (to Edmund *Gosse, 11 June 1918). Preferring an evocative generality, Conrad was also presumably conscious that for his fictional republic he had drawn upon histories of several diverse South American countries—Mexico, Colombia, Venezuela, Paraguay, and Argentina—and used an eclectic mixture of existing place names: Sulaco is in Honduras, Zapiga in Chile, Esmeraldas in Ecuador, and Azuera, Punta Mala, and Rincon in Panama.

While *Nostromo*, as 'an achievement in mosaic', may initially seem to deny the reader and its characters any secure historical and temporal reference points, it is increasingly possible—with the help, for example, of Martin *Decoud's synoptic letter to his sister in Part II, chapter 7—to reassemble chaotic events into a causal sequence and devise a largely coherent chronology of Costaguana's history. Watts's two helpful chronologies (1993: 171–3) place its central events, not in the 1870s as mentioned in Conrad's letter to Gosse, but during a period from 1888 to 1891, with the closing episodes taking place in 1900.

The several studies of Conrad's documentary sources tend to emphasize the extraordinary geopolitical vividness of Conrad's created Latin American world, sometimes attempt to give an actual map of Costaguana (as in Watts 1993: 174–5), and admire the prescience of his diagnosis of 19th-century South American politics. In a similar spirit, Conrad's friend R. B. Cunninghame *Graham, judging the novel's title to be 'damned bad', felt that it would have been more evocative to call it *Costaguana* (quoted in *LCG*, 159), while Arnold *Bennett preferred to think of it as *Higuerota* (*CCH*, 161). By contrast, some readings of the novel have suggested that it is more useful to consider Costaguana as a fictional disguise or displacement for historical and political concerns essentially European, ranging from Morf's view that Costaguana is a mirror image of Polish history—'it is the Polish history of the years 1814 to 1867 all over again' (1976: 300)—to Peter Smith's interesting suggestion that socio-political Costaguana is 'a little Europe with its history intact but its memories gone' (*Public and Private Value: Studies in the Nineteenth-Century Novel* (CUP, 1984), 188). More recent *Marxist readings pay less attention to fictional Costaguana as an exercise in geopolitical reconstruction than as an ideological configuration which, it is claimed, reveals a writer 'in whom a *Western* view of the non-Western world is so deeply ingrained that it blinds him to other histories, other cultures, other aspirations' (Edward Said, 'Through Gringo Eyes', *Harper's Magazine* (April 1988), 71). See also Ugo Mursia, 'The Fictional State of Costaguana', *L'Époque Conradienne* (1979), 85–107.

Cracow. The medieval Polish capital was Conrad's home from 1869 to 1874, when it was part of Austrian *Poland. Soon after arriving there in February 1869, his father Apollo *Korzeniowski died, his funeral on 26 May occasioning a patriotic demonstration, with the 11-year-old Conrad at the head of a procession of several thousand people. His father was buried at the city's Rakowicki Cemetery and memorialized on his gravestone as 'the victim of Muscovite tyranny'. Conrad lodged at three places in the city, the first at 6 Poselska Street with his father; the second at a *pension* for boys run by Ludwik Georgeon at 47 Floriańska Street; and the third with his maternal grandmother Teofila *Bobrowska at 9 Szpitalna Street.

Details of Conrad's daily life and education during his Cracow years remain shadowy. After a period attending preparatory classes organized in the Georgeon *pension*, he may have been a pupil at the prestigious St Anne's Gymnasium (as he several times claimed in later life), or at St Jacek's Gymnasium; for some of this period, he was certainly placed under a private tutor, Adam Marek *Pulman, a medical student at the Jagiellonian University. An application to the City Council by his grandmother in 1872 to obtain the freedom of the

city for her beloved 'Konradek' was granted only on condition that he acquire Austrian nationality, although efforts to bring this about were unsuccessful. In this same year, Conrad, aged 14, first announced his desire to leave Poland for the *sea. He later said in 'Poland Revisited': 'It was in that old royal and academical city that I ceased to be a child, became a boy, had known the friendships, the admirations, the thoughts and the indignations of that age. It was within those historical walls that I began to understand things, form affections, lay up a store of memories and a fund of sensations with which I was to break violently by throwing myself into an unrelated existence' (*Notes*, 145).

Conrad's trip to Poland with his wife Jessie and their two sons in the summer of 1914, his first visit to his homeland for more than twenty years, involved a sentimental pilgrimage to a city he had not seen for four decades: 'I felt so much like a ghost that the discovery that I could remember such material things as the right turn to take and the general direction of the street gave me a moment of wistful surprise' (ibid. 164). If for Conrad the journey was a *recherche du temps perdu*, for his sons it was intended as an important initiation, designed to let them 'see something of the Polish life and visit Cracow . . . before they grew too old to care for the early associations of their father's life' (*JCKH*, 61). During his stay, Conrad met several old friends and revisited the city's historic landmarks—the great Market Square with its massive St Mary's Church, the Florian Gate, the Grunwald Monument in Matejko Square, and Wawel Castle. He also visited the Jagiellonian University Library, which yielded a precious contact with some of his father's surviving manuscripts, and made a pilgrimage to his father's grave where 'for the only time in his life, Borys saw his father kneel down and pray' (*JCC*, 399). The Conrads' visit to the city was suddenly cut short after five days by the outbreak of the *First World War, when they decided to make the short journey to unmilitarized territory in the mountain resort of *Zakopane. Conrad's moving recollections of his return to Cracow can be found in 'First News' and 'Poland Revisited' (*Notes*). See also Andrzej Braun, 'Cracow in the Life of Joseph Conrad', in Moore (ed.) 1992: 49–56.

Crane, Stephen (1871–1900), American writer and journalist. Stephen Crane was introduced to Conrad by S. S. *Pawling in October 1897, some months after Crane's arrival in England. Then in his mid-twenties, Crane and his partner Cora Howarth (1865–1910), an ex-brothel-keeper turned journalist, had arrived in London from Greece, where they had been covering the Graeco-Turkish War. Strangers in England and short of money, the couple were taken in hand by Edward *Garnett, who found them a home at Ravensbrook in Oxted, Surrey. They later lived at a nominal rent in Brede Place, a large and crumbling 14th-century manor house in east Sussex. With his talent for friendship, Crane gathered around him many of the writers who were already Conrad's friends—not only Garnett, but also Ford Madox *Ford, Henry *James, Edwin Pugh, and H. G. *Wells. He also had several friends whom Conrad did *not* like, and in his later reminiscences Conrad referred to a possible weakness in Crane's character that prevented him from freeing himself from a retinue of worthless admirers.

Before their first meeting, Conrad, who had already read and admired Crane's *The Red Badge of Courage* (1895), anticipated that he would like Crane enormously, and he was not disappointed. At that meeting, the pair wandered around *London streets for several hours in absorbed discussion, with Crane at one point requesting that Conrad should tell him all about Balzac's novels. Conrad was immediately charmed by the simplicity and directness of a young man whose eyes seemed to carry the secret of his personality, 'very steady, penetrating blue eyes, the eyes of a being who not only sees visions but can brood over them to some purpose' (*Notes*, 50). As writers, they quickly discovered a common bond in their insatiable interest in making the reader 'see' and the possibilities of literary

*impressionism. Soon after their meeting, Conrad wrote to Garnett of Crane's 'The Open Boat' (1897): 'His eye is very individual and his expression satisfies me artistically. He certainly is *the* impressionist and his temperament is curiously unique. His thought is concise, connected, never very deep—yet often startling. He is *the only* impressionist and *only* an impressionist' (*CL*, i. 416). Although Conrad was later to express even greater dissatisfaction with Crane's lack of 'depth', the latter's example figures very importantly at one stage in Conrad's evolving attitude towards impressionism as a visual aesthetic, and it has often been claimed that the influence of *The Red Badge of Courage* can help to explain the fresh departure in subject matter and style announced in *The Nigger of the 'Narcissus'*, which Crane read in proof (see Peter L. Hays, 'Joseph Conrad and Stephen Crane', *Études anglaises*, 31 (1978), 26–37). Increasing closeness between the two men also brought with it the possibility of a *collaboration—on a play to be called *The Predecessor*—although the project never seems to have been more than a playful extension of their developing friendship.

That friendship, interrupted in April 1898 by Crane's departure for the *Spanish-American War as a correspondent, resumed in 1899 with regular meetings, trips in a boat the two men had acquired, and a light-hearted collaboration with other writers on an entertainment called *The Ghost*, which was performed at Brede Place during the Christmas season of 1899. Some four months later, Conrad, hearing that Crane was terminally ill with tuberculosis, visited him in Dover, two weeks before his death. In 'Stephen Crane as a Source for Conrad's Jim', *Nineteenth-Century Fiction*, 38 (1983), 78–96, Nina Galen, noting that Crane died during the composition of *Lord Jim*, suggests that the Conrad–Crane friendship may provide a catalyst for the bond between *Marlow and *Jim, helping also to explain the novel's inner logic and its elegiac mood. In his later years, Conrad wrote three appreciations of Crane and his work: 'Stephen Crane: A Note without Dates' (*Notes*), 'His War Book' (on *The Red

Badge of Courage) and 'Stephen Crane' (*Last Essays*). For a general survey, see Elsa Nettels, 'Conrad and Stephen Crane', *Conradiana*, 10 (1978), 267–83.

'Crime of Partition, The'. Conrad's final intervention on behalf of the Polish cause, this essay was written in the second half of December 1918, only two months after the end of the *First World War. It was published in the *Fortnightly Review*, 105 (May 1919), 657–9, and collected in *Notes on Life and Letters* in a revised form. According to J. H. Stape, in '"The Crime of Partition": Conrad's Sources', *Conradiana*, 15 (1983), 219–26, Conrad was indebted to two specific texts: Lord Eversley's *The Partitions of Poland* (1915) and Józef H. *Retinger's pamphlet *La Pologne et l'équilibre européen* (1916). It should also be noted that in 1917 Conrad read *Problems of Central and Eastern Europe* (1917) sent to him by its author, Roman Dmowski, who was General Józef Piłsudski's ideological opponent and head of the Polish delegation at the Versailles Peace Conference in 1919.

The wide fears that Conrad had expressed on Armistice Day—'Great and very blind forces are set free catastrophically all over the world' (*LL*, ii. 211)—assume a more specific form in the essay's concern with the question of future Polish autonomy within the context of Europe's post-war reconstruction. 'The Crime of Partition' was written at a time when the fate of the newly constituted *Poland was still critically uncertain, since the Versailles Peace Conference had not yet taken place and recognition of a sovereign Poland had not been formalized. Conrad had justifiable anxieties about official British policy, since both Prime Minister Lloyd George and his Foreign Secretary Balfour were known to be unsympathetic to an independent Poland. Conrad also feared that the invitation to *Russia to attend the conference might result in an ugly compromise: 'The mangy Russian dog having gone mad is now being invited to sit at the Conference table, on British initiative!' (*LL*, ii. 217).

First addressing the *Polish question in its historical setting, Conrad's essay soon moves on to more recent events, arguing that the nature of the Polish national temperament and the nation's political traditions, both strongly linked with the West, make its independence 'a political necessity and a moral solution' (128): 'The only course that remains to a reconstituted Poland is the elaboration, establishment, and preservation of the most correct method of political relations with neighbours to whom Poland's existence is bound to be a humiliation and an offence. Calmly considered it is an appalling task, yet one may put one's trust in that national temperament which is so completely free from aggressiveness and revenge. Therein lie the foundations of all hope' (131). A revised typescript of the essay, dated 12–27 December 1918, is held at the Beinecke Rare Book and Manuscript Library, Yale University.

Curle, Richard [Henry Parnell] (1883–1968), author, editor, and journalist. Richard Curle was a close friend in the last decade of Conrad's life and co-executor of his estate after his death. Curle was born in Scotland, the third son of a Melrose lawyer and landowner who had eleven children. In 1905 he took a job with the publishing firm of Kegan Paul in *London, and began to publish essays and studies of George Meredith. He first met Conrad in 1912, at one of the Thursday meetings of Edward *Garnett's circle at the *Mont Blanc Restaurant. The friendship developed and became lasting, with Curle perhaps filling the gap left by Conrad's rupture with Ford Madox *Ford. While making use of Curle's links with the press and basking in the younger man's adulation, Conrad also enjoyed Curle's company and valued his practical sense. In 1914 Curle published a book-length appreciation of Conrad's work, *Joseph Conrad: A Study* (Kegan Paul, Trench, Trübner). He was active as a journalist in South Africa in 1916–18, and spent most of 1920 in Burma and the Malay States. *The Arrow of Gold* was dedicated to Curle, who became a regular guest of the Conrads after 1919, and happened to be visiting at Oswalds when Conrad died on 3 August 1924.

Together with Ralph *Wedgwood, Curle served as co-executor of Conrad's estate for twenty years until 1944, when its management was transferred to Conrad's younger son John and the law firm of Withers. Curle prepared Conrad's final novel *Suspense* for publication in 1925, and arranged for private limited editions of Conrad's *Congo Diary* and of the notes that Conrad had inscribed in books he had given to Curle. He also helped Conrad's widow Jessie to organize the sale of her husband's library. Most of his own extensive Conrad collection was sold at *auction in 234 lots by the American Art Association in New York on 28 April 1927. Curle's many essays and articles devoted to Conrad culminated in the publication of two volumes in 1928: an edition of Conrad's *letters (*CTF*), and a narrative account of his friendship with Conrad (*LTY*). Although Curle was originally quite close to Jessie Conrad and helpful to her in the immediate aftermath of her husband's death, he later disapproved of her extravagance, but he remained close to John Conrad, with whom he maintained an extended correspondence. Curle's many publications include novels and critical works, travel literature, and handbooks about book-collecting and stamp-collecting. He later specialized in entomology, becoming a Fellow of the Royal Entomological Society of London in 1947. Most of Curle's papers are now held at the Lilly Library, Indiana University.

D

Daily Mail. See ANDERSON, JANE; 'AS-CENDING EFFORT, THE'; 'CENSOR OF PLAYS: AN APPRECIATION, THE'; 'CHRISTMAS DAY AT SEA'; 'CONFIDENCE'; 'FRIENDLY PLACE, A'; 'HAPPY WANDERER, A'; 'LEGENDS'; 'LIFE BEYOND, THE'; *MIRROR OF THE SEA: MEMORIES AND IMPRESSIONS, THE*; NORTHCLIFFE, LORD; 'SECRET SHARER, THE'; 'SILENCE OF THE SEA, THE'; THOMAS, EDWARD; 'TRADITION'.

Dante Alighieri (1265–1321). As in the works of Charles Baudelaire, Arthur Rimbaud, and other French Symbolists whom Conrad read and admired, allusions to Dante's *Inferno* often figure in his writings in order to evoke conditions of unending suffering and stagnant despair. Predictably, many of these appear in his *letters with reference to his own position as a writer consigned to suffer the 'infernal' torment of literary creation: 'I am one of those who are condemned to run in a circle,' says Conrad of himself (*CL*, ii. 243). Elsewhere, he echoes *Inferno*, iii. 9: 'And one returns to one's nightmare . . . It is like that. "Abandon all hope" you who, by love and by hate, seek to give body to a few inconsequential shades' (*CL*, iii. 53). Other Dantean references in his letters serve to picture a wider, more public hell-scape, as in the description of modern political Europe: 'We have passed t[h]rough the gates where "lasciate ogni speranza" [abandon all hope] is written in letters of blood and fire, and now the gate is shut on the light of hope' (*CL*, i. 12). Among the several Dantean allusions in his fiction, a description of the retreating Napoleonic army in 'The Warrior's Soul' is the most vivid: 'I have seen it stream on, like the doomed flight of haggard, spectral sinners across the innermost frozen circle of Dante's Inferno, ever widening before their despairing eyes' (*Tales of Hearsay*, 1).

A more long-standing debate concerns the importance of Dante's *Inferno* as a major intertext in 'Heart of Darkness', which at one point includes *Marlow's explicit reaction: 'it seemed to me I had stepped into the gloomy circle of some Inferno' (*Youth*, 66). Robert O. Evans, in 'Conrad's Underworld', *Modern Fiction Studies*, 2 (1956), 56–62, counters a previous reading by Lillian Feder in 'Marlow's Descent into Hell', *Nineteenth-Century Fiction*, 9 (1955), 280–92, in which she had argued that Conrad uses parallels with the traditional voyage to Hades in Virgil's *Aeneid* in order to create 'an image of hell credible to modern man' (281). Evans's reading gives importance to Dante's work as *the* main intertext in the story, with Marlow assuming the role of Virgil, Dante's guide through hell. According to this view, the story's structure and cosmology systematically emulate those of the *Inferno*, with all of Conrad's 'pilgrims' corresponding to specific categories of Dantean sinners and Marlow's journey involving a progress towards a satanic *Kurtz who occupies its innermost circle. Evans's reading, however, seems as problematically limited as the one it seeks to replace and is notably closed to the possibility that Conrad, like T. S. Eliot in 'The Love Song of J. Alfred Prufrock' (1915) and *The Waste Land* (1922), may significantly modify and even invert Dantean schemata to achieve an ironic point: for example, the depiction of Marlow's traumatic meeting with the *Intended—whose house in sepulchral *Brussels has been regarded as the innermost point of hell (Stark 1974)—may be seen as exploiting a coldly ironic inversion of Dante's triumphant culminating union in the *Paradiso* with his own Intended, Beatrice.

Quite apart from the question of influence, Dante's work can provide a fruitful means of entry into some of the tale's interpretative cruxes. As Watts points out (1977: 136–7), Dante's conception of hell contains the possibility of a teasing paradox, since while the morally nondescript are consigned to the Inferno's dreary limbo, more active sinners—presumably like Kurtz—acquire a privilege, and even a heroic dignity, by virtue of the extremity of their damnation. Resting upon the Jansenist conception of the primacy of evil and the implication that the 'criminal' hero can discover in the ultimacy of evil redemptive possibilities not open to the average pilgrim of the world, such a paradox bears upon the difficult question of how the 'damned' Kurtz can be said by Marlow to have achieved a 'moral victory paid for by innumerable defeats' (151). From yet another point of view, the question of Conrad's allusions to Dante's *Inferno* and other epic underworlds in 'Heart of Darkness' relates to the wider issue raised by post-colonial critics, of whether and how far this work implicitly follows the long-standing Western tradition of representing Africa as 'dark' and demonic.

Darwinism. The evolutionary ideas of Charles Darwin (1809–82), published in *The Origin of Species* (1859) and *The Descent of Man* (1871), flew in the face of the religious belief in the special creation of species by offering overwhelming evidence for the existence of a principle of natural selection. Evolution by natural selection—or descent with modification, as Darwin sometimes calls it—depends upon three broad facts: the 'struggle for life' (summed up in Herbert Spencer's phrase 'survival of the fittest'), variation, and inheritance. Darwin's theories, which significantly helped to expand the role of empirical science, synthesized the work of many previous naturalists, and stand as the culmination of Victorian evolutionary thought. It was, for instance, Malthus's *Essay on the Principle of Population* (1798) that first suggested to Darwin the mechanism of natural selection. Nonetheless, just as 'evolution' and 'Darwinism' have become interchangeable terms, so it is to him that the conflict between science and religion has been attributed.

When Conrad began writing *Almayer's Folly* in the autumn of 1889, less than twenty years after the publication of Darwin's *The Descent of Man*, one of the books to which he turned for source material was Alfred Russel *Wallace's The Malay Archipelago* (1869), which became one of his favourite books. Wallace's travels in the Amazon Basin and the Malay Archipelago led him to develop the idea of natural selection independently of Darwin. His own *Contributions to the Theory of Natural Selection* (1870) amplified Darwin's *The Origin of Species*, and it was Darwin's receipt of a paper from Wallace expressing ideas identical to his own that prompted him to complete *The Origin of Species* for publication.

Conrad's response to Darwinism can be gauged from his presentation of humanity as an extension of the natural world, driven by the same impulse to survive. In *Almayer's Folly*, for instance, Nina and Dain's vows to each other are spoken against a symbolic backdrop of the evolutionary struggle of forest plants 'climbing madly and brutally over each other in the terrible silence of a desperate struggle towards the life-giving sunshine above' (71). Similarly, Conrad's sardonic comment upon colonialism becomes clear when *Almayer's belief in his racial superiority is placed within the context of evolutionary theory. In this light, the novel's final depiction of Almayer as being led around by his pet monkey Jack undermines his claim to superiority, suggesting instead that the European has actually *descended* the evolutionary ladder. Conrad's fiction also dramatizes the will-to-survive in 'Falk', whose protagonist eats human flesh in order to keep himself alive.

In *The Descent of Man*, Darwin played into the hands of late 19th-century white-supremacists with his suggestion that some races (many of which he refers to as 'savages') can be regarded as sub-species, and that the moral sense that distinguishes man from other species has found its highest expression among Caucasians. So, for instance, John Westlake could argue in *Chapters on the Principles of International*

Law (1894) that 'uncivilized' parts of the world should be annexed by advanced powers. It has been claimed that Kurtz's injunction, 'Exterminate all the brutes!' (*Youth*, 118), not only stands as the maxim of 19th-century European colonialism but has its roots in the evolutionary science of Darwin's *The Origin of Species* with its claim (in chapter 6) that 'At some future period not very distant . . . the civilized races of man will almost certainly extermi- nate and replace throughout the world the savage races'. In his vision of colonialism, Conrad repeatedly undermines European claims to racial superiority by unsettling the binary opposition between 'savage' and 'civilized'. Instead, he suggests that Western morality is relative, based on little more than convention, and kept in place by 'the holy terror of scandal and gallows and lu- natic asylums' (*Youth*, 116). Perhaps most devastatingly, where Conrad does identify a continuum from 'savage' to 'civilized', it tends to undermine the claims of the latter by revealing its kinship with the former. Thus, Decoud can argue that the 'bar- barism' of the past, which 'went about yelling, half-naked, with bow and arrows in its hands', persists in the present, albeit wearing 'the black coats of politicians' (*Nostromo*, 231). See O'Hanlon (1984) and Hunter (1983) for full-length studies of Conrad and Darwinism.   AHS

Daudet, Alphonse (1840–97), French writer. Alphonse Daudet was one of Con- rad's 'youthful enthusiasms', an author from whose work he could evidently quote by heart, and to whom in 1895 he even thought of sending a copy of his first novel, *Almayer's Folly*, as 'an act of homage': 'Do you think', he asked Marguerite *Porad- owska, 'it would be foolish of me to send him my book—I who have read all his, in all weathers?' (*CL*, i. 202). According to Ford Madox *Ford's testimony (*JCPR*, 103), Conrad was in 1892 'immensely fas- cinated' by Daudet's *Jack* (1876), while Ém- ilie *Briquel recorded in her 1895 journal that Conrad had advised her to read Daudet's *Fromont jeune et Risler aîné* (1874) and *Le Nabab* (1877). In early 1898, shortly

after Daudet's death, Conrad wrote an obituary tribute (see 'ALPHONSE DAUDET'), which reveals that he had also read the *Tartarin* stories, *Les Rois en exil* (1879), *L'Immortel* (1880), and *Sapho* (1884). Significantly, Conrad's 1898 article also in- dicates that his 'Daudet worship' (*CL*, i. 202) was at this stage tempered by a clearer perception of his shortcomings as an artist: 'He was not a great artist, he was not an artist at all, if you like—but he was Al- phonse Daudet, a man as naïvely clear, honest, and vibrating as the sunshine of his native land' (21). The likely truth is that Conrad's youthful ardour for Daudet's works was, at a formative stage in his liter- ary career, decisively overtaken by a more powerful admiration for the technical craftsmanship of *Flaubert and *Maupas- sant. Hence Daudet seems to have exerted little influence upon Conrad's fiction, al- though Ford felt that *Almayer's Folly* was 'written too much in the style of Alphonse Daudet' (*JCPR*, 16), while Graver (4) de- tected Daudet's impact in 'The Black Mate' (*Tales of Hearsay*).

Davray, Henry-Durand (1873–1944), a French journalist, critic, and translator. H.-D. Davray first made personal contact with Conrad through H. G. *Wells around 1899. In that same year, Davray received a grateful letter from Conrad thanking him for his recent complimentary review of *The Nigger of the 'Narcissus'* in the *Mercure de France*, in which, comparing Conrad to Gustave *Flaubert, Davray praised him for his un-English attention to the craft of fiction, and claimed him as 'one of ours' (*CL*, ii. 186). As editor of the *Mercure*'s 'Col- lection of Foreign Authors' series, Davray translated a number of British authors— including George Meredith, Rudyard *Kipling, and Wells—and soon wished to include Conrad. In early 1902, he expressed an interest in translating *Tales of Unrest* and *Typhoon and Other Stories*, and also hoped to undertake further works. While not all of these ambitions materialized, Davray translated 'Karain' (*Tales of Unrest*) and *The Secret Agent*, and in February 1908 was granted Conrad's permission to oversee French translation rights to all of his work, a task later taken over by André *Gide. Davray's contribution to the promotion of Conrad's reputation was thus quite considerable, and he was one of the first critics to stress the importance of Conrad's French inheritance. He also performed some of the functions of a literary agent, regularly noted the publication of Conrad novels in the *Mercure*, and on the writer's death wrote an eloquent obituary, 'Joseph Conrad', *Mercure de France*, 175 (1 October 1924), 32–55.

Dawson, Alec John (1872–1951) and his brother **Ernest** (1884–1960). Alec and Ernest Dawson lived in Rye, Sussex, and, from about 1901 onwards, 'were very real friends of the [Conrad] family' (*JCTR*, 76), whom they visited on their powerful motorcycle and side-car. In connection with their army duties, both men had travelled in India and the Far East, and so shared a common source of interest with Conrad. They were also both authors, Ernest having contributed travel reminiscences to *Blackwood's Magazine*. In 1923, Conrad supplied a foreword to Alec Dawson's *Britain's Life-boats: The Story of a Century of Heroic Service* (1923), reprinted in *CDOUP*, 107–8. The brothers remained in contact with Conrad until his death and attended his funeral. See also Ernest Dawson, 'Some Recollections of Joseph Conrad', *Fortnightly Review*, 130 (1 August 1928), 203–12, excerpted in *JCIR*, 213–15.

Dawson, [Francis] Warrington (1878–1962), born in Charleston, South Carolina, the son of a wealthy newspaper-owner. Warrington Dawson was a successful international journalist and aspiring novelist when through E. L. *Sanderson he arranged to meet Conrad in May 1910. Then recovering from a breakdown, the lonely and depressed Conrad was probably flattered by the hero-worship accorded him by this young American admirer, who since 1899 had lived in France and 'had a special taste and talent for conversing with the great and near-great' (Randall (ed.), 4).

Soon after their meeting, Conrad read Dawson's two published novels, *The Scar* (1906) and *The Scourge* (1908), and subsequently helped to revise and promote his work. For his part, Dawson became one of the first of Conrad's younger disciples, his numerous lectures on 'A Great Contemporary—Joseph Conrad' contributing to the growing legend surrounding the writer. He later claimed to have influenced Conrad's portrayal of the *de Barral case in *Chance* by providing him with information about the celebrated fraud and downfall of Frédéric and Thérèse Humbert in Paris in 1903. Their personal relations were closest during 1913–14, when Dawson frequently visited Capel House and, in the spring of 1914, rented nearby Gill Farm to be a close neighbour. Even the requirements of cordial friendship could not, however, persuade Conrad to respond positively to Dawson's invitation to join the Fresh Air Art Society, a high-minded movement influenced by Max *Nordau and devoted to countering what its founder-members regarded as a pervasive degeneracy in the Modernist arts by an appeal to the 'laws of health' and the 'Oneness of Life'. Conrad's powerfully critical letter of 20 June 1913 finds him hard-pressed to maintain polite equanimity. In response to the Society's fourteen articles of faith, he offered a devastating critique of fixed creeds in general and particular, voicing the belief that 'the artist[']s salvation is in fidelity, in remorseless fidelity to the *truth of his own sensations*. Hors de là, point de salut [Beyond there, no salvation].' He also witheringly pointed out that there 'are millions of perfectly healthy people who are stupid, for whom all art other than oleograph reproduction is morbid' (*CL*, v. 238–9). After 1914, Dawson became an invalid and was unable to leave his Versailles home. The two men maintained a friendly correspondence, with Conrad acceding to Dawson's requests to cobble together extracts from his letters into prefaces for his novels. Some of Dawson's characteristics may later have found their way into the portrait of the South Carolinian Captain J. M. K. Blunt in *The Arrow of Gold*. Dawson dedicated *The Pyramid* (1922) and *Adventure in the Night* (1924) to Conrad. For a detailed 'Account of the Friendship' between the two men, see Randall (ed.), 3–123.

de Barrals, the. Despite his foreign-sounding name, de Barral, the villain of *Chance*, is a half-Scottish financier born in Bethnal Green who began his career as a junior clerk in an East End dock company. He becomes 'the Great de Barral', amassing a fabulous fortune as the proprietor of the Orb Deposit Bank, the Sceptre Mutual Aid Society, and the Thrift and Independence Aid Association, which attract depositors by advertising the virtue of thrift and promising interest rates of 10 per cent. The collapse of these institutions leads to scandalous bankruptcy proceedings, at the end of which de Barral is convicted of fraud and sentenced to seven years in prison. Upon his release, his daughter Flora arranges for him to join her in Captain *Anthony's ship, the *Ferndale*, but de Barral, eager to take revenge on his enemies, despises the ship as only another form of incarceration and determines to get Flora away from Anthony.

As a child, Flora had been installed with her mother at the Priory, a mansion adjoining the village where Carleon Anthony lived, and here made the acquaintance of Mrs Fyne. After his wife's death, de Barral placed Flora in Hove, a suburb of Brighton, where the Fynes observed with dismay how Flora's unscrupulous governess Eliza was plotting to marry the wealthy heiress off to a 'nephew' named Charley. The governess's scheme is foiled by the collapse of de Barral's empire only a few days before Flora's 16th birthday, whereupon the governess insults and abandons her brutally. E. E. Duncan-Jones has suggested that Flora and her governess may owe something to Henry *James's famous story *The Turn of the Screw* (1898), in which another Flora finds herself at the mercy of a hired governess (see 'Some Sources of *Chance*', *Review of English Studies*, 20 (1969), 468–71). Conrad's Flora finds temporary refuge with the Fynes, but is then claimed, on her

father's orders, by an odious cousin, a cardboard-box manufacturer in *London's East End. She twice runs away, and Mrs Fyne tries to find other employment for her. A damsel in distress, Flora is ultimately rescued thanks to her chance encounters with *Marlow, Captain Anthony, and Powell.

Conrad also explicitly compares the de Barrals to 'Figures from Dickens' (162), and resemblances have been noted especially with fathers and daughters in *Dickens's *Dombey and Son* (1848) and *Little Dorrit* (1855–7), and with the great swindle described in Anthony Trollope's *The Way We Live Now* (1875). In 'Conrad, Ford, and the Sources of *Chance*', *Conradiana*, 7 (1976), 207–24, Thomas C. Moser examines a number of historical sources for de Barral, among them Whitaker Wright, whose Globe Financial Corporation, known simply as the 'Globe', defaulted in 1900, resulting in a lengthy and scandalous trial. An hour after he was sentenced, Wright committed suicide by swallowing prussic acid. Moser suggests that de Barral's blue eyes and puffy cheeks may have been borrowed from Ford Madox *Ford, and registers a number of similarities between *Chance* and Ford's *The Good Soldier* (1915).

deconstructive approaches. In Barbara Johnson's well-known definition, '*Deconstruction* is not synonymous with *destruction* . . . It is in fact much closer to the original meaning of the word *analysis*, which etymologically means "to undo"—a virtual synonym for "to de-construct." The de-construction of a text does not proceed by random doubt or arbitrary subversion, but by the careful teasing out of warring forces of signification within the text' (*The Critical Difference* (Baltimore: Johns Hopkins UP, 1980), 5). A deconstructive reading of a text might be thought of as oppositional reading: it exposes the text's internal instabilities, inconsistencies, and contradictions in order to reveal disunity beneath apparent unity (whereas more traditional styles of close reading tend to have the opposite intention, seeking to demonstrate underlying unity beneath the apparently disunified text). Deconstruction is the practical application of the theory known as 'post-structuralism', which had as its starting point Jacques Derrida's 1966 lecture 'Structure, Sign and Play in the Discourse of the Human Sciences'. Here, Derrida, a French philosopher, argued that in the 20th century the tradition of Western thought has been 'decentred': points of fixity that had obtained thus far, such as the white, Western norms or 'centres' that determine everything from dress codes to intellectual outlook and against which alternatives can be detected and judged as 'other', have been eroded (through such causes as advances in science, the barbarism of war, and intellectual and artistic revolutions). As a result, there are no longer any absolutes or guaranteed facts, but only interpretations, each of which lacks the stamp of authority. Although, in his critique of the hierarchical oppositions that have provided the basis for Western thought, Derrida's deconstruction was aimed primarily at philosophical works, literary critics have been quick to adopt the rigour, scepticism, and playfulness of his methods.

To demonstrate the text as 'decentred', a deconstructive approach 'reads the text against itself' in order to reveal the presence of latent meanings that threaten the expressed meaning, and so demonstrate an inherent instability of meaning within the text. Such an approach seeks evidence of textual discontinuities or 'faultlines'—such as breaks, aporias, impasses, or contradictions—which may provide evidence of a concealed meaning of which the text itself is seemingly unaware. One might thus think of deconstruction as the attempt to engage with the text's 'unconscious' dimensions. So, for example, a deconstructive reader who finds the word 'guest' in a text might exploit the fact that this word is etymologically cognate with the Latin word *hostis*, meaning enemy: the apparently positive word 'guest' represses an unconscious or suppressed negative aspect that destabilizes and threatens its surface meaning. Another tactic employed by deconstructionists is to analyse a text's binary

oppositions (such as male/female or light/dark) in order to show how it reverses their customary polarity—so female rather than male may be the privileged term. Behind such a reversal lies not only the desire to destabilize the individual binary opposition, but also the 'decentring' of the ideological hierarchy on which it relies.

J. Hillis Miller's essay '*Heart of Darkness Revisited*' (in Murfin (ed.) 1989) offers an example of how this approach can be applied to Conrad's fiction. Miller begins by speculating upon whether 'Heart of Darkness' constitutes an 'apocalyptic' text (prompted by the title of Francis Ford Coppola's *film version, Apocalypse Now). His confessedly 'roundabout' approach first leads him to identify the novel as a parable, whose characteristic feature is to use a realistic story in order to express another reality or a truth not otherwise expressible. Recalling that *apocalypse* means 'unveiling', Miller connects apocalyptic and parabolic narratives through their shared intention to illuminate, to 'unveil that which has never been seen or known before' (210), and then proceeds to read the text—which, after all, also 'seemed to throw a kind of light', according to *Marlow (*Youth*, 51)—in terms of these two generic classifications. The narrator's distinction between the different kinds of yarns told by seamen is then shown to be a distinction between simple tales and parables. (Miller indulges, too, in the playful inventiveness of deconstructionists when he observes that describing Marlow's tales in terms of their 'likeness' to misty haloes homonymically recalls the German word for parables, *Gleichnis*.) Examining the relationship between kernel and nut, Miller identifies the relation of story to meaning in simple tales as metonymic synecdoche; by contrast, parables involve metaphorical synecdoche. Such use of figures is typical in post-structural criticism, as is Miller's subsequent speculation about whether the figurative nature of Marlow's language serves only to carry us further away from the meaning of experiences.

The terms used in the novella to describe Marlow's method of narration, in which an invisible mist will yield a visible haze, raise questions about the efficacy of parabolic narration. Then, in an argument which simultaneously and subtly questions the boundary between biblical and literary narrative (and anticipates the removal of the boundary between literature and criticism later in the essay), Miller likens Marlow's tale to Jesus's story of the sower, in which more will be given to those who already have and taken from those who have not. He argues that both have ultimately to do with the efficacy of parable, and especially with its paradoxical qualities: 'If you can understand the [biblical] parable you do not need it. If you need it you cannot possibly understand it. You are stony ground' (214); similarly, 'if we see the darkness already, we do not need "Heart of Darkness". If we do not see it, reading "Heart of Darkness" or even hearing Marlow tell it will not help us' (214). Such inversion precipitates a sequence of reversals, through which the text is shown to defer its 'unveiling' indefinitely.

Like parables and apocalyptic narratives generally, 'Heart of Darkness' is shown both to promise revelation and demonstrate that revelation is impossible: 'The novel is a sequence of episodes, each structured according to the model of appearances, signs, which are also obstacles or veils. Each veil must be lifted to reveal a truth behind which always turns out to be another episode, another witness, another veil to be lifted in its turn' (218). The text, whose subject is, purportedly, the 'unveiling' of dark truth, is shown in Miller's reading to yield only the illumination of its own 'continuing impenetrability' (224).   AHS

Decoud, Martin, a prominent character in *Nostromo*, born in *Costaguana and godson of Don José Avellanos. Martin Decoud has for most of his life lived with his family in Paris where he has studied law and dabbled in literature. Approximately 28 years old at the time of his return to Costaguana, the 'idle boulevardier' (152) makes a delayed appearance in Part II, chapter 3 and dominates the middle chapters of the novel. One of Conrad's most

complex characters, he is a compound of irreverent Frenchified dandy, repressed romantic, intellectual libertine, and—as events show—public servant. During the country's period of unrest, the sceptically withdrawn Decoud surprises himself by the extent to which he becomes involved in events as editor of the Ribeirist journal, lover of Antonia Avellanos, and originator of the idea that the Occidental Province of *Sulaco should secede from the rest of Costaguana and become an independent republic. With *Nostromo, he is entrusted with smuggling the silver across the Golfo Placido. When their lighter collides with a rebel troopship in the darkness, they are forced to run aground on the nearest island and conceal the silver there. Left alone on the island for several days, the oppressed Decoud commits *suicide.

As with most of Conrad's major characters, Decoud is the product of richly composite sources. Richard F. Burton's *Letters from the Battlefields of Paraguay* (1870) mentions a journalist in Paraguay named Don Juan Decoud who probably supplied the name for Conrad's character (a name possibly attractive for its nearness to the French *découdre,* 'to unpick or unstitch'). A more important source was Anatole *France's portrait of Prosper *Mérimée in *La Vie littéraire* (1888–92), which offered Conrad a blueprint of a deracinated and self-defeating intellectual libertine, whose entire life was a playing-out of multiple selves destructively at odds with each other—the romantic and the sceptical, the sentimental and egocentric, the ascetic and the cultivated sensualist. (For a study of Conrad's handling of this Francian source material, see Knowles 1979.)

A good deal of critical debate has centred on possible similarities between Decoud and Conrad himself—or at least the younger Conrad in his dandyishly 'French' phase—and their effect upon a novel that, on the one hand, values Decoud as a historian and bitingly sceptical commentator but, on the other, appears sharply to repudiate his scepticism by devising a punishingly lonely and faithless death for him. F. R. Leavis was one of the first critics to note the close relationship between creator and created character: 'Decoud may be said to have had a considerable part in the writing of *Nostromo*; or one might say that *Nostromo* was written by a Decoud who wasn't a complacent dilettante' (200). Following upon Leavis, Guerard famously went on to explain Decoud's sudden death by introducing the notion of surrogacy: 'The characterization obviously belongs with those in which a writer attempts to separate out and demolish a facet of himself; attempts to condemn himself by proxy' (199). Guerard believes that if the novel leaves the impression that Decoud has been unfairly treated, it is because the later ordeal devised for the Frenchman and Conrad's triumphantly final judgement upon him seem more like a concerted attack upon a conventional dandy figure than a fair test upon the sensitive individual who evolves in the course of the action. Ray (1984) offers a useful synopsis of the variety of 'autobiographical' explanations of Decoud's career and fate, and extends the notion of surrogacy important in so many of them to Conrad's own ordeal of creativity. Ray argues that through Decoud, Conrad could confront the pull towards annihilation involved in his own creative endeavour, the former's suicide allowing him 'to continue writing by enabling him to recognize, anticipate, and even purge the threat which is latent in his own literary practices' (58). For a lively and penetrating view of the Conrad–Decoud relationship, see Joyce Carol Oates, '"The Immense Indifference of Things": The Tragedy of Conrad's *Nostromo*', *Novel*, 9 (1975), 5–22.

dedications. 'A dedication, for me, is a serious thing. It is an offering of my thoughts given in affection and esteem to someone whose friendship I consider a good fortune and a privilege,' wrote Conrad to T. Fisher *Unwin in 1896, in the mistaken belief that an advertisement was to be placed opposite the dedication of *An Outcast of the Islands* (*CL*, i. 261). The main body of Conrad's dedications provides a record of his 'affection and esteem' for

family members and long-standing friends, some of whom often worked together to provide him with an indispensable support system in times of illness, financial difficulty, or creative stasis. They are (in order of book publication): Tadeusz *Bobrowski (*Almayer's Folly*), E. L. *Sanderson (*An Outcast of the Islands*), Edward *Garnett (*The Nigger of the 'Narcissus'*), G. F. W. *Hope and his wife (*Lord Jim*), Jessie Conrad (*Youth*), R. B. Cunninghame *Graham (*Typhoon*), John *Galsworthy (*Nostromo*), Katherine Sanderson (*The Mirror of the Sea*), H. G. *Wells (*The Secret Agent*), Harriet *Capes (*A Set of Six*), Hugh *Clifford (*Chance*), Ralph *Wedgwood and his wife (*Within the Tides*), Perceval *Gibbon and his wife (*Victory*), Borys Conrad (*The Shadow-Line*), Richard *Curle (*The Arrow of Gold*), and G. *Jean-Aubry (*The Rover*). In some cases, the dedication of a work to a close friend might include Conrad's gratitude for services rendered on behalf of that work: hence, Clifford was associated with *Chance* for his help in securing its American serial publication, and Garnett with *The Nigger of the 'Narcissus'* because that story represented the high point of his early services to Conrad.

Four dedicatees form a special group by virtue of their peripheral position in the Conrad circle or by the specialized significance of the dedication: Adolf P. *Krieger, one of the writer's friends from his earliest *London years, was linked with *Tales of Unrest*, but since their relationship was at that time in the process of dissolving, Conrad's dedication to Krieger 'for the sake of old days' may represent an attempt to placate his friend; Carlos *Marris had helped to prompt Conrad's return to Eastern subjects in *'Twixt Land and Sea* and was rewarded with its dedication, although the two men had met only once; the American writer Agnes *Tobin (*Under Western Eyes*) was a family friend, but only for a very short period; and Frederic C. *Penfield (*The Rescue*) was being thanked for very specific help in securing the Conrads a permit to leave *Poland after the outbreak of the *First World War.

Conrad's habitual practice of dedicating his works inevitably draws attention to the question of omissions and exclusions. Posthumously published volumes apart, only *A Personal Record* and *Notes on Life and Letters* were left undedicated. He presumably felt that since both volumes dealt with matters personal to his 'life and letters', they qualified as his own special offspring. Another order of omissions applies to close friends and relations who were not singled out for dedications. Whether by design or accident, Conrad did not dedicate volumes to such friends as Ford Madox *Ford (although *Romance* was co-dedicated to their wives and *The Inheritors* to their elder offspring), Marguerite *Poradowska, Henry *James, William *Rothenstein, Arthur *Marwood, to his younger son John, or to the memory of his parents, or indeed to any other Pole apart from his uncle Tadeusz Bobrowski.

Ideally a simple and private matter between author and dedicatee, a small number of dedications seem to have involved Conrad in a good deal of circumspect manœuvring in his dealings with friends and publishers. For example, he originally planned to dedicate the *Youth* volume to Graham, but deferred to the wishes of his publisher William *Blackwood, a high Tory to whom Graham's socialism was anathema. Conrad then contemplated W. E. *Henley as a possible dedicatee, but finally changed his mind in favour of his wife Jessie, with Graham having to await his next published volume. In later life, Conrad promised John *Quinn that *The Arrow of Gold* would be dedicated to him, but then reverted to an earlier promise to assign it to Curle and instead promised Quinn the forthcoming *Suspense*. Shortly after making this revised offer, relations between the two men soured and then petered out, with *Suspense*, the novel upon which Conrad was working at his death, left undedicated. The dedication of *The Secret Agent* to Wells is probably one of the most curious in its combination of admiration and teasing irony. Conrad took care to write to Wells reproducing the contents of his unusually elaborate dedication,

explaining that he wished to assign 'This Simple tale of the XIX Century' to his friend, who was also being linked in the dedication to 'what the perfect Novelist should be—Chronicler[,] Biographer and Historian' (*CL*, iii. 461). Since, however, this novel may be a partial satire of the technological and socialist future outlined in Wells's post-1900 works, it probably offers an unusual example of a work ambiguously suspended between dedication and interrogation, Conrad offering with one hand what he ironically takes away with the other.

Works dedicated to Conrad include: Galsworthy's *Jocelyn* (1898) and *In Chancery* (1920); Constance *Garnett's translation of Ivan *Turgenev's *A Desperate Character* (1899); Graham's *Progress* (1905); Ford's *The Fifth Queen* (1906); Gibbon's *Margaret Harding* (1911); Stephen *Reynolds's *How 'Twas* (1912); Edward *Thomas's *Walter Pater* (1913); E. L. Grant Watson's *When Bonds are Loosed* (1914); Violet Hunt's *The House of Many Mirrors* (1915); Arthur *Symons's *Figures of Several Centuries* (1916); John Powell's musical composition *Rhapsodie nègre* (1917); Curle's *Wanderings* (1920); Clarence E. Andrews's *Old Morocco and the Forbidden Atlas* (1922); Cecil Roberts's *A Tale of Young Lovers: A Tragedy in Four Acts* (1922); Hugh *Walpole's *The Cathedral* (1922); F. Warrington *Dawson's *The Pyramid* (1922) and *Adventure in the Night* (1924); and André *Gide's *Voyage au Congo* (1927).

delayed decoding. Ian Watt first coined this critical term in a 1972 lecture, 'Pink Toads and Yellow Curs: An Impressionistic Device in *Lord Jim*', in Jabłkowska (ed.) 1975: 11–31, and incorporated it into his later full-length study *Conrad in the Nineteenth Century* (Chatto & Windus, 1980) to describe a feature of impressionistic narrative seemingly peculiar to Conrad's early works. A form of deferred explanation, delayed decoding is 'the verbal equivalent of the impressionist painter's attempt to render visual sensation directly'. The technique 'combines the forward temporal progression of the mind, as it receives messages from the outside world, with the much slower reflexive process of making out their meaning' (176, 175). Two examples cited by Watt are when *Marlow recounts his belated understanding of (i) the explosion of the *Judea* in 'Youth' (*Youth*, 22–3) and (ii) the attack upon his boat in 'Heart of Darkness' (ibid. 111–12). Watt goes on to discuss the device within the context of late 19th-century literary and pictorial *impressionism, seeking out its broader philosophic and aesthetic traditions in the writings of David Hume, Walter Pater, and Stephen *Crane.

Watt's formulation has had a fruitfully diverse afterlife, in one direction prompting a search for more specific literary precedents. Other critics have considerably expanded its application, notably Cedric Watts, who, regarding delayed decoding as a powerful tool for creating effects of defamiliarization, claims that to 'be aware of the technique ... is to discover the secret of much vivid, immediate writing by Conrad and by others' (1993: 116). In a number of books and articles, Watts extends its range beyond local descriptive effects to embrace large-scale narrative sequences. Thus, in *The Deceptive Text: An Introduction to Covert Plots* (Harvester, 1984), which includes a pithy discussion of 'Conrad and Delayed Decoding' (43–6), he connects the device with varieties of 'covert' plotting, defined as 'a concealed plot-sequence' in which some of 'its elements are conspicuous, but the connections between them are not, either because of authorial strategies of reticence and elision or because they are occluded by the conspicuous linkages of the overt plot' (1). Watts includes Conrad's fiction among a number of largely Modernist works, where a problematic 'covertness' ambushes and dallies with the reader, so transforming the process of forward reading into a sustained act of backward decoding. A later critic, Jakob Lothe, also frequently draws upon Watt's formulation in his application of a more systematic narrative theory to Conrad's works and notes: 'For [Gérard] Genette, the term which approximates to delayed decoding is "completing analepsis", which "comprises the

retrospective sections that fill in, after the event, an earlier gap in the narrative"' (30 n.)).

Yet a third group of critics has moved beyond the general terms of impressionism to consider more specific turn-of-the-century phenomenologies with which Conrad's practice can be aligned. For example, Martin Bock, in 'The Sensationist Epistemology in Conrad's Early Fiction', *Conradiana*, 16 (1984), 3–18, aims to refine Watt's definition by using assumptions drawn from Ernst Mach's *Contributions to the Analysis of Sensations* (1897), whose 'sensationism', he argues, offers the most appropriate frame for understanding Conrad's delayed structuring of events and apprehension. A significant dissenting note to Watt appears in Bruce Johnson's 'Conrad's Impressionism and Watt's "Delayed Decoding"', in Murfin (ed.) 1985: 51–70. Like Bock, Johnson invokes a turn-of-the-century phenomenology, represented here by Edmund Husserl and developing gestalt psychology, although with markedly different emphases: he avers that Watt, in overvaluing the act of decoding, ignores a basic purpose of impressionism—that of returning to the 'primitive' eye and a condition of 'aboriginal sensation before concepts and rational categories are brought to bear' (53).

Delestang, César (1796–?), head of the *Marseilles shipping firm C. Delestang et Fils. César Delestang was Conrad's first employer upon his arrival in *France in 1874, engaging him to make three voyages to the *Caribbean in Delestang ships (see SHIPS AND VOYAGES). Delestang *père* and his wife, in their late seventies when Conrad knew them, appear to be the family members described in *A Personal Record*. There, Delestang emerges as having a 'thin bony nose, and a perfectly bloodless, narrow physiognomy clamped together as it were by short formal side-whiskers' and as being 'such an ardent—no, such a frozen-up, mummified Royalist that he used in current conversation turns of speech contemporary, I should say, with the good Henri Quatre' (124, 125); his wife,

Marguerite-Thérèse, a haughty and imperious woman who always reminded Conrad of Lady Dedlock in Charles *Dickens's *Bleak House* (1853), is recalled as having once said to him: '*Il faut, cependant, faire attention à ne pas gâter sa vie* [After all, one must take care not to spoil one's life]' (126). Since Conrad does not specify whether his main contacts were with Delestang *père* or his son Jean-Baptiste, who had taken over the running of the firm, it is not always possible to gain an accurate picture of his contacts with the family. However, 'de Korzeniowski', as he seems to have been styled, regularly mingled in gatherings at the Delestang family salon, which brought together local supporters of the Bourbon dynasty as well as persons involved in the *Carlist activities later described in *The Mirror of the Sea* and *The Arrow of Gold*. Conrad quarrelled with Jean-Baptiste Delestang in 1877, although the shipowner later supplied a generous testimonial of the young seaman's services while in his employment.

Dent, J[oseph] M[allaby] (1849–1926), Conrad's main British publisher in the later part of his career. J. M. Dent was described by Edward *Garnett in the 1890s as the quintessential self-made man, 'an original East End bookbinder ... with an ambition, a rosy face and a long black beard' (quoted in Ernest Rhys, *Everyman Remembers* (Dent, 1931), 237). That ambition had led to the foundation in 1888 of the J. M. Dent publishing house, which evolved in 1909 into J. M. Dent & Sons, a family business that included Dent's eldest son Hugh Railton (1874–1938). In 1913, the year after he had published Conrad's *'Twixt Land and Sea*, Dent entered into negotiations with the writer at a time when the latter was caught up in contractual difficulties with the *Methuen Company. In his correspondence of February 1913, Dent apologized to Conrad for not being able to serialize *Chance*—'One seems to be reading almost at the same time Plato and Meredith, Conrad and Laurence Sterne— a most delightful combination, and infinitely sane'—but assured him that he

was 'very keen indeed' to get Conrad's future books into his 'clutches'. As a result, Conrad signed a three-book contract with Dent, also attracted no doubt by the publisher's offer to 'advance some money on account of these three books' (*CL*, v. 177, 178).

Dent went on to publish *Within the Tides*, *The Shadow-Line*, *The Rescue*, and *Notes on Life and Letters*, as well as the posthumous *Suspense* and *Last Essays*. Although Conrad found Dent something of a 'humbug' (*CL*, v. 688), he maintained friendly relations with the publisher and his son, and in later life, on visits to *London, would often step in to see Dent at his Aldine House headquarters. He was rightly impressed by the commercial acumen of a firm that during the Edwardian period had marketed a wide range of moderately priced fiction in its 'libraries', including the Temple Classics Library, the Wayfarer's Library (advertised as embracing 'all that is healthy, clean and good in the field of modern literature'), and the ubiquitous Everyman's Library (with its famous motto, 'Everyman, I will go with thee, and be thy guide'). Dent certainly helped to guide Conrad's fiction into a new age of industrial publishing. He was responsible for bringing out second English editions of *Youth* (1917), *Lord Jim* (1917) and *Nostromo* (1918), reissued Conrad's works in his various 'libraries', and entertained long-term plans to publish a popularly priced *collected edition of Conrad's works, which materialized in the form of Dent's Uniform Edition (1923–8). After the death of both Dent and Conrad, the firm continued to publish Conrad in Dent's Collected Edition (1946–55), a reissue of the earlier Uniform Edition. See *The House of Dent, 1888–1938* (Dent, 1938), by Hugh R. Dent, who became head of the firm in 1926. The Dent company was sold to Weidenfeld and Nicolson in 1988, and its extensive archive is now held at the Wilson Library, University of North Carolina at Chapel Hill.

Dickens, Charles (1812–70). 'Books are an integral part of one's life,' wrote Conrad in *A Personal Record* (73), and none was more so to him than the fiction of Charles Dickens, which always evoked his warmest affection. Dickens's *Nicholas Nickleby* (1839) had the talismanic significance for Conrad of a work that first introduced him to English imaginative literature, although he read it in Polish translation. A reading of *Hard Times* (1854), a work his father translated, probably soon followed. Chief among his early favourites, however, was *Bleak House* (1853), 'a work of the master for which I have such an admiration, or rather such an intense and unreasoning affection, dating from the days of my childhood, that its very weaknesses are more precious to me than the strength of other men's work. I have read it innumerable times, both in Polish and in English' (ibid. 124). Dickens is recalled here as less of an influence in the conventional sense than a long-standing personal English friend, who had not only amused the isolated young Conrad but presumably also spoken intimately to his orphan's sensibility, since so many of his own works deal with abandoned or psychologically orphaned children. When, years later, Conrad gave his first public *interview as a writer, it was largely concerned with his beloved Dickens and headlined in the Cardiff *Western Mail* (1 January 1897) as 'A New Novellist [*sic*] on Dickens: Mr Joseph Conrad's Opinion on Dickens' (reprinted in *CUFE*, 172–7).

Conrad's debt to Dickens, observes Hawthorn, is 'too extensive and too profound ever to be more than inadequately charted' (1990: 136). One teasing complication in such an endeavour is that Conrad is never explicit about the 'weaknesses' he found in Dickens and how they counted for him as a writer who dissociated himself from many of the practices of the 'national English novelist' (*Last Essays*, 132). Another is the possibility that the very longevity of his attraction for Dickens was likely to have encouraged in Conrad the writer a detached wariness of his powerful predecessor's example. While his works incorporate recognizable Dickensian effects—sparkling caricature, grotesque effects, and comic visualization—they are invariably boldly announced and overtly savoured,

the product of the respectful *pasticheur*, and introduced as a form of conscious and overt homage to the Victorian writer or employed to give his work a recognizable English appeal. Elsewhere, there may even be an element of the affectionate joke or pun in Conrad's play with Dickens, as when he shows Captain *MacWhirr in 'Typhoon' with his Dickensian gamp or assigns the name 'Toodles' to one of his characters in *The Secret Agent*. In these cases, pastiche and playfulness signify the measure of Conrad's detachment from Dickens, one allowing him to keep his cherished predecessor at arm's length in order to develop more stringently impersonal forms and styles.

Most critics agree that two Conrad novels in particular, *The Secret Agent* and *Chance*, suggest a powerful creative engagement with Dickens's legacy. Significantly, both have *London settings and incorporate, even while they modify, the rich urban mythologies associated with *Bleak House*. *The Secret Agent* in particular evokes a cityscape as part-jungle and part-subaqueous world in a way remarkably similar to the one Conrad associated with Dickens, 'that wonder city, the growth of which bears no sign of intelligent design, but many traces of freakishly sombre fantasy the Great Master [Dickens] knew so well how to bring out by the magic of his understanding love' (*Notes*, 152). In addition to many effects of 'freakishly sombre fantasy', the novel also exhibits a marked Dickensian relish for the grotesque in its treatment of the anarchists and includes several characters who appear to have forebears in *Bleak House*: *Stevie and the crossing-sweeper Jo, Chief Inspector Heat and Inspector Bucket, Sir Ethelred and the Lord High Chancellor, and Toodles and almost any of the anonymous bureaucratic functionaries in the novel.

For fruitfully dissimilar approaches to the Conrad–Dickens relationship, see Robert L. Caserio, 'Joseph Conrad, Dickensian Novelist of the Nineteenth Century: A Dissent from Ian Watt', *Nineteenth-Century Fiction*, 36 (1981), 337–47, who argues that the reader should look to Dickens's novels as the most apposite context for realizing the '*Victorian* Conrad' (338); Hawthorn (1990: 135–40) for a view of *Chance* that sees Conrad as re-examining critically Dickens's myths and ideas about women; and Hugh Epstein, who ranges widely and perceptively over the Conrad canon in his '*Bleak House* and Conrad: The Presence of Dickens in Conrad's Writing', in Moore *et al.* (eds.) 1997: 119–40.

dictation. Conrad was by all accounts a good storyteller, and like most people he found it easier to speak than to write. G. F. W. *Hope remembered the seaman's yarns that were exchanged during sailing parties on Hope's yawl, the *Nellie*, and *Marlow's narratives are also examples of such yarns. Ford Madox *Ford heard many of Conrad's tales in this way, and was probably the first to recognize the importance of recording them. As Ford later recalled: 'Indeed a great part of his *Mirror of the Sea* was just his talk which the writer took down in a shorthand of his own extemporising, recalling to Conrad who was then in a state of great depression, various passages of his own relating' (*JCPR*, 30).

When Conrad's chronic gout affected his wrists and left him unable to write, he was forced to rely on dictation as a means of producing text. His typist, Lilian M. *Hallowes, was originally hired in 1904 as a copyist, but she was also quite capable of taking dictation, especially when Conrad was under time pressure (*CL*, iv. 137). She often wrote *letters on his behalf (usually by hand) when he was unable to wield a pen, and many of his later business letters were dictated to her and then corrected or amplified by Conrad in ink, with the curious result that the text becomes a palimpsest in which both the corrected and uncorrected versions remain visible. After *The Arrow of Gold* (1919), the literary works of Conrad's later years were for the most part dictated directly to Miss Hallowes. In an important sense, she became an unsung co-producer of his work, supplying at least the first version of spelling and punctuation. Although sound technology existed at the time, no recordings were ever made

of Conrad's voice, but it is possible at times to recover a sense of his accent from the mistakes made by Miss Hallowes. In a draft chapter of *Suspense*, for example, she first typed 'lover's fears', then deleted the words with the thick blue pencil used for immediate corrections and typed 'lower police spheres', indicating that she had at first misunderstood Conrad's pronunciation (typescript at Mary Baldwin College, folio 347).

Both Jessie Conrad and Richard *Curle witnessed a strange experiment in dictation near the end of Conrad's life (but evidently before the last week of June 1924, when Miss Hallowes left on holiday). Jessie recalled: 'For several weeks before his death, he managed with great labor to write himself and adopted the method of reading out loud as he wrote, so that it could be typewritten at the same time. That, of course, was very tiring, but he persevered to the last for love of his art' (*New York Times*, 17 September 1925, 8). Curle could not remember if this unusual practice was used for first drafts or revisions, but suggested that the 'idea probably was to give him the visual sense of what he was doing while enabling him to have the benefit of that clear contemplation which comes from dictating' (*LTY*, 70).

Doña Rita. Rita de Lastaola, the central figure in *The Arrow of Gold*, first appears as the subject of a discussion between Mr Mills and Captain Blunt, in which each has a different view of her. The riddle of her character is the mystery at the centre of the narrative, and the novel is constructed as a dramatization of the efforts of various men (including the narrator) to understand her. A Basque peasant girl, Rita de Lastaola was sent from Lastaola to Paris to stay with her uncle, an orange merchant in Passy. In Paris she meets the painter and art collector Henry Allègre: she poses for him, becomes his companion, and inherits his fortune. This wealth gives her influence, but not respect, in political circles in Paris. After Allègre's death, she has an affair with Don Carlos in Venice, as a result of which she also becomes an influential figure in

*Carlist politics. She is courted by Captain John Blunt, who is interested in her wealth, but cannot reconcile himself to her character. M. *George falls in love with her and lives with her for six months before she disappears.

The complex Rita has the 'terrible gift of familiarity', but she can also 'put in an instant an immense distance between herself' (25) and others. The key to her changeable and elusive character is the fear she manifests and acknowledges, associated with her cousin Ortega. The end of the narrative reveals how her childhood relationship with Ortega produced her hysterical and dissociated personality. The reader's perception of Rita is further obscured by the rhetoric, the fantasies, and the projections that the male characters generate around her. Jerry Allen (52–4) suggests that Rita was based on Don Carlos's mistress Paula de Somoggy, although their relationship did not begin until 1877, after the end of the Second Carlist War. Don Carlos's wife Doña Margarita, whom he married in February 1867, may also be among the possible sources for Rita.   RH

Donkin, a dirty and ragged cockney seaman from London's East End in *The Nigger of the 'Narcissus'* who joins the ship in Bombay, bears some resemblance to a wider family of exploitative vagabonds present in Conrad's early fiction. However, in *The Nigger of the 'Narcissus'*, Conrad's early *sea story, he is a vagabond with a more precise social definition as a rogueseaman and working-class demagogue who enters into the hierarchical order of shipboard life and violates its most precious sanctities. In a community where actions speak louder than words, Donkin's loquacity is repeatedly condemned as 'filthy'; he is further depicted as being 'solitary and brooding over his wrongs' (32) and so an enemy to the crew's corporate life, as a habitual malingerer who is a stranger to the *work ethic, and a perpetually 'whining' critic of authority.

Certain problems attach to the opening presentation of Donkin. In a long, setpiece description by an apparently omniscient narrator (9–14), strident polemic combines with heavy sarcasm and an element of demonization to translate into a less than subtle caricature of Donkin as a type of modern agitator as conceived by a stiffly conservative imagination. As such, he soon becomes a whipping-boy for all newly emergent working-class ideologies and their liberal sympathizers: 'The pet of philanthropists and self-seeking landlubbers. The sympathetic and deserving creature that knows all about his rights, but knows nothing of courage . . . The independent offspring of the ignoble freedom of the slums full of disdain and hate for the austere servitude of the sea' (11). As Watt comments, the result is a 'somewhat overwrought parody of the socialist attempt to achieve equality and justice by mobilising working-class solidarity' (1980: 110), including presumably that kind of solidarity represented by the formation in 1887 of the National Amalgamated Sailors' and Firemen's Union.

If Donkin's subsequent role is largely circumscribed by his part in Conrad's most conservative political fable, he is nevertheless allowed a colourfully 'filthy' cockney voice (Conrad's first exercise in demotic English) and a vivid presence as the ship's malign predator. He also gains added complexity through the contrast he makes with the strong, silent Singleton and especially through his uneasy association with *Wait, since together they represent a twin threat to the crew's stability: Wait attacks their inner security, while Donkin exploits the fact of Wait's illness in an attempt to incite a mutiny. At the story's conclusion, Donkin—defeated by the forces of order, chastened, but essentially unchanged—attracts a final polemical aside: 'And Donkin, who never did a decent day's work in his life, no doubt earns his living by discoursing with filthy eloquence upon the right of labour to live. So be it! Let the earth and the sea each have its own' (172).

Don Quixote, the self-invented knight errant and hero of Miguel de Cervantes Saavedra's masterpiece (Part I, 1605; Part II, 1612), offered Conrad an image of his own behaviour in leaving a non-existent *Poland to go to *sea, and also serves as a model for the idealism or folly of many of his characters. Conrad first read Cervantes as a child, in an abridged Polish or French translation (*A Personal Record*, 70–1). At the top of the Furca Pass in the Swiss Alps, when his tutor Adam Marek *Pulman realized that young Conrad could not be persuaded to abandon his project of going to sea, he dismissed the matter by saying: 'You are an incorrigible, hopeless Don Quixote. That's what you are.' As Conrad recalled, 'I was only fifteen and did not know what he meant exactly. But I felt vaguely flattered at the name of the immortal knight turning up in connection with my own folly' (ibid. 44).

In *The Rescue*, when Mrs *Travers learns that Immada is a princess, she draws the conclusion that Tom *Lingard must be a knight, and D'Alcacer extends the allusion by describing him as a 'descendant of the immortal hidalgo errant upon the sea' (142); in the event, Lingard's dreams of restoring Hassim to power in Wajo indeed prove to have been quixotic. In *Nostromo*, Martin *Decoud invokes the image of Don Quixote to explain the history of *Costaguana, telling Don José Avellanos: 'There is a curse of futility upon our character: Don Quixote and Sancho Panza, chivalry and materialism, high-sounding sentiments and a supine morality, violent efforts for an idea and a sullen acquiescence in every form of corruption' (171). In *The Secret Agent*, Conrad gave the Assistant Commissioner 'a long, meagre face with the accentuated features of an energetic Don Quixote' (115). This description of the Assistant Commissioner, who is preparing to disguise himself and sally forth to solve the *Greenwich mystery on his own, may also owe something to Conrad's friend R. B. Cunninghame *Graham, a quixotic politician and ardent Hispanist who cultivated a remarkable physical resemblance to Cervantes's hero and even served as a model for a series of illustrations. Conrad often addressed him in letters as 'Don Roberto'. In *Montpellier Conrad engaged a Spanish tutor so that he could read *Don Quixote* in

the original (to J. B. *Pinker, 15 January 1907; cf. *CL*, iii. 409). In 1910, in his review 'A Happy Wanderer' (*Notes*), Conrad compared the author of *Quiet Days in Spain*, C. Bogue Luffman, to the immortal hidalgo who 'became converted . . . from the ways of a small country squire to an imperative faith in a tender and sublime mission' (61).

Later in his career, Conrad came to know a number of 'real' knights, and in May 1924 the 'incorrigible Don Quixote' was offered a knighthood of his own by the Labour Prime Minister Ramsay MacDonald. Conrad immediately and graciously declined the offer, but without explaining his refusal. Najder speculates that accepting a British knighthood might have looked to Conrad like a renunciation of his ancient heritage as a member of the Polish *szlachta* class (*JCC*, 488). Much as Conrad enjoyed playing the part of the English country gentleman, Karl is perhaps nearer the mark in suggesting that it was important to Conrad to avoid becoming institutionalized as a novelist, and to preserve his free standing as an outsider (*JCTL*, 881). Cedric Watts (1993: 67–74) discusses the 'Hamlet/Don Quixote' dichotomy in Conrad's life and work.

Dostoevsky, Fyodor [Mikhailovich]

(1821–81). Fyodor Dostoevsky, the famous Russian novelist, is generally acknowledged as a major influence on Conrad's work, especially on *Under Western Eyes*, even though Conrad vigorously denied any affinity with Dostoevsky and professed an intense dislike for his work. Richard *Curle recalled: 'There was no name in literature that Conrad detested more than that of Dostoievsky, and usually the mere mention of it drove him into a fury' (*LTY*, 16). *Psychoanalytic critics have suggested that the very strength of Conrad's protests lends credence to the charge of influence. As Jeffrey Berman puts it: 'Dostoevsky was Conrad's Lucifer but he was also a mirror, a secret sharer, a Rorschach test of his own projective innermost self' ('Introduction to Conrad and the Russians', *Conradiana*, 12 (1980), 6). Carabine has argued that Conrad's aversion to Dostoevsky was in reaction to an author whose Messianic nationalism was diametrically opposed to the no less rigid radical patriotism espoused by Conrad's father ('Conrad, Apollo Korzeniowski, and Dostoevsky', in Carabine 1996: 64–96).

Unlike the 'Westernizer' Ivan *Turgenev, who influenced Conrad both directly and through his impact on Gustave *Flaubert and Henry *James, Dostoevsky was an ardent 'Slavophile' who often disparaged Poles and felt no sympathy for their national aspirations. As against the elegance and balance of Turgenev's work, Dostoevsky (like Tolstoy) appeared to Conrad's 'master' Henry James as an author of 'loose, baggy monsters', although the subsequent publication of Dostoevsky's notebooks has revealed that he was a far more careful craftsman than was realized in Conrad's day.

Despite Conrad's own reservations, many of his closest friends were fascinated by Russian literature and by Dostoevsky, especially Edward *Garnett and his wife *Constance, whose translations of the works of Dostoevsky, Chekhov, Tolstoy, and Turgenev first made them accessible to English audiences. When Garnett sent Conrad a copy of *The Brothers Karamazov*, the first of her Dostoevsky translations, he complimented her translating skills but described the novel as 'terrifically bad and impressive and exasperating', adding: 'I don't know what D stands for or reveals, but I do know that he is too Russian for me. It sounds to me like some fierce mouthings from prehistoric ages' (*CL*, v. 70). There is no evidence that Conrad could read Russian fluently, nor is there any record of Russian books in his personal library. In a vehement rejection of the idea of 'Slavonism' in his works, Conrad insisted in 1922 that 'as a matter of fact I never knew Russian', and he added: 'The few novels I have read I have read in translation. Their mentality and their emotionalism have been always repugnant to me, hereditarily and individually' (*LL*, ii. 289). Dostoevsky's works were unavailable in English at the time he wrote *Under Western Eyes*, but Conrad could have read them in French or

possibly Polish translation. His friend and translator André *Gide published a volume of essays on Dostoevsky in 1923. Russell West's study of *Conrad and Gide: Translation, Transference and Intertextuality* (Amsterdam: Rodopi, 1996) contains helpful bibliographical references to materials on Conrad and Dostoevsky.

Both authors shared an interest in the theme of the doppelgänger, as expressed particularly in Dostoevsky's novella *The Double* and Conrad's story 'The Secret Sharer' (*'Twixt Land and Sea*). *Under Western Eyes* has often been compared with Dostoevsky's *Crime and Punishment*, but Paul Kirschner argues that it was also influenced by *A Raw Youth* (1875), which Conrad probably read in French translation; see 'The French Face of Dostoyevsky in Conrad's *Under Western Eyes*', *Conradiana*, 30 (1998), 24–43, and Kirschner's substantial introduction to the Penguin Classics edition of *Under Western Eyes* (1996).

Doubleday, F[rank] N[elson] (1862–1934). F. N. Doubleday, whose initials formed the basis of his nickname 'Effendi', was Conrad's main American publisher after 1913. He began his career in publishing at a very early age in 1877 with Charles Scribner's Sons before forming a partnership with S. S. *McClure from 1897 to 1900. Doubleday, McClure published the first American edition of *Lord Jim* and, with William *Heinemann, helped to subsidize Conrad during his protracted trials with *The Rescue*. During the period 1912–14, Doubleday, then president of Doubleday, Page, took a renewed interest in bringing out Conrad's works on a commercially successful basis in *America. The company's publication of *Chance* in 1914 was accompanied by an aggressive publicity campaign, which included the formation of a 'Conrad Committee', with pressure put upon Conrad (which he resisted) to make a promotional visit to New York in 1914. As a result of these efforts, the American edition of *Chance* sold over 10,000 copies in the first week of publication. With the help of two enthusiastic employees, Alfred A.

Knopf and Eugene F. Saxton, the company went on to play a major role in establishing the writer's subsequent reputation in the United States.

In 1914, Doubleday, Page set about acquiring American rights to Conrad's novels for a *collected edition, the eventual 'Sun-Dial' edition, which began to appear in 1921. Unfailingly courteous in his direct contacts with Doubleday during this period, Conrad's letters to his agent J. B. *Pinker reveal a growing wariness—and even suspicion—of the American company and their frankly commercial motives. A protracted wrangle in 1918 about the exact number of sets to be printed for the collected edition led Conrad and his agent to agree that future Doubleday, Page arrangements would need to be scrutinized carefully. In 1923, Doubleday masterminded Conrad's promotional visit to America, when the author stayed with 'Effendi' and his second wife Florence at Effendi Hill, their home in Oyster Bay, Long Island, undertook a tour of New England, and addressed 'fellow' employees at Doubleday's Garden City headquarters. The publisher's high-powered publicity campaign ensured that the 'famous' Joseph Conrad was widely interviewed and his movements reported in the American press. See also Doubleday's 'Joseph Conrad as a Friend', World Today (London), 52 (July 1928), 145–7.

Douglas, [George] Norman (1868–1952), polymath, traveller, author of the celebrated novel South Wind (1917), and homosexual adventurer. Norman Douglas was a close friend of Conrad's during the period 1905–17. Like Conrad, he had a cosmopolitan background: of Scottish descent, he was brought up in Austria and Germany, travelled widely in the diplomatic service, and later resided in Italy. At the time of their first meeting in Capri in 1905, Douglas had only published anonymously and was intent on furthering his literary career. Conrad subsequently played a substantial part in launching Douglas as a writer, reading his work-in-progress, giving advice ('This is a counsel

of wisdom. A novel is the shortest way to a living. Before all imitate no one!!' (CL, iv. 51)), recommending his writings to publishers, and establishing contacts for him with the *English Review, of which Douglas became assistant editor (1912–15).

Conrad's services to the restless and unconventional Douglas were also of a more private kind. In August 1911, Douglas arrived at the Conrads' *Kent home desperately ill with malarial fever and needed ten days' nursing at Capel House and Ashford Hospital. The Conrads also oversaw the education of Douglas's son Robin and gave him a home—and, in Jessie, a 'Mum'—during his school vacations (see Robin Douglas, 'My Boyhood with Conrad', Cornhill Magazine, 66 (1929), 20–8). In November 1916, Douglas's increasingly unhampered sexual adventurism led to his being charged with indecent assault upon a schoolboy, an episode that provoked Conrad's exasperated comment: 'I wish to goodness the fellow had blown his brains out. He has been going downhill for the last 2 years and I did once or twice ask him most seriously to consider his position. But it was impossible to do anything for him. Lately he has been avoiding us all' (CL, v. 684). With Douglas held in custody for a week before being granted bail, Conrad faced the problem of protecting 14-year-old Robin from the effects of the scandal. A trial was only averted when, in January 1917, Douglas jumped bail and left England permanently, so remaining true to one of his deepest habitual impulses: 'Burn your boats! This has ever been my system in times of stress' (Mark Holloway, Norman Douglas: A Biography (Secker & Warburg, 1976), 102). After this episode, the friendship between the two men came to an end. See also Frederick R. Karl, 'Joseph Conrad, Norman Douglas, and the English Review', Journal of Modern Literature, 2 (1971–2), 342–56.

'Dover Patrol, The'. Written in July 1921 at the request of Lord *Northcliffe, this celebration of the contribution of local merchant seamen to the war effort was first published in The Times (27 July 1921), 11–12,

the day on which the Prince of Wales unveiled the Dover Patrol Memorial on the
Dover coast. It was published as a limited-
edition *pamphlet and collected in *Last Essays*. Conrad's revised draft, a typescript
dictated to his typist Miss *Hallowes and
dated 27 July 1921, is held at the British Library, and a smaller fragment is held at the
Beinecke Rare Book and Manuscript Library, Yale University.

'Duel, The'. Conrad's first Napoleonic
fiction appeared in *Pall Mall Magazine*
from January to May 1908 (illustrated by
W. Russell Flint), and was included as the
fifth and longest (at 31,000 words) of the
stories in *A Set of Six* (1908) with the added
title 'A Military Tale'. In the United States it
was published under the title 'The Point of
Honor', first in *Forum* from July to October
1908, and then as a book by McClure
(illustrated by Dan Van Sayre Groesbeck).
It appeared again as a separate volume
from the Garden City Publishing Co. in
1924.

'The Duel' is the story of two cavalry
officers who fight an obsessive and seemingly unwarranted series of duels during
the years of the Napoleonic Wars. In 1801,
Lieutenant Gabriel Florian Feraud, a hot-
tempered and low-born southerner from
Gascony, first takes offence when Lieutenant Armand D'Hubert, an urbane, aristocratic northerner, is sent to confine him
to quarters for having injured a civilian in
a duel. Feraud insists on fighting with
D'Hubert immediately, and both are
wounded. Some time later, they fight a formal duel with seconds and duelling-
swords, at the end of which D'Hubert is
injured. D'Hubert's colonel, frustrated at
his inability to get to the bottom of the affair, orders a one-year truce, in the course
of which D'Hubert is promoted to captain.
This promotion has the effect of prolong-
ing the truce, since challenging or receiving
a challenge from a subordinate is an offence 'amenable to a court-martial' (203).
When Feraud is similarly promoted after
the battle of Austerlitz (December 1805), he
immediately challenges D'Hubert, and
they bloody each other with cavalry sabres

until their seconds stop the duel. Separated
by the fortunes of war and the requirements of the army, the two meet again after
the battle of Jena (October 1806) and fight
on horseback outside the town of Lübeck.
D'Hubert enters the duel with forebodings
of death, but Feraud is wounded almost
immediately. The disastrous retreat from
Moscow in the winter of 1812 again brings
Colonels Feraud and D'Hubert together,
but instead of duelling they make common
cause against the Cossacks. After the battle
of Waterloo (1815), the calumny spread by
General Feraud to the effect that General
D'Hubert 'never' loved the Emperor
inadvertently helps D'Hubert to adapt to
the Bourbon Restoration. Upon overhearing this slander, D'Hubert visits Joseph
Fouché, the Minister of Police, to ask that
Feraud's name be removed from a list of
Bonapartist officers facing trial.

D'Hubert retires to the country and is
about to marry a young girl chosen by his
sister when he meets Feraud's seconds,
who have come to offer D'Hubert a final
challenge with pistols. D'Hubert and Feraud meet at dawn, and D'Hubert survives
Feraud's two shots, but refuses to take Feraud's life. The duel is ended, and D'Hubert
realizes that he owes his adversary the felicity of knowing that his young fiancée loves
him enough to have run 2 miles (3 km)
barefooted when she learned of the duel. In
gratitude, D'Hubert secretly provides
Feraud with an income for the rest of his
life.

Conrad's letters indicate that he began
'The Duel' in *Montpellier in December
1906 or January 1907 and finished it in
April. He told his agent J. B. *Pinker that he
first thought of calling it *The Masters of
Europe: A Military Tale* (*CL*, iv. 60). The
story is based on a famous series of duels
fought by two French army officers, which
first appeared in English in *Harper's Magazine* in September 1858. It describes how
two captains of hussars named Fournier
and Dupont fought a series of duels beginning in Strasbourg in 1794 and ending in a
duel with pistols in 1813 in which Dupont,
who was engaged to be married, spared
Fournier's life in return for a promise to

end the hostilities. This article is reprinted in J. DeLancey Ferguson's 'The Plot of Conrad's "The Duel"', *Modern Language Notes*, 50 (June 1935), 385–90. The immediate source for the *Harper's* article was an account published a few months earlier in the Parisian magistrates' journal *L'Audience* (2: 71, 18 June 1858; see Donald Cross's note in the *TLS*, 15 August 1968, which also mentions other references to the duellists). Hans van Marle has identified an earlier version of the story in Alfred d'Alembert, *Le Duel* (1853), and references to Fournier and Dupont can be found in various Napoleonic memoirs and books about duelling. It remains strange that the story of these duelling hussars should not have appeared in print until 40 years after the duels ended. The reactionary attitudes described at the end of Conrad's story may also remind readers of the atmosphere evoked in Balzac's novella *Le Colonel Chabert* (1832). A detailed, comparative study of the historical sources of Conrad's tale remains to be written.

Conrad had difficulty placing the story, which was generally better received in *America, where reviewers praised its clarity and directness. British reviewers were more patronizing: Robert Lynd described it as 'an excellent example of Mr. Conrad's whimsical, half humorous, decorative method'; another found it 'tedious through its unnecessary length'; and a third suggested that 'Irony at once becomes

heavy and vulgar when used with a lack of breeding' (*CCH*, 212–18). Conrad answered his reviewers privately in a letter to Edward *Garnett of 21 August 1908, in which he implied that the story of the duellists had enabled him to trace a fictional history of the First Empire, a subject to which he would return in his final novels: 'I did conscientiously try to put in as much of Napoleonic feeling as the subject could hold. This has been missed by all the reviewers, every single one being made blind by the mere tale' (*CL*, iv. 106–9). In 'Conrad's "The Duel": A Reconsideration', *The Conradian*, 11 (1986), 42–6, J. H. Stape suggests that the meaning of the story lies not in Napoleonic history but in 'the salvation-by-woman theme that so much preoccupied nineteenth-century art' (45).

In 1977 'The Duel' was filmed as *The Duellists*, directed by Ridley Scott and starring Harvey Keitel as Feraud and Keith Carradine as D'Hubert. Acclaimed for its historical accuracy and beautiful photography, the film ends by emphasizing the resemblance between the isolated and embittered Feraud and the Emperor Napoleon, 'whose career had the quality of a duel against the whole of Europe' (165). Allan Simmons analyses various aspects of fidelity in Conrad's Napoleonic films in Moore (ed.) 1997: 120–34.

The manuscript of 'The Duel' (one-third of which is typescript), dated 4 April 1907, is at the Philadelphia Free Library.

E

editions. See COLLECTED EDITIONS; IL-
LUSTRATIONS; SERIALIZATION; TRANSLA-
TIONS.

'End of the Tether, The'. Obliged to
supply William *Blackwood with a third
and final story of some 40,000 words for
the volume that became *Youth: A Narrative,
and Two Other Stories*, Conrad began writing this novella in March 1902, after he and
Ford Madox *Ford had finished their joint
work on *Romance*. Conrad described the
story to Edward *Garnett as 'heartbreaking
bosh' (*CL*, ii. 424), and Ford may have
helped considerably with its production,
acting as general factotum and amanuensis
especially after much of the manuscript of
the second instalment was burnt on 23 June
1902, when an oil lamp exploded (although
Najder has doubts about the amount destroyed: see *JCC*, 283). Conrad had to re-
construct the lost material and struggled
thereafter to meet his serial deadlines. Finished by mid-October, the story eventually
ran to some 55,000 words and was still
being serialized in *Blackwood's Magazine*
(July to December 1902) when it was published in November in the *Youth* volume.
Early reviewers bestowed high praise on
'Youth' but had little to say about the two
other stories, and over the years 'Heart of
Darkness', the central story, has proved an
increasingly difficult act to follow.

Sherry (*CEW*, 198–205) has suggested
that Captain Henry Ellis, Master-Attendant in *Singapore during Conrad's visit
there, served as a primary model both for
Captain Eliott, the Master-Attendant in
Conrad's tale, and for the story's central
figure, Captain Henry *Whalley. Before he
began writing the story, Conrad described
it as 'the sketch of old Captain Loutit' (*CL*,
ii. 193), referring to Captain Thomas Louttit, the master of the *Duke of Sutherland*
just before Conrad joined the ship in 1878.
Whalley was originally called Loutit in the
manuscript, the surviving pages of which,
now at the Beinecke Rare Book and Manuscript Library, Yale University, show no
trace of fire damage.

The story opens as Captain Whalley,
with the help of a native serang, brings his
coasting steamer, the *Sofala*, up to cross the
shallow bar of Batu Beru along the Sumatra coast in the Strait of Malacca. Once famous as 'Dare-devil' Harry Whalley in the
days of fast clipper ships, with an island
and a passage named after him, Captain
Whalley has outlived the heroic age of sail
to become a 67-year-old widower whose
only daughter Ivy lives in Melbourne,
*Australia, with her ne'er-do-well hus-
band. Stranded as a sturdy relic of the past
in a modern commercial (but unnamed)
Singapore in which he finds 'hardly any
room to exist' (177), Whalley loses his savings in a bank crash and is forced to sell his
small ship, the *Fair Maid*, to supply his distant daughter with funds to open a boarding house. In the course of a long walk on
the Esplanade just after the sale, Captain
Whalley encounters the Master-Attendant,
his old friend Captain Ned Eliott, who is
seeking a new master for the *Sofala*. This is
no easy task, because the ship is owned by
her unsavoury chief engineer, a compulsive
gambler and 'mutinous sort of chap' (204)
named Massy, who bought the ship with
his second-prize winnings from the Manila
lottery and treats his captains so badly that
Captain Eliott has advised him to find one
willing to invest something in the ship.
That night, Whalley invests what is left of
his savings in the *Sofala* with the understanding that in three years the entire sum
will be refunded to him or his daughter 'in
case of anything' (214), although repay-
ment can be postponed for one year if
Whalley should leave the ship before the
end of his term.

The *Sofala* narrowly misses running
aground on the bar at Batu Beru, which

confirms the ambitious mate, Mr Sterne, in his suspicions that something is wrong with the captain's eyes. He tries to inform Massy, but is rudely rebuffed and waits to use the discovery to his own best advantage. That evening at dinner Whalley confesses to Mr Van Wyk, the resident trader in Batu Beru, that he is going blind but must finish this last voyage in order to collect his daughter's savings. Van Wyk seals Sterne's lips with a promise to have him appointed master once Whalley has finished the trip. Massy, blind to the Captain's dilemma and enraged at having to pay back money he has already lost in the lottery, decides to wreck the ship and claim the insurance. He places bits of iron in his coat and hangs it near the compass to throw the ship off course and cause it to run aground. Massy forgets about low tide, and the ship strikes a reef. Whalley, discovering Massy's trick, decides to go down with his ship and transfers the bits of iron to his own pockets.

Critics have often seen 'The End of the Tether' as a story of old age which complements the 'Youth' of the first story and the experience of *Marlow and *Kurtz in 'Heart of Darkness'. Whalley's obsessive concern with his daughter's welfare recalls *Almayer's relation to Nina in Conrad's first novel, *Almayer's Folly*. Comparisons have also been made between Whalley's sacrifice for his ungrateful daughter and the cases of *Shakespeare's *King Lear* or Balzac's *Le Père Goriot*. Perhaps the bleakness of its theme has prevented critics from appreciating the rich humour of the story, with its cast of assorted fools and grotesques whose various follies blind them to their most immediate experience: Whalley's physical blindness is equalled by his inability to see that he has lost his daughter; the odious Massy is too blinded by raging greed to see that the captain is blind; and the silent second engineer can only speak his mind when he is roaring drunk. Schwarz (1980: 119–30) discusses the story as a 'great tale of the complex problem of ageing, and of the broader problem of man's movement through time' (119). In 'Conrad's "Unreal City": Singapore in "The End of the Tether"' (in Moore (ed.) 1992:

85–96), J. H. Stape compares details of Captain Whalley's long walk with Conrad's experience of Singapore.

England. Conrad first touched English soil at Lowestoft on 10 June 1878 and spent most of the next fifteen years in the *British Merchant Service before devoting himself to the life of writing upon which his fame rests. In each of his careers Conrad can be seen to have contributed towards the life of his adopted country: he sailed under the Red Ensign as a British sailor in the last great phase of empire; and, as an author, his early writing quickly earned comparisons with his contemporaries Rudyard *Kipling and Robert Louis *Stevenson, while his subsequent place in the canon of English literature was assured when the influential critic F. R. Leavis (1948) identified Conrad as the successor to Jane Austen, George Eliot, and Henry *James, in the 'great tradition' of the English novel. As a remark he made to David *Bone in 1923 demonstrates, Conrad never lost sight of the fact that his British status depended upon a conscious decision: 'I am more British than you are. You are only British because you could not help it' (quoted in *Landfall at Sunset* (Duckworth, 1955), 160). In 1886, the year in which Conrad was naturalized, he claimed: 'When speaking, writing or thinking in English the word Home always means for me the hospitable shores of Great Britain' (*CL*, i. 12). In the mind of the Anglophile Pole, England was always associated with liberty. Tadeusz *Bobrowski, Conrad's uncle and guardian, expressed his wish to see his young ward take up British citizenship and become 'a free citizen of a free country' (*CPB*, 88). For his part, Conrad speaks with evident pride of the liberty 'which can only be found under the English flag' (*CL*, ii. 230).

Conrad's patriotism is evident in his writings in such scenes as the paean to Britain at the end of *The Nigger of the 'Narcissus'*, published in the year of Queen Victoria's Diamond Jubilee. More subtly, this patriotic ideal is represented in the combination of *work ethic and solidarity in

'Youth', where the motto of the *Judea*, 'Do or Die', reflects the determination of the all-English crew. But the expression in Conrad's fiction of his evident love of his adopted country is generally tempered with realism. For instance, when Hollis presents Karain with the Jubilee sixpence depicting Queen Victoria in 'Karain: A Memory', he tells him: 'She commands a spirit, too—the spirit of her nation; a masterful, conscientious, unscrupulous, unconquerable devil . . . that does a lot of good—incidentally . . . a lot of good . . . at times' (*Tales of Unrest*, 49). Curiously, those who flaunt their status as Englishmen in the fiction—like *Donkin, or Martin Ricardo in *Victory*—are presented unsympathetically. At times, Conrad's comments upon England in his *letters are tinged with nostalgia for its lost political influence and values. Writing to Roger *Casement in December 1903, he says that 'in the old days England had in her keeping the conscience of Europe' (*CL*, iii. 96), while the setbacks suffered by the Conservatives in the general election of 1885 evoke the sweeping comment: 'England was the only barrier to the pressure of infernal doctrines born in continental back-slums. Now there is nothing!' (*CL*, i. 16). In 'Heart of Darkness', *Marlow subtly challenges England's insularity when he mentions that his relations live on the Continent 'because it's cheap and not so nasty as it looks, they say' (*Youth*, 53). Usually, though, Conrad's attitude towards England is one of evident affection. In a letter to Edmund *Gosse from Capri in April 1905, he complained about the slow progress of his writing abroad thus: 'It's all very well for Englishmen born to their inheritance to fling verse and prose from Italy back to their native shores. I, in my state of honourable adoption, find that I need the moral support, the sustaining influence of English atmosphere even from day to day' (*CL*, iii. 227). There is also something delightful in Conrad's humorously professing himself 'scandalized' by Christopher Sandeman's 'unpatriotic choice of disease' in 1917 (*LL*, ii. 183): Sandeman had caught German measles!

Conrad's sense of his own national identity balances his identification with his adopted country with his continued allegiance to *Poland. In a letter of 5 December 1903 to Kazimierz Waliszewski, a Polish historian, Conrad famously defined himself as 'homo duplex': 'Both at sea and on land my point of view is English, from which the conclusion should not be drawn that I have become an Englishman. This is not the case. Homo duplex has in my case more than one meaning' (*CL*, iii. 89). That said, it is interesting that during his visits to *Champel, Conrad passed himself off as an Englishman (see *JCC*, 176–8). The idea of Conrad as 'duplex' extends to the presentation of cultures in his first novel, *Almayer's Folly*, where he reveals himself to be Janus-faced, both confirming and challenging imperial assumptions, perhaps reflecting his national status as both insider and outsider. Similarly, 'Amy Foster' (*Typhoon*) dramatizes the plight of a young Slavic immigrant to England. Conrad spent most of his writing life in the southeast corner of England, where he forged enduring friendships with many of the most brilliant writers and personalities of the day, including John *Galsworthy, R. B. Cunninghame *Graham, H. G. *Wells, Henry James, and Ford Madox *Ford. He also knew such international figures as George Bernard Shaw, Bertrand *Russell, André *Gide, and Maurice Ravel. Inevitably, his English friendships gave Conrad a sense of belonging. In March 1897, he referred to a letter he had received from Helen Watson, Ted *Sanderson's fiancée, as representing 'a high assurance of being accepted, admitted within, the people and the land of my choice' (*CL*, i. 347). Conrad was taken up and supported by the literary establishment both artistically—in the advice and encouragement he received from Edward *Garnett, for instance—and materially in the form of literary *grants: for instance, the Royal Literary Fund awarded him £300 in 1902 (about five times the annual salary of an adult male) and £200 in 1908, while he received £500 from the Royal Bounty Special Service Fund in 1905. In 1910 Conrad was awarded a Civil List

Pension of £100 per annum (which his improved financial circumstances enabled him to renounce in 1917). Official recognitions of his work included the offer of honorary degrees from various universities and, in May 1924, the offer of a knighthood from the Prime Minister, Ramsay Mac-Donald, all of which he declined.

Although, as many of his contemporaries testify, Conrad never fully mastered English pronunciation, he repeatedly voiced his love of—one might almost say his seduction by—the English language. Recalling his first encounter with the language in *A Personal Record*, he refers to English as 'the speech of my secret choice, of my future, of long friendships, of the deepest affections, of hours of toil and hours of ease, and of solitary hours too, of books read, of thoughts pursued, of remembered emotions—of my very dreams!' (136). He told Hugh *Walpole in June 1918: 'You may take it from me that if I had not known English I wouldn't have written a line for print in my life' (*LL*, ii. 206). It was thus doubly painful to him when critics pointed to the 'foreignness' of his writing. In response to a review of *The Secret Agent* that praised his art as being 'alien to our national genius' (*CCH*, 195), Conrad complained to Garnett: 'I've been so cried up of late as a sort of freak, an amazing bloody foreigner writing in English' (*CL*, iii. 488). Conrad maintained that he 'had to work like a coalminer in his pit quarrying all my English sentences out of a black night', and he pronounced himself 'too English' for one American magazine (*CL*, iv. 112, 307). He was particularly stung by Robert Lynd's review of *A Set of Six*, which described him as 'without either country or language' (*CCH*, 211), and responded by questioning Lynd's competence in a letter to Garnett and asking mischievously: 'Couldn't someone speak to him quietly and suggest he should go behind a counter and weigh out margarine by the sixpennyworth?' (*CL*, iv. 108). Such attacks were rare, and Conrad could also on occasion profess himself 'the spoiled child of the critics' (*CL*, ii. 313). Nonetheless, the 'duplex' nature of his national identity which had dogged him

through life followed him to the grave: despite the fact that he had spent half his lifetime living and writing in England, Virginia *Woolf still referred to Conrad as 'our guest' in the obituary she wrote for the *Times Literary Supplement* on 14 August 1924.   AHS

English Review, The. Ford Madox *Ford founded this monthly literary journal in 1908 with the financial backing of Arthur *Marwood, the practical assistance of his assistant editor Douglas Goldring, and considerable help and moral support from Conrad, in whose Someries *home the first issue of the journal was put together in readiness for its December début. Caught up in the excitement of Ford's venture, Conrad interrupted his work on *Under Western Eyes* to compose a series of autobiographical sketches, 'Some Reminiscences' (later collected and retitled *A Personal Record*), and two book reviews for its early issues. He may also have suggested the periodical's name and almost certainly helped to fashion its manifesto, which, in an accompanying circular, promised a journal for 'grown-up minds', its contents marked by 'either distinction of individuality or force of conviction, either literary gifts or earnestness of purpose, whatever the purpose may be—the criterion of inclusion being the clarity of diction, the force of' the illuminative value of the views expressed'.

An inspired and talented editor, Ford succeeded in bringing together the work of older writers (Thomas Hardy, H. G. *Wells, Henry *James, and Conrad) with the best of a younger generation (Ezra Pound, D. H. Lawrence, Norman *Douglas, and Wyndham Lewis). Brief though its life was under Ford's editorship, the *English Review* was the finest literary review of its day. However, with his sudden access to power and prestige Ford seems, by common consent, to have fallen prey to an intoxicated sense of self-importance, becoming, according to Wells, 'a great system of assumed personas and dramatized selves' (1934: ii. 617). New complications in his private life led to serious strains in his hitherto close relationship with Conrad, who by April 1909 was objecting to Ford's 'mania for managing the universe, worse even in form than in substance' (*CL*, iv. 214–15). In July 1909, what Conrad regarded as Ford's high-handed audacity in questioning the completeness of his contribution to the *English Review* caused their decisive estrangement. Not long after, in December 1909, when the journal was in debt to the tune of £2,800 and acquired by a new owner, the financier Sir Alfred Mond, Ford's brief reign as editor ended. Conrad continued to contribute to the journal under Ford's successor, Austin Harrison. In 1937, the journal was absorbed into the *National Review*.

English teacher. See TEACHER OF LANGUAGES.

epigraphs. Jessie Conrad commented that 'Conrad's title-page quotations had always a close and direct relation to the contents of the book itself, and . . . often expressed the mood in which the work was written' (*JCKH*, 49). All of the volumes of Conrad's fiction published during his lifetime have epigraphs, with the exception of *The Secret Agent*. Further, his chosen epigraphs were from dead authors, with the exception of those for *Under Western Eyes*, '*Twixt Land and Sea*, and *The Shadow-Line*. Watts comments that 'sometimes an epigraph implies Conrad's knowledge of the [original] context and invites the reader to apply both the quoted phrases and their context to the Conradian novel or tale, while at other times it seems to have been chosen in a more casual way for its immediate thematic associations' (1989: 45). Whatever their origin, all of Conrad's epigraphs serve a powerfully proleptic function in evoking in time-honoured, aphoristic form the dominant moral, social, and philosophic postulates in his fiction.

Almayer's Folly: 'Qui de nous n'a eu sa terre promise, son jour d'extase et sa fin en exil?' [Which of us has not had his promised land, his day of ecstasy, and his end in exile?]. This extract is taken (in slightly misquoted form) from the 24 April 1852 entry in the *Journal intime* (published 1883–7) of Henri-Frédéric Amiel, a Protestant professor of philosophy at the University of Geneva. It occurs in a passage in which Amiel laments the evanescence of youthful dreams of immortality and the inevitability of disillusionment in adult life, as exemplified in the fate of Moses. Watt argues that the Amielian context makes the epigraph 'more appropriate to Conrad's youthful romantic reveries than to Almayer's more material aspirations' with the effect that 'in the novel this imputed universality of theme hardly stands up to examination' (1980: 66). This judgement underestimates, however, the way in which Amielian resonances extend beyond *Almayer to embrace, for example, Captain Tom *Lingard's expectation of 'the promised land' (8), Dain's sensation of entering through the 'gates of paradise' (73), and Nina Almayer's flight to the anticipated paradise of Dain's Bali.

An Outcast of the Islands: 'Pues el delito mayor | Del hombre es haber nacito' [For man's greatest crime is that he was born]. These lines, with a slight misspelling, are from Pedro Calderón de la Barca's play with a Polish setting *La vida es sueño* (Life is a Dream; 1635), i. ii. However, Conrad probably found them in Arthur *Schopenhauer's *Die Welt als Wille und Vorstellung* (1818; expanded 1844), vol. i, book iv, where, after quoting Calderón's lines, Schopenhauer continues: 'Why should it not be a crime, since, according to eternal law, death follows upon it? Calderón has merely expressed in these lines the Christian dogma of original sin.'

The Nigger of the 'Narcissus': '. . . My Lord in his discourse discovered a great deal of love to this ship.' According to Conrad, he spotted these words in a volume of Samuel Pepys's *Diary* (first published 1825) in Henry *James's library, while awaiting his host. As Pepys's entry for 30 March 1660 indicates, his 'Lord' was his cousin and employer Sir Edward Montagu. The 'ship' in question was the *Nazeby* in which the exiled King Charles II returned to England on the restoration of the monarchy in 1660. Watts points out that in addition to its obvious aptness as a eulogy, 'the epigraph may serve to emphasize the conservative implications of a text which describes the failure of an attempt to subvert the captain's authority and to foment mutiny aboard the *Narcissus*. As traditional rule was restored, after turmoil, to "the ship of state", so traditional order is restored, after turmoil, to the ship *Narcissus*' (1988: 133).

Tales of Unrest: 'Be it thy course to busy giddy minds | With foreign quarrels.' Drawn from Henry IV's last speech to his son Hal in *Shakespeare's 2 Henry IV* (1597), IV. v. 213–14, these lines may have appealed to Conrad as a way of evoking the rhetorical effect of his own 'unrestful' and largely 'foreign' tales upon a conventionally minded audience.

Lord Jim: 'It is certain my conviction gains infinitely the moment another soul will believe in it.' So reads the first English edition, although for 'my', the later Dent's Collected Edition reads 'any', possibly the result of a compositorial error. This aphorism originally belongs to Novalis (pseudonym of Friedrich von Hardenberg) and fragment 153 of his *Das allgemeine Brouillon* (1794), where Novalis explains the power of indirect quotation. In translation, the passage reads: 'It is certain that an opinion gains greatly, as soon as I know that someone is convinced by it: it acquires veracity.' However, according to Watt (1980: 40 n.), it is probable that Conrad was using Thomas *Carlyle's translation of this aphorism in *On Heroes, Hero-Worship, and the Heroic in History* (1841), Lecture II. While the epigraph has an obvious link with the comfort *Jim derives from sharing his story with *Marlow, it may also embrace the author's needed relationship with the reader through the created novel, since in *A Personal Record* Conrad again uses this aphorism, adding: 'And what is a novel if not a conviction of our fellow-men's existence strong enough to take upon itself a form of imagined life clearer than reality and

whose accumulated verisimilitude of selected episodes puts to shame the pride of documentary history?' (15).

Youth: '. . . but the Dwarf answered: "No, something human is dearer to me than the wealth of the world."' Originally Conrad planned to preface this volume with lines from John Keats's *Endymion* (1818) and a dedication to his socialist friend R. B. Cunninghame *Graham but, deferring to his Tory publisher William *Blackwood, he transferred both dedication and epigraph to the *Typhoon* volume. The *Youth* collection was instead dedicated to Jessie Conrad and bore a new inscription from Grimm's *Tales* (1812–22). When questioned by the puzzled Jessie about the new choice, Conrad apparently replied that it had been selected 'not [with reference] to the text, but to the dedication [to her] alone' (*JCKH*, 49). The implications of the epigraph are interestingly spelled out in Claude-Nöel Thomas's note to the Pléiade edition of *Conrad: Œuvres* (Paris: Gallimard, 1985), ii. 1248–9.

Typhoon: 'Far as the mariner on highest mast | Can see all around upon the calmest vast. | So wide was Neptune's hall . . .' These lines, slightly misquoted, come from John Keats's *Endymion* (1818), III. 866–8. See the previous entry.

Nostromo: 'So foul a sky clears not without a storm.' As the proofs of the novel indicate, Conrad originally chose—no doubt for its mainly ironic application—an extract from Sir Walter Scott's 'The Lay of the Last Minstrel' (1805), III, stanza 2: 'Love rules the court, the camp, the grove.' His final choice from Shakespeare's *King John* (1590), IV. ii. 109, was presumably intended to link the political treachery and instability of John's troublesome reign with that of Charles *Gould's *Sulaco. The epigraph may also reflect upon the mood of Conrad's own 'troublesome' composition.

A Set of Six: 'Les petites marionnettes | Font, font, font | Trois petits tours | Et puis s'en vont' [The little puppets | Do, do, do |

Three quick turns I And then are gone]. This French nursery rhyme is a variation on one of the *Chansons lointaines* (1841) of the Swiss writer Juste Olivier. The version used by Conrad is, however, almost certainly derived from Anatole *France's 'M. Guy de Maupassant et les conteurs français' in *La Vie littéraire* (2nd series), where France sees in this rhyme a perfect crystallization of *Maupassant's view of life. For Conrad's own pleasure in watching marionettes and their 'impassibility in love[,] in crime, in mirth, in sorrow', see *CL*, i. 419.

The Mirror of the Sea: 'for this miracle or this wonder troubleth me right gretly' (title-page). This epigraph derives from Geoffrey Chaucer's translation of Boethius' *De Consolatione Philosophae*, book IV, prose vi, 2–5, where it concludes the speaker's plea to the spirit of philosophy 'to unwrappen the hid causes of thinges and to discovere me the resouns covered with derknesses'. The work itself carries a further motto—on the theme of mutability—from Chaucer's 'The Franklin's Tale' 1160–1: 'And shippes by the brinke comen and gon, I And in swich forme endure a day or two.'

The Secret Agent has no epigraph, but Conrad supplied one for H.-D. *Davray's 1912 French translation, using words spoken by the *Professor in the novel (309): 'Madness and despair! Give me that for a lever, and I'll move the world.'

Under Western Eyes: 'I would take liberty from any hand as a hungry man would snatch a piece of bread.' This novel and *The Shadow-Line* are the only ones in the canon to employ words from the text itself as a motto. In this case, Conrad uses Natalia *Haldin's words (135), although in slightly misquoted form. In 'Speech and Writing in *Under Western Eyes*', in Sherry (ed.) 1976: 119–28, Avrom Fleishman considers the significance of this misquotation in relation to the novel's preoccupation with documents, the processes of transmission, and the status of spoken and written language.

'*Twixt Land and Sea*: 'Life is a tragic folly I Let us laugh and be jolly I Away with melancholy I Bring me a branch of holly I Life is a tragic folly.' Conrad's friend Arthur *Symons composed this stanza after reading 'A Smile of Fortune', one of the stories collected in the volume.

Within the Tides: '. . . Go, make you ready.' From Hamlet's speech to the players in Shakespeare's *Hamlet* (1601), III. i. 45. The epigraph and its original context foreshadow both a leading theme of the collection—the spectacle of characters who, like dramatic players, act out a variety of conventional roles—and its intended effect upon the reader, that of awakening 'guilty' recognition.

Chance: 'Those that hold that all things are governed by fortune had not erred, had they not persisted there.' From Sir Thomas Browne's *Religio Medici* (1642), part 1, section 18. In 'The Epigraph of Conrad's *Chance*', *Nineteenth-Century Fiction*, 9 (1954), 209–10, Bruce Harkness points out that Browne proceeds to say that such believers in fortune would not have erred if they had recognized that behind the workings of chance lies a divine pattern, so that 'all things begin and end with the Almighty'. Harkness argues that the epigraph renders the novel's title ironic and confirms that 'the basis of the novel, far from being a representation of accidental occurrences, is the reverse of chance'. In reality, he concludes, a powerful determinative causality is at work in the novel.

Victory: 'Of calling shapes, and beckoning shadows dire, I And airy tongues that syllable men's names I On sands and shores and desert wildernesses.' From John Milton's *Comus* (1634), the epigraph recalls a moral and philosophic allegory from which the novel appears to borrow some of its generic features. More specifically, Milton's work prefigures through Comus, his 'rout of monsters', and their assault upon the lady both the representation of Mr *Jones's animal-like companions and the subsequent challenge to *Lena's chastity and courage. Milton's poem, like *Victory*, also echoes Shakespeare's *The Tempest.*

The Shadow-Line: 'Worthy of my undying regard' (title-page). Conrad explained that these words 'are quoted from the text of the book itself [100]; and, though one of my critics surmised that they applied to the ship, it is evident . . . that they refer to the men of that ship's company' ('Author's Note', p. viii). The story carries a further motto from Charles Baudelaire's sonnet 'La Musique' in *Les Fleurs du mal* (1857): '—
. . . D'autres fois, calme plat, grand miroir I De mon désespoir' [At other times, dead calm, the large mirror of my despair]. Pointing out that the epigraph contains one of Conrad's favourite metaphors, that of the 'mirror' of the sea, Stanisław Modrzewski, in 'Conrad's Idea of Culture in *The Shadow-Line*', *CON-texts*, 1 (1997), 41–4, offers a subtle analysis of the epigraph's reverberations.

The Arrow of Gold: 'Celui qui n'a connu que des hommes polis et raisonnables, ou ne connait pas l'homme, ou ne le connait qu'a demi' [He who has known only polite and rational men either does not know mankind or only knows half of it]. Borrowed from Jean de La Bruyère's 'De l'homme', *Les Caractères* (1688), although with accents missing, this epigraph might serve as a rubric for the whole of Conrad's work.

The Rescue: '"Allas!" quod she, "that ever this sholde happe! I For wende I never, by possibilitee, I That swich a monstre or merveille mighte be!"' In Watts's words, these lines from Geoffrey Chaucer's 'The Franklin's Tale', 1342–4, 'invoke a tale of trust and generosity which provides a potent and bitterly ironic counterpoint to Conrad's narrative of incommunication, frustration and betrayal' (1989: 45). See also Joel R. Kehler, 'A Note on the Epigraph to Conrad's *The Rescue*', *English Language Notes*, 12 (1975), 184–7.

The Rover: 'Sleep after toyle, port after stormie seas, I Ease after warre, death after life, does greatly please.' This epigraph, from Edmund Spenser's *The Faerie Queene*

(1590), I. ix. 40, is part of an address by Despaire soliciting the Red Crosse Knight to commit suicide, a context that Conrad clearly did not want the reader to recall. The words appear on Conrad's gravestone in Canterbury cemetery. See also Eloise Knapp Hay, 'Joseph Conrad's Last Epigraph', *Conradiana*, 2: 3 (1970–1), 9–15.

Epstein, Jacob (1880–1959; knighted 1954), sculptor. Jacob Epstein undertook his famous bust of Conrad, now at the National Portrait Gallery, London, in the last year of the author's life. In March of that year Conrad watched the sculpture take shape: 'The bust of Ep. has grown truly monumental. It is a marvellously effective piece of sculpture, with even something more than masterly interpretation in it' (*CTF*, 233). The National Portrait Gallery in London refused the original casting of Epstein's Conrad bust, although a slightly damaged casting was later accepted. In his later recollections *Let There Be Sculpture: An Autobiography* (Joseph, 1940), 89–94, extracted in *JCIR*, 168–71, the sculptor gave an extended pen-portrait of the aged Conrad as 'courtly and direct' in manners, but one whose 'neurasthenia forced him at times to outbursts of rage', concluding: 'He was crippled with rheumatism, crochety, nervous, and ill. He said to me, "I am finished."' They conversed about some of Conrad's literary antipathies—including Herman Melville, whom Conrad accused of knowing 'nothing' about the sea, George Meredith, and D. H. Lawrence, who in Conrad's view had started promisingly but gone wrong ('Filth. Nothing but obscenities'). For Henry *James, on the other hand, he had 'unqualified admiration'. As against Conrad's own declarations (in the 'Author's Note' to *A Personal Record* and elsewhere), Epstein claimed that Conrad 'said it was a toss up at one time whether he would write in English or French'.

examinations (merchant service). During the 1880s Conrad the seaman underwent successive examinations for the certificates of second mate, first mate, and master, although he did not pass all of them at the first sitting. Administered by the Marine Department of the Board of Trade, these examinations all took place at St Katherine's Dock House, Tower Hill, London E1. *A Personal Record* (chapter 6) contains Conrad's later recollection of his 'ordeals' but makes no mention of his failures; he also draws upon his examination experiences in 'Outside Literature' (*Last Essays*) and the opening pages of *Chance*. The form and content of the examinations, all of which combined an oral and a written test, were set out in *Notice of Examinations of Masters and Mates and Engineers under the Merchant Shipping Act of 1854* (1870) and show the increasingly sophisticated knowledge of navigation and seamanship needed by Conrad to pass each examination. Several volumes owned or mentioned by Conrad indicate the kinds of textbooks he used to prepare himself: *Captain Alston's Seamanship* (new edn., 1871; first pub. 1860 as Alfred Henry Alston, *Seamanship*), Robert White Stevens, *On the Stowage of Ships and their Cargoes* (1858), and *Seamanship Both in Theory and Practice* (1807).

In preparation for his second-mate's examination in 1880, Conrad, aged 22, took a tutorial course under John Newton, head of the Navigation School in Dock Street, London E1, and author of standard handbooks on seamanship. Candidates for the examination were required to have completed at least four years' service at *sea. In his application, Conrad appears to have misrepresented his previous service: as Najder points out, 'the entire duration of his service [in French ships] amounted to thirteen months and five days, not [as he submitted] three years' (*JCC*, 65). With Captain James Rankin as his examiner, he passed his examination on 28 May 1880, much to his uncle Tadeusz *Bobrowski's 'profound pleasure' (*CPB*, 64). Najder further comments that from Conrad's point of view 'the most difficult condition to meet must have been that "foreigners must prove to the satisfaction of the Examiners that they can speak and write the English language sufficiently well to perform the duties required of them on board a British vessel"' (*JCC*, 66).

On 17 November 1884, Conrad, aged 26, made an attempt at the first-mate's examination, open to candidates with five years' service at sea. He failed, having been found wanting on the Day's Work section of the navigation test. On 3 December 1884, he passed the examination successfully, with Captain Peter Thompson as examiner.

On 28 July 1886, Conrad, aged 28, made his first attempt to meet the more demanding requirements of the master's examination, open to candidates with six years' service at sea. He was unsuccessful, having been found wanting in arithmetic and again on the Day's Work section of the navigation test. Najder comments: 'In view of the fact that Korzeniowski was certainly not unintelligent, one cannot help suspecting that the roots of the problem were his inadequate knowledge of English and his foreign origin' (*JCC*, 91). Just over three months later, he successfully re-sat his master's examination and received his precious signed blue slip (dated 11 November). For one of these examinations, Conrad seems to have had a Captain Sterry as examiner.

Tadeusz Bobrowski was quick to greet his nephew as the 'Ordin. Master in the British Merchant Service!! May he live long!!' (*CPB*, 113), although Conrad did not go on to take the Extra Master's examination and achieve a yet higher qualification as Bobrowski hoped. The account in *A Personal Record* recreates with hindsight something of the symbolic importance the 28-year-old attached to his newly won status. With his recent *naturalization, it marked an important and decisive stage in his cultural passage into English life: 'It was a fact, I said to myself, that I was now a British master mariner beyond a doubt.' In 'mastering' a profession, he also felt that he had answered the charges that some had made about his departure from *Poland in 1874 and so 'vindicated' himself 'from what had been cried upon as a stupid obstinacy or a fantastic caprice' (120). For further details, see Hans van Marle, 'Plucked and Passed on Tower Hill: Conrad's Examination Ordeals', *Conradiana*, 8 (1976), 99–109, and Meyers, 65–73.

F

Falk. The eponymous hero of 'Falk', Christian Falk is a bearded and Herculean Scandinavian tug-boat owner who is driven to cannibalism. By presenting Falk at the outset of the story as the narrator's 'enemy' (*Typhoon*, 147), Conrad employs a form of *delayed decoding, the effect of which is to transform Falk into a troublesomely unknown quantity, frustrate the reader's desire for simple certitudes, and prompt the question of whether the primitive life-principle embodied in an apparently unsociable 'strange beast' (213) like Falk can be reconciled with any conception of what is 'naturally' human. When, at the end of the story, Falk is suddenly identified as an unwilling transgressor and taboo-breaker, his confession shocks only the 'world proof' (156): for the reader, by contrast, Falk's confession locks into place the story's developing juxtaposition between the depth and intensity of the primitive urge for self-preservation and narrow bourgeois habits, which, as the story ironically shows through two German characters Hermann and *Schomberg, often disguise an egotism more meanly self-regarding than Falk's. Essential to the challenge Falk projects is his ambiguous position at the axis-point of colliding value-systems: classical (as centaur and man-beast (162)), *Darwinian (the stronger animal who survives at the expense of the weaker), *Nietzschean (as 'a tall man, living in a world of dwarfs' (213)), and bourgeois (through his desire for respectability, home, and marriage). From a point of hindsight, even Falk's name appears to be a form of teasing provocation in conflating 'Christian' with suggestions of lordly predatoriness (Swedish *falken*, 'falcon').

'Falk: A Reminiscence', a novella of 26,000 words, was written immediately after 'Typhoon' during the first three months of 1901. The story did not attract any magazine publishers, being one of only two Conrad stories (along with 'The Return') to suffer this fate. Edwardian editors were either offended by its subject matter or disliked the fact that the young unnamed girl in the story (Hermann's niece) was not allowed to utter a single word. The story was first published in 1903 in the *Typhoon* volume.

Events in 'Falk' are narrated by an experienced sea captain in a *Thameside inn who looks back to the difficult circumstances that attended his first command in *Bangkok. Frustrated by numerous checks and delays, the young captain of that time finds some relief by visiting the *Diana*, the floating home of a German sea captain (Hermann), his family, and niece. Hermann's young niece has attracted Falk, a Scandinavian owner of the only tug-boat on the river. The narrator-captain cannot move his ship without Falk's services, but Falk, thinking him a rival for the girl's hand, adamantly refuses to undertake the task. At one point Falk actually abducts the *Diana* and at another he works behind the young captain's back to ensure that he cannot hire an alternative pilot. During a significant confrontation with Falk in *Schomberg's hostelry, the narrator assures him that he has no designs on Hermann's niece and agrees to become an ambassador and go-between for Falk and the young girl. The surprise ending to the tale coincides with Falk's momentous confession: that some years previously, when on board a stranded and distressed ship, he was driven to eating human flesh. Although Hermann and his wife are shocked and cannot bear the sight of Falk, his niece, 'olympian and simple . . . the siren to fascinate that dark navigator' (239), proves to be a soulmate and marries him.

The story illustrates Conrad's characteristic method of grafting together different kinds of sources. The events surrounding the young narrator-captain's difficulties in making a departure from Bangkok are loosely based upon Conrad's own experiences of first command in the *Otago* in the same port in 1888. By contrast, for details of Falk's cannibalism Conrad probably drew upon historic accounts such as he might have read in *The Times* (7 November 1884), 11, which reported the case of two seamen who, afloat in an open boat for many days, killed a ship's boy and (with a third seaman) ate his flesh. Their death sentences were later commuted to six months in jail after a defence which included the argument that 'there was an inevitable necessity that one life should be sacrificed in order that the other three might be saved, and . . . they were justified in doing so in selecting the weakest'.

Although not generally numbered among Conrad's finest stories, 'Falk' has attracted some lively and appreciative commentary, especially from critics who respond to the part played by astringent comedy and the use of contrasting value-systems in making up what Kirschner aptly describes as a 'philosophical black comedy' (1990: 18). Conrad himself summarized its provocative central point thus: 'The idea: contrast of commonplace sentimentality and the uncorrupted point-of-view of an almost primitive man (Falk himself) who regards the preservation of life as the supreme and moral law' (*CL*, ii. 402). The story's unsettling effect does not simply rest with the suggestion that Falk's transgressive 'crime' of eating human flesh is, in reality, the natural operation of the *Darwinian law of the survival of the fittest. More provocatively, events reveal this same law to be acted out in all aspects of Falk's composition, his powerfully centaur-like maleness, his sexual desire, monopoly of trade on the river, pursuit of Hermann's niece (which is described as an ancient chase), and his quest for a secure home. Nor is the contrast between the powerfully 'primitive' Falk and world-proof citizens like Hermann and his wife a settled one. The images of gastronomy pervading all aspects of the tale imply the presence of

suppressed or disguised hungers beneath even the most conventional forms of bourgeois life. Such images are also used to make a playfully self-reflexive joke upon the writer himself, since the story's opening Thameside frame also establishes a link between eating and the primitive urge to tell stories and make narratives. Although the young narrator-captain seems mainly important as an intermediary who serves the larger serio-comic ends of the story, he has been treated as a figure of interest in his own right and regarded as yet another of Conrad's young initiates whose narrative 'becomes his personal tribute to purity of passion in a world infested by duplicity and hypocrisy' (Schwarz 1980: 103).

While using a taboo subject to unsettle and tease, 'Falk' also makes certain concessions to an Edwardian magazine audience. Its unusual encouragement to endorse a transgressor like Falk is accompanied by a more conventional invitation to withdraw sympathy from Schomberg and Hermann, two Germanic villains who have their roots in the stock types of popular writing. The story's ending is also of a more popular kind since, instead of returning to the Thameside frame, Conrad prefers the secure note of a marriage between Falk and Hermann's niece, and, with it, the suggestion that the young unnamed woman, a 'tamer of strange beasts' (213), has been the agent of Falk's salvation. See also Bruce Johnson, 'Conrad's "Falk": Manuscript and Meaning', *Modern Language Quarterly*, 26 (1965), 267–84, and Tony Tanner, '"Gnawed Bones" and "Artless Tales": Eating and Narrative in Conrad', in Sherry (ed.) 1976: 17–36. The manuscript is held at the Beinecke Rare Book and Manuscript Library, Yale University, and a typescript at Texas Tech University, Lubbock.

'Familiar Preface, A'. In Conrad's letter to the American collector John *Quinn of 11 December 1913, offering to sell him the manuscript for £20, he described 'A Familiar Preface' as the 'best piece of purely abstract English I ever wrote' (*CL*, v. 313). As well as painting an autobiographical picture of his twin lives, both as an Anglo-Pole and as a sailor-turned-author, Conrad's 'Preface' (which was signed 'J.C.K.', the 'K' standing for 'Korzeniowski', Conrad's family name) addresses the motivation for writing a work such as *A Personal Record*, in which he stands revealed to his public. As he says, while an artist stands confessed in his work, he remains yet 'a figure behind the veil; a suspected rather than a seen presence'; in *A Personal Record*, by contrast, 'there is no such veil' (p. xiii). It constitutes 'a personal note in the margin of the public page' of his fiction (p. xv).

'A Familiar Preface' begins by asserting the claims of felt or intuitive truth over those of reason and arguing that the sound of a word, rather than the argument to which it contributes, carries its persuasive appeal. In this, Conrad expands upon ideas about the role of the artist he had expressed in the 'Preface' to *The Nigger of the 'Narcissus'*. This claim serves to introduce the source of much of his artistic inspiration: his own past. To this end, Conrad's claim that 'One's literary life must turn frequently for sustenance to memories and seek discourse with the shades' (p. xv) provides a rationale for the work to follow. Next, Conrad addresses the criticism that he eschews open displays of sentiment in his autobiographical writing by arguing that his reserve is less a matter of emotional restraint than a safeguard necessary to the dignity of one's work: 'There can be nothing more humiliating than to see the shaft of one's emotion miss the mark of either laughter or tears' (p. xvi). This restraint combines with the belief that unchecked emotion may lead to the loss of self-control which, as 'the first condition of good service' (p. xvii), was a conviction he had acquired during his seafaring years. Here, and throughout *A Personal Record* generally, Conrad emphasizes the consistency and coherence of his lives as seaman and artist, implying that the former provided a basis for the latter. Nor is Conrad's attitude to displays of emotion to be taken as a weakness, for he claims: 'An historian of hearts is not an historian of emotions, yet he penetrates further, restrained as he may

be, since his aim is to reach the very fount of laughter and tears' (p. xix).

One of Conrad's important claims in the later part of 'A Familiar Preface' has attracted considerable attention: 'Those who read me know my conviction that the world, the temporal world, rests on a few very simple ideas; so simple that they must be as old as the hills. It rests notably, among others, on the idea of Fidelity' (p. xix). In keeping with the attempt to integrate his past and present lives, this sentiment stresses the importance of tradition, especially in the face of what he perceives to be the force of disruptive and irresponsible change: 'At a time when nothing which is not revolutionary in some way or other can expect to attract much attention I have not been revolutionary in my writings. The revolutionary spirit is mighty convenient in this, that it frees one from all scruples as regards ideas' (p. xix). So, against the 'fanaticism and intolerance' of revolutionary optimism, fidelity offers a form of inherited stability. 'A Familiar Preface' does not explicitly identify the 'few very simple ideas' of Conrad's creed, but in a letter to a Japanese admirer during the summer of 1911, when he was writing this preface, he wrote: 'As to my view of life it is contained in my books which are the sincere expression of my thoughts and feelings. . . . I respect courage, truth, fidelity, self-restraint and devotion to the ancient ideals of mankind; and I am sorry that, like most men, I fail in the practice of these simple virtues' (*CL*, iv. 457). The 25-page manuscript of 'A Familiar Preface' was sold for $700 at the auction of Quinn's collection in 1923. It is now held in the Berg Collection, New York Public Library.   AHS

feminist approaches. The male narrator in 'Because of the Dollars' reflects a common attitude in Conrad's fiction when he claims: 'Ours . . . was a bachelor crowd; in spirit anyhow, if not absolutely in fact. There might have been a few wives in existence, but if so they were invisible, distant, never alluded to' (*Within the Tides*, 175). Conrad is often described as 'a man's writer' because his novels deal with subjects traditionally supposed to be the preserve of men, including the European male's colonial 'burden', the *British Merchant Service, and politics, and endorse a code of conduct at once chivalric, stoical, and sceptical. This masculine focus was actively supported by early criticism. For instance, in a contemporary review, *The Nigger of the 'Narcissus'* was praised because 'There is not a petticoat in all Mr Conrad's pages' (*CCH*, 88). Similarly, in the 1950s, the *'achievement-and-decline' interpretation of Conrad's writing career, propounded by Moser (1957) and Guerard (1958) in particular, held that Conrad's decline as a novelist was linked to his increasing preoccupation with the 'uncongenial subject' of women and sexual relationships in his late fiction. Conrad's comment to Edward *Garnett about 'The Secret Sharer' is significant in this context: 'On the other hand the Secret Sharer, between you and me, is *it*. Eh? No damned tricks with girls there. Eh? Every word fits and there's not a single uncertain note' (*CL*, v. 128). Much of the fiction certainly excludes or silences women in a manner that is, at times, provocative, as when *Marlow distinguishes between men and women in *Chance*: 'As to honour—you know—it's a very fine mediaeval inheritance which women never got hold of . . . In addition they are devoid of decency' (63). Hardly surprisingly, Marlow later confesses: 'I am not a feminist' (146). It was, thus, fitting and timely that feminist criticism should turn its attention to Conrad's work and to the presentation of women within this 'man's world'.

In its present form, feminist literary criticism—whilst indebted to a tradition of thought and action that stretches back at least as far as Mary Wollstonecraft's *A Vindication of the Rights of Women* (1792)—is directly descended from the 'women's movement' of the 1960s, which began the process of questioning the authority and coherence of images of women in literature and revealing the narrative strategies used to disempower women. A feminist reading of a text is typically one that examines the representation of women in order to expose the underlying power relations to which they are subjected, and to challenge the strategies used to define women as 'other', or a 'lack', or part of 'nature'. Feminist critics have also exploited the close connection between feminism and postcolonialism in their readings: in post-colonial theory, the colonized subject rather than woman is characterized as 'other', but the strategies of subjugation are comparable. Hence, patriarchy, colonialism, racism, and sexism may be conflated, and colonialism comes to be seen as a hypermasculine construct that subordinates not just persons of colour but also women.

Three novels in particular in the canon have lent themselves to feminist rereadings: 'Heart of Darkness', *Under Western Eyes*, and *Chance*. Of these, the first has received the most rigorous attention. In her essay '"Too Beautiful Altogether": Patriarchal Ideology in *Heart of Darkness*' (in Murfin (ed.) 1989: 179–95), Johanna M. Smith argues that when Marlow describes *Kurtz's African mistress as an embodiment of the jungle, he fuses patriarchal and imperialist ideology: 'As the patriarchal ideology intends with its power of image-making to distance and hence conquer the woman's body, so the imperialist ideology intends with its power for good to distance and conquer the mysterious life of the jungle. And both the savage woman and the jungle are momentarily silenced by Marlow's images of them. As these images interrupt the movement of the narrative, however, they create gaps by which the reader can see the impossibility of such ideological containment' (186). In 'The Exclusion of the Intended from Secret Sharing in Conrad's *Heart of Darkness*', *Novel*, 20 (1987), 123–37, Nina Pelikan Straus casts a wider net, drawing on psychoanalysis and reader-response theory to argue that Marlow's tale is directed at a male 'reader-participator': 'these words are understood differently by feminist readers and by mainstream male commentators' (129). The artistic conventions of the novel are 'brutally sexist' (125), catering for the needs and desires of *male* readers and extending into the sexism perpetuated by the masculinist tradition of Conradian critics. Thus, Marlow's lie, a 'chivalric, albeit ironic, sacrifice', which excludes the *Intended from the truth (and thus the male world), simultaneously excludes female readers unless they 'are willing to suspend their womanliness far enough to forever disassociate themselves from the women characters in *Heart of Darkness*' (129). But Straus does find a role for the woman reader: arguing that Marlow's protectiveness of Kurtz's secret stems from unexpressible homocentric, but not necessarily homosexual, love (itself offering a paradigm of the male critic's relationship with Conrad), she claims that the 'guarding of secret knowledge is thus the undisclosed theme of *Heart of Darkness* which a woman reader can discover' (134).

In the characters of Peter *Ivanovitch, in *Under Western Eyes*, and, more particularly, Mrs *Fyne, in *Chance*, Conrad addresses the issue of feminism in both its political and social forms. In 'Feminism–Antifeminism in *Under Western Eyes*', *Conradiana*, 5: 2 (1973), 56–65, Maureen Fries argues that Conrad 'never treated women with more justice than in *Under Western Eyes*' (64). She maintains that while Peter Ivanovitch uses feminism as merely another anarchist weapon, Conrad is much closer to the spirit of feminism in his attitude to Natalia *Haldin and especially to Sophia Antonovna, whom Fries regards as 'the most individually and antistereotypically drawn of any woman in the tradition of the nineteenth-century political novel which begins with Stendhal' (63). The case of *Chance*, however, is less clear. Published in 1913, the novel clearly captured the topical spirit of feminism, which contributed to its success in the market place, and the sexual ideas of the militant feminist Mrs Fyne may reflect those of Sylvia Pankhurst. Mrs Fyne herself is satirically portrayed as an exploitative and possibly lesbian dogmatist who, together with the malicious governess, is responsible for Flora *de Barral's insecurities. Nowhere is Mrs Fyne's hypocrisy better illustrated than when she tries to thwart Flora's chances of success after the latter has espoused her very own

'feminist doctrine' (58). The fact that Flora's salvation comes through first Captain *Anthony and then Powell adds to the impression that this is an anti-feminist novel. As part of the advance publicity for the *serialization of *Chance* in the *New York Herald*, Conrad wrote: 'I aimed at treating my subject in a way which would interest women. That's all. I don't believe that women have to be written for specially as if they were infants' (*CL*, iv. 531–2). Yet, in the novel, when Marlow says that 'women . . . so often resemble intelligent children' (171), his expressed idea of purity cannot be separated from the implied idea of immaturity and dependence upon men. Conrad's portrayal of Carleon Anthony owes much to Coventry Patmore, the Victorian poet whose 'The Angel in the House' sentimentalized the Victorian wife and mother. The fact that Anthony, like Peter Ivanovitch, idealizes women in public whilst tyrannizing over them in private suggests that part of the novel's intention is to attack outmoded patriarchal attitudes toward women. To Hawthorn, *Chance* is flawed by Conrad's doubts and hesitations about feminism: 'narrative hesitations seem traceable back to ideological contradictions or confusions: it is as if Conrad's inability to decide what he believes gets in the way of the . . . narrative clarity' (1990: 140–1).

In the first book-length study of Conrad's work from a feminist perspective, Nadelhaft (1991) claims that 'Conrad wrote through the critical eyes of his women characters' (12). While this seems to overstate the case, she does demonstrate how the women in Conrad's Malay fiction pose a significant challenge to the dominance of white European colonialism and, by extension, to the social and political order of western Europe: 'Through narrative strategies, female characterizations, and reference to his own marginal status, Conrad found means to express in works prized by patriarchal culture a consistent and profound criticism of that very culture' (12).

Conrad's writings, like those of many male authors, often marginalize women, reveal familiar masculine fears in their presentation, and depict marriage as a trap to be avoided. These traits provide valid targets for feminist criticism; but Conrad's fiction itself exposes the connivance and hypocrisy of male dominance, and, with corrosive cynicism, debunks the claims of a patriarchy which results in the marital servitude of wives like Mrs Schomberg in *Victory* and Joanna Willems in *An Outcast of the Islands*. Conrad's recognition of the plight of women is dramatized in his neglected short story 'The Return', where the wife asserts to her husband: 'I've a right—a right to—to—myself' (*Tales of Unrest*, 185). AHS

films. By the end of the 20th century, almost 90 film or television adaptations were based on works by Joseph Conrad, ranging from melodramatic silent films to Francis Ford Coppola's classic *Apocalypse Now* and to the live, low-budget drama of 'TV theatre'. They also display a wide variety of film genres, from action/adventure epic to picaresque satire, and from historical costume drama to topical spoof. Many of these films were made not in Hollywood but in Europe, and some of them by well-known directors like Alfred Hitchcock, Ettore Scola, Ridley Scott, and Andrzej Wajda. Orson Welles, who wrote three Conrad filmscripts, apparently felt that Conrad's stories were ideal for the cinema, requiring little or no adaptation: 'I don't suppose there's any novelist except Conrad who can be put directly on the screen' (Orson Welles and Peter Bogdanovich, *This is Orson Welles* (HarperCollins, 1993), 262). But although Welles adapted 'Heart of Darkness' twice for radio, he failed to put any of his own Conrad films on the screen, and he conceded paradoxically: 'There's never been a Conrad movie, for the simple reason that nobody's ever done it as written' (ibid. 32).

The difficulty of doing Conrad 'as written' is not so much a matter of exotic settings or the technical requirements of gales and typhoons as it is essentially the problem of Conrad's indirect and often ironic narration. Films can present narratives in action, but they have difficulty 'showing'

the act of narrating from a perspective other than that of the camera, which, as the point of view from which the pictures are presented, tends to occupy the position of the narrator in a fictional work. In the succinct phrase of George Bluestone, 'Where the novel discourses, the film must picture' (*Novels into Film* (Berkeley and Los Angeles: University of California Press, 1957), 47). Films must show us *Kurtz or *Verloc or *Razumov visually, but cannot reproduce the way in which we see their respective situations through the ironic lens of Conrad's narration. In film, characters are usually obliged either to speak for themselves or to mime their thoughts, so that much of Conrad's *irony is carried over into explicit dialogue, with varying degrees of success. Without Conrad's verbal irony, works like *The Secret Agent* or *Victory* tend to appear far more melodramatic on the screen than they do on the page.

Conrad was first approached by filmmakers as early as 1913, when he was asked by the London office of Pathé Frères Cinema to consider reproducing some of his novels or stories on the 'cinematograph'. In 1915 Conrad's agent J. B. *Pinker negotiated the sale of the 'moving picture rights' for *Romance* to Fiction Pictures, Inc. for the sum of $500, although the film did not materialize and the option expired. Four years later, Conrad received $20,000 from Lasky-Famous Players (a forerunner of Paramount) for the film rights to *Romance*, *Lord Jim*, *Chance*, and *Victory*, and three of these four films were actually made.

A largely pecuniary interest in film inspired Conrad to try his own hand at scriptwriting, and in September 1920, with Pinker's help and the added incentive of $1,500 from the Lasky company, he produced a silent film adaptation of his story 'Gaspar Ruiz' entitled *Gaspar the Strong Man*. Conrad thus became the first major English novelist to have written a film scenario. Although Lasky rejected the 'film-play'—it was never filmed, and was published only in Italian translation—Conrad continued to be interested in film, lecturing on the subject of 'Author and Cinematograph' during his visit to *America in

May 1923. His manuscript notes for this lecture, held at the Lilly Library, Indiana University, have been transcribed by Arnold T. Schwab in 'Conrad's American Speeches and his Reading from *Victory*', *Modern Philology*, 62 (1965), 342–7.

Five silent Conrad films were made, of which three survive (viewing copies at the Library of Congress or the George Eastman House, Rochester, NY). The first of these was Maurice Tourneur's *Victory* (1919), which Conrad apparently saw with Pinker when it played in Canterbury, followed by *Lord Jim* (1925), *The Silver Treasure* (*Nostromo*, 1926, now lost), *The Road to Romance* (*Romance*, 1927, now lost), and *The Rescue* (1929, with 'vocal chorus numbers'). The advent of sound at the end of the 1920s left film-makers with the problem of how to deal with foreign audiences, and one solution devised by Paramount involved re-shooting a number of selected films on a common set with five foreign teams of actors and directors. William Wellman's adaptation of *Victory* as *Dangerous Paradise* (1930) was one of ten Paramount films chosen for this experimental project, and five separate versions (in French, German, Italian, Polish, and Swedish) were produced in assembly line fashion at specially constructed studios in Joinville, near Paris. The films were badly received, the experiment failed, and Wellman's original film is apparently the only one to have survived.

The first Conrad films were all exotic romances made in Hollywood, but the relatively grim realities of the 1930s brought Conrad's more political fictions to the screen, albeit in a romantic mode, with Alfred Hitchcock's *Sabotage* (*The Secret Agent*) and Marc Allégret's *Razumov* (*Under Western Eyes*) both released in 1936. (Hitchcock also made a film called *The Secret Agent*, based not on Conrad but on stories by Somerset Maugham.) Both films are in modern dress, with motor-cars and machine-guns, yet despite their political overtones, Hitchcock's film is basically a love story between Winnie *Verloc and a detective named 'Ted' who bears no resemblance to Conrad's Inspector Heat or the Assistant Commissioner, while Allégret's film portrays a guilty, love-stricken Razumov who thanks Nikita in the end for putting him out of his misery. The part of Mikulin was played by Jacques Copeau (a playwright and friend of André *Gide), with whom Conrad had exchanged letters in 1924.

In 1939 Orson Welles, then aged 24 and already notorious as the perpetrator of a Halloween radio broadcast of H. G. *Wells's *The War of the Worlds* that convinced many Americans that Martians had invaded New Jersey, was invited to Hollywood by RKO studios and given unprecedented *carte blanche* to make a film. He chose 'Heart of Darkness', and devised a radical solution to the problem of narration by having the camera (and thus the viewer) play the part of *Marlow. He also found a visual correlative for the accumulating horror of Kurtz by showing the dense jungle becoming increasingly bleak and blasted as the boat moves upriver, so that Kurtz is finally discovered in a desolate swamp, in a hut raised on poles and covered with skulls. In the end, budget overruns and other difficulties caused the project to be cancelled, and Welles made *Citizen Kane* instead. Script summaries and other materials from the 'Heart of Darkness' project can be found in the Welles Collection at the Lilly Library, Indiana University.

After the Second World War, the first Conrad film to make extensive use of location film footage was Carol Reed's *Outcast of the Islands* (1952), although most of it was filmed either in Sri Lanka or in London studios. A 1950 BBC production of 'The Secret Sharer' was the first Conrad adaptation made for television, followed by live-performance American versions of 'Heart of Darkness' in the rubric of *Camera Three* (1955) and *Playhouse 90* (1958; Kurtz was played by Boris Karloff, famous for his role as the Frankenstein monster: 'The horror!'). The advent of television forced film companies to offer something more than black-and-white drama: *Laughing Anne* (1953) was in full colour, and also used actual footage from Malaya.

American television closed the colour gap by 8 April 1960, when Conrad's *Victory* was presented by CBS as an offering of *The Art Carney Show*, with Carney playing the part of *Heyst.

In 1965 Richard Brooks adapted *Lord Jim* for the wide screen, producing a swash-buckling adventure film shot in Cambodia, in which Peter O'Toole followed his recent success as *Lawrence of Arabia* with a similar portrayal of *Jim. The ethnic complexities of Conrad's novel are replaced here with film stereotypes: Eli Wallach is cast as a French version of the bandit Calvera in *The Magnificent Seven* who, as 'The General', stands in for Conrad's Sherif Ali; while *Jewel, played by Israeli actress Daliah Lavi, does not learn English meekly from Jim, but serves the class struggle by teaching English and French at the village school. A far more subtle and unduly neglected Conrad film from the same period is Terence Young's operatic adaptation of *The Rover* (1967), with Anthony Quinn and Rita Hayworth, filmed on Elba, and especially memorable for the music of Ennio Morricone. The following year, Ettore Scola made a lively satirical adaptation of 'Heart of Darkness', filmed partly in Angola and released under the breathtaking title of *Riusciranno i nostri eroi a ritrovare l'amico misteriosamente scomparso in Africa?* (Will our Heroes Succeed in Finding the Friend Who Has Mysteriously Disappeared in Africa?). In Scola's film, Kurtz does not die, but jumps off the rescuing ship and swims back to stay with his African people instead of returning to the vapid social horrors of Rome.

Numerous European television productions and co-productions were made in the 1970s, but only three notable films: Andrzej Wajda's *Smuga cienia* (*The Shadow-Line*, 1976), filmed as an autobiographical tale in strange pastel colours; Ridley Scott's lavish and historically detailed *The Duellists* ('The Duel', 1977); and Francis Ford Coppola's controversial Vietnam War version of 'Heart of Darkness' as *Apocalypse Now* (1979), easily the best known of all Conrad adaptations, and one that has achieved classic status in film studies for its innovative sound and visual design. A documentary about the making of *Apocalypse Now* entitled *Hearts of Darkness: A Filmmaker's Apocalypse* appeared in 1991. At the other end of the scale, the most ludic and ludicrous of all Conrad films is easily Jonathan Lawton's low-budget 1988 spoof of 'Heart of Darkness' as *Cannibal Women in the Avocado Jungle of Death* (also available as *Piranha Women*), in which actress and former *Playboy* bunny Shannon Tweed is sent into the 'avocado jungle' of southern California to rescue 'Dr Kurtz', a radical feminist turned cannibal played by the 'queen of the B-films', Adrienne Barbeau.

Film director David Lean died before he could realize a film adaptation of *Nostromo*, but in the 1990s, under competition from film, television offered a number of high-quality and large-scale Conrad adaptations: a BBC version of *The Secret Agent* in 1992, and in 1997 a multinational epic television version of *Nostromo* filmed in Colombia, again with music by Ennio Morricone. Nicolas Roeg's made-for-TV *Heart of Darkness* (1994) was filmed in Belize but otherwise follows Conrad's plot more closely than any of the previous adaptations. Harold Pinter's screenplay version of Conrad's *Victory* was never filmed but is available in *The Comfort of Strangers and Other Screenplays* (Faber, 1990); and Christopher Hampton's adaptations of *The Secret Agent and Nostromo* are also in print (Faber, 1996). Hampton's own film version of *The Secret Agent* (1996) cast Bob Hoskins as Verloc, Gérard Depardieu as Tom Ossipon, and Robin Williams as the *Professor. Conradian 'type-casting' may be evident in a number of cases where actors have appeared in more than one film: Otto Matiesen played character roles in the lost silent film versions of both *Nostromo* and *Romance*; Oscar Homolka was the sinister Verloc in Hitchcock's *Sabotage* and the company doctor in a *Playhouse 90* episode based on 'Heart of Darkness'; James Mason played both the protagonist of 'The Secret Sharer' (*Face to Face*, 1952) and Gentleman *Brown in Brooks's *Lord Jim*; French actor Christian Marquand was the French lieutenant in *Lord Jim* and also played in a

French colonial scene that was cut from *Apocalypse Now* (but is excerpted in the documentary *Hearts of Darkness*); Harvey Keitel lost the role of Coppola's Marlow-figure Willard after one week of shooting, but returned to play Feraud in *The Duellists*; and Albert Finney has played both Joseph Fouché in *The Duellists* and Dr *Monygham in *Nostromo*.

The 'film canon' of Conrad's works is oddly different from his literary canon. The most frequently filmed of all Conrad's works is not 'Heart of Darkness' but *Victory*, which has inspired roughly one film for every decade since 1919, not counting Jerzy Skolimowski's *The Lightship* (1985), which is sometimes deemed a Conrad film but is actually an adaptation of a novella by the German author Siegfried Lenz. The film canon also contains curious omissions: although *Chance* was the novel that first made Conrad famous, and Lasky purchased the film rights in 1919, no film version of *Chance* has been made.

Some of the practical and artistic difficulties encountered in bringing Conrad to the screen are chronicled by Adam Gillon 1994: 145–82. Two book-length studies of Conrad films are available: Gene D. Phillips, *Conrad and Cinema: The Art of Adaptation* (New York: Peter Lang, 1995), and Gene M. Moore (ed.), *Conrad on Film* (CUP, 1997), the latter equipped with a comprehensive international filmography.

finances. Conrad's financial affairs appear to have been in a state of crisis throughout his adult life, from his early feckless years in *Marseilles, when he fell into debt (either through ill-advised investment or gambling or both) and made a half-hearted attempt at *suicide, to his final years when he was a well-known presence on the literary scene earning a respectable income from his pen. Even at this stage of what by most financial yardsticks could be accounted a highly successful career, he would nonetheless ritually complain to friends of near-penury and a lack of ready cash.

While Conrad's earnings during his *sea years were modest, the wages of seamen

were directly regulated by market forces and influenced, to some extent, by the nascent union movement. Conrad, however, enjoyed the good fortune of having his salary constantly topped up by an allowance from his uncle Tadeusz *Bobrowski. (A legacy totalling approximately £1,600 on Bobrowski's death in 1894 soon evaporated in ill-fated South African investments.)

Having been constrained by macroeconomic shifts in supply and demand to abandon a career at sea in 1894, Conrad after some initial false starts, such as managing a *London warehouse, embarked on a prolonged period of financial incertitude in opting for authorship, always a career of unpredictable returns, particularly so at its inception, when an audience must be found and won over. During the opening years of his writing life, moreover, he married and became a father, taking on responsibilities that increased his financial worries. Bouts of genuine ill *health and depression, to which he was regularly subject, affected his capacity to maintain a steady income, and this strain in turn engendered neurotic symptoms that further affected his ability to deal with practical matters. By January 1899, at a time when he was producing work that would win him a place in world literature, he was, by the sympathetic assessment of David S. *Meldrum, his editor at *Blackwood's, making somewhat less than £300 a year, which even in rural *Kent allowed for no extravagances and made living in London, according to Meldrum, 'impossible' (Blackburn (ed.), 40). On the other hand, perspective is offered by raw statistics: the average annual income in England shortly after 1900 has been varyingly calculated as between £56 and slightly over £90. While such a rough figure does not account for class differences and personal expectations, Conrad was in the upper percentiles of wage-earners from the beginning of his writing career.

He nonetheless established a pattern of overspending and borrowing, with the result that perceived as well as actual need frequently dogged him. He seems almost to have engineered some of his financial crises in order to test the loyalty and generosity of his friends. He lost the friendship of Adolf P. *Krieger in this fashion but cemented that with John *Galsworthy, on whose deep pockets he made demands from the late 1890s until at least 1910. Unplanned expenditures inevitably led to major crises: the collapse of Conrad's bank, William Watson & Co., in 1904 was wholly beyond his control, but it exacerbated an already difficult situation since it required him at short notice to settle a £200 overdraft. How much his pattern of insecurity and dependence may owe to the extreme instability of his childhood is open to speculation. William *Rothenstein thought that the pattern of extravagance was established during Conrad's sea years: 'he was like a sailor between two voyages, ready to spend on land what he couldn't aboard ship' (ii. 44). Self-induced pressures, while they engineered occasional physical collapse and severe mental tension, at other times seem to have engendered bouts of almost frenzied productivity.

While he may often have exaggerated his shaky economic condition, he was for the first decade or so of his career in a genuinely precarious position as he lurched from crisis to crisis, without a contingency fund for emergencies. In 1900, when Conrad engaged J. B. *Pinker as his agent, he made the first serious effort to place his finances on a surer footing and freed himself from marketing his work. Previously acting as his own agent, he had done himself no favours, squandering precious energies on firming up *contracts and courting *publishers. For instance, lacking previous experience in the publishing world, he had sold the copyright of *Almayer's Folly* outright to T. Fisher *Unwin, at the time apparently a sound move but one that in the end proved short-sighted, since it deprived him of royalties from 1895 until 1921, when arrangements with Unwin allowed for its inclusion in his *collected edition.

Desperate to clear his debts, Conrad would resort to various strategies, juggling competing claims and occasionally placing himself in an awkward position with both friends and professional colleagues. In late 1900, for instance, having taken out a life insurance policy for £1,000, he asked his publisher William Blackwood to stand surety for a £200 loan against it, in a characteristic interjection of intimate private matters into a business relationship.

From the outset of his career until the runaway financial success of *Chance* in 1913, Conrad won critical esteem but not popular success. The acclaim of the literary establishment was useful, however, in making him eligible for government resources available to struggling writers of special merit: in July 1902 he received a *grant of £300 from the Royal Literary Fund with the support of Henry *James; in March 1905, the efforts of Edmund *Gosse and S. S. *Pawling culminated in his receiving a Royal Bounty Fund grant of £500 (administered by Henry *Newbolt and William Rothenstein) to help him sort out his troubled financial affairs; and in August 1910, he was granted an annual Civil List Pension of £100, which he relinquished only in June 1917.

Years of slogging and relative insecurity were, however, the norm, with only brief periods of respite. Conrad nevertheless declined to compromise his artistic aims or to abandon what he considered his real work for temporary stopgaps, and was spared 'the degradation of daily journalism' (*CL*, ii. 34), which may have loomed as a possibility at the start of his writing life. By 1910, however, years of makeshift solutions resulted in large accumulated debts. These were the result of his wildly over-optimistic estimates of potential earnings and a chronic inability to meet deadlines. Circumstances beyond his conscious control finally united to bring him to a financial and mental breaking point, with outstanding debts to Pinker having swollen to £2,700. Their angry breach of January 1910 and a consequent two-year estrangement seem, from the perspective of hindsight, inevitable.

With the success of *Chance*, Conrad's career entered a new phase, offering increased opportunities for the sale of new work at higher prices and the chance to relaunch earlier writing to a wider and eager public. He was able to recycle his work in various forms, sometimes being paid twice or more for it. For example, he could sell his manuscripts and typescripts to John *Quinn and Thomas J. *Wise, both keen collectors of Conradiana. After *serialization in England and America, collection in book form came as a matter of course. This was sometimes followed by *translation. The de luxe collected edition, aside from the *'Author's Notes' specifically written for it, occasioned little work. To take a single example of this process of multiple payment: 'Stephen Crane: A Note without Dates', a 1,000-word essay written in 1919, earned £10 from the *London Mercury* and $40 from the *Bookman* upon publication. Conrad sold a typescript to Wise for £10; the piece was reprinted in *Notes on Life and Letters* in 1921; and that volume was in turn included in Doubleday's and Heinemann's collected editions.

At the close of his career, the sums Conrad brought in by his writing, both new and recycled, were, if not staggering, very good indeed. Figures for only part of his income from 1919 to 1921 are revealing. In 1919, he received £1,200 for serial rights to *The Arrow of Gold*; £3,080 for the sale of film rights to four of his novels; £200 from Wise for permission to print limited-edition *pamphlets of his occasional writings and £80 for manuscript materials; and he shared in the proceeds from the successful stage version of *Victory* by Basil Macdonald *Hastings. In 1920, *The Rescue* earned him nearly £3,000 for serial rights; sales of manuscript materials netted approximately £460; and for a complete set of Wise and *Shorter pamphlets he received $1,750 from Quinn. In 1921, *Notes on Life and Letters* garnered £250 from Dent and, after taxes, $980 from Doubleday, and the sale of the collected edition brought Conrad's total receipts to £10,000 (not including, presumably, the private sale to Wise of manuscript materials, which amounted to at least £300). By his own calculation, his pre-tax income for 1921 was £4,264, against fixed expenditures (housing and maintenance, salaries, and allowances to his family) of £2,301. These sums are placed in perspective by the fact that in 1924, the year of Conrad's death, the average annual income in England was approximately £210. On the other hand, the psychological factors at play are impossible to determine. Conrad could not look forward to a pension or to 'retirement'; he no doubt felt pressures to maintain himself and family in a style appropriate to his social class; and he was under unrelenting stress to produce saleable work to provide daily bread and to ensure the welfare of his wife and children after his death.

Conrad's actual and non-fixed expenses for his later years are difficult to calculate precisely. He never owned a *home, preferring, it seems, to live in rented houses. Treatment and hospitalization for Jessie Conrad during these years were costly, but Conrad did not stint on it, placing his wife under the care of a titled surgeon, Sir Robert *Jones. There were private nurses as well as costs related to her recuperation in private nursing homes in London, Liverpool, and Canterbury. His younger son, John, was provided with a public school education, private tutoring, and a period in *France for him to learn the language. Conrad generously contributed to the education of his wife's relatives and also assisted Jessie Conrad's mother as well as Karola *Zagórska financially. His last ten years witness a comfortably genteel style of life culminating in residence at Oswalds, a large country mansion maintained by servants and gardeners. Among other amenities was a chauffeured motor-car and membership in the Royal Automobile Club, and London stays were usually at Brown's Hotel in Mayfair. The gross value of his estate at his death as reported by *The Times* of 17 November 1924 amounted to £20,045 (net £17,054).

The subject of money, which punctuates Conrad's day-to-day correspondence with his friends and permeates his *letters to his publishers and Pinker, is pursued in his fiction, sometimes under the influence of Balzac and *Dickens. Financial ambition, speculation, and outright theft figure in the plots of *Almayer's Folly*, *An Outcast of the*

Islands, and 'Heart of Darkness', while 'The End of the Tether' and *The Secret Agent* dramatize the problems of earning a living, economic insecurity, and the threat of financial ruin. 'Typhoon' broaches the subject of greed; while ill-gotten wealth and its corrosive influence are principal thematic interests in *Nostromo* and *Chance*.

The question of what happened to the bulk of Conrad's earnings has never been systematically investigated or satisfactorily answered. Early editions of Conrad's letters discreetly censor out such ungentlemanly topics as his loans from Galsworthy and exact figures of earnings. In the 1940s, the Conrad estate denied the Indianapolis lawyer Fred Bates Johnson permission to publish 125 letters from Conrad to Pinker because they dealt with financial matters; Johnson's interest in the issue of Conrad's financial affairs is broached in his brief 'Notes on Conrad's Finance', *Indiana Quarterly for Bookmen*, 3 (1947), 27–30.

Conrad's financial affairs are treated in Karl's *JCTL* and Najder's *JCC*. Watts's 1989 study focuses on the economics of Conrad's literary life but is hobbled by its lack of archival research and mainly useful in suggesting areas for further enquiry. Watts's 'Marketing Modernism: How Conrad Prospered', in Ian Willison *et al.* (eds.), *Modernist Writers and the Marketplace* (Macmillan, 1996), 81–8, covers some of the same ground. Carabine (1996) interestingly, if passingly, raises issues related to Conrad's finances.   JHS

fin de siècle. The phrase *fin de siècle* is normally applied to the last two decades of the 19th century, when traditional social, moral, and artistic values were in transition. With particular reference to the arts, it is often used synonymously with 'decadence'. William Sharp's description of the 1890s identifies its prevailing ethos: 'A great creative period is at hand, probably a great dramatic epoch. But what will for one thing differentiate it from any predecessor is the new complexity, the new subtlety, in apprehension, in formative conception, in imaginative rendering' (quoted in Holbrook Jackson, *The Eighteen Nineties* (Pen-

guin, 1939), 26–7). The closing years of a century, like all anniversaries, seem to invite a reappraisal of our place in time and a consequent 'quickening of life', in Holbrook Jackson's phrase (15). Jackson referred to the closing decade of the 19th century as 'not, primarily, a period of achievement, but rather of effort: suggestive, tentative, rather than formative. Its relics are moods, attitudes, experiments; fantastic attenuations of weariness, fantastic anticipations of a new vitality; an old civilization a little too conscious of itself and the present, and a little too much concerned for its future' (10). As reflected in the arts, the *fin de siècle* was characterized by a conception of the world in aesthetic terms, as a spectacle, which in turn prompted a critique of middle-class morality. No one better exemplified the aestheticism of the period, both in his art and his writing, than the wit and playwright Oscar Wilde, whose essay 'The Soul of Man under Socialism' (1891) stressed the links between aestheticism and individualist as opposed to collectivist socialism. A sense of exhaustion, reflective of the collapsing Victorian world-order, was a further characteristic of the period. Thus, in Wilde's *The Picture of Dorian Gray* (1890), when Lord Henry murmurs '*Fin de siècle*', his hostess replies knowingly, '*Fin du globe*'.

According to Frederick R. Karl, Conrad's first novel, *Almayer's Folly*, 'manifests the language, the tones, the characteristic rhythms, and most of the mannerisms of *fin de siècle* literature' (1960: 91). He argues that the novel affords a prose counterpart to the 'primeval drowsiness' in the 1890s poetry of W. B. Yeats, 'the siftings of the pre-Raphaelites', and the verse of Arthur *Symons, which, Jessie Conrad claimed, was 'almost the only verse that [her] husband read . . . with any real appreciation and pleasure' (*JCHC*, 154). The themes of breakdown and (literal) decadence in *Almayer's Folly*, together with the emphasis upon dream, torpor, and, above all, the imagery of languor, help to support the sense that this is a novel fully attuned to its decade. In particular, the mannerisms in the many descriptive passages, with their slow rhythms, conjure up the sense of primeval drowsiness: 'Before going down to his boat Babalatchi stopped for a while in the big open space where the thick-leaved trees put black patches of shadow which seemed to float on a flood of smooth, intense light that rolled up to the houses and down to the stockade and over the river, where it broke and sparkled in thousands of glittering wavelets, like a band woven of azure and gold edged with the brilliant green of the forests guarding both banks of the Pantai' (131). Here, Babalatchi's contemplative pause is conveyed in a sentence whose long open vowels suggest highly self-conscious styling. Subsequent criticism has extended this concern with Conrad's presentation of *fin de siècle* exhaustion. For instance, in *Exotic Memories: Literature, Colonialism and the Fin de Siècle* (Stanford UP, 1991), Chris Bongie sees Conrad's over-wrought prose in 'The Return' (*Tales of Unrest*) as an attempt to relate the troubled Hervey marriage to the world-weary perspective of decadentism. As an extension of such ideas, Padmini Mongia's reading of *Lord Jim* offers an insight into tensions resulting from *fin de siècle* colonial and gender anxieties (see 'Ghosts of the Gothic: Spectral Women and Colonized Spaces in *Lord Jim*', *The Conradian*, 17: 2 (Spring 1993), 1–16). See also NORDAU, MAX.   AHS

'First News'. Conrad's brief recollection of his sensations in *Cracow on hearing of the outbreak of the *First World War in the first days of August 1914 was written at John *Galsworthy's request for publication in a Ministry of Pensions journal of which he had become editor in April 1918. Probably finished during May of that year, the essay was published in *Reveille: Devoted to the Disabled Sailor & Soldier*, 1 (August 1918), 16–19 under the title of 'The First News', later retitled and collected in *Notes on Life and Letters*. As often occurs in Conrad's occasional writings, his reminiscence departs from the chronology of actual happenings, events being either misremembered or perhaps deliberately rearranged and conflated for literary effect. The essay

movingly counterpoints Conrad's re-immersion in his private Polish past on his first visit to his homeland for over twenty years with a public *Poland suddenly thrown into total confusion by the threat of war: 'I saw in those faces the awful desolation of men whose country, torn in three, found itself engaged in the contest with no will of its own and not even the power to assert itself at the cost of life. All the past was gone, and there was no future, whatever happened' (178). Tear-sheets from *Reveille* were sold in 1925, but their present location is unknown. See also 'POLAND REVISITED'.

'First Thing I Remember, The'. Conrad's brief response to a poll organized by *John O'London's Weekly* and involving 'the Prime Minister and many other famous men and women' appeared on 10 December 1921. He offers both an early physical memory—that of the 3-year-old boy being rubbed with snow as a treatment for frostbite—and a visual one of his mother seated at the piano. The note is reprinted in *CDOUP*, 98–9.

First World War. At the outbreak of the First World War in August 1914, Conrad, aged 56, found himself with his family stranded in Austrian *Poland and directly witnessing the first stages of militarization. He returned home to suffer a prolonged period of illness, his description of which provides a characterizing rubric for his steadily darkening mood throughout the war: 'I am painfully aware of being crippled, of being idle, of being useless with a sort of absurd anxiety, as though it could matter to the greatness of the Empire' (*CL*, v. 427). Caught in the toils of a drab and uncreative 'sick-apathy' (*CL*, v. 424), Conrad increasingly spoke in the tones of a man prematurely ageing with each successive month, and by February 1916 confessed to feeling a 'strangely useless personality' whose 'mentality seems to have gone to pieces' (*CL*, v. 553). Various reasons come into play to explain this state of mind. By early 1916, Conrad's elder son Borys, aged 18, was on active service and a source of constant nagging worry to his parents. Daily life at their Capel House *home became increasingly lonely as the war progressed, broken only by long visits to *London, where Jessie Conrad required repeated surgery on her knee. Conrad's own ill *health left him with a sense of frustrated uselessness at not being able to participate directly in the war effort. Although he briefly considered military enlistment in February 1916, he soon realized that his age and lameness would prevent him from making any significant contribution: 'I have been affected mentally and physically more profoundly than I thought it possible. Perhaps if I had been able to "lend a hand" in some way I would have found this war easier to bear. But I can't. I am slowly getting more and more of a cripple—and this too preys on my mind not a little' (*CL*, v. 559–60). In the event, his involvement with the war effort was indirect and limited. By agreement with the Admiralty, he undertook some tours of Royal Naval Reserve bases in late 1916, agreed to write propaganda pieces, and, at the urging of Józef H. *Retinger, also submitted 'A Note on the Polish Problem' to the Foreign Office. Conrad's sense of an impending ending and cataclysm was further intensified, according to his wife, by the fact 'that the war brought back even more vividly than ever his tragic early life and . . . that for a long time before his death he felt the call of his native land' (*JCKH*, 16).

The impact of war upon Conrad the creative writer forms an important chapter in the account of his later development. The overall evidence provided by his wartime *letters, with their insistent valedictory patterns, lends some support to the *achievement-and-decline view of his career which regards his works after 1918 as symptoms of creative weariness and exhaustion. By common consent *The Shadow-Line*, written at the beginning of the war, is a very considerable work, but Conrad wrote little else of substance during the war apart from two short stories, 'The Warrior's Soul' and 'The Tale' (*Tales of Hearsay*). While he did remain busy—planning future *collected editions, writing *'Author's Notes', and helping with plans for the stage *Victory*—he felt unable to commit himself to any full-length work until *The Arrow of Gold* in 1917, a novel that effects a retrospective escape into his *Marseilles youth. Physical frailty, spiritual malaise, and creative dearth increasingly combined to make Conrad feel that the broken and war-torn Europe mirrored the terms of his own disintegration. In May 1917, he described himself to Edward *Garnett: 'I am like you my dear fellow; broken up—and broken in two—disconnected. Impossible to start myself going, impossible to concentrate to any good purpose. Is it the war—perhaps? Or the end of Conrad, simply? I suppose one must end, someday, somehow. Mere decency requires it' (*LFC*, 270). But elsewhere the sense of creative disablement is extended to include the impact of war upon *all* endeavours in literary art: 'It seems almost criminal levity to talk at this time of books, stories, publication. This war attends my uneasy pillow like a nightmare. I feel oppressed even in my sleep and the moment of waking brings no relief' (*CL*, v. 439). During 1918, a significant change occurred in Conrad's method of composing his fiction: he ceased to write by hand and began dictating his work directly to a secretary for typing. From a point of hindsight, the event might be seen as a resonant valedictory moment, a setting-down of the pen, during a year in which, according to G. *Jean-Aubry, he became 'haunted by the idea of his approaching end and wanted to set himself straight with the future' (1957: 274).

These wartime sentiments form part of a wider context for the achievement-and-decline debate. Conrad's sad lament echoes representatively at the time, shared by other members of an older generation of writers with strong roots in the 19th century, who endured the war from a position of helpless inactivity and felt it to be a comprehensive defeat for the liberal conscience. In 1915, Henry *James also speaks with Conrad, and for their generation: 'The war has used up words; they have been weakened; they have deteriorated like motor-car tyres; they have during the last six months been, like millions of other things, more overstrained and knocked about and voided of the happy semblance than in all the long ages before and we are now confronted with a depreciation of all our terms, or, otherwise speaking, a loss of expression, through increase of limpness, that may well make us wonder what ghosts will be left to walk' ('Henry James's First Interview', New York Times Magazine (21 March 1915), 4). James died in 1916 and thus did not survive as a 'ghost'. Outliving him by nearly a decade, Conrad felt increasingly 'overstrained and knocked about' as his literary generation was in the process of making way for a group of younger writers —T. S. Eliot, James Joyce, Ezra Pound, and Virginia *Woolf—whose work would represent a new phase of post-war Modernism. For helpful perspectives, see Berthoud's 'Introduction: Autobiography and War', 1986: 7–24; Celia M. Kingsbury's '"Infinities of Absolution": Reason, Rumor, and Duty in Joseph Conrad's "The Tale"', Modern Fiction Studies, 44 (1998), 715–29, in a special issue of that journal devoted to 'Modernism and Modern War', and Schwarz's chapter on Conrad's wartime fiction (1982: 81–104). Peter Buitenhuis's The Great War of Words: Literature as Propaganda 1914–18 and After (Batsford, 1989) includes Conrad and Ford Madox *Ford in a detailed survey of Great War propaganda.

Flaubert, Gustave (1821–80). The French novelist 'with enormous moustaches and a thundering voice' hovers not simply over the tenth chapter of Almayer's Folly, as Conrad fancifully recollected in A Personal Record (3), but over much of his early and mid-period writing. His comment to Hugh *Walpole that 'my Flaubert is the Flaubert of St. Antoine and Ed[uca-tion]: Sent[imentale]: and that only from the point of view of the rendering of concrete things and visual impressions' (LL, ii. 206) is a singularly ungenerous acknowledgement of his large debts to 'the last of the Romantics' (A Personal Record, 3). Flaubert's fiction was a fundamental influence on Conrad: it shaped his conception of the novel as an art form; informed his idea of a narrative authority founded on impersonality and authorial absence; provided models for characters; and served as a source for direct verbal as well as larger *borrowings. While Conrad commented on other major 19th-century French writers in his letters and in his essays 'Anatole France', 'Guy de Maupassant', and 'Alphonse Daudet', his restrained taciturnity about Flaubert is significant: the methods and interests of his fiction in themselves form an extended commentary on Flaubert's art.

Conrad's inheritance from Flaubert was twofold. He received various techniques from him, and a view of the novel as a vehicle for ideas, in contrast to prevalent English attitudes towards fiction as an entertainment or pastime that only incidentally achieved intellectual significance. By these lights, the novelist was neither an entertainer desiring to amuse (the pose of Thackeray) nor a social reformer cajoling or seducing his audience into embracing a political or ideological position (an aim of *Dickens), but a craftsman dedicated to the search for structural coherence and a carefully wrought prose style adapted to the expression of his ideas. The 'Preface' to The Nigger of the 'Narcissus', whatever its tangled quarrel with *impressionism, is indebted to Flaubert for its emphasis on commitment to le mot juste and on the visual impact as aims of fiction.

The works of Conrad's early phase, in particular Almayer's Folly, The Nigger of the 'Narcissus', and Lord Jim, owe much to Madame Bovary (1857), Salammbô (1862), and Trois contes (1877) for their narrative modes. Rejecting the confidential and intrusive narrator and the intricate sub-plotting of the high Victorian novel, Conrad derived his basic structural principles from Flaubert's famous notion of the godlike artist, constantly present yet removed from his creations and refraining from active comment on their doings. Conradian narrative, however, evades the more austere implications of this detachment through its dependence on *irony and the use of a characterized narrator such as *Marlow as a substitute for the narrator-commentator.

Conrad's clearest debt to Flaubert for characters is to *Madame Bovary*. The two quintessential romantics, *Almayer and *Jim, and, to a lesser extent, the self-deluded Captain *Whalley of 'The End of the Tether', avatars of an extreme and even dangerously exaggerated individualism, suffer from an inflated conception of the value of the self, a condition that commentators have named *Bovarysme*. (Flaubert himself was indebted to Cervantes's *Don Quixote* (1605–15) for this psychological type.) Conflict with the demands of everyday life and the constraints of bourgeois morality enmesh such dreamers, whose subsequent struggles with an unsympathetic world inevitably end in defeat.

Conrad's other debts for characters are perhaps less obvious. If, in Ian Watt's well-turned phrase, 'Almayer is a Borneo Bovary' (1980: 51), then Babalatchi, the wily statesman of *Almayer's Folly* and *An Outcast of the Islands*, is a Borneo Homais. Resembling Flaubert's self-seeking pharmacist in his lack of ideals and corrosive pragmatism, Babalatchi, like Cornelius in *Lord Jim*, serves as a foil to the unworldly dreamer he conspires to ruin. In 'An Outpost of Progress', the conception of Kayerts and Carlier, fools lost in enigmas, owes a debt to *Bouvard et Pécuchet* (1881), and the central female characters of 'Amy Foster', 'To-morrow', and *The Secret Agent* in their bemused passivity before life are partly modelled on Félicité of 'Un cœur simple' (1877). *The Nigger of the 'Narcissus'* pays a more complex homage to Flaubertian method in continuing the experimental mode of *Salammbô*. Taking a group as its protagonist, the novella handles its crew of seamen in ways pioneered by Flaubert in his treatment of his novel's Roman and Carthaginian troops.

Since 1915, when Hugh Walpole judged the influence of Flaubert on Conrad to be 'unmistakeable' (*Joseph Conrad* (Nisbet, 1916), 78), the topic of Conrad's indebtedness to Flaubert has received considerable critical attention. The most comprehensive discussions are by Yelton (1967) and Her-

vouet (1990), the latter surveying the Conrad–Flaubert relationship under the categories 'Unity', 'Selection', Impersonality', 'Visibility', and the 'Mot Juste'. Among specific studies are Wallace Watson's '"The Shade of Old Flaubert" and Maupassant's "Art Impeccable (Presque)": French Influences on the Development of Conrad's Marlow', *Journal of Narrative Technique*, 7 (1977), 37–56, and Lawrence Thornton's 'Conrad, Flaubert, and Marlow: Possession and Exorcism', *Comparative Literature*, 44 (1982), 146–56.   JHS

'Flight'. This brief essay records Conrad's feelings about his only experience of flying, involving a short trip in a biplane from Yarmouth over the North Sea on 18 September 1916 during a wartime tour of Norfolk naval bases. It was probably written in late May 1917 at the request of B. Macdonald *Hastings, who was in close touch with Conrad during 1916–17 about his dramatization of *Victory* and who, as a member of the Royal Flying Corps, edited one of its journals. The article was published in the *Fledgling: The Monthly Journal of the No. 2 Royal Flying Corps Cadet Wing*, 1 (June 1917), 17–18, and collected in revised form in *Notes on Life and Letters*. Its original title, 'Never Any More: A First and Last Flying Experience', emphasizes the way in which the experience left Conrad feeling the effects of his age and echoes the final sentences of the essay: 'I would never go flying again. No, never any more—lest its mysterious fascination, whose invisible wing had brushed my heart up there, should change to unavailing regret in a man too old for its glory' (212). The present location of the manuscript, last auctioned at the Parke-Bernet Galleries in New York in 1940, is unknown.

Flora. See DE BARRALS, THE.

Ford, Ford Madox (1873–1939), known also as Ford Madox Hueffer, English man of letters. Ford Madox Ford was Conrad's closest literary friend and his collaborator from 1898 to 1909. The author of more than 80 books in his own right, Ford is chiefly remembered for his novels *The Good*

Soldier (1915) and the 'Tietjens tetralogy' known collectively as *Parade's End* (1924–8). Ford and Conrad collaborated on *The Inheritors* (1901), *Romance* (1903), and the novella *The Nature of a Crime* (written 1906, published 1909). In addition, Ford supported Conrad as an amanuensis and editor, and was a ready and willing source of ideas, advice, and practical help. Conrad's story 'Amy Foster' is based on an anecdote that Ford recorded in *The Cinque Ports* (1900), and Conrad credited Ford with the idea for *The Secret Agent*. Ford encouraged Conrad to commit his memoirs to paper; he took down portions of *The Mirror of the Sea* in his private shorthand from Conrad's dictation; and he commissioned for the *English Review* the autobiographical essays later published as *A Personal Record*. Ford also helped Conrad to adapt 'To-morrow' for the stage as *One Day More*, and he may have written one instalment of *Nostromo* (the first part of Part II, chapter 5) when Conrad was unable to meet a deadline.

Jessie Conrad never liked Ford, and Conrad's friendship also cooled after 1909 as a result of the scandal attending Ford's love affairs and his financial difficulties with the *English Review*; but Ford's profound devotion to Conrad remained unwavering, despite his caricatures of Conrad and other literary acquaintances in *The Simple Life Limited* (1911). Allusions to Ford's notorious 'unreliability' have been common in Conrad scholarship for many years, together with charges that Ford exaggerated his own importance to Conrad, but the surviving documentary evidence has validated many of Ford's claims. The determined efforts of Ford scholars like Sondra J. Stang in the 1980s and Max Saunders in the 1990s have resulted in a serious reassessment of Ford's work, highlighting his importance to modern English letters generally and to Conrad studies in particular.

Born Ford Hermann Hueffer, Ford grew up surrounded by famous Pre-Raphaelite artists and men of letters, and was closely acquainted with members of the Garnett and Rossetti families. (The Rossettis were his cousins, since a maternal aunt had married William Michael Rossetti.) Ford's German father Francis Hueffer came from an important publishing family in Münster. A champion of *Schopenhauer and Wagner, he emigrated to England and became music critic for *The Times*. Ford's maternal grandfather was the artist Ford Madox Brown, whose altruism and artistic devotion were for Ford a lifelong source of inspiration: he dedicated his first novel to his beloved grandfather, his next major work was a memorial biography, and he honoured Ford Madox Brown throughout his life by choosing to assume various forms of his name.

Ford attended Pretoria House school in Folkestone, where classes were held in French, English, and German on successive days. Leaving school at the age of 17, he began his writing career with the publication of two volumes of children's fairy tales. In 1892 he began courting Elizabeth ('Elsie') Martindale (1877–1949), sending her a ring for her sixteenth birthday on 3 October (he would be 19 in December). Her father opposed their engagement, and fifteen months later, in March 1894, they staged a romantic elopement that provoked the first of the public scandals to plague Ford's social career.

There are various accounts of how Conrad and Ford first met, but the idea of *collaboration apparently originated in Conrad's concern that he could not write fast enough to support himself and his family. Conrad's friend and literary mentor Edward *Garnett may have been the first to suggest collaboration with Ford as a way of increasing Conrad's productivity, and the idea was also supported by William Ernest *Henley, the editor of the *New Review*. Fluency was never Ford's problem; Conrad produced only one novel in the seven years between the publication of *Nostromo* and *Under Western Eyes*, while during the same period Ford wrote eleven. In 1898, among other current projects, he had two novels in rough draft that he was willing to submit to Conrad's scrutiny. Thus began a decade of close friendship and co-operation: Ford lent Conrad money (which was never fully repaid), sublet Pent Farm to the Conrads, helped Conrad with his writings in various ways, and in general made Conrad the full beneficiary of the rule of life that he had learned from his grandfather: 'Beggar yourself rather than refuse assistance to any one whose genius you think shows promise of being greater than your own' (Ford, *Memories and Impressions* (New York: Harper, 1911), 219). Conrad, for his part, tried Ford's patience but taught him invaluable lessons in the art of writing: how to be more precise and dramatic, and to keep ever in mind the need for **progression d'effet*, the doctrine that every word should move the story forward toward its conclusion. Ford would never forget the groans he wrung from Conrad by reading aloud *Seraphina*, the first draft of *Romance*. A decade later, Ford would pass some of these same lessons on to Ezra Pound.

Ford's casual, bohemian manners made life difficult for Jessie Conrad. When he would arrive suddenly without warning, she felt obliged to abandon her domestic routine and prepare her hair and clothing in order to receive her husband's guest in proper style. She never forgave Ford for what she considered his chronic abuse of her husband's hospitality, and in letters and memoirs published after Conrad's death, she steadfastly rejected Ford's claims and impugned his motives, publicly attacking his own memorial volume as a 'detestable book' in which Ford ignobly sought to take credit for her husband's labours (*PL*, 251).

In 1908 Ford founded the *English Review*, a short-lived but brilliant venture to which Conrad promised to contribute autobiographical essays along the lines of *The Mirror of the Sea*. That same year, Ford began an affair with Violet Hunt that would have disastrous repercussions, ultimately ruining his relations not only with Conrad but also with Henry *James and Arthur *Marwood. Ford and Elsie had led separate lives after she left Winchelsea in 1907 with their two children, ostensibly for the sake of her health, which was endangered by extramarital complications,

including an enduring fondness between Ford and Elsie's elder sister Mary. By 1909 Ford was hoping to marry Violet Hunt if he could obtain a divorce from Elsie. Under the strain of serious personal and editorial problems, Ford behaved erratically. As Conrad described the situation to his agent J. B. *Pinker, 'he has quarrelled with every decent friend he had; has nearly made mischief between me and some of my best friends, and is, from all accounts, having a most miserable time himself' (*CL*, iv. 266). All contact between Conrad and Ford ceased for twenty months, from July 1909 until March 1911, and when their correspondence resumed, it would henceforth always be Ford who took the initiative. When Elsie proved unwilling to go through with a divorce, Ford went abroad and returned with the implausible and unsubstantiated claim that he had obtained a divorce in Germany.

Remarkably, some of Ford's most memorable fictions date from this difficult period, including *A Call* (1911) and *The Good Soldier* (1915). In *The Simple Life Limited* (1911), Ford caricatured the Fabians and revolutionaries gathered around Edward Garnett at his country home near Limpsfield, Surrey, and parodied Conrad in the figure of the novelist Simon Brandson (born Simeon Brandetski), the author of *Clotted Vapours*. Ford's marital embarrassments would not be overcome until he emerged from the trenches of the *First World War, suffering the after-effects of gas attacks and memory loss, but ready to change his name and begin a new life. By becoming Ford Madox Ford, he simultaneously rejected his German patrimony and freed himself nominally from all claimants to the title of Mrs Hueffer. An attempt by Elsie to resume relations with the Conrads in 1920 met with a cold rebuff.

Ford settled in Paris after the war and founded a second journal, the *transatlantic review*, in which he published the works of a new generation of writers including Djuna Barnes, John Dos Passos, Ernest Hemingway, James Joyce, Ezra Pound, Jean Rhys, and Gertrude Stein. Ford also wrote to Conrad to ask about publishing their

1906 collaborative novella, *The Nature of a Crime* (Conrad claimed to have forgotten its existence, but consented to write a brief preface). In May 1924 Conrad and Ford agreed that their collaborations would be included in *collected editions of Conrad's works but not of Ford's, in return for which Ford would receive a proportionate half-share of Conrad's royalties, plus full rights and royalties for any French or other European *translations of *The Inheritors* and *Romance*. Upon hearing of Conrad's death, Ford immediately wrote *Joseph Conrad: A Personal Remembrance* (1924), an impressionistic and eloquent tribute to their friendship, with a history of their collaboration and a detailed account of the literary techniques and principles they cultivated. Ford's historical novel *A Little Less Than Gods* (1928) is also a tribute to Conrad in the form of posthumous collaboration, producing a curious sequel to Conrad's *Suspense*. In an introductory note, Ford recalled that he and Conrad had long ago planned to collaborate on a novel set in Napoleonic times. With Conrad's death, Ford decided to commemorate their collaboration in a novel that deals with the same historical situation, although Ford gave his fictional characters different names.

After the failure of the *transatlantic review* and an amicable separation from Australian-born artist Stella Bowen, Ford left Paris for Provence, and also began to spend more time in the United States, where he was eventually awarded an honorary doctorate of letters and a professorship at Olivet College in Michigan. The last decade of his life, shared with the Polish-American artist Janice Biala, was devoted chiefly to panoramic works in which he celebrated the altruistic chivalry of the troubadour and the virtues of the kitchen gardener who is able to live from the products of his own labour. Ford fell ill during a return to France by boat, and died in Deauville in June 1939.

The interest of Ford's work for Conrad scholars is by no means limited only to their collaborative works or to Ford's memories of working with Conrad. Ford held that the task of the writer was to serve as the historian of his or her own times. The chronicles of English life and customs that he produced during his years of association with Conrad provide a rich and varied sense of the cultural environment in which they lived and worked. These studies include *The Cinque Ports* (1900), an anecdotal history of five coastal towns in Kent and Sussex, and three studies of urban and rural life entitled *The Soul of London* (1905), *The Heart of the Country* (1906), and *The Spirit of the People* (1907), published collectively in the United States as *England and the English* (1907). Ford also wrote a suffragette pamphlet and contributed regular *feuilletons* to a number of periodicals, in which he addressed political and social issues ranging from the meaning of Toryism to the morality of dancing. His 'sociological' works were extended to Germany with a monograph on Hans Holbein (1905) and *High Germany* (1912), and he wrote contrasting studies of German and French culture in support of the Allied effort in the First World War. His love of the Mediterranean became increasingly evident in later works such as *A Mirror to France* (1926) and *Provence* (1938). Ford recorded his impressions of American culture in *New York Essays* and *New York is Not America* (both 1927), and *The Great Trade Route* (1937). He was unable to find a publisher for a three-volume history of the modern world, but his drafts of the first volume have been edited and published posthumously as *A History of Our Own Times* (1988). Ford's final work was a magisterial survey of literary history entitled *The March of Literature: From Confucius to Modern Times* (1939).

There has never been a collected edition of Ford's works, most of which have been out of print for decades. A remarkably readable and informative bibliography of Ford's works and secondary criticism was compiled by David Dow Harvey in 1962 (reprinted 1972), and a selection of letters was edited by Richard M. Ludwig in 1965. Students of Ford's life would do well to start with his own memoirs, set down in volumes like *Ancient Lights and Certain*

New Reflections (1911), *No Enemy* (1929), *Return to Yesterday* (1931), and *It Was the Nightingale* (1934). Ford's biographers include Douglas Goldring, his assistant on the *English Review*, who remembered working with Ford in *South Lodge* (1943) and *The Last Pre-Raphaelite* (1948). Other biographies have been written by Frank MacShane (1965), Arthur Mizener (1971), Thomas C. Moser (1980), and Alan Judd (1990). By far the most extensive and thorough biography is Max Saunders's *Ford Madox Ford: A Dual Life* (2 vols., OUP, 1996). For a general overview of the collaborations, see John A. Meixner, 'Ford and Conrad', *Conradiana*, 6 (1974), 157–69. Their work on *Romance*, the most extensive and thoroughly shared of the collaborations, is examined by Raymond Brebach in *Joseph Conrad, Ford Madox Ford, and the Making of 'Romance'* (Ann Arbor: UMI Research Press, 1985). Electronic texts and other information on the collaborations are available on the Internet at <www.hevanet.com/demarest/jcfmf/index 2.html>.

The Carl A. Kroch Library at Cornell University holds a vast collection of Ford's letters and papers. A second major resource is the collection of Edward Naumburg Jr, now in the Princeton University Library, and much of Ford's correspondence with Conrad is at the Beinecke Rare Book and Manuscript Library, Yale University.

'Foreword' to *A Hugh Walpole Anthology*. Conrad composed this appreciative note to an anthology of writings by his younger friend Hugh *Walpole in March 1921, during his stay in *Corsica. It appeared when the volume was published by J. M. *Dent in 1922. It is reprinted in *CDOUP*, 100–1.

'Foreword' to A. J. Dawson, *Britain's Life-boats: The Story of a Century of Heroic Service*. Written in 1923, this brief eulogy to the Royal Life-boat Institution accompanied an introduction by the Prince of Wales when A. J. *Dawson's volume was published by Hodder & Stoughton in 1923. It is reprinted in *CDOUP*, 107–8.

'Foreword' to A. S. Kinkead, *Landscapes of Corsica and Ireland*. This brief note was written at the request of the Irish artist Alice S. Kinkead, nicknamed 'Kinkie' (1871–1926), whom the Conrads had met during their stay in *Corsica in early 1921. To her request for a preface to her catalogue of 53 paintings, Conrad, then back in England, replied that he had little enthusiasm for Corsica, preferring it more in Miss Kinkead's pictures than in actuality, and did not know Ireland at all, but that he would nevertheless send her a brief contribution. She soon became a frequent visitor to Oswalds and made *portraits of Conrad and Jessie. Written quickly soon after her first visit to Oswalds in late June 1921, Conrad's foreword appeared when the catalogue was published by the United Arts Gallery (London) in November of that year. It is reprinted in *CDOUP*, 96–7. A corrected typescript is held at the Beinecke Rare Book and Manuscript Library, Yale University.

frame-narrative. This term is commonly applied to a type of story in which one narrative is embedded within—or 'framed' by—another. In Britain, the technique can be traced back at least as far as Chaucer's *Canterbury Tales*, and occurs in such diverse forms as the dramatic monologues of Tennyson and Browning, and the multiple narration of Charlotte Brontë's *Wuthering Heights* (1847). Conrad may well have encountered a corresponding Polish variety of this technique in the *gawęda* or 'literary yarn'. This is generally a loose, informal narrative, involving an intermediary narrator, and told in the manner of a reminiscence. The convention of a tale-within-a-tale was used by writers whose work Conrad admired, such as *Turgenev, *Maupassant, Rudyard *Kipling, and H. G. *Wells. 'Heart of Darkness' (1899) offers the best-known example of Conrad's use of this technique: *Marlow's monologue is framed by the narrative of the unnamed narrator, who then becomes part of a listening audience whose presence is implied throughout the story. Conrad had experimented with this technique before 'Heart of Darkness', as 'The Lagoon' (1896), 'Karain' (1897), and, in particular, 'Youth' (1898) all demonstrate.

Most obviously, the use of frame-narrative calls attention to the role of the reader by dramatizing the presence of the narratee. The self-conscious emphasis upon the link between the tale and its recipient at this moment in Conrad's career may owe something to his developing sense of an English audience. Thus, while 'Karain' was published in *Blackwood's Magazine* (November 1897), it was not written with the magazine in mind. 'Youth', by contrast, was written specifically for *Blackwood's* and suggests that Conrad may have dramatized the frame-narrative in response to this new readership. In both 'Youth' and 'Heart of Darkness' (also published in *Blackwood's*), Marlow addresses an audience of professionals (the director of companies, the lawyer, the accountant) with whom he shares 'the bond of the sea' (*Youth*, 45). Frame-narrative thus dramatizes the connection between the tale and its recipients, and thus emblematizes the reciprocal relationship between the author and his readers that Conrad identified in a letter of August 1897: 'one writes only half the book; the other half is with the reader' (*CL*, i. 370). To Watt, the embodied audience in 'Heart of Darkness' restores 'the old friendly commerce of oral storyteller and the listening group' (1980: 213). This identification of the frame-narrator as a friend of Marlow's confers upon the ensuing tale the status of a personal experience conveyed to friends. In this, the frame-narrative in 'Heart of Darkness' is markedly different from that in 'Youth', where the frame-narrator is not even sure how Marlow 'spelt his name' (3). Watts views the relationship between teller and hearer that frame-narrative affords in terms of social custom. Noting that Marlow's narratives involve a story told by one British gentleman to others, he claims that the technique thus dramatizes 'the social customs of an age of gentlemen's clubs and semi-formal social gatherings at which travellers would meet to compare notes and exchange yarns about foreign experiences' ('Heart of

Darkness', in Stape (ed.) 1996: 46). Although Conrad continued to use the technique in subsequent works—*Lord Jim*, 'Falk', *Under Western Eyes*, and *Chance*—the convention appears in its most flexible form in 'Heart of Darkness'.

This novella's use of frame-narrative has a number of interpretative consequences. As Watts argues, the interaction between outer and inner narratives 'demonstrates that we are dealing with a tale which is largely *about* the telling of a tale: about the responsibilities and difficulties of seeing truly, judging fairly and expressing adequately' (1977: 27). The fact that Marlow's narrative is framed by the narrative of one of his listeners advertises, through the disjunction between private and social experience, the subjective and relative nature of perception that is such a feature of Modernist narrative. In Marlow's own words: 'it is impossible to convey the life-sensation of any given epoch of one's existence—that which makes its truth, its meaning—its subtle and penetrating essence' (82). Thus, frame-narrative implies a rejection of full narratorial or authorial understanding and, instead, self-consciously highlights the process of interpretation. Then, just as this technique confers upon the frame-narrator a dual identity, as narrator of the frame-narrative and narratee of the Marlow narrative, so the juxtaposition between the frame and the embedded narratives suggests both contiguity and separation: since Marlow is identified with the group who form his audience, we are invited to suspect them of some knowing complicity in the darkness of which he speaks, and yet since he is separated from them, their presence connotes detachment, scepticism, and a rejection of full understanding. In other words, frame-narrative serves to dramatize the incompleteness of the experience.

It is possible to interpret the frame-narrative as being at variance with Marlow's narrative, as Lothe does when he claims that 'the personal narrator's opening remarks indicate a more unproblematic, simplifying attitude to the text's main thematic concerns than that of Marlow, whose story he transmits' (1989: 23). But it is also possible to see the frame-narrator as creating the conditions for our interpretation of the embedded narrative. He warns us to expect 'one of Marlow's incomplete experiences' (51) and goes some considerable way to introducing Marlow's narrative technique. His absorption with the 'brooding gloom' strikes the keynote in the novella. Even before Marlow emerges from the frame to take over the tale, *London is transformed from 'the greatest' town on earth into a 'monstrous town' (45, 48). In the same vein, the frame-narrative subtly undermines the Victorian truism about the sun never setting on the British Empire by means of a skilful paragraph break: 'The dreams of men, the seed of commonwealths, the germs of empires. | The sun set' (47). Thus, the frame does more than simply throw the Marlow narrative into stark relief: it prefigures effects of the Marlovian narrative and employs images that Marlow will take up and expand. Whether one argues that the outer and inner narratives are in agreement or in opposition, the presence of the frame-narrative ensures a dialogue between the story's different narrational levels. This dialogue between embedding and embedded narratives both obscures the margin between them and suggests that the frame cannot contain Marlow's narrative. To use Samuel Beckett's celebrated image of Marcel Proust's narrative, the whisky bears a grudge against the decanter. Paradoxically, the frame-narrative helps to emphasize the openness of the Marlow narrative.

AHS

France. Conrad's avowal that 'of all the countries in Europe it is with France that Poland has most connection' (*A Personal Record*, 121), whatever its slight historical idealization, offers a key to the deep connection he himself felt with France. When he arrived in *Marseilles in 1874 for some three years, punctuated by absences in the *Caribbean, it was to a culture long admired and envied in his homeland. He already spoke French idiomatically, having learned it, as did Poles of the *szlachta* class, in his childhood; and he read it fluently,

French books figuring as a matter of course in the library of his father Apollo *Korzeniowski, who had translated Victor Hugo's *Les Travailleurs de la mer* (1866). After his Marseilles years, he remained linked to the country by his 'aunt' Marguerite *Poradowska, who moved to Paris, and Conrad occasionally visited the capital when their friendship was at its most intense (up to 1895). Later, drawn to the country for its congenial cultural atmosphere, better climate, and lower prices, Conrad was to pass the six months of his honeymoon and early marriage on the Brittany coast in 1896, to sojourn in *Montpellier with his family (mid-February to mid-April 1906 and mid-December 1906 to mid-May 1907), to stay in *Corsica with his wife Jessie to soak up atmosphere for *Suspense* (early February to the end of March 1921), and to make a final brief visit in September 1923 to Le Havre to arrange for lodgings in which his son John could learn good French. In 1922, he considered spending some months of each year in France in order to reduce his taxes.

Aside from these personal connections, the intellectual and literary culture of France was essential to Conrad's writing, extending to direct *borrowing, the most obvious if not always most honest form of *hommage*, and profoundly shaping his attitudes towards fiction, especially through Gustave *Flaubert, as an art requiring discipline and dedication. France provided settings for 'The Idiots' (Brittany), 'The Duel' (Strasbourg, Paris, and the Midi), 'An Anarchist' (Paris), *The Arrow of Gold* (Marseilles), and *The Rover* (Toulon and the Giens peninsula), while Conrad's fascination with the Napoleonic era, partly inspired by Stendhal, permeates *Suspense*. Conrad imbibed contemporary French writing, closely reading and commenting on Guy de *Maupassant, Alphonse *Daudet, Anatole *France, and Marcel Proust, and establishing contact, through André *Gide, with the writers of the *Nouvelle Revue Française* circle.

Conrad's love affair with France was not one-sided. Almost from the beginning of his career his work was reviewed in major

French periodicals and championed by significant writers, including Paul Claudel and Valéry *Larbaud. The *translation of his writings into French as his books appeared, and then in a *collected edition under Gide's guidance, was an endeavour that deeply engaged his interest and helped cement his friendship with G. *Jean-Aubry, through whom he maintained contact with things French and, in 1922, met Paul Valéry and Maurice Ravel. Conrad's literary and cultural connections with France are extensively explored by Hervouet (1990).   JHS

France, Anatole (pen-name of Jacques Anatole François Thibault, 1844–1924), French novelist and essayist awarded the Nobel Prize for Literature in 1921. Anatole France was judged by Conrad in 1904 to be a writer of 'princely' gifts, remarkable for the combination of 'critical temperament' and 'creative power' (*Notes*, 39, 41). France's influence upon Conrad the writer—first evident in *Nostromo* (1904) and culminating in *Victory* (1914)—forms an important strand in his later French legacy.

'Conrad's cult of Anatole France was not a case of artistic love at first sight, but a maturing intellectual appreciation,' writes Kirschner (1968: 229), one of the first critics to examine the close relationship between Conrad and his famous contemporary. Conrad first made contact with France's work in 1894 through a reading of *Le Lys rouge* (1894), which at that time left him wholly unmoved. His admiration for France slowly but decisively strengthened during the next fifteen years, when he read virtually everything of the Frenchman's writings, including his occasional journalism collected in the four-volume *La Vie littéraire* (1888–92). During this period Conrad also wrote two appreciative reviews of France's *Crainquebille* (1904) and *L'Île des Pingouins* (1908), and in January 1907 was even keen to send the French author a copy of his first review (*CL*, iii. 405).

Unlike the impact of *Flaubert and *Maupassant, which occurred at the very beginning of Conrad's literary career and constituted a form of discipleship, France's

influence was of a later date, slower in effect, and more diffuse. It is not for that reason of lesser importance, but simply different and more difficult to describe. For one thing, it is predominantly the *intellectual* quality and sceptical probity of France's work that attracted Conrad in 1904 when he stressed that the 'proceedings of France's thought compel our intellectual admiration' (*Notes*, 39–40). It is also necessary to add as a qualification that France probably attracted Conrad in different ways and for different reasons at various stages of his career. Some Conradian debts to France suggest that the latter was at times a *maître à penser*, a decisive and formative influence upon Conrad's way of regarding the world. Elsewhere, it seems truer to say that France's ideas appealed to Conrad because he had his own reasons for looking at the world in a way similar to France: hence, what he sometimes takes over are not attitudes and beliefs, but primarily aphorisms and imagery that supplement his own deeply held convictions. Again, another reason for Conrad's intellectual attraction to France may be that the latter, as a writer sensitively attuned to the mood of the times, acted as a spokesman for, and gave Conrad access to, a whole body of late 19th-century opinion.

While, as Hervouet has shown (149–64), a wide range of France's works impacts upon Conrad's writing, it is possible to discern certain important patterns of influence. France's *La Vie littéraire* stands out as a major formative influence, a work that, in Sylvère Monod's apt formulation, 'seems to have played for Conrad the part that the wrecked ship played for Robinson Crusoe: he returned to it again and again, and always came back laden with valuable, even vital objects and materials' ('Editing Conrad . . . for Whom?', in Curreli (ed.), 33). Among the valuable objects Conrad took from France's four-volume collection of essays were scores of aphorisms, generalizations, and *obiter dicta* on life and art that often appear in his fiction and non-fiction as more or less directly translated *borrowings. From this same source, Conrad derived significantly more valuable spoils in the form of germinating ideas for parts of *Nostromo* and *Victory*. In the case of the former, France's portrait of the French writer Prosper *Mérimée as *homo duplex* seems to have provided Conrad with a suggestive blueprint for Martin *Decoud as a type of sceptical *désillusionné* whose multiple potential selves are destructively and fatally at odds with each other. For *Victory*, Conrad again returned to *La Vie littéraire*, borrowing from France's portrait of Benjamin Constant, the early 19th-century French writer, for important details of Axel *Heyst's father's philosophic nihilism and its corrosive power. In both novels, these influences are supplemented by yet more from other Francian works, notably *Le Lys rouge*, the novel that had made no impact upon him in 1894 but from which in later life, according to G. *Jean-Aubry (1930: 12), he could quote large sections by heart: France's heroine Thérèse in that novel is a major shaping force in the presentation of *Lena in *Victory*.

The mutually enriching work of a small group of critics has yielded some tentative sense of the patterns of dependency underlying these borrowings and influences. Kirschner observes that 'where women and love were concerned, [Conrad] was willing to take the word of Anatole France' (1968: 235). Focusing upon France's part in helping Conrad to fashion the careers of Decoud and Heyst, Knowles (1979) discerns an equally profound Conradian attraction for France's treatment of the early Romantic *désillusionné* and the dangerous maladies associated with life-denying scepticism. Hervouet summarizes these and other findings, but adds to them plentiful evidence to show how Conrad, a reluctant literary critic, habitually depended in his non-fictional writings upon France's *obiter dicta*. (*Note*: this entry incorporates material written by Owen Knowles for the introduction to chapter 7 of Yves Hervouet's 1990 study in the course of preparing Hervouet's posthumous typescript for the press.)

'Freya of the Seven Isles', a novella of some 28,000 words, was written between 26 December 1910 and 28 February 1911. It was published in the *Metropolitan Magazine* (New York, April 1912) and the *London Magazine* (July 1912) before appearing as the third and final story in *'Twixt Land and Sea* with the ironic subtitle 'A Story of Shallow Waters'. As Conrad explained to Edward *Garnett, the story was based on what he remembered (prompted by Captain Carlos *Marris, to whom *'Twixt Land and Sea* was dedicated) of the fate of the ship *Costa Rica* (*CL*, iv. 469).

The story is set against the background of the commercial and political rivalry between the Dutch and the English for control of the Malay Archipelago. Freya, the beautiful daughter of a Danish tobacco planter named Nelson (or Nielsen), is passionately in love with an English trader named Jasper Allen, the owner and master of the wonderful brig *Bonito*. Freya's father is fearful of the Dutch 'authorities', as represented by Lieutenant Heemskirk, the commander of a patrol boat called the *Neptun*. Heemskirk becomes a jealous rival for Freya's affections, but there is clearly no contest: the handsome Jasper, who is like 'a flashing sword-blade' (158), loves Freya as he loves his white and agile ship, while the brutal and 'cylindrical' (163) Heemskirk is described as 'that beetle' (188).

Freya, worried that her father will oppose the match, plans to elope with Jasper on the day after her 21st birthday, and tries meanwhile to keep Jasper and Heemskirk out of each other's way. On Jasper's last visit to Nelson's Cove before the date arrives, Heemskirk sees Freya kissing Jasper. After Jasper leaves, Heemskirk, maddened by jealousy, makes advances to Freya, and she slaps his face. Her father enters and assumes that Heemskirk, who is raging with pain and fury, must be suffering a sudden attack of toothache. The following morning, Heemskirk sees Freya blowing kisses to Jasper as he sails off in the *Bonito*.

Heemskirk then stalks Jasper's brig and plots his revenge. He detains the *Bonito* near Carimata and discovers that, without his master's knowledge, Jasper's alcoholic mate Schultz has sold the ship's firearms to the local natives. Heemskirk tows the

Bonito to Makassar, but he releases the tow-rope so that the brig runs aground on Tamissa reef at high tide, where it can never be refloated (a similar episode is also mentioned in *The Rescue*, 101). His heart broken by Heemskirk's treachery and the loss of his ship, Jasper goes mad and spends the rest of his days staring at the wreck. The 'sensible' Freya wastes away and dies.

The story of Freya is narrated by a steamer captain, a friend of Jasper and the Nelson family who is privy to Jasper's plan to elope with Freya. He leaves Seven Isles (the actual Pulau Seribu, off the coast of Sumatra) before the crucial scenes occur, and learns of them only later (and rather implausibly) when Freya's father visits *London. The plot is obviously melodramatic: Jasper, his brig, and the Nelsons are all fair and elegant, as against the black and mechanistic Heemskirk, who is like 'a grotesque specimen of mankind from some other planet' (165). The characters are drawn from classical comedy, as the narrator acknowledges by referring to Freya's father as a 'comedy father' and describing Freya's maid Antonia as 'like the faithful camerista of Italian comedy' (184). Yet despite these operatic elements, the story is unusually bleak even by Conrad's standards: the lovers and the brig are ruthlessly destroyed, while the villainous Heemskirk gets off scot-free. The unrelieved gloom of the ending may explain why two periodicals rejected the story in 1911. In his 1920 'Author's Note' to *'Twixt Land and Sea*, Conrad mentions a letter he had received from one American reader whom the story had made 'quite furiously angry' (p. ix).

'Freya of the Seven Isles' has been adapted twice for television, first in Poland (1968) and again as a French-German-Italian co-production (1972). The complete original manuscript is preserved at the Philadelphia Free Library, and a complete typescript is held at the Berg Collection, New York Public Library.

'Friendly Place, A'. Written to support an appeal for funds to repair and refurbish the Well Street London Sailors' Home, near Tower Hill, London E1, this brief essay was published in the *Daily Mail* (10 December 1912), 8, and collected in *Notes on Life and Letters*. Conrad's contribution, designed to add a 'personal note' to the campaign, recalls his last visit to the Sailors' Home eighteen years previously to see a seaman friend, 'Old Andy' (Claes Anderson, the Norwegian sailmaker in the *Torrens*), and draws upon his own contacts with the establishment between 1878 and 1894 as testimony to its long record of useful public service. The manuscript is held at Smith College, and a typescript in the Berg Collection, New York Public Library.

'Future of Constantinople, The'. Originally published as a letter in *The Times* (7 November 1912), 5, the first part of this piece addresses the question of Constantinople's fate after the end of the First Balkan War, which began in October 1912. In it, Conrad proposes that in future peace negotiations the city should be granted an independent status consonant with its traditions as a 'spiritual capital' to Muslims and Christians alike, and be placed under the joint guarantee of all the Balkan powers, as 'the fit object of Europe's care' (*Last Essays*, 49). The second part, written on 7 November 1912, was prompted by an invitation from the *Daily News and Leader* for Conrad to expand upon his *Times* letter, although the piece did not appear in the *Daily News* and has not been located in print elsewhere. Here, he defends himself from the charge of being an ideologue and restates his belief in an independent Constantinople. His interest in the Balkan War was no doubt partly aroused by the departure of his friend Perceval *Gibbon for the Bulgarian front as a war correspondent. Conrad was also particularly alert, as the later part of the essay shows, to Russian involvement in the Balkans. Both letters were later collected with minor revisions in *Last Essays*. No pre-publication documents are known.

Fynes, the. In *Chance*, John Fyne and his wife Zoe are acquaintances whom *Marlow meets in the country while on holiday. Mr Fyne, a civil servant in the Home

Office, is 'a serious-faced, broad-chested, little man' and an 'enthusiastic pedestrian' with 'a horror of roads' (37). He is the author of 'Tramp's Itinerary', a guidebook to the footpaths of England. Mrs Fyne is the daughter of the aristocratic and tyrannical poet Carleon Anthony, and the sister of Captain Roderick *Anthony. Captain Anthony escapes from his despotic father to sea, while Mrs Fyne escapes into a militant 'feminism', publishing 'a sort of handbook for women with grievances . . . a sort of compendious theory and practice of feminine free morality' (65–6). They have three daughters, but Mrs Fyne takes a more particular and possibly lesbian interest in the various 'girl-friends' she collects, the most

important of whom is Flora *de Barral. Watts (1989: 118–19) has suggested that in her ideas about sexuality, Mrs Fyne may have been meant as a satirical portrait of the feminist activist Sylvia Pankhurst (1882–1960).

Conrad often seems, perhaps unconsciously, to play with the sound of fine/Fyne, as when Marlow protests that 'no Fyne of either sex would make me walk three miles . . . on this fine day' (135); when Mrs Fyne has 'the fine ear of a woman' (169); or when, just after showing Marlow her letter to Mrs Fyne announcing her elopement with Captain Anthony, Flora comments, 'I have had a fine adventure' (444).

G

Galsworthy, John (1867–1933), novelist, dramatist and short-story writer. John Galsworthy was in his mid-twenties and trained for the legal profession when, as a passenger in the *Torrens* on her homeward passage from Adelaide in 1893, he first met Conrad, then serving as her first mate. He and his fellow Harrovian E. L. *Sanderson had been to Australia and then to the South Seas in quest of Robert Louis *Stevenson: they missed Stevenson, but found Conrad. From that meeting developed two of the longest and most equable friendships of Conrad's life.

As the senior man and the first to be published, Conrad provided his younger friend with a literary role model and played an important part in getting Galsworthy's fiction noticed when in 1897 he began writing under the pseudonym John Sinjohn. Conrad also read Galsworthy's early work-in-progress, including the manuscripts of *Jocelyn* (1898), *A Man of Devon* (1901), and *The Island Pharisees* (1904), and advised, probed, and debated with a writer very different from himself. He was also strongly sympathetic to Galsworthy's awkward personal position—in 1895 he had formed a relationship with Ada Galsworthy (née Pearson, 1864–1956), the wife of a first cousin, with whom he was forced to maintain a respectable façade until she was free to secure a divorce and marry him in 1905. Ten years of close friendship lie behind Conrad's *dedication of *Nostromo* to Galsworthy in 1904, when he also wrote a review of the latter's *The Island Pharisees* in 'A Glance at Two Books' (*Last Essays*), and a preface to Ada Galsworthy's translation of *Maupassant. A review of Galsworthy's *The Man of Property* (1906) under the title 'John Galsworthy' (*Last Essays*) followed in 1906. In that same year Conrad named his younger son John in honour of his friend. The faithful and good-natured Galsworthy reciprocated with constant emotional support, considerable financial help, hospitality at his *London homes, and even proofreading. He also undertook a general survey of Conrad's works in 'Joseph Conrad: A Disquisition', *Fortnightly Review*, 83 (April 1908), 627–33, reprinted in *CCH*, 203–9. The most tangible product of his support arrived in 1910 when, after a campaign that Galsworthy had pursued for two years, Conrad was granted an annual Civil List Pension of £100 (see GRANTS AND AWARDS).

Although the two men could sustain each other's literary endeavours in practical ways, Conrad soon realized that Galsworthy as a writer represented everything that he was not: Galsworthy was financially secure, remarkable for his speed of composition, able to appeal to a ready-made middle-class audience, and likely to achieve popular success. Such differences served to bring home to Conrad a sharper vision of his own marginality and insecurity as a writer who, in many ways a stranger to English social and literary traditions, was perpetually forced to struggle with all the things that Galsworthy could take for granted. As Conrad came to see, these differences were also symptomatic of a more fundamental polarity. To the richly cosmopolitan Conrad, with his schooling in the Flaubertian tradition of *le mot juste*, Galsworthy's work seemed typical of the 'national' English tradition in fiction—earnest and humanitarian, preoccupied with the types and issues of genteel society, and indifferent to technical refinement. Indeed, Conrad may well have agreed with the general tenor of Edward *Garnett's assessment: 'Truth to say Mr. Galsworthy is an excellent fellow, a good Briton and one neither stiff nor prejudiced ... [but he] sees things always through the eyes of a Clubman who carries England with him wherever he goes' (quoted in Jefferson, 110). On rare occasions, Conrad openly betrayed a hint of impatience at the narrowness of Galsworthy's inherited limitations as a liberal reformist: 'The fact is you want more scepticism at the very foundation of your work. Scepticism the tonic of minds, the tonic of life, the agent of truth—the way of art and salvation. . . . You seem . . . to hug your conceptions of right or wrong too closely' (*CL*, ii. 359). Elsewhere, he pinpointed Galsworthy's identity as 'a humanitarian moralist' as both his greatest asset—in making him an 'Idol of the Public'—and the greatest potential danger to his development 'because your art will always be trying to assert itself against the impulse of your moral feelings' (*CL*, iv. 115, 116).

By 1906, Galsworthy had made the transition from apprentice to professional writer, finding his own direction as a novelist with *The Man of Property* (the first of the Forsyte series) and as a dramatist with *The Silver Box*. Although he later gained a public recognition that eluded Conrad (being awarded the Nobel Prize for Literature in 1932), his reputation began to wane from the 1930s onwards. After Conrad's death in 1924, he wrote one of the most sensitive obituary tributes, 'Reminiscences of Conrad: 1924', collected in Galsworthy 1927, and excerpted in *JCIR*, 62–3. See also H. V. Marrot, *The Life and Letters of John Galsworthy* (1934), and Frederick R. Karl, 'Conrad–Galsworthy: A Record of their Friendship in Letters', *Midway*, 9 (1968), 87–106.

Garnett, Constance [Clara] (née Black, 1862–1946), translator of Russian literature. Constance Garnett first met Conrad through her husband Edward *Garnett in 1895. She had been a brilliant student in classics at Cambridge and had worked as a librarian at the People's Palace in London's East End before her marriage to Garnett in 1889. With him, she created at their Cearne home in Limpsfield, Surrey, a meeting place for writers, artists, anarchists, Fabians, and émigré Russians. The couple had an open marriage, which enabled Garnett to sustain a lifelong relationship with the artist Ellen ('Nellie') Heath, and left Con-

stance free to forge an independent direction. She began to learn Russian in 1892 and visited Russia in 1894, the prelude to a long career devoted to translating the major modern Russian writers, including *Turgenev, *Dostoevsky, Tolstoy, Gogol, and Chekhov.

Like her husband, she responded warmly to Conrad who, from the mid-1890s onwards, received presentation copies of her translations, one of them—Turgenev's *A Desperate Character* (1899)—being dedicated to him. Through her translations, Conrad was thus during his writing career regularly reading or rereading Russian literature. In the period 1895–1900, for example, he received over ten volumes of Turgenev's fiction and in 1917 commented: 'Turgeniev for me is Constance Garnett and Constance Garnett *is* Turgeniev. She has done that marvellous thing of placing the man's work inside English literature and it is there that I see it—or rather that I *feel* it' (*LFC*, 269). As a Pole with a strong antipathy to most things Russian, he did not, however, share the Garnetts' ardent Russophilia or the widespread Russomania which Constance Garnett's translations helped to foster in British literary circles. Hence in 1912, Conrad had strong qualms about her choice of Dostoevsky for translation—'It sounds to me like some fierce mouthings from prehistoric ages'—and upon receiving her version of *The Brothers Karamazov* he wrote to Garnett that 'the man's art does not deserve this good fortune' (*CL*, v. 70–1). See also Richard Garnett, *Constance Garnett: A Heroic Life* (1991).

Garnett, Edward [William] (1868–1937), influential critic, man of letters, publisher's reader, and nurturer of such literary talents as D. H. Lawrence, Edward *Thomas, and John *Galsworthy. Edward Garnett was a key influence in Conrad's early career after their first meeting in 1894 when, as reader for T. Fisher *Unwin, he recommended *Almayer's Folly* for publication. From then until about 1900, the priceless Garnett was always at hand as sympathetic friend and mentor: he

performed for Conrad many of the duties
of an unofficial literary agent in addition to
being a 'creative' reader of his early work-
in-progress and a regular reviewer of his
fiction. The high point of his services as a
book-surgeon occurred during an early
crisis in Conrad's career in 1896–7. During
this period, Garnett helped to nurse him
through the ordeal attending two abandoned works, *The Rescuer* and *The Sisters*,
and then instigated Conrad's move towards the writing of *sea fiction (*The Nigger of the 'Narcissus'*) as a way of expanding
his British audience. Simultaneously, he
helped Conrad to sever his connection
with Unwin and steered him towards new
publishing connections with William
*Heinemann and William *Blackwood.
'All the good moments—the real good
ones in my new life I owe to you . . . You
sent me to Pawling—You sent me to
Black^ds—when are You going to send me
to heaven?' Conrad wryly commented in
1897 (*CL*, i. 378). In addition, Garnett, attracted to Conrad's foreignness, generally
provided the isolated writer with access to
a wider English social elite with some bohemian fringes as well as to useful personal
and literary contacts, including Conrad's
first meeting with his future collaborator
Ford Madox *Ford. Little wonder, then,
that Conrad chose to dedicate *The Nigger
of the 'Narcissus'*, an important landmark
in his career, to Garnett, and in changing
the name of a character in that novella
from Sullivan to Singleton, he was also
probably paying polite tribute to Garnett's mother, whose maiden name was
Singleton.

The greater distance between the two
men after about 1900 did not derive from
any personal difference, although Conrad
often reacted adversely to Garnett's keen
Russophilia and did not like the Russian
circle that gathered around Edward and his
wife Constance at their Cearne home. As
Garnett himself realized, Conrad had by
1900 forged his own complex craft, was
committed to a future in literature, had acquired a professional agent in J. B. *Pinker,
and no longer needed the sort of literary
midwifery that Garnett had previously

supplied. Indeed, the association between
the two men forms one strand in a wider
recurrent pattern in Garnett's career, originating in his tendency to live vicariously
through the creative trials of a number of
beginning writers who, after his careful
nurturing, would then leave the nest for
independent flight. During the period
1902–16, Conrad's friendship with Garnett
continued in a more relaxed and intermittent way, with Conrad still in contact with
him through the *Mont Blanc literary
circle and able to repay some of his literary
debt by reading Garnett's plays and joining
in the latter's quarrel with drama censorship (see 'CENSOR OF PLAYS: AN APPRECI-
ATION').

A later stage in their relationship developed about 1916, with a renewal of the
kind of emotional and professional intimacy that had marked their early friendship. In 1917, Conrad readily agreed to
supply a preface to Garnett's *Turgenev: A
Study* (see 'TURGENEV') and, not long after,
resumed the practice of consulting Garnett
about his work-in-progress, sending him
both *The Rescue* and *Suspense*. In 1923, he
eloquently summarized his debt to the
age's most complete bookman: 'Straight
from the sea into your arms, as it were.
How much you have done to pull me together intellectually only the Gods that
brought us together know. . . . All I had in
my hand was some little creative gift—but
not even one single piece of "cultural" lug-
gage. I am proud after all these years to
have understood you from the first' (*LFC*,
326–7). In that same year, Conrad fittingly
presented Garnett with a Polish translation
of *Almayer's Folly*, inscribed with the date
of their first meeting 30 years earlier. In
Letters from Conrad: 1895 to 1924 (LFC)
Garnett collected the writer's numerous
letters to him and supplied a moving introductory reminiscence.

As a result of this important friendship
with the Garnetts, Conrad naturally came
to be on intimate terms with other members of their family. In his early *London
days, he occasionally met Garnett's father
Richard (1835–1906), the Keeper of Printed
Books at the British Museum, and often

mixed in literary circles that included Edward's sister Olive (1871–1957). Edward's elder brother Robert Singleton (1866–1932), a senior partner in the law firm of Darley, Cumberland, looked after Conrad's literary interests during his breakdown in 1910. Edward's son David (1892–1981), later a novelist linked with the Bloomsbury Group, recalled the Garnett–Conrad era in *Memoirs: The Golden Echo* (1953) and *Great Friends: Portraits of Seventeen Writers* (1979).

Garnett's relations with Jessie Conrad were probably never more than respectfully polite. He always entertained serious private doubts about her suitability as Conrad's wife, and in 1896 may have tried to dissuade Conrad from marrying a woman intellectually and socially his inferior. On the publication of Jessie's second memoir about her late husband (*JCHC*) in 1935, Garnett reacted explosively to what he regarded as a vindictive and common-minded portrait. He wrote angrily to her on 11 July 1935: 'I think it the most detestable book ever written by a wife about her husband . . . In publishing this detestable book you have betrayed Conrad's trust in you. I judge that no friend of his will wish to see you again' (*PL*, 256). Carolyn G. Heilbrun's *The Garnett Family* (1961) and George Jefferson's *Edward Garnett: A Life in Literature* (1982) provide useful portraits of Garnett, his home at the Cearne as a literary centre, and his place in Edwardian literary life. See also Cedric Watts, 'Edward Garnett's Influence on Conrad', *The Conradian*, 21: 1 (1996), 79–91.

'Gaspar Ruiz'. In March 1923, Conrad informed R. B. Cunninghame *Graham that he had found the 'seed' for 'Gaspar Ruiz' in Captain Basil Hall's *Extracts from a Journal Written on the Coasts of Chili, Peru, and Mexico, in the Years 1820, 1821, 1822* (Edinburgh: Constable 1824): 'The original of G. Ruiz is a man called Benavides, a freelance on the southern frontier of Chile during the wars of the revolution' (*LCG*, 196). Conrad had presumably read Hall as part of his South American research for *Nostromo*. After finishing this long novel in

autumn 1904, Conrad's fascination with the pirate Vicente Benavides led him to compose a tale entitled 'Benavides' for the monthly *Strand Magazine* (which had requested a short story from him). The tale was sent to his agent J. B. *Pinker in mid-November 1904 with a letter in which Conrad suggested 'a Benavides cycle' of three tales (*CL*, iii. 181). Subsequent letters to Pinker reported progress on the second and third 'Benavides' tales, although these were eventually serialized not in the *Strand* but, as 'Gaspar Ruiz', in *Pall Mall Magazine* (July–October 1906) and collected in *A Set of Six*.

Subtitled 'A Romantic Tale', the story is set in Chile during the war for independence from Spanish rule and tells of a simple, humane man, of enormous physique and strength, who is unjustly condemned as a deserter by the republicans and sentenced to death. Surviving the firing squad, he escapes and is nursed back to health by a young aristocratic woman with royalist sympathies and a desire to be revenged upon republicans for ruining her family. Gaspar evades recapture by the republicans under the command of General Robles through the intervention of a timely earthquake, during which his great strength enables him to save the lives of the woman and the general. For this latter act, Gaspar is pardoned and rises to a position of responsibility in the republican forces. But, spurred on by the woman who has now become his wife (and by whom he now has a daughter), Gaspar leads a successful uprising against the republicans before leaving with his guerrillas to conduct a war of revenge. So great is this desire for revenge that, even when told that the Spanish are withdrawing from the continent of South America, he vows that he will 'persist in carrying on the contest against Chile to the last drop of blood' (50–1). The war against Gaspar takes on a new intensity when General Robles's victorious forces return to Chile, having assisted in the struggle to liberate Peru from Spanish rule. Through an act of treachery, the republicans capture Gaspar's wife and daughter. In the rescue attempt, Gaspar acts as a human gun-carriage to support a cannon-barrel that has lost its mount, and, when the defences of the imprisoning fort are breached, his back is broken. Just before he dies, his wife Erminia declares her love for him. Then, while being escorted to Santiago as a prisoner, she throws herself to her death into a chasm, leaving the child, named after her mother, to be brought up as the adopted daughter and heiress of the narrator, General Santierra.

Although many critics and readers have agreed with Conrad's own negative judgement on the story ('I know I shall get several additional centuries of Purgatory for that tale' (*CL*, iv. 128)), there is a welcome attempt by Paul Kirschner, in 'Conrad's Strong Man', *Modern Fiction Studies*, 10 (1964), 31–6, to show how even a lesser Conrad story 'throws an unusual light on the way a great creative imagination worked' (31). Conrad returned to 'Gaspar Ruiz' in the autumn of 1920 when, with Pinker, he used it as the basis for a 'film-play', *Gaspar the Strong Man*.   AHS

Gaspar the Strong Man, an adaptation of 'Gaspar Ruiz' (*A Set of Six*) for the silent cinema, is Conrad's only 'film-play' and remains a curiosity not only as the first *film adaptation ever written by a major English author, but also as the only one of Conrad's creative works that has never been published—at least not in English, although a translation of the manuscript draft appeared as 'L'uomo forte' in *Opere varie*, the fifth volume of Ugo Mursia's Italian edition of Conrad's *collected works, *Tutte le opere narrative di Joseph Conrad* (Milan: Mursia, 1982), 673–706.

In 1919 Conrad's agent J. B. *Pinker arranged the sale of the film rights to four of his novels to Lasky-Famous Players (a forerunner of Paramount), and Conrad received $20,000 for work he had already done. Offered an additional $1,500 from Lasky Players for an original screenplay, he chose the subject of 'Gaspar Ruiz' at the suggestion of his wife Jessie, and also perhaps because the story is packed with vivid action, including a firing squad, an earthquake, a political assassination, a siege and

battle, and a suicidal plunge into the abyss. Conrad and Pinker agreed to produce the scenario in *collaboration, but were not quite sure how to do it; their research included watching a silent film version of Victor Hugo's *Les Misérables* at the London Pavilion on 27 August 1920. Three days later, the Conrads left for a three-week holiday at the Great Eastern Hotel in Deal, *Kent, and Pinker joined him for the final week (14–21 September) to work on their 'film-play'. Conrad later described their working method to Pinker's son *Eric: 'Father held the pen while I with the book before me suggested the wording depicting the episodes from the film point of view. We discussed each scene, and after settling it I spoke the description and Father wrote down the agreed text' (quoted in Moore (ed.) 1997: 36). However, this account is contradicted by the manuscript itself, which is exclusively in Conrad's handwriting and is prefaced by a detailed note for Thomas J. *Wise (to whom Conrad sold the manuscript on 3 November for £105) certifying it as the complete first draft from which Conrad, by 29 October, had dictated a final version to Miss *Hallowes. In April 1921, the 'film-play' was rejected by Lasky's representative Robert MacAlarney on the grounds that it would be 'weak commercially' (ibid. 41).

Adapting 'Gaspar Ruiz' for film was essentially a matter of finding visual equivalents for Conrad's narrative with the help of explanatory intertitles, but with only the most rudimentary vocabulary available for stage-directing an essentially static camera. Conrad's 'film-play' is thus divided into two sections: dramatic action, which he labelled 'Picture', and written intertexts, which he called 'Screen'. The idea that some pictures should be 'Close-up' seems to have occurred to him as an afterthought, since the term appears only in handwritten annotations to the typescript. Conrad follows his own plot closely, but adds an extra scene to establish Gaspar's great physical strength, in which Gaspar rescues Doña Erminia from being crushed by a falling tree. For the rest, relatively subtle signs in the narrative are rewritten as grand and necessarily visual gestures for the screen, expressed with the raw emotion of 19th-century theatre: where an astonished sergeant in the story 'remained standing with his mouth open as if overtaken by sudden imbecility' (*A Set of Six*, 14), in the 'film-play' he angrily throws his hat to the ground and stamps his feet. At times, Conrad invokes a kind of artistic shorthand, inviting the film-makers to employ conventional stereotypes, as when General Robles is to be shown listening to General Santierra's tale 'with appropriate facial play', or a firing squad is instructed to carry out an execution 'with the usual forms customary for that sort of thing'; one scene even requires a vulture to land very close to Gaspar's head before settling on a pile of dead bodies 'in a characteristic attitude' (cited in Moore (ed.) 1997: 40).

Gaspar the Strong Man has been neglected in Conrad studies, and has even been thought not to have survived (*JCC*, 456); but the manuscript has been at the Beinecke Rare Book and Manuscript Library, Yale University, since 1938 and the typescript is at the Case Library, Colgate University. Further details on Conrad as a scriptwriter are given in Moore (ed.) 1997: 31–47.

Geneva. Conrad visited Geneva on four occasions, the first three times on his own and the last time with his family. He first visited the city in 1891, in search of convalescence in the wake of his *Congo experience. This visit lasted from 21 May to 14 June and set the pattern for his three further visits. On each occasion, he stayed at the Hôtel-Pension de la Roseraie at *Champel-les-Bains, in the outer suburbs of Geneva and ideally located for him to take the baths at the hydrotherapy establishment across the road. The *pension*, a large four-storeyed building, stands on the River Arve, half an hour's walk from the centre of town. Hydrotherapy was a favoured cure for nervous ailments, and, as Conrad complained to Marguerite *Poradowska, in May 1891, 'my nerves are disordered' (*CL*, i. 77). Writing to her again on 3 June 1891, he pronounced himself 'much

better, if not altogether cured' (*CL*, i. 82). During his first visit, Conrad worked on chapter 7 of *Almayer's Folly*. His second stay three years later lasted from 7 August to 6 September 1894, and again he wrote to Poradowska of the beneficial effects of hydrotherapy. It was during this visit that Conrad began work on the short story 'Two Vagabonds', which would develop into his second novel, *An Outcast of the Islands*. See also HEALTH.

Soon after the publication of *Almayer's Folly*, Conrad made a third journey to Geneva from 2 May to 30 May 1895, again for hydrotherapy. During this visit, he met and became friendly with the Briquels, a family from Lorraine, who were also staying at La Roseraie and whom he took sailing on Lake Leman. Drawing on Émilie *Briquel's diary of this period, Najder (*JCC*, 176–91) speculates upon the possibility of a brief romantic attachment between Conrad and Émilie, then aged 20, which was ended by her engagement to a local doctor in February 1896. Najder also makes the interesting point that during his visits to Champel, Conrad passed himself off as an Englishman. At this time, Conrad was still working on *An Outcast of the Islands*, for which Émilie's brother Paul suggested a number of *epigraphs. Ten years later, Conrad made his fourth and final visit to Geneva, from 15 May to 19 August 1907. When his elder son Borys developed whooping cough on a family holiday in *Montpellier, Conrad took the family to Geneva for a course of water treatment for Borys and himself. Borys passed the whooping cough on to his younger brother John, and then himself developed pleurisy and rheumatic fever. As a result of the children's illnesses, the Hôtel-Pension de la Roseraie was initially closed to the Conrads, and so the family stayed at the Hôtel de la Poste in central Geneva before moving to Champel on 23 May. In the course of this stay, Conrad was busy with revisions to *The Secret Agent*, during which he added all of chapter 10 and significantly expanded chapters 11 and 12.

In 'Making You See Geneva: The Sense of Place in *Under Western Eyes*' (*L'Époque*

Conradienne (1988), 101–27), Paul Kirschner argues that Conrad relies on his memories of the city to describe Geneva in *Under Western Eyes*, which was begun in December 1907, shortly after his final visit. Meticulously comparing Conrad's references to Geneva in *Under Western Eyes* with period maps and sources, Kirschner reveals how an intricate network of topographical connections provides a subtext to reinforce and parallel the narrative events. To take a single example, he shows that the Boulevard des Philosophes, on which the Haldin women occupy a house in the novel, is situated midway between Geneva's Russian Orthodox Church to the north, and 'La Petite Russie' to the south, the quarter where the Russian Social Democratic Labour Party had its address and where V. I. Lenin stayed on his visit to the city in 1905. As this neighbourhood is a mere few hundred yards from the Hôtel-Pension de la Roseraie, it seems unlikely that Conrad would not have known of its political reputation. Thus, Kirschner argues that Conrad has located the women, themselves divided between the old religion and the new, 'midway between the two implacably opposed Russian spiritual centres in Geneva: the Orthodox church and the headquarters of Lenin' (108). Conrad's knowledge of the city was such that he could adapt its features to his thematic ends. For instance, when *Razumov composes his report to Mikulin it is beneath the statue of one of Geneva's favourite sons, Jean-Jacques Rousseau, whose intellectual legacy is keenly felt in the novel.

The picture of Geneva in *Under Western Eyes* is largely negative, in order to convey the view of the Russian exiles themselves, to whom it is 'indifferent and hospitable in its cold, almost scornful toleration—a respectable town of refuge to which all these sorrows and hopes were nothing' (338). As a response to this portrayal, when the Genevese erected a plaque on the Hôtel-Pension de la Roseraie to commemorate Conrad's four visits, they included on it the inscription: 'Geneva Despecta Suscipiens' (Geneva is scorned giving shelter). However, as Kirschner's efforts demonstrate, Conrad's intimate knowledge of the city, reflected in *Under Western Eyes*, is itself the sincerest form of tribute to the shelter it afforded him. AHS

Genoa, the main seaport of Italy, provided the setting for Conrad's Napoleonic novel *Suspense*. Conrad may have visited the city during his time in *Marseilles, but his first definite sight of it was in December 1879, when he was an ordinary seaman in the steamer *Europa* bound from *London to various Mediterranean ports, of which Genoa, at that time a city of some 163,000 inhabitants, was the first. His next documented visit to Genoa occurred unexpectedly in October 1914, when the August declarations of the *First World War found him trapped with his family in the Austrian zone of former *Poland. After two months of uneasy refuge in *Zakopane, and with the help of Frederic C. *Penfield, the American ambassador representing British consular affairs in Vienna, Conrad finally obtained permission to leave Poland. He proceeded to Vienna, Milan, and Genoa, now with a population of 272,000, where he spent three days before embarking for England on 24 October.

In between his two visits, Conrad had read the *Mémoires* (1907) of the Comtesse de Boigne (1781–1866), which gave him the idea of situating his 'Mediterranean novel' in Genoa in the days just before *Napoleon's return from Elba at the end of February 1815. Many of the landmarks mentioned in *Suspense* may have been based on his impressions of 1914, such as the Molo Vecchio, where Cosmo Latham first meets Attilio, or the Palazzo Rosso (also called the Palazzo Brignoli, Conrad's mistake for Brignole) rented by the Comte de Montevesso, which is now an art museum on the via Garibaldi. Where Conrad and his family stayed in Genoa is not known, but the Piazza della Nunziata bears the closest resemblance to the location of Cosmo Latham's hotel. For a discussion of these topographical references, see Ugo Mursia, 'Notes on Conrad's Italian Novel: *Suspense*' (trans. Mario Curreli), in Moore (ed.) 1992: 269–81.

'Geography and Some Explorers'. At the invitation of J. A. Hammerton, Conrad agreed in October 1923 to write a general preface for Hammerton's new and lavishly illustrated serial publication *Countries of the World*. Composed in early November and finished by mid-month, it appeared under the title of 'The Romance of Travel' in *Countries of the World*, 1 (February 1924), pp. xviii–xxviii, and was published in America in the *National Geographic Magazine*, 45 (March 1924), 239–74. The *National Geographic's* founding editor, Gilbert Grosvenor, would have liked more articles from the author, although Conrad declined, explaining that he knew 'very little of the historical aspect of exploration' and could only deal with its 'picturesque aspect' (13 March 1924). With a new title, the essay was later collected in *Last Essays*.

Written some nine months before Conrad's death, the essay provides him with the occasion for a nostalgic evocation of his youthful attraction to the heroic legends surrounding famous explorer-adventurers and of the influence of 'the romance of travel' in his own evolution. While the essay's informing logic is a personal and sentimental one, Conrad also sketches in a history of exploration that turns upon a contrast between the 'fabulous' and 'militant' phases of geographic enquiry. The second of these phases finds him trying to distinguish between, on the one hand, explorers whose 'only object was the search for [geographical] truth' and whose purity of intention gave them a heroic dimension; and, on the other, forms of conquest 'prompted by an acquisitive spirit, the idea of lucre in some form, the desire of trade or the desire of loot, disguised in more or less fine words' (10). Although this distinction between militant geography and imperial conquest is difficult to sustain—as emerges in Conrad's depiction of the 17th-century Dutch navigator Abel Tasman (8)—it does in fact largely underpin the essay's structure and enables Conrad to rescue a tradition of 'blameless' geographical exploration (3), in which he claims a humble share for himself through his voyage in the *Otago* to *Mauritius via the Torres Strait in 1888.

Noting Conrad's interest in the semantics of the word 'adventurer', Hawthorn remarks that Conrad's more mature use of the word 'displays a clear awareness of the fact that European men engaged in what seemed like boys' adventures could in fact be adventurers engaged in dubious activities in the service of imperialism', and he adds: 'Whenever the romantic in Conrad dominates the realist in him, the negative elements in the semantics of "adventurer" tend to be suppressed' (1990: 207, 208). If these 'negative' elements are generally underplayed in the essay, they nevertheless surface in the account of his experiences in the *Congo, an episode that underlies 'Heart of Darkness'. He recounts that as a young boy he had put his finger on 'the then white heart of Africa' on a map (16), imagining it as a place of 'worthy, adventurous and devoted men . . . conquering a bit of truth here and a bit of truth there' (13), and he resolved that he would some day follow these explorers. The reality turned out to be very different: 'But there was . . . only the unholy recollection of a prosaic newspaper "stunt" and the distasteful knowledge of the vilest scramble for loot that ever disfigured the history of human conscience and geographical exploration' (17). Crimes such as these do not, however, appear to weaken Conrad's faith in the 'picturesque aspect' of heroic geographical exploration, and he concludes with an effusive eulogy to 'men great in their endeavour and in hard-won successes of militant geography; men who went forth each according to his lights and with varied motives, laudable or sinful, but each bearing in his breast a spark of the sacred fire' (21). The manuscript and the first typescript are held at the Beinecke Rare Book and Manuscript Library, Yale University; the second typescript, with a revised carbon copy, is held in the Berg Collection, New York Public Library; and a fourth typescript, edited by the *National Geographic Magazine* staff, is in the National Geographic Society Archives (Washington, DC). See Ray Stevens, 'Conrad, Gilbert Grosvenor, *The National Geographic Magazine*, and "Geography and

Some Explorers"', *Conradiana*, 23 (1991), 197–202.

'George, Monsieur', the name used by the protagonist of *The Arrow of Gold*. A 'young gentleman' who has come to *Marseilles and 'pretended rather absurdly to be a seaman', he divides his time between 'a bohemian set' (who have given him the nickname 'Young Ulysses') and 'the people of the Old Town, pilots, coasters, sailors' (5). He also has access to the ultra-legitimist salon of a Marseilles banker, which brings him into contact with Mr Mills and Captain John Blunt, who recruit him to run guns for the *Carlists. The novel opens as M. George has just returned from his 'second West Indies voyage' (8). Mills and Blunt engage his interest in *Doña Rita de Lastaola, a former lover of Don Carlos, and as soon as M. George meets her, he falls in love with her and commits himself to the Carlist cause. M. George and his friend Dominic purchase 'a fast sailing craft' (90) and smuggle guns to the Carlists. As M. George becomes more closely involved with Doña Rita, he finds himself condemned to a 'purgatory of hopeless longing and unanswerable questions' (155) and also comes into conflict with Captain Blunt.

In the final part of the novel, Doña Rita leaves Marseilles for Paris, upon which M. George throws himself into his 'unlawful trade' with 'a sort of desperation' (254). When the Carlist position in Spain deteriorates and the gun-running ends in shipwreck. M. George returns to Marseilles, where he finds Doña Rita and learns the secret of the 'fear' (56) that has dominated her character. For the next six months, they withdraw from Marseilles to a small house in the Maritime Alps. M. George returns briefly to Marseilles and hears that Blunt has been spreading rumours about him. He and Blunt fight a duel, and M. George is wounded. He is nursed by Doña Rita, but, before he recovers, she disappears. Like Conrad's account of similar events in *The Mirror of the Sea*, the adventures of M. George reflect his own youthful experiences in Marseilles during the period 1874–8.   RH

Germany. 'I have a reasoned hatred of the Prussians for their policy of extermination and for the way they despise us' (*CUFE*, 200). So spoke the writer of Polish origin in an *interview of 1914 with another Pole, with whom he shared an inherited and ingrained animus towards Prussia which, in 1772 at the instigation of Frederick the Great, had begun the process of annexing a large portion of *Poland. Conrad's political essays, collected in *Notes on Life and Letters*, are similarly unforgiving in their colourful condemnation of Prussia as an arrogant and bullying partner-in-crime with *Russia in this historical outrage. One of these, 'Autocracy and War' (1905), looks back to this history of subjection; it also addresses the state of Europe at the beginning of the 20th century and registers Conrad's fear of the unified Germany that had come into being in 1871, with its increasingly aggressive foreign policy and commitment to *Weltpolitik*: '*Le Prussianisme—voilà l'ennemi!*' (114). Conrad's inherited distrust of 'Germanism' was, however, by the turn of the century being amply confirmed by evidence of military and political aggressiveness in post-Bismarckian Germany and coincided with growing international distrust of that country's intentions: thus, in 1899, the writer of Polish origin was very close to popular British opinion in his belief that the Boer War was 'not so much a war against the Transvaal as a struggle against the doings of German influence' (*CL*, ii. 230).

Conrad's treatment of German national types in his fiction—the captain of the *Patna* in *Lord Jim*, Hermann in 'Falk' (*Typhoon*), *Hirsch in *Nostromo*, and *Schomberg in *Lord Jim*, 'Falk', and *Victory*—suggests a studied effort to keep his 'reasoned hatred' at arm's length and avoid the crude anti-German vilification present in much popular Edwardian literature. Instead, grotesque caricature or lampoon prevails as a way of highlighting national traits, but invariably in a form conveying a topical sense of the malevolent purpose and suppressed aggression that attended 'the doings of German influence'. For example, a generalized reference in 'The End of the Tether' to a fleet or 'squad of confounded German tramps' who 'prowled on the cheap to and fro along the coast . . . like a lot of sharks in the water ready to snap up anything you let drop' (*Youth*, 205–6) characteristically combines images of predatoriness, military force, and vagabondage as a way of evoking the new phenomenon of German commercial encroachment in Far Eastern waters. The treatment of the German merchant Hirsch in South American *Costaguana in Nostromo* again employs a comedy of grotesque national stereotype, in this case supplemented by more crudely defamatory references to Hirsch as a Jew and salesman of dynamite, in order to represent German expansionism abroad as a force for evil and to devise a conflict mentioned by Conrad in an earlier letter: 'If one could set the States & Germany by the ears! That would be *real fine*' (*CL*, ii. 81). Above all, the evolving conception of the character of Schomberg, who appears three times in Conrad's fiction during the period from 1900 to 1914, clearly shows the writer interacting with a wider and progressively more powerful anti-German sentiment in pre-*First World War Britain. In the process of developing from a conventional comic buffoon in 'Falk' into the threateningly grotesque 'Teuton' in *Victory*, Schomberg's 'deeper passions come into play,' Conrad remarked, 'and thus his grotesque psychology is completed at last': 'I don't pretend to say that this is the entire Teutonic psychology; but it is indubitably the psychology of a Teuton' ('Note to the First Edition', p. viii).

The creator of Schomberg was, however, also responsible for the sympathetic *Stein in *Lord Jim*, a clear exception to the general family of Germans in Conrad's fiction and testimony to his ability to transcend an inherited animus. Significantly, the Bavarian-born Stein is represented as upholding a European tradition of political idealism that led him to participate in the 1848 Revolution and forced him to escape from Germany after its failure. He is therefore an honourable exile, a spokesman for the

wisdoms of *Goethe and *Shakespeare as well as the heir of a central tradition of German Romanticism, with no desire to 'annex' anything but scientific knowledge of butterflies and beetles (206).

Although many *translations of Conrad's works have been produced in Germany, there is no significant tradition of German Conrad criticism. The most incisive piece of writing to have emerged from Germany is still Thomas Mann's appreciative introduction to a 1926 German translation of *The Secret Agent* (English version in Watt 1973: 99–112). See also Paul Wohlfarth, 'Joseph Conrad and Germany', *German Life and Letters*, 16 (1963), 81–7, and Spittles, 104–12.

Gibbon, [Reginald] Perceval (1879–1926), known to Conrad, his good friend, by the nickname 'Salvator' (the title-figure of one of Gibbon's novels) and to Conrad's young sons as 'Uncle Reggie'. Educated in Germany, Perceval Gibbon had worked as a merchant seaman in British, French, and American ships before pursuing a double career as man of letters and widely travelled war correspondent. With their common roots as former seamen, Conrad and Gibbon enjoyed other links: they had both become writers and contributors to *Blackwood's Magazine*, shared J. B. *Pinker as literary agent, and were family men living in *Kent. Although Conrad had forewarned his wife Jessie about Gibbon's sharp tongue and outspokenness before she met him, she was fascinated by his 'intense virility' and 'unconscious brutality', but could also recall numerous other people who were 'apprehensive of some rather malicious attack' from Gibbon the 'fighting male' (Jessie Conrad, 'A Personal Tribute to the Late Perceval Gibbon and Edward Thomas', *Bookman*, 78 (1930), 323, 324). From 1908, Gibbon, his wife Maisie, and their two daughters were good personal friends of the Conrads, both families spending several holidays together. The relationship between the two men was particularly close during the writing of *Under Western Eyes* when, for example, Gibbon read the existing manuscript and allowed

Conrad access to his 'Russian notes' (*CL*, iv. 269). In the novel's wake (1910–13), the extrovert Gibbon was always on hand to provide Conrad with moral support—and physical diversion, in the form of hair-raising rides on the pillion of his powerful motorcycle. In the spring of 1913 the two men developed a plan to collaborate on a play based upon one of Gibbon's African stories, although the project did not materialize.

A close and developing friendship lies behind Gibbon's dedication of *Margaret Harding* (1911) to the Conrads (as well as his penning of two *Bookman* articles of 1911 and 1912 on his friend's work) and Conrad's dedication of *Victory* to the Gibbons in 1914: 'no words and no silences', Gibbon wrote to Conrad in a wartime letter, 'can affect the friendship and affection which I have for you and yours. That is one thing which is assuredly "au dessus de la melee" and of any melee' (*PL*, 120). During the war, Gibbon was a correspondent and later a member of the British Intelligence Service in Italy, keeping the Conrads in touch with Borys Conrad's movements at the war-front. He also, according to Józef H. *Retinger, confirmed Conrad's deepest anti-Russian prejudices by telling 'sanguinary stories about the horrors he had seen, and he spoke most critically of the Russian methods of conducting warfare' (75). In later years, after his marriage had failed, Gibbon lived in Jersey where 'he had deliberately abandoned, or had been abandoned by, all his other friends and was living in rather squalid loneliness' (*MFJC*, 61) and where, after Gibbon's death, Conrad's presumably many letters to him were destroyed by fire during the German occupation of the Channel Islands. This loss of materials has been a serious hindrance in forming a detailed portrait of one of Conrad's most important friendships.

Gide, André[-Paul-Guillaume] (1869–1951). Conrad's friendship with France's future Nobel Laureate for Literature of 1947 was mainly an epistolary one. The two writers first met at Capel House in July 1911, under the friendly aegis of the American poet and translator Agnes *Tobin. Other meetings occurred in December 1912 and June 1918. While Gide had heard of Conrad from the poet Paul Claudel, apparently as early as 1905, the first meeting cemented an enthusiasm that took tangible forms in the ensuing decade: Gide actively championed Conrad's work among writers of his circle, translated 'Typhoon' in 1917, and painstakingly oversaw the *translation of his writings for an edition published by Éditions de la Nouvelle Revue Française. In gratitude for promoting his reputation in *France, Conrad bestowed on Gide a set of his *collected edition.

Often concerned with matters relating to the translation of Conrad's work, the correspondence between the two writers was marked by various ceremonious courtesies that included sending books to one another and the exchange of year-end greetings. It suffered a major crisis in the autumn of 1919 over the translation of *The Arrow of Gold*. Work had already begun when Conrad expressed a wish that G. *Jean-Aubry be assigned to translate it, objecting that Gide's team of translators consisted mainly of women who, Conrad lamely argued, were incapable of understanding his writing. Loyal to his professional obligations and badly misreading Conrad's mood, Gide instigated an almost hysterical outburst from Conrad, who angrily insisted on the rightness of his views. Despite the inconvenience and wounded by Conrad's abrasive tone, Gide deferred to Conrad's wishes. The friendship seemingly weathered the crisis; but the two writers missed rare later opportunities to see one another, Gide making no effort while he was in England and Wales during 1920 to contact Conrad, and Conrad doing likewise when travelling through northern *France en route to *Corsica in January 1921. In September 1923, when briefly in Le Havre to arrange tutoring for his son John, Conrad descended unannounced on Gide's Normandy home only to find him abroad. Conrad professed to admire *Les Caves du Vatican* (1914) and *Le Journal sans dates* (1919) and read *La Symphonie pastorale* (1919). Gide's editorial obligations and commitments to his own work prevented him from writing a planned study of Conrad, and he managed only a sensitive appreciation for the collection of obituary tributes organized by Jacques Rivière for the December 1924 issue of the *Nouvelle Revue Française*. Other forms of homage were his selection of an epigraph from *Lord Jim* for Book V of *Les Faux-Monnayeurs* (1926) and the *dedication of *Voyage au Congo* (1927) to Conrad's memory.

Frederick R. Karl's 'Conrad and Gide: A Relationship and a Correspondence', *Comparative Literature*, 39 (1977), 148–71, analyses the friendship's vicissitudes. Sylvère Monod's *face-en-face* edition *Typhoon/Typhon* (Paris: Gallimard, 1991) and 'Deux traductions du *Typhoon* de Conrad', *Bulletin des amis d'André Gide*, 21 (1993), 577–92, and J. H. Stape's 'The Art of Fidelity: Conrad, Gide, and the Translation of *Victory*', *Journal of Modern Literature*, 17 (1990), 155–65, focus on Gide as a translator of Conrad. Various facets of the literary relationship are explored by Walter C. Putnam III in *L'Aventure littéraire de Joseph Conrad et d'André Gide* (Saratoga, Calif.: Anima Libri, 1990) and by Russell West in *Conrad and Gide: Translation, Transference and Intertextuality* (Amsterdam: Rodopi, 1996). JHS

'Glance at Two Books, A'. Conrad finished this review of John *Galsworthy's *The Island Pharisees* and W. H. *Hudson's *Green Mansions* (both 1904) on 2 March 1904 for *Pall Mall Magazine*, but it was apparently suppressed by an editor and never appeared in his lifetime. It was first published posthumously in *T.P.'s and Cassell's Weekly* (1 August 1925) 475, 494, and later collected in *Last Essays*. Conrad's treatment of these two writers is shaped by his wider sense of the contrasting traditions to which they belong, with Galsworthy representing the 'national English novelist' who, driven by powerful feeling, is 'always at his best in denunciations of institutions, of types or of conventionalised society' (132). Hudson, by contrast, belongs to Conrad's own preferred tradition of the impartial and craftsmanly worker in prose

devoted to 'rendering the external aspects of things' (134). The revised typescript, dated 2 March 1904, is held at Colgate University. See also 'JOHN GALSWORTHY'.

Goethe, Johann Wolfgang von (1749–1832). Although Conrad maintained in 1913 that he had 'never read a line of the Great Man' either in the original or in translation (*CL*, v. 174), he does in fact include an extract in the original German from Goethe's play *Torquato Tasso* (1790) in *Lord Jim* (chapter 20), and there is also an allusion to *Faust* (1808) in a post-1913 work, *The Arrow of Gold*. In addition, Conrad could hardly have avoided meeting Goethe's enormous influence and legacy in indirect ways: on 14 May 1917, he attended a performance of Charles Gounod's opera *Faust* (1859) at *London's Garrick Theatre, and one of his favourite novels, Anatole *France's *Le Lys rouge* (1894), ends with a climax set against the background of a performance of Goethe's best-known work. The influence of France's novel upon *Victory* in particular may help to explain the latter's pervasive Goethean tonalities, felt in the Mephistophelean presence of Mr *Jones and the final *Walpurgisnacht* that enfolds *Samburan. As long ago as 1932, Alice Raphael suggested that *Victory* was the *Faust* of 'our generation' (*Goethe the Challenger* (Cape, 1932), 44).

Most critical attention has, however, been given to Goethe's possible impact upon *Lord Jim*. In 'Conrad, Goethe, and the German Grotesque', *Comparative Literature Studies*, 13 (1976), 60–74, Peter Firchow offers grounds for connecting the German *Stein in *Lord Jim* with Goethe and detects other Goethean elements in the novel's treatment of the grotesque. Paul Kirschner's later study 'Conrad, Goethe and Stein: The Romantic Fate in *Lord Jim*', *Ariel*, 10 (1979), 65–81, discovers many suggestive consonances in theme, structure, and imagery between *Lord Jim* and Goethe's *Torquato Tasso* and *The Sorrows of Young Werther* (1774). Through Stein, whom Kirschner sees as the novel's oracular spokesman and possibly its 'real tragic figure' (79), Conrad implicitly acknowledges 'an eminently Goethean and a traditional German theme: the tempting abyss between the gift of imagination and the ordinary demands and consolations of life' (71–2). Finally, Batchelor, observing that 'Jim and Heyst belong to a dramatic pattern that is very rare in the English novel' in dying voluntarily 'for idealistic reasons', notes the powerful precedent of Goethe's *Werther* in establishing 'the suicide of the protagonist as a romantic *motif*' (1988: 170).

Goorall, Yanko, the central tragic figure in 'Amy Foster' (*Typhoon*). Yanko Goorall is one of only two Polish characters in Conrad's fiction (the other being the title-character of 'Prince Roman') and is identified by the author in a letter as 'an Austro-Polish highlander' (*CL*, ii. 401), from the 'eastern range of the Carpathians' (121). 'Yanko' is a dialect form of 'Janek', the diminutive of 'Jan' (John), while 'Goorall' corresponds to the Polish *góral* or 'highlander'. An Anglicized form of Yanko's given name is inherited by his son Johnny, 'which means Little John' (142).

The nature and centrality of Yanko's ordeal in the story were originally signalled in the tale's two working titles, 'A Castaway' and 'The Husband'. While emigrating from his Polish homeland to *America, Yanko is shipwrecked off the English coast, suffers an intolerable ostracism in a provincial *Kent community, and later, as a married man, is deserted by his English wife Amy when he falls ill and deliriously reverts to his native language. In Yanko's experience of cultural and linguistic alienation as a 'lost stranger' in *England (113), many critics have discerned elements of Conrad's own spiritual autobiography as a Polish exile living in an adopted country. However, as Watts points out, 'Yanko Goorall is no Korzeniowski but a holy fool, an innocent and ignorant Slavic peasant', and the product of various literary sources ('Introduction', Joseph Conrad, *Typhoon and Other Tales* (Oxford World's Classics, OUP, 1986) p. xiii). Some of these may, appropriately, be of Polish origin and include the popular literary stereotype of the Carpa-

thian *góral* and the 19th-century Polish emigrant-tale (Busza, 224–30).

Gosse, Edmund [William] (1849–1928; knighted 1925), literary historian, author of the semi-autobiographical *Father and Son* (1907), and an influential figure in the Edwardian literary establishment. Edmund Gosse played a minor and indirect part in shaping Conrad's early career. As one of the first readers of *Almayer's Folly* in manuscript in 1894, he possibly advised the author to submit it to the publisher T. Fisher *Unwin. His most substantial contribution to Conrad's career occurred between 1902 and 1905 when, as Librarian of the House of Lords and Secretary of the Royal Literary Fund, he organized subsidies and grants for the needy Conrad, playing an important part in arranging for him to receive £500 from the Royal Bounty Special Service Fund in 1905 and helping to conduct the sensitive subsequent negotiations with the testy writer. Gosse remained a friend and admirer of Conrad's work and was a moving force in securing a Civil List Pension for the writer in 1910 (see GRANTS AND AWARDS). In 1916, he purchased a William *Rothenstein portrait of Conrad, which he later presented to the National Portrait Gallery, London. Conrad was among 200 signatories to a congratulatory message sent to Gosse in 1919 on his 70th birthday. Shortly after Conrad's death, Gosse made his final assessment on him in a letter to André *Gide, stating that 'we have lost Conrad, a beautiful figure. But he had said all he had to say, and went on writing in order to make money. He will live in half a dozen of his early books' (quoted in Ray 1988: 20).

Gould, Charles, a leading character in *Nostromo*, of English descent but born in South American *Costaguana. Charles Gould inherits the San Tomé silver mine which has brought about the deaths of his uncle and father. After several years in Europe, he returns in his mid-twenties with his new wife *Emilia determined to make a 'serious and moral success' (66) of the mine. So powerful does the silver become that Gould becomes uncrowned 'King of

Sulaco' and a figure increasingly obsessed by the fixed idea of bringing justice to the country. However, during a phase of political instability he is forced to throw the power of the mine behind a new president-dictator, upon whose overthrow it becomes the object of a power struggle between warring factions.

In a novel where national identity is of key importance in determining our responses, Gould's Englishness is consistently stressed as one of the determining features of his personal and political traditions. Although Gould (like his creator) does not speak English with a correct accent, he is depicted in all other respects as the quintessential middle-class liberal English gentleman abroad. Early descriptions present him as dressed in leather leggings, a Norfolk flannel jacket, and with flaming moustaches, all suggesting 'an officer of cavalry turned gentleman farmer' (71). While some characters admire Gould's English, rock-like quality of character, their opinions are adjusted by a more sceptical omniscient narrator who connects Gould's persistently held Anglo-Saxon manner with more serious limitations. Proud to emulate his Uncle Harry who 'remained essentially an Englishman in his ideas' and would tolerate 'no nonsense' (64), he is characteristically aloof and tight-lipped in situations requiring moral commitment; unintrospective, he is driven by a suppressed idealism that, on some occasions, gives him the appearance of a man blindly muddling or blundering through difficulties and, at other times, of someone who believes his ideas to be right because they belong to a 'no-nonsense' Englishman. Several commentators have also noted that Gould's generalized view of the relationship between moral and material success involves a form of humane capitalism associated with the English tradition of *laissez-faire* economics set out in Adam Smith's *The Wealth of Nations* (1776). Englishness is also a crucial part of Charles's defining personal ancestry, since he belongs to the third generation of Goulds who all maintain strong connections with their homeland, have all taken English wives, and who, in

their involvements in South America, appear to labour under a tragic curse. Characteristically, Gould impulsively chooses to defy this curse, and his final punishment for doing so is to enter into a full consciousness of the heritage he has chosen to ignore: 'After all, with his English parentage and English upbringing, he perceived that he was an adventurer in Costaguana, the descendant of adventurers enlisted in a foreign legion, of men who had sought fortune in a revolutionary war, who had planned revolutions, who had believed in revolutions' (365). See also Berthoud 1978: 104–7, Watt 1988: 52–61, and Hampson, 152–7.

Gould, Emilia, an Englishwoman and wife of Charles *Gould in *Nostromo*. Emilia Gould meets her future husband in Italy, where she has been staying with her aunt. Attracted to Charles and moved by his grief at his father's death, she agrees to marry him and share in his life's work, the task of redeeming the San Tomé mine in South American *Costaguana. Like many female characters in Conrad's fiction, she is destined to be sacrificed on the altar of her male partner's increasing obsessiveness, and the history of her married life during the turbulent period covered by the novel is dispiriting: she is childless, unable to attract her husband away from his devotion to the mine, and finally finds herself alone and estranged. She eventually takes a place among a community of women in the novel who have all lost or been deserted by the males in their lives, their prototype being Emilia's old aunt who, mourning her dead Italian husband who has given up his life for his country, lives 'a still, whispering existence, nun-like in her black robes' in a ruined palace (60).

Critics who read the novel for its moral patterns and significances tend to find in Emilia one of the 'fine consciences' celebrated in Conrad's essay on Henry *James (*Notes*, 17). Berthoud speaks of her as a secular saint who 'dispenses a kind of redemptive grace': 'What she has tried to uphold, with her simplicity and charm, is not a principle, or a system, or an ideology, but the life of the moral imagination'—all qualities, Berthoud adds, that associate 'her special gift with the art of the novelist himself' (1978: 129). Such a judgement, however, is probably more generous than the full and subtly mixed textual evidence warrants.

If Mrs Gould is characterized by a capacity for gently humane irony, then so too is Conrad in his treatment of her. His sympathetic *irony derives from the perception that her 'feminine' qualities are the source of both her strengths and limitations, and that these limitations are at least partly defined by her position as a late Victorian middle-class Englishwoman abroad. Admiration is thus tempered by the perception that Mrs Gould, however instinctively insightful she may be, is forced to play out the more restricted role of a Victorian 'angel in the house'. *Nostromo* dramatizes a sharp disjunction between the locus of man's *work (the mine) and the woman's sphere (the Casa Gould), where Emilia is invariably to be found, like a lady in a medieval castle, or 'the good fairy' (520), or 'hostess of all the Europeans in Sulaco' (63). While she is a lively questioner of her husband's motives and aims, she nevertheless plays the part required of her as a late Victorian Englishman's wife: she is supportive, practised in the arts of self-abnegation, and finally—to her own cost—joins her husband in his schooled silence. Moreover, from a point of hindsight, her contacts with the public world through her charitable work in *Sulaco's schools and hospitals (189) can be seen to conform to the kinds of philanthropy allowed to the middle-class woman of her time: she is, in brief, increasingly presented as the novel's version of Florence Nightingale, a ministering nurse in the 'hospital' of the Casa Gould (233–4). For contrasting views, see Berthoud 1978: 128–30; Watt 1988: 52–61; and Rebecca Carpenter, 'From Naiveté to Knowledge: Emilia Gould and the "Kinder, Gentler" Imperialism', *Conradiana*, 29 (1997), 83–100.

Graham, R[obert] B[ontine] Cunninghame (1852–1936), pioneer socialist,

writer, Scottish nationalist, and traveller. R. B. Cunninghame Graham instantly attracted Conrad when they first met in 1897. The uniquely fraternal character of their lifelong friendship impressed many in the Conrad circle. For example, Richard *Curle observed: 'In each other's company they appeared to grow younger; they treated one another with that kind of playfulness which can only arise from a complete, unquestioning, and ancient friendship. I doubt whether the presence of any man made Conrad happier than the presence of Don Roberto' (quoted in West 1932: 114). On several occasions in his letters, Conrad himself attempted to explain his attraction to Graham, describing him as 'the most alive man of the century' (*CL*, ii. 286), and 'one of the few men I *know*— in the full sense of the word—and knowing cannot but appreciate and respect—abstractedly as human beings. I do not share his political convictions or even all his ideas of art, but we have enough ideas in common to base a strong friendship upon' (*CL*, ii. 165).

At the time of their first meeting, Conrad was an unknown fledgling writer and 'Don Roberto' a charismatic public figure. After an early period working in South America in an attempt to rescue the family fortunes, Graham had succeeded to the family estate in 1883. Thereafter, he began a career in politics, being elected as a Liberal Member of Parliament for North-West Lanarkshire (1886–92), imprisoned for six weeks after the 'Bloody Sunday' riots in Trafalgar Square (1887), well known for his outspoken socialist opinions, and often affectionately caricatured as in George Bernard Shaw's *Arms and the Man* (1894). At the time of his first meeting with Conrad, Graham had lost his seat in Parliament, begun a career as a writer, and become active in the emergent socialist movement: he campaigned vigorously and controversially on behalf of many oppressed groups and was a biting critic of Western expansionism. In later life Graham, according to some scholars the rightful king of Scotland, became involved with the cause of Scotland's independence.

The first contact between the two men occurred when Graham, having been impressed by the serial version of 'An Outpost of Progress', wrote to congratulate Conrad. A meeting soon followed, supplemented by further correspondence, with Conrad quickly falling into the warmly informal address 'Cher ami' and soon able to chide Graham in a puckish way about his atrocious, scarcely legible handwriting. In its form, the characteristic Conrad letter to 'Don Roberto' in the early stages of their friendship is an unmistakably distinctive play and blend of different registers and *languages: it invariably takes the form of what Conrad on one occasion called the 'polyglot epistle' (*CL*, ii. 5) that veers back and forth between English and French languages, and is liberally peppered with Spanish exclamations. Cedric Watts summarizes the basis of their developing friendship in the late 1890s as follows: 'Both were aristocratic adventurers, men of action and travel who had turned to writing after years of taxing labour in far regions; both had strong sympathies with nations lacking autonomy and with colourful but vanishing cultures; and both, consequently, were acute critics of territorial and economic imperialism. In temperament, each was a blend of Don Quixote and Hamlet, of self-sacrificing idealism and pyrrhonistic scepticism; and both, as writers, were keen to exploit oblique, deceptive, and impressionistic narrative methods and to relish the ironies that stem from vivid racial, cultural, and geographical contrasts' (*Conrad and Cunninghame Graham* (Joseph Conrad Society, UK, 1978), 7).

The Conrad–Graham correspondence between 1897 and 1904, in which they discuss each other's work, contemporary political events, the history of imperialism, and their own differences of outlook, prompted some of Conrad's richest and most revealing *letters. It shows two secure friends bouncing off each other's opinions and, while arguing from opposing political corners, often being surprised into recognizing fundamental similarities between themselves. For his part, Graham seems to have argued the case for active socialist commitment, challenging Conrad to defend his philosophic pessimism or even nihilism. In response, Conrad, fascinated by Graham's combination of aristocratic heritage and revolutionary politics (a combination possibly reminding Conrad of his father Apollo *Korzeniowski), provocatively countered with a radical Hobbesian view of society as essentially criminal, so challenging Graham to question the meaning of his social idealism and even sometimes hinting at the possibility that his friend 'was more a cynic than an idealist, whose socialism was a form of contempt for a feeble aristocracy' (*Rothenstein, ii. 44).

These letters, as well as Graham's own writings, were part of the rich matrix out of which Conrad's works between 1897 and 1904 grew. As Watts points out, Graham's attack on British imperialism in 'Bloody Niggers' (*Social-Democrat*, 1 (1897), 104–9), which Conrad read in 1898, rests upon ironic parallels between Roman and modern forms of foreign conquest strongly reminiscent of the extended historical synopsis at the beginning of 'Heart of Darkness'. At key points in the writing of this story, Conrad seems to have had Graham in mind as his ideal reader and originally wished to dedicate the *Youth* volume to him, although he changed his plan and instead assigned the *Typhoon* collection to his friend in 1903. Historical manifestations of imperialism also inform Conrad's letters to Graham about the *Spanish-American War and, in turn, find their way into the texture of *Nostromo*. Other suggestions for Conrad's South American novel may come from histories lent to him by Graham or from Graham's own writings, as in the case of suggestions for Giorgio *Viola from Graham's 'Cruz Alta' in *Thirteen Stories* (1900). If Sherry's conjecture is correct (*CWW*, 149), then Graham may also have provided a partial model for Charles *Gould in that novel.

The warmth and intimacy of the Conrad–Graham relationship remained constant. In 1917, Conrad wrote to Graham telling him proudly of his son Borys's exploits as a soldier. His intimation that Borys had turned out to be like Graham was not facile flattery, but expressed a lifetime's admiration for Graham's combination of gentlemanly values, democracy of feeling, and a 'divine indignation which is a gift of the gods' (*LCG*, 186). After Conrad's death, Graham wrote a moving tribute, 'Inveni Portum', reproduced in *JCIR*, 230–5. He also helped Curle to compile the contents of the posthumous *Tales of Hearsay* and wrote an introduction to the volume. For further details on the engrossing relationship between a product of the Polish *szlachta* and a son of the Scottish landed gentry (who died in Buenos Aires), see the 1979 biography of Graham by Watts and Davies, and Watts's introduction to *LCG*.

grants and awards. H. G. *Wells's wry comment in a letter of 1904 to Arnold *Bennett that the impecunious Conrad 'ought to be administered by trustees' was sharply prophetic of the general character of his desperate financial position between 1902 and 1914. Before 1902, the needy Conrad had largely relied on helpful friends and an informal support system to ease his financial burdens. But after 1902, the legacy of debts from that earlier period was compounded by several further financial crises and meant that Conrad, despite being heavily subsidized by his agent J. B. *Pinker, required the help of public grant-awarding bodies, one of these involving officially appointed trustees.

The first of these occasions arose in early 1902 when Conrad's acute financial problems prompted S. S. *Pawling to write on his behalf to Edmund *Gosse. Gosse in turn set about organizing a Royal Literary Fund award (formally granted in July) of £300 for him, securing letters of support from Mrs Craigie and Henry *James, who feelingly characterized Conrad's work as 'of the sort greeted more by the expert & the critic than (as people say,) by the man in the street' (*PL*, 36). A further crisis arrived in 1904 when spiralling debts, medical bills, the catastrophic failure of his bank Watson & Co., and a fifteen-month struggle with the composition of *Nostromo* left Conrad

on the 'verge of insanity' (*CL*, iii. 129). William *Rothenstein drew Conrad's case to the attention of Henry *Newbolt, a committee member of the Royal Bounty Special Fund, the result being that in March 1905, with the Prime Minister's approval, he was awarded £500 from the Fund.

Initial euphoria at hearing the news soon changed to gathering anger as Conrad realized what it entailed. He had, in fact, misconceived its nature, believing that a large amount of money would be forthcoming at once, whereas the award was expressly intended to promote the recipient's permanent benefit by being held in trust or for the purchase of a life insurance policy. The news that two trustees (Newbolt and Rothenstein) had been appointed to administer the award further dismayed Conrad, who complained to Gosse, the Fund's secretary, that the 'whole affair has assumed an appearance much graver and more distressing than any stress of my material necessities: the appearance of "Conrad having to be saved from himself"—the sort of thing that casts a doubt on a man's sense of responsibility, on his right feeling, on his sense of correct conduct' (*CL*, iii. 246–7). He was further angered to hear that the trustees might employ a solicitor to help administer the award, thus threatening to turn his financial distress into something resembling a public case of bankruptcy. Subsequent exchanges and wrangles with the two well-intentioned trustees saw the volatile Conrad oscillating between an extreme of hysterical outrage at the implied assumption that he was an untrustworthy bohemian and, on the other hand, a painfully studied humility as it became clear that Newbolt and Rothenstein were trying to serve his best interests. Eventually, the trustees agreed to pay Conrad's pressing debts without the assistance of a solicitor. The total allowed for immediate payment of debts was £260, with the remainder of the award being paid in instalments of £15 to £20 until April 1906.

In March 1908, at a time when Conrad was convulsively at work on *Under Western Eyes* and his debts to Pinker were again mounting sharply, he applied for a further

Royal Literary Fund award, with letters of support from John *Galsworthy, H. G. Wells, and J. M. *Barrie. By April, he received a grant of £200. Almost a year later, in January 1909, Galsworthy began marshalling support and actively lobbying to secure a regular annual source of income for Conrad in the form of a Civil List Pension, an award from the Prime Minister's discretionary fund available to needy recipients who had rendered service to the Crown or the nation by their achievements in science, art, literature, or other fields. After an unsuccessful application on Conrad's behalf in 1909, success arrived the next year in August 1910 with the award of an annual stipend of £100, which he relinquished only in June 1917. See also FINANCES.

Greenwich Royal Observatory. This famous institution, situated in Greenwich Park in the Greater London borough of Greenwich on the River *Thames, figures centrally in *The Secret Agent*. Adolf *Verloc, *agent provocateur*, is advised by his employer, Mr Vladimir, to select a bomb-target that will seem purely gratuitous but also attack one of the most sacrosant fetishes of the day—science. His advice is to commit an outrage against 'Astronomy' and to go for 'the first meridian' (37) by bombing the Royal Observatory at Greenwich. The subsequent narrative shows how the plot misfires when Verloc's young brother-in-law and assistant *Stevie is accidentally blown to pieces by the exploding bomb, leaving the Observatory itself unscathed. In his choice and development of this subject, Conrad was drawing selectively upon an actual bomb plot in 1894 that had placed the Royal Observatory at the centre of a public debate about law, order, and the question of 'foreign' *anarchist activity in Britain. In February of that year, Martial Bourdin, a French anarchist, attempted to blow up the Observatory. As a result of an accidental explosion, Bourdin was fatally injured before reaching his target and was found in horribly mutilated condition by a park official. Rushed to hospital, he died half an hour later, leaving the

popular press to debate the significance of a shocking terrorist 'mystery'. In thus giving his novel an obliquely topical relevance to one of the best-known anarchist events of late Victorian England, Conrad teasingly evokes memories and fears in his audience of an event that, in its attempted assault upon social order, was both worryingly typical—in its issue of 23 April 1895, the magazine *All the Year Round* remarked that 'dynamite outrages . . . have become a sort of institution in the land' (135)—and, in this case, opaquely mysterious.

'The silence was profound; but it seemed full of noiseless phantoms . . . in whose invisible presence the firm, pulsating beat of the two ship's chronometers ticking off steadily the seconds of Greenwich Time seemed to me a protection and a relief.' So speaks a seaman in 'Karain: A Memory' (*Tales of Unrest*, 40), explicitly invoking Greenwich as a sacrosanct symbol of civilized order. In yet another way, Mr Vladimir's choice of the Royal Observatory as such a symbol or 'fetish' is an appropriately topical one for a novel set in the 1880s. In 1884, discussions were taking place in Washington, DC, in an attempt to establish an International Time Zone System, the main problem being to decide which country would be selected to host the prime world meridian, the designating point for the world's time/space infrastructures. As David Leon Higdon points out, the decision to choose Greenwich was, in some measure, 'an imperialist gesture' by Britain and *America, one of whose representatives supported the choice on the grounds that 'the observatory was placed in the middle of a large park in the control of the Government, so that no nuisance can come near it without their consent' ('Conrad's Clocks', *The Conradian*, 16: 1 (1991), 7). *The Secret Agent* unsettles the reader by its unconventional handling of narrative chronology; but, with this context in mind, it can also be seen to use the Royal Observatory to engage with the wider contemporary politics of time and space, and to play with public perceptions of temporality that were still dramatically changing when the novel appeared in 1907.

'Guy de Maupassant'. This essay originated in Ada Galsworthy's request for a preface to her translation of selected *Maupassant short stories, with which Conrad assisted her. Written during May–June 1904, it appeared as the foreword to *Yvette and Other Stories* (Duckworth, 1904), later served to preface Ada Galsworthy's translation of *Mademoiselle Fifi* (Four Seas, 1919), was issued as a privately printed pamphlet in that same year, and was collected in *Notes on Life and Letters*. Although Conrad had for many years read Maupassant's work devotedly and pondered it at length, he appears to have had difficulty in writing the essay. Under these circumstances, as Hervouet shows (140–1), he looked for assistance to Anatole *France's essay 'M. Guy de Maupassant critique et romancier' in *La Vie littéraire* (1888–92), many of whose main emphases —upon Maupassant's austere 'impersonality', scrupulous attention to fact, artistic honesty, and intense Frenchness—recur in Conrad's appreciation. While Conrad clearly valued France as a *maître à penser*, he nevertheless conveys both his warm respect for Maupassant's greatness as an artist and his own personal sense of having inherited Maupassant's demanding legacy, that of the tradition of *le mot juste*: 'His proceeding was not to group expressive words, that mean nothing, around misty and mysterious shapes . . . His vision by a more scrupulous, prolonged and devoted attention to the aspects of the visible world discovered at last the right words as if miraculously impressed for him upon the face of things and events' (28). Proofs of the privately printed pamphlet are held at the Lilly Library, Indiana University.

H

Haldin, Natalia, Victor *Haldin's sister, the handsome, grey-eyed heroine of *Under Western Eyes*, who wins *Razumov's deep admiration and ultimately drives him to confess his duplicity. Natalia Haldin, who mourns the death of her brother and looks after her grieving mother in *Geneva, represents all that is morally positive and altruistic about revolutionary activity. Conrad recognizes this by citing one of her remarks as the *epigraph to the novel: 'I would take liberty from any hand as a hungry man would snatch a piece of bread' (135, slightly misquoted in the epigraph). This remark reverses the lesson of the cynical Grand Inquisitor in *Dostoevsky's *The Brothers Karamazov*, who argues that in the end, the peoples of the world will renounce their freedom for the sake of food. Natalia Haldin is among Conrad's most successfully virtuous female creations, inspiring love in everyone she meets, including both Razumov and the English *teacher of languages. Her very name, Haldin, sounds like *Heldin*, German for 'heroine'. Critics have noted that the qualities for which she is praised, such as her deep voice and her intrepid gaze, are more commonly associated with men than women.

Responding to a complaint from Edward *Garnett's sister Olivia that Miss Haldin was too static and undeveloped, Conrad explained that he needed a 'pivot for the action to turn on' and that 'She had to be the pivot. And I had to be very careful because if I had allowed myself to make more of her she would have killed the artistic purpose of the book: the development of a single mood.' He conceded that 'Still I need not have made Miss Haldin a mere peg as I am sorry to admit she is. Result of over caution' (*CL*, iv. 489–90). The evolution of Miss Haldin during the process of composition of the novel is examined by Carabine 1996: 128–73.

Haldin, Victor. In *Under Western Eyes*, Victor Haldin is a former student turned terrorist bomber who kills Minister of State de P—(along with a number of bystanders and horses) on a St Petersburg street before seeking shelter in *Razumov's room. Conrad told John *Galsworthy (*CL*, iv. 9) that Haldin's attack was based on the assassination of the tsarist Minister of Internal Affairs Vyacheslav von Plehve on 15 July 1904 by Igor Sazonov, a member of the Socialist Revolutionary (SR) party. Wounded in the explosion, Sazonov was arrested and given a life sentence; he later committed suicide in a Siberian prison by dousing himself with kerosene and setting himself on fire. The attack on Plehve was masterminded by the notorious police spy and SR terrorist Yevno Azev (1869–1918), whom Conrad may also have used as a model for the double agent Nikita. Avrom Fleishman has noted that the details of Haldin's attack more closely resemble those of the assassination of Tsar Alexander II in 1881 (219). Conrad was at sea in the *Loch Etive* at the time of the murder, but may have read newspaper accounts. Betrayed by Razumov, Haldin is tortured and hanged, but his memory is revered by his mother and sister *Natalia and the revolutionaries in *Geneva.

Haldin plays a crucial role in the novel, since the 'disruption' (34) of his sudden appeal transforms Razumov's life into a choice of nightmares. When his first effort to help Haldin fails, Razumov thinks of him as a 'pestilential disease' (32) and decides to deliver him up to the police. He steps through a hallucinatory image of Haldin's body lying in the snow, only to learn later that 'You don't walk with impunity over a phantom's breast' (362). Haldin's ghost, in the esteem of the Genevan revolutionaries and the devotion of his sister Natalia, continues to haunt

Razumov as the emblem of his betrayal. In confessing his secret to Natalia Haldin, Razumov charges her brother with having 'stolen the truth of my life from me, who had nothing else in the world' (359). In the end, Razumov realizes that by betraying Haldin he has betrayed himself: 'In giving Victor Haldin up, it was myself, after all, whom I have betrayed most basely' (361).

Hallowes, Lilian Mary (1870–1950). Lilian Hallowes was Conrad's secretary and typist for the last twenty years of his life, and the unsung co-creator of the original drafts of his late works. Engaged by Conrad's agent J. B. *Pinker in the spring of 1904 to help with *Nostromo* while Conrad was plagued with gout and influenza and his wife was recovering from a recent knee injury, 'Miss Hallowes' soon became a discreet and intermittent but familiar member of the household. At starting wages of 25 shillings a week (*CL*, iii. 126), she would often be called upon to answer *letters on Conrad's behalf or transcribe corrections when he was 'laid up' with illness.

No photographs of Miss Hallowes have been located, but Conrad's son Borys remembered her as 'a tall willowy female . . . with a supercilious manner and a somewhat vacant expression. She also had very thick long brown hair which she wore in an insecurely anchored bun on the nape of her long neck, which used to wobble about as she moved, in a most intriguing manner and finally disintegrate, leaving her hair free to cascade over her shoulders—usually at the most inappropriate and embarrassing moments' (*MFJC*, 14). Conrad's first impression was that she was 'a most goodnatured, useful girl' (*CL*, iii. 125). She joined him and his family during their long stay on Capri in 1905 and their visit to *Corsica early in 1921.

Unlike Jessie Conrad, Miss Hallowes was able to take *dictation, and Conrad increasingly adapted to this method of composition. After 1917, much of his literary work and most of his letters were typed by Miss Hallowes directly from his dictation, and the significance of her contribution as a co-creator of his texts has long been over-

looked by Conrad scholars. According to Jessie, she 'used to declare that proofs would be found imprinted on her heart when she died' (*JCHC*, 228). Her notebook with information on *contracts and *manuscripts has been published in *The Conradian*, 25: 2 (2000), 205–44 (originally at the Bodleian Library, shelfmark MS.Eng.Misc. e.578). After Conrad's death, Miss Hallowes wrote to Eric *Pinker to ask if she might be allowed to have the Corona *typewriter she had used in her work with Conrad. It is not known if her request was granted, but an ancient Corona typewriter is still in the possession of the Conrad family.

'Happy Wanderer, A'. This review of C. Bogue Luffmann's *Quiet Days in Spain* (1910) was one of four written in July 1910 at the invitation of Lindsay Bashford, literary editor of the *Daily Mail*, who towards the end of June had offered Conrad a regular Saturday review-column. It appeared in the *Daily Mail* (23 July), 8, and was collected in *Notes on Life and Letters*. Conrad soon found the task of reviewing popular books uncongenial and sustained the column for only three issues. An exercise in affectionate banter that borrows elements from *Don Quixote* (1605, 1615), this review of a genteel traveller whose 'quiet days require no fewer than forty-two of the forty-nine provinces of Spain to take their ease in' (64) also offers a foretaste of the comic treatment applied to the peripatetic *Fyne in *Chance*. No pre-publication documents are known.

Harlequin, the. This is the name by which *Kurtz's Russian companion or disciple at the Inner Station in 'Heart of Darkness' is generally known in Conrad criticism. *Marlow never refers to him by these words, but most often as 'the Russian', although the man's brightly patched clothing reminds Marlow of a harlequin, or of someone who 'had absconded from a troupe of mimes' (126). The Harlequin's patchwork garb is often taken as a visible symbol of his cosmopolitan origins: although he is definitely Russian, he speaks and reads English and is supplied by a Dutch trading house. His multicoloured costume recalls the map of Africa seen by Marlow in the Company's offices, which is 'marked with all the colours of a rainbow' (55). The manager at the Central Station considers the Harlequin a 'miserable trader' and an 'intruder' (100), and fears him as a rival for the Company's ivory.

Most of the information Marlow obtains about Kurtz's life at the Inner Station comes from the voluble Harlequin, who introduces himself as the wayward son of an arch-priest in the government of Tambov who ran away to sea and ended up roaming the jungle before coming under the influence of Kurtz (123). The Harlequin is fantastic but considerate, and serves to mediate between Kurtz and Marlow. His exaggerated respect for his visionary and mind-expanding master can be seen as a burlesque comment on Marlow's own need to identify himself with Kurtz.

The validity of the Harlequin's comments about Kurtz has been challenged by Todd G. Willy in 'The "Shamefully Abandoned" Kurtz: A Rhetorical Context for *Heart of Darkness*', *Conradiana*, 10 (1978), 99–112. The second Norton Critical Edition of 'Heart of Darkness' (1971) contains a brief anthology of essays (248–61) on the Harlequin in the context of the roles of the Fool, royal jester, and court buffoon.

Harmsworth, Alfred Charles William. See NORTHCLIFFE, LORD.

Hastings, Basil Macdonald (1881–1928), a minor essayist and dramatist whose best-known play *The New Sin* (1912) had some success on the London stage. B. Macdonald Hastings approached Conrad in early 1916 with a plan to dramatize *Victory*. During the next three years until the play was performed in 1919, Conrad oversaw the project, assisted Hastings with the adaptation and casting, attended rehearsals, and thought of collaborating with him on an original play, set in Italy, about a faked painting by an old master. During the First World War, Hastings enlisted in the army but was later a commissioned officer in the Royal Flying Corps and edited its monthly paper, the *Fledgling*, in which Conrad's essay 'Flight' (*Notes*) appeared in 1917. From 1924, Hastings was drama critic for the *Daily Express*. His reminiscences in *Ladies Half-Way* (1927), extracted in *JCIR*, 222–4, give further details of their *collaboration and throw light on Conrad's habitual attitudes to the *theatre and actors. See also VICTORY: A DRAMA.

health. Conrad was afflicted with a great variety of ailments throughout his life, and complained about them frequently in his *letters. In spite of chronic attacks of gout, malaria, neurasthenia, and at least one major nervous breakdown, he nevertheless managed in three creative decades to produce some 30 volumes of fiction and memoirs, plus a correspondence comprising at least 5,000 letters. As he told David S. *Meldrum in 1902, 'perhaps true literature (when you "get it") is something like a disease which one feels in one's bones, sinews and joints' (*CL*, ii. 368).

Conrad's first reported illness occurred during the journey with his parents from *Warsaw into exile in *Vologda, when as a child of 4 he fell seriously ill with pneumonia, and was treated with leeches and calomel. Both his parents contracted tuberculosis in Vologda, and after his mother's death, young Conrad was often sick, not only with specific ailments like German measles, but also from headaches and nervous attacks of an epileptic sort (*JCC*, 24 and 502 n. 64). Conrad's father also described a recurrent gastric complaint: 'urinary sand forms in his bladder, causing continuous cramps in the stomach' (ibid. 26). Conrad's education was irregular not only because of his need to attend his dying father, but also because of the uncertain state of his health. In the summer after his father's death in May 1869, Conrad's maternal grandmother took him to Wartenberg (Bavaria) for his first water cure, establishing a therapeutic habit that Conrad would often have occasion to repeat, usually at *Champel-les-Bains, near *Geneva.

Young Conrad's doctors recommended fresh air and exercise, and felt that a stay at the seaside might cure him. The need for a coastal climate was among the several factors leading to Conrad's decision to go to *sea, where he would find the ultimate 'water cure' for his childhood maladies in a maritime career that spanned nearly twenty years. His early attempts in *Marseilles to obtain regular employment in French vessels were frustrated by his status as a Russian subject, and he apparently attempted *suicide in March 1878, later disguising the shameful episode by claiming to have fought and lost a duel. Conrad's son John remembered seeing scars on his father's chest that may have dated from this period (*JCTR*, 181). Conrad recovered rapidly, and his health apparently improved once he entered the *British Merchant Service, although illnesses and handicaps play an important role in his maritime fictions, from the mortal illness of James *Wait in *The Nigger of the 'Narcissus'* to the disease-ridden ship in *The Shadow-Line.* Conrad was struck by a falling object during heavy seas on an 1887 voyage to *Java in the *Highland Forest* and the ensuing symptoms led to his hospitalization in *Singapore, an episode he later recalled in *Lord Jim.*

The six months Conrad spent in the *Congo in 1890 seriously and permanently undermined his health. He suffered from bouts of malarial fever and dysentery, and was so sick that he had to be carried the 200 miles from Matadi back down to the coast. After his return to Europe he complained of swollen legs and anaemia, and spent the following March in the German Hospital in Dalston (London) with what he described to Marguerite *Poradowska as rheumatism in his left leg and neuralgia in his right arm (*CL*, i. 72). On the advice of his doctor, Conrad travelled in May to Champel-les-Bains, near Geneva, for a course of hydrotherapy. This evidently brought some relief, although he continued to experience strange attacks of weakness that he attributed to the shattered nerves resulting from his Congo experience (*CL*, iv. 88). He returned to Champel in 1894 and 1895, and went there again in 1907 when both his children were seriously ill.

Najder has argued that the nervous and physical ailments that plagued Conrad

throughout his writing career can be understood as the psychosomatic signs of chronic pathological depression of a neurotic kind, with occasional psychotic episodes (*JCC*, 144–5). Conrad's nervous complaints impeded his efforts to meet deadlines and commitments, and to support his family; they were an expression of his constant worry and a reason to worry all the more. One such episode apparently occurred during his honeymoon in Brittany in 1896 when, frustrated by his difficulties with *The Rescuer*, he suffered a recurrence of malarial fever that left him delirious and raving in Polish. Conrad described his condition in a letter to Edward *Garnett of 2 June 1896: 'I have long fits of depression, that in a lunatic asylum would be called madness. I do not know what it is. It springs from nothing. It is ghastly. It lasts an hour or a day; and when it departs it leaves a fear' (*CL*, i. 284).

Conrad regularly described his physical symptoms as 'rheumatism' or 'neuralgia', early bouts of which caused his arms and legs to swell, while later episodes seem mainly to have affected his hands and feet. Gout was not identified as the culprit until 1898, when Conrad first complained to R. B. Cunninghame *Graham in January that 'gout or some other devil' had rendered his wrist powerless (*CL*, ii. 29). By late November the diagnosis was more definite, when Conrad was unable to walk for three days due to 'some kind of gout' (*CL*, ii. 122). Gout occurs when the concentration of uric acid in the blood increases to the point where crystals are precipitated, which settle in the joints and cause acute pain. Uric acid is a normal by-product of the metabolism of nucleic acid, and high levels in the blood indicate an insufficient quantity of the enzymes needed for metabolism. This shortage can be a result of excessive protein in the diet (not unlikely, given the hearty recipes in Jessie Conrad's cookbooks), an inherited biochemical anomaly, a complication of kidney disease, or some combination of these factors. In Conrad's case, the 'urinary sand' mentioned as a childhood problem may signal a predisposition to gout, and

Conrad often linked his condition with the malaria he had contracted in the Congo. In this connection, Richard *Curle spoke of 'more than thirty years of auto-intoxication from that malarial gout contracted in the Congo in the early '90s' (*LTY*, 217).

In Conrad's day there was no cure for gout. The treatments available to his doctors included aspirin, thymionic acid, and colchicum, an extract from the poisonous winter crocus. These medications had no effect on uric acid levels, although they may have calmed his nerves. Frustrated by his inability to 'cure' Conrad's condition, Dr Robert D. Mackintosh, Conrad's primary physician from 1909 to 1921, occasionally supplied him with experimental potions (*CL*, v. 594). According to Jessie, Dr Mackintosh became convinced in 1918 that Conrad's 'gout' was actually caused by his bad teeth, and urged him to see a 'first-rate dentist' and have them pulled (quoted in *JCC*, 433). Conrad also experimented with cures of his own. Józef H. *Retinger recalled that '[Arthur] *Marwood, or maybe somebody else, told him once about the old-fashioned mode of carrying raw potatoes on his person, with the idea that they would collect all the poisonous fluid accumulated in his body. Conrad maintained for a long time that the remedy was really efficacious' (60). Nevertheless, he was usually obliged to wait for the crystals to dissolve naturally, spending days confined to his bed or 'hobbling' painfully around.

The role of stress on metabolism, and thus on gout, is still not fully understood, but Conrad certainly saw his own gout as a malady provoked by nervous tension. He told Edward Garnett in March 1899: 'I am literally lame. Gout. Brought on by—by—by agitation, exasperation, botheration' (*CL*, ii. 176). It often affected his wrist, leaving him unable to write and forcing him increasingly to resort to *dictation. Miss Lilian *Hallowes was hired as a secretary and typist in 1904 to help with *Nostromo*, and served Conrad intermittently for the next twenty years, often answering letters or transcribing corrections on his behalf. The 'original' manuscripts of Conrad's literary work after 1919 are, with few exceptions, the versions typed by Miss Hallowes directly from his dictation.

At the end of January 1910, after years of unrelenting personal stress and problems with his *finances, and only a few days after delivering the manuscript of *Under Western Eyes* to his agent J. B. *Pinker, Conrad suffered a complete physical and mental breakdown that left him prostrate and delirious, swollen with severe gout, ranting in Polish, and conversing with the characters in his novel. (For his wife's account of this ordeal, see *JCHC*, 140–7.) Conrad's own diagnosis was of 'gout in the abdominal muscles', and Dr Clifford Hackney treated the condition 'exclusively with sour milk and thymionic acid' (*CL*, iv. 322). For three months, Conrad was confined to bed and allowed visits only from his closest friends. He was unable to resume normal social life until after the move from Aldington to Capel House in June 1910.

Chronic ill health was exacerbated by financial worries and the knowledge that his writing was the family's only source of income. Moreover, the health of the entire family was precarious: Jessie Conrad had dislocated her knee as a child, and a fall on a London street in 1904 left her permanently disabled with knee injuries; she walked with the aid of crutches, and endured a seemingly endless series of treatments and surgical consultations, with major knee operations on 24 November 1904, 27 June 1918, 2 December 1919, 31 March 1920, and 13 June 1924. Conrad's sons were often seriously ill: Borys was prone to lung infections, and during a stay in *Montpellier in 1907 he apparently managed to contract whooping cough, pleurisy, and rheumatic fever all at once. The fact that Conrad and Borys both contracted severe influenza in the summer of 1918 may have helped to protect them against the notorious pandemic that began in the autumn and ultimately claimed more than twenty million lives.

Despite many chronic problems that frequently made it impossible for him to work, Conrad lived to the age of 66. When Conrad arrived in New York in May 1923, artist Walter *Tittle noted in his diary that he 'is now coughing a great deal and suffering with asthma. He looked very tired and weak, and walked slowly' (quoted in Richard P. Veler, 'Walter Tittle and Joseph Conrad', *Conradiana*, 12 (1980), 96). In the spring of 1924, the sculptor Jacob *Epstein remembered him as 'crippled with rheumatism, crotchety, nervous and ill' (*JCIR*, 169). In the summer, Conrad found himself more alone than usual; Jessie was in a nursing home recovering from a knee operation until 24 June, and Miss Hallowes was away on vacation. Conrad complained of chest pains during a car-ride on 2 August, and on the following morning he died suddenly from a heart attack.

For a psychosomatic interpretation of Conrad's work, see Paul Wohlfarth, 'Der kranke Joseph Conrad' (The Sick Joseph Conrad), *Sudhoffs Archiv für Geschichte der Medizin und der Naturwissenschaften*, 41 (1957), 68–77. Meyer's psychoanalytic biography (1967) discusses Conrad's works in terms of his childhood traumas and fears. In 'Conrad and Calomel: An Explanation of Conrad's Mercurial Nature', *Conradiana*, 23 (1991), 151–6, M. J. McLendon suggests that the treatment of Conrad's childhood ailments with large doses of calomel (mercurous chloride) could have left him permanently afflicted with mercury poisoning, which would help to explain the frequent lack of correspondence between the symptoms he reported and the usual signs of gout.

'Heart of Darkness'. Conrad's most famous and most controversial story is based on his voyage up the *Congo River in 1890. A novella of nearly 40,000 words, it is frequently anthologized as a classic of high Modernism, and its title has become a media byword for the horrors of famine or war, although the story itself deals only obliquely with these issues. The story of *Marlow's quest for *Kurtz has provoked strong responses and been subjected to a wide variety of readings, interpretations, and adaptations into other media. H. L. Mencken praised its 'perfection in design which one encounters only rarely and miraculously in prose fiction' (Keating,

100), and Ford Madox *Ford hailed it as 'the most impassioned unveiling of the hidden springs of human hypocrisy, greed, bloodlust—and of course heroism!—that the pages of any book have ever recorded' (1938: 93). In 1973 the Nigerian writer Chinua Achebe challenged the story's canonical standing on the grounds that 'Conrad was a bloody racist' (Hamner (ed.), 124), while Adam Hochschild maintains that 'Heart of Darkness' is 'one of the most scathing indictments of imperialism in all literature' (146).

Begun in December 1898, the story was finished by early February 1899 and published as 'The Heart of Darkness' in three consecutive monthly issues of *Blackwood's Magazine* from February to April 1899. It first appeared in book form as the first of the two 'other stories' in *Youth: A Narrative, and Two Other Stories*, published by William Blackwood & Sons in Edinburgh on 13 November 1902, and by McClure, Phillips in New York on 8 February 1903.

'Heart of Darkness' opens at sunset with Marlow in the company of four friends aboard the yawl *Nellie* at anchor in the *Thames estuary awaiting the turn of the tide. Marlow suddenly observes that *London, its glorious history notwithstanding, has also been one of the 'dark places of the earth' (48). A vivid sketch of a Roman commander who goes mad from isolation and despair prefigures the story of Kurtz. Marlow reminds his listeners that he had once turned 'fresh-water sailor' (51), and describes how he found employment with a continental company to replace a steamboat captain in the Congo who had been killed by natives. After meeting the director of the Company in the 'sepulchral city' (*Brussels) and having his skull measured by the company doctor, Marlow sets off for Africa. At the 'seat of government' he transfers to another steamer for the voyage to the first company station, where he is struck by the contrast between the immaculate linen of the Company's chief accountant and the misery of natives forced to work in chains and left to die in a 'grove of death'. From the accountant, Marlow first hears the name of Kurtz, a 'remarkable man' upriver at the Inner Station. Ten days later, Marlow departs with a caravan of 60 men to walk the next 200 miles (320 km) to the Central Station, which he reaches fifteen days later, only to find that his steamboat has sunk. Marlow has reason to suspect that the manager of the Central Station, who 'inspired uneasiness' (73), is deliberately trying to delay the relief of Kurtz, who is reported to be ill. Marlow spends three months raising and repairing his steamer, and finally sets off upriver in the company of four or five traders and a crew of Africans. At a deserted hut, Marlow finds a note exhorting him to 'Hurry up' and to 'Approach cautiously' (98), together with a manual on seamanship with illegible notes in the margins. After a night of thick fog in which human sounds are heard in the jungle, the steamer is attacked and its native helmsman is killed with a spear. Marlow, convinced that Kurtz is dead, proceeds to the Inner Station, where he is welcomed by a strange Russian dressed like a *harlequin. Kurtz is brought out on a stretcher and addresses the natives who have emerged from the jungle. He is brought on board, but that night Marlow finds him missing from his cot and discovers him trying to crawl back to the campfires of his native subjects. The steamship departs the following day with Kurtz on board, while the natives line the shore and a 'wild and gorgeous apparition of a woman' (135) bids Kurtz farewell. He dies on the journey downriver, whispering his famous last words: 'The horror! The horror!' (149). Marlow, nearly dead himself, returns to the 'sepulchral city' and decides, six months later, to return Kurtz's letters to his *Intended. In a heavily funereal atmosphere, Marlow mentions that he was present at Kurtz's death. When the Intended asks to know Kurtz's last words, Marlow 'lays the ghost of his gifts at last with a lie' (115) by telling her that Kurtz's last words were her name.

The biographical and historical background of the story was first examined in detail by G. *Jean-Aubry in *Joseph Conrad in the Congo* (1925–6). This pioneering study has been superseded by Sherry's

CWW, which remains the most comprehensive account of Conrad's movements and encounters in the Congo, supplemented with essays by Hunt Hawkins. A comparison of 'Heart of Darkness' with Conrad's actual experience in the Congo reveals a number of interesting differences. Conrad was recommended not only by his 'aunt' Marguerite *Poradowska but by various shipping agents whose letters (see *PL*, 5) led to a first interview with Albert *Thys in Brussels in November 1889, several months before his first visit to the Poradowskis. Conrad left for the Congo at the end of April 1890, catching the steamer *Ville de Maceio* at Bordeaux, her last European port of call. After numerous stops along the African coast, she arrived at Boma on 12 June. Marlow has little to say about this 'seat of government', but a deleted passage in the typescript contains a bleak description of the town with its new hotel and a special steam-tramway constructed to carry colonial bureaucrats between their offices and the hotel restaurant. Like Marlow, Conrad continued his journey to Matadi (the company station) in a coasting steamer with a Scandinavian skipper. In the small, leatherbound *Congo Diary* that he began keeping in Matadi, Conrad registered the pleasure of meeting Roger *Casement and the uneasiness inspired by the other Europeans he encountered: 'Think just now that my life amongst the people (white) around here cannot be very comfortable. Intend avoid acquaintances as much as possible' (*CDOUP*, 7).

On the trek from Matadi to Stanley Pool (Kinshasa, the Central Station), Conrad came upon the unburied corpses of several natives and a skeleton tied to a post, and was asked to administer first aid to a boy who had been shot in the head. When he arrived at Stanley Pool after 36 days on the trail, he found that Freiesleben's steamer, the *Florida*, had hit a snag and needed repairs. Instead of waiting, Conrad continued his journey upriver in the *Roi des Belges*, whose young captain, Ludvig Rasmus Koch, pointed out obstacles and soundings that Conrad duly recorded in a second notebook labelled the 'Up-river book'. Unlike Marlow's slow progress to the heart of darkness, the *Roi des Belges* reached her destination quickly, covering the 1,000 miles (1,600 km) upstream in less than a month. Marlow describes the journey as a return to prehistoric times, or at least to the Roman conquest of Britain at the dawn of the Christian era, but the actual river was not quite so utterly isolated as his tale suggests. At the time of Conrad's journey, some eleven steam vessels belonging to various companies were disturbing the waters of the Congo. Stanley Falls (Kisangani, Kurtz's Inner Station) was not just a hacked-out clearing but a small permanent settlement with offices, warehouses, workers' quarters, vegetable plantations, a jail, and even a hospital. The King's representative, the Resident, had a house made of stone—perhaps for protection against the Arabs, whose control of the ivory and slave trade in the eastern parts of the Congo Free State aroused fierce indignation in the newspapers of the 'civilized' world.

The company agent at Stanley Falls, Georges Antoine Klein, was sick with dysentery when Conrad arrived. He was brought aboard the *Roi de Belges*, but died on the voyage downstream, and was buried just outside the Christian graveyard at Tchumbiri Station. Conrad's manuscript shows that Kurtz was originally named Klein. In *CWW*, Sherry presents evidence to suggest that the attempted rescue of Klein was probably incidental to the main business of the journey, namely to repair a larger troop-carrying steamer disabled by a snag. When Captain Koch fell ill on the journey downstream, Conrad replaced him as master for ten days, until he was well enough to resume command. Back in Kinshasa, Conrad also succumbed to fever and dysentery, and returned to *England thoroughly demoralized and complaining of numbness and paralysis in his limbs.

Reviewers seemed unsure what to make of the middle story in the *Youth* volume, which was not an immediate success. Edward *Garnett called it a 'psychological masterpiece' and hailed it as 'the high-water mark of the author's talent' (*CCH*, 132); but John Masefield expressed a more general opinion when he complained that 'the author is too much cobweb' (ibid. 142). Its fame spread only gradually, and the first translations did not appear until 1924, the year of Conrad's death. In the following year, T. S. Eliot called attention to the story's symbolic potential by taking the line 'Mistah Kurtz—he dead' as the epigraph to his poem 'The Hollow Men'. F. R. Leavis (1948) complained of Conrad's 'adjectival insistence', his obsessive overuse of negative modifiers like 'implacable' or 'inscrutable' or 'unspeakable' which deny the possibility of a more precise meaning. Later critics have viewed this same lack of precision as a positive strength for its power to evoke and maintain a dreamlike atmosphere, in which Marlow's journey upriver to confront his alter ego in Kurtz is also a struggle with the limits of language. Watt (1980) has shown how Conrad's impressionistic method involves a local process of *'delayed decoding' in which the reader shares in Marlow's momentary inability to grasp what is happening (as when the 'little sticks' flying about the boat turn out to be arrows). The decoding of the manager's 'covert plot' to destroy Kurtz is discussed by Watts (1984). Structuralist and deconstructionist critics have analysed the importance of Kurtz as an absent or 'hollow' centre for the story's meaning (see Tzvetan Todorov, 'Knowledge of the Void: *Heart of Darkness*', *Conradiana*, 21 (1989), 161–72), or the ways in which Marlow's narrative is an 'unreadable report' (Peter Brooks in *Reading for the Plot* (Oxford: Clarendon, 1984), 238–63).

In the 100 years since the story first appeared, the shifting attentions of literary critics have swung like a pendulum between text and context, from studies that explore the formal or inherent features of the text to studies claiming that its meaning depends primarily on its place in human culture or history. Marlow's insistence that the 'horror' is not limited to Africa has sometimes had the effect of encouraging critics to dismiss the specific circumstances of the Congo and to consider Kurtz's situation as emblematic of the alienation of modern man or the meaninglessness of

Western civilization. Marlow thus journeys not into Africa but into the self, from the control of the cultivated superego to the barbarism of the id, or from the surface of civilization down into a classical underworld, to confront Kurtz as a second self in the guise of Lucifer or Faust. Claude Lévi-Strauss has claimed that for Amazon tribes 'a frog is good to think', because its amphibious shapes can assume a variety of totemic meanings. In a similar fashion, the ambiguous 'horror' of Kurtz's last breath has been good for Conrad readers to think, and has provided a rich field for speculation about the return to the womb, the fall from grace, or the aporias of language.

Angered by the cultural solipsism and arrogance of such abstractions, the Nigerian writer Chinua Achebe launched an unrestrained attack on 'Heart of Darkness' in 1975 ('An Image of Africa', first published in the *Massachusetts Review*, 18 (1977), 782–94) charging that it was the work of a 'bloody racist' who showed too little sympathy for the oppressed to warrant his high standing in the canon of Western literature. Achebe argues that in human and historical terms, Marlow's discomfort at having to lie for Kurtz does not count for much when measured against the real sufferings of Africans in places like the 'grove of death'. The 'Achebe controversy' has been an important stimulus to certain kinds of Conrad criticism, and the continuing debate serves to confirm the relevance of the story in discussions of multiculturalism and post-colonial discourse. In the wake of Achebe's attack, *feminist and gender critics have also called attention to the ways in which the story can be seen to patronize and denigrate not only black Africans but also women.

During a visit to Conrad's home in 1910, the American composer and pianist John Powell offered to adapt the story for an *opera libretto; on Conrad's advice, he chose instead to write *Rhapsodie nègre* (1917) as a piece for piano and orchestra. 'Heart of Darkness' has also inspired numerous adaptations for radio, *film, television, and *theatre. Orson Welles twice dramatized the story in half-hour radio

shows broadcast on 6 November 1938 and 13 March 1945. He also planned to adapt it as his first Hollywood film, but faced the classic problem of how to film a first-person narrative. His radically innovative solution involved turning Marlow into a 'subjective camera', so that the viewer would see all the events through Marlow's eyes. When the project ran over budget and was cancelled, Welles made *Citizen Kane* instead. Forty years later, film director Francis Ford Coppola transplanted 'Heart of Darkness' from Africa to Vietnam in *Apocalypse Now* (1979) and turned Marlow's rescue effort into a mission to 'terminate' Kurtz 'with extreme prejudice'. Nicolas Roeg's 1994 video adaptation follows Conrad's text more closely, but none of the adaptations to date has situated the 'horror' of Kurtz's situation in the historical circumstances of the Congo: Welles's radio broadcasts compared Kurtz with Hitler; Coppola turns Conrad's story into an ambiguous commentary on the Vietnam War; and Roeg's film updates the story by stressing its cruelty to animals and developing Marlow's friendship with the helmsman.

The criticism available on 'Heart of Darkness' is vast, but readers may wish to begin with Watt (1980) or with Watts's chapter on the novella in Stape (ed.) 1996. Other useful guides include Harold Bloom (ed.), *Joseph Conrad's 'Heart of Darkness'* in the Modern Critical Interpretations series (New York: Chelsea House, 1987), and Anthony Fothergill, *Heart of Darkness*, Open Guides to Literature (Milton Keynes: Open UP, 1989). Of the many editions available, the third Norton Critical Edition (ed. Robert Kimbrough, 1988) contains valuable background information, while the *Heart of Darkness* volume edited by Ross C. Murfin in the series Case Studies in Contemporary Criticism (Boston: Bedford Books, 1989) approaches the story from a variety of critical perspectives.

What survives of the original manuscript is at the Beinecke Rare Book and Manuscript Library, Yale University, and an important typescript fragment is in the Berg Collection, New York Public Library.

Heinemann, William [Henry] (1863–1920), English publisher. William Heinemann founded his firm in 1890 and during its first decade compiled a remarkable fiction list that included Robert Louis *Stevenson, Rudyard *Kipling, H. G. *Wells, as well as Conrad's The Nigger of the 'Narcissus'. From 1895 to 1897 Heinemann also published the New Review, whose editor, W. E. *Henley, had accepted The Nigger of the 'Narcissus' for serial publication before its appearance as a Heinemann volume. With F. N. *Doubleday, Heinemann also helped to subsidize Conrad during his trials with The Rescue. At the turn of the century, Conrad was thus simultaneously committed to two British publishers, being newly connected to William *Blackwood, but having a prior personal obligation to the 'awfully decent' Heinemann who, in Conrad's words, had 'nothing to show for his decency but a few receipts for moneys paid out and half a novel which is hung up, to ripen' (CL, ii. 261). He resolved this division of loyalties by bifurcating his commitments: while Blackwood published his *Marlow stories, Heinemann brought out The Inheritors and Typhoon. In 1921, the Heinemann firm, in which Doubleday had taken over a majority share on Heinemann's death, co-published with Doubleday, Page the first *collected edition of Conrad's works. See also PAWLING, SYDNEY SOUTHGATE.

Henley, William Ernest (1849–1903), poet and critic. W. E. Henley was also an influential editor and patron whose decision to publish the serial version of The Nigger of the 'Narcissus' in the New Review (1897) marked an important breakthrough in Conrad's early career. Having previously heard that Henley had been unable to 'read more than 60 pages of the immortal work', Almayer's Folly (CL, i. 211), Conrad was naturally elated at having conquered the 'affectionate Pontiff' of the influential New Review. Several critics have plausibly argued that the strains of militant Toryism, anti-liberal sentiment, and lyrical patriotism in The Nigger of the 'Narcissus' were deliberately devised to flatter the ebullient Henley's right-wing opinions and to emulate the journal's masculine, imperial, and staunchly oligarchic stance. Some support for this view comes from Conrad himself in a confession that The Nigger of the 'Narcissus' was written 'with an eye on him [Henley]—and yet with no idea whatever that it would ever meet his eye' (CL, iii. 115). Whether by accident or design, many features of the novella's political allegory—for example, its emphasis upon strong leadership and the strictly hierarchical nature of the ship's society—chime in with both the general mood of celebratory patriotism in 1897, Queen Victoria's Diamond Jubilee year, and the Henleyism that so determined the political character of the New Review. In Watts's view, The Nigger of the 'Narcissus' 'offers, from the whole of Conrad's output, probably the clearest instance of a text ideologically modified by the immediate circumstances of magazine publication' (1989: 70). Surprisingly, the two men never met, although in October 1898 Conrad consulted Henley in a long letter on the subject of his *collaboration with Ford Madox *Ford (CL, ii. 106–10), considered dedicating the Youth volume to him in 1902, and associated himself with the Henley Memorial in 1904. For his part, Henley seems to have arrived at his own bluff estimation of Conrad's importance: 'Conrad is a Swell: he is a damned swell; you know, I sometimes think Conrad is the damnedest swell we've got' (quoted in JCIR, 214). See also Todd G. Willy, 'The Conquest of the Commodore: Conrad's Rigging of "The Nigger" for the Henley Regatta', Conradiana, 17 (1985), 163–82; and Peter McDonald, 'Men of Letters and Children of the Sea: Conrad and the Henley Circle Revisited', The Conradian, 21: 1 (1996), 15–56, reprinted in his British Literary Culture and Publishing Practice (CUP, 1997), 22–67.

'Henry James: An Appreciation'. This tribute to the literary 'artist' whom Conrad regarded as the greatest living novelist writing in English was composed after he had completed Nostromo and finished by mid-October 1904. It first appeared in the North American Review, 180 (January

1905), 102–8, and was reprinted in revised form in the same journal in April 1916 to mark James's death. It was later collected in *Notes on Life and Letters*. The reasons that prompted Conrad to write the essay are not known, nor is it certain that James read it, since the essay is nowhere mentioned in his writings.

Some readers have found Conrad's 'appreciation' to be disappointingly generalized (he alludes passingly to only two of James's works, 'The Art of Fiction' (1884) and *The Ambassadors* (1903)) or belletristic in manner—in the words of one critic 'lofty and orotund to an almost mock-heroic degree, its insights half-hidden by its rhetoric' (Graham, 4). In later life, Conrad tried to explain the approach he had taken: 'And after all the article was professedly "An Appreciation" nothing more —nothing less. I didn't write like a professional critic would write. I spoke of his art in a large relation, as a fellow writer . . . The sheer great art of it, where not so much the mind as the soul finds its expression' (*CL*, v. 595). As Conrad indicates, the essay is best regarded as essentially an *evocation* of James's greatness and inexhaustible artistic energy, a combination of formal eulogy and prose poem in which the very manner of the writing flatters 'the Master' by emulating his arabesque imagery and stylistic niceness.

Ultimately, the essay seems valuable less for what it tells us about James than for its insight into Conrad's sense of his own 'large relation' to James and the kind of modernity the latter stands for. As Karl remarks, Conrad probably used the essay as a way of expressing his own artistic code and renewing the insights expressed in his 1897 'Preface' to *The Nigger of the 'Narcissus'*: 'Nearly every phrase about James reverberates back to Conrad: the need for a symbolic art, the use of art as a way of resisting a short-lived reality, the reliance on form as a means of expressing circumstance and character, the expression of the truth of fiction over the record of history.' (*JCTL*, 571–2).

A notable feature of the essay is the striking *self*-confidence that allows Conrad to generalize powerfully upon the significance of the Jamesian achievement. At the moment in his career when *Nostromo* is a finished accomplishment, his address to 'the Master' is less that of the shrinking disciple than of the confident fellow pioneer, who implicitly positions himself in relation to the salient features of James—his role as 'the historian of fine consciences', an exponent of 'infinite complication and suggestion' (17), and a writer who has developed an open-ended type of fiction (18)—and silently aligns himself with the traditions of modern high art that James has helped to inaugurate. The manuscript is held at the Beinecke Rare Book and Manuscript Library, Yale University. See also Allan Simmons, 'Conrad on James: Open-Endedness and Artistic Affiliation', in Carabine *et al.* (eds.) 1998: 97–112.

Heyst, Axel, the protagonist of Conrad's *Victory*. Axel Heyst was described by Baines as 'perhaps the most interesting, and certainly the most complex' of all Conrad's characters because of the Jamesian subtlety of his consciousness, but also as 'the only three-dimensional character in the book' (397). Critics who dismiss *Victory* as overly melodramatic generally concede that its main interest lies in its portrayal of Heyst; H. M. Daleski, for example, finds the presentation of Heyst 'Virtually the sole interest of *Victory*' (in Murfin 1985: 107).

The son of a disillusioned Swedish expatriate, Heyst grows up in *London. Leaving school at the age of 18, he decides to avoid all serious human contact by deliberately choosing to live as a 'drifter'. Ever courteous and gentlemanly, he earns the reputation of a 'queer chap' in the Malay Archipelago. With Morrison, he founds the Tropical Belt Coal Company with headquarters on the remote island of *Samburan, where he continues to live after Morrison's death. Heyst's ascetic lifestyle is thoroughly disrupted by his encounter with *Lena in *Schomberg's hotel in Surabaya. He takes Lena back with him to his island, and finds himself torn between his feelings for her and a manner of life based on his father's dictum that 'he who forms a tie is lost' (199–200).

In his 'Author's Note' to *Victory*, Conrad declined to identify where he first met the original of Heyst on the grounds that 'a marked incongruity between a man and his surroundings is often a very misleading circumstance' (p. xi). However, in his reply of 3 June 1917 to a young correspondent who had inquired about dramatizing the novel, Conrad placed this encounter in the same hotel in Saint-Thomas (West Indies) where the 'Author's Note' relates his first sight of the original of Mr *Jones. In 'Axel Heyst and the Second King of the Cocos Islands', *English Studies* 44 (1963), 443–7, G. J. Resink suggests that Heyst may have been modelled on a member of the Ross family who ruled the Cocos Islands, as described in Hugh *Clifford's *Heroes of Exile* (1906).

In the manuscript Heyst was first called Augustus Berg, which perhaps too closely resembled 'Schomberg', Heyst's vindictive antagonist. The pronunciation of 'Heyst' varies by country of origin or critical predilection. Some critics rhyme it with 'Christ' in accordance with Heyst's role as the 'saviour' first of Morrison and then of Lena, while others have noted a prelapsarian link with the German verb *heissen*, 'to be named'. However, the name could also be a homonym for 'haste'. Critics have been divided about whether Heyst's devotion to his father's ideal of detachment is a pose or an essential part of his being, but they are united in regarding the division against himself provoked by his interest in Lena as the defining and tragic feature of his character.

Hirsch. A secondary character in *Nostromo*, this Jewish hide merchant of German origin, a 'little hook-nosed man from Esmeralda' (203), makes contact with many leading characters and serves a number of functions as a catalysing agent, representative of foreign 'material interests', victim-figure, and sacrificial scapegoat. He first appears in Part I, chapter 5, when, attempting to gain the support of Charles *Gould for his business ventures, he represents one of the many foreign commercial

forces at work in *Costaguana. He reappears in Part II, chapter 8 as a desperate stowaway hidden (a punning link with his occupation as a hide merchant?) in the lighter taking Martin *Decoud, *Nostromo, and the silver to the Isabels. An account of Hirsch's subsequent capture by Sotillo (Part III, chapter 2) is soon followed by a scene in which his hanging corpse, 'disregarded, forgotten, like a terrible example of neglect' (435), oversees the interview between Dr *Monygham and Nostromo (Part III, chapter 8) and climaxes in a retrospective dramatization of his torture and death (Part III, chapter 9).

A critical controversy has developed around the question of whether and how far Conrad's treatment of Hirsch involves an element of vindictive *anti-Semitism. The impersonal narrator's opening description of the German-Jewish trader contains a strong vein of casual and unfeeling stereotyping—he is said to have a 'hooked beak' (202), speaks in a 'strange, anxious whine', uses Spanish 'like some sort of cringing jargon' (201)—many of which epithets continue to appear when Hirsch, again the 'hook-nosed' individual (270), is a stowaway on board the lighter. Cumulatively, these labels tend to imply that Hirsch's physical and moral traits are racially innate and typical of any 'enterprising Israelite' (205). A further problem is that a similar kind of anti-Semitic vilification constitutes part of the torture inflicted by Sotillo—'Speak, thou Jewish child of the devil' (448)—upon a character at this stage coldly and non-committally labelled 'Señor Hirsch'. In response to charges of authorial anti-Semitism, some critics point to the treatment of Hirsch's death—sympathetically dramatized from the sufferer's point of view and allowing him a final heroic moment when he defiantly spits into his torturer's face (449)—as a strongly mitigating factor. Such evidence can, however, point in a converse direction: that is, the momentary dignity allowed to the dying Hirsch may, by contrast, largely serve to emphasize how coldly stereotypical has been the treatment of the living Hirsch. For differing views, see 'The

Merchant of Esmeralda: Conrad's Archetypal Jew', in Gillon 1976: 163–82, Daleski, 121–2, and Verleun 1978: 180–229.

'His War Book'. This preface to a new Heinemann edition of Stephen *Crane's *The Red Badge of Courage* (1895) was written hastily and finished on 29 March 1923. Published posthumously in 1925, it was later collected in *Last Essays*. The essay provided Conrad with an occasion to recall the initial impact or 'detonation' caused by the appearance of Crane's 'masterpiece' of 1895 and to re-examine the nature of his *impressionism, his 'gift for rendering the significant on the surface of things' (119) and of 'welding analysis and description in a continuous fascination of individual style' (124). The manuscript is held at the British Library and a revised typescript at Dartmouth College. See also 'STEPHEN CRANE' and 'STEPHEN CRANE: A NOTE WITHOUT DATES'.

homes and lodgings. As the son of political prisoners and an orphan by the age of 12, Conrad's early life in *Poland unfolded against a background of wandering exile from one temporary place of stay to another, none of them holding the promise of rootedness and permanency normally associated with the idea of 'home'. A seaman for twenty years, Conrad later discovered a spiritual home in the traditions of the *British Merchant Service, but in physical terms he was inevitably a bird of constant passage: he had scores of temporary lodgings, ranging from quarters on board numerous merchant ships to a variety of shore-lodgings and Sailors' Homes in different parts of the world. By contrast, his writing life was more settled, although it too embraced a further eight residencies, all rented rather than owned.

After his birth in *Berdyczów in the *Ukraine, Conrad's first home was in Derebczynka in Podolia (for one year) where Apollo *Korzeniowski, his father, had been an estate-manager since 1852; his financial failure in 1858 forced the family to move to Żytomierz (for two years). By May 1861 Apollo had moved to *Warsaw and was joined there by his wife Ewa and their

young son in October, the family occupying a flat at 45 Nowy Świat, which was also used as a secret meeting place for the first gatherings of the revolutionary Committee of the Movement. In May 1862, Apollo and Ewa were sentenced to exile for their clandestine anti-Russian activities and, with their son, escorted to enforced residence among a larger community of Polish exiles in *Vologda, 300 miles (480 km) northeast of Moscow, where they lived for seven months in a one-storey wooden house on Kozlinaja (now Uritski) Street. In January 1863, the family was permitted to move to a small house on the outskirts of Chernikhov (near Kiev), where, two years later, Conrad's mother died. For three years thereafter, 'home' for the young boy consisted of a bleakly isolated life with his melancholy father as though 'in a cloister' (*CUFE*, 102), interrupted only by visits to see his grandmother in the country or by stays in Kiev for medical treatment. In February 1868, the seriously ill Apollo and his son were allowed to move to *Lwów (11 Szeroka Street) in Galicia, the most liberally governed part of former Poland. In February 1869, three months before his death, Apollo moved to *Cracow with his son, residing at 6 Poselska Street. After his father's death, Conrad was first placed in a boarding house for boys run by Ludwik Georgeon, a veteran of the 1863 insurrection, at 47 Floriańska Street, Cracow. His more settled Cracow home, from late 1870 to May 1873, was with Teofila *Bobrowska, his maternal grandmother and one of his officially appointed guardians, in her flat at 9 Szpitalna Street. For a period of ten months in 1873–4, he returned to Lwów to be looked after by his father's distant cousin Antoni Syroczyński, who ran a boarding house for boys orphaned by the 1863 insurrection.

After leaving Poland in 1874, Conrad had lodgings during at least one of his three years in *Marseilles in a small boarding house owned by a Joseph Fagot (whose wife acted as landlady) at 18 rue Sainte, a street parallel to the eastern side of the Old Port and close to the Opera House. Through his connection with the British

Merchant Service, Conrad's main land-base after 1878 shifted to *London. On his first long shore-leave in 1880, he began the year in lodgings at Tollington Park, near Finsbury Park, London N4, and then in May he rented rooms in the home of William Ward at 6 Dynevor Road, Stoke Newington, N16. In 1889, he took rooms at 6 Bessborough Gardens, Pimlico, London SW1, where he began *Almayer's Folly*, his first novel. Sometime before September 1891, he moved to new lodgings at 17 Gillingham Street, near Victoria Station, London SW1, which remained his base until his marriage in March 1896.

Najder remarks of Conrad that as a writer prone to long periods of depression his 'frequent changes of home were usually symptoms of a search for a psychological regeneration; to each move he attached hopes of improvement, in regard to his own work as well as general living conditions' (*JCC*, 364–5). The newly married Conrads had their first two homes in Stanford-le-Hope, an Essex village 5 miles (8 km) north of Tilbury and near the *Thames estuary. Conrad was initially attracted to the village in 1896 by the prospect of living near his oldest English friends, G. F. W. *Hope and his wife, and of resuming with Hope their long-standing tradition of taking boat-trips together. After a six-month stay in a semi-detached villa in Victoria Road—which Conrad damned as 'a jerry-built rabbit hutch' (*JCHC*, 44)—the Conrads made the short move in March 1897 to Ivy Walls Farm, a spacious Elizabethan house on the edge of the Essex marshes and the birthplace of their first son Borys. Associated by Jessie with the most difficult year of their married life, Ivy Walls was in her mind linked with the dawning realization that her husband 'must be feeling the isolation from men of his own standard of intellect' (ibid. 50).

Their next home, Pent Farm, an old and isolated farmhouse in Postling, near Hythe, *Kent, was sublet to the Conrads by Ford Madox *Ford in October 1898, at an annual rent of £30, and remained their home until September 1907. Residence there brought Conrad nearer to Ford as well as a congenial literary community living in south-east England—notably H. G. *Wells, Henry *James, and Stephen *Crane—and also allowed him close proximity to the *sea (with Hythe only 3 miles (5 km) away). It also saw an expansion in the members of the household: in 1898, Nellie Lyons, faithful maid to the Conrads for twenty years; in 1904, Lilian M. *Hallowes, Conrad's secretary; in 1905, Elena Wright, a cousin of Jessie's, as typist and companion to Jessie; and in 1906, the birth of John Conrad, their second son. At Pent Farm, Conrad had his first opportunity to play the role of English country squire, although eventually, as Najder observes, he probably developed mixed feelings about the place: 'Jessie later came to regard the years spent at the Pent as the happiest of her married life. Conrad did not share her view. In his mind the Pent must have been associated primarily with incessant grind and mounting debts. But it was at Pent Farm that Conrad wrote the books ['Heart of Darkness' to *The Secret Agent*] that establish his greatness and determine his position' (*JCC*, 289). A ruinously expensive family trip to the Continent in 1907 left Conrad heavily in debt and intent upon leaving the 'damnably expensive' Pent, although ironically his next home proved to be an even greater financial burden.

In September 1907, the Conrads moved from Pent Farm to Someries, a Bedfordshire farmhouse situated on the Luton Hoo estate of Sir Julius Wernher, let at an annual rent of £60. Just before moving in, the novelist described its situation: 'It is in Bedfordshire 40 minutes from St Pancras. . . . It is 2½ miles [4 km] from Luton: a farmhouse of a rather cosy sort without distinction of any kind, but quite 500 ft [150 m] above the sea—which is what we both want' (*CL*, iii. 472–3). Despite the advantage of being close to London during the eventful period when Ford was establishing the *English Review (the first issue of which was partly edited and put together at Someries), Conrad soon came to dislike the house and increasingly felt exiled there. Almost immediately after the move, when household debts began to mount, he also began to realize that Someries was too expensive to maintain.

In March 1909, after only eighteen months in Luton, the Conrads moved permanently back to Kent, first for fifteen months in Aldington, near Hythe, where Ford had arranged for them to rent four small rooms above a butcher's shop at an attractively cheap annual rent of £30. Little else was attractive about this 'odious' hole, in close proximity to the butcher's slaughter-house and curing shed. These lodgings provided Conrad with a small windowless cubicle for a study and were the setting for the most traumatic year of his writing career—his break-up with Ford, the ordeal of finishing *Under Western Eyes*, his mounting financial difficulties, and his subsequent breakdown. As Conrad's *letters indicate, the physical meanness of Aldington constantly mirrored back to him the desperation of his position and prospects at that time.

An escape arrived in June 1910 with a move to Capel House, a roomy 17th-century farmhouse in Orlestone, near Ashford, Kent, with an annual rent of £45. Conrad observed: 'It may be folly to take it—but it's either that or a breakdown. . . . I require perfect silence for my work—and I can get that there' (*CL*, iv. 330). No greater contrast with Aldington could be imagined: only 8 miles (13 km) from Pent Farm, in an isolated position, and surrounded by extensive woodland, Capel House and its 'sylvan wilderness' were immediately 'sympathetic' to Conrad (*CL*, iv. 364). His friend Warrington *Dawson described the writer's cosy and crowded study thus: 'The desk people saw—& the special table at which he wrote—The paper-knife made by Borys—The arm-chair in which he rested or smoked, but a straight, hard, uncomfortable chair to write in "and keep myself awake"' (quoted in Randall (ed.), 39). At Capel House in 1912, the family also acquired its first motor-car, 'the puffer', a second-hand Cadillac, a foretaste of the more lavish style of living they enjoyed after the dramatic upturn in Conrad's financial position with the popular success of *Chance* in

1914. The family home during the whole of the *First World War, Capel House saw the beginnings of the many friendships—notably with Richard *Curle, G. *Jean-Aubry, Hugh *Walpole, and Józef H. *Retinger—that sustained Conrad in his later years. He might well have been content to end his days there had it not been that in 1918 its new owner wanted the house for his own immediate use and gave the Conrads six months' notice. On their departure in March 1919, they took up temporary residence until early October in Spring Grove, a furnished 17th-century manor in Wye, near Ashford, Kent, until they moved to Conrad's last home seven months later.

Situated in Bishopsbourne, near Canterbury, Oswalds was the last and largest of the Conrads' residences, its annual rent of £250 being almost six times higher than that for Capel House. Conrad liked the Georgian house itself, but not its situation—in a hollow enclosed by woods that did not offer any larger view. Spacious, elegant, with a household staff, or 'crew' as Conrad called them, that included a butler/valet (Arthur Foote), chauffeur (Charles Vinten), cook (Sophie Piper), housemaids (Vinten's two sisters), gardeners, and a full-time nurse-companion (Audrey Seal) for Jessie, Oswalds became a place of pilgrimage for the numerous friends and admirers of the ageing novelist, its large drawing room the scene of musical evenings and quite lavish weekend gatherings. For further details, see Borys Conrad, *Joseph Conrad's Homes in Kent* (Joseph Conrad Society, UK, 1978). See also FINANCES.

honours and prizes. The literary culture to which Conrad and his fellow writers belonged did not offer numerous large and prestigious literary prizes such as those available to later 20th-century authors. His only literary prize of 50 guineas was awarded in January 1899 when the *Academy* 'crowned' *Tales of Unrest* as one of the most distinctive books of the previous year. Conrad's involvement in later life with the world of public honours was largely a record of repeated polite refusals. Offers of honorary degrees by the universities of

Oxford, Cambridge, Durham, Liverpool, Edinburgh, and Yale during the 1920s were all firmly declined: 'I am perfectly determined to have nothing to do with any academic distinction' (*LL*, ii. 298). Karl has justifiably commented that one reason for these refusals was because, in Conrad's view, 'they distracted the reader from what he really was—an author proving himself in the sole way he could, on paper, in the privacy of his own room, working along the lines of what was uniquely his' (*JCTL*, 882).

A wider sense of what was 'uniquely his' came into play when, in 1919, Conrad learned that members of the Athenaeum Club were unofficially supporting Rudyard *Kipling and himself as possible recipients of the Order of Merit, the highest honour open to a British writer. Conrad commented: 'It is the sort of thing one could not refuse. But I feel strongly that K. is the right person, and that the O. M. would not perhaps be an appropriate honour for me who, whatever my deepest feelings may be, can't claim English literature as my inheritance' (to J. B. *Pinker, 15 February 1919). Speaking here perhaps as *homo duplex*, Conrad's refusal derives from his sense of owning a literary tradition wider and more diverse than the 'national English novelist' (*Last Essays*, 132). As he had written to a fellow Pole in 1903: 'Both at sea and on land my point of view is English, from which the conclusion should not be drawn that I have become an Englishman. . . . Homo duplex has in my case more than one meaning' (*CL*, iii. 89). Conrad's delicate awareness of his anomalous position in relation to his host country complicated by a residual allegiance to his *Polish heritage may also lie behind his refusal in 1924 of the offer of a knighthood from the Labour Prime Minister J. Ramsay MacDonald. To the Prime Minister's offer, he replied on 27 May 1924 that 'as a man whose early years were closely associated in hard toil and unforgotten friendships with British working men, I am specially touched at this offer being made to me during Your premiership'. There is no evidence to suggest that Conrad turned down the honour because it was being made by a socialist govern-

ment; he was simply being consistent in declining all offers of a merely 'national' kind from the British establishment. Nor did his repeated refusals derive from any false modesty. On the contrary, one possible award, significantly the most international, did attract him—the Nobel Prize. From 1919 onwards, he harboured the persistent hope of securing a Nobel award, which he regarded as 'less in the nature of an honour than a reward' (to Pinker, 15 February 1919). Despite efforts on his behalf by French and Swedish admirers, however, this most prestigious 'reward', for which he was never officially nominated, eluded him.

Hope, George Fountaine Weare

(1854–1930), a lifelong non-literary friend whom Conrad first met in January 1880. G. F. W. Hope was a former *Conway* boy (i.e. one who had trained on the famous sail training ship) and merchant navy officer who had sailed in the *Duke of Sutherland* three years before Conrad. As a director of several companies and owner of a leisure craft, a yawl called the *Nellie*, in which Conrad enjoyed trips along the *Thames estuary in the early 1890s, Hope and his friends, W. B. Keen (an accountant) and T. L. Mears (a lawyer), provided the models for the group of auditors in the *frame-narratives of 'Youth' and 'Heart of Darkness'. In the frame-narratives of two later works, 'Falk' and *Chance*, Conrad also draws upon his convivial Thameside meetings with the three men.

Jessie Conrad described the Hopes as 'Conrad's oldest English friends' and as offering 'the first English home that had been opened to him'; she also recalled Conrad's telling her, presumably around 1895, that 'now his uncle was dead, Mr. and Mrs. Hope, as far as feelings could go, were the nearest relations he had in the world' (*JCKH*, 41). Hope was one of Conrad's sureties when he petitioned to become a British subject (1886) and also a witness at his wedding (1896). After their honeymoon, the Conrads settled in Stanford-le-Hope, Essex, in order to be close neighbours of the Hopes, with the two men continuing their tradition of regular sailing on the nearby Thames. According to John Conrad, they enjoyed playing the role of old salts: 'they were both captains, they both had beards, and they both liked talking about the sea and ships' (*JCTR*, 23); by 1899 they were also both leisure-boat owners, since Hope sold his small sailing boat *La Reine* to Conrad and Stephen *Crane. The part Hope played in Conrad's financial disaster of 1896—involving the loss of his shares in a South African gold mine—is obscure, although Hope appears to be the 'unfortunate' friend who, with Conrad, suffered heavily when the venture collapsed (*CL*, i. 292). After the Conrads moved from Stanford in 1898, they never lost contact with the Hopes. Conrad dedicated *Lord Jim* to them in 1900 'with grateful affection after many years of friendship' and also finished *Nostromo* in their Stanford home in August 1904. Earlier, in 1890, the Hopes had named one of their sons Conrad. Hope's memoir of his early contacts with Conrad, entitled 'Recollections of Joseph Conrad's Early Days in England and at Sea', has been published in *The Conradian*, 25: 2 (2000), 1–56. The typescript is held at the Harry Ransom Humanities Research Center, University of Texas at Austin.

Hudson, W[illiam] H[enry] (1841–1922), writer and naturalist, born in Argentina of American parents. W. H. Hudson came to England in 1869 and wrote a number of South American romances and essays on rural England that were championed by Edward *Garnett and R. B. Cunninghame *Graham. After their first contact in March 1899, he and Conrad met periodically—mainly in Garnett and *Mont Blanc circles—and perhaps shared a feeling of being at the periphery of the Edwardian literary establishment. Conrad read and admired Hudson's work, had a special liking for *Idle Days in Patagonia* (1893), and remained a permanent admirer of his style. In 'A Glance at Two Books' (*Last Essays*), he reviewed *Green Mansions* (1904) in the year of its publication, comparing Hudson to *Turgenev and admiring 'the presence of a fine and sincere, of a deep and pellucid personality' (136). Hudson's opinion of Conrad's work was evidently less favourable. In 1904, he begged to differ from the critical praise lavished on *Nostromo*, while in 1914 he found the *Marlow of *Chance* a 'bore' and the ending of the novel 'hugely comical' in its melodrama (*PL*, 96). On the occasion of Hudson's death in 1922, Conrad commented: 'I was not intimate with him but I had a real affection for that unique personality of his with its, to me, somewhat mysterious fascination' (*LCG*, 194); 'there was,' he wrote elsewhere, 'nothing more *real* in letters—nothing less tainted with the conventions of art' (*LFC*, 314).

Hueffer, Ford Madox. See FORD, FORD MADOX.

I

'Idiots, The'. This was the first short story Conrad ever wrote, composed during his honeymoon on the coast of Brittany. Conrad's wife Jessie corroborates his brief account in the 'Author's Note' to *Tales of Unrest* of how the story was inspired by the sight of retarded siblings along the road from Lannion to Île Grande. In the context of Conrad's recent marriage, this lurid tale of deformity, sexual coercion, and homicide appears an odd subject; but Jessie, who typed up the manuscript, apparently never thought it strange, and even expressed a fondness for it, claiming that 'Much of our Ile Grande life is in that short story, for which Conrad had . . . an unreasonable contempt' (*JCKH*, 38). Completed in May 1896, this tale of some 9,200 words was rejected by both *Cosmopolis* and *Cornhill* magazines before appearing in *Savoy*, 6 (October 1896), 11–30. It was published as the second of the five *Tales of Unrest*.

The story begins in the manner of Guy de *Maupassant, with a traveller who notices the orphaned children and pieces their story together from local informants. He relates how Jean-Pierre Bacadou, a farmer near Ploumar, returns from military service to marry and raise sons to help maintain the family farm. The twin sons born to Bacadou and his wife Susan turn out to be 'simple', as does their third son, but Bacadou insists on having more children in the hope of securing a normal heir. He says poignantly: 'When they sleep they are like other people's children' (62). In desperation, the republican Bacadou tries going to mass; but his fourth child, a girl, is like the others. Bacadou blasphemes and blames his wife, who 'could not rear children that were like anybody else's' (68). One autumn evening, Mme Levaille receives a sudden visit from her daughter Susan, who, ashamed of her reputation as the 'mother of idiots' and fearful of damnation, confesses to having killed her

husband with a pair of scissors to avoid yet another pregnancy. Brutally rejected by her own mother and pursued by the ghost of her dead husband, Susan flees towards the coast. Millot, a seaweed-gatherer, tries to rescue her, but she confuses him with the ghost and falls to her death in the waves.

In the 'Author's Note' to *Tales of Unrest*, Conrad dismissed the story as an 'obviously derivative piece of work' (p. vii), and critics since Edward *Garnett have detected the influence of Maupassant in both its setting and the manner of its *frame-narration. Breton references were identified by Anatole Rivoallan in *Nouvelle Revue de Bretagne* (September–October 1949; English translation as 'Joseph Conrad and Brittany', *The Conradian*, 8: 2 (1983), 14–18). Modern re-evaluations begin with Schwarz (1980: 24–5), who argues for an ironic reading in which the real 'idiots' of the story are the inflexible farmers who, after the wedding, sprawl drunkenly along the roads in attitudes later assumed by the children. The publishing context of the story is discussed by Robert W. Hobson and William S. Pfeiffer in 'Conrad's First Story and the *Savoy*: Typescript Revisions of "The Idiots"', *Studies in Short Fiction*, 18 (1981), 267–72. The resemblances between 'The Idiots' and Maupassant's 'La Mère aux monstres' are examined by Gene M. Moore in Moore *et al.* (eds.) 1997: 49–58. The corrected typescript prepared by Jessie Conrad (without the last page) is held at the Beinecke Rare Book and Manuscript Library, Yale University.

'Il Conde', Conrad's only Italian story prior to *Suspense*, offers an ironic gloss to the proverb 'See Naples and die', which is used as its epigraph. It appeared in *Cassell's Magazine* in London in August 1908 (illustrated by Cyrus Cuneo) and in *Hampton's Magazine* in New York in February 1909 (illustrated by G. W. Peters), and was subtitled 'A Pathetic Tale' and reprinted as the sixth and last story in *A Set of Six* (1908).

The story, some 6,000 words long, is told in the manner of Guy de *Maupassant, by a narrator who describes his encounter with a fellow hotel guest in Naples, a sensitive, elderly, central European gentleman familiar to the hotel staff as 'Il Conde'. (Conrad later acknowledged that the word was misspelled, since the Italian for 'Count' is 'Conte', not 'Conde'.) The Count suffers from rheumatism, from which he can find relief only on the shores of the Bay of Naples. The narrator is obliged to leave Naples to look after a friend who has fallen ill in Taormina, and when he returns ten days later, he finds the Count devastated by an 'abominable adventure'. After dinner, Il Conde explains how, on the evening after the narrator's departure, he went to the gardens of the Villa Nazionale and happened to share a table with a moody, well-dressed young stranger of the 'South Italian' type. Strolling later in the darkness of a nearby path, Il Conde is robbed by the young stranger, who threatens him with a knife. Thanks to his foresight, Il Conde loses only a small amount of money and a cheap watch; but he finds the experience shattering. He goes to the Café Umberto to calm himself, remembering that he also has a 20-franc gold piece for emergencies. The young stranger is also there, and noticing that Il Conde pays with gold, he insults and threatens him. Il Conde learns that the stranger is a student and the leader of a powerful 'Camorra', a secret organization, so that his life is henceforth in danger, and he will have to forsake his beloved Bay of Naples for ever.

It is tempting to think that Conrad might have begun 'Il Conde' in *Montpellier in March 1906, since he mentions an unnamed 'next story' in a letter to his agent J. B. *Pinker in which he also complains of having lost his pocketbook (*CL*, iii. 321–2). This is unlikely, however, since Conrad told Ada Galsworthy that he wrote the story in ten days immediately after finishing the serial version of *The Secret Agent* (*CL*, iv. 104). This would place its composition in November 1906; and the manuscript is

dated as having been finished on '4th Dec.' In his 1920 'Author's Note' to *A Set of Six*, Conrad described the story as 'an almost verbatim transcript of the tale told me by a very charming old gentleman whom I met in Italy' (p. v). This gentleman was probably Count Zygmunt Szembek (1844–1907), a Polish aristocrat whom Conrad met in Capri early in 1905. Conrad's letters to Szembek indicate that the Count was especially fond of Conrad's 7-year-old son Borys. The story was written while Szembek was still alive, but published in book form only after his death.

Critical appreciation of 'Il Conde' has varied widely, depending largely on the extent to which readers have found occasion to question the reliability of the two narrators. Readers have often felt that Il Conde's account of his 'abominable adventure' (274) is inadequate as an explanation of his moral devastation, and have sought to base their interpretations on other, less obvious frames of reference. Frederick R. Karl, for example, sees the Count as symbolic of the old, civilized order of Europe threatened by a new generation of 'political gangsters' represented by the menacing young thief (1960: 206–9). In 'The Self-Deceiving Narrator of Conrad's "Il Conde"', *Studies in Short Fiction*, 6 (1969), 187–93, Daniel R. Schwarz cites evidence of the narrator's lack of objectivity. Two essays published in the same issue of *Conradiana* in 1975 make a compelling case for reading the story as a tale of homosexuality and shame: in 'Conrad's "Il Conde": "A Deucedly Queer Story"', *Conradiana*, 7 (1975), 17–25, Douglas A. Hughes argues that Il Conde is 'actually a lonely, vulnerable pederast who becomes involved in a sordid incident' (18); and in 'Il Conde's Uncensored Story', Theo Steinmann provides additional evidence for reading 'Il Conde' as a story of homosexuality that would have been deemed unacceptable if told in a straightforward manner (ibid. 83–6). This view draws support from the reputations of Naples and Capri as sites for sexual encounters, and may also reflect Conrad's friendship with Norman *Douglas, whom he first met in Capri in 1905.

The original manuscript of 'Il Conde' is in the Robert H. Taylor Collection, Firestone Library, Princeton University.

illustrations. Conrad's literary career coincided with an unparalleled explosion, both in Britain and America, in the production of popular illustrated magazines and monthlies. With an insatiable need for short fiction and serial stories, most of them aspired to combine text with 'a picture on every page' (Pound, 30). From 1890 onwards, the highest technical and production standards were set in America by *Harper's* and *Scribner's*, which hired some of the finest American illustrators for their elaborate artwork. Following their style, the typical British magazine of the time, such as the *Strand Magazine* or *Pall Mall Magazine*, employed an art director who oversaw a team of busy and versatile illustrators, some resident jobbing draughtsmen, but others accomplished freelance artists like Sidney Paget, who worked with A. Conan Doyle in the creation of Sherlock Holmes, Gordon Browne (son of Hablot K. Browne, Dickens's illustrator), and H. R. Millar, an illustrator of Shakespeare's comedies. Magazine artwork thus flourished as never before, used as a means to attract the eye and sell copy, but also at its best inspired by the belief 'that art exists not for the intellectual enrichment of the few but for the frank enjoyment of all' (ibid. 36). After the *First World War, the art of magazine illustration inevitably began to wane as the practice of serialization itself gradually declined.

Generally, the illustrations that accompanied Conrad's serialized novels and short fictions in magazines do not evoke much comment from the author, although to H.-D. *Davray he confessed in March 1908 that illustrations by W. Russell Flint for *Pall Mall Magazine*'s serialization of 'The Duel' made him 'sick' every time he saw them (*CL*, iv. 58), and a month later he complained to H. G. *Wells that he felt he had had 'no luck' with the illustrators so far chosen for his work (*CL*, iv. 77). An altogether more serious protest took place in 1918, when he objected to the quality of the

artwork produced by Dudley Hardy for *Land & Water*'s serialization of *The Rescue*. In a long, angry letter of 12 December 1918 to the editor, he presented himself as 'a man whose work has been illustrated in many publications for upward of 15 years and who, as an artist himself in another medium, has always been treated by his illustrators with a certain amount of consideration' and complained bitterly about the illustrator's representation of Tom *Lingard: 'The whole thing is false enough to set one's teeth on edge; and of unpardonable ugliness. . . . What does he mean by sticking a fur cap on the head of Lingard? What is it—a joke? . . . And what is that face? (Lingard is a man with a beard—I say so)—that face which says nothing, which suggests no type, might belong to a hotel waiter or a stock broker.' Interestingly, Conrad also outlines the kind of unspoken contract he expects to find between writer and magazine illustrator, significantly thinking of himself as a pictorial artist in prose and calling upon the 'loyalty which is due from a conscientious artist to the conceptions of another': 'I have preserved to this day a sentiment of real gratitude for the sympathy of workmanship, for the honest effort to render in another medium —if not all the details or even the hard facts, then the spirit of my conception.' Such effort, Conrad adds, requires of illustrators a careful reading of the text and a response to it 'according to their temperament, but always with skill & knowledge'.

In this same letter, Conrad invokes the example of some of his previous successful illustrators, specifying the *Harper's Magazine* group (Anton Otto Fischer, Wolcott Hitchcock, Thornton Oakley, W. J. Aylward), *Metropolitan Magazine*'s team (Clifford W. Ashley, Frederic Dorr Steele, H. J. Mowat), and David B. Waters's finely executed illustrations for *Pall Mall Magazine*'s presentation of *The Mirror of the Sea* in 1905. Elsewhere, he expressed admiration for the artwork of Gunning King in the *Illustrated London News*'s version of 'Amy Foster' in 1901. Chief among his favourites was, however, Maurice Greiffenhagen (1862–1931), who illustrated 'Typhoon' for

Pall Mall Magazine in 1902, 'The Inn of the Two Witches' for the same magazine in 1913, and who was brought in to work with a team of illustrators on *The Rescue* after Conrad's complaint in 1918. Conrad said in his 1919 'Author's Note' to *Typhoon* that as an illustrator Greiffenhagen combined 'the effect of his own most distinguished personal vision with an absolute fidelity to the inspiration of the writer' (p. ix). Greiffenhagen's several drawings for 'Typhoon' are models of their kind, tactfully chosen to evoke key moments in the narrative and sharply responsive to the spirit of the text. For example, the first instalment had three drawings; the first two (*Pall Mall Magazine*, 26 (1902), 95, 99) are sensitive visual portraits of Captain *MacWhirr's 'stiff and uncouth smartness' and everything that goes with it: watch-chain, heavy boots, tight-fitting shore-togs, bowler hat, 'fiery metallic gleams' (3) on his cheeks, and, of course, his unfurled umbrella. The third—of the Chinese coolies—is equally evocative, illustrating the *Nan-Shan's* human cargo under the caption, 'The sun, pale and without rays, poured down a leaden heat, and the Chinamen were lying prostrate about the decks' (*Pall Mall Magazine*, 103).

Illustrations and visual advertisement as elements in the high-powered packaging and marketing of Conrad's fiction became more important in his later career, reaching a climax with the American serialization of *Chance* in the *New York Herald*. This was preceded by advance notices, interviews, and portraits of the author, and the promise of a serial lavishly illustrated by L. A. Shafer. Packaging also played a part in the illustration on the book's dust-jacket, of which Edward *Garnett said: 'the figure of the lady on the "jacket" of *Chance* (1914) did more to bring the novel into popular favour than the long review by Sir Sidney Colvin in *The Observer*' (*LFC*, p. xx). In showing a handsome middle-class woman seated on a ship's deck turning to receive a shawl being proffered by a dashing and genteel naval officer who stands solicitously over her, the cover was presumably designed to assure cultivated Edwardians that the story combined sea narrative and romantic interest in a way designed to appeal to male *and* female readers.

An interesting insight into Conrad's view of the general differences between his habits of visualization as a writer and those of the illustrator emerges from two 1917 letters to the American publisher and collector W. T. H. Howe. In the first (20 April) he points out that 'neither my people nor the situations in my novels lend themselves to pictorial grouping'. In the second (16 August) he explains at greater length: 'It's the static quality of a grouping that disconcerts my imagination. When writing I visualise the successive scenes as always in motion—a flow of closely linked events; so that when I attempt to arrest them in my mind at any given moment the first thought is always: that's no good! And I get discouraged.' Partly recalling the emphasis on visual plasticity, colour, and movement proclaimed in the 'Preface' to *The Nigger of the 'Narcissus'* (p. ix), Conrad's views here help to explain not only his lingering dissatisfaction with static illustration in general, but also his growing interest in the possibility of seeing his novels adapted as motion pictures (see FILMS).

impressionism. Reacting to the adverse criticism that greeted his painting *Impression: soleil levant*, which was first exhibited in Paris 1874 (and from which the Impressionist school of painters probably acquired their name), Claude Monet remarked haughtily: 'Poor blind idiots. They want to see everything clearly, even through a fog!' This response locates the basis of impressionism in the perceiving consciousness rather than the object perceived. In 1891, Conrad had visited Marguerite *Poradowska in the Paris apartment of her cousin Dr Paul Gachet and found the walls hung with Impressionist paintings. (When Gachet's collection was given to the Louvre it included paintings by Cézanne, Monet, Renoir, and Van Gogh.) Writing to her after his visit, he said of the apartment: 'It had a nightmarish atmosphere, with its paintings of the Charenton school' (*CL*, i. 84). 'Charenton' referred to the lunatic asylum near Paris;

but as Gene M. Moore argues in 'Conrad, Dr. Gachet, and the "School of Charenton"', *Conradiana*, 25 (1993), 163–77, the paintings to which Conrad objected were not primarily Impressionist works (and not by Van Gogh), but portraits by and of actual patients in Parisian asylums. Nevertheless, Conrad's doubts about impressionism also found expression in a letter to Edward *Garnett concerning Stephen *Crane: 'His eye is very individual and his expression satisfies me artistically. He certainly is *the* impressionist and his temperament is curiously unique. . . . He is *the only* impressionist and *only* an impressionist' (*CL*, i. 416). If Conrad was not enthusiastic about the school from the first, his two essays on Crane reveal an increasing sympathy towards impressionism. Although acknowledging the phrase as Garnett's, Conrad's tribute to Crane in *Last Essays* declares him to have been the 'chief impressionist of the age' (111), and in his 1919 essay in *Notes on Life and Letters* he went even further, describing Crane as 'a wonderful artist in words' whose 'impressionism of phrase went really deeper than the surface' (50). According to Eloise Knapp Hay, Conrad's attitude towards impressionism changed as he became increasingly familiar with the movement through the writings of Walter Pater and Ferdinand Brunetière ('Impressionism Limited', in Sherry (ed.) 1976: 54–64).

In his 'Preface' to *JCPR*, Ford Madox *Ford describes the book as 'the writer's impression of a writer who avowed himself impressionist' (6). While Conrad was notoriously resistant to any attempts to identify him with particular artistic movements or 'isms', his 1897 'Preface' to *The Nigger of the 'Narcissus'* is impressionist in nature: not only does it stress Conrad's commitment to the visual arts—'My task which I am trying to achieve is, by the power of the written word, to make you hear, to make you feel—it is, before all, to make you *see*' (p. x)—but defines art generally as 'an impression conveyed through the senses' (p. ix). In July 1923 he described to Richard *Curle the literary 'effects' he was seeking in terms immediately suggesting the general aims of impressionism: 'As a matter of fact, the thought for effects is there all the same (often at the cost of mere directness of narrative), and can be detected in my unconventional grouping and perspective, which are purely temperamental and wherein most of my "art" consists. This, I suspect, has been the difficulty the critics felt in classifying it as romantic or realistic. Whereas, as a matter of fact, it is fluid, depending on grouping (sequence) which shifts, and on the changing lights giving varied effects of perspective' (*LL*, ii. 317).

With their recurrent emphasis upon a truth or phenomenon obscured by mist or shadow, Conradian narratives involve the mobility of perspective or misting of clarity one associates with viewing an Impressionist painting. In his review of *An Outcast of the Islands*, H. G. *Wells wrote that Conrad's 'style is like river-mist; for a space things are seen clearly, and then comes a great grey bank of printed matter, page on page, creeping round the reader, swallowing him up' (*CCH*, 73). According to Guerard, who interprets *Lord Jim* as 'Conrad's first great impressionist novel' (126), the aesthetic principles of the Impressionist painters lie behind the techniques Conrad employs to convey the sense of imprecision and haze. Guerard argues that the oscillating combination of sympathy and judgement in *Lord Jim* serves to establish radical new alignments between writer and reader in a manner that is impressionist. In this reading of the novel, Conrad's intention is that of impressionism generally: 'to achieve a fuller truth than realism can, if necessary by "cheating"; and to create in the reader an intricate play of emotion and a rich conflict of sympathy and judgment, a provisional bafflement in the face of experience which turns out to be more complicated than we ever would have dreamed' (126–7).

By contrast, Watt (1980), plays down the influence of impressionism on Conrad. None the less, he coins the term *'delayed decoding' to describe the technique by which Conrad illustrates the gap between immediate impression and later conscious interpretation. So, for example, during the attack on the steamer in 'Heart of Darkness', *Marlow's (and the reader's) first impression that 'sticks, little sticks, were flying about' needs to be revised: 'Arrows, by Jove!' (*Youth*, 109, 110). In Watt's terms, Marlow's 'decoding' of the situation has been 'delayed'. But, as Bruce Johnson notes, this technique is used in some form by all impressionists since they inevitably privilege impression over understanding. In fact, Johnson goes even further, claiming that Watt's emphasis upon 'decoding' is at odds with Conrad's interest in the integrity of sensations, and arguing that instances of delayed decoding, such as the sticks/arrows example, typically imply 'not so much an initial misunderstanding that will subsequently "clear up" as they do an initial unguarded perception whose meaning may be far more revealing to the reader than the subsequent "decoding"' ('Conrad's Impressionism and Watt's "Delayed Decoding"', in Murfin (ed.) 1985: 57). This recalls Conrad's claim to Garnett, in 1896, that, whereas other authors 'know something to begin with', he has as his starting point only his 'impressions and sensations of common things' (*CL*, i. 289). To some critics, Conrad's impressionism inhibits rather than enables his fiction. In '*Heart of Darkness*: Anti-Imperialism, Racism, or Impressionism?', *Criticism*, 27 (1985), 363–85, Patrick Brantlinger, for instance, argues that the anti-imperialist message in 'Heart of Darkness' is rendered ambiguous and elusive by the novel's impressionism.

AHS

influences on other writers. The specific nature of influence is often problematic, but there can be little doubt that Conrad, as a defining figure of literary Modernism with a remarkably international background and range, continues to influence both readers and writers throughout the world. His works have been translated into more than 40 languages, from Albanian and Yiddish to Korean and Swahili. The importance of his work was recognized by his literary friends and contemporaries such as Norman *Douglas, Ford Madox *Ford, John *Galsworthy, André *Gide, and Henry *James, and also by subsequent generations of writers as different from him, and from one another, as William S. Burroughs, T. S. Eliot, William Faulkner, Alberto Moravia, V. S. Naipaul, and Redmond O'Hanlon, to name only a few. 'Heart of Darkness' has become a cultural byword signifying the 'horror' at the heart of modern Western civilization. Some of Conrad's works have initiated major literary subgenres: *The Secret Agent* and *Under Western Eyes* are among the very first novels about spies who cannot come in from the cold, and *Nostromo* is the first panoramic epic of South American *colonialism. The life and works of Conrad have inspired *films, *operas, journeys, websites, sculptures, *comic books, Conrad societies and *journals, and countless academic books and articles. His novels even serve as hotel wallpaper in the title story of Howard Norman's *Kiss in the Hotel Joseph Conrad and Other Stories* (1989).

T. S. Eliot contributed immensely to the spread of Conrad's influence by taking 'Mistah Kurtz—he dead' as the epigraph to his poem 'The Hollow Men' (1925). Eliot had planned to use *Kurtz's 'The horror! the horror!' as the epigraph to *The Waste Land* (1922), but was dissuaded by his friend and volunteer editor Ezra Pound. Ernest Hemingway, for his part, preferred reading Conrad to reading Eliot, but found Conrad hard to reread, and saved his works for occasions 'when the disgust with writing, writers and everything written of and to write would be too much'. Once, on a trip to Canada, Hemingway stayed up all night reading the serial version of *The Rover*, and regretted it the morning after: 'I had hoped it would last me the trip, and felt like a young man who has blown his patrimony' (*By-Line: Ernest Hemingway*, ed. William White (New York: Bantam, 1968), 114–15). F. Scott Fitzgerald claimed that the idea of using Nick Carraway as the narrator of *The Great Gatsby* came from reading Conrad. When Conrad visited *America in May 1923, Fitzgerald and Ring Lardner paid tribute to Conrad with a drunken dance performed on the lawn of

F. N. *Doubleday's Long Island estate, where Conrad was staying, only to be escorted off the premises by a caretaker. William Faulkner's two favourite books were *Moby Dick* and *The Nigger of the 'Narcissus'*, and he read Conrad regularly. His acceptance speech for the 1949 Nobel Prize bears a striking resemblance to Conrad's 1904 essay on Henry James (*Notes*). Malcolm Lowry registered his respect for Conrad's achievement in an eloquent sonnet written in 1940. Jorge Luis Borges's short story 'Guayaquil' (in *Doctor Brodie's Report*) is a historical fantasy based on *Nostromo*, and Borges entitled one of his poems 'Manuscript Found in a Book of Joseph Conrad'.

Conrad's influence has by no means always been positive: Edmund Wilson dismissed *Under Western Eyes* as 'about the worst-told story I have ever read' and 'a masterpiece of mishandling' (*Letters on Literature and Politics, 1912–1972*, ed. Elena Wilson (New York: Farrar, Straus & Giroux, 1977), 367). Graham Greene stopped reading Conrad around 1932 because, as he put it, 'his influence on me was too great and too disastrous' (*In Search of a Character* (Harmondsworth: Penguin, 1968), 31); he persevered in this abstinence for 25 years before taking up 'Heart of Darkness' and going to the *Congo to gather material for what eventually became the novel *A Burnt-Out Case*. Vladimir Nabokov, irritated by frequent comparisons with his multilingual Polish predecessor, begged to 'differ from Joseph Conradically' (*Strong Opinions* (Weidenfeld & Nicolson, 1973), 56–7). References to Conrad and phonic echoes of his name recur with pathological insistence in Jerzy Kosinski's last novel, *The Hermit of 69th Street: The Working Papers of Nobert Kosky* (1991). Most famously of all, the Nigerian novelist Chinua Achebe attacked Conrad as a 'bloody racist' in a lecture first published in 1977, thus igniting the so-called 'Achebe controversy' that continues to inform and inflame Conrad criticism.

From the time of Ford's satirical portrait of Conrad as Simeon Brandetski in *The Simple Life Limited* (1911), Conrad's life as well as his works have provided inspiration to other writers who have used him as a character or even adopted him as the protagonist of their own works. Two such *vies romancées* are by Polish authors. Leszek Prorok's *Smuga Blasku* (The Radiant Line, 1982) is a fictionalized account of Conrad's romantic involvement with two young ladies in *Mauritius, while Wacław Biliński's *Sprawa w Marsylii* (The Affair in Marseilles, 1983) dramatizes the story of his attempted *suicide in *Marseilles. Neither work is available in English translation, but excerpts from both appear in Gillon 1994: 87–112; and Prorok's novel is also discussed by Stefan Zabierowski in *The Conradian*, 9 (1984), 90–9. The most experimentally interesting of these fictional biographies is James Lansbury's *Korzeniowski* (Serpent's Tail, 1992), which examines 'The Secret Sharer' via a variety of genres including letters, memoirs, a poem, a mini-play in two acts, a newspaper advertisement, and even a fictional Freud's own analysis of the story as 'a case of male inversion'. The historical Conrad also makes a brief cameo appearance as a gun-runner in Gabriel García Márquez's novel *Love in the Time of Cholera* (trans. Edith Grossman (New York: Knopf, 1988), 320).

Conrad had a greater personal experience of 'Third World' populations than most writers of his time, and the protagonists of his first two novels, Kaspar *Almayer and Peter *Willems, are memorable examples of the moral degeneracy of *colonialism founded on racial prejudice. It is therefore not surprising that Conrad's influence has been deeply felt by writers who have sought to chronicle the human history of colonies and the struggles of those seeking a *modus vivendi* between the rights and claims of native traditions and the access to a larger world available through Western technologies and means of communication. For some, like Achebe, Conrad remains hopelessly Eurocentric and racist, while others have found in his works a subtle and complex mixture of cultural awareness and imperialist blindness. Although writers like V. S. Naipaul and Edward Said greatly admire Conrad's achievement, Naipaul has characterized *Lord Jim* as an 'imperialist' novel with a 'racial straggler' for a hero, and Said has described a similar imperialist bias in *Nostromo*.

Conrad has had a profound influence on African novelists writing in English. Jacqueline Bardolphe has claimed that in the work of the Kenyan novelist Ngugi Wa Thiong'o, 'Conrad's work is not an "influence" but a fundamental intertext ... in such a determining way that the two major novels (*A Grain of Wheat* (1967) and *Petals of Blood* (1977)) are "parodies" in the full sense that they provide readings of Conrad' ('Ngugi wa Thiong'o's *A Grain of Wheat* and *Petals of Blood* as Readings of Conrad's *Under Western Eyes* and *Victory*', *The Conradian* 12 (1987), 32). V. S. Naipaul has traced the history of his readings of Conrad in an eloquent essay entitled 'Conrad's Darkness', and paid a major fictional tribute to Conrad with *A Bend in the River* (1979), which essentially retells the story of 'Heart of Darkness' from the 'other side', from the perspective of Muslim and Hindu colonialism on the east coast of Africa. Many of the narrator's comments seem to respond directly to Conrad's *Marlow: 'If it was Europe that gave us on the coast some idea of our history, it was Europe, I feel, that also introduced us to the lie. Those of us who had been in that part of Africa before the Europeans had never lied about ourselves ... we were people who simply did what we did. But the Europeans could do one thing and say something quite different; and they could act in this way because they had an idea of what they owed to their civilization. It was their great advantage over us' (*A Bend in the River* (New York: Vintage, 1980), 16–17). Naipaul, in his own career, has also had to relive Conrad's struggle for recognition as an English novelist despite his foreign origins, and like Conrad, he has often met with misunderstanding and disapproval from both sides: Third World ideologues have criticized him for his dreary portrayals of the garbage and litter of the colonies and for his enigmatic desire to enact the life of an English gentleman, while Western critics find it difficult to accept him other than as a Third World writer whose aspirations to 'arrival' are dismissed as a presumptuous dereliction of his duty to his 'own' people. This situation closely resembles Conrad's struggles to gain acceptance as an English writer and to be respected as more than merely a curious case of linguistic and cultural assimilation.

Every great novel is both unique and exemplary, and at least three of Conrad's masterpieces have come to stand as models for novelistic subgenres. The river voyage of 'Heart of Darkness', which is also a descent into inner darkness, recurs in works including *Los pasos perdidos* (The Lost Steps, 1953) by the Cuban novelist Alejo Carpentier, *Palace of the Peacock* (1960) by the Guyanese novelist Wilson Harris, and *Deliverance* (1970) by the American writer James Dickey. It has also inspired two Swedish works: *Färd med Mörkrets hjärta* (Journey with Heart of Darkness, 1987) by Olof Lagercrantz, and *Utrota varenda jävel* (Exterminate All the Devils, 1992) by Sven Lindqvist. The theme of the river also recurs explicitly in the title of a Dutch novel by Mineke Schipper, *Conrads rivier* (Conrad's River, 1994). 'Heart of Darkness' has also provided inspiration for a number of science-fiction novels, most explicitly in Robert Silverberg's *Downward to the Earth* (1970); and Elaine L. Kleiner has spoken up for *The Inheritors* as a genre-inspiring model in 'Joseph Conrad's Forgotten Role in the Emergence of Science Fiction', *Extrapolation*, 15 (1973), 25–34.

As the first epic novel of colonial Latin America, *Nostromo* prefigures the panoramic chronicles of writers like Carpentier, Márquez (Colombia), Mario Vargas Llosa (Peru), and Augusto Roa Bastos (Paraguay). The silver mine in *Costaguana is both mythical and material, demonic and economic; and Conrad's portrayal of the conflict between dreams and 'material interests' precedes the development of 'magical realism' as a technique for rendering a sense of history and cultural identity specific to post-colonial Latin American conditions. The mixture of moral ambiguity, political intrigue, and domestic squalor in Conrad's two novels of espionage, *The Secret Agent* and *Under Western Eyes*, has found a lasting echo in the spy fictions of W. Somerset Maugham, Graham Greene, and especially John Le Carré. Although credit for founding the novel of espionage must be shared to some extent with the creator of Sherlock Holmes and with other early studies of international intrigue like *Dostoevsky's *The Possessed* (1872) or Erskine Childers's *The Riddle of the Sands* (1903), the turbid world of counter-espionage was first explored by Conrad's half-hearted double agents who are caught in a Cold War between their emotional attachments and their political duties, and who ultimately do not know where their final allegiance lies. In Le Carré's *The Honourable Schoolboy*, the middle novel of the 'Smiley Trilogy' (1974–80), the protagonist Jerry Westerby reads Greene and Conrad in Saigon; while 'Charlie', 'Joseph', and 'Kurtz' appear as names or code-names for the characters in *The Little Drummer Girl* (1983).

Conrad's example has inspired not only writers but also travellers who have taken his experiences as an excuse to follow in his footsteps either morally or geographically. In an essay entitled 'The Conrad of my Generation', Polish author Jan Józef Szczepański described the extraordinary impact of Conrad's works on young readers in the Polish resistance under the Nazi occupation. In at least one instance, Conrad's influence proved fatal: in a story called 'Przypadek' ('The Accident'), based on a true event, Szczepański describes how a young fugitive from the Gestapo was inspired by the ethical imperatives of *Lord Jim* to return home to retrieve a compromising document, and was captured and executed.

Many writers have followed Conrad's footsteps to the Congo: André Gide in 1925–6, Alberto Moravia in 1943, Graham Greene in 1959, and Redmond O'Hanlon around 1990. The first scholarly attempt to study Conrad's works against the historical context of his travels was undertaken by John Dozier Gordan, who travelled to *Borneo in 1939 in search of Conrad's

*Sambir but went to the wrong settlement (see Gordan, 36). He was unable to correct his mistake, and after the Second World War it was learned that a diary kept by the original Charles *Olmeijer had disappeared when the Japanese opened bank safes in Samarinda in 1942. In two companion volumes (*CEW* and *CWW*), Norman Sherry unearthed much valuable information about the historical originals of Conrad's characters and settings, although he worked mainly in *Singapore and *Bangkok, and never visited Borneo or Africa. At about the same time, Andrzej Braun travelled to various Conradian sites in Borneo and *Java, visited Sumatra, and published an account of his journey in a series of articles entitled *Śladami Conrada* (In Conrad's Footsteps (Warsaw: Czytelnik, 1972); excerpts in English are available in *Conradiana*, 4: 2 (1972), 33–46 and 5: 2 (1973), 86–94). The German dramatist Horst Laube describes a similar journey to Sambir in *Zwischen den Flüssen: Reisen zu Joseph Conrad* (Between the Rivers: Journeys to Joseph Conrad, 1982). *In Search of Conrad* (1991) is an account by journalist and travel writer Gavin Young of his own Conrad-inspired excursions in the Malay Archipelago. Conrad's footsteps have been followed not only by intrepid literary scholars, but also by writer-adventurers who have been less interested in the details of Conrad's works than in the natural world they evoke. British naturalist Redmond O'Hanlon is the author of a study of Conrad and Darwin, and Conrad's influence pervades his travel volumes *Into the Heart of Borneo* (1984) and *Congo Journey* (1996). Andrew Eames borrowed a title from Conrad for his *Crossing the Shadow Line: Travels in South-East Asia* (1986).

Conrad's influence also takes non-literary forms and has been expressed in a wide variety of other media. Since the appearance of Maurice Tourneur's first silent film of *Victory* in 1919, more than 80 film and video versions of Conrad's works have been made by directors including Alfred Hitchcock, Andrzej Wajda, and Francis Ford Coppola. During his own lifetime, Conrad was by no means averse to the propagation of his work in other, more lucrative forms: he adapted *The Secret Agent* and two short stories for the stage, and wrote a 'film-play' based on his own short story 'Gaspar Ruiz'. Conrad's cinematic influence sometimes extends beyond those films devoted directly to the adaptation of his works: many of the experimental techniques that Orson Welles planned to use in a film version of 'Heart of Darkness' appear in *Citizen Kane* (1941), the film he made instead. British director Ridley Scott, who filmed 'The Duel' as *The Duellists* (1977), has also paid tribute to Conrad by naming the space-freighters in his *Aliens* series the *Nostromo* and the *Sulaco*. The importance of Conrad's impact on film can hardly be underestimated, since many more people will see famous films like Coppola's *Apocalypse Now* (1979) than will ever read the stories on which they are based.

Another important form of influence, and one hitherto neglected in Conrad scholarship, is propagated by the 'classic' comic books addressed primarily to children. Comic-book versions of *Lord Jim* and *The Secret Agent* have been published in the United States and the United Kingdom. Dan Malan, the author of *The Complete Guide to Classics Illustrated* (1992), notes that the 'Classics Illustrated' edition of *Lord Jim* was reprinted in English at least five times between 1957 and 1975, and foreign-language editions were published in ten other countries, including Brazil, Finland, and Mexico. Although the amount of 'Conrad' surviving in such adaptations is highly questionable, many younger readers of the 1960s and 1970s will first have encountered his influence in this form.

The extent and variety of Conrad's appeal is perhaps a result of the rare combination of the remarkable range of his experience with a fathomless but not pitiless *irony. Conrad was one of the first Western writers to give voice to the claims and aspirations of non-Western peoples. His own lack of a national homeland led him to speak for a larger constituency, and the essential statelessness of his own condition is reflected in the wide variety of

national types that people his fictions. The protagonists of his first two novels are Dutch colonials, *Nostromo is a South American immigrant of Italian origin, *Razumov is an uprooted Russian, and Axel *Heyst is of Swedish descent. Adolf *Verloc's background is obscurely continental, and 'all Europe' contributed to the making of *Kurtz. Although Conrad was in many ways an ardent Anglophile, his work embodies a lifelong commitment to the recognition voiced in the 'Author's Note' to *Almayer's Folly* that 'there is a bond between us and that humanity so far away' (p. viii).

Conrad's extensive influence on modern Polish literature is the subject of Stefan Zabierowski's *Dziedzictwo Conrada w literaturze polskiej XX wieku* (The Legacy of Conrad in Twentieth-Century Polish Literature (Cracow: Oficyna Literacka, 1992)). Influences on American literature and culture have been compendiously catalogued by Robert Secor and Debra Moddelmog in *Joseph Conrad and American Writers: A Bibliographical Study of Affinities, Influences, and Relations* (Westport, Conn.: Greenwood, 1985). See also Jeffrey Meyers, 'Conrad's Influence on Modern Writers', *Twentieth Century Literature* 36 (1990), 186–206; all of *Conradiana*, 22: 2 (Summer 1990), which was devoted to 'The Influence of Conrad'; and Gene M. Moore, 'Conrad's Influence', in Stape (ed.) 1996: 223–41.

For information on the many literary and cultural influences that affected Conrad's work, see the entries named in the Classified Contents List under 'Conrad's influences and sources' and 'Places associated with Conrad's life and writings', and also the entries on BORROWING; BRITISH MERCHANT SERVICE; POLISH INHERITANCE; READING; and WORK ETHIC.

'Informer, The', a story of anarchists. 'The Informer' was published in *Harper's Magazine* in December 1906 (illustrated by Wolcott Hitchcock) before appearing as the second of six stories in *A Set of Six* (1908) with the subtitle of 'An Ironic Tale'. Begun immediately upon the completion of 'An Anarchist' in December 1905, it was finished by 11 January 1906, shortly before Conrad began work on the tale that would become *The Secret Agent*, his most extended study of the world of *anarchism.

An intricate *frame-tale of some 9,000 words in the style of *Maupassant, 'The Informer' is narrated by a collector of Chinese bronzes and porcelain who receives, from a friend in Paris who 'collects acquaintances' (73), a letter of introduction to Mr X, who turns out to be not only a fine connoisseur of bronze and porcelain but also a notorious revolutionary writer, 'the greatest destructive publicist that ever lived' (74). In the course of an elegant dinner, the narrator dares to question Mr X about the contrast between the starving proletariat of his polemics and the luxury in which he lives. Mr X denies the contradiction, and claims that his revolutionary activities are also supported by 'amateurs of emotion' among the 'idle and selfish class' (78). To prove his point, he tells the story of a young bourgeoise who had given her house in London's Hermione Street (a fictitious address) to a group of anarchists who make bombs on the top floor and print propaganda in the basement. When the 'centre' in *Brussels realizes that the group contains an informer, Mr X decides to stage a mock police raid in Hermione Street to flush him out. During the raid, 'Comrade Sevrin', who is in love with the young woman, is shocked to discover her presence in the basement. Fearful for her safety, since the whole building may be blown up by the unpredictable *Professor upstairs, Sevrin gives himself away. The young lady rejects him with a melodramatic gesture, and he commits suicide by swallowing a capsule of poison. When the narrator complains later to his Parisian friend about Mr X's abominable cynicism, the friend replies that 'he likes to have his little joke sometimes' (102). Generations of later readers have shared the narrator's inability to see the 'joke' in Mr X's story.

Conrad's letters indicate that he began 'The Informer' in the last days of 1905 and finished it by 11 January 1906 (*CL*, iii. 209, 308). Early reviewers ranked the story among the weakest in *A Set of Six*, and

found themselves unable to fathom the ironies announced in its title. Sherry argues that Conrad drew much of the material for the story from Ford Madox *Ford, whose three Rossetti cousins, Olive, Arthur, and Helen, experimented with explosives and published anarchist literature from their London home at 3 St Edmunds Terrace (*CWW*, 210–18). Conrad thought of calling the story 'Gestures' (*CL*, iii. 305), and Mr X's repeated emphasis on 'gestures' may reflect Conrad's inability to take seriously the precocious anarchism of the Rossetti children. Renato Prinzhofer has suggested that Mr X may owe something to the French novelist and anarchist Georges Darien (Georges-Hippolyte Adrien, 1862–1921); see 'Il signor X e il delatore: un'ipotesi e una fonte per "The Informer"' (Mr X and the Informer: A Conjecture and a Source for 'The Informer'), *Joseph Conrad Society Newsletter (Italy)* 5 (1977), 8–12. Margaret Scanlan discusses the subversive use of language in the story in 'Language and Terrorism in Conrad's "The Informer"', *Conradiana*, 27 (1995), 115–22.

Conrad sent the manuscript of 'The Informer' to John *Quinn in May 1912 to compensate for the loss of 'Karain', which went down with the *Titanic*. It is now at the Rosenbach Museum and Library, Philadelphia.

Inheritors: An Extravagant Story, The. An allegorical or satirical novel of some 66,000 words, *The Inheritors* (1901) was the first product of Conrad's *collaboration with Ford Madox *Ford (then Ford M. Hueffer). Its particular mixture of political satire with sentimental romance and futuristic fantasy makes it difficult to describe. Ford's biographer Max Saunders has called it 'a curious hybrid work, mingling a political *roman à clef* with a Wellsean science-fiction fantasy of futuristic invasion' (i. 118). The sentimental plot is based on the narrator's mawkish infatuation with a tough-minded, clear-headed girl from the 'Fourth Dimension'. Najder has defined the 'theoretical (because not developed) theme of the book' as 'the inevitable defeat of political idealism when confronted with pragmatism' (*JCC*, 260). Thomas C. Moser has called the novel 'a neurotic portrait of a neurotic hero' (*The Life in the Fiction of Ford Madox Ford* (Princeton UP, 1980), 46). In the appendix to *The Nature of a Crime*, Ford remembered his collaboration with Conrad as a friendly contest in which Conrad tried always to 'key up' his material while Ford wanted to 'key down'. Ford's low-key approach seems to have carried the day in the case of *The Inheritors*, which, as he said, 'remains a monument as it were of silver-point, delicacies and allusiveness' (appendix to *The Nature of a Crime*, 97).

By the turn of the century Ford had published three children's books, two collections of verse, a biography of his grandfather Ford Madox Brown, and an anecdotal history of the Cinque Ports along the coasts of Kent and Sussex, but only one previous novel, *The Shifting of the Fire*, which had appeared in 1892 when he was 18 years old. He began writing *The Inheritors* in the summer of 1899, during an interval in his work with Conrad on *Seraphina* (which eventually became *Romance*). By October, he had enough material to show Conrad, who was then busy with *Lord Jim*. Conrad apparently found the effect of the first few chapters 'remarkably weird' (*CL*, ii. 234). Although he did not say so, the weirdness may have had to do with the way in which *The Inheritors* imitates both the language and the subject of Conrad's 'Heart of Darkness', which was appearing in *Blackwood's Magazine. Conrad confided to Edward *Garnett that Ford took the novel far more seriously than he did (*CL*, ii. 257). He made Ford rewrite most of the chapters two or three times over, but Conrad's own share of the actual writing was minimal, far smaller than in the case of *Romance*. Ford later described the nature of Conrad's contributions to *The Inheritors* in detail (see especially *JCPR*, 134–42). As he put it, 'Conrad's function in the *Inheritors* . . . was to give to each scene a final tap' (ibid. 136), for example by giving one of the characters a final, memorable remark that summed up its meaning.

No evidence of the novel's serialization has ever been found, although serial possibilities were under discussion (*CL*, ii. 256, 258), and the existence of a serial edition might help to account for the delay between Conrad's mention in March 1900 that *Heinemann had accepted the novel (*CL*, ii. 256) and the signing of a formal agreement on 28 February 1901, almost a year later (Cagle, 61). The novel was published by McClure, Phillips on 23 May 1901 in New York, and by Heinemann on 26 June 1901 in London, using electroplates from the American setting. The authors dedicated the novel to their own 'inheritors'—Conrad's son Borys and Ford's newborn daughter Christina—but the dedication page in the first American printing contained an embarrassing error ('To Boys & Christina'), and some of the first English copies appeared without a dedication leaf. Ford gives a humorous account of their visit to the London offices of Heinemann to protest about the problems with the dedication (Keating, 78).

The Inheritors begins at Canterbury Cathedral, where the narrator, a well-born and unsuccessful novelist named Arthur Etchingham Granger, encounters a dazzling young woman with oddly free manners (the narrator at first thinks she is American) who claims to inhabit the Fourth Dimension. She explains that the Fourth Dimensionists are destined 'fatally' to inherit the earth from mere three-dimensional mankind, just as the latter inherited it from the relatively two-dimensional Choctaw. In effect, Granger feels 'colonized' by the girl's superiority, and she closes the conversation with a political prophecy: 'You will see how we will bring a man down—a man, you understand, with a great name, standing for probity and honour' (13).

Granger has been commissioned to write a series of weekly biographical sketches for Fox's newspaper, the *Hour*, designed to 'get the atmospheres' of various literary and political celebrities. He learns that the newspaper is funded by the Duc de Mersch, who is using it to generate British support for his 'Greenland system' and to obtain British funds for the Trans-Greenland railway he plans to build. As Granger puts it, 'the British public was to be repaid in casks of train-oil and gold and with the consciousness of having aided in letting the light in upon a dark spot of the earth' (32). 'Greenland' clearly stands here for the *Congo Free State, and the Duc de Mersch for the Belgian King Leopold II, whose railway into the Congo was completed in 1898 at the cost of thousands of lives. The Conservative leader (and future Prime Minister) Arthur Balfour is represented by Churchill, who invites the narrator to collaborate with him on a biography of Oliver Cromwell. Fox is based on the newspaper baron Alfred Harmsworth (later Lord *Northcliffe), the villainous Gurnard on Joseph Chamberlain, Lea on Edward *Garnett, Jenkins on Ford's grandfather Ford Madox Brown, and Polehampton on Conrad's first English publisher, T. Fisher *Unwin. Conrad found some amusement in the attempts of readers to identify the originals of the other characters, such as the pompous novelist Callan, who could be based on Henry *James, Hall Caine, or the Scottish novelist S. R. Crockett (*CL*, ii. 344–5).

At a certain point, in return for a further commission from Polehampton, Granger is sent to Paris to write one of his 'atmospheres' as an 'energetically engineered boom' (87) in praise of the Duc de Mersch as a State Founder. Once he has delivered the mendacious article to the Paris newspaper office, Granger's increasingly snobbish and self-indulgent language begins to reveal offensively *anti-Semitic and racist aspects of his character. Granger finds the Fourth Dimensionist girl ahead of him at every turn, passing herself off as his sister and gaining more intimate and familiar access to important people than does Granger himself. She enlists the help of Granger's aunt to establish a Legitimist salon in the Faubourg Saint-Germain that becomes a hotbed of conspiracies. At one of their meetings, Conrad himself makes an appearance as the brilliant journalist Radet, a 'nomad of some genius' who has written an exposé of 'Greenland' in lan-

guage that, as Granger says, 'set me tingling with desire . . . for the fine phrase, for the right word' (110). Granger's 'pseudo-sister' engineers the suicide of de Mersch's financier and shocks Granger by announcing that her part in bringing about an 'inevitable' future requires that she marry Gurnard. The narrator returns to England, where the spreading news of the Greenland scandals eventually brings about the downfall of Churchill, the death of Fox, and the return of the narrator to obscurity.

Conrad received personal compliments on the novel from both John *Galsworthy and Marguerite *Poradowska (*CL*, ii. 342), but most reviewers were not enthusiastic, appreciating the novel's satirical subtlety but complaining that it was overly allegorical and never quite seemed to come to life. When a writer for the *New York Times Saturday Review* discussed the book as if it were Conrad's work only, and described it as a satire on English traditions, Conrad responded with a rather formal and extravagant letter to the editor in which he explained it as an 'experiment in collaboration' designed to 'point out forcibly the materialistic exaggeration of individualism, whose unscrupulous efficiency it is the temper of the time to worship' (*CL*, ii. 347–8). In 1911, after his friendship with Ford had cooled, Conrad claimed that he did not even own a copy of *The Inheritors*, and avowed that 'this book has no importance among my works' (*CL*, iv. 411). Ford described it later as 'a thin collaboration with no plot in particular' (*JCPR*, 53), and added that it was 'a political work, rather allegorically backing Mr. Balfour in the then Government; the villain was to be Joseph Chamberlain who had made the [Boer] War. The sub-villain was to be Leopold II, King of the Belgians, the foul—and incidentally lecherous—beast who had created the Congo Free State in order to grease the wheels of his harems with the blood of murdered negroes' (ibid. 133–4).

As against Conrad's public claim that the point of the novel was to satirize the 'materialistic exaggeration of individualism' (*CL*, ii. 348), Robert Green has argued to the contrary that Ford, who considered himself a Tory and a traditionalist (like the later protagonist of his *Parade's End*), was trying to satirize not 'individualism' but the heartless collectivism of political programmes (like the Fabian Society of Beatrice and Sidney Webb, or the Social Imperialism of the Earl of Rosebery) that advocated a combination of domestic social reform with the pursuit of imperialism abroad (see *Ford Madox Ford: Prose and Politics* (CUP, 1981)). Many of the political allusions and references, like the 'keys' to the characters, have by now become sufficiently historical to require a good deal of explanation, but no annotated edition of the novel has been printed. Even in its own day, the novel's satirical impact was weakened by the social arrogance of Granger's narrative. His racist and anti-Semitic remarks will strike modern readers as gratuitous and inexcusable, and he shows an appalling lack of interest in the details of the policies he deplores or in the people he meets. The only passion of which he seems capable is his sentimental infatuation for the Fourth Dimensionist girl. He readily admits he is no humanitarian, and remains quite indifferent to the sufferings of the natives of 'Greenland': 'One supposes that that sort of native exists for that sort of thing—to be rooted out by men of goodwill, with careers to make' (110). Similarly, those ruined by the scandal are for him 'just the material to make graveyards' (199). As the girl herself finally tells him, 'All these people were nothing to you. . . . And, even now, it is only yourself that matters' (210). The romantic plot is thus at odds with the political plot, while the science-fiction elements remain undeveloped beyond the suggestion that the girl comes from an advanced race that is callous and immoral—hardly a convincing thesis given Granger's own lack of feeling and his willingness to prostitute his literary talent.

The Inheritors contains many verbal echoes of Conrad's other works, almost as if Ford were showing Conrad how thoroughly he had steeped himself in them and was teasing his new collaborator to acknowledge or comment on them. Verbal allusions to 'Heart of Darkness' are abun-

dant: there are references to the 'horrors' of barbarism and the 'Système Groënlandais' (110, 183); London is 'an immense blackness' (46); and Granger even cites the same biblical passage as *Marlow's aunt when he observes that the colonists are 'proving themselves worthy of their hire' (110). There are other Conradian *'borrowings' as well: de Mersch's French mistress insults him with '*Peeg, peeg*', just as Nina Almayer taunts Peter *Willems in *An Outcast of the Islands* (97), and *Lord Jim* comes to mind when Granger describes himself as 'one of us' (55). The idea of the 'Fourth Dimension' also echoes H. G. *Wells's *The Time Machine* (1895).

The Inheritors has always occupied a marginal place in the canons of both Conrad and Ford. It has been omitted from some *collected editions of Conrad's works, and from important reference works like the Conrad *concordances or the review collections in the Critical Heritage series (in which the corresponding Ford volume reprints only Conrad's letter to the *New York Times* (*CL*, ii. 346–9)). It has received more attention from Ford scholars than from Conradians, who usually consider *Romance* the most interesting and rewarding of the collaborations. However, Conrad's name has kept the novel from disappearing entirely, and paperback editions published in 1985 and again in 1991 may indicate a modest revival of interest. The novel has never been adapted for film or television, and no pre-publication versions of the text are known to survive.

'Inn of the Two Witches: A Find, The'. An untypical Conradian exercise in a Gothic 'bogey story' (*CL*, v. 151), this 10,500-word tale was written during a break in the composition of *Victory* in December 1912. Published in *Pall Mall Magazine* (March 1913), 335–52, it was collected in *Within the Tides*. The tale's climax employs the machinery of a four-poster bed with a destructive movable canopy like the one Wilkie Collins had used in 'A Very Strange Bed' published in *Household Words* (1852). In his 'Author's Note' Conrad asserted that he did not know Collins's story and instead invoked an alternative source in the form of details he had come across about a bed 'discovered in an inn on the road between Rome and Naples at the end of the 18th century' (p. ix).

Set in northern Spain at the time of the Peninsular War, the tale follows the horrifying experiences of a young naval officer, Edgar Byrne, who goes in search of his friend and mentor Tom Corbin and who, while staying at an inn occupied by two witches and a young devil-woman, narrowly avoids being suffocated by the movable canopy of his bed and suffering the same fate that has befallen his older friend. The tale carries across from *Victory* the spectacle of an isolated individual confronted by a triad of evil figures, although such a comparison largely serves to underline the degree to which the tale makes concessions to popular magazine machinery: in particular, the evil females—two leering witches 'affiliated to the Devil' and a younger 'Satanic girl' (151) who is impulsively given to rattling a pair of castanets—derive from a conventional chamber of horrors. By contrast, the later treatment of a young man's initiation into the unknown, his isolated test, and threatened breakdown under stress is altogether more gripping. Conrad also employs a formal convention familiar in this kind of genre piece, that of the lost historical document recovered (the 'find' signalled in the story's title), and uses a framing narrator-editor to mediate Byrne's original account as a third-person narrative. See also Barbara H. Solomon, 'Conrad's Narrative Material in "The Inn of the Two Witches"', *Conradiana*, 7 (1975), 75–82, and Schwarz 1982: 26–8. The manuscript is held at the Rosenbach Museum and Library, Philadelphia, and a typescript at the Beinecke Rare Book and Manuscript Library, Yale University.

Intended, the, *Kurtz's betrothed. The Intended appears in the final scene of 'Heart of Darkness' when *Marlow, six months after his return from Africa, delivers Kurtz's letters to her in the 'sepulchral city' (*Youth*, 152) of *Brussels. Kurtz's ghostly presence haunts this encounter,

which culminates when Marlow answers the Intended's question about Kurtz's last words with a sentimental lie. As Conrad explained to his publisher William *Blackwood, 'the interview of the man and the girl . . . makes of that story something quite on another plane than an anecdote of a man who went mad in the Centre of Africa' (*CL*, ii. 417). The romantic cult of death espoused by the grieving Intended complements and reinforces Marlow's contention in the opening scene that Europe is also 'one of the dark places' (48).

The refined and civilized Intended is often compared with the 'barbarous and superb woman' (146) in the *Congo whose tragic farewell gesture of uplifted arms is repeated in the Intended's interview with Marlow. The Intended may be based to some extent on the figure of Marguerite *Poradowska, whose husband died only two days after Conrad arrived to visit them in Brussels (she also figures as part-model for the 'aunt' in the story).

In the wake of Achebe's attack upon racial attitudes in the story, some *feminist critics have faulted 'Heart of Darkness' for its denigration and suppression of women like the Intended: see, for example, Johanna M. Smith, '"Too Beautiful Altogether": Patriarchal Ideology in *Heart of Darkness*', in Murfin (ed.) 1989: 179–95; and Nina Pelikan Straus, 'The Exclusion of the Intended from Secret Sharing', in Jordan (ed.), 48–66.

interviews. Strongly protective of his personal and literary privacy, Conrad gave relatively few interviews, preferring, as he once said, 'to be judged by his books alone'. Only later in life, when he was sought after as an internationally known writer or pressed into service by his *publishers, did he agree to undergo the ritual of being interviewed. Even on his 1923 trip to *America, one interviewer noted: 'He grows restless under questioning, especially when asked about his literary methods, his characters and plots. . . . He chafes visibly at any invasion of his literary privacy. And he has sufficient human irascibility to make you feel not a little uncomfortable when you step beyond the bounds of tact in an interview' (quoted in *JCIR*, 181). Within limits, Conrad's interviews can provide helpful insights into his wide *reading, methods of work, and chameleon personality, but sometimes these limits are very marked. The writer's impatient 'chafing'—and the element of polite role-playing he employed to disguise it—suggests one reason why the substance of his interviews should be treated with some scepticism: nervous of appearing *en pantoufles*, he can often be found to retreat into polite generality or, more commonly, play the parts expected of him by over-reverential questioners. The authenticity of Conrad's interviews is further limited by the fact that his actual words were rarely reproduced verbatim, but, following the convention of the time, reported and assimilated into the interviewer's own continuous narrative.

Conrad gave his first interview in late 1896 when he went to Cardiff to stay with Joseph *Kliszczewski and was interviewed by Arthur Mee for the *Western Mail* (1 January 1897). Entitled 'A New Novellist [*sic*] on Dickens: Mr Joseph Conrad's Opinion on Dickens', the interview is of interest in confirming Conrad's lifelong admiration for *Dickens: 'His is not high art, but it conveys an exceedingly fine sense of humanity. I fancy that Dickens will never cease to be one of the masters: he is inimitable, and much more accessible to the general mind than Thackeray. He did not give a new form to English, but he used it as it had never been used before, and his very defects help to make up his greatness.' It seems, however, that Conrad was 'most indignant' that details of his Polish origins—given to the interviewer by the Kliszczewskis—were also published: 'In Conrad's view the spreading of information about his background would be highly detrimental to the popularity of his books and might even undermine his very means of subsistence' (*CUFE*, 177).

A significant interview of June 1897 with Wincenty Lutosławski, a Polish philosopher and nationalist, is less important for what it reveals of Conrad than for its

impact in *Poland when it appeared as an article on 'The Emigration of Talent' in *Kraj*, 12 (1899; reprinted in *CUFE*, 178–81). To a large extent, Conrad's position as a Polish émigré was used—and misrepresented—by Lutosławski to support his thesis that Polish writers should follow Conrad's example 'and master the English language, which is universally known, and write for their living in English instead of Polish'. His essay contains only one attempt to render Conrad's own words. In response to the question 'Why don't you write in Polish?', the writer is said to have answered: 'I value our beautiful Polish literature too much to bring into it my clumsy efforts, but for the English my gifts are sufficient and secure me my daily bread.' This attempted compliment to Polish traditions and the modest reference to 'daily bread' counted for little when set against Lutosławski's crude defence of talented Poles who, in his view justifiably, escaped a penurious life in Poland and lived abroad as a way of 'stuffing one's pockets' or went to America to 'amass millions' (*CUFE*, 178–9). Unsurprisingly, Lutosławski's article immediately attracted a hostile reaction in the form of a riposte by the Polish novelist Eliza *Orzeszkowa who, in her article 'The Emigration of Talent' in *Kraj*, 16 (1899; reprinted in *CUFE*, 182–92), accused Conrad and his unscrupulous kind of having betrayed Poland to seek sources of wealth elsewhere.

This heated controversy in Poland, news of which probably soon reached Conrad, must have strengthened his habitual wariness of giving interviews other than those of a strictly promotional kind. His next significant one was not until nearly twenty years later, with another Pole, Marian Dąbrowski, in 1914 (*CUFE*, 196–201). Conducted in Polish, it is not without some value in showing Conrad's sense of kinship with Polish writers and his attitude to the wartime condition of Poland—'I can't think of Poland often. It feels bad, bitter, painful. It would make life unbearable' (ibid. 201). Ultimately, however, its most powerful insights are into the potency of the Conrad legend by this date and its effect upon an intensely susceptible admirer, who tremulously announced: 'I would like to talk with you like one Pole to another; I would like to hear from you many beautiful, firm words, commandments; I would like to find in the English writer the immortality of Poland' (ibid. 199).

Two late interviews also merit attention, the first with Ernest Rhys in November 1920 and published as 'An Interview with Joseph Conrad', *Bookman* (NY), 56 (1922), 402–8, a version of which is extracted in *JCIR*, 131–5, and the second with R.-L. Mégroz in November 1922 and printed in the latter's *Joseph Conrad's Mind and Method: A Study of Personality in Art* (Faber, 1931; extracted in *JCIR*, 208–11). Both interviewers find Conrad in expansively genial mood and introduce the contents of the interviews with vivid pen-portraits of the ageing writer. With Rhys, Conrad discussed his methods of work and mentioned a wide range of other writers from Rabelais and Cervantes to Anthony Trollope and George Bernard Shaw. Mégroz, interviewing Conrad at a Mayfair hotel on the opening night of the stage version of *The Secret Agent*, seems to have encouraged the writer to range over a number of issues connected with his life and letters—his early Polish experiences, British politics in the 1890s, his methods of work, and, revealingly, his early problems with the English language: 'The phonetics of English is indeed a dismal thing for foreigners' (33). One vignette to emerge involves the amusing image of Conrad attempting to learn English by studying John Stuart Mill's *Principles of Political Economy* (1848): 'It was most interesting, but also it was an excellent soporific—Mill charms your mind into sleep' (32). Among his revered British writers, Conrad mentioned Charles Dickens, Dr Johnson, John Keats as his favourite poet, and Jeremy Taylor.

Conrad's promotional visit to *America in May 1923, masterminded by his American publisher F. N. *Doubleday, involved the novelist in giving several group interviews and press conferences. These often yield interesting *obiter dicta* and insights

into Conrad's reading, although they are sessions of a promotional or celebratory kind and sometimes seem tailored to supply the listening journalists with eye-catching headlines—'Americans Kind, So Why Lecture?', 'Conrad, in Light and Shadow, Talks of Crane and Hardy and the Paleness of Words', and so on. For a useful compendium of Conrad's American interviews, see *JCIR*, 175–201. Ray's comprehensive annotated bibliography of Conradian interviews and reminiscences (1988) supplies invaluable guidance to lesser-known examples.

irony. Although irony can simply be a local effect confined to a sentence or paragraph, it is also, and in some works is primarily, a mode of vision determining and structuring overall meaning. While irony is a prominent feature of the Western literary tradition and notably informs the writings of many of Conrad's predecessors and models, including Charles *Dickens, Gustave *Flaubert, and Anatole *France, it is also one of the defining characteristics of literary Modernism. Conrad's reliance on it as a vehicle for developing and shaping his thematic materials is fundamental, as Kenneth Graham has observed: 'Conrad's irony is as unsparing and voracious as Kurtz's open mouth, and he finds himself continually in the intellectually intolerable, but imaginatively exciting, position of subverting by dramatic irony the values, language, and concepts he also upholds by irony' ('Conrad and Modernism', in Stape (ed.) 1996: 215).

Ironic effects, whatever their functions in a specific text, depend upon an especially intimate negotiation between author, audience, and culture, since irony involves the exposure of a discrepancy in the manifest content, whether linguistic or situational, in order to establish, by connotation and indirection, the priority of a latent content. It is thus not surprising that irony is at times misread or simply missed, since its coding relies upon a shared, highly sophisticated experience not only of language but also of a cultural ethos.

In high Modernism generally, and throughout Conrad's canon, irony is a mode of perception deriving from a realization that the human experience is quintessentially disjunctive: the aspiration to 'meaning', motivating day-to-day behaviour and embodied in cultural products, lacks external validation and is denied by the most basic conditions of existence, which are physical and non-rational. Irony, which corrodes fixed perspectives and core societal values, ultimately undermines confidence in the communicative and mediating potentials of language itself. Indeed, any Modernist or post-modernist writer is inherently in an ironic situation since the attempt at meaningful expression, the very activity that defines the writer socially and in terms of self-identity, is unremittingly and inevitably frustrated by the innately unreliable materials used for its assertion. Conrad dramatizes this conundrum by employing narrative strategies that dissociate the contents from the method of their conveyance. (Captain *Mitchell in Nostromo is a prime example of such an unreliable narrator.)

In Conrad's writings, irony is a distancing device employed to prevent the reader's sympathetic identification with a situation or character, and a means by which the viewpoint of the narrator or author is only obliquely revealed. Conrad's ironic techniques run a gamut of possibilities from irony of tone, achieved by positioning even a single word so as to subvert a conventional expectation, to such large-scale effects as irony of situation and dramatic irony. They range from the elusive tonal variation directing or colouring an interpretation to the relatively obvious and the exaggerated. A classic example of verbal irony would be the final sentence of 'The End of the Tether'. On its surface it asserts Ivy's love for her dead father—'But she had loved him, she felt she had loved him after all' (Youth, 339)—yet its sense pulls in the contrary direction, registering the pathos of emotional deprivation, Ivy's and her father's, as well as the need for an illusion to protect Ivy from fully realizing her own alienation. The reader who shares with the author the knowledge that the sentence is a *borrowing from Flaubert's Madame Bovary (1857) appreciates still other ironies. Conrad's treatment of physical grotesqueness in The Secret Agent offers an example of a blunter use of ironic sarcasm to control the reader's response. The reform of society, itself evidently laudable, is neglected by those charged with it—Sir Ethelred toys with the regulation of fisheries—and is left to a group of misfits, who would improve society by destroying it. While this situation is in itself highly ironic, the irony is complicated by recourse to animal imagery that puts a *Darwinian perspective on the anarchists: unfit for survival, they are incapable of altering 'things as they are'. These ironies typically involve a series of disjunctions between 'what should be' and 'what is', between surface reality and the actual state of affairs. The novel also offers a classic example of dramatic irony: a knowledge of *Stevie's death, withheld from certain characters but possessed by the reader, foments tension and establishes complicity between the reader and narrating agent.

Another aspect of Conradian irony is that characters with a vein of irony in their make-up seem to receive authorial approval (the gently ironic Mrs *Gould of Nostromo, for example), while those who do not are subjected to questioning (*Jim, for instance, who is unable to perceive the shafts *Marlow directs at him); although those who habitually indulge in sceptical irony (like Martin *Decoud) often meet an untimely end. As Hervouet (1990) points out, Conrad borrows from Anatole *France the formula 'irony and pity' as the properly humane authorial response to human problems and character types.

Irony is so pervasive in Conrad's writings that it is usually discussed in the context of a particular work. Useful general perspectives are offered by Anthony Winner in Culture and Irony: Studies in Joseph Conrad's Major Novels (Charlottesville: University of Virginia Press, 1988), and by Paul B. Armstrong in 'The Politics of Irony in Reading Conrad', Conradiana, 26 (1994), 85–101.   JHS

Islam. The *Patna* episode in *Lord Jim* is based on the famous scandal surrounding the *Jeddah*: in 1880, while on a voyage from *Singapore to Mecca, some 900 Muslim pilgrims were abandoned by their European crew who deserted the ship, believing that she was sinking. Reports of this scandal, which initiated a marine inquiry in Aden, a debate in the Singapore Legislative Assembly, and a question in the House of Commons, obviously contributed to the popular interest in Islam in Victorian Britain during the second half of the 19th century. Such interest was fuelled by the opening of the Suez Canal in 1869, by the British occupation of Egypt in 1882, by reports of Islamic fanaticism which had resulted in the death of General Gordon at Khartoum (just five years before Conrad went to the *Congo) and of the Jihad, or Holy War, against infidels called by the Mahdi. Conrad's contact with Arabs—and thus his exposure to the religion of Islam—extended from his travels in Eastern seas to his contact with the Congo 'Arabs' at Stanley Falls. The Arab with whom Conrad probably had most to do was Syed Mohsin bin Salleh Al Jooffree, the owner of the *Vidar*, in which he served as first mate during the period 1887–8. Set against this background, Conrad's early Malay fiction is rendered more believable and more exotic by references to Islam, the region's predominant religion. His knowledge of Muslim customs includes their having to pray to Mecca at certain times of the day, not eating the flesh of a pig or consuming alcohol, and the practice of marrying up to four wives. He knew too of the pilgrimage to Mecca and the title 'Hadji' thus acquired.

Apart from his first-hand experience, Conrad's sources for the Islamic religion (which virtually disappears from his fiction after *Lord Jim*) are literary. Writing to William *Blackwood in 1898, Conrad says: 'I never did set up as an authority on Malaysia. I looked for a medium in which to express myself', and he goes on to claim that the 'little characteristic acts and customs' he includes have their origin in 'undoubted sources—dull, wise books' (*CL*, ii.

130). His main source was Sir Richard Burton's *Personal Narrative of a Pilgrimage to El-Medinah and Meccah* (1855–6), with which, Hans van Marle argues, Conrad 'was demonstrably familiar enough . . . to know bits of it more or less from memory' ('Conrad and Richard Burton on Islam', *Conradiana*, 17 (1985), 139).

In his essay 'Geography and Some Explorers', Conrad mentions the importance of Burton upon his formative imagination: 'the very latest geographical news that could have been whispered to me in my cradle was that of the expedition of Burton and Speke' (*Last Essays*, 14). In his study of Conrad's religion John Lester traces a range of correspondences between Burton's *Narrative* and Conrad's Malay trilogy of novels. At one level, this indebtedness entails mere verbal echoing of phrases, but it extends also to Conrad's use of Muslim traditions. Thus, Burton records how 'After touching the skin of a strange woman, it is not lawful in El Islam to pray without absolution. For this reason, when a fair dame shakes hands with you, she wraps up her fingers in a kerchief or in the end of her veil' ((Longman, 1885–6), ii. 47 n.); in *An Outcast of the Islands*, when he meets *Aïssa, 'Abdulla glanced at her swiftly for a second, and then, with perfect good breeding, fixed his eyes on the ground. She put out towards him her hand, covered with a corner of her face-veil' (131). Nor was Burton Conrad's only source for Islamic customs: another book to which Conrad habitually turned was *The Malay Archipelago* (1869) by the British naturalist Alfred Russel *Wallace.

Lester suggests that 'Islam is used in the early works not only to give an exaggerated reflection of Christian failings but also to act as . . . a way of presenting the faults of religion without incurring the wrath of Christian Victorians' (58). Thus Conrad might be seen to exploit typical European prejudices about Arabs as violent or dishonest in order to comment critically upon western Europeans. In his 'Author's Note' to *Almayer's Folly*, Conrad speaks of 'a bond between us and that humanity so far away' (p. viii), and he capitalizes on this bond to cast the Malay islanders as a satirical mirror of European habits. Thus, at the end of *Almayer's Folly*, having gazed at the dead Almayer, 'this Infidel he had fought so long and had bested so many times', Abdulla departs, his prayer-beads clicking in his hands, 'while in a solemn whisper he breathed out piously the name of Allah! The Merciful! The Compassionate!' (208). Giving instructions for translating the work into Polish, Conrad emphasized that Abdulla 'recites the well-known formula mechanically' (*CPB*, 287). This automatism recalls the no less mechanical relationship of 'the proper Mrs Vinck' with her religion in *Almayer's Folly*: when potential suitors are attracted to Nina rather than her own daughters, Mrs Vinck's protective 'Protestant wing' is hastily withdrawn (41). Islam is thus an important element in Conrad's depiction of colonial 'Others' who, through their actions and prejudices, make visible the hypocrisy of European colonists and traders. While Conrad's use of Islam points up Christian failings, there is no intention of perpetuating a religious (or racial) hierarchy, nor of privileging one faith above another. The death of the old warrior Omar el Badavi in *An Outcast of the Islands* is accompanied by the ironic comment that 'the fierce spirit of the incomparably accomplished pirate took its flight, to learn too late, in a worse world, the error of its earthly ways' (214). As Conrad claims: 'I am content to sympathize with common mortals, no matter where they live . . . Their hearts—like ours—must endure the load of the gifts from Heaven: the curse of facts and the blessing of illusions, the bitterness of our wisdom and the deceptive consolation of our folly' ('Author's Note', *Almayer's Folly*, p. viii).   AHS

Ivanovitch, Peter. Peter Ivanovitch, the 'great feminist' in *Under Western Eyes*, has a patronymic instead of a surname. As *Razumov is Kirylo Sidorovitch, Cyril son of Isidor, so Peter Ivanovitch is Peter son of John. The celebrated 'heroic fugitive' and author of a book describing his spectacular escape from Siberia with a length of heavy chain attached to his leg, Peter Ivanovitch is the most imposing of the *Geneva revolutionaries. His biography borrows from the lives of the exiled anarchists Mikhail Bakunin (1814–76) and Peter Kropotkin (1842–1921), and similar characters can be found in works by *Dostoevsky and *Turgenev. Maureen Fries considers the contradictory and hypocritical *feminism of Peter Ivanovitch in the context of Sergei Nechaev's *Catechism of Revolution* in 'Feminism–Antifeminism in *Under Western Eyes*', *Conradiana*, 5: 2 (1973), 56–65. In 'From *Razumov* to *Under Western Eyes*: The Case of Peter Ivanovitch', *Conradiana*, 25 (1993), 3–29, Keith Carabine traces the sources and evolution of Peter Ivanovitch through the composition of the novel, and suggests that his feminism may owe something to Tolstoy. In 'The Feminism of Peter Ivanovitch', *Conradiana*, 29 (1997), 113–22, Gordon Spence identifies other possible Russian sources, including the theological writings of Vladimir Solovyov.

Jacques, William Henry (1869–93). W. H. Jacques was a passenger in the *Torrens* in 1892–3 when he met Conrad, the ship's first mate. Jacques had graduated from Cambridge in 1891 and, like a number of the *Torrens*'s passengers, was making the trip to *Australia for his health. As described in *A Personal Record*, Conrad 'on a sudden impulse' (15) asked his new acquaintance whether he would care to read his manuscript of the still-unfinished *Almayer's Folly*. Jacques thus became Conrad's 'very first reader', whose subsequent judgement that the novel was 'distinctly' worth finishing left Conrad feeling 'as if already the story-teller were being born into the body of a seaman' (17). As Conrad later realized, he had erred in saying that Jacques died in Australia or on his return journey in another ship; in fact, largely confined to his cabin, he sailed back to England in the *Torrens* with Conrad and died from consumption two months after arriving home.

James, Henry (1843–1916), American novelist, short-story writer, and man of letters. Henry James was at the height of his reputation when Conrad sent him an effusively inscribed copy of *An Outcast of the Islands*, his second novel, in 1896. James soon reciprocated with a copy of *The Spoils of Poynton* (1897), after which, in February 1897, the two writers met for the first time at the *London Reform Club. From a point of hindsight, this meeting carries a resonant symbolism, since it involved two fellow pioneers of early Modernism, who, in their cosmopolitan backgrounds, literary inheritances, and artistic ideals, shared many underlying consonances. It also brought together two refined and subtle individuals who, almost inevitably, were always to have a difficult personal relationship. The awkwardly constrained formality of their early correspondence (much of it in French, with James addressed as 'Cher Maître') seems to have extended into the later personal contact between two men, who, although fairly close neighbours, were uneasily aware of their inhibiting cultural and temperamental differences. Looking back in 1914 on his personal relationship with Conrad, James deemed it a decidedly 'rum' one (*PL*, 97).

Outwardly, their contact and mutual regard reached its height at the turn of the century, when Ford Madox *Ford moved to Winchelsea and, in turn, brought Conrad closer to James's home at Lamb House in Rye (see HOMES AND LODGINGS). In 1902, James readily supported efforts to secure a Royal Literary Fund award for Conrad, writing to Edmund *Gosse that he 'has been to me, the last few years, one of the most interesting & striking of the novelists of the new generation' (ibid. 36). James's response to Conrad seems, however, to have been complicated by ambivalences and hidden constraints that sometimes bordered on duplicity. An element of professional jealousy, a wariness of Conrad's volatile 'Slavonic' temperament, and the tendency to allow a class-based or 'metropolitan' condescension to spill over into his judgements of Conrad may help to account for the fact that while outwardly effusive in his admiration, James seems privately to have entertained severe reservations about Conrad's work. In conversation with others he referred to Conrad's *Marlow as 'that preposterous master mariner' (*JCPR*, 161), and elsewhere he is reported to have 'objected to the narrator mixing himself up with the narrative in "The Heart of Darkness" & its want of proportion; said that we didn't really get hold of Kurtz after all the talk about him', preferring "The End of the Tether" to "Heart of Darkness" (Diary of Olive Garnett, 5 January 1903).

By contrast, Conrad's early letters show him to be reading and staunchly championing James the 'cosmopolitan' artist, whom he soon came to regard as the greatest living writer in English (according to Conrad, his first contact with James's novels was as early as 1891, with a reading of *The American* (*CL*, iv. 161)). In an eloquent letter to John *Galsworthy of March 1899 Conrad mounted a sustained 'defence of the "Master"' as 'the most civilised of modern writers'. Drawing examples from James's *The Lesson of the Master* (1892), *The Real Thing and Other Stories* (1893), and *Terminations* (1895), he stressed that James's technical sophistication was not to be equated with that of the cerebral and unfeeling *homme du monde*: 'Technical perfection unless there is some real glow to illumine and warm it from within must necessarily be cold. I argue that in H. J. there is such a glow and not a dim one either' (*CL*, ii. 174, 175). Indeed, some critics have argued that James's 'The Turn of the Screw', which Conrad read and admired in October 1898, may have exerted a strong influence on the *frame-narrative and general rhetorical character of the Marlow stories, written soon after the appearance of James's tale (see Roger Ramsey, 'The Available and the Unavailable "I": Conrad and James', *English Literature in Transition, 1880–1920*, 2 (1971), 137–45). The full extent of Conrad's admiration for James's work appears in his sympathetic, if also somewhat florid and generalizing essay of 1904, 'Henry James: An Appreciation' (*Notes*), which, in the course of defending James as 'the historian of fine consciences' (17), communicates a genuine sense of kinship with many of James's social and artistic ideals. Summarizing the nature of this early Jamesian inheritance, Watt claims that during the late 1890s 'it was probably James's example which, more than anything else, helped Conrad to evolve his mature technique [the invention of Marlow] at a crucial stage in his development' ('Conrad, James and *Chance*', in Mack and Gregor (ed.), 305).

More marked divergences of opinion between the two writers arose in their later careers. In 1913, Conrad confessed to Bertrand *Russell that he preferred James's

middle period to the novels from *The Golden Bowl* (1904) onwards, whose falling off he attributed to the practice of dictation (Knowles 1990: 142). James's reservations surface in two *Times Literary Supplement* articles of March–April 1914, 'The Younger Generation' (revised as 'The New Novel' in *Notes on Novelists with Some Other Notes* (1914) and extracted in *CCH*, 263–70). Here, respectful praise for Conrad's art in general mixes with drily humorous criticism of *Chance*, a novel that emulates, but may also slyly parody, Jamesian techniques. James's negative view of *Chance* as 'a porcupine of extravagant yet abnormally relaxed bristles' (ibid. 270) was, Conrad later admitted, 'the *only* time a criticism affected me painfully' (*CL*, v. 595). In a letter to Edith *Wharton of 27 February 1914, James offers an even more dismissive postscript to his published comments on *Chance*: 'This last book happens to be infinitely more practicable, more curious and readable, (in fact really rather *yieldingly* difficult and charming), than any one of the last three or four impossibilities, wastes of desolation, that succeeded the two or three final good things of his earlier time' (*PL*, 97). For comparative studies of the two writers, see E. K. Brown, 'James and Conrad', *Yale Review*, 35 (1945), 265–85, Elsa Nettels, *James & Conrad* (Athens: University of Georgia Press, 1977), Watt 1980: 200–14, and Daniel J. Schneider, 'James and Conrad: The Psychological Premises', *Henry James Review*, 6 (1984), 32–8.

Java. Conrad made a single visit to the Indonesian island of Java in 1887 as first mate in the *Highland Forest*. During the voyage there he sustained a back injury, probably being hit by a falling spar. When the ship arrived in the Semarang roads on 20 June, he was advised by a local doctor to go to *Singapore for treatment in hospital; accordingly, after some ten days on board, he signed off on 1 July, leaving Semarang in the SS *Celestial* the next day. Conrad often alludes incidentally to Java in his fiction—for example, in *Lord Jim* *Stein's house is located in Semarang—but only once, in *Victory*, does he substantially develop a

Java setting. The events of the first part of the novel in *Schomberg's hotel—including *Heyst's meeting with *Lena and the arrival of Mr *Jones and his two henchmen—are represented as taking place in Surabaya, the chief city and port in eastern Java. The typescript of the novel indicates that Conrad originally identified this city as Semarang but later changed all of these references to Surabaya—apart, that is, from two instances (15, 58) where allusions to Semarang apparently escaped his eye.

Jean-Aubry, G[érard] (né Jean-Frédéric-Émile Aubry, 1882–1950), a cultured French man-of-letters active in literary and musical circles in London and Paris. G. Jean-Aubry first met Conrad in May 1918 with an introduction from André *Gide. At that time engaged in a French translation of *Within the Tides*, he became an ardent admirer, a regular member of the Conrad circle, and—after the author's death—the leading editor and translator of his work.

Conrad's son John remembered Jean-Aubry as follows: 'Everyone was most careful not to make any remarks that might be misconstrued as being critical of him [Conrad] when Jean Aubry came. He was so serious, always on his dignity and prone to take umbrage at the least provocation and always impeccably attired, seemingly for ever flicking invisible specks of dust or hairs from his clothes. Occasionally he would smile at a joke but I do not remember ever seeing him laugh' (*JCTR*, 205). Probably not widely liked by other members of the Conrad circle, the earnest Jean-Aubry offered the author contact with the French language and culture that he admired, helped to renew his ties with *France, and introduced him to Maurice Ravel and Paul Valéry. Jean-Aubry's subsequent activities as a writer and regular lecturer on Conrad must have suggested to the author that here was a Boswell-like disciple who was equipped to be a future biographer and undertake the task of fashioning his life and work for posterity. As affection between the two men developed

into friendship, Jean-Aubry became more integrated into the Conrads' daily life, spending numerous weekends at their *Kent homes, helping them on one occasion to choose a piano, accompanying them part of the way on their journey through France in 1921, and joining the search to find John a French tutor in 1923. For his part, Conrad reciprocated by warmly championing his younger friend's causes—as when he supported him as a translator of *The Arrow of Gold* in preference to the female translator chosen by Gide—and in 1923 dedicated his French historical novel *The Rover* 'in friendship' to Jean-Aubry, perhaps assigning its central character *Peyrol the given name Jean in his honour.

Designated by Conrad to be his first biographer, Jean-Aubry went on to compile the two-volume *Joseph Conrad: Life and Letters* (Heinemann, 1927). His other publications include *Joseph Conrad au Congo* (Mercure de France, 1925; translated 1926), *Twenty Letters to Joseph Conrad* (Curwen Press, 1926), *Lettres françaises de Joseph Conrad* (Paris: Gallimard, 1930), *Vie de Conrad* (Paris: Gallimard, 1947; translated as *The Sea Dreamer: A Definitive Biography of Joseph Conrad* (Allen & Unwin, 1957)), numerous articles on Conrad's life and work, and some eleven translated volumes of his fiction.

While it is difficult to overestimate Jean-Aubry's achievement in making primary Conrad materials available, promoting the author's posthumous reputation, and securing him a wider audience in France, time has also revealed that his labours suffer from various shortcomings. Sylvère Monod has remarked that, as a translator, Jean-Aubry was 'less infallible than most': 'There are relatively few downright mistakes in interpretation, but there are all kinds of other defects in his translations: unsatisfactory or awkward phrasings, addition of words to cushion French sentences with, omission of words, phrases, and whole sentences. That occurred increasingly as Jean-Aubry grew older' ('On Translating Conrad into French', *The Conradian*, 9 (1984), 71). Again, possibly because of shortage of funding, his pioneer edition of *Life and Letters* was hurried in its later stages, with the result that its biographical interchapters, translated into English by Desmond MacCarthy, dwindle into perfunctory survey. As an editor of Conrad's letters, Jean-Aubry engages in a degree of silent censorship about such matters as Conrad's finances and intimate family problems; he also frequently normalizes Conrad's style and punctuation. With some justice, John Conrad adds that Jean-Aubry's 'lack of humour and impatience when questioning people could well have been the reason for the somewhat "dry" treatment of *The Life and Letters* which could have been so much more entertaining had he troubled to listen to friends who knew my father before he did' (*JCTR*, 205).

Jewel and her 'strange uneasy romance' (283) with *Jim in the *Patusan section of *Lord Jim* embody two recurring motifs in Conrad's fiction—the 'knightly' rescue by a European male of a childlike woman in distress (often a woman of mixed racial origins, who is then christened anew by the male) and the subsequent severance of their 'marriage' by what the woman regards as her betrayal by the man's obsessive commitment to refined Western ideals. This pattern unfolds in Patusan, when Jim, intent upon rescuing a Eurasian woman from her 'extravagantly awful' life (304), gives her the name of a precious material object, makes himself responsible for her happiness, and subsequently leaves her embittered as he 'goes away from a living woman to celebrate his pitiless wedding with a shadowy ideal of conduct' (416).

A Eurasian woman who feels herself to be excluded by gender and *race from many of the European male assumptions that bond together *Marlow and Jim, Jewel acquires a powerfully challenging alternative voice. Her carefully depicted history explains her credentials. When Marlow first introduces her love affair with Jim, he comments enigmatically that 'visible in its background [was] the melancholy figure of a woman, the shadow of a cruel wisdom

buried in a lonely grave, looking on wistfully, helplessly, with sealed lips' (275–6). This woman is Jewel's dead mother, a Eurasian who has twice been betrayed by European men—first by her father and then by her first husband, a high colonial official whose career ended under a cloud. With her mother, Jewel shares an obvious bond, since both are abused by her mother's second husband Cornelius, and Jewel will feel herself to be the betrayed victim of another man under a cloud, Jim. Jewel's voice, born out of this tradition of female suffering, may be regarded as 'unsealing' her mother's lips in order to voice a protest against the cruel fate that 'fastens upon the women with a peculiar cruelty' (277). The height of Jewel's challenge arrives in chapter 33 when her confrontation with Marlow leaves him feeling that 'the familiar landmarks of emotions' (312) in his world have been obliterated and that her powerful challenge has 'driven' him out of his 'conception of existence, out of that shelter each of us makes for himself to creep under in moments of danger, as a tortoise withdraws within its shell' (313). As Nadelhaft has aptly commented: 'What Marlow experiences here, in Conrad's astonishing risk of his narrator's representative stance, is the splitting open of the world as he knows it' (54). The novel's final paragraph again reminds the reader that Jim's is not the only catastrophe to have occurred: as Jewel herself had predicted earlier, she is left alone and bereft, 'leading a sort of soundless, inert life in Stein's house' (416–17).

Jim, or 'Lord Jim' as he is later named, the title-character of Conrad's novel of 1900, is one of the writer's most resonant and enigmatic creations. On some occasions, *Marlow—his friend, mentor, and the narrator of his story—is drawn to consider Jim as a 'simple' young man or as typical of his 'kind'. And some of the details in the opening chapters do appear to offer temporary access to a type: Jim is a decent, middle-class, English parson's son who, after a course of light holiday reading, becomes so charmed by the images of the heroic life that he impulsively commits himself to the sea and trains to be a seaman as the means to fulfil his heroic aspirations. Such a type has often figured in boys' colonial adventure stories, which typically go on to show how such youthful impulses translate into decisive action and to celebrate the English hero's capacity for fair play, effective colonial rule, and honourable achievement.

The nearness of Jim's aspirations to stereotypical story-book dreams—some of them probably harboured by Conrad himself as a young boy in *Poland—almost guarantees that this fictional character is unlikely to remain a simple, uncomplicated type. Even on his first appearance, Jim the 'ship-chandler's water-clerk' presents visible evidence of a young man with a tortured relationship to his fabricated self-image. He misses the traditional height of the hero by being 'an inch, perhaps two, under six feet'. The 'spotlessly neat' and 'immaculately white' appearance Jim presents to the world seems to be as much the extension of an inner necessity as his 'dogged self-assertion which had nothing aggressive in it'; while Jim 'advances straight' at other people, he does so with 'a slight stoop of the shoulders', as if weighed down, and with a 'fixed from-under stare' (3). As Jim's life-history develops, he comes to figure in an unusually constructed narrative. His experiences do not unfold according to the laws of simple causal sequence traditionally present in the adventure story, nor does the novel named after him ever simply endorse his belief that the world offers open possibilities for youthful English adventurers. On the contrary, a teasingly unchronological narrative initially presents Jim as a puzzle (who is he and why has he assumed the name 'Jim' as an incognito?), then emulates the logic of predicament (when Jim tells the narrator Marlow of his first crisis on board the *Patna* and challenges him to believe that he was unfairly tested by events), and finally deepens into open-ended irresolution with Jim's death in *Patusan. As a character, Jim is thus born out of crisis and apparent failure, a young man perpetually 'under a cloud', whose very identity for the reader

involves not only elusive questions of right and wrong, but the wider problem of 'How to be' (213). The entire trajectory of Jim's life as projected by the narrative is itself part of this problem, since it shows a young man moving Eastwards towards the remote country of Patusan in order to make what he imagines to be a fresh start only to discover that his life threatens to fall into the pattern of a circle of repeated crisis.

The main sources out of which Conrad built his central character's experiences are similarly unsettling in their contrasting implications. The novel's later section in which Jim becomes Lord Jim, the unofficial ruler of Patusan, owes a heavy debt to histories and memoirs of James *Brooke, the Indian-born Englishman who, as a young man, had adventured his way to Sarawak, become the first white rajah, and existed as a legend in his own lifetime. Outwardly, Brooke the legendary hero might be seen to correspond to Jim's most powerful yearnings and perhaps also to echo Conrad's own 'boyish' admiration for the Rajah of Sarawak by virtue of 'the greatness of his character and the unstained rectitude of his purpose' (to Lady Margaret *Brooke, 15 July 1920, in *LCG*, 210). But the sources for the first part of the story derive from very different materials in the form of the 'pilgrim ship episode' mentioned in Conrad's 'Author's Note' (p. viii). One of the notorious maritime scandals of the 1880s, the episode had involved the desertion of the *Jeddah*, a ship carrying 953 pilgrims to Mecca, by her European captain and officers in the belief that the ship was sinking. The ship's first mate was Augustine Podmore *Williams, who, like Jim, was the last to leave the ship and later with his captain had to submit to an inquiry, where he was severely reprimanded; after the inquiry he remained in the Far East, working as a water-clerk. If these two sources broadly anticipate Jim's progress from *Patna* to Patusan, they also exist in the novel's presentation of Jim's predicament as a permanent ambiguity woven of irreconcilable opposites: legend and scandal, the aristocratic 'lord' and the clumsy 'charging bull' (3), the fluttering butterfly and the crawling beetle.

The complexity we impute to Jim as a character is inseparable from the nature of the interest taken in him by the presiding narrator Marlow. His quest to piece together a narrative of Jim's life and then divine its inner meaning partly involves him in sifting through a number of contradictory judgements and seeking the appropriate position from which to judge Jim. Since Marlow is always in ethical transit, so too is Jim as an object of attention who perpetually stands at the axis-point of conflicting and shifting value-systems. The most dramatic of these arrives when Marlow consults the German *Stein, who is responsible for the suggestion that Jim be sent to Patusan. Prior to this point Jim has largely been judged against legal and professional codes of conduct, represented by the maritime inquiry and Marlow's own sense of fitting seamanly conduct. The Romantic ironist Stein's meditation in chapter 20 sympathetically relocates Jim's dilemma within a wider context of possibly doomed idealistic striving and a family that includes *Shakespeare's Hamlet, *Goethe's Torquato Tasso, and perhaps Stein himself.

Marlow's shifting position has its formal correlative in a novel always ambiguously suspended between competing genres. As a very 'literary' novel, partly taking its quality from Jim's devotion to story-book images of heroism, Lord Jim may be regarded as an enquiry into the kind of literary genre to which Jim's life-experiences belong. Stein implicitly posits an analogy between Jim, Hamlet, and high tragedy, but these connections jostle uncomfortably with frequent intimations of 'low comedy' (101) and issue in a prevailing note of the mock-epic, by which Jim stands revealed as more like a credulous *Don Quixote. At other times, Marlow holds out the promise that Jim is a protagonist in a Bildungsroman, according to the conventions of which he may be expected to grow into full adulthood, slowly mature, and reach a satisfying social accommodation. But this possibility coexists with several others: sometimes, for example, Jim is regarded as resembling a Romantic artist, like Goethe's Torquato Tasso, who is consigned to suffer a permanently ill-adjusted relationship with his society and belongs essentially to the genre of the 'portrait of the artist as a young man'; elsewhere, as a mythlike figure of eternal youth he seems most fitted for the Romantic lyric (Watt suggests that Lord Jim may have originally been conceived as a 'Song of Innocence' (1980: 269)). But at every point, too, there are suggestions that the pattern of his life may follow the laws of the more mundane naturalistic novel, in the light of which Jim's career can be seen to unfold as a puppet-like acting-out of ideals that he has uncritically ingested from the most popular of cultural forms, the colonial adventure stories of his youth, and internalized as his own. Predictably, Jim has attracted a very substantial body of commentary. See Tanner; Batchelor (1988); Watt (1980); Ross C. Murfin, Lord Jim: After the Truth, Masterwork Studies (New York: Twayne, 1992); and, as an example of a more 'resistant' critique, Robert Ducharme's 'The Power of Culture in Lord Jim', Conradiana, 22 (1990), 3–24.

'John Galsworthy'. Conrad quickly wrote this review of *Galsworthy's The Man of Property (1906) during a stay in *Montpellier, sending it off on 20 March 1906. It was published under the title of 'A Middle-Class Family' in Outlook (31 March), 449–50. In 1920, when Conrad was revising his essays for collection in a single volume, he forgot that he had written the piece and failed to include it in Notes on Life and Letters. By way of apology to Galsworthy for its omission, Conrad had the piece published in *pamphlet form, but its book appearance had to await Last Essays. On finishing the essay in 1906, Conrad wrote to Galsworthy to apologize for what he called an 'inept and benighted' performance (CL, iii. 322). The essay is awkwardly suspended between Conrad's desire to help market the book of a close friend by writing a bland 'notice', his fear of being thought by other literary friends to have indulged in mere puffery, and his urge towards a more candid opinion of a book about which he apparently entertained serious doubts. In the end, the very inertness of some of the writing—'Mr. Galsworthy remains always a man, whether he is amused or moved' (130)—and its accompanying belletristic evasiveness must have left Galsworthy deeply uncertain and disappointed. Proofs corrected by Conrad are held at the Lilly Library, Indiana University, and at Colgate University.

Jones, Mr, the assumed name of one of Conrad's least endearing villains, the diabolical nemesis of Axel *Heyst in *Victory*. Mr Jones arrives in Surabaya accompanied by his 'secretary' Martin Ricardo and an ape-like servant named Pedro. Describing himself as 'plain Mr. Jones' and as a 'gentleman at large' (103), Mr Jones has the tall, thin stature and cavernous eyes of a ghoul. He is acutely and outrageously misogynous; the very mention of women makes him physically ill. Conrad never fully explained this aversion (which Ricardo also fails to understand), and a number of critics have assumed that Mr Jones must be homosexual. Richard Ruppel has described him as the 'only absolutely unequivocal homosexual in Conrad's fiction' ('Conrad and the Ghost of Oscar Wilde', *The Conradian*, 23: 1 (1998), 22), although very little about the dubious Mr Jones would appear to be 'absolutely unequivocal'. Geoffrey Galt Harpham puts the case more strongly, claiming that Jones 'is plainly, even caricaturally, homosexual—he despises women, keeps a paid lover, wears makeup, and troubles Heyst with insinuations about their common "tastes"' (118–19). Harpham also notes Conrad's evasive reference to Jones's 'mentality' in the 'Author's Note': 'I will say nothing as to the origins of his mentality because I don't intend to make any damaging admissions' (p. xii).

Using threats of arson and violence to be carried out by Ricardo, Mr Jones sets up gambling tables in *Schomberg's hotel until he is lured away to *Samburan by Ricardo's story of Heyst's unprotected wealth. Ricardo omits all mention of *Lena's presence on the island, and Mr

Jones's realization that Ricardo has tricked him leads directly to the novel's catastrophic conclusion, in which Mr Jones dies a characteristically ambiguous death, either drowning accidentally or committing suicide.

Mr Jones and his associates have often been dismissed as melodramatic caricatures, but the many ambiguities attending his name, his sexual identity, and his motives make him a rather unusual stage villain. In a sense he represents a counterpart to Heyst, as a man whose fundamental boredom results not from a Heyst-like 'detachment' but from an active life of crime and misdemeanour.

Jones, Robert (1857–1933; knighted 1917), Jessie Conrad's surgeon from late 1917 onwards. Robert Jones was the most prominent British orthopaedic surgeon of his day and author of many pioneering books in the field. He was attached to the Royal Southern Hospital in Liverpool, where he also ran a private clinic in Nelson Street. Jones performed several difficult operations on Jessie's leg—in 1918, 1919, 1920, and 1924—in an attempt to repair the damage done by her previous surgeons. Conrad spent most of December 1919 in Liverpool while Jessie was treated at the clinic, and the Conrads returned to Liverpool in September 1922 for a weekend stay and trip to north Wales with Jones, who by that time had become a family friend. He was exactly the same age as Conrad, a conservative with strong liberal convictions, and unfailingly optimistic in his personal and professional attitudes. According to his biographer, however, his dislike for modern fiction was 'instinctive and constitutional . . . the novels of his friend Conrad he found difficult to follow after a long day's work' (Frederick Watson, *The Life of Sir Robert Jones* (Hodder & Stoughton, 1934), 287).

Joseph Conrad. The veteran training ship *Joseph Conrad* sailed under three flags and made a famous round-the-world voyage as a floating memorial to Conrad before mooring permanently at Mystic Seaport, Connecticut, in 1947. Built in

Copenhagen in 1882 and named the *Georg Stage* as a memorial to the young son of Frederik Stage, a prominent shipowner, the 111-foot (34-m) vessel, one of the smallest full-rigged ships to be built in modern times, was designed to accommodate 80 boys in training for the Danish merchant service. In her first 52 years of service, more than 4,000 cadets sailed in her for six-month training courses in the Baltic and North Seas. Run down by a British freighter in 1905, the *Georg Stage* sank, with the loss of twenty-two young lives. She was raised and repaired, and soon resumed her career.

The vessel was retired and about to be broken up when Captain Alan J. Villiers bought her in 1934. Renamed the *Joseph Conrad*, the ship was adorned with a wooden figurehead in Conrad's image designed by Bruce Rogers (a friend of T. E. *Lawrence), who also designed a number of Conrad's books for Crosby Gaige in New York (see Ton Hoenselaars and Gene M. Moore, 'Joseph Conrad and T. E. Lawrence', *Conradiana*, 27 (1995), 3–20). Under the British flag, Captain Villiers took the ship on a 58,000-mile voyage around the world that lasted more than two years. He described the voyage in *Cruise of the Conrad* (Hodder & Stoughton, 1937), and in the *National Geographic Magazine*, 71 (February 1937), 220–50.

In 1936 the ship was purchased by the American tycoon George Huntington Hartford, who added a modern engine and used her for three years as a private yacht. Under his ownership, the *Joseph Conrad* was matched against the *Seven Seas* in a square-rigged ship race from the United States to Bermuda and back, with each ship winning one leg. In 1939 the *Joseph Conrad* was transferred by Hartford to the United States Maritime Commission and continued in service as an American training ship until 1945. After two idle years she became, by act of Congress, the property of Mystic Seaport. Film footage of the ship under full sail was used in *Face to Face*, a film adaptation of 'The Secret Sharer' together with Stephen *Crane's 'The Bride Comes to Yellow Sky', produced by Hartford in 1952.

The *Joseph Conrad* is on exhibition at Mystic Seaport, where she continues to serve as a training ship in addition to providing accommodation for groups taking part in the Seaport's educational programmes. See Villiers's 'The Age of Sail Lives on at Mystic', *National Geographic Magazine*, 134 (August 1968), 220–39, and MUSEUMS AND MEMORABILIA.

journals, organizations, and study centres. The most senior of the specialist Conrad journals, *Conradiana*, was founded in 1968 and evolved into *Conradiana: A Journal of Joseph Conrad Studies* when its publication was taken over by Texas Tech University Press in 1971. Appearing thrice yearly, this international journal is devoted to, and welcomes, 'essays on all aspects and periods of the life and works of Joseph Conrad' and also contains valuable reviews and bibliographies. Information is available from: Texas Tech Press, Sales Office, Texas Tech University, Lubbock, TX 79409–1037, USA. Constituted in 1974, the Joseph Conrad Society of America publishes *Joseph Conrad Today: The Newsletter of the Joseph Conrad Society of America*, which appears biannually and carries short articles, reviews, abstracts, and information about its sessions at the yearly convention of the Modern Language Association of America. Further details are available from: The Joseph Conrad Society of America, c/o Department of English, Florida State University, Tallahassee, FL 32306–1580, USA.

Established in 1973, the Joseph Conrad Society (UK) soon found a home at the Polish Social and Cultural Association (POSK) in Hammersmith, London W6. Here, the 'Joseph Conrad Centre' acts as its administrative base and houses a library of Conrad materials bringing together the Society's and POSK's non-lending collection of first and later Conrad editions as well as a large selection of journals, monographs, and translations of Conrad's works. The contents of the library are listed in a catalogue available from the Polish Library at POSK. *The Conradian: Journal of the Joseph Conrad Society (UK)*, initially a modest newsletter, has evolved into a respected international journal published biannually by Editions Rodopi of Amsterdam with articles on all aspects of Conrad's life and work, conference proceedings, and reviews. In addition, the Society hosts an annual international conference, normally held on the first weekend in July at POSK. Information is available from: The Honorary Secretary, Joseph Conrad Society (UK), c/o The Polish Social and Cultural Association, 238–46 King Street, Hammersmith, London W6 0RF.

For many years, Conrad scholars and students in *Poland organized their activities under the auspices of the Society of Friends of the Central Maritime Museum of Gdańsk, in 1972 becoming known as the Polish Conrad Club. Despite formidable political and economic difficulties, the Club developed a distinctive identity through its numerous activities within Poland and its increasing links with societies in other countries. Its journal, the *Conrad News* (1976–95), contained articles, reviews, and surveys of work in Poland, and performed a valuable service in making various Polish Conrad materials and studies more widely available to English readers. In 1994, this organization was reconstituted as the Joseph Conrad Society (Poland), based at the Conrad Centre, Wojewódzka Biblioteka Publiczna, Targ Rakowy 5/6, 80–806 Gdańsk, Poland. Its earlier journal has evolved into *CON-texts: The Journal of the Joseph Conrad Society (Poland)*, which, while continuing the editorial policy of its predecessor, now also welcomes contributions from Conrad scholars at large and promises to be more international in character. The Polish Society's further plans involve the creation of a centre for Conrad materials based at the Wojewódzka Biblioteka Publiczna in Gdańsk.

Founded in 1975, *L'Époque Conradienne*, the annual bilingual journal of the Société Conradienne Française, publishes articles, proceedings of its occasional conferences, and reviews. Information is available from: Société Conradienne Française, Faculté des Lettres et des Sciences Humaines, Campus Universitaire de Limoges-Vanteaux, 39E rue Camille-Guérin, 87036 Limoges, France. The Scandinavian Joseph Conrad Society, founded in 1984, is active in hosting international conferences and produces occasional bulletins from: c/o Post Box 12 16, S-221 05 Lund, Sweden.

The Center for Conrad Studies in the Institute of Bibliography and Editing, Kent State University, holds a wide variety of primary and secondary materials to support the editing of the Cambridge Edition of the Works of Joseph Conrad. Scholars wishing to consult the collection should contact: The Chief Executive Officer, Cambridge Edition of Joseph Conrad, 1118 Library, Kent State University, PO Box 5190, Kent, OH 44242–0001, USA. Another study centre, the Ugo Mursia Memorial Collection at the University of Pisa, has a large non-lending collection of first and later editions of Conrad's texts, along with standard critical works, and scholarship in Italian. The contents of the collection are listed in *Catalogo della collezione conradiana di Ugo Mursia*, compiled by Flavio Fagnani (Mursia, 1984). Scholars wishing to consult the collection should contact: Professor Mario Curreli, Department of English, University of Pisa, via S. Maria, Pisa 56126, Italy. During the period 1974–80 the Joseph Conrad Society (Italy), based at the study centre in Pisa, published several annual newsletters in Italian containing news items, reviews, bibliographical studies, and information on *film and television adaptations. At the end of each year since 1995, the Tokyo Conrad Group has published a bilingual newsletter with summaries of its meetings, conference reports, and a bibliography of Conrad studies in Japan. Further information is available from Yoko Okuda, Atomi College, Otsuka 1–5–2, Bunkyo-ku, Tokyo 112–0012, Japan.

K

'Karain: A Memory' was first described to Edward *Garnett on 7 February 1897 as 'A Malay thing. It will be easy to write' (*CL*, i. 338); by 24 March it had become 'that infernal story' (*CL*, i. 346). Conrad's correspondence reveals the importance of Garnett's assistance with the story. As Conrad acknowledged to Garnett on 14 April 1897 (the same day that he sent the completed tale to T. Fisher *Unwin): 'it is Your advice that had reshaped it and made it what it is' (*CL*, i. 352). The tale, for which Conrad received £40, was published in the November issue of *Blackwood's Magazine*, initiating his fruitful five-year collaboration with William *Blackwood, and it appeared as the first of the five *Tales of Unrest*.

The story is narrated by an anonymous member of a gun-running trio who recalls how, with his partners Hollis and Jackson, he once smuggled guns to Karain, a Malay chief engaged in territorial disputes. An assured and haughty ruler, Karain is constantly attended by his old sword-bearer. A friendship develops between the smugglers and Karain during the course of two years of trading with him, and he generally visits them aboard their ship after dark and recounts tales of his past. On their final visit (because the trade is becoming too risky), Karain does not come to visit them, and they learn of the death of his attendant. Then, on the night before their departure, he startles them by arriving unannounced, having swum out from the shore, and proceeds to tell them how he is haunted by the ghost of Pata Matara, his closest friend, whom he killed.

When Matara's sister eloped with a Dutchman, bringing dishonour on the family, Karain joined his friend on his 'obscure Odyssey of revenge' (40). By the time the pair eventually tracked down their quarry, Karain had become so obsessed with his mental image of the girl that he saw himself as her protector and, when the

moment for revenge came, he killed Matara to save her life. In consequence, Karain was haunted by the ghost of his friend until he met the old man whose presence exorcized Matara's ghost and who became his sword-bearer. When this protection is removed by the sorcerer's death, Karain is, once again, haunted by the ghost, and he begs the gun-runners either to take him with them to *England where people 'live in unbelief' or to give him 'some of your strength—of your unbelief . . . A charm!' (44). Hollis provides Karain with a Western talisman, a Jubilee sixpenny piece bearing the image of Queen Victoria, telling him: 'She commands a spirit, too—the spirit of her nation; a masterful, conscientious, unscrupulous, unconquerable devil' (49). The coin succeeds in exorcizing Matara's ghost and Karain returns to lead his people. As an epilogue to the tale, the narrative concludes with a chance encounter in *London between Jackson and the narrator outside a gun-shop on the Strand, where, Jackson confesses, the hustle and bustle of city life seems less real to him than Karain's story.

'Karain' was Conrad's first substantial *frame-narrative and Conrad's use of this technique here has been seen by some critics to anticipate its use in *Lord Jim*; see, for example, Bruce Johnson, 'Conrad's "Karain" and *Lord Jim*', *Modern Language Quarterly*, 24 (1963), 13–20. Busza (209–15) examines the influence of Adam *Mickiewicz's ballad 'The Ambush' on 'Karain'; and in 'Ghostwriting (In) "Karain"', *The Conradian*, 18: 2 (1994), 1–16, Mark Conroy discusses the tale as a ghost story. The manuscript of 'Karain' was sold to the American collector John *Quinn, but went down with the *Titanic in 1912 on its way to New York.   AHS

Kazimierówka. The Bobrowski family estate, presided over from 1850 by Conrad's uncle and guardian Tadeusz *Bobrowski, was situated at Oratów, near Lipowiec in *Ukraine. After his departure from *Poland in 1874, Conrad twice visited his uncle at Kazimierówka, in 1890 and 1893, and his later reminiscences in *A Personal Record* telescope the events of both visits in a moving description of his return to a landscape and house associated with his earliest formative impressions. Further glimpses of the 32-year-old Conrad on his 1890 visit can be found in Jan Perłowski's reminiscences in 'On Conrad and Kipling' (*CUFE*, 155–7). During the ,1917 October Revolution, Kazimierówka—then in the hands of one of Bobrowski's nephews, Stanisław Bobrowski (1865–1939)—was burnt down, and all of Conrad's many *letters to his uncle were destroyed.

Keating, George Thomas (1892–1976), a New York businessman and avid book collector. George Keating assembled and catalogued one of the most extensive collections of original and printed Conrad materials, now housed at the Beinecke Rare Book and Manuscript Library, Yale University. Keating, who grew up in the Hell's Kitchen area of New York, was in the eighth grade when the death of his father forced him to leave school and go to work. He took a job as a messenger boy for Moore and Munger, a firm dealing in clay and paper products, and worked his way up through the ranks, eventually becoming a partner in the company before he retired and moved to Claremont, California. An omnivorous reader, Keating collected autographed books and manuscripts in a variety of areas. His Conrad collection began with inscribed copies of the *pamphlets printed by Clement K. *Shorter and Thomas J. *Wise, supplemented with items that came on the market following the John *Quinn sale in 1923 and, after Conrad's death, from the Hodgson, Richard *Curle, and Edward *Garnett sales, plus a number of items from Wise's Ashley Library. Keating published a lavish catalogue of his collection entitled *A Conrad Memorial Library: The Collection of George T. Keating* (Garden City, NY: Doubleday,

Doran, 1929), with many illustrations and special introductions to specific works written by G. *Jean-Aubry, Jessie Conrad, Ford Madox *Ford, John *Galsworthy, Edward Garnett, H. M. Tomlinson, and others. When Keating donated his collection to Yale University in 1938, additional purchases of items from Wise's collection and other sources were catalogued in a special issue of the *Yale University Library Gazette*, 13: 1 (July 1938). With an income supplemented by investments in oil under the guidance of his boyhood friend Joseph Zeppa, Keating was able to assemble several other important collections, eventually placing them in university libraries. His collection of some 17,000 rare operatic recordings is also at Yale, and a collection of some 1,250 original musical scores and manuscripts is at Stanford University. A small but select collection named 'Battles and Leaders of the Civil War' is now at the Huntington Library, San Marino, California. In 1967 his collection of more than 800 autographed or inscribed volumes dealing with the First and Second World Wars was transferred to the Fondren Library at Southern Methodist University, Dallas, Texas, as the Joseph Zeppa Collection of War, Diplomacy, and Peace, which for a time also included Keating's autograph manuscript of the last two chapters of 'The Planter of Malata'. Keating described his collections in 'Born a Collector', *The Cabellian: A Journal of the Second American Renaissance*, 2 (1971), 83–6.

Kent. For most of his professional writing career, Conrad lived in a succession of *homes in the county commonly known as 'the garden of England'. The family's move to their first Kentish home at Pent Farm in 1898 brought him close to the *sea, provided the rural peace and isolation essential for his work, and, most importantly, gave him easy access to his new collaborator, Ford Madox *Ford, as well as a larger group of literary friends. This group was always a loose association of sharply contrasting and cosmopolitan individuals, and Nicholas Delbanco's attempt to argue, in *Group Portrait* (Faber, 1982), that five writers living in Kent and Sussex at the turn of the century—Conrad, Ford, Henry *James, Stephen *Crane, and H. G. *Wells —formed a coherent group or movement comparable to the Bloomsbury Group or the Paris circle of writers in the 1920s is largely unpersuasive. During Conrad's early years at Pent Farm, Kent provided him with a setting for two short stories, 'Amy Foster' and 'To-morrow' (*Typhoon*). Based upon the Dungeness part of the Kentish coast, the fictional Colebrook of these stories is the setting for two bitingly critical portraits of English provincial life, 'Amy Foster' describing the unsympathetic reception given to a young Slavic castaway who comes to live in the Kentish country-side. The coast of Kent figures largely in Ford's history of *The Cinque Ports* (1900), and it also provides the setting for the first three chapters of Conrad and Ford's novel *Romance*.

Ernest *Dawson recalled that Conrad on one visit to Canterbury looked at the cathedral and remarked: 'I often forget that I am not an Englishman' (quoted in Ray (ed.) 1988: 29). In the last years of his life, Conrad's sense of his English identity seems to have incorporated a strong feeling for regional Kent as a long-standing home where he had put down roots, raised a family, and acquired the social identity of a gentleman-squire. To one visitor to his home in 1922, he styled himself a 'Kentish-man' (ibid. 40), and to another in 1923, he 'would branch off into praises of what was now unmistakably his own country' and was full of admiration for the 'British good sense [that] always prevailed in Kent' where he cherished his home 'within sound of Canterbury's bells' (ibid. 193, 194).

The rhythms of the Conrads' social life in the early 1920s were closely connected with Canterbury: the city's annual August Cricket Week provided an opportunity for house parties, while Conrad made weekly visits from his home at Oswalds to the town, calling at his tobacconist and Gontran Goulden's bookshop before taking refreshments at the Fleur-de-Lys Inn. Upon his death in 1924, Conrad's name acquired its permanent link with Canter-

bury. After a funeral mass at St Thomas's Roman Catholic Church during the August Cricket Week, he was buried at the public cemetery on Westgate Court Avenue. Edward *Garnett commented: 'To those who attended Conrad's funeral in Canterbury during the Cricket Festival of 1924, and drove through the crowded streets festooned with flags, there was something symbolical in England's hospitality and in the crowd's ignorance of even the existence of this great writer. A few old friends, acquaintances and pressmen stood by his grave' (quoted in *JCC*, 491). Conrad's connection with the area is also remembered by a small permanent exhibition of Conrad memorabilia at the Canterbury Heritage Centre.

Kipling, [Joseph] Rudyard (1865–1936), novelist, patriotic poet, and champion of the Empire. Rudyard Kipling was a leading British writer when Conrad's first novel was published in 1895. To be styled 'the Kipling of the Malay Archipelago' (*CCH*, 69) or repeatedly linked with Kipling, as Conrad was, might well have been a source of some satisfaction to the fledgling writer. Moreover, these early comparisons between Kipling and the author of *The Nigger of the 'Narcissus'* were not entirely unfounded. Kipling's belief in 'the Law' as a bracing and masculine social ideal can be likened to the Conradian belief in the precious qualities of loyalty, fidelity, and trust nourished by the strict hierarchy of shipboard life, a hierarchy sanctioned by tradition and accepted by all as in their best interests: common to both writers at some points is a stress upon the honourable discipline of the *work ethic, solidarity within the male group, and vigilant devotion to the facts of daily life.

However, in most essential matters, including the kind and degree of their commitment to such a code, the two writers seem very different, as is evident in the contrast between two of their stories that appeared in the *Cosmopolis* magazine in 1897: Kipling's 'Slaves of the Lamp' and Conrad's 'An Outpost of Progress' (*Tales of Unrest*). Again, on the subject of the Boer

War, Conrad wrote in October 1899: 'There is an appalling fatuity in this business. If I am to believe Kipling this is a war undertaken for the cause of democracy. C'est à crever de rire [It's enough to make you die laughing]' (*CL*, ii. 207). While Conrad's own sense of his difference from Kipling's politics is marked, he never shared the violent animus of Edward *Garnett and R. B. Cunninghame *Graham, for whom Kipling the apologist for empire was '*the* enemy . . . *the genius of all we detest*' (quoted in *LCG*, 20). Conrad responded more ambivalently to Kipling the writer; he may have distrusted his outlook, but he respected his technical skill and craftsmanship: 'Mr Kipling has the wisdom of the passing generations—and holds it in perfect sincerity. Some of his work is of impeccable form and because of that little thing he shall sojourn in Hell only a very short while. He squints with the rest of his excellent sort. It is a beautiful squint; it is an [*sic*] useful squint. And—after all—perhaps he sees around the corner?' (*CL*, i. 369–70). A *Saturday Review* article by Arthur *Symons in 1898 (extracted in *CCH*, 97–8) critical of both Kipling's *Captains Courageous* (1897) and Conrad's *The Nigger of the 'Narcissus'* seems to have provoked Conrad into writing a short article on Kipling for *Outlook* (*CL*, iii. 32–4), and although the article was not published and the manuscript is lost, it presumably defended Kipling's work. He visited Kipling at his Burwash home in August 1904, sent him an inscribed copy of *The Mirror of the Sea* two years later, and received an admiring reply.

Kipling's high regard for Conrad as a writer as well as his sense of him as a 'queer fellow' emerges in 'On Conrad and Kipling', a 1928 interview with Jan Perłowski (*CUFE*, 150–70). Claiming that the secret of Conrad's appeal to the English was through his very strangeness and foreignness, Kipling likens his work to 'an excellent translation of a foreign author' (162). He instances *The Nigger of the 'Narcissus'* as 'more Russian than English' and *Lord Jim* as evidence of Conrad's 'spiritual alienation' (163). See also John A. McClure, *Kipling and Conrad: The Colonial Fiction* (Cambridge, Mass.: Harvard UP, 1981) for a comparative study arguing that Conrad's *Polish background and 'principled despair' (93) allow him sceptical insights into the imperial adventure unavailable to Kipling.

Kliszczewski, Joseph Adolf Spiridion (1849–1932), the son of an émigré Pole who left Poland after the 1830 insurrection and worked as a watch-maker in Cardiff. Brought into contact with the Kliszczewskis through a fellow Pole, Conrad first visited them in May 1885 and immediately became friendly with Joseph, who ran the family business. His five letters from *Singapore and Calcutta to Joseph during the period 1885–6 are the first extant examples of his written English. They thank his friend for sending him English newspapers, outline his plans for making 'a fresh start in the world', and reveal a glimpse into his early political position, here taking the form of a stiffly conservative antipathy to 'the rush of social-democratic ideas' throughout Europe (*CL*, i. 13, 16). In 1896, Conrad took Jessie to spend their first Christmas as a married couple with the Kliszczewskis in Cardiff. On this occasion Joseph, a devoted Polish patriot, seems to have unwittingly provoked Conrad by suggesting that the writer should 'use his talent to glorify Poland's name and to depict in his novels the unhappiness of his native land', to which Conrad is said to have replied: 'Ah, mon ami, que voulez-vous? I would lose my public' (*CUFE*, 175). No letters to the family seem to have survived after 1898, although Kliszczewski later received from Conrad an inscribed copy of *Lord Jim*.

Korzeniowski, Apollo (1820–69) and **Ewa** (née Bobrowska; 1832–65), Conrad's parents, who gave their lives to the cause of Polish national independence. The Korzeniowskis were originally from near Poznań, but had been settled for centuries in Podolia as members of the *szlachta* or landowning nobility. The Korzeniowski lands were confiscated following the unsuccessful November rising of 1831, but the

Bobrowskis continued to hold estates producing wheat and sugar beets. Until recently, Conrad scholars have generally followed Tadeusz *Bobrowski in contrasting the hot-headed, romantic Korzeniowskis with the relatively rational and prudent spirit of the Bobrowskis. Although true enough of Conrad's father and uncle, this generalization fails to acknowledge the extent to which Tadeusz Bobrowski's siblings, and especially Conrad's mother, played an important part in the preparations for the January uprising of 1863.

Apollo Korzeniowski attended school at Żytomierz and went to the University of St Petersburg, although there is no evidence that he took a degree. After five years of resistance from the Bobrowskis, Apollo and Ewa Korzeniowski were finally married in Oratów, the family estate of Ewa's grandfather, on 4 May (new style) 1856. Apollo, who brought no capital to the marriage, took up a position as estate manager in Łuczyniec, and then leased a farm in Derebczynka. These efforts soon proved unsuccessful; his real passion was for literature and political agitation. The extent to which the cause of Polish independence governed every aspect of his life is reflected in the very title of the poem he wrote on the occasion of the baby Conrad's christening: 'To my son born in the 85th year of Muscovite oppression' (*CUFE*, 32). He translated Victor Hugo's *La Légende des siècles*, wrote poetry of a religious and patriotic sort, and produced two satirical verse comedies: *Komedia* (Comedy, 1855) and *Dla miłego grosza* (For the Love of Money, 1859). In 1860 he moved to Żytomierz to devote his full attention to literature and to political agitation.

In the spring of 1861 he moved to *Warsaw, ostensibly to launch a journal called *Dwutygodnik* (The Fortnightly), modelled on the French *Revue des Deux Mondes*, but actually to lead the radical 'Red' faction in preparing what would become known as the January uprising. Ewa and young 'Konradek' had remained behind, but joined him in October. The underground Committee of the Movement, the kernel of a future national government, was formed in

their apartment on 17 October. Three days later, Korzeniowski was arrested on four counts of criminal activity, the authorities apparently unaware of the full extent of his involvement in plans for the insurrection. In May 1862, after six months of imprisonment in the Warsaw Citadel, the Korzeniowskis were sentenced to exile in the province of Perm. At the request of the provincial governor, one of Korzeniowski's former schoolmates, they were diverted to *Vologda, in the *Russian province of the same name.

The hardships of life there—of which Conrad retained only a 'vaguely sinister impression' (*CPB*, 264)—quickly undermined the health of his parents, and they were granted permission to move south to Chernikhov, in north-east *Ukraine, where they first learned of the defeat of the January rising. Conrad's mother was granted a three-month 'medical leave' to visit relatives in Nowochwastów, but her health continued to decline. She died in Chernikhov on 18 April 1865, aged 32.

In December 1867, Apollo, busily translating *Shakespeare (*A Comedy of Errors* and *The Two Gentlemen of Verona*), *Dickens (*Hard Times*), and Hugo (*Les Travailleurs de la mer*), received a permit to go abroad, to Madeira or Algiers. He used this liberty to take his son only as far as Austrian *Poland, settling first in *Lwów and then in *Cracow, where he hoped to found a new journal appropriately called *Kraj* (Homeland). When Apollo died at the age of 49 on 23 May 1869, his funeral was the occasion of a great patriotic demonstration in which Conrad walked at the head of a procession of several thousand mourners. Conrad's recollections of this day are described in *A Personal Record* and 'Poland Revisited' (*Notes*).

Bobrowski's habit of contrasting the impetuous Korzeniowskis with the relatively calm and reasonable Bobrowskis has encouraged critics to examine Conrad's work for traces of the strains and struggles resulting from these opposing family traits. The idea of nationhood and of national honour was not to be taken lightly in Russia's western provinces in the 19th century, and an understanding of the resulting claims on Conrad's emotional solidarity may help to explain the forces that drove him abroad to seek foreign nationality.

Addison Bross surveys Conrad's father's political ideas in their historical context in 'Apollo Korzeniowski's Mythic Vision: *Poland and Muscovy*, "Note A"', *The Conradian*, 20 (1995), 77–102. The psychological and intellectual legacy of both parents is described in Najder's chapter on 'Joseph Conrad's parents', 1997: 18–43.

Krieger, Adolf Philip (*c*.1850–1918), an American of German origin, first met Conrad when they were fellow lodgers at Tollington Park, near Finsbury Park, *London N4, in early 1880, the starting point of a staunch fifteen-year friendship. Married in 1881, Adolf Krieger then moved to Stoke Newington, London N16, where Conrad also lodged between 1881 and 1886. Krieger reappears frequently at key points during Conrad's early life in London. As a partner in Barr, Moering & Co, a firm of shipping agents, he found temporary work for Conrad in the company's warehouse, and during the period 1883–6 the pair contemplated forming a business partnership, with Conrad receiving £350 from his uncle Tadeusz *Bobrowski to secure a share in the Barr, Moering Company, although nothing came of these plans. Later, Krieger assisted Conrad to obtain release from Russian nationality (1889), used his influence to help him find a job in the *Congo, and arranged treatment for him at the German Hospital, Dalston, after his return from Africa (1891), as well as serving as witness at his wedding (1896).

Krieger also acted as intermediary for the allowance paid by Tadeusz Brobowski to his nephew, and around 1896 lent Conrad a substantial amount of his own money. These unpaid debts (evidently of about £180, although possibly larger) appear to have caused his estrangement from Conrad, who in 1897 wrote to Edward *Garnett: 'I am going through the awful experience of losing a friend. . . . But when life robs one of a man to whom one has pinned one's faith for twenty years the wrong

seems too monstrous to be lived down' (*CL*, i. 416–17). This 'awful experience' almost certainly prompted Conrad to dedicate *Tales of Unrest* to Krieger ('for the sake of old days') as a way of placating his erstwhile friend. Under financial obligation to Krieger for several years, he was still in correspondence with him about their affairs in 1904, when he also sent him a copy of *Nostromo* with a signed dedication 'from his affectionate friend'. Sherry has plausibly argued that the burly and taciturn Krieger later served as part-model for Adolf *Verloc in *The Secret Agent* (*CWW*, 325–34).

Kurtz, the ivory trader at the Inner Station in 'Heart of Darkness', is one of Conrad's most powerful and enigmatic creations. Of all the characters in 'Heart of Darkness', only *Marlow and Kurtz are named; all the other characters are defined by their functions or relations, as aunt, company director, chief accountant, helmsman, or the *Intended. Marlow tells us that 'All Europe contributed to the making of Kurtz' (*Youth*, 117): his mother was half-English, his father half-French, and he was educated partly in England, so that he speaks not French but English with Marlow. He possesses many remarkable qualities: he writes and paints, is 'essentially a great musician' (153), and in politics he 'would have been a splendid leader of an extreme party' (154). However, once Kurtz finds himself alone in the *Congo, he becomes corrupt and murderously obsessed with power. His fall from civilized values is apparent in his draft report to the International Society for the Suppression of Savage Customs, which ends with a scrawled note: 'Exterminate all the brutes!' (118). Kurtz is often regarded as a Faustian overreacher, a devil, or the embodiment of the savage and unrestrained id, and the nature of his relation to Marlow and to the Intended has generated a vast amount of criticism. Kurtz becomes the private goal of Marlow's journey, since Marlow hopes to hear Kurtz's voice explain the 'idea' behind the abuses of colonial rule. When Marlow arrives at the Inner Station, he finds Kurtz's voice nearly extinguished, and Kurtz has few lines of dialogue in the story, which culminate in his famous dying words, 'The horror! The horror!' (149).

Critics have also tried to identify an original on whom Kurtz could have been based. The obvious candidate is Georges Antoine Klein, the chief of the 'Inner Station' at Stanley Falls who was ill when Conrad arrived and died on the return trip downriver. Klein's name (German for 'small') may well have suggested the name of Kurtz ('short'), but there is no record of his having possessed any other remarkable qualities. Sherry has identified Kurtz with an intrepid and highly successful ivory trader named Arthur Hodister, who was beheaded by an Arab chieftain two years after Conrad had left the Congo (*CWW*, 98–118). In 'An African Encounter, a British Traitor, and *Heart of Darkness*', *Conradiana*, 27 (1995), 123–34, Jane Ford traces the links between Kurtz and the solitary and enigmatic Roger *Casement, who was accustomed to roaming the jungle alone for weeks on end with only two bulldogs and a native carrier for company. Adam Hochschild (1998) shows that Conrad could have encountered other Kurtzes in the course of his journey, such as Guillaume van Kerckhoven, a police officer in charge of the strategic riverside fortress of Basoko, who paid his native soldiers a bounty of five brass rods for every human head they brought him, or Léon Rom, a station chief at Stanley Falls whose flower-bed was decorated with the severed heads of 21 victims of his displeasure, including women and children. Rom painted as a hobby, and some of his works can be seen at the Museum of Central Africa in Tervuren, Belgium.

L

'Lagoon, The'. Belonging to Conrad's earliest period, this 5,700-word tale was composed in the summer of 1896 during his stay in Brittany and published in the prestigious *Cornhill Magazine* (January 1897). It was later collected in *Tales of Unrest*. The tale draws heavily upon the Malay setting of *Almayer's Folly* and *An Outcast of the Islands*: it was, says Conrad, 'a tricky thing with the usual forests[,] river—stars —wind[,] sunrise, and so on—and lots of secondhand Conradese in it' (*CL*, i. 301). Later, the tale achieved unexpected prominence through Max *Beerbohm's clever parody of its impalpabilities in *A Christmas Garland* (1912).

'The Lagoon' is a tale-within-a-tale, in which an unnamed European seaman-narrator listens to a tale told by his friend Arsat, who for many years has lived with his wife close to a 'lagoon of weird aspect and ghostly reputation' (189). Arsat's account of crime and remorse concerns an event that occurred some years earlier when, with the help of his brother, he had run off with the servant girl of his ruler, pursued by guards. At a crucial moment when his brother cried for help, Arsat failed to respond, choosing instead to escape with the girl and leaving his brother to die. Ever since that time, he has been stricken by doubt and self-remorse at having ignored his brother's repeated cries for help: 'I heard him calling my name again with a great shriek . . . and I never turned my head' (201). Freed now by the death of his wife, he talks of returning home to avenge his brother's murder, although it is difficult to know whether he will make that return since the end of the story—which has occasioned a good deal of critical debate (see Graver, 27–8)—leaves him ambiguously staring 'beyond the great light of a cloudless day into the darkness of a world of illusions' (204).

Generally regarded by critics as one of Conrad's more conventional and derivative tales, 'The Lagoon' has often been used, as in Richard Ruppel's '*The Lagoon* and the Popular Exotic Tradition', in Carabine *et al.* (eds.) 1993: 177–87, to anatomize the overelaborate *fin de siècle* styles, operatic dialogue, and overwrought landscape descriptions that the developing writer was soon to outgrow. But some readers agree with Guerard's more positive verdict that even the most commonplace magazinish elements in Conrad's early fiction can be imaginatively inhabited in a way that gives them new power. He describes the tale as 'an eccentric dream, and one that touches on several of Conrad's lasting preoccupations' (65)—exile from one's homeland, the difficult choice between two powerful allegiances, the betrayal of a fraternal bond, and the permanent remorse that haunts the transgressor. Critics intent upon following the development of Conradian narrative have also been drawn to the tale as offering his first rudimentary exercise in *frame-narrative. Fraser (27–30) follows Conrad's first attempt to transform the 'told-tale' convention of 19th-century adventure fiction, noting the way in which he insinuates an underlying relationship between the central figure and the listener (28), while Schwarz argues that 'The Lagoon' forms a first stage 'in the development of the introspective and meditative voice' leading to the emergence of *Marlow (1980: 27). A corrected and revised typescript is held at the Beinecke Rare Book and Manuscript Library, Yale University.

languages. Conrad was thoroughly trilingual in Polish, French, and English, and Józef H. *Retinger recalled that when he lost his temper, he 'swore furiously in three languages' (55–6). A substantial knowledge of French was not uncommon among major English writers of Conrad's time, and some were comfortable in Italian (like Henry *James) or German (like Ford Madox *Ford) as well; but the unusual course of Conrad's life exposed him to a far greater variety of languages than other writers of his generation, and the extent to which multiple languages figure actively and constantly in his literary creations is without parallel in modern English literature.

Although he spoke Polish infrequently after leaving his homeland at the age of 16, his command of the language remained 'grammatically perfect with an amazingly rich vocabulary, [and] had still the intonation of the district of Poland to which he belonged' (ibid. 56). He grew up speaking Polish with his immediate relatives, but the margins of his childhood would have been filled with the sounds of other languages, including Russian, Yiddish, Ukrainian, and perhaps local Ruthenian dialects. The novels (in French) of his 'aunt' Marguerite *Poradowska convey a strong sense of the mixed ethnic groups and languages of the world into which Conrad was born. The fact that his father Apollo *Korzeniowski was translating works of *Shakespeare, *Dickens, and Victor Hugo into Polish would also have reinforced Conrad's sense of the multilingual nature of his world. Polish elements in Conrad's style are examined by Mary Morzinski in *The Linguistic Influence of Polish on Joseph Conrad's Style* (Lublin: Maria Curie-Skłodowska University, 1994), and a comprehensive survey of Conrad's *Polish inheritance is provided by Busza (1966).

Lamenting his own children's lack of linguistic talent, Conrad told his wife Jessie that he could read French at the age of 5 (*JCKH*, 6), and in *A Personal Record* he gave full credit for this accomplishment to Mlle Durand, his French tutor at Nowochwastów: 'In three months, simply by playing with us, she had taught me not only to speak French but to read it as well' (65). By the age of 10, he claimed to have read much of Victor Hugo and other French Romantics (ibid. 70). According to Henry-Durand *Davray, Conrad could speak French 'with

great ease and no trace of an accent' (quoted in *JCC*, 245), while Ford recalled that in conversation with Henry James, 'Conrad spoke with extraordinary speed, fluency and some incomprehensibility, a meridional French with a strong Southern accent' (1932: 31). Ford's judgement is confirmed by G. *Jean-Aubry, who noted that Conrad spoke French 'with absolute grammatical correctness' and 'an accent so perfect that it never betrayed his Polish descent', although he acknowledged that 'At most a slight meridional accent could be observed in his pronunciation of certain words'. Jean-Aubry even detected 'a very strong French accent' in Conrad's English (*LL*, i. 160). His written French was also fluent, but far from error-free. René Rapin's edition of Conrad's letters to Marguerite Poradowska (Geneva: Droz, 1966) is preceded by a systematic examination of the solecisms and irregularities in his written French. A thorough survey of Conrad's French is provided by Yves Hervouet in a two-part essay, 'Joseph Conrad and the French Language', consisting of a descriptive essay in *Conradiana*, 11 (1979), 229–51, followed by a catalogue of Conrad's Gallicisms in *Conradiana*, 14 (1982), 23–49. See also Hervouet's full-length study of French literary and cultural influences on Conrad's work (1990).

In his 'Author's Note' to *A Personal Record*, Conrad sought to answer critics and reviewers who were puzzled by his adoption of English as an artistic medium. He declared that if there had been a choice, it was made by the language itself: 'English was for me neither a matter of choice nor adoption. The merest idea of choice had never entered my head. And as to adoption —well, yes, there was adoption; but it was I who was adopted by the genius of the language, which directly I came out of the stammering stage made me its own so completely that its very idioms I truly believe had a direct action on my temperament and fashioned my still plastic character' (p. v). Nevertheless, Conrad did not encounter the genius of English on a regular basis until he first shipped out in British vessels at the age of 20, and his own spoken

English remained a constant source of social embarrassment. When Conrad was in the final throes of *Under Western Eyes* in January 1910 and his exasperated agent J. B. *Pinker protested that Conrad 'did not speak English' (*CL*, iv. 334), the remark caused a breach that took many months to heal and was among the factors leading to a nervous breakdown in which Conrad held delirious conversation with his characters in Polish. On the occasion of a public lecture and *reading in New York in May 1923, Conrad's host, publisher F. N. *Doubleday, positioned secretaries to record Conrad's comments in shorthand, but the experiment failed when his heavily accented English proved to be incomprehensible. Even Conrad's faithful secretary of many years, Lilian M. *Hallowes, could occasionally be misled by his accent, as when, in a fragment of *Suspense* taken down from Conrad's dictation, she typed 'lover's fears', then deleted the words with the blunt blue pencil he used for immediate corrections and continued with 'lower police spheres' (typescript at Mary Baldwin College, folio 347).

English, French, and Polish are by no means the only languages to figure in Conrad's works. The first words of Conrad's first novel are not in English but in Malay: 'Kaspar! Makan!'—'Kaspar! Come and eat!' (*Almayer's Folly*, 3); and his last novel, *Suspense*, is sprinkled with Italian phrases, many of them misspelled. Conrad's greatest works are characterized by his ability to create ironic situations in which characters share a common language but nonetheless profoundly misunderstand each other (like Winnie and Adolf *Verloc in *The Secret Agent*, or Flora *de Barral and Captain *Anthony in *Chance*). This double-edged use of English has a strong parallel in other situations where the characters are unable to understand each other's languages. In *Almayer's Folly*, English is explicitly marked as a secret language to be used to prevent others from understanding (53): *Almayer is surprised when Nina speaks English to him (46), since they usually speak Malay, and he reacts with delight when sailors from a Dutch frigate fill his

bungalow with the 'unusual sounds of European languages' (35). In Part III of *The Rescue*, Tom *Lingard visits Mr Travers's schooner-yacht *Hermit* and is soon joined by Pata Hassim and his sister Immada, so that Lingard is obliged to carry on two conversations at once in two different languages in the midst of two mutually uncomprehending parties. When the sailing master of the *Hermit* mistakes the couple for local fisherfolk and addresses them insultingly in pidgin English, Hassim asks Lingard, 'Why did the little white man make that outcry?' (136); and just as Mrs *Travers awakens from her inertia long enough to notice the childlike beauty of Immada, the latter, realizing that the stranded Europeans are not of Lingard's party, shouts 'Let them die!' (143). Although the entire scene is described in English, Conrad dramatically exploits the various ways in which the characters embody mutually incomprehensible attitudes in their different languages. The problem of linguistic exile is also poignantly dramatized in 'Amy Foster', where the castaway Yanko *Goorall dies of grief when his English wife refuses to let him teach their son his own language.

Conrad uses a wide variety of means to signal the presence of foreign phrases in his English texts. For example, in *Lord Jim* the French lieutenant who has rescued the *Patna* later tells *Marlow his story in French. When Marlow retells it to English listeners, he interrupts the lieutenant's translated discourse with parenthetical samples of the original French. When the Malay helmsman who testifies at the *Patna* inquiry creates a sensation by launching into a passionate proclamation of his vast experience at sea, Marlow remembers only 'a lot of queer-sounding names, . . . names of forgotten country ships, names of familiar and distorted sound' (99), and Conrad does not bother to remind us that the helmsman is actually speaking Malay and has outrun his interpreter, so that only the proper names remain comprehensible. *Stein speaks English, which he learned 'in Celebes—of all places!' (233), rather than his native German, with the result that his

English is heavily influenced by Conrad's impression of German word-order and accent. The master of the brigantine who delivers *Jim to the mouth of the river below *Patusan speaks an English filled with malapropisms, which 'seemed to be derived from a dictionary compiled by a lunatic' (238). The colonial advantage of English over other modes of communication helps Jim to plead the case of Gentleman *Brown to the elders of Patusan, to whom Jim reports that he has spoken with Brown 'in the language of his own people, making clear many things difficult to explain in any other speech' (391).

In many instances where Conrad's characters must realistically be conversing in a linguistic milieu that is not English—and often speaking languages that Conrad did not know—the problem is silently overlooked or obscured, from the Dutch and native languages of the Malay novels to the Spanish of *Nostromo*, the Russian of *Under Western Eyes*, the French of *The Rover*, and the Italian of *Suspense*. At times Conrad's *narrators seem endowed with a linguistic competence that stretches the bounds of credibility: in *Romance*, for example, John Kemp uses expletives in French and Italian although he barely speaks Spanish. Scenes in foreign languages are often translated silently into English, and the problem of language is often left unmarked—as when we learn, for example, that *Razumov 'did not even know English' (*Under Western Eyes*, 287). The English *teacher of languages who narrates the story claims to be translating Razumov's secret diary into English, but the language of many important scenes from which Razumov is absent remains unclear. When Natalia *Haldin gives the English teacher her long account of her visit to the Château Borel, is she speaking English, and translating the Russian remarks of others into English, or is she speaking Russian and leaving the translation to him? Such questions may not matter to most readers, but this 'language problem' serves at least as a reminder of the remarkable extent to which Conrad's texts reflect the multilingual aspects of all dialogue.

Conrad's works often contain allusions to the impossibility of expressing oneself in language: as the English teacher who narrates *Under Western Eyes* puts it, 'Words, as is well known, are the great foes of reality' (3). Another casual remark by Marlow in *Lord Jim* carries devastating linguistic implications: 'the power of sentences has nothing to do with their sense or the logic of their construction' (75). In an intricate and suggestive study of Conrad's presentation of narrative, Edward Said has claimed that 'Conrad's fate was to have written fiction great for its presentation, and not only for what it was presenting. He was misled by language even as he led language into a dramatization no other author really approached. For what Conrad discovered was that the chasm between words saying and words meaning was *widened*, not lessened, by his talent for words written' ('Conrad: The Presentation of Narrative', *Novel*, 7 (1974), 116). The 'self-conscious' aspects of Conrad's use of language are explored by Jeremy Hawthorn (1979). For a stimulating survey of Conrad's relation to language and the history of this issue in Conrad criticism, see Martin S. Ray, 'The Gift of Tongues: The Languages of Joseph Conrad', *Conradiana*, 15 (1983), 83–109, and this same critic's 'Language and Silence in the Novels of Joseph Conrad', *Conradiana*, 16 (1984), 19–46.

Larbaud, Valéry-Nicolas (1881–1957), French writer. Valéry Larbaud first met Conrad in July 1911 on a visit to Capel House with André *Gide and Agnes *Tobin. As Najder points out, this visit represented 'one of the signs of recognition accorded Conrad by young French writers converging round the *Nouvelle Revue Française*' (*JCC*, 372). Not long after, Conrad read Larbaud's *Journal intime d'A. O. Barnabooth* (1913) and responded with warm admiration and 'a little bit of professional envy' (*CL*, v. 310). A review by Larbaud of Conrad's prefaces in *Revue de France*, 1 (15 May 1921), 423–8, shows the width of his Conradian reading and his interest in Conrad's methods of writing (he judges the technically sophisticated *Chance* to be the author's most representative work). In 1924, Larbaud contributed a photograph of Conrad, Gide, and himself taken at Capel House in 1911 to a special memorial number of *Nouvelle Revue Française* devoted to Conrad.

Lastaola, Rita de. See DOÑA RITA.

Last Essays. Published posthumously, this volume collects a selection of Conrad's essays, letters to the press, and other miscellaneous items, and, with the earlier *Notes on Life and Letters* (1921), brings together most of his non-fictional writings. It was published by J. M. *Dent in Britain on 3 March 1926, and by Doubleday, Page in America on 26 March 1926. Although most of the collected items are meditative reminiscences written and published after 1921, a few pieces belong to earlier times, notably 'The Congo Diary', 'Cookery', 'John Galsworthy', 'A Glance at Two Books', 'The Future of Constantinople', and 'The Unlighted Coast'. The volume's compiler, Richard *Curle, explained in his introduction that the first six essays—including 'Legends', the piece on which Conrad was working at his death—were grouped together because they would have formed part of a companion-volume to *The Mirror of the Sea* that Conrad had been planning and may thus be considered 'the shadowy nucleus of a projected work' (p. iv). See Ray Stevens, 'A Milch-Cow's Overview of Sailing Ships and Other Conradian Narrative Perspectives in the Lighter Later Essays', in Carabine *et al.* (eds.) 1992: 263–78.

Laughing Anne is a two-act adaptation of Conrad's own short story 'Because of the Dollars' (*Within the Tides*). 'Laughing Anne' was the title given to the short story on its first publication in *Metropolitan Magazine* (September 1914). Conrad adapted it for the stage in the second half of 1920. In a letter to G. *Jean-Aubry of 10 December 1920, he described it as 'a play for Grand Guignol (English), 2 acts, 3 scenes. It will play forty minutes' (quoted in *JCC*, 457). The play was first performed on 15 June 2000, when a production directed by Richard J. Hand

opened at the University of Glamorgan in Wales before touring to Birmingham, UK, and to a Conrad conference in Lubbock, Texas.

Act I begins on the back verandah of the Macao Hotel, where Hollis and 'good Davy' Davidson, having met after many years, have just lunched and are remembering old times. During the course of these reminiscences, which, unbeknown to them, are being overheard by Fector, they recall Laughing Anne with affection as 'a good sort too', and Davidson reveals that his next voyage will be 'a dollar-collecting trip'. Left alone, and dozing after Hollis's departure, Davidson is startled by the appearance of Laughing Anne, who relates something of her life since being cast off by Harry the Pearler: she and her young son Tony are currently living with Bamtz 'in a little native place . . . where no white man ever comes'. In response to her request, Davidson agrees to include Bamtz on his trading route in future. Following Davidson's departure, Bamtz tells Fector that he is to be a 'merchant' and that Captain Davidson will be calling on him in a month's time. Fector quickly sees the means of stealing the dollars that Davidson will have on board. He tells his two accomplices, Nakhoda and the Man Without Hands, what he has heard and they plan to ambush Davidson when he comes to visit Bamtz.

The first scene of Act II is set in Bamtz's hut where Davidson arrives to find the trio of desperadoes playing cards with Bamtz, and Tony ill with a fever. As Davidson attends to Tony, Anne reveals the men's purpose to rob him. The ringleader, the Man Without Hands, makes Anne tie a weight to his right stump: his plan is to rob Davidson, and then do away with his accomplices before leaving with Anne and the booty. Davidson leaves to sleep aboard the *Sissie* assured that Anne will try to warn him of the attack by laughing. The second scene depicts the foiled robbery. The Man Without Hands sends his henchmen off to gather the dollars while he attempts to murder the sleeping Davidson. Discovering that Davidson is not in his hammock, he realizes that the plot has been discovered and immediately suspects Anne of treachery. The other three men flee while he kills Anne and is then shot by Davidson, who takes Tony aboard his ship. The play ends with four of his Malay sailors preparing to take Anne's body aboard for a burial at sea.

The 56-page manuscript of the play is held in the British Library, and a three-page typescript with Conrad's 'Characters in *Laughing Anne*' is at Colgate University. The play was first published, together with *One Day More*, by J. Castle, London, in October 1924, with an introductory essay by John *Galsworthy. See Paola Pugliatti, 'From Narrative to Drama: Conrad's Plays as Adaptations', in Curreli (ed.), 297–316.

AHS

Lawrence, T[homas] E[dward] (1888–1935), the controversial soldier and scholar known as 'Lawrence of Arabia' for his exploits in organizing Arab opposition to the Turks during the *First World War. T. E. Lawrence was a devoted reader of Conrad's works, and shares with Conrad the distinction of having declined the offer of a knighthood. Conrad and Lawrence met once at Oswalds, on 18 July 1920, at a time when Conrad had just begun work on *Suspense* and Lawrence was revising the second of three drafts of his magisterial history of the Arab Revolt, *Seven Pillars of Wisdom* (1926). Lawrence's copy of *Lord Jim* is inscribed 'T.E.L., Paris 1919', which suggests that he may have been reading Conrad's novel as he was writing the first draft of his remarkable exploration of the moral ambiguities of *colonialism; in many respects, Lawrence's life as a leader of Arabs was similar to *Jim's situation in *Patusan.

Lawrence was accompanied to Oswalds by Conrad's old friend R. B. Cunninghame *Graham, but the meeting was the result of a letter Lawrence had written on 20 March to F. N. *Doubleday, Conrad's American publisher, with comments that Doubleday had forwarded to Conrad: 'He's absolutely the most haunting thing in prose that ever was: I wish I knew how every paragraph he writes . . . goes on sounding in waves, like the note of a tenor bell, after it stops. It's not built on the rhythm of ordinary prose, but on something existing only in his head, and as he can never say what it is he wants to say, all his things end in a kind of hunger, a suggestion of something he can't say or do or think' (*The Letters of T. E. Lawrence*, ed. David Garnett (Cape, 1938), 301–2). Sir Herbert Baker, an architect who had made the attic of his office in Westminster available to Lawrence as a quiet refuge in which to write, later reported that Lawrence had asked Conrad about his literary methods: 'when meeting Conrad he probed him on the methods of his craft; Conrad admitting but little conscious design' (A. W. Lawrence (ed.), *T. E. Lawrence by his Friends* (Cape, 1937), 250). Hugh *Walpole, who was also present that weekend at Oswalds, recorded in his diary that Conrad and Lawrence had talked 'of printing and the Crusades' (Rupert Hart-Davis, *Hugh Walpole: A Biography* (Macmillan, 1952), 195). Two years after their meeting, Conrad sent Lawrence an inscribed copy of *The Mirror of the Sea*, and their mutual friend Sydney Cockerell, the curator of the Fitzwilliam Museum at Cambridge, sent Lawrence a copy of *The Rover* as a Christmas gift.

The reclusive Lawrence maintained an extensive correspondence which included not only statesmen and writers but also printers and crusaders of various kinds. In 1934 Alan Villiers purchased the full-rigged sailing ship *Joseph Conrad for a voyage round the world. When printer and designer Bruce Rogers made a wooden figurehead for the ship in Conrad's image, Lawrence was reminded of Conrad's appearance in the garden at Oswalds: 'What I shall always remember is his lame walk, with the stick to help him, and that sudden upturning of the lined face, with its eager eyes under their membrane of eyelid. They drooped over the eye-socket and the sun shone red through them, as we walked up and down the garden' (*Letters*, ed. Garnett, 843). For more details of the relationship, see Ton Hoenselaars and Gene M. Moore, 'Conrad and T. E. Lawrence', *Conradiana*, 27 (1995), 3–20, or *Journal of the T. E. Lawrence Society*, 5 (1995), 25–44.

'Legends'. Conrad's last piece of writing, over which he laboured painfully during July 1924 when his secretary Miss *Hallowes was on holiday, was left unfinished at his death on 3 August. It was published posthumously in the *Daily Mail* (15 August 1924), 8, with a prefatory note by Richard *Curle and a facsimile of 'The Last Written Page' of the manuscript. The essay and facsimile were collected in *Last Essays*. Although the first part of the article displays a tonic scepticism about the status of legends, this scepticism later tends to evaporate when Conrad goes on to extol the vocational legends that have arisen around the merchant sailing fleet during the period 1850–1900 and to upbraid a reviewer for his reference to a 'timid' seaman. 'What is a "timid member" of a crew?' Conrad asks rhetorically (47). Najder cites this essay as evidence that the 'farther Conrad's sea years receded into the past, the more he idealized not only ships but seamen' (*JCC*, 162). The manuscript is held at the Pierpont Morgan Library, New York.

Leggatt, the captain's mysterious double in 'The Secret Sharer', is the first mate of the *Sephora* who causes the death of a crewman during a storm and then escapes to be given secret shelter by the unnamed captain of another ship. Sherry (*CEW*, 256–60) cites three sources for the story, the most obvious of which, as Conrad acknowledged in his 'Author's Note' to *'Twixt Land and Sea*, is a notorious incident that occurred in the famous tea clipper *Cutty Sark* in 1880, when the first mate, Sydney Smith, struck and killed a black seaman named John Francis and was then helped to escape by Captain Wallace (who served as the primary model for Captain Brierly in *Lord Jim*). Smith was later captured and imprisoned, but worked his way back up to become tanker captain, finally dying in 1922 at the age of 73 (Guerard, 29). Leggatt's culpability is mitigated in Conrad's story, and his guilt does not deter the captain from giving refuge to his fellow 'Conway boy'.

Critics of the story have long been divided over the issue of how to understand Leggatt. Is he a sinner or a saint? A criminal, or an ideal self-image? A Cain who murders a brother seaman, or an Abel who is symbolically killed by the captain when he escapes into the sea? A monitory projection of the captain's unrestrained libido, or a catalyst who helps the novice captain through a rite of initiation into responsibility? In a letter to John *Galsworthy, Conrad responded with shock and indignation to one reviewer's description of Leggatt as a 'murderous ruffian', and added, 'I feel altogether comforted and rewarded for the trouble he has given me in the doing of him. For it wasn't an easy task. It was extremely difficult to keep him true to type first as modified to some extent by the sea-life and further as affected by the situation' (*CL*, v. 121– 2). Cedric Watts has examined the role of Leggatt as a mirror image of the captain in 'The Mirror-Tale: An Ethico-structural Analysis of Conrad's "The Secret Sharer"', *Critical Quarterly*, 19 (1977), 25–37. Leggatt's role as a doppelgänger or alter ego has generated an impressive array of psychological studies in which he has been understood as 'a symbolic manifestation of the captain's unconscious' (Ressler, 82), or as a means by which the captain enters the 'symbolic order' described by Jacques Lacan.

Critics in gay studies and queer theory have stressed the homosocial or homosexual nature of the bond between the captain and Leggatt. In 'Deep Fellowship: Homosexuality and Male Bonding in the Life and Fiction of Joseph Conrad', *Journal of Homosexuality*, 4 (1979), 379–87, Robert Hodges describes the story as 'an allegory of coming out' (385) and considers the sexual overtones of Leggatt's role as the captain's 'lover'. A more original and provocative exploration of the story's homoerotic subtext informs James Lansbury's novel *Korzeniowski* (Serpent's Tail, 1992).

Lena is the name given by Axel *Heyst to the heroine of *Victory* at her own request. When he realizes that he does not know her name, she says, 'They call me Alma. . . . Magdalen too. It doesn't matter; you can call me by whatever name you choose' (88).

Lena is a violinist in Zangiacomo's itinerant Ladies' Orchestra until Heyst, captivated by her voice and sympathetic to her plight, rescues her from *Schomberg's hotel in Surabaya and takes her away to *Samburan. Like Heyst, Lena never knew her mother. Her father was a musician in small theatre orchestras in England until alcohol and a paralytic stroke left him in a home for incurables and launched her on her wanderings.

Lena's intensely emotional and intuitive love for Heyst stands in sharp contrast to his own doubts and hesitations. In keeping with often-noted parallels, she has been compared with the biblical Eve, with Mary Magdalene, and with *Shakespeare's Miranda from The Tempest. Edward W. Said has suggested that Conrad may have derived the name 'Alma' through Flaubert from the Arabic alemah, a learned woman (Orientalism (New York: Random House, 1978), 186). Cedric Watts (1993, 193) notes that 'Alma' is both a Spanish and Italian noun meaning 'soul', and also a Latin adjective meaning 'kind or nourishing', as in the phrase alma mater.

Lena's selfless efforts to save Heyst from the three villains leads ultimately to her temptation of Ricardo and her sacrificial Liebestod. Conrad chose the chapter describing her death for the occasion of a unique public lecture and *reading from Victory before an audience of 200 people in New York on 10 May 1923, and reported to his wife that 'There was a most attentive silence, some laughs and at the end, when I read the chapter of Lena's death, audible snuffling' (LL, ii. 310).

letters. The most important scholarly event in Conrad studies during recent years has been the continuing publication of The Collected Letters of Joseph Conrad, edited by Frederick R. Karl and Laurence Davies, and published by Cambridge University Press. When complete, the edition will probably yield nine volumes and include some 5,000 extant letters, over a third of them previously unpublished. The edition is also an achievement in recovery work of another kind, since it restores to their original forms many letters that were tactfully censored, normalized in style and punctuation, or carelessly transcribed by G. *Jean-Aubry and other early editors. At the most obvious level, Conrad's letters offer a compelling personal record very different in range and kind from his public autobiography of that name. Conrad wrote the first of his letters—a short note in Polish to his father—in May 1861 when he was 3½ years old and his hand was probably guided on the paper by his mother; his last was composed in late July 1924, just before his death. In a letter of February 1896 to Edward *Garnett, Conrad remarked: 'I can be deaf and blind and an idiot if that is the road to my happiness—but I'm hanged if I can be mute. I will not hold my tongue! What is life worth if one can not jabber to one's heart['s] content?' (CL, i. 262). So, Conrad's letters can occasionally 'jabber' animatedly, but more characteristically communicate the perils of intense solitude; they express a flashingly cosmopolitan sensibility, can be written in English, French, or Polish, and show something of his struggles with two adopted *languages; they offer a detailed portrait of the modern writer's life, both in its private and professional dimensions; and, above all, they indicate Conrad's extraordinary talent for lifelong friendships. In a presentation copy of his edition of Conrad letters (CTF) now held at the Polish Library, London, Richard *Curle wrote in 1928: 'Although Conrad disliked the labour of letter-writing, yet he wrote an astonishing number. He loved to keep in touch with his friends by means of the written word and . . . all bear the stamp of his unique personality.'

Correspondence was a natural and regular form of communication for Conrad. Since for most of his writing life he lived in rural *Kent, both his friendships and business dealings needed to be sustained by letter. There are over 1,300 extant letters alone to his agent J. B. *Pinker, to whom in later life he would often write twice a day. Other large collections of letters are to intimate friends such as Edward Garnett, R. B. *Cunninghame Graham, John *Galsworthy, and Richard Curle. Even during a busy day of composition, Conrad invariably made time, often in the late hours, to write to his friends. These late-night letters, especially during Conrad's middle years (1898–1910), are sometimes movingly desperate calls as if from a great distance and seem to bear an intimate connection to the rhythms of his creative process, offering the isolated writer the opportunity to unburden the frustrations of the working day and to seek needed human contact, albeit through indirect epistolary means. On many other days, Conrad wrote several letters at one sitting, so allowing an insight into how the sensitive letter-writer adapted and modulated a common subject in relation to his various addressees.

For most of his life, Conrad wrote his letters by hand, the handwriting itself often a gauge to the state of his health, presenting on some occasions visible evidence of the gouty hand that could barely control the pen. The conventionally printed Conrad letter is, in other respects, sometimes only an approximate translation of the revealing physical evidence presented by the manuscript itself, with its deletions, hasty postscripts, and second thoughts squeezed along the margins. After 1918, the form of Conrad's letters is markedly different, since almost all of his business letters and even some of his personal ones were dictated to his secretary Lilian M. *Hallowes for typing. The presence of a listening intermediary undoubtedly alters the prevailing character of Conrad's later letters, but this is not always the case, since in some of them a lengthy, more informal handwritten postscript characteristically follows the typed portion of the letter. Throughout his life Conrad rarely kept any copies of his letters, apart from those occasions when he was engaged in important business matters, in which case he would sometimes have a copy made for his agent to read and check. Some of these copies still survive and present revealing evidence of the working relationship between writer and agent.

Conrad's letters survive in a variety of forms. Some original documents now missing or unlocated only exist through copies made by another hand, or printed versions, or extracts published in auction house catalogues. The majority of the letters published in the *Collected Letters* are, however, based on existing manuscripts of a widely dispersed kind, with a small percentage privately owned and the remainder housed in North American and European libraries and archives. The largest holdings are in the United States, notably in the Berg Collection and the Miscellaneous Manuscripts Division at the New York Public Library (the Pinker collection, letters to John *Quinn, and others), the Beinecke Rare Book and Manuscript Library, Yale University (letters to Marguerite *Poradowska, Ford Madox *Ford, and others), the Harry Ransom Humanities Research Center at the University of Texas at Austin (notably Henry *James, Hugh *Walpole, and Norman *Douglas), the Lilly Library, Indiana University (the Richard Curle collection), the William R. Perkins Library at Duke University (F. Warrington *Dawson and Sidney *Colvin), and the Firestone Library, Princeton University (F. N. *Doubleday correspondence). In Europe there are substantial holdings of Conrad letters at the British Library (Thomas J. *Wise, Edmund *Gosse, and others), the National Library of Scotland in Edinburgh (the William *Blackwood letters), and the Bibliothèque Littéraire Jacques Doucet in Paris (André *Gide correspondence). Despite the magnitude of Conrad's extant correspondence, there are potentially important letters missing from the published record, some of which may eventually come to light, but others of which are known to be irrecoverable. The most important in the latter group are the numerous letters Conrad wrote from all over the world as a seaman to his uncle Tadeusz *Bobrowski, which were destroyed when Bobrowski's home burned down in 1917. Fortunately the other side of the correspondence—Bobrowski's letters to Conrad—has survived and is published in Najder's *CPB*. Yet another serious loss, again by fire, but this time during the Second World War in Jersey, is Conrad's correspondence to his close friend Perceval *Gibbon. The possible recovery of other letters known to have existed—for example, from Conrad to Marguerite Poradowska between 1895 and 1900, G. F. W. *Hope, W. H. *Hudson, Edward *Thomas, Edwin Pugh, and Sir Robert *Jones—will require assiduous researchers and long periods of systematic detective work.

Conrad's letters were written in three languages—Polish, French, and English—although the *Collected Letters* edition reproduces only the last two. Letters in French are supplied in their original forms with translations, but Polish originals are omitted in favour of English translations. The greater privacy and spontaneity involved in the act of writing letters allows for some revealing glimpses into Conrad's changing linguistic situation. The editorial decision not to correct Conrad's spelling errors and faulty syntax makes it possible to follow his habitual struggle with some of the finer points of English grammar and spelling. The letters from the period 1885–95 in particular reflect his movement between two languages, the English he was in the process of learning and the French that had been his second language for many years. Letters of 1885–6 to Joseph Spiridion *Kliszczewski offer the first extant examples of his command of written English, and those to Marguerite Poradowska of his written French. The extended correspondence with Poradowska is especially revealing in other ways: it contains virtually all that is known directly of Conrad when he was writing his first novel *Almayer's Folly* and shows him moving towards a more formal literary register, emulating the ornate French neo-Romantic styles associated with the tradition of *la belle page*.

The juxtaposition of different kinds of epistolary voice in the volumes of the *Collected Letters* can itself surprise the reader into new recognitions. Public, private, professional, formal, and informal letters often appear in quick succession in any one sequence and sometimes recall the changing registers and perspectives characteristic of Conrad's fiction. Of most direct interest to the student of his works are those letters with a bearing on the sources, evolution, and germinating ideas in his written works. Another large body during the first ten years of his career (1895–1905) emerge as resonant tales of unrest, remarkable for their view of the writer's commitment as a Faustian pact and 'Une chose néfaste [an ill-fated thing]' (*CL*, ii. 409). Unlike Henry James's letters, Conrad's epistolary recreation of the pressures and labours of literary creation do not generally emerge from the calm centre of the writer's workshop. The most revealing of them are written after a day's exhausting labour and take the form of self-sustaining 'performances' in response to problems of psychic energy and motivating conviction—the lack, the expenditure, and the desired renewal of creative momentum. What the letters tell us about Conrad's official attitudes is often secondary to their value as a record of the eccentricities of the Conradian creative process and the writer's attempt to cope with what it involves: a perpetual struggle with erratic temperamental imperatives, writer's block, real or psychosomatic illness, and 'unprofessional' dreaming suddenly released by an energizing rebound into writing. These and other obstacles, both real and self-enforced, often cover whole sequences of letters and present themselves not so much as an interruption of creative rhythms as conditions that seem strangely essential to them.

Of the letters published for the first time in the collected edition the greatest number by far is to J. B. Pinker, Conrad's agent, friend, informal banker, and factotum, suggesting that the time will soon be ready for a much-needed specialized study of their twenty-year relationship. Numerous other letters in the 'professional' category (to publishers and editors, and others on contracts, earnings, and publication decisions) also point to the possibility of a comprehensive study of Conrad's literary life as grounded in the conditions and conventions of late Victorian and Edwardian publishing. Equally significant is the restoration of Conrad's more public missives to the complete epistolary range, in the form of several letters about maritime events and disasters, and, most vitally, the occasional public letter with an important bearing on his artistic creed, as in his long missive to the *New York Times* 'Saturday Review' of 2 August 1901 which offers one of his finest short statements about the 'fundamental truth of fiction' and concludes: 'Fiction, at the point of development at which it has arrived, demands from the writer a spirit of scrupulous abnegation. The only legitimate basis of creative work lies in the courageous recognition of all the irreconcilable antagonisms that make our life so enigmatic, so burdensome, so fascinating, so dangerous—so full of hope' (*CL*, ii. 348, 349).

The edition of the *Collected Letters* itself provides indispensable resources for the Conrad student. After a somewhat uncertain start in volume i, the texts and datings of the letters are as definitive as such things can be, and detailed annotation, especially good on biographical matters, invariably brings with it a secondary kind of archival richness. Each volume includes a detailed chronology, introduction, short biographies of Conrad's correspondents, description of editorial procedures, illustrations, and indexes. The 'General Editor's Introduction' in volume i provides a welcome overview, surveying previous collections of letters; the nature and scope of the unpublished correspondence and how it broadens the picture of some of Conrad's most important friendships; textual and editing problems; and principles of selection. There is also an attempt to define Conrad's various letters by kind and several thoughtful insights into how they relate to the body of his fiction.

Until the completion of the *Collected Letters*, Conrad students and specialists will still need to consult the second volume of G. Jean-Aubry's *Joseph Conrad: Life and Letters* (Heinemann, 1927) supplemented by other individual collections of Conrad's letters to Cunninghame Graham (*LCG*), Richard Curle (*CTF*), William Blackwood (ed. Blackburn), F. Warrington Dawson (ed. Randall), Edward Garnett (*LFC*), Polish friends (*CPB*), and French correspondents in Jean-Aubry's edition of *Lettres françaises* (Paris: Gallimard, 1930).

The sheer bulk and variety of Conrad's letters being made available in the *Collected Letters* call out for closer and more sharply focused studies of the correspondence. Karl comments, 'Conrad was not a self conscious correspondent. Yet since he wrote 3500 [*sic*] letters, we cannot dismiss their significance as the *obiter dicta* of a writer committed to other means of expression. On the contrary their importance must be measured in terms of what they suggest to us about Conrad's mind at any given stage of his career, as well as what, by direct comment and implication, they tell us about his novels and stories. Conrad is frequently not a writer whom one can approach directly, and the indirection, as it were, of his correspondence becomes of a piece with the man' (*CL*, i. p. xxxiv). A beginning was made by Edward Said in *Joseph Conrad and the Fiction of Autobiography* (Cambridge, Mass.: Harvard University Press, 1966), which ambitiously brings together fiction and letters in a study of the spiritual history of an alienated and self-exiled Polish writer living and writing in another country. Said argues that Conrad's letters show explicitly what is implicit in the fiction—that is, the stages in a continuing process of self-authentification forged through the creative act itself, but also coming to include the construction of a public identity. But Said's study did not create a decisive momentum, and it is still common to find the letters treated as a repository of Conrad's fixed beliefs, or valued as merely instrumental in passing from his life to his work, or consigned to the margins of the canon. In 'Echoes, Pictograms, Triangulations: Conrad's *Collected Letters* at Mid-Career', *L'Époque Conradienne* (1988), 5–9, Laurence Davies, one of the editors of the *Collected Letters*, offers a lively invitation to consider a set of alternative questions: how are the letters to be regarded as literary phenomena? How much personation do we find in them and how much impersonation? In what sense do the contents of the *Collected Letters* change the nature or definition of the Conrad canon? Should one in this respect speak of a continuum, or is it more likely, as Batchelor has argued, that 'much of the depressive's agony is channelled into his letters, which are characterized by self-pity, self-reproach, manipulation, lamentation and (less often) aggression' and that the 'hysterical, attention-seeking and dependent part of Conrad's personality displayed in the letters was split off . . . from the artist' (1994: 45)?

These and other questions are broached in a quartet of exploratory essays collected under the title 'The Conrad Letters', edited by J. H. Stape, *Conradiana*, 23 (1991), 5–58. In the first essay, 'Listening for the Silences: Lacunae and Restraints in Conrad's Letters', Laurence Davies argues that Conrad's letters 'are not only valuable for what they tell us about Conrad's life and work but form part of that work themselves' (7). Frederick R. Karl's 'Letters into Biography' examines the way in which the pattern-making biographer will often seem to do violence to the internalized, hybrid, and multi-dimensional letter: 'The letter is it-self a free spirit working through the writer's imagination; for the biographer, on the other hand, it becomes that ominous thing labelled a "document"—obviously quite a different order of being from a free spirit' (18). In 'Conrad's Correspondence: A Literary Dimension', Owen Knowles explores possibilities for treating Conrad's 'letters as literature' in the light of more theoretical studies and the 'written self' of autobiography. He uses a characteristically dark letter of 1899 to show how, in his pursuit of an intractable self, Conrad emulates the strategies of Symbolist autobiography already developed in 'Heart of Darkness', these practices raising larger questions about both the artefactual nature of Conrad's letters and their relation to his fiction. In 'For the Record: Letters to and about Conrad', J. H. Stape discusses the unfortunate consequences arising from the convention of publishing the major writer's correspondence in splendid isolation from the epistolary occasions in which they are grounded, arguing that letters to Conrad serve to 'contextualize his experience' in several ways. The supporting evidence for many of Stape's claims is available in the form of an edition of correspondence to and about Conrad (*PL*), edited by Stape and Owen Knowles.

'Life Beyond, The'. This review of Jasper B. Hunt's *Existence after Death Implied by Science* (1910) was one of four written in July 1910 at the invitation of Lindsay Bashford, literary editor of the *Daily Mail*, who towards the end of June had offered Conrad a regular Saturday review-column. It appeared in the *Daily Mail* (16 July), 8, and was collected in *Notes on Life and Letters*. Conrad soon found the task of reviewing popular books uncongenial and sustained the column for only three issues. The slightest of his *Daily Mail* reviews, this piece finds Conrad tilting sarcastically at modern science's claim to be able to affirm a spiritual immortality. For the phrasing of his concluding vision of modern religious perplexity, he was heavily indebted to two essays by Anatole *France in *La Vie littéraire* (see Hervouet, 142–3). No pre-publication documents are known.

Lingard, James (1862–1921), William *Lingard's nephew. Jim Lingard left England for the *Netherlands East Indies around 1876. After serving in his uncle's ships, he joined Charles *Olmeijer as William Lingard's trading agent in Berau (Conrad's *Sambir) on the Pantai River in north-east *Borneo. Lingard, who spoke Malay like a native, was in Berau at the time of Conrad's visits in 1887, and remained on the Pantai for the rest of his life. Captain James Craig, the master of the *Vidar*, later told Conrad's first biographer G. *Jean-Aubry that his crew had dubbed Lingard 'Lord Jim' because of 'the swaggering manner he assumed, when meeting our ship' (*LL*, i. 97). Although disputing Craig's assertion, Sherry argues that Jim Lingard provided a model for the second half of *Lord Jim* (*CEW*, 135–8). Lingard married a woman named Siti and had six children, one of whom, Mrs C. C. Oehlers, a schoolteacher in Singapore, was interviewed by Sherry in 1962.

Lingard, Tom, an English trader and adventurer whose courage and seamanship earn him the Malay nickname of 'Rajah Laut' or 'King of the Seas'. Tom Lingard is the protagonist of *The Rescue*, and episodes of his later life are recounted in the other novels of Conrad's so-called 'Malay trilogy', *An Outcast of the Islands* and *Almayer's Folly*. Tom Lingard is apparently based primarily on stories Conrad would have heard about seaman-trader William *Lingard, or on his nephew *Jim, whom Conrad could have met in *Borneo; and other details may have been inspired by the lives of Rajah James *Brooke and Captain John Dill Ross. Lingard was born about 1825, since he is 'about thirty-five' at the time of the action of *The Rescue*, which takes place five years after the Crimean War of 1853–6 (*The Rescue*, 9, 20). He came originally from Devon: 'this Brixham trawler-boy, afterward a youth in colliers, deep-water man, gold-digger, owner and commander of "the finest brig afloat"' (ibid. 78). Since he tells *Almayer that he and Captain Craig were 'shipmates in the forties' (*An Outcast of the Islands*, 190), Lingard may have been sailing the Eastern seas in the 1840s, the heroic age of the Rajah Brooke, with whom he is implicitly compared in the opening pages of *The Rescue*. He was prospecting for gold in California in 1849, and apparently obtained the money to purchase his first ship (called the *Flash* in *An Outcast of the Islands* and the *Lightning* in *The Rescue*) in the gold-fields of Victoria, *Australia, in 1851 (ibid. 195). We are told that once he was master of his own ship: 'after a very few years there was not a white man in the islands, from Palembang to Ternate, from Ombawa to Palawan, that did not know Captain Tom and his lucky craft' (ibid. 13). Like Brooke, Lingard's larger-than-life reputation as 'Rajah Laut' was earned in 'desperate fights with the Sulu pirates' (*Almayer's Folly*, 7).

The Rescue describes Lingard's plans to organize and arm a Malay force to depose the Dutch-supported native rulers in Wajo (Celebes, now Sulawesi) and restore his exiled friend Hassim to power. This adventurous scheme is frustrated when a European schooner runs aground opposite Lingard's secret base of operations on the

'Shore of Refuge', on the south-west coast of Borneo. The embarrassments attending Lingard's efforts to 'rescue' the Europeans culminate in the violent deaths of Hassim and his sister Immada.

Lingard's reputation apparently survives the fiasco dramatized in *The Rescue*, perhaps because most of the native chiefs are killed when Jörgenson blows up the *Emma*. In any event, he moves the main focus of his trading and prospecting to the north-east coast of Borneo, where he discovers a secret passage into the Pantai River and establishes the first permanent trading settlement at *Sambir (*An Outcast of the Islands*, 200). Lingard has a lifelong penchant for collecting human strays and orphans, providing the girls with a Western education and the boys with spouses or a start in business. After one of his early encounters with Sulu pirates, he adopts an orphaned pirate girl, provides for her education in a convent in *Java, and later arranges her marriage to Almayer, who hopes thereby to gain a share in Lingard's fortune (ibid. 162). In similar fashion, Lingard helps a destitute young Peter *Willems to find employment with Mr Hudig in Macassar, and Willems unwittingly marries Hudig's unacknowledged daughter (ibid. 189). When Willems is fired for theft, Lingard rescues him again and deposits him in Sambir as Almayer's assistant. Willems, seduced by *Aïssa, betrays Lingard's secret passage to the Arabs; and Lingard's efforts to reunite Willems with his secret family ultimately lead to Willems's death at the hands of the jealous Aïssa. Almayer bitterly laments the consequences of Lingard's 'infernal charity' toward 'Cat, dog, anything that can scratch or bite; as long as it is harmful enough and mangy enough' (ibid. 161).

In *An Outcast of the Islands*, Lingard's enthusiastic dream of finding gold or diamonds in the interior of Borneo inspires confidence in Almayer, who suffers the isolation of Sambir for the sake of a share in Lingard's wealth that will guarantee the future of his beloved daughter Nina. But Lingard's prospecting expeditions are unsuccessful, and he spends the profits of his legitimate trade on his long and mysterious journeys into the interior. Lingard is almost the only survivor of his last expedition, returning 'aged, ill, a ghost of his former self' (*Almayer's Folly*, 26). He 'kidnaps' Nina from Sambir to have her educated in *Singapore, and then returns to Europe, ostensibly to raise more money, but he disappears and is never heard from again.

Lingard, William (1829–88), a celebrated English adventurer and trader whose exploits provided Conrad with a primary model for Captain Tom *Lingard in the 'Malay trilogy'. Known as 'Rajah Laut' or 'King of the Sea', William Lingard was the first Western trader to discover a regular passage into the Pantai River on the northeast coast of *Borneo, and the first to establish a permanent trading settlement there at Berau.

John Dozier Gordan and Jerry Allen have collected information about Lingard in Borneo, and Sherry has done research in *Singapore, but the record of his life remains sketchy. He was sailing the Eastern seas as early as 1848, but as Sherry notes (*CEW*, 90–1), he does not appear in Singapore documents until 1861, when he is described as 'a merchant of Lombock' and captain of the brig *Nina*. In November 1864, Lingard married Johanna Carolina Olmeijer (an aunt or cousin of Charles *Olmeijer, the original of Conrad's *Almayer) in Singapore; they apparently had two daughters, and she travelled with Lingard on his later voyages. When the owner of the *Nina*, Francis James Secretan, died in 1864, Lingard was named co-executor of his will and guardian of his two children. In 1867, while sailing the *Coeran* along the east coast of Borneo, Lingard gave assistance to the Dutch steamship *Reteh* which had run aground, and was later honoured for his services by being named an Officer of the Order of the Netherlands Lion. In 1870 Lingard placed Charles Olmeijer, his relative by marriage, in charge of the trading station at Berau (Conrad's *Sambir). Around 1875, Lingard was joined by two nephews who arrived from England, Joshua and James *Lingard: Joshua later

became a sea captain, while James was with Olmeijer in Berau at the time of Conrad's visits in the autumn of 1887. In a letter to W. G. St Clair, Conrad said that 'Old Lingard was before my time but I knew slightly both his nephews, Jim and Jos' (ibid. 317). Lingard's trade in rattan and gutta-percha suffered from his refusal to consider switching from sail to steam; the steamer *Vidar*, on which Conrad served as first mate, was owned by Lingard's Arab competitors. St Clair's account of meeting 'Old Lingard' on a voyage in early 1887 (ibid. 115) apparently provides the last direct testimony of his movements. Like Conrad's 'King Tom', he returned to England and died there.

Lombroso, Cesare (1836–1909), an Italian physician, psychiatrist, and criminologist. Cesare Lombroso believed that 'criminal degenerates', epileptics, and idiots' could be recognized and categorized by such physical features as the shape of their ears or lips; his best-known work is *L'uomo delinquente* (1875). 'Lombroso is an ass', says the terrorist Karl Yundt in *The Secret Agent* in response to Ossipon's comments that the lobes of *Stevie's ears identify him as a Lombrosan 'degenerate'. Yundt goes on to call Lombroso 'this imbecile who has made his way in this world of gorged fools by looking at the ears and teeth of a lot of poor, luckless devils' (47). Although he is dismissed as something of a crank today, along with the 'physiologies' that fascinated the Victorians, Lombroso's views were influential in their time. His classification of various criminal types by means of physical anthropology can be recognized as a late 19th-century attempt to bring the rigours of science to bear upon the field of criminology.

Sherry (*CWW*), Hunter (1983), and Watts (1997) have demonstrated correspondences between Lombrosan 'types' and Conrad's presentation of the anarchists in *The Secret Agent*, where they are often used to ironic effect. Alone with Winnie in the train carriage, Ossipon 'gazed at her, and invoked Lombroso, as an Italian peasant recommends himself to his favourite saint.

He gazed scientifically. He gazed at her cheeks, at her nose, at her eyes, at her ears... Bad!... Fatal! . . . Not a doubt remained... a murdering type' (297). But, with superb irony, the precise description of Ossipon's physical attributes identifies him, in Lombrosan terms, with a whole range of social degenerates. Ossipon is described thus: 'A bush of crinkly yellow hair topped his red, freckled face, with a flattened nose and prominent mouth cast in the rough mould of the negro type. His almond-shaped eyes leered languidly over the high cheek-bones' (44). But, in Gina Lombroso Ferrero's account of her father's ideas, *Criminal Man: According to the Classification of Cesare Lombroso* (New York: Putnam's Sons, 1911), she says that, according to Lombroso, the nose of a born thief is often of a 'flattened negroid character'; violators of women have lips 'protruding, as in negroes'; swindlers have 'curly and woolen hair'; and many congenital criminals have such Mongoloid features as oblique eyes and prominent cheekbones (15–18). That Ossipon is unconsciously hoist with his own petard suggests that Conrad's *irony in the novel extends to this particular 'science', Ossipon's own sacrosanct fetish. As Robert Hampson argues: 'The ironic treatment of Ossipon's faith in Lombroso is thus of a piece with the radical scepticism that pervades *The Secret Agent* and with the novel's own anarchic subversion of systems' ('"If you read Lombroso": Conrad and Criminal Anthropology', in Curreli (ed.), 326).

Debate continues as to whether Conrad actually read Lombroso's work or knew of his views only through indirect sources. However, as one of the major criminologists of the period, his ideas informed its central debates. For instance, between 1899 and 1907, *Blackwood's Magazine* carried four long editorial articles on anarchists which seem to rely on Lombroso's classification of anarchists as criminal degenerates, and these may have provided Conrad with a source. In the best overview of the debate, Hampson traces Conrad's use of Lombroso beyond *The Secret Agent* (1907) into *Chance* (1913), where, for instance,

*Marlow says of *de Barral: 'A pressman whom I knew told me "He's an idiot". Which was possible. Before that I overheard once somebody declaring that he had a criminal type of face; which I knew was untrue' (85). Gina Lombroso Ferrero says that, to her father, 'idiocy, epilepsy and genius, crimes and sublime deeds were forged into one single chain' (288). Knowing this, is it merely coincidence that Carleon Anthony 'seized with avidity upon the theory of poetical genius being allied to madness, which he got hold of in some idiotic book everybody was reading a few years ago' (184)? And might that 'idiotic book' be by—or related to—Lombroso? Conrad's view of Lombroso's ideas seems consistently sceptical. In *Chance*, Marlow describes himself to Mrs Fyne as a 'physiognomist', claiming: 'on the principles of that science a pointed little chin is a sufficient ground for interference' (151). Not recognizing that she is being teased, she asks whether he is serious, and Marlow's reply is unequivocal: 'That science is farcical and therefore I am not serious' (152).   AHS

London. Having first set foot on English soil in Lowestoft on 10 June 1878, Conrad immediately travelled to London. Throughout his career in the *British Merchant Service, the city, capital of the richest and most powerful country in the world, provided a logical place for him to seek maritime employment. Writing to Marguerite *Poradowska in March 1894, he says: 'I am looking for a job, and I dare not leave London now for fear of missing an opportunity' (*CL*, i. 150). After signing off the *Europa* early in 1880, Conrad's first address in London was at Tollington Park, a street near Finsbury Park, N4. In May that year he rented a flat from William Ward at 6 Dynevor Road, Stoke Newington, N16. Then, in May 1889, after a lengthy period of service in Far Eastern and *Australian waters, he took rented rooms in Bessborough Gardens, Pimlico, SW1, where he began writing *Almayer's Folly*. Finally, in mid-1891, he rented rooms at 17 Gillingham Street, near Victoria Station, SW1, which was to be his last London base.

Conrad's early years in London were lonely years for the immigrant Pole, and he recalls how he 'explored the maze of streets east and west in solitary leisurely walks without chart and compass' (*A Personal Record*, 68). So profound were the memories of these early walks that, when Conrad based *The Secret Agent* in the city, they threatened to dominate the novel. As he confesses in his 'Author's Note': 'I had to fight hard to keep at arms-length the memories of my solitary and nocturnal walks all over London in my early days, lest they should rush in and overwhelm each page of the story' (p. xiii). Conrad's love of walking in London is confirmed in his essay 'Stephen Crane' where he recalls meeting *Crane for the first time and how 'that first long afternoon . . . had a character of enchantment about it. It was spread out over a large portion of central London' (*Last Essays*, 104). In *Chance*, *Marlow reflects Conrad's spirit of urban exploration when he confesses to 'playing the vagabond in the streets of a big town till the sky pales above the ridges of the roofs' (52). London was intimately bound up with Conrad's personal and professional lives: here he met, courted, and married Jessie George, having proposed, according to her, on the steps of the National Gallery (*JCHC*, 12); and it was in the London literary market place of publishers and agents that he earned his living. Conrad's letters reveal frequent visits to London to see friends— for instance, at the Tuesday lunches organized by Edward *Garnett at the *Mont Blanc Restaurant in Gerrard Street, which Hilaire Belloc, G. K. Chesterton, John *Galsworthy, and Edward *Thomas among others also attended—and for Jessie to receive medical attention for her knees (which she damaged in a fall in London during a family visit to the capital in 1904).

Conrad's early fiction typically portrays London from a sailor's perspective. Thus, it is through the eyes of a returning sailor that the city is seen at the end of both 'Karain: A Memory' (*Tales of Unrest*) and *The Nigger of the 'Narcissus'*, while 'Heart of Darkness' begins with a view of the city from the deck of the *Nellie*. As the *Narcis-sus* journeys up the *Thames towards her berth, the outskirts of London are presented in images of clutter and grime, immediately replacing the images of freedom and isolation associated with the *sea voyage: 'On the riverside slopes the houses appeared in groups—seemed to stream down the declivities at a run to see her pass, and, checked by the mud of the foreshore, crowded on the banks. Further on, the tall factory chimneys appeared in insolent bands and watched her go by, like a straggling crowd of slim giants, swaggering and upright under the black plummets of smoke, cavalierly aslant' (163). The image of the chimneys, in particular, may owe something to *Dickens's description of Coketown in *Hard Times* (1854). Viewing London from a sailor's perspective in 'Heart of Darkness' reinforces the novella's colonial theme by subtly reminding the reader of the city's place at the heart of the British Empire, whence 'the ships and the men . . . had sailed from Deptford, from Greenwich, from Erith—the adventurers and the settlers' (*Youth*, 47). The presence of London is conjured up, too, during the homeward voyage of the *Narcissus* in the various references to the East End: in Wait's memories of a 'Canton Street girl' and of 'swaggering up the East India Dock Road' (149), for instance, or the nicknames and descriptions of *Donkin, which include 'Whitechapel', 'that cheeky costermonger chap', and 'East End trash' (13, 21, 45).

The incompatibility of sea and city values is made palpable in the form of money and it is significant that, at the end of the novel, the narrator loses sight of the crew of the *Narcissus* outside the Mint. In London, and out of their element, the returning sailors feel alienated by the welter of city life and disoriented by the randomness of the buildings, as when the narrator and Jackson meet in the Strand at the end of 'Karain: A Memory' amid 'the broken confusion of roofs, the chimney-stacks, the gold letters sprawling over the fronts of houses' (54). The anonymity of London life is made even more forcefully in 'The Return' (*Tales of Unrest*) where Alvan Hervey walks home past 'all the innumerable houses with closed doors and curtained windows' (135), which seems to anticipate T. S. Eliot's 'Preludes' (1915), and where the Herveys' social circle 'grew steadily, annexing street after street. It included also Somebody's Gardens, a Crescent—a couple of Squares' (122). London is at its darkest and most alienating when the jilted Alvan Hervey looks out on 'the damp and sooty obscurity over the waste of roofs and chimney-pots . . . He saw an illimitable darkness, in which stood a black jumble of walls, and, between them, the many rows of gaslights stretched far away in long lines, like strung-up beads of fire. A sinister loom as of a hidden conflagration lit up faintly from below the mist, falling upon a billowy and motionless sea of tiles and bricks' (126). Thus, while 'The Return', with its metropolitan setting, is markedly different from Conrad's other early sea tales, its use of London as a locale anticipates Conrad's sustained presentation of the city in *The Secret Agent* (1907) and *Chance* (1913).

These two novels reflect Conrad's intimate knowledge of London in the precision of their locations. Thus, the sweep of the city in *The Secret Agent*, Conrad's first metropolitan novel, includes the 'furnished apartments for gentlemen near Vauxhall Bridge Road' (6); the salon of Michaelis's patroness in Piccadilly; Adolf *Verloc's shop at 32 Brett Street, Soho; and Whitehall and Westminster; while *Chance* is, if anything, even more precise in measuring *de Barral's financial rise by his topographical shift from east to central London: from 'lending money in a very, very small way in the East End to people connected with the docks' (70) to offices in 'a small street off the Strand' (79). Conrad's sense of London is present too in the many journeys contained in each narrative—like Verloc's walk to the (Russian) embassy—which not only provide urban counterparts to the voyages in the sea fiction but whose use of topography provides an external indicator of the inward psychology of the characters. Thus Verloc's impressions of the metropolis say as much about the state of his perceiving consciousness as about the city perceived: on his way to the

embassy the city exhibits 'the majesty of inorganic nature'; later it is transformed into 'the enormity of cold, black, wet, muddy, inhospitable accumulation of bricks, slates, and stones' (14, 56). Similarly, the Eastern Hotel where Flora meets Captain *Anthony is located 'at the bifurcation of two very broad, mean, shabby, thoroughfares' (197), which have been identified as the East India and West India Dock Roads.

Conrad's depiction of London is simultaneously a reflection of his personal experience of the city and a testament to the literary heritage within which he worked. Inevitably, his presentation of the city contains echoes of *Dickens, who, as Conrad's essay 'Poland Revisited' suggests, provides a subtle link between his own youth in *Poland and his careers of sailor and writer. Here, Conrad recalls his first visit to London and calling at a shipping office which occupied 'a Dickensian nook of London, that wonder city, the growth of which bears no sign of intelligent design, but many traces of freakishly sombre phantasy the Great Master knew so well how to bring out by the magic of his understanding love. And the office I entered was Dickensian too' (*Notes*, 152). *The Secret Agent* especially seems indebted to Dickens for its view of London. Winnie *Verloc's impression of the city as a town 'of marvels and mud' (270) and the Assistant Commissioner's 'descent into a slimy aquarium from which the water had been run off' (147) echo the London of *Bleak House* (1853), which Conrad claimed to have read 'innumerable times' (*A Personal Record*, 124), while the inanimate piano suddenly bursting into life and the cab journey across London, from Soho to the almshouses at the southern end of the Old Kent Road, carry traces of Dickensian grotesquerie and farce.

In 1905, two years before the publication of *The Secret Agent*, Conrad's friend and collaborator Ford Madox *Ford published *The Soul of London*, which Conrad praised warmly (see *CL*, iii. 241). For an extensive treatment of Conrad's knowledge of London, see Robert Hampson, '"Topographical Mysteries": Conrad and London', in

Moore (ed.) 1992: 159–74. See also the essays by Hugh Epstein and Martin Ray in the same volume for a discussion of possible influences on Conrad's depiction of London in *The Secret Agent*. AHS

Lord Jim: A Tale. Described in Conrad's 'Author's Note' as 'a free and wandering tale' (p. viii), *Lord Jim* (1900) was first meditated and its opening chapters sketched out before the composition of 'Heart of Darkness' but then set aside until after the completion of this famous novella. *Lord Jim* also enjoys a secure place as one of Conrad's masterpieces, generally regarded by critics as containing some of his finest writing; the *tour de force* for which all his earlier stories are a preparation; the most revealing of his fictional autobiographies; a test case for more recent theoretical preoccupations with gender, nationality, and post-coloniality; and a work 'of extraordinary modernity, standing at the end of the nineteenth century and at the beginning of the twentieth as a kind of milestone' (Batchelor 1994: 112).

The novel's first four chapters offer a synoptic, if selective view of *Jim's early life. The son of a decent, middle-class English parson, Jim is so charmed by images of the heroic life presented to him through his light reading that he impulsively commits himself to a seaman's life as the means to fulfil his romantic aspirations. However, as a young trainee, he fails to live up to his idealized conception of himself and subsequently discovers at sea little of the glamour for which he yearns. After a period of hospitalization in the Far East, Jim, in his mid-twenties, enlists as first mate in the *Patna*, but, after a mysterious maritime crisis in the Arabian Sea (17) that has found him again wanting and left him 'under a cloud' ('Author's Note', p. ix), he moves restlessly from one mundane job to another in search of anonymity.

From chapter 5, his story is taken up by the English master mariner *Marlow, who has become fascinated with Jim. In an after-dinner narration (which continues until chapter 36), Marlow pieces together from a wide variety of sources and testi-

monies the events on board the *Patna* that have brought Jim to a court of inquiry. With a cargo of 800 pilgrims bound from *Singapore to Mecca, the *Patna*, 'a local steamer as old as the hills, lean like a greyhound, and eaten up with rust worse than a condemned water-tank' (13–14), apparently strikes a submerged object and threatens to sink. When the unscrupulous German master and the white members of the crew decide to save their own skins and take to a lifeboat, Jim is at first a removed onlooker, but events—or so he later argues—conspire against him and compel him towards actions for which he does not feel himself fully responsible. George, the third engineer, collapses with a heart attack; but the absconding crew nevertheless shout for George to join them in the lifeboat and leave the unsuspecting pilgrims to their fate. His heroic aspirations notwithstanding, Jim finally jumps and finds himself in the lifeboat. Contrary to expectations, the *Patna* survives unharmed and is towed by a French gunboat to Aden. The crew members in the lifeboat are rescued by an eastbound British steamer and taken to an unnamed port (Bombay), where they learn of the *Patna*'s survival. The captain disappears, and Jim is left to face an official inquiry alone, between the sessions of which he tells his personal story to Marlow. The cancellation of Jim's mate's certificate only partially satisfies his need to rehabilitate himself. He has also to live with the private consciousness of disgrace, a matter of absorbing concern to Marlow, who becomes involved in the 'fundamental why' (56) behind events that took place on board the *Patna*.

During the following three years Jim is perpetually in transit, 'a rolling stone' (197) who, pursued by malign gossip, retreats eastwards 'towards the rising sun' (5). Eventually, with the help of Marlow's German friend *Stein, Jim is established as manager of Stein's trading post in *Patusan, a remote settlement (in north-west Sumatra) that seems to offer him a sanctuary from the accusing world. By defeating the Arab trader Sherif Ali and successfully defying the authority of the villainous

Rajah Allang, Jim restores peace within the Patusan community on behalf of the elderly chief Doramin. He also enjoys the close friendship of the chief's son, Dain Waris, and the devoted love of *Jewel, the Eurasian stepdaughter of his corrupt predecessor Cornelius. So powerful and respected does Jim become as Patusan's virtual ruler that he is called Tuan (or Lord) Jim. The narrator's translation of 'Tuan' as 'Lord' (5) is singularly solemn and eloquent, since the Malay term is commonly equivalent to 'sir' or 'mister' or 'boss'. Eventually, at the point where Jim seems to have 'achieved greatness' (225), the second main crisis of his life arises when Patusan is invaded by Gentleman *Brown and his gang. More than two years after the evening of Marlow's long narration, the 'privileged man', an Englishman who had been one of his listeners, receives from Marlow a package containing details of Jim's final catastrophe (chapters 36–45). While Jim's social duty to the Patusan community seems to require that he destroy Brown, he is susceptible to Brown's appeal and finally arranges for him to leave Patusan unharmed. In the course of their departure Brown and his henchmen murder Dain Waris and some of his followers. Jim has pledged his own life to guarantee the safety of the Patusan community, and chooses to redeem his pledge (and his lost honour) by walking to his death, to be shot by the grieving Doramin.

The novel's earliest origins can be traced to a 28-page fragment entitled 'Tuan Jim: A Sketch' pencilled into a leather-bound album originally owned by Conrad's maternal grandmother Teofila *Bobrowska and sold by Jessie Conrad to the Houghton Library, Harvard University, in July 1925. Its text, corresponding roughly to the novel's first three chapters, seems to confirm Conrad's statement in his 'Author's Note' that his 'first thought was of a short story, concerned only with the pilgrim ship episode; nothing more' (p. viii), although there are hints in this ur-version of later developments in Jim's life in a remote Eastern country. Probably written in the spring of 1898 (although an earlier date is possible,

and one as far back as 1896 has been suggested), this 'Sketch' was laid aside and evidently not taken up again until Conrad was asked for a story by William *Blackwood in mid-1898. 'Tuan Jim: A Sketch' is reprinted in *Lord Jim: An Authoritative Text, Backgrounds, Sources*, ed. Thomas C. Moser, Norton Critical Edition, 2nd edn (New York: Norton, 1996). Eloise Knapp Hay considers its importance in the evolution of the final novel in '*Lord Jim*: From Sketch to Novel', *Comparative Literature*, 12 (1960), 289–309.

Conrad's first extant reference to *Lord Jim* appears in a letter to Edward *Garnett of 28 May or 4 June 1898 (*CL*, ii. 62), in which he described it as a future 20,000-word story planned for publication in *Blackwood's Magazine* and to be collected with 'Youth' and other pieces in a volume of short stories. By early June, Conrad, presumably having resurrected his earlier 'Sketch', sent an eighteen-page sample of the new story to Blackwood's London office. Its composition was then delayed for a full year during which he composed 'Heart of Darkness' and *collaborated with Ford Madox *Ford on *The Inheritors*. Conrad committed himself single-mindedly to the 'Jim story' in July 1899, sending Blackwood's '3 chap:^{rs} 31 pp.' and now estimating a work of 'fully 40000 words' (*CL*, ii. 184).

Once Conrad had begun composition in earnest, *Lord Jim* gradually turned into the first spectacular example of what he later termed a 'runaway' novel—a work originally conceived as a short story but which, batch by batch of manuscript, gradually developed and expanded until it far exceeded its original scope. Late in his life, he described the process as one of pursuing his subject for the length of a novel 'without being able to overtake it . . . It's like a chase in a nightmare,—weird and exhausting' (*LL*, ii. 339–40). In the case of *Lord Jim*, the chase occupied an entire year, with Conrad regularly assuring his publisher that the end was in sight, only to find that it still, apparently, eluded him. By the time it was finished in July 1900, the work ran to more than 130,000 words and its *serialization took up space in fourteen monthly issues of *Blackwood's*, from October 1899 to November 1900. At the time the first instalment appeared, Conrad anticipated that only five such instalments would be needed for the entire story (*CL*, ii. 208), although Blackwood may have found grounds for apprehension in Conrad's slightly later proviso: 'I do suffer at times from optical delusions (and others) where my work is concerned' (*CL*, ii. 230). In January 1900, Conrad wrote repeatedly to his publisher assuring him that he was nearing its end, and on 12 February he declared that with the completion of chapter 20, he would need only two more chapters to finish. As Ian Watt points out, since chapter 20 covers Marlow's meeting with Stein, Conrad was even at this late stage presumably 'still not thinking of giving the Patusan episode any extensive treatment, let alone the twenty-four chapters it eventually received' (1980: 260). On Conrad's behalf, Blackwood's literary adviser, David *Meldrum, apologized to his employer for the work's growing length but insisted that it was a 'great story' and that 'in the annals of *Maga* [*Blackwood's Magazine*] half a century hence it will be one of the honourable things to record of her that she entertained "Jim"' (Blackburn (ed.), 86). Faithful to its original plan, the Blackwood firm began setting type for the projected volume of short stories in mid-April. By mid-May, however, the publisher informed Conrad that since the story was going to run to at least 31 chapters and take up 320 pages (with the addition of what Blackwood imagined to be another ten pages or so), it would have to be brought out as a separate volume. Conrad agreed that the work would 'be (it seems incredible) of, apparently, 100000 words' (*CL*, ii. 271), although even this proved to be a conservative estimate. He was aware that the story had 'run away' with him and needed to be brought to a close, and its composition proceeded quickly, at an average rate of more than 10,000 words per month. He went on to revise the serial text for book publication, some of these revisions being made at the very last minute for the first British edition, entitled *Lord Jim: A Tale*,

published by Blackwood on 9 October 1900. The first American edition, under the title *Lord Jim: A Romance*, was published by Doubleday, McClure on 31 October.

Lord Jim evolves out of a rich matrix of personal, historical, and literary sources. The fact that its presiding narrator Marlow is approximately 43 years old (the same age as Conrad at the time of writing) and that Jim was born around 1859 (two years later than Conrad's own year of birth) has confirmed many critics in the belief that the work is one of its creator's most revealing autobiographical fictions. In a novel notable for its doublings and mirror reflections, Jim's romantic ambitions are comparable to the young Conrad's quixotic desire to go to *sea, and his life also imitates the 'standing jump' that consigned Conrad to a form of exile and left him open to repeated charges of having betrayed the traditions of his homeland. One biographer goes so far as to detect a triple self-portrait in the novel: 'Jim is his younger self's youthfulness, uncertainty, guilt, ambition and idealism; Marlow is ... the Englishman that Conrad would have liked to have been; and Stein is, in a sense, Conrad as he actually was ... not "one of us" but an exotic stranger speaking broken English, a wise foreigner with an adventurous past' (Batchelor 1994: 110). The main historical source for Jim's career in the first part of the novel was Augustine Podmore *Williams, an Englishman based in the Far East who was involved in a widely reported maritime scandal of 1880. A clergyman's son like Jim, Williams was first mate in the *Jeddah*, a steamship carrying 953 pilgrims bound from Penang (Malaya) to Mecca. When on 8 August the ship hit bad weather and developed a leak in her hull, she was abandoned by her European captain and crew, who believed her to be sinking and knew that her lifeboats were inadequate. Williams was the last crew member to leave the ship, although, unlike Jim, he did not jump but was thrown overboard by the pilgrims. When it was later discovered that the *Jeddah* had survived, the ship's captain and Williams figured prominently in a maritime inquiry, after which, barred from a sea career, Williams worked as a water-clerk in Singapore and married a local Eurasian girl (for further details of the novel's 'Eastern' sources, see Sherry, *CEW*, 41–86; and Hans van Marle and Pierre Lefranc, 'Ashore and Afloat: New Perspectives on Topography and Geography in *Lord Jim*', *Conradiana*, 20 (1988), 109–35). Conrad's depiction of the one-man empire established by Jim in Patusan incorporates two further sources. Jim *Lingard, nephew of William *Lingard, the 'King of the Seas' and the benevolent paternalist in east *Borneo who had provided a part-model for Tom *Lingard in Conrad's first two novels, probably suggested Jim's name and other features of his situation in Patusan. In addition, the life of James *Brooke, the first Rajah of Sarawak, provided a blueprint for Jim's accession to benevolent rule in Patusan but may also have sharpened Conrad's sense of how Jim was also a faltering or even 'failed Brooke' (see Andrea White, 'Conrad and Imperialism', in Stape (ed.) 1996: 189). At one point in the narrative, when Stein gives him a ring as a talisman to identify him in Patusan, Jim comments, 'It's like something you read of in books' (233–4). In part a mythical narrative, *Lord Jim* is grounded not only in the 'light holiday literature' (5) of Jim's childhood but also in a literary community of transcendent dreamers ranging from Cervantes's *Don Quixote through Romantic poetry to Gustave *Flaubert's Emma Bovary, as well as in works and authors central to the evolution of Western mythology: classical tragedy, the Bible, *Shakespeare, and *Goethe. These literary sources also include Conrad's own earlier work, in relation to which *Lord Jim* stands as a richly organized coda and summation.

Two months after publication, Conrad commented: 'I am the spoiled child of the critics' (*CL*, ii. 313). The characteristic note of most reviews was one of admiring, if slightly bewildered wonderment at the strange mechanics of a work that had brought Conrad 'at once into the front rank of living novelists' (*CCH*, 120). One of those living novelists was Henry *James, who wrote to Conrad with effusive con-gratulations and who also provided one early reviewer with a means to characterize the combination in *Lord Jim* of popular story and refined artistic novel: 'If Mr. Henry James had a consummate knowledge of life at sea and in the Pacific Coast towns and settlements, he would write a novel very like *Lord Jim*. Is this praise or blame? Granting the supreme talent of Mr. James, would it be rightly or wrongly devoted to analysing the soul behind the rough-and-tumble life of a sailor and a ship-chandler's water clerk? Is it well for us to be reminded that such persons may be as infinitely complicated, as civilisedly degenerate as any dweller in refined and sophisticated circles?' (*CCH*, 126). Meldrum was delighted that his predictions for the novel had been realized, and went on to ensure that the first print run was followed by a second in December 1900 on the grounds that the Blackwood firm could not 'afford to let *Lord Jim* go out of print' because Conrad was 'a man whose coming into his own may take very long but is bound to result one day' (Blackburn (ed.), 116). Meldrum also summarized the prevailing tenor of the book's reception: 'I wish I could say that he would ever be "popular" . . . but he is too good for that. On the other hand, it would seem that over "Lord Jim" he is coming into his own quicker than so "unfashionable" and clever an author . . . [has] any right to expect in these days' (ibid. 122).

After Conrad's death, two works of the 1930s helped to strengthen *Lord Jim*'s special place in the Conrad canon. In his influential psychoanalytic study, Morf held it to be significant that *Lord Jim* appeared in the same year as Sigmund Freud's *The Interpretation of Dreams*: '*Lord Jim* is unique amongst Conrad's books. It is perhaps not his best, but his most intimate. . . . In *Lord Jim*, Joseph Conrad exteriorized, in a symbolic form, the deepest conflicts that arose from the dualism Polish-English within himself' (1930: 165–6). In Joseph Warren Beach (*The Twentieth Century Novel: Studies in Technique* (New York: Appleton-Century-Crofts, [1932])), Conrad found an American admirer who, predominantly interested in his technical rhetoric, regarded the handling of point of view and disrupted chronology in Lord Jim as striking evidence of Conrad as 'the most restless and ingenious experimenter of his time' (337). However, when the novel underwent a major reassessment during the period 1940–60, it attracted more divergent responses. In Britain, the highly influential F. R. Leavis energetically championed Conrad's reputation, but was also instrumental in shaping the widespread opinion that Lord Jim was a flawed work. He judged that the novel did not 'deserve the position of pre-eminence among Conrad's works often assigned to it' largely on the grounds that after its first part ('good Conrad'), 'the romance that follows, though plausibly offered as a continued exhibition of Jim's case, has no inevitability as that; nor does it develop or enrich the central interest, which, consequently, eked out to provide the substance of a novel, comes to seem decidedly thin' (189, 190). In his 1952 study, Douglas Hewitt, another British critic, found the two parts of the novel to be organically connected, but nevertheless detected a pervasive and unsatisfactory 'muddlement' resulting from the fact that Conrad's 'feelings are too deeply and too personally involved for him to stand above the bewilderment in which he places Marlow' (39). By contrast, American critics during this period were more ambitious, versatile, and positive in their claims. Morton Dauwen Zabel, in 'Joseph Conrad: Chance and Recognition', Sewanee Review, 53 (1945), 1–22, employing very different emphases from Leavis, encouraged readers to regard Conrad's major works, including Lord Jim, as 'always more than the sum of his conscious motives and critical intelligence' (12) and, in their preoccupation with 'the test and opportunity of fundamental selfhood' (5), as belonging spiritually with those of Thomas Mann, André *Gide, and Franz Kafka. Dorothy Van Ghent, in her chapter on Lord Jim in The English Novel: Form and Function (New York: Holt, Rinehart & Winston, 1953), 229–44, maintained that Conrad approached, but also memorably diverged

from, a model of classical tragedy: what intervenes between Conrad's attitude toward the story of Jim and the attitudes of Aeschylus and Sophocles is 'modern man's spiritual isolation from his fellows' (232). The model of classical tragedy is complicated by the ambiguities of relative judgement which, in Conrad's novel, finally put 'both the law and the self to question' (244). Albert J. Guerard's seminal work of 1958, which helped to set the critical agenda for many years, shows a pluralist and eclectic critic seeking to define the 'psychomoral' richness of Conrad's work and outlining the richly dualistic nature of Conrad's vision as a tragic pessimist. For this critic, all of the writer's characteristic qualities are evident in Lord Jim, a work given a memorable technical reading as an *impressionist novel which, in its rich and oscillating combination of sympathy and judgement, establishes radically new alignments between writer and reader: as an innovative kind of 'art novel', Lord Jim forces upon the reader 'an active, exploratory, organizing role' and presents itself as a work requiring second and subsequent readings. With its emphasis less on the novel's communicable meanings than upon the indeterminate responses called into play through Marlow's agency, Guerard's reading foreshadows the more specialized *narratological, *Bakhtinian, and reader-response approaches later applied to the novel.

As a difficult 'classic' of modern literature, the novel has attracted several studies of a more introductory kind aimed at the general reader's needs. Tanner's monograph of 1963 was followed by several others offering explication of difficult cruxes (such as the Stein episode, the Jim–Gentleman Brown confrontation, and the ending of the novel) and attempting to summarize its leading themes. Watt (1980: 254–356), Batchelor (1988), and Ross C. Murfin (in Lord Jim: After the Truth, Masterwork Studies (New York: Twayne, (1992)) offer contextually rich and detailed studies, the first arguing that the treatment of the friendship between Marlow and Jim 'goes far to explain why Lord Jim has become the cherished and enduring work it is' (338); while the second regards Conrad himself to be the best guide to the novel's essential subject in his claim that it follows 'the acute consciousness of lost honour' ('Author's Note', p. ix). Other general studies include Berthoud's elegant chapter (1978: 64–93), Stape's compact survey of the novel (Stape (ed.) 1996: 63–80), and Moser's Norton Critical Editions (1968 and 1996), which include a selection of contextual documents, contemporary reviews, and later criticism.

An essential element of continuity between criticism of the 1960s and subsequent studies has been the emergence of more overtly political readings of *Lord Jim*. The process was begun in Irving Howe's chapter on Conrad in *Politics and the Novel* (1957) and continued in Hay's 1963 study of the political Conrad with her question, 'What is it about *Lord Jim* that no one has adequately explained?' (p. vii). By way of response, she and other critics went on to argue that Conrad's preoccupation with social cohesion lends an inherently political dimension to works which, in Hay's words, dramatize 'the iron necessities imposed on nonpolitical individuals by political or quasi-political circumstances' (84). These approaches added a number of fresh emphases to *Lord Jim* criticism, leading to interpretations more issue-based and contextualized than many previous ones, sometimes less sympathetic to Jim's 'fine sensibilities' (177), and with greater attention to the social damage created by 'Lord Jim' in the Patusan section of the novel.

Since the mid-1970s, the politicization of literary studies allied to the tendency of critics to read oppositionally or 'against the grain' of established classics has seen no lessening in the centrality of *Lord Jim*. On the contrary, the attraction of the novel for *feminist, post-colonial, *deconstructive, and *Marxist approaches testifies to the part played by the work in strengthening Conrad's reputation as 'our contemporary'. Owen Knowles's *An Annotated Critical Bibliography of Joseph Conrad* (Hemel Hempstead: Harvester Wheatsheaf, 1992) and Batchelor (1988) offer useful guides to more recent *Lord Jim* criticism, a represen-

tative selection of which can be found in Harold Bloom (ed.), *Joseph Conrad's Lord Jim: Modern Critical Interpretations* (New York: Chelsea House, 1987). For the history of *film versions of *Lord Jim*, see Moore (ed.) 1997. Major portions of the manuscript are held at the Rosenbach Museum and Library, Philadelphia, and smaller fragments are held at the Henry E. Huntington Library, San Marino, Calif., and at the British Library, London. Additional materials can be found at the Lilly Library, Indiana University, and in the Berg Collection, New York Public Library. The manuscript of the 'Author's Note' is at the Beinecke Rare Book and Manuscript Library, Yale University.

'Loss of the *Dalgonar*, The'. Written in mid-October 1921, this short piece on matters of seamanship was originally published as a letter to the editor of the *London Mercury* (December 1921), and was later collected in *Last Essays*. In his brief letter, Conrad responds to an article in the journal's September issue entitled 'A True Story: Log and Record of the Wreck of the Ship *Dalgonar* of Liverpool, bound from Callao to Taltal', concerning the sinking of the *Dalgonar* during a gale in October 1913 and the rescue of her crew members by a French ship, the *Loire*. After a first part devoted to correcting errors in the transcription of the *Dalgonar*'s log record, Conrad goes on to offer an admiring tribute to the 'seamanlike resolution' (83) of the *Loire*'s crew. A corrected typescript and fair copy were sold at the Hodgson sale in 1925, but their present location is unknown.

Lucas, Edward Verrall (1868–1938), essayist, anthologist, and biographer of Charles Lamb. E. V. Lucas was introduced to Conrad by Edward *Garnett in 1895. As a journalist and editor in the 1890s, he played a quietly helpful part in furthering Conrad's early career, working with Garnett to establish publishing contacts for him, reviewing his fiction in positive terms, and promoting his work in general. He acted as advisory reader at *Methuen for many years, helping to secure Conrad as a Methuen author during the period from 1906 to 1915, and became chairman of the company in 1925.

Lwów. In December 1867, some 28 months after the death of his wife, Conrad's father Apollo *Korzeniowski was granted a permit to leave *Poland with his 10-year-old son for Algeria or Madeira. However, Apollo's ill health and a shortage of money led them instead to settle in Lwów, the capital of Austrian *Poland, where from February 1868 they resided for a year, at 11 Szeroka (later Kopernik) Street in the centre of the city. Despite the greater freedom there, Apollo's patriotic expectations were sadly disappointed by the air of 'semi-torpid floundering'. He found the city devoid of any 'great idea', almost totally lacking in 'Polishness', and characterized by a Germanized population who 'snarled' at each other over trivialities: 'Few peoples in Europe can boast of such freedom of expression as they have here today; but what of it if the *word* has long since died in them and only empty phrases remain for barking and growling at each other?' (*CUFE*, 113, 115). For similar reasons, Apollo seems to have distrusted the local schools and so hired a private tutor in an attempt to bring up his son 'not as a democrat, aristocrat, demagogue, republican, monarchist, or as a servant and flunkey of those parties—but only as a Pole' (ibid. 113). Jadwiga Kałuska, whose parents entertained Apollo and his son around this time, recalled the 'wreck of a human being accompanied by the motherless boy . . . [whose] every action

was coloured with love for his unhappy motherland'. Already producing his own literary pieces, Conrad diverted Jadwiga and her brother with a number of short plays he had written, the main theme of which involved 'battles with the Muscovites', one of them called 'The Eyes of King Jan Sobieski' (ibid. 138, 139). By the end of their stay in Lwów, Conrad's father, increasingly ill and suffering from the acute inner pain of a defeated idealist, appears to have been resigned to dying.

Four years after Apollo's death in *Cracow on 23 May 1869, Conrad returned to Lwów, where his guardian had arranged for him to live and be educated. For a period of ten months in 1873–4, he lodged with his father's cousin Antoni Syroczyński, who ran a boarding house for boys orphaned by the 1863 insurrection. As remembered by friends and relatives, the 16-year-old Conrad, prone to headaches and nervous attacks, was precociously bright and independent: 'Intellectually he was extremely advanced but he disliked school routine, which he found tiring and dull; he used to say that he was very talented and planned to become a great writer. Such declarations, coupled with a sarcastic expression . . . used to shock his teachers and provoke laughter among his class-mates'; he also 'read a lot, mostly about travel . . . used to attend lectures given by university professors at the Town Hall', and enjoyed *reading *Wędrowiec,* a popular *Warsaw weekly magazine (ibid. 136, 140). In the autumn of 1874, he left Lwów to return to Cracow.

M

McClure, Samuel Sidney (1857–1949), one of Conrad's early American *publishers. Samuel McClure had founded a newspaper syndicate and *McClure's Magazine* before establishing his first publishing company in 1897. With various partners, including F. N. *Doubleday, he published several of Conrad's works in *America during the period 1900–4, including the *Youth* volume and *Lord Jim* as well as the fruits of his *collaboration with Ford Madox *Ford, *The Inheritors* and *Romance*. Robert McClure, the London agent for his brother, had many dealings with Conrad during the early part of his career when he was struggling unavailingly to finish *The Rescue*, the American book rights of which had been acquired by the McClure firm.

MacWhirr, Captain, master of the *Nan-Shan* in 'Typhoon'. He takes his name from Captain John McWhir, a 34-year-old Irishman under whom Conrad had served in the *Highland Forest* in 1887 and who is remembered in *The Mirror of the Sea* (5–6). According to Conrad's 'Author's Note', specific debts are, however, less important than the fact that the fictional MacWhirr was 'the product of twenty years' of his sea life: 'Conscious invention had little to do with him' (*Typhoon*, p. vi).

One of Conrad's most unusual characters by virtue of his unthinking and prosaic ordinariness, MacWhirr is an interesting antithesis to the waywardly imaginative Lord *Jim in the novel preceding 'Typhoon'. Although by comparison MacWhirr may seem excessively 'simple', he nevertheless figures in a novella of considerable technical complexity, since in Conrad's perilous world a short-sighted trust in the straightforwardness of 'facts' can be as potentially hazardous as its opposite, embodied in this story in the youthful first mate Jukes. Bringing over from *Lord Jim* the technique of multiple choric figures

and following MacWhirr's progress from shore to sea, Conrad's tale yields a sense of paradox and multiple truth: the quality of literal-minded pragmatism that leads MacWhirr to endanger his ship by insisting that she meet the typhoon head-on is the very same quality that ensures her survival during the storm and guarantees that justice for the coolie passengers is done at the close. In 'MacWhirr and the Testimony of the Human Voice', *Conradiana*, 7 (1975), 45–50, Christof Wegelin broaches these paradoxes in developing a view of the captain as a type of 'absurd fool', whose heroism is born of the occasion but also limited by it, and who is at once foolish and admirable in the face of an indifferent natural world.

manuscripts and archival collections. All but a few of Conrad's surviving manuscripts, typescripts, and other documents are accessible to scholars in library or archival collections in the United States or the United Kingdom. Some items are in the possession of an increasingly small number of private collectors, and some *letters continue to be held as keepsakes in the possession of the families of their addressees. A number of literary works have been lost or destroyed, like the manuscript of 'Karain', which was on board the *Titanic*. (Conrad sent John *Quinn the manuscript of 'The Informer' to make good the loss.) Other documents have gone missing, like the manuscript of *The Sisters*, which disappeared in New York after it was used in the preparation of the 1928 Crosby Gaige edition (see Tom Schultheiss, 'The Search for "The Sisters": A Chronology of Ownership', *Conradiana*, 3: 1 (1970–1), 26, 50, 68, 90, 92). Nevertheless, pre-publication materials exist in some form for nearly all of Conrad's works.

Although outdated, Gordon Lindstrand's bibliographical survey of Conrad's literary manuscripts published in three issues of the second volume of *Conradiana* in 1969–70 (2: 1, 23–32; 2: 2, 105–14; and 2: 3, 155–62) remains the only complete printed location register of Conrad manuscripts and typescripts, amplified and rectified in more recent bibliographical articles by Donald W. Rude and others. There is no published calendar of Conrad's letters, but roughly half of them (2,665 letters, up to 1916) have been published since 1983 in the first five volumes of *The Collected Letters of Joseph Conrad*. A selection from the other side of the correspondence is available in *A Portrait in Letters: Correspondence to and about Conrad*, ed. J. H. Stape and Owen Knowles (Amsterdam: Rodopi, 1996), which contains a calendar and location register of some 700 extant letters addressed to Conrad. The location and identification of Conrad items has been greatly stimulated by two major publishing projects currently under way at Cambridge University Press: a critical edition of Conrad's complete works in 30 volumes, and the above-mentioned complete edition of Conrad's letters in at least eight volumes.

The survival of so many of Conrad's working papers is due in the first instance to the sentimental vigilance of his wife Jessie, who kept his papers in the deep drawers of an old yellow press and thus preserved them from the fires that consumed most of Conrad's incoming correspondence. Tokens of Conrad's presence began to acquire a market value well before *Chance* made him a public celebrity, and autograph hunters began to approach him for his 'precious signature' as early as 1904 (*CL*, iii. 190).

In 1911, at the suggestion of Agnes *Tobin, the New York lawyer and art collector John Quinn entered into a gentleman's agreement with Conrad to purchase his original 'first draft' manuscripts, beginning with *An Outcast of the Islands* and 'Freya of the Seven Isles' (*CL*, iv. 475). By the following summer, Conrad had sold all of his complete manuscripts to Quinn and began to offer him less orderly materials, such as the heavily revised manuscript of *Under Western Eyes*. Quinn eventually

came to own virtually all of the surviving pre-publication documents from Conrad's early and middle career. Money was no object; Quinn was willing to pay whatever Conrad might ask, but Conrad found it socially difficult to demand higher prices as his popularity increased.

In 1919 Conrad's American publisher F. N. *Doubleday asked Quinn to donate a hundred or more manuscript pages to be laid into specially printed copies of the 'Sun-Dial' (limited) Edition, but Quinn wisely kept his collection intact. The correspondence between Conrad and Quinn became sparse after the summer of 1920, and despite Quinn's repeated efforts to arrange a meeting, Conrad was unable to see him during his American tour in May 1923. In November, forced to vacate his New York apartment and short of funds to support his growing interest in French art, Quinn put his Conrad collection up for sale along with some 12,000 other items. The Conrad manuscripts were the most successful items in the sale, earning Quinn a return of eleven to one on his investment and evoking some wry and bitter comments from Conrad. Dr A. S. W. Rosenbach of Philadelphia spent some $72,000 at the sale; he purchased the manuscript of *Victory* for $8,600, at that time the highest price ever paid for the manuscript of a living author. A typescript of *Almayer's Folly* that Quinn had bought for £5 (about $25) in 1912 fetched $650 at the Quinn sale; in 1970, together with a typescript of *Chance*, it was priced at $25,000. By the end of the 20th century, Conrad manuscripts were valued at roughly $1,000 dollars per page (see AUCTIONS AND SALES).

In spite of his understanding with Quinn, by October 1918 Conrad had begun selling currently available items to Thomas J. *Wise for ready cash, including the manuscript of *The Rescuer* (abandoned in 1898) and a typescript of *The Arrow of Gold*. Conrad later told Ford Madox *Ford that he was worried about exposing his papers to the risk of German submarines during the *First World War (1933: 310). Perhaps Conrad could also believe that his new practice of *dictation altered the nature of his productions and thus released him from his arrangement with Quinn. In any event, Wise's purchases could be made quickly and discreetly, without the bother of transatlantic correspondence or currency and insurance transactions. Their dates and amounts were recorded with other contractual matters in a notebook kept by Conrad's secretary Lilian M. *Hallowes (*The Conradian*, 25: 2 (2000), 205–44; Bodleian Library, shelfmark MS.Eng.Misc. e.578 or microfilm WM 7693). Wise gained an extra advantage by offering to purchase Conrad's productions in advance, speculating in creations that did not yet exist or were as yet unfinished. Wise could consider himself something of an expert in non-existent editions, since by this point in his career he had already corrupted the bibliographical record with about 100 literary forgeries. He was Conrad's first bibliographer, and reprinted limited editions of a number of Conrad's shorter works in *pamphlet form, but Wise has never been charged with any Conrad forgeries. By the time he met Conrad, he could easily afford to play by the rules. His forgeries were not exposed until 1934, ten years after Conrad's death, and when Wise died three years later, his widow sold what remained of his 'Ashley Library' to the British Library. Wise had his manuscripts sturdily bound in lavish red or blue morocco bindings, making it difficult for modern scholars to decipher marginal comments that disappear into the binding. The hand-lettered title-pages of these sumptuous volumes resemble certificates of authenticity, although the dates and descriptions are often wrong, as, sometimes, are Conrad's own notes written for Wise on the occasion of a sale. Thanks partly to the monopolies of Quinn and Wise, collectors became so eager to obtain Conrad's 'latest' that trial copies sometimes surfaced as spurious first editions and required a good deal of explaining.

Most of Conrad's library and the literary papers left at his death were auctioned by his widow through the well-known firm of Hodgson & Co. (London) on 13 March 1925: two manuscripts, about 50 typescripts, and some ten sets of proof sheets went on the block. In October 1924, Conrad's friends and literary executors met in London to co-ordinate their various efforts to publish the last of Conrad's work and editions of his letters. Many of their own papers later found their way into various public collections, especially in the United States: G. *Jean-Aubry's papers are now at the Beinecke Rare Book and Manuscript Library, Yale University; Richard *Curle's at the Lilly Library, Indiana University; and more than one thousand of Conrad's letters to J. B. *Pinker and his sons are in the Berg Collection, New York Public Library. Materials relating to Conrad can also be found in the Ford Madox Ford archives at Cornell and Princeton Universities. After Conrad's death, his literary estate was placed in the care of his executors, Richard Curle and Ralph *Wedgwood, where it remained until 1946, when trusteeship of the estate passed to Conrad's son John. The Curle papers at the Lilly Library contain information on the early years of the estate. For the period from 1946 until 1974, the year when works published during Conrad's lifetime entered the public domain, scholars can consult John Conrad's papers at the Canterbury Heritage Museum in *Kent, which also holds a number of books owned by Conrad and other *memorabilia.

The largest single collection of Conrad materials is the *Keating Collection held at the Beinecke Rare Book and Manuscript Library, Yale University, whose many items include manuscripts of 'Heart of Darkness' and *Under Western Eyes* and more than 100 letters in French from Conrad to Marguerite *Poradowska. Other major archival collections in the United States include those of the Rosenbach Museum and Library in Philadelphia (with the manuscripts of Conrad's first two novels, *Lord Jim*, *Nostromo*, and *The Secret Agent*); the Berg Collection, New York Public Library (a manuscript of *Chance* and a complete typescript of *Suspense*); the Case Library, Colgate University (Conrad's correspondence with Basil Macdonald *Hastings and other items purchased by Henry Colgate at the Quinn sale); the Widener Library at

Harvard University (the sketch 'Tuan Jim' and Conrad's Congo diaries); the Harry Ransom Humanities Research Center at the University of Texas at Austin (the manuscript of *Victory*); and the Lilly Library, Indiana University (pamphlet proofs and a comprehensive collection of printed editions). The library of Texas Tech University houses a few manuscripts and an important collection of Conrad editions. The Conrad Study Center associated with the Institute for Bibliography and Editing at Kent State University, Ohio, supports the Cambridge Edition of the Works of Joseph Conrad with a large collection of materials in photocopied and digital form in addition to printed editions, and an attractive website at <http://www.library.kent.edu/speccoll/center.html>.

The only major archival collection of Conrad manuscripts outside the USA is that of the British Library in London, which holds most of the Conrad items from Wise's Ashley Library, including the manuscript of *The Rescuer*, typescripts of the stage versions of *Laughing Anne* and *The Secret Agent*, and the original typescripts of *The Rover* and *Suspense*. There are two Conrad *study centres in Europe. The Polish Social and Cultural Association (POSK) in Hammersmith, London, houses both a Conrad library and a Polish library, and holds a number of Conrad's letters to John *Galsworthy. The Centro di Studi Conradiani at the University of Pisa, Italy, houses a collection of Conrad editions, translations, and secondary materials first assembled by Ugo Mursia.

Conrad has been posthumously fortunate in his librarians. John Dozier Gordan, the author of *Joseph Conrad: The Making of a Novelist* (1940), was from 1951 to 1968 curator of the Berg Collection, to which he added many Conrad items. William R. Cagle, former curator of the Lilly Library, has prepared the most extensive bibliography of Conrad first editions available to date, although it remains unfinished and unpublished (photocopies of Cagle's draft typescript, which stops in 1923 with *Laughing Anne*, are available at cost from the Lilly Library). In addition to Conrad *bibliographies, useful archival information can often be found in exhibition and sales catalogues. In particular, the two-volume catalogue of the Raymond M. Sutton Jr Collection (David J. Holmes Autographs, nos. 9 and 10, 1985) contains much information not available elsewhere. The catalogue of the Robert C. Findlay Collection of Joseph Conrad (Randall House Catalogue 27, Santa Barbara, California, 1993) is richly illustrated with reproductions of the dust-jackets of many Conrad first editions.

Marlow. The best known of Conrad's storytellers, Marlow narrates four of Conrad's works: 'Youth', 'Heart of Darkness', *Lord Jim*, and *Chance*. His given name, 'Charlie', is mentioned only in 'Heart of Darkness' (53, 59). He has often been seen as Conrad's autobiographical alter ego, since his narratives are based on Conrad's own experiences in the ill-fated *Palestine* ('Youth') or in the *Congo ('Heart of Darkness'). At the same time, Conrad and Marlow differ fundamentally in their ethnic background (Marlow is an Englishman, without Slavic origins) and their marital status (Marlow never marries, and becomes increasingly misogynist). In the 'Author's Note' written in 1917 for the collected edition of *Youth*, Conrad took the occasion to respond to speculations about Marlow's function as 'a clever screen, a mere device, a "personator," a familiar spirit, a whispering "dæmon"' (p. v). He explained: 'The man Marlow and I came together in the casual manner of those health-resort acquaintances which sometimes ripen into friendships. This one has ripened. For all his assertiveness in matters of opinion he is not an intrusive person. He haunts my hours of solitude, when, in silence, we lay our heads together in great comfort and harmony; but as we part at the end of a tale I am never sure that it may not be for the last time' (p. vi).

Marlow's voice is always mediated by a frame-narrator who remains anonymous, as the unidentified fifth member of the party aboard the *Nellie*, or one of the after-dinner listeners in *Lord Jim*, or as Marlow's nameless friend in *Chance*. In other words,

Marlow is exclusively an oral narrator, and his statements are converted into readable form by a member of his audience. The orality of Marlow's text is at times problematic: when citing the testimony of the French lieutenant in Lord Jim, does he interrupt himself to speak aloud the parenthetical French passages given in the text? Does he 'do' German or other accents, as suggested by the spellings in the text (for example, Lord Jim, 41–2, 199)? In Chance, is Marlow consciously aware of his own punning references to the name of Fyne? And, as reviewers of Lord Jim were quick to notice, how can he possibly speak for so long without a break? In his 1917 'Author's Note' to Lord Jim, Conrad answered this last charge with the implausible (and testable) assertion that 'all that part of the book which is Marlow's narrative [31 of its 45 chapters] can be read through aloud, I should say, in less than three hours' (p. vii).

The four Marlow narratives in Conrad's canon were written in approximate chronological order as events in Marlow's (and Conrad's) life, although Marlow is still in the East when he narrates the story of *Jim, so that it may actually be the first of his tales to be told. Moreover, unlike the other tales which are told on specific occasions, Marlow tells the story of Jim 'many times, in distant parts of the world' (33), and his faithful listener has prepared what amounts to a composite version for the novel, in a narrative mode that Gérard Genette, speaking of Marcel Proust, has described as 'pseudo-iterative', where statements presented as typical or recurring are nevertheless rendered in such detail as to preclude the realistic possibility of exact repetition. As against the relatively simple narrative situations of 'Youth' (in a *Thamesside tavern) or 'Heart of Darkness' (aboard the anchored Nellie), the longer novels develop a range of narrative modes and weave together materials from a longer span of time. Thus, in Lord Jim, Marlow hears Captain Jones's account of Brierly's death 'more than two years' (64) after Brierly's suicide, and Marlow meets the French lieutenant 'more than three years' (149) after the Patna inquiry. Mar-

low's oral narrative ends before the arrival of Gentleman *Brown in *Patusan, and the denouement of Jim's story is provided in the form of various documents which Marlow forwards 'more than two years later' (337) to a 'privileged reader' (351) in an unnamed *London, evidently an earlier listener—or the earlier listener—who has taken an interest in Jim's case.

If the identity of Marlow warrants the assumption that his faithful scribe or 'narratee' is the same from story to story, it may thus be a minor anachronism that in 'Youth' the listening frame-narrator is uncertain about the proper spelling of Marlow's name (and many a critic has shared this uncertainty, confusing Conrad's Marlow with Christopher Marlowe or with Raymond Chandler's Philip Marlowe). Marlow is 42 years old when he narrates 'Youth', in which he recalls how, at the age of 20, in hopes of seeing the 'real' East beyond the colonial ports of *Australia, he gave up a berth as third officer in a 'crack Australian clipper' and signed on the barque *Judea* as second mate for a voyage to *Bangkok with a cargo of 600 tons of combustible English coal (4). When the ship sinks off the coast of Sumatra, Marlow is given his 'first command' in the form of one of the ship's three small boats, in which he youthfully wants to make land all by himself ahead of the others. After many days of rowing and steering, Marlow finally sees the East, and with this vision in the final pages of 'Youth' he bids farewell forever to the confidence and endurance that were once his birthright as a young man thirsty for adventure. Conrad was 40 when he wrote the story, but he was five years older than Marlow when the Palestine sank under similar circumstances in March 1883.

'Heart of Darkness' is narrated by an older and wearier Marlow who is haunted by the horrors he has witnessed in the Congo, and who realizes that the 'dark places of the earth' (48) include central London as well as central Africa. He has also become less patient with his interlocutors, and his narration is not only the story of his African adventure as a 'fresh-water sailor' but also a bitter confession to having fallen under the spell of *Kurtz and having lied to escape from it. Marlow says that this African episode came at a time when he had satisfied his curiosity about the East, having 'just returned to London after a lot of Indian Ocean, Pacific, China Seas—a regular dose of the East—six years or so' (51). He and his companions in the *Nellie* are united by what the frame-narrator calls 'the bond of the sea' (45), but unlike the director of companies, the lawyer, and the accountant, who have gone on to other careers, Marlow is the only one of the five who still 'followed the sea' (48). Nevertheless, his ordeal in the Congo, which he describes as 'the farthest point of navigation and the culminating point of my experience' (51), has left him with 'sunken cheeks, a yellow complexion, a straight back, an ascetic aspect' (46), and a Kurtz-like resemblance to a Buddha or an idol. Marlow's role in 'Heart of Darkness' has generated a large amount of criticism in the wake of Guerard's assertion that 'the story is not primarily about Kurtz or about the brutality of Belgian officials but about Marlow its narrator' (37).

The frame-narrator of 'Heart of Darkness' says that unlike the sedentary life of most sailors, Marlow was a 'wanderer' (48); but by the time of *Chance*, Marlow has not only left deep-water sailing but has become remarkably sedentary and averse even to walking for exercise in the country, where he regularly rents a cottage to spend his holidays. The precise nature of Marlow's post-maritime career is never explained, but he is sometimes suddenly 'called to town on business' and 'detained in town from week to week' (46), and he tells *Fyne that he 'had business at the Docks' (191). More surprisingly, in *Chance* Marlow daydreams vaguely about marriage (136, 150), and joins in a lengthy verbal duel with Mrs Fyne, who credits him with 'sagacity' while he continually mocks her feminist convictions. For no apparent reason, Marlow seems to take as deep an interest in Flora *de Barral as he once took in Jim, and his curiosity is hard to square with the irritation provoked in him by women. As he puts it: 'For myself it's towards women that I feel vindictive mostly, in my small way' (150). Marlow's misogynist comments, far more frequent in *Chance* than in 'Heart of Darkness', have given rise to a number of *feminist studies of this novel which first brought Conrad success with American readers but which critics have generally not considered one of his best works. See also FRAME-NARRATIVE.

The literature on Marlow is vast, including studies of the various works in which he appears. A general overview is provided by Alan Warren Friedman in 'Conrad's Picaresque Narrator: Marlow's Journey from "Youth" through *Chance*', in Zyla and Aycock (eds.) 17–39, and by Pierre Vitoux in 'Marlow: The Changing Narrator of Conrad's Fiction', *Cahiers Victoriens et Édouardiens*, 2 (1975), 83–102. See also the anthology *Marlow*, ed. Harold Bloom, in the Major Literary Characters series (Broomall, Pa.: Chelsea House, 1992).

Marris, Carlos Murrell (1875–1910). Born in New Zealand. Carlos Marris was for several years a master mariner in the Far East. He converted to Islam in order to marry a Malay princess with whom he lived in Penang. While on a visit to England for medical treatment, the retired captain wrote to Conrad on 18 July 1909. His letter brought the writer up to date with more recent history in the Malay Archipelago, assured him of the popularity of his Malay stories in the East, pressed him to write more of their kind, and wondered if they might meet. This correspondence, along with the meeting that followed in early September, reactivated Conrad's memories of the Far East and prompted him to return to Eastern material in *'Twixt Land and Sea*, in which one story, 'Freya of the Seven Isles', grew out of an anecdote told to him by Marris. Conrad later dedicated *'Twixt Land and Sea* to Captain Marris 'in memory of those old days of adventure'. For Marris's letters to Conrad, see *PL*, 66–70, 71–2.

Marryat, Frederick (1792–1848), British naval captain and author, a major role model and literary influence on Conrad. Like Conrad, Frederick Marryat went off to sea as a youth and worked his way up to a captaincy before retiring to take up his pen. Conrad paid tribute to Marryat and to James Fenimore *Cooper in an essay of 1898, 'Tales of the Sea' (*Notes*). He praised the 'natural glamour' of Marryat's temperament, and described his work in terms that could also be applied to Conrad: 'His novels are not the outcome of his art, but of his character' (53). According to Ford Madox *Ford, Marryat's novels were the source of 'the strongest influence on the life of Conrad—on his literary life, on his travels, and on the manner in which he took up his difficult and glorious literary career' (*JCPR*, 252).

The second son of an MP for Sandwich and a German-American mother, Marryat was such a difficult student that his father arranged for him to enter naval service at the age of 16 on board the frigate *Impérieuse*, under Lord Cochrane, in 1806. Admiral Nelson's recent victory over a combined French and Spanish fleet at Trafalgar had established the supremacy of the English navy over *Napoleon's forces in the Mediterranean and largely confined the French fleet to their ports, and so Marryat's frigate was employed in enforcing the blockade, controlling privateers, and occasionally raiding ships in enemy ports. He took part in a number of such encounters, and was promoted to commander in 1815 at the age of 23. He married in 1819, was on patrol in the South Atlantic off St Helena when Napoleon died in 1821, and later served in the East Indies. Following the success of his autobiographical first novel, *The Naval Officer; or, Scenes and Adventures in the Life of Frank Mildmay* (1829), he resigned his commission to devote himself to literature. His Napoleonic novels of idealistic young men in the British navy include *Peter Simple* (1834), *Jacob Faithful* (1834), and *Mr Midshipman Easy* (1836). For several years Marryat served as editor of the *Metropolitan Magazine*, in which many of his works first appeared. In 1837 he travelled to the United States and Canada, where he remained for two years and volunteered for service with British forces engaged in putting down a rebellion of the French population in Quebec. With *Masterman Ready; or, The Wreck of the 'Pacific'* (1841), Marryat turned his attention to children's books, and is now most often remembered as the author of *Children of the New Forest* (1847). His last years were spent on his estate in Langham, Norfolk.

We do not know in what language Conrad first encountered the works of Captain Marryat, but the freshness and energy of Marryat's style and the romance of the naval service described in his works already appealed to Conrad as a child, and may well have been among the factors prompting his own desire to go to *sea. Many of Conrad's own early and late works, from the first version of *The Rescue* and *Romance* to the *Napoleonic fictions with which he ended his career, follow directly in the tradition established by Marryat. Although these works, like those of Marryat, are often dismissed by academics as less than serious literature, the popularity of C. S. Forester's 'Horatio Hornblower' series and the Napoleonic fictions of Patrick O'Brian suggests that the adventurous world of naval warfare continues to delight English-speaking readers to this day.

Marseilles. Conrad resided in this ancient port city on the Mediterranean Sea from October 1874 until April 1878. The arrival of the 16-year-old Korzeniowski at Marseilles railway station after a long journey via Vienna, Zurich, and Lyons was itself a symbolic moment in signalling his victory over family opposition to his determination to go to *sea. The staging ground for the sowing of wild oats and of his first professional endeavours, the city left a mark on both him and his fiction: the setting of *The Arrow of Gold*, it influences the atmosphere of *Nostromo* and *The Rover*. By his own retrospective and at times highly coloured account in *A Personal Record*, Conrad appears to have immediately embraced the town's pleasures, from its rich food, to its café life, *theatre, and *opera. Having made what he called a 'standing jump out of his racial surroundings and associations' (121), Conrad, whatever the steadier perspective of adulthood, felt released from the constraints imposed by well-meaning guardians and experienced an excited awareness of new possibilities.

The contrasts between this vibrant Mediterranean port and his previous experience were themselves vivid: the busy quays of the Vieux-Port literally incarnated the long-caressed dream of going to sea; the city's warmer climate and cosmopolitan sophistication must have come as a relief from a *Poland blighted by decades of political and cultural domination; the city was larger than any he had previously lived in; and there were the usual first deep, almost greedy, gulps of fresh air on embarking upon an independent adult life. Even the shift of language offered freedom from a troubled individual and communal past and an escape into a new identity. (Conrad's spoken French was henceforth to be marked by southern inflections acquired during his time in Marseilles.) The transformation from provincial to would-be *boulevardier* almost cries out for the myth-making it received in due course in *The Mirror of the Sea* and *A Personal Record*; the experience was also to prove predictably overwhelming as initial elation shaded first into casual self-indulgence and then into outright excess.

Conrad's separation from his Polish past, like many such breaks, was neither instantaneous nor complete, arrangements having been made by his guardian Tadeusz *Bobrowski to provide an unofficial mentor in Wiktor Chodźko, a seaman of Polish extraction living outside Toulon. In the event, Chodźko played two roles: maintaining links with the language and culture Conrad had left behind him, and serving as a bridge to the beckoning future, more tangibly shaped by Chodźko's friend Baptistin Solary, a former sailor engaged in the shipping business, who provided contact with the port's pilot association and the firm *Delestang et Fils, Conrad's first employer.

Marseilles was witness to and, in some sense, occasion for the major events of Conrad's late adolescence: his initiation into a trade, first on the Mediterranean coast and then in voyages to the French

*Caribbean; a period of youthful hero-worship of the Corsican sailor Dominique *Cervoni; the initial stirrings of romantic involvement; and, possibly, a spate of smuggling and gun-running. Freedom from old inhibitions and the plunge into new circles proved a heady mixture, culminating in overspending, eventual indebtedness, and, in early 1878, a half-hearted attempt at *suicide, followed by his concerned uncle's arrival and Conrad's departure not long after for a career in English *ships. All these events leave their traces in his fiction, and, with the exception of the attempted suicide (later disguised as a duel), form set-pieces in his autobiographical writings. In these, facts freely mingle with exaggeration and outright invention, with, from one perspective, a certain ironic appropriateness, since Marseilles itself was the first stage on which Conrad was quite literally invited to reinvent himself.

However much larger than life in Conrad's recounting, his period in Marseilles was obviously a formative one. Not only did he gain professional experience with seasoned veterans of the Mediterranean coast, but his very failures made him more mature and gave him a greatly needed perspective on his financial and personal situations. The ready assimilation of new experience was also later to stand him in good stead, and he may have been more cautious about forming associations. How much the young Pole with money in his pocket might have been an easy mark for his more savvy French companions is a moot question; but from the knowing Mme Delestang, with whom he appears to have mildly flirted (although she was in her seventies), to the overly enthusiastic Baptistin who greeted him on his arrival, there are reasons to suspect that his *naïveté* did not go unnoticed.

Corroborating evidence for some of Conrad's claims about his Marseilles experience is wanting, but Hans van Marle's meticulous archival research sifts fact from fabrication in 'Young Ulysses Ashore: On the Trail of Konrad Korzeniowski in Marseilles', *L'Époque Conradienne*, 2 (1976), 22–34, and 'An Ambassador of Conrad's

Future: The *James Mason* in Marseilles, 1874', *L'Époque Conradienne*, 14 (1988), 63–7.   JHS

Marwood, Arthur Pierson (1868–1916), a close friend of Conrad's from 1906 until his premature death. The younger son of a Yorkshire baronet, Arthur Marwood had emerged from Clifton and Trinity College, Cambridge, as a talented mathematician, although he was prevented from completing his degree by ill health. An invalid with tuberculosis of the bladder, he was never able to pursue a career and lived the quiet life of a gentleman-farmer in *Kent. Through Ford Madox *Ford, who revered Marwood as a living embodiment of the enlightened Tory gentry, he met Conrad in 1906. According to Ford, the burly and large-framed Marwood used to say of himself when set beside Conrad's small, nervous figure: 'We're the two ends of human creation: he's like a quivering ant and I'm an elephant built out of meal-sacks!' Extremes like these counted for little when measured against Conrad's and Ford's admiration for the subtle intelligence and encyclopedic mind that made Marwood 'a man of infinite benevolence, comprehensions and knowledges' (1933: 208).

In 1908, Marwood put up £2,000 to help start Ford's *English Review* and became his brother-in-arms in the new literary venture, helping to administer the journal and contributing to it 'An Actuarial Scheme for Insuring John Doe against All the Vicissitudes of Life'. A crisis in relationships occurred in April 1909 when the ugly complications of Ford's marital problems entangled Marwood in a way that led him to break off all relations with Ford and also contributed to the decisive breach between Conrad and Ford that soon followed. Upon hearing of Ford's affair with Violet Hunt, his outraged wife Elsie, probably in an effort to provoke a counter-jealousy in Ford, claimed that Marwood had made sexual advances to her. Deeply troubled by Elsie's efforts to involve the Conrads in the maelstrom of domestic crisis and distressed on Marwood's behalf, Conrad

wrote to Ford protesting against the 'atmosphere of plots and accusations and suspicions' being created and warning him that if he did not mend his ways, he would find himself 'at forty with only the wrecks of friendships at your feet' (*CL*, iv. 222, 223).

On the demise of his friendship with Ford, Conrad's relations with Marwood, then his near-neighbour, became even closer. From 1909 until Marwood's death in 1916, he was one of the novelist's most regular visitors, the 'real Wise Man of the Age' (*CL*, v. 464) with whom Conrad could regularly discuss his work and sound out his ideas: he was, said Conrad, 'a great reader with a profound knowledge of literature, in whose judgement I have an absolute confidence; a man whose critical instinct is of marvellous justness' (*CL*, v. 278). The paucity of documentary evidence prevents a detailed assessment of the character of this important friendship or the extent of Marwood's influence on Conrad's literary life, but there is no reason to doubt Jessie Conrad's view that 'my husband would always accept his criticism, if not exactly without argument, at least with a reasoned and considered one. I can trace Arthur Marwood's influence in most of the books written during the period of his close friendship' (*JCHC*, 117). Marwood also provided a partial model for Christopher Tietjens in Ford's *Parade's End* tetralogy (1924–8).

Marxist approaches. The school of thought known as 'Marxism' was founded by the German political philosopher Karl Marx (1818–83) and the German sociologist Friedrich Engels (1820–95). A materialist (as opposed to an idealist) philosophy, the aim of Marxism is to bring about a classless society, based on the common ownership of the means of production, distribution, and exchange. The basic model of society from a Marxist viewpoint consists of an economic 'base' (the means of production, distribution, and exchange) and a 'superstructure' (the 'cultural' world of ideas, art, religion, and law) determined by this base. Man's life is thus determined by his relations to the means of economic production, and literature is similarly conditioned by the economic, social, and political circumstances in which it is produced. Marxists view history as a class struggle, inspired by competition for economic, social, and political advantage. Typically, Marxist literary critics distinguish between the overt and implicit content of a text and try to relate the implicit content to basic Marxist preoccupations (such as the class struggle). Further, in order to demonstrate how the text is determined by an economic base, they often relate the textual content to the author's social class, to the historical moment at which it was produced, and to the social assumptions of the time in which it was 'consumed' or read. Perhaps the most influential figure in recent Marxist criticism has been the French theoretician Louis Althusser (1918–90), who claimed that, despite the relationship between economics and culture, art retains some independence from economic forces. Looking beyond the base/superstructure model, Althusser thus broadened the Marxist view of literature from being a product of the economic base to being more subtly reflective of indirectly operating socio-economic forces which also serve to maintain the status quo. A helpful way of visualizing the Marxist approach is to adapt the title of Fredric Jameson's *The Political Unconscious: Narrative as a Socially Symbolic Act* (Methuen, 1981): beneath the overt meaning of a text lies a repressed political ideology on which it depends, its unconscious, susceptible or open to analysis. Jameson's influential Marxist interpretation of *Lord Jim* and *Nostromo* (206–80) has inspired others, among them Terry Collits in 'Imperialism, Marxism, Conrad: A Political Reading of *Victory*', *Textual Practice*, 3 (1989), 303–22.

With their emphasis upon individuals caught up in the larger forces of imperial history and economics, by which their lives are determined and over which they have no control, Conrad's fictions have attracted a good deal of Marxist criticism. For instance, from the outset, in *Almayer's Folly* and *An Outcast of the Islands*, he

demonstrated with characteristic scepticism the substratum of economic and political self-interest beneath idealistic or pious rhetoric. Through his friendship with R. B. Cunninghame *Graham—described by Engels as 'Communist, Marxian, advocating the nationalisation of all means of production' (quoted in Watts and Davies, 89)—one senses a new maturity in Conrad's political thinking. By the time Conrad wrote *Nostromo*, with its emphasis upon 'material interests', he was closely involved with themes and ideas pertinent to a Marxist view of the world. *Sulaco's history is economically determined. However much characters claim to be influencing events, they are demonstrably at the mercy of both the means of production and international economic forces. And, finally, the political process is shown to be sustained by, and biased towards, the wealthy. As Charles *Gould says: 'Only let the material interests once get a firm footing, and they are bound to impose the conditions on which alone they can continue to exist' (84). The novel's presentation of the progress of Sulacan society through various stages, from feudalism to capitalism, similarly endorses the Marxist notion of history. In particular, the suggestion at the end of the novel of discontent in the workforce looks forward to the historical phase where the internal contradictions of capitalism will lead to its overthrow. That Conrad is not totally persuaded by the Marxist view, however, is evident from his unsympathetic presentation of the Marxist agitator at the bedside of the dying *Nostromo. Asking whether Nostromo has any 'dispositions' to make as the 'rich must be fought with their own weapons' (562), he resembles nobody so much as *Donkin waiting at the deathbed of James *Wait, in *The Nigger of the 'Narcissus'*, for his chance to steal Wait's money. According to one Marxist reading, Conrad's critique of capitalism in *Nostromo* is, however, counterbalanced by its implication in the very values it criticizes: the novel 'acknowledges a possibly debilitating paradox at the heart of its own project in that it attempts to analyse the historical development of capitalism and its correlative colonialism while being itself a strand within the discourse of capitalism/colonialism and hence disposed to endorse its values' (Jim Reilly, *Shadowtime: History and Representation in Hardy, Conrad and George Eliot* (Routledge, 1993), 143). In this sense, Marxism comes to resemble *deconstructive approaches in its attempts to show that, despite appearances, texts are threatened or disrupted by latent inconsistencies and contradictions.

In 'Marxism and Ideology: Joseph Conrad, *Heart of Darkness*' (in Douglas Tallack (ed.), *Literary Theory at Work: Three Texts* (Batsford, 1987), 181–200), Steve Smith adopts an Althusserian approach and starts by noting a contradiction: the colonial exploitation *Marlow encounters in the *Congo is only such within the context of humanism, but humanism is the very ideology used to justify the colonial venture. (Marlow's frequent, if ironic, references to the colonizers as 'philanthropists' reveal his awareness of this frame of reference.) Marlow's understanding of the workings of the colonial economy—'a stream of manufactured goods, rubbishy cottons, beads, and brass-wire set into the depths of darkness, and in return came a precious trickle of ivory' (68)—prompts Smith to claim that the narrator's discourse 'foregrounds that revealing incongruity between the rhetoric and the reality of colonialism' (187). Smith next examines the character of Marlow himself, particularly his own economic plight and the historical forces to which he is subject. Marlow's sense of disorientation in the Congo is held to mirror his status as a displaced ocean-going seafarer. He thus straddles two worlds: he is both the sea captain, aloof from the social world implied by his cargo, and the fresh-water pilot caught up in the hectic colonialist trade. To Smith, 'Marlow can thus be considered in relation to a whole mode of production that predates the frenzied colonialist penetration of the African continent and which is now threatened, or profoundly transformed, by its arrival' (189). Thus 'Heart of Darkness' is concerned with the struggle that ensues when one mode of production and its ideology is overlaid on another,

older one. Smith probes this conflict to argue that it offers a space for a critique of the colonial system and, thus, that the narrative carries an implicit unease with the ideological assumptions of colonialist exploitation. But such unease is manifest in the narrative itself rather than in Marlow, whose destruction of the postscript to *Kurtz's report, in particular, renders him, in Smith's reading, aloof from the unpalatable realities of history and politics.   AHS

Maupassant, Guy de (1850–93), French novelist and author of short stories, one of Conrad's most important literary *influences. Like Conrad, Guy de Maupassant was a sailor, although his voyages were limited to the Mediterranean and the coast of his native Normandy; and like Conrad, Maupassant was a master of the *mot juste* and the use of *frame-narratives.

Maupassant first appears in Conrad's correspondence in a letter addressed to Marguerite *Poradowska in August 1894 from *Champel-les-Bains (near *Geneva), in which Conrad reported that he was reading Maupassant 'with delight' (*CL*, i. 171). Given his location, it is strange that he does not mention (unless he was unaware) that Maupassant had stayed at the very same hydropathic establishment at Champel in the summer of 1891, apparently arriving just after Conrad's departure for *London. Maupassant's health was at that time already in serious decline, and by all accounts, his erratic behaviour at Champel was likely to have been remembered. Maupassant shared with Conrad a deep fondness for Mediterranean sailing, and his adventures along the French Riviera were recorded in *Sur l'eau* (On the Water, 1888).

In the autumn of 1894, Conrad told Poradowska that he was afraid of being too much under the influence of Maupassant (*CL*, i. 185). In 1902 Ford Madox *Ford mentioned to Conrad that his wife Elsie was thinking of translating some of Maupassant's stories, and Conrad responded with advice: 'Let her bear in mind that there are three requisites for a good translation of M. Imprimis she must be idiomatic, secundo she must be idiomatic, and lastly she must be idiomatic. For in the idiom is the *clearness* of a language and the language's force and its picturesqueness—by which last I mean the picture-producing power of arranged words' (*CL*, ii. 435). In the event, Conrad corrected the proofs of *Stories from Maupassant* (Duckworth, 1903) with Elsie's translations and a preface which Ford contributed to the volume (*CL*, iii. 49–50). In recommending the collection to Henry-Durand *Davray for review, Conrad noted that he was 'astonished at the Maupassantesque style one can give to English prose' and added that 'the English of the translation is perfectly idiomatic, entirely pure' (*CL*, iii. 54).

The idea of Maupassant translations by writers' partners apparently proved so appealing that John *Galsworthy's companion Ada soon followed Elsie's lead with eleven more stories, *Yvette and Other Stories* (Duckworth, 1904), this time with a preface by Conrad later reprinted in *Notes on Life and Letters* as 'Guy de Maupassant'. Conrad was aware that these translations would help to bring to the attention of the English reading public the works of an author with a reputation for cynicism, cruelty, and sexual perversion, and so in his preface he is at pains to praise Maupassant for his courage and honesty. Moreover, the translation volumes apparently also served as semiotic emblems of the marital difficulties of their translators: Elsie was listed as 'E.M.' on the title-page of her volume, using the initials of her maiden name, Elsie Martindale, although she was married to Ford. Conversely, the title-page of Ada Galsworthy's translation listed her curiously both as 'A.G.' and as '(Mrs. John Galsworthy)', although at that time she was legally still the wife of Galsworthy's cousin Arthur.

Conrad's fondness for Maupassant, and the strong similarities between their works, have long been obvious in a general way to Conrad's reviewers and critics. Kirschner (1968) was the first scholar to recognize the importance of these influences. Following his pioneering work, Hervouet (1990) examines Conrad's *'borrowings' from Maupassant in detail, juxtaposing passages to show remarkable textual parallels between Conrad's 'The Return' (*Tales of Unrest*) and Maupassant's *Bel-Ami* (1885), between *Nostromo* and 'L'Héritage' (1884), and between *The Secret Agent* and 'Ce Cochon de Morin' (1883), one of several favourite Maupassant tales of which Ford and Conrad are said to have known 'immense passages' by heart (*JCPR*, 36). Additional links between Conrad's 'The Idiots' and Maupassant's 'La Mère aux monstres' are traced by Gene M. Moore in Moore *et al.* (eds.) 1997: 49–58. As Hervouet's magisterial study demonstrates, Maupassant's influence on Conrad was pervasive: he was indeed 'saturated with Maupassant' (*CL*, iii. 54), as he told Davray. Conrad not only Anglicized Maupassant's stories by correcting the proofs of Elsie Hueffer's translations, but he also Anglicized passages and segments of Maupassant into his own writings throughout his career, including virtually an entire paragraph of *Fort comme la mort* (1889) that reappears in English in the manuscript of *Victory* (126). The stylistic accuracy and vividness of Maupassant's prose, together with his penchant for frame-narratives and the poignancy of his anecdotes, appealed greatly to Conrad and left an indelible mark on his work.

Mauritius. In 1888, Conrad, as master of the *Otago*, spent seven weeks (30 September–21 November) on this island in the Indian Ocean. The 30-year-old 'Captain Korzeniowski' who stayed in the island's capital Port Louis was recalled some 40 years later by a local charterer, Paul Langlois, who, after describing his somewhat dandyish external appearance, goes on: 'As to his character: a perfect education; very varied and interesting conversation—on the days when he felt communicative, which wasn't every day. The man who was to become famous under the name Joseph Conrad was quite often taciturn and very excitable. On those days he had a nervous tick in the shoulder and the eyes, and anything the least bit unexpected—an object dropping to the floor, a door banging—would make him jump. Today we would call him a neurasthenic; in those days one said a neurotic' (quoted in *JCC*, 110). Through two Frenchmen, Gabriel and Henri Renouf, Conrad was introduced to the household of Louis Edward Schmidt, one of the colony's senior officials, and seems to have mixed in his family circle, making excursions to the Jardin des Pamplemousses and inviting the family for tea aboard the *Otago*. The household included Schmidt's sister-in-law, the 26-year-old Eugénie Renouf, for whom Conrad developed a romantic attachment and to whom, a couple of days before his departure, he proposed marriage. On learning that she was already engaged, the disappointed suitor left the island, determined never to return. Conrad's 1910 short story 'A Smile of Fortune' ('*Twixt Land and Sea*) depicts the unhappy romantic entanglements of a young sea captain in Mauritius and, in its generally unflattering view of Port Louis society, appears to draw upon the Schmidt household in its description of 'the S— family' as 'one of the old French families, descendants of the old colonists; all noble, all impoverished, and living a narrow domestic life in dull, dignified decay. . . . The girls are almost always pretty, ignorant of the world, kind and agreeable and generally bilingual . . . The emptiness of their existence passes belief' (34–5).

Although Conrad later claimed that the story was not based on personal experience, he seems nevertheless to refract through it much of his own troublesome romantic involvements with Eugénie and possibly another Mauritian girl. In the story, the narrator meets and flirts with Alice Jacobus in the exotic garden of her father, a ship chandler. Later local research has uncovered the possibility that Conrad, like the narrator, also developed a romantic interest in Alice Shaw, a 17-year-old Mauritian girl whose father, a shipping agent, owned the only rose garden on the island. In the light of Conrad's own Mauritian experiences, this bitter short story may, as Najder remarks, represent a form of retrospective 'emotional revenge' (*JCC*, 111) upon a society and its women who, in the words of the story's narrator, had made

him 'the object of unkind and sarcastic comments' and injured his reputation (81); like Conrad, who resigned his command of the *Otago* on his arrival in *Australia, the narrator also decides to leave his ship and return to Europe. Conrad's experiences in Mauritius later provided subject matter for the Polish writer Leszek Prorok in his novel *Smuga Blasku* (The Radiant Line, 1982).

Meldrum, David Storrar (1864–1940), literary editor at Blackwood's London publishing office and himself a writer. David Meldrum urged Conrad's work upon the attention of William *Blackwood and, as both friend and mentor of the author, was sympathetically involved in overseeing the early fruits of his major period (1897–1902), notably the *Youth* volume and *Lord Jim*. One of the select group of early readers to appreciate Conrad's stature as a writer, Meldrum considered the publication of *Youth* to be a momentous event for the Blackwood firm, 'the most notable book we have published since George Eliot', and urged Blackwood to realize that 'in the annals of *Maga* [**Blackwood's Magazine*] half a century hence it will be one of the honourable things to record of her that she entertained "Jim"' (Blackburn (ed.), 172, 86). Throughout this six-year period, the patient and supportive Meldrum continued to mediate between Conrad and Blackwood, and valued the former's opinion of his own literary efforts in *The Conquest of Charlotte* (1902). Although Conrad ceased to be a Blackwood author in 1902, he maintained cordial relations with Meldrum, who went on to become a partner in the firm in 1903 before retiring in 1910.

memorabilia. See MUSEUMS AND MEMORABILIA.

'Memorandum on the Scheme for Fitting Out a Sailing Ship'. In response to an approach in mid-July 1920 from Lawrence Holt, junior partner of the family-managed Ocean Steam Ship Company of Liverpool (*PL*, 159–60), Conrad readily agreed to supply comments of a general nature on the design and running of a five-masted barque that the company was proposing to build for the training of cadets. Attracted equally by the prospect of a fee and by the opportunity to return imaginatively to his own nourishing maritime traditions, he drafted the piece by 24 July. The memorandum was first printed posthumously in *Last Essays*.

Responding to the Company's desire to 'impart to the venture the fullest measure of highest artistry, of the spirit of romance and of high endeavour' (*PL*, 159), Conrad devised a training programme based upon the 'old traditions' he associated with the golden age of the sailing ship between 1850 and 1880 (69): it combines elements of his own experience in the *Torrens* with features of a 19th-century *Conway* training programme (such as *Jim undertakes in Lord Jim). To the charge that such a scheme is hopelessly outdated in an age of steam, Conrad draws an analogy between the 'classical practice of the sea' and the training afforded by a classical education, which, although having little practical application, gives to the public schoolboy 'a more liberal conception of his attitude to life and a strong inner feeling of that continuity of human thought, effort and achievement which is such an inspiring and at the same time such a steadying element in national existence, and in the corporate life of any body of men pursing a special calling' (*LL*, ii. 246). Unfortunately, nothing came of Holt's scheme, which was abandoned during the depression of trade that soon followed his negotiations with Conrad. The first draft, a revised typescript dated July 1920, is held at the British Library; the second revised typescript survives in a private collection.

merchant service. See BRITISH MERCHANT SERVICE.

Mérimée, Prosper (1803–70). Both John *Galsworthy and G. *Jean-Aubry testified to Conrad's admiration for the works of this French novelist and short-story writer, Jean-Aubry reporting (1924: 41) that Bizet's operatic treatment of Mérimée's *Carmen* prompted Conrad in later life to feel that some of his own works (especially *Nostromo*) might be suitable for lyrical adapta-

tion. More direct literary influences from the French writer's life and letters have also been detected in Conrad's work. Knowles (1979) has shown how details of Mérimée's career as given in Anatole *France's portrait in *La Vie littéraire* (2nd series) have an important formative impact upon Conrad's conception and treatment of Martin *Decoud's life and death in *Nostromo*. In France's diagnosis of Mérimée as a deracinated intellectual libertine and *homo duplex* whose entire life was a record of potential selves destructively at odds with each other, Conrad seems to have derived a suggestive blueprint for the type of maladjusted Romantic sensibility that afflicts Decoud, the fashionable Parisian *boulevardier*, devoted lover, unwilling man of action, and sceptic. Indeed, Conrad's celebrated epitaph for Decoud which begins 'What should he regret?' (498) virtually follows verbatim France's description of Mérimée which, in translated form, reads: 'What should he regret? He had never recognized anything but energy as virtue or anything but passions as duties. Was not his sadness rather that of the sceptic for whom the universe is only a succession of incomprehensible images?' Knowles also argues that Conrad's heavy reliance upon this diagnosis of Mérimée's terminal despair may help to explain an element of uncertainty in the treatment of Decoud's collapse and death, which has disturbed a number of critics. In another study of affinities between the two writers, Knowles suggests that Conrad's 'The Planter of Malata' (*Within the Tides*) adapts motifs from one of Mérimée's most famous short stories, 'La Vénus d'Ille' (1837), and concludes: '"The Planter of Malata" has the interest of a technical experiment and the strength of a narrative myth which, in its carefully designed contrasts, borrows many of the qualities of Mérimée's "La Vénus d'Ille". In counterpointing the primitive and civilized to show how a myth fulfils itself destructively in modern conditions, the latter anticipates a familiar Conradian theme' ('Conrad and Mérimée: The Legend of Venus in "The Planter of Malata"', *Conradiana*, 11 (1979), 183).

**Methuen, Algernon Methuen Mar-
shall** (né Stedman, 1856–1924; baronetcy
1916). Algernon Methuen founded his London publishing firm in 1889 and was soon
publishing writers such as Oscar Wilde,
Rudyard *Kipling, R. L. *Stevenson, and
Hilaire Belloc. After an unsuccessful attempt to secure Conrad as a Methuen
author in early 1899, he became Conrad's
main British publisher during the period
1906–15, bringing out *The Mirror of the Sea,
A Set of Six, The Secret Agent, Under Western Eyes, Chance,* and *Victory.* Relations
between the author and the Methuen
Company were never smooth and, by 1911,
Conrad expressed dissatisfaction with both
the firm's handling of his fiction and
Methuen's personal treatment of him: 'He
had the impudence to advise me what to
write. I prefer to deal with men who know
better than to talk like that to an author
who has always stood on his own feet, quite
alone both in vision and expression' (*CL,*
iv. 503). In 1913, the awkward relationship
between writer and publisher was even
more severely tested by a prolonged contractual wrangle and deteriorated to a
point where the company communicated
with Conrad only through his agent J. B.
*Pinker. A severance followed upon the
publication of *Victory* in 1915, when Conrad turned to J. M. *Dent as his main
British publisher. See also CONTRACTS and
PUBLISHERS.

Mickiewicz, Adam (1798–1855). Conrad's early knowledge of this celebrated
Polish Romantic poet is confirmed by Jadwiga Kałuska, with whom the young Conrad spent his holidays in Lwów. She tells of
how 'he knew long passages from *Pan
Tadeusz* and Mickiewicz's "Ballads" by
heart' (*CUFE,* 139). Under his father's tu-
ition, the young Conrad's education had a
marked literary bias. In an interview with
Marian Dąbrowski, Conrad said that what
his English critics ultimately found 'incomprehensible, inconceivable, elusive' in
his writing could be identified as his 'Polishness' which he took from Mickiewicz
and Juliusz Słowacki: 'My father read *Pan
Tadeusz* aloud to me and made me read it

aloud. Not just once or twice. I used to prefer *Konrad Wallenrod, Grażyna*' (*CUFE,*
199). Nonetheless, according to Józef H.
Retinger, a battered copy of *Pan Tadeusz*
was one of the few personal items surviving Conrad's career as a sailor, and one
which 'he never tired of rereading' (*Conrad
and his Contemporaries: Souvenirs* (Minerva, 1941), 96).

Mickiewicz was born in an easterly part
of old Poland which had fallen to Russia
three years earlier. His literary career began
in 1822 with the publication of a collection
of ballads, soon followed by a collection of
poems, containing fragments of a fantastic
drama, *The Forefathers,* and the short
historical poem *Grażyna* (1828). These volumes reflect the first powerful expression
in Poland of the prevailing Romantic
movement in Europe and, in particular,
Mickiewicz's enthusiasm for Byron, whom
he read in the original. In 1823 Mickiewicz
was arrested and banished to Russia, where
he spent six years and met many of the
most eminent men of letters in Russia, including Pushkin, who admired his work.
During his exile, he published *Konrad Wallenrod* (1828), a verse tale of a Lithuanian
chief who, realizing that he cannot defend
his people against the Teutonic Knights,
contrives to join their order and, eventually, lead them to destruction. After leaving
Russia in 1829, Mickiewicz travelled to Italy
where his residence in Rome brought
about a rebirth of his Catholic faith that
strongly affected his later writings.

Mickiewicz joined the Great Emigration
of Poles implicated in the 1830 insurrection
and fled to Paris where he spent most of
the rest of his life. Although the uprising
failed, it inspired him during the next four
years to write *Forefathers' Eve* (1832), which
expresses the anguish of a nation in defeat
through a kind of Christian Prometheus,
the patriotic martyr Konrad; *The Books of
the Polish Nation and of the Polish Pilgrimage* (1832), a quasi-religious work intended
to bring comfort to Polish exiles; and *Pan
Tadeusz* (1834), his greatest poem and also
his last significant work. The central theme
of the poem is the age-old conflict between
Pole and Muscovite and, as in *Konrad*

Wallenrod, the hero of *Pan Tadeusz*, Father Robak, strives to atone for past misdeeds through heroic service to his country. After its publication, Mickiewicz became increasingly absorbed by a religious mysticism that caused him to turn aside from poetry. In 1854, with the outbreak of the Crimean War, he journeyed to Constantinople hoping to organize a Polish legion to fight against Russia. He died there of cholera in 1855, his death providing parallels with that of Lord Byron. Mickiewicz's remains, first laid to rest in Paris, were transferred to his own country in 1890 and placed in the cathedral in Cracow.

Busza (1966) has clearly demonstrated Conrad's literary debt to Mickiewicz. For instance, he shows how the central episode in 'Karain: A Memory' (*Tales of Unrest*) echoes one of Mickiewicz's ballads, 'The Ambush', and how other ballads in the collection may have been used as sources for other elements in the tale. He also demonstrates that Conrad's only Polish story, 'Prince Roman' (*Tales of Hearsay*), uses echoes from the work of the Polish poet. But Conrad's debt to Mickiewicz may be even more intimate than intellectual, for while the first two of his given names, Józef Teodor, are derived from maternal and paternal grandfathers respectively, his third name, Konrad, was made popular in Poland by two heroes in Mickiewicz's poems: the eponymous hero of *Konrad Wallenrod* and the main character of *Forefathers' Eve*, who changes his name from Gustaw to Konrad in response to his mystical awareness that he is charged with the power to free Poland from Muscovite tyranny. Thus, through Mickiewicz, Conrad's very name is invested with the political ideals of his nation.   AHS

Mirror of the Sea: Memories and Impressions, The.

This volume collects a number of essays on the *sea life—reminiscences, anecdotal episodes, and historical subjects—that Conrad composed intermittently over a period of some eighteen months in 1904–5. The idea for such a collection originated in January 1902 in Conrad's notion that he might do 'some

autobiographical matter about Ships, skippers, and an adventure or two' (*CL*, ii. 368). This idea recurred in February 1904 at a time when, immersed in the composition of *Nostromo* and desperately short of money following the collapse of his bank, Conrad needed to produce saleable copy as quickly as possible. At this time staying in *London, Conrad was probably urged to take up the idea by Ford Madox *Ford, who remained on hand for some weeks to stimulate Conrad's recall of his sea memories and assist in the production of the papers by taking them down in shorthand at Conrad's *dictation—for which tasks he was later paid a fee. Conrad wrote to his agent J. B. *Pinker that he could 'dictate that sort of bosh without effort at the rate of 3000 words in four hours' (*CL*, iii. 112) and explained the nature of his planned 'papers': 'Essays—impressions, descriptions, reminiscences[,] anecdotes and typical traits—of the old sailing fleet which passes away for good with the last century. Easy narrative style' (*CL*, iii. 114). The appeal of the project for Conrad lay in its simplicity: apart from some research for the paper on Admiral Nelson, it demanded little background *reading and could be taken up during regular breaks from his main preoccupation, *Nostromo*.

With Ford's help, Conrad speedily produced six papers by mid-March 1904: 'Landfalls and Departures', *Pall Mall Magazine* (January 1905); 'Emblems of Hope', published as 'Up Anchor', *Pall Mall Magazine* (February 1905); 'The Fine Art', *Pall Mall Magazine* (April 1905); 'The Weight of the Burden', *Harper's Weekly* (17 June 1905); 'Overdue and Missing', published as 'Missing', *Daily Mail* (8 March 1904) and 'Overdue', *Daily Mail* (16 November 1904); and 'The Grip of the Land', published as 'Stranded', *Daily Mail* (2 December 1904).

By mid-April three more papers had been prepared: 'The Character of the Foe', published as 'Gales of Wind', *Pall Mall Magazine* (March 1905); 'Rulers of East and West', *Pall Mall Magazine* (May–June 1905); and 'In Captivity', published as 'Her Captivity', *Blackwood's Magazine* (September 1905). Although in May Conrad assured his agent that he was confident he 'could get the Mirror of the Sea ready in six weeks' (*CL*, iii. 136), he spent the next few months wholly absorbed in finishing *Nostromo* and produced only two more sea papers during the remainder of 1904: 'The Faithful River', published as 'London River: The Great Artery of England', *World's Work and Play* (December 1904), and 'Cobwebs and Gossamer', published as 'Tallness of the Spars', *Harper's Weekly* (10 June 1905). Conrad returned to the series in July 1905 and added: 'Initiation', published as 'Initiation: A Discourse Concerning the "Name" of Ships and the Character of the Sea', *Blackwood's Magazine* (January 1906); 'The "Tremolino"', published as 'The Sea of Adventure: Some Chapters in Autobiography', *Tribune* (22–5 January 1906), 'The Heroic Age', published as 'Palmam qui meruit ferat, 1805–1905', *Standard* (21 October 1905); and 'The Nursery of the Craft', published for the first time in the book edition of *The Mirror of the Sea*. Conrad revised the essays and determined their final order for book publication in March 1906, and a month later he settled upon a title, having rejected the idea of calling it *A Seaman's Sketches* on the model of *Turgenev's A Sportsman's Sketches* (1852). *The Mirror* was published by Methuen in Britain and by Harper in America on 4 October 1906.

Najder advises the reader that to appreciate it fully 'it is best to read *The Mirror* not knowing, or else forgetting, how the volume originated and its parts got assembled: simply, to read the book as a whole' in order to enjoy 'so many statements of the author's essential beliefs' (1988: pp. vii, viii). However, this advice leaves the volume strangely remote from the conditions that went into the making of what is in many ways Conrad's most frankly commercial Edwardian work and minimizes the reader's difficulties in adjusting both to its mixed contents and the highly variable quality of the writing.

Many readers have felt, with some justice, that Conrad's claim in his later 'Author's Note' that *The Mirror* was designed to offer 'a very intimate revelation' and 'a true confession' of 'the inner truth of almost a lifetime' (pp. ix, x) is misleadingly ambitious. Purportedly semi-autobiographical, *The Mirror* is severely reticent about many of the most significant facts of Conrad's life: it makes little mention of his *Polish background or of the underlying reasons why he took up a sea career and finally abandoned it. In addition, the 'impressions and memories' of his own sea life are coloured and decorated to such a degree that the work's relation to the actual facts of his life is at times very slight indeed. Sometimes, factual inaccuracy is a matter of small detail, as when Conrad transforms his only command at sea into the plural form, or protests that he never sailed as a passenger. At another extreme, there is a more pervasive mixture of potential fact, wishful dreaming, and nostalgic myth-making, as when he broaches the episode—so troublesome to later biographers—of his avowedly 'real' youthful involvement with gun-smuggling in the *Tremolino* during his *Marseilles years.

The fiction-writer's licence to rework, embroider, and transform the materials of his or her own experiences is so marked in *The Mirror* that it is ultimately unrewarding to regard it as a work 'rooted' in the details of Conrad's own life or as an expression of his 'philosophy of life'. A more helpful approach to its generic features can be made by noting its similarity to an earlier autobiographical fiction like 'Youth'. When, in 1902, Conrad first conceived the scheme of writing a collection of sea papers, he felt that they would turn out to be eminently suitable for *Blackwood's* and wrote to David *Meldrum, its literary editor, describing them as follows: '*Youth* style upon the whole only not with the note of Youth in it but the *wonderfulness* of things, events, people,—when looked back upon. . . . Of course it shall be "fiction" in the same sense that *Youth* is fiction' (*CL*, ii. 368). The linking of *The Mirror* with the manner of 'Youth' is significant here. In the short story of 1898, Conrad had cultivated a popular 'English' appeal by projecting details of his own sea life through the middle-aged Englishman *Marlow's address to a listening audience, shaping them into a nostalgic reminiscence of a vanished world and transforming the crew's struggle to save the *Judea* into an epic chronicle. 'Tempi passati,' exclaims the narrator in *The Mirror* (57), echoing earlier Marlovian tones and drawing upon that same vein of popular nostalgic feeling that Conrad had mined in 'Youth', his first story written for *Blackwood's*. *The Mirror* is, in many ways, an important document in the Conrad canon, although not for the reasons often adduced: its importance lies in what it indicates about the ease with which Conrad could by this stage in his career improvise upon his British persona and employ *Blackwood's* conventions in order to write quickly for popular audiences. William *Blackwood did in fact accept two of the papers, 'Initiation' and 'In Captivity', for his magazine, although he thought the latter paper to be 'perhaps not Mr Conrad at his best' (Blackburn (ed.), 184).

While Conrad later came to think highly of *The Mirror*, insisting that it be placed before *A Personal Record* in the volume of reminiscences included in later *collected editions, there is evidence to suggest that in 1906 he was aware of certain uncomfortable ironies in *The Mirror*'s contemporary reception. Written at a time when Conrad was engaged on his most ambitious novel and seeking to dispel the image of himself as a sea writer, he was nevertheless trapped by financial need into exploiting the popular appeal of sea material in a form that he basically regarded as jobbing occasional work. His attempt certainly produced the desired reaction. In letters to him about the book, E. V. *Lucas and John *Galsworthy confessed to having wept over its contents, while Ada Galsworthy praised Conrad as the 'high-priest of the sea' and *The Mirror* as its 'Bible' (*PL*, 54–6). Reviewers also maintained the hyperbolic note, delighted at being able to pigeon-hole Conrad in simple terms: 'When Mr Conrad writes of the sea his work is a pure delight' (*Athenaeum*, 27 October 1906, 513). According to the *Spectator*'s reviewer, the volume contained 'the whole soul of a man who has known the deeps of sea mysteries, who has sought them as a lover, with joy, and rever-

ence, and fear' (1 December 1906, 888–9), a eulogy echoed in the *Literary Digest*'s judgement that Conrad's 'high gift of imagination, held in abeyance by a clear, rational perception, has enabled him to impart a vivid idea of the wonder and charm of the Infinite as expressed by its most potent symbol, the ocean' (10 November 1906, 685). Flattering though these reviews were, Conrad soon became sceptical of their underlying implications when he realized that *The Mirror* had strengthened the very image of 'Conrad the high priest of the sea' that he was seeking to escape: 'There are those who have seized the occasion to kick poor *Nostromo* . . . Beneath this chorus of praise, I can hear in a murmur: "Keep to the open sea. Do not land!" They want to exile me to the middle of the ocean. . . . They will be well and truly cheated' (*CL*, iii. 372).

Although varying types of unity have been claimed for *The Mirror*, readers of the time clearly enjoyed its untaxing medley of popular subjects and styles. Three of the papers—'The Faithful River', 'The Heroic Age', and 'The "Tremolino"'—were originally commissioned by journals for special occasional purposes and included in the volume to swell its contents. But in other respects the volume's fifteen chapters and 49 sections constitute a very diverse mixture of subjects, embracing voyage anecdote, technical essay, set-piece description, autobiographical reminiscence, and historical elegy. Its registers are also varied and undemanding, ranging from the informal armchair address ('Here is Conrad talking of the events and feelings of his own life as he would talk to a friend' (*CL*, iii. 133)) to the openly belletristic. All of the subjects, moreover, were designed to draw upon various aspects of the conventional historical and patriotic myth of the English as a seagoing and imperial nation at a time when *Germany was attempting to challenge their traditional supremacy. The clearest example of Conrad's adeptness in striking a chord of popular feeling was the paper on Admiral Nelson that provides *The Mirror* with its grand climax: it was written specifically for, and first published on, 21 October 1905, the occasion of the Trafalgar centenary, along with scores of other similar articles and eulogies. In other respects, many of Conrad's subjects tapped areas already known to the Edwardian reading public through the works of Henry *Newbolt, John Masefield, or Alfred Noyes (whose blank verse epic *Drake* appeared in 1906), including the mythology of the world's winds, the imperial glamour of the *Thames, the romance of the Mediterranean, and the symbolism of landfall and departure.

Robert Foulke has persuasively argued (*Joseph Conrad Today*, 6 (1981), 165, 167) that if *The Mirror* has an encompassing genre, it is not that of the reminiscence or autobiography, but of the elegiac memorial to figures and ships now gone, notably the heroic figure of Nelson, but also including the vanished age of sail. As he notes, Conrad characteristically presents himself as an emblem- or relic-seeker, rescuing people and objects from the 'Valley of Oblivion' (30) or 'the yesterday of the sea' (7) and using the discourse of the funeral elegy or historical eulogy as an appropriate ceremonial form. Behind this appeal lies a mythology deeply rooted in the Edwardian consciousness and its literature: that is, the nostalgic pastoral myth of the golden age represented, on the one hand, by a simpler, pre-industrial, and heroic age; and, on the other, by the symbol of the devoted stoic brotherhood, with its precedent in Alfred Tennyson's 'Ulysses' (1842). In this process, the materials of Conrad's own earlier life at sea are inevitably epicized and assimilated into a myth pleasingly familiar to his Edwardian readers.

It is fair to say that *The Mirror* does not now hold the high position it once enjoyed, and critical opinion has tended to reverse Conrad's judgement on the relative merits of his two volumes of autobiographical reminiscences. Yet it does shed considerable light on a point of bifurcation in the writer's middle career, when he was compelled to divide his energies between slowly germinating major work and occasional, readily marketable pieces. See Avrom Fleishman, '*The Mirror of the Sea*: "Frag-

ments of a Great Confession"', *L'Époque Conradienne* (1979), 136–51, and Sylvère Monod, 'Conrad and Kipling: Two Reticent Autobiographers', *The Conradian*, 12 (1987), 122–37.

The manuscript of 'The Weight of her [*sic*] Burden' (in Ford's shorthand) and a typescript of 'The Heroic Age' are held at the Beinecke Rare Book and Manuscript Library, Yale University. Manuscripts of 'Initiation' and 'The Inland Sea' (the latter equivalent to 'The Nursery of the Craft' and 'The "Tremolino"') are at the Rosenbach Museum and Library, Philadelphia. Typescripts of the 'Author's Note' are held at Yale, at Bryn Mawr University, and in the Fales Library, New York University.

Mitchell, Captain Joseph, or 'Fussy Joe' as he is nicknamed. Captain Mitchell is an elderly English former sea captain who superintends the *Sulaco branch of the Ocean Steam Navigation Company in *Nostromo*. His is one of the first voices to be heard at the beginning of the novel, when, as a long-standing resident in *Costaguana and direct witness of many of its main crises, he presents himself as a historical guide and temporarily provides a fixed point in a bewilderingly chaotic South American country. It soon becomes clear, however, that his primary role is that of the comically obtuse commentator and historian, a variant of what Henry *James calls the *ficelle* or choric appendage. In Mitchell's case, the comic effect produced by his being 'utterly in the dark, and imagining himself to be in the thick of things' (112) shows him to be a recognizable national and professional type, embodying what Edward *Garnett described as 'the wooden-headed unimaginativeness of the Britisher' (*CCH*, 176). He is also presented as the well-meaning but pompous seaman ashore who, in the face of events that fail to correspond to his idea of the shipshape, can only resort to the equivalent of sensational newspaper headlines: 'Almost every event out of the usual daily course "marked an epoch" for him or else was "history"' (112–13).

Mitchell's most significant appearance occurs in Part III, chapter 10. Several years older and even more pompously garrulous, he is enlisted to narrate the history of Sulaco's more recent development to an anonymous distinguished visitor, who, listening 'like a tired child to a fairy tale' (487), hears a rambling anecdotal narrative of the part played by history's villains and heroes in the 'memorable' evolution of Costaguana into the 'Treasure House of the World' (480). Conrad's tactic of abandoning the role of omniscient historian at this crucial point and allowing 'Fussy Joe' to act as guide tends to cast considerable ironic doubt upon the latter's version of Sulaco's successful 'progress' and to complicate the vision of historical development implied at the novel's ending: is the society presented through Mitchell and others in the final chapters preferable to that at the beginning, or has Sulaco merely undergone a depressingly familiar historical cycle? Garnett believed the latter to be the case and felt that the narrative 'should have ended with the monologue of Captain Mitchell and the ironic commentary of Dr. Monygham on the fresh disillusionment in store for the *régime* of "Civilisation" planted by European hands on the bloodstained soil of the Republic of Costaguana' (*CCH*, 177).

Mont Blanc, a French restaurant at 16 Gerrard Street in Soho, London W1, where informal literary gatherings convened in an upstairs room on Tuesday lunchtimes. A frequent meeting place for G. K. Chesterton and Hilaire Belloc from 1900, the Mont Blanc was chosen by Edward *Garnett and Edward *Thomas because of its central location and cheapness. Garnett was at that time a reader for Duckworth's and used the gatherings to nurse his literary contacts. Garnett and Thomas were always present, and other participants included Muirhead Bone, W. H. Davies, John *Galsworthy (occasionally), Perceval *Gibbon, W. H. *Hudson, Ford Madox *Ford, Arthur *Marwood, Stephen *Reynolds, and H. M. Tomlinson. In 1908, the Mont Blanc provided a forum for discussions about founding the *English Review. Conrad was an infrequent visitor to luncheons at the Mont Blanc (which bore the same name as

the first ship he had sailed in as a young seaman), but he met several new friends there, including Richard *Curle and Edward Thomas. The restaurant was later renamed the Taglionis, and is currently incorporated into a larger oriental restaurant. A lively account of the Mont Blanc luncheon club appears in Jefferson, 128–42.

Montpellier. With his family, Conrad spent two working holidays during the period 1906–7 in this southern French city, staying a total of seven months. The first trip to Montpellier, a location chosen for its warm winter climate and reputation as a medical centre, was primarily intended to improve Borys's poor health and to give Jessie, then pregnant, a restful break. The family set off on 9 February 1906 for a two-month stay, lodging at the Hôtel Riche & Continental in Montpellier's main square, the Place de la Comédie, where they arrived on 12 February to find 'the whole town an amazing mixture of carnival and political riots going on at the same time' (*CL*, iii. 316). The first stay coincided with the germination and first batches of manuscript for a new novel, The Secret Agent, at this point called 'Verloc', which Conrad worked on in Le Peyrou Gardens. The Conrads left for home on 16 April.

The second and longer stay began eight months later, when Conrad, fatigued and depressed after completing the serial version of The Secret Agent, decided to seek in Montpellier winter sunshine and conditions for working on Chance. Travelling via Paris, the Conrads arrived at the same hotel in Montpellier on 18 December 1906 for what proved to be a five-month stay. As Conrad relaxed, reread his favourite French authors, and began taking lessons in Spanish, his work lay dormant, and on 8 January he reported: 'Work at a standstill. Plans simply swarming in my head but my English has all departed from me' (*CL*, iii. 403). Many of these plans were connected with a projected Napoleonic novel, which he researched in the city library. His only piece of creative work in Montpellier was an offshoot of these same Napoleonic interests, the short story 'The Duel' (*A Set of*

Six), finished on 11 April. The family made excursions to Palavas-sur-Mer, visited the church at Maguelone, and attended a performance of Bizet's *Carmen*. Conrad befriended a local painter, Louis-Charles Eymar, although apparently without telling him that he was a writer. The two frequented the still-extant Café Riche, where, Eymar recalled, Conrad would sit very near the orchestra and observe a young and attractive girl musician, who, Conrad later maintained, was a model for *Lena in Victory*. The visit was complicated when Borys contracted measles followed by a mysterious lung infection variously diagnosed as bronchitis, pneumonia, and possibly tuberculosis. By mid-March, Conrad decided upon a change of climate for Borys and prepared to leave for *Geneva. On the eve of departure (14 May), Borys caught whooping cough and passed it on to his 9-month-old brother John. There began what Conrad later called 'a ghastly time—from the 15th May to the 15th July' (*CL*, iii. 458). Ida R. Sée, Borys's tutor in Montpellier, published her reminiscences in 'Joseph Conrad à Montpellier', *Le Petit Méridional*, 6 September 1924.

Monygham, Dr, a 50-year-old English medical doctor in *Nostromo*. Dr Monygham appears briefly at an early point in the novel but is then held in abeyance until Part III, when he emerges as a leading, if not dominating, character during the Sulacan war of secession. Exposition in Part III, chapter 4 makes clear the reasons for his physical disfigurement (a limping walk, twisted shoulders, and scarred face) and psychological wounds. A long-standing resident in *Sulaco, Monygham suffered extreme torture during the earlier regime of the autocratic Guzman Bento and his partner-in-crime Father Beron. Under torture, Monygham broke down and committed what he felt to be a betrayal (although it is a largely imaginary one). He has lived for many years as an outcast and sour misanthrope, wandering in the country, with a perpetual sense of failure that 'makes truth, honour, self-respect, and life itself matters of little moment' (373). A first stage in his

rehabilitation is effected by Emilia *Gould, who secures for him a position as chief medical officer to the San Tomé mine and whom he comes to worship from afar. Although this worship threatens to become a dangerously fixed obsession, it nevertheless leads him to discover a capacity for loyal and committed action that, in turn, explains his readiness for 'dirty work' during the crisis in Sulaco: he lies to Sotillo at a crucial point, thereby gaining time for the Sulacan forces, and helps to engineer *Nostromo's ride to Cayta. The end of the novel sees the language of physical and spiritual rebirth applied to Monygham. In public terms he has become Inspector-General of State Hospitals in the new Sulacan republic and, in Captain *Mitchell's words, a 'big-wig' (481). Hobbling around 'more vivaciously' (505), he is freshly dressed and now nearly free of the recurring dreams of his earlier torture (508). It is perhaps fitting that he should be allowed to voice a final moral epitaph upon the novel's action: 'There is no peace and no rest in the development of material interests. They have their law, and their justice. But it is founded on expediency, and is inhuman; it is without rectitude, without the continuity and the force that can be found only in a moral principle' (511).

Conrad's account of Monygham's sufferings is indebted to G. F. Masterman's lengthy description in *Seven Eventful Years in Paraguay* (1869) of his own imprisonment and cruel torture. A physician and surgeon in Asunción, Masterman was twice arrested and endured long periods of captivity, after which, in considerable mental and physical distress, he made a false confession to secure his release. As is common in Conrad's work, borrowed details are developed in ways more rich and varied than are suggested by the original source. In particular, Monygham's rehabilitation in Part III—for which there is little precedent in Masterman—is rendered especially complex by its structural proximity to contrasting life-histories, particularly those of Martin *Decoud and Nostromo. Monygham is born as a fictional character at the moment when Decoud disappears from the action, and he enters the public sphere at a time when Nostromo is intent upon withdrawing from it. While Nostromo and Decoud undergo two versions of a process of disintegration and dispossession, Monygham presents an important variation: initially robbed of self-belief and acutely conscious of lost honour, he manages to find a decisive release from a prison largely of his own making, and repossesses himself anew. See also Watt 1988: 64–5, and Ressler, 64–8.

Morrell, Lady Ottoline Violet Anne

(née Cavendish-Bentinck, 1873–1938), socialite and literary patron who was known as 'Ottie' to her Bloomsbury Group friends. Lady Ottoline Morrell presided over celebrated artistic circles at her London home at 44 Bedford Square, London WC1, and, during the post-First World War decade, at Garsington Manor, near Oxford. With an introduction from Henry *James, she first visited Conrad at Capel House in *Kent in August 1913 and responded extravagantly to the 'wonderful' literary giant: 'He made me feel so natural and very much myself, that I was almost afraid of losing the thrill and wonder of being there, although I was vibrating with intense excitement inside' (quoted in Gathorne-Hardy, 241). She also arranged a September meeting between Conrad and Bertrand *Russell, whose hero-worship of the novelist she helped to fire. See also Knowles 1990.

museums and memorabilia. There is no Conrad museum centred upon one of the writer's *homes comparable to the *Dickens House Museum in London or Rudyard *Kipling's Burwash home. The main public exhibition of Conrad memorabilia is to be found in the Heritage Centre in Stour Street, Canterbury, in a medieval building that was formerly the Poor Priests' Hospital. Here, a selection of objects from the writer's last home, Oswalds, reminds the visitor of Conrad's connections with *Kent and forms a small but attractive permanent display: it includes his writing-table and chair, pens, an ashtray, portraits, photographs, first editions, and books belonging to him and his wife Jessie.

Another museum is in the process of formation in part of the regional museum in Terechowa, some 6 miles (10 km) from Conrad's birthplace in *Berdyczów, in *Ukraine. Andrzej Braun describes it as follows: 'Several rooms are devoted to Conrad and are dotted with pieces of furniture from his era, nineteenth-century noblemen's utensils, reproductions of old photographs connected with the Bobrowski and Korzeniowski families, photographs illustrating Conrad's travels and works, a few collected editions in Polish and in the original. There is no astounding discovery here, but one can feel a certain reverent care' ('In the Home Village of Conrad', *Conrad News* (1992), 52).

Joseph Conrad *study centres in London, Gdańsk, and Pisa as well as merchant navy institutions also serve as repositories for Conrad memorabilia. Unfortunately, one material symbol of his sea career and first command, the *Otago* (see SHIPS AND VOYAGES), lies in a state of terminal wreckage on the banks of the Derwent River, above Hobart in Tasmania. However, her steering-wheel is preserved in HQS *Wellington*, the floating Thameside headquarters of the Honourable Company of Master Mariners, on Victoria Embankment, London WC2. Several larger museums display a range of exhibits that reflect interestingly upon Conrad's traditions, notably the National Historical Museum and Adam *Mickiewicz Museum in *Warsaw, and the National Maritime Museum in Greenwich, with its replicas, models, and photographs of many of the sailing ships associated with Conrad, including the *Cutty Sark*, which is on public display. Although she was never directly associated with Conrad, the sail training ship *Joseph Conrad* is similarly displayed in Mystic Seaport, Connecticut.

Many of the writer's *homes and lodgings in Poland and *England are now identified by commemorative plaques, but they can also be found as far afield as *Australia (on Sydney's Circular Quay), *Singapore (in the Raffles Hotel—in which, contrary to legend, the writer never stayed), *France (the Conrads' honeymoon lodgings in

Brittany), and Switzerland (at the Hôtel-Pension de la Roseraie in *Champel-les-Bains, *Geneva). See also PORTRAITS AND OTHER IMAGES.

'My Best Story and Why I Think So'.
At the request of the editor of *Grand Magazine* to contribute to its 'Best Story' series, Conrad sent a short note to his agent J. B. *Pinker on 4 January 1906, despite having qualms at being identified with other writers who had appeared in the series

(such as Robert Hichens, Jerome K. Jerome, and Morley Roberts). His brief note nominating 'An Outpost of Progress' (*Tales of Unrest*), on the grounds that it 'aimed at a scrupulous unity of tone' and demanded the utmost 'severity of discipline' to keep the tale within its preconceived limits, appeared in *Grand Magazine*, March 1906. It is reprinted in *CDOUP*, 82–3.

myth criticism. See ARCHETYPAL APPROACHES.

N

Napoleon Bonaparte (1769–1821), the 'Man of Destiny' who crowned himself Emperor of the French and redrew the map of Europe, was a defining figure in Conrad's cultural heritage. He figures as a commanding presence in the 19th-century novels of Balzac, Stendhal, Thackeray, and Tolstoy. By the turn of the 20th century, his legend in English literature often found expression in a comic or satirical mode, as in G. K. Chesterton's first novel, *The Napoleon of Notting Hill* (1904), or in H. G. *Wells's *Tono-Bungay* (1909), where Edward Ponderevo is described as 'The Napoleon of domestic conveniences'. For Conrad, however, Napoleon was never a figure of fun. In 'Autocracy and War' (*Notes*), he described him as 'a sort of vulture', and added that the 'subtle and manifold influence for evil of the Napoleonic episode as a school of violence, as a sower of national hatreds, as the direct provocator of obscurantism and reaction, of political tyranny and injustice, cannot well be exaggerated' (86).

From the frigate service described in the works of Captain *Marryat that he read as a child to the historical novels that marked the final phase of his own career, the Napoleonic period continued to preoccupy Conrad and provide him with material for many of his own creations. As Richard *Curle recalled, 'Conrad had always been interested in naval tactics, and I daresay there were few people who had studied more minutely the naval side of the Napoleonic wars' (*LTY*, 197). He was also an avid reader of memoirs of the Napoleonic period; Ford Madox *Ford recalled that Conrad's 'power of consuming memoirs always appeared to me fantastic—and although I had read a good deal, he must have read five times as much' (1932: 194).

Many Poles without a country saw Napoleon's victories over the powers that had partitioned *Poland as a chance to re-constitute their vanished homeland, and a minimal Poland was briefly reconstituted under Napoleon as the Duchy of Warsaw. Conrad's paternal grandfather Teodor Korzeniowski fought in Napoleon's army, and his maternal great-uncle Nicholas Bobrowski had been driven by hunger to make a meal of a dog during Napoleon's catastrophic retreat from Moscow in the winter of 1812, a débâcle described in *A Personal Record* as 'the greatest military disaster of modern history' (35) and dramatized in two of Conrad's stories, 'The Duel' (*A Set of Six*) and 'The Warrior's Soul' (*Tales of Hearsay*).

Conrad's fascination with the age of Napoleon led him to contemplate writing a historical 'Mediterranean novel' as early as 1902, but twenty years would pass before the idea would be realized in his last two novels: *The Rover*, set on the Giens peninsula near Toulon in the years 1796 and 1804, and *Suspense*, set in *Genoa in February 1815, on the eve of Napoleon's return from exile for the final Hundred Days that ended at Waterloo. Conrad took his Mediterranean project as an occasion for serious research, consulting books about Napoleon in the town libraries of *Montpellier and Ajaccio (in *Corsica). On 7 June 1920, just before he began the actual writing of *Suspense*, he visited the British Museum to find information about Napoleon on Elba, using a set of application slips that his friend G. *Jean-Aubry had prepared for him. His notes show that he submitted only two of the slips, consulting works by by Marcellin Pellet and by André Pons de l'Hérault in addition to the memoirs of Sir Neil Campbell. Conrad's notebook and the application slips are now held at the Beinecke Rare Book and Manuscript Library, Yale University; the complete list of 21 books is printed together with a transcription of the original text of Conrad's notes in an appendix to Jean-Aubry's French translation of *Suspense* as *Angoisse* (Paris: Gallimard, 1956), 348–53.

Conrad's story 'The Duel' opens with the remark that Napoleon's 'career had the quality of a duel against the whole of Europe' (165), and this grand international duel provides a historical setting for a series of duels fought between two of his officers, one of whom, Feraud, remains totally devoted to the Emperor. 'The Warrior's Soul' links an encounter between a young Russian named Tomassov and a French officer named De Castel in Paris with a second meeting during the retreat from Moscow, but makes no direct reference to Napoleon. In *The Rover*, the false papers for which Peyrol dies are devised on orders given in a letter signed 'Bonaparte' (113). The title of *Suspense* signifies the state of tension occasioned throughout Europe at the possibility that the Emperor might grow restless and return from Elba; and the Italians, like the Poles, saw his advent as an opportunity to claim a nation state of their own. Napoleon's looming presence offstage sets the tone for the entire novel, and he also makes a cameo appearance when Adèle d'Armand, the Countess de Montevesso, tells Cosmo Latham of the one occasion on which she met him (146–7), in a scene borrowed literally from the *Memoirs of the Comtesse de Boigne* (1907). Conrad has been accused of plagiarizing from the Boigne memoirs, but his treatment of Napoleon may also be viewed as a sign of artistic discretion and of respect for the historical record; see Hans van Marle and Gene M. Moore, 'The Sources of Conrad's *Suspense*', in Moore *et al.* (eds.) 1997: 141–63.

It is surely no accident that towards the end of his career Conrad chose to return to the Mediterranean coast that had nourished the dreams of his youth. Once he had finished *The Arrow of Gold*, his most directly autobiographical novel, and had then completed *The Rescue* after a twenty-year interruption, the combination of Napoleonic history with Mediterranean scenery enabled him to prolong his lingering sojourn in a time and place that were entirely congenial to his creative imagination.

narratological approaches. Narratology, the study of narrative, first emerged from the context of French structuralism in the 1960s in an effort to develop a systematic poetics of storytelling. From the beginning, a distinction was apparent between those who, following the earlier work of Vladimir Propp, hoped to elaborate an underlying structure or 'narrative grammar' true for all narratives, and others who, in the wake of Viktor Shklovsky and the rhetorical tradition, extended and refined the methodology available for the exploration of narrative 'devices' such as the presentation of time, perspective, and narrative voice. Gérard Genette's systematic study of Proust, *Figures III* (1972), applied grammatical categories to larger discursive units and opened up a realm of narrative analysis based on new terms and distinctions. The decade following the publication of Genette's study was a narratological golden age, with important contributions by Seymour Chatman, Dorrit Cohn, Gerald Prince, Shlomith Rimmon-Kenan, Meir Sternberg, and others, and the Jerusalem-based journal *Poetics Today* (since 1979) providing a forum for narratological debate. By 1990, the first wave of discovery had passed; many narratologists, beginning to feel constrained by their own formalisms, found themselves unable to answer the radical challenge to the validity of 'structural' solutions that became the hallmark of post-structuralism and deconstructionism. Although currently out of fashion, narratology continues to make available a precise and systematic critical vocabulary for the analysis of complex narrative situations of the kind often found in the works of Conrad.

Students of the temporal aspects of Conrad's fictions, or his use of multiple levels of narration, have often found Genette's terminology useful. Mary Sullivan has examined 'Conrad's Paralipses in the Narration of *Lord Jim*', *Conradiana*, 10 (1978), 123–40; and Watt (1980: 295) adopts Genette's analepsis and prolepsis in a discussion of time in *Lord Jim*. Linda M. Shires supplements Watt's discussion in 'The "Privileged" Reader and Narrative

Methodology in *Lord Jim*', *Conradiana*, 17 (1985), 19–30. Genette's approach has for some reason proved especially popular among Conradians in Norway, providing Lothe (1989) with a 'primary theoretical basis' (6) from which he proceeds to explore various modes of Conradian narrative. In a study which complements and parallels Lothe's work, Hawthorn (1990) examines modes of represented speech in Conrad's narratives in order to identify the relations between literary form and moral content. Hawthorn has also compiled *A Glossary of Contemporary Literary Theory* (3rd edn., Arnold, 1998), with definitions and illustrations of many narratological terms. In *The Art of Fiction* (Secker & Warburg, 1992), David Lodge illustrates the notion of 'intertextuality' by examining echoes of Samuel Taylor Coleridge's 'The Rime of the Ancient Mariner' in *The Shadow-Line* (98–101). Genette's concept of 'focalization' is applied by Allan H. Simmons in '"Conflicting Impulses": Focalization and the Presentation of Culture in *Almayer's Folly*', *Conradiana*, 29 (1997), 163–72.

narrators. Conrad's mastery of ironic and indirect narration has long been recognized as one of the hallmarks of his fiction, and many of his fictions are presented as oral narratives. As Edward Said has noted, 'Narratives originate in the hearing and telling presence of people to each other. In Conrad's case this is usually true whether or not the narratives are told in the first person' ('The Presentation of Narrative', *Novel*, 7 (1974), 120). His narrators typically bring with them a meditative frame which transforms apparently conventional 'action' stories into moral and philosophical enquiries. Apropos of *Chance*, Henry *James described this particular form of narrative omniscience as 'a prolonged hovering flight of the subjective over the outstretched ground of the case exposed' (*CCH*, 267). Conrad's complex perspectival techniques often make it difficult to assign responsibility for particular attitudes to a specific narrating voice, and the obliquities thus generated

make it possible for him to evoke a variety of storytelling modes, including historical adventure (*The Rescue*, 'Heart of Darkness'), hearsay (*Lord Jim*), and gossip (*Victory*). In the four stories narrated by *Marlow, an unidentified 'frame-narrator' introduces Marlow and records his spoken words; and although most critics speak of Marlow as the narrator of these tales, his entire narrative is mediated by this unobtrusive amanuensis. Conrad's fondness for multiple narrators was perhaps inspired by his reading of *Maupassant, and Conrad's works gave F. Scott Fitzgerald the idea of using Nick Carraway as the first-person narrator of *The Great Gatsby*.

Some of Conrad's first-person narratives are relatively unproblematic in terms of the identity of the narrator: *The Shadow-Line*, for example, or 'The Secret Sharer', which Guerard called 'Conrad's most successful experiment by far with the method of nonretrospective first-person narration' (27). Conrad's three *collaborations with Ford Madox *Ford all employ first-person narrators, while Conrad's own early and late works tend towards an all-purpose, generally omniscient, and frequently ironic third-person narrative voice, as do his two major 'political' works, *Nostromo* and *The Secret Agent*. In *Nostromo*, the versatile narrative voice encompasses various competing versions of the history of *Costaguana.

Conrad's 'mixed' narratives have received considerable attention from critics because of the problem of 'authority' that arises when first-person narrators seem to lay claim to the omniscience characteristic of third-person narration. In *The Nigger of the 'Narcissus'*, for example, the narrator is evidently a nameless member of the crew, yet he is able to describe private scenes (like the final scene between *Wait and *Donkin) at which he was not present. This problem is examined by John Lester in 'Conrad's Narrators in *The Nigger of the "Narcissus"*', *Conradiana*, 12 (1980), 163–72; by David Manicom in 'True Lies/False Truths: Narrative Perspective and the Control of Ambiguity in *The Nigger of the "Narcissus"*', *Conradiana*, 18 (1986), 105–18; and by Bruce Henricksen, *Nomadic Voices:*

Conrad and the Subject of Narrative (Urbana: University of Illinois Press, 1992), 23–46. An interesting and wide-ranging discussion of the narrator of 'Falk' is provided by Tony Tanner in '"Gnawed Bones" and "Artless Tales": Eating and Narrative in Conrad', in Sherry (ed.) 1976: 17–36.

In his 1917 'Author's Note' to *Lord Jim*, Conrad took the occasion to respond to critics who had protested that Marlow's oral narrative is simply too long to be plausible: 'They argued that no man could have been expected to talk all that time, and other men to listen so long' (p. vii). Conrad wryly suggested that 'refreshments' would have been available; but the conflict between the realism required of first-person narrators and the stamina and omniscience of Conrad's yarn-spinners has often been the subject of critical scrutiny. For example, in *Chance*, how does Marlow know what Flora *de Barral's governess is thinking (106–7), or the private thoughts of Captain *Anthony (347)? Marlow also strains credibility beyond the breaking point by claiming to have 'heard all the details which really matter in this story' (443) from Flora in the space of a single late afternoon.

Inconsistencies like these have sometimes been taken as an indication of the narrator's unreliability, or worse. For example, in 'Secrets and Narrative Sequence' (in *Essays on Fiction, 1971–82* (Routledge & Kegan Paul, 1983), 133–55), Frank Kermode concludes that the English *teacher of languages who narrates *Under Western Eyes* is 'the father of lies, a diabolical narrator' (153), a view rebutted by Carabine 1996: chapter 6. Although Conrad strenuously denied having been influenced by *Dostoevsky, the impossible omniscience of the English teacher is remarkably similar to that of Stepan Trofimovitch Verhovensky, the narrator of Dostoevsky's *The Possessed* (1872). In some works, the line between first- and third-person narration is drawn more clearly: in *Victory*, for example, an introductory first-person account of *Heyst's reputation is followed by an omniscient perspective on events in *Samburan and their aftermath; and in *The Arrow*

of Gold, Monsieur *George's manuscript is edited and framed between two 'Notes' supplied by a knowledgeable but anonymous narrator.

In *Bakhtinian terms, Conrad's narratives are sites of 'heteroglossia' in which multiple narrating voices strive to understand an issue, often in different languages, and always in a dialogic relation with one another and with the reader. For a more detailed overview of the techniques employed by Conrad's narrators, see Werner Senn, *Conrad's Narrative Voice: Stylistic Aspects of his Fiction* (Bern: Francke, 1980).

naturalization. When in 1868 Conrad left the *Ukraine, a part of *Poland annexed by *Russia since 1793, and went with his father to settle in Austrian Poland, he did so as a Russian subject. He never considered the possibility of returning to the Ukraine after his father's death, since as the son of a political prisoner he would have been harassed and liable to military conscription in the Russian army for a maximum of twenty years. On the other hand, the efforts of his guardian Tadeusz *Bobrowski from 1872 onwards to obtain Austrian nationality for the young boy were unsuccessful, because Conrad had not been officially released from Russian allegiance and because Austrian law required an uninterrupted domicile of ten years in the country. These legal difficulties, compounded by Conrad's inner sense of exile from his homeland, must have strengthened his youthful compulsion to leave Poland for *Marseilles. In entering France in 1874 as a Russian subject without official permission to live and work abroad, he faced two complications: first, he could not safely return to the Ukraine to see his relatives, and, secondly, his employment in French ships was rendered problematic by new regulations in the French merchant navy requiring crew members to have completed national service in their own country.

In the summer of 1877, Bobrowski corresponded with him about the varied possibilities for naturalization open to him, including French, Swiss, and British. In

1883, at a time when Conrad had served almost four years in British merchant ships (where no special permits were required for the enlistment of foreigners), the question of petitioning for British nationality again arose at a meeting between the 25-year-old Conrad and his uncle. Bobrowski donated a sum of money to cover the requisite legal costs, and from this point onwards constantly pressed his nephew to take his maritime *examinations and seek naturalization, in his view two crucial stages in the young man's progress towards a successful and secure career. Although Conrad pursued his examinations, he did not respond to his uncle's promptings about naturalization until 1886, by which time he seems to have become inwardly convinced of its rightness: 'When speaking, writing or thinking in English the word Home always means for me the hospitable shores of Great Britain' (*CL*, i. 12). In the summer of 1886, a year of important decisions, he sat for his master's examination (unsuccessfully) and applied for British nationality. On 2 July, aged 28, he filed the petition, with four English friends as sureties: G. F. W. *Hope (one of his earliest English contacts), E. A. Poole (provisions merchant), John Newton (his tutor for his second-mate's examination), and John Weston (manager of the Well Street Sailors' Home). The police report following upon his petition—'Applicant who is about 30 years old, stated that he left Russia when he was 12 years old. He has been 10 years in the *British Merchant Service, and now holds an appointment as chief mate'—contained three misrepresentations: Conrad was in fact 10 when he left for Austrian Poland, had served in British ships for only eight years, and had never been a chief mate. His application accepted, he became a British subject on 19 August 1886. A final stage arrived on 2 July 1889 when, after application to the Russian Embassy in London, Conrad's release from the status of Russian subject was officially gazetted. The way was paved by 1890 for his first visit to the Ukraine in sixteen years, now as a fully fledged British subject freed from allegiance to Russia.

Nature of a Crime, The. This work is the last and by common consent the least important of Conrad's *collaborations with Ford Madox *Ford. Almost entirely Ford's work, this story of some 15,000 words was apparently written in Winchelsea in May 1906 (while Conrad was at work on *The Secret Agent*) and first published in Ford's *English Review* in April and May 1909 under the pseudonym 'Baron Ignatz von Aschendrof' (one of Ford's numerous personae, derived from the name of his German ancestor Anton Wilhelm Aschendorff, the founder of a publishing house in Münster). Both Ford and Conrad evidently forgot about the story until years later, when Ford needed material for a new journal he was founding in Paris. He reminded Conrad of their collaboration on 'Story of a Crime', and although Conrad told Ford that he found it 'introspective and somewhat redolent of weltschmerz' and even 'somewhat amateurish' (*JCTL*, 896, 609), he did not object to its publication in the first two numbers of the *transatlantic review* (January and February 1924), accompanied by prefaces written by each of the collaborators. Ford also added an appendix entitled 'A Note on "Romance"', in which he described his collaboration with Conrad on the earlier novel and cited passages to illustrate the stylistic differences between them. With the double preface and the appendix, *The Nature of a Crime* appeared in book form (Duckworth; Garden City, NY: Doubleday) on 26 September 1924, less than two months after Conrad's death (albeit with a typographical error in the appendix to the American edition which reversed the attributions of passages of *Romance*, so that Conrad's words appear as Ford's and vice versa). The story has not been included in *collected editions of Conrad's work, but is reprinted with his preface in *CDOUP* (117–51).

The work takes the form of a rambling and self-consciously suicidal letter addressed by a wealthy and neurotic businessman to his mistress on holiday in Rome. For years the mistress's husband Robert, with the narrator's connivance, has been drugging himself with the sedative chloral hydrate, although the narrator has secretly arranged for the dose to be progressively reduced in order to 'cure' him of his dependence. The narrator faces imminent disgrace with the discovery that for nine years he has been enriching himself with funds stolen from the estate of young Edward Burden's father, of which he is the sole trustee. Burden is soon to be married, at which point control of the estate will revert to him and the narrator's peculations will be discovered. When Burden confesses to the narrator that he has been having an affair and wants to tell his fiancée, the narrator replies sadistically, 'My good Edward, you are the most debauched person I have ever met' (*CDOUP*, 132). Edward borrows money from the narrator, and in the end the narrator finds himself 'reprieved' by the discovery that Edward has used the money to renegotiate the terms of his arrangement with his fiancée's solicitors so that the narrator's stewardship of the Burden estate will remain secret. The story ends when the narrator asks his mistress to choose between living with him, in which case he will work to repay the money he has embezzled, or rejecting him, in which case he will carry out the romantic *Liebestod* he has been threatening, by drinking poison from a ring.

Ford identified the story as one his grandfather, the Pre-Raphaelite artist Ford Madox Brown, used to tell about 'one of his wealthy Greek art patrons who, imagining himself to be ruined, wrote a letter to his mistress to the effect that he was going to commit suicide rather than be detected in a fraudulent bankruptcy and then found that bankruptcy could be avoided' (1932: 194). An early sketch of the novella prior to Conrad's involvement survives in the form of an unpublished typescript draft (at the Kroch Library, Cornell University) of 'The Old Story' by 'Daniel Chaucer', one of Ford's favourite pseudonyms. During the time of the collaboration, Ford described the story to his wife Elsie as 'awful piffle', although at least one early letter from Ford to Elsie is written in similar tones of morbidly romantic self-consciousness (Saunders, i. 65, 210). The opening lines of the story are also used in the first verse of Ford's poem 'Views'.

For the most part, Conrad's collaboration was apparently in the form of suggestions given viva voce to Ford, who would read his manuscript aloud. In a copy of the novel inscribed to George T. *Keating, Ford claimed that several pages of chapter 1 (from the paragraph beginning 'The stress of every secret emotion' to the first mention of the mouse) were contributed by Conrad; and a three-page manuscript in Conrad's hand corresponding to the ending of chapter 5 (from the paragraph beginning 'Even to the dullest of men') is in the Keating Collection at Yale University (Keating, 348, 448). The typescript and several pages of galleys used for the *transatlantic review* are now in the Naumburg Collection at Princeton University.

Jessie Conrad claimed that her husband thought the story 'too trivial to be reprinted' but that he agreed to Ford's request to avoid an argument (*JCKH*, 152). Baines dismissed the story as 'a worthless trifle' (351); and Najder calls it 'a piece of kitsch produced for money' (*JCC*, 321), though it never produced any income. Critics have been unable to take it seriously beyond brief mention when the collaborations are described, or in connection with Ford's efforts to revive his contact with Conrad after the *First World War. One exception is Eric Meyer's '"The Nature of a Text": Ford and Conrad in Plato's Pharmacy', *Modern Fiction Studies*, 36 (1990), 499–512.

Netherlands East Indies. The area exploited by the Dutch East India Company, roughly equivalent to present-day Indonesia, provided a cultural and geographical setting for many of Conrad's novels and stories, including *Almayer's Folly*, *An Outcast of the Islands*, *Lord Jim*, *Victory*, *The Rescue*, 'Karain', 'The Lagoon', 'The End of the Tether', and 'Because of the Dollars'. Conrad's own direct experience of the region was limited to a week he spent in Muntok (Bangka Island, off the east coast of Sumatra) following the sinking of the *Palestine* in March 1883, and to the last four months of 1887, when he made four trading trips as first mate in the *Vidar* (an English vessel owned by a wealthy Singapore Arab), stopping briefly in ports of call in *Borneo (now Kalimantan) and Celebes (present-day Sulawesi), before signing off the ship in January 1888. Although Semarang, Surabaya, and Macassar are used as settings in his novels and stories, there is no evidence that Conrad ever visited Surabaya or Macassar, and he spent only ten days in the Semarang roads in June 1887 with a mysterious back injury, awaiting transport to hospital in *Singapore.

The history of the East Indies is one of waves of immigration from the west: Hindu traders and Buddhist monks were followed by Arab traders in the 14th and 15th centuries, so that by the end of the 16th century *Islam was the dominant religion in most of the islands. The first European traders were the Portuguese and Spanish, followed by the Dutch in 1596 and the English in 1610. When the Dutch East India Company (the Verenigde Oost-Indische Compagnie, or VOC) was dissolved in 1799, control of the Indies was assumed by the Dutch government, although it was interrupted from 1811 to 1815 when Sir Stamford Raffles responded to *Napoleon's annexation of the Low Countries by extending British control over the Dutch territories. After the Napoleonic Wars ended, Dutch and English spheres of influence were defined by the Treaty of 1824, in which the Dutch recognized British sovereignty over Singapore and agreed to share Borneo along lines corresponding roughly with the current boundary between Indonesia and Malaysia. In practice, European control was often vague or nonexistent, and some of the more remote parts of the islands witnessed a continuing commercial rivalry in which British traders often operated in areas officially under Dutch control.

The effects of these successive waves of traders and colonists are evident in Conrad's novels: the 'original' inhabitants, like the Dyaks of Borneo or the Alfuros of *Heyst's *Samburan, have been driven inland or into the outlaw condition of piracy;

trading is in the hands of Malays (often Bugis or Wajo immigrants from the east) and local Arabs, while English traders like Tom *Lingard operate out of Singapore in the Dutch sphere of influence. Both the English and the Dutch used local conflicts as a means of increasing their influence: Sarawak, on the western coast of Borneo, became 'English' when James *Brooke, a British subject, was named its rajah as a reward for helping local rulers; and in *The Rescue*, Conrad describes the efforts of Tom Lingard to restore the exiled Pata Hassim to power in Wajo (Celebes) after he was ousted in a coup sponsored by the Dutch. Conrad understood that 'Trading . . . was the occupation of ambitious men who played an occult but important part in all those national risings, religious disturbances, and also in the organized piratical movements on a large scale which, during the first half of the last century, affected the fate of more than one native dynasty and, for a few years at least, seriously endangered the Dutch rule in the East' (*The Rescue*, 68).

The main centres of Dutch administrative power were the cities along the northern coast of *Java: the capital, Batavia (modern Jakarta), where the 'Great White Ruler' (*An Outcast of the Islands*, 179) lived and where *Almayer spent his boyhood; Semarang, *Stein's place of residence in *Lord Jim*, and where the future Mrs Almayer is taught to be civilized in a convent; and Surabaya, where Axel Heyst in *Victory* does his banking and rescues *Lena from *Schomberg's hotel. The corresponding base of English influence was Singapore, where Lingard does his military shopping in *The Rescue* and later sends Nina Almayer to school. In the more remote parts of the archipelago, the effective or relative control of the Dutch and the British was often uncertain. The 'Shore of Refuge' on the southwest coast of Borneo is one such no man's land, where, in *The Rescue*, Jörgenson hides the fugitive Belarab from the Dutch authorities and Lingard prepares his armed expedition against Wajo. When Mr Travers, on a voyage designed to 'expose' the Dutch colonial system, is stranded in the midst of the anti-Dutch forces assembled by Lingard, he expects help from Singapore, or from a passing British or Dutch warship, and finally announces that 'This coast . . . has been placed under the sole protection of Holland by the Treaty of 1820 [*sic*]' (147). In the event, Lingard's loyalty to Hassim is sacrificed to his feelings for Mrs *Travers, even though, in England, class barriers would have made their relationship socially impossible. After the fiasco dramatized in *The Rescue*, Lingard discovers a secret entrance to a river in Dutch territory on the east coast of Borneo, and founds the settlement of *Sambir, where for years he enjoys a monopoly of the local trade under the local management of his Dutch protégés Almayer and Peter *Willems, who both trained as clerks working for 'Mr Hudig' in Macassar. When Willems betrays Lingard's secret passage and brings the Arabs into Sambir, Almayer, although himself a Dutchman, runs up the Union Jack as a way of invoking the protection of the power behind Lingard. When Almayer tells Lingard of Abdulla's hoisting a makeshift Dutch flag at the other end of the settlement, Lingard exclaims indignantly, 'But, hang it all! . . . Abdulla is British!' (*An Outcast of the Islands*, 179); and when the Arab intruders demand obeisance to the flag, the 'Chinaman' Jim-Eng refuses: 'Said he was an Englishman, and would not take off his hat to any flag but English' (182). Almayer not only trades in rattan and gutta-percha but is also involved in gun-running; when his Arab rivals betray him to the authorities in Batavia, a Dutch frigate is sent to investigate.

Critics have often assumed that *Patusan in *Lord Jim* is simply Sambir under another name, and indeed the various trading factions in Patusan resemble those of Sambir; but as Hans van Marle has shown ('The Location of Lord Jim's Patusan', *Notes and Queries*, NS 15 (1968), 289–91), the settlement is located not in east Borneo but in north-west Sumatra, where Stein's trading firm 'was the only one to have an agency by special permit from the Dutch authorities' (227). Like Lingard, *Jim is an English interloper in Dutch ter-

ritory, and his nemesis arrives in the form of Gentleman *Brown, another colonial 'straggler' (224).

Multiple nationalities also play an important role in *Victory*: the English-educated Swede Axel Heyst becomes a trader for the Dutch firm of Tesman Brothers in Surabaya, but after rescuing the Englishman Morrison from the Portuguese authorities in Dili (on Timor), he enters into a partnership to establish the Tropical Belt Coal Company on the remote island of Samburan somewhere in the Java Sea. When the company fails, its liquidation is listed in both *Amsterdam and *London. The round island is so remote as to be a world unto itself, although the native Alfuros on its western coast build a barrier to protect themselves from the 'sudden invasion of Chinamen' (179) imported to work the mine. The villains are similarly mixed: Mr *Jones is ostensibly English, Pedro is Colombian, and Martin Ricardo's nationality is never specified. The fact that Samburan is in Dutch territory appears of no importance, except that Heyst's banking and social ties are all with Java rather than Singapore.

For more details about the role of the Netherlands East Indies in Conrad's fictions, see Florence Clemens, 'Conrad's Malaysian Fiction' (unpublished Ph.D. dissertation, Ohio State University, 1937); Sherry, *CEW* (although he conflates Patusan with Sambir); and especially G. J. Resink, 'The Eastern Archipelago under Joseph Conrad's Western Eyes', in *Indonesia's History between the Myths: Essays in Legal History and Historical Theory* (The Hague: W. van Hoeve, 1968), 305–23, 385–7.

Newbolt, Henry [John] (1862–1938; knighted 1915), originally a barrister and later the author of rousing nautical and patriotic ballads, naval historian, and editor of the *Monthly Review* (1900–4). Henry Newbolt first met Conrad in 1904. Shortly after, in 1905, the two men became involved with each other in an unexpectedly difficult way. A committee member of the Royal Literary Fund, Newbolt was in May of that year appointed co-trustee with William *Rothenstein to administer the £500 grant awarded to Conrad from the Royal Bounty Special Service Fund. He engaged with the prickly Conrad in a month-long negotiation about procedures for paying the award and then acted as cautious purse-holder until April 1906 (see also GRANTS AND AWARDS). Once the heat of early negotiations had died down, Conrad corresponded more equably with Newbolt, enquired about writing for the *Monthly*, and read Newbolt's *The Year of Trafalgar* (1905) as part of his research into Admiral Nelson's life for 'The Heroic Age', a *Mirror of the Sea* paper. Their correspondence lapsed in 1906 when Newbolt's trusteeship came to an end. The latter recalled his involvement with Conrad's financial crisis of 1905 in his *My World as in my Time: Memoirs of Sir Henry Newbolt, 1862–1932* (Faber, 1932), excerpted in *JCIR*, 115–20.

New Historicist approaches. The term 'New Historicism' was coined by the American critic Stephen Greenblatt in his book *Renaissance Self-Fashioning: From More to Shakespeare* (1980). The critical approach it signifies depends upon a parallel reading of literary texts and their contemporary historical texts. Traditionally, the approach of literary critics to history has been to treat it as a background or context for the literature it produced. In this way, literary texts were regarded as emerging from a particular historical moment to assume an ahistorical, timeless existence. In essence, New Historicism reinstates the historical moment in the interpretation of a literary text by emphasizing its inextricable and intimate relationship with this moment. The paradox inherent in the term 'New Historicism' thus extends to its approach. Rather than privileging or 'fore-grounding' the literary text, by treating the historical text as 'background', as is usually the case, New Historicists give equal weight to literary and non-literary texts so that they are seen to be mutually revealing: historical sources and texts now provide co-texts rather than contexts. To achieve this, New Historicists regard history as a narra-

tive that, like literature, organizes experience into meaningful patterns. Although history is, thus, denuded of its objectivity, it is not simply seen as fictional; rather, non-literary historical documents are seen to behave in a similar manner to literary documents. Erasing the dividing line between history and literature means that a literary event, such as the staging of a Shakespeare play, can be read as a political act, while an historical event, such as the coronation of Elizabeth I, can be interpreted in terms of its staging as a dramatic spectacle. Typically, a New Historical approach juxtaposes a literary text with contemporary non-literary texts in order to read the former in terms of the latter and, by treating the historical sources with parity, attempts to read the text anew by detaching it from the weight of previous criticism. A series of dialogues is seen to define the relationship between history and literature, in which the literary work is related to the period of its composition, and to the histories of the reader (which will differ depending upon nationality, gender, and age). The focus of New Historicism tends to be ideological: its concern with patriarchy, state power, and colonialism allies it to other theoretical positions such as feminism, Marxism, and post-colonialism, on which it freely draws.

In his essay 'Henry James: An Appreciation' (1905), Conrad relates fiction and history thus: 'Fiction is history, human history, or it is nothing. But it is also more than that; it stands on firmer ground, being based on the reality of forms and the observation of social phenomena, whereas history is based on documents, and the reading of print and handwriting—on second-hand impression. Thus fiction is nearer truth. But let that pass. A historian may be an artist too, and a novelist is a historian, the preserver, the keeper, the expounder, of human experience' (*Notes*, 17). Brook Thomas approaches Conrad's fictional presentation of colonial history in 'Heart of Darkness' by way of this claim in order to establish a contemporary non-literary co-text and to claim Conrad himself as a proto-New Historicist. Reminding us that 'no history can relate the past as it really was because our histories will always be influenced by our present perspective' and that 'the rhetoric the historian adopts shapes and determines his representation of the past' ('Preserving and Keeping Order by Killing Time in Heart of Darkness', in Murfin (ed.) 1989: 239), Thomas then contrasts the 19th-century view of history, as an organic and continuous progress through time, with the discontinuities apparent in Conrad's presentation of history in 'Heart of Darkness': *Kurtz clearly unsettles the historical narrative of enlightened progress, while the novel's indirect narrative structure eschews any clear, unbiased view of history by advertising itself as a structure.

Thomas next sees the text's chronological and perspectival disruptions as symptomatic of the impossibility of stating its truth directly, and he grounds this in the revisionist view of history as Euro-centred, paradoxically forced on the West by its own imperialism. This decentring of the Western historical narrative has deconstructive consequences as *Marlow's tale about Kurtz is transformed into a tale about himself and as the narrative about the colonized 'Other' comes to reveal more about the colonizer. A key issue for New Historicists is whether the literature of a period subverts or helps to sustain the prevailing ideologies of its time. In this respect, Conrad's tale of a journey to Africa, which is simultaneously a journey into Europe's past and a journey into each human being's primitive psyche, 'subverts prevailing European values, offering a "counter-memory" to the belief in rationality and progress. On the other hand, by merely inverting the narrative Conrad remains within a Eurocentric logic' (248). The tale is caught in a historical bind: it helps to reveal the horror at the heart of darkness while serving to keep it at bay. Shifting his focus, Thomas points out that the *work ethic both provides the saving power which keeps the horrors of *colonialism at bay and sustains the colonial enterprise through the enforced labour of the Africans. But whereas Marx, who viewed history as the history of labour, expounded human experience in order to change it, Conrad's novelist-as-historian expounds it to very different effect, becoming, in Thomas's reading, its 'preserver' and 'keeper' by pointing to its prehistoric, unchanging nature.   AHS

Nietzsche, Friedrich (1844–1900), the first philosopher to confront fully the consequences of Western man's loss of faith in religion. In his 'Introduction' to Thus Spake Zarathustra (1883–5), Friedrich Nietzsche announced: 'God is dead! . . . I teach you the Superman.' If there is no transcendent God, then, according to Nietzsche, man chooses his own values, morality, truth, and standards of every kind to meet his needs. To this end, Nietzsche advocates an absolute scepticism towards past conventions and inherited concepts which, he claims, have enslaved mankind. In their appeal to a common denominator, these concepts have created generalized 'herd values' for the mass of mankind and quashed the individualism that marks the great man. Thus, for instance, Nietzsche, himself the son of a Lutheran minister, attacked the institution of Christianity for fostering such values as compassion and loving one's neighbour, believing that adherence to them diminished and dishonoured one's selfhood, one's élan vital. An extension of this is Nietzsche's belief in the Übermensch or Superman, a human being whose natural impulses have not been repressed by the (artificial) codes and values of society. Such emphasis upon individual rules makes Nietzsche antagonistic towards the Kantian Categorical Imperative, while his belief in a 'will to power' sets him at odds with his early mentor and fellow sceptic, Arthur *Schopenhauer. Whereas Schopenhauer believed that the 'Will' was the source of man's unhappiness, Nietzsche sees it as the source of man's strength. In essence, his approach, which radically questions the foundations of Western thought, criticizes all appeals to shared belief and traditional sanction, and advocates that the great man should be a law unto himself.

Edward *Garnett's article on Nietzsche in the *Outlook* (8 July 1899) prompted Conrad to comment disparagingly on 'The mad individualism of Niet[z]sche' (*CL*, ii. 188). Further insight into Conrad's attitude can be gained from his correspondence with the Belgian novelist and poet André Ruyters, who had sent Conrad his volume *Le Mauvais Riche* (1907), in which he tries to reconcile the ideas of Christianity with those of Nietzsche. Writing to thank Ruyters for the volume in March 1913, Conrad says: 'The problem of life is just not so simple. I suspect you know that as well as I do. The great minds (I am thinking of Nietzsche) don't notice it. Their job is not to look too closely' (*CL*, v. 204). In 'The Crime of Partition' Conrad is even more critical, associating Nietzsche with the morality of 'Germanic Tribes' (*Notes*, 124–5), placing him within the context of the Poles' hatred of their German oppressors. Nonetheless, from the outset, critics recognized Nietzschean strains in Conrad's work. For example, a contemporary review of *The Inheritors*, in the *Daily Chronicle* of 11 July 1901, pointed to a connection between the Fourth Dimensionists and Nietzsche's *Übermensch*, and, when commenting on the book's reviews in a letter to Ford Madox *Ford of 23 July 1901, Conrad himself refers to the 'overman' as 'what Niet[z]sche's phil*phy* leads to' (*CL*, ii. 344).

Seeking a philosophical basis for Conradian scepticism, more recent critics have seen him as adopting either a Schopenhauerian stance (Kirschner 1968) or a Nietzschean stance (Erdinast-Vulcan). While Conrad's work may be open to such elements of Nietzschean thought as the idea that morality is a fragile human construction perpetuated to enslave mankind, that the *Übermensch* offers an alternative to the herd mentality, and that the universe is empty and meaningless, these convictions are often voiced by characters who do not enjoy their author's sympathy. Examples include the crew's feelings for James *Wait in *The Nigger of the 'Narcissus'*, which renders them 'highly humanised, tender, complex, excessively decadent . . . as though we had been over-civilised, and rotten' (139);

the *Professor's claim, in *The Secret Agent*, that 'the great multitude of the weak must go . . . Every taint, every vice, every prejudice, every convention must meet its doom' (303); and the character of Heyst senior, in *Victory*, the 'destroyer of systems, of hopes, of beliefs', who proclaims that 'men love their captivity. To the unknown force of negation they prefer the miserably tumbled bed of their servitude' (175, 220). Erdinast-Vulcan argues that, rather than representing the 'decline' which critics (following Moser) have identified, Conrad's late novels reflect his view that the world is merely a text, a fiction, lacking ultimate truth, and thus represent his 'surrender to the radical scepticism of the Nietzschean outlook which he had managed to keep at bay throughout the best part of this creative career' (145). But, while Conrad's fiction clearly flirts with Nietzsche's ideas, its overall vision resists being defined as Nietzschean. For example, in *The Nigger of the 'Narcissus'* Conrad steadfastly resists the temptation to transform Captain Alistoun into a Nietzschean *Übermensch*. Instead, whilst deprecating the divisive effect of the crew's pity for Wait, Alistoun is shown to share something of their sympathy. In this he recalls Conrad's belief stated in 'A Familiar Preface' that 'the world, the temporal world, rests on a few very simple ideas; so simple that they must be as old as the hills. It rests notably, among others, on the idea of Fidelity' (*A Personal Record*, p. xix). See also Edward Said, 'Conrad and Nietzsche', in Sherry (ed.) 1976: 65–76.   AHS

Nigger of the 'Narcissus', The. This sea story of 1897 can, despite its international cast of characters, safely be called Conrad's first English novel: not only is the *Narcissus* sailing home to *England, but the novel's celebration of life at *sea is simultaneously a celebration of the traditions of its creator's adopted homeland. Henry *James's view is typical of the affection in which the novel is held: '*The Nigger of the "Narcissus"* is in my opinion the very finest & strongest picture of the sea and sea-life that our language possesses—the masterpiece in a whole class' (*PL*, 36).

The narrative begins in Bombay harbour as the crew of the *Narcissus* gather in the forecastle on the evening of her homeward voyage to London. Amid the uproar, *Donkin arrives. Having fled the brutality in his previous (American) ship and now destitute, he quickly preys on the crew's sympathies. At the roll-call, he is cheeky to Mr Baker, the first mate, much to the amusement of other crew members. The roll-call is thrown into further confusion by the late arrival of James *Wait, the 'nigger' of the title, who introduces himself by his surname, which Baker interprets as a command. As the crew settle down to sleep for the night, Singleton, 'a lonely relic of a devoured and forgotten generation' (24), tightens the ship's brake as she moves slightly in the breeze. The new and potentially disruptive forces aboard the ship, represented by Donkin and Wait, are thus offset by an image of stability and duty. When Wait asks Singleton about conditions aboard the *Narcissus* he is told: 'Ships are all right. It is the men in them!' (24)

The *Narcissus* begins her journey the following morning and is soon being driven southwards by the monsoon winds. The subversive influence of James Wait upon the cheerfulness and unity of the sailors is soon evident. He manifests symptoms of illness, and the forecastle is virtually transformed into his sick bay, from where he tyrannizes over the crew who, ironically, wait upon him hand and foot, 'base courtiers of a hated prince' (37). Wait's complaints about the quality of his food lead Belfast to steal the officers' Sunday pie from the galley, an act which shakes confidence in the rule of law and authority on board. Wait's subsequent ingratitude leads Belfast to attack him, but Wait's coughing quickly puts an end to the assault. Donkin's insubordination continues, earning Mr Baker's rough justice, as a result of which he loses one of his front teeth. But in the forecastle he alone is openly abusive to James Wait, and yet Wait appears to like him. The crew suspect that they are being duped: 'all our certitudes were going' (43). In order to counteract Wait's influence upon the crew, Mr Baker

suggests to the captain that he be moved from the forecastle, and a sick bay is eventually fitted up for him, where the crew continue to wait on him.

When the *Narcissus* runs into stormy seas off the Cape of Good Hope, the crew abandon the forecastle just before the ship is toppled onto her side and the forecastle flooded. They want to cut the masts in an attempt to right the ship, but Captain Allistoun refuses their demands, a decision accepted by all except Donkin. A rescue party succeeds in rescuing the trapped Wait despite enormous difficulties. For their pains, they are merely berated by Wait for not having rescued him sooner. While the crew tend to expect the worst, Mr Baker believes that the ship is beginning to right herself. Even now, Wait tyrannizes over the crew: as Belfast shivers because he has put his own oilskin and coat over him, Wait complains about not being able to breathe. But Podmore typifies the resilience of the crew in the face of the storm when he succeeds in making coffee for the men, declaring defiantly: 'As long as she swims I will cook' (84). When the Captain orders the exhausted crew to 'Wear ship!' they respond heroically and get sail on the ship. Gradually the *Narcissus* rights herself and begins to steer. In direct contrast to Donkin, who is reprimanded for not pulling his weight, Singleton stands at the helm, where he has remained throughout this ordeal. Fittingly, the tribute to him is simple: 'He steered with care' (89).

The crew's efforts to put sail on the ship and to pump her out prove successful, and she at last steers properly. Only after these duties are performed do the men return to the forecastle, now 'a place of damp desolation' (94). As the *Narcissus* speeds northwards, the crew recount their ordeal in self-aggrandizing stories, while Donkin, with his 'picturesque and filthy loquacity' (101), works on the crew's steadily growing sense of their own importance to demonstrate to them how undervalued they are. The crew continue to congregate around Wait who, with Donkin officiating, is invested with the status of 'a black idol' (105), and held up by Donkin as an example of how authority can be outwitted. Donkin admits to Wait that he is using him as an example to incite the crew and, for his part, Wait confesses that he has feigned illness on previous ships and got away with it.

After Donkin's departure, Wait wakes from a tormented vision to find that Podmore has brought him a pot of tea. Spurred on by a vision of his own, the evangelical Podmore, in the grip of religious fervour, attempts to save the soul of James Wait, whose cries for help are answered by the three officers. Wait, clearly terrified by this reminder of his impending death, proclaims himself fit enough to recommence work immediately, but Allistoun refuses, accusing him of shamming his illness throughout the voyage. Mayhem ensues during which Donkin throws a belaying pin at Captain Allistoun, an action from which the crew dissociate themselves, telling him: 'We ain't that kind!' (123). In the forecastle afterwards, Singleton introduces the superstitious idea that Wait will only die in sight of land. Donkin is now rejected by the crew. When Captain Allistoun addresses the crew the following morning he criticizes their inefficiency—'your best is no better than bad' (134)—before forcing the unwilling Donkin to replace the belaying pin.

The final chapter opens with the crew shown washing clothes, in a calm which the narrative exploits to offer a summary of attitudes towards Jimmy Wait through the first-person narrator ('we'). There is no longer any doubt among the crew that James Wait is dying. Although they continue to dissemble to him, they are no longer taken in: 'He was so utterly wrong about himself' (139). Belfast's devotion to Jimmy reveals all the dangers of unthinking sympathy, as he is belligerent towards anyone suspected of not feeling deeply enough about the dying man. When the island of Flores is sighted, Donkin, whose only prospect ashore is 'a bad pay-day' (147), recalls Singleton's superstition that Wait will die in sight of land, and he visits Wait to rob him. As Donkin prepares to leave the cabin, Wait dies in a final effort to remonstrate with him. Wait's death robs the crew of an important bond—the

'respectable bond of a sentimental lie' (155) —and they become increasingly short-tempered with each other, earning the rebuke of Belfast, who is especially affected by Wait's death. Mr Baker conducts the funeral service during which Wait's corpse seems reluctant to leave the *Narcissus* and has to be assisted by Belfast before it slides off its planks and into the sea. Almost immediately, a breeze springs up, as if to confirm Singleton's superstition.

Running before a fair breeze, the *Narcissus* enters the English Channel a week later. The eulogistic description of *England that follows, during which it is described as 'the great flagship of the race' (163), celebrates its maritime history while reflecting the upbeat mood of the returning sailors. Nonetheless, the image of land becomes progressively disenchanting as the *Narcissus* enters and is towed up the River *Thames: the sense of freedom and light of the sea are replaced by the clutter and grime of an industrial landscape. Such images culminate in the claim that 'She had ceased to live' (165), as the *Narcissus* docks. Excited and dressed in ill-fitting shore clothes, the crew come together the next day at the shipping office to receive their pay and seem out of place on land. The opposition between land and sea values is starkly presented through the pay-clerk's contempt for the crew. Singleton, for instance, is dismissed as 'a disgusting old brute'. Significantly, Donkin, in better clothes and possessed of an 'easy air' (169), is the only one with whom the clerk converses. Given a bad discharge by Captain Allistoun, Donkin renounces the sea and is in turn renounced by the crew. After his departure, they go off to the Black Horse public house for a farewell drink. On the pavement outside the Mint, the same sailors who weathered the storm off the Cape seem strangely vulnerable. The narrator does not join them. Instead, as he watches them disappear, the narrative concludes with his tribute to his erstwhile shipmates, a valediction tempered by his comment: 'I never saw them again' (172).

In response to Edward *Garnett's suggestion, in the wake of *Almayer's Folly*

(1895) and *An Outcast of the Islands* (1896), that he write a novel of the *sea, Conrad began work on 'The Rescuer', telling Garnett in March 1896: 'You have driven home the conviction and I *shall* write the sea-story' (*CL*, i. 268). But this particular 'sea-story' was soon abandoned and, instead, in mid-1896, Conrad began *The Nigger of the 'Narcissus'*, which he described to T. Fisher *Unwin as 'a respectable shrine for the memory of men with whom I have, through many hard years lived and worked' (*CL*, i. 308–9). The novella's initial subtitle, 'A Tale of the Forecastle', advertises Conrad's focus as the group of able-bodied and ordinary seamen who constitute the crew of the *Narcissus*, those quartered in her forecastle: it is to them that Conrad constructs this 'shrine'.

The Nigger of the 'Narcissus' recounts the story of a homeward voyage of the *Narcissus* from Bombay to England. The tale is grounded in the reality of Conrad's own personal experiences in the *Narcissus* and other ships. The real *Narcissus* was registered at Greenock in 1876, and her record shows that she made approximately one overseas voyage per year. Conrad joined her as second mate for the journey home, which began in Bombay on 5 June 1884 and ended in Dunkirk on 16 October. (The 'Agreement and Account of Crew' of the *Narcissus* is held at the National Maritime Museum, Greenwich.) During the voyage, one crew member, Joseph Barron, died on 24 September 1884. G. *Jean-Aubry recalled a comment made by Conrad shortly before his death: 'I do not write history, but fiction, and I am therefore entitled to choose as I please what is most suitable in regard to characters and particulars to help me in the general impression I wish to produce. Most of the personages I have portrayed actually belonged to the crew of the real *Narcissus*, including the admirable Singleton (whose real name was Sullivan), Archie, Belfast, and Donkin. I got the two Scandinavians from associations with another ship' (*LL*, i. 77).

The story was serialized in the *New Review* (August–December 1897). On 9 August 1897 Conrad wrote to R. B. Cunning-

hame *Graham, urging him to read the book rather than the serial version, because 'The instalment plan ruins it' (*CL*, i. 372). Following its final serial instalment, Conrad appended an 'Author's Note' that was subsequently printed as a pamphlet on various occasions before appearing as a *'Preface' to the American (Doubleday, Page) edition of the novel in 1914. The 'Preface' was first printed in England in the Heinemann edition of 1921. Many critics have come to view this 'Preface' as Conrad's artistic manifesto.

On 29 July 1897, a copyright edition of just seven copies of *The Nigger of the 'Narcissus': A Tale of the Forecastle* was printed in Britain by Heinemann: five of these were deposited in British libraries, and the remaining two were presented to Mrs Richard Garnett, Edward's mother, and to W. H. *Chesson. The novel was published by Dodd, Mead in America on 30 November 1897 as *The Children of the Sea: A Tale of the Forecastle*. In a letter to Alfred A. Knopf of 20 July 1913, Conrad referred to the American title as 'absurdly sweet' (*CL*, v. 257). He consented to the change of title under protest, commenting in an inscribed copy of *The Children of the Sea*: 'The argument was that the American public would not read a book about a "nigger"' (Smith, 8). The original title was subsequently restored. British publication followed on 2 December 1897, when the novel was issued by Heinemann.

Early reviewers were exercised by the lack of incident in the story, but they praised its realism. Anticipating such criticism, Conrad wrote to Garnett in November 1896: 'As to the lack of incident, well —it's life. The incomplete joy, the incomplete sorrow, the incomplete rascality or heroism—the incomplete suffering' (*CL*, i. 321). W. L. Courtney's review in the *Daily Telegraph* compared the novel with Stephen *Crane's *The Red Badge of Courage* (1895), saying that Conrad 'has determined to do for the sea and the sailor what his predecessor had done for war and warriors' (*CCH*, 86). Many years later Conrad wrote of the two books, in his introduction to Thomas Beer's *Life of Stephen Crane*:

'Stephen Crane dealt in his book with the psychology of the mass—the army; while I—in mine—had been dealing with the same subject on a much smaller scale and in more specialized conditions—the crew of a merchant ship, brought to the test of what I may venture to call the moral problem of conduct' (*Last Essays*, 95). The modern quality of the novel was also quickly recognized. An anonymous review in the *Daily Chronicle* pointed to its modern qualities, noting that it was unique among sea tales: 'There may be better tales of the sea than this, but we have never read anything in the least like it' (*CCH*, 89). This same reviewer heralded the critical debate to follow by advertising the novel's narrative method: 'the value of the book lies in the telling, and not in the events of the tale' (ibid. 90). Subsequent debate has focused on Conrad's 'violation' of a consistent point of view in the novel's movement between omniscient narration and first-person narration.

Few critics have failed to comment upon the unstable narrative authority in *The Nigger of the 'Narcissus'*. The narrating voice shifts in the novel between a detached, third-person, omniscient narrator and a first-person narrator who is one of the crew. Thus, the narration begins in the third person, then gives way to a first-person plural narrator ('we') who is a member of the crew (for instance, he takes part in the rescue of Wait during the storm), and, after the voyage, switches into the first-person singular: 'As I came up I saw [Charley's mother]' (170). To complicate matters, even within this continuum there are additional varieties of narrative authority, as when the omniscient perspective is suddenly restricted. For instance, after he has stolen Wait's money, Donkin's face is described as having 'a pink flush—perhaps of triumph' (154). The use of such variable perspective in the novel has provided one of the cruxes of Conradian criticism. Guerard, for instance, criticizes Conrad's 'violation' of point of view: 'We need only demand that the changes in point of view not violate the reader's larger sustained vision of the dramatized experience. . . . But

serious violation does occur twice: when we are given Wait's broken interior monologues' (107). But Watt, while recognizing that Conrad's handling of point of view 'involves many difficulties', defends his right to flout 'the modern shibboleth of a consistent point of view' (1980: 102).

Recent criticism has also examined the novel's presentation of politics and *race. Fleishman (1967) considers its status as a political tale and, citing as evidence Conrad's comments about 'Well-meaning people' who represented sailors as 'whining over every mouthful of their food; as going about their work in fear of their lives' (25), argues: 'This scorn of well-meaning "liberals" and of whining workers generates the plot and makes this Conrad's most didactic political tale.' He goes on to say that, in our age, it is difficult not to read *The Nigger of the 'Narcissus'* as a parable of both class conflict and racial attitudes: 'one can see the Negro, James Wait, and the rabble rouser, Donkin, as co-conspirators for the support of public opinion' (129). Miriam Marcus explores the metaphorical implications of Wait's fatal disease in 'Writing, Race, and Illness in *The Nigger of the "Narcissus"*', *The Conradian*, 23: 1 (1998), 37–50.

Wait's very appearance reflects both the dilemma he poses to the crew and the contradiction in their own attitudes. For instance, despite his size, Wait is physically infirm. Furthermore, the racism that underlies the crew's derogatory description of Wait as a 'nigger' is continually frustrated by their deference and servility towards him. That 'nigger' is a term of abuse is clear from Wait's (similarly racist) reaction to it: 'You wouldn't call me nigger if I wasn't half dead, you Irish beggar!', he says to Belfast (79–80). Hawthorn claims that Wait provides a focus for Conrad's own ideological contradictions and uncertainties and those of his age: 'Conrad's artistic instinct led him to choose the figure of the Negro as the central character in this work with good grounds, for if anything symbolized contradiction and unclarity in the late Victorian popular mind it was the figure of the Negro' (1990: 102). Recent editions published in the Oxford World's Classics, Penguin, and Everyman series (edited respectively by Jacques Berthoud, Cedric Watts, and Allan Simmons) provide excellent introductions and useful apparatus.

In a letter of 1912 to the American collector John *Quinn, in which Conrad offered him the 194-page manuscript of the novel for £80, he described *The Nigger of the 'Narcissus'* as 'the story by which, as a creative artist, I stand or fall, and which, at any rate, no one else could have written. A landmark in literature' (*CL*, v. 145). The manuscript is now held in the Rosenbach Museum and Library, Philadelphia. An incomplete typescript is at Colgate University.   AHS

Noble, Edward (1857–1941), a seaman-friend whose literary ambitions Conrad encouraged at a time in 1895 when he himself was first gaining a foothold in the literary establishment. Conrad commented at length upon Edward Noble's first manuscript and passed it on to Edward *Garnett in an effort to help the aspiring writer towards publication. His letters to Noble of 1895 contain one of the earliest expressions of his already demanding artistic creed, with its emphasis upon the importance of the 'poetic faculty', the strenuous quest for *le mot juste*, and the need for the writer's fidelity to his independent vision: 'Everyone must walk in the light of his own heart's gospel. No man's light is good to any of his fellows. That's my creed—from beginning to end' (*CL*, i. 252, 253). Noble's *Shadows from the Thames* (1900) was the first of his many published works.

Nordau, Max [Simon] (né Südfield; 1849–1923), of Hungarian birth. Max Nordau studied medicine and established himself as a physician in Budapest and (from 1886) in Paris. In 1898, Conrad received from Nordau, via R. B. Cunninghame *Graham, a written tribute probably referring to *The Nigger of the 'Narcissus'* and wryly commented that 'Praise is sweet no matter whence it comes', although he added: 'He *is* a Doctor and a Teacher—no doubt about it' (*CL*, ii. 121). This praise came from a cultural pundit now chiefly remembered as 'the Jeremiah of *fin de siècle*' (Watts and Davies, 27) and author of *Degeneration* (Heinemann, 1895; first published in Berlin in 1892 as *Die Entartung*), a pseudo-scientific diagnosis of cultural decline and cult book of the 1890s. Dedicated to Cesare *Lombroso, Nordau's work extended Lombroso's study of degeneracy as manifested in criminal types into a sensationally apocalyptic and often lurid diagnosis of the decline of 'modern' European artistic culture, which he styled the *fin de siècle*, an epoch 'in which all suns and stars are gradually waning, and mankind with all its institutions and creations is perishing in the midst of a dying world' (3). Most of this epoch's artistic 'creations', Nordau avers, are symptoms of mental degeneration in their creators, who are in turn products of a culture marked by atavistic regression, entropy, exhaustion, and rampant egomania. Nordau's heated castigation of Tolstoy, Ibsen, *Nietzsche, *Zola, Huysmans, Baudelaire, Wagner, and the exponents of *impressionism ('The degenerate artist who suffers from *nystagmus* or trembling of the eyeball' (27)) is accompanied by a full array of apocalyptic imagery—the Dusk of the Nations, the Twilight of the Gods, and the Modern Antichrist—in order to suggest that the *fin de siècle* is but a short step away from *fin du globe*: we stand, Nordau warned his readers, 'in the midst of a severe mental epidemic; of a sort of black death of degeneration and hysteria, and it is natural that we should ask ourselves on all sides: "What is to come next?"' (537).

As many commentators have pointed out, *Degeneration* can itself be regarded as symptomatic rather than diagnostic, an instance of the hysterical egomania and cloudy mysticism that it purports to find elsewhere. Despite (or sometimes because of) this, Nordau's work had a considerable effect upon an 1890s literary culture preoccupied with his question of 'What is to come next?' Some of the decade's more monstrous literary births—Bram Stoker's Dracula, H. G. *Wells's Dr Moreau, and Conrad's *Kurtz—bear testimony to the influential power of Nordau's figurings of a degenerate modernity, as William Greenslade shows in *Degeneration, Culture and the Novel, 1880–1940* (CUP, 1994). For his part, Conrad seems to have responded to *Degeneration* with characteristic ambivalence. On the one hand, he is unlikely to have given much credence to a work—possibly the cult-book described as 'idiotic' in *Chance* (184)—that sought to consign an entire community of late 19th-century European writers to the asylum, and in 1913 he would have nothing to do with Warrington *Dawson's pressure upon him to join the Fresh Air Art Society, a society inspired by Nordau-like principles and devoted to restoring a bracingly extrovert health to modern literature. Nevertheless, there is some evidence to suggest that Conrad, as an analyst of 'excessively decadent' states of mind in the crew of the *Narcissus*, or of forms of grotesque atavistic regression in his colonial and urban fiction, was attuned to the apocalyptic force of *Degeneration* and adapted it for ends that were sometimes symbolic and sometimes satiric. In 'Conrad, Nordau, and Other Degenerates: The Psychology of *The Secret Agent*', *Conradiana*, 16 (1984), 125–40, Martin Ray usefully summarizes previous work on Conrad's possible indebtedness to Nordau in the course of proposing that *Degeneration* is an important source for character types in *The Secret Agent*, including the anarchist group as well as the 'degenerate' *Stevie. Ray's final conjecture that Nordau may also have provided Conrad with 'a *perspective* on his subject' (139) and encouraged a type of reflexive irony that allows for pity (and even self-pity) seems more tendentious. See also O'Hanlon, 48–52, and Griffiths's chapter on 'Nordau's *Degeneration* and Lombroso's Atavism in *Heart of Darkness* and "Falk"' (153–78).

Northcliffe, Lord. Alfred Charles William Harmsworth (1865–1922), first Baron (1905), later Viscount (1918) Northcliffe, a powerful newspaper magnate and pioneer of mass circulation journalism, first met Conrad in 1916. Having founded the *Daily Mail* (1896) and the *Daily Mirror* (1903),

Northcliffe had by that date also added to his vast empire *The Times*, whose editorial columns he used to further his political ideals and ambitions. Although Ford Madox *Ford stated (*JCPR*, 139) that in *The Inheritors* (1901) Northcliffe had been represented as one of the 'powers of evil' (evidently in the character of Fox), Conrad's later personal contacts with the man produced a markedly different response. His friendship with 'the Napoleon of Fleet Street' developed during the *First World War and was no doubt cemented both by their mutual admiration of Jane *Anderson and by Conrad's fascination with Northcliffe's power as press lord, shaper of policy during the war, and Director of Enemy Propaganda. Friendship with Northcliffe also made Conrad the object of the magnate's largesse and patronage: in March 1918, Northcliffe rewarded him with 250 guineas for his *Daily Mail* article 'Tradition' (*Notes*), and in that same month, when Conrad was elected to the Athenaeum Club, the newspaper magnate paid his £40 membership fee. On the occasion of Northcliffe's death, Conrad commented that he had found him 'absolutely genuine': 'He had given me one or two glimpses of his inner man which impressed me . . . After all that fortune was not made by sweating the worker or robbing the widow and the orphan' (*LCG*, 194). See also Reginald Pound and Geoffrey Harmsworth, *Northcliffe* (1959).

Nostromo. The title-character of Conrad's novel of 1904, an Italian and former seaman who has been persuaded by his fellow Italian Giorgio *Viola to give up the sea and better himself in *Sulaco, is introduced fleetingly in the early chapters. He has been hired by Captain *Mitchell to be captain of the Oceanic Steam Navigation Company's lightermen and caretaker of its jetty. Partly modelled on the charismatic *Corsican sailor Dominique *Cervoni whom Conrad had known in *Marseilles and celebrated in *The Mirror of the Sea*, the Nostromo or 'Capataz de Cargadores' of the first half of the novel offers the occasion for a sceptical enquiry into the mystique of popular heroism and hero-worship. Hungry for prestige, the apparently 'incorruptible' Nostromo becomes a willing servant of the San Tomé mine as its 'universal factotum' (44), culminating in his involvement in helping to remove the silver from Sulaco and his 'famous' ride to Cayta to save the country from rebel forces. Later in the novel, when Nostromo realizes that the treasure of his famous name is false coin and that he has been manipulated by his masters, he undergoes a painful birth into a condition that he can only describe as a 'betrayal' (418). Becoming a private citizen intent on securing the hidden silver for himself, he offers the most literal example of the corruptive power of 'material interests'. For details of Nostromo's later career, Conrad was indebted to a second main source in the form of Frederick Benton Williams's *On Many Seas: The Life and Exploits of a Yankee Sailor* (1897). This work offered him access to the story of a seaman Nicolo, an audacious thief and rascal who, entrusted with large amounts of silver by a Panamanian steamship company, proceeded to hide and appropriate the treasure for himself and, like Nostromo, grow rich very slowly.

As a functionary and talisman for the San Tomé mine, Nostromo can be glimpsed fleetingly at several points in the early narrative, but his three extended appearances are in the concluding phases of the novel's three parts. At the end of Part I, he appears on horseback at the town festival and crystallizes the mood of heady intoxication just after the inauguration of the railway in Sulaco. At the end of Part II, Nostromo is alone in the waters of the dark Golfo Placido, swimming back to a Sulaco whose fate, like his own, is precariously balanced. The novel's final climax is reserved for his death and Linda Viola's mourning of her dead lover. Although some critics have argued for Nostromo as the novel's main centre of attention, Conrad himself denied his importance, asserting in one of his letters that he 'is nothing at all—a fiction—embodied vanity of the sailor kind—a romantic mouthpiece of "the people" which (I mean the "people")

frequently experience the very feelings to which he gives utterance. I don't defend him as a creation' (*CL*, iii. 175). Among his many functions, Nostromo is a valuable aid to the reader, serving as an emblematic coda for each of the novel's changing phases and having an exemplary force in finally embodying the fate of the entire country.

Some of these emblematic functions are signalled in the the character's varying names. The word *nostromo* is the Italian for 'boatswain' (which was the character's position when he arrived in Sulaco). However, another meaning emerges from Mitchell's mispronunciation of the Italian *nostro uomo* or 'our man', which Teresa Viola complains of as being 'properly no word' (23) and takes to symbolize Nostromo's desire to be a favourite with the English in Sulaco. Nostromo's full name is Giovanni (or Gian') Battista Fidanza. His given name Giovanni Battista ('John the Baptist') holds the potential for considerable irony since, as Watts explains, 'John the Baptist prepared the way for Jesus Christ and was thus the inaugurator of the Christian era; Nostromo prepares the way for the control of Sulaco by the economic imperialists and is thus an inaugurator of its capitalistic era' (1993: 195), or, as Martin *Decoud puts it, he is the 'active usher-in of material implements for our progress' (191). In the last part of the novel, Nostromo, now a private citizen, calls himself Captain Fidanza, so retaining an Anglicized version of the Spanish 'Capataz' in conjunction with his birth name, *fidanza* being the Italian word for 'trust' or, in certain contexts, 'misplaced trust'.

As in *Lord Jim*, the Conradian interest in the growth of legendary reputations as signalled by the bestowal of titles and names forms part of a wider probing of the mystique of popular heroism, in this case through a character whose very being rests upon outward recognition and the prestige conferred by titles. The sardonic description of Nostromo at the town festival reminds the reader of just how many titles the Italian has acquired: 'The circle had broken up, and the lordly Capataz de Cargadores, the indispensable man, the tried and trusty Nostromo, the Mediterranean seaman come ashore . . . rode slowly towards the harbour' (130). On the one hand, Nostromo lives among a community always ready to confer upon him the status of popular hero and whose fetishization of the 'Capataz de Cargadores' Nostromo himself shares and treats as a form of treasure. But, on the other, he is the servant of a capitalist enterprise in which titles are used in order to assert ownership over its servants and identify their functions. When, at one point, Nostromo, in debate with Teresa Viola, heatedly claims that a 'good name' is 'a treasure', she finds a simpler truth behind his fine metaphor and responds, 'They have been paying you with words. Your folly shall betray you into poverty' (257), so reminding him that in latter-day Sulaco words themselves have been commodified and may turn out to be little more than false coin. As Parry aptly comments, although Nostromo may not figure as the novel's central character, his name functions as a 'totalising' metaphor, 'signifiying essential themes in the fiction's myriad political and ethical discussions' (102). See also Watt 1988: 65–9; Hampson, 145–52; and Josiane Paccaud-Huguet, 'Nostromo: Conrad's Man of No Parentage', *The Conradian*, 18: 2 (1994), 65–75.

Nostromo: A Tale of the Seaboard. Described by Conrad as his largest canvas and often considered his masterwork, *Nostromo* (1904) is one of the most experimental novels of the early Modernist period. This panoramic epic is set in the imaginary South American republic of *Costaguana, with the majority of events taking place in *Sulaco, capital of the Occidental Province, during a period of history from the mid-1880s to 1900. *Nostromo* centres upon the effects of 'material interests', as symbolized by the San Tomé silver mine, in simultaneously shaping the country's modern destiny and the largely unhappy lives of those caught up in historical events.

Charles *Gould, of English descent, returns to the country of his birth, Costaguana, to take up ownership of the San Tomé silver mine left to him by his late father. A member of a family whose two previous generations have worked and died in the country, Charles sets aside his father's warning that the mine is cursed and commits himself to making it a working success as a way of bringing 'rational' political and economic evolution to a country plagued by a long series of civil wars and rapacious governments. With him, he brings a new wife, Emilia *Gould, and the financial sponsorship of a wealthy American backer, Mr Holroyd.

As the renovated mine becomes increasingly profitable and attracts more foreign developers, there eventually comes a point when Gould makes a bold and dangerous move to secure its long-term security by throwing the power of the mine behind the presidency of Don Vincente Ribiera, an enlightened dictator who is mandated 'to establish the prosperity of the people on the basis of peace at home' and by honouring foreign debts (141). During a period of some eighteen months, Sulaco enjoys considerable political stability: the growing influence of the mine during this period encourages the building of a railway in order to open up Sulaco to the wider world. Ribiera's presidency suddenly comes to an end when the head of armed forces, General Montero, and his brother Pedrito stage a coup in Santa Marta and force Ribiera to flee to Sulaco, where mob rule is already spreading. Rioting Monterist rebels try to seize the San Tomé mine, and Sulaco is cut off for a fortnight. Now desperate, Gould decides to ship the silver away from Sulaco in a lighter to a part of the coast where it can be picked up by a European vessel and transported to safety.

The task is given to two men. One of these, Martin *Decoud, is a young man who (like Gould) has returned to the Costaguana of his birth after several years living abroad. Falling in love with his childhood girlfriend Antonia Avellanos, the sceptical Decoud has surprised himself by becoming centrally involved in the country's political crisis and is already responsible for the proposal that Sulaco should secede from the republic of Costaguana.

The other man chosen to save the silver is *Nostromo, the Capataz de Cargadores and a 'universal factotum' (44) of the mine, who feeds off the prestige he earns as a popular hero and sees the expedition as one of his most desperate exploits. These unlikely partners transport the silver by boat across the Golfo Placido but, their lighter having been involved in a collision with a rebel troopship, they decide to hide the silver on an island, the Great Isabel. Decoud remains there alone, while Nostromo swims back to Sulaco. Now disillusioned and feeling that he has been betrayed by his masters, Nostromo undertakes one final dangerous mission with his 'historic' journey to Cayta to persuade General Barrios to relieve Sulaco, the success of which puts an end to the rebellion and enables Decoud's plan for secession to be realized.

The later stages of the novel show the country entering its 'modern' phase, enjoying a rapidly developing material progress, with a new president, Don Juste Lopez. Whatever success is claimed for the country in Captain *Mitchell's long commentary in Part III, chapter 10 is, however, rendered ambiguous by events themselves. Decoud, we learn, has been unable to withstand his utterly isolated situation on the Great Isabel island and has committed *suicide. Other major characters have died, or, like the Goulds, are the victims of a mine that has become 'a monstrous weight' (221). Moreover, there are signs of unrest in the country. While the Occidental Republic enjoys its wealth, the rest of Costaguana suffers poverty and oppression. Antonia Avellanos believes that the country should reunite, but others argue that such a move would be likely to meet with resistance from the foreign interests that now effectively control the country; the Archbishop of Sulaco, Father Corbelàn, predicts another revolution if Sulaco refuses to acknowledge its responsibilities to the poor of Costaguana.

During this phase of later history, Nostromo, having severed his connection with the mine and now known as Captain Fidanza, fosters the belief that the silver has been sunk and gradually enriches himself

from the hidden treasure. When a lighthouse is built on the Great Isabel, Nostromo arranges that Giorgio *Viola be made lighthouse keeper so that he may continue his visits under pretence of courting one of Viola's daughters. He is engaged in a second duplicity, since while being betrothed to Giselle Viola, he is increasingly attracted to her sister Linda. On one of his clandestine visits to the buried treasure, Nostromo is mistaken by Giorgio for an intruder and fatally shot. On his deathbed he confesses his theft to Mrs Gould, who guards his secret and does not wish to hear about the location of the silver in the belief that it should be 'lost for ever' (560). The novel closes with the spectacle of Linda Viola mourning the dead Nostromo whose 'genius . . . dominated the dark gulf containing the conquests of treasure and love' (566).

Conrad began composing *Nostromo* at the end of 1902, at this time envisioning it as a short story 'belonging to the "Karain" class of tales' (*CL*, ii. 448) and, in January 1903, as something 'silly and saleable' (*CL*, iii. 4). By 23 March, he seemed fairly confident that the work would take the form of a 60,000- or 70,000-word novella (*CL*, iii. 27), with a subject 'concerned mostly with Italians' in a South American republic, and with Giorgio Viola envisaged as one of the leading characters (*CL*, iii. 34). Reporting on 4 June that 'Nostromo grows; grows against the grain by dint of distasteful toil . . . but the story has not yet even begun' (*CL*, iii. 40), Conrad probably realized that the die was cast and that he was committed to a work of far greater proportions than he had originally conceived. Between September and December 1903, when the 'atrocious misery of writing' (*CL*, iii. 61) was compounded by depression and illnesss, Conrad's letters began to employ images more appropriate to a novel of existential ordeal: 'I . . . am absolutely out of my mind with worry and apprehension of my work. I go on as one would cycle over a precipice along a 14 inch plank. If I falter I am lost' (*CL*, iii. 80). By December, when he had written 566 manuscript leaves and was still eight months away from completion, he groaned: 'It has been a most disastrous year for my work. If I had written each page with my blood I could not feel more exhausted at the end of this twelvemonth' (*CL*, iii. 100).

The climax of Conrad's distress occurred in the first three months of 1904 when, with the serialization of *Nostromo* having begun in January, he was very far from completion. At this time, mounting debts after the failure of his bank, growing tiredness, and a complicated series of illnesses meant that he had to rescue his financial position by writing more saleable items in parallel with *Nostromo*. Thus at one point in early 1904, he was writing the novel during the day, dictating reminiscences to Ford Madox *Ford in the evening, and also cobbling together a one-act play out of an earlier short story. Afflicted by gout and nervous depression, Conrad had to rely on Ford in other ways. The latter seems to have composed—or at least acted as scribe for—a section of *Nostromo* (manuscript pages 588–603; a fragment of Part II, chapter 5). In late June, approaching the end of composition, Conrad complained of a lack of energy: 'I work desperately but slow—much too slow for the situation. . . . I dare do nothing. Either my soul or my liver is very sick. . . . And I am tired, tired, as if I had lived a hundred years' (*CL*, iii. 147). In an effort to complete the novel, his only recourse during the last month of composition in August 1904 was to work eighteen hours each day. He finally finished a draft of the novel in a 'half delirious state' (*CL*, iii. 164) during a frantic weekend at the end of this month, when writing was completed at the home of G. F. W. *Hope in Stanford-le-Hope, Essex. For a detailed account of the chronology of composition see Mario Curreli, 'The Writing of "Nostromo"', in Jabłkowska (ed.) 1979: 47–67.

Nostromo was serialized in *T.P.'s Weekly* from 29 January to 7 October 1904. In September 1904, Conrad began revising the serial version in preparation for book publication. He considerably expanded Part III, in particular amplifying the Nostromo–Giselle relationship, while also making some cuts in the earlier parts of the novel. The World's Classics edition of *Nostromo*, ed. Keith Carabine (OUP, 1984), usefully makes available the original serial ending. Conrad continued to tinker with the text of *Nostromo* in later life, with the result that the first edition contains descriptive passages missing from later editions. The book version of the novel, dedicated to John *Galsworthy, was published by Harper on 14 October in Britain and 23 November in America.

While Conrad's later 'Author's Note' identifies some of the main sources out of which *Nostromo* grew, it does not anticipate their prodigious scope and variety or the process by which they came together. Whether or not Conrad ever fleetingly visited Central or South America is still an open question, but even if he did, it would hardly have afforded him more than glimpses of the continent. Conrad's 'Author's Note' hints at important sources apparently far removed from any obvious South American connection. For example, the novel's subject activated personal memories of his charismatic friend Dominique *Cervoni from Conrad's *Marseilles years in the mid-1870s. Similarly, parts of the novel are rooted in the emotional hinterland of Conrad's youthful years in *Poland, leading some Polish critics to claim that in *Nostromo* a South American country functions as a disguise or displacement for historical and political concerns belonging essentially to 19th-century *Poland. More specifically, Conrad's 'first love' as an adolescent in Poland seems to have provided a model for the novel's Antonia Avellanos ('Author's Note', p. xiv). This source also lends weight to the supposition that Antonia's lover, Martin Decoud, may refract some of the traits of the younger Frenchified and sceptical 'de Korzeniowski' of his *Marseilles days. *Nostromo* is, however, mainly the product of Conrad's prodigiously varied reading. At one extreme, he found elements of a pattern for Nostromo's later career in a colourful and popular story, *On Many Seas: The Life and Exploits of a Yankee Sailor* (1897) by Frederick Benton Williams; at another extreme, he discovered germinating hints for episodes and characters in some of his favourite French writers— Gustave *Flaubert, Guy de *Maupassant, and Anatole *France. In response to the enormous challenge of creating a fictional South American country needing to be named and populated, and given a local colour, geography, and history, Conrad consulted a number of historical memoirs (see READING), more orthodox histories like the classic accounts of Spanish involvement in South America by W. H. Prescott, works by his friend R. B. Cunninghame *Graham, and contemporary newspapers. The ways in which Conrad incorporated his immense reading in the final novel has an important critical bearing on its final character and structure. The 'Author's Note' playfully introduces *Nostromo* as a documentary history based on the *History of Fifty Years of Misrule*, a work written by one of the novel's characters, Don José Avellanos. This play with the boundaries of fiction and history does serve to emphasize *Nostromo*'s character as a book largely constructed out of other books of a very mixed nature and one that, in Fogel's words, often conducts 'a dialogue with a number of energetic works usually not mentioned' (97). Looking back on the novel's structure many years later, Conrad described it as 'an achievement in mosaic' (to Edmund *Gosse, 11 June 1918), presumably emphasizing the variety and discreteness of its parts but also suggesting the synthetic quality of its final design. Cedric Watts (1995: p. xvii) uses the image of the palimpsest or 'layered' creation to evoke the way in which some of the characters can be found to bring with them 'traces' of a former life in other widely different works. Other commentators have described Conrad's handling of source materials by drawing upon metaphors of fusion and assimilation, although Fogel makes the interesting point that given the diversity produced by modern imperialism in Costaguana, Conrad may also have exploited his various sources as a 'variegate hodgepodge held together only by his own openly arbitrary force as a novelist' (98). For extended studies of *Nostromo*'s sources, see Sherry's *CWW*, 147–201, Hervouet, 83–95, and Watts (1990 and 1993).

Although Conrad later described the initial reception of *Nostromo* as 'the blackest possible frost' (*CL*, v. 139), he was probably referring to its lack of widely popular impact, since the positive reviews far outweighed the negative. Nevertheless, of all of his novels *Nostromo* brought home to him the chastening recognition that in the competitive world of the Edwardian book market good critical reviews did not necessarily guarantee commercial success, or, as an *Independent* reviewer succinctly put it, 'Conrad fascinates a circle of the elect, but bores others' (9 March 1905, 557). Among the second group were the uncomprehending *Black and White* reviewer who complained, 'I do not understand . . . what truth of life Mr. Joseph Conrad intended to represent when he decided to write *Nostromo*', and the *Review of Reviews* reader's dismissal, 'Then there is Mr. Conrad's *Nostromo*, though it is hardly up to the level of his previous work' (*CCH*, 166). But the most disheartening review must have been the *Times Literary Supplement*'s which, after upbraiding Conrad for having made 'a novel of a short story' in which 'the drama is overwhelmed by the machinery', went on to pronounce that 'we think that the publication of this book as it stands is an artistic mistake' (ibid. 164). As usual it was Edward *Garnett, Conrad's friend and mentor, who, in his first signed review of Conrad, penned a sensitive and uncompromising vindication of *Nostromo* in the *Speaker* and helped to create the taste by which Conrad could be understood. He claimed the novel as an achievement in high art 'which is not in the power of any English contemporary novelist to touch', greeting 'the working unity and harmonious balance of his fascinating gifts' (ibid. 174), a view increasingly shared by 'a circle of the elect', including Arnold Bennett who in 1912 judged *Nostromo* to be 'the finest novel of this generation (bar none)' (ibid. 161).

Garnett's judgement was largely to prevail during the period 1945–60 when

Conrad's works became a subject of critical study in British and North American academe. Four influential British critics, F. R. Leavis, Douglas Hewitt, Arnold Kettle, and E. M. W. Tillyard, pressed the claims of *Nostromo* as Conrad's finest achievement, at the same time asking questions or expressing reservations that made up the terms for a first stage of serious debate. Leavis (1948) and Hewitt (1952) championed the novel in the process of downgrading *Lord Jim*, although Leavis tempered his admiration for *Nostromo* as one of the great novels of the English language with the reservation that 'the reverberation of *Nostromo* has something hollow about it; with the colour and life there is a suggestion of a certain emptiness' (200). In *An Introduction to the English Novel*, ii: *Henry James to the Present Day* (Hutchinson University Library, 1953), Kettle, a leading *Marxist critic, expressed his admiration for the moral honesty and political insight of what he took to be Conrad's greatest work, but with the not unexpected reservation, which many later Marxist critics have shared, that 'it is the failure to recognise in its full theoretic and moral significance the process of imperialism that leads to the element of mistiness in *Nostromo*' (78). In *The Epic Strain in the English Novel* (Chatto & Windus, 1958), Tillyard took an appreciative interest in the novel's expansive geography, tragic theme, and politics as evidence of its epic scope, judging it finally to be a 20th-century classic and offering the acute aside that *Nostromo* may be about western Europe rather than South America. In the United States, the novelist and critic Robert Penn Warren ambitiously hailed the novel as the writer's masterwork in an essay finely responsive to Conrad's concerns and attitudes as a philosophic novelist. He also inaugurated a debate on the vision of historical development implied by the novel's ending, claiming that the society presented in the closing pages is preferable to that at the beginning ('*Nostromo*', *Sewanee Review*, 59 (1951), 363–91). Disagreeing with this judgement on the novel's ending, Albert J. Guerard balanced high praise for the novel with two severe judgements: that Nostromo was 'the lost subject of the book' (204) and that *Nostromo* markedly fell off in quality in its last third: 'What . . . would be lost if we simply lopped off those last two hundred pages?' (204).

Nostromo's arrival as a modern 'classic' has ensured its centrality in subsequent general studies of modern fiction and Conrad criticism. As a work that, in Berthoud's words, 'has acquired some notoriety as a novel that one cannot read unless one has read it before' (1978: 97), it has also attracted a number of short critical studies written with the general reader in mind. The chapter in Berthoud's own study serves the student and general reader well in isolating a debate structure underlying the novel's obliquities of presentation. Of the other short studies, Watt's (1988) is the most accessible in its sampling of sources, techniques, characters, and criticism, while Watts's two introductions (1990 and 1993) are flexibly organized, wide-ranging, and informative (in providing, for example, helpful synopses of sources, maps of Sulaco, and chronologies).

There has been no lessening of interest in *Nostromo* in post-1960 decades, although the kinds of preoccupation and terms of debate brought to it are very different from those of the 1945–60 period. The dramatic shifts in critical practice from the 1970s onwards have brought to centre-stage postmodern interests in the ideologies of reading, *deconstructive approaches, post-colonial and Marxist theory, and *narratology, all of which have entailed a corresponding shift in the objects of attention: from notions of mimesis to the self-referential or culturally produced; from the humanistic concern with individual characters to the phenomenology of voice and how fiction 'voices' itself; from the apparent stability of the author-centred *œuvre* to the text as encoding culturally significant faultlines, internal contradictions, and aporias. As a novel that, in Fleishman's words, 'marks the fulfilment of Conrad's political imagination' (161) and engages directly with the processes of modern history and the emergence of high capitalism, *Nostromo* has taken its place as one of the most important test-cases or sounding-boards for contemporary political readings and other forms of critical practice.

A good introduction to these practices for the beginning reader is Jordan's collection of essays in the Macmillan New Casebook series, an anthology designed for the late 20th-century classroom and helpfully prefaced with an 'Introduction: Reading Conrad'. Jordan's selection of extracts rightly introduces two important critics who have helped to shape the character of contemporary approaches to *Nostromo*. Fredric Jameson's ambitious metacommentary in *The Political Unconscious: Narrative as a Socially Symbolic Act* (Methuen, 1981) has been particularly influential in its fusion of materialist and post-structural methodologies. *Nostromo* figures centrally in Jameson's attempt to devise a Marxist narrative grammar by which to approach the literary text in an age of high capitalism and in order to probe the text's formal structures as symptoms of the containment and suppression of history by ideology. A second form of metacommentary, Edward Said's *Beginnings: Intention and Method* (Baltimore: Johns Hopkins University Press, 1975), brings together refined deconstructive practice and historical analysis in an approach to *Nostromo* as 'a novel about political history that is reduced, over the course of several hundred pages, to a condition of mind, an inner state' (110) and has similarly influenced a generation of younger critics. For a trenchant political reading of *Nostromo* strongly influenced by Jameson's approach, see Parry's *Conrad and Imperialism: Ideological Boundaries and Visionary Frontiers* (1983). The contents of the Conrad-based journals, *Conradiana* and *The Conradian*, reflect the main changes in post-1970 critical practice and offer a wide variety of approaches to *Nostromo*, including post-colonial, reader-response, *Bakhtinian, and *feminist.

The manuscript of *Nostromo* is held at the Rosenbach Museum and Library, Philadelphia. The largest extant typescript is at the Beinecke Rare Book and Manuscript Library, Yale University, together with manuscript and typescript fragments, including fifteen pages in Ford's hand. A second major typescript (equivalent to Part III, chapters 1–7) is at the Henry E. Huntington Library, San Marino, California. The manuscript and typescript of the 'Author's Note' are both at Yale.

'Note on the Polish Problem, A'. Written in June 1916 for circulation at the British Foreign Office, this memorandum was drafted at the request of his friend Józef H. *Retinger, who had previously helped to awaken Conrad's concern for the political fate of wartime *Poland and persuaded him to join forces in internationalizing the Polish problem. Retinger worked closely with Conrad on the essay, claiming to have supplied him with a rough draft. It was received at the Foreign Office on 15 August 1916, and a few days later the two men met with George Russell Clerk, head of the Foreign Office's War Department, for discussion. Drawing the main thrust of its argument from Retinger's memorandum *La Pologne et l'équilibre européen* (1915), Conrad's note asserts the value of 'Polonism' as an 'advanced outpost of Western civilisation': 'Polonism has resisted the utmost efforts of Germanism and Slavonism for more than a hundred years. Why? Because of the strength of its ideals conscious of their kinship with the West. Such a power of resistance creates a moral obligation which it would be unsafe to neglect' (*Notes*, 138, 137). It goes on to argue that in order to secure permanent stability in Europe, a strong Poland—under the joint protectorate of Britain and France, and 'with the fullest concurrence of Russia' (140)—should be re-established. Officials at the Foreign Office responded with varying degrees of scepticism. Clerk pointed out that the proposals could only be acted upon if they were to come from Poland and met with the agreement of all Polish parties. Other officials found the memorandum 'impossible', 'impractical', and a 'hopeless solution', with Lord Grey, the Foreign Secretary, judging: 'Quite impossible. Russia would never share her interest in Poland with Western Powers' (quoted in *JCC*, 417). The memorandum first appeared as a privately printed pamphlet (1919) before being collected in *Notes on Life and Letters*. The manuscript, dated June 1916, is held at the Rosenbach Museum and Library, Philadelphia; the typescript received at the Foreign Office (Public Records Office) and a second typescript (private collection) survive.

Notes on Life and Letters. This volume collects many of Conrad's essays, reviews, and other occasional pieces from the period 1898–1920 and, with the posthumous *Last Essays*, brings together most of his non-fiction writings. In 1920, Richard *Curle was delegated to collect the texts of these essays and reviews, which by mid-July of that year were ready for Conrad to revise. Substantially completing this task by late September, he finished the 'Author's Note' on 9 October. The volume was published by J. M. *Dent in Britain on 25 February 1921, and by Doubleday, Page in America on 22 April 1921.

As early as 1905, Conrad had conceived of a volume that would bring together his existing occasional writings under the tentative title *Action and Vision* (*CL*, iii. 200), although the plan came to nothing. When the suggestion for such a collection was made by J. M. Dent in 1919, Conrad was initially diffident, but eventually came to regard the project as a means of establishing the canon of his works for posterity and a necessary act of valediction before his death—'the leaves fall, the water flows, the clock ticks' ('Author's Note', p. vi). His own description of the volume's contents as presenting 'Conrad literary, Conrad political, Conrad reminiscent, Conrad controversial' (pp. v–vi) accurately reflects the loose unity of the collection. The first group embraces several essays on such writers as Henry *James, Hugh *Clifford, Frederick *Marryat, James Fenimore *Cooper, Alphonse *Daudet, Anatole *France, Guy de *Maupassant, Stephen *Crane, and *Turgenev; the second a number of essays on the *Polish question; the third several recollections of his earlier Polish youth and *sea life; and the fourth essays on contemporary events and issues, including such subjects as the *Titanic disaster of 1912, other maritime accidents, and *theatre censorship.

The volume occasioned E. M. Forster's famous comment, made in a *Nation and Athenaeum* review of March 1921, that 'These essays do suggest that he [Conrad] is misty in the middle as well as at the edges, that the secret casket of his genius contains a vapour rather than a jewel; and that we need not try to write him down philosophically, because there is, in this particular direction, nothing to write' (*CCH*, 346). While Forster's charge has prompted a number of general defences of Conrad's fiction, J. H. Stape is largely alone in testing its more specific validity in relation to *Notes on Life and Letters*. In 'Establishing Identities: Exile and Commitment in Conrad's Non-Fiction Prose', *English Literature in Transition, 1880–1920*, 31 (1988), 53–63, he chooses a fruitfully different direction, arguing that the real value of the essays lies in what they reveal of complex balances and tensions between Conrad's 'Life' and 'Letters', and in his social position as a writer generally. Notably, he suggests that 'Conrad's non-fiction prose represents an attempt to reconcile the exile necessarily required by artistic endeavor with commitment to the community and to daily life' (53), so allowing him to remain faithful to a conception of writing essentially activist in nature. Moreover, he posits that Conrad, as a man and writer who stood at the margins of native British traditions, found in his occasional essays a way of establishing an identity as 'an artist-spokesman fulfilling the public role of middle-class man of letters' (54). See also Andrzej Busza, 'The Rhetoric of Conrad's Non-fictional Political Discourse', *Annales de la Faculté des Lettres et Sciences Humaines de Nice*, 34 (1978), 159–70.

O

'Observer in Malaya, An'. Following an enthusiastic review of *Tales of Unrest* in the *Academy*, its editor, C. L. Hind, asked Conrad to review *Studies in Brown Humanity* (1898) by Hugh *Clifford, then a British Resident in Malaya. Conrad received the book on 15 April 1898 and sent his review on the next day. It was published in the *Academy*, 53 (23 April 1898), 441–2, and revised for inclusion in *Notes on Life and Letters*. While generous to Clifford's services as a public servant abroad and to the sureness of his knowledge of Malay life, Conrad was mainly lukewarm about his literary gifts and concluded with the unvarnished judgement that 'to apply artistic standards to this book would be a fundamental error in appreciation' (60). This review, soon followed by an article on Conrad's work by Clifford, led to a meeting between the two men and an exchange of letters in which they debated the merits of their differing literary constructions of the Malay world. They later became enduring friends. No pre-publication documents are known.

'Ocean Travel'. Conrad composed this essay during his voyage to *America in the *Tuscania* (21 April–1 May 1923), and on arriving in New York sent the manuscript to Richard *Curle, who oversaw its publication in the London *Evening News* (15 May 1923). It was collected in slightly revised form in *Last Essays*. One of a group of late essays concerned with the evolving psychology and history of travel, this one pursues the changed ethos of modern seafaring, a topic already taken up in Conrad's two essays on the *Titanic*. Its original title, 'My hotel in mid-Atlantic', points to both the older Conrad's increasingly sentimental attachment to the vanished myths of the age of the sailing ship and his sardonic disapproval of changes that, to his eyes, had made the modern passenger vessel a 'marvel of applied science' on its technical side (35) and 'an unpleasantly unsteady imitation of a Ritz Hotel' in its social atmosphere (36). David *Bone, Conrad's friend and master of the *Tuscania*, observed with some surprise that during his voyage Conrad was unimpressed by the 'manifest efficiency' of the liner's equipment and the new breed of seaman: 'Strangely, for one so understanding and cultured in himself, it was the "gentility" and apparent confidence of the new ship manners that seemed to disquiet him the most' (*Landfall at Sunset: The Life of a Contented Sailor* (Duckworth, 1955), 157). The manuscript, dated 29 April 1923, is held at the Harry Ransom Humanities Research Center, University of Texas at Austin.

Olmeijer, William Charles (1848–1900), a *Java-born Dutch Eurasian whom Conrad met on four visits to Berau in east *Borneo between September and December 1887. Olmeijer provided the prototype for Kaspar *Almayer, a leading character in Conrad's first two novels, *Almayer's Folly* and *An Outcast of the Islands*. As Conrad later wrote in *A Personal Record*, 'if I had not got to know Almayer pretty well it is almost certain there would never have been a line of mine in print' (87). While Conrad here seems extravagantly generous to a real-life source, it is nevertheless probable that he was 'haunted' by the man whose surname he appropriated for his fictional character. Some of the reasons for this fascination may be discerned in the type of personality who emerges from the pages of *A Personal Record*—an exiled outcast 'lost to the world' (88), a 'Borneo Bovary' (Watt 1980: 51), and the victim of a disablingly fixed idea. Research has revealed that from Olmeijer, Conrad also borrowed the outline of a personal history: Olmeijer was related by marriage to Captain William *Lingard (who figures in the Malay novels as Tom *Lingard); went to Berau around 1869 to manage Lingard's trading post; built himself a large house which he neglected; and, like Almayer, boasted of being the only possessor of a flock of geese on the east coast of Borneo. The historical Olmeijer seems also to have been preoccupied with thoughts of gold: he went inland from Berau in 1877 to prospect, and applied for his last prospector's permit in 1890.

As Conrad openly acknowledged in *A Personal Record*, hints derived from the original Olmeijer and his plight were subjected to a freely inventive process. One necessity imposed upon him was that of devising a slow and lingering death for a protagonist in *Almayer's Folly* whose historical prototype was still living when the novel was published. He also admitted to draping the Dutchman in 'the royal mantle of the tropics' and 'the very anguish of paternity' (88). Again, the family unit over which Olmeijer presided was quite different from that of the fictional Almayer. The latter is a Caucasian of Dutch parentage, a country-born colonial, and not a Eurasian like the original Olmeijer; Mrs Almayer is a Malay of Sulu origin, and not—like her historical original—the Eurasian daughter of a Dutch colonial soldier; where the Almayers have a single daughter, the Olmeijers parented a total of eleven children, many of whom did not survive beyond adolescence. Such differences have the obvious effect of heightening Almayer's plight as an isolated derelict. They also serve to emphasize the racial differences between the Almayers and make the family unit itself a microcosm and representative test-case. Crucial to this test-case is the fact that Almayer, unlike his historical counterpart, is involved in a racially mixed marriage, from which there arises a complex of issues relating to miscegenation. As Gail Fraser has suggested, the treatment of mixed-race marriage in Conrad's fiction generally is original and provocative, having an important representative function in revealing 'the logic of racial myths and phobias—the imaginative and emotional constructs that inform imperialist ideology' ('Empire of the Senses: Miscegenation

in *An Outcast of the Islands*', in Carabine *et al.* (eds.) 1993: 127). Thus, Conrad's boldness in highlighting the flinty issue of Almayer's mixed marriage—and its effects upon his wife and daughter Nina—goes some way to making *Almayer's Folly* and *An Outcast of the Islands* original social-problem novels with a distinctively colonial character.

One Day More. Conrad drafted this one-act stage adaptation of his short story 'Tomorrow' (*Typhoon*) in *London during early 1904, while at work on *Nostromo* and in close contact with Ford Madox *Ford. Composition was finished in late February, and by late March a French version by an unknown hand was also in existence. Conrad sent the first draft to Sidney *Colvin, who suggested revisions and became a prime mover in its eventual production, and later drafts to J. M. *Barrie, Arnold *Bennett, Beerbohm Tree, and George Bernard Shaw, who was responsible for cutting and trimming the play. All of the pre-production revisions by Conrad and others seem to have been devoted to making the play's methods of exposition more subtle, thus necessitating the cutting from its early drafts of a fish-hawker, who had replaced the barber of the original short story, in order to make its five scenes a proper dramatic correlative for what Conrad in a stage-note called 'the varied groupings of the characters with the consequent changes in the mental and emotional atmosphere of the situation' (Kirschner (ed.) 1990: 271).

At the point where contracts were being signed in 1905, questions about the play's authorship arose and gave rise to divergent explanations from Conrad and Ford. The latter had had links with the original 'Tomorrow' story, and there is further evidence—in the form of a 43-page playscript of the first part of *One Day More* in Ford's hand (held at Cornell University)—to suggest that he may have been involved in the play's composition as well. However, Kirschner's examination of Ford's manuscript (ibid. 267–9) leads him both to conclude that the play is essentially Conrad's and to support the latter's version of its provenance as explained to Colvin: 'The facts are that Hueffer a good and dear friend helped me by spending a whole day in taking out the dialogue of [the] story in a typewritten extract for my use and reference. The play, as can be shown by the MS, has been written entirely in my own hand . . . I've always looked upon the play as mine' (*CL*, iii. 236).

Mounted by the Stage Society, the play ran for one evening and two matinee performances as an afterpiece to Laurence Alma-Tadema's *The New Felicity* at the Royalty Theatre, London, between 25 and 27 June 1905, with leading parts taken by Constance Collier and J. L. Estrange. Although Conrad was heartened by praise from Shaw and other friends, he generally felt that his first exercise in playwriting had not been a success and quickly returned to finishing *Nostromo*. *One Day More* was staged only occasionally during Conrad's lifetime. Its first French performance was apparently a version by P.-H. Raymond-Duval which opened at the Théâtre des Arts in Paris on 14 April 1909. In a letter of 1919, Conrad reported that the play had also been 'performed in three English towns, in Paris, and also (for a week) in Chicago' (*LL*, ii. 225). *One Day More* was published in the *English Review* (August 1913) and in limited editions in London (1917 and 1919) and New York (Doubleday, Page, 1920). It was issued in *Laughing Anne & One Day More: Two Plays by Joseph Conrad* by John Castle in Britain in October 1924, and by Doubleday, Page in America in May 1925. Its most recent reprinting is in Kirschner's Penguin edition of *Typhoon and Other Stories* (1990: 267–94). The manuscript is held in the Berg Collection, New York Public Library. See also 'TO-MOR-ROW'.

opera. According to G. *Jean-Aubry, Conrad 'often found delight in recalling the evenings he had spent in days gone by, about 1875, at the Marseilles Opera . . . and he retained a very correct impression of Meyerbeer's or Verdi's operas, as well as of Offenbach's operettas' (1924: 38–9). Opera

is mentioned frequently in Conrad's works, especially in his Malay fictions. In *Almayer's Folly*, Babalatchi soothes the spirits of Lakamba by playing him an aria from Verdi's *Il trovatore* on a hand-cranked organ (88–9). Opera is also a subject of conversation between Mrs *Travers and Tom *Lingard in Part V of *The Rescue*, where it betokens both the romance and the artificiality of their relationship. Leaving Belarab's stockade on Lingard's arm was for Mrs Travers like 'walking on a splendid stage in a scene from an opera'. Lingard tells her that he once saw an opera in Melbourne, and although he cannot recall its name, it seemed to him 'More real than anything in life' (300–1).

The Virginia pianist and composer John Powell was apparently the first musician to contemplate transforming one of Conrad's works into an opera. During a visit to Conrad's *home in 1910, he suggested that Conrad consider preparing an opera libretto based on 'Heart of Darkness'. Conrad frowned and left the room without speaking, and on that visit the subject was not broached again. Several years later, when Powell received a commission for a large work, he wrote to Conrad, who replied that 'he believed it would be impossible to put the whole in dramatic form, and suggested that the material might better be used as the theme of a symphonic poem' (Randall, 60 n.). Powell eventually wrote a piece for piano and orchestra called *Rhapsodie nègre* that premièred at New York's Carnegie Hall in March 1917. He later recalled that when he played the piece for Conrad on the piano at Oswalds on 3 July 1920, Conrad said to him: 'Ever since I began to write, it has been my highest ambition to have one of my stories made into an opera' (ibid. 61 n.).

Conrad's favourite opera was Georges Bizet's *Carmen* (1875), which he first encountered in *Marseilles and claimed to have seen fourteen times (Galsworthy, 82). He gave Émilie *Briquel a piano score of the opera, and turned the pages while she played and perhaps sang (*JCC*, 179). According to Conrad's son Borys, he could whistle airs from *Carmen* and from Pietro

Mascagni's *Cavalleria rusticana* (1890), and the family dog was named Escamillo after Bizet's Toreador. In his later and better documented years, Conrad was an occasional opera-goer. On a weekend visit to *London, he took Jessie to see Charles Gounod's *Roméo et Juliette* (1867) at the Shaftesbury Theatre on 8 October 1915 (*CL*, v. 517); and eighteen months later, on 14 May 1917, he attended a performance of Gounod's *Faust* at the Garrick Theatre. Towards the end of his life Conrad met several composers in person, including Karol Szymanowski, who visited him at Oswalds in December 1920, and Maurice Ravel, who performed in the London home of the singer Mme Alvar in early July 1922. Conrad heard Ravel again on 17 April 1923, just before his trip to *America, in the course of which he discussed the *'Polish question' with composer Ignacy Paderewski.

According to Jean-Aubry, Conrad considered *Nostromo* the most suitable of all his works for adaptation as a lyrical drama (1924: 41). The relation of grand opera to *Nostromo* is further explored by E. C. Bufkin in 'Conrad, Grand Opera, and *Nostromo*', *Nineteenth-Century Fiction*, 30 (1975), 206–14. In 'Opera in Conrad: "More Real than Anything in Life"', *Studies in the Literary Imagination*, 13 (1980), 1–16, Frank Baldanza usefully reviews the operas performed in Marseilles in 1874–8 when Conrad was there between voyages.

Conrad's own works have inspired no fewer than four operas, two in Polish and two in English, all of which were first performed in the decade between 1966 and 1977. *Jutro* ('To-morrow'), a musical drama in one act by the Polish composer Tadeusz Baird, with a libretto by Jerzy S. Sito, was written during the period 1964–6 and first performed in the Teatr Wielki (Great Theatre) at the Warsaw International Festival of Contemporary Music. Baird's only operatic work, it premièred on 18 September 1966, produced by Witold Rowicki, directed by Aleksander Bardini, and with music conducted by Jan Krenz. On 11 April 1974, a video adaptation of Baird's opera was broadcast in Warsaw, with Mieczysław Nowakowski conducting the Great Sym-

phony Orchestra, and the original singers doubled with actors. A piano score was published in 1967 and a full score in 1983, both by PWN in Cracow. The Poznań National Symphony Orchestra also released a recording of the opera directed by Renard Czajkowski (SXL stereo nr 1057). An unpublished Ph.D. dissertation by Jeremy Lee Carter entitled 'The Interplay of Musical and Dramatic Structures in "Jutro," an Opera by Tadeusz Baird' (Washington University, 1984) describes the music as 'largely derived from the interaction of a small group of trichords which coalesce and produce a twelve-tone series' although 'dodecaphony is not the governing principle of the work'. Carter also noted what he called 'anti-Soviet dimensions' in the libretto. His thesis includes an English translation of the libretto and an interview with Baird in 1981, the last year of the composer's life.

Under Western Eyes, an opera in three acts by South African composer John Joubert, with a libretto by Cedric Cliffe, was composed in 1965–7 and given its world première by the New Opera Company at St Pancras Town Hall, London, on 29 May 1969, as a part of the Camden Festival. Joubert's second full-length opera after *Silas Marner* (1961), it was conducted by Leon Lovett and broadcast on BBC Radio 3 on 10 August 1969. A review by Paul Kirschner appeared in *Conradiana*, 3: 3 (1971–2), 50–3. As Joubert explained in the programme notes, 'in order to achieve the necessary translations into operatic terms some scenes and characters have had to be abandoned, some conflated, and some newly invented'. There is no English *teacher of languages, Peter *Ivanovitch, or Mme de S—; and *Razumov sings a final duet with Tekla even after his eardrums have been destroyed.

In 1915 Conrad told his agent J. B. *Pinker: 'I think *Victory* may make a libretto for a Puccini opera anyhow' (*CL*, v. 452). Fifty-five years would pass before the opera by Richard Rodney Bennett in three acts, with a libretto by Beverley Cross, opened at the Royal Opera House, Covent Garden, on 13 April 1970. Bennett's fourth opera and the first ever to be commissioned for the Royal Opera by the Friends of Covent Garden, it was produced by Colin Graham, designed by Alex Stone, and conducted by Edward Downes. There were plans to tour with Georg Solti to West Berlin and perhaps Munich. The opera was revived at Covent Garden for a second series of performances in May 1972 with many of the original singers in the main roles. A number of photographs and documents concerning the production are held at Covent Garden.

Lord Jim, a musical drama in three acts by Romuald Twardowski, won the Prince Pierre de Monaco Prize for the best opera of 1973. The prologue was first performed in the autumn of 1972 by the Pomeranian Philharmonic Symphony Orchestra in Bydgoszcz, with tenor Piotr Trella and the 'Arion' choir under the direction of J. Radwana. The second interlude was performed on 18–19 January 1974 in Gdańsk by the Baltic Philharmonic Orchestra under the direction of Z. Chwedczuka. A partial score was published by PWN (Cracow) in 1976, and the Cracow Symphony Orchestra, under the direction of Mieczysław Nowakowski, released a phonograph recording of Interlude II. The complete opera opened on 16 July 1977, performed by the National Philharmonic Orchestra of the Baltic in Gdańsk under the direction of Maria Fołtyn.

organizations. See JOURNALS, ORGANIZATIONS, AND STUDY CENTRES.

Orzeszkowa, Eliza (1841–1910), Polish novelist and patriot. Eliza Orzeszkowa wrote a scathing attack on Conrad in an article on 'The Emigration of Talent' in the Polish weekly *Kraj*, 16 (23 April 1899; reprinted in *CUFE*, 182–92). It was composed in response to an earlier article of the same title in *Kraj*, 12 (26 March 1899, reprinted in *CUFE*, 178– 81) by Wincenty Lutosławski, who had interviewed Conrad in June 1897. Lutosławski had been generally sympathetic to the emigration of outstanding talents from *Poland, although in crudely misrepresenting Conrad's material situation as an émigré, he unwittingly exposed him to the possibility of unfair at-

tack in Poland. In her heated counter-assault, Orzeszkowa singled out Conrad as having ignominiously deserted his country, betrayed his patriotic duties, and besmirched a famous name: 'I must say that this gentleman, who writes popular and very lucrative novels in English, has almost caused me a nervous breakdown. My gorge rises when I read about him. . . . It is even hard to think about it without shame.' Conrad probably read Orzeszkowa's article soon after its publication, a probability that has led some critics to surmise that it may have had an immediate effect in drawing him towards the subject of desertion, flight, and expiation in *Lord Jim*, which in 1899 was in its early stages. Some measure of the outrage and pain Orzeszkowa's attack caused to Conrad's delicate Anglo-Polish sensibility can be gauged by his refusal on his 1914 visit to Poland to read anything by the 'hag' who had earlier vilified him (*CUFE*, 187–8, 214 n.). See also INTERVIEWS.

Outcast of the Islands, An. Conrad's second novel (1896) is also the middle volume of the 'Malay trilogy' that in fictional chronology begins with *The Rescue* and ends with *Almayer's Folly*. Ostensibly an exotic tale of passionate interracial seduction and adultery, the novel describes the events that led to the arrival of Arab traders in the village of *Sambir around 1872, some fifteen years before the time of *Almayer's Folly*. Approximately 105,000 words long, it is also one of Conrad's most bitterly ironic studies of *racism, *colonialism, and the complexities of ethnic and religious politics at the local level.

The outcast of the title is Peter *Willems, an ambitious and unscrupulous young sailor from Rotterdam who jumps ship in Semarang and is taken up as a protégé by Tom *Lingard. Although he is 'hopelessly at variance with the spirit of the sea' (17), the boy shows promise, and with Lingard's help rises eventually to become the confidential clerk of Hudig & Co. in Macassar. The novel opens on the night of Willems's 30th birthday, as we learn that he has stolen money from his employer to cover his gambling debts, but has by this time secretly repaid almost all of it. The opening paragraph is an elaborately wrought and deeply ironic depiction of Willems's arrogance and self-delusion: he is contemptuous of his half-caste wife Joanna and their baby son, but glories in the awe and respect shown him necessarily by her poor relatives, who depend on him for their support. When his 'idiotic indiscretion' is discovered two days later and Hudig fires him, Willems returns home to reap the bitter harvest of his years of abuse. In despair, he is found at the harbour by Lingard, who reveals that Willems's wife Joanna is actually Hudig's illegitimate daughter. Lingard decides to give Willems another chance by taking him along up his secret river to Sambir and leaving him with *Almayer until the scandal in Macassar blows over.

The scene then shifts to Sambir three months later, where the one-eyed Babalatchi, a Malay adventurer and politician, is plotting to use Willems to break the monopoly of Lingard by bringing Arab traders into the river. Willems, contemptuous of his isolation and of Almayer, has meanwhile fallen under the spell of the beautiful *Aïssa, the daughter of Omar el Badavi, once the dreaded leader of the Brunei rovers but now a blind invalid. Torn between his sense of racial superiority and the power of Aïssa's sensuality, Willems finally succumbs to her charms, surrendering to her what he imagines to be 'the unstained purity of his life, of his race, of his civilization' (80).

The second part of the novel opens five weeks later as Willems, distraught at the disappearance of Aïssa two days earlier, asks Almayer to help him establish a second trading post across the river. Almayer rejects his appeal, but informs him that Aïssa and her father are living in Lakamba's campong (village) 14 miles (22 km) downstream. Frustrated by Almayer's refusal to support him, Willems threatens to betray Lingard's secret river passage to the Arabs. The scene then shifts to Lakamba's compound, where first Willems arrives and then Syed Abdulla, the Arab trader, with whom Willems agrees to share his knowledge of the secret passage. That evening, Aïssa's blind father, who hates Willems, attempts to murder him with a kris, but is restrained by his daughter, upon whom he pronounces a curse. Aïssa refuses to stay with Willems, but promises to wait for his return with Abdulla.

Part III takes up the story about six weeks later, when Lingard, delayed by the loss of his brig, has at last returned to Sambir in a schooner and learns from Almayer of the recent unfortunate developments. Willems indeed piloted Syed Abdulla's barque and her crew of 'Sumatra men' into Sambir. He then demanded supplies from Almayer, who refused him, counting on support from the Rajah Patalolo across the river; but Patalolo, weary of the intrigues of white men, wants only to visit Mecca before he dies. After witnessing how Patalolo's stockade was invaded and disarmed by Willems the following morning, Almayer ran the Union Jack up his flagstaff for 'protection'. The next morning, Willems and Lakamba hoisted a makeshift Dutch flag at the other end of the settlement and compelled all passers-by to salaam to it. Jim-Eng, Willems's Chinese neighbour, refused to salaam to any but a British flag, and sought refuge with Almayer from an angry mob led by Willems. In the ensuing confrontation, Jim-Eng grabbed Almayer's revolver and fired into the crowd, with the result that both Jim-Eng and Almayer were immediately overpowered. At Willems's orders, Almayer was sewn up in his own hammock 'like a bale of goods' and subjected to the murderous taunting of Aïssa. To Babalatchi's dismay, Willems also ordered Almayer's entire stock of gunpowder to be dumped in the river. Since then, Almayer has not seen Willems. Lingard reveals that he has brought Willems's wife and son with him, planning to reunite the family and take them all away to make a new start in Palembang. Almayer despairs of his situation, but Lingard, while building a fragile house of cards to amuse Almayer's little daughter Nina, describes his plans to make them all rich with gold from the interior (a dream expanded in *Almayer's Folly*).

In Part IV, Lingard visits Lakamba's campong in search of Willems, but finds Babalatchi instead, who invites Lingard into his hut and delicately suggests that Lingard ambush Willems from a window. Lingard instead goes to see Willems, and when Aïssa tries to hold him back, he promises her that he will spare Willems's life. Willems appears and tries to blame Aïssa for all that has happened. Lingard strikes him, bloodying his nose, then condemns him to remain forever in Sambir. As Lingard departs, a thunderstorm breaks.

The final section, Part V, begins a few days later as Almayer, worried about Willems's continued presence on the river, hatches a plot to help him escape. He arranges for Joanna to be taken to Lakamba's campong, then dispatches a slow whaleboat to alarm Lingard, and directs his own boat into a narrow channel where it becomes stuck when the tide ebbs. When Joanna arrives to join Willems and get away, Aïssa finds them and realizes that Willems is married to a 'Sirani [i.e. Christian] woman' and has a son. When he tries to take the revolver from her, she kills him. An epilogue 'many years later' (while Nina is staying with the Vincks in *Singapore) parodies and subverts the preceding narrative of romance and tragedy, as an aggrieved and gin-sodden Almayer tells an itinerant Romanian orchid-hunter how Aïssa was eventually 'tamed' by Almayer's daughter Nina and given a place to live among his serving girls.

Like its predecessor and sequel *Almayer's Folly*, the novel was based on Conrad's brief experience in eastern *Borneo as first mate of the *Vidar* in the autumn of 1887, when he traversed 'Lingard's Passage' and made four trading visits to the Malay settlement of Berau, on the Pantai River, the model for 'Sambir' and the place where he first met William Charles *Olmeijer, the prototype of Kaspar Almayer. In his 'Author's Note' written in January 1919, Conrad traced the origin of the novel back to a remark made by Edward *Garnett after the publication of *Almayer's Folly* in April 1895: 'You have the style, you have the tempera-

ment; why not write another?' However, Conrad's letters to Marguerite *Poradowska indicate that he had begun writing the novel in *Geneva in August 1894, before his first meeting with Garnett. It was originally conceived as a short story entitled 'Two Vagabonds: A Tale of the Islands', in which the vagabonds were apparently Willems and Babalatchi. At the end of October he complained to Poradowska that M[argaret Louisa] Woods had 'stolen' his title by publishing a book called *The Vagabonds*, so he was forced to find another one (*CL*, i. 183). Conrad finished the novel in thirteen months, writing the date of its completion, 14 September 1895, on the last page of the manuscript, but announcing to Garnett 'the sad death of Mr Peter Willems late of Rotterdam and Macassar who has been murdered on the 16th inst at 4 p.m. while the sun shone joyously and the barrel organ sang on the pavement the abominable Intermezzo of the ghastly Cavalleria' (*CL*, i. 245). Although the writing went relatively smoothly, Conrad was not pleased with the way the novel ended. He shared Garnett's satisfaction with chapter XXIII (equivalent to the first two chapters of Part V), but agreed with Garnett that the final chapter (originally XXIV, equivalent to Part V, chapters 3 and 4) was a 'dismal failure' (*CL*, i. 246).

An Outcast of the Islands was first published in England by T. Fisher *Unwin on 4 March 1896, and in New York by D. Appleton about 15 August. Conrad never corrected proofs for the American edition, which was silently censored. Not only was 'damn' twice amended to 'blast', but some twenty passages conveying the sensuality of Willems's attraction to Aïssa were omitted, most of them from Part II, chapter 6, including lines such as: 'his eyes looked at the modelling of her chin, at the outline of her neck, at the swelling lines of her bosom, with the famished and concentrated expression of a starving man looking at food' (140–1).

Initial reviews were appreciative, complaining of the density of Conrad's style but admiring his ability to evoke the lush, sweltering atmosphere of the tropics.

The most influential of the notices was probably that by H. G. *Wells published in the *Saturday Review* (16 May 1896), which, despite some severe criticism of Conrad's over-elaborate rhetoric, concluded that the novel was, 'perhaps, the finest piece of fiction that has been published this year' (*CCH*, 75). In 1897, Conrad sent an effusively inscribed copy of the novel to Henry *James, who reciprocated with an inscribed copy of his own most recently published work, *The Spoils of Poynton* (1897).

Until recently, most readers and critics have understood *An Outcast of the Islands* as an exotic tale of love and corruption in the jungle, although some with personal experience of Malay life (like Hugh *Clifford) have found its characters unconvincing. The novel has often been cited in connection with *Almayer's Folly*, but has seldom received consideration as an independent work. In *Conrad żywy* (The Living Conrad, B. Świderski, 1957), 181–92, Wit Tarnawski argued that the novel was underestimated, but linked its pervasive theme of betrayal to Conrad's own 'treason complex' at having betrayed his *Polish origins. In 'Conrad's First Battleground: *Almayer's Folly*', *University of Kansas City Review*, 25 (1959), 189–94, Leo Gurko contrasted the intense vitality of the jungle and the river with Willems's own inertia, and argued that the jungle was a perfect setting for his downfall. In 'Conradiaanse interraciale vriendschappen' ('Interracial Friendships in Conrad', *Forum der Letteren* 6 (1965), 35–44), G. J. Resink noted that the Asian partners in such friendships are usually of a higher social class than their white counterparts, which works to counterbalance the superiority felt by the whites. The insight of the blind Omar el Badavi and the one-eyed Babalatchi could also be contrasted with the moral astigmatism of white characters like Willems, Almayer, and Lingard. In '*An Outcast of the Islands*: A New Reading', *Conradiana*, 2: 3 (1969–70), 47–58, R. A. Gekoski argued that the novel is centred not on Willems and Aïssa but on Lingard. An orthodox *Marxist interpretation of the novel as a critique of 'bourgeois reality' was published in Rus-

sian in Perm (USSR) by M. T. Krugliak in 1972.

Critical recognition of the merits of *An Outcast of the Islands* as an independent and self-sufficient work of art has been slow to arrive for several reasons. As a sequel (or 'prequel') to *Almayer's Folly*, it has often been mined for evidence concerning issues that pertain chiefly to Conrad's first novel or to the so-called 'Malay trilogy' as a whole. Since the 1960s, both works have suffered from the credence accorded to Thomas C. Moser's *achievement-and-decline thesis, in which Conrad's earlier and especially his later works are deemed vastly inferior to the masterpieces of his middle and 'major phase'. In this context, the novel has sometimes been viewed as an earlier and (therefore) less successful version of *Lord Jim*.

The tendency to regard the novel as a melodramatic tale of sultry passion in the tropics was visibly strengthened by the success of Carol Reed's film *Outcast of the Islands* (1952), which scholars have often hailed as the best of all Conrad film adaptations. Reed shot most of the film in Ceylon (Sri Lanka), and transformed the mixed-race wives of Willems and Almayer into stereotypical Victorian ladies wearing sunbonnets to protect their fair complexions, perhaps in an effort to highlight the racial and sexual 'otherness' of Aïssa. These and other changes are discussed by Catherine Dawson and Gene M. Moore in 'Colonialism and Local Color in *Outcast of the Islands* and *Lord Jim*' (Moore (ed.) 1997: 104–19). An Italian film and television adaptation of *Un reietto delle isole* (1979) followed Conrad's plot and characterization more closely than Reed, but location filming near Madras lent a strangely Indian style to costumes and backgrounds.

In the wake of the work of Jacques Lacan, Edward W. Said, and others, critics have recently begun to examine *An Outcast of the Islands* in terms of its representation of an ethnic or feminist Other, and to appreciate the novel not primarily in terms of its white male characters, but from the 'other' side, from a native or female perspective. In 'Women as Moral and Political

Alternatives in Conrad's Early Novels', in Gabriela Mora and Karen S. Van Hooft (eds.), *Theory and Practice of Feminist Literary Criticism* (Ypsilanti, Mich.: Bilingual, 1982), 242–55, Ruth L. Nadelhaft argues that women of mixed race like Aïssa challenge Western male insularity and domination and provide alternatives to the morality of imperialism (see also Nadelhaft 1991). Heliéna Krenn (1990) refutes charges that Conrad was racist and sexist by exploring the contrasts developed in his use of native and white characters, noting especially the strength and integrity of mixed-race women like Aïssa and Joanna Willems, and observing that Lingard's betrayals come increasingly into focus through the reverse chronology of the trilogy. As against the recent tendency to view the female characters in a positive light, J. H. Stape, in a wide-ranging and provocative introduction to the Oxford World's Classics edition of the novel (ed. J. H. Stape and Hans van Marle, OUP, 1992), argues that Aïssa's 'reading of the colonial situation is a characteristic splitting-off and projection of the negative upon the Other, with the outsider as a convenient scapegoat for one's own moral inadequacies and failures' (p. xv). In *Joseph Conrad and the Adventure Tradition* (CUP, 1993), Andrea White argues that while Lingard is typical of the idealistic heroes of adventure fiction, Willems is an anti-hero whose devastating misadventures effectively subvert and 'deconstruct' the image of colonialism propounded in the novels of R. M. Ballantyne, H. Rider Haggard, and the early works of Robert Louis *Stevenson. This approach has been further developed by Linda Dryden in '*An Outcast of the Islands*: Echoes of Romance and Adventure', *The Conradian*, 20 (1995), 139–68.

Conrad's manuscript of *An Outcast of the Islands* is held at the Rosenbach Museum and Library, Philadelphia. A manuscript of the 1919 'Author's Note' is at the Henry E. Huntington Library, San Marino, California, and two typescripts are at the Detroit Public Library. To date, the only comprehensive study of textual issues in the novel is Mary Gifford Belcher's unpublished Ph.D. dissertation 'A Critical

Edition of *An Outcast of the Islands*' (Texas Tech University, 1981), available from UMI microfilms (Order Number 8202068). Conrad's revisions have been described briefly by Elmer Alindogan Ordoñez in *Notes and Queries*, NS 15 (August 1968), 287–9, and at greater length in his *The Early Joseph Conrad: Revisions and Style* (Quezon City: University of Philippines Press, 1969). A proof of the 1921 Heinemann Limited Edition setting is at Hofstra. A copy of a 1914 edition of the novel was used by Conrad in 1916 to correct the text for the collected edition (see *CL*, v. 572, 575), but it has not been located since it was last sold at auction in 1924.

'Outpost of Progress, An'. One of the earliest of Conrad's short stories, this 10,000-word tale was written in July 1896 during Conrad's stay in Brittany and first published in *Cosmopolis* (June–July 1897). It was later collected in *Tales of Unrest*. The work provided the occasion for a first contact between Conrad and R. B. Cunninghame *Graham, who, having read and admired the serial, wrote to Conrad and evidently contrasted it favourably with Rudyard *Kipling's 'Slaves of the Lamp', which had preceded it in *Cosmopolis*. Conrad's own high opinion of his story led him in 1906 to nominate it as his best on the basis of its 'scrupulous unity of tone' and 'severity of discipline' (*CDOUP*, 83).

The story centres on the spectacular downfall of two incompetent representatives of a European trading company, Kayerts and Carlier, who are left to administer a remote 'outpost of progress' in Africa. Under their charge are a Sierra Leonean clerk, Makola, or 'Henry Price' as he is also known, his family, and ten African workers. Over a period of several months, the ineffectual Kayerts and his assistant Carlier struggle unavailingly to adjust to their new surroundings. Then, through the business acumen of Makola, their ten African workers are sold to a group of itinerant slave-dealers in exchange for ivory. Kayerts and Carlier, at first shocked in a conventionally high-minded way, gradually ease their consciences by blaming

Makola, while eventually persuading themselves that the ivory is the company's legitimate property. Deserted by the fearful local tribes, the isolated station becomes the setting for the swift downfall of the ironically styled 'pioneers of trade and progress' (93). After a quarrel over some sugar for their tea, Kayerts accidentally shoots Carlier. He then commits suicide by hanging himself on the cross that marks the grave of his predecessor. When the company manager arrives, he is confronted by Kayerts's body, dangling from the cross as if standing to attention and putting out 'a swolled tongue' (117) at his superior.

Soon after the story's completion, Conrad drew attention to its nearness to his *Congo experiences of 1890: 'All the bitterness of those days, all my puzzled wonder as to the meaning of all I saw—all my indignation at masquerading philanthropy—have been with me again, while I wrote' (*CL*, i. 294). That the finished story succeeds in sustaining a coolly satiric detachment is testimony to Conrad's ability to distance himself rigorously from those memories, a process helped by his adoption of a tone of tight-lipped impassibility associated with *Flaubert and *Maupassant. Published in Queen Victoria's Diamond Jubilee year, the work offered its first readers—apparently to Cunninghame Graham's delight—a mordantly ironic counterblast to European fictions about the *colonial mission in Africa.

While Conrad in his 1919 'Author's Note' described the story as being 'the lightest part of the loot I carried off from Central Africa' (p. vii) and so encouraged the view that it was largely an appendage to, or dry-run for, 'Heart of Darkness', it has increasingly attracted attention as a finely crafted story in its own right. Lothe (45–56) has written appreciatively of its sustained *irony and control of omniscient perspective. Hawthorn regards it as 'qualitatively new' in the context of Conrad's early fiction, admiring its uncompromising analysis of the mechanisms of imperialism and finding in it 'the work in which Conrad first achieves a full maturity of vision and execution which is both technical and in-

tellectual, a work in which the reader feels in the company of a major talent' (1990: 159).

With several of Conrad's earlier fictions, 'An Outpost' dramatizes the large spectacle of the European abroad, removed from the familiar constraints of the Western 'crowd', isolated in the wilderness, and suffering spectacular degeneration and death. Here, however, that predicament is shaped by an acutely political awareness, since the story's focus is less upon two individuals than the representative imperial fictions that arrive in Africa with these two carefully chosen types, a bureaucrat and a soldier. Conrad's sarcastic exposure of 'masquerading philanthropy' partly involves a transposing of imperialist clichés into incongruous settings, as occurs in the title itself. The story's more iconoclastic ironies result from a thoroughgoing reversal of European imperialist discourses. A traditional Western view of African peoples as ungovernable 'children', indistinguishable from each other, and subject to superstition is dramatically upturned, since events show Kayerts and Carlier to be like 'children . . . in the dark' (89), 'indistinguishably alike' to the Africans (95), and prisoners of their own fetish in the form of the ivory-store. The two pioneers arrive in Africa voicing the conventional view that as 'superior' Europeans they have the right and duty to civilize 'backward' peoples, but further ironies emerge when it transpires that, as two failed rejects from Europe, they are happy to cultivate failure, content with their fellowship in idleness, and oblivious to the civilized litter they leave around an increasingly inefficient trading-post. The Sierra Leonean Makola plays an essential part in uncovering the pretence hidden by their fine rhetoric: he knows what their European masters really want—full inventories, plentiful supplies of ivory, and increasing profits.

Now being established as one the finest stories of the writer's earliest phase, 'An Outpost' is remarkable for its mining of what Arnold Bennett most valued in Conrad's work, its 'rich veins of dark and glittering satire and sarcasm' (*Letters of Arnold*

Bennett, ed. James Hepburn (OUP, 1968), ii. 321). The manuscript of the story is held at the Beinecke Rare Book and Manuscript Library, Yale University.

'Outside Literature'. Composed just before it was published, this essay appeared under the title of 'Notices to Mariners' in the *Manchester Guardian Weekly*, 7 (November 1922), 453, and was collected in *Last Essays*. Written in praise of the 'ideal of perfect accuracy' and technical precision of informational Notices to Mariners, the essay finds Conrad correspondingly sceptical about the language of literature and its dangerous capacity for mystification: 'I never learned to trust it. I can't trust it to this day. . . . A dreadful doubt hangs over the whole achievement of literature' (43). While the 'dreadful doubt' expressed here has a precedent in Conrad's earliest *letters, it may also echo a pervasive attitude to language in much post-*First World War writing, with its shared apprehension that, as Henry *James put it. 'The war has used up words; they have been weakened; they have deteriorated like motor-car tyres . . . and we are now confronted with a depreciation of all our terms' ('Henry James's First Interview', *New York Times Magazine* (21 March 1915), 4). Nevertheless, Conrad sustains a playfully ambivalent perspective, since he is aware of what a merely technical register excludes—'All means of acting on man's spiritual side are forbidden to that prose' (39–40)—and, paradoxically, eulogizes 'unliterary language' (39) in an essay of considerable linguistic sophistication. The first draft, a revised typescript dictated by Conrad, is held at the Beinecke Rare Book and Manuscript Library, Yale University.

P

pamphlets. The first limited-edition pamphlets of Conrad's work to appear in his lifetime resulted from an agreement made by Conrad first with Clement R. *Shorter in late 1916 and then with Thomas J. *Wise two years later to reprint certain of his articles and short pieces. During the period 1917–19, Shorter produced six pamphlets in editions limited to 25 copies each, with Wise following suit during 1919–20 with two series of ten pamphlets each. The venture, a frankly commercial one designed to exploit Conrad's growing international reputation and recycle his work for a collectors' market, yielded substantial double rewards for the author; he was paid handsomely by Shorter and Wise for the right to republish and also received substantial returns from the sale of the pamphlets reserved for him: for example, for a complete set of pamphlets John *Quinn in 1920 sent Conrad a draft for the sum of $1,750. In the order of their publication, the Shorter and Wise pamphlets were as follows:

The Shorter Pamphlets
One Day More: A Play in One Act (1917)
The First News (1918)
'*Well Done!*' (1918)
The Polish Question: A Note on the Joint Protectorate of the Western Powers and Russia (1919)
The Tale (1919)
London's River (1919)

The Wise Pamphlets
First Series
Autocracy and War (1919)
Henry James: An Appreciation (1919)
Tradition (1919)
Some Reflexions, Seamanlike and Otherwise, on the Loss of the Titanic (1919)
Some Aspects of the Admirable Inquiry into the Loss of the Titanic (1919)
The Shock of War: Through Germany to Cracow (1919)

To Poland in War-Time: A Journey into the East (1919)
The North Sea on the Eve of War (1919)
My Return to Cracow (1919)
Guy de Maupassant (1919)

Second Series
The Lesson of the Collision: A Monograph upon the Loss of the 'Empress of Ireland' (1919)
Anatole France (1919)
Tales of the Sea (1919)
Books (1920)
Anatole France: 'L'Île des pingouins' (1920)
Confidence (1920)
Alphonse Daudet (1920)
Prince Roman (1920)
An Observer in Malay (1920)
The Warrior's Soul (1920)

When in 1920 Conrad refused Quinn permission to print two pamphlets, his reason was that he had been 'drawn into this very unwillingly and want[ed] now to stop it dead' (18 March 1920). Yet he clearly recognized the commercial advantages in republishing desirable rarities and later had no qualms in allowing Richard *Curle to market limited editions of his shorter pieces, with both men sharing the profits. In 1922, Curle secured Conrad's agreement to print a small private edition of *Travel: A Preface to 'Into the East': Notes on Burma and Malaya, by Richard Curle*. With Curle's help, there later followed *The Dover Patrol: A Tribute* (1922), *The Black Mate: A Story* (1922), *John Galsworthy: An Appreciation* (1922), *The 'Torrens': A Personal Tribute* (1923), and *Geography and Some Explorers* (1924). On the appearance of the penultimate item, Conrad commented to Curle: 'It is only fair that you should participate in things which are put in my way by you, especially this windfall, for which certainly I have not done a stroke of work' (*CTF*, 214). One further by-product of the

Shorter and Wise ventures was that in 1919 they revived Conrad's interest in collecting his occasional papers in a volume and facilitated the gathering of items for inclusion in *Notes on Life and Letters*. For details, see J. H. Stape, '"Conrad Privately Printed": The Shorter and Wise Limited Edition Pamphlets', *Papers of the Bibliographical Society of America*, 77 (1983), 317–32; reprinted in revised form in Curreli (ed.), 93–109.

'Partner, The'. Composed intermittently during the last three months of 1910, this 11,500-word short story was published in *Harper's Magazine* (November 1911), 850–65, and later collected in *Within the Tides*. The 'partner' of the title is Cloete, an American confidence trickster or 'Yankee fiend' (125), who arrives in *England and attempts to inveigle his co-partner George Dunbar in a plot to wreck a ship for insurance money in order to allow them to invest in a patent-medicine company. Through the machinations of Stafford, a villain hired by Cloete to undertake the 'tomahawking' of the ship, the plot tragically misfires: the captain of the ship, George's brother Harry Dunbar, is murdered by Stafford, his widow left mentally unbalanced, and Cloete finally disappointed when he is cheated of the immense fortune that an investment in Parker's Lively Lumbago Pills might have brought.

Written during a period when Conrad was still recovering from a physical and nervous breakdown, the tale might be regarded as one which testifies to its own limitations, since it puts the entire narrative into the mouth of a rugged stevedore and dramatizes his listener as a professional magazine-writer who, at the end of the story, openly confesses that 'it would have been too much trouble to cook it for the consumption of magazine readers' (128). Yet this is less an admission of idleness than a conscious recognition on the writer's part of the dressed-up literary fare which he habitually 'cooks' for magazine readers. Interestingly, then, the tale makes an intermittent attempt to reflect upon both 'the process by which stories—stories for periodicals—were produced' (90) and

the 'silly heads' (91) for which they are written. It does so by handing the narrative over completely to the 'rough' stevedore in order to suggest that his kind of narration—the raw material out of which magazine stories are built—is both stranger than such fiction and has a direct power which would be lost in the acceptably 'cooked' products of the potboiler. The latter would have 'transposed [the story] to somewhere in the South Seas': 'For it is too startling even to think of such things happening in our respectable Channel in full view, so to speak, of the luxurious continental traffic to Switzerland and Monte Carlo' (128). The tale has attracted some critical attention, and Batchelor (1994: 222), who regards it as 'an interesting and under-regarded narrative experiment', makes the point that Conrad's use of a plot involving commercial chicanery and a quack patent medicine touches upon a popular Edwardian subject that H. G. *Wells also employs in *Tono-Bungay* (1909). The manuscript is held at the Rosenbach Museum and Library, Philadelphia.

Patusan. A real-life pirate settlement in Sarawak appropriately provides the name for the setting of the second part of *Lord Jim*. Borrowed from Henry Keppel's *Expedition to Borneo* (1846), one of the 'dull, wise books' (*CL*, ii. 130) Conrad drew on for the novel's local colour, the place name neatly evokes a comparison with the *Patna*, the ship of the first part of the novel. The course of Gentleman *Brown's voyage in chapter 38 establishes its geographical locale as the Teunom (or Tenom) River area of north-west Sumatra; but numerous topographical details, including its protected riverine location miles from the sea coast and two prominent hills, are drawn from north-east *Borneo's Berau River region. Conrad knew the area from his four voyages in 1887 in the *Vidar*, which provided him with the settings of *Almayer's Folly* and *An Outcast of the Islands*, where he gives the locale the name of *Sambir. The Patusan chapters divide the novel into two roughly equal halves, but critical consensus has been that the romance elements introduced in this section—the love affair with *Jewel, the elevation of *Jim into a mythic hero, and the confrontation with evil in the form of the emblematic Gentleman Brown—match neither the narrative complexities nor thematic depths of the first part. Some of the weaknesses of this section, if such they be, may derive from the novel's unplanned growth during *serialization.

A striking feature of Conrad's fictional Patusan is the precision of geographical and natural detail, rivalling that of the *Sulaco of *Nostromo*; another is its extreme isolation. Both are used for symbolic purposes as this remote backwater becomes, like *Heyst's island in *Victory*, a staging-ground for classical tragedy. Hoping to find a haven from the world, Jim initially romanticizes Patusan as a refuge that affords him the chance to redeem a lost conception of himself, mainly on his own terms, only to find, ironically, that the world seeks him out even there. Patusan is subject to shifting and even opposing projections. Jim's personalized idealization of it as an opportunity contrasts with *Marlow's final vision of it as hermetically sealed off, hedged by the 'primeval smell of fecund earth' (331); and this view differs from Gentleman Brown's exclusively practical assessment of Patusan's prosperity in terms of his own needs.

As a colonial setting, Patusan is remarkably diverse in its ethnic complexion: the indigenous groups are mainly relegated to the background, whereas the main players in the local economy and its politics are outsiders, including not only Jim, but Cornelius, a 'half-caste' Malacca Portuguese placed in Patusan, like Jim himself, by the German merchant *Stein, and extending to Doramin and his Bugis, immigrants from the southern Celebes. The intense rivalry for control of the local economy among Rajah Allang, Sherif Ali, and Doramin obliquely and ironically mirrors great power competition for economic hegemony in South-East Asia, a struggle relegated to the novel's periphery and more central in the earlier Malay fiction. Gentleman Brown, a forthright plunderer,

represents one pole of colonialism—naked aggression, rapacity, and outright theft (albeit for survival); Jim, modelled here on James *Brooke, embodies its potentially more benign side as a bringer of light and the rule of law. The advantages he gives to Patusan are, however, sharply questioned by the novel's denouement: the death of a charismatic leader typically leaves a polity founded on his unique power without institutions for continuing governance. Frequently conceived, as in Jim's case, in the non-rational terms of magic and myth, this power disperses upon death. Hence, with Jim's end Patusan appears doomed to further cycles of political chaos, economic insecurity, and violence. The novel's conclusion serves two ends: it iconoclastically dismantles the platitudes of heroic *colonialism, and articulates Conrad's radical scepticism about political commitments as a means of securing basic individual and communal needs. Lacking a historic past, Jim's rule is necessarily heirless, a theme treated in 'Autocracy and War', and, as in 'Heart of Darkness', civilization is a mere 'flicker' and, from an anti-utopian perspective, anomalous.

Hans van Marle and Pierre Lefranc's detailed 'Ashore and Afloat: New Perspectives on Topography and Geography in *Lord Jim*', *Conradiana*, 20 (1988), 109–35, supersedes earlier discussions of Patusan's geographical location.   JHS

Pawling, Sydney Southgate (1862–1922), partner in William *Heinemann's London publishing firm. Sydney Pawling first met Conrad in December 1896 at a meeting arranged by Edward *Garnett. In the process of helping Conrad to secure a new publisher, Garnett had previously arranged for Pawling to show *The Nigger of the 'Narcissus'* to W. E. *Henley for serialization in the *New Review*, a monthly published by Heinemann, and for the firm to consider it for book publication as well. By the time of their first meeting, the publishing future of *The Nigger of the 'Narcissus'* was, thanks to Pawling, virtually secure. The connection with Pawling, who went on to acquire British book rights of *The

Rescue for Heinemann, temporarily freed the writer from the wearisome business of selling his fiction in the market place; through his new contact, Conrad was also introduced to Stephen *Crane. An 'excellent fellow' and lifelong friend, the trusty Pawling could always be relied on for professional advice and support, as when in 1902 he wrote a long memorandum to Edmund *Gosse in support of the move to secure Conrad a Royal Literary Fund award (see GRANTS AND AWARDS). He also oversaw publication of Heinemann's *Collected Edition of Conrad's works in 1921.

Penfield, Frederic Courtland (1855–1922), American ambassador in Vienna from 1913 to 1917. Frederic Penfield was during the First World War responsible for handling the diplomatic interests of Britain, France, Italy, and Japan in Austria-Hungary. Acting as the Conrads' intermediary when war was declared during their 1914 visit to *Poland, he helped to secure funds and permits enabling them to leave *Zakopane in Austrian Poland for Vienna. By good fortune, Penfield 'had been for many years one of the legion of Conrad's admirers, and therefore his interest in being of service to the novelist was just that much greater, and a warm friendship sprang up between them immediately' ('Conrad in Poland', *Bookman* (NY), 46 (February 1918), 659). Several years later, Conrad dedicated *The Rescue* (1920) to Penfield.

Perse, Saint-John (pen-name of Marie-René-Auguste-Alexis Saint-Léger Léger, 1887–1975), French poet and diplomat awarded the Nobel Prize for Literature in 1960. Saint-John Perse visited Conrad in the summer of 1912 with an introduction from Agnes *Tobin and stayed for a few days. Perse recalled in several later letters and reminiscences his memorable meeting with 'the most humane man I have met in literary circles' and vividly remembered conversations that embraced the works of *Dostoevsky, *Turgenev, Herman Melville, Edward Lear, Molière, and Émile *Zola. The only note of criticism to appear in Perse's reminiscences is a reference to Con-

rad speaking in '*épouvantable* [dreadful] French' (*JCIR*, 221), a rare criticism of his spoken French.

Personal Record, A. At the end of 'A Familiar Preface', Conrad expressed his hope and his aim in writing this work of reminiscence: his hope was that the pages would yield 'at last the vision of a personality; the man behind the books'; and his aim was 'to give the record of personal memories by presenting faithfully the feelings and sensations connected with the writing of my first book and with my first contact with the sea' (p. xxi). Writing to E. V. *Lucas in June 1909, Conrad declared of *A Personal Record*: 'I know that the form is unconventional but it is not so casual as it seems. It has been thought out.... My case (as before the public) being not only exceptional but even unique I felt that I could not proceed in cold blood on the usual lines of an autobiography' (*CL*, iv. 247). A month later, he informed Ford Madox *Ford that the work 'expresses perfectly my purpose of treating the literary life and the sea-life on parallel lines with a running reference to my early years' (*CL*, iv. 263).

Conrad begins *A Personal Record* with the observation, 'Books may be written in all sorts of places' (3), and illustrates this claim by recounting how he began writing the tenth chapter of *Almayer's Folly* in his cabin aboard the *Adowa* in Rouen harbour in December 1893, while he was serving as her second mate. After he had written a single sentence, he was interrupted by the arrival of the banjo-playing third mate. This interruption occasions a retrospective account of the circumstances that led to his serving in the *Adowa*. He tells how, through the efforts of Captain Froud, the secretary of the London Shipmasters' Society, and through his own ability to speak French fluently, he was employed by the 'ephemeral France-Canadian Transport Company' (6). Noting that the impulse to abandon his career as a seaman for that of a writer had not yet signalled itself, Conrad again interrupts the narrative in order to sketch how he began writing *Almayer's Folly* in his Belgravia lodgings in *London.

Returning to the *Adowa* narrative, he recalls that, although the ship had been chartered to carry French emigrants from Rouen to Canada, the company's plans failed to materialize and she never left Rouen. As this aborted voyage marked the end of Conrad's professional career as a seaman, the interconnected *Adowa* and *Almayer's Folly* narratives serve to convey the sense of his transition between two careers.

The growth of Conrad's first novel *Almayer's Folly*, whose manuscript was begun in 1889 and finished in 1894, provides a parallel to his changing fortunes and the development of his career during this time. After his visit to Africa in 1890—which fulfilled his childhood assertion 'When I grow up I shall go *there*' (13)—the first seven chapters of the manuscript were completed; the conclusion of its chapter 8 is associated in his mind with his subsequent convalescence and hydrotherapy in *Champel-les-Bains, *Geneva, in 1891; and the ninth is linked with his temporary job as a warehouse manager in London in that same year. Then, during a voyage to *Australia in the *Torrens*, in which Conrad served as first mate between November 1891 and July 1893, the unfinished manuscript of *Almayer's Folly* had its first reader in a 'young Cambridge man' (15), W. H. *Jacques, who, in response to Conrad's query, pronounced it 'Distinctly' worth finishing (17). Fittingly, embedded within his account of the manuscript's development, Conrad offers a definition of the novel: 'And what is a novel if not a conviction of our fellow-men's existence strong enough to take upon itself a form of imagined life clearer than reality and whose accumulated verisimilitude of selected episodes puts to shame the pride of documentary history?' (15).

Having used the tale of 'the wandering MS.' (22) of *Almayer's Folly* to introduce aspects of his two careers, sailor and author, Conrad then recounts how, 'advanced now to the first words of the ninth chapter' (19), it travelled with him on a visit to his uncle in *Ukraine in 1893 and was almost lost in Berlin. Now, the narrative focus shifts to Conrad's Polish descent, particularly the fate of his family under 'the oppressive shadow of the great Russian Empire' (24). The manner in which Conrad finds traces of his childhood memories in the characters and incidents of his Ukraine visit is analogous to the manner in which *A Personal Record* generally traces the formative influences of the past on the present, or the life on the art.

Continuing the narration of his Ukraine visit and the memories of childhood it evokes, chapter 2 affords Conrad the opportunity to introduce his uncle and 'the wisest, the firmest, the most indulgent of guardians' (31), Tadeusz *Bobrowski, who, in turn, speaks of other family members, such as Conrad's mother and his aunt, Teofila *Bobrowska. He then recalls Mr Nicholas B[obrowski], his grandfather's brother, who served under *Napoleon in the Russian campaign of 1812. In particular, Conrad recounts how, during the retreat from Moscow, Mr—later Captain—Nicholas B was driven by hunger to eat dog, a family tale which made an indelible impression on the young boy. Although his reaction to the tale is still one of 'childish horror', Conrad recognizes that this act of self-preservation is nevertheless a form of 'patriotic desire'. This episode leads him to confront the charge of 'desertion' made against himself by 'men of unstained rectitude' for leaving Poland as a young man to make his life elsewhere. Conrad's response is that no charge of faithlessness 'ought to be lightly uttered': 'The part of the inexplicable should be allowed for in appraising the conduct of men in a world where no explanation is final' (35).

Lamenting the fact that it 'would take too long to explain the intimate alliance of contradictions in human nature which makes love itself wear at times the desperate shape of betrayal', Conrad invokes *Don Quixote, 'the patron saint of all lives spoiled or saved by the irresistible grace of the imagination', to argue that this same imaginative spirit, responsible for so much greatness, nonetheless meant that 'he was not a good citizen' (36, 37). He then remembers how his persistent desire to go to *sea led his tutor, Adam Marek *Pulman, to declare him 'an incorrigible, hopeless Don Quixote' (44) during a walking holiday in the Swiss Alps in 1873, when Conrad had refused to be dissuaded from his maritime ambitions. Conrad's resolve in the face of his tutor's arguments is depicted as coinciding with a chance meeting with an English traveller striding purposefully at the head of a small caravan. In essence, after the opening chapter's concern with the relationship between Conrad's life and his art, the theme of the second chapter is fidelity: fidelity to oneself and fidelity to one's nation.

In chapter 3, the narrative returns to Nicholas B, Conrad's great-uncle, and recounts how he was the last man to cross the bridge over the River Elster after the battle of Leipzig (in 1813). Conrad maintains that his great-uncle's wound in the heel unites him with Achilles and Napoleon himself. Nicholas B joined the army of the newly established Polish Kingdom as a lieutenant, but at the news of the *Warsaw uprising of 1830 (which Conrad dates as 1831) and before his first campaign, the entire regiment was exiled to *Russia. Nicholas B, now a captain, was sent to Astrakhan, where he spent three years. Declining to serve in the Russian army, Captain Nicholas B was retired on half-pension. But not even in retirement, as a tenant on the estate of a friend, could he escape the attention of the Russians since Cossacks, in the process of quelling the 1863 uprising, visited the farm in his absence and, before departing, ransacked the outbuildings and removed the firearms, an example followed by the local peasants, who proceeded to ransack the house, searching for money. Among their booty was a tin box containing the ex-soldier's two military crosses of the Legion of Honour and For Virtue, and his Legion of Honour Patent. Nicholas B 'broke down completely' (63) at the news of this loss and, although the crosses were subsequently found, he never recovered in the two years of life left to him from the loss of the parchment. Conrad's memories of Nicholas B, which serve to link the life of his family to the life of the nation, are bound up with memories of exile, that of

his great-uncle but also that of his mother and himself—and he ends the chapter with his memory of their departure as they prepared to return to exile after a three-month leave. Its closing words are poignantly simple: 'Each generation has its memories' (67).

Chapter 4 is devoted to Conrad's encounter with the man who would be immortalized as the eponymous dreamer in *Almayer's Folly*. The chapter opens with the observation that, although he had not set out with the ambition of becoming an author, once he 'had done blackening over the first manuscript page' of the novel, 'the die was cast' (68–9). Next he continues the narrative, broached in the first chapter of *A Personal Record*, of how he started writing *Almayer's Folly* while lodging in Bessborough Gardens, London. Conrad first saw Kaspar *Almayer, actually William Charles *Olmeijer, a Dutch Eurasian living in *Borneo, from the bridge of an island steamer the *Vidar*, in which Conrad served as first mate. He recalls how, during this visit to the settlement of Tanjung Redeb on the Berau River, a Bali pony was delivered to Almayer. Trying to fathom Almayer's reasons for wanting the pony, which he could not ride and which the island terrain made impractical for use, Conrad concludes: 'With Almayer one could never tell. He governed his conduct by considerations removed from the obvious, by incredible assumptions, which rendered his logic impenetrable to any reasonable person' (76). The narrative recounts the struggle to secure the pony, winching it overboard and onto the jetty, where Almayer's failure to control it led to the pony fleeing into the morning mist still wearing the canvas sling used to land it. On its recapture, at the cost of the ship's best quartermaster who was disabled by a kick to the shoulder, the crew earned no thanks from Almayer: 'Both remorse and gratitude seemed foreign to Almayer's character' (84). Conrad's account reveals how Almayer's eccentricity extended to his apparent reluctance to open his letters and to his owning 'The only geese of the East Coast' (85). It is during these revelations that Conrad makes his famous claim about the importance of meeting Almayer: 'if I had not got to know Almayer pretty well it is almost certain there would never have been a line of mine in print'. The chapter ends with a rhetorical apostrophe in which Conrad imagines meeting Almayer in the Elysian fields and having to account for 'convert[ing] your name to my own uses' (87).

So improbable does Conrad deem his becoming an author that he speculates (chapter 5) on the broader laws governing the fate of mankind: 'The ethical view of the universe involves us at last in so many cruel and absurd contradictions, where the last vestiges of faith, hope, charity, and even of reason itself, seem ready to perish, that I have come to suspect that the aim of creation cannot be ethical at all. I would fondly believe that its object is purely spectacular.' Whatever else this spectacle may occasion, it is 'never for despair'. Rather, since 'the unwearied self-forgetful attention to every phase of the living universe reflected in our consciousness may be our appointed task on this earth' (92), such speculation allows Conrad to claim for the prose artist of fiction—'which after all is but truth often dragged out of a well and clothed in the painted robe of imaged phrases'—a place in mankind's attempt to make sense of 'a purely spectacular universe' (93). Thus he justifies simultaneously the art of fiction and his own status as an author, one of the 'many humble retainers' in the 'fair courtyards of the House of Art' (94). Nor is this merely self-justification. Literary criticism, too, has its place here for, as Conrad claims, 'as long as distinguished minds are ready to treat it in the spirit of high adventure, literary criticism shall appeal to us with all the charm and wisdom of a well-told tale of personal experience' (96).

Characteristically, the accident of Conrad's becoming an author is inextricably linked to his choice of career and country. Thus, the inherent spirit of 'romance' in fiction echoes the desire that inspired him to go to sea, while the 'adventure' of the best literary criticism has links with Englishness: 'For Englishmen especially . . . a task, any task, undertaken in an adventurous spirit acquires the merit of romance' (96). Conrad devotes the second half of the chapter to the problems of literary composition and, in particular, to how he was interrupted during the composition of *Nostromo* so that the banalities of polite conversation swept away the entire imaginary world of *Costaguana he had been painstakingly constructing. This anecdote, in which 'the profane world' (97) intrudes heedlessly into the world of art, concludes with Conrad comparing his devotion to the craft of fiction to the devotion of the family dog, and observing that his uninvited and departing visitor can know nothing of either 'the secret terms of self-imposed tasks' or 'the pain that may lurk in the very rewards of rigid self-command' (105).

The last two chapters concentrate on Conrad's initiation into sea life rather than his career as a writer. Chapter 6 starts by briefly contrasting the literary criticism he has received as an author with the 'quarterdeck criticism' (109) at sea. This in turn introduces the 'sea appreciations' or references he has received from the various masters under whom he served, all of which testify to his 'strictly sober' character (111). Nor was such sobriety a feature only of his maritime career for, as Conrad claims: 'I have tried to be a sober worker all my life—all my two lives' (112). Then, stressing the importance of sobriety to the Maritime Department of the Board of Trade, Conrad goes on to describe each of his three *examinations, for the certificates of second mate, first mate, and, finally, master. While Conrad claims to have made a 'deliberate choice' well before he went to sea that 'if I was to be a seaman then I would be a British seaman and no other' (119), biographical evidence would not appear to support this. He then describes how he took a 'standing jump out of his racial surroundings and associations' (121) by going to *Marseilles to pursue a career as a sailor. His early training, what he calls his 'sea-infancy' (124) under the pilots in Marseilles, is vividly recaptured, as is his acquaintance with Mme Delestang who, he recalls, urged him to take care not to waste his life.

The final chapter opens with Conrad's recollection of how he meditated deeply upon this warning throughout the evening and before going out for his final moonlit service cruise as the guest of the Marseilles pilots. The anecdote is clearly designed as an answer to Mme Delestang, and the fact that the narrative occasionally strays into the present tense helps to underscore both the intimacy with which the moment is recollected and the intensity of Conrad's commitment to these formative experiences. He also dwells upon the sense of tradition and comradeship among the sailors, and the anecdote provides an apt conclusion to *A Personal Record* since it was during this last cruise that Conrad first touched an English ship, the *James Westoll*. The actual moment is recorded in terms faintly erotic: 'when I bore against the smooth flank of the first English ship I ever touched in my life, I felt it already throbbing under my open palm' (137). This sensuous communion leads to the image of the Red Ensign, with which the book closes, but it is also linked to the English language, for, as Conrad recalls just before this: 'for the very first time in my life, I heard myself addressed in English—the speech of my secret choice, of my future, of long friendships, of the deepest affections, of hours of toil and hours of ease, and of solitary hours too, of books read, of thoughts pursued, of remembered emotions—of my very dreams!' (136). The conclusion of *A Personal Record* emphasizes the literary purpose and the nation towards which Conrad's sea career in the service of the Red Ensign has led him.

On 18 September 1908, Conrad revealed to his agent J. B. *Pinker that he would be contributing 'a series of papers' to Ford's *English Review. 'These are to be intimate personal autobiographical things under the general title (for book form perhaps) of the Life and the Art' (*CL*, iv. 125). Subsequently, he explained to Pinker that he intended to 'make Polish life enter English literature', and suggested that, since his literary reputation was becoming 'more

clearly defined with every published vol[ume]', this was 'the psychological moment' for the success of such a book (*CL*, iv. 138). The text was serialized in the *English Review*, under the title *Some Reminiscences*, from the (inaugural) December 1908 issue until June 1909. The first *English Review* paper provided the basis for a pamphlet published under the title *Some Reminiscences* by Paul R. Reynolds (New York) in 1908 to secure the American copyright. The first British book edition of *Some Reminiscences* was published by Eveleigh Nash in 1912, and contained 'A Familiar Preface', signed 'J.C.K.', the 'K' standing for Korzeniowski and thus identifying his Polish descent. In the same year, the first American edition, also containing 'A Familiar Preface', was published by Harper under the title *A Personal Record*. Conrad wrote 'A Familiar Preface' in summer 1911 and his 'Author's Note' to the volume in September 1919. The title used for the first American edition was adopted in the second English edition of the book, published by Nelson in 1916. No manuscripts or typescripts survive, with the exception of a single handwritten page now held at Syracuse University.

While outwardly offering itself as an autobiography, *A Personal Record* is a very 'fictional' one in its use of disrupted chronology, teasingly juxtaposed digressions, and variable points of view. As Najder suggests: 'The result is a splendid piece of personal mythology' (1997: 104). The work can also be read as Conrad's answer to such critics as Robert Lynd who argued that Conrad was 'without either country or language' and that 'the works of Joseph Conrad translated from the Polish would . . . have been a more precious possession on English shelves than the works of Joseph Conrad in the original English' (*CCH*, 211). Such criticism must have reminded Conrad of the controversy in the late 1890s, when the Polish novelist and nationalist Eliza *Orzeszkowa charged him with draining away 'the life blood from the nation in order to pass it on to the Anglo-Saxons . . . just because they pay better' (*CUFE*, 188). Thus, *A Personal Record* might be said to 'answer' both his Polish *and* English critics: on the one hand, Conrad implicitly rejects Orzeszkowa's charge by his expression of fidelity to his Polish past; and on the other, he responds to Lynd's charge by demonstrating the relevance of his formative experiences to his choice of becoming an English writer. For a detailed discussion, see J. M. Kertzer, 'Conrad's Personal Record', *University of Toronto Quarterly*, 44 (1975), 290–303. See also POLAND and POLISH INHERITANCE.

AHS

Peyrol. From his first appearance at the port of Toulon dressed in the colours of the French flag, Jean Peyrol, the title-character of *The Rover*, has the emblematic function of representing *France itself. His return in late middle age to the scenes of his childhood after long years at sea, some as a Brother of the Coast, a lawless freebooter in the eastern oceans, is a reconciliation with his native land. But thrust into the turmoil of the French Revolution and its turbulent aftermath, Peyrol finds his desire for quiet withdrawal from society frustrated by the necessity of long-deferred commitment, first to those surrounding him, and then, at the sacrifice of his life, to France. At Escampobar, the remote old farmhouse where he establishes his first and last true home high above the sea, Peyrol is with time compelled to take on a variety of roles. As the friend of old Catherine and companion of Michel; as father-protector of *Arlette, for whom he feels a romantic attraction that he realizes must be suppressed; as the antagonist of Citizen Scevola, the psychotic anarchist; and as mentor and example to Lieutenant Réal, whom Arlette loves, the old seaman finds himself implicated in ties that provide him with sufficient reasons for living and dying.

These various calls on his feelings transform the solitary and alienated figure of the novel's opening into a man of 'large heart', rooted in place and community. Under the tutelage of friendship and love, the key-words of Peyrol's destiny become reconciliation, commitment, and sacrifice to an ideal; and his heroic death, defending

France from its English enemies and protecting Arlette's love for Réal, is an act of loyalty and a *Jim-like keeping of faith with an ideal. Much as Escampobar's residents alter Peyrol, he, in turn, changes them: he bequeaths to the traumatized Arlette an internal calm, symbolized by her love for Réal, and to the prematurely world-weary Réal an awakening to life; he accords hope and dignity to Michel by his friendship; and in confining Scevola aboard his doomed tartane he puts an end to the spirit of division and bloodlust that had possessed France. Peyrol's own final transformations, first into solar hero—he dies in his boat at sunset, his purpose accomplished and victory assured—and then into genius of place, as sentinel watching over the peace and prosperity of his adoptive family, suggest the novel's reaching out towards myth.

While Peyrol's first name may pay a compliment to Conrad's friend of his late years G. *Jean-Aubry, the character draws on, and recollects, Conrad's *Marseilles companion and shipmate Dominique *Cervoni. Peyrol is also a finely shaded self-portrait of Conrad in his later years, subject to the pull of a romantic attraction to Jane *Anderson and an affectionate devotion to his cousin Aniela *Zagórska, and as the seaman-turned-landsman wistfully seeking rest after a long career and taking a last farewell of the Mediterranean haunts of his youth.

JHS

phrenology. A pseudo-science based on the belief that the personality is reflected in the specific shape of the skull, phrenology was founded at the end of the 18th century by German anatomist Dr Franz Joseph Gall (1757–1828) and his associate Johann Gaspar Spurzheim (1776–1832). Now long discredited, it was still taken quite seriously throughout the 19th century right up to Conrad's time, and references to phrenology appear in 'Heart of Darkness' and *The Secret Agent*.

Conrad's first encounter with phrenology may have been in the third chapter of Captain *Marryat's *Mr Midshipman Easy* (1836), where Easy's father requires the nursemaid Sarah to submit to a phrenological examination before employing her to nurse the baby, just as in 'Heart of Darkness' *Marlow's head is measured by a company doctor before he goes out to the *Congo. Both Marryat and Conrad are ironic about the value of the exercise. This head-measuring episode has been linked with a strange request that Conrad received from his uncle Tadeusz *Bobrowski on behalf of Dr Izydor Kopernicki, a Polish anthropologist who wanted Conrad to collect a dozen native skulls and dispatch them to the Museum of Craniology in *Cracow (*CPB*, 74). However, comparative craniology is not the same as phrenology, and Conrad may also have remembered the phrenological heads in the collection of Dr Paul-Ferdinand Gachet, which he could have seen when he passed through Paris to visit his 'aunt' Marguerite *Poradowska on 15 June 1891 (see Gene M. Moore, 'Conrad, Dr. Gachet and the "School of Charenton"', *Conradiana*, 25 (1993), 163–77). The heads in Dr Gachet's collection were plaster casts of the decapitated heads of guillotined criminals like Pierre-François Lacenaire, on which the phrenological zones were often marked for purposes of instruction, as if to show that the owner of the head was obviously a criminal 'type'.

Studies of 'criminal man' by the Italian criminologist Cesare *Lombroso and of 'degeneracy' by the Hungarian Max *Nordau brought increased interest to the possible applications of phrenology as a means of identifying criminals or other human types, such as geniuses. Conrad's own characterizations often reflect these classifications: for example, *Kurtz's 'lofty frontal bone' (*Youth*, 115) is, in Lombrosan terms, a sign of genius. As John E. Saveson has shown in 'Conrad, *Blackwood's*, and Lombroso', *Conradiana*, 6 (1974), 57–62, Lombroso's classifications were common in articles about anarchists published in *Blackwood's Magazine* at the turn of the century. In effect, phrenology sought to describe the mind by means of the shape of the skull, while Lombroso and Nordau explored the diagnostic value of visible facial features such as lips or ear-lobes. In *The Secret Agent*, Tom Ossipon invokes Lombroso to identify *Stevie as a 'degenerate' (46) and Winnie *Verloc as a 'murdering type' (297), but the joke is on Ossipon, whose own facial features are those of a Lombrosan rapist and murderer. For a survey of the significance of phrenology in British culture, see Roger Cooter, *The Cultural Meaning of Popular Science: Phrenology and the Organization of Consent in Nineteenth-Century Britain* (1984).

Pinker, Eric Seabrooke (1891–1973), J. B. *Pinker's elder son. Eric Pinker joined his father's literary agency on leaving school in 1908 and later served in the First World War, being awarded the Military Cross for bravery in September 1917. Returning to the agency, he took over the firm's management after his father's death in 1922 and became Conrad's agent for the last two years of the writer's life. Moving to New York in 1926, Eric set up the American branch of the firm, leaving his younger brother Ralph (1900–59) in charge of the London office. The company was liquidated in 1939 when Eric admitted to embezzling $139,000 of his clients' royalties and was sentenced to a term of two-and-a-half to five years in New York's Sing Sing prison. A similar fate simultaneously overtook his brother Ralph, who, found guilty of malpractice and misappropriation of funds, was sentenced to Wormwood Scrubs prison.

Pinker, James Brand (1863–1922), one of the first literary agents in London, who represented Conrad's interests for over twenty years. A Scotsman by birth, J. B. Pinker began his working life as a clerk in Tilbury Docks before entering the world of journalism through the *Levant Herald* in Constantinople and then, in London, through *Black & White*, and as editor of *Pearson's Magazine*. In 1896, he started a Granville House literary agency in Arundel Street, London WC2, presenting himself in the *Literary Year-Book* at this time as follows: 'Mr. Pinker has always made a special point of helping young authors in the early stages of their career, when they need most the aid of an adviser with a thorough knowledge of the literary world and the publishing trade.' By 1900, when the association between Conrad and Pinker began, the astute agent was outstripping his chief rival, A. P. Watt, in the quality of his clientele, which included Arnold *Bennett, H. G. *Wells, Stephen *Crane, Henry *James, and Ford Madox *Ford. Although much maligned as a 'mere' tradesman by authors of the day, the astute Pinker was superbly attuned to the changing economic climate of the 1890s publishing market and served the interests of several 'difficult' writers with a skilful blend of shrewdness, tact, generosity, and long-suffering.

These qualities were certainly needed in the early stages of his long association with Conrad, who in 1900 was regarded by Pinker (and regarded himself) as an uncertain professional risk. In a relationship where the volatile Conrad required Pinker to play many parts—friend, generous banker, father-figure, general factotum—tension and mutual exasperation were unavoidable. Underlying many of these tensions was a potential problem created by the new marketing strategies Pinker brought into Conrad's professional life as a writer. Before Pinker's arrival, Conrad had enjoyed supportive personal relationships with individual publishers such as William *Heinemann and William *Blackwood, who were indulgently sympathetic to the vagaries of his methods of work, which could include writer's block, broken deadlines, and the phenomena of 'runaway' stories and debts. On taking over as Conrad's agent, Pinker advised him to drop the idea of fixed commitment to an individual publisher and enter the burgeoning late Victorian publishing market as a free-bargaining writer. Even with Pinker to guide him, Conrad was ill-fitted to survive such a cut-throat market, committed as he was to a form of experimental novel, the unpredictable gestation of which involved an enormous amount of energy, time, and living costs. One of his solutions to the problem of mounting debts was to rely upon his agent's generosity and borrow heavily on the strength of future payments and royalties. Pinker's patience in the face of his client's mushrooming debts was remarkable, but not as limitless as Conrad sometimes seems to have demanded. With yet more financial burdens placed upon him in 1904, Conrad was increasingly driven to a second solution, that of bifurcating his writing life between serious projects and saleable journalistic material in an effort to respond to market conditions, buy himself time for more important projects, and make a move to pacify Pinker. Thus, at one period during the writing of *Nostromo* in 1904, he resembled a hectic juggler, composing the novel during the daytime, dictating reminiscences to Ford in the evening, nursing an injured wife, and in spare intervals cobbling together a one-act play out of an earlier story.

These mounting and converging pressures help to explain why Conrad's relationship with Pinker, from 1904 to 1910, was fraught with underlying tension. In 1904, Pinker, distressed by a public rumour that he kept his client under tight financial control, requested Conrad to scotch it immediately. During this period, further medical costs, household bills, and expenses incurred by the Conrads on stays abroad required Pinker to supply large advances. In 1907, the desperate Conrad asked his agent to help him 'settle down . . . on an economical basis' (*CL*, iii. 460), but then he became increasingly resentful at having to justify all of his expenses and resisted Pinker's efforts to link his payments to fixed amounts of delivered copy. The inevitable crisis arrived when Pinker's patience snapped in December 1909 at a time when Conrad owed him £2,700. By that date, he had been labouring painfully for over two years on *Under Western Eyes*, constantly assuring Pinker that its end was in sight, and yet perversely and high-handedly (in Pinker's view) demanding his agent's agreement when he interrupted *Under Western Eyes* to write for the *English Review*. Pinker firmly pointed out that he could advance no more money unless *Under Western Eyes* were finished within a fortnight. Threatening to throw the manuscript into the fire, Conrad soon had an explosive row with his agent, which led to a two-year estrangement.

Restored in 1912, their relationship matured into genuine friendship. With the dramatic upturn in Conrad's financial fortunes after 1914, he could begin to settle his debts and meet his long-suffering agent's right to 10 per cent of his literary earnings. The two men met weekly, spent weekends at each other's homes, shared family holidays, and even collaborated on a screenplay, *Gaspar the Strong Man*, in autumn 1920. By 1916, Conrad had come to realize that his relationship with Pinker far transcended the client–agent bond: 'those books which, people say, are an asset of English literature owe their existence to Mr Pinker as much as to me. For 15 years of my writing life he has seen me through periods of unproductiveness[,] through illnesses[,] through all sorts of troubles. . . . But the fact remains that P was the only man who backed his opinion with his money, and that in no grudging manner' (*CL*, v. 619). Pinker's sudden death in New York in 1922 deeply affected Conrad: 'Twenty years' friendship and for most of that time in the constant interchange of the most intimate thoughts and feelings created a bond as strong as the nearest relationship' (*LL*, ii. 265). After his death, Pinker's thriving literary agency was taken over by his sons *Eric and Ralph. For a survey of the 1,300 extant letters between the author and his agent, see Frederick R. Karl, 'Conrad and Pinker', in Sherry (ed.) 1976: 156–73. See also Watts 1989: 85–9.

'Planter of Malata, The', a tale of unrequited infatuation, written in November and December 1913 during a break from Conrad's work on *Victory*. Some 25,000 words in length, it was published in the June and July 1914 issues of *Metropolitan Magazine* (New York) before appearing as the first of four stories in *Within the Tides*.

The story opens in an editorial office in an unnamed 'great colonial city' (3) that was identified in the manuscript as Sydney, *Australia. Geoffrey Renouard has just returned from solitary life on his silk planta-

tion in Malata and has encountered Felicia Moorsom and her philosopher father at a dinner-party the previous evening. The lovely Miss Moorsom has returned from England in search of her fiancé Arthur, who was disgraced in a financial scandal and disappeared, but whose name has meanwhile been cleared. The news arrives that Arthur has been working incognito as 'Mr Walter', Renouard's assistant in Malata; and Renouard has neglected to mention to anyone that Arthur died in an accident just before Renouard's departure for the city. He takes the Moorsoms back with him to Malata and arranges for his native assistants to pretend that Mr Walter is away on a trip, but the 'ghost' of the dead Arthur haunts both the natives and the visitors. Finally Renouard confesses to Felicia both Arthur's death and his love for her. When she leaves the island, Renouard remains there alone after dismissing his plantation crew. When his friend the Editor arrives a month later, only Renouard's jacket and sarong are found, indicating that the Planter of Malata must have drowned himself by swimming out into the open sea.

In his 'Author's Note' to *Within the Tides*, Conrad described the story as 'a nearly successful attempt at doing a very difficult thing', and he agreed with critics who found that the final scene between Felicia and Renouard 'destroyed to a certain extent the characteristic illusory glamour of their personalities' (p. viii). Critics have generally tended to dismiss the story as a sentimental melodrama or a failed romance. The manuscript indicates that Conrad occasionally had trouble writing the name 'Renouard', and this symptom, together with the similarity between the names 'Renouard' and 'Renouf', leads Meyer (1967) to the psychoanalytic conclusion that the story was a masochistic return to Conrad's failed courtship of Eugénie Renouf in *Mauritius in 1888. In '"The Planter of Malata": Renouard's Sinking Star of Knowledge', *Conradiana*, 8 (1976), 148–62, Joel R. Kehler reviews earlier criticism (*Within the Tides* is not included in *CCH*) and discusses the sense in which the story can be seen as a variation on the themes of *Victory*. Despite Conrad's disavowal of medieval subjects in his 'Author's Note', Owen Knowles sees the story as a free adaptation of Prosper *Mérimée's 'La Vénus d'Ille' (1837) in 'Conrad and Mérimée: The Legend of Venus in "The Planter of Malata"', *Conradiana*, 11 (1979), 177–84. In 'Conrad's Heart of Emptiness: "The Planter of Malata"', *Conradiana*, 18 (1986), 180–92, Juliet McLauchlan argues that the tale is 'finer and more interesting than has so far been allowed' (180), and uses a close reading of the text to demonstrate that it is 'pre-eminently not a love story' but, on Renouard's part, one of 'ultra-romantic delusion' (185), while Felicia herself remains indifferent and superficial. In '"The Planter of Malata": A Case of Creative Pathology', *Conradiana*, 26 (1994), 187–200, Daphna Erdinast-Vulcan diagnoses the story as an 'inferior' and 'generically schizophrenic' work with a problematic and imbalanced structure (188). In sum, scholars have valued 'The Planter of Malata' not as a love story but as a ghost story, in which the solitary Renouard falls in love with an illusory image of the living Felicia only to find himself thwarted by the ghost of her first lover.

The manuscript is held in the Berg Collection, New York Public Library, and the typescript at the Beinecke Rare Book and Manuscript Library, Yale University. A manuscript of the last two chapters was last recorded as the property of George T. *Keating. One page of carbon typescript is held at Texas Tech University, Lubbock.

Poland: historical outline. The documented history of Poland as an independent state begins in 965 with the Catholic baptism of its first historical ruler, Mieszko I, and of his subjects. Ever since, Poland has remained the easternmost country with a Latin alphabet, strong links with papal Rome, and active participation in the great European intellectual currents of the Renaissance, Reformation, and Counter-Reformation. The Romanesque, Gothic, and Baroque styles reach only as far as the eastern frontiers of old Poland.

While its western border changed little from the 14th to the 18th century, Poland expanded eastwards. Topographically, it lies mostly within the huge East-Central European plain stretching from Brandenburg deep into *Russia. The Carpathian Mountains flank it from the south, the Baltic Sea from the north. In the late 14th century, vast territories of the Grand Duchy of Lithuania, inhabited by Lithuanians, Belorussians, and Ruthenians (now called Ukrainians), were joined to Poland as the result of a royal marriage between the Lithuanian Grand Duke Iogaillas (who assumed the name of Władysław Jagiełło) and the Polish Crown Princess Jadwiga. This marital union founded the Jagiellonian dynasty, which ruled Poland for 183 years. The Union of Lublin (1569) linking ethnic Poland ('the Crown') with Lithuania-Belorussia and *Ukraine established a multinational commonwealth of three nations in which Poland was culturally dominant. For nearly two centuries, Poland remained the largest country of continental Europe.

Its sole ruling class was the *szlachta*, or landed nobility and gentry combined, with no legal distinction between the two groups and no hereditary titles. The *szlachta* made up about 6 per cent of the population, from 8 to 10 per cent in ethnic Poland, and were endowed with far-reaching individual and civic liberties, among them the *neminem captivabimus* dating from 1430, the equivalent of habeas corpus; the right to elect the king (hence the official name of the *Rzeczpospolita* or Republic, or more appropriately, Commonwealth); and the election of provincial and national parliaments with the exclusive right to levy taxes and declare war. The country was long renowned for its ethnic and religious tolerance, particularly remarkable at a time of great religious wars in Europe, to which a large Jewish population (since the 14th century) and many names of French, German, and Scottish origin can testify. Towns and cities, harbouring many burghers of foreign extraction, had the right to self-government, but their economic and political role was curtailed by the landowning *szlachta*, who were also dominant in cultural affairs. The capital, originally in Gniezno and after 1320 in *Cracow, was moved in 1609 to *Warsaw; other important urban centres included the capital of the Grand Duchy of Lithuania (now Vilnius), Lwów, Poznań, and the multinational port of Gdańsk.

Polish science came to the European forefront with Copernicus (Mikołaj Kopernik, 1473–1543), while political theory found an internationally influential exponent in Andrzej Frycz Modrzewski (1503–72). Polish as a literary language supplanted Latin early in the 16th century, and Polish poetry immediately flourished in the work of Jan Kochanowski (1530–84).

Since the mid-13th century, Poland had repeatedly played the role of defender of the eastern frontiers of Europe against invasions by Tartars and Ottoman Turks. Its geopolitical position earned Poland the sobriquet of the 'bulwark of Christianity', confirmed in 1683 by the lifting of the Turkish siege of Vienna by an army under the command of King Jan III Sobieski. The political system, with a strong component of subsidiarity in the structure of government and stress on unanimity in the adoption of parliamentary measures (the *liberum veto*), severely limited the central powers of the king and the administrative cohesion of the state. At the same time, these liberties stood in sharp contrast to the autocratic rule of Poland's neighbours. The Ukrainian rebellion of the mid-17th century and the ensuing annexation of eastern Ukraine by Russia marked the beginning of a decline. Towards the end of the 18th century, the lands of the Polish Commonwealth were divided in three consecutive partitions. In 1772, Austro-Hungary, Prussia, and Russia annexed large territories of the south, north-west, and north-east. On 3 May 1791, the Polish parliament or *Sejm* adopted the first written constitution in Europe: a liberal document which extended basic civic privileges to burghers and Jews, while at the same time strengthening the government and the army. This act prompted the second partition of Poland in 1793, in which Prussia and

Russia carved further territories from the western and eastern parts of the country. The third and final partition occurred in 1795, and the first Polish Republic was extinguished in spite of a desperate defence mounted by the Polish army commanded by Tadeusz Kościuszko.

Conditions in the three annexed parts of Poland varied. The Russian part was by far the largest, with Warsaw as its capital. The tsars assumed the title of kings of Poland, and the western territories incorporated in the third and final partition became known as 'the Kingdom', and until 1864 enjoyed a degree of legal and administrative autonomy from Russia proper. However, the entire country suffered from political backwardness and the rigidity imposed by autocratic rule, while Russia remained an empire in which the centre was less developed than many dependencies (such as Finland, Latvia, and Poland itself).

The Austro-Hungarian Empire was a multinational and far less centralized structure. After 1865, Poles in the Austrian zone enjoyed extensive cultural and even political autonomy, with their own school system and two universities. Several Poles held high positions in the Vienna parliament and government.

The Prussian part of Poland was the smallest, and the authorities in Berlin implemented a strategy of political and economic domination, together with attempts at cultural Germanization. The standard of living was the highest of the three partition zones, and industry most modern. In spite of discrimination, Poles learned how to organize themselves for the defence of their social and economic interests; but no degree of national autonomy was tolerated.

Following the failure of attempts to restore an independent Poland by means of an alliance with *Napoleon I, Poles staged a series of unsuccessful insurrections throughout the 19th century (in 1830–1, 1846, 1848, and in the January uprising of 1863–5) against foreign, and chiefly against Russian, domination. Harsh repressions followed, in which tens of thousands of 'rebels' were deported to exile in Siberia.

The role of the non-existent national institutions was largely taken over by literature. After the defeat of the November uprising of 1830, a 'Great Emigration' of Poles brought to the West, and mainly to France, thousands of officers and soldiers, leading poets like Adam *Mickiewicz and Juliusz Słowacki, artists like Frédéric Chopin, and representatives of independence movements of all political shades (see POLISH QUESTION and POLISH INHERITANCE).

The most important political and intellectual developments in Poland towards the close of the 19th century took place in the Russian and Austro-Hungarian zones. While the dominant mood among the Polish moneyed classes was one of some sort of accommodation with the three partitioning powers, clandestine socialist leaders, and especially Józef Piłsudski, preached in the 1890s that the Polish proletariat must have its own independent state. The 1905 Revolution that shook the very foundations of tsarist power in Russia also strengthened a strong national undercurrent in Poland. Later, with the permission of the Austrian authorities, Piłsudski founded a paramilitary organization that would come to play a vital role as a cadre of the future Polish army.

The reborn independent Poland was proclaimed on 11 November 1918, with Piłsudski as head of state. Within three months the first parliamentary elections were held under universal suffrage; in March 1921 a new constitution was adopted, guaranteeing legal equality to all citizens and giving strong powers to the Sejm. Meanwhile, Poland had to fight for virtually all its frontiers in a fierce and dramatic war with the Soviet army. A stunning Polish victory at the gates of Warsaw in August 1920 decided the results of this war, which was supposed to carry the revolution on towards *Germany.

The new Poland was much smaller than the territory prior to the partitions, with an irregular shape and complex borders. While a few million Poles remained on the other side of its frontiers, about 30 per cent of the population was made up of ethnic minorities: Ukrainians, Belorussians, Germans, and Jews (about 10 per cent of the total population). The new state had to be built on territory devastated by multiple German, Russian, and Austrian offensives, after a war in which about 15 per cent of the population had perished, from three segments with differing legal codes and administrative traditions, non-compatible road and railway networks, and no school system. In 1922 the first president, the former émigré scientist Gabriel Narutowicz, who had been elected with the support of representatives of the minorities, was assassinated by a nationalist fanatic in the gravest political murder in Poland's history.

Gdańsk (Danzig) was a 'free city' ruled by its mostly German inhabitants, so Poland began in 1922 to build its own seaport in nearby Gdynia, which became the home port of the merchant fleet and the navy, while Conrad came to be recognized as the foremost cultural patron of Polish seamanship and maritime literature.   ZN

'Poland Revisited'. The essay had its origin in an offer made through F. N. *Doubleday in America in mid-October 1914 by the Saturday Evening Post for some war articles to be written by Conrad when he returned home after being trapped on the family's visit to *Poland at the outbreak of the *First World War. During Conrad's absence, J. B. *Pinker was simultaneously negotiating for British newspaper publication. Returning home in early November 1914, Conrad fell ill and was unable to do any writing, with the result that drafting, revision, and rewriting continued until as late as February 1915. The essay was first published in the Daily News Leader in four parts, on 29 and 31 March, and 6 and 9 April 1915. In America, it was rejected by the Saturday Evening Post and was published in the Boston Evening Transcript in three instalments on 3, 10, and 17 April 1915. It was collected in revised form in Notes on Life and Letters.

The essay is one of Conrad's most sophisticated in its fusion of inner autobiographical record, impressionistic narrative strategy, and symbolic geography. Like

Wordsworth in his meditation upon his return to Tintern Abbey after a five-year absence, Conrad represents himself as a pilgrim or time-traveller returning to his homeland after a long separation. Through the agency of a reactivated memory, he is engaged in a quest for origins and for the moral pattern that has given his life both meaning and continuity. While the other members of the Conrad family see the visit to Poland as an expedition in space, it is for the writer himself a *recherche du temps perdu* and 'a journey in time, into the past' (149) enabling him to retrace in reverse a journey he had made many years earlier: from the writer's present home in *England, through *London, across the North Sea, and back to *Cracow where he had lived as a young boy. 'It was', Conrad comments, 'like the closing of a thirty-six-year cycle' (154). Hence, much of the essay reproduces a cyclical pilgrimage through a landscape of memory, in which the pilgrim seeks to discover the sense of a unified self, one at the same time inseparable from the communal values that have variously sustained him as a Pole, a seaman, and an English writer. This vision of continuity even extends from Conrad's own past into a future generation, since he is accompanied by his two 'English' sons, who may discover a meaning for themselves in their father's return to his origins: 'I trusted to the fresh receptivity of these young beings in whom, unless Heredity is an empty word, there should have been a fibre which would answer to the sight, to the atmosphere, to the memories of that corner of the earth where my own boyhood had received its earliest independent impressions' (146).

Almost inevitably, Conrad's awareness of the unrestful world of 1914 means that his 'retracing of footsteps on the road of life' (163) is no simple unbroken recollection in tranquillity. Using narrative discontinuities common in his fiction, Conrad increasingly juxtaposes the fruits of his private quest with the realities of an outer world teetering on the brink of a world war. So, while the return journey from Poland via Venice, Milan, and *Genoa, and then through the Mediterranean to Eng-

land, should similarly have offered further adventures in personal retrospection, it stubbornly refuses to do so: 'On that searoute I might have picked up a memory at every mile if the past had not been eclipsed by the tremendous actuality . . . But what were to me now the futilities of an individual past?' (172, 173). This final question also movingly hangs over the whole literary enterprise of using 'words' and artistry to recapture a 'mere' chapter of personal history in a world 'desecrated by violence, littered with wrecks, with death walking its waves, hiding under its waters' (155). See Andrzej Busza, 'Reading Conrad's *Poland Revisited*, *Cross Currents: A Yearbook of Central European Culture*, 6 (1987), 159–71. The manuscript is held at the Beinecke Rare Book and Manuscript Library, Yale University; a corrected and revised carbon-copy typescript of Part I and corrected ribbon-copy typescripts of Parts III and IV also survive in the Berg Collection, New York Public Library, and Bryn Mawr College. See also 'FIRST NEWS'.

Polish inheritance. Conrad's Polish inheritance can be seen and studied on several levels, most directly in his use of *language. The imprint of Polish syntax, Polish use of adverbs, and the rhetorical rhythm of Polish prose has been detected in Conrad's writings. Polish is a highly inflected language, which allows for greater flexibility in word-order and syntax. The influence of Polish on Conrad's English is, however, often difficult to distinguish from the influence of French, his second language.

A second level of influence involves Conrad's familial memories and traditions. He must have been conscious of being the son of distinguished parents, although he probably underestimated the political role of his father. His paternal inheritance included writing as a profession: Apollo *Korzeniowski was a mediocre poet, and rather better as a playwright and translator, but was above all a very well-read intellectual, an admirer and translator of *Dickens and *Shakespeare. Conrad was born into a family of ardent patriots, and both his parents sacrificed their lives to the idea of a free and socially just *Poland. So did his uncle Stefan Bobrowski, one of the chief leaders of the January 1863 uprising. Conrad's uncle and guardian Tadeusz *Bobrowski was also a devotee of duty, but differently conceived. He advocated political compromise, and ultimately became resigned, embittered, and pessimistic as to his country's future. Family lore was supplemented in Conrad's mind by reminiscences of many friends and acquaintances whose lives followed similar lines, and 19th-century Polish history provided him with source material for 'Prince Roman' (*Tales of Hearsay*). Although Conrad apparently did not attend school regularly, his education in Poland followed the established programme. He had to study Latin and German, and the list of required readings contained the essential works of classical antiquity.

The most powerful element of Conrad's Polish literary inheritance was the work of the great Romantic poets, Adam *Mickiewicz (1798–1855), Juliusz Słowacki (1809–49), and Zygmunt Krasiński (1812–59). Their Romanticism was of the continental kind, saturated with the spirit of communal and especially national responsibilities. But the consciousness of the public function of literature was already present in the work of Jan Kochanowski (1530–84), the first great personality of Polish poetry. The conflict between individual and communal interests, or between fidelity to a cause and personal happiness, was typical of the Polish poetry and prose avidly absorbed by the young Conrad. Among the more characteristic forms of popular fiction was the *gawęda*, a tale told by an individual narrator who was often also one of the protagonists involved. Echoes of the works of Polish Romantics, both in the form of concrete motifs and in the shape of moods and imagery, have been noticed in Conrad's fiction and also in his non-fictional pieces. The evident parallels between the plot of Stefan *Żeromski's *Dzieje grzechu* (The Story of a Sin, 1908) and Conrad's *Victory* are the most notable instance of the direct influence of later Polish literature.

Following the partitions of Poland at the end of the 18th century, literature was called upon to perform many of the functions of non-existent national institutions, and provided the main cultural bond unifying the country divided by imposed frontiers. This communal role tallied with the Romantic idea of a work of art as a deed, as an act at the same time artistic and moral. In Mickiewicz's supremely characteristic drama *Dziady* (Forefathers' Eve, 1832), the main protagonist Gustaw, a lonely, egocentric individual, highly self-conscious and brandishing his unhappy love under the pressure of political persecution by the Russians, becomes transformed into the Romantic patriot Konrad (to whom Konrad Korzeniowski owed his given name). Konrad's exceptional imagination and sensibility lead him to assume major social responsibilities; as he declares, 'My name is Million, because I love and suffer for millions'. Such linkage of individual morality with communal duty fully agrees with the traditions of the chivalric ethos, which has prevailed in Poland—and not only in literature—since the 16th century. The values of fidelity and honour are stridently celebrated in Polish poetry, drama, and fiction. A long history of mainly defensive wars against Tartars, Turks, Russians, and Swedes offered ample opportunity for both the preaching and the practice of these ideals. Polish culture contains a strong tradition of admiration for military service and armed exploits. The landed *szlachta* saw themselves as the cultural scions of the heroes of the *Iliad* and the *Aeneid*, and as embodiments of the values of medieval chivalry.

After the partitions of Poland, the struggle for liberty became the supreme duty of all Poles, ennobling all those who took up the cause, whatever their social background. The entire Polish moral and cultural tradition was steeped in the mythology of duty performed against all odds; fidelity, even to evidently lost causes; and honour, to be defended, and if lost, to be regained even at the cost of one's own life (which is the essential element of the plot of Mickiewicz's best-known work, his great epic *Pan Tadeusz*, 1834).

This Polish 'inheritance' is not to be understood as something consciously accepted or conveyed; for Conrad, it meant rather something bequeathed, available, and certainly accessible somewhere in the back of his mind. Another element of this legacy was the memory of the political reality of partitioned Poland. Eliza *Orzeszkowa (1841– 1910), a leading Polish novelist and one of the country's recognized moral authorities, attacked Conrad sharply in 1899 for 'desertion' and dereliction of his patriotic duty. Conrad was hurt, and responded to the attack obliquely in *A Personal Record*, declaring: 'No charge of faithlessness ought to be lightly uttered' and contemplating 'the intimate alliance of contradictions in human nature which makes love itself wear at times the desperate shape of betrayal' (35–6). Before the *First World War, Conrad apparently considered the cause of full Polish independence to be lost, but as 'Autocracy and War' (*Notes*) shows, the issue was one he continued to ponder. This sense of an inherited catastrophe, both personal and communal, was also a part of his mental background. See also Najder's 'Introduction', *CPB*, 1–31.

ZN

Polish question. The partitioning of the Commonwealth of *Poland, a country with a tradition of over eight centuries of statehood bolstered by a well-developed national culture, was perhaps the greatest political catastrophe of 18th-century Europe. The partitions provoked an immense intellectual and emotional reaction both in Poland and in other countries, and have remained a subject of debate ever since. Were they mainly a consequence of the internal weakness of the country, of the rampant 'Polish anarchy'? This claim, voiced by conservative German and Russian historians and politicians, was echoed by Polish critics of the power of the *szlachta*, or landed gentry. Or were the partitions, as Thomas Babington Macaulay and Jules Michelet maintained, the result of an uneven conflict between a more liberal and democratic Poland and three neighbouring centralized autocracies? Was it a demonstration of the natural selection of the fittest, and thus, as Karl Marx thought, a 'crime' against the progress of Europe towards liberty?

The fact that the three powers of Austria-Hungary, Prussia, and *Russia shared a common interest in quashing Polish aspirations, and that *France, a traditional ally of Poland, could play the Polish card at will, greatly influenced European diplomatic manœuvres throughout the 19th century. At the Congress of Vienna, Tsar Alexander I proposed the restoration of Poland as a separate entity, joined to Russia in a personal union. This move was blocked by Viscount Castlereagh, supported by Metternich and Talleyrand; they opted instead to maintain a 'balance of powers', which remained the guiding principle of British diplomacy through the time of Lloyd George, and one unsympathetic to Polish independence. Expressions of support for the Polish cause by Napoleon III only helped to stimulate closer cooperation among the three partitioning powers. Still, Polish hopes of obtaining 'Western' support for their aspirations remained high between the 1830 July Revolution in Paris and the defeat of France by the Prussians in 1870.

As it seemed unreasonable to count on a simultaneous victory over three stronger partitioning powers, most Polish patriots tied their hopes to the idea and force of 'progress', which would ultimately bring about the collapse of autocratic monarchies and produce an international brotherhood of free and friendly democracies. This faith in progress helps to explain the presence of Polish volunteers on the barricades of most European social revolutions and in the wars of national liberation in the 19th century, including the Paris Commune of 1871, whose commanders included Jarosław Dąbrowski, a Polish émigré, a veteran of the January 1863 uprising against the Russians, and a friend of Conrad's uncle Stefan Bobrowski.

As the most oppressive and backward occupying power, Russia remained for

Poles the principal foe, against whom two major insurrections were directed in 1830 and 1863. The former involved a war that lasted for nearly a year, with several pitched battles; while the latter signalled a two-year campaign of fights and skirmishes between the regular Russian army and Polish, Lithuanian, and Belorussian guerrillas, most of them poorly armed and inexperienced. The immediate losses were heavy, and in both cases there followed a period of reprisals, with numerous executions, massive confiscations of landed estates, and the banishment of thousands of insurgents, their families, and sympathizers to the depths of Russia. These terrible and futile losses caused much criticism among less 'romantically' disposed Poles. These could be divided between 'appeasers' who tended to accept the fact of foreign rule as ineluctable, or to be changed only by an act of Providence, and the 'positivists' who did not renounce the aim of independence but stressed the necessity for 'organic' groundwork: education, mutual assistance, and economic development. The less patient 'activists' believed mainly in armed resistance, which required conspiratorial preparations. 'Reasonable' leaders, like Marquis Aleksander Wielopolski, who tried in vain to satiate the aspirations of his compatriots by obtaining concessions from Tsar Alexander II in the areas of education and local administration, had their role undercut by the axiomatic conviction of the tsars that was expressed in a letter from Nicholas I to his brother the Grand Duke Constantine in 1831, when the latter was viceroy of Poland: it is either us or them; either Russia or Poland has to perish. The liberal Alexander II opened a dialogue with delegates from the *szlachta* in 1856 by saying, 'Messieurs, point de rêveries'—'Gentlemen, no daydreaming'. In January 1863, in an attempt to prevent his radical opponents from fomenting an uprising, Wielopolski ordered the compulsory conscription of Poles into the Russian army. The insurrection erupted anyway, but at the worst possible time of year, and shortly afterwards, Wielopolski was summarily dismissed by Alexander II. The uprising was suppressed,

but when the underground National Government (initiated by Conrad's father Apollo *Korzeniowski in 1861) announced the unconditional emancipation of the peasantry, the Tsar, not to be outdone, freed the peasants in his 'Polish Kingdom' on terms more favourable than in the rest of his empire. The uprisings caused untold misery, but kept the national spirit very much alive. Throughout Poland, responsibility for tending this spirit was assumed by literature and the arts; Chopin's music has been described as 'cannons hidden among bouquets of flowers'. Political thought was nurtured by émigrés, and after 1865 also in the Austrian zone of Poland.

During the *First World War, Poles had to serve in the armies of their occupying powers, and were thus made to fight against each other. To drum up popular support and attract volunteers, first Russia (1914) and later Germany (1916) published manifestos promising Poles the reconstruction of their own country, but these obviously self-serving proclamations aroused little enthusiasm. It was American President Woodrow Wilson who, first in his 'State of the Union' speech of January 1917 and again in his famous list of fourteen points proclaimed on 8 January 1918, demanded 'a united, independent, and autonomous Poland with free, unrestricted access to the sea'. In March 1917, the new provisional government of Russia recognized Poland's right to independence (albeit in a military alliance with Russia).

The simultaneous collapse of the three partitioning empires created the opportunity for which Poles had been waiting. They were prepared for it, both politically and organizationally, although they had to build all central institutions up from scratch. The Versailles Conference, at which the Polish cause was supported mainly by France, Italy, and the United States, approved what had been in practice accomplished by the new government in Warsaw headed by Józef Piłsudski, and also gave Poland direct access to the Baltic Sea through the Polish Corridor.

Conrad refers to the 'Polish question' marginally in 'Autocracy and War' and more directly in 'A Note on the Polish Problem' (1916) and 'The Crime of Partition' (1919), all of which are collected in *Notes on Life and Letters*. The 'Note' was prompted by Józef H. *Retinger, a Pole living in London who had befriended Conrad and helped to awaken his concern for the fate of wartime Poland. Strongly influenced by Retinger's *La Pologne et l'équilibre européen* (1916), the 'Note' was sent to the British Foreign Office in London, where Conrad and Retinger were subsequently interviewed. The 'Polish question' is also addressed in a number of Conrad's letters, including one to Edward *Garnett of October 1907: 'You remember always that I am a Slav (it's your *idée fixe*) but you seem to forget that I am a Pole. You forget that we have been used to go to battle without illusions. . . . We have been "going in" these last hundred years repeatedly, to be knocked on the head only' (*CL*, iii. 492).　　　ZN

Poradowska, Marguerite (née Gachet; 1848–1937), Conrad's distant cousin by marriage and one of his closest friends in the immediate pre-literary years of his career. Marguerite Poradowska served as the primary model for *Marlow's 'aunt' in 'Heart of Darkness', and was possibly also a model for the *Intended. She was also the first novelist of Conrad's acquaintance, and his surviving *letters to her (110 letters in French, most of them written between 1890 and 1895) provide the most comprehensive first-hand account of the period before Conrad left the *sea to take up the pen.

The Gachets were originally from Lille, but Marguerite's father Émile Gachet had moved to *Brussels in 1835 and earned a reputation as a distinguished medieval scholar and palaeographer. His daughter Marguerite, a celebrated beauty, shocked the family by marrying Aleksander Poradowski, a first cousin of Conrad's maternal grandmother and a veteran of the 1863 uprising, and moving with him to Galicia (now *Ukraine). Although the couple returned to Brussels in 1884 for the sake of her health, the exotic customs and manners of the many ethnic and religious groups in the vicinity of Lwów provided a rich cultural background for most of her romantic novels and adaptations, whose subtitles often signal this 'sociological' interest: *Yaga, esquisse de mœurs ruthènes* (Yaga: A Sketch of Ruthenian Ways, 1887); *Demoiselle Micia, mœurs galiciennes* (Miss Micia: Galician Ways, 1888–9); *La Madone de Busowiska, mœurs houtsoules* (The Madonna of Busowiska: Hutsulian Ways, 1891). Her works, appearing regularly in the *Revue des Deux Mondes*, the most prestigious of the Parisian literary journals, received extravagant praise from Conrad, who also recommended them to Ford Madox *Ford.

Conrad first met Poradowska in February 1890, when he stopped in Brussels on his way back to the Ukraine for the first time in sixteen years. Conrad's cousin Poradowski had been in poor health, and died just two days after Conrad's arrival; this circumstance doubtless intensified the relationship between Conrad and the beautiful widow, whom he always addressed in letters as his 'dear Aunt'. They also met briefly on several occasions in Brussels and Paris. In July 1894, while *Almayer's Folly* was under consideration by T. Fisher *Unwin, Conrad, worried about a rejection, suggested to Poradowska that they prepare a French version for the *Revue des Deux Mondes*, 'not as a translation but as a collaboration' (*CL*, i. 165). After Conrad's letter to her of 11 June 1895, a hiatus of nearly five years occurs in the surviving correspondence. Evidence in other letters (*CL*, i. 428) indicates that they continued to correspond, suggesting that Poradowska either lost or for some reason destroyed the missing letters. Since the beginning of this period coincides with Conrad's interest in Émilie *Briquel in *Champel (who volunteered to translate *Almayer*; see *CL*, i. 235) and his renewed contact with his future wife Jessie George in *London, critics have speculated that he may also have courted Poradowska, whose other suitors included Charles Buls, the mayor of Brussels.

The widowed Poradowska divided her time between Brussels, Lille, and an apartment in Paris. The final years of her life were spent on her nephew's estate at the Château de Montgoubelin, Saint-Benin d'Azy, Nièvre. Conrad's letters to Poradowska are held at the Beinecke Rare Book and Manuscript Library, Yale University.

portraits and other images. With his rugged features, Vandyke beard, and heavy-lidded eyes, Conrad was a favourite subject of artists, sculptors, photographers, and caricaturists. He was also a talented amateur artist in his own right; several of his ink sketches, preserved by his wife Jessie, are reproduced by Meyer (1967).

The earliest known portrait of Conrad is by Ellen M. ('Nellie') Heath, Edward *Garnett's partner and a pupil of Walter Sickert. It was undertaken at Garnett's home, the Cearne, in one three-hour sitting on 4 March 1898, and Garnett presented it to the Leeds City Art Gallery in 1935. Conrad's reported verdict was that the painting 'bore a strong resemblance to his father' (*LFC*, p. xvii; a black-and-white reproduction serves as the frontispiece to Stape (ed.), 1996). In August 1903 William *Rothenstein secured Conrad's agreement to be included in a series of portraits of notable literary figures. Rothenstein's visit to Conrad's house at the Pent resulted in two drawings: one in pastel (now in the National Portrait Gallery, London, and reproduced as plate 1 in *CL*, iii.) and another in chalk. In December 1902, Conrad sat for a portrait by George Sauter (1866–1935), John *Galsworthy's brother-in-law, and another sitting followed in February 1904 (*CL*, ii. 469; *CL*, iii. 111).

The increasingly creased and angular features of the eminent writer attracted many artists and caricaturists, especially with the wider popularity he enjoyed after the publication of *Chance* in 1914. On 23 August of that year, while Conrad was waiting in the mountain town of *Zakopane for permission to return from Austrian *Poland to England, he sat for a crayon portrait by Dr Kazimierz Górski, a physician (reproduced in Sherry 1972: 102). In January 1918 Conrad met Percy Anderson at the Carlton Hotel in London, and

Anderson painted his portrait later in the year (National Portrait Gallery, London).

The American artist Walter *Tittle first met Conrad in 1922 and, soon on friendly terms, was fortunate to arrange a number of sittings during the last two years of the writer's life. Two oil paintings, two lithographs, and a copper dry-point etching remain from these sessions. Tittle's best-known oil portrait of Conrad, painted in January 1924, was presented by George T. *Keating to Yale University in 1948. The lithograph reproduced on the cover of *Conradiana* since 1971 was obtained by the National Portrait Gallery in 1931. The following year the same museum unveiled a replica of the oil portrait which Tittle had prepared for use as the frontispiece to Keating's catalogue. Conrad seems to have been especially fond of Tittle's portraits, selecting one of them as frontispiece for the first volume of Dent's Collected Edition of his works. See Richard P. Veler, 'Walter Tittle and Joseph Conrad', *Conradiana*, 12 (1980), 93–104. Tittle's papers, including an unpublished autobiography and extensive diaries, are held at Wittenberg University, Springfield, Ohio.

In May 1923, Scottish artist Muirhead *Bone accompanied Conrad to *America on board the *Tuscania*, under the command of his brother David. Bone made several dry-point etchings of Conrad both on the voyage and during his stay, one of which, showing Conrad with David Bone, was used as a frontispiece for the English edition of *Suspense* in 1925; another is reproduced in Sherry 1972: 110. The woodcut portrait of Conrad reproduced on the cover of *The Conradian* since 1985 is by Muirhead Bone.

In 1924 Max *Beerbohm, who had parodied Conrad's prose style in *A Christmas Garland* (1912), included Conrad among a series of caricatures called 'The Young Self and the Old Self' which also included such notables as Byron, Rossetti, and Millais. The idea behind the series was to show the subject simultaneously in youth and in old age, and to allow the two 'selves' to exchange a few words. In Beerbohm's watercolour, the young Conrad speaks a gibberish meant to be Polish, to which the old Conrad, bearded and monocled, responds in French and English (privately owned, reproduced in *Conradiana*, 4: 1 (1972), 62). Another caricature by Quiz was published in *Saturday Review*, 4 October 1922 (in Sherry 1972: 109). Shortly before Conrad's visit to America, a drawing by Gordon Stevenson appeared on one of the first covers of *Time* magazine (7 April 1923).

The first sculptural representation of Conrad was a bust by American artist Jo Davidson (1883–1952), for which Conrad posed in March 1916. Conrad described it to his agent J. B. *Pinker as 'a fine piece of work, really. As to the likeness I am not so sure' (*CL*, v. 566). While Conrad was sitting for Davidson in his London studio on 11 March, photographer Alvin Langdon Coburn, famous in literary circles for the atmospheric photographs used as frontispieces for the New York Edition of the works of Henry *James, 'came into the studio too and took about a dozen shots' (*CL*, v. 566). Davidson's autobiography, *Between Sittings* (1951), has a chapter on Conrad. Davidson's bust was later purchased by Edmund *Gosse and presented to the National Portrait Gallery; Coburn's negatives are now at the George Eastman House, Rochester, NY.

Sculptor Jacob *Epstein visited Oswalds in March 1924 and made a head and a bust of Conrad in bronze, one of which is now at the National Portrait Gallery. Conrad's sittings are vividly described in *Epstein: An Autobiography* (1955). Australian sculptress Dora Clarke made two sculptural images of Conrad: a statue in Burmese haldu wood of Conrad 'as a ship's prow' (reproduced in *JCHC*, facing p. 257; now at the Seamen's Institute, New York), and a memorial plaque above the door of the meeting hall in Bishopsbourne, *Kent. Photographs of Clarke posing with her works are held in the Conrad collection at the Canterbury Heritage Museum. In 1934 designer Bruce Rogers was asked to provide an actual figurehead in Conrad's image for the *Joseph Conrad*, which Alan Villiers was then outfitting for a voyage

round the world; a photograph is reproduced in *Conradiana*, 27 (1995), 16. More recent sculptures include a bust by Alfons Karny that stood in the lobby of the Wielki Teatr (Great Theatre) in *Warsaw before it was moved to the Conrad Gallery of the Maritime Museum in Gdańsk. A massive stone monument to Conrad is in nearby Gdynia.

The first surviving images of Conrad and his family are in the form of studio photographs, including the earliest known picture of Conrad as a child of 5, taken by Stanisław Kraków in *Vologda and reproduced recto and verso in *JCC*. Later studio photographs include one taken by W. Rzewuski in *Cracow in 1874, shortly before Conrad's departure for *Marseilles, and another taken by Otto Bielefeldt during Conrad's meeting with his uncle Tadeusz *Bobrowski in Marienbad in 1883. He also had a studio portrait taken around the time of his marriage in March 1896.

In later years, family snapshots also became possible, but Conrad would still have studio photographs taken on special occasions. In 1904 George Charles Beresford made a handsome sepia platinotype portrait of Conrad (National Portrait Gallery). When Conrad's American publisher Alfred A. Knopf, then working for F. N. *Doubleday and busily advertising *Chance*, requested a portrait, Conrad arranged to visit Will and Carine Cadby at their studio in Borough Green, Kent, where, on the morning of 20 September 1913, they 'took 18 negatives of my celebrated person' (*CL*, v. 284). Conrad distributed copies of these photographs to his friends, and one of them is reproduced in Sherry 1972: 65. The Cadbys also visited Capel House to take a number of family photographs, and John Conrad recalled how much his father 'disliked being posed' (*JCTR*, 62).

Some 'Conrad' photographs are of questionable authenticity: one, reproduced and discussed by Jeremy Hawthorn in *The Conradian*, 16: 2 (1992), 38–45, shows a bearded figure in a crowd awaiting survivors of the *Titanic disaster at the railway station in Southampton on 29 April 1912; another, published by Claudine Lesage in *Magazine* *littéraire* (March 1992), 27, purports to show Conrad posing with Edith *Wharton and Paul Bourget on the Giens peninsula near Toulon in 1921. There is no corroborating evidence of Conrad's presence on either occasion. In the final years of his life, formal photographic portraits of Conrad were made by T. and R. Annan and Sons and by Malcolm Arbuthnot. There is apparently no *film footage of Conrad, which is somewhat surprising given that by the end of Conrad's life the silent cinema was booming, and Conrad was keenly interested in film. In 1957, to mark the centennial of Conrad's birth, *Poland issued two commemorative postage stamps designed and engraved by Stefan Łukaszewski, showing Conrad in profile and the *ship *Torrens* under full sail. See also Jeffrey Meyers, 'Joseph Conrad: An Iconography', *Bulletin of Bibliography*, 47 (1990), 33–4.

'Preface' to *The Nature of a Crime*. In October 1923 Ford Madox *Ford invited Conrad to contribute to the *transatlantic review*, a new journal he was about to launch in Paris. Conrad declined the offer, but his reply contained friendly recollections of Ford's earlier editorship of the *English Review*. This enterprise had actually been among the causes leading to the cooling of their relations in 1909, but Ford was so pleased with the tone of Conrad's letter that he reproduced one page in facsimile as the frontispiece to his 1924 memorial tribute, *JCPR*. Ford asked Conrad's permission to reprint their last *collaboration from the *English Review*, the title of which Ford misremembered as 'Story of a Crime', and Conrad agreed to write a brief preface for publication together with one that Ford would write.

Conrad's brief note describes *The Nature of a Crime* as 'a piece of work in the nature of an analytical confession (produced *in articulo mortis*, as it were)' (*CDOUP*, 117), and basically dismisses it as a failure, of interest only for the nostalgia it evokes. As Ford later claimed, this brief and grudging tribute to their collaboration was the last piece of work to be finished by Conrad before his death on 3 August. The manuscript of Conrad's 'Foreword', signed and dated 14 May 1924, is held at the Beinecke Rare Book and Manuscript Library, Yale University, together with a typescript. The typescript used for the *transatlantic review* is held in the Naumburg Collection, Princeton University.

'Preface' to *The Nigger of the 'Narcissus'*. Despite its claims to be 'simply an avowal of endeavour' (p. ix), it is hardly surprising that this 'Preface' has subsequently come to be seen as Conrad's artistic manifesto, containing as it does the celebrated passage in which he states his literary aim thus: 'My task which I am trying to achieve is, by the power of the written word to make you hear, to make you feel—it is, before all, to make you *see*. That—and no more, and it is everything. If I succeed, you shall find there according to your deserts: encouragement, consolation, fear, charm—all you demand—and, perhaps, also that glimpse of truth for which you have forgotten to ask' (p. x).

In its opening paragraph, the 'Preface' claims that the purpose of art is 'to render the highest kind of justice to the visible universe, by bringing to light the truth, manifold and one, underlying its every aspect', and then proceeds to claim that art differs from other truth-seeking endeavours, such as science. While both confront the same 'enigmatical spectacle' of life, it is the artist who 'speaks to our capacity for delight and wonder, to the sense of mystery surrounding our lives'. The concern of art—and indeed its appeal—is communal: it reflects a human rather than a scientific truth which has its basis in such ties of fellowship as 'the solidarity in dreams, in joy, in sorrow, in aspirations, in illusions, in hope, in fear, which binds men to each other, which binds together all humanity' (pp. vii, viii). Developing this idea of fellowship, Conrad goes on to define fiction as 'the appeal of one temperament to all the other innumerable temperaments whose subtle and resistless power endows passing events with their true meaning' (p. ix). While art's appeal may be to the senses, its means are necessarily grounded in practicalities since, given the author's tools, 'the old, old words, worn thin, defaced by ages of careless usage', it is only through his dedication to craftsmanship, to the 'perfect blending of form and substance' and the 'unremitting never-discouraged care for the shape and ring of sentences', that his appeal can succeed (p. ix). According to Jacques Berthoud, Conrad's famous declaration enacts the very process it defines: 'Sensory perception ("to make you hear") merges into affective engagement ("to make you feel"), which in turn yields to visionary perception ("to make you see")' (1984: 181). Artistic endeavour is thus visionary in impulse: 'To snatch in a moment of courage, from the remorseless rush of time, a passing phase of life' in order to 'reveal the substance of its truth—disclose its inspiring secret' (p. x). But its aim—like its inspiration—is, finally, communal: 'at last the presented vision . . . shall awaken in the hearts of the beholders that feeling of unavoidable solidarity . . . which binds men to each other and all mankind to the visible world' (p. x). As Berthoud notes, 'if there is a necessary connection between "visionary truth" and "human solidarity" it is because the latter is the test of the former' (181).

Conrad completed the 'Preface' in August 1897 and sent it to Edward *Garnett for his scrutiny: 'I want you not to be impatient with it and if you think it at all possible to give it a chance to get printed' (*CL*, i. 375). When Heinemann refused to publish the 'Preface' with the novel, Conrad offered it to W. E. *Henley, editor of the *New Review*, where *The Nigger of the 'Narcissus'* first appeared in serial form. Following the final instalment of the novel in December 1897, the 'Preface' appeared as an 'Author's Note'. This version omits a number of passages from Conrad's original. These were restored when the 'Preface' was subsequently printed, at Conrad's instigation, as a pamphlet in November 1902, although it omits a single paragraph to which Garnett had objected. Thereafter, the 'Preface' was printed in *America, first as an essay, entitled 'The Art of Fiction', in *Harper's Weekly* (13 May 1905), and then

with 'To My Readers in America' in April 1914 by Doubleday, Page as a promotional handout for their first publication of *The Nigger of the 'Narcissus'* in 1914 (which contained the 'Preface'). It first appeared in England as a 'Preface' to the Heinemann Collected Edition of 1921.

The ten-page manuscript is held in the Rosenbach Museum and Library, Philadelphia, and a typescript at Colgate University. See also Watt 1980: 76–88, who argues that Conrad's 'Preface' belongs to a tradition of Romantic criticism and, in its concern with the psychology of creation and the social function of art, may be likened to Wordsworth's position in the preface to the *Lyrical Ballads* (1798). AHS

'Preface' to *The Shorter Tales of Joseph Conrad*. This brief preface was written to introduce an anthology of short stories first proposed by F. N. *Doubleday in early 1924. Initially dubious about a medley that would wrench his stories from their original contexts, Conrad eventually became involved in selecting the contents (eight of his 29 short stories) and title. He also suggested writing a preface himself, partly as a way of making the volume commercially attractive to the bibliophiles and the general reader alike. One of Conrad's last completed pieces before his death, the preface was finished on 5 May 1924 and appeared posthumously when the anthology was published on 30 October 1924. It was subsequently collected in *Last Essays*. The essay offers a backward glance at the directive impulses underlying his entire writing life, including the 'first paper boats in the days of my literary childhood' (142). He also takes the opportunity to refute the popular image of him as a writer of the *sea. These stories, he avers, 'deal with feelings of universal import . . . I modestly hope that there are human beings in them, and also the articulate appeal of their humanity so strangely constructed from inertia and restlessness, from weakness and from strength and many other interesting contradictions' (143–4). See also Donald W. Rude, 'Conrad as Editor: The Preparation of *The Shorter Tales of Joseph Conrad*', in

Zyla and Aycock (eds.), 189–96. The manuscript and the first two revised typescripts are held at the Beinecke Rare Book and Manuscript Library, Yale University, a third revised typescript in the Berg Collection, New York Public Library, and a fourth revised typescript at Dartmouth College.

'Prince Roman'. Conrad completed this 8,000-word story on 25 September 1910, using materials originally designed for, but finally withheld from, *A Personal Record*. It first appeared in the *Oxford and Cambridge Review* (October 1911), was later reprinted as a limited-edition *pamphlet, and was collected in *Tales of Hearsay*.

The only work in the Conrad canon to make direct use of *Polish historical materials, 'Prince Roman' is based on the true story of a 19th-century Polish aristocrat and patriot, Prince Roman Sanguszko (1800–81), whom Conrad as a small boy had seen briefly. Detailed source material about this figure was readily available to him in Tadeusz *Bobrowski's *Memoirs* (1900), where the Prince emerges as an exemplary model of honourable conduct and patriotism, a 'highly respected, worthy and generally revered man of unrivalled integrity, noble-mindedness and strength of character' (*CUFE*, 8). Primarily an exercise in national hagiography, Conrad's story preserves the main elements in the life of the historical patriot-hero. After the death of his young wife, the Prince rejects the luxury of private grief, resigns his position in the Russian Guards, and, changing his name to Sergeant Peter, singleheartedly commits himself to the sacred struggle for Polish independence. When he is later captured, brought to trial, and questioned by one of his sympathetic judges, who suggests that excessive grief has caused him to join the rebels, the Prince replies proudly that he enlisted from conviction. Condemned to Siberian exile for 25 years, he returns home deaf and frail, but unbroken in spirit, and still devotes himself to a life of exemplary public service.

Although many of the formal and thematic aspects of 'Prince Roman' are accessible to non-Polish readers, it holds an added resonance when placed in the context of Polish historical and literary traditions. An act of historical piety in which, unusually, there is no trace of Conradian *irony, 'Prince Roman' emulates some of the qualities of Polish Romantic literature in its celebration of a patriot who, in subordinating the claims of private suffering to national responsibilities, exemplifies a combination of military honour, chivalric response, and communal obligation. Andrzej Busza comments: 'Conrad's main purpose here is neither self-revelation, nor discovery, nor analysis, nor description; it is rather—in a broad sense of the word—translation. The text represents an attempt to give English expression to Polish structures—stylistic, narrative, ideological. . . . To put it simply: in "Prince Roman" Conrad tries to tell a Polish story in a Polish way' ('St. Flaubert and Prince Roman', *L'Époque Conradienne* (1980), 19). Among the tale's mosaic of Polish materials, he identifies the so-called *żywot* or 'life' of heroic martyrdom and sacrificial patriotism, the *gawęda*, a familiar oral form in Polish literature, and several specific motifs and allusions (particularly to Adam *Mickiewicz's poetry) linking the tale to early Polish Romantic literature. See also Busza, 231–8, and Alina Nowak, '*Prince Roman*: An Attempt at Interpretation', *Conrad News* (1995), 5–19.

'Princess and the Page, The'. First published only in 1988, this 1,400-word fairy tale has a somewhat mysterious provenance. Either Conrad's translation of a French text that has not come to light or, less likely, his original work passed off as a translation, it appears to derive from the very beginning of the writer's career. Prepared by Conrad as a document for private presentation, the manuscript (held at the Beinecke Rare Book and Manuscript Library, Yale University) subtitles the story 'A True Fairy Tale for Grown-up Princesses', while two typescripts (held at Yale University and the Harry Ransom Humanities Research Center, University of Texas at Austin) omit this subtitle, but are each clearly labelled as a 'Translation by Joseph

Conrad'. A 1928 auction catalogue of Edward *Garnett materials describes the manuscript as 'said to be a translation from the French' and as given to Garnett by Conrad 'probably in Autumn of 1896'. The manuscript was first printed by David Leon Higdon and Donald W. Rude in '"The Princess and the Page": An Unpublished Conrad Manuscript', *Nineteenth-Century Literature*, 43 (1988), 235–43. For this sad little tale about a lovelorn page who sacrifices himself so that a spoiled and ungrateful princess may live, Higdon and Rude aptly invoke a wider 1890s literary context when 'the British reading public witnessed an unexpected interest in and publication of numerous *Kunstmärchen* or art fairy tales' (240). They further link the tale to the possibility that Conrad's activities in *London in the early 1890s included a job at an Oxford Street translation agency. Despite its uncertain provenance, Higdon and Rude regard the tale as a significant addition to Conrad's very earliest canon, notably in anticipating later Conradian themes: 'The ideal and the real remain constantly at odds in the tale, as they often do in Conrad's stories and novels.' In particular, they note the motifs of the narcissistic male 'so blinded by his enchantment with a woman purified into an ideal that he is unable to see the realities surrounding him' and the catastrophic effect upon him of a destructive, indeed devouring, woman. Overall, they propose, the work's multi-level, 'grown-up' ironies suggest that this is an art fairy tale 'written against the grain of the genre' (242–3).

prizes. See HONOURS AND PRIZES.

Professor, the, the most absolutely radical and fearless of Conrad's anarchists in *The Secret Agent*, a sallow and bespectacled maker of bombs who provides *Verloc with the device that kills *Stevie. He is physically insignificant, but the force of his character and the incorruptible logic of his nihilism make him one of the most formidable and memorable of Conrad's characters. A former chemistry student, he is passionately committed 'To the destruc-

tion of what is' (306), and devotes his life to the quest for a perfect detonator. He is perhaps the first suicide bomber in fiction, since he protects himself from capture by wiring his own body with a bomb that can be detonated in twenty seconds, and no one doubts his determination to use it. He appears briefly but importantly in Conrad's story 'The Informer' (*A Set of Six*): when Mr X stages a mock police raid in Hermione Street (a fictional address in *London), everyone is afraid that the Professor will blow up the entire house, and Sevrin's fear for the life of his beloved drives him to reveal himself as the informer. As the ironic narrator of *The Secret Agent* puts it, 'The Professor had genius, but lacked the great social virtue of resignation' (75). Like *Kurtz in *Heart of Darkness*, the Professor wants to exterminate all those who are too weak to survive. His weapon is 'death, which knows no restraint' (68); and he detests the *London crowds which remind him that mankind may prove too multitudinous to be dealt with in this summary and comprehensive fashion. Mr X says that he was eventually hoist with his own petard, perishing 'in a secret laboratory through the premature explosion of one of his improved detonators' (88).

Various historical figures have been suggested as sources for the Professor, from Ford Madox *Ford's young cousin and neighbour Arthur Rossetti to the Irish terrorist Luke 'Dynamite' Dillon. In 'Conrad's Anarchist Professor: An Undiscovered Source', *Labor History* (New York), 18 (1977), 397–402, Paul Avrich reproduces a speech given by an American anarchist who called himself Professor Mezzeroff, first printed in the *Alarm* (Chicago) of 13 January 1885, in which Professor Mezzeroff prided himself on his ability to make explosives from 'tea and similar articles of food from the family table' (401). This Professor also carried his home-made trinitro-glycerine bombs around with him in his pocket and in the horse-drawn streetcars. This source, supported by casual references to America in the first conversation between the Professor and Comrade Ossipon

(60), implies that the Professor may be American; in Christopher Hampton's 1996 film version of the novel, the Professor was played (without screen credit) by American actor Robin Williams. *The Secret Agent* was dedicated to H. G. *Wells, and in 'Conrad's Invisible Professor', *The Conradian*, 11 (1986), 35–41, Martin Ray examines the possible influence of the protagonist of Wells's *The Invisible Man* (1897) on the character of the Professor.

progression d'effet. According to Ford Madox *Ford, this term figured centrally in his discussions with Conrad during their *collaboration on *Romance* in 1901: 'In writing a novel we agreed that every word set on paper—*every* word set on paper— must carry the story forward and, that as the story progressed, the story must be carried forward faster and faster and with more and more intensity. That is called *progression d'effet*, words for which there is no English equivalent' (*JCPR*, 210).

Although the term is probably too widely inclusive to serve as a critical tool, it nevertheless points interestingly to the powerful influence of Gustave *Flaubert, who occasionally uses it in his correspondence. For Flaubert, as for his two excited disciples, it evokes characteristics of a new type of narrative that gains its effects through stringent regard for *le mot juste*, the pursuit of singleness of effect—'one embroilment, one set of embarrassments, one human coil, one psychological progression', as Ford described it (1921: 88)— and a rigorous selection of detail that contributes to an increase in the tempo and intensity of narrative pace. Robert F. Haugh, one of the few critics to apply the term to Conrad's fiction, offers the following definition: 'The term . . . embraces growth, movement, heightening of all elements of the story: conflict and stress if it is a dramatic story; intensity and magnitude of image if it is a poetic story; complexity of patterns; balance and symmetry; evocations in style used for mood and functional atmosphere' (*Joseph Conrad: Discovery in Design* (Norman: University of Oklahoma Press, 1957), 7).

The term seems especially useful in approaching some of Conrad's more 'poetic' stories from the pre-1900 phase of his career, such as *The Nigger of the 'Narcissus'* and 'Heart of Darkness'. The early rendering of the *Narcissus*'s crew as they excitedly gather in the forecastle in preparation for voyage offers a beginning that, in its cascading imagery and patterned colour symbolism, anticipates 'the tempo of the whole performance' (*JCPR*, 171). The coda of 'Heart of Darkness', when *Marlow, accompanied by omnipresent memories of his meeting with *Kurtz, goes to meet the *Intended, rests upon what Ambrosini describes as a method of extending 'the tension produced by rhythm, rhetoric and imagery to its breaking point' (115).

'Protection of Ocean Liners'. This essay was prompted by the sinking of the Canadian Pacific liner *Empress of Ireland* after a collision with a Norwegian collier, the *Storstad*, in the treacherously foggy St Lawrence River on 29 May 1914, with the loss of 1,024 lives. Conrad's response was written by 3 June and published in the *Illustrated London News*, 144 (6 June 1914), 944, under the title 'The Lesson of the Collision'. In it, he claims that, unlike the *Titanic* disaster, the collision was a genuine casualty of the sea for which no one could be held to blame, understandable though the desire to apportion blame might be in a modern world that instinctively places its trust in 'the mere power of material contrivances' (*Notes*, 251). He goes on to recommend a more traditional preventive measure, the use of cork fenders as protective padding around the sides of all vessels: 'It certainly won't look very pretty but I make bold to say it will save more lives at sea than any amount of the Marconi installations which are being forced on the shipowners on that very ground—the safety of lives at sea' (256). Correspondence followed the publication of Conrad's article, and another letter by him on the subject, dated 8 June, appeared in the *Daily Express* (10 June 1914), 4. Both items were later collected in revised form in *Notes on Life and Letters*. No pre-publication documents are known; the manuscript of the *Daily Express* letter (private collection) and a typed transcription of the *Daily Express* printing made for Conrad's revision for *Notes on Life and Letters* (Stanford University) survive. His views challenged from yet another quarter, Conrad wrote a further letter on the *Empress of Ireland* catastrophe, published in the London *Globe* (13 June 1914), 5, but uncollected in *Notes on Life and Letters* or *Last Essays*. For the text of the letter, see *CL*, v. 388–90.

'Proust as Creator' is the title given to Conrad's comments in a letter to Marcel Proust's first English translator, Charles Kenneth Scott-Moncrieff, in 1922, which were included as Conrad's contribution to a memorial volume. Najder reprints the text in *CDOUP* (105–6), introducing it as 'Conrad's only extended comment about any major twentieth-century writer' and as 'one of the most original critical pieces which Conrad ever wrote' (ibid. 104). On 21 November 1922, three days after Proust died in Paris, Conrad wrote: 'I've lately read nothing but Marcel Proust' (*LL*, ii. 287). On that very day, Conrad's erstwhile friend and collaborator Ford Madox *Ford attended Proust's funeral at the church of Saint-Pierre-de-Chaillot. Sir John Collings Squire invited Conrad to take part in a collective tribute to Proust, to which he replied that he 'had heard first of Proust either in 1913 or 1914'—probably in connection with the publication in 1913 of *Du côté de chez Swann*, the first volume of *À la recherche du temps perdu*—and praised him for 'disclosing to us a past like nobody else's and thus adding something memorable to the general experience of mankind' (to J. C. Squire, 30 November 1922). In the event, Squire's project did not materialize, but Conrad had given some thought to the matter, and when Scott-Moncrieff approached him in December for a contribution to a memorial volume, he reworked the ideas he had expressed to Squire, emphasizing that Proust's art was 'absolutely based on analysis. It is really more than that. He is a writer who has pushed analysis to the point when it becomes creative'

(*CDOUP*, 105). When Scott-Moncrieff visited Conrad at Oswalds and sought his help in finding an English equivalent for the resplendent title of Proust's second volume, *À l'ombre des jeunes filles en fleurs*, Conrad apparently suggested *In the Shade of Blossoming Youth* or *In the Shade of Young Girls in Bloom* (*LL*, ii. 292–3). 'Proust as Creator' was first published in *Marcel Proust: An English Tribute*, ed. C. K. Scott-Moncrieff (Chatto & Windus, 1923), 126–8. A two-page typescript is held at the Beinecke Rare Book and Manuscript Library, Yale University.

psychoanalytic approaches. Based upon theories developed by Sigmund Freud (1856–1939), psychoanalysis investigates the relationship between the conscious and the unconscious elements of the mind. While Freud did not invent the concept of the unconscious mind, his name has become inextricably linked to its study through his argument that the decisive motivating forces in our lives are unconscious ones. As its vocabulary of 'repression', 'sublimation', 'displacement', and 'condensation' suggests, the practice of psychoanalysis consists in unearthing—in order to confront—the fears and conflicts assumed to lie buried in the unconscious. Often the existence of these repressed fears and conflicts is signalled in some coded or disguised form, as in the form of a dream, which needs to be translated by the psychoanalyst. Having initially viewed the human psyche as divided into a conscious and an unconscious, Freud later came to suggest the 'id', the 'super-ego', and the 'ego' (corresponding, roughly, to the unconscious, the conscience, and the conscious personality which mediates between them). The analogy between psychoanalysis and literary criticism is obvious: literature may be seen to share with the unconscious the fact that it does not tend to communicate explicitly; instead its meaning is conveyed in the more implicit form of images, symbols, and metaphors. Thus, the practice of psychoanalytic criticism, like the practice of the psychoanalysis, examines the relation between the overt meaning of a text and its covert meaning. In the same way that a psychoanalyst might interpret a single dream-image as an example of condensation within which a number of people, events, or meanings are represented, a psychoanalytic critic may interpret a metaphor as if it were a dream condensation. In this sense, a text may be said to have an 'unconscious' which it is the task of literary criticism to identify and translate. Psychoanalytic criticism can embrace both the artist and the art, since the unconscious motives in a text may be attributed either to the author of the work (in which case the text may be read as a projection of authorial repressions) or to its characters.

There is no evidence to suggest that Conrad encountered Freud's writings directly before 1921 when, during a holiday on *Corsica, he met H.-R. Lenormand, a young French playwright and disciple of psychoanalysis, who lent him some of Freud's works and urged him to psychoanalyse such characters as *Jim and *Almayer. Lenormand records that, although Conrad confessed that he had long been fascinated by the father–daughter relationship, he excused himself as being 'only a teller of tales' with no desire to analyse *Almayer's Folly* from this perspective, saying: 'I have no wish to probe the depths. I like to regard reality as a rough and rugged object over which I can run my fingers. Nothing more' (quoted in Stallman (ed.), 4). Conrad, who spoke of Freud 'with scornful irony', returned the books apparently unread and urged Lenormand to write a novel about 'the decline of men who had arrived at certitude' (7). Despite Conrad's protestations, however, the psychological concerns of his fiction were bound to attract psychoanalytic approaches. That such concerns were evident from the beginning is clear from Edward *Garnett's (unsigned) review of the *Youth* volume, in which he says: 'the art of "Heart of Darkness"—as in every psychological masterpiece—lies in the relation of the things of the spirit to the things of the flesh, of the invisible life to the visible, of the sub-conscious life within us, our obscure motives

and instincts, to our conscious actions, feelings and outlook' (*CCH*, 132).

In his highly influential work, Guerard (1958) interpreted *Marlow's journey in 'Heart of Darkness' as 'a spiritual voyage of self-discovery' and saw Marlow himself as a 'projection of whatever great or small degree of a more irrecoverable Conrad' (38). Exploiting the story's dream-references, Guerard argues that the narrative 'takes us into a deeper region of the mind' where Marlow's encounter with *Kurtz translates variously into a confrontation with his 'double', a 'facet of the unconscious', and the 'Freudian id' (42, 39). As early as 1930, Gustav Morf, in *The Polish Heritage of Joseph Conrad*, had interpreted Conrad's fiction as coded 'confessionals' for his desertion of *Poland. This approach was extended by Meyer (1967), who argued that Conrad's art provides a compensatory revision of traumas in his life. This practice of treating the work as coded autobiography and using it to psychoanalyse the author has exerted a powerful influence. For instance, in his discussion of 'The Secret Sharer', Robert Rogers argues that between the young Captain and his 'secret sharer', *Leggatt, are projections of the various conflicts in their author's psyche 'between loyalty and rebellion, patriotism and exile, maturity and youth, order and passion, realism and idealism, and so on' (*A Psychoanalytic Study of the Double in Literature* (Detroit: Wayne State University Press, 1970), 43). In similar vein, Karl claims: 'The seeming disparity between Marlow's moderation and Kurtz's anarchy is a good objective correlative of divisions Conrad sensed within himself' (*JCTL*, 488). In a subsequent essay, 'Introduction to the *Danse Macabre*: Conrad's *Heart of Darkness*', Karl argues that what Conrad meant by 'darkness' was what his contemporary, Freud, meant by 'unconscious'. Thus, in Marlow's nightmare experience, the jungle 'runs parallel to our anxieties, becomes the repository of our fears' (in Murfin (ed.) 1989: 132). For one of the best general introductions to this topic, see Barbara Johnson and Marjorie Garber, 'Secret Sharing: Reading Conrad Psychoanalytically',

College English, 49 (1987), 628–40, which helpfully outlines various psychoanalytic approaches, from those dealing with the pathology of the author to Lacanian criticism, testing their possibilities on 'The Secret Sharer'.   AHS

publishers. The following checklist gives details of the first British and American publishers of Conrad's novels, volumes of short stories, and collections of essays in chronological order of publication. Unless otherwise indicated, the year of American publication is identical with that of the British.

	BRITISH	AMERICAN
Almayer's Folly	Unwin, 1895	Macmillan
An Outcast of the Islands	Unwin, 1896	Appleton
The Nigger of the 'Narcissus'	Heinemann, 1897	Dodd, Mead
Tales of Unrest	Unwin, 1898	Scribner's
Lord Jim	Blackwood, 1900	Doubleday, McClure
Youth: A Narrative and Two Other Stories	Blackwood, 1902	McClure, Phillips
Typhoon		Putnam, 1902
Typhoon and Other Stories	Heinemann, 1903	
Falk, Amy Foster, To-morrow		McClure, Phillips, 1903
Nostromo	Harper, 1904	Harper
The Mirror of the Sea	Methuen, 1906	Harper
The Secret Agent	Methuen, 1907	Harper
A Set of Six	Methuen, 1908	Doubleday, Page, 1915
Under Western Eyes	Methuen, 1911	Harper
A Personal Record	Nash, 1912	Harper
'Twixt Land and Sea	Dent, 1912	Hodder & Stoughton, Doran
Chance	Methuen, 1914	Doubleday, Page
Victory	Methuen, 1915	Doubleday, Page
Within the Tides	Dent, 1915	Doubleday, Page
The Shadow-Line	Dent, 1917	Doubleday, Page
The Arrow of Gold	Unwin, 1919	Doubleday, Page
The Rescue	Dent, 1920	Doubleday, Page
Notes on Life and Letters	Dent, 1921	Doubleday, Page
The Rover	Unwin, 1923	Doubleday, Page
Suspense	Dent, 1925	Doubleday, Page
Tales of Hearsay	Unwin, 1925	Doubleday, Page
Last Essays	Dent, 1926	Doubleday, Page

Although Conrad cultivated an early aristocratic disdain for publishers and often felt victimized by their hard-nosed commercial attitudes, his main antipathy as a young writer was to the time-consuming task of selling his works in the literary market place. While such negotiations inevitably bred a certain cynicism, Conrad was nevertheless very fortunate during the 1890s in being able to take advantage of a late Victorian business culture that still allowed the author to have a friendly and personal relationship with his publisher. As Watts points out, even Conrad's first publisher, the coldly professional and tight-fisted T. Fisher *Unwin, 'met the author personally, encouraged him to maintain his literary ambitions, provided exceptional publicity, and entered into a detailed postal discussion of Conrad's future works' (1989: 52). Conrad was even more fortunate in being taken up by two paternalistic gentlemen-publishers—William *Heinemann and William *Blackwood—each of whom was willing to act as financial sponsor, friend, mentor, and literary agent to the fledgling writer; and he simultaneously enjoyed the personal support of many others linked to the trade—including Edward *Garnett, W. H. *Chesson, E. V. *Lucas, S. S. *Pawling, David *Meldrum, and Perceval Graves.

The pattern of Conrad's relationships with publishers changed in two major ways during his career. By engaging J. B. *Pinker as his literary agent in 1900, Conrad was largely released from the burden of personally marketing his fiction. But this great advantage also brought with it a set of new economic pressures, since he also lost that network of supportive relationships and financial sponsorship provided by individual publishers. With Pinker as his middle-man, he became but one writer among many in a competitive and increasingly industrialized Edwardian market place, having to work to deadlines and survive economically without the cushioning effect of sympathetic individual publishers.

The second major change occurred during Conrad's middle career (from 1906 onwards), when he signed the first of several long-term *contracts. After the publication of *The Mirror of the Sea* by *Methuen, Conrad contracted in 1906 to supply Methuen with three novels; when this commitment expired with the publication of *Victory* in 1915, he was ready to fulfil another long-term contract previously made with J. M. *Dent. The situation with regard to American publishers was similar. After a series of American publishers up to 1904, Conrad's position was first regularized through his steady commitment from 1904 to 1912 to the Harper firm, which he valued because it paid well. Then, in 1914, with the publication of *Chance*, his main American publisher became Doubleday, Page. Dent and Doubleday, Page became the two main shaping influences in Conrad's later career. They were attractive to him for several reasons, not least because he was on cordial terms with their owners; both companies, he also felt, marketed his fiction in an efficiently modern way and, in their willingness to commit themselves to *collected editions, were sensitive to his long-term reputation. In his last years, Conrad was pressed unwillingly into a contract with

Unwin, his very first publisher. With the plan to bring out a collected edition of Conrad's works, Unwin was invited to cede his copyright on Conrad's earliest fiction. Unwin responded that he would do so only on condition that the author return to the Unwin fold: hence from 1919 onwards, Unwin brought out *The Arrow of Gold*, *The Rover*, and the posthumous *Tales of Hearsay*. See also Watts 1989, which includes a useful appendix on 'The Power of the Proprietor' (135–7).

Pulman, Adam Marek (1846–?), Conrad's private tutor in *Cracow from 1870 to 1873. Adam Pulman was a student in medicine at the Jagiellonian University, graduating in 1875. His duties also included escorting the young boy on three summer visits to Krynica, a resort-town in the Carpathian Mountains. In May 1873, Conrad, sent to Switzerland for his health, was again accompanied by Pulman on a three-month trip that also took them to Bavaria, *Austria, and northern Italy. According to Conrad's later reminiscences, Pulman was given the mission of dissuading him from the 'romantic folly' of leaving *Poland to go to *sea but, after long arguments, capitulated to his young charge with the words: 'You are an incorrigible, hopeless *Don Quixote. That's what you are' (*A Personal Record*, 43, 44). Pulman and his wife later settled in Sambor, Galicia, where he practised medicine.

Q

Quinn, John (1870–1924), a wealthy New York commercial and financial lawyer of Irish descent, patron of the arts, and collector, who purchased the first of many manuscripts from Conrad in August 1911 when the latter was desperately short of money. This first sale—of the manuscripts of *An Outcast of the Islands* and 'Freya of the Seven Isles'—brought Conrad a welcome £60. On condition that John Quinn did not disperse his collection of Conradiana, the author was happy to continue selling items exclusively to a patron who invariably agreed to pay the prices asked by him. A large cache of Conrad materials, including the manuscripts of *Almayer's Folly, Under Western Eyes, Chance,* and *Victory,* thus formed a keystone in the American collector's celebrated private collection that also came to include manuscripts of W. B. Yeats, Ezra Pound, T. S. Eliot, and James Joyce.

Although the two men never met, they corresponded regularly over a number of years in a series of *letters covering such public matters as the *Titanic* disaster, the *Polish question, the *First World War, and the trial and execution of Roger *Casement. In 1916, Quinn also pressed Conrad to make a lecture tour of *America to strengthen his already growing reputation there. The later breach in their relationship was anticipated in 1918, when Conrad reneged on his gentleman's agreement with Quinn by selling manuscripts to a new and willing buyer, Thomas J. *Wise, to whom he wrote on 10 December 1918, 'I am afraid Quinn will want to take my scalp when he hears of our transactions.' Unbeknown to Quinn, Conrad continued to engage in transactions with Wise. Relations with his American patron descended into further muddle in May 1919 when Conrad, having impulsively assured Quinn that *The Arrow of Gold* would be dedicated to him, finally held to an earlier promise to assign it to Richard *Curle and reserved for Quinn the dedication of the forthcoming *Suspense*— 'a bigger thing in every way' (3 May 1919). To Quinn's justified outrage when he discovered in September 1919 that he had been competing with Wise for Conradiana, Conrad, acknowledging that the moral right lay with Quinn, could only respond with feeble prevarication, claiming that money from Wise was more quickly available than money sent from New York.

On his May 1923 trip to America, Conrad avoided meeting Quinn. That autumn the latter, partly out of personal grievance but partly because he was also seriously ill and wished to settle his affairs, arranged to sell his Conrad collection. At a spectacular series of *auctions in New York's Anderson Galleries in November 1923, the 228 items for which Quinn had paid Conrad $10,000 yielded a sum in the region of $110,000. The American collector resisted accusations of profiteering and rejected suggestions that part of the proceeds should go to the author. Realizing that he had no justifiable grounds for complaint, Conrad remained philosophical and even managed to turn the publicity surrounding the auction to his personal advantage: 'Yes, Quinn promised to keep the MSS. together—but the mood passes and the promise goes with it. But did you ever hear of anything so idiotic as this sale? . . . People who never heard of me before will now know my name. Others who have never been able to read through a page of mine are convinced that I am a great writer' (*LFC,* 328). See also B. L. Reid, *The Man from New York: John Quinn and his Friends* (1968).

Quixote, Don. See DON QUIXOTE.

R

race/racism. In a polemical lecture delivered at the University of Massachusetts in February 1975, the Nigerian novelist and critic Chinua Achebe accused Conrad of being 'a bloody racist'. The lecture was first published in *Massachusetts Review*, 17 (1977), 782–94, and has been subsequently printed in revised form (where the charge was meliorated to 'thoroughgoing racist'). Focusing on the presentation of Africa and Africans in 'Heart of Darkness', Achebe argues that Conrad's version of the 'heart of darkness plagues us still. Which is why an offensive and totally deplorable book can be described . . . as "among the half dozen greatest short novels in the English language"' ('An Image of Africa', in Hamner (ed.), 126). He maintains that Conrad presents the Africans as dehumanized embodiments of evil and so reduces Africa 'to the role of props for the break-up of one petty European mind' (12), thereby confirming 'the need . . . in Western psychology to set Africa up as a foil to Europe, as a place of negations at once remote and vaguely familiar, in comparison with which Europe's own state of spiritual grace will be manifest' (3). Achebe's attack, which challenges the comfortable and widespread reading of Conrad's novel as a polemic against the prevailing racist attitudes of its time, has probably provoked more debate than any other single piece of Conrad criticism. Other writers from the so-called 'Third World' have defended the tale's racial attitudes, finding them to be more enlightened than Achebe allows. For instance, in 'Out of Darkness: Conrad and Other Third World Writers', *Conradiana*, 14 (1983), 173–87, the Ugandan critic Peter Nazareth argues that the narrative demonstrates the erosion of *Marlow's 'inherited racist framework through the direct experience of Africa, through reflection on that experience, and through the telling of the story' (177). Nazareth goes so far as to

suggest that Achebe's hostility to 'Heart of Darkness' is symptomatic of a post-colonial attitude: 'the explanation is that once Conrad helped colonials break out, some of them looked back and found him unnecessary' (182).

Whatever the validity of Achebe's conclusions, race has proved to be a central issue in Conrad studies both because of the fact that, in his colonial fiction, Conrad drew upon his travels in the last era of imperial expansion, and because of the emergence of a body of critical theory known as post-colonialism. A post-colonial reading of a Western text seeks to show how its construction of the colonial 'other' rests upon Eurocentrism, the conscious and unconscious processes by which Europe and European cultural assumptions are accepted as normal, natural, and universal. Post-colonial critics are also concerned with the politics of representation, arguing that, in the grand narrative of empire, the colonized are reduced to characters in someone else's story—the story told by the colonizer—and have no story or voice of their own. In essence, the impetus behind this cultural criticism is neatly summarized in Achebe's argument that 'the fundamental theme [that] must . . . be disposed of . . . is that African people did not hear of culture for the first time from Europeans; that their societies were not mindless but frequently had a philosophy of great depth and value and beauty, that they had poetry and, above all, they had dignity' ('The Role of the Writer in a New Nation', in G. D. Killam (ed.), *African Writers on African Writings* (Heinemann, 1973) 8).

Conrad was profoundly affected by what he saw in the *Congo Free State in 1890, and he transformed these experiences into 'Heart of Darkness', 'An Outpost of Progress', and 'Geography and Some Explorers'. Lady Ottoline *Morrell records that, during her first visit to Conrad, 'He spoke of the horrors of the Congo, from the moral and physical shock of which he said he had never recovered' (quoted in *JCC*, 388). Conrad also told Edward *Garnett: 'before the Congo I was a mere animal' (Baines, 119). What he saw, at first hand, were the horrors of racism manifest in the excesses of colonialism, and his writings served as an indirect contribution to the international campaign to protest against the cruelties in the Congo. For instance, he wrote to Roger *Casement in December 1903: 'there exists in Africa a Congo State, created by the act of European Powers where ruthless, systematic cruelty towards the blacks is the basis of administration . . . Of course You may make any use you like of what I write to you' (*CL*, iii. 97). E. D. Morel, the leader of the Congo Reform Association, in a letter to A. Conan Doyle on 7 October 1909 called 'Heart of Darkness' simply 'the most powerful thing ever written on the subject'. Conrad's novella was published in 1899, the year Rudyard *Kipling wrote 'A Song of the White Men', which claimed that it is 'well for the world when the White Men drink | To the dawn of the White Man's day!' and spoke of colonial expansion in terms of White Men going 'to clean a land'. Some of Marlow's attitudes may seem patronizing to a later audience, but in an age when Britain was competing for its share of African territory, the condemnation of racial exploitation in 'Heart of Darkness' was bravely interrogative and ideologically subversive.

Although 'Heart of Darkness' has attracted most of the critical attention focused on issues of race and racism, Conrad's concern with racial prejudice is evident in his earliest fiction. Given the exotic setting of his first novel, *Almayer's Folly*, the repeated classification of it by early reviewers as a 'romance' was perhaps inevitable, as were the frequent comparisons with Kipling and Robert Louis *Stevenson, and through them with the tradition of boys' adventure stories and 'escape literature' represented by writers like G. A. Henty and Rider Haggard. But this latter identification is misleading, for Conrad casts a far colder eye on the nature

of European involvement in—and administration of—overseas countries. Conrad's early Malay fiction seems crucial in forging a passage from the 'naïve' tradition of imperial fiction to a new kind of sceptical and interrogative colonial novel. Far from simplistically contrasting European with native, *Almayer's Folly* demonstrates that the same impulses motivate different racial groups and that the real distinction between them is simply that, when it comes to trade, the Malays are less inhibited than their European counterparts. As Nina sees it, both orientals and occidentals pursue 'the uncertain dollar in all its multifarious and vanishing shapes. To her resolute nature, however, after all these years, the savage and uncompromising sincerity of purpose shown by her Malay kinsmen seemed at last preferable to the sleek hypocrisy, to the polite disguises, to the virtuous pretences of such white people as she had had the misfortune to come in contact with' (43). Repeatedly, the narrative shows *Almayer caught in the morass of his own self-condemning racist contradictions. For instance, when Abdulla visits Almayer with an offer to buy Nina as 'a favourite wife' for his nephew Reshid, the supremacist Almayer hypocritically excuses Nina on the grounds that she is unworthy to belong to Reshid's harem, being but 'an infidel woman' (45). This is not to suggest that traces of the period's more conventional attitudes to race are not evident; but the narrative reflects sharp doubts about the supremacy of the European, and, in doing so, threatens the inflexible distinctions born of racist assumptions. Significantly, the very possibility of a 'happy ending' in the novel depends upon Almayer abandoning his racial prejudices and fleeing with Nina and Dain: 'What if he should let the memory of his love for her weaken the sense of his dignity? . . . What if he should suddenly take her to his heart, forget his shame, and pain, and anger, and—follow her! What if he changed his heart if not his skin and made her life easier between the two loves that would guard her from any mischance!' (192). Of course, Almayer does not surrender to this impulse, but his tragedy is shown to rest upon his failure to do so.

Since imperialism was motivated largely by dreams of wealth, race was one of its sustaining ideas. Nineteenth-century science, in the form of *Darwin's theory of natural selection, provided a basis for a theory of race which could be put to the service of imperial expansion and the 'white man's burden'. In his notorious formulation in 'Recessional', Kipling depicted non-European races as 'lesser breeds without the law'. By contrast, Conrad's presentation of such characters as Almayer, *Willems, and *Kurtz soon undermines the savage/civilized distinction and, with it, the racial hierarchy that it sustains. Any attempt to evaluate Conrad's attitude to race and racism needs to take account of the pervasive scepticism with which it is presented. For instance, Willems's love for *Aïssa exposes the paradoxical dualism in colonial thought whereby the colonized subject is both debased and idealized, while *Jim's 'civilizing mission' in *Patusan is undone by a fellow European.

Any consideration of possible racism in Conrad's works would do well to take into account the example of *The Nigger of the 'Narcissus'* (1897), which, despite its provocative title, has remained popular with readers for more than a century. When the novel was first published in America (by Dodd, Mead in 1897), its title was changed to the more acceptable *The Children of the Sea*. Conrad consented to the change under protest, referring to the American title as 'absurdly sweet' (*CL*, v. 257). The new title was occasioned not by racial sensitivity alone but by 'material interests': in an inscribed copy of *The Children of the Sea* Conrad recorded that 'The argument was that the American public would not read a book about a "nigger"' (Smith, 8). In *The Nigger of the 'Narcissus'* such instances of racism within the multiracial forecastle as *Donkin's belligerence towards the uncomprehending Wamibo illustrate the threat posed by racist attitudes to the unity of the crew. But it is through James *Wait, the 'nigger' of the title, that the crew are made to confront the hypocrisy underlying

their own prejudices. For instance, the racism that underlies the crew's derogatory description of James Wait as a 'nigger' is constantly contradicted by their deference and servility towards him. That Conrad intends the word 'nigger' as a term of abuse is clear from Wait's (similarly racist) reaction to it: 'You wouldn't call me nigger if I wasn't half dead, you Irish beggar!' (79–80). Conrad's decision to make Wait a negro is a masterstroke: whilst his presence in the forecastle reflects the historical fact that there were thousands of racially diverse sailors in the *British Merchant Service in the late 19th century, the crew's attitudes to Wait—such as Donkin's shocked reaction to Wait's memory of his white 'Canton Street girl' (149)—allow Conrad to address the colonial prejudices and ideological hypocrisies of Victorian England. See also Watts 1993, and his '"A Bloody Racist": About Achebe's View of Conrad', *Yearbook of English Studies*, 13 (1983), 196–209; Ian Watt, 'Conrad's *Heart of Darkness* and the Critics', *North Dakota Quarterly*, 57 (1989), 5–15; and Allan Simmons, 'Introduction', in *Almayer's Folly* (Wordsworth, 1999).   AHS

Razumov. Kirylo Sidorovitch (Cyril son of Isidor) Razumov, the protagonist and implicit narrator of most of *Under Western Eyes*. Razumov is a third-year student in philosophy in St Petersburg when Fatality enters his room in the person of Victor *Haldin, who is seeking refuge after having assassinated the Minister of Internal Affairs. Razumov's name derives from the Russian noun *razum*, meaning reason, mind, or intellect. He is without a family (although he is apparently a natural son of Prince K—), and considers himself thoroughly apolitical, seeking only to distinguish himself by winning a Silver Medal. Frustrated in a half-hearted effort to help the fugitive escape, Razumov betrays Haldin to the police, and discovers that by doing so he has become their creature. Councillor Mikulin sends him to spy on the revolutionaries in *Geneva, but Razumov, exhausted by the demands of his false position and shamed by the naïve good faith of Natalia *Haldin, is soon driven to confess his betrayal and cleanse his guilty conscience.

The striking similarities between Razumov's situation and that of Raskolnikov, the protagonist of *Dostoevsky's *Crime and Punishment*, have received extensive critical commentary, although Conrad's access to Dostoevsky's works was probably through French translation. The motives and consequences of Razumov's betrayal of Haldin are examined by Tony Tanner in 'Nightmare and Complacency: Razumov and the Western Eye', *Critical Quarterly*, 4 (1962), 197–214. The autobiographical aspects of the novel have led critics to interpret Razumov in terms of Conrad's own complex feelings about the loyalties that dominated his childhood. In an early *psychoanalytic study, *The Polish Heritage of Joseph Conrad* (Sampson Low, 1930), Gustav Morf regarded Razumov's secret anguish as emblematic of Conrad's own repressed guilt at having betrayed the cause of Polish independence to which both his parents sacrificed their lives. For a later approach along similar lines, see Peter Stine, 'Joseph Conrad's Confessions in *Under Western Eyes*', *Cambridge Quarterly*, 9 (1980), 95–113. In 'The French Face of Dostoyevsky in Conrad's *Under Western Eyes*: Some Consequences for Criticism', *Conradiana*, 30 (1998), 24–43, Paul Kirschner makes a compelling textual case for the influence of Dostoevsky's novel *Podrostok* (A Raw Youth, 1975), which Conrad could have read in a 1902 French translation. Among many parallels noted by Kirschner, Dostoevsky's adolescent hero Arcade Macarovitch Dolgorouki is also the unrecognized son of an aristocrat.

reading. 'Books are an integral part of one's life,' Conrad commented in *A Personal Record* (73), an autobiographical reminiscence that evokes the way in which books attracted him in different ways and for different reasons at various stages of his life. As a young boy living in *Poland, Conrad found both solace and escape from a lonely life in the many alternative worlds opened up by sea stories and travel litera-

ture. During his twenty years at *sea, he read omnivorously during long, uneventful voyages and shore-leaves. As a writer, reading was as natural to him as breathing, an essential part of the creative process and the writer's life. Books provided Conrad the writer with access to a community of fellow artists, supporting traditions to take the place of those he had moved away from, germinating hints for short stories and episodes in his longer fiction, authenticating local details for his overseas fiction, and materials for creative *borrowing. The talismanic and symbolic importance of books, writers, and acts of reading in marking the important formative stages of a developing life is often represented obliquely in his writings. For example, *Marlow's initiation into the adult seaman's world in 'Youth' is accompanied by a simultaneous initiation, represented by his acquiring three books—Lord Byron's works, Thomas Carlyle's *Sartor Resartus* (1836), and Frederick Burnaby's *Ride to Khiva* (1876). Conrad's reminiscence of his own evolution from seaman to writer in *A Personal Record* is especially significant in its paralleling of the life lived and the books read. It takes the form of a pilgrimage in which significant stages are always magically signalled by remembered books and writers. The work begins with an image of Conrad during his last days as a seaman busily engaged in composing his first novel, *Almayer's Folly*, aboard the *Adowa* in Rouen. By coincidence, this northern French city was, he notes, also the birthplace of Gustave *Flaubert and the setting for scenes in *Madame Bovary* (1857), so that 'the kind Norman giant with enormous moustaches' (3) seems to preside as father-figure and guardian over Conrad's literary birth. Key stages in his life are then remembered in connection with the writers who had vitally helped to shape a literary destiny: notably Charles *Dickens as a friend to his youth, but also Cervantes's famous character *Don Quixote, who is associated with his early romantic wish to go to sea and invoked by his tutor in the course of trying to persuade the young boy to abandon his plan of leaving Poland. The chapters portraying the very first impulse to write the story that eventually developed into Conrad's first novel are again notable for a talismanic literary presence: the act of putting pen to paper followed upon a probable reading of Anthony Trollope, possibly signifying to the later writer a magical indicator of his future vocation as a novelist writing in English.

A special difficulty in attempting to compile a brief and compact account of Conrad's 'reading' lies partly in the fact that it was so prodigious as to demand a sizeable volume to itself. R. B. Cunninghame *Graham echoed the testimony of many others when he described Conrad as having 'a mind steeped in the modern literature of Europe, especially in that of France' (Preface, *Tales of Hearsay*, p. ix). Richard *Curle said of Conrad: 'It was part of his inbred unself-conscious courtesy that he always seemed to take it for granted that one knew as much as he did and had read all the obscure memoirs he had read—he was one of the widest-read men, one of the fastest and most tenacious readers, I ever met' (quoted in Adam Curle, *The Last of Conrad* (Joseph Conrad Society, UK, 1975), 8–9). An additional problem is that while much is known about Conrad's revered writers and his habit of reading 'professionally' for his fiction, it is not always possible to specify when or where he made contact with certain works and writers. Although he read avidly throughout his life, he kept no formal diary or commonplace book to indicate specific times and volumes. In an area where comprehensiveness would be an unrealizable ideal, it is at least possible here to indicate the *kinds* of reading undertaken by Conrad at various stages of his life. Further help is available for interested students in David W. Tutein (comp.), *Joseph Conrad's Reading: An Annotated Bibliography* (West Cornwall, Conn.: Locust Hill Press, 1990) and Hans van Marle's review-article, 'A Novelist's Dukedom: From Joseph Conrad's Library', *The Conradian*, 16: 1 (1991), 55–78, which adds nearly 200 items missing from Tutein's volume.

Conrad's early life unfolded within a cosmopolitan literary and linguistic atmosphere that soon encouraged him to dabble in writing, master French, and, above all, become 'a great reader' (*A Personal Record*, 70). It is not known at what precise age he began to read Polish works, but he told his wife Jessie that he could read French at the age of 5 (*JCKH*, 6), and at the age of 6 received from his uncle Tadeusz *Bobrowski a copy of A. E. Saintes's *Les Anges de la terre* (1844). Partly through his father's work as a translator, he had easy access to examples of several national literatures, including Polish Romantic literature through Adam *Mickiewicz and Juliusz Słowacki, whose poetry he read and recited aloud. His early reading quickly expanded to include translations of several British and American writers, including *Shakespeare (*The Two Gentlemen of Verona* (1594)), Sir Walter Scott, Frederick *Marryat, James Fenimore *Cooper, Charles Dickens (*Nicholas Nickleby* (1839), *Bleak House* (1853), and *Hard Times* (1854)), W. M. Thackeray, as well as extensive travel literature by Richard Burton, H. M. Stanley, Mungo Park, and Sir Leopold McClintock. At this stage in his life, these authors and books no doubt served to alleviate Conrad's childhood isolation and presented him with consoling 'friends'; they also provided him with the terms by which to imagine, however quixotically, a possible future outside his Polish homeland. Referring to his adolescent reading, Conrad later observed that 'if [his] . . . mind took a tinge from anything it was from French romanticism perhaps' (*LL*, ii. 289), and his earliest reading of French writers included Alain-René Lesage (*Gil Blas* (1717–35)), Alfred de Vigny, Louis Garneray (*Voyages, aventures et combats* (1853)), and Victor Hugo, whose *Les Travailleurs de la mer* (1866) provided his first introduction to sea literature. In addition to Cervantes (*Don Quixote* (1605–15)), the young Conrad also read Ivan *Turgenev (*A Nest of Gentlefolk* (1858) and *Smoke* (1867)). Later in life, he mentioned that as a boy he was also 'steeped in classicism to the lips' (*CL*, ii. 289).

Although little is known of what Conrad read during his twenty-year sea career, it was, according to Ford Madox *Ford, spectacularly varied. At one extreme, it included popular Victorian favourites like Mrs Henry Wood and Mary Braddon, and at another, Gustave Flaubert and Guy de *Maupassant (*JCPR*, 93, 94). When in 1878 Conrad began working on British *ships and adopted a *London shore-base, his English reading during the next decade was connected with the acquisition of the English language. He is reported by his son John to have said in later life: 'I never use a dictionary. If I want to know what a word means I read till I find out how it's used. Then I know' (quoted in Ray 1988: 46). Whether Conrad held to this principle in his early efforts to learn English is not known, but, as with many language-learners, he appears to have relied heavily on his reading. He first made contact with the language through newspapers—in particular the *Standard*, which he read on his first arrival in Lowestoft—and then maintained regular contact with British newspapers and magazines, some sent to him abroad and others seen overseas, such as the *Singapore Free Press* and the *Straits Times*. But clearly everything read by Conrad during his years in British ships—from John Stuart Mill's *Principles of Political Economy* (1848), through Lord Byron and Henry *James, to Mrs Braddon, Israel Zangwill, and Mark Twain—served to introduce him to the workings and potentials of the English language.

During Conrad's later sea years, when he was engaged in writing the work that would later become his first novel *Almayer's Folly*, he, like most fledgling writers, used his reading to discover supporting literary traditions as well as, in his case, the sense of kinship with a congenial family of writers that might replace the communities he had left. An important pattern to emerge during these years was his increasing preference for, and commitment to, French writers and their more strenuous artistic traditions. There exist numerous testimonies from his friends that, in John *Galsworthy's words, he 'was ever more at home with French literature than with English' (79). When in 1899 the French critic H.-D. *Davray reviewed *The Nigger

of the 'Narcissus' in France and claimed Conrad as 'one of ours', Conrad responded: 'The phrase "who is one of ours" touched me, for truly I feel bound to France by a deep sympathy' (*CL*, ii. 186). As early as 1879, he seems to have made a first contact with Flaubert through *Salammbô* (1862), and in 1892 was rereading *Madame Bovary* with 'respectful admiration' (*CL*, i. 111), almost certainly soon followed by *L'Éducation sentimentale* (1870), *Trois contes* (1877), and *Bouvard et Pécuchet* (1881). The other object of his early admiration was Maupassant, whom he was reading 'with delight' in 1894 ·(*CL*, i. 171). Later that year, he reported: 'I fear I may be too much under the influence of Maupassant. I have studied *Pierre et Jean* [1888]—thought, method, and all—with the profoundest despair. It seems nothing, but it has a technical complexity which makes me tear my hair. One feels like weeping with rage while reading it' (*CL*, i. 184–5). Other evidence suggests that during the period of his early writing career he had also read *Mademoiselle Fifi* (1883), *Bel-Ami* (1885), and a wide range of Maupassant's short stories. According to Ford Madox Ford, the admiration he and Conrad shared for Flaubert and Maupassant provided an essential keystone to their *collaboration which was first meditated in 1898: 'But that which really brought us together was a devotion to Flaubert and Maupassant. We discovered that we both had *Félicité*, *St.-Julien l'Hospitalier*, immense passages of *Madame Bovary*, *La Nuit*, *Ce Cochin de Morin*, and immense passages of *Une Vie* by heart' (*JCPR*, 36). Other references from his letters or specific echoes in his fiction indicate a wider reading into such French authors and works as Alphonse *Daudet, Pierre Loti's *Le Roman d'un spahi* (1881), Anatole *France's *Le Lys rouge* (1894) which meant 'nothing' to him (*CL*, i. 171), Émile *Zola's *La Débâcle* (1892) and *Lourdes* (1894), and probably works by Charles Baudelaire, François Rabelais, and Balzac. Conrad's early appetite for French literature created a pattern that remained with him for life. While his devotion to Flaubert and Maupassant remained undimmed, he continued to be a prodigous reader of French literature, later revising his opinion of Anatole France and also admiring the work of Prosper *Mérimée, André *Gide, Valéry *Larbaud, and, in later life, Marcel Proust. For further details on Conrad's reading of French writers, see Hervouet, especially 233–56.

When Conrad the apprentice writer gave up the sea and settled permanently in Britain in 1894, he was immensely fortunate in the kind of initial foothold he secured in the literary establishment. Had he attempted to make his way into the profession via Grub Street, he would almost certainly not have survived. In the event, he was taken up, and his path eased, by several influential literary friends—Edward *Garnett, E. V. *Lucas, Edmund *Gosse, and S. S. *Pawling. Nevertheless, as a relative stranger to British audiences and their literary tastes, Conrad needed to develop his English reading in order to understand the nature of the literary market place within which he would be working. Of his early professional insecurity in relation to these markets, Garnett commented that in 1897 Conrad was in a 'state of protracted tension and anxiety as to the saleability of his work' and went on, in a sparkling vignette, to characterize this anxiety in relation to Conrad's reading of a Grub Street product: 'I remember Conrad one day when he was very depressed at his lack of popular success throwing down some miserable novel by Guy Boothby which he vowed he would imitate, saying: "I can't get the secret of this fellow's manner. It's beyond me, how he does it!"' (*LFC*, pp. xxix, xxx). The evidence presented in Conrad's *letters suggests that he quickly developed an antenna-like sensitivity to features of the late Victorian English literary world. For example, as early as 1895, he seems to have acquired a sense of the range and quality of the numerous literary magazines of the day, and several of his letters during the period 1895–6 contain knowledgeable references to the *Yellow Book*, the *Cornhill*, and other magazines. He also read a wide range of Grub Street fiction and pondered the source of its popularity, and expanded his 'English' reading in other ways essential to

the making of the professional writer: he occasionally read in order to write a review, scrutinized reviews of his own work, and—in the case of his connection with *Blackwood's Magazine*—undertook a preparatory course of reading in order to explore the magazine's conventions and ethos. A Christmas letter of 1898 to Aniela Zagórska in Poland is interesting in showing the extent of Conrad's growing familiarity with the world of recent English letters: it finds him giving a knowledgeable summary of the preceding year's new novels and mentioning works by Grant Allen, Marie Corelli, Hall Caine, Rudyard *Kipling, J. M. *Barrie, George Meredith, Theodore Watts-Dunton, and H. G. *Wells.

Borys Conrad recalled that after about 1905 his father read mainly non-fiction (*MFJC*, 74), but in fact such reading seems to have been a feature of Conrad's literary life from its inception and essential to the construction and authentification of his various overseas works, as Sherry has shown in studies of Conrad's Eastern and Western worlds (see *CEW* and *CWW*). To his publisher William *Blackwood, he wrote in 1898 that his early Malayan world rested on numerous 'dull, wise books' and went on to say: 'In *Karain*, for instance, there's not a single action of my man (and [a] good many of his expressions) that can not be backed up by a traveller's tale—I mean a serious traveller's' (*CL*, ii. 130). The most important of these 'travellers' for his earliest fiction was A. R. *Wallace and his *The Malay Archipelago: The Land of the Orang-Utan and the Bird of Paradise* (1869), an account of his eight-year exploration of the *Netherlands East Indies on behalf of the Royal Geographical Society, dedicated to Charles Darwin. A constant companion of Conrad's from the mid-1890s onwards, Wallace's book supplied numerous details on Malay natural life, social culture, and religious practices for a wide range of his novels (see Amy Houston, 'Conrad and Alfred Russel Wallace', in Moore *et al.* (eds.) 1997: 29–48). Other sources for his earliest fiction included Major Frederick McNair's *Perak and the Malays: 'Sarong' and 'Kris'* (1878), Captain Rodney Mundy's *Narrative* of Events in Borneo and Celebes, down to the Occupation of Labuan: From the Journals of James Brooke (1848), and numerous other memoirs connected with James *Brooke, the first Rajah of Sarawak. Many of Conrad's Islamic terms and his references to Muslim beliefs can be traced to Richard F. Burton's Personal Narrative of a Pilgrimage to El-Medinah and Meccah (1855–6).

The South American world in Nostromo (1904), with its mixed nationalities, cultures, and languages, similarly entailed a prodigous amount of reading. At one extreme, Conrad used a number of South American histories and memoirs to name the people and places in his fictional world; but more significantly, those sources also offered hints about how the fictional *Sulaco might be populated, local colour secured, and the historical action developed in order to achieve what Henry James calls 'solidity of specification'. Hence, behind the making of the novel exist a whole series of ur-texts, such as G. F. Masterman's Seven Eventful Years in Paraguay: A Narrative of Personal Experience amongst the Paraguayans (1869), Edward B. Eastwick's Venezuela: or Sketches of Life in a South American Republic; with the History of the Loan of 1864 (1868), Ramón Páez's Wild Scenes in South America; or, Life in the Llanos of Venezuela (1863), Richard F. Burton's Letters from the Battle-Fields of Paraguay (1870), Alexander Dumas the Elder's translation of Mémoires de Garibaldi (1860), Frederick Benton Williams's On Many Seas: The Life and Exploits of a Yankee Sailor (1897), and material from newspapers and magazines of the time on current events in Colombia and Panama. Some sense of the range and wealth of Conrad's reading of non-fiction as a mature writer is conveyed in Ford's description: 'Conrad had read every imaginable and unimaginable volume of politicians' memoirs, Mme de Campan, the Duc d'Audiffret Pasquier, Benjamin Constant, Karoline Bauer, Sir Horace Rumbold, Napoleon the Great, Napoleon III, Benjamin Franklin, Assheton Smith, Pitt, Chatham, Palmerston, Parnell, the late Queen Victoria, Dilke, Morley. . . . There

was no memoir of all these that he had missed or forgotten—down to Il Principe or the letters of Thomas Cromwell' (JCPR, 59). Of almost lifelong interest to Conrad the writer were volumes connected with the Napoleonic era that he absorbed in connection with his long-held ambition to write a historical novel: 'All his life Conrad was a student of the Napoleonic era. He had absorbed the history, the memoirs, the campaigns of that period with immense assiduity and unflagging interest' (Curle, 'Introduction', Suspense, p. vi).

How did Conrad the 'student' gain access to the books, 'dull', 'wise', and others, that he needed to consult for his work? Conrad's own personal library was sizeable, and at his death was estimated by Richard Curle to have included over 1,000 books, although only some 630 of these have been identified. A documentary record of the contents of Conrad's library can be found in the auction catalogue accompanying the sale of his books in 1925, Hodgson & Co., London, A Catalogue of Books, Mss., and Corrected Typescripts from the Library of the Late Joseph Conrad, auction of 13 March 1925. A list of books drawn up by Conrad's executors and dated 30 August 1924 (held at the Bodleian Library) lists a proportion of these volumes in large categories and offers some indication of Conrad's habitual tastes and needs: French novels (78 volumes), Navy Records (24), Nelson's novels, apparently the Nelson series of cheap editions (120), Galsworthy (32), Henry James (24), Turgenev (15), and Hugh *Walpole (3). As his letters indicate, he also relied upon his literary friends to lend him the many volumes he needed for his work. In a letter of 1903 during his early composition of Nostromo, he exclaimed to Ford, 'Oh! for some book that would give me picturesque locutions[,] idioms, swear words—suggestive phrases on Italy' (CL, iii. 28), and went on to ask him to send a volume on the life of Garibaldi. Garnett, Cunninghame Graham (with his large library of South American literature), and Sidney *Colvin were also regularly called upon to supply required books. Some of Conrad's needs, especially for material in connection with his long-meditated Napoleonic novel, could only be supplied by libraries. He was a member of the London Library from 1897, and is known in 1920 to have used the British Museum Library, and also, when on working holidays abroad, libraries and local archives in *Montpellier, Capri, and *Corsica.

As a professional writer, Conrad gave generous amounts of time to reading manuscripts and works by members of his circle and other friends. He thus regularly read works by Marguerite *Poradowska, Edward Garnett, W. H. *Hudson, Ford Madox Ford, Cunninghame Graham, Hugh *Clifford, H. G. Wells, Henry James, Arnold *Bennett, F. Warrington *Dawson, and André Gide. He was also regularly helpful to beginning writers like Edward *Noble, Norman *Douglas, Stephen *Reynolds, and Helen Sanderson, so offering them some of the services that Garnett had performed for him in his early career. Conrad also received scores of presentation copies from authors of the day (which he may have read very selectively) and was often solicited by beginning writers, like the seaman-author David *Bone, to give an opinion on their work.

After leaving Poland in 1874, Conrad seems to have lost contact with Polish literature of the later 19th century. Aniela *Zagórska recorded that on his arrival in Poland for a visit in 1914, he knew little of contemporary Polish authors other than Stefan *Żeromski and Kazimierz Przerwa-Tetmajer. He made up for this deficiency during his stay, devouring 'almost all that was worth reading in fiction and drama' (*CUFE*, 214), including further works by Żeromski, whom he also met, Stanisław Wyspiański, Bolesław Prus, and Wacław Sieroszewski. In later years, Conrad's library was regularly supplemented by Polish volumes—by, for example, Andrzej Strug, Zofia Kossak-Szczucka, and Aleksander Fredro—sent to him by Aniela Zagórska. He was also in regular touch with the work of playwright Bruno Winawer, one of whose plays he *translated into English.

All of the existing evidence suggests that Conrad remained a voracious reader in later life, when, for example, he was ambitiously preparing materials for his last two historical novels, *The Rover* and *Suspense*. In 1922, he wrote to Curle: 'I do read biography and memoirs. History has a fascination for me. Naval, military, political' (*CTF*, 140). One later pattern of reading was, however, the inevitable consequence of his growing international stature as a writer whose works were regularly reprinted and his career crowned with the publication of *collected editions. These enterprises meant that the older Conrad was almost inevitably involved in systematically rereading his own works with a view to revising them or in order to furnish them with *'Author's Notes'. The preparation of collected editions for an English-speaking audience and translations for French and Polish audiences meant that from about 1916 he was engaged in a prolonged return to his own past work, re-immersing himself in his own fiction on several fronts and in different *languages. From 1914 onwards, he was also reading critical estimates of his work by such admirers as Richard Curle (1914), Wilson Follett (1915), Hugh Walpole (1916), Ruth M. Stauffer (1922), and Ernst Bendz (1923), and even corresponding with some of them about their views.

Varied glimpses can be gained of Conrad the more relaxed reader at various stages of his life. John Conrad's reminiscences offer attractive vignettes of a father who often shared his younger son's reading, either by secretly appropriating his *Boy's Own* annual or by reading aloud to him: 'He admired Edward Lear and would spend whole evenings reading the *Nonsense Songs and Stories*, and he was also very fond of the Lewis Carroll books' (*MFJC*, 84). Conrad's short note on 'The Books of my Childhood' (*CDOUP*, 77) lists the authors he had enjoyed with his elder son Borys—the brothers Grimm, Hans Christian Andersen, and Edward Lear. For an insight into the kinds of authors Conrad had for bedside reading, John is again helpful with his description of the 'library' table at the foot of Conrad's bed: 'There were several piles of books ... W. W. Jacobs for light reading, de Maupassant, Flaubert, Galsworthy, Cunninghame Graham, various periodicals and a book, which has always been a mystery to me, *Out of the Hurly Burly* by Max Adler' (*MFJC*, 149). Other bedside books for repeated browsing were Wallace's *The Malay Archipelago* and W. H. Hudson's *Idle Days in Patagonia* (1893), with *La Vie parisienne* and *Punch* reserved for lighter browsing.

readings. See SPEECHES AND READINGS.

Rescue: A Romance of the Shallows, The. Chronologically the first novel in the so-called 'Malay trilogy', *The Rescue* (1920) describes an episode from Tom *Lingard's early years. The character of Lingard is based in part on the life and fame of the Rajah James *Brooke, while, as Conrad told William *Blackwood, the story of the 'rescue' was derived from a variety of historical figures and sources (*CL*, i. 381–2). Long neglected as a romantic 'failure', *The Rescue* nevertheless remains one of Conrad's most complex explorations of the nature of fidelity between members of different races, cultures, and genders.

Conrad's second longest work (at nearly 135,000 words), *The Rescue* is also unique as a novel whose composition spans almost the entire course of Conrad's literary career. Begun (as *The Rescuer*) before Conrad's honeymoon on Île Grande (Brittany) in March 1896, the novel required what Conrad called 'a special mood difficult to attain and still more difficult to preserve' (*CL*, ii. 166). Its composition was often interrupted for the sake of other opportunities and commitments, when Conrad's early successes led to invitations he could not afford to refuse. With the help of S. S. *Pawling, Conrad sold the American serial rights to the novel to S. S. *McClure in March 1898, but was unable to meet the deadline he had proposed. Frustrated by his lack of progress, he even considered that a return to the *sea might be beneficial, and journeyed to Glasgow in September 1898 to explore the possibility of obtaining a command. By that time, *The Rescue* had reached a point corresponding roughly to the third and fourth chapters of Part IV.

Conrad's *letters bear witness to the constancy of his intention to return to the novel and finish it, but it was not until 1916 that he finally took up the task. He had the abandoned pages copied and subjected them to severe cutting before proceeding to write the remainder of the story, which was again interrupted for *The Arrow of Gold* (July 1917 to June 1918). The last words of *The Rescue* were dictated on 25 May 1919, some 23 years after it was begun. It was serialized in England in *Land and Water* (30 January–31 July 1919) and in the United States in the first issues of a new journal, *Romance* (November 1919 through May 1920). The first book edition was published by Doubleday, Page in Garden City, New York, on 21 May 1920, and by J. M. Dent and Sons in London in August 1920. It contained an *epigraph from Chaucer's 'Franklin's Tale' and a *dedication to Frederic C. *Penfield, the American Ambassador in Vienna who had helped to 'rescue' the Conrads from being trapped in *Poland by the outbreak of the *First World War in August 1914.

The Rescue opens with Tom Lingard's brig *Lightning* lying becalmed at sunset near Carimata, off the western coast of *Borneo. The action is set about the year 1860, some five years after the Crimean War (20). A row-boat approaches the *Lightning* in the dark, and her commander, Mr Carter, reports that the private schooner-yacht *Hermit* has been stranded for four days on a mud flat. Lingard decides to go to the ship's rescue, but Carter is surprised at the vehemence of his reactions. The next section takes the form of a flashback explaining how Lingard has spent the past two years mustering a volatile coalition of native forces for an armed expedition to restore his friend Hassim to power in Wajo (Celebes, now Sulawesi), to be launched from Belarab's secret settlement on the 'Shore of Refuge', near the spot where the *Hermit* has stranded. Lingard has purchased arms from a Yankee trader in *Singapore, and stores them in the *Emma*, a derelict ship in the care of old Captain Jörgenson.

Arriving at the *Hermit*, Lingard is treated with arrogant scorn by Mr Travers, who considers him a worthless adventurer interested only in salvage or ransom. That evening, while Travers and Mr d'Alcacer are taking a stroll on a sandbank, Lingard returns and secretly explains his situation to Mrs *Travers, urging her to convince her companions to accept the relative safety of his brig. During this long and passionate conversation, Travers and d'Alcacer are kidnapped from the sandbank by Daman's Illanun pirates, who are eager to plunder the stranded yacht. Lingard evacuates the crew of the *Hermit* to his own ship, and the next day, accompanied by Mrs Travers, he negotiates the transfer of the two 'prisoners' to his custody aboard the *Emma*. Carter, left in command of Lingard's brig and unaware of Lingard's delicate situation, destroys the Illanun praus and sets about refloating the *Hermit*. Lingard, whose word has been broken by Carter's action, is obliged to return the hostages to Belarab's stockade. Meanwhile, Hassim and his sister Immada journey to Belarab to enlist his help. On their return, they are captured by followers of Belarab's rival Tengga, but Hassim dispatches Jaffir to give Lingard an emerald ring as a signal of his distress. Jaffir reaches the *Emma* while Lingard is negotiating with Belarab; Jörgenson entrusts the delivery of the ring to Mrs Travers, but does not explain to her fully what it means. She finds Lingard in Belarab's stockade, but mistrusts Jörgenson and fails to deliver the ring. While waiting in vain for 'King Tom' to make a move, Jörgenson is approached by an envoy from Tengga requesting a parley. Jörgenson insists that the meeting be held on board the *Emma*, where, once the company is assembled, he leaps into the hold with a lighted cigar and blows up the ship. Lingard and the former hostages are returned to their ships by Belarab, and before he dies of his wounds, Jaffir delivers the Rajah Hassim's last message to Lingard, telling him to 'forget everything' (450). After bidding a bitter farewell to Lingard on the sandbank near Jaffir's grave, Mrs Travers throws the ring into the ocean.

Early reviewers praised the way in which the sustained poetic atmosphere of the story creates a heightened sensitivity to words and impressions, but expressed reservations about the static and debilitating love story between Lingard and Mrs Travers. In a patronizing review in the *Times Literary Supplement*, Virginia *Woolf suggested that Conrad was simply too old to be a 'romantic' writer (*CCH*, 332; see also her diary entry for 23 June 1920). This preoccupation with the 'romantic' aspects of the story has coloured most of its critical history, with many post-war critics following F. R. Leavis in regarding the novel as an over-long 'Grand Style staging of the conflict between Love and Honour' that is 'boring in its innocence' (1948: 210–11). In '"The Rescuer" Manuscript: A Key to Conrad's Development—and Decline', *Harvard Library Bulletin*, 10 (1956), 325–55, Thomas C. Moser cited unpublished fragments from the original manuscript to argue that it was Conrad's inability to deal with the 'uncongenial subject' of love that made it difficult for him to finish the novel. A later critic, Eloise Knapp Hay (1963), pays more attention to the political and historical dimensions of the story, and the ways in which it anticipates *Lord Jim*, although she characterizes Lingard oddly as 'the paragon of a pure politician' (97) and agrees with earlier critics that his virility ultimately comes to 'nothing more than a frustrated and frustrating sex appeal' (96). As against this dismissive tradition, Robert Caserio's '*The Rescue* and the Ring of Meaning' (in Murfin (ed.) 1985: 125–49) revalues the novel and notes that for writers of Conrad's generation, the idea of 'romance' involved not only 'romantic' love but an adventurous and uncorrupted way of life based on a sense of freedom from oppression, as exemplified by the novels of Sir Walter Scott and by the revolutionary traditions of Conrad's *Polish inheritance.

By deploring the naïve childishness of Lingard's ambition to restore his native friends to their position and focusing almost exclusively on Lingard's 'love affair' with Edith Travers, critics have in effect aligned themselves with Travers in refusing to take seriously the human claims of the non-European characters. Mrs Travers can only understand the world of the novel in terms of an opera or a ballad, and has no choice but to use Lingard to rescue her husband; while Lingard, who has devoted himself to the cause of Hassim and Immada, is suddenly called upon to sacrifice this commitment for the sake of arrogant European intruders who live for nothing beyond their own social images of themselves. The nature of this contrast is effectively dramatized in the scene where Lingard first boards the *Hermit*, when Hassim and Immada arrive and a double conversation ensues, one in English and the other in Malay. Mrs Travers emerges from her lethargy to admire the childlike 'prettiness' of Immada, while the princess, as soon as she realizes that the Europeans are strangers to Lingard, triumphantly shouts, 'Let them die!' (143). Mrs Travers comes eventually to understand that Lingard's quest for the freedom of the exiles is indeed a matter of life and death, but she is unable to face the consequences. She tells Lingard, 'You are always coming to me with those lives and those deaths in your hand' (355). Although Conrad does not make the point explicitly, the stranding of the *Hermit* also illustrates the foolishness of Westerners who sail along unknown coasts without proper knowledge or guidance, since it remains unclear who is actually in charge of the *Hermit*, and in practice the responsibility seems to be divided between Mr Travers (who owns the yacht but is apparently no sailor), the ineffectual sailing master, and the resourceful second mate Mr Carter. Critics have sometimes blamed Mrs Travers for provoking the final catastrophe by choosing not to deliver Hassim's ring to Lingard, and this twist of plot has sometimes been attributed to Conrad's putative misogyny. But Lingard absolves Mrs Travers of guilt, and under the circumstances, without his brig and without help, it is by no means clear what he would have been able to do to help his Wajo friends even if the ring had been delivered. Lingard finds himself in a classic 'double bind' across racial lines: he cannot permit the Europeans to be killed and their yacht plundered (not only on moral grounds,

but also because he knows that the destruction of the Europeans would provoke reprisals from the British or the Dutch that would destroy Belarab's refuge), yet his efforts to rescue the Europeans increasingly compromise his authority in the eyes of the natives, and make it impossible for him to maintain the coalition that he has assembled to help Hassim and Immada. In order to negotiate with Daman and Belarab, Lingard is also forced to leave his brig, the source of his fighting strength, outside the lagoon in charge of a subordinate; and although his 'word' is powerful, Carter's actions in attacking the Illanun praus expose his weakness and put him in an impossible position. The moral and practical complexity of Lingard's divided loyalty recalls *Jim's difficulty in dealing with Gentleman *Brown, and can be seen as emblematic of the colonial dilemma faced by many of Conrad's protagonists. This dilemma is summarized in a passage of *The Rescuer* manuscript involving a 'Mr. Wyndham' (a real historical figure; see *CL*, i. 382) not included in the final versions of the novel. Mr Wyndham warns Lingard against getting involved with natives, since such encounters can only end by bringing 'remorse to you, misfortune to them. Always. It's fatal.'

A lavish 'semi-silent' Hollywood film version of *The Rescue* appeared in 1929, starring Ronald Colman as Lingard and Lily Damita as Edith Travers. The only known copy of this film is held at the George Eastman House, Rochester, NY. The original manuscript of 1896–8 is now in a bound volume at the British Library (Ashley 4787). Later materials include a Doubleday typescript now in the Berg Collection, New York Public Library, and another corrected typescript in two bound volumes at the Case Library, Colgate University, which also holds the original typescript of Conrad's 'Author's Note'. Heavily corrected proofs of the serial version published in *Land and Water* are at the Beinecke Rare Book and Manuscript Library, Yale University.

Retinger, Józef H[ieronim] (1888–1960), a Polish literary scholar active in

Parisian literary and political circles, who first met Conrad in late 1912. Their meeting was arranged by Arnold *Bennett, who introduced Józef Retinger as follows: 'To me the idea of ardent young artistic people like R[etinger] carrying on a political campaign is chiefly comic. He has so. far as I know, no understanding whatever of politics. But these generous impulses must be humoured' (*PL*, 88). Earlier that year, the cosmopolitan Retinger had arrived in London to enlist British support for the cause of *Poland's independence under a constitutional monarch, supervised a Polish Bureau in Arundel Street, London WC2, and quickly took steps to make contact with his compatriot Conrad. He and his wife Otylia (née Zubrzycka; 1889–1984) soon became good friends with the Conrads, although Retinger was initially disappointed to find that Conrad 'refused to meet any more Poles' and exhibited an 'attachment' for his homeland that was 'objective, passive, and reticent' (Józef H. Retinger, *Conrad and his Contemporaries: Souvenirs* (Minerva, 1941), 119, 116).

Friendship with the Retingers served gradually to kindle Conrad's interest in revisiting Poland for the first time in over twenty years. At the invitation of Otylia's mother, the Conrad family and the Retingers travelled on a holiday to Poland in the summer of 1914, a visit that coincided with the outbreak of the *First World War. Subsequently, Retinger continued to try to quicken Conrad's feeling for the political fate of wartime Poland, persuaded him to help internationalize the country's dilemma, and worked closely with him on 'A Note on the Polish Problem', which was prepared for the British Foreign Office in 1916 and led to an interview there. Conrad's 'Note' and his 1918 essay 'The Crime of Partition' (both in *Notes on Life and Letters*) owe a heavy debt to Retinger's pamphlet on the future of Poland, *La Pologne et l'équilibre européen* (1916). During Retinger's war years in Paris, the political and the amorous were closely intertwined. In 1917, the year in which the Retingers had a daughter, he began an affair with Jane *Anderson that resulted in the break-up of his

first marriage and 'landed him in considerable trouble and affected his health' (John Pomian, *Joseph Retinger: Memoirs of an Eminence Grise* (Brighton: University of Sussex Press, 1972), 38).

A victim of his own political inexperience, Retinger was in 1918 deported by the French government and became *persona non grata* in Allied countries. From Spain, he pleaded for help from Conrad, who sent him £50 and solicited Hugh *Walpole to use his influence to obtain permission for Retinger to return to England: 'The question for me is to save this, in many respects, lovable human being broken in health and fortune from perishing miserably as if abandoned by God and men. . . . If we could get him over here we would look after him' (31 August 1918). However, according to Retinger, his association with Jane Anderson, whom he followed to America after the war, eventually caused a 'certain estrangement' from Conrad (83), although he omits to explain why and how. Subsequently, he lived and travelled widely in Mexico and the United States, where, in poor health, friendless, and rootless, he found himself, in his own words, 'living the life of a personage in Conrad's novels' (154). Later, Retinger returned permanently to the European political arena and, at the outbreak of war in 1939, devoted himself to the service of the exiled Polish government, achieving significant political influence as friend and personal aide to General Władysław Sikorski. He published an evocative but often unreliable memoir, *Conrad and his Contemporaries: Souvenirs* (Minerva, 1941). Otylia Retinger's reminiscences of Conrad are reprinted in *CUFE*, 201–10. Retinger's papers are held at the library of the Polish Social and Cultural Association (POSK), and the Sikorski Institute, both in London.

'Return, The'. Fresh from the serial success of *The Nigger of the 'Narcissus'*, Conrad first mentioned this 20,000-word *'London story' in April 1897 (*CL*, i. 351). He proceeded to struggle painfully with its composition over the summer months of that year, and, upon finishing it in

September, confessed: 'I have a physical horror of that story. . . . It has embittered five months of my life. I hate it' (*CL*, i. 386). In response to Edward *Garnett, who read and criticized the manuscript, Conrad raged against what he saw as his own artistic wrongheadedness: 'Well! Never more! It is evident that my fate is to be descriptive and descriptive only. There are things I *must* leave alone' (*CL*, i. 387). 'The Return' did not attract any magazine publishers, being one of only two Conrad stories (along with 'Falk') to suffer this fate. It was first published in 1898 in *Tales of Unrest*. In his 1919 'Author's Note', Conrad continued to denigrate the story, calling it a 'left-handed production' and describing how a recent rereading of it had produced in him the 'material impression of sitting under a large and expansive umbrella in the loud drumming of a furious rainshower' (p. viii).

Although roundly dismissed by many critics and judged by one to be 'Conrad's worst story of any length, and one of the worst ever written by a great novelist' (Guerard, 96), 'The Return' represents a significant, and certainly audacious, early attempt on Conrad's part to move away from exotic Malay settings to something decidedly nearer to the genteel English drawing room. 'I wanted to give out the gospel of the beastly bourgeois,' he said (*CL*, i. 393) about a story which finds the ultra-respectable Alvan Hervey returning to his London home one evening after work to find that after five years of marriage his wife has run off and left him for a newspaper-editor. She, lacking the courage of her convictions, returns home on that same evening to confront her outraged husband, who, as the narrative unfolds, is so shocked by what he discovers about his bruised ego and defeated manhood that he finally runs from the house, never to return. Conrad's study of the 'beastly bourgeois' is literally enacted in a story that uses a varied bestiary (Hervey as a sleek animal or prowling tiger) in order to suggest the atavistic brutality underlying the polite socially created identity, a phenomenon vividly described by Harold Pinter as 'the

weasel under the cocktail cabinet'. Conrad's story also attempts an early exercise in what has later become better known as 'Pinterese', a form of dialogue seeking to register mimetically the submerged logic of inner breakdown through indeterminate pause, agitated repetition, and broken fragments. Ambitiously, he dramatizes Hervey's collapse in terms of his growing linguistic failure to structure an appalling silence and in a way requiring the reader to be unusually sensitive to such paralinguistic features as tone, pause, stress, and silence as indicators of submerged feeling that Hervey dare not articulate: 'One doesn't usually talk like this—of course—but in this case you'll admit . . . And consider—the innocent suffer with the guilty. . . . I don't want to say any more . . . on—on that point—but, believe me, true unselfishness is to bear one's burdens in—in silence' (164, 165).

Although several commentators have regarded the story as a misplaced and best-forgotten attempt to emulate a Jamesian subject matter, 'The Return' calls for a re-assessment in relation to the developing continuities of Conrad's own early fiction. Although not the right-hand production he had wished for, the story's experiments with a more naturalistic kind of dialogue provide a striking anticipation of the 'dubious stammers' in which *Jim habitually expresses himself (*Lord Jim*, 155); Hervey's half-fascinated revulsion for his wife's supposed infidelity offers a domestic version of the moral 'horror' that *Marlow will later experience in the presence of *Kurtz; and the handling of the couple's marital isolation (for which some critics have found a precedent in Henrik Ibsen's *A Doll's House* (1879)) looks forward to the more severely ironic treatment of the *Verlocs' marital estrangement in the final chapters of *The Secret Agent*. There are welcome attempts to reassess the story in Dale Kramer's 'Conrad's Experiments with Language and Narrative in "The Return"', *Studies in Short Fiction*, 25 (1988), 1–12, and William Bonney's 'Contextualizing and Comprehending Joseph Conrad's "The Return"', *Studies in Short Fiction*, 33 (1996),

77–90. The manuscript is held in the Berg Collection, New York Public Library.

Reynolds, Stephen (1881–1919). Stephen Reynolds was, when Conrad first met him in 1907, a promising young Edwardian prose writer who had published very little. After an abortive attempt to start a writing career in Paris in 1903, he developed a fascination with the lives of the Devon fishing communities and settled in Sidmouth in 1906. His recreation of that life forms the substance of his two best works, *A Poor Man's House* (1908) and *Alongshore* (1910). Through Edward *Garnett, his first mentor, Reynolds gained an entry into the London literary establishment, soon meeting Ford Madox *Ford and Conrad. Ford championed the unpublished writer and secured for him a post as assistant editor on the *English Review*, although the two eventually quarrelled over payment for Reynolds's novel *The Holy Mountain* (1910) which was serialized in the journal. Reynolds found a more reliable source of emotional and artistic support in Conrad, whose sea fiction he admired enormously. For his part, Conrad may have seen in Reynolds's situation as a young, struggling novelist a reflection of his own early career. His letters to Reynolds during their brief, but close, connection show the older writer reading Reynolds's work-in-progress and encouraging him to keep his artistic 'torch burning bright—and to hold it high' (*CL*, iv. 135). Becoming one of the circle of young admirers gathered around Conrad between 1907 and 1912, Reynolds wrote an essay on 'Joseph Conrad and Sea Fiction', which is finely responsive to the gifts that allowed Conrad to produce 'novels *of* the sea, as opposed to novels *about* the sea' (*Quarterly Review*, 217 (1912), 165). See also J. D. Osborne, 'Conrad and Stephen Reynolds', *Conradiana*, 13 (1981), 59–64.

Romance. A picaresque adventure novel set in the *Caribbean in the 1820s, *Romance* (1903) is the longest, most thoroughly integrated, and most successful of Conrad's *collaborations with Ford Madox *Ford. As Conrad described the story to his agent J. B. *Pinker, 'There's easy style, plenty of action, a romantic atmosphere and a happy ending after no end of real hair's breadth escapes.' As usual, the popular genre served Conrad as a basis for something more, which he described as 'a serious attempt at *interesting, animated Romance*' (*CL*, ii. 366). Despite his protestations that the novel was not a work of boys' literature, most critics have found it difficult to take the novel seriously as a work of art, and have used it primarily as a means to explore the mechanics of the Conrad–Ford collaboration.

Romance is a first-person memoir narrated by John Kemp, a well-born, chivalrous Kentish boy in desperate quest of 'Romance'. Conrad called the novel 'a Straight romantic narrative of adventure where the hero is a Kent youth of good birth, the heroine a Spanish girl, the scene in England, Jamaica, Cuba, and on the sea—the personages involved besides Hero and Heroine smugglers, planters, sailors and authentic pirates' (*CL*, ii. 366). Kemp's first glimpse of 'Romance' comes in the person of his Spanish cousin Carlos Riego, who is in love with his sister Veronica. She, however, is engaged to be married to Ralph Rooksby, who engages Kemp to take his place in helping Riego and his surly comrade Tomas Castro, who are being sought by the Bow Street runners, to flee the country. Kemp is caught by the runners and rescued by Jack Rangsley, the leader of the local free traders, who terrifies the runners (and Kemp) with a mock execution by hanging them over the edge of what they believe to be a high cliff—thus introducing literally the 'cliff-hanging' motif that recurs throughout the novel. The smugglers arrange with the mayor of Hythe for the escape of Kemp and the fugitives under the drunken guidance of Rangsley's uncle. Kemp rows Carlos and Castro in a sinking row-boat to rendezvous with the *Thames*, on which they make good their escape to Jamaica.

During the voyage, a second mate named Nichols warns Kemp against his companions and describes Rio Medio as a hotbed of pirates licensed by Mexican letters of marque to prey upon Englishmen.

The strong man of the island is a renegade Irish rebel named Patrick O'Brien, the villain of the tale, a judge of the marine court in Havana and a hater of Englishmen. He has the ear of Carlos's uncle, Don Balthasar Riego, and wants also the hand of his daughter Seraphina. Through priests, O'Brien also controls the mob of *Lugareños*, 'the lowest outcasts of the island' (163) outside the Casa Riego, where one of two warring factions is led by Manuel-del-Popolo, a piratical bard whose name and vanity curiously anticipate those of Conrad's 'Man of the People', *Nostromo.

After two years of uneventful work in Kingston, Kemp rescues a friend but publicly embarrasses Admiral Rowley by striking one of his councilmen, Mr Topnambo. Ford claimed that it was at this point, when John Kemp attacks Mr Topnambo and thus allies himself with the Separationists who favour union with the United States, that the novel assumed a political dimension and Conrad suddenly felt that a 'third person' was writing, one who was neither himself nor Ford (*JCPR*, 45). Kemp is obliged to flee Jamaica, and O'Brien tries to recruit him on the common ground of resistance to *England. Kemp threatens to denounce O'Brien and is kidnapped for transport to Rio Medio. Seraphina helps him to escape by boat, and he is taken up by the *Breeze*. He is then re-kidnapped by Tomas Castro in a pirate attack led by Manuel-del-Popolo. Eventually Kemp arrives in Rio Medio to find Carlos dying in despair over how to protect Seraphina from O'Brien. Kemp falls in love with Seraphina; he refrains from killing O'Brien but expels him from the mansion. From Havana O'Brien sends a priest to incite the populace to demand the infidel *Inglez*. A bullet from the crowd kills Don Balthasar, and Carlos witnesses a symbolic marriage between Kemp and Seraphina from his deathbed. Like Captain *Anthony in *Chance*, Kemp cannot believe himself worthy of Seraphina's love. Funeral ceremonies make it possible for Kemp and Seraphina (and Castro, who has sworn to protect Kemp from harm) to escape from Rio Medio. After a good many alarums and excursions in the fog, the trio

rescue an English ship, the *Lion*, from a pirate attack led by Manuel-del-Popolo. To Carlos's great disgust, Kemp misses a chance to kill Manuel, who dives overboard to escape.

The *Lion* is bound for Havana, where O'Brien rules. Kemp agrees to a plan to find shelter on the mainland while the *Lion* proceeds to Havana, then to rejoin the ship after she has been searched by O'Brien, and return to England (where Castro is still wanted on a warrant). Castro is caught by the *Lugareños* and dies in the ravine; Manuel also falls to his death, but Kemp and Seraphina eventually make their rendezvous with the *Lion* in Havana harbour. Captain Williams is at that moment frolicking on land, and Kemp volunteers to fetch him. He is caught by O'Brien and handed over to the English authorities as Nikola el Escoces, an infamous and murderous pirate from Nova Scotia (the actual Nikola is Nichols, the second mate of the *Thames*).

Tried for piracy at the Old Bailey, Kemp tries to save himself from death by telling his story, which is the story of *Romance*. Exhausted, he awaits the verdict when Captain Williams suddenly arrives at the last moment to save him from the gallows. Kemp finds happiness with Seraphina and writes his memoirs as a romantic tribute to his lost youth.

The idea of a novel about smugglers occurred to Ford as early as 1896, perhaps inspired by the material he was collecting for *The Cinque Ports* (1900). As he recalled in *Return to Yesterday* (1932: 195), the idea of a novel about pirates was first suggested to him by Richard Garnett, Keeper of Printed Books at the British Museum, the father of Edward *Garnett and an old family friend. Garnett sent Ford to the Reading Room for materials on Aaron Smith, 'the last pirate ever to be tried at the Old Bailey' (*JCPR*, 47), who was acquitted in 1824. Smith's account was entitled *The Atrocities of the Pirates: Being a Faithful Narrative of the Unparalleled Sufferings Endured by the Author during his Captivity among the Pirates of the Island of Cuba; with an Account of the Excesses and Barbarities of those Inhuman

Freebooters (1824). Ford was also familiar with the account of Smith's adventures published by Charles *Dickens in his magazine *All the Year Round*, entitled 'Cuban Pirates: A True Narrative' (1870). He read 'a vast number of Jamaica newspapers of the "twenties"' which showed the island to be 'an ant-heap of intrigue by what were called Secessionists' (ibid. 47). Conrad told William *Blackwood that 'All the details of the political feeling in Jamaica (about 1821) are authentic' (*CL*, ii. 339). Ford later recalled that the characters of Tomas Castro and Seraphina were also modelled upon two contemporary visitors to the Pent Farm: the Portuguese Consul-General, Don Jaime Batalha Reis, and his daughter Celeste (1932: 140).

Conrad first heard the story of *Seraphina* when Ford read it aloud to him from his manuscript at Pent Farm in the autumn of 1898, soon after they first met. Ford has described how Conrad began to groan and writhe in his chair. He felt that Ford had failed to extract from his subject 'every drop of blood and glamour' (*JCPR*, 29), and offered to help. Ford was familiar with the Kentish smugglers of Part I of the novel, but Conrad's knowledge of the *sea would prove invaluable once Kemp had set sail for the Caribbean. The practical difficulty lay in piling up sufficient perils for John Kemp to keep him maximally 'hangable'.

Despite financial worries, Conrad and Ford were remarkably productive during the four years they worked together on *Romance*. Between the autumn of 1898 and the spring of 1902, Conrad had abandoned *The Rescue* but written *Lord Jim* and two volumes of stories, including 'Heart of Darkness', 'The End of the Tether', 'Typhoon', and 'Amy Foster'. During the same period, Ford was working on a novel about Oliver Cromwell and a biography of Henry VIII; he published *The Cinque Ports*, a topographical history in which the Romney smugglers who appear in *Romance* are also mentioned, and a novel called *The Benefactor*. They had also published their first collaboration, *The Inheritors*.

Immediately upon finishing *Lord Jim* in July 1900, Conrad travelled to Belgium to join Ford for a holiday devoted to the completion of *Romance*, but Borys's illness and Conrad's own ill temper meant that little work was done. Ford says that he and Conrad abandoned *Seraphina* after two and a half years 'because the problem of how to get John Kemp out of Cuba had grown too difficult' (*JCPR*, 117). In July 1901 they asked Pinker to forward the first, second, and fourth (now fifth) parts of the novel to *Blackwood's Magazine*, whose editor, David S. *Meldrum, had published Ford's *The Cinque Ports* and serialized Conrad's *Lord Jim* only the previous year. Conrad expected the novel to be accepted, but Meldrum's recommendation to Blackwood was lukewarm; he considered *Seraphina* an uneasy blend of 'Hueffer's story and Conrad's telling' (quoted in Blackburn (ed.), 131). In Ford's view, Conrad had actually been more involved with the structure and he with the style, but in the version submitted to Blackwood, Ford had been primarily responsible for both. Blackwood rejected it without waiting to read Part III.

Conrad was working on other materials for Blackwood at that time but, his confidence shaken by the rejection, he embarked on a thorough revision of Part III, entitled 'Casa Riego', and the elaboration of Part IV, 'Blade and Guitar'. The novel was growing too long for *serialization, and Conrad, assuming that 'from the moment Kemp is kidnapped the thing is satisfactory' (*CL*, ii. 395), set about cutting material from Parts I and II. Conrad and Ford were in general agreement about the final division of labour: Ford was chiefly responsible for Parts I, II, and V; Conrad for Part IV; and they shared the credit for Part III. Basically, Ford contrived all the scenes set in England and Jamaica, plus the pirate attack on the *Breeze* and the 'burial stuff' of Kemp's escape from the Casa Riego at the end of Part III. Conrad was responsible generally for seamanship and editing, and specifically for Part IV.

The American publisher S. S. *McClure was willing to serialize a shortened version, but Ford was angry with McClure, accusing the company of delaying payments for *The Inheritors*. In the end *Romance* was never serialized. It was published by Smith, Elder in London in October 1903, with extra copies printed for Bell's Indian and Colonial Library, published by George Bell & Sons in London and Bombay. The American edition was published by McClure, Phillips in New York in March 1904, with illustrations by Charles R. Macauley. A reader's report of 25 September 1903 has survived in the Macmillan Archives in the British Library. The Macmillan reader rejected *Romance* for qualities that might elsewhere be interpreted as strengths: 'the affectation of the style, the extraordinary minuteness of the details, and the variety, complexity, and breathlessness of the situations'. It seems that in their efforts to keep John Kemp maximally 'hangable', Conrad and Ford may have succeeded too well, since the reader complained of the 'unnecessary amount of adventure' (quoted in David Leon Higdon, 'The Macmillan Reader's Report on *Romance*', *Modern Fiction Studies*, 30 (1984), 275).

Like *An Outcast of the Islands* and *The Rescue*, *Romance* can be read as an astute commentary on cultural stereotypes that explores the power and corruption of colonial politics. The novel is also an extended meditation on the idea of 'Romance'—a term for which, as Ford noted, there is no French equivalent—that had inspired many literary works familiar to Conrad and Ford in childhood, from *Don Quixote* to Frederick *Marryat's fiction (the names of Seraphina and O'Brien also occur in Marryat's novel *Peter Simple*, 1834). Conrad and Ford had dedicated *The Inheritors* to their own heirs, Borys and Christina respectively, and they continued the joke by dedicating *Romance* to their wives, Elsie and Jessie. *Romance* may well be, as Jefferson Hunter has claimed, 'the most self-consciously romantic Edwardian novel of them all' (80).

For Conrad, a measure of cultural cross-fertilization was an essential ingredient of *Romance*. As he told Blackwood, he and Ford felt that this book would be different from other romances because 'the feeling of the romantic in life lies principally in the glamour memory throws over the past and

arises from contact with a different race and a different temperament; so that the Spanish girl seems romantic to Kemp while that ordinary good young man seems romantic and even heroic not only to Seraphina but to Sanchez [the original name for Carlos] and Don Riego too' (*CL*, ii. 339). The novel is filled with a sense of love and danger arising from interracial encounters, not unmixed with ethnic caricatures and racial slurs. The Spanish-speaking characters also mix their English with expletives in French or Italian, but they seem to concur in their appreciation of British courage, as embodied chiefly in the hero, while deploring the cowardice of the *Lugareños*, the corruption of the Spanish, and the fanatical passions of Irishmen like O'Brien.

The novel shows the English and Spanish struggling to maintain control of their colonies against a rising tide of nationalism and demands for secession and independence. As in *Nostromo*, which Conrad began writing immediately after *Romance*, national interests can take strangely European forms: O'Brien rules Cuba for the Spanish and makes war on the English with American-built schooners, while employing a Nova Scotian as his chief pirate henchman. The forms and terms of warfare between small ships have not changed since Elizabethan times. Slavery was still legal (it was not abolished in Jamaica until 1833, effective 1838), and torture still standard practice: the maniacal bard Manuel threatens to cut off Castro's eyelids and point him towards the sun.

Early readers and reviewers were generally sceptical of Conrad and Ford's effort to collaborate and unimpressed with its results. Writing to thank Ford, who had sent him a copy of *Romance*, Henry *James said that he could not read it immediately, but that 'it looks like a store of romance to keep on the shelf like one would keep a large chunk of bride cake for earnest but interspaced and deliberate degustations' (*PL*, 43). *Romance* has rarely been studied as a work of art in its own right, perhaps because of its double authorship. As Ford put it, 'the critics of our favoured land do not believe in collaboration' (*JCPR*, 28). After Ford's own recollections of their work on *Romance* published in *JCPR* and in the 'Note on *Romance*' printed as an appendix to *The Nature of the Crime*, other major studies of the novel include Richard James Herndon, 'The Collaboration of Joseph Conrad with Ford Madox Ford' (unpublished Ph.D. dissertation, Stanford, 1957); John Hope Morey, 'Joseph Conrad and Ford Madox Ford: A Study in Collaboration' (unpublished Ph.D. dissertation, Cornell, 1960); and Raymond Brebach, *Joseph Conrad, Ford Madox Ford, and the Making of 'Romance'* (Ann Arbor: UMI Research Press, 1985).

Conrad's first film contract was signed in 1915 with Fiction Pictures Inc. for the 'moving picture rights' to a film version of *Romance*. This film was never made, but the rights were sold again in 1919, and in 1927 MGM produced a silent seven-reeler entitled *The Road to Romance*, starring Ramon Novarro and Marceline Day, no copies of which appear to have survived.

Surviving manuscript materials include Ford's early draft of *Seraphina* and other Ford materials at the Carl A. Kroch Library, Cornell University, and manuscript portions of Parts III and IV in Conrad's hand with other items at the Beinecke Rare Book and Manuscript Library, Yale University. Two sets of proofs, one corrected by Conrad and the other by Ford, are in a bound volume at Colgate, which also holds other related fragments and materials.

Rothenstein, William (1872–1945; knighted 1931), painter and principal of the Royal College of Art (1920–35), one of Conrad's most devoted friends. Born in Bradford, Yorkshire, William Rothenstein studied art at the Slade School, London, and then at the Académie Julian in Paris, where he made contact with Whistler, Degas, and Pissarro. According to Max *Beerbohm, Rothenstein 'wore spectacles that flashed more than any other pair ever seen. He was a wit. He was brimful of ideas. . . . He knew everyone in Paris. He knew them all by heart. He was Paris in Oxford' (*Seven Men* (Heinemann, 1919), 4–5). From 1898, he specialized in painting celebrities, including Conrad, who sat for him in 1903. The *portrait made from this first sitting is now held at the National Portrait Gallery, London.

Originating in a shared sympathy for each other's artistic aims, their warm and lasting friendship developed through Rothenstein's efforts to find subsidies and organize loans for the needy Conrad during his *Nostromo* period. 'Poor Conrad', he commented, 'was always in difficulties over money. His books brought him insufficient for his needs; needs which were perhaps not quite so simple as he believed them to be. There was an extravagant side to Conrad, characteristic, I thought, of his former profession; he was like a sailor between two voyages, ready to spend on land what he couldn't aboard-ship' (Rothenstein, ii. 44). Rothenstein was most active on his behalf in the summer of 1904, when he succeeded in easing Conrad's immediate financial difficulties by securing him a loan of £150 to which he added £50 of his own. Intent upon helping Conrad to seek a more permanent solution to his pressing needs, Rothenstein also drew his case to the attention of Henry *Newbolt, a committee member of the Royal Literary Fund. When, in March 1905, Conrad received £500 from the Royal Bounty Special Service Fund, Rothenstein was appointed co-trustee with Newbolt to administer the award (see GRANTS AND AWARDS).

Subsequently, the Conrads visited the Rothenstein family's London home on a regular basis. Conrad also attended the artist's soirées, making contact with other painters in his circle such as Augustus John, and frequently visited the artist's exhibitions. Rothenstein and his wife Alice were among the mourners at Conrad's funeral in 1924. For further details, see Rothenstein's *Men and Memories: Recollections of William Rothenstein, 1900–1922* (Faber, 1932), excerpted in *JCIR*, 143–6.

Rover, The. First intended for a collection of short stories, *The Rover* (1923) quickly absorbed Conrad's interests, expanded beyond its planned length, and eventually displaced *Suspense*, the long meditated 'Mediterranean novel' (*LL*, ii. 337) on which he had been working. Conrad began dictating *The Rover* to his secretary Miss *Hallowes in early October 1921. Problems with his *health caused some interruptions during writing, but its composition was mainly untroubled. However, as he neared a conclusion, Conrad experienced some anxiety, reporting to Edward *Garnett: '*The Rover* has ceased to rove—and be damned to him. You have no idea how that fellow and a lot of other crazy creatures that got into my head have also got on my nerves. I have never known anything like this before. I have been infinitely depressed about a piece of work, but never so exasperated with anything I have had to do' (*LJC*, 313). As was the case with *Lord Jim*, another short story that unexpectedly grew into a novel, he apparently discovered his conclusion only at a very advanced stage. Having reached the beginning of chapter 11 in late May 1922, he anticipated a conclusion in one additional chapter. Four more were to come, and from early June to mid-July he produced these in a sudden burst of creativity.

Publication of the novel was delayed in order to secure its *serialization in America. After the William Randolph Hearst consortium declined it, arrangements were made for its appearance in New York's *Pictorial Review*, a popular, mass-circulation women's magazine where it was published in four instalments, from September to December 1923, with illustrations by Mead Schaeffer. The serial text was subjected to extensive house-styling and editing, particularly with respect to its paragraphing. Doubleday, Page, and Company of New York published a limited edition on 30 November and a trade edition on 1 December. The first English edition was published by T. Fisher *Unwin on 3 December 1923. Conrad dedicated the novel to his French friend and first *biographer, G. *Jean-Aubry, and may have named his title-character after him in a gesture of affectionate friendship. He wrote no 'Author's Note' to the novel, which is prefaced with a significant *epigraph from the speech of

Despaire in Spenser's *Faerie Queene* (1590): 'Sleep after toyle, port after stormie seas, I Ease after warre, death after life, does greatly please.' The lines, which in context counsel suicide, were inscribed on Conrad's own tombstone.

The novel opens in the port of Toulon in 1796 at a historic turning point for the French Revolution. Revolutionary fervour is on the wane; *Napoleon is on the verge of becoming a major political force; and *France and England are at war. The first action in the novel is a deeply symbolic one: Master-Gunner Jean *Peyrol, arriving, after numerous vicissitudes, to deliver an English prize-ship to the Port Office, lowers his ship's anchor in Toulon Harbour. He quickly notes the many changes that have occurred in his native land after a 40-year absence, many spent as a lawless freebooter in the Eastern seas. Regarded with suspicion by the port authorities, eager to hide a fortune in coins discovered aboard his prize-ship, and having in any case decided to retire from his long and adventurous life at sea, Peyrol soon distances himself from the troubled political and social scene by quietly wandering off to the nearby Giens peninsula, the scene of his childhood.

Finding a resting-place at a remote old farmhouse, Peyrol becomes intimately entangled in the emotional lives of the farm's inhabitants. Its royalist owners, who were killed during reprisals for Toulon's delivery to the English and Spanish fleets in 1793, have left the farm to their daughter *Arlette. The young woman, haunted by the past, suffers from a spiritual malaise that at moments vents itself in a restless anxiety and vagueness of focus that resemble mental instability. Unable to exorcize the murder of her parents and the trauma of her own participation in the sanguinary acts in which they met their deaths, she is also plagued and tormented by 'Citizen' Scevola Bron. A fanatical Jacobin of morbid and highly excitable temperament, Scevola gave full rein to his sadistic bloodlust during the Revolution, but as political stability slowly returns to France his discontent and marginalization increase. The watchful efforts of Arlette's Aunt Catherine, a sympathetic and caring guardian but one insufficiently strong to rid Escampobar Farm of Scevola, have failed to neutralize him as a hovering sexual menace.

The full effect of Peyrol's presence is registered only with the beginning of chapter 4, set in 1804, eight years after the events of the first three chapters and not long before Napoleon's coronation. Peyrol, now aged 64, has broken completely with his wandering past, making enduring commitments to a place as well as to individuals. An English blockade of Toulon endangers these ties, as the larger outside world that he so deliberately left behind him begins to intrude upon his existence. The arrival at Escampobar of Lieutenant Eugène Réal, a young officer charged with monitoring the actions of the English and later entrusted with a secret mission authorized by Napoleon himself, is another presence Peyrol must contend with. Orphaned by the Revolution, Réal is an isolate, disconnected from life and lacking ties either of love or friendship. The English also threaten Escampobar's fragile dynamics when Mr Bolt, recalling his friendly relationship with the farm's owners, convinces Captain Vincent to put a party ashore at night to explore the possibilities of re-establishing contact with the royalist couple he once knew. On arriving at the farm, Bolt immediately senses that things at the farmhouse have changed greatly, abandons his plans, and returns to his boat; but he must confess to his captain that he has lost one of his men. Sam Symons, struck on the head by Peyrol, is confined in the cuddy of a tartane that Peyrol has lovingly restored to seaworthiness. Safely moored in a protected cove, the tartane is the abode of Michel, a homeless man whom Peyrol has befriended and to whom he gives refuge. Michel keeps a nervous watch on the English intruder.

Inevitably drawn to one another, Arlette and Réal fall in love, an event that heightens the already tense emotional situation at Escampobar. Raving with jealousy, the possessive Scevola plots Réal's death to rid himself of a perceived rival. For his part Peyrol, whose essentially platonic affection for Arlette is nonetheless tinged by an erotic element, becomes a father-figure increasingly abandoned by a beloved surrogate daughter for the love of a younger man. The love affair is no ordinary one, however; and Réal, although he is forced to acknowledge to himself his love for Arlette, frets that he has fallen in love with a mere 'Body without mind' (214). He experiences intense pangs of guilt about his erotic attraction, and even goes so far as to contemplate suicide. His acceptance of a dangerous mission to deceive the English is partly an effort to return to the calls of duty and discipline, but it is also an attempt to escape the commitment that his feelings for Arlette represent. In the event, Peyrol removes this choice from Réal, substituting himself to perform the young man's mission, and in doing so, bequeaths to Arlette a younger, vigorous replacement for his ageing self.

During a night of feverish and mysterious activity at the farmhouse and aboard the tartane a number of events occur more or less simultaneously. Believing that Réal is hidden aboard the tartane, Scevola goes off, pitchfork in hand, to murder him; he is, however, confined in the cuddy by Symons, who has managed to make his way out of it. He escapes and is rescued by a search party that Captain Vincent has sent to find him. Arriving back from Toulon, Réal discovers Arlette in his room, learns of Scevola's plot to kill him, and confesses his love. Catherine, however, warns Réal to abandon Arlette who, as she claims, is destined 'for no man' (225). Peyrol meanwhile keeps careful watch on the farm as events continue to unfold.

Forced to accept that the time has come for the younger generation, Peyrol turns half-willingly towards death, replacing Réal on the dangerous and heroic mission for France. Aboard his tartane, Peyrol deftly plays decoy to the *Amelia*, convincing her officers that his attempted evasion betokens an important official mission. As the English ship gives chase to the tartane, the old rover, drawing upon the skills honed during years of seamanship, succeeds in creating the illusion of an attempt to avoid capture. After a long chase, the English corvette finally fires on her antagonist, shooting down all on board. Along with the bodies of the wizened sea-dog Michel and Scevola are found the faked dispatches designed to mislead the English about French naval strategy in Egypt and the East. Captain Vincent conveys the documents to Admiral Nelson himself, delivering an account of the chase. The *Amelia*'s crew give a respectful farewell to the worthy seaman and skilful adversary, sinking the tartane as the sun sets into the Mediterranean. The novel concludes with a brief coda, set some years after the battle of Trafalgar, and showing that peace has again returned to France. Venturing into Toulon once more, Catherine prays for Peyrol's soul in the reopened churches, while Mme and M. Réal look back affectionately on the old seaman of 'large heart' (286) who, though he allowed them to realize their happiness, will forever remain an enigma to them.

The sources of the novel lie in Conrad's *reading as well as in his personal experience. In addition to drawing on the scenes of his young adulthood in *Marseilles and the South of France and on a more recent stay in *Corsica in early 1921, *The Rover* is crafted out of, and uses to effect, many of the same materials that he had at hand for *Suspense*. There is specific *borrowing from Louis Garneray's *Voyages, aventures et combats* (1853) and a more general call on the history of the famous French privateer Robert Surcouf. Some critics have seen a vicarious working-out of the aged Conrad's attraction to the young and vivacious American journalist Jane *Anderson in the relationship of Peyrol and Arlette. Based in part on Dominique *Cervoni, a figure Conrad admired during his youthful days in Marseilles, Peyrol is perhaps the most convincingly drawn of Conrad's late characters, having psychological roundness and amplitude partly because he is so enmeshed in a particularized setting. He is also obviously a finely shaded self-portrait of the older Conrad himself, facing the closure of his career and life, yet still swayed by the world's demands and concerned about the legacy, both personal and artis-

tic, that he will leave behind him. The admiration for Peyrol's seamanship in a final outing against a much respected adversary, and his sacrifice of himself for others, are themes with personal resonance that Conrad poignantly develops.

Conrad was aware of Peyrol as a self-projection, commenting to John *Galsworthy, who had professed to like the novel, that he had 'wanted for a long time to do a seaman's "return" (before my own departure) and this seemed a possible peg to hang it on' (*LL*, ii. 339). There may also linger in the affectionate leave-taking of Peyrol some of the loss and distress that Conrad must have experienced on the death of his agent and old friend J. B. *Pinker, which occurred during the novel's writing. Whatever these personal sources, Peyrol is also a figure of mythic proportions resembling some of the sea-dogs of James Fenimore *Cooper, a writer Conrad admired in his boyhood. Emblematic of France herself—his first appearance on the scene is in the red, white, and blue of the tricolour—Peyrol is also a solar hero, a Phoebus or Helios figure who first appears at dawn and dies at the close of day, and his body is respectfully committed to the *sea at sunset as the tartane is sunk.

The novel's contemporary reception was mixed. At a time when the experimental writings of James Joyce and Virginia *Woolf were coming into fashion, the novel appeared to be a throwback to an earlier kind of fiction, the limits of which had already been explored. Critics thus tended to complain about flagging inventive energies, and what Conrad himself characterized as a 'note of disappointment' (*LL*, ii. 337) in the novel's reception presaged the decline his reputation saw in the 1930s and 1940s. Various aspects of the novel, in particular the characterization of Peyrol and the vivid long chase of the ending, did, however, win praise. It later enjoyed a certain vogue as a 'boys' book' and was required reading for a generation of secondary school students in Britain. A *film version appeared in 1967.

The Rover returns to a number of ideas Conrad had addressed in his earliest work, including solidarity and community, commitment and solipsistic isolation, politics and national identity. Activist engagement and mortality are also among the novel's major themes. To these he adds a sympathetic and affecting treatment of ageing and maturity, as Peyrol bids a graceful farewell to active life and then to the world. Perhaps the most compelling theme is the belated realization of oneself—a task undertaken by Peyrol, Arlette, and Réal—and a reconciliation with the world not so much as it might be but as it fundamentally is. This conservative, even anti-romantic theme of fidelity to one's surrounding community and, ultimately, to one's nation and culture, finds a corollary in the novel's direct narrative methods. Eschewing the narrative complexity so characteristic of Conrad's earlier works, *The Rover* represents a soothing of nervous energies and a confident grounding of the artist-spokesman in the simpler concerns of the human community rather than in abstract problems. This affirmative gesture, made after years of turmoil, both personal in the case of Conrad and communal in the case of war-weary England, is, however, carefully qualified, as the dark realities of mental disintegration, self-destruction, and political and social anarchy remain vivid threats in the background. Conrad concedes that these forces are not amenable to defeat, but they can be held in check by dint of constant and determined effort. His main point here is a restating of his fundamental conviction of the essential fragility of civilization, a theme that haunts his entire output.

The novel's political and social themes are developed concurrently with the themes of love and friendship. The relationship between Arlette and Peyrol is handled subtly, with Peyrol's paternal affection providing the disturbed young woman with the emotional security she requires in order to find herself, to ground her personality in the exterior world, and to make ties in it. The theme of friendship is likewise worked out in the sympathy established by Peyrol and Catherine, and in Peyrol's avuncular affection for Michel.

Erotic tensions trouble a number of the relationships. Mainly hinted at, Peyrol's sexual interest in Arlette is displaced into the distorting mirror of Scevola, whose neurotic and latently violent interest is an attempt to dominate the young woman. Although Réal's puritanical rejection of passion is at times simply melodramatic, the eventual attachment of the young couple plays a significant symbolic role in suggesting how love brings about an awareness of the value of, and need for commitment, and it fulfils the generic requirements of comedy as the younger generation emerges to take control from the passing older one. Catherine's frigidity, the history of her youthful obsession for a priest (a celibate by vocation), and her refusal to release Arlette from the world of women to the world of men are yet further changes rung on the themes of sexual passivity, misdirected erotic interest, and puritanical self-control. A motif of voyeurism and overly alert gazing also pervades the novel—the French watch the movements of the English ships, Scevola jealously spies on Arlette, Catherine watches out for Scevola—and the sexual gaze forms part of this pattern of observation and observing the observer. A *psychoanalytic criticism of a Freudian inclination might see the novel's concern with Scevola's ritual bloodletting as a covert treatment of detumescence, with its attendant frustrations finding ultimate relief in a linkage between *eros* and death. A covert incest motif might also be discerned in the relationship between Peyrol, the surrogate father, and Arlette, the surrogate daughter.

The political ideas raised in the novel are given somewhat muted treatment. This is partly a matter of its temporal setting. The great events of the French Revolution have already occurred, and the novel concentrates on the shadowy aftermath of extreme social and political upheaval and on the reconstruction of social and personal life. The depiction of aberrant personality in Scevola reworks some of the raw materials Conrad had drawn upon for the anarchists of *The Secret Agent* and the revolutionary fanatics of *Under Western*

Eyes. As in the former novel, Conrad to some extent undermines a potentially serious point by treating it not wholly seriously. Edward Garnett, a friend of more radical political tendencies, perceptively objected of Scevola that 'such a bloodthirsty ruffian should be formidable, in all his relations,—& he fades away steadily before our eyes, like a revolutionary scarecrow' (*PL*, 225).

Conrad's deeply rooted hostility to revolution as a means of bringing about change in the body politic may have originated partly in his childhood experience of orphanhood and his own 'abandonment' by parents who had committed their lives to the cause of *Poland's freedom. Whatever its emotional basis, his attitude is complicated by a profound scepticism towards political solutions to the problem of community. The novel once again places his faith in shared values and traditions as the true binding forces of nationhood, ideas addressed more directly in such essays as 'Autocracy and War' and 'The Crime of Partition' (*Notes*). While Conrad was fascinated by Napoleon and the Napoleonic period, his antipathy to France's national hero contrasts with his admiration for Nelson, the hero of Trafalgar. The novel's sympathies for France and its culture are, however, readily apparent, but the work also partly acts to affirm an English identity towards the close of Conrad's life. It may also respond, if only very obliquely, to the Bolshevik Revolution in *Russia, the predatory forces of which were active at the time of the novel's writing, and to the slow and continuing alteration of English society in the wake of the *First World War.

Along with Conrad's other late fictions, *The Rover* has never received much critical attention. As reviewers noted, it suffers from a surfeit of plotting, especially in later chapters, and sometimes fails to justify the elaboration of action with thematic weight. (The laboriously worked out subplot of Symons's entrapment and escape is a case in point.) The novel's technical conventionality has disappointed other readers. *The Rover* nonetheless has decided strengths, not only in the portrait of Peyrol

but also in the descriptions of place and the long chase of the conclusion.

Andrzej Busza's 'Introduction' to the World Classics edition of *The Rover*, ed. Andrzej Busza and J. H. Stape (OUP, 1992), is a critically sophisticated and subtle analysis of the novel. The relevant chapters of Geddes (1980) and Schwarz (1982) offer sympathetic evaluations, and the following commentaries remain of interest: W. R. Martin, 'Allegory in Conrad's *The Rover*', *English Studies in Africa*, 10 (1967), 186–94; Avrom Fleishman, 'Conrad's Last Novel', *English Literature in Transition*, 12 (1969), 189–94; David Leon Higdon, 'Conrad's *The Rover*: The Grammar of a Myth', *Studies in the Novel*, 1 (1969), 17–26; and H. F. Lippincott, 'Sense of Place in Conrad's *The Rover*', *Conradiana*, 6 (1974), 106–12.

A mixed batch of eleven typescript pages and holograph leaves is held at the Beinecke Rare Book and Manuscript Library, Yale University; a 'first draft recopied' typescript, dated October 1921–July 1922, at the Berg Collection, New York Public Library; and a 'complete and final copy' typescript, dated 14 October 1922, at Colgate University.   JHS

Russell, Bertrand [Arthur William] (1872–1970; third Earl (1931)), British philosopher, mathematician, and in 1950 Nobel Laureate. Bertrand Russell first met Conrad on a visit to Capel House on 10 September 1913 through Lady Ottoline *Morrell, who had been introduced to the novelist a month earlier. At that time undergoing a personal crisis and embroiled in a complicated relationship with Lady Ottoline, Russell responded with particular intensity to the 'wonderful' Conrad and the spell of his 'inward pain & terror' (quoted in Knowles 1990: 142). In sharing the effect of this 'thrilling' meeting with Lady Ottoline, Russell almost certainly displayed an element of self-dramatizing hero-worship for the benefit of his lover, the terms of whose strenuous Conrad-worship Russell compulsively echoed.

While Conrad may eventually have tired of these displays, he and Russell seem initially to have struck a mutual chord, with the philosopher responding tremulously to the novelist's view of 'civilized and morally tolerable human life as a dangerous walk on a thin crust of barely cooled lava which at any moment might break and let the unwary sink into fiery depths' (*Portraits from Memory and Other Essays* (Allen & Unwin, 1956), 82). A few days after their first meeting, Conrad visited Russell in Cambridge, after which for a short period they regularly exchanged their recent publications. An additional reason for their closeness in 1913–14 was that the philosopher wanted the writer's opinion of his earliest attempt at creative writing, *The Perplexities of Paul Forstice* (published posthumously in 1972). Their year-long friendship lapsed in 1914, probably through Russell's adoption of a new 'hero' in D. H. Lawrence, although contact revived briefly in 1921, when the philosopher wrote to Conrad asking his permission to name his son after him. While an immediate bond seems temporarily to have linked a philosopher with creative ambitions and a novelist of philosophic dimensions, the most powerful insights offered by Russell's testimony are ultimately into the growing legend surrounding Conrad in 1913 and its effect upon an intensely susceptible admirer. Russell's retrospective (and still dramatically over-coloured) view of what Conrad meant to him can be found in his *Portraits from Memory* and *Autobiography, 1872–1914* (Allen & Unwin, 1967). See also Edgar Wright, 'Joseph Conrad and Bertrand Russell', *Conradiana*, 2: 1 (1969–70), 7–16, and Knowles 1990.

Russia. In the light of the sufferings of both his family and his nation at the hands of Russian overlords, it is unsurprising that Conrad's private correspondence should reveal a consistently antagonistic attitude towards Russia and things Russian, and, in particular, that it should refute the charge of any Russian influence on his writing. For instance, in his letter of January 1924 to Charles Chassé, who, like other critics, had referred to his 'Slavonism', Conrad writes: 'it would have been more just to charge me at most with "Polonism." Polish tempera-

ment, at any rate, is far removed from Byzantine and Asiatic associations.' He adds that the main task of Polish life was 'the struggle for life against Asiatic despotism at its door'. His formative influences, Conrad argues, were 'purely Western', as 'Poland has absorbed Western ideas, adopted Western culture, sympathized with Western ideals and tendencies'. Furthermore, he claims not to know the Russian language and 'next to nothing of Russian imaginative literature, except the little I have been able to read in translations' (*LL*, ii. 336). Writing to Olivia Garnett about *Under Western Eyes*, Conrad says: 'I know extremely little of Russians. Practically nothing. In Poland we have nothing to do with them. One knows they are there. And that's disagreeable enough' (*CL*, iv. 490).

In Conrad's public writing, Russia is addressed with a bitterness recalling his father Apollo *Korzeniowski's polemical memoir 'Poland and Muscovy' (1864; *CUFE*, 75–88). In 'Autocracy and War', Conrad describes Russia as 'a yawning chasm open between East and West; a bottomless abyss that has swallowed up every hope of mercy, every aspiration towards personal dignity, towards freedom, towards knowledge, every ennobling desire of the heart, every redeeming whisper of conscience' (*Notes*, 100). In the same essay, Russia is associated with 'the moral corruption and mental darkness of slavery' (92). Some of this antagonism is manifest in the portrayal of Russians in Conrad's fiction. Thus, the villain in *The Secret Agent* is the sinister Russian diplomat Mr Vladimir, while *Kurtz's gullible admirer and apologist in 'Heart of Darkness' is the Russian *harlequin. In his 'Author's Note' to *Under Western Eyes* Conrad says of the characters: 'The oppressors and the oppressed are all Russians together; and the world is brought once more face to face with the truth of the saying that the tiger cannot change his stripes nor the leopard his spots' (p. x). Nonetheless, given his critical attitude towards Russia, it is a testament to his artistic integrity that in this novel he attempts to render the complexity of its national character by discriminating between the autocrats and the revolutionaries. In Conrad's own words, his subject is 'not so much the political state as the psychology of Russia' (p. vii).

Despite Conrad's protestations, subsequent criticism has sought to argue that his attitude towards Russia may be more ambivalent than he himself ever admitted. Regarding his ignorance of the Russian language—he told Edward *Garnett 'I don't even know the alphabet' (*LL*, ii. 192)—some critics like Morf (1976) take Conrad at his word, while others are more sceptical. Marcus Wheeler, for instance, suggests that 'it stretches credibility to suppose that a boy who later . . . revealed quite exceptional linguistic abilities, did not acquire any Russian' (*Joseph Conrad Today*, 3 (1978) 94). Conrad was equally vehement in his condemnation of *Dostoevsky, saying of *The Brothers Karamazov* (1880) in 1912: 'It's terrifically bad and impressive and exasperating. Moreover, I don't know what D stands for or reveals, but I do know that he is too Russian for me. It sounds like some fierce mouthings from prehistoric ages' (*CL*, v. 70). Yet, as a host of critics have noted, the connections between *Under*

Western Eyes and *Crime and Punishment* (1866) testify to Conrad's intimate knowledge of Dostoevsky's novel. It is as if, through *Razumov, Conrad sought to 'answer' Dostoevsky's text: whereas, in *Crime and Punishment*, Raskolnikov is contrasted with Razumihin, an average man with a healthy conscience, in *Under Western Eyes* Conrad sets up an internal polemic between the two novels by creating, in Razumov, a Razumihin-figure corrupted by politics. Kirschner says that 'Conrad's antipathy to Dostoevsky, like many antipathies, carries a strong suggestion of secret kinship' (1968: 252), while Andrzej Busza sees a parallel between Conrad's relationship with Russia and *Marlow's relationship with Kurtz: 'On the one hand, Conrad despises and is repelled by the monstrous "Russian Soul"; on the other, he is fascinated by it' ('Rhetoric and Ideology in Conrad's *Under Western Eyes*', in Sherry (ed.) 1976: 108). However complicated such an analysis of Conrad's private responses might seem, his public attitude towards Russia and Russians never wavered. See also Jeffrey Berman, 'Introduction to Conrad and the Russians', *Conradiana*, 12 (1980), 3–12, and Carabine 1996.   AHS

S

sales. See AUCTIONS AND SALES.

Sambir. The actual source for the fictional Sambir, the setting of Conrad's first two novels, *Almayer's Folly* and *An Outcast of the Islands*, remained unidentified during his lifetime, although one clue survives in *Almayer's Folly* through what is presumably an inadvertent reference to Sambir as 'Brow' (42). Research by later critics has revealed that Sambir's physical geography is closely based upon the remote coastal region of Berau in north-east *Borneo (present-day Kalimantan). Conrad visited Berau four times while serving in the *Vidar* between September and December 1887, although, as Sherry points out, the total length of his stay there was unlikely to have exceeded twelve days or so (*CEW*, 139). Divided into the two sultanates of Gunung Tabur and Sambaliung, Berau's 8,550 square miles (22,160 square km) cover the drainage basins of two rivers, the Kelai and Segah, which unite to form the Berau River at a confluence some 35 miles (60 km) from the sea. This latter river is called the Pantai in Conrad's first two novels, although strictly speaking the Muara Pantai is the southernmost passage of the Berau estuary. In both novels, Sambir is also the name given to the region's main settlement at the confluence of the two rivers, which was and still is known as Tanjung Redeb.

At Berau, Conrad became acquainted with William Charles *Olmeijer, the prototype of the fictional *Almayer. He probably also made contact with James *Lingard, nephew of the influential Captain William *Lingard, one of the first European traders to establish a permanent commercial base in the area, manager of the trading firm for which Olmeijer worked, and a model for Conrad's Tom *Lingard. In the 'Author's Note' to *An Outcast*, Conrad also claimed to have met in Berau the original of that novel's central figure, Peter *Willems,

identified by Allen (224–5) as a young, penniless, and alcoholic Dutchman, Carel de Veer, who at one point had quarters in Olmeijer's house and undertook odd jobs for him. By the time Conrad came to write *Almayer's Folly* and *An Outcast of the Islands*, he had undoubtedly supplemented his first-hand impressions and memories of the area with extensive *reading of what he later called 'undoubted sources—dull, wise books' (*CL*, ii. 130), notably such travel narratives as A. R. *Wallace's *The Malay Archipelago* (1869) and Major Frederick McNair's *Perak and the Malays* (1878), from which he garnered a more detailed picture of the region's natural history, varied ethnic groups, and their social and religious practices. He also consulted a Malay dictionary for many words that he professed to have 'forgotten': 'I don't put . . . much language-colour in my books, but I like to be correct' (*CL*, i. 276–7).

The portrait of Sambir also includes an interesting attempt to sketch out a wider colonial history appropriate to the temporal settings of *Almayer's Folly* (set in the mid-1880s) and *An Outcast of the Islands* (around 1872). For example, in the first novel Almayer's declining fortunes are linked with specific historical changes in the region, involving the formation of the British Borneo Company in 1881, which was granted a royal charter to govern and administer a large area of north Borneo. Its formation, we are told in the novel, affects even 'the sluggish flow of the Pantai life' and prompts Almayer, in a fit of extravagant hope, to build his new house (33). Following upon the company's formation, extended border disputes between the British and the Dutch led the latter to strengthen their territorial position in north-east Borneo and culminated in 1884 with the setting up of a joint British-Dutch commission to investigate the whole boundary question. This strengthening of

Dutch control in the region is presented as shaping Sambir's evolving colonial history and marks an important turning point in the erosion of Almayer's hopes, because, as an agent in the British firm of Lingard and Co. in Sambir, he justifiably expects his trading interests to prosper under British influence. Under the Dutch, on the other hand, Almayer can expect more hostile treatment since, as he hears from the chief of the Dutch Commission, 'the Arabs were better subjects than Hollanders who dealt illegally in gunpowder with the Malays' (36). For maps of the region, photographs, and extended commentary, see Sherry's chapter 'An Eastern River' in *CEW*, 119–38, Allen, 187–240, and Ron Visser, 'An Out-of-the-Way Place Called Berau', *The Conradian*, 18: 1 (1993), 37–47. Gavin Young's *In Search of Conrad* (Hutchinson, 1991) provides an absorbing account of his retracing of Conrad's footsteps in Borneo.

Samburan. Various attempts have been made to find a specific Eastern location for this fictional island, the setting for Axel *Heyst's ordeal in *Victory*. Samburan or 'Round Island' is described as a 'little' island, with deposits of coal, surrounded by 'a tepid, shallow sea' (4), and 50 hours of sailing-time north-east of *Java's Madura (168). Its nearest neighbour is an 'indolent' volcano, visible 'just above the northern horizon' (4), and when Heyst looks southward out to sea, he observes what he takes to be a 'native craft making for the Moluccas' (190). Of the suggestions so far offered, Hans Lippe's nomination—the island of Bejaren or Biaro in the Sangihe Islands chain, near the northern entrance to the Celebes Sea—fulfils many, although not all, of the required features ('The Geographic Position of Samburan Island in *Victory*', *The Conradian*, 16: 1 (1991), 51–4). The probable truth is that Samburan, like many other Conrad settings, is essentially a composite construction, drawn from scattered personal memories and numerous printed sources.

For most readers, symbolic geography is likely to be of foremost importance in a work that an early reviewer described as 'a struggle between the spiritual powers of the universe temporarily incarnate in a little group of human beings on a lonely Pacific island' (*CCH*, 288). Subtitled 'An Island Tale', *Victory* is the summation of Conrad's preoccupation with isolated hermitages and island retreats, notably in a group of short stories written just before the longer novel of 1915—'A Smile of Fortune', 'Freya of the Seven Isles' (*'Twixt Land and Sea*), and 'The Planter of Malata' (*Within the Tides*). It also implicitly recalls a long tradition of island or retreat literature, including such works as *Shakespeare's The Tempest* (1611) and Daniel Defoe's *Robinson Crusoe* (1719). If, however, the novel occasionally alludes to the ceremonies of past island literature in suggesting the utopian possibilities of self-realization through withdrawal, the idyllic blessings of a prelapsarian Eden, and the sanctity of the ivory tower, it quickly deflates them by its ironic placing of Samburan within a recognizably latter-day world of trade, crass commercialism, and greedy opportunism. As Lee M. Whitehead observes: 'The major themes of the novel are suggested . . . in images that evoke the history of ascetic withdrawal, the mountain and the island, and in an image, the sea, that no longer suggests inexhaustible and unexplored possibility as it did for the Romantics, but is a trackless expanse over which men have established roadways . . . and which, in the immediate neighborhood, suggests tepidness, passionlessness, and delusion' ('"An Island is but the Top of a Mountain": Isolation and Solidarity in Conrad's *Victory*', *L'Époque Conradienne* (1980), 89). The image of Samburan quickly attracts some of Conrad's most potent ironies. 'An island is but the top of a mountain', the narrator comments (4), stressing that the island draws attention to itself by its very isolation; further, remote Samburan exists in a world where even the smallest islands are subject to forms of sophisticated mapping and is represented on one of them as 'the central spot of the Eastern Hemisphere', with heavy lines radiating from it 'in all directions' (23), hence inviting a ferocious invasion by three emissaries from the outside world. In this process, Conrad may be felt to parody and even invert most of the assumptions of traditional island literature. In contrast to *The Tempest*, Conrad's island drama culminates in violent, widespread death and suggests a 'tragedy of the absurd' (Lodge, 199); unlike Defoe's island, the setting for Crusoe's successfully practical and mercantilist endeavour, Samburan is the scene of a failed colonial business venture, with Heyst the ex-manager of the defunct Tropical Belt Coal Company. The combined effect of these ironic reversals suggests that *Victory*, along with Robert Louis *Stevenson's *The Ebb-Tide* (1894) and H. G. *Wells's *The Island of Dr Moreau* (1896), belongs essentially to a distinctively modern tradition of dystopian island literature continuing in William Golding's *Lord of the Flies* (1954).

Sanderson, Edward Lancelot (1867– 1939). Edward Sanderson was John *Galsworthy's travelling companion in March 1893 when the two men, returning from a fruitless tour of the South Pacific in search of Robert Louis *Stevenson, sailed back from Australia to Europe in the *Torrens* and met Conrad, then serving as the ship's first mate (see SHIPS AND VOYAGES). From this meeting developed two of the longest and most equable friendships of Conrad's life.

A Cambridge graduate, Sanderson initially trained for the Church, but a weak constitution led him to accompany Galsworthy to hospitable South Pacific climes, after which he became an assistant master in the family's Anglican preparatory school in Elstree, Hertfordshire. From 1893 until his marriage in 1896, Conrad regularly visited 'Ted' in Elstree where he found abundant hospitality, the boisterous company of a large family (Ted had thirteen brothers and sisters), and a cultivated haven where he was encouraged to complete *Almayer's Folly*. Sanderson played an active part in helping Conrad to prepare his first novel for publication. During the *Torrens* voyage, he had listened to Conrad reading from a draft of the novel and later, with his mother Katherine, had a hand in polishing

the completed manuscript, and was also nominated by Conrad to oversee the proofs. Later, Conrad dedicated *An Outcast of the Islands* to Sanderson and *The Mirror of the Sea* to his mother, 'whose warm welcome and gracious hospitality extended to the friend of her son cheered the first dark days of my parting with the sea'.

In 1898, Sanderson married Helen Mary Watson (1875–1967), daughter of the Sheriff Substitute of Dumfries and Galloway, Scotland, whose vivacity and lively intelligence always attracted Conrad. After serving in the Boer War, Sanderson was joined by his wife in Africa, where he remained until 1910 for his health, working first for the Transvaal Education Department and then as Town Clerk of Nairobi. During their stay Helen, under the name Janet Allardyce, contributed sketches of African life to *Scribner's Magazine* and sent her work to Conrad for his opinion. On returning to England, Sanderson succeeded a brother-in-law as headmaster at Elstree Preparatory School and remained a devoted friend of Conrad's. The latter always seems to have identified his early contacts with the Sandersons as a precious initiation into hospitable English social and familial values that he could increasingly associate with the idea of *home. He later commented: 'I've been warmed, moved, and made to feel welcome under that ... roof of the Sandersons, as in no other place on earth' (to Helen Sanderson, 28 January 1918).

Schomberg, a hotel-keeper and notorious gossip, makes a brief appearance in *Lord Jim* and 'Falk', and sets in motion the catastrophic events of *Victory*. With his obscure, downtrodden wife, Wilhelm Schomberg 'came out East directly after the Franco-Prussian War' of 1870 (*Victory*, 96); his military manner suggests that he may have been a lieutenant in the Reserve. 'He was by profession a hotel-keeper, first in Bangkok, then somewhere else, and ultimately in Sourabaya' (20). In chapter 19 of *Lord Jim*, Jim boards at Schomberg's hotel in *Bangkok for six months during his employment with Yucker Brothers. In the manuscript of *Victory*, Schomberg's hotel was first located in Semarang. It was moved to Surabaya in revision, but the change was not implemented consistently, resulting in a confusing anatopism at the opening of Part I, chapter 7 (58), where the hotel is suddenly placed in Semarang. In *Lord Jim*, Schomberg is described as 'a hirsute Alsatian of manly bearing and an irrepressible retailer of all the scandalous gossip of the place' (198). The narrator of *Victory* calls him a 'noxious ass' (20). In a colourful but thoroughly unreliable memoir called *The Seas Were Mine* (New York: Dodd, Mead, 1935), Howard Hartman identified Conrad's Schomberg with a *Singapore tavern-keeper named Dutchy Scharlberg, whose customers were said to include Conrad and Jim *Lingard, the primary model for *Lord Jim*; extracts from Hartman's book appear in *Conradiana*, 1: 2 (1969), beginning p. 44. Many aspects of Hartman's account are demonstrably incorrect, and his lively Conradian anecdotes have never been corroborated; see Alan Villiers, 'Grave Doubts about Hartman', *Conradiana*, 3: 2 (1971– 2), 54–5.

Schopenhauer, Arthur (1788–1860), German philosopher and the author of *Die Welt als Wille und Vorstellung* (1819; expanded 1844). Arthur Schopenhauer was, according to John *Galsworthy, a particular object of interest to Conrad at the turn of the century and 'used to give him satisfaction' (121). Conrad also belonged to a generation of writers in the 1890s who could hardly have avoided being exposed to the impact of the charismatic German philosopher whose 'voice' echoed throughout Europe in the later part of the century as ubiquitously as *Kurtz's through the African jungle in 'Heart of Darkness'. The philosopher's radical pessimism and the association of genius and madness in his life and writings meant that the whole question of his legacy was obsessively troublesome to writers of the *fin de siècle*, who were often called his 'children'. Conrad's exposure to Schopenhauer was likely to have been direct—through a reading of his work—and indirect, through his con-

tact with the writings of others, such as Guy de *Maupassant, who had been strongly influenced by the German philosopher. There is evidence to suggest, for example, that Conrad knew Maupassant's short story 'Auprès d'un mort' (Beside a Dead Man, 1883), in which Schopenhauer is memorialized as having 'overturned beliefs, hopes, poetry, idle fancies, destroyed the aspirations and laid waste the trust of souls, killed love, abolished the idealised worship of women, exploded the illusions of the heart, accomplished the most gigantic labour of scepticism that has ever been achieved'. Conrad had almost certainly read also William Wallace's short biography *The Life of Arthur Schopenhauer* (1890), and probably met the philosopher's influence in several other indirect ways: for example, through Ferdinand Brunetière's 'La Philosophie de Schopenhauer et les conséquences du pessimisme', *Revue des Deux Mondes*, 102 (1890), 210–21, Cesare *Lombroso's *The Man of Genius* (1891), and Max *Nordau's *Degeneration*, which describes Schopenhauer as having fathered the entire *fin de siècle* community of 'the degenerate and insane', his 'pre-destined disciples' ((Heinemann, 1895), 20).

Schopenhauer's more popular essays are frequently echoed in Conrad's dark *letters of the mid-1890s, with their emphasis on life as a 'masquerade' and a condition of 'ever becoming—never being' (*CL*, i. 267, 268). This latter phrase constantly appears in Schopenhauer's work to signify the only fixed law in a world in which all is flux, constant motion, and an expression of the imperishable Will, whose concern is not with the individual but the preservation of the species. It could be argued that much of Conrad's work in the late 1890s represents an attempt both to indulge and grapple with one of Schopenhauer's core beliefs, again echoed in Conrad's letters—'Life knows us not and we do not know life' (*CL*, i. 17)—and with its corollary that human existence, a fundamentally ironic riddle, is a constant ordeal to stave off the consciousness that 'life has *no true and genuine value* in itself, but is kept *in motion* merely through the medium of needs and illusions' (*On Human Nature*, ed. Thomas Bailey Saunders (Allen & Unwin, 1897), 44).

The issue of Conrad's relationship to Schopenhauer and the traditions of 19th-century pessimism he sponsored has long been a lively and contentious one. The case for a link was forcefully argued by Kirschner (1968), who detected the influence of Schopenhauer in Conrad's 1897 'Preface' to *The Nigger of the 'Narcissus'*, and by Johnson (1971), whose chapters on Conrad's early fiction present the picture of a writer whose sense of life as a 'riddle'—'that mysterious arrangement of merciless logic for a futile purpose', as *Marlow puts it in 'Heart of Darkness' (*Youth*, 150)—is significantly shaped by Schopenhauerian postulates. A substantial body of later criticism and research, including Mark Wollaeger's *Joseph Conrad and the Fictions of Skepticism* (Stanford, Calif.: Stanford University Press, 1990) and Cedric Watts's valuable gleanings in his notes for the Everyman edition of *Victory* (Dent, 1994), suggest new and fruitful ways of approaching the question of Conrad's Schopenhauerian legacy.

'Man is at bottom a savage horrible beast. We know it, if only in the business of taming and restraining him which we call civilisation. Hence it is that we are terrified if now and then his nature breaks out. Wherever and whenever the locks and chains of law and order fall off and give place to anarchy, he shows himself for what he is' (*On Human Nature*, 18–19). This dark intuition from Schopenhauer's essay on 'Human Nature', with its obvious relevance to 'Heart of Darkness', suggests that the German philosopher may be a key formative influence in shaping the cosmology of Conrad's novella. In *Fictional Structure and Ethics: The Turn-of-the-Century Novel* (Athens: University of Georgia Press, 1990), William J. Scheick makes a well-argued and thoughtful case for regarding 'Heart of Darkness' as offering a substantially 'Schopenhauerian world' and Conrad's 'most pronounced experiment with Schopenhauerian aesthetics' (115). In '"Who's Afraid of Arthur Schopenhauer?": A New Context for *Heart of Darkness*',

Nineteenth-Century Literature, 49 (1994), 75–106, Owen Knowles concurs, but for very different reasons. He discovers a new shaping context for Kurtz, the Promethean outlaw-philosopher and ubiquitous 'voice', not in Schopenhauer's own writings but in the secondary myths, legends, and icons that endowed the great philosopher with a potent cultural afterlife during the period from 1870 to 1900. Focusing, for example, on Marlow's pose as a 'meditating Buddha' (*Youth*, 162), Knowles claims that it links with an icon widely used in the later 19th century to characterize the German philosopher as a European Buddha, who had incorporated the teachings of the Upanishads into his work.

sea, the. Conrad's philosophy of life is intimately connected with his maritime experiences and his attitudes towards the sea. As he wrote in a letter to William *Blackwood in August 1901: 'A wrestle with wind and weather has a moral value like the primitive acts of faith on which may be built a doctrine of salvation and a rule of life. At any rate men engaged in such contests have been my spiritual fathers too long for me to change my convictions' (*CL*, ii. 354). Similarly, in his 'Author's Note' to *The Mirror of the Sea*, acknowledging these 'fathers' as 'the ultimate shapers' of his character, convictions, and destiny, he pays tribute to 'the imperishable sea, to the ships that are no more, and to the simple men who have had their day' (p. x).

The importance of the sea and navigation to island Britain across the centuries has ensured that it has been transformed into a national myth. Nowhere is this better reflected than in the rich literature of the sea. Thus, in the 1890s, Conrad's sea literature took its place alongside that of James Froude, Henry *Newbolt, and Alfred Noyes. As Berthoud says: 'by the end of the nineteenth century the sea had become a national obsession' (1984: p. viii). That said, it remains surprising how *few* British novelists of the sea there are before this period. For the origins of sea fiction as a distinct form one has to look to America. The naval supremacy of America in the first half of the 19th century (before the Civil War put such a drain on her capital spending) gave rise to a literature about the sea that included James Fenimore *Cooper's *The Pilot* (1823) and Herman Melville's *Moby-Dick* (1851). As Tony Tanner argues, while Joseph Conrad is the greatest writer of sea stories in the language, 'it was American writers who effectively invented, and developed, the sea story as a separate and recognizable genre' (*The Oxford Book of Sea Stories* (OUP, 1994), p. xvii).

Conrad offers an insight into his attitude towards sea fiction when he distinguishes between two of his predecessors, the English writer Captain Frederick *Marryat (1792–1848) and his American contemporary James Fenimore Cooper (1789–1851), in his essay 'Tales of the Sea' (*Notes*). According to Ford Madox *Ford, Conrad 'in his misty youth . . . read with engrossment Marryat and Fenimore Cooper, and so sowed the seeds of his devotion to England' (*JCPR*, 68). While Conrad applauds Marryat's sea tales for their 'disclosure of the spirit animating the stirring time when the nineteenth century was young', his judgement is that these tales ultimately present the sea as incidental: 'To this writer of the sea the sea was not an element. It was a stage, where was displayed an exhibition of valour, and of such achievement as the world had never seen before' (53). By contrast, Conrad argues, sea-fiction became an art with Cooper: 'For James Fenimore Cooper nature was not the framework, it was an essential part of existence. . . . In his sea tales the sea inter-penetrates with life; it is in a subtle way a factor in the problem of existence' (55).

Drawing upon his first-hand experiences in the *British Merchant Service, Conrad's contribution to the sea literature of his adopted country is simultaneously an extension and a reinforcement of its national myth of the sea. For example, 'Youth' opens with the claim: 'This could have occurred nowhere but in England, where men and sea interpenetrate, so to speak— the sea entering into the life of most men, and the men knowing something or every-

thing about the sea, in the way of amusement, of travel, or of bread-winning' (*Youth,* 3). Similarly, at the conclusion of *The Nigger of the 'Narcissus'*, he describes *England as 'A ship mother of fleets and nations! The great flagship of the race; stronger than the storms! and anchored in the open sea' (163). Adapting T. S. Eliot, Conrad's sea fiction may be said to purify the dialect of his adopted tribe.

Generally speaking, the body of writing about the sea, stretching back as far as *The Odyssey*, has been marked by a number of recurrent and recognizable elements, concerns, and motifs. These include: the tradition of adventure; the romance of life under sail; the use of the actual voyage as a metaphor for a journey from one state of experience to another; and the untameable might of the ocean. The romantic and escapist idea of sea travel as adventure for adventure's sake is soon dispelled in *The Mirror of the Sea*, where Conrad identifies the prosaic and practical skills of seamanship that form 'the moral side' of such 'bread-winning' (24). The sea is always a means of earning a livelihood, and this commercial emphasis unites his sea fictions with the national history. But Conrad's sea tales also repeatedly celebrate the sea at the expense of the land, actively promoting its attraction over the tawdriness of life ashore. For instance, the further inland the *Narcissus* sails at the end of *The Nigger of the 'Narcissus'*, the more she is stripped of her beauty and glory, until finally berthed, 'a swarm of strange men, clambering up her sides, took possession of her in the name of the sordid earth. She had ceased to live' (165). Thus Conrad's fiction manages to preserve the romance of the sea without losing sight of the reality of seamanship.

The sea journeys undertaken in Conrad's fiction repeatedly advertise themselves as voyages of initiation. Thus, in the wake of the great storm in *The Nigger of the 'Narcissus'*, the narrator concludes: 'from that time our life seemed to start afresh as though we had died and had been resuscitated' (99–100), while *Marlow prefaces his tale in 'Youth' with the assertion that 'there are those voyages that seem ordered for the illustration of life, that might stand for a symbol of existence' (*Youth*, 3–4). Nowhere is the idea that the sea voyage stands as an image of life itself more clearly expressed than in Conrad's opening words in *The Mirror of the Sea*: 'Landfall and Departure mark the rhythmical swing of a seaman's life and of a ship's career. From land to land is the most concise definition of a ship's earthly fate' (3). Canto 4 of *Childe Harold's Pilgrimage* contains Byron's famous statement about the ocean: 'Man marks the earth with ruin—his control | Stops with the shore; upon the watery plain | The wrecks are all thy deed' (4. 179). Writing about the sea necessarily, if obviously, reveals the ocean as a vast, elemental force and, correspondingly, both the freedom and danger associated with a life at sea. Conrad's fiction reveals a fascination with the individual, tested to the limits of his endurance, called upon to proclaim his moral toughness. For this, the sea offers the perfect antagonist, and, in the sailors' battle for existence against arbitrary natural forces, we find one of the definitive images of the modern condition. Conrad repeatedly demonstrates that, however anthropomorphically presented, the sea is indifferent to the men who sail on her in a 'close dependence upon the very forces that, friendly to-day, without changing their nature, by the mere putting forth of their might, become dangerous to-morrow' (*The Mirror of the Sea*, 71–2). Their shared predicament encourages and demands the fellowship of the craft between sailors dependent upon each other, a fellowship that is tested through the obligations and responsibilities of sea life. As Singleton says in *The Nigger of the 'Narcissus'*: 'Ships are all right. It's the men in them!' (24). In Conrad's sea fiction, the worth of these men is measured by the duties they perform and how they confront their weaknesses in the face of trials.

To Conrad, the world of the sea cannot be understood as merely an inflected form of life on land. Rather it offers a wholly different form of knowledge, complete with its own signifying system and test of truth.

That the world of the sea has its own unique concepts is revealed in the precision of nautical language that renders these stories convincing yet mysterious to the ordinary reader. A grammar, founded on duty and solidarity, then articulates these concepts into the system within which they acquire meaning and purpose, which is why, in *The Nigger of the 'Narcissus'*, Captain Allistoun forces *Donkin to replace the belaying pin, restoring it to its rightful place within this system. The discrete world of the sea has its own definitive codes and laws, allowing *Leggatt to say: 'you don't see me coming back to explain such things to an old fellow in a wig and twelve respectable tradesmen . . . What can they know whether I am guilty or not—or of *what* I am guilty' (*'Twixt Land and Sea*, 131). See Robert Foulke's 'Life in the Dying World of Sail, 1879–1910', *Journal of British Studies*, 3 (1963), 105–36, for a careful survey of the final era of sailing ships that measures fiction against fact, highlighting the idealizing myths present in the works of retired seamen-writers, including Conrad. William E. Messenger, in 'Conrad and his "Sea Stuff"', *Conradiana*, 6 (1974), 3–18, discusses Conrad's movement towards sea fiction in the early part of his career.   AHS

Secret Agent, The. This work of 1907 is now generally recognized as one of Conrad's greatest masterpieces, and as the first modern novel of counter-espionage. Conrad's only novel to be set almost entirely in *London, *The Secret Agent: A Simple Tale* is a profoundly ironic study of the ways in which domestic relations and political ideologies reflect and corrupt each other.

The secret agent of the title is ostensibly Adolf *Verloc, a purveyor of disreputable wares whose primary source of income is the secret-service fund of a foreign (Russian) embassy that has employed him for eleven years to monitor and report on the activities of anarchist groups with names like the International Red Committee or the Future of the Proletariat. Verloc also serves as an unpaid informer to the police in the person of Chief Inspector Heat. Verloc is a soft pornographer, indolent and bourgeois, who sees his mission in life as the protection of the social mechanism that guarantees him a comfortable livelihood for a minimum of effort. He has married his former landlady's daughter *Winnie, and taken her brother and mother with their furniture into the bargain. Verloc is unaware that Winnie married him only for the sake of securing a place for her hypersensitive brother *Stevie. Winnie is thus also the secret agent of her brother's interests. Other characters in the novel, like the Assistant Commissioner or Chief Inspector Heat, similarly mix private motives with professional duties. Although it seems unusual that an anarchist like Verloc should be married, all the members of Verloc's regular anarchist circle are supported by women: the obese 'ticket-of-leave apostle' Michaelis owes his social standing to the interest of a Lady Patroness, the disgusting Karl Yundt has a disgusting female companion, and young Tom Ossipon is a notorious chaser of skirts. With the notable exception of the nihilistic *Professor, it is hard to take Conrad's anarchists seriously as terrorists.

The story opens as Verloc answers a summons from Mr Vladimir, the First Secretary of the Embassy, who reproaches him for his idleness and gives him one month in which to carry out a bomb attack on the *Greenwich Royal Observatory intended to shock the British authorities into adopting a tougher policy against anarchists. The fourth chapter skips to a month later in the Silenus Restaurant, where Ossipon and the *Professor discuss a bomb outrage at Greenwich that morning in which a man (presumed to be Verloc) has been blown to bits. The main action of the novel follows the course of this long and eventful day in a sequence of interlocking scenes: the Professor encounters Chief Inspector Heat in an alley; Heat reports to the Assistant Commissioner at the headquarters of the Special Crimes Department; and the Assistant Commissioner visits Sir Ethelred at the Ministry. Chief Inspector Heat wants to take the bomb outrage as a warrant for arresting Michaelis, unaware that Michaelis enjoys the social protection of the Lady

Patroness, who is also a close friend of the Assistant Commissioner's wife. The Assistant Commissioner decides to protect Michaelis and preserve his own domestic tranquillity by having Heat removed from the case and disguising himself for a visit to Verloc's shop. At this point a flashback (chapter 8) describes the earlier departure of Winnie's mother to an almshouse in a ramshackle cab drawn by an ill-used horse whose pathetic condition awakens Stevie's sense of the world's cruelty and injustice.

The remaining chapters constitute one of the most memorable dramatic sequences in all of Conrad's work. Verloc returns home late and shivering, having withdrawn all his money from the bank. When the bell rings, Winnie assumes that the Assistant Commissioner is one of her husband's clients from the Continent. While Verloc is confessing to the Assistant Commissioner in a nearby hotel, Chief Inspector Heat pays his own visit to Verloc's shop in Brett Street (a fictitious address in Soho) and shows Winnie a piece of cloth removed from the remains of the bomb victim, which she recognizes as the address label she had sewn in Stevie's coat to keep him from getting lost on visits across town to his mother. When Verloc returns, she eavesdrops on the conversation between Verloc and Heat and realizes that Stevie has been blown to bits. With masterful pacing, at this point Conrad inserts a proleptic tenth chapter describing the Assistant Commissioner's visit to the Lady Patroness later that evening, where he meets Mr Vladimir and informs him of Verloc's confession and its consequences. Meanwhile, devastated by Stevie's death, Winnie is oblivious to Verloc's attempts to justify himself and to plan an escape; when he calls her to come to him on the sofa, she stabs him with a carving knife. Fearing the gallows, she runs out into the street and encounters Tom Ossipon, who promises to help her escape before he realizes that she has just killed her husband. He takes her money and abandons her just as the boat train for the Continent is leaving the station. An epilogue ten days later shows Ossipon visiting the Professor, troubled to the point of obsession by a newspaper account of the mysterious suicide of a lady passenger on a Channel ferry.

In his 'Author's Note' written in 1920, Conrad explained that the idea for the novel originated in a comment made by an 'omniscient' friend (Ford Madox *Ford) about a bomb attack on Greenwich Observatory on 15 February 1894 in which an anarchist named Martial Bourdin had blown himself up: 'Oh, that fellow was half an idiot. His sister committed suicide afterwards' (p. x). Norman Sherry's research has shown that although Bourdin may indeed have been the dupe of other anarchists, his sister and brother-in-law lived on into the 1930s and were remembered by Helen Rossetti Angeli as 'a bad lot' (*CWW*, 322). In *A History of our Own Times*, ed. Solon Beinfeld and Sondra J. Stang (Bloomington: Indiana UP, 1988), Ford claimed that Bourdin was inspired to perpetrate the Greenwich bombing by the terrorist and *agent provocateur* Yevno Azev (1869–1918), who also masterminded the assassination of the tsarist minister Plehve that Conrad used in *Under Western Eyes* (84). Ford was apparently mistaken: Azev was a police spy by 1894, but he was then studying engineering at the Karlsruhe Polytechnic Institute, and there is no evidence that he was ever in England; see Richard E. Rubenstein, *Comrade Valentine* (1994).

After completing 'An Anarchist', 'The Informer', and 'The Brute' (*A Set of Six*) in the winter of 1905–6, Conrad took his pregnant wife and ailing son to the south of *France for a two-month holiday. They settled into the Hôtel Riche & Continental in *Montpellier in February 1906, where Conrad immediately began work on a short story provisionally entitled 'Verloc'. A month later he saw it as a 'longish story' of about 18,000 words (*CL*, iii. 320); by the time Conrad returned with his family to England in mid-April, he had drafted the first three chapters and changed the title. Work on the novel continued at Pent Farm; during a fortnight in Winchelsea in Ford's vacant cottage, the Bungalow; and at John *Galsworthy's flat in Addison Road, Kensington, which the Conrads occupied for

two months prior to the birth of their younger son John. One of the main sources of inspiration for the Assistant Commissioner, Sir Robert Anderson's *Side-Lights on the Home Rule Movement* (1906), appeared while Conrad was in Winchelsea.

In the meantime, Conrad's agent J. B. *Pinker managed to place *The Secret Agent* with the American periodical *Ridgway's: A Militant Weekly for God and Country*, where from 6 October to 15 December 1906 it appeared, with the customary half-tone illustrations, simultaneously in New York and thirteen other cities 'between advertisements for Johnson's revolvers (five dollars each), ten-cent cigars, washing machines and the unexpurgated works of Balzac' (Watts 1989: 105). Neither Conrad's novel nor the advertisements was sufficient to keep the periodical from folding in February 1907. Conrad worked under pressure to complete the serial instalments on time, and finished this first version of the novel on 3 November. He described the *Ridgway's* text to Pinker as 'an extended, uncorrected copy' (*CL*, iii. 364) and offered to shorten Pinker's typescript by several thousand words for the sake of serial publication. Conrad clearly saw the serial version as a provisional, streamlined version of the text with a necessarily hasty ending. As he told Pinker, 'Ridgways are sending me their rag. It's awful—and it don't matter in the least.' He went on to note that 'they are "editing" the stuff pretty severely' (*CL*, iii. 369). The editors at *Ridgway's* had cut and rearranged Conrad's text freely in an effort to clarify dialogue or action, or simply to fit the instalments neatly onto the allotted pages.

Once the serial version was done, Conrad set the novel aside for several months to work on other projects. He took his family back to Montpellier in December and moved on to *Champel, Switzerland, in early May. He had asked his publisher *Methuen to send him galley slips to use in revising *The Secret Agent*, and was unpleasantly surprised when page proofs arrived in Champel in mid-May, complaining to Pinker that the added expense and smaller margins of page proofs would force him to curtail the extensive revisions he had planned. Nevertheless, with his children ill and in need of constant nursing, Conrad revised the proofs rapidly, adding chapter 10 (including the scene between the Assistant Commissioner and Mr Vladimir) and elaborating the ending to include much more of Winnie's story. The serial version was expanded to half its length again, and revisions were finished by the end of July. With the added subtitle of 'A Simple Tale' and a *dedication to H. G. *Wells, the first editions were published by Methuen in London on 12 September 1907 and by Harper's in New York about two days later.

Conrad's relations with Methuen were further strained when the publisher took Conrad's remark that 'when it is prepared for "book form" it will be 68,000 words in length—or perhaps even more' (*CL*, iii. 371) as a warrant for excluding *The Secret Agent* from the terms of Conrad's *contract of 1905, which required three novels and defined a novel as a work of at least 75,000 words. As Conrad told Pinker, 'I am not a draper to measure my stuff to the exact yard' (*CL*, iv. 50). In fact, the Methuen edition of *The Secret Agent* contains some 92,000 words.

Intensely Edwardian in its preoccupation with topical issues such as degeneracy and anarchism, *The Secret Agent* is also perhaps the best example in all of Conrad's works of a novel that was ahead of its time. Conrad seemed generally pleased with it, but he warned his friends against taking it too seriously, or reading it for its political or social content. As he told John *Galsworthy, 'The whole thing is superficial and it is but a tale. I had no idea to consider Anarchism politically—or to treat it seriously in its philosophical aspect' (*CL*, iii. 354); and he refused a request from Methuen for a descriptive note on the grounds that the novel was 'purely a work of imagination. It has no social or philosophical intention' (*CL*, iii. 371). Conrad admitted to R. B. Cunninghame *Graham that 'It had some importance for me as a new departure in genre', and he explained its 'technical intention' as 'a sustained effort in ironical treatment of a melodramatic subject'; yet he insisted that 'All these people are not revolutionaries—they are shams' (*CL*, iii. 491). Jacques Berthoud examines Conrad's seeming compulsion to trivialize the novel in an invigorating chapter in Stape (ed.) 1996: 100–21.

The merits of the novel were slow to find recognition. Reviews were mixed, with most readers complaining of the excessive analysis to which the characters are subjected, or the complicated organization of the narrative, or the general lack of amusement in the tale. In his column in the *Nation* (28 September 1907), Edward *Garnett praised Conrad for having given English readers access to 'those secrets of Slav thought and feeling which seem so strange and inaccessible in their native language' (*CCH*, 191). Although Conrad's anarchists are refugees from the Continent, they are not necessarily of Slavic origin; strictly speaking, the only representative of 'Slav thought and feeling' in the novel is Mr Vladimir, who is not an anarchist. Conrad disliked being cast in the role of an exotic polyglot Slav, but he replied with praise for Garnett's intuition that Winnie's mother was the real heroine of the story, and agreed with Garnett that the Verlocs suffer from a 'hidden weakness in the springs of impulse' that leaves them unable to act (*CL*, iii. 487).

The Secret Agent was a typical Conradian *succès d'estime*, applauded by his literary friends but not widely acclaimed by the general readership. It was more popular in England than in America: some 5,000 copies of the English edition were sold in 1907, but sales declined thereafter and it was not reprinted until 1914; the first American edition of 4,000 copies was not reprinted until 1919. In all, the English edition of *The Secret Agent* was printed thirteen times during Conrad's lifetime, totalling over 41,500 copies (Cagle, 128).

Despite Thomas Mann's appreciative introduction to a 1926 German translation (English version in Watt 1973: 99–112), the novel did not win full academic recognition until Leavis proclaimed it 'indubitably a classic and a masterpiece' (209) and hailed the final scene between the Verlocs as 'one of the most astonishing triumphs of genius in fiction' (214). With the arrival of the Cold War and the increasing popularity of spy fiction and film, critics came to admire Conrad's prescience in linking the ambiguous world of counter-espionage with domestic treachery. The novel has figured prominently in critical attempts to understand Conrad's own politics. Howe praised the 'brilliantly original' (99) character of Verloc, but found Conrad's irony too corrosive to permit the development of positive values: his 'ironic tone suffuses every sentence, nagging at our attention to the point where one yearns for the relief of direct statement almost as if it were an ethical good' (101). Eloise Knapp Hay (1963) argued that *England appears in the novel as 'the highest example of political rectitude' (255); while Avrom Fleishman (1967) describes the novel as 'a dramatic portrayal of the sociological concept of "anomie"—radical disorder in the social structure and consequent personal dislocation' (212). These and other studies have often discussed the role of symbols like the triangle of Verloc's secret name or Stevie's drawings of circles, or recurring images like the descriptions of London scenery in terms of a jungle or an aquarium.

A detailed account of the textual history of *The Secret Agent* is available in the critical edition prepared by Bruce Harkness and S. W. Reid (CUP, 1990). A more concise and still useful account is by Emily K. Dalgarno, 'Conrad, Pinker, and the Writing of *The Secret Agent*', *Conradiana*, 9 (1977), 47–58. The historical events and personalities underlying *The Secret Agent* have been examined by Norman Sherry in *CWW*. A number of reviews and essays on the novel by critics including John Galsworthy, Thomas Mann, F. R. Leavis, and J. Hillis Miller are reprinted in Watt's casebook (1973). An annotated checklist of critical articles from 1960–73 was published by Robert W. Stallman in *Conradiana*, 6 (1974), 31–45. The relationship with H. G. Wells has been examined by Frederick R. Karl in 'Conrad, Wells, and the Two Voices', *PMLA* 88 (1988), 1049–65, and by Martin Ray in 'Conrad, Wells, and *The Secret*

Agent: Paying Old Debts and Settling Old Scores', *Modern Language Review*, 81 (1986), 560–73. The role of London in *The Secret Agent* is discussed in four of the essays in Moore (ed.) 1992.

Conrad adapted *The Secret Agent* for the stage, and ten performances were given at the Ambassadors Theatre, London, from 2 to 11 November 1922. Among the spectators was Alfred Hitchcock, who in 1936 directed the first and most famous adaptation of the novel as *Sabotage*, released in America under the title of *The Woman Alone* (Hitchcock's film *The Secret Agent*, released earlier the same year, was based not on Conrad but on stories by Somerset Maugham). Five film or video adaptations have been made in the United Kingdom since 1967, the most ambitious of which was a 1992 three-hour BBC adaptation that was also broadcast in the United States in the public television series 'Masterpiece Theatre'. Two essays in Moore (ed.) 1997 examine aspects of Hitchcock's film, and a third looks 'behind the scenes' of the BBC production with the help of its producer, Colin Tucker. The latest film version (1996) was written and directed by Christopher Hampton (the script was published by Faber in 1996), and features Gérard Depardieu as Ossipon and Robin Williams as the Professor. Other film or video adaptations were made in Poland (1974) and Italy (1978), and a Franco-German co-production of 1981 relocated Verloc in Montmartre. Other forms of adaptation include a futuristic Classics Illustrated *comic book designed by John K. Snyder III (Chicago: Berkley, 1991) and a large-format edition of Sylvère Monod's French translation lavishly illustrated with drawings by Miles Hyman (Paris: Gallimard 'Futuropolis', 1991).

The novel has also been mentioned in connection with Theodore Kaczynski, the so-called 'Unabomber' whose home-made letter bombs killed two people and injured more than ten others in the United States between 25 May 1978 and 10 December 1994. The Unabomber's quest for a 'perfect detonator' may have been inspired by Conrad's Professor, as reported in a 'Dateline

NBC' broadcast on 16 April 1996 and in Serge F. Kovaleski's article in the *Washington Post*, 9 July 1996, pages A1 and A6.

The manuscript of *The Secret Agent* is held at the Rosenbach Museum and Library in Philadelphia, and the original typescript of the 'Author's Note' at the Beinecke Rare Book and Manuscript Library, Yale University.

Secret Agent: A Drama, The. Conrad's own adaptation of his 1907 novel marks the culmination of his efforts as a dramatist. It ran for ten performances at the Ambassadors Theatre, *London, from 2 to 11 November 1922 and was published in both a four-act and a three-act version. Conrad worked on the adaptation over a period of three years, beginning in late 1919, in the wake of the unexpected success of Basil Macdonald *Hastings's stage adaptation of *Victory*. By 11 November, Conrad had finished the second of four acts and had met with theatrical producer Frank Vernon to discuss problems of staging. A draft of the entire four-act version of the play was completed by 15 March 1920. Whereas Hastings had taken liberties with the plot of *Victory*, Conrad decided not to alter the basic plot of his earlier novel, but to take up the challenge of rendering as much of the story as possible in scenic form. As he told John *Galsworthy, 'I've managed to ram everything in there except the actual cab-drive' (*LL*, ii. 238).

The stage demanded far greater respect for the unities of time and space than did the novel. The adaptation opens with the departure of Winnie *Verloc's mother, after which Mr Vladimir visits Adolf *Verloc's shop to remind him of their earlier meeting at the Embassy. Act II is set in the Silenus Restaurant and the offices of the Special Crimes Department, and Act III in the drawing room of Lady Mabel (the Lady Patroness of the novel). The final act takes place entirely in Verloc's shop, where Tom Ossipon steals Winnie's cash and rushes out the door only to be caught by one of Inspector Heat's detectives, who returns with him to find Winnie gone mad, raving about 'blood and dirt', when suddenly the

*Professor arrives. If the plot of the novel had to be 'rammed in' to fit the stage, the removal of the ironic narrator's voice was, conversely, a process of denudation. Conrad described the process of adaptation to his agent J. B. *Pinker as one of 'stripping off the garment of artistic expression and consistent irony which clothes the story in the book' to reveal 'a merely horrible and sordid tale' (*LL*, ii. 233–4); the same metaphor recurs in his 1920 'Author's Note' to the collected edition of the novel. Years earlier he had described his 'technical intention' in the novel as a sustained effort in the ironical treatment of a melodramatic subject (*CL*, iii. 491). Once the narrative irony had been stripped away, the subject reverted inevitably to melodrama.

In December 1920, the play was taken on option for a year by actor-manager Norman McKinnel. By this time Conrad, who had once hoped for a popular success with the novel, was privately expressing his doubts about whether the play would be appreciated. As he told fellow playwright Chistopher Sandeman, 'I foresee for it a "frost" modified—or tempered—by a certain amount of curiosity on the part of a small section of the public: with the conclusion on the part of the critics that "Conrad can't write a play"' (*LL*, ii. 253). Conrad hoped at best for a *succès de curiosité* from a public that knew him chiefly as a novelist.

In the autumn of 1921, McKinnel's option having expired, the play was taken up by J. Harry Benrimo of the Ambassadors Theatre (London WC2). For practical reasons, the original four-act structure was reduced to three acts by turning Act III into scene 3 of Act II. As Conrad explained to Polish playwright Bruno Winawer, 'The play was presented in Three Acts, the Drawing-room Act becoming the Third Scene of Act Second, and the Fourth Act being then called the Third. That certainly gave a better balance to the composition' (*CPB*, 283). Conrad was actively involved in the production, and made pen-and-ink sketches of the design of the five sets. He witnessed three rehearsals, including the dress rehearsal, but did not attend any of the regular performances. Following the first performance, he made some cuts, including some lines of the Professor and Heat in Act II, explaining to Winawer that he was 'very glad to do it, because these two parts were so badly cast that the less those people had to do and say the better, I thought, it would be for the play as a whole' (*CPB*, 283). The Professor was played by Clifton Boyne, and Heat by Jevan Brandon-Thomas; H. St. Barbe West played the part of Verloc, and Winnie was played by Miriam Lewes. Apparently the audience shared Conrad's opinion of the acting, and the play closed after only ten performances. R. L. Mégroz, who interviewed Conrad in a London hotel room while Conrad's wife Jessie was attending the opening night, commented that 'many people feel that The Secret Agent was badly cast and, with one or two exceptions, not very well played' (*A Talk with Joseph Conrad and a Criticism of his Mind and Method* (Elkin Mathews, 1926), 29–30.

Conrad had translated Bruno Winawer's short play from Polish to English (*The Book of Job*) in 1921, and Winawer returned the favour by translating The Secret Agent into Polish and helping to arrange for its performance in Poland; *Tajny agent* opened at the Teatr Bagatela in *Cracow on 23 March 1923.

Fifty-two copies of the four-act version of The Secret Agent were privately printed for the author by H. J. Goulden in Canterbury in 1921, and the three-act version appeared in a limited-subscription edition of 1,000 copies printed by T. Werner Laurie in London in 1923. The first regular edition of the play (in four acts) was in *Three Plays* (Methuen, 1934).

Conrad's dramatic adaptations have been largely neglected by his critics and biographers. The few available studies include James Kilroy, 'Conrad's "Succès de Curiosité": The Dramatic Version of The Secret Agent', *English Literature in Transition, 1880–1920*, 10 (1967), 81–8; Robert S. Ryf, '*The Secret Agent* on Stage', *Modern Drama*, 15 (1972), 54–67; William C. Houze's unpublished Ph.D. dissertation 'Philosophy, Politics, and Morality in The Secret Agent as Novel and Play: A Comparative

Study' (Syracuse University, 1980, Order No. 8026365), excerpted as '*The Secret Agent* from Novel to Play: The Implications of Conrad's Handling of Structure', *Conradiana*, 13 (1981), 109–22; and Amy Houston, 'Joseph Conrad Takes the Stage: Dramatic Irony in *The Secret Agent*', *The Conradian*, 23: 2 (1998), 55–69.

The original four-act draft of *The Secret Agent: A Drama* was sold to T. J. *Wise and is at the British Library, London. Other typescripts, fragments, and proofs are at Colgate University. Conrad's set designs (in the Berg Collection, New York Public Library) have been reproduced by Daniel E. Lees in *Conradiana*, 8 (1976), 253–6.

'Secret Sharer, The'. Conrad's most famous and frequently anthologized short story was composed rapidly in early December 1909 during a break in his work on *Under Western Eyes*. Some 15,000 words long, it was first published in *Harper's Magazine* (New York) in August and September 1910, illustrated by W. J. Aylward, before appearing as the second of three stories in *'Twixt Land and Sea*, subtitled 'An Episode from the Coast'.

Narrated by a young captain entering upon his first command, the story concerns a fugitive doppelgänger who is given refuge on the captain's ship as his secret guest. The captain is mistrusted by his crew and feels a stranger in his own (unnamed) ship, which is becalmed at the head of the Gulf of Siam. Alone on deck late one night, he is surprised to find a naked man floating in an aura of phosphorescence at the bottom of a rope ladder. *Leggatt, the swimmer, is the first mate of the *Sephora*; he killed an insolent seaman in a moment of anger during a hurricane, and was being transported to *Bangkok for trial when he escaped. The captain feels a mysterious sympathy for Leggatt, a fellow '*Conway* boy' (101) who learned to sail on the famous training ship. The captain gives Leggatt clothing and hides him in his cabin, and when Captain Archbold of the *Sephora* arrives the following day in search of the fugitive, the young captain shows him the ship without revealing Leggatt's presence.

Four days later, on the voyage southward, the captain devises a plan for Leggatt's escape that involves sailing perilously close to the islands on the eastern side of the Gulf on the dubious pretext of picking up land breezes. When the captain finally orders the ship brought about, Leggatt secretly escapes overboard. His hat floating in the water signals to the captain that the ship is being blown backwards (making sternway); the captain shifts the helm to save the ship, and this reckless act of bravado wins him the respect of the crew.

Conrad received his first command in the Gulf of Siam in 1888, and the first voyage of the *Otago* provided material for both 'The Secret Sharer' and *The Shadow-Line*. As Conrad acknowledged in his 'Author's Note' to *'Twixt Land and Sea*, 'The Secret Sharer' was also inspired by an actual incident that occurred in the famous tea clipper *Cutty Sark* in September 1880. Unlike Captain Archbold, the real Captain Wallace helped his prisoner to escape and committed suicide soon afterwards. (Conrad used Wallace as a model for Captain Brierly in *Lord Jim*.) Details of these historical events can be found in Basil Lubbock's *The Log of the 'Cutty Sark'* (1924) and in *CEW*. The *Cutty Sark* can now be visited at the National Maritime Museum in Greenwich, but the documentation on public display makes no mention of Captain Wallace or this shameful incident.

Conrad told his agent J. B. *Pinker that the story was written in only eight days, and informed both John *Galsworthy and Perceval *Gibbon that it took ten days. In '"The Secret Sharer": A Note on the Dates of its Composition', *Conradiana*, 19 (1987), 209–13, Keith Carabine analyses evidence from the composition of *Under Western Eyes* to determine when the story was written. Conrad explained to Pinker that it was written in response to an offer from Lindsay Bashford, the literary editor of the *Daily Mail*, for a series of brief sketches that could provide Conrad with much-needed extra income. Although Conrad's maid was ill at the time, he was himself enjoying a brief period of unusually good health; as he told Pinker, 'I am now feeling as well as I have not felt since the Lord Jim days—which were the last good ones' (*CL*, iv. 298, 310). Conrad was unable to choose a title for the story, and asked Pinker to select one from among several candidates: 'The Secret Self', 'The Other Self', or 'The Secret Sharer', although he thought the last one 'may be *too* enigmatic' (*CL*, iv. 300). The enigma of Pinker's choice is enhanced by a grammatical ambiguity, since the word 'secret' can be understood either as an adjective or as part of a compound noun, suggesting in the first case a hidden double and in the second a sharer of secrets. As Conrad's letters show, Pinker was predictably upset with Conrad for spending a week on a new story at a time when the finishing of *Under Western Eyes* should have had first priority. Conrad complained to Perceval Gibbon and to John Galsworthy that Pinker was threatening to 'stop short' if he did not finish *Under Western Eyes* within a fortnight, and he spoke of flinging the manuscript in the fire (*CL*, iv. 302). In the event, a full draft of the novel was ready within a month, by 26 January 1910, at which point a major rupture erupted between Conrad and his agent for which the argument over 'The Secret Sharer' had been merely a rehearsal. Conrad was pleased with the story, and confided his satisfaction to Edward *Garnett: 'the Secret Sharer, between you and me, is *it*. Eh? No damned tricks with girls there. Eh? Every word fits and there's not a single uncertain note. Luck my boy. Pure luck' (*CL*, v. 128). When Edith *Wharton wrote to suggest that Conrad consider translating the story into French, he declined on the grounds that 'the thing . . . is so particularly English, in moral atmosphere, in feeling and even in detail—n'est-ce pas?' (*CL*, v. 152). In the event, *'Twixt Land and Sea* was translated into Swedish (1914) and Danish (1919) before the first French translation appeared in 1921.

The ambiguities announced in the story's title also pervade the moral dilemma dramatized in its plot. The young captain represents the law on board his ship, and is therefore obliged to assist other captains to see that justice is done. Instead of following the book of standard procedure, he allows a personal sympathy to corrupt his proper behaviour, and exposes himself to great risk both legally and professionally by assisting a fugitive criminal to make good his escape. On the other hand, Leggatt's appeal is so humanly irresistible, and his crime so thoroughly mitigated by extenuating circumstances, that the captain becomes involved with his plight and feels as if he himself might have behaved in the same way. The conflict between the strict letter of the law represented by Captain Archbold and the spirit of a more intimate justice represented by the captain's efforts to aid his unfortunate double is one of the major cruxes in interpretation of the story, which largely depends on how one understands the captain's motives, the question of whether or not Leggatt's homicide is justifiable, and the nature of the intense bond that unites the two men.

'The Secret Sharer' has been read from a wide variety of analytic perspectives and occasioned a great many exercises in criticism designed for classroom use. As a story involving covert doubles, it has proved particularly amenable to psychological approaches. Redefining Conrad's canon in terms of *achievement and decline, Moser (1957) considers the story as the last work of the 'major Conrad' (2) and as a study of evil (embodied in Leggatt) that Conrad later reworked less intensely and more affirmatively in The Shadow-Line. Guerard (1958) hailed the story as (together with 'Heart of Darkness' and The Shadow-Line) 'among the first and best . . . symbolist masterpieces in English fiction', and described it in terms of Jungian psychology as an instance of the *archetypal myth of the 'night journey' involving 'a risky descent into the preconscious or even unconscious' (14–15). In 'The Secret Sharer', this myth assumes the characteristically Conradian form of 'an act of sympathetic identification with a suspect or outlaw figure, and the ensuing conflict between loyalty to the individual and loyalty to the community' (24). In Jungian terms, the captain's successful liberation of Leggatt,

and his release from the guilt associated with hiding him, signals the successful integration of the captain's personality through an intense encounter with the dark forces of his secret self. A range of *psychoanalytic approaches to the story, from Freud to Lacan, are helpfully surveyed and compared by Barbara Johnson and Marjorie Garber in 'Secret Sharing: Reading Conrad Psychoanalytically', *College English*, 49 (1987), 628–40.

Much of the ambiguity of the story results from the character of Leggatt, who has been seen by critics as either a sinner or a saint, a Cain or a Moses, a 'homicidal ruffian' (102) or an image of fertility or rebirth. The story is told by the captain in the first person, and some critics have deemed his account unreliable, and consider Leggatt a projection of his own madness. Early criticism tended to emphasize the symbolic and moral aspects of the story, often coupling it with The Shadow-Line as a tale of initiation or a rite of passage derived from corresponding events in Conrad's life. Similarities have also been noted with Lord Jim, where the protagonist is a parson's son like Leggatt, and a ship named the Sephora is mentioned in chapter 13. A number of critical essays were collected in a casebook edited by Bruce Harkness entitled Conrad's Secret Sharer and the Critics (Belmont, Calif.: Wadsworth, 1962). Three years later, Harkness published an article poking fun at archetypal criticism by arguing that the secret of the story lies in its 'Hyacinthine' homosexuality (see 'The Secret of "The Secret Sharer" Bared', *College English*, 27 (1965), 55–61). Some readers took the parody seriously, and the story has come increasingly to be appreciated as a masterful study in homosocial bonding or in more or less repressed homosexual desire. James Lansbury's experimental novel *Korzeniowski* (Serpent's Tail, 1992) explores these aspects of the story in a variety of styles and modes.

Mirror imagery in the story has been analysed by Cedric Watts in 'The Mirror-Tale: An Ethico-structural Analysis of Conrad's "The Secret Sharer"', *Critical Quarterly*, 19: 3 (1977), 25–37. Noting that the captain refers to Leggatt literally as 'my double' some eighteen times in the story, along with many other references to 'my other self' or 'my secret self', Joan E. Steiner discusses the significance of the double and usefully summarizes previous criticism in 'Conrad's "The Secret Sharer": Complexities of the Doubling Relationship', *Conradiana*, 12 (1980), 173–86.

The outlaw Leggatt's sudden appeal to the captain for help strongly resembles the appeal addressed to *Razumov by the fugitive Victor *Haldin in *Under Western Eyes*. In 'Conrad's "The Secret Sharer": Affirmation of Action', *Conradiana*, 16 (1984), 195–214, Steve Ressler examines the story as a 'romantic counterpart' (195) to the tragedy of *Under Western Eyes*, and argues that the confidence Conrad gained by writing the story quickly was essential in making it possible for him to finish the longer and far more troublesome novel, although it did not save him from the major nervous breakdown that followed its completion. Problems posed by literary allusion are explored in Mark A. R. Facknitz's 'Cryptic Allusions and the Moral of the Story: The Case of Joseph Conrad's "The Secret Sharer"', *Journal of Narrative Technique*, 17 (1987), 115–30. James Hansford provides a refreshing and original close reading in 'Closing, Enclosure and Passage in "The Secret Sharer"', *The Conradian*, 15: 1 (1990), 30–55. A lucid explanation of the ship's complex manœuvres at the end of the story can be found in a note appended to Cedric Watts's edition of *Typhoon and Other Tales* (OUP, 1986). The perennial susceptibility of 'The Secret Sharer' to a wide variety of critical approaches is evident from its inclusion as the second Conrad volume (after *Heart of Darkness*) in the series Case Studies in Contemporary Criticism, edited by Daniel R. Schwarz (Boston: Bedford Books, 1997), where the text is presented together with critical essays written from five different perspectives: psychoanalytic criticism, reader-response criticism, *new historicist criticism, *feminist and gender criticism, and *deconstruction.

The first video adaptation of any of Conrad's work was a BBC version of 'The Secret Sharer' made in 1950. In 1952 the story was filmed by Huntington Hartford as the first half of a 'duo-drama' called *Face to Face*, together with James Agee's adaptation of Stephen *Crane's short story 'The Bride Comes to Yellow Sky'. Other film or video adaptations have been made in Italy (1967), Poland (1967), the USA (1972), and France (1988).

The manuscript of 'The Secret Sharer' is now in the Berg Collection, New York Public Library, and a 1924 sketch by Conrad of a scene from the story is at the Beinecke Rare Book and Manuscript Library, Yale University.

serialization. While serialization is often thought of as a dominant feature in the shaping and marketing of the mid- and late-Victorian novel, it remained a vital force in publishing throughout the whole of Conrad's career, and both his short fiction and novels first appeared in serial form. He was, however, both by temperament and working methods singularly ill-equipped for the very real constraints that serialization imposed upon a long work. It demanded a methodical approach to literary production, a thorough mapping out in advance of plotting and characterization (with an eye, moreover, to where breaks would fall), a careful control over word-counts and chapter length, and an ability to write to tight deadlines. By Anthony Trollope's dictum, 'the author should see the end of his work before the public sees the commencement'. Conrad's methods of composition flew in the face of this caution, and it is only a slight exaggeration to say that the early history of the serialization of his writing comprises a tale of nearly missed catastrophe, extreme frustration, and almost constant tension, and unplanned growth as stories and novels ran away with him. The crudity of the conclusions of the serial versions of *Nostromo* and *The Secret Agent* bear witness to his struggles to write to ready-made formulae and a strict schedule. Conrad attempted to skirt these problems by asserting to himself, his agent, and *publishers the primacy of his book text, by planning for extensive revision and rewriting for book publication, and, as regards his novels, by bowing to the necessity of delivering to his public work that was unpolished and, in some sense, 'unfinished'. By inclination, he nonetheless attempted to impose his high artistic standards even where necessity required their compromise. With some justification he could vent the anguished cry 'If one only could do without serial publication!' (*CL*, ii. 260) as he neared the completion of *Lord Jim*; but he could not do without it, and despite the form's fundamental uncongeniality to his particular talent, he buckled down to it. His experience with serialization later in his career was, on the whole, considerably happier, since by then he had learned only to see into print work that was in its final stages of completion.

The economic factor in all this was primary since serialization paid extremely well, especially as Conrad's fame and popularity grew after 1913, the landmark year of *Chance*. The serialization of *The Arrow of Gold* earned him a fee of £1,200 and *The Rescue* £2,200. It was, however, almost from the outset of his career essential to managing his *finances since it meant, except for revisions at the book stage, double payment for the same creative effort.

The publication of Conrad's short stories in serial form was on the surface mainly untroubled. At times he fretted over where a division had to occur, and he wished to exert more control over this than publishing practice customarily allowed for. He also had to submit to his work being embellished with *illustrations of varying quality and pertinence to the text. Magazine publication engaged him at times in a complicated juggling act to secure American copyright, since failure to do so would result in financial loss, as happened in the case of 'Youth', which was scheduled to appear in the *Atlantic Monthly* but was barred from doing so because of copyright problems. The more far-reaching effect of the magazine serialization was to place restrictions on the topics that could be handled and to limit the method of treatment: middle-of-the-road subject matter and the

happy ending ruled the form. 'Falk', a story dealing with cannibalism and sexual desire, was never serialized, and only on a third attempt did 'The Idiots' find its way into print in Arthur *Symons's highbrow *Savoy*. (Prudishness extended even to the use of realistic language: the somewhat salty expressions given to the seamen in *The Nigger of the 'Narcissus'* came in for criticism by reviewers, and euphemisms appear somewhat more frequently in works written after it.)

Conrad's willingness to experiment in his short fiction declined as he discovered that it proved difficult to place. He simply could not afford the price of failing to conform, and his more stable associations with establishment periodicals, first with *Blackwood's Magazine* and then with *Pall Mall Magazine*, suggest a practical concession to marketing realities. Writing for a known audience was a much safer bet than attempting to place work after it was written. In the event, Conrad's connection with *Blackwood's* was not only personally rewarding but highly successful artistically; that with *Pall Mall Magazine*, on the other hand, tended to encourage the writing of potboilers. After J. B. *Pinker began managing Conrad, his work was placed in America through the New York agent Paul R. Reynolds. Although this brought immediate financial rewards with a given piece going to the highest bidder, the long-term consequences of this arrangement were that Conrad could establish no continuous relationship with a specific magazine editor or readership.

The directions Conrad's short fiction might have taken had he enjoyed a completely free hand are impossible to determine. The negative effect of serialization can, however, be observed in the case of 'The End of Tether', which might have been better had it been simply shorter. No evidence suggests that Conrad intentionally spun out his basic materials in order to make more money—like his Victorian predecessors, he was paid by the word—but he was undoubtedly aware that judicious pruning would have entailed a smaller cheque.

With the exception of *Almayer's Folly* and *An Outcast of the Islands,* all of Conrad's novels appeared in serial form (details are provided in the individual entries). Circumstances of composition and publication differed somewhat in each case. *Lord Jim,* which began as a short story, evolved into a lengthy novel as writing and serialization proceeded hand-in-hand; the composition of *The Secret Agent* was hurried on in order to oblige its serial publisher; at the wise insistence of the *New York Herald, Chance* was virtually finished when its serialization began. *The Rover* proved difficult to place, and book publication was even delayed in order to accommodate its serial appearance. Conrad generally did not see proofs for work published serially in America, and did not usually do so for that published in England. The general neglect by English reviewers of serialized novels led to a certain insouciance on his part, whether feigned or genuine, about serial versions, and he could write to Philippe Neel, one of his French translators: 'Il me serait indifférent si l'on imprimait une ligne sur trois, au hasard, ou même en commençant par la fin' [I wouldn't care if they printed one line out of three, by chance, or even began with the ending] (*LF*, 177).

The progress of 'Heart of Darkness' through composition and serial printing set a pattern that Conrad repeated with *Lord Jim*: he sold it before it was finished; it grew beyond his expectations and those of his indulgent publisher; he systematically revised promised completion dates to compensate for overly optimistic estimates of his ability to produce; and tension inexorably mounted as he was forced to furnish copy. Even in its serial form *Lord Jim* is remarkably free from the blemishes that might have ensued from such a method of composition; and the respect that William *Blackwood extended to his demanding writer played a crucial role in permitting the novel to grow Topsy-like as it did. More surprising is the fact that its conclusion was repeatedly envisaged and repeatedly deferred. It appears that at a very late stage of composition Conrad foresaw bringing

the novel to a close with *Marlow's final glimpse of *Jim on *Patusan in chapter 35. The Gentleman *Brown episode and Jim's tragic death were not conceived until about mid-May 1900, and then required two full months of writing. The serial ending proved typically to be a draft, and Conrad's compulsive desire to polish and revise resulted in a number of significant changes in book proofs where he modified the characterization of Gentleman Brown so that the encounter for Jim became a psychological test rather than an allegorical battle with evil incarnate.

The serial endings of *Nostromo* and *The Secret Agent* similarly suffer from the pressures of hasty composition, and are essentially roughed-out sketches to be worked up after serial publication. While Conrad managed to salvage the conclusion to *The Secret Agent,* he never fully removed from *Nostromo* the negative effects of its serialization. Having finished the draft of the novel in a 'half delirious state' (*CL*, iii. 164), he was forced almost immediately to set about revising for book publication and, in the main, did so rather lightly. By critical consensus, the results of these strained efforts mar his largest canvas. Another bout of revision for the 1917 edition saw him attempting to correct the earlier damage inflicted by forced and speedy revision; at this late stage of his career, he was a different writer from the one he had been in 1903–4, and some of his changes problematize the text in ways similar to the revisions Henry *James made for the New York Edition of his work.

The serialization of Conrad's fiction contributed to complicating his texts. In addition to being house-styled, his prose was occasionally altered by editors eager to correct his grammar or smooth out his idiom. Since Conrad revised for book publication on serial tear-sheets, almost invariably without recourse to his manuscripts or revised typescripts, alterations made during serial production were passed along to later editions. The serial forms have thus had a long afterlife; while the Cambridge Edition will as far as possible strive to restore Conrad's own forms, those of the serials will continue to influence Conrad's texts.

No full-scale study of the effects of serialization on Conrad's writing has been undertaken. Gail Fraser's 'The Short Fiction', in Stape (ed.) 1996: 25–44, deals masterfully and in a brief compass with some of the general consequences of serial publication. Peter McDonald's 'Men of Letters and Children of the Sea: Conrad and the *Henley Circle Revisited', *The Conradian*, 21: 1 (1996), 15–56, examines the shaping of *The Nigger of the 'Narcissus'* for a specific editor and audience. Ernest W. Sullivan's *The Several Endings of Joseph Conrad's 'Lord Jim'* (Joseph Conrad Society, UK (1984)) and Dwight H. Purdy's 'Conrad at Work: The Two Serial Texts of *Typhoon'*, *Conradiana*, 19 (1987), 99–119, offer model close studies of individual serial texts.

The World's Classics edition of *Nostromo*, ed. Keith Carabine (OUP, 1984), and the Cambridge Edition of *The Secret Agent*, ed. Bruce Harkness and S. W. Reid (CUP, 1990), usefully make available the original serial endings of these novels. Everyman's centennial-year edition of *The Nigger of the 'Narcissus'*, ed. Allan Simmons (Dent, 1997), and Cedric Watts's *The Heart of Darkness* (Dent, 1995) adopt the serial versions as copy-texts and draw attention to variants with the first English editions.

JHS

Set of Six, A. First planned by Conrad in October 1907, this volume brings together six stories written during the period 1905–7—'Gaspar Ruiz: A Romantic Tale', 'The Informer: An Ironic Tale', 'The Brute: An Indignant Tale', 'An Anarchist: A Desperate Tale', 'The Duel: A Military Tale', and 'Il Conde: A Pathetic Tale'—all of which had previously appeared in magazines. It was published by *Methuen in Britain on 6 August 1908. 'The Duel' was brought out separately in America by S. S. *McClure in October 1908 as *The Point of Honor: A Military Tale*. The American edition of *A Set of Six* appeared considerably later, published by Doubleday, Page on 15 January 1915, with a specially written 'Author's Note' (*CDOUP*, 89–90). Conrad's description of the volume's contents to his British publisher as 'stories of incident—action—not of analysis . . . just stories in which I've tried my best to be *simply entertaining*' (*CL*, iv. 29–30) hardly does them justice. *A Set of Six* is, in fact, one of his most varied collections, deriving from a period between *Nostromo* and *The Secret Agent* which, as he recalled in the 'Author's Note' to *The Secret Agent*, 'was attended by a very intense imaginative and emotional readiness' (p. ix). Its contents embrace diverse settings and interests (South American, *Napoleonic, maritime, and political), tonal qualities (as signalled by the subtitles), and short-story forms. Conrad's response to the generally favourable contemporary reviews of the volume, a selection of which is reprinted in *CCH*, 210–26, appears in a long letter to Edward *Garnett. (*CL*, iv. 107–8). Among modern critics, Fleishman, who reads all of these tales with the exception of 'The Brute', as 'incisive views of modern political life', makes the highest claim for them to date as 'worthy to stand with the three great political novels' (143). See also Addison C. Bross, '*A Set of Six*: Variations on a Theme', *Conradiana*, 7 (1975), 27–44.

Shadow-Line, The. This short novel of some 40,000 words, published in 1917, was Conrad's most substantial piece of writing during the *First World War. A letter to Eugene F. Saxton of August 1915, in which Conrad refers to the impending enlistment of his own son Borys, captures the authorial mood during the novella's composition: 'Everybody we know has lost someone—except Sir Hugh [*Clifford] whose son has been wounded and now is gone out again —a dear boy—both he and his father feel only to be killed. They all go. My boy's turn will be coming presently to start off. The shadow lies over this land. This is a time of great awe and searching of hearts and of resolute girding of loins' (*CL*, v. 500). This quiet apprehension typifies Conrad's comments on the war, which he refused to see in terms of jingoistic ideals. As he told John *Quinn: 'We are fighting for life first, for freedom of thought and development in whatever form next' (quoted in *JCC*, 424). To Conrad the war was primarily a nation's struggle for survival and, in *The Shadow-Line*, he explores in miniature the nature of such a struggle. As Berthoud puts it: 'Its protagonist . . . is taught that he could not have survived the ordeal to which he is exposed without a full reciprocity of dependence between himself and his crew. This lesson may seem banal enough; yet Conrad shows that it supports the entire edifice of human life' (1986: 14).

On the opening page of the novella, the narrator announces the principle which the narrative then proceeds to develop: 'One goes on. And the time, too, goes on— till one perceives ahead a shadow-line warning one that the region of early youth, too, must be left behind' (3). The narrator recalls how, in 'an Eastern port' (4) and having suddenly grown disillusioned with life at sea, he resigned from his position as first mate in a steamship under the command of Captain Kent. While waiting for a homeward-bound mail boat, he checked into the Officers' Sailors' Home rather than a hotel, unwilling to accept his status as 'a mere potential passenger' just yet (8). At the Officers' Home the narrator meets the 'Chief Steward', whom he regards as a 'failure' (9), Captain Giles, whom he knows slightly as an expert 'in intricate navigation' in the waters of the Archipelago (12), and the self-important Hamilton, whose persistent refusal to settle his bill makes him the bane of the Chief Steward's existence. Clearly interested by the narrator's decision to throw up his berth, Captain Giles notes, by way of a subtle warning, how sailors can 'go soft mighty quick' in the East where life is 'made easy for white men' (14).

The following day, having discovered that the narrator has no employment to return to in *England and has not yet paid his passage-money, Captain Giles reports that an official communication from Captain Ellis, the harbour master, was delivered to the Officers' Home that morning. Directed by Captain Giles, the narrator confronts the Chief Steward and discovers that the letter advertises a captaincy, for

which the Steward has begged Hamilton to apply, wanting to be rid of him. Urged on by Captain Giles, the narrator hastens to the Harbour Office to apply for the command himself and, clearly expected, he is ushered into the office of Captain Ellis and duly appointed as 'the right man for the job' (31). Back at the Officers' Home and alone in his bedroom, the narrator admits his commitment to the sea: 'I discovered how much of a seaman I was, in heart, in mind, and, as it were, physically—a man exclusively of sea and ships; the sea the only world that counted, and the ships the test of manliness, of temperament, of courage and fidelity—and of love' (40). Captain Giles's parting advice is that the Gulf of Siam is a 'funny piece of water', and to keep to the east side of it, as the west side is dangerous (44–5). That same evening he sails in the steamer *Melita* for *Bangkok, where his first command, a sailing ship, awaits him, her previous master having died. Throughout the passage to Bangkok, the *Melita*'s captain, an embodiment of the 'spirit of modern hurry' (46), is mocking in his attitude towards the young novice. In Bangkok harbour the young captain sees his command for the first time and rapturously pronounces her 'a high-class vessel, a harmonious creature in the lines of her fine body, in the proportioned tallness of her spars . . . like some rare women, she was one of those creatures whose mere existence is enough to awaken an unselfish delight. One feels that it is good to be in the world in which she has her being' (49). Like the Captain himself, the ship is never named.

Aboard his new ship, the Captain muses upon her previous masters and views himself as part of 'a dynasty; continuous not in blood, indeed, but in its experience, in its training, in its conception of duty, and in the blessed simplicity of its traditional point of view on life' (53). Nonetheless, he is keenly self-conscious of his inexperience during his discussion with Mr Burns. At first taciturn, the mate becomes more voluble when talking about the eccentric violin-playing previous captain whose negligent behaviour suggested that he was intent upon destroying his own ship. After the Captain's burial at sea, at the entrance to the Gulf of Siam, Mr Burns took temporary command of the ship and brought her in to Bangkok. Unsurprisingly, the new Captain views his predecessor's actions as 'a complete act of treason' (62).

The ship's departure is delayed due to poor health among the crew. First, the steward dies and then Mr Burns is moved to the local hospital, having developed a raging fever. From his sickbed, he pleads with the Captain not to be left behind when the ship sails. On board, too, there is infirmity and the Captain learns that, despite his healthy appearance, Ransome, the cook, has a weak heart, 'a deadly enemy in his breast' (68), and must be spared heavy duties. Curiously, Ransome is the only member of the crew who is unaffected by fever. By now impatient to get under way with his first command and deciding that the sea, 'pure, safe, and friendly' (70), will restore his crew, the Captain sets sail, having restored the still ailing Mr Burns to his cabin. Bangkok, which had appeared 'gorgeous and dilapidated' (48) on his arrival, now strikes the Captain as merely 'Oriental and squalid' (72).

Anchored a mile outside the bar, the Captain looks forward to the sea breezes which will blow away 'the steaming heat of the river' (73), but the first day brings only calm, which Mr Burns blames on the malevolent influence of the former Captain, the 'old man' (74). Progress southwards across the Gulf of Siam is tortuously slow and, to compound matters, the Captain discovers that the ship has not left sickness behind her as the crew start to fall ill with tropical fever. In the ship's medicine chest, the Captain finds a letter from the doctor warning of the probable return of tropical illness and suggesting that he put his trust in the ship's supply of quinine rather than in the beneficial effects of sea air. From his sickbed, Mr Burns blames the unusual weather conditions which becalm the ship on the malignant supernatural influence of the 'old man' buried 'right in the ship's way . . . out of the Gulf' (83). Although sceptical of his mate's interpreta-

tion, the Captain's own use of phrases such as 'the evil spell held us always motionless' (83) and 'Only purposeful malevolence could account for it' (87) sustains the possibility of a supernatural influence at work on the ship.

Only the Captain and Ransome remain untouched by the fever which 'played with us capriciously very much as the winds did' (85). The energy expended by the men in their efforts to take advantage of any slight winds saps their already weakened strength, and the Captain comes to view his quinine supply as 'more precious than gold' (88). Weighing out doses of this 'unfailing panacea' (88) one morning, he discovers that the remaining bottles are filled not with quinine but with some replacement powder. Mr Burns's theory is that the previous Captain sold the ship's quinine supply. Haunted by guilt for not checking the quinine supply, the Captain decides to change course for *Singapore. Extracts from the Captain's diary of the time confirm his sense of hopelessness on this 'death-haunted command' where his every order, obeyed by 'a tottering little group', is issued with 'a pang of remorse and pity' (98). Between the state of the crew and the meteorological conditions, this 'first command' is characterized by the lack of opportunity to command. The crew's solidarity, endurance, and unreproachful attitude make them, in the Captain's phrase (which Conrad used as an *epigraph for the novel), 'worthy of my undying regard' (100). The Captain records in his diary how all of his life before this voyage seems like 'a fading memory of light-hearted youth, something on the other side of a shadow' (106). Alone in his cabin, he experiences a moment of extreme self-doubt and is reluctant to return on deck to face the imminent storm with his weakened crew, recording in his diary: 'I am no good' (107). But, when called, he responds 'briskly' (108), and takes the lead in hoisting the mainsail, assisted by the few crewmen still able to work and, unbeknown to him, Ransome, who is clearly weakened by his exertions.

As the rain begins to fall, and with the ship still becalmed, the defiant Mr Burns crawls onto the deck 'to scare the old bully-ing rascal' through a 'provoking, mocking peal' of laughter (116, 119) and, though he faints from the exertion, almost immedi-ately 'the spell of deadly stillness' (119) is broken and wind fills the sails. From now on the ship makes good progress but, with her crew overcome by their exertions, she is 'a ship without a crew' (123). With most of the crew fever-stricken, it is left to the Cap-tain, Ransome, and Mr Burns to bring the ship into Singapore harbour after her three-week journey from Bangkok. As the crew are removed to hospital, the young Captain sees each one as 'an embodied re-proach of the bitterest kind' (129). Ashore, he confesses to Captain Giles: 'I feel old' (131). Captain Giles offers the advice that 'one must not make too much of anything in life, good or bad' and 'a man should stand up to his bad luck' (131, 132). When Captain Giles hears that the Captain will be shipping a new crew and intends to leave at daybreak the next day, he offers the simple commendation: 'You'll do' (132). Returning to his ship, the Captain reluctantly dis-charges Ransome, who has asked to be paid off, clearly worried that his recent exertions might have overtaxed his heart. The tale ends with Ransome descending the com-panion steps 'in mortal fear of starting into sudden anger our common enemy it was his hard fate to carry consciously within his faithful breast' (133).

The earliest reference to the story that was to become *The Shadow-Line* occurs in a letter to William *Blackwood of February 1899, where Conrad mentioned two stor-ies, entitled 'First Command' and 'A Sea-man', which 'creep about in my head' but have yet 'to be caught and tortured into some kind of shape' (*CL*, ii. 167). Although Conrad continued to mention this story over the next year and a half, nothing came of it. Sixteen years later, in February 1915, Conrad wrote to his agent J. B. *Pinker: 'I propose to write a story for the Met[ropoli-tan Magazine]: It's an old subject some-thing in [the] style of Youth. I've carried it in my head for years under the name of First Command' (*CL*, v. 441). By 18 March, Conrad had found a new title: 'By the way

the title will be: *The Shadow-line* it having a sort of spiritual meaning' (*CL*, v. 458). On 15 December 1915, Conrad announced to Pinker that the tale was completed. It was *serialized in the *English Review (Sep-tember 1916–March 1917) before being published as a volume by J. M. Dent in England in March 1917; the first American edition, by Doubleday, Page, followed a month later. Conrad sold the manuscript of *The Shadow-Line* to the American col-lector John *Quinn, describing it in a letter of 24 December 1915 as 'a sort of auto-biography—a personal experience—dra-matized in the telling—the MS of which amounts to about 200 pp of pen and ink and a few (about 30) or so of type' (*CL*, v. 543). In the Quinn sale of 1923, the 235 manuscript leaves and 74 leaves of type-script fetched $2,700.

While *The Shadow-Line* is not 'exact autobiography', as Conrad informed Sid-ney *Colvin (*LL*, ii. 182), it is substantially based on Conrad's experiences of his own first command, as Sherry (*CEW*) has shown. Having signed off the *Vidar* in Singapore on 4 January 1888 and while staying in the Sailors' Home, Conrad was offered and accepted his only command, the *Otago*, on 19 January. He joined the ship, whose captain had recently died, in Bangkok on 24 January. The *Otago*'s voyage to *Australia was beset with problems: her departure from Bangkok was delayed until 9 February, and then calms in the Gulf of Siam and illness aboard forced her to stop at Singapore (after a voyage lasting three weeks), in order to replenish her medical supplies and take on fresh crew members before continuing her journey on 2 March.

The novel is dedicated to Conrad's eldest son Borys, who had enlisted in September 1915 and was attached to the Mechanical Transport Corps. He became a second lieu-tenant and suffered shell-shock during the closing months of the war. The dedication reads: 'To Borys and all others who like himself have crossed in early youth the shadow-line of their generation | With Love'. In his 'Author's Note' of 1920, Conrad universalizes his subject—'the change from youth, care-free and fervent, to the more self-conscious and more poignant period of maturer life' (p. vi)—by placing the recreation of his own first command within the historical context of 'the supreme trial of a whole generation' (p. vi). The novella's subtitle, 'A Confession', emphasizes the autobiographical nature of Conrad's sources. He told Helen Sanderson that 'it is a piece of as strict autobiography as the form allowed' (*LL*, ii. 195), and described it to Colvin as 'experience . . . transposed into spiritual terms—in art a perfectly legitimate thing to do, as long as one preserves the exact truth enshrined therein' (*LL*, ii. 183). This concern is underscored in a March letter to Colvin, in which Conrad claims that, throughout his writing life, his concern has been 'with the "ideal" value of things, events and people. That and nothing else' (*LL*, ii. 185).

Conrad wrote to Pinker in December 1915: 'The story is by no means bad for what it is' (*CL*, v. 541). An unsigned review in the *Nation* on 24 March 1917 judged that it was 'written at Mr. Conrad's fullest imaginative stretch' and praised the author's 'elfin power of mingling the natural with the supernatural' (*CCH*, 307). Although Conrad maintained that the tale contained no metaphysical dimension, early reviewers thought otherwise, and it is notable that in his 'Author's Note' he defends the 'enchantment' of life: 'The world of the living contains enough marvels and mysteries as it is; marvels and mysteries acting upon our emotions and intelligence in ways so inexplicable that it would almost justify the conception of life as an enchanted state' (p. v). Not all of the early reviews were favourable. For instance, the *Bookman* called it 'scarcely one of Mr Conrad's big achievements', suggesting that it was 'the work of Mr Conrad the sea-captain rather than Mr Conrad the psychologist' (*CCH*, 309). In early 1917, Conrad confessed to Pinker that one review of *The Shadow-Line* claiming that it reflected the *English Review*'s 'taste for the morbid' had upset him 'very much' (*LL*, ii. 181). However, after the lead later given by F. R. Leavis's essay on the novella ('Joseph Conrad', *Sewanee Review*, 66 (1958), 179–200), subsequent reviewers have generally interpreted *The Shadow-Line* as the masterpiece of the last phase of Conrad's writing life.

As critics have noted, the novella resonates with such familiar Conradian themes as the solidarity and interdependence of the crew, man's struggle with the sea which ultimately reveals something of his moral fibre, and the idea of the sea voyage as an initiation into the burden of command. Criticism has been divided over whether the novel is affirmatory: to many critics, the redemptive quality of work and the recognition of the young captain's bond with his fellow sailors are themselves redemptive, while others argue that the protagonist's dependence upon others, coupled with the sickness and death in the tale, render the conclusion more ambiguous. Among the approaches which interpret the novel allegorically is Guerard's *psychoanalytic interpretation, in which he argues that the novel dramatizes an immobilizing depression, with the sea voyage standing for a night journey into the self, where the irrational (Burns) and the rational (Ransome) are at war (1958: 29–33). Alongside Berthoud's excellent contextual essay on the work (1986), two important further studies of the novel are Ian Watt's 'Story and Idea in Conrad's *The Shadow-Line*', *Critical Quarterly*, 2 (1960), 133–48, and Jeremy Hawthorn's wide-ranging 'Introduction', '*The Shadow-Line*', World's Classics (OUP, 1985), pp. vii–xxv. The manuscript and typescript of the novel are in the Beinecke Rare Book and Manuscript Library, Yale University.   AHS

Shakespeare, William (1564–1616). Shakespeare's work first entered into Conrad's life, at least passingly, during his childhood, his father Apollo *Korzeniowski having translated *A Comedy of Errors* (1594) and *The Two Gentlemen of Verona* (1594) into Polish. It remains unclear, however, whether Conrad read any of Shakespeare's plays or poetry in translation or the original before arriving in England in 1878. Shakespeare's ineluctable centrality to European culture suggests, however, the likelihood of Conrad's having come into contact with his work before that date, and that *Jim takes a copy of Shakespeare to *Patusan offers a hint. Conrad, who bought a volume of Shakespeare before the *Palestine* left for the Far East, undoubtedly became familiar with the writings of England's national playwright—'your great poet' (213) as *Stein, who quotes from *Hamlet* (1601), calls him in *Lord Jim*—during the years of his transition from roving seaman to English writer. At this period he would also have encountered the bardolatry that was so much a feature of late Victorian culture. It seems likely that he encountered Shakespeare mostly from reading rather than in theatrical performance, an art form, with the exception of *opera, that he seems generally to have found unsympathetic; and his knowledge of the canon, as constructed from allusions in his fiction and letters, appears to have centred on the great tragedies. (In March 1914, he read A. C. Bradley's *Shakespearean Tragedy*.) The imprint of Shakespeare on Conrad's writing extends from passing allusion or casual *borrowing to a full-scale dialogue with the playwright's ideas. Among English writers only *Dickens had a comparable impact on his fiction.

Lord Jim is perhaps the most Shakespearian of Conrad's works. Passing allusions are made to *Hamlet*—the famous 'To be, or not to be' soliloquy is quoted and the phrase 'undiscovered country', also from that speech, resonates complexly—but Conrad's more profound debt lies in the construction of his hero's character. Jim's self-interrogation, his youthful confrontation with the vertigo of mortality, his suspension between the ideal and the real and love, are quintessentially Hamletian problems. Jim's quandary at the moment of his jump replicates, at a distance, the Hamletic moment of self-torturing doubt and indecision. The sense of a self riven by division and suspended between possibilities, as well as Jim's reluctant engagement with quotidian reality, whatever Conrad's debts to *Flaubert here, owes much to 19th-century interpretations of Hamlet's character. The novel's tragic denouement is, in some sense, a psychological version of Hamlet's

duel with Laertes, as Gentleman *Brown takes his revenge against the world and Jim attains, at least in many critical readings, the status of tragic hero and emblematic figure of a sensitivity too fine for this world. *Marlow, at least partly, takes on the role of Horatio, acting as Jim's witness and elegist, charged with justifying his friend's actions and personality. There are likewise significant Hamletian echoes in *The Shadow-Line*, in which the young captain is haunted by the ghosts of his professional predecessors.

The *epigraph finally selected for *Nostromo*—'so foul a sky clears not without a storm'—from *King John* (1590) (a discarded possibility from Sir Walter Scott's 'Lay of the Minstrel' (1805) played up the novel's love interest) throws emphasis on its politics. The recurrent pattern of order and discord also recalls the history plays, in particular the Henry IV and Henry VI cycles, where civil strife, ambition, and power intrigues dominate the action. The novel's sheer amplitude allows a Shakespearian scale of treatment of these themes. The epigraph for *Tales of Unrest* is from *2 Henry IV*, IV. v. 213–14: 'Be it thy course to busy giddy minds | With foreign quarrels.'

Analogies may also be found between Captain *Whalley of 'The End of the Tether' and King Lear. Shut up in their own worlds, Whalley and Lear share a physical blindness that symbolizes a self-absorption and self-deception so complete that they literally shut out the surrounding world. Both old men also attempt to fend off mortality, refusing to recognize their inability to control the Wheel of Fortune, a Renaissance commonplace that the story variously evokes as the wheel of the Manila lottery and the steering-wheel of the *Sofala*. The victim of hubris, Whalley-as-Lear is mainly an ironic portrait, since the story offers no redemptive possibilities; and Whalley, although he appears belatedly to discover the vast scale of his self-betrayal, is simply defeated, deprived of the tragic grandeur and terrible dignity that Lear's insights afford him in his dying moments. In her casual emotional indifference to her father's sacrifice, Ivy, though she is no active predator, more closely resembles Goneril and Regan than the faithful Cordelia for whom Whalley mistakes her.

A number of critics have found a pervasive Shakespearian presence in *Victory*, which, broadly, rewrites *The Tempest* (1611); and some commentators have likewise found echoes of the Caliban–Prospero antagonism in 'Heart of Darkness'. The novel's island setting, trio of villains, and, perhaps, its heroine have analogues in Prospero's island of exile, while its mixed allegorical and realistic modes also make a nod towards the play. Caliban's deep hostility to Prospero's values and the antagonism between civilized order and anarchic self-seeking are motifs in the *Heyst–*Schomberg and Heyst–*Jones relationships. Lacking both the vitality and hard-won wisdom of Shakespeare's magus, Heyst's Prospero is, like Whalley's Lear, mostly an ironic figure. He nonetheless has transformational powers, straying sufficiently far from his quietist moorings to offer *Lena a refuge from her troubled situation and love of a kind. Its paternal aspects echo Prospero's love, which involves the moral education of his daughter Miranda.

Necessarily putting to one side Shakespeare's comic genius, Conrad may be seen as approaching a Shakespearian scope in his moral and philosophical concerns: his writings range over large tracts of fundamental human experience including love, politics, the problem of self-knowledge, and the burden of mortality. And like Shakespeare's universe, Conrad's lacks a fixed reference point in religious belief, although questions of morality and ethics form the very centre of his interests.

Of the relatively large body of critical writing on this subject the following are essential: David Lodge, 'Conrad's *Victory* and *The Tempest*: An Amplification', *Modern Language Review*, 59 (1964), 195–9; Adam Gillon (1976); Eloise Knapp Hay's 'Lord Jim and *le Hamlétisme*', *L'Époque Conradienne*, 16 (1990), 9–27; and John Batchelor's 'Conrad and Shakespeare', *L'Époque Conradienne*, 18 (1992), 125–51.   JHS

ships and voyages. The following entries give details of the ships in which Conrad served and the voyages he undertook during his sea career, 1874–94.

Mont-Blanc, three-masted wooden barque of 394 tons, built 1853, owned by César *Delestang et Fils of Marseilles.

First voyage. Conrad, aged 17, joined his first ship on 8 December 1874, sailing as a passenger when the *Mont-Blanc*, under Captain Sever Ournier and with a crew of eleven, departed from *Marseilles on 15 December bound for Martinique in the *Caribbean. She arrived in the Saint-Pierre roads, Martinique, on 6 February 1875 for a seven-week stay. She began her homeward passage on 31 March, via the Straits of Gibraltar (5 May), arriving back in Marseilles on 23 May after a five-and-a-half-month voyage.

Second voyage. Conrad, aged 17, signed on as a *novice* or ship's boy at a monthly wage of 35 francs. Under Captain Jean-Prosper Duteil and with a crew of twenty, the *Mont-Blanc* departed from Marseilles on 25 June 1875 for Martinique in the Caribbean and arrived in the Saint-Pierre roads on 31 July. Leaving Saint-Pierre on 23 September, she stopped over at Saint-Thomas, now Virgin Islands (27–8 September), and Cap-Haïtien, Haïti (1 October–1 November), arriving in Le Havre on 23 December after a six-month voyage.

Saint-Antoine, three-masted wooden barque of 432 gross tonnage, built 1870, owned by J. M. Cairo of Nantes.

Conrad, aged 18, signed on in *Marseilles as 'M^{tre} *d'hôtel*' or steward at a monthly wage of 35 francs. Under Captain Casimir Antonin Stanislas Escarras and with a crew of 13, the *Saint-Antoine* departed from Marseilles on 10 July 1876 bound for Martinique in the *Caribbean. Among her crew members were Dominique *Cervoni and César *Cervoni, only very distantly related but both from the same Corsican village, who later figured in Conrad's memoirs and fiction. Entries in the ship's crew list indicate beyond doubt that on arriving in Martinique (18 August) the *Saint-Antoine* stayed in the

Saint-Pierre roads and did *not*, contrary to Conrad's intimations, visit ports in Colombia and Venezuela. It remains possible that Conrad absented himself from ship temporarily, but visits to South American ports would only have been possible in regular mail steamers, not under sail, in order to be back in time to join the ship for her return to *France. Five weeks later, on 25 September, she left Saint-Pierre, stopping over at Saint-Thomas, now Virgin Islands (27 September–12 October), and at Port-au-Prince (26 October–28 November) and Miragoâne, Haïti (5–23 December). She then began her homeward run, passing the Straits of Gibraltar (27 January 1877), arriving in Marseilles on 15 February after a seven-month voyage. For further details about Conrad's Caribbean voyages, see van Marle 1991.

Mavis, steamer of 764 gross tonnage, built 1872, owned by J. V. Gooch of London.

Conrad, aged 20, after payment of a 500-franc deposit, boarded ship in *Marseilles on 24 April 1878 as unofficial apprentice. Under Captain Samuel William Pipe and with a crew of eighteen, the *Mavis*, a British steamer, reached Malta on 26 April and left the same day for Constantinople, arriving on 2 May, on her way to Kerch in the Crimea; she passed through the Straits of Kerch on 6 May, bound for Yeysk on the Sea of Azov. After a seven-week voyage, the *Mavis* arrived in Lowestoft on 10 June when Conrad first set foot in *England.

Skimmer of the Sea, three-masted coasting schooner of 215 gross tonnage, built 1855, owned by Joseph Saul of Lowestoft.

Conrad, aged 20, signed on as ordinary seaman in Lowestoft on 11 July 1878 at a monthly wage of one shilling. Under Captain William Cook and with a crew of six, he made three round trips from Lowestoft to Newcastle, signing off on 23 September after almost eleven weeks of service. Conrad later commented: 'In that craft I began to learn English from East Coast chaps each built as though to last for ever, and coloured like a Christmas card. . . . Good school for a seaman' (*CL*, ii. 35).

Duke of Sutherland, full-rigged wooden sailing ship of 1,047 gross tonnage, built 1865, owned by Daniel Louttit of Wick, Scotland.

Conrad, aged 20, signed on as ordinary seaman on 12 October 1878 at a monthly wage of one shilling. Under Captain John McKay and with a crew of 25, the *Duke of Sutherland* departed from *London on 15 October bound for *Australia via the Cape of Good Hope; she passed the Cape on 26 December, and arrived in Sydney on 31 January 1879. During her five-month stay in port, Conrad remained on board acting as night-watchman. She departed from Sydney on 5 July with a crew of 27, sailed via Cape Horn, and arrived back in London on 19 October after a one-year voyage. In *The Mirror of the Sea*, Conrad commented that the *Duke of Sutherland* belonged to a group of clippers that 'knew the road to the Antipodes better than their own skippers' (120). For a photograph of the ship, see Sherry 1972.

Europa, iron steamer of 676 gross tonnage, built 1862, owned by the London Steamship Company.

Conrad, aged 22, signed on as ordinary seaman on 11 December 1879 at a monthly wage of £3 5s. Under Captain Alexander Munro and with a crew of 21, the *Europa* departed from *London on 12 December for the Mediterranean, via Penzance. She passed through Dover on 14 December and called at *Genoa, Livorno, Naples, the Greek port of Patras, the island of Cephalonia, and the Sicilian ports of Messina and Palermo. The *Europa* returned to London on 30 January 1880, with Conrad signing off the same day and completing a seven-week voyage.

Loch Etive, full-rigged iron sailing ship of 1,287 gross tonnage, built 1877, owned by James Aitken of Glasgow.

Conrad, aged 22, signed on as third mate, his first berth as an officer, on 21 August 1880 at a monthly wage of £3 10s. Under Captain William Stuart and with a crew of 27, the *Loch Etive* departed from *London on 22 August bound for *Australia, crossed the equator (28 September), and arrived in Sydney on 24 November. Departing from Sydney on 11 January 1881, she arrived back in London on 25 April, completing an eight-month voyage. For photographs of the ship, see Allen; Visiak; and Sherry 1972.

Palestine, wooden barque of 427 gross tonnage, built 1857, owned by John Wilson of London.

Conrad, aged 23, signed on as second mate on 19 September 1881 at a monthly wage of £4. Under Captain Elijah Beard and with a crew of thirteen, the *Palestine* departed from *London on 21 September bound for *Bangkok. Stopping over at Gravesend until 1 October, she took almost three weeks to reach Newcastle after meeting violent gales (18 October) and remained there six weeks to load her cargo of coal. Departing from Newcastle on 29 November, the ship lost her sails and sprang a leak in the English Channel (24 December) and, with the crew refusing to continue, put back to Falmouth, where she underwent repairs for eight months. Conrad decided to stay with the ship as a way of accumulating service in preparation for his first mate's *examination. She departed from Falmouth for Bangkok with a new crew of twelve on 17 September 1882. Spontaneous combustion led to the ship's catching fire (12 March) and caused a coal-gas explosion (14 March), forcing the crew to abandon ship in Bangka Strait, off Sumatra. The crew took to boats and next day reached Muntok on Bangka Island. From there (21 March) they were taken in the SS *Sissie* to *Singapore, where, on 2 April, a marine court of inquiry exonerated the master, officers, and crew from all blame. Discharged on 3 April, after eighteen months of service, Conrad remained in Singapore until mid-April when he sailed home via the Suez Canal as a passenger. The *Palestine*'s erratic and ill-fated progress later formed the basis of the narrative in 'Youth', where the ship is renamed the *Judea*. For a photograph of the ship, see Visiak.

Riversdale, full-rigged sailing ship of 1,490 gross tonnage, built 1865, owned by L. H. McIntyre of Liverpool.

Conrad, aged 25, signed on as second mate on 10 September 1883 at a monthly wage of £5 5s. Under Captain Lawrence Brown McDonald and with a crew of 23, the *Riversdale* departed from *London on 13 September bound for India, stayed over in Port Elizabeth, South Africa (7 December–9 February), and arrived in Madras on 6 April 1884 after a seven-month voyage. Given a bad-conduct record by the captain (against which he later successfully appealed), Conrad was relieved of his position and officially discharged on 17 April. He travelled overland to Bombay and obtained a berth in the *Narcissus* there. See also Geoffrey Ursell, 'Conrad and the "Riversdale"', *Times Literary Supplement* (11 July 1968), 733–4.

Narcissus, full-rigged iron sailing ship of 1,336 gross tonnage, built 1876, owned by Robert R. Paterson & Company of Greenock, Scotland.

Conrad, aged 26, signed on as second mate in Bombay on 28 April 1884 at a monthly wage of £5. Under Captain Archibald Duncan and with a crew of 24, the *Narcissus*, later memorialized in the title of Conrad's early sea story, departed on 5 June for Dunkirk via the Cape of Good Hope. Joseph Barron, an able seaman and possibly an American Negro, died at sea on 24 September. Passing St Helena on 19 August, the *Narcissus* arrived in Dunkirk on 16 October, Conrad signing off the next day after service of five and a half months. For photographs and drawings of the ship, see Allen, and Najder's *JCC*. Further helpful information about the *Narcissus* can be found in 'Note on the Crew', *The Nigger of the 'Narcissus'*, ed. Allan Simmons, Everyman edition (Dent, 1997), 146–53.

Tilkhurst, full-rigged iron sailing ship of 1,570 gross tonnage, built 1877, owned by W. R. Price & Company of London.

Conrad, aged 27, signed on as second mate in Hull on 24 April 1885 at a monthly wage of £5. Under Captain Edwin John Blake and with a crew of 36, the *Tilkhurst* departed on 27 April for Indian ports, first stopping over at Penarth (13 May–10 June) to collect cargo, and arriving in *Singapore on 22 September. From there (19 October) she sailed for Calcutta, arriving on 19 November. Departing from Calcutta on her homeward passage on 12 January 1886, she sailed via St Helena and arrived in Dundee on 16 June after a fourteen-month voyage. For photographs of the ship, see Allen; Sherry 1972; and Karl, *JCTL*.

Falconhurst, full-rigged iron sailing ship of 1,997 gross tonnage, built 1883, owned by W. R. Price & Company of London.

Conrad, aged 29, signed on as second mate on 28 December 1886 at a wage of £5. Under Captain Richard Jones and with a crew of eighteen, the *Falconhurst* left *London on the same day for Penarth, where Conrad signed off on 2 January 1887 after five days of service. There he heard from his London agent of a vacant berth as chief mate in the *Highland Forest* and, not having signed up for a second voyage in the *Falconhurst*, returned to London in order to join the ship in *Amsterdam. See also Edmund A. Bojarski and Harold Ray Stevens, 'Joseph Conrad and the *Falconhurst*', *Journal of Modern Literature*, 1 (1969–70), 197–208.

Highland Forest, iron barque of 1,040 gross tonnage, built 1884, owned by Crane, Colvil & Company of Glasgow.

Conrad, aged 29, obtained a position in the temporarily captainless *Highland Forest* and supervised her loading in *Amsterdam in January 1887, before officially signing on as first mate on 16 February at a monthly wage of £7. Under Captain John McWhir and with a crew of 21, the *Highland Forest* departed Amsterdam for *Java on 18 February. On the voyage Conrad sustained a back injury, probably being hit by a falling spar. When the ship reached the Semarang roads (20 June), he was advised by a local doctor to go to *Singapore for treatment. He signed off on 1 July after a four-month voyage, sailed in the SS *Celestial* the next day, and arrived in Singapore on 6 July.

Vidar, iron screw steamer of 304 gross tonnage, built 1871, owned by Syed Mohsin bin Salleh Al Jooffree Steamship Company of Singapore.

Conrad, aged 29, signed on as first mate in *Singapore on or about 20 August 1887. Under Captain James Craig and with a crew of fifteen, the *Vidar* made four trading trips between Singapore and small *Netherlands East Indies ports on *Borneo and Celebes (present-day Sulawesi). Destinations included Banjarmasin, Pulau Laut, Donggala, Samarinda, Berau, and Bulungan, with the last two—on the east coast of Borneo—probably being main ports of call. The Malay settlement of Tanjung Redeb on the Berau River later provided the basis for the fictional *Sambir of Conrad's first two novels. He resigned his berth in Singapore on 4 January 1888 after four and a half months of service. For a drawing of the ship, see Allen.

Otago, iron barque of 367 gross tonnage, built 1869, owned by Henry Simpson & Sons of Adelaide.

Conrad, aged 30, was engaged as master of the *Otago*, his only permanent command, at a monthly wage of £14, in *Singapore on 19 January 1888. He joined the ship in *Bangkok on 24 January for her voyage to *Australia. Departure being delayed until 9 February, the ship with a crew of ten then took three weeks to reach Singapore, where she stopped over for fresh medical supplies and new crew members. Departing on 2 March with a crew of ten, she met heavy gales on the way south and did not arrive in Sydney until 7 May. The *Otago* departed from Sydney on 22 May for a round trip to Melbourne, where she remained for a month (6 June–7 July), arriving back in Sydney on 11 July. On 7 August, Conrad departed for *Mauritius, sailing via the Torres Strait, and arriving in Port Louis, Mauritius, on 30 September. After a seven-week stay, the *Otago* departed on 21 November for Melbourne, arriving there on 4 January 1889. Leaving Melbourne on 13 February on what was expected to be the first stage of a journey to Port Elizabeth in South Africa, the *Otago* proceeded to Minlacowie, South Australia (22 February–21 March). A change in the owners' plans then brought her back to Adelaide (26 March). At the end of March, Conrad decided to resign his command, and on 3 April sailed via the Suez Canal for Europe as a passenger in the SS *Nürnberg*, arriving back in England on 14 May. Events and experiences from Conrad's fourteen-month connection with the *Otago* provided the basis for *The Shadow-Line* and 'A Smile of Fortune' ('*Twixt Land and Sea*). For photographs of the ship, see Allen; *CEW*; Sherry 1972; and *JCC*. The rotting hulk of the ship is still moored on the Derwent River, outside Hobart, Tasmania. The *Otago*'s steering-wheel is in the possession of the Honourable Company of Master Mariners and held at their headquarters, HMS *Wellington* on the *Thames Embankment.

Roi des Belges, wood-burning steamer of 15 tons, built 1887, owned by the Société Anonyme Belge pour le Commerce du Haut-Congo of Brussels.

After being interviewed in late 1889 by Albert *Thys of the Société Anonyme Belge pour le Commerce du Haut-Congo, Conrad, aged 32, was finally appointed in *Brussels (29 April 1890) to take charge of the company's *Congo river steamer, the *Florida*, whose previous captain had been murdered by tribesmen. First disembarking in Africa on 12 June, Conrad eventually arrived at Kinchasa (2 August) to find that the *Florida* had been wrecked on 18 July. He left Kinchasa for the upriver passage to Stanley Falls on 3 August in the *Roi des Belges*, serving first as supernumerary under Captain Ludvig Rasmus Koch, and arrived there on 1 September. When Captain Koch fell ill, Conrad was appointed acting master (6 September) for part of the return passage from Stanley Falls to Kinchasa which began on or by 8 September. The *Roi des Belges* reached Kinchasa on 24 September, when Conrad terminated his seven-week connection with the ship. Over the next three months Conrad, suffering severe illness, made a slow journey back to the coast: on 23 October he was in Fumemba, on 27 October heading for Manyanga, and on 4 December reached Matadi, soon sailing from Boma back to Europe. Conrad's experiences in the *Roi des Belges* form part of his traumatic Congo

ordeal that subsequently demanded expression in 'Heart of Darkness' (*Youth*). For photographs of the ship, see *CWW*; Sherry 1972; *JCTL*; and *CL*, i.

Torrens, full-rigged composite passenger clipper of 1,334 gross tonnage, built 1875, owned by A. L. Elder & Company of London.

First voyage. Conrad, aged 33, signed on as first mate in *London on 19 November 1891 at a monthly wage of £8. Under Captain Walter Henry Cope and with a crew of 34 and five apprentices, the *Torrens* departed from London on 21 November bound for *Australia. She called at Plymouth to collect passengers (departing 25 November), reached Cape Finisterre on 10 December, and arrived in Adelaide on 28 February 1892. She departed from Adelaide on 10 April, calling at Capetown (18–30 June) and St Helena (14–18 July), arriving in London on 2 September, with Conrad signing off the next day after a voyage of almost ten months.

Second voyage. Conrad, aged 34, signed on as first mate in London on 22 October 1892 at a monthly salary of £8. Again under Captain Cope and with a crew of 34 and six apprentices, the *Torrens* departed on 25 October for Australia, called at Plymouth (29–31 October) to collect passengers, crossed the equator (4 December), and arrived in Adelaide on 28 January 1893. Departing from Adelaide on 23 March, she called at Capetown (18–21 May) and St Helena (7–12 June), and arrived in London on 26 July, with Conrad signing off on the 27th after a nine-month voyage. In 'The *Torrens*: A Personal Tribute' (*Last Essays*), Conrad remembered his own service in the ship. For photographs of the vessel, see Allen; Karl's *JCTL*; Najder's *JCC*; and *CL*, i. For a fuller factual record of Conrad's service in the *Torrens*, see Stape and van Marle 1995.

Adowa, iron steamer of 2,097 gross tonnage, built 1882, owned by Fenwick & Company of London.

Conrad, aged 35, was confirmed as second mate on 26 November 1893, joining the ship the following day. Chartered by the newly organized Franco-Canadian Transport Company to carry emigrants from France to Montreal and commanded by Captain Frederick Paton, the ship with a crew of 24 left *London on 1 December and arrived in Rouen on the River Seine on 4 December. She remained idle when the company's plans did not materialize. After a fruitless wait, the *Adowa* departed from Rouen on 10 January and arrived back in London two days later, with Conrad signing off on 17 January 1894, marking the end of his professional sea career. For a photograph of the ship, see *JCC*.

Shorter, Clement K[ing] (1859–1926), editor and bibliophile. Clement Shorter first entered Conrad's sphere in summer 1898 when, as editor of the *Illustrated London News*, he acquired the serial rights of *The Rescue* for his journal and held Conrad to an October 1898 deadline. Trapped in an unavailing struggle to finish the novel, Conrad could not meet Shorter's successive deadlines and eventually disappointed him altogether when he abandoned the novel in early 1899. In autumn 1916, Shorter reintroduced himself to Conrad and soon after proposed a profitable publishing scheme that involved bringing out a series of Conrad's miscellaneous shorter works in limited-edition *pamphlets of 25 copies, all signed by the author. Beginning with Conrad's play *One Day More*, Shorter published six pamphlets between 1917 and 1919. Conrad's separate negotiations with Thomas J. *Wise in 1918 for the publication of a second series of pamphlets may have left Shorter feeling unfairly treated, and it was he who informed the American collector John *Quinn that Conrad had reneged on his gentleman's agreement with Quinn and was selling his manuscripts and typescripts to Wise.

'Silence of the Sea, The'. This newspaper article was composed in early September 1909, some six weeks after the date of the event it comments on, the sudden capsizing in heavy seas of the *Waratah*, a new passenger and cargo ship of 9,339 tons, with the loss of 211 passengers two days after she had left Durban, South Africa, on 26 July 1909. At the time of Conrad's composition, the ship was still posted as 'overdue', so providing him with the occasion to meditate on the various dangers and cruel mysteries of the modern sea and to offer the consoling moral that until there was evidence about the ship's fate to the contrary 'we must never say die'. The article, published in the *Daily Mail* (18 September 1909), 4, is reprinted in *CDOUP*, 84–8. See Paul Kirschner, 'Conrad: An Uncollected Article', *Notes & Queries*, 213 (1968), 292–4.

Singapore. Between 1883 and 1888, Conrad as a sailor made several visits to Singapore. Founded as a European settlement in 1819 by Stamford Raffles, the city by Conrad's time had become the rapidly expanding capital of the Straits Settlements, with a population of over 175,000. His periods of residence in the city left rich and varied impressions for the later novelist. While there, he obviously made direct contact with the life of the large colonial metropolis and its bustling crowd of races, seamen, and local personalities. Through harbour gossip, informal anecdote, and local newspapers, he also picked up a good secondhand knowledge of Eastern maritime history—the widely reported *Jeddah* and *Cutty Sark* episodes, for example—and its well-known figures—such as William *Lingard and A. P. *Williams—who were assimilated into his fiction. Inevitably, then, Singapore is a recurrent presence in Conrad's Far Eastern stories as a large commercial port, a 'thoroughfare to the East' (*Lord Jim*, 12), and a colonial metropolis (for example, in *Almayer's Folly* it is the setting for Nina's initiation into 'Christian teaching, social education, and a good glimpse of civilized life' (42)). As a frequent locale in his Eastern fiction, Singapore 'strengthens the sense of authenticity and generates . . . the sense of a meta-narrative—a large imaginative territory, closely related to actuality, from which all the individual existent narratives seem to arise as selections' (Watts and Hampson, 355).

Referring to the city's more specific legacy, Sherry comments: 'Under the guise of "an Eastern port", Singapore is the scene of the action in many of his Eastern novels, or at least of parts of these novels' (*CEW*, 175). In *Lord Jim*, Singapore is the unnamed port where *Jim is hospitalized and the port of departure for the *Patna*, but it is *not* the location for the *Patna* inquiry, which is set in Bombay. Sherry also points out that the small portion of the city best known to Conrad was the Esplanade, 'the oldest part, the area about the sea-front with which any sailor would become acquainted', situated between two buildings, the Sailors' Home (just behind St Andrew's Cathedral) and the Harbour Office (on the east side of the Singapore River). This sea-front area as it existed in the 1880s is sketched with most intricate detail in the walk taken by Captain *Whalley at the beginning of 'The End of the Tether' (*Youth*), a story that also indicates Conrad's quite detailed knowledge of the city's colonial history. As J. H. Stape has pointed out, this work offers Conrad's most explicit political comment on late 19th-century colonial Singapore as shaped by European material interests and intrusive colonization, a 'new' city 'precariously balanced, emptied at its very core of meaningful connexion with the peoples inhabiting it and longing for a past it never experienced' ('Conrad's "Unreal City": Singapore in "The End of the Tether"', in Moore (ed.) 1992: 90). The opening section of *The Shadow-Line* draws upon details of Conrad's stay in Singapore in 1887–8 prior to his taking command of the *Otago* and finds the young narrator moving between the opposite poles of the Sailors' Home, with its 'tomb'-like atmosphere (9), and the Harbour Office, the setting for his recall to responsible maritime life. For further details of the presence of the city in Conrad's fiction and a map of central Singapore in the 1880s, see Sherry's chapter 'An Eastern Port: Singapore', *CEW*, 173–94. Hans van Marle's 'Jumble of Facts and Fiction: The First Singapore Reaction to *Almayer's Folly*', *Conradiana*, 10 (1978), 161–6, reprints two interesting Singapore responses to Conrad's first novel from the *Straits Times* (January 1896).

Sisters, The. After writing *Almayer's Folly* (1895) and *An Outcast of the Islands* (1896), Conrad commenced work on this novel in the autumn of 1895. He abandoned the 'cherished aspiration' (*CL*, i. 268) in the following spring in response to adverse comments from Edward *Garnett, who advised him to think of writing a tale of the sea. Not included in any of the *collected editions of Conrad's work, the fragment was first published in 1928 in the *Bookman* (New York) with an introductory essay by Ford Madox *Ford called 'Tiger, Tiger'. In the same year, Crosby Gaige (New York) also published a limited edition of *The Sisters* in book form. The first European edition of the fragment was published by Ugo Mursia (Milan) in 1968 together with Ford's essay, and in a bilingual facing-page edition as *The Sisters/Le sorelle* (1990), ed. Mario Curreli. The novella was included (without Ford's essay) in *CDOUP*, 45–70.

The seven chapters of *The Sisters* introduce two unconnected narrative strands. The first four chapters follow the fortunes of a young Ruthenian painter, Stephen, who leaves his homeland to travel through western Europe 'on his search for a creed', but finds 'only an infinity of formulas' (*CDOUP*, 45). Stephen's decision to become a painter thwarts the expectations of his father, who had hoped his son would become a government official. For his part, Stephen's father has risen to become 'a merchant of the first guild—a very rich man', while always remaining 'the peasant' (38, 40). With his parents dead, and leaving his brother to take over the family business, Stephen's share of the inheritance leaves him in very comfortable circumstances. Nonetheless, his European quest continues until, having become increasingly disillusioned, he sets up a studio in the courtyard of a house owned by an orange merchant named José Ortega, on the outskirts of Paris, in the district of Passy.

The second narrative, which occupies the last three chapters of the fragment, focuses upon Rita Ortega. After the deaths of their parents, Rita and her sister Theresa are looked after by their uncle, a fanatical priest who believes he is living in 'a world inhabited by damned souls' (61). As the marriage of their other uncle, José Ortega, is childless, Rita is sent from her village in the Basque country to Paris to be brought up by him and his wife as their daughter. When the sentimental José offers to take both sisters, the priest refuses, believing that Theresa 'had dispositions . . . a sacred spark that must be nursed into a flame' (63). Ortega's wife Dolores, described as 'a strange product of ignorance and shop-keeping instincts' (64), dominates her husband and, it is suggested, bullies Rita, describing her as an 'Unruly minx' (66–7). To counterbalance his wife's influence, Ortega arranges that Rita should spend part of her time with the Malagon family, where 'Rita, tamed under the heavy hand of Dolores, was softened by the peaceful influences of a commonplace and happy home' (67), and where she enjoys the 'fierce friendship' of Adéle Malagon. Rita's growing up is thus informed by the influences of two very different households. At this point, the fragment ends, but, as Stephen's studio is in a pavilion in the courtyard of the Ortega house, the two narrative strands were obviously destined to be connected.

According to Ford, the tale was to have been about incest: 'Stephen was to have met, fallen in love with and married the elder sister. The younger sister, failing in the religious vocation that her uncle the priest desired her to have was to come to Paris and to stay with the young couple in Stephen's pavilion, the tyrannous character of her aunt being such that she could not live with the orange merchant and his wife. The elder sister proving almost equally domineering Stephen was to fall before the gentler charm of the younger. And the story was to end with the slaying of both the resulting child and the mother by the fanatic priest' (quoted in *The Sisters/Le sorelle* (Milan: Mursia, 1990), 36, 38). Baines, who finds the fragment 'bizarrely stilted and lifeless', dismissed this outline on the grounds that, as Ford 'had not even noticed the similarities between *The Sisters* and *The Arrow of Gold* his comments are not worth much' (167, 168). Ford's notorious unreliability has led subsequent critics to take much the same view.

Several parallels between *The Sisters* and *The Arrow of Gold* (1919) suggest that the fragment acted as the seed for the later novel. These mainly involve the character of Rita in each work. For instance, both are born of peasant stock in the Basque country, which they leave for cosmopolitan sophistication, and both have a sister (Theresa/Therese) who is religious and an uncle who is a fanatical priest. Coincidentally, the interest in tracing possible autobiographical material relating to Conrad's days in *Marseilles in *The Arrow of Gold* extends to *The Sisters*. Noting that the action of *The Sisters* was to have taken place in Passy, where Conrad's 'aunt' Marguerite *Poradowska rented an apartment, Najder says: 'It may be only a coincidence, but one cannot help noticing that Conrad began writing *The Sisters* in autumn 1895, during the "discreet" stage of his relationship with Poradowska and before he proposed to Jessie—and then stopped writing it shortly before his marriage' (*JCC*, 183 n.).

Conrad sent the 39-page manuscript of *The Sisters* to John *Quinn on 18 July 1913, saying that it had been 'abandonned [*sic*] in despair of being able to keep up the high pitch . . . I think it would have been an impossible novel for the public—at the time' (*CL*, v. 255–6). Receiving £20 for the fragment, Conrad suggested that Quinn might publish it after his death 'as a literary curiosity—and the blessed critics will babble about it'. *The Sisters* was the single manuscript Quinn kept back from the auction of his Conradiana in 1923. Although, in this same letter to Quinn, Conrad calls *The Sisters* 'a novel which should have been about a painter', which suggests that Stephen was to have been its central character, in subsequent letters he refers to the fragment as *The Sisters* or *Thérèse*, indicating a slightly different focus for the work. The location of the manuscript is unknown; see Tom Schultheiss, 'The Search for "The Sisters": A Chronology of Ownership', *Conradiana*, 3: 1 (1970–1), 26, 50, 68, 90, 92). See also Najder, '*The Sisters*: A Grandiose Failure', in Curreli (ed.), 111–26.   AHS

'Smile of Fortune, A'. A novella of some 25,000 words, 'A Smile of Fortune' was written in the summer of 1910 and was the first work to emerge from Conrad's pen during his recovery from the nervous breakdown that followed the completion of *Under Western Eyes*. It was first published as a 'complete novel' in a single issue of the *London Magazine* in February 1911, and was reprinted, with the added subtitle of 'Harbour Story', as the first of three stories in *'Twixt Land and Sea* (1912).

The narrator of the tale is a young captain who has been instructed to use his own judgement in managing his ship's business. The owners have given him a letter of recommendation to a Mr Jacobus in 'Pearl of the Ocean', the harbour of a tropical island where he intends to load a cargo of sugar. No sooner does his ship arrive than he is visited by a merchant named Jacobus, who brings him breakfast on board and offers to provide him with various commodities and services. The visitor turns out to be Alfred Jacobus, the brother and business rival of Ernest Jacobus, the wealthy merchant to whom the captain had been recommended.

The captain gradually learns more and more about Alfred Jacobus, who is mysteriously shunned by the local population. Alfred's wealthy brother Ernest proves to be rude and arrogant, and unpleasantly abusive to a mulatto boy who is apparently his illegitimate son. This impression brings the captain closer to Alfred Jacobus, and when his voyage is threatened by a shortage of bags in which to load sugar, he accepts an invitation to visit Jacobus's home. There he encounters Alice, a mysteriously silent and isolated girl who is later identified as the illegitimate daughter of Jacobus and a 'circus-woman' (37).

Alice captivates the captain with her disdainful manners and her thick black hair, and he spends many evenings in her company in the fairy-tale atmosphere of a verandah overlooking a magnificent garden. The narrator finally overcomes her passivity and showers kisses on her, but the girl runs away and the narrator realizes that Jacobus has probably seen them. (A parallel scene occurs in 'Freya of the Seven Isles' when Heemskirk sees Freya kissing Jasper Allen.) A deal is struck whereby the captain will receive the sugar bags in return for accepting a cargo of potatoes. When Alice returns to find a slipper she lost in her retreat, the captain bids her farewell and seems oddly and suddenly disenchanted. In a final 'smile of fortune', the potatoes fetch a surprisingly high price upon delivery in *Australia.

Reviewers generally liked the story when it was first published in *'Twixt Land and Sea*, but academic critics have often found it frustrating and enigmatic; it has been compared with fairy tales and with *Shakespeare's *The Tempest*. Based on Conrad's own experiences in *Mauritius in 1888, the story examines the relations between business affairs and love affairs. In his psychoanalytic biography, Bernard C. Meyer (1967) traced the origins of the story to Conrad's relationship with Mlle Eugénie Renouf in Mauritius. Following Albert J. Guerard (1958: 51), critics have often understood the story as a demonstration of the corrupting influence of the land on a seaman who abhors trade. This aspect is explored by William Lafferty in 'Conrad's "A Smile of Fortune": The Moral Threat of Commerce', *Conradiana*, 7 (1975), 63–74. Conrad conveys the moral and social atmosphere of life in a remote island society that reacts in opposite ways to the illegitimate offspring of two brothers: Alfred Jacobus, the eager merchant who ruined himself for love of a circus performer, is forced to hide his daughter and live as a pariah in the same town where his wealthy brother is free to behave brutally to his own unacknowledged mulatto boy. The father–daughter theme bears comparison with *Almayer's Folly*, while the scenes between the captain and Alice anticipate the sedentary love affair depicted in *The Arrow of Gold*. The influence of Maupassant, in particular the resemblance of Conrad's Alice to Francesca from 'Les Sœurs Rondoli', has been noted by Paul Kirschner 1968: 220–9, and by Yves Hervouet 1990: 112–18.

'A Smile of Fortune' has never been filmed, although parts of it were incorporated into a French-German-Italian television version of *The Shadow-Line* made in 1972. The complete manuscript and typescript of the story are held at the Berg Collection, New York Public Library, and a partial typescript is at the Beinecke Rare Book and Manuscript Library, Yale University.

'Some Reflections on the Loss of the *Titanic*'.

In response to the century's most famous maritime disaster—the collision of the new and supposedly 'unsinkable' White Star liner *Titanic* with an iceberg in the North Atlantic and her dramatically swift sinking just after midnight on 15 April 1912, with the loss of over 1,500 lives—Conrad quickly planned an article in the form of a 'personal sort of pronouncement, thoughts, reminiscences and reflec[t]ions inspired by the event with a suggestion or two' (*CL*, v. 56). After unsuccessfully negotiating with *Nash's Magazine* and the *American*, Conrad offered to write a piece on the disaster for the *English Review*, whose editor, Austin Harrison, responded favourably. Much of the composition took place on the night of 24–5 April. The essay was published in the *English Review*, 11 (May 1912), 304–15, and was later revised for inclusion in *Notes on Life and Letters*.

Distressed by the catastrophe, the 'good press' given to it, and the 'Bumble-like proceedings' (213, 214) of the United States Senate Inquiry that had begun on 19 April, Conrad seems to have felt an unusually urgent need to unburden his feelings in print. In contrast to the sensationalist media exploitation of the event as an occasion for promulgating popular myths and defending vested interests, Conrad's polemic derives its sombre power from his detached position as a conservative seaman-historian. His is a distinctively personal and human voice speaking on behalf of dead brother-seamen who, betrayed by the so-called 'unsinkable' *Titanic* and forgotten in the media's 'babble', have no voice of their own: 'Thus they are gone, and the responsibility remains with the living who will have no difficulty in replacing them by others, just as good, at the same wages'

(224–5). As J. H. Stape has shown, the motifs of collision and historical loss inform the essay's rhetoric more generally and help to explain its structure of colliding oppositions: 'The modern era—represented by journalistic opportunism, the quest for speed, an emphasis on the commercial and mechanical, and impersonality—confronts what Conrad delineates as a code of values inherited from the past, a life regulated by and dependent upon devotion to a traditional and exacting craft with an emphasis on individual effort and respect for community. . . . The central opposition is between two kinds of faith: that in the material world opposed to one that, in Conradian terms, is just as real and significant but intangible and complex' (1988: 63, 64). Such rhetoric also allows for a number of tonal variations, ranging from acerbic satire of fatuous modern 'sea-leviathans' (228) to simple elegy for traditions of seamanship now gone for good. The loss of the *Titanic* involved Conrad in a personal way also, since the manuscript of his short story 'Karain: A Memory' (*Tales of Unrest*), bound for John *Quinn, the American collector, went down with the ship. For details of Conrad's second *Titanic* essay, see 'Certain Aspects of the Admirable Inquiry into the Loss of the *Titanic*'. The manuscript was destroyed by the printers after setting.

Spanish-American War.

This short-lived war of 1898, together with other instances of *Weltpolitik* in turn-of-the-century Central and South America, attracted Conrad's continued interest and may well have prompted his turning towards a South American subject in *Nostromo* in 1902 and helped to shape the novel's final character. The war resulted in Spain's losing the final remnants of its colonial empire—Cuba, Puerto Rico, and the Philippines—to the United States. If these international events signalled the unambiguous eclipse of Spain as an imperial power, they also marked the emergence of the United States as an expansionist force. The issues raised by international events in 1898 recur in *letters between Conrad and

R. B. Cunninghame *Graham, whose *Saturday Review* articles (1898–1901) on the war and its significance were known to Conrad, who seems to share Graham's critical attitude towards the United States: 'If one could set the States & Germany by the ears! That would be *real fine*. I am afraid however that the thieves shall agree in the Philip[p]ines. The pity of it! Viva l'España! Anyhow' (*CL*, ii. 81). Another dramatic instance of American expansionism in Central America occurred while *Nostromo* was being written. In November 1903, the United States intervened with military support in Panama to lend weight to Panama's secession from Colombia. The Hay–Bunau–Herrán Treaty of that month ensured the future construction of the Panama Canal and also gave the United States control over a 10-mile (16 km) Canal Zone and the right to intervene anywhere else in the new republic. In the following month, Conrad asked Graham what he thought of 'the Yankee Conquistadores in Panama', adding, 'Pretty, isn't it' (*CL*, iii. 102). Almost simultaneously, Conrad's interest in events in Panama was strengthened by his contacts with Santiago Pérez Triana, Colombian Envoy Extraordinary in London and Madrid and a partial model for Don José Avellanos in *Nostromo*, whose view of the ill effects of foreign 'highway robbers and land thieves' in South America (*LCG*, 207) may have encouraged Conrad to develop wider political themes in the novel.

Conrad's representation of *Costaguana testifies both to the waning influence of the Spanish in South America and to the emergence of a new capitalist dynamic with its origins in the United States. The crucial turning point in the country's contemporary history arrives when Charles *Gould makes an alliance with a San Francisco magnate, Holroyd. Although he appears only briefly, Holroyd, a 'great personage' (79), is evoked as a symptomatic national type. The product of many composite influences, an uncritical servant to the belief that the United States is 'the greatest country in the whole of God's Universe' (77), and a patron of the 'purer forms of

Christianity' (80), he speaks in the tones of an acolyte in the service of a high, impersonal mission: 'We shall be giving the word for everything: industry, trade, law, journalism, art, politics, and religion, from Cape Horn clear over to Smith's Sound, and beyond, too, if anything worth taking hold of turns up at the North Pole. . . . We shall run the world's business whether the world likes it or not. The world can't help it—and neither can we, I guess' (77). Through Holroyd, who regards 'his own God as a sort of influential partner' (71) and Costaguana as a plaything, Conrad diagnoses a new aggressive Americanism associated with a form of global capitalism irresistible in its force and amoral in character. Unsurprisingly, at the end of the novel, the birth of a more modern phase in *Sulaco's history is signalled when 'an international naval demonstration . . . put an end to the Costaguana–Sulaco War . . . [and] the United States cruiser, *Powhattan*, was the first to salute the Occidental flag' (487). See Watts's 'A Note on the Background to "Nostromo"', in *LCG*, 37–42, and Spittles, 91–104.

speeches and readings. A constitutional nervousness about formal public speaking led Conrad to decline almost all invitations that involved him in addressing large audiences. The exceptions occurred in the last five years of his life. He gave his first public speech in Liverpool on 16 December 1919 at a University Club gathering in honour of the *British Merchant Service, with David *Bone there to give support. According to Bone, he 'spoke of the resolute character of seamen with whom he had sailed in his sea days under square sail' (154). On 17 April 1923, he also delivered a brief congratulatory speech (reprinted in *CDOUP*, 109–12) at the 99th annual meeting of the Royal National Life-Boat Institution of Great Britain at the Aeolian Hall, *London.

More public speaking was required of Conrad on his 1923 visit to *America, organized by his American publisher F. N. *Doubleday. Before leaving, he prepared a series of notes that would act as the basis for two talks, one to 'fellow' employees at the Doubleday, Page headquarters in Garden City, New York, on 5 May 1923, dealing with his long-standing association with the firm. The second part no doubt provided the basis for Conrad's introduction to his reading of the chapter describing *Lena's death in *Victory* to an audience of some 200 people at the Manhattan home of Mrs Curtiss James on 10 May. Entitled 'Author and Cinematograph', this second section was, as he said in a letter to Eric *Pinker, intended to show that 'the imaginative literary art being based fundamentally on scenic motion, [is] like a cinema; with this addition that for certain purposes the artist is a much more subtle and complicated machine than a camera, and with a wider range, if in the visual effects less precise' (*LL*, ii. 302). Although Conrad had earlier, in 1920, professed a dislike for the 'cinematograph'—'The Movie is just a silly stunt for silly people' (*CTF*, 114)—his American speech shows his growing receptiveness to cinematography and its power to create 'moving' images; perhaps he chose to read from *Victory* because it had already been adapted both for the stage and silent screen (see FILMS). While Conrad deemed the evening at Mrs Curtiss James's home a brilliant success, Doubleday, who introduced the proceedings, thought differently, feeling that 'the occasion nearly killed him [Conrad], because of his extreme nervousness' ('Joseph Conrad as a Friend', *World Today*, 52 (July 1928), 147). Conrad's handwritten notes for this talk are held at the Lilly Library, Indiana University. The text of 'Author and Cinematograph' is transcribed in Arnold T. Schwab, 'Conrad's American Speeches and his Reading from *Victory*', *Modern Philology*, 62 (1965), 342–7.

Stein, a 'wealthy and respected merchant' (202), appears only twice in the dramatic action of *Lord Jim*, but, as a resonant oracular 'voice', is crucially significant in the development of its themes and meanings. Modelled partly on the naturalist Alfred Russel *Wallace, a scientific collector of butterflies and beetles in the Malay Archipelago, and partly on a German-born collector of tropical species for the Leiden Museum, a Dr Bernstein whom Wallace encountered in his travels, Stein may also owe something to Conrad's reading of *Goethe. Sherry suggests in *CEW*, that the character's name derives from Dr Bernstein's. Critics have noted that *Stein* means 'stone' or 'rock' in German.

Stein serves various significant functions and acts to counterbalance the views of *Jim offered by other characters who witness or comment upon his personality and destiny. At once an archetypal Old Wise Man and father confessor to whom *Marlow goes for advice about an intractable problem, Stein is also a chastened figure whose full experience of vicissitude complements the over-exuberant youthfulness of Jim. He is also by turns an artist-priest engaged in a lifelong commitment to order and meaningful coherence, a scientist in quest of ever-elusive truths, an idealist whose adventures, failures, and missed opportunities have taught him the full value as well as the limitations of the practical, and a vicarious father-figure offering to an errant child unquestioning affection and hard-won understanding.

Stein's life-experience of adventure and love, of failure and disappointment, is mirrored and paralleled by Jim's, and thus offers crucial, and sometimes distancing, perspectives on Jim's situation. Frustrated by the defeat of the revolutionary movement of 1848 in his native Bavaria, Stein is forced to become a wanderer and expatriate before he eventually takes up residence in Semarang, at the time of the novel a major port on the *Java Sea, where he earns his livelihood in various mainly unspecified but not particularly romantic trading activities. (That Cornelius, the beetle, serves as his agent suggests his own compromise with the ways of the world.) Before settling into this mode of life, Stein had taken to himself a native wife and befriended a high-ranking Malay, both of whom die as victims of a struggle for power and wealth. The outlines of the romantic episodes of Stein's life are, with variations, repeated in Jim's own. Stein and

Jim also share a capacity and deep need for the exercise of imagination. Stein gives vent to this in his scientific work, which gives him intense aesthetic pleasure as well as fame in the small circles that value the expansion of human knowledge, whereas Jim applies his abilities to the reform of *Patusan.

The placement of the Stein chapter, chapter 20, at roughly the centre of the novel, gives it, in the view of some critics, a uniquely privileged and even symbolic position. As the history of the novel's writing establishes, however, the chapter's centrality is a fortuitous accident. At a number of stages in composition, and even at a very advanced point in it, Conrad predicted a conclusion only to defer it. However great Stein's role in arranging Jim's practical problems by sending him as his agent to Patusan, his oracular pronouncements on Jim's case are carefully and subtly qualified by light imagery at the very moment he makes them, and by the growing insubstantiality of his physical presence. Like those of other judges of Jim's case—the French Lieutenant, for instance—Stein's is a partial view based upon fragmentary and second-hand knowledge. His diagnosis of Jim as a Romantic is, as Marlow realizes, as much a self-diagnosis as a pronouncement upon an individual whom, at that point, he 'sees' only through Marlow's perspective. Hedged by careful qualification, not least the Chinese-box method of narration, Stein's vatic judgement and ambiguous and syntactically tortured statement 'In the destructive element immerse' (214) have tempted more than one unwary reader to settle upon him as a fixed and unerringly reliable means for evaluating Jim. By contrast, the symbolic play of light imagery against the backdrop of dead things, classified and meticulously ordered, point to yet another turn of the kaleidoscope in which Jim can be fleetingly viewed. The close parallels between Stein and Jim add signal interest to this perspective, but the workings of the novel as a whole also indicate that no single view adequately accounts for the variety and depths of even so 'simple' an individual as Jim.

Conrad's introduction of the Hamlet–Jim analogy through Stein is not incidental. While this may partly reflect mid- and late 19th-century Germanic bardolatry that led German scholars to speak of 'our *Shakespeare', it more importantly establishes a prism through which Stein views Jim's case as that of a young man for whom reality itself is deficient, and who is thereby fated to die in his confrontation with it. Stein is also significantly connected with Jim in death, both through the talismanic ring (the very emblem of a friendship bridging the large, if ultimately arbitrary, difference of race) he entrusts to him that leads to his death, and through Stein's realization at the novel's close that his own departure from life cannot be long delayed. This final poignant insight permits Conrad to complete a range of mythic references (including the *senex/puer* archetype): the death of the hero necessarily engenders, as classical tragedy witnesses, the deaths of others in a symbolic cataclysm that presages the end of the world.

Tanner's discussion of Stein and the symbolic role of his collection of butterflies and beetles remains essential reading, especially 39–44. Paul Kirschner, in 'Conrad, Goethe and Stein: The Romantic Fate in *Lord Jim*', *Ariel: A Review of International English Literature*, 10 (1979), 65–81, suggestively places Stein in the context of German Romanticism. Richard C. Stevenson provides a valuable close reading of the novel's most significant crux and its surrounding critical debate in 'Stein's Prescription for "How to be" and the Problem of Assessing Lord Jim's Career', *Conradiana*, 7 (1975), 223–43.   JHS

'Stephen Crane'. The last and longest of Conrad's three articles on Stephen *Crane was written in March 1923 as a preface to Thomas Beer's biography *Stephen Crane: A Study in American Letters* (New York: Knopf, 1923). It was collected in *Last Essays*. Encouraged by Edward *Garnett to cooperate with Beer, Conrad recalls with affectionate detail his first memorable meeting in *London with the American writer, their early sense of artistic affinity (see IMPRESSIONISM), desultory plans to collaborate on a play, and their close but brief friendship during the period 1897–1900. Garnett, an early champion of Crane's work, also figures prominently in the reminiscence, with Conrad quoting approvingly from his 1898 *Academy* article on Crane. The manuscript, dated 23 March 1923, is held at the University of Virginia; the revised typescript and galley proofs are held at Yale University's Sterling Memorial Library. See also 'STEPHEN CRANE: A NOTE WITHOUT DATES' and 'HIS WAR BOOK'.

'Stephen Crane: A Note without Dates'. Written at the invitation of Peter F. Somerville for publication in the *Englishman*, this short essay was completed sometime before 30 September 1919. When Somerville's plans to revive his wartime journal fell through, Conrad instructed his agent J. B. *Pinker to send it to J. C. Squire, who in August had invited a contribution for his new periodical. The essay was first published in *London Mercury*, 1 (December 1919), 192–3, and collected in *Notes on Life and Letters*. Written almost twenty years after *Crane's death, the first of Conrad's three essays on his erstwhile friend conveys warm appreciation of Crane as man and writer, although with some surprisingly severe reservations: Conrad mentions an 'ignorance of the world at large' that did not obstruct Crane's imaginative grasp of facts, comments that his death 'was a great loss to his friends, but perhaps not so much to literature', and refers to a possible weakness of character that prevented Crane from freeing himself from a retinue of 'worthless' admirers and caused Conrad a good deal of 'secret irritation' on his visits to see him (50–1). Two corrected and revised typescripts of the essay survive (Beinecke Rare Book and Manuscript Library, Yale University, and the Harry Ransom Humanities Research Center, University of Texas at Austin). See also 'STEPHEN CRANE' and 'HIS WAR BOOK'.

Stevenson, Robert Louis [Balfour] (1850–94), Scottish novelist and essayist. R. L. Stevenson had an enormous popular following at the time of his death, one year

before the publication of Conrad's first novel, *Almayer's Folly*. Conrad was invariably touchy about Stevenson, no doubt envying the size of his audience, but also resentful that he was constantly linked by reviewers with Stevenson as an exotic 'romance-writer', and decidedly angry when his agent J. B. *Pinker held up Stevenson as the model of an agent's dream-client, a 'literary' man who was also a commercial and popular success. On one occasion, Conrad responded grandly: 'I am no sort of airy R. L. Stevenson who considered his art a prostitute and the artist as no better than one' (*CL*, ii. 371).

Conrad's reaction against the tradition of 'naïve' romance that Stevenson's early works helped to sponsor may be discerned in his very earliest Malay fictions. Here, in modifying, complicating, and demystifying the materials of the exotic adventure novel, his work seems excitingly disobedient in producing what has been called 'a fiction of reversals': 'That fiction would be about the failure of action to relieve mental anguish, the devastating isolation of the hero, the corruption of heroism for political purposes, and the puniness of human action when set against the mindless immensity of nature' (Hunter 1982: 128). However, Stevenson's late works—*The Wrecker* (1892), *The Beach at Falesá* (1893), and *The Ebb-Tide* (1894)—combine romance elements unusually with a developing psychological intensity, an interest in lawless European and American outcasts who create havoc in the South Pacific islands, and a growing political awareness of colonial exploitation. These late works may have attracted Conrad and exerted a considerable influence on *Lord Jim* and *Victory*. Hence a contemporary *Pall Mall Gazette* reviewer of *Lord Jim* could ask pertinently: 'When Jim, the burly German Captain, and his two engineers come up from the sea . . . we are faintly conscious of some old familiar acquaintances. Is it out of *The Wrecker* that these people have strayed; or is it, perhaps, *The Ebb-Tide* that has been brought to our recollection?' (*CCH*, 122). For responses to this and other questions about the Conrad–Stevenson relationship, see Batchelor (1988: 29–31), Cedric Watts, 'The Ebb-Tide and Victory', Conradiana, 28 (1996), 133–7, and Hugh Epstein, 'Victory's Marionettes: Conrad's Revisitation of Stevenson', in Carabine et al. (eds.) 1998: 97–112.

Stevie, Winnie *Verloc's brother in The Secret Agent, is inadvertently blown up by the bomb that Adolf *Verloc gives him to place against the walls of *Greenwich Observatory. A hypersensitive and 'peculiar' youth, Stevie's radical innocence serves to expose the blindness and folly of the other characters in the novel. His naïve goodness is most fully displayed during the famous cab-ride in Chapter 8, when his pity for the driver's horse leads him to conclude that it's a 'Bad world for poor people' (171). Verloc generally ignores Stevie's existence and never realizes that his wife Winnie married him only to provide a home for her beloved brother, who is incapable of taking care of himself. Tom Ossipon, who prides himself on his knowledge of science, sees Stevie as a classic 'degenerate' (and remains unaware that his own physiognomy is that of *Lombroso's criminal type). Stevie's 'Lombrosan' characteristics are discussed by Martin Ray in 'Conrad, Nordau, and Other Degenerates: The Psychology of The Secret Agent', Conradiana, 16 (1984), 125–40. Stevie gives the impression of being quite young, and was portrayed in Hitchcock's film Sabotage as a cheerful and heedless boy; but Aaron Fogel (147, 270 n. 3) has observed that Stevie must be at least 21 years old, since he sets off some rockets and catherine wheels at the age of 14, before Winnie's engagement to Verloc, and the Verlocs have been married for seven years by the time of the bomb plot. His historical prototype, Martial Bourdin, who blew himself up near Greenwich Observatory on 15 February 1894, was described as about 30 years old, and may also have been the dupe of his brother-in-law (see CWW, 228–47). Like the other characters in the novel, Stevie is also a 'secret agent', albeit unwittingly, not only because he carries the bomb for Verloc but also because Winnie married Verloc only as a way of providing for him.

study centres. See JOURNALS, ORGANIZATIONS, AND STUDY CENTRES.

suicide. During the 1950s the emergence of certain items of Tadeusz *Bobrowski's correspondence to a Polish friend, Stefan Buszczyński—notably his letter of March 1879 (CPB, 175–9)—revealed a startling fact hidden from previous biographers: that in early March 1878, Bobrowski was called to *Marseilles because his 20-year-old nephew had attempted 'to take his life with a revolver'. He added: 'Let this detail remain between us, as I have been telling everyone that he was wounded in a duel' (177). Conrad himself sustained this wounding-by-duel version of events in his later semi-fictional depiction of his Marseilles years in The Mirror of the Sea and The Arrow of Gold. It also seems to have been the version he communicated to his wife, sons, and closest friends.

Bobrowski's more prosaic account suggests that after difficulties concerning his status in French ships, financial setbacks over a proposed smuggling expedition, and an indiscreet gambling episode in Monte Carlo, the errant young man returned to Marseilles virtually penniless and, while awaiting one of his creditors, attempted suicide by shooting himself in the chest, although without serious injury. 'Suicide', Conrad later wrote in Chance, 'is very often the outcome of mere mental weariness— not an act of savage energy but the final symptom of complete collapse' (183). On arriving in Marseilles, Bobrowski found his nephew out of bed and mobile, and spent a fortnight settling his debts: he was, after all, 'not a bad boy, only one who is extremely sensitive, conceited, reserved, and in addition excitable' (CPB, 177). Shadowy though the details are, they seem to indicate that Conrad's suicide attempt was essentially a desperate plea for attention and help rather than a serious attempt to end his life, as may be obliquely confirmed by a comment to Marguerite *Poradowska of December 1894: 'One talks . . . but then one lacks the courage. There are those who talk like that of suicide. And then there is always something lacking, sometimes strength, sometimes perseverance, sometimes courage.... What remains always cruel and ineradicable is the fear of finality. One temporizes with Fate, one seeks to deceive desire, one tries to play tricks with one's life. Men are always cowards. They are frightened of the expression "nevermore"' (*CL*, i. 191).

Numerous critics have pointed to the frequency and importance of suicide and variant forms of self-destruction in Conrad's fiction. While *The Sisters* refers to suicide as 'the unpardonable crime' (53)—that is, a mortal sin according to Roman Catholic theology—other novels suggest a powerful wish to defend or justify the act as a legitimate response to unbearable life, or a positive act of self-sacrifice, or as the outcome of 'bewildered thinking which makes the idea of non-existence welcome so often to the young' (*Chance*, 183). Jeffrey Berman's *Joseph Conrad: Writing as Rescue* (New York: Astra Books, 1977) considers the omnipresence of the self-destructive urge in Conrad's fiction and develops in largely Freudian terms a view of his art as both cathartic and, eventually, liberating in allowing the writer to displace negative urges onto a fictional surrogate in order to effect a psychic 'rescue'. There are absorbing discussions of Lord *Jim, Martin *Decoud, *Razumov, and Axel *Heyst as offering mechanisms for self-rescue in the context of the underlying paradox that, whatever the perils involved for Conrad, 'nothing more fully liberated his creative powers nor more effectively sustained his private and professional life than the subject of self-destruction' (25). Ray 1984 offers a helpful study of Decoud's suicide in *Nostromo* and its place in the Conradian ordeal of creativity, while in 'Measures of the Heart and of the Darkness: Conrad and the Suicides of "New Imperialism"', *Conradiana*, 14 (1982), 189–98, Todd G. Willy makes fruitful use of perspectives drawn from Émile Durkheim's *Suicide: A Study in Sociology* (1897) to examine the presentation of acts of suicide in Conrad's late Victorian imperial fiction.

Sulaco. The main setting for events in *Nostromo*, Sulaco is the chief port and town in an imaginary South American province of the same name, a province which by the end of the novel has seceded from the Republic of *Costaguana and reconstituted itself as the Occidental Republic of Sulaco. The location of Sulaco corresponds roughly to a part of the Pacific seaboard near the present border of Ecuador and Colombia, although Conrad may have taken the place name from the port of Sulaco in Honduras.

A vivid panoramic view of the town's harbour and its coastal setting emerges vividly in the novel's opening chapter. Thereafter, brief impressionistic vignettes gradually give a more detailed and coherent picture of Sulaco's urban design, which, as Jacques Berthoud points out, corresponds to the rectilinear design of the prototypical Hispanic-American city ('The Modernization of Sulaco', in Moore (ed.) 1992: 147–8). Sulaco consists of a vast central square—the Plaza Mayor ('Twice the area of Trafalgar Square' (476))—with its large fountain and statue of Charles IV of Spain. The square is bisected on its northerly side by a long avenue leading to the harbour, the Calle de la Constitución, on which can be found the Casa *Gould and the Casa Avellanos. Leading off from its southerly end, another avenue runs to the town's land gate and then to the San Tomé mine. Around the square are clustered most of the buildings that provide the novel's recurring locations—the Amarilla Club, the *Porvenir* newspaper office, Anzani's stores, the Cathedral, the Intendencia, and the Cabildo. If the early Sulaco acts as an evocative indicator of an early formative phase of Spanish colonization, then the changed town produced by a later phase of history speaks of the waning or erasure of the Spanish and the birth of a more modern phase of colonial history coinciding with the influence of Anglo-American capitalism. The town's changing architecture, with its erasures, added formations, and transformations, thus serves the reader as a guide to the recent geopolitical bearings of the republic. Captain *Mitchell's description in Part III, chapter 10 reveals that the colonnaded part of the town's square has been burned down, the statue of Charles IV demolished (possibly to be replaced by 'a marble shaft commemorative of Separation, with angels of peace at the four corners, and bronze Justice holding an even balance, all gilt, on the top' (482)), and Spanish buildings replaced by new ones—two American bars, the Sulaco National Bank, old properties taken over by the railway company, and a new and enlarged Ocean Steamship Navigation headquarters. As Berthoud notes, during this more modern phase, the disappearing vestiges of Spanish architectural influence have themselves become objects of historical nostalgia to some of the characters. For useful maps of Sulaco, see Watts 1993: 174–5.

Suspense. This novel of historical intrigue is set in *Genoa in 1815, just before *Napoleon's return from Elba for the Hundred Days that ended at Waterloo. Nearly 81,000 words in length, it is commonly described as Conrad's 'last, unfinished' novel, and generally ignored in Conrad studies or disparaged as a derivative fragment. Conrad began work on this long-promised 'Mediterranean novel' with a visit to the British Museum in June 1920 to consult memoirs of Napoleon on Elba. With Parts I and II drafted, work was interrupted by the sudden death of Conrad's agent J. B. *Pinker in New York in February 1922; and it was then set aside for the sake of Conrad's other Napoleonic novel, *The Rover*. Conrad frequently mentioned plans for *serialization, but the novel remained unpublished at the time of his death in August 1924. In the posthumous division of editorial labour that followed Conrad's death, his friend and co-executor Richard *Curle assumed responsibility for the publication of *Suspense*. He purchased the typescript 'scraps' left in Conrad's possession from Thomas J. *Wise, who had bought the 'first draft' of the novel in advance, and prepared the novel for print. Curle said later: 'I felt that I had to bring it out as it was, with scarcely an alteration from the written text' (*LTY*, 108).

Five different editions of *Suspense* appeared in 1925: an English serialization in

Hutchinson's Magazine (February–August); an American serial version in the *Saturday Review of Literature* (27 June–12 September); the first American edition, titled *Suspense: A Napoleonic Novel*, by Doubleday, Page on 15 September; the first English edition by J. M. Dent & Sons on 16 September; and finally in October a 'copyright edition' printed and published by Bernhard Tauchnitz in Leipzig.

References to the project of a 'Mediterranean' novel appear in Conrad's correspondence as early as 1902 (*CL*, ii. 423), although the plot and setting were not immediately clear to him. In 1905 Conrad wrote to Pinker from Capri to report that his novel would treat 'the struggle for Capri in 1808 between the French and the English' (*CL*, iii. 219). He again wrote to Pinker from *Montpellier in 1907 to say that he had discovered in the atmosphere surrounding Napoleon's exile on Elba 'a theme for a Mediterranean novel with historical interest, intrigue and adventure' but still needed to find its 'moral pivot' (*CL*, iii. 409). By 1911 he was hoping to begin work on the novel as soon as he finished *Chance*. The following year he told Pinker: 'I have the *story* itself. The question is of the setting. I hesitate between the occupation of Toulon by the fleet—the Siege of Genoa—or Napoleon's escape from Elba' (*CL*, v. 10). By May 1912, he seemed to have decided on Elba, but was uncertain whether to tell the story in the first or third person (*CL*, v. 64). Eventually Toulon would find its way into *The Rover*, and Conrad combined the other two options in *Suspense*, placing the novel in Genoa in the nervous days just before Napoleon's return from Elba on 26 February 1815. By the autumn of 1912 Conrad was daydreaming of a return to the Mediterranean and of having it ready for publication by 1914, in time for the centenary of Napoleon's exile (*CL*, v. 120). He planned to spend 1913 at work on it, but *Victory* proved difficult to complete. Visiting *Poland with his family in the summer of 1914, Conrad was caught 'behind enemy lines' when the *First World War erupted in August, and the complications of his return to England forced him to spend an unscheduled ten days in Vienna and a few days in the last half of October in Milan and Genoa. This unplanned visit to Genoa may also have contributed details to the 'Mediterranean novel', although no references to the project appear in Conrad's correspondence until 1918.

The memoirs of the Comtesse de Boigne (1781–1866), published in 1907 in French and in English, finally provided Conrad with the 'moral pivot' he needed for his 'Mediterranean novel'. In effect, Conrad took the Comtesse de Boigne as a model for his own heroine, changing her name slightly from Adèle d'Armand to Adèle d'Osmond and incorporating details of her background and her encounters with Napoleon literally into his own work. She was in Genoa at the moment of Napoleon's 'escape' from Elba, and although this particular episode is mentioned only briefly in her memoirs, it provided Conrad with the setting and situation he needed. Conrad has been accused of plagiarizing her work, but one could argue that the settings and circumstances adapted from her memoirs for the sake of historical authenticity are ultimately far less important than the fictional and imaginary elements with which he elaborated and developed her story, altering her family circumstances (her husband was not in Genoa, for example) and introducing new characters and an entirely original plot. Curiously, Conrad's *'borrowings' from the Comtesse de Boigne follow the language of the English translation so closely as to suggest that he had that version at hand (see Hans van Marle and Gene M. Moore, 'The Sources of Conrad's *Suspense*', in Moore *et al.* (eds.) 1997: 141–63.

The story of *Suspense* follows the actions of Cosmo Latham, a young English veteran of the Peninsular War who takes advantage of Napoleon's exile on Elba to make a grand tour of previously inaccessible parts of the Continent. On his first day as a tourist in Genoa, a city under Austrian occupation, Cosmo strolls down to the harbour at sunset and follows an interesting stranger (Attilio) to a tower at the end of the Molo Vecchio. The stranger encourages

him to leave, but Cosmo stubbornly remains and eventually helps him to transmit secret documents to boatmen waiting below at the foot of the tower. Back in his inn, Cosmo is informed of the tense political situation by his worried valet, Spire. Cosmo has been asked by his father, Sir Charles Latham, to present his greetings to the Marquis d'Osmond, who had sought refuge from the French Revolution with his daughter at the Lathams' country estate in Yorkshire. The Marquis d'Osmond is now the restored French monarchy's ambassador to the Kingdom of Sardinia. He lives in the Palazzo Rosso (also called the Palazzo Brignoli) with his daughter Adèle, who had agreed to marry the Comte Helion de Montevesso during their exile in *London in order to secure the welfare of her parents.

Cosmo visits the Palazzo Rosso the following day, and has a long conversation with Adèle. He is invited to return that evening, when he meets Adèle's charming father and her unpleasant husband, as well as a strangely intense Italian girl named Clelia. Cosmo learns that the social life of Genoa is overshadowed by the suspense attending the results of the Congress of Vienna and troubled especially by the looming and restless presence of Napoleon on nearby Elba. The next morning, Cosmo meets another Englishman at his hotel, Dr Martel, who senses that Cosmo may be in some danger from the easily jealous Montevesso. Cosmo spends that afternoon writing a letter to his sister Henrietta, and realizes that his meeting with Adèle has deprived him of all desire to travel. At supper Dr Martel warns him to leave Genoa. Back in his room, he thinks of Adèle as 'the awed recollection of a prophetic vision' (195), and a strangely intense vision of a woman with a dagger in her breast drives him out into the streets. The following morning, Dr Martel becomes worried about Cosmo's disappearance, and makes enquiries at the Palazzo Rosso. In the fourth and final part of the novel, we learn that Cosmo, retracing the path he had taken in the opening chapter, returns to the harbour and becomes caught up in the dramatic efforts of the courier Attilio to escape capture by the police. Cosmo is himself captured, but is then freed with Attilio's help. They make good their escape thanks to an old boatman who rows them to their rendezvous with a ship apparently bound for Elba, although the effort costs the old boatman his life.

The surviving documents show that Conrad wrote the novel chronologically, but that at some point he reversed the order of the final two chapters. The novel thus ends with a complete chapter, and the last chapter on which Conrad was working was Part III, chapter 3, the penultimate 'morning-after' chapter (chronologically the last) which describes the reactions of others to Cosmo's disappearance.

When it first appeared, *Suspense* was heavily publicized as an unfinished fragment, and the elegies and tributes that had followed Conrad's death the previous summer were repeated in reviews lamenting that the great author did not live to finish his final masterpiece. Although Jessie Conrad strictly forbade anyone to presume to write an ending, the American serial version published in the *Saturday Review of Literature* called for readers to participate in a contest to write a summary of how the novel should end, and the winning entries were published in the magazine. Another such contest was held when G. *Jean-Aubry's French *translation of *Suspense* (finished in Paris during the Nazi occupation) was serialized in 1946 in the periodical *Climats: hebdomadaire de la communauté française*.

The novel contains hints of an ancient love affair in Italy between Cosmo's father, Sir Charles Latham, and Adèle's mother, and critics have often drawn the conclusion that Cosmo and Adèle are actually brother and sister. There are explicit references to Adèle's 'filial affection' (22) for Sir Charles, and to his returning her affection 'as though she had been another daughter of his own' (36). This 'incest theme' helps to explain Sir Charles's unusual generosity to the d'Osmonds in their exile, his concern at the news of Adèle's marriage to the 'upstart' Montevesso, and the strangely intense intimacy that Cosmo and Adèle feel for each other upon first meeting as adults in Genoa. This theme also provides a link with Conrad's earlier unfinished novella *The Sisters*.

Ford Madox *Ford claimed that Conrad's 'Mediterranean novel' was originally planned as the subject of a *collaboration, and he took Conrad's death as an occasion to write his own fictional sequel to *Suspense* in the form of a novel called *A Little Less Than Gods* (1928). In Ford's novel, the English protagonist (here renamed George Feilding) finds himself caught up in Napoleon's return from Elba at a moment just after the end of *Suspense*, and the later parts of the novel have to do with the legend of the mock execution of Napoleon's Marshal Ney in Paris. The 'incest theme' hinted at in Conrad's novel is made fully explicit in Ford's pseudo-sequel.

Once the wave of initial reviews had passed, *Suspense* sank into a deep critical oblivion relieved only rarely by reviews of new translations or rediscoveries of the borrowings from the Comtesse de Boigne. This neglect was sanctioned and intensified by the *'achievement-and-decline thesis' propounded by Moser (1957), according to which, as the last of the late works reflecting a decline in Conrad's creative energy, *Suspense* was dismissed as an utter and negligible failure, of interest only for its 'incest theme' and the passages taken from the Comtesse de Boigne. In the wake of Moser's devastating critique, *The Rover* has frequently supplanted *Suspense* as *de facto* the 'last' of Conrad's novels; and even studies devoted to Conrad's later works (for example, those by Geddes (1980) and Schwarz (1982)) have treated *Suspense* as a relatively insignificant afterthought. The very existence of the English serial version in *Hutchinson's Magazine* was forgotten for many years and rediscovered only in 1993.

In an important sense, all of Conrad's novels after *The Shadow-Line* (with the exception of *The Rescue*) are 'Mediterranean' novels that treat historical subjects taking place along the coasts of *France, Italy, or Spain. Moser claimed that *Suspense* contains 'none but the most obvious historical details' (203), but the critical neglect of *Suspense* may also be due to the fact that Conrad presupposes a degree of familiarity with Napoleonic history that is becoming increasingly rare, especially in its relation to the early history of Italian nationalism.

Typescripts of *Suspense* are held at the British Library and the Berg Collection, New York Public Library. Curle's 'scraps' were sold at auction in 1927, and these fragments are now held at Colgate University; the Lilly Library, Indiana University; Mary Baldwin College; and the Beinecke Rare Book and Manuscript Library, Yale University. For a descriptive survey, see Hans van Marle and Gene M. Moore, 'The Crying of Lot 16: The Drafts and Typescripts of Conrad's *Suspense*', *Papers of the Bibliographical Society of America*, 88 (1994), 217–26.

Sutherland, John Georgeson (1871–?), Commander in the Royal Naval Reserve in charge of minesweeping vessels during the *First World War at Granton Harbour, Scotland. John Sutherland captained HMS *Ready*, in which Conrad made a ten-day voyage in November 1916. Conrad had responded to the Admiralty's invitation to join the *Ready*, the first sailing ship to be commissioned for active service during the war, for her tour of duty in the North Sea. Sailing from Granton under Norwegian colours and disguised as a merchant vessel to lure out German submarines, the ship (unofficially renamed the *Freya* in Conrad's honour) had an uneventful voyage and arrived back unscathed in Bridlington. Later, Sutherland wrote an entire book about the voyage, *At Sea with Joseph Conrad* (Grant Richards, 1922), despite the fact that Conrad in a candid letter to Sutherland—which he used as a foreword to the book—expressed the view that he did not think that memories of the voyage 'were worth preserving in print' (10). Writing to Richard *Curle, Conrad characterized Sutherland's book more forthrightly as 'preposterous bosh' (*CTF*, 151).

Symons, Arthur [William] (1865–1945), poet, critic, and author of the influential *The Symbolist Movement in Literature* (1899). Arthur Symons was a leading figure in the British aesthetic movement of the 1890s, when he contributed to the *Yellow Book* and edited the *Savoy*, in which he published Conrad's 'The Idiots' (*Tales of Unrest*) in 1896. Two years later, a *Saturday Review* article by Symons praising a translation of d'Annunzio at the expense of volumes by Conrad and Rudyard *Kipling (extracted in *CCH*, 97–8) provoked Conrad into writing a short essay on Kipling (the contribution was not published, and its text has not come to light). Conrad and Symons began to correspond in August 1908, when the latter sent a draft of an essay on Conrad to the author, probably the forerunner of an article published in *Forum* (1915) and the basis of a later short study, *Notes on Joseph Conrad with Some Unpublished Letters* (Myers, 1925). To that 1908 draft Conrad wryly responded: 'I did not know that I had "a heart of darkness" and an "unlawful" soul ... [and] that I delighted in cruelty and that the shedding of blood was my obsession' (*CL*, iv. 100). Their friendship, coinciding with a period when both men suffered severe nervous collapses, was particularly important for the ailing Symons, whose breakdowns involved extended hospitalization in a private London asylum. As near-neighbours in *Kent, the two men met fairly regularly during the period 1909–12, with Conrad helping to console and encourage the depressed Symons. However, given the fragile state of his own nervous constitution in 1909–10, Conrad's involvement with Symons was necessarily guarded, and John Conrad remembered that 'my father rather tended to keep him [Symons] at "arms length" and he never became a close friend. He seemed to me to be a lonely person who lacked the ability to become a companion' (*JCTR*, 60). Conrad used a stanza Symons had written after reading 'Freya of the Seven Isles' as an *epigraph for '*Twixt Land and Sea*.

T

'Tale, The', the only one of Conrad's stories to deal explicitly with the *First World War. While his elder son Borys was serving in the trenches of the western front, Conrad participated in the war effort by touring naval bases and travelling with coastal vessels in the autumn of 1916. In mid-September he spent two days in the minesweeper *Brigadier*, but it was not until shortly after he had completed 'The Tale' on 30 October that he spent twelve days in the 'Q-ship' HMS *Ready*, which posed as a neutral vessel and sailed under false colours in the hope of luring German submarines into open waters. A detailed account of this voyage, which bears an uncanny resemblance to the mission described in Conrad's story, was later published by the ship's master, Captain J. G. *Sutherland, as *At Sea with Joseph Conrad* (Grant Richards, 1922). 'The Tale', some 6,700 words in length, first appeared in the *Strand Magazine* (October 1917), with illustrations by C. M. Padday. In 1919 Clement K. *Shorter printed a private pamphlet edition limited to 25 copies, and it was included as the third of four stories in the posthumous *Tales of Hearsay*.

The story opens as an anguished conversation between an unnamed man and woman seems to be nearing its end. In response to the woman's ironic request for a story, the man relates a wartime episode in which the Commanding Officer of a naval vessel 'in the early days of the war' (63) was driven by thick fog to take shelter in a cove, only to discover there a suspicious vessel under the command of a neutral Northman. The Commanding Officer inspects the ship and interrogates the Northman, and soon becomes convinced that the Northman has been provisioning enemy submarines. Frustrated by the absence of positive proof, the Commanding Officer tests his hypothesis by expelling the Northman from the cove and giving him a false

course that will wreck the ship on a hidden ledge of rock, in the certainty that the Northman will disobey instructions and thus reveal his treachery. As it happens, the Northman follows the prescribed course and steams out to his death, with the loss of the ship and the entire crew. In the end, the narrator reveals to the listening woman that he was himself the Commanding Officer who realized too late that he will never know if he was right about the Northman, since his test established only that the Northman was unfamiliar with that stretch of coast, not whether or not he was delivering contraband. The woman pities the Commanding Officer and embraces him, but he rejects her sympathy and departs.

Even in the context of other Conrad stories, this tale is morally ambiguous in the extreme, contrasting the age-old bond of the 'fellowship of the sea' with the political loyalties demanded by nations at war, and exploring the possibility of moral conduct in an uncertain and fog-bound realm beyond the pale of established custom or international law. The implicit relevance of the tale to its narrative frame suggests that the narrator and his interlocutor may also have been involved in an adventure beyond the bounds of conventional morality, but the narrator's confession of his war-crime fails to achieve therapeutic catharsis or moral clarity.

The moral desolation of 'The Tale' is perhaps unique in Conrad's *œuvre*, but critics have noted its similarity to a war-story by Rudyard *Kipling first published in September 1915, 'Sea Constables', which also treats the theme of neutrality. The narrative complexity of 'The Tale' has appealed especially to *narratological approaches, and several such studies have devoted entire chapters to exploring its Chinese-box structure of tales within tales: for example, William Bonney in *Thorns & Arabesques: Contexts for Conrad's Fiction*

(Baltimore: Johns Hopkins UP, 1980); Jakob Lothe (1989); and Hawthorn (1990). Vivienne Rundle's '"The Tale" and the Ethics of Interpretation', *The Conradian*, 17: 1 (1992), 17–36, usefully summarizes and extends earlier criticism. The manuscript of 'The Tale' is now in the Berg Collection, New York Public Library.

Tales of Hearsay. This volume had its origin in Conrad's plan of January 1922 for a collection bringing together miscellaneous short stories already published in magazines but with the addition of *The Rover*, at that time in an early stage of composition and conceived as a long short story. When *The Rover* later grew to novel length, the planned volume was set aside. It was eventually published posthumously by T. Fisher *Unwin in Britain and by Doubleday, Page in America on 23 January 1925. Richard *Curle, the volume's editor, worked closely with R. B. Cunninghame *Graham, who supplied a moving introduction and advised Curle on the title and contents, persuading him to exclude *The Sisters*, a fragment from Conrad's early career. In his preface, Graham described the collection as embracing 'the first and the latest of the author's work' (p. viii), so remaining faithful to Conrad's plan of collecting in volume form what he regarded as his 'first' piece of writing, 'The Black Mate'. Also included are 'The Warrior's Soul', 'Prince Roman', and 'The Tale'. Graham further explained in a note to the volume that its title was 'one which Conrad long had in his mind for a future volume of short stories' (p. xvi).

'Tales of the Sea'. No details are known about the writing of this essay, although it was probably composed shortly before its publication in the *Outlook*, 1 (4 June 1898), 560–1. It was later revised for inclusion in *Notes on Life and Letters*. Conrad affectionately celebrates the work of two writers, Frederick *Marryat and James Fenimore *Cooper, to whose books he had 'surrendered' as a small boy and who who had shaped his early adventurous impulse towards a life at sea. In part an exercise in reaffirming the truth of his early sensations, the essay

also shows Conrad the sea writer positioning himself in relation to two contrasting predecessors, one English (a vigorous and manly 'writer of the Service' (54)) and one American (notable for his 'profound sympathy' and 'artistic insight' (57)), who, in his view, have given sea literature its defining and nourishing traditions. The essay's affirmation of the rightness of youth's uncritical 'surrender' to heroic sea literature is not a final one, and in *Lord Jim*, a work written about the same time, Conrad probes the more harmful effects of the youthful hero's enslavement to the myths of light literature. No pre-publication documents are known.

Tales of Unrest. Conrad's fourth published volume brings together five short stories written during the years 1896–7— 'Karain: A Memory', 'The Idiots', 'An Outpost of Progress', 'The Return', and 'The Lagoon'—all but 'The Return' previously serialized. It was published by Scribner's in America on 26 March 1898, and by T. Fisher *Unwin in Britain on 4 April 1898. Marking the end of Conrad's early publishing connection with Unwin, the book's final contents silently reflect their deteriorating relationship. Originally Conrad had planned to include *The Nigger of the 'Narcissus'*, but Unwin's failure to offer him decent terms for the story and Conrad's consequent determination to seek a better home for it elsewhere led him to withdraw the novella and supply Unwin with two substitutes, 'Karain' and 'The Return'. The varied fruits of two years' work, his first collection of short stories represents an important watershed in other respects. While still partly drawing upon Malay material, it marks the opening stage of Conrad's learning to write for popular magazines. As he told Unwin, 'in that book I come nearer to the popular notion of tale-telling than in any previous work of mine' (*CL*, ii. 48). The collection also marks an expansion of subjects to include African material as well as a middle-class domestic drama set in *London, and shows Conrad developing personalized narrative voices and relative perspectives. Contemporary reviewers, including Edward *Garnett, used both *Tales of Unrest* and *The Nigger of the 'Narcissus'* as occasions for surveying Conrad's early career more broadly and to measure the quality of his 'arrival' as a developing writer. A selection of contemporary reviews is included in *CCH*, 101–10. More formal recognition for *Tales of Unrest* came in 1899 when the *Academy* awarded Conrad his sole literary prize by 'crowning' the volume with a 50-guinea award, as one of the best books of the previous year.

teacher of languages. The English teacher who narrates *Under Western Eyes* understands that 'Words, as is well known, are the great foes of reality' (3). With such disclaimers, he offers the reader what purports to be an edited and translated version of a secret document that he has difficulty describing: 'The document, of course, is something in the nature of a journal, a diary, yet not exactly that in its actual form' (4). The teacher is not Russian, but learned Russian as a child of 'parents settled in St. Petersburg' (187). As an expatriate living in *Geneva, he maintains contact with members of the Russian community, and is employed by Natalia *Haldin as an English tutor. Although *Razumov sees him as English, referring to him as 'the officious Englishman' (199) and 'an old Englishman' (360), the narrator claims to speak as a 'Westerner' (141, 329) more generally. His linguistic skills give him access to the international world of the revolutionaries, yet he remains acutely aware of his own 'European remoteness' from the world of the Haldins.

His motives for making Razumov's story accessible to Western eyes are never entirely clear, and his obvious infatuation with Miss Haldin adds to the reader's doubts about the adequacy of his presentation of Razumov's text. Early reviewers and critics seemed relatively unaware of the teacher's obtrusiveness, or accepted his contradictions in good faith. In 'Nightmare and Complacency: Razumov and the Western Eye', *Critical Quarterly*, 4 (1962), 197–214, Tony Tanner has described him as impercipient and incredulous, and as 'a vague

peripheral fatuous presence', yet felt that despite these shortcomings he was 'honest and objective' and 'scrupulously fair in his handling of evidence' (199). Later critics have been less tolerant of the narrator's weaknesses, charging him with being unreliable, incompetent, or even diabolical. The effects of his unreliability are discussed by Robert Secor in 'The Function of the Narrator in *Under Western Eyes*', *Conradiana*, 3: 1 (1970–1), 27–38. Among the numerous articles by Daniel R. Schwarz whose titles begin with 'The Significance of' is one entitled 'The Significance of the Language Teacher in Conrad's *Under Western Eyes*', *Journal of Narrative Technique*, 6 (1976), 101–15. The teacher's expansive sense of 'Genevan' time and space is contrasted with Razumov's compressed 'Petersburg' chronotope in Gene M. Moore's 'Chronotopes and Voices in *Under Western Eyes*', *Conradiana*, 18 (1986), 9–25. The role of the language teacher is also discussed by Keith Carabine in Stape (ed.) 1996: 122–49, and in his major study (1996) of the novel's composition.

Thames, River. 'Conrad first approached London from its amazing other end, going up a great, silver-grey estuary between sixty miles of docks, all with seagoing ships lying shoulder to shoulder, like fish in thick shoals. And he was confronted with grandiosities, evidences of wealth, of steadfastness, courage, enterprise, and justice, in a world where the first and last of virtues is the quality of shipshapeness. So for Conrad that metropolis was the Port of London and, as an afterthought, he might have conceded that you might reasonably style it the Port and City of London. For some years that remained his naive psychology.' Despite its condescension and inaccuracy (Conrad did not first approach *London along the River Thames, but on a prosaic train from Lowestoft to Liverpool Street Station), this description by Ford Madox *Ford (1938: 85) provides a useful reminder that, as a matter of biographical fact, much of Conrad's life as a British merchant seaman was closely involved with the Thames. As a beginning writer, too, he chose to live close to G. F. W. *Hope in an Essex village near the river in order to continue their tradition of sailing in its estuary.

Ford also rightly diagnoses a strain of sentimental patriotism attaching to some of Conrad's literary constructions of the Thames. It is most marked in a section of *The Mirror of the Sea* devoted to 'The Faithful River', which was originally entitled 'London River: The Great Artery of England' and tailored for publication in a popular journal, the *World's Work and Play*, in December 1904. Here, grandiosity and rhetorical pomp unite in Conrad's rehearsal of conventional national and historical traditions associated with the Thames as a symbol of imperial Britain: it is a river with 'the glamour conferred by historical associations' and 'a romantic stream flowing through the centre of great affairs' (113, 114). Drawing upon Thames mythologies that would not be out of place in Elizabethan literature, Conrad intensifies such 'glamour' by a form of pastoral mythology which compares sailing ships as they enter London docks with 'a flock of swans kept in the flooded backyard of grim tenement houses' (110) and a wild bird 'put into a dirty cage' (111). Cedric Watts has commented: 'If pastoral poetry is sentimental to the extent that it veils the economic dependence of the rural world on the requirements of the urban world, so Conrad's maritime version . . . is sentimental to the extent that it veils the dependence of maritime life on the commercial activities of the city' ('Conrad and the Myth of the Monstrous Town', in Moore (ed.) 1992: 20). An earlier story, *The Nigger of the 'Narcissus'*, which appeared in Queen Victoria's Diamond Jubilee year, does not wholly escape such sentimentality in its closing vision of England as 'A ship mother of fleets and nations! The great flagship of the race', while the *Narcissus*, '[s]horn of the glory of her white wings' (163), is finally imprisoned within the 'soulless walls' of London's docklands (165).

What Ford does not sufficiently emphasize is Conrad's increasing tendency to use conventional Thames mythology in order to question and subvert commonly accepted patriotic notions of Englishness. Thamesside settings figure in several of his *frame-narratives and serve to invoke familiar images of English decency, communality, and historical security that are later questioned by complications thrown up by their inset stories. Such an effect is probably most marked in 'Heart of Darkness', where a grandiose early eulogy presents a vision of the nation's historical origins as intimately wedded to the Thames as an imperial waterway: 'What greatness had not floated on the ebb of that river into the mystery of an unknown earth! . . . The dreams of men, the seed of commonwealths, the germs of empires' (*Youth*, 47). This vision belongs not to *Marlow, the central narrator, but to the anonymous narrator who introduces him, and it is one that Marlow immediately destabilizes and undercuts. His opening meditation sees the river not as a point of departure for the makers of the British Empire, but as 'one of the dark places of the earth' (48), a place of arrival for the Romans who conquered ancient Britain: the Thames is no longer the centre of the civilized world, but stands on its outermost frontier, at 'the very end of the world', a wilderness, and place of 'savages' (49). In this process, Marlow reverses a conventional patriotic view of English history by locating its origins in the ancient confrontation between 'a decent young [Roman] citizen' and the 'utter savagery' of the Thames swamplands (50). By the very end of the story, which returns to the Thames setting, even the anonymous narrator seems to have accepted Marlow's spatio-temporal adjustments to the river's genealogy: there, he repeats a formulation he had used in his earlier paean—'the tranquil dignity of a waterway leading to the uttermost ends of the earth' (46–7)—but significantly omits any reference to the river's 'dignity' and adds that the Thames 'flowed sombre under an overcast sky— seemed to lead into the heart of an immense darkness' (162).

theatre. In his attitudes to the theatre and actors, Conrad admitted to being 'avowedly a prejudiced person' with an 'ineradicable mistrust of the theatre as destroyer of all suggestiveness' (*CL* iv. 432). To R. B. Cunninghame *Graham he confessed in 1897 to wanting to write a play as his 'dark and secret ambition', and yet remorselessly inveighed against actors: 'I can't conceive how a sane man can sit down deliberately to write a play and not go mad before he has done. The actors appear to me like a lot of *wrongheaded* lunatics pretending to be sane. Their malice is stitched with white threads. They are disguised and ugly. To look at them breeds in my melancholy soul thoughts of murder and suicide—such is my anger and my loathing of their transparent pretences' (*CL*, i. 419). This is no passing prejudice, since Conrad's scornful *hauteur* still vigorously persisted ten years later: 'Though I detest the stage I have a theatrical imagination—that's why perhaps I detest the stage—that is the actors who mostly poor souls, have no imagination' (*CL*, iv. 218).

As Baines points out (290), it is difficult to find the basis for this inbuilt hostility, since Conrad confessed in 1897 to Graham that he had not seen a play 'for years'. Indeed, despite the fact that he persisted in wanting to write for the stage, Conrad repeatedly maintained that the theatre offered an inferior artistic practice from which he had little to learn, and he would rarely attend a theatrical performance. As a young man in *Marseilles, he seems to have seen plays by Augustin Eugène Scribe and Victorien Sardou. Later, friendship with John *Galsworthy involved him in attending many of the latter's plays. Even when he was more involved with dramatic projects after 1916, his theatre-going did not notably increase, although during the *First World War he went to see performances of *Shakespeare's *Hamlet* and Henrik Ibsen's *Ghosts*. His one notable intercession in matters theatrical had little to do with any practical involvement in theatre: in 1909, at Edward *Garnett's request, he wrote 'The Censor of Plays: An Appreciation' (*Notes*), an essay sharply critical of drama censorship.

Some of Conrad's negative attitudes to the theatre appear to be those characteris-

tic of the prose writer engaged in adapting his own work for the stage who cannot overcome the proprietorial sense that the work 'belongs' to him and that his first commitment is to the integrity of the original. Perhaps one reason why Conrad preferred marionettes to actors (*CL*, i. 419) is that they are essentially rigorously controlled creatures who respond to the manipulator's guiding hand. This is not to say that his own stage adaptations—*One Day More*, *The Secret Agent*, and *Laughing Anne*—lack dramatic qualities. The problem is, as B. Macdonald *Hastings said of Conrad's *One Day More*, that while it 'has a definite technique . . . it has no stagecraft', and he continues: 'The truth of the matter is that his mental attitude, prompted by his temperament, did not allow him to appreciate what is theatrically significant' (quoted in *JCIR*, 223), This sentiment partly echoes Conrad's own to Hastings: 'You can have no conception of my ignorance in theatrical art. I can't even *imagine* a scenic effect' (25 January 1917). Only perhaps in later life did Conrad mellow into a degree of humility when, having come into contact with sensitive directors and actors, he could conceive of himself as working with, rather than against, stage conventions. In November 1919, one such director, Frank Vernon, gently but firmly corrected Conrad's sense of the theatre as a hierarchy extending downwards from the God-like figure of the author: 'it was a particular and important point you made when you insisted that one is dependent on the actors. That is true, but it is equally true that an acted play is the result of collaboration, the three chief collaborators being Author, Actors and Audience' (*PL*, 144). A brief, but stimulating view of Conrad's attitudes to the theatre can be found in John Galsworthy's 'Preface to Conrad's Plays' (1927), 128–35. See also Paola Pugliatti, 'From Narrative to Drama: Conrad's Plays as Adaptations', in Curreli (ed.), 297–316.

Thomas, [Philip] Edward (1878–1917), poet and essayist. Edward Thomas first met Conrad in 1910 at one of the regular *Mont Blanc gatherings in *London. Soon after, the latter enlisted his help as a ghost-writer who would, if required, help with some reviews he was writing for the *Daily Mail*. After graduating from Oxford in 1900, Thomas had earned his living by reviewing, criticism, and occasional prose until, prompted by encouragement from the American poet Robert Frost and support from Edward *Garnett, he turned to writing poetry. A near-neighbour of Conrad's in *Kent, Thomas dedicated his *Walter Pater* (1913) to Conrad and kept in touch with him during the early years of the *First World War, when Conrad also lent unofficial support to Thomas's application for a Civil List Pension. Their friendship was cut short by Thomas's death at the battle of Arras. For the poet's account of one of his visits to Conrad's *home, see *JCIR*, 217–18.

Thys, Albert (1849–1915) was the managing director of the trading company that sent Conrad to the *Congo in 1890. He appears briefly in 'Heart of Darkness' as 'The great man himself' who 'was five feet six . . . and had his grip on the handle-end of ever so many millions'. *Marlow says that his interview lasted only 'about forty-five seconds' (*Youth*, 56), but in fact Conrad met Thys more than once, for a first interview in November 1889 and again the following spring before his departure for Africa. Conrad's employer, the Société Anonyme Belge pour le Commerce du Haut-Congo (Belgian Limited Trading Company for the Upper Congo), was one of some half-dozen interlinked companies created by Thys, a former staff officer, for the development and exploitation of King Leopold's personal colony. Thys spent many months in the Congo between 1887 and 1893, and is credited with having opened up the Congo by building a railway over difficult terrain from Matadi to Stanley Pool. Construction of the line was just beginning when Conrad arrived in the Congo, and his steamship carried the first cargo of rails and sleepers. This project took eight years to complete and cost thousands of African lives, as witnessed in Conrad's description of the chain-gangs and

dying labourers in 'Heart of Darkness'. Conrad's business *letters to Thys are included in *CL*, i, and Thys's commercial activities are summarized in Gene M. Moore, 'The Colonial Context of Anti-Semitism: Poradowska's *Yaga* and the Thys Libel Case', *The Conradian*, 18: 1 (1993), 25–36.

***Titanic* disaster.** Conrad was deeply stirred by news of the *Titanic*'s sinking in the North Atlantic on 15 April 1912, and publicly responded to the event with indignation and scarcely controlled dismay. He first sought a venue for expressing his opinion on the disaster in *Nash's Magazine* and William Randolph Hearst's *American*, but both would have involved delayed publication, and he declined to wait. In the end, he made three pronouncements: a lengthy statement in a special *Titanic* issue of the London newspaper the *Budget* on the weekend of 20–1 April, and two full-length essays, 'Some Reflexions, Seaman-like and Otherwise, on the Loss of the *Titanic*' and 'Certain Aspects of the Admirable Inquiry into the Loss of the *Titanic*'. No copy of the *Budget* has been located, and Conrad's comment apparently survives only in quotation, whether complete or in extract is unknown, in New York's *Literary Digest* (4 May 1912, 925). The essays appeared in the May and July issues of the *English Review and were later collected in *Notes on Life and Letters*. Conrad's second article on the affair was partly a reply to John *Quinn, who had defended the American Senate's investigation, and an occasion to address topics raised by the official British inquiry.

Conrad's statements express concern about four issues: the inadequacy of the Board of Trade's regulations for public safety at sea; what he considered the exaggerated size of the ship; its luxurious appointments, which required a large non-professional contingent of service personnel untrained to cope with maritime emergencies; and the general journalistic sensationalism, first in advertising the *Titanic*'s vaunted 'unsinkability' and then in reporting on the disaster itself. The issues deeply stirred Conrad both as a professional seaman and a professional writer, and he levelled his key charge of irresponsibility, in effect a dereliction of duty, at the Board of Trade and the press. In the case of the Board of Trade, the government department responsible, under the Privy Council, for regulating commercial activities, he inveighed against singularly outdated regulations; and he attacked the press for concocting 'facts' and a cynical abuse of language in falsifying emotions for purposes of increasing circulation figures.

Conrad's attack on the hastily convened inquiry authorized by the American Senate is unflinching. In the first instance, he questioned its jurisdictional authority, the disaster having taken place in international waters and involving a ship of British registry under the command of persons of British nationality. He also severely faulted its lack of specialist expertise in nautical matters. On the whole, he considered the investigation motivated by a need for catharsis from the frenzied emotional climate stirred up by the American press rather than a properly constituted professional undertaking. The official British inquiry was more conservatively structured, partly guided by a desire to avoid offending powerful vested interests close to home. Later commentators have suggested that Conrad was on the wrong side of history in his attack on the Senate's investigation, which, in the event, was the more even-handed and comprehensive of the two. Although the British inquiry was held in *London and open to the public (Leonard and Virginia *Woolf, for instance, attended some of its sessions), Conrad apparently did not do so. Given his vehement complaints about the fundamental unreliability of journalism, there is some irony in his having formed his views exclusively from press reports, particularly those in *The Times*.

See Stape (1988) for a study of Conrad's essays on the *Titanic*. Jeremy Hawthorn's *Cunning Passages: New Historicism, Cultural Materialism and Marxism in the Contemporary Literary Debate* (Arnold, 1996), 87–157, treats Conrad's reactions to the sinking in a contextualized study of literary responses to the disaster.   JHS

Tittle, Walter Ernest (1883–1966), American illustrator and portraitist. Walter Tittle produced two oil paintings, two lithographs, and a dry-point etching of Conrad after their first meeting in July 1922 (see PORTRAITS AND OTHER IMAGES), and helped persuade Conrad to make his 1923 trip to *America, where Tittle was the first to greet him on his arrival in New York. Conrad had a special liking for Tittle's portraits, believing that they showed him 'as the rough old sea-dog' that he was, and chose one of them as the frontispiece for Dent's *Collected Edition of his works. Tittle took great pride in his friendship with Conrad, kept a detailed diary about their meetings, continued to see Jessie Conrad after her husband's death, and wrote several reminiscences (Tittle's 'The Conrad who Sat for Me' (1925) is reprinted in *JCIR*, 153–63). In 1931, a copy of Tittle's best-known oil painting of Conrad was acquired by the National Portrait Gallery, London, while in 1948, the original was presented to Yale University Library. See also Richard P. Veler's 'Walter Tittle and Joseph Conrad', *Conradiana*, 12 (1980), 93–104, which includes generous extracts from Tittle's unpublished autobiography and diary.

Tobin, Agnes (1864–1939), a minor American poet and translator of Petrarch with a fascination for meeting famous writers. Agnes Tobin numbered among her friends Alice Meynell, Edmund *Gosse, Ezra Pound, and W. B. Yeats (who hyperbolically described her as the best American poet since Walt Whitman). With Arthur *Symons, she first visited Capel House in 1911 and made an immediate impact upon Conrad, who not long after dedicated *Under Western Eyes* to his new friend 'who brought to our door her genius for friendship from the uttermost shore of the west'. She provided Conrad with an introduction to John *Quinn, a wealthy New York lawyer and collector who during the next five years or so bought many of his *manuscripts and typescripts; she also brought the French novelist André *Gide to Conrad's Capel House *home.

'To-morrow'. Composed during the first half of January 1902 under the title of 'The Son' and needing to be cut by 2,000 words for its serial printing, this 10,000-word story gave Conrad 'no end of trouble': it was, he said, '"Conrad" adapted down to the needs of a magazine. By no means a potboiler; on the contrary' (*CL*, ii. 373). The story appeared in *Pall Mall Magazine*, 27 (1902), 533–47, and was collected in *Typhoon*. Little is known about its sources, although the germinating idea seems to have come from Ford Madox *Ford, to whom Conrad wrote about it: '*All your* suggestion and *absolutely my* conception' (*CL*, ii. 372). The story's title relates to the obsessional belief of old Captain Hagberd, retired, that his long-lost son Harry will return 'to-morrow'. As his obsession strengthens, Hagberd draws Bessie Carvil, the passive daughter of a domestic tyrant, into the fantasy that she and Harry will be married upon his son's return. When Harry finally does turn up, his father, in what seems like a parodic inversion of the biblical parable of the returning prodigal son, refuses to recognize him; Harry, having in the meantime learned of the scheme to marry him off, eventually disappears to resume his life as an adventurer. Hagberd is left 'shouting of his trust in an everlasting to-morrow' (277), while Bessie feels robbed, humiliated, and despairing. In 1904, Conrad adapted the story for the stage under the title *One Day More*.

An unjustly neglected tale, 'To-morrow' is a stark and haunting companion-piece to another story in the same collection, 'Amy Foster', with which it shares the stuffy provincial setting of fictional Colebrook and an interest in the psychopathy of everyday domestic existence or 'life around the hearth' (*CL*, ii. 402), here represented by two kinds of paternal 'madness': on the one hand, the crazed domination of the blind patriarch Carvil, and, on the other, the delusional *idée fixe* of Hagberd, whose life is permanently arrested by 'the disease of hope' (248).

A striking feature of the story is its sympathetic focus upon Bessie Carvil as a type of unmarried woman of her time who, trapped within a domestic prison, is starved of any vision of freedom other than that offered by marriage. She is cruelly robbed even of that fantasy by the males around her, and the final description of Bessie returning to her domestic imprisonment incorporates a sombre allusion to *Dante: 'She . . . began to totter silently back towards her stuffy little inferno of a cottage. It had no lofty portal, no terrific inscription of forfeited hopes—she did not understand wherein she had sinned' (276). As Kirschner (1990: 24) remarks, in 'To-morrow' the imaginative pattern of 'Amy Foster' is reversed since, in contrast to Amy, Bessie as a woman and provincial insider is the tragic victim, while the seafaring adventurer and outsider Harry departs a free man. Looking back in 1919 on his conception of Bessie, Conrad observed that she was 'absolutely the first conscious woman-creation in the whole body of my work' (*LL*, ii. 225). The manuscript of the story is held in the Berg Collection, New York Public Library, and a typescript at the Rosenbach Museum and Library, Philadelphia.

'Torrens: A Personal Tribute, The'. Through Richard *Curle, Conrad received an invitation in August 1923 from F. A. Hook, the owner and editor of *Blue Peter*, to complement a coloured illustration of the *Torrens* that was to appear in the September 1923 issue with a personal remembrance of the ship in the next number. His contribution was duly published in the October issue of *Blue Peter* under the title 'A Clipper Ship I Knew' and collected in *Last Essays*. The essay occasions a moving recollection in tranquillity of a ship in which Conrad had served some 30 years earlier (see SHIPS AND VOYAGES). Its opening and closing mood is that of elegiac pathos. Professing an unfamiliarity with 'the spirit of the [present] age' (22), Conrad images himself as the last representative seaman of a sailing vessel now gone: her launching in 1875 coincided with his own initiation into Mediterranean waters; she was also associated with the end of his career; and her final demise in *Genoa in 1910, with 'body . . . broken up' (28), acts as a generalizing *memento mori*. A wider maritime history is also involved, since from a point of hindsight Conrad uses the *Torrens* to symbolize a moment when sailing ships simultaneously reached a point of perfection and were irrevocably doomed. As in *The Nigger of the 'Narcissus'* with its final invocation to 'a shadowy ship manned by a crew of Shades' (173), Conrad here comes to rest with the implication that an act of memory has momentarily rescued the ship from oblivion. For a detailed factual recreation of Conrad's service in the *Torrens*, see Stape and van Marle 1995. The manuscript, dated 29 August 1923, is held at the Beinecke Rare Book and Manuscript Library, Yale University, and a revised typescript at Boston Public Library.

'Tradition'. At Lord *Northcliffe's request and for a generous fee of 250 guineas, Conrad dictated this tribute to the efforts of British merchant seamen during the *First World War and sent it to J. B. *Pinker on 4 March 1918 for publication in the *Daily Mail* (8 March 1918), 2. He later revised it for inclusion in *Notes on Life and Letters*. Initially invoking Leonardo da Vinci's views on the sanctity of *work, Conrad celebrates the risky war effort readily undertaken by the *British Merchant Service, and concludes with an illustrative narrative of heroism at sea. For this narrative, the record of an actual event in September 1917 when the indomitable Captain William Leask managed to save his crew after his ship, the *St Margaret*, was torpedoed in the North Atlantic, Conrad drew upon a written account of events by the ship's chief engineer Frank Russell. A corrected and revised typescript (Beinecke Rare Book and Manuscript Library, Yale University) and a clean carbon-copy typescript (Berg Collection, New York Public Library) survive. See also J. H. Stape, 'Conrad's "Certain Steamship": The Background of "Tradition"', *Conradiana*, 16 (1984), 236–9.

translations. Conrad was familiar with translation from his earliest childhood, since his father, Apollo *Korzeniowski, in addition to his journalistic and political activities, was a prolific translator of works by *Shakespeare (*A Comedy of Errors* and *The Two Gentlemen of Verona*), Charles *Dickens (*Hard Times*), and Victor Hugo (*Le Roi s'amuse* and *Les Travailleurs de la mer*). As a child, Conrad was an avid reader of translations in Polish or French, including the manuscripts of his father's translations, works by Sir Walter Scott and William Makepeace Thackeray, and an 'excellent' Polish version of Dickens's *Nicholas Nickleby* which left him amazed at 'how well Mrs. Nickleby could chatter disconnectedly in Polish and the sinister Ralph rage in that language' (*A Personal Record*, 71). Translation is also an important element in many of Conrad's works, often involving the silent Anglicization of languages that Conrad did not know: the characters in Conrad's first two novels, *Almayer's Folly* and *An Outcast of the Islands*, express themselves not in English but in Malay or Dutch; the company agents and managers in 'Heart of Darkness' speak not English but French (although *Kurtz speaks English with *Marlow); and *Under Western Eyes* is presented explicitly (but implausibly) as the English *teacher's translation of *Razumov's Russian diary. Conrad also produced one explicit translation of his own, of *Księga Hioba* (*The Book of Job*) by Polish playwright Bruno Winawer, who returned the favour by translating Conrad's stage version of *The Secret Agent* into Polish. In 1920 Conrad also translated G. *Jean-Aubry's article 'Joseph Conrad's Confessions' from French into English (*JCC*, 457).

Conrad's own works have been translated into more than 40 languages. Virtually complete *collected editions are available in French, Italian, and Polish; all but a few of his works are available in German; and many have been translated into Japanese and Spanish. *Lord Jim* is the most widely translated of all Conrad's works, with versions in 29 languages by 1995, including Finnish (1930), Portuguese (1940),

Romanian (1964), Arabic (1970), Catalan (1978), and Malayalam (1983). 'Heart of Darkness' follows in second place; although it was not translated at all in Conrad's lifetime (the first translations, into French, Italian, and Dutch, date from 1924), by 1989 there were translations into 24 languages including Russian (1926), Hebrew (1954), Estonian (1963), and Turkish (1984). Conrad is still unavailable in Urdu; and only 'Heart of Darkness' has been translated into Albanian (1983), Chinese (1970), and Swahili (1972). The selections are often curious and seemingly accidental: only 'Typhoon' (1950) has been translated into Latvian, and only 'Falk' (1951) and 'Typhoon' (1961) into Greek. Of Conrad's 'Malay' works, only *Almayer's Folly* (1967) is available in Malay, and Arabic translations are limited to 'Youth' (1959) and *Lord Jim* (1970). *Nostromo* and *Under Western Eyes* have never been translated into Dutch, nor has *The Mirror of the Sea*, despite its description of *Amsterdam, nor *The Rescue* despite its setting in the former *Netherlands East Indies. Even though 'Falk' and *The Shadow-Line* are set partly in *Bangkok, the 60 million citizens of Thailand have never had access to Conrad in their own language. Conrad's Basque readers know him as the author of 'Karain' (1980), 'Youth' (1985), and *The Shadow-Line* (1989); in Icelandic he is known only for 'Typhoon' (1946) and *The Nigger of the 'Narcissus'* (1949). For some strange reason, the only work ever translated into Yiddish is 'Gaspar Ruiz' (1928).

The first translation of Conrad's work was the Polish translation of *An Outcast of the Islands* by Maria Gąsiorowska that ran as a *serialization in the *Warsaw *Tygodnik mód i powieści* (Weekly of Fashion and Fiction) from January to June 1897. As Conrad told Edward *Garnett, 'They have heard of me in Poland, through Chicago (of all the God-forsaken places)' (*CL*, i. 316). *Lord Jim* was translated by Emilja Węsławska as early as 1904, and Gąsiorowska's translation of *The Secret Agent* appeared in 1908. Helena Janina Pajzderska's translation of *Under Western Eyes* was serialized in the Warsaw journal *Świat* in 1917. In a letter of

10 April 1920, Conrad gave Aniela *Zagórska his 'best and completest authority and right' to translate all his works into Polish, with responsibility 'to give or to refuse permission and to decide all matters concerned herewith' (*CPB*, 261), and later that year he formally extended her authority to include copyright on Russian translations as well. Under her direction, the first collected edition of Conrad's works in translation began appearing from 1923, eventually comprising 22 volumes, at least ten of which she translated herself.

From the very beginning of his writing career, Conrad was concerned with the possibility of publishing in French as well as (or instead of) in English. In July 1894, more than two months before his first novel was accepted for publication by T. Fisher *Unwin, he had suggested to Marguerite *Poradowska that they prepare a French version of the text, 'not as a translation but as a collaboration' (*CL*, i. 165), for the Parisian *Revue des Deux Mondes*, to which she was a regular contributor. The following spring (*Almayer's Folly* was published on 29 April) he was still trying unsuccessfully to generate French interest in his work; but in July he gently declined Émilie *Briquel's offer to translate the text, presumably because he had doubts about her competence in English (*CL*, i. 236). Poradowska apparently completed a translation of 'An Outpost of Progress' (*CL*, ii. 401) that was never published; the first French translation of *Almayer's Folly* (by Geneviève Séligmann-Lui) did not appear until 1919. In April 1902, Henry-Durand *Davray offered his services as a French translator, and the first of Conrad's works to appear in French was Davray's version of 'Karain' published in the *Mercure de France* (1906), followed by a translation of *The Nigger of the 'Narcissus'* by Robert d'Humières in 1909.

Davray's work proceeded slowly, and by 1915 Conrad accepted an offer from André *Gide to supervise the translation of his works into French for publication by Gallimard and the *Nouvelle Revue Française*. Gide, an early admirer of Conrad's work, had first met him through Agnes *Tobin in

1911. He published his own translation of 'Typhoon' in 1918, although the story had already been translated by Joseph de Smet in 1911 (see the essays by Daniel Durosay and Sylvère Monod in the *Bulletin des Amis d'André Gide* (1993), 'Autour de *Typhon*'). A bilingual edition of *Typhoon/Typhon* with Gide's translation on facing pages and an introduction by Monod was published by Gallimard in 1991.

Conrad's own knowledge of French, and his earlier involvement with translations of *Maupassant into English, was at times a source of complications. Gide invited Isabelle Rivière, the sister of novelist Alain-Fournier and wife of publisher Jacques Rivière, to translate *Victory*, but when Conrad saw samples of her work, he protested that it was not idiomatically correct (*CL*, v. 590). Gide defended her against Conrad, but complained in his private diary about her 'childish theories' of literal translation. The dispute was resolved when Philippe Neel was brought in to assist her with the translation. A similar contretemps arose in 1919 when Gide assigned the translation of *The Arrow of Gold* to Madeleine Octavie Maus even though Conrad had warmly recommended G. *Jean-Aubry, whom Gide had introduced to Conrad the previous year (see Gabrijela and Ivo Vidan, 'Further Correspondence between Joseph Conrad and André Gide', *Studia Romanica et Anglica Zagrabiensia*, 29–32 (1970–1), 523–36). Jean-Aubry would eventually produce not only the first Conrad biography and general collection of *letters, but some eleven volumes of translations of Conrad into French. Gide's involvement in making Conrad available in French has received considerable attention from scholars. An early overview is Frederick R. Karl's 'Conrad and Gide: A Relationship and a Correspondence', *Comparative Literature*, 29 (1977), 148–71. The problems associated with the translation of *Victory* are discussed by J. H. Stape in 'The Art of Fidelity: Conrad, Gide, and the Translation of *Victory*', *Journal of Modern Literature*, 17 (1990), 155–65. Russell West's comprehensive study, *Conrad and Gide: Translation, Transference and Intertextuality* (Amster-

dam: Rodopi, 1996), contains a useful bibliography.

Sylvère Monod, the veteran translator of Conrad and Dickens who has edited the works of both authors for the magisterial French collected editions published in the Bibliothèque de la Pléiade (Gallimard), discusses some of the special difficulties confronting French translators in 'On Translating Conrad into French', *The Conradian*, 9 (1984), 69–80. The amply annotated Pléiade edition (5 vols., 1982–92) contains either new or refurbished translations of Conrad's works. Since its publication, yet another translator has emerged in Odette Lamolle, who has translated Conrad privately for her own pleasure since the early 1930s, when she first read *Lord Jim*. Ten novels and stories in Lamolle's translations have been published by Éditions Autrement in Paris.

The first translation of Conrad into Italian was 'The Idiots', which appeared in a bilingual series edited by J. E. Mansion and published in London by Harrap's and in New York by Brentano's in 1920. Most of Conrad's canonical works were available in Italian by the end of the 1920s, but the first scholarly edition was the work of Ugo Mursia, whose *Tutte le opere narrative di Joseph Conrad* (5 vols., 1967–82) is the most complete of the foreign collected editions, including even a translation of Conrad's 'film-play' *Gaspar the Strong Man* as *L'uomo forte*, which is to date the only published edition of this work. Mursia's efforts have been continued by Mario Curreli, who has published numerous translations and editions.

Although Conrad does not figure strongly in German literary criticism, most of his works have been available in various German translations since the 1920s. The translation of *The Secret Agent* by Ernst W. Freissler in 1926 contained an introduction by Thomas Mann (available in English in Watt 1973: 99–112).

The Secret Agent was translated into Russian as early as 1908, followed over the next twenty years by most of the major novels and stories, including a five-volume edition of *Selected Works*. Inscribed copies of

Under Western Eyes often contained Conrad's claim that many inexpensive editions of the novel were printed in Russia before the October Revolution of 1917, but apparently none of these editions has survived, and it may be that Conrad was confusing 'editions' with the print runs of newspapers in which the novel was serialized. In 'Conrad in Russian (1912–1959)', *Conradiana*, 14 (1982), 57–62, Eugene Steele, citing the work of Russian bibliographer Yuri Kagarlitsky, makes impressive claims for the availability of Conrad's works printed in Russian translation: over 50,000 copies printed in 1925, and over 70,000 in 1926 and in 1927. These volumes were occasionally reprinted or newly translated, but no new Russian translations appeared during the 30 years from 1928, when Mark Volosov's translation of *Nostromo* was published in Leningrad, to 1958, when M. E. Abkina's translation of *The Mirror of the Sea* appeared in Moscow. None of Conrad's works written after 1917 has been translated into Russian.

*Bibliographical information on translations of Conrad's works before 1955 is listed in Kenneth A. Lohf and Eugene P. Sheehy's *Joseph Conrad at Mid-Century: Editions and Studies, 1895–1955* (Minneapolis: University of Minnesota Press, 1957), and in one section of Theodore G. Ehrsam's *A Bibliography of Joseph Conrad* (Metuchen, NJ: Scarecrow Press, 1969). See also Yasuko Shidara, 'Japanese Translations of Conrad's Works, 1914–1995', *Tokyo Conrad Group Newsletter*, 2 (1996), 4–7.

transtextual narratives. Cedric Watts first coined this critical term in *The Deceptive Text: An Introduction to Covert Plots* (Brighton: Harvester, 1984) to describe certain family connections that occur in Conrad's works when a narrative sequence spans two or more texts and often brings with it repeated characters and settings. Watts's coinage is closely related to the more traditional term *roman-fleuve*, used to signify a series of novels, each of which exists as a separate work in its own right, but all of which are interrelated by their overriding chronicle form. The vogue for such chronicles was established in the 19th century with Balzac's series *La Comédie humaine* (1833–47) and followed in different ways in Émile *Zola's *Les Rougon-Macquart* (1871–93), Anthony Trollope's Barsetshire novels, and Thomas Hardy's Wessex novels.

Although Conrad's works do not belong to the tradition of the *roman-fleuve*, some of them possess transtextual connections common to the form. The most obvious of these appear in the so-called 'Malay trilogy' —*Almayer's Folly*, *An Outcast of the Islands*, and *The Rescue*—which dramatizes the life history, in reverse chronological order, of Captain Tom *Lingard. As Vernon Young points out, to read the works as a trilogy is to become aware of the boldness of Conrad's overall conception and the possibility that they form 'a tragedy in three acts' dramatizing 'first the consequences and later the inceptions of Tom Lingard's benevolent despotism'. Nevertheless, he adds, the attempt to read transtextual connections in the trilogy may obscure more than it reveals. The Lingard series, unlike the 19th-century *roman-fleuve*, has a reverse chronology and so does not offer the traditional historical continuity of the chronicle series. Again, since a period of over twenty years separates the composition of the first two works from the completion of the third, *The Rescue* (1920), the trilogy may ultimately be more revealing of the changing interests and quality of Conrad's work over two decades ('Lingard's Folly: The Lost Subject', *Kenyon Review*, 15 (1953), 522).

The appearance of the narrator *Marlow in four of Conrad's works—'Youth', 'Heart of Darkness', *Lord Jim*, and *Chance* —also allows for the possibility of following transtextual connections in what may be regarded as a tetralogy. At the beginning of 'Heart of Darkness', the first narrator echoes the previous story, 'Youth', when he says, 'Between us there was, as I have already said somewhere, the bond of the sea' (*Youth*, 45), and so implicitly invites the reader to regard the two works as stages in a continuous spiritual development. The narrator Marlow is unlike Conrad (in being permanently unmarried, for example), but also like him in being shown to grow older in a way paralleling his creator's own developing life. Hence the 'tetralogy' bears upon the Conradian preoccupation with 'the three ages of man' (*LL*, ii. 338) in embracing the youthful Marlow's experiences in the *Judea*, the middle-aged man's recounting of his earlier experiences in 'Youth' and 'Heart of Darkness', and the older, sage-like Marlow of *Chance*. Alan Warren Friedman's 'Conrad's Picturesque Narrator: Marlow's Journey from "Youth" through *Chance*', in Zyla and Aycock (eds.), 17–39, treats the Marlow works as a 'multi-volume' in the Proustian manner and traces such continuities and changes. Yet more transtextual possibilities emerge in a group of stories all deriving from Conrad's own experience of first command following upon his joining the *Otago* in *Bangkok 1888–9. These stories of untested young men and their ordeal of initiation— 'Falk', 'The Secret Sharer', and *The Shadow-Line*—include so many repeated settings and characters that they inevitably offer themselves as variations of a theme.

The idea of transtextual—or intertextual—echoing can also be applied in suggestive ways to other kinds of family relationship between stories in the canon. For example, Conrad's habits of composition often involved him in interrupting a longer work in order to compose non-fiction or short stories. Thus, during the writing of *Under Western Eyes* (1908–10), he broke off the longer work to compose 'The Black Mate' (*Tales of Hearsay*), 'The Secret Sharer' (*'Twixt Land and Sea*), and papers for *A Personal Record*; again, while composing *Victory* during the period 1910–12, he similarly diverted his energies into a small satellite of shorter works, including 'The Planter of Malata' and 'Because of the Dollars' (*Within the Tides*). While such families of works do not explicitly use repeated characters or settings, they are nevertheless rooted in a distinctive creative phase and generate the sense of a large meta-narrative, from which core-problems are developed in different directions and sometimes to alternative endings.

The works written during the painfully prolonged composition of *Under Western Eyes* offer particularly intriguing transtextual possibilities. Set in *Russia and dealing with *Razumov's conscience-stricken ordeal after informing upon a fellow student, *Under Western Eyes* engaged the deepest tensions within Conrad's *Polish inheritance as well as his constituted identity as *homo duplex*. The power of the novel's subject to attack and 'haunt' him during its two-year composition can also be measured by consulting its satellite works, which, in the case of 'The Secret Sharer', recapitulate themes of self-division and the double life, and, in the case of *A Personal Record*, prompted the writer to return to his own earlier background of Messianic and revolutionary traditions. As an example of how such subterranean connections and links may be developed, Ressler's study of 'The Secret Sharer' argues that the story is a 'romantic counterpart to the tragic *Under Western Eyes* and shaped by its creator's need to find relief in a confident rendering of life's possibilities that did not dilute his more deeply felt tragic knowledge' (81). The quest for such relief, he argues, can be detected in the tale's diminished scepticism and its emphasis on courageous action that springs from psychological rather than moral imperatives.

'Travel'. Written in the last week of July 1922 as a preface to Richard *Curle's *Into the East: Notes on Burma and Malaya* (1923), this piece was later collected in *Last Essays*. For its subject Conrad turned to travel books in general and to a theme underlying many of his later non-fictional writings, the evolving psychology and history of travel. At the basis of the essay is a genealogy of geographical travel, elaborated more fully in 'Geography and Some Explorers' (*Last Essays*), that identifies two geographical epochs: fabulous and militant. Sharply contradictory feelings are in evidence, since while Conrad celebrates an earlier age of selfless heroic exploration, he must sadly acknowledge the effects of an increasingly 'militant' geography in desacralizing the world. The demystifying effect of scientific enquiry, the growth of European colonization, the spread of trade that resulted in the opening of the Suez Canal in 1869, and the emergence of global tourism—all combine to usher in a different world, 'girt about with cables, with an atmosphere made restless by the waves of ether, lighted by that sun of the twentieth century under which there is nothing new left now, and but very little of what may still be called obscure' (88). In part a nostalgic lament for the world known to Conrad through his treasured boyhood reading and own travel experiences, this essay raises issues that bear upon a later cultural and geographical debate 'in which conventional accounts of spatial boundaries and hierarchies are under challenge in all sorts of ways' (Felix Driver, 'Geography Triumphant? Joseph Conrad and the Imperial Adventure', *The Conradian*, 18: 2 (1994), 111). The first revised typescript, dated 1 August 1922, is held at the Beinecke Rare Book and Manuscript Library, Yale University; the second revised typescript, assigned the same date, is held at the Rosenbach Museum and Library, Philadelphia. See also 'OCEAN TRAVEL' and 'GEOGRAPHY AND SOME EXPLORERS'.

Travers, Edith, in *The Rescue,* the wife of the diplomat Martin Travers, whose yacht *Hermit* becomes stranded on a mudbank off the 'Shore of Refuge' on the south-west coast of *Borneo. In addition to her husband, an intolerant and self-important snob, Mrs Travers is attended by Mr d'Alcacer, a Spanish gentleman who was invited along on the voyage for the sake of his conversation. Tom *Lingard, rudely rebuffed by Mr Travers when he arrives to take charge of the rescue operation, returns that night and has a long and secret conversation with Mrs Travers, to whom he feels he can speak openly about his efforts to restore the Rajah Hassim and his sister Immada to power in Wajo. Mrs Travers belongs to a series of courageous but unhappily married heroines in Conrad's works, including Emilia *Gould in *Nostromo* and Adèle de Montevesso in *Suspense,* whose devotion to their husbands is beyond ques-

tion, but who are nevertheless grateful for the attentions of other men. Mrs Travers and Lingard become fascinated with each other: she with the directness and simplicity of an adventurous man of action, and he with a woman who represents a level of society to which he had no access in *England, although he has become a 'King' in the meantime. When Mr Travers and d'Alcacer are kidnapped by Daman's pirate forces, Mrs Travers insists upon joining Lingard in his efforts to negotiate their release, and she dresses herself in the native clothing that Lingard had prepared for Immada. The special status she claims has the effect of 'emasculating' Lingard in the eyes of both his followers and his enemies; and in his efforts to rescue the Europeans he is forced to leave his brig, the source of his fighting strength, in charge of a subordinate. When Hassim and Immada also become prisoners but manage to dispatch Jaffir to Lingard with an emerald ring betokening their distress, Mrs Travers is asked to deliver the ring to Lingard, but she fails to do so and thereby provokes the catastrophe in which Hassim and Immada are blown up in the *Emma*. Critics have sometimes taken this resolution of the plot as a sign of Conrad's supposed misogyny; but even if the ring had been delivered, it remains uncertain how Lingard could have freed his Wajo friends and kept his mission intact.

'Turgenev'. At Edward *Garnett's request, Conrad readily agreed to contribute a preface to his *Turgenev: A Study* (1917), and the essay was written at Conrad's home on 7–8 May 1917 with Garnett in attendance. It was collected in *Notes on Life and Letters.* Expanding upon views he had communicated to Garnett in late April 1917 (*LFC*, 268–71), Conrad pays a generous tribute to *Turgenev's cosmopolitanism, the balance of national and universal traits in his life and writings, his humanism, and his political liberalism. However, as in many of Conrad's other scattered statements on Russian literature, the essay is complicated by a strangely obsessive rejection of *Dostoevsky and the type of

Russianness with which he is associated. The characterization of Turgenev as a 'Western' artist congenial to the English-speaking world is influenced—indeed even shaped—by Conrad's recurrent need to use that writer as a bulwark against, and a stick to beat, the 'convulsed terror-haunted' and Slavonic Dostoevsky (48). Hence, Conrad's rhetoric works to de-Russianize Turgenev by locating him within a larger non-Russian context, from which Dostoevsky, as the creator of incomprehensible Russian 'monsters', is outlawed: 'All his [Turgenev's] creations, fortunate and unfortunate, oppressed and oppressors are human beings, not strange beasts in a menagerie or damned souls knocking themselves to pieces in the stuffy darkness of mystical contradictions. They are human beings, fit to live, fit to suffer, fit to struggle, fit to win, fit to lose' (47). Thus heatedly demonized and apparently exorcized, the Dostoevsky constructed by the essay nevertheless tends to emerge with the charismatic force of a dangerous, but tempting, Mephistopheles. The manuscript (Beinecke Rare Book and Manuscript Library, Yale University) and a revised typescript (Dartmouth College) survive.

Turgenev, Ivan [Sergeyevich] (1818–83), Russian novelist. Ivan Turgenev was for Conrad an 'incomparable artist', who, by virtue of his Westernness, was especially valued as a humane contrast and antitype to the haunted and 'too Russian' *Dostoevsky. Having first read Turgenev's *A Nest of Gentlefolk* (1858) and *Smoke* (1867) as an adolescent in *Poland, Conrad reimmersed himself in this writer's works during the early part of his literary career (1895–1900) when he regularly received Constance *Garnett's pioneering translations of Turgenev, on which he later commented: 'Turgeniev for me is Constance Garnett and Constance Garnett *is* Turgeniev. She has done that marvellous thing of placing the man's work inside English literature and it is there that I see it—or rather that I *feel* it' (*LFC*, 269). Her co-pioneer in 'Englishing' Turgenev was her husband Edward *Garnett, Conrad's early literary

mentor, who supplied prefaces to all of the volumes. His advocacy of Turgenev was inseparable from his championing of the kind of novel that he believed the Russian novelist (and with him, Conrad) had helped to create: the 'most serious and significant of all literary forms . . . the novel shares with poetry today the honour of being the supreme instrument of the great artist's skill' (Introduction to *The Jew and Other Stories* (Heinemann, 1899), p. ix). When Garnett brought the prefaces together for publication in 1917, Conrad readily agreed to write an introduction (see 'TURGENEV') and described the Russian writer in terms comparable to those he reserved for his revered favourites, *Flaubert and *Maupassant.

Given Conrad's continuing intimacy with Turgenev's works, it would be surprising if there were *not* pervasive consonances and affinities between the two writers, some of which may be detected in the overall forms and character typologies in Conrad's fiction. As an example of the first, Conrad regarded *The Mirror of the Sea* as a work 'in the spirit of Turgeniev's Sportsman's Sketches' and even contemplated titling it *A Seaman's Sketches* (*CL*, iii. 132). With regard to the second, both Kirschner (1968: 241–2) and Watts (1993: 67–74) suggest that Conrad could hardly have been unaware of Turgenev's basic division of mankind into two fundamental types as signalled in his influential 1860 lecture 'Hamlet and Don Quixote: The Two Eternal Human Types', types often felt in Conrad's work with a pivotal force that Turgenev anticipates when he describes them as 'the twin antitypes of human nature, the two poles of the axle-tree on which that nature turns' (ibid. 68). Watts also points out the likely appeal for the creator of Martin *Decoud, *Razumov, and Axel *Heyst of the conception of the 'superfluous man' as embodied in Turgenev's Lermontov in 'The Diary of a Superfluous Man' (1850) and other 19th-century Russian writers (ibid. 65–6). Kirschner (1968: 240–52) offers the fullest and most systematic assessment of the differences and affinities between the two writers, and identifies specific links between *Lord Jim* and *Rudin* (1855), and *Under Western Eyes* and *Smoke* and *On the Eve* (1860). See also Marcus Wheeler, 'Turgenev and Joseph Conrad: Literary and Philosophical Links', *Slavonic and East European Review*, 61 (1983), 118–24.

'Twixt Land and Sea: Three Tales. Originally conceived in August 1910 with the provisional title *Tales of Experience*, this volume collects three short stories written during the period 1909–11—'A Smile of Fortune', 'The Secret Sharer', and 'Freya of the Seven Isles'—all previously published in magazines. It was brought out by J. M. *Dent in Britain on 14 October 1912 and by Hodder & Stoughton, Doran in America on 3 December 1912. According to Conrad, the stories had 'a common character— something slightly different from any short stories I ever wrote. It's my second manner, less forcible, more popular than the Typhoon set and in another tone than the [Set of] Six' (*CL*, iv. 503–4). In his 1920 'Author's Note', he also stressed their geographical unity as stories 'of the Indian Ocean with its off-shoots and prolongations north of the equator even as far as the Gulf of Siam', thereby underlining his turning away, after *Under Western Eyes*, from Western to Eastern subjects, a movement partly inspired in autumn 1909 by Captain Carlos *Marris, a visitor from the Far East, to whom the collection was dedicated. He also invokes both a personal and a professional context. The volume is 'the book of a man's convalescence' (p. vii), with two of the stories written during a period of recovery from his 1910 breakdown; and in retrospect it also signposted for Conrad a marked change in the fortune of his fiction with the popular reading public. The richly enigmatic story 'The Secret Sharer', composed before Conrad's breakdown, stands apart from some of these contexts, with its links both to *Under Western Eyes* and to the more intimate side of Conrad's maritime life. For a selection of contemporary reviews, see *CCH*, 251–8.

typewriters. At the turn of the century, the term 'typewriter' could refer to a typist as well as a machine for typing. In this sense, Conrad's first 'typewriter' was his wife Jessie, whom he first met when she was working 'as a "Typewriter" in a business office of the American "Calligraph" company' (*CL*, i. 265). During their honeymoon in Brittany, Jessie used what she remembered as a 'strange little typewriter called the Marriott' to prepare typed copy of Conrad's 'The Idiots'. This was actually a Merritt typewriter, and she has described its mechanism: 'It had a sliding bar containing the type, and was worked with a striker. You had to slide the bar about and stamp the letter by pressing the striker . . . but you had to be extremely careful how you moved that bar, because if you went ever so little too far, all the type would fall on the floor' (*JCKH*, 31). After the birth of their son Borys in January 1898, Jessie was less available for typing, although she was still helping as late as 1913 (*CL*, v. 301); on very rare occasions, Conrad apparently even did some of his own typing (*CL*, ii. 208).

The Nigger of the 'Narcissus' was the last of Conrad's works to be typed by Jessie on the Merritt. This machine was followed by 'a monolithic typewriter called a Yost' that she was unable to lift without help (*MFJC*, 12–13); Jessie herself remembered it as the 'mighty Yost' (*JCKH*, 43). Around 1910 she obtained 'one of the earliest portables, a Blick' (i.e. a Blickensderfer; *MFJC*, 13), which she used until about 1917. In October 1900, J. B. *Pinker became Conrad's literary agent and assumed responsibility for the preparation of multiple typed copies. Conrad's earliest surviving typed letter, sent to several publishers to notify them that Pinker was henceforth his agent, dates from 16 February 1903 (*CL*, iii. 19). In 1904 Pinker hired Lilian *Hallowes to serve as Conrad's resident typist, and Miss Hallowes remained in Conrad's service intermittently for the next twenty years, after 1917 typing most of his fictional work directly from *dictation. In January 1905, Conrad reported to Pinker from Capri that 'Miss Hallowes . . . has got a machine of her own now' (*CL*, iii. 211). The typewriter on which Conrad's later works were composed was a Corona portable model, possibly the one still in the possession of Conrad's grandson Philip.

It is possible to recognize not only the fonts of various machines but also the formatting 'signatures' of Conrad's typists: Jessie Conrad uses a variable number of spaces for paragraph indentation and tends to run words off the right-hand margin, while Miss Hallowes regularly indents five spaces in literary manuscripts (or sometimes ten spaces in letters) and usually respects the right margin. Conrad's late works display a routine in which Miss Hallowes's 'original' typescript would first undergo correction by Conrad and then be sent to Pinker, who would arrange to have multiple clean copies retyped, at least one of which would be returned to Conrad for further revision.

An understanding of Conrad's typescripts and the nature of his handwritten revisions is essential to the establishment of his texts. It seems unlikely that Conrad —whose own spelling and punctuation were inconsistent—would have dictated spelling or punctuation to Miss Hallowes. The punctuation of his later works is thus her immediate creation in the first instance, produced under time pressure, and subject to Conrad's subsequent review and correction, which often introduced new inconsistencies. Conrad's typed letters often take the nowadays curious form of openly edited texts, where the original wording remains clearly visible beside or beneath his handwritten amendments.

'Typhoon'. Conrad's first reference to this novella was apparently in a letter to David *Meldrum of 14 February 1899 where he refers to a still-unwritten story as '"Equitable Division" (a story of a typhoon)' (*CL*, ii. 169) and as possibly suitable for *Blackwood's Magazine*. Almost a year later, in January 1900, the unwritten story—at this point called 'A Skittish Cargo' (*CL*, ii. 237)—was further delayed while Conrad finished *Lord Jim*. It was not begun until October 1900, when he sent William *Blackwood a specimen, anticipated a story of some 12,000 words, and

described it to his agent J. B. *Pinker as 'quite the thing that finds room in Xmas numbers' (*CL*, ii. 295). By the time of its completion in January 1901, 'Typhoon' had evolved into a novella of 28,000 words. It was serialized in Britain in *Pall Mall Magazine* (January–March 1902) with some finely crafted *illustrations by Maurice Greiffenhagen, and in America in *Critic* (February–May 1902). The two serial texts are considered in detail in 'Conrad at Work: The Two Serial Texts of *Typhoon*', *Conradiana*, 19 (1987), 99–119, where Dwight H. Purdy illuminatingly follows the process of revision undertaken by Conrad for the British serial and concludes that 'some wonderful criticism of Conrad is to be found in Conrad's revisions' (117). Conrad reluctantly allowed the story to be published separately by Putnam's in the United States in 1902, but later complained that he had not seen the proofs and that it had been 'set up from an uncorrected MS' (*CL*, ii. 466). In Britain, the story was collected in the *Typhoon* volume of 1903.

The novella's first chapter introduces Captain *MacWhirr and the British crew of the steamer *Nan-Shan* prior to her departure with 200 coolies from an unnamed Eastern port for Fu-Chau on the south China coast. A selective and affectionately comic introduction to the quintessentially British sea captain's physical appearance, habitual manner, and background prevents the reader from making any easy judgement on him: he is humane, physically stalwart, a stickler for detail, and admired by the ship's owner for his efficiency, but also dully prosaic, literal-minded, apparently oblivious to the world's more sinister dangers, and with 'just enough imagination to carry him through each successive day, and no more' (4). Other perspectives upon MacWhirr—by his wife and family, the youthful first mate Jukes, and the chief engineer Solomon Rout— add to the prevailing impression of the captain as a Chaplinesque figure, with tightly fitting suit and gamp. Once at sea (chapter 2), the *Nan-Shan* is faced by signs of unusually worsening weather which may portend a typhoon. Consulting a manual of seamanship, MacWhirr refuses to follow the standard textbook regulations and insists, to Jukes's disquiet, that the ship must face the coming bad weather 'plain and straight' (88). Chapters 3 and 4 portray the gathering tumult of the typhoon and its danger to the ship's very existence, contrasting Jukes's growing nervous apprehension with MacWhirr's grim determination. At the end of chapter 4, a further crisis arrives when the 200 coolies 'come adrift' in their between-deck quarters and begin to fight over their scattered dollars. On Mac-Whirr's decisive command, Jukes and a small company of the crew succeed in restoring order (chapter 5) just as the ship herself heads towards the height of the typhoon. This climax, which takes place on Christmas Day, is not described. Set some days later, chapter 6 shows the *Nan-Shan* having escaped 'the Great Beyond, whence no river ever returns to give up her crew to the dust of the earth' (91) and arriving at her destination. A narrative postscript is largely handed over to Jukes who, in a letter to a friend, tells how on arrival in port MacWhirr insisted upon redistributing the dollars to the coolies in equal shares, and who concludes the story: 'I think that he [MacWhirr] got out of it very well for such a stupid man' (102).

As in *The Nigger of the 'Narcissus'*, many of the tale's main sources belong to Conrad's own past *sea life. MacWhirr, he comments, 'is the product of twenty years of life. My own life' ('Author's Note', p. vi), the captain's name being borrowed from an actual Irish captain, John McWhir, under whom Conrad had served in the *Highland Forest* in 1887 and who is remembered in *The Mirror of the Sea* (5–6). The episode of the fighting coolies appears to have been based on an actual event about which Conrad had heard through *Singapore harbour-gossip during his stays there in the first half of the 1880s.

First reviewers were virtually unanimous in praising the story as a storm-piece and as one of the finest examples of its kind—Quiller Couch thought it 'a small masterpiece' (*CCH*, 156)—although many also pointed out that in comparison to

Conrad's previous novel, *Lord Jim*, 'Typhoon' was a more modest and limited genre study. It found its first eloquent champion in F. R. Leavis who, in the course of devising a canon of Conrad's major works in *The Great Tradition* (1948), built part of his main thesis around the story, using it to downgrade *Lord Jim* and claiming that it revealed Conrad as, above all, 'the laureate of the Merchant Service, the British seaman happily doubled with the artist' (190). Leavis argued that the strength of the story lay not in the description of the storm, but in Conrad's treatment of Mac-Whirr and the crew, and he praised Conrad's ability to represent 'ordinariness' as a form of 'heroic sublimity' (185).

The way in which Conrad's art functions in modulating between the ordinary and the heroic has exercised many later critics. An unusual story in the canon by virtue of the central character's unthinking literalness and even, on occasions, denseness, 'Typhoon' presents the reader with ample evidence to endorse Jukes's dismissal of MacWhirr: 'There are feelings this man simply hasn't got—and there's an end of it' (98). This evidence would include the fact that, in expostulating against Jukes's use if images and treating written words as if they were 'worn-out things, and of a faded meaning' (15), MacWhirr sets himself in opposition to the very foundations of Conrad's art in 'Typhoon' and elsewhere. However, the novella moves beyond such condescendingly easy judgements, partly by its implicit querying of whether the youthfully 'animated' Jukes (97) has earned the right to dismiss the captain in the way that he does, and partly by the use of warmly Dickensian comedy which, as Kirschner has admirably shown, gathers affection for the ordinary MacWhirr and by which he is 'defined and vindicated' (1990: 6). In other ways, the novella is Janus-like in its perspectives. The main structural contrast in the tale between the stolid Captain MacWhirr and the imaginative young mate is not simply a means to denigrate MacWhirr's unimaginativeness, but also an invitation to question its opposite in a young man who desperately needs the support and strength that MacWhirr has to offer during the typhoon. The reader is further pressed into revaluing the captain's apparent inadequacies by the emerging paradox that the quality of unmoving stubbornness that so limits him in matters of difficult choice is the very same quality that, during the stress of the typhoon, makes him such a rock-like presence. During the storm itself, moreover, MacWhirr takes on a significant representative quality as the ship's commander whose 'voice', as both a response to the typhoon and an expression of command, enacts 'a point of view that . . . put[s] all that elemental fury into its proper place' ('Author's Note', p. vi). In these episodes, MacWhirr's bearing is less that of the 'perfectly satisfactory son of a petty grocer in Belfast' (4) than of a doughty John Bull, who is confident that although the *Nan-Shan* flies a Siamese flag, she nevertheless embodies the *British Merchant Service traditions of fair play, courage, and resistance in adversity. That the final confrontation with the typhoon takes place on Christmas Day—a detail easily missed, since it is mentioned only briefly in chapter 6—is perhaps partly symbolic, but also possibly ironic, since the tale implies that 'Christmas', an incidental event in the dangerous battle with the indifferent sea, is mainly a construction of the comfortable hearth and home.

Some later critics have served to complicate Leavis's view of the relative merits of *Lord Jim* and 'Typhoon' by arguing that the novella's richly paradoxical presentation of MacWhirr is, in fact, considerably indebted to the novel about *Jim that preceded it. Both stories incorporate a crisis at sea involving a large human cargo and a ship threatened by extreme weather conditions. It can also be helpful to regard MacWhirr as Jim's antitype, the former's pragmatic devotion to the eloquence of facts standing in sharp contrast to the errant Bovaryism of his younger opposite. Both works begin with a teasingly speculative physical description of their main figures and both then employ the varying testimony of plural narrators. Hence, although 'Typhoon' may initially seem to

offer a 'simple' character, its methods are by no means straightforward: from *Lord Jim*, the novella inherits a mock-epic quality as well as a pervasive interrogative note, present in the early pages through references to MacWhirr's 'mysterious side' (4) and in the narrator's tendency never to present a view of his prosaic dullness, as imaged, for example, in his 'clumsy black boots', without some qualifying sense of the captain's humane integrity, as signalled by his hair, which is 'fair and extremely fine' (3). The tale further frustrates any simple judgement of MacWhirr by enlisting as a main commentator a young man, Jukes, whose proneness on one occasion to 'do-nothing heroics to which good men surrender at times' (51) inescapably reminds the reader of the earlier Jim. For helpful and varied commentary, see T. A. Birrell, 'The Simplicity of *Typhoon*: Conrad, Flaubert and Others', *Dutch Quarterly Review of Anglo-American Letters*, 10 (1980), 272–95; Christof Wegelin, 'MacWhirr and the Testimony of the Human Voice', *Conradiana*, 7 (1975), 45–50; and Joseph Kolupke, 'Elephants, Empires, and Blind Men: A Reading of the Figurative Language in Conrad's "Typhoon"', *Conradiana*, 20 (1988), 71–85. Both manuscript and typescript (private collection) survive.

Typhoon and Other Stories. This volume collects four stories written during the period 1900–2—'Typhoon', 'Amy Foster', 'Falk', and 'To-morrow'—all but 'Falk' previously serialized. It was published by *Heinemann in Britain on 22 April 1903. In America, 'Typhoon' had been published as a separate volume by Putnam on 4 September 1902, with the other three stories appearing in a later collection entitled *Falk, Amy Foster, To-morrow: Three Stories* by McClure, Phillips in late September 1903. In Conrad's opinion, the separate publication of 'Typhoon' in America spoiled for transatlantic readers what had been planned as a unified quartet. Addressing the question of the volume's unity, Kirschner helpfully shows how the collection represents a fresh departure after the *Marlow stories of Conrad's *Blackwood's* period, and how it emerges from the writer's altered sense of his past and present vocations to form a meaningful literary phase between *Lord Jim* and *Nostromo*. Not printed in the order of their writing, the stories have been re-organized, he suggests, in a way that presents 'a chiaroscuro of sea and land life in an alternating rhythm of hope and despair', with 'Typhoon' and 'Falk' implicitly linked as two relatively optimistic sea stories in contrast to two land stories, 'Amy Foster' and 'To-morrow', with a common *Kent set-

ting and a central figure who 'either perishes in despair or is condemned to domestic slavery, mocked by the "hopeful madness" of a fixed idea'. In Kirschner's view, this reorganization also points to important biographical correlatives, 'the seesaw mental struggle of a man pining for lost freedom while doggedly mooring himself to an existence that must often have seemed to combine hopeless slavery and hopeful madness' (1990: 14). For a selection of contemporary reviews, see *CCH*, 143–58.

U

Ukraine. The origins of Kievan Ruś precede those of *Russia, and Moscow itself was founded by a Kiev prince. Internecine struggles in the 12th century between Ruthenian and Russian princedoms, followed by Mongol invasions in the 13th century, inhibited the development of stable state structures in the territories which now constitute Ukraine. Most of these territories, including Kiev itself, were absorbed by the expanding Grand Duchy of Lithuania in the latter half of the 14th century. Soon afterwards, Lithuania was joined with *Poland in a dynastic union, institutionalized in 1569 as the Union of Lublin, which gave the Ukrainian *szlachta* (landed gentry) and the clergy the same privileges as those of their Polish counterparts. The failure of the Polish *szlachta* to honour the promised liberties led to a bloody rebellion under the leadership of Bohdan Chmielnicki (himself born of Polish parents), who in 1654 at Pereyaslav declared eastern Ukraine subject to Russian rule, thus foreclosing for 300 years the formation of an autonomous Ukraine.

Since then, Ukraine has consisted of three parts: eastern, central, and western. The eastern part was promptly incorporated into Russia. The central part, which until the end of the 18th century formed part of the multi-ethnic Polish Commonwealth, had a strong Polish minority in the towns and a dominant Polish landowning class. Conrad was born in central Ukraine, at a time when the Polish cultural presence was becoming increasingly constrained by censorship and other administrative restrictions. There were no Polish or Ukrainian schools; all instruction was in Russian.

Western Ukraine, part of the Polish 'Crown' since the 14th century and incorporated into the Austro-Hungarian Empire after the partitions of Poland, had its capital in *Lwów, a lively, multinational city that at the turn of the 19th century was second only to *Warsaw as a centre of Polish intellectual and cultural life.

The eastern territories of the Polish Commonwealth, sparsely populated and with huge tracts of fertile soil, had to be defended until the early 18th century against frequent Tartar and Ottoman Turkish inroads. These open lands attracted not only adventurous and combative members of the *szlachta*, but also innumerable Polish peasants fleeing from serfdom, and townsfolk seeking better opportunities. There was no clear-cut political division between Poles and Ruthenians (Ukrainians); the commonly used formula *gente Ruthenus natione Polonus*—Ruthenian by descent, Polish by nationality—reflected the fact that being 'Polish' meant to feel oneself a citizen of the multinational Polish Republic. However, most Poles were Roman Catholics, while Ukrainians were either Orthodox or Uniates.

The Polish Commonwealth was an imperfect federal state with fairly extensive civil liberties. Ukrainians coming under Russian rule discovered that Russia was, in contrast, a thoroughly centralized autocracy. Eastern Ukraine was fully integrated within the Russian empire, and the partitioning of Poland, which gave Russia power over almost all of Ukraine, was presented by official Russian historians as an act of recovery of their tsars' patrimony. In the 19th century, Ukrainian, which Russians regarded as a corrupt dialect of their own language, was banned from schools and offices, and only religious books could be published in it.

The revival of the Ukrainian national spirit dates from the mid-19th century and owes a debt to Polish Romanticism. Ukrainian patriots have seen themselves as a nation distinguished from the Russians by their historical links to western Europe, and by the individualism of their people, their attachment to personal liberties, and their preference for federalism over centralism. These inclinations are linked to the past they share with Poles, and the struggle for Ukrainian national independence was greeted with sympathy by many mid-19th-century Polish democrats, among them Conrad's father Apollo *Korzeniowski. In his poems, circulated clandestinely, and in political articles published anonymously abroad to bypass official censorship, he sharply criticized Polish landowners for putting class above national interests, and profit above patriotic duty. He visualized the future free Poland as a country where Ukrainians would enjoy social and national equality.

Poles considered Russia the most dangerous enemy of Ukrainian independence, but as a result of religious, cultural, and especially social divisions, compounded by the haughty contempt of the Polish *szlachta* for the Ukrainian peasantry, and perhaps most of all by shrewd Russian political manœuvres and provocations, by the 20th century the Ukrainian masses turned sooner against the Poles than against the Russians. This tendency was strengthened by communist agitation directed at the landowning 'exploiters' and intensified by the spread of the Russian Revolution to Ukraine in 1918–19. Hundreds of manors were burnt to the ground, among them *Kazimierówka, the estate of Conrad's uncle and guardian Tadeusz *Bobrowski, owned at the time by Conrad's uncle Stanisław Bobrowski, himself a socialist who spent several years in a Russian prison. Conrad's *letters to his relatives were also destroyed.

The violent battle for Lwów, won by Poles in 1918 (who were a majority in the city itself, with Ukrainians predominantly a rural population), marked the most significant event in Polish–Ukrainian relations in the aftermath of the *First World War. A military pact signed in April 1920 by Polish head of state Józef Piłsudski and Ukrainian leader Semyon Petliura allied an independent Ukraine with Poland in a common struggle against the Soviets. Poland managed to repel the enemy, but the Ukrainian masses remained passive.

The Ukrainian Soviet Socialist Republic, established in 1924, was autonomous in name only. See also Najder, 'Conrad and Ukraine: A Note', *The Conradian*, 23: 2 (1998), 45–54.   ZN

Under Western Eyes. Conrad's 'most deeply meditated novel' (*CL*, v. 695) and the site of his closest encounter with 'the very soul of things Russian' (*CL*, iv. 8), *Under Western Eyes* is generally regarded as the most complex and autobiographical of his political fictions. Planned as a short story initially titled 'Razumov', it grew eventually to 1,351 pages of manuscript, and proved the most painful and difficult of all Conrad's novels to write. He worked on the manuscript for more than two years, from December 1907 to January 1910, during a period of poor health, increasing debts, relentless anxieties, and damaged friendships. These difficulties, compounded by the effort of wrestling with the Russian spectre that had haunted his childhood, ultimately shattered Conrad's nerves and led to a serious physical and psychological breakdown, reflected in a six-week hiatus in his correspondence and a breach in his relationship with his agent J. B. *Pinker. In his first letter after the crisis, Conrad told John *Galsworthy, 'I feel all crumpled up beyond all hope [of] being ever smoothed out again' (*CL*, iv. 321). His double perspective as an émigré looking back upon 'things Russian' is manifest in the 'double authority' of the narrative of *Under Western Eyes*, which has tested the interpretative mettle of readers and critics representing a wide variety of school and approaches.

The story of *Razumov is introduced by a *teacher of languages in *Geneva who claims to have based his account on documents written by the protagonist, which he undertakes to present to 'Western eyes'. The story proper begins in St Petersburg, where Razumov, a third-year student in philosophy, returns to his lodgings to find that Victor *Haldin, who has just killed a Minister of State and a number of bystanders with a terrorist bomb, expects Razumov to hide him and help him to escape. Razumov agrees to visit the driver Ziemianitch to arrange for Haldin's flight, but when he finds the driver hopelessly drunk, he beats him and then betrays Haldin to Prince K—, whom he believes to be his own natural father. Haldin is arrested, tortured, and hanged. Razumov's room is ransacked by the police, and he is summoned before Councillor Mikulin. When Razumov tries to leave, or 'retire', Mikulin asks him, 'Where to?'

The scene then shifts to Geneva, where the teacher of languages describes the reactions of Haldin's mother and sister *Natalia to the news of his death. The 'heroic fugitive' and 'great feminist' Peter *Ivanovitch, the cynosure of the local revolutionaries, informs Natalia Haldin of Razumov's arrival in Geneva. A fortnight later, the language teacher finds Miss Haldin on the Promenade of the Bastions, and she tells him of her visit to the Château Borel and her meeting with Tekla, Peter Ivanovitch's sympathetic and long-suffering secretary. They are interrupted by Razumov, and when Miss Haldin leaves to rejoin her mother, Razumov walks off with the teacher, who makes a futile effort to engage Razumov in conversation before leaving him, at the end of Part II, standing on a bridge staring down at the rushing waters of the source of the Rhône.

The 'day of many conversations' (237) that occupies the rest of the novel begins several weeks later, when the teacher again encounters Miss Haldin on the Promenade of the Bastions. Earlier on this day Razumov has visited the Château Borel and met Mme de S— and Peter Ivanovitch. He then becomes involved in a long and difficult conversation with Sofia Antonovna on the grounds of the château, in the course of which he learns of the suicide of Ziemianitch, which provides him with an unexpected alibi by solving the mystery of why Haldin failed to make good his escape. Razumov walks back to town, encountering Julius Laspara on the way, who urges him to 'write!' Taking this as his cue, Razumov wanders to the Île Rousseau and composes his first secret report to the authorities under the Western eyes, as it

were, of the great philosopher. While Razumov is writing, the teacher of languages opens Part IV of his narrative by resuming the St Petersburg narrative at the point where it broke off at the end of Part I. He describes the circumstances under which Razumov was given his mission to Geneva, in part because of Councillor Mikulin's promotion to director of general police supervision over Europe.

Having finished and mailed his report, Razumov returns to his rooms and writes in his diary. Meanwhile, the teacher of languages encounters Natalia Haldin in search of Razumov, since her mother has just learned of his presence in Geneva and wishes to see him at once. Returning to the Haldin apartment after a long quest on foot, they are surprised to find Razumov already there. His fifteen minutes with Haldin's mother have affected him like 'the revenge of the unknown' (340); fleeing, he finds Natalia in the ante-room and confesses to her his betrayal of her brother. He returns home to conclude his secret diary with a second version of this confession (the only part of the diary to be directly quoted by the narrator), then walks through drenching rain to Laspara's house to make a public confession to the assembled revolutionists. The conspirators decide to allow Razumov to leave, but the brutal Nikita (who turns out later to be a police spy, as Razumov senses) first deafens him by bursting his eardrums. Unable to hear, Razumov is run over by a tram the following morning. He returns to Russia, where Tekla devotes the remainder of her life to caring for him.

Conrad's first reference to 'Razumov' was apparently in a letter to Pinker of 4 December 1907, the day after his 50th birthday, when he interrupted his slow progress on *Chance* to begin a short story 'about the revolutionist who is blown up with his own bomb' (*CL*, iii. 513). The idea began to grow in Conrad's mind, and a month later he was describing it to Marguerite *Poradowska as a novella, and to Galsworthy and Pinker as an effort to confront the very soul or essence of 'things Russian' (*CL*, iv. 9, 14–15, 22). In this original version, Conrad planned for Razumov to marry Natalia Haldin and have a child whose resemblance to her dead brother would ultimately lead Razumov to confess his betrayal. By the time the novel was published, Razumov would be driven to confess by the accumulating pressures of a single day.

In September 1908, Lilian *Hallowes was re-engaged as a typist and charged with preparing a clean copy of 'Razumov', which by then amounted to 'at least 62 thou[sand] words' (*CL*, iv. 133). Conrad completed drafts of Part I and much of Part II by the autumn of 1908 (*JCC*, 345). During this period he was also writing his memoirs of *Poland for publication in Ford Madox *Ford's new journal the *English Review*. (Ford's role as a source of information for the novel is described by Thomas C. Moser in 'Ford Madox Hueffer and *Under Western Eyes*', *Conradiana*, 15 (1983), 163–80.) In March 1909 the Conrads moved from Someries to rented rooms above a butcher's shop in Aldington. Conrad's labours to complete the novel are chronicled by David Leon Higdon and Robert F. Sheard in '"The End is the Devil": The Conclusions to Conrad's *Under Western Eyes*', *Studies in the Novel*, 19 (1987), 187–96. When he interrupted work on the novel in December 1909 to write 'The Secret Sharer' (in which *Leggatt's appeal to the captain echoes Haldin's appeal to Razumov in the opening scenes of *Under Western Eyes*), Pinker's disapproval of what he considered Conrad's misuse of precious time, combined with a threat to withdraw support from Conrad unless the novel were finished in a fortnight, left Conrad fuming and threatening to throw the manuscript into the fire (*CL*, iv. 302). A draft of the entire novel, cut back to some 113,000 words, was finished by 26 January 1910, at which point Conrad argued with Pinker and suffered a mental breakdown in which he 'spoke all the time in Polish' or repeated 'snatches of orders in an Eastern language' (*JCHC*, 143). Recovering in March, he revised the text in April and May before moving from Aldington to Capel House (both in Kent) in June. From December 1910 to October 1911, serial versions appeared in

both the *English Review* and the *North American Review*. Conrad sent pages of the English serial version to Methuen to be reset for the English edition, which was revised in proof and published on 5 October 1911. Two weeks later, on 19 October, Harper & Brothers in New York published the unrevised American serial text as a book. The stages of the novel's composition have been traced in detail by Emily K. Izsak [Dalgarno] in '*Under Western Eyes* and the Problem of Serial Publication', *Review of English Studies*, NS 23 (1972), 429–44, and by Roderick Davis in '*Under Western Eyes*: "The Most Deeply Meditated Novel"', *Conradiana*, 9 (1977), 59–75. Neither Izsak nor Davis had access to the typescript of the novel, which was in private hands until 1977. The typescript and its role in the work's composition are discussed by David Leon Higdon in his contribution to David R. Smith (ed.), *Joseph Conrad's Under Western Eyes: Beginnings, Revisions, Final Forms* (Hamden, Conn.: Archon, 1991). Much of the material in these studies has been superseded by Carabine (1996).

As happened so often in Conrad's career, *Under Western Eyes* received high praise from his fellow artists and critics but did not sell very well. Early reviewers applauded its psychological penetration and dark evocation of the atmosphere of 'things Russian'; but as Conrad commented in the 'Author's Note' to '*Twixt Land and Sea*, 'there is no denying the fact that "Under Western Eyes" found no favour in the public eye' (p. vii). Ford considered it Conrad's greatest masterpiece. In an article published in the December 1911 issue of the *English Review*, he spoke eloquently of Razumov's struggle to redeem his personal honour—a theme of particular importance to Ford at this time of crisis in his own life. Another reviewer observed that Conrad was uniquely situated to interpret the mysteries of the East for the benefit of Westerners, and claimed that the novel 'helps us to understand Turgeniev and Dostoievsky with greater clearness' (*CCH*, 234).

In *The Great Tradition* (1948), a landmark work of criticism that launched Conrad's modern academic reputation,

F. R. Leavis had little to say about *Under Western Eyes*. The first substantial appreciation of the novel was an introductory essay (1951) by Morton Dauwen Zabel, later reprinted under the title 'The Threat to the West', which placed the novel squarely in the context of Russian history and saw it as a prescient warning to the West of the need for moral decision. During the Cold War, Western critics naturally paid more attention to the political dimensions of Conrad's works, and often hailed *Under Western Eyes* as a fictional expression of the condemnation of Russia expressed in 'Autocracy and War' (1905) and in his 1920 'Author's Note'. The popularity of this approach eventually provoked Tony Tanner to counter that 'Too much insensitive criticism has charged the book with being a crude and embittered anti-Russian tract' ('Nightmare and Complacency: Razumov and the Western Eye', *Critical Quarterly*, 4 (1962), 198). Nevertheless, Avrom Fleishman argues that the novel can be read as 'Conrad's critique of Russian obscurantism' (1967: 224).

The setting and style of Part I are especially reminiscent of *Dostoevsky, whose works Conrad may have read in French translation. When Constance *Garnett sent him a copy of *The Brothers Karamazov*, the first of her thirteen Dostoevsky translations, in 1912, Conrad replied: 'I don't know what D stands for or reveals, but I do know that he is too Russian for me. It sounds to me like some fierce mouthings from prehistoric ages' (*CL*, v. 70). Later that same year he told Edward *Garnett's sister Olivia that 'the fact is that I know extremely little of Russians. . . . I crossed the Russian frontier at the age of ten. Not having been to school then I never knew Russian' (*CL*, iv. 490). The nature and extent of Dostoevsky's unacknowledged influence are difficult issues to resolve. Although Conrad vehemently denied any Russian influence on his writings, *Under Western Eyes* has long been considered the most 'Dostoevskian' of his works. The Russian reception of the novel is discussed by Roderick Davis in 'Under Eastern Eyes: Conrad and Russian Reviewers', *Conradiana*, 6 (1974), 126–30. Yves Hervouet surveys the influence of French literature in 'Conrad's Debt to French Authors in *Under Western Eyes*', *Conradiana*, 14 (1982), 113–25. Some critics, among them Gustav Morf and E. H. Visiak, have understood Razumov's 'betrayal' as an expression of Conrad's own guilt at having abandoned his native country and language. Andrzej Busza takes a more nuanced and pluralistic approach in 'Rhetoric and Ideology in Conrad's *Under Western Eyes*', in Sherry (ed.), 105–18. Paul Kirschner discusses both Russian and French literary influences on the novel in 'The French Face of Dostoyevsky in Conrad's *Under Western Eyes*: Some Consequences for Criticism', *Conradiana*, 30 (1998), 24–43, where he makes a strong case for the influence of *Un adolescent*, a 1902 French translation of Dostoevsky's *Podrostok* (A Raw Youth, 1875) that Conrad could have read.

In Conrad's novel, two narrators compete for the attentions of the heroine, while each appears as a character in the other's story. Razumov's story is recorded in the 'secret diary' that Natalia Haldin receives in the mail and later gives to the teacher of languages, who takes on the task of translating and 'editing' it in order to render 'things Russian' comprehensible to Western eyes. But the narrator's voice is unstable; he often assumes the characteristics of an omniscient narrator who reports things he has no plausible way of knowing. Razumov dislikes the narrator, but remains subject to his mediation, and only the final words of his diary are quoted directly. The many parallels between Razumov and the narrator, and their relation to the author, figure in Penn R. Szittya's 'Metafiction: The Double Narration in *Under Western Eyes*', *English Literary History*, 48 (1981), 817–40. Frank Kermode's essay 'Secrets and Narrative Sequence', first published in *Critical Inquiry* 7 (1979, reprinted in *Essays on Fiction 1971–82* (Routledge, 1983)), offers a subtle and original reading of the novel's problems of narration.

The double-voiced authority of the narrative is further complicated by the double roles played by most of the characters. Nothing in this novel is what it seems:

Peter Ivanovitch preaches *feminism while rudely abusing and tyrannizing Tekla; the ghoulish Mme de S— plots revolution in order to wreak revenge on the 'thieves' of the ruling family, not to help a proletariat whose vulgarity she despises. Peter Ivanovitch and Sophia Antonovna tolerate Mme de S— only for the sake of her wealth, but she dies intestate. Given Razumov's secretly false position, even the simplest remarks or the most innocent queries are filled with unintentional implications. Razumov speaks in taunts and riddles so as not to reveal himself utterly. The use of doublings as a structural principle is examined by Claude Thomas in 'Structure and Narrative Technique of *Under Western Eyes*', *Studies in Joseph Conrad* (Montpellier: Université Paul Valéry, 1975), 205–21.

Research for a critical edition of *Under Western Eyes* has inspired a number of detailed studies of the novel's composition and the history of its publication. Five such essays are collected in Smith's *Joseph Conrad's Under Western Eyes: Beginnings, Revisions, Final Forms*. David Leon Higdon has discussed the manuscript, the typescript, and *collected edition texts of the novel in a series of important essays. Keith Carabine (1996) provides a detailed discussion of composition and is especially critical of Kermode's essay 'Secrets and Narrative Sequence', which he calls a 'wild account of the narrator's diabolism' (208 n.). Paul Kirschner's studies of Conrad's use of Russian materials and the topography of Geneva have appeared in *L'Époque Conradienne* (1988, 101–27), in Moore (ed.) 1992: 223–54, and in his substantial introduction and notes to the 1996 Penguin edition of *Under Western Eyes*.

Marc Allégret's *film adaptation of *Under Western Eyes* in 1936 as *Razumov* ('*Sous les yeux d'Occident*') took substantial liberties with Conrad's plot and told the story of Razumov as a romantic melodrama in which Razumov attempts suicide but is nursed back to health by Natalia at an Alpine resort. Haldin was played by Jean-Louis Barrault, and the sinister Mikulin by Conrad's admirer and correspondent Jacques Copeau. In 1969 John Joubert's *opera based on *Under Western Eyes* premièred in London, in which Razumov sings a final duet with Tekla after his eardrums have been destroyed. A 1975 BBC-TV adaptation by Stuart Burge starred Roger Rees as Razumov. An Italian television version, *Con gli occhi dell'Occidente*, was made in 1979. A dramatic adaptation by Zygmunt Hübner and Michał Komar entitled *Spiskowcy* (Conspirators) was performed at the Teatr Powszechny in Warsaw in 1980 and first broadcast on Polish television in 1983.

The manuscript of *Under Western Eyes*, whose former owners include John *Quinn and Jerome Kern, is at the Beinecke Rare Book and Manuscript Library, Yale University. A nearly complete typescript and a smaller manuscript fragment are at the Philadelphia Free Library. The Beinecke Library also has a typescript of Conrad's 'Author's Note' to the novel.

'Unlighted Coast, The'. In response to an invitation by the Admiralty in September 1916 to join such writers as Rudyard *Kipling, Arnold *Bennett, and A. Conan Doyle in writing wartime propaganda, Conrad agreed to combine a series of tours of British ports with some articles on the work of the Royal Naval Reserve. Probably written in December 1916, 'The Unlighted Coast' was not released by the Admiralty and remains the only 'official' piece from Conrad's pen. The Admiralty was clearly unhappy with his brooding meditation on his experiences of the previous month in the North Sea aboard HMS *Ready*. Beginning with an evocation of omnipresent darkness reminiscent of 'Heart of Darkness', the article—as Najder observes—contains 'no trace of propaganda and not even much optimism' (*JCC*, 422). The essay had to await posthumous publication in *The Times* (18 August 1925), 13–14, and was later collected in *Last Essays*. The location of the manuscript, the copy-text for the 1925 pamphlet *Admiralty Paper*, edited by Jerome Kern, is unknown; the first revised typescript is held at Dartmouth College; the second typescript, sent to the Admiralty, seems not to have survived.

Unwin, T[homas] Fisher (1848–1935), founder of the Unwin publishing house in 1882, who brought out Conrad's first novel (*Almayer's Folly*) and two other of his early volumes (*An Outcast of the Islands* and *Tales of Unrest*) during the period 1895–8. Shrewdly responding to the changing economic climate of book-publishing in the 1890s, T. Fisher Unwin had fashioned a highly competitive company with a reputation for discovering and marketing promising new authors. This was partly due to the professional flair Unwin had acquired through a long apprenticeship in the book trade, and partly to the skilful team he had brought together, including the brilliant Edward *Garnett as reader and David Rice as chief salesman. Always alert to new market possibilities, the company developed enterprising fiction series such as the 'Pseudonym Library' and the 'Overseas Library' as rubrics within which a whole range of promising new authors, including Conrad, could be profitably marketed to a growing middle-class reading public.

Conrad's delight at having his first novel published by Unwin was soon qualified. First, he found that Unwin's notoriously cold and humourless manner made it impossible to have a personal relationship with him: 'I never know what to write to that man. He numbs me like an electric eel', Conrad wrote to Unwin's own valued employee, Garnett (*CL*, i. 281). More seriously, Conrad discovered that while Unwin's hard bargaining might be acceptable to the beginning author, it was not so to the writer whose entire financial survival had

come to rest upon the rewards he could get for his work. Money matters thus forced them into confrontation: in late 1896, Conrad found Unwin's terms for his work-in-progress unacceptable, and, when he could not get an improved offer, took steps to find an alternative publisher (William *Heinemann) for *The Nigger of the 'Narcissus'*, while allowing Unwin to publish *Tales of Unrest*. In these negotiations Conrad was supported, indeed steered, by Garnett, who had no great love for publishers as a species and always sided with the needs of the writer. From this point onwards Unwin seems to have aroused what Conrad called his 'Private Devil', and in one letter he goes so far as to style him 'the animal' (*CL*, ii. 406). In *The Inheritors*, Unwin was represented as Polehampton, a cultural philistine for whom books are merely marketable commodities.

The plan to bring out a *collected edition of Conrad's works later in his career raised the awkward problem of acquiring copyrights from a variety of publishers, Unwin included. The latter did not relinquish material in which he held copyright easily and, as part of an overall agreement for the collected edition, ceded his claim only on condition that Conrad return to the Unwin fold: hence from 1919 onwards Unwin brought out *The Arrow of Gold*, *The Rover*, and the posthumous *Tales of Hearsay*. Not to be outdone, he also set about planning his own Adelphi 'uniform' edition of Conrad's works, published in five volumes in 1923. See also Philip Unwin, *The Publishing Unwins* (1972).

V

Verloc, Adolf. The protagonist of the planned short story that became *The Secret Agent* is a half-hearted anarchist who lives by betraying his fellow revolutionaries both to a foreign embassy and to the *London police. Verloc spent five years in a French prison for stealing artillery designs, not from political motives but under the influence of what he calls a 'fatal infatuation' (21). He is essentially without political convictions, and wishes only to preserve society from disruption so that he can continue his indolent and effortless life in a disreputable Soho shop that serves as a meeting place for anarchists. When Mr Vladimir, his primary employer, demands that he perpetrate a bomb outrage, his life is thrown into a fatal turmoil. Conrad never makes it clear why Verloc should require anyone's help to place a small bomb by the walls of *Greenwich Royal Observatory; but Verloc's desperate search for an accomplice inevitably leads him by default to *Stevie, who stumbles with the bomb and is blown to bits. When Verloc's wife *Winnie finds out that Verloc has thus been the secret agent of her brother's murder, she stabs him to death. Verloc anticipates many characters in the genre of spy fiction in that he is unwittingly trapped in a complex and false position: he no longer knows which side he is on, and can lay claim neither to political nor to domestic solidarity.

Verloc's given name, Adolf, has been discredited by modern history in ways that Conrad could not have foreseen, but it was also the name of one of his earliest English friends, Adolf P. *Krieger. Verloc's surname echoes that of Eugène François Vidocq (1775–1857), the French detective and double agent whose life and memoirs are also reflected in the arch-criminal Vautrin of Balzac's *La Comédie humaine*. Other possible sources for Verloc are discussed by Norman Sherry in *CWW*, 317–29.

Verloc, Winnie. The heroine of *The Secret Agent*, Winnie Verloc sacrifices her own happiness to provide for her young brother and consoles herself with the thought that 'things do not stand much looking into' (177). Her husband *Adolf never suspects that she married him only to provide a home for her dependent brother *Stevie. When her mother makes a comparable sacrifice after seven years by moving to an almshouse so as not to jeopardize Stevie's place in the Verloc household, this altruistic act paradoxically generates a fatal series of events. As Conrad explained in his 'Author's Note' of 1920, he discovered the dramatic potential of Winnie's 'maternal passion' (p. xii) only in the course of writing the novel, which increasingly becomes an account of her descent into despair and madness. She is the secret agent of her brother's survival, and the devastating force of her reaction to his death exposes the other revolutionaries (except the *Professor) as mere humbugs and shams. This difference in character is evident in the epilogue in which Tom Ossipon, who has basely betrayed her and stolen her money, remains unable to fathom the 'impenetrable mystery' (307) of her suicide.

Victory: A Drama, an adaptation of Conrad's novel *Victory: An Island Tale* by Basil Macdonald *Hastings, was performed at the Globe Theatre, London, from 26 March until 6 June 1919.

In April 1916, Conrad learned that actor-manager Henry Brodribb Irving (1870–1919) was interested in staging an adaptation of *Victory* for the Savoy Theatre. Once he had ascertained from his agent J. B. *Pinker that he was under no obligation to an earlier would-be adapter (whose name he could not remember, and who had meanwhile gone off to Australia on tour), Conrad accepted Irving's recommendation that Hastings be engaged to adapt the play. Conrad insisted that Hastings receive full credit for his adaptation, although at Hastings's invitation he contributed many suggestions regarding scenery and costumes, and even drafted several new scenes of dialogue. Some 40 letters to Hastings testify to Conrad's interest in the production.

This correspondence shows that it was Conrad himself who first gave the story a melodramatic 'happy ending' in which *Heyst and *Lena survive to live happily ever after. The correspondence also contains a number of interesting comments concerning the character of Mr *Jones, a role that Irving himself intended to play. Conrad's explanation of Mr Jones's 'woman-hate' makes no mention of homosexuality (which would have been socially dangerous and unwise, as the treason trial of Roger *Casement demonstrates); instead Conrad described Mr Jones as 'at bottom crazy' (*CL*, v. 653). But Mr Jones continued to trouble both Hastings and Irving, until at last Irving decided to play the part of Heyst instead, necessitating major revisions to the text. Conrad recommended the young actress Catherine Willard to Irving, who interviewed her but did not give her a part. Late in 1917, Irving decided to abandon the project altogether, apparently somewhat to the relief of Conrad and Hastings.

Negotiations followed with the actress Lillah McCarthy, who wanted to play the part of Lena, and with the American producer John Cromwell, whose interest in *Victory* would not be realized until more than twenty years later, with the release of his film version in 1940 under wartime circumstances similar to those of the novel's first appearance in 1915. Finally, in February 1919, the actress Marie Löhr acquired the rights to Hastings's adaptation and signed an agreement to produce and direct the play, and to appear in the role of Lena. She put it into rehearsal immediately. Conrad was offered a box for opening night, 26 March, but he felt unwell, having moved *homes the previous day from Capel House (in Bishopsbourne) to Spring Grove

(in Wye). Jessie Conrad later claimed that he never saw the play, but Marie Löhr recalled that he had been present at three of its 83 performances. The part of Heyst was played by Murray Carrington, Mr Jones by W. Gayer Mackay, Ricardo by Sam Livesey, and *Schomberg by Charles Garry. The music, performed by the Carlton Mason Quintet, included several short pieces by Camille Saint-Saëns.

Although it was the most popular of all Conrad adaptations for the stage, it has received little attention from Conrad scholars. Seven contemporary reviews are listed in Theodore G. Ehrsam's bibliography. Robert S. Ryf traced the history of the project in 'Conrad's Stage *Victory*', *Modern Drama*, 7 (1964), 148–60. Both Ryf and Ehrsam mention a prompt copy held in the Manuscript Department of Samuel French, Ltd., in London in 1964, but the company reports that it was lost with other papers during a move to new offices. Identical typescripts of the play, with photographs of the sets and other materials, are held in the Billy Rose Theater Collection, New York Public Library, and at the Lilly Library, Indiana University. The play has been published in *The Conradian*, 25: 2 (2000), 87–176.

Victory: An Island Tale. Conrad's last major novel to be set in the Malay Archipelago, *Victory* (1915) is among his most allusive and reflective creations. It has also proved the most amenable of all his works to various forms of adaptation: on stage, on *film, and as an *opera. Perhaps its perennial appeal has to do with the elemental nature of the story, in which a stoic and much-maligned gentleman rescues a damsel in distress and carries her off to the tropical paradise of his secluded island, where they live happily until their idyll is disrupted by the arrival of a trio of desperadoes.

The novel, some 116,000 words long, opens with a portrait of Axel *Heyst, a reticent and courteous English-educated Swede who for fifteen years has drifted and occasionally traded among the islands between Saigon and New Guinea. Heyst rescues Captain Morrison and his ship from the clutches of the Portuguese port authorities in Delli (Dili, Timor), after which Morrison takes him along on his voyages. Heyst enters into a partnership with Morrison to establish the Tropical Belt Coal Company, with its central station on the 'Round Island' of *Samburan in the *Java Sea. After Morrison's death in England and the liquidation of this short-lived venture, Heyst continues to live alone on Samburan. *Schomberg, a Teutonic hotel-keeper in Surabaya, feels an instinctive hatred for Heyst, and spreads malicious gossip to the effect that Heyst robbed and even murdered his former partner.

After living alone on Samburan for more than a year and a half, Heyst journeys to Surabaya in Captain Davidson's steamship. When Davidson returns three weeks later to take Heyst back to his island, he finds that Heyst has already departed for Samburan with *Lena, a violinist from Zangiacomo's touring ladies' orchestra whom Schomberg had been trying to seduce.

In Part II, the story of this chivalrous and unlikely rescue is told by an omniscient narrator who provides insight into Heyst's reactions and Schomberg's smouldering resentment. Shortly after Heyst's departure, a man calling himself Mr *Jones arrives in Surabaya with his fellow desperadoes, a vicious knife-wielding former seaman named Martin Ricardo and an ape-like servant named Pedro. They set up an illegal gambling operation in Schomberg's 'music room', using his *table d'hôte* as a decoy. Schomberg, angry and intimidated, finally engineers their departure from Surabaya by telling Ricardo of the wealth to be found on Heyst's island. Ricardo does not inform Mr Jones that a woman is living with Heyst on the island.

Part III shifts the scene to Samburan, where, after more than three months together, Heyst and Lena are beginning to understand the nature of their relationship. Just as Heyst assures Lena that nothing can disturb their isolation, Wang, Heyst's Chinese servant, bursts in to announce that he has sighted a boat with three white men. Jones, Ricardo, and Pedro arrive weakened by thirst, and Heyst settles them in an unused office building. That night, he discovers that his pistol is missing.

Part IV opens two mornings later, and the rest of the events follow in the course of this long, eventful day in a classic example of Conradian *progression d'effet*. Ricardo, unable to restrain his savage curiosity, creeps into Heyst's bungalow and surprises Lena. Her vigorous resistance to his assault convinces Ricardo that she is 'one of his own sort', and he enlists her in the plot to rob Heyst. Lena, choosing her words carefully, helps Ricardo to escape through a window just as Heyst returns. Wang, aware of Ricardo's visit, is convinced that Heyst is doomed, and announces that he is leaving (although they normally converse in Malay, this exchange is apparently in pidgin English). Heyst reports to Jones that he can no longer be held responsible for Wang, who is armed and at large, and Jones insists that Pedro replace Wang as Heyst's servant. Heyst then goes with Lena to the mountain barrier erected by the Alfuro natives to protect them from 'civilization', and asks that Lena be allowed to pass to the safety of the other side; but Wang refuses. Heyst and Lena return to the bungalow, and Ricardo joins them for supper, asking that Heyst speak with Mr Jones that evening. Heyst agrees on condition that Pedro not be left at the bungalow. He bids farewell to Lena, dressing her in dark clothing and asking her to hide in the forest until she sees a signal from him. While Heyst visits Mr Jones, Lena does not hide but remains determined to save Heyst by disarming Ricardo, removing the 'very sting of death' (399). She manages to get her hands on Ricardo's dagger (a Pyrrhic 'victory' reflecting the novel's title); but Heyst and Mr Jones arrive at just that moment, and Mr Jones shoots, grazing Ricardo's head but mortally wounding Lena. In a rapid finale, Davidson suddenly arrives, Lena dies, Wang shoots Pedro, Mr Jones shoots Ricardo and then drowns, and Heyst sets fire to the bungalows and dies in the blaze that consumes Lena's body. The final word is pronounced by Davidson: 'Nothing!'

Victory began life as a short story called 'Dollars' in the wake of the *Titanic* disaster in April 1912, but the story was slow to develop. By late June Conrad had written only 3,000 words (*CL*, v. 80), but the pace increased through the summer as he submitted instalments of what he called 'the D novel' to his agent J. B. *Pinker in batches of 3,000 words typed by his wife Jessie. By October he estimated that he had written 'about 28 thou[sand]' (*CL*, v. 110), and by June 1913 he had reached 70,000 words or some 350 typescript pages (*CL*, v. 242). The subtitle of 'An Island Story' was added in October (*CL*, v. 288). Pinker arranged for American *serialization in *Munsey's Magazine* (New York) with delivery promised for the end of April, so that through the early months of 1914 Conrad was working hard to finish the text. Although the manuscript bears the completion date of 29 May 1914, Conrad's letters indicate that he was busy with typescript revisions until mid-July, just before the Conrads left for a family visit to *Poland. The title of *Victory* first appears in Conrad's extant correspondence on 1 July (*CL*, v. 396); as he explained to John *Galsworthy, 'there seems to be a fashion just now for short titles and apparently I have been unconsciously influenced; for I *could not* think of anything else' (*CL*, v. 406). The American serial version appeared in a single issue of *Munsey's Magazine* in February 1915, but Conrad was unhappy with the liberties taken with his text, complaining to Pinker that 'they have cut, transposed and altered the paragraphing more than I can stand' (*CL*, v. 435). The first American edition, based not on the *Munsey's* text but on a corrected typescript, was published by Doubleday, Page on 26 March. The English first edition, published by Methuen, was printed by May, but unexpectedly large export orders created a shortage of domestic issues, and efforts to redress this imbalance led to a complex series of pre-publication printings and reprintings, which are described in William R. Cagle's unpublished Conrad bibliography. Methuen's colonial issue was

published on 10 August, and the domestic issue on 24 September. Meanwhile, the English serial version was appearing in the London *Star* from 24 August to 9 November. A Swedish translation by Elin Palmgren, *Seger*, was published in Stockholm the following year.

Critical reactions to *Victory* have always been mixed. Some have found the plot and the characters altogether too melodramatic, while others have admired the way in which these romantic elements are transformed into something rich and strange. John Galsworthy was disappointed, and Harriet M. *Capes (whose anthology of excerpts entitled *Wisdom and Beauty from Conrad* was published in London that same year) expressed her dislike directly to Conrad (*CL*, v. 538). The American novelist Jack London, who had admired Conrad's work for years, wrote from Honolulu to say that *Victory* had swept him off his feet and cost him a night's sleep. Some of the early reviewers called Heyst a 'Hamlet of the South Seas', and many were struck by the curious mixture of horror and comedy in the treatment of the villains. The volume sold well, if not as well as *Chance*, and has generated substantial and steady critical attention.

In Thomas C. Moser's *achievement-and-decline thesis, *Victory* stands as the first clear proof of Conrad's decline, a judgement seconded by Albert J. Guerard and Bernard C. Meyer. Champions of the novel like F. R. Leavis acknowledge that it cannot be ranked with *Nostromo* or *The Secret Agent*, but they appreciate its importance as a philosophical meditation on the Conradian themes of isolation and solidarity. The manuscript has received serious attention from Frederick R. Karl in *JCTL* and in a later essay entitled '*Victory*: Its Origin and Development', *Conradiana*, 15 (1983), 23–51, in which Karl shows how, in the course of revision, Conrad deleted roughly one-sixth of the text to make it less realistic and specific. As against previous critics, Karl is convinced that *Victory* 'is the culmination of Conrad's achievement, not the first stage in his decline' (49 n. 1). Another comprehensive and suggestive study is

Tony Tanner's 'Joseph Conrad and the Last Gentleman', *Critical Quarterly*, 28 (1986), 109–42, which examines the novel as a study of 'gentlemen' in the context of Darwin and evolutionary theory.

Heyst is explicitly described as a latter-day Adam, and the trio of villains are distinctly diabolical. Parallels with the Bible and *Shakespeare have long been noted: Heyst's hesitations have often been compared with those of Hamlet, and Samburan with Prospero's island in *The Tempest*. The links with Shakespeare are discussed by Adam Gillon in 'Joseph Conrad and Shakespeare, Part Four: A New Reading of *Victory*', *Conradiana*, 7 (1975), 263–81. Similarities have also been noted with works by *Dickens, Melville, and Emerson, with Robert Louis *Stevenson's *The Ebb-Tide* (1894), H. G. *Wells's *The Island of Doctor Moreau* (1896), and even with Vladimir Nabokov's *Lolita* (1955). Scholars have also recognized the extent to which *Victory* 'borrows' from Polish and French sources. Katherine Haynes Gatch suggested that Heyst's name and much of his character may owe their origins to *Axël*, a visionary novel (1890) and play (1894) by Villiers de l'Isle-Adam ('Conrad's Axel', *Studies in Philology* 48 (January 1951), 98–106). Andrzej Busza (1966: 216–23) has described the similarities between *Victory* and Stefan *Żeromski's 1908 novel *Dzieje grzechu* (The History of a Sin). Paul Kirschner (1968) has shown that entire passages in *Victory* are translated almost literally from Guy de *Maupassant's 1889 novel *Fort comme la mort*—some of which, although later deleted from the manuscript in revision, leave little doubt that Heyst and Lena are indeed meant to make love in the gap between chapters 4 and 5 of Part III. These and other textual 'borrowings' are examined by Hervouet (1990: 122–35), who greatly admires Conrad's skill as a translinguistic bricoleur, calling *Victory* 'undoubtedly his most philosophical work' and 'second only to *Under Western Eyes* in its extraordinary allusiveness' (133). The novel has also been subjected to a wide variety of approaches, from symbolic and allegorical readings to *archetypal, *Marxist, and *feminist interpretations. For example, in 'Imperialism, Marxism, Conrad: A Political Reading of *Victory*', *Textual Practice*, 3 (1989), 303–22, Terry Collits examines the novel in the wake of Fredric Jameson's Marxist interpretation of *Nostromo* and concludes that it represents Conrad's 'most far-reaching insight into the meaning of modern imperialism' (322).

Perhaps because of its Edenic setting and the elemental melodrama of its plot, *Victory* has become the most amenable of all Conrad's works to expression in other media, inspiring a stage play, an opera, and nearly a dozen film or television adaptations. A dramatic adaptation by Basil Macdonald *Hastings (incorporating suggestions by Conrad) ran for more than 80 performances in 1919, marking the most commercially successful of all efforts to put Conrad on stage. The first Conrad film ever made was a silent version of *Victory* directed by Maurice Tourneur and released the same year as the stage play. Conrad apparently saw both these productions; and for the only occasion on which he ever gave a public *reading from his own works, during his American tour in May 1923, he chose to read the death of Lena. In 1930 a 'talking' adaptation of *Victory* directed by William A. Wellman, entitled *Dangerous Paradise*, was among ten Paramount films chosen for reworking in multiple foreign-language versions in studios built especially for the purpose in Joinville-le-Pont, near Paris. (Although a copy of *Dangerous Paradise* has survived, the versions made in Italian, Polish, French, German, and Swedish have apparently all been lost.) In 1940 John Cromwell, who had negotiated in 1918 for the rights to produce Hastings's staging of *Victory*, directed a film version starring Fredric March as (Hendrik) Heyst, Betty Field as Alma, and Cedric Hardwicke as Mr Jones. A live television production made by NBC in 1960 for the American series *The Art Carney Show*, with Art Carney playing Heyst, was the first television adaptation of Conrad to be made in colour. In 1970 Richard Rodney Bennett's operatic version of *Victory* premièred at the Royal Opera House, Covent Garden. Film-maker Peter

Bogdanovich reports that in the autumn of 1971 Orson Welles prepared a screenplay based on *Victory* called *Suriname*, but it was never filmed (see *This is Orson Welles* (HarperCollins, 1993), pp. xxv, 441). Another unfilmed screenplay of *Victory* was prepared by playwright Harold Pinter in 1982 and published in *The Comfort of Strangers and Other Screenplays* (Faber, 1990, 165–226). Jerzy Skolimowski's 1985 film *The Lightship* is often thought to be based on *Victory*, since its villains bear a strong resemblance to the evil trio in Conrad's novel; but Skolimowski's adaptation was based in the first instance not on Conrad but on a novella by German author Siegfried Lenz. A German film version of *Victory* entitled *Des Teufels Paradies* (The Devil's Paradise), directed by Vadim Glowna, was released in 1986. Another French–German co-production of *Une victoire*, starring Willem Dafoe, Irène Jacob, and Sam Neill, was filmed in 1995.

The manuscript of *Victory* is at the Harry Ransom Humanities Research Center, University of Texas at Austin. The original 'first copy' typescript was donated by F. N. *Doubleday to the Berg Collection, New York Public Library; and a nearly complete carbon copy with Conrad's holograph corrections is at the Philadelphia Free Library. Corrected proofs of the 1924 Methuen edition were offered for sale in 1925, but their present location is unknown.

Viola family. Giorgio Viola (the old 'Garibaldino') and his family are among the first characters to be introduced in *Nostromo* when, during a period of rioting, they are shown trapped inside Giorgio's hotel, the 'Albergo d'Italia Una'. The family members go on to play a crucial part in the fate of their fellow Italian, *Nostromo. Giorgio is responsible for encouraging the Genoese seaman to try his shore luck in *Sulaco and unofficially adopts him as a 'son'. Giorgio's wife Teresa contributes to a major trial of choice for Nostromo when, upon her dying request that he fetch her a priest, he refuses her appeal, and thereafter feels himself under a curse. At the end of the novel, Giorgio and his two daughters are intimately linked to the circumstances of Nostromo's death. When secretly wooing one of Giorgio's daughters while being publicly betrothed to the other, Nostromo is accidentally shot by old Giorgio, at this stage a lighthouse keeper and virtually blind.

The course of Giorgio's life—one of almost permanent exile from Italy—has largely followed that of his hero Garibaldi, under whom he has served both in Montevideo and later in Italy. At a point in 1903 when Conrad still conceived *Nostromo* as a short story about an Italian community in South America in which 'Giorgio shall take a good space' (*CL*, iii. 28), he consulted historical accounts of Garibaldi's life. By a characteristically Conradian process of transference, Giorgio is also endowed with many of Garibaldi's attributes (his white beard and leonine hair, his anticlericalism, as well as his devotion to a dying wife). Conrad was also indebted for some details of Giorgio's situation to his friend R. B. Cunninghame *Graham's 'Cruz Alta', a tale in Graham's *Thirteen Stories* (1900), which features a certain Enrico Clerico, also a follower of Garibaldi, an Italian immigrant in Paraguay, and a storekeeper.

The placing of the Viola family at the opening of the novel serves a powerfully proleptic function. Represented as a Messianic disciple of lost political causes and a sad, drifting relic of an irrecoverable heroic past, Giorgio the defeated idealist attracts considerable sympathy. But, as Verleun remarks, he is an unambiguous political portent of 'the ousting of . . . true liberalism from South America', and his relegation to the island of Great Isabel later in the novel constitutes a form of banishment from 'the continent he fought for' (1978: 230). The opening sketch of his relationship with Teresa, largely the history of a man whose wife has been sacrificed to his fixed obsessions, overshadows almost every relationship in the novel, being explicitly linked to the tragic history of Emilia *Gould's aunt (60) but also anticipating the landscape of pain awaiting most of the other women in the novel.

visual arts. In his 1897 'Preface' to *The Nigger of the 'Narcissus'*, Conrad made his celebrated claim: 'Fiction—if it at all aspires to be art—appeals to temperament. And in truth it must be, like painting, like music, like all art, the appeal of one temperament to all the other innumerable temperaments . . . Such an appeal to be effective must be an impression conveyed through the senses . . . It must strenuously aspire to the plasticity of sculpture, to the colour of painting, and to the magic suggestiveness of music—which is the art of arts' (p. ix). With its probable echoing of Walter Pater's belief expressed in *The Renaissance* that 'All art constantly aspires towards the condition of music', Conrad's claims would be immediately recognizable to his late nineteenth-century contemporaries as a variation of the growing interest in the synthesis and cross-fertilization of the arts. From 1850 onwards, the theory and practice of numerous artists—including Richard Wagner, Charles Baudelaire, Eugène Delacroix, and Impressionist painters —developed in response to the possibility that the art of the future would have a composite identity in its fusion of possibilities from the several arts of music, painting, sculpture, and literature. According to the Russian film-maker Sergei Eisenstein, the growth of modern cinema played a vital role in bringing about this synthesis: 'The problem of the synthesis of the arts is of vital concern to cinematography. Men, music, light, landscape, colour and motion brought into one integrated whole by a single piercing emotion, by a single theme and idea—this is the aim of modern cinematography' (quoted in John Stokes, *Resistible Theatres: Enterprise and Experiment in the Late Nineteenth Century* (Elek, 1972), 104).

Since the very early reviews of Conrad's work, it has become commonplace to find analogies for some of his fictional effects in the techniques of visual art: he is often regarded as an *'impressionist', 'painterly' writer, or an 'artist in prose'. Some of these labels should, however, be used with a degree of caution. Although several attempts have been made to suggest that

Conrad was directly attuned to the developing artistic movements of his time, there is little evidence to support this claim. According to Richard *Curle, 'it cannot be said that either music or painting was in any degree essential to him . . . and in all his conversations with me I have no recollection of his talking, save casually, about pictures' (*LTY*, 128). In response to a request from Grace Willard in 1916, Conrad refused to compose a piece on the visual and plastic arts: 'I really don't know enough about art in general and sculpture in particular to write anything which could be of the slightest use. I haven't the words for it— and frankly I don't want to expose my ignorance' (*CL*, v. 601). He had connections with members of the William *Rothenstein circle and came to know such artists and sculptors as Jo Davidson, Alice S. Kinkead, Walter *Tittle, and Jacob *Epstein, although there is no record of his being a regular gallery visitor, and his letters and works contain only a small handful of passing references to artists—the 'Charenton school', Jean-François Millet, J. M. Whistler, El Greco, Dante Gabriel Rossetti, Ford Madox Brown, and Auguste Rodin. While several of Conrad's own sketches show him to be a competent graphic artist, they are of a conventional kind—some have been described as '"sexy" pictures done in the style of "naughty" French magazines' (Meyer, 327–8)—and were probably undertaken to entertain his wife Jessie during the early years of their marriage.

As Yves Hervouet has suggested, while analogies between Conrad and the visual arts have produced many valuable studies, 'they fail to present the technical innovations of Conrad and Ford in an accurate historical perspective, since most of their theories and practices, whether evolved before they met or in the course of their collaboration, derived primarily from the fictional and critical models offered by Flaubert and Maupassant' (191). He goes on to argue that the most important visual techniques in Conrad's work have their precedent in the two French writers, through whose fiction he gained access to the wider late nineteenth-century interest in a synthesization of the arts. Ford Madox *Ford explained: 'There was painting before Cézanne and there has been painting since Cézanne, but the objectives of the two modes of painting have scarcely any connection. A similar caesura is observable in the aesthetics of creative writing. There was writing before Flaubert; but Flaubert and his coterie opened, as it were, a window through which one saw the literary scene from an entirely new angle. Perhaps more than anything else it was a matter of giving visibility to your pages: perhaps better than elsewhere, Conrad with his "It is above all to make you see!" [*sic*] expressed the aims of the New World. And your seeing things became an integral part of your story' (*The March of Literature: From Confucius' Day to our Own* (New York: Dial Press, 1938), 802). For interesting studies of the analogies between Conrad and nineteenth-century art and artists, see Geddes's chapter on '*The Arrow of Gold*: The Detailed Manner of a Study'; Donald R. Benson, 'Impressionist Painting and the Problem of Conrad's Atmosphere', *Mosaic*, 22 (1989), 29–40; and Wendy B. Faris, 'The "Dehumanization" of the Arts: J. M. W. Turner, Joseph Conrad, and the Advent of Modernism', *Comparative Literature*, 41 (1989), 305–26.

Vologda, in the *Russian province of the same name, an ancient and insalubrious town some 300 miles (480 km) north of Moscow, was the place of banishment to which Conrad was transported with his condemned parents from *Warsaw under strict police escort. In a bitterly ironic letter written shortly after their arrival on 11 June 1862, his father described Vologda as 'a huge quagmire stretching over three versts, cut up with parallel and intersecting lines of wooden foot-bridges, all rotten and shaky under one's feet'. He noted that 'The air stinks of mud, birch tar and whale-oil', and described the two most important aspects of the local civilization as 'police and thieves' (*CUFE*, 66–8).

At that time, Vologda had a population of some 17,000, including a number of Polish exiles from the uprisings of 1830, 1846, and 1848. Apollo *Korzeniowski seems to have taken refuge in a stubborn internal exile within this community, wearing only Polish clothing, refusing to speak anything but Polish to the Russian authorities, and dividing his time between prayer and political discussions with his fellow exiles. As he told his cousins, 'Vologda as such does not exist for us' (ibid. 67). The family lived in 'Deviatkov's house', a one-storey wooden structure that once stood at what is now 62 Uritski Street.

Conrad was only 4 years old when he arrived in Vologda, and he seems to have retained no clear memory of the town, which is rarely mentioned in his memoirs or letters. However, the earliest known image of Conrad is a photograph taken in Vologda at the studio of Stanisław Kraków (reproduced in *JCC*) that was sent to his maternal grandmother with a note on the back in Polish, the earliest example of Conrad's handwriting: 'To my dear Granny who helped me send pastries to my poor Daddy in prison—grandson, Pole-Catholic, and *szlachcic* [i.e., of the *szlachta*, or land-owning gentry], Konrad.'

The climate, consisting of a brief 'green winter' of rain alternating with a long 'white winter' of freezing cold, soon affected the family's health, and on 2 October they were granted permission by the Governor of Vologda to move south to Chernikhov, in *Ukraine, although the state of their health and the poor condition of the roads delayed their departure until January.

Vologda continued to serve as a place of exile and punishment long after Conrad's day; its prison is mentioned in the first volume of Aleksandr Solzhenitsyn's *Gulag Archipelago* (1973). For further historical information, see Viktor Borisov's essay in Moore (ed.) 1992: 39–48.

voyages. See SHIPS AND VOYAGES.

W

Wait, James, a negro sailor from St Kitts, who joins the *Narcissus* in Bombay for her homeward voyage to *London in *The Nigger of the 'Narcissus'*. Hints thrown out by Conrad himself (*LL*, i. 77) have prompted speculation that Wait's original was George White, an able seaman from Barbados who served with him in 1878–9 in the *Duke of Sutherland* (*LL*, i. 77), but he may also owe something to other seamen with whom Conrad served—a certain Thomas Walters from St Kitts in the *Palestine*, and Joseph Barron, possibly an American negro, who died on the homeward voyage of the *Narcissus*.

With his 'calm, cool, towering, superb' presence and his opening pronouncement 'I belong to the ship' (18), Wait has understandably evoked a rich variety of symbolic and *archetypal readings, variously reminding critics of the biblical story of Jonah, the cursed seaman of S. T. Coleridge's 'The Rime of the Ancient Mariner' (1798), a spectre of death, or a manifestation of malign evil. Wait's very name carries a varied symbolic potential. When he first utters his name at the roll-call, it sounds like a command or provocative challenge to 'wait' and instantly produces confusion among the crew. As a malingerer, he then becomes connected with acts of waiting, since his ostentatious illness throws the crew into constant perplexity, forcing them both to wait upon him and to wait for his death. In all of these functions, his name is also homophonous with a 'weight' or 'burden' that delays the ship and is not released until, with his death, the *Narcissus* rolls 'as if relieved of an unfair burden' (160).

In his introduction to the 1914 reprinted American edition of *The Nigger of the 'Narcissus'*, Conrad described Wait as 'merely the centre of the ship's collective psychology and the pivot of the action', so redirecting attention from Wait's symbolic character to his functions as catalyst and manipulator of the crew's ultimately narcissistic fears and doubts. As Hampson has observed, Wait's presence enables Conrad to explore 'the mechanisms people employ to avoid direct awareness of their own mortality and the errors into which this self-deception leads them'. But Wait is considerably more than 'merely' a catalyst in this process, since, as Hampson also observes, 'he is not only equivocating with the crew, he is also equivocating with himself', by adopting a pretence of dying in order to put away from his consciousness the fact that he is actually fatally ill (103, 104). Paradoxically, he is both the manipulator and the victim of his pretended illness.

A more pressing issue for some readers has involved the question of how far Conrad falls into the casual *racist stereotypes of his day in his use of the term 'nigger' (which is recognized in the story as pejorative) and in his recourse to such descriptions of Wait as having 'a face pathetic and brutal, the tragic, the mysterious, the repulsive mask of a nigger's soul' (18). Just before American publication of the novella in 1897, Conrad had himself to face this issue, since his publisher there requested a change of title on the grounds, as Conrad later put it, 'that the American public would not read a book about a "nigger"' (quoted in Smith, 8). In the event, the American title became *The Children of the Sea: A Tale of the Forecastle*, while in Britain its title remained *The Nigger of the 'Narcissus'*, prompting one reviewer to call it 'the ugliest conceivable' (*CCH*, 85). In 'Racism, or Realism? Literary Apartheid, or Poetic Licence? Conrad's Burden in *The Nigger of the "Narcissus"*', in Robert Kimbrough (ed.), *Joseph Conrad: The Nigger of the 'Narcissus'* (Norton, 1979), 358–68, Eugene B. Redmond argues that 'Conrad makes James Wait a whipping-boy for his and Europe's insecurities and moral hang-ups'

(362). For contrasting responses to this issue, see Watts 1988: pp. xxiv–xxvii, and Hawthorn 1990: 101–32.

Wallace, Alfred Russel (1823–1913). Alfred Russel Wallace's *The Malay Archipelago, The Land of the Orang-Utan and the Bird of Paradise* (1869), a vivid account of his journeys of scientific exploration in *Borneo and other islands of the Dutch East Indies during 1854 and 1862, influenced Conrad's Malay fiction in providing characters, incidents, and general atmosphere. According to Richard *Curle, the book was Conrad's 'favourite bedside companion', frequently reread and resorted to as an authority on matters related to tropical landscapes and nature ('Joseph Conrad: Ten Years After', *Fortnightly Review*, 142 (1934), 189–99). As well as a source book, it was also an *aide-mémoire* used by Conrad to revive his memories of his own much more limited experience in South-East Asia. Wallace himself is mentioned in *The Secret Agent* (118).

Conrad's first direct *borrowings from Wallace are the Commissie and Anak Agong in *Almayer's Folly*. The buffalo stampede scene in chapter 6 of *An Outcast of the Islands* also reworks an incident described by Wallace: the community's fear of Wallace as a white man and the breaking away of buffaloes from their halters is transformed to emphasize *Willems's profound alienation from the Bugis among whom he 'unnaturally' resides. The novel also relies upon Wallace's descriptions of tropical flora and fauna. *The Malay Archipelago* likewise provided some background details for the Shore of Refuge in *The Rescue*.

Wallace's influence on *Lord Jim* is deeper and more wide-ranging. Wallace himself, whom Conrad greatly admired as an intrepid pioneer explorer, provides a historical model for aspects of *Stein. Wallace amassed enormous collections of tropical species, particularly of butterflies and beetles, and his scientific curiosity, allied to an aesthetic appreciation of natural phenomena, is echoed in Stein's enthusiasm for the works of nature. More generally, Wallace's extreme dedication to the discovery of scientific truth through patient observation and painstaking analysis, his classifying bent, and his sympathetic scrutiny of the inhabitants of the regions he travelled through seemingly mark Stein's approach to discovering truths about human nature in his 'study' of *Jim. In this respect, Wallace may also obliquely influence the portrayal of *Marlow, who likewise seeks to order the observations that he has randomly gathered.

Among specific borrowings in *Lord Jim* are Conrad's conflation of two incidents from *The Malay Archipelago* for the description of Stein's capture of a rare butterfly while armed. The Dutch scientist mentioned in passing in chapter 20 draws on a Dr Bernstein, a German-born naturalist who collected specimens for the Leiden Museum. The descriptions of Doramin's wife and retainers in chapter 25 are indebted to the narrative of Wallace's encounter with the Rajah of Goa (Gowa in the southern Celebes), and Wallace's description of James *Brooke supplied significant materials for the character of Jim in the *Patusan chapters.

Florence Clemens in 1937 and Sherry in *CEW* pioneered the topic of Wallace's impact on Conrad. Hans van Marle's explanatory notes to the World's Classics edition of *An Outcast of the Islands*, ed. J. H. Stape and Hans van Marle (OUP, 1992), and Amy Houston's 'Conrad and Alfred Russel Wallace', in Moore *et al.* (eds.) 1997: 29–48, further pursue this topic. Conrad's copy of Wallace's *The Malay Archipelago* is in the Canterbury Heritage Museum.   JHS

Walpole, Hugh [Seymour] (1884–1941; knighted 1937), novelist, one of a group of young admirers who gathered around Conrad in his later years. Born in New Zealand and educated in England, Hugh Walpole worked as a schoolmaster before becoming a freelance writer in 1909. With a considerable talent for self-promotion and an insatiable urge to connect himself with literary celebrities, Walpole in that year became a protégé and close companion of Henry *James, a connection that ensured him entry into the best literary circles. In 1909, A. C. Benson commented on Walpole in his diary: 'But it must be very surprising to have Henry James fall in love with you, to go everywhere, to meet everybody, to be welcomed by all the best literary men of the day—Wells, Max Beerbohm, Gosse etc to have a dinner given you at the Reform etc—he must have a great deal of ballast!' (quoted in Seymour, 193).

In *Joseph Conrad* (Nisbet, [1916]) Walpole wrote an early and sympathetic appreciation of Conrad's fiction, although the two did not meet until January 1918, just after Walpole had returned from wartime service in Russia. By then, Walpole was already a prolific novelist and had won a measure of popular success. From 1918, he was a regular visitor to Conrad's *Kent *homes, usually arriving 'all smiles and friendliness' and was well liked by the Conrad family generally, although John Conrad remembered that he was 'a bit inclined to gossip, which JC didn't approve of' (*JCTR*, 203). Conrad read and admired Walpole's two Russian novels, *The Dark Forest* (1916) and *The Secret City* (1919), and wrote a preface to *A Hugh Walpole Anthology* (1922). In turn, Walpole dedicated *The Cathedral* (1922) to Conrad. By 1928, four years after Conrad's death, the mocking Walpole wrote unflatteringly about his erstwhile hero: 'Conrad never said anything very interesting in his last years; he was too preoccupied with money and gout. He was only thrilling when [in great pain] he lost his temper and chattered and screamed like a monkey' (quoted in Hart-Davis, 286). See Rupert Hart-Davis, *Hugh Walpole: A Biography* (Macmillan, 1952), excerpted in *JCIR*, 135–9.

'Warrior's Soul, The'. First mentioned in a letter of December 1915, this 7,500-word story occupied Conrad during the early months of 1916, under the working title 'The Humane Tomassov'. Completed by mid-April, it was published in *Land & Water* (March 1917), later appeared as a limited-edition *pamphlet, and was collected in *Tales of Hearsay*. Conrad derived a leading suggestion for the story from Philippe-Paul de Ségur's *Un aide de camp de Napoléon (de 1800 à 1812): mémoires du Général Comte de Ségur* (1895).

Set against the background of Napoleon's retreat from Moscow in 1812, the story is, as Najder remarks (*JCC*, 410), an unusual one for Conrad in its unexpectedly sympathetic treatment of the Russian military characters who dominate the narrative. An aged Russian officer recalls an episode during the Napoleonic struggles concerning his subaltern, the young, idealistic, and humane Tomassov, who, before the war, had spent some time in Paris mixing in genteel circles and worshipping at the feet of a Parisian *grande dame*. There he had been saved from arrest by a forewarning from de Castel, a gallant French officer, and so incurred a debt of honour. During the later battle with the retreating French, Tomassov takes a prisoner only to realize that it is de Castel, who, professing to have lost his warrior's courage and honour, begs Tomassov to fulfil his debt and kill him. Confronted by a claim that offends his deepest humanity, Tomassov finally shoots de Castel: it is 'one warrior's soul paying its debt a hundredfold to another warrior's soul by releasing it from a fate worse than death—the loss of all faith and courage' (26).

An unjustly neglected tale, 'The Warrior's Soul' has presented itself to later readers as a sombre period-piece and an offshoot of Conrad's lifelong interest in *Napoleon. Original readers of March 1917, who were soon to read of the carnage at the battle of Arras in their newspapers, were more likely to see it as a tale with an inescapable relevance to events then taking place on the Continent and embodying a bleak anti-war elegy. In this respect, 'The Warrior's Soul' displays interesting similarities with Conrad's earlier war story, *The Shadow-Line*, notably in the way that Tomassov the soldier, like the narrator of the earlier sea story, is engaged in crossing the shadow-line from romantic innocence to clear-eyed understanding. The main difference between the two is that whereas *The Shadow-Line* had been dedicated to Conrad's son Borys as a sign of the author's solidarity with, and hope for, the younger generation of soldiers, the more sombre 'The Warrior's Soul' imagines an infinitely more tragic awakening confronting the young Tomassovs of the *First World War. With some justice, Schwarz argues that all of the value-systems present in the work— the romantic worship of women, the Christian concept of a benevolent universe, and the chivalric conception of honour—are shown to be rendered futile by modern warfare. He adds: 'The grotesque irony is that, to fulfill his role as an Abel figure and thus be his brother's keeper, Tomassov must be a Cain figure and murder his brother' (1982: 99, 100). The manuscript and typescript are held at the Beinecke Rare Book and Manuscript Library, Yale University; a second typescript is held at Texas Tech University, Lubbock.

Warsaw. Conrad's only period of residence in Warsaw was as a young boy when, from early October 1861 to May 1862, he lived with his parents at 45 Nowy Świat, in a building on the city's main street which is now marked by a commemorative plaque. Twenty-eight years later, in February 1890, he stayed in the city for a couple of days on the way to visit his uncle in *Ukraine, and called at the offices of *Słowo* ('The Word'), a conservative journal, where he left his card and an 'announcement'—possibly about the recent death of Aleksander *Poradowski, who had written articles for the journal. He again passed through the city in August 1893, probably simply to change trains, and it seems unlikely that his later picturesque account of that brief stay can be accurate: 'When I was in Poland 5 years ago and managed to get in contact with the youth of the university in Warsaw I preached at them and abused them for their social democratic tendencies' (*CL*, ii. 158).

'Things here have not changed: constant arrests and hardly any men released . . . The town is sad, black and silent: people suffer for the victims, whose number grows daily. . . . Only the Citadel's iron gate is daily surrounded by crowds: so serious, griefstricken and mournful that it is neither possible nor proper to think only of one's own suffering' (*CUFE*, 61). The symbolism of Warsaw and its Citadel as evoked here by Conrad's mother in January 1862 shares something of the oppressive horror of William Blake's poem 'London'. At this time both she and her husband were awaiting trial, accused by the Russian authorities of unlawful revolutionary activity, with Conrad's father already imprisoned in the Citadel where he would remain until his military trial in May 1862.

The resonant symbolism of a city 'sad, black and silent' was, of course, unavailable to her 4-year-old son. If Warsaw formed the material of his first shadowy impressions, it was only later, with the advantage of hindsight, that he came to realize the stark, dangerous realities underlying them and arrived at a sense of the city as a political centre and symbol of foreign oppression. The giant moving figures disappearing into the 'immense space' of his parents' house in Nowy Świat were, he later learned, members of the underground Committee of the Movement whose clandestine meetings his father organized at their home; his shadowy mother was, in reality, dressed in 'the black of the national mourning worn in defiance of ferocious police regulations' ('Author's Note', *A Personal Record*, p. x). When, in later life, Conrad contemplated Warsaw's Citadel, it was with something of his mother's earlier mournful apprehension of its meaning as political prison, symbol of Poland's oppression, and inescapable inheritance for someone of his generation: 'my Father was imprisoned in the Warsaw Citadel, and in the courtyard of this Citadel—characteristically for our nation—my childhood memories begin' (*CL*, i. 358). See also Zdzisław Najder, 'Conrad's Warsaw', in Moore (ed.) 1992: 31–8.

Wedgwood, Ralph Lewis (1874–1956; knighted 1942), a member of the celebrated family of potters and brother of the politician Lord Wedgwood, who met Conrad in 1913 through Richard *Curle. After graduating from Cambridge, Ralph Wedgwood followed a career in railway administration and later became Chief General Manager of the London & North Eastern Railway Company (1921–39); during the First World War, as Director of Docks, he held the rank of brigadier-general. In July 1914, Conrad finished *Victory* at the Harrogate home of Wedgwood and his wife Iris Veronica (née Pawson, 1886–1982), and he later acknowledged their hospitality by dedicating *Within the Tides* to them. With Curle, Wedgwood also acted as a co-executor of Conrad's will. Dame Veronica Wedgwood, the distinguished historian, recalled her own childhood impressions of Conrad and described the bond between her father and the writer as follows: 'My father admired Conrad's writing and unusual personality and history, and Conrad probably admired my father's intelligence and cultural and intellectual interests. (He had been an "Apostle" at Cambridge.) . . . As a young child I was impressed by what seemed an exotic personality with beautiful if overelaborate manners and a funny accent' (quoted in Meyers 279).

'Well Done!' Written in late July and early August 1918 as a way of covering current expenses, the essay was published in instalments on three successive days in the *Daily Chronicle* (22–4 August 1918), and revised for inclusion in *Notes on Life and Letters*. In it, Conrad acknowledges the valuable part played by the *British Merchant Service during the *First World War and then modulates into a eulogistic prose poem extolling the *work ethic, spirit of service, seamanship, and national sentiment that have gone into the making of the Merchant Service's unspoken historical traditions. A set of galley proofs for the *Daily Chronicle* setting survives at the Beinecke Rare Book and Manuscript Library, Yale University, with Conrad's revisions for *Notes on Life and Letters*.

Wells, H[erbert] G[eorge] (1866–1946). H. G. Wells and Conrad first made contact by an exchange of letters in 1896 when Wells, then a rising novelist, reviewed *An Outcast of the Islands* in the *Saturday Review* (reprinted in *CCH*, 79–80). Conrad was flattered by the generally favourable

notice, but bristled privately at some of Wells's criticisms. Their more active friendship began in 1898 when, Conrad having moved to a new *home in *Kent, they became near-neighbours, discussed each other's work, and maintained regular personal and epistolary contact until at least 1906.

A long-standing—and decidedly unresonant—view of the relationship between Conrad and Wells has emphasized their profound and unbridgeable differences, from Baines's assertion in 1960 that 'two men more different in outlook and temperament could scarcely be conceived' (232) to Najder's judgement that Conrad's 'admiration and amity' for Wells give 'the impression of being directed at a representative of a different biological species' (*JCC*, 317). Such views do not correspond to Conrad's more positive view of their relationship as one that survived—and even thrived—on differences; nor do they throw light on the productive literary consequences of their increasing coolness towards each other from 1905 onwards.

The period from 1898 to 1905 represents the high point of their relationship. One indicator of their imaginative closeness is signalled by their mutual echoing of each other's work—in Conrad's case, through likely echoes in 'Heart of Darkness' of *The Time Machine* (1895), *The Invisible Man* (1897), and *The War of the Worlds* (1898), as well as a very obvious debt in his collaborated work with Ford Madox *Ford, *The Inheritors* (1901), to Wells's scientific romances in general. Ultimately, however, specific debts are less important than the fact that their turn-of-the-century fiction grows out of a similar cultural terrain and inherits a number of shared *fin de siècle preoccupations. In '*Heart of Darkness* and the Early Novels of H. G. Wells: Evolution, Anarchy, Entropy', *Journal of Modern Literature*, 13 (1986), 37–60, Patrick A. McCarthy convincingly argues for significant consonances between the two writers during the 1890s on the basis of their handling of psychological, social, evolutionary, and other scientific issues. Viewing the ideas raised in T. H. Huxley's 'Romanes Lecture' (1893) as their common intellectual property, he offers valuable insights into how the two writers, despite their differences, were 'united by their Victorian (and anti-Victorian) inheritance' (60).

During the period from 1906 to 1909 their social, artistic, and political differences became more marked, as is evident in a series of letters indicating Conrad's mounting impatience with Wells's utopianism and socialist reconstruction. For his part, Wells probably became privately more and more derisive about what he regarded as the comically solemn earnestness with which Conrad and Ford pursued the way of High Art and *le mot juste*. The probable impact of these differences upon Conrad's work has produced two lively essays centred upon *The Secret Agent* (1907), which Conrad *dedicated to Wells as 'the historian of the ages to come'. In Martin Ray's view, Conrad's novel is predominantly a thinly veiled satire on the technological and socialist future outlined in Wells's *Mankind in the Making* (1903) and *A Modern Utopia* (1905), and marks the final breach between the two writers, 'with Conrad paying old debts in the dedication while settling old scores in the text which follows' ('Conrad, Wells, and *The Secret Agent*: Paying Old Debts and Settling Old Scores', *Modern Language Review*, 81 (1986), 561). In '*The Secret Agent* under Edwardian Eyes', *The Conradian*, 16: 2 (1992), 1–17, Dwight H. Purdy argues that Ray's view is unduly one-sided in ignoring the more positive debt *The Secret Agent* owes to Wells. Purdy's view is more consonant with the interesting diagrammatic version of their relationship drawn by Conrad for Wells in a letter of September 1903 (*CL*, iii. 62): 'Our differences are fundamental but the divergence is not great.——Graphically our convictions are like that

Not like this:

After 1909, their friendship seems to have markedly cooled. There are thinly disguised caricatures of Conrad in *Tono-Bungay* (1909) and *Boon* (1915), and in 1918 Conrad was quite explicit about his philosophic quarrel with Wells: 'The difference between us, Wells, is fundamental. You don't care for humanity but think they are to be improved. I love humanity but know they are not!' (quoted in Rupert Hart-Davis, *Hugh Walpole: A Biography* (Macmillan, 1952), 168). Wells's final word appeared in an unflattering version of their relations in 1934 in his *Experiment in Autobiography*: 'We never really "got on" together. I was perhaps more unsympathetic and incomprehensible to Conrad than he was to me. I think he found me Philistine, stupid and intensely English' (ii. 618). See also Robert G. Jacobs, 'H. G. Wells, Joseph Conrad, and the Relative Universe', *Conradiana*, 1: 1 (1968), 51–5; Frederick R. Karl, 'Conrad, Wells, and the Two Voices', *PMLA* 88 (1973), 1049–65; and Linda Anderson, *Bennett, Wells and Conrad: Narrative in Transition* (Macmillan, 1988).

Whalley, Captain Henry, the elderly protagonist of 'The End of the Tether' (collected in *Youth*). He is the former 'Daredevil' Harry Whalley of clipper-ship fame who, in an effort to provide for his daughter, invests in a steamship command under terms which allow him to retrieve his investment after three years, but require him to wait an extra year (and to risk losing everything) if for any reason he should fail to complete his three-year term. When he discovers that he is no longer fit to command, Whalley hides his disability from his crew (including the owner, Mr Massy) and depends on the help of his native serang.

Before he wrote the story, Conrad described it as 'the sketch of old Captain Loutit' (*CL*, ii. 193), a reference to Captain Thomas Louttit, the master of the *Duke of Sutherland* just before Conrad joined the ship in 1878. Whalley was originally called Loutit in the manuscript. Sherry has suggested that Captain Henry Ellis, Master-Attendant in *Singapore during Conrad's visit there, served as a primary model both for Captain Whalley and for Captain Eliott, the Master-Attendant in Conrad's tale (*CEW*, 198–205).

Critics have compared Whalley with the protagonist of Balzac's *Le Père Goriot* (1835) and with Kaspar *Almayer, the doting father of Conrad's first novel. However, the mainspring of Whalley's predicament, for Conrad at least, has less to do with paternal sacrifice than with the 'deterioration' that begins with his failure to be candid with his old friend Captain Elliott. As Conrad explained to David S. *Meldrum: 'A character like Whalley's cannot cease to be frank with impunity. . . . The pathos for me is in this that the concealment of his extremity is as it were forced upon him. Nevertheless it is weakness—it is deterioration' (*CL*, ii. 441).

Wharton, Edith [Newbold] (née Jones, 1862– 1937), American novelist and friend of Henry *James, who first entered Conrad's sphere with a letter to him in December 1912 from Paris, where she had lived since 1907. According to one of her biographers, she had in 1912 'discovered' Conrad and went on to acquire all of his works (R. W. B. Lewis, *Edith Wharton: A Biography* (Constable, 1975), 331). She later made contact with him in connection with her unflagging support for the European war effort. Through James, she approached Conrad in 1915 in order to solicit from him a contribution to *The Book of the Homeless*, an anthology she was compiling to raise funds for the American Hostels for Refugees and for the Children of Flanders Rescue Committee. Despite some cooling in Conrad's relationship with James over the latter's lukewarm response to *Chance* in a *Times Literary Supplement* review of 1914 (in which James had compared Conrad unfavourably to Edith Wharton), Conrad readily agreed, sending her the essay 'Poland Revisited' and donating the manuscript for auction in New York where John *Quinn purchased it. With a commendatory letter from General Joffre and an introduction by Theodore Roosevelt, *The Book of the Homeless* appeared in 1916, with a dazzling list of contributors, including Sarah Bernhardt, Jean Cocteau, John *Galsworthy, Thomas Hardy, Henry James, Igor Stravinsky, W. B. Yeats, and with artwork by Max *Beerbohm, Cézanne, Monet, and others. The last exchange of letters between the two writers in October 1917 finds Conrad thanking Wharton for sending him a copy of her latest novel, *Summer* (1917).

Willems, Peter, the anti-hero of *An Outcast of the Islands*, a memorable embodiment of the colonial mentality and one of Conrad's most despicable creations. Conrad described him to Marguerite *Poradowska as 'an ignorant man who has had some success but neither principles nor any other line of conduct than the satisfaction of his vanity' (*CL*, i. 185). The son of a Rotterdam shipping clerk, Willems jumps ship in Semarang roads at the age of 16, and is taken up by Tom *Lingard, who eventually finds him a job as clerk for the merchant Hudig in Macassar. Willems marries Joanna, a woman of Portuguese descent who is actually Hudig's illegitimate daughter; vainglorious and thoroughly racist, he tyrannizes his wife and their 'pale yellow child' (3), who seems to be sexless and is always referred to as 'it'. Willems steals from his employer to pay his gambling debts, and has nearly replaced the entire sum when, on his 30th birthday, he is caught and summarily dismissed. Once again Lingard comes to his aid, placing him with *Almayer in *Sambir, where he falls under the spell of the sultry *Aïssa and becomes, in the words of one early reviewer, 'drunk with the poison of passion' (*CCH*, 68). Her influence over him is exploited by the local Malays so that Willems betrays Lingard's secret passage to Arab traders, who break Almayer's trading monopoly. Lingard renounces his protégé, and when Aïssa realizes that Willems is about to rejoin his 'Sirani' (Christian) wife and child, she shoots him.

In his 1919 'Author's Note' to the novel, Conrad described his impressions of the prototype of Willems at Sambir, whom he found interesting not in himself but 'by his dependent position, his strange, dubious status of a mistrusted, disliked, worn-out European living on the reluctant toleration of that Settlement hidden in the heart of the forest-land, up that sombre stream which our ship was the only white men's ship to visit' (p. ix). Jerry Allen has identified the original of Willems as Carel de Veer, 'an alcoholic with a defective hand' (224–5) who arrived as the assistant of a German trader and took a native wife.

Willems's lack of redeeming moral value has made it difficult for critics to explain the point of the story, which has often been read merely as a sequel or 'prequel' to *Almayer's Folly*. In 'An Outcast of the Islands: A New Reading', *Conradiana*, 2: 3 (1969–70), 47–58, R. A. Gekoski argues that the real hero of the story is not Willems but Tom Lingard, and suggests that the novel should have ended at the conclusion of Part IV. This was evidently the opinion of Carol Reed, whose 1952 *film, with actor Trevor Howard in the role of Willems, omits the fifth and final section of the novel.

Williams, Augustine Podmore (1852–1916), an English merchant seaman who was involved in one of 'the most famous [maritime] scandals in the East of the 1880's' (*CEW*, 41), upon which Conrad drew for the main outlines of the *Patna* episode in *Lord Jim* and for some details in 'The Secret Sharer' (*'Twixt Land and Sea*). On 19 July 1880, the SS *Jeddah*, under Captain Joseph Lucas Clark and with Augustine Williams as first mate, left Penang for Jeddah with 953 pilgrims bound for Mecca on board. The ship hit bad weather, developed a leak in her hull, and on 8 August was abandoned by her captain and European officers, who believed her to be sinking and knew that her lifeboats were inadequate. Landing in Aden, they reported the ship and all her passengers to be lost. However, the *Jeddah* appeared in port the next day, with the pilgrims on board, having been towed into Aden by another ship. After a marine court inquiry, the *Jeddah*'s captain had his certificate suspended for three years, and Williams was severely reprimanded. The 'pilgrim ship episode' provided an event that, as later described by Conrad, 'could conceivably colour the

whole "sentiment of existence" in a simple and sensitive character' ('Author's Note', *Lord Jim*, p. viii).

The close similarities between Williams and *Jim include the following: like his fictional counterpart, Williams was one of five sons of a clergyman; the 28-year-old first mate was the last officer to leave the *Jeddah* and figured prominently in the inquiry; his career as a merchant seaman having been ruined, he remained in the Far East, working as a water-clerk; and he married a Eurasian. The changes Conrad made to the story of the disaster are also significant: for example, the *Jeddah* was a relatively new ship, while the *Patna* is rusty and 'as old as the hills' (13); Williams, a more active agent in events aboard the *Jeddah* than is Jim aboard the *Patna*, did not jump from his ship but was thrown overboard by the pilgrims; and, again in contrast to Jim, he remained in *Singapore after the court inquiry and became a prosperous and respected figure in the city. Conrad's changes to the story of the disaster are, in Batchelor's words, 'marked and substantial' and 'have the effect of "internalizing" it, of emphasizing the relentless pressure of Jim's imagination and consciousness as against the violent aspects of the physical emergency' (1988: 63, 62). Sherry, who believes that Conrad may have met Williams in Singapore in 1883 (when the *Jeddah* was still afloat and in harbour), devotes two chapters to Conrad's handling of his source material in *CEW*, 41–86, and prints transcripts relating to the *Jeddah* inquiry held in Aden in August 1880 (299–311).

Wise, Thomas James (1859–1937), a commodities broker, a book collector, a bibliographer, an unofficial bookseller, the promotor of many literary forgeries, a vandal, and a thief. He was also the creator of the 'Ashley Library', named after his address at 52 Ashley Road, Crouch Hill (London N19), which eventually became known as one of the world's finest private collections of English books and manuscripts.

Wise first came into contact with Conrad through Richard *Curle in autumn 1918, when he purchased the original manuscript of *The Rescue* and received Conrad's permission to replace Clement K. *Shorter as a printer of limited-edition *pamphlets. Wise's printer, Richard Clay & Sons of Bungay, Suffolk, eventually prepared two series of ten pamphlets, the first between December 1918 and April 1919 and the second between November 1919 and January 1920. By 1920 Wise had not only replaced Shorter as a printer of pamphlets for collectors, but had also supplanted New York lawyer John *Quinn as the primary buyer of Conrad's books, manuscripts, and typescripts, sometimes purchasing them even before they were written. His acquisitions included the 'original First Copies' of *The Rover* and *Suspense*, Conrad's *translation *The Book of Job*, his dramatic adaptation of *The Secret Agent*, and his 'film-play' *Gaspar the Strong Man*. Conrad's secretary Lilian M. *Hallowes kept a record of these transactions in a notebook (*The Conradian*, 25: 2 (2000), 205–44; Bodleian Library, Oxford University, shelfmark MS. Eng.Misc.e.578 or microfilm WM 7693). Wise also prepared the first catalogues and bibliographies devoted exclusively to Conrad and had them privately printed in limited editions. Conrad items were included in volumes i, x, and xi of *The Ashley Library*, and Wise described his Conrad holdings in *A Bibliography of the Writings of Joseph Conrad* (1920; 2nd edn., 1921) and in *A Conrad Library: A Catalogue of Printed Books, Manuscripts and Autograph Letters by Joseph Conrad, Collected by Thomas J. Wise* (1928). Wise visited Conrad at Oswalds in August 1920, and was among the mourners at Conrad's funeral.

His forgeries had begun many years earlier, in connection with his involvement in various London literary organizations like the Shelley Society and the Browning Society. Together with Henry Buxton Forman (1842–1917), a Post Office official and an editor of Keats and Shelley, Wise would arrange for these societies to sponsor publication of facsimile editions of small works by their authors. Wise and Buxton then began to meet the demands of a growing market by printing and selling forged pamphlet editions of works by Shelley, Brown-

ing, Swinburne, *Dickens, *Kipling, and others, which were introduced into the market over a period of years, allegedly as previously unknown editions printed in limited numbers for private circulation among their authors' friends. No presentation copies ever turned up, but suspicions were aroused by events like the discovery after Forman's death of no fewer than five mint copies of the supposedly rare first edition of George Eliot's *Agatha*, all uncut and unopened.

There is no evidence to suggest that any of Wise's Conrad materials are less than genuine, although in his Conrad bibliographies he dared to describe certain 1913 first editions of *Chance* as probable forgeries, and he may well have pulled an excessive number of 'proofs' for some of his limited-edition Conrad pamphlets. The income gained from the sale of forged pamphlets supported Wise's collection of genuine works, which he was not beyond supplementing with pages removed from library copies. He authenticated his own fabrications by a variety of means: with elaborate stories of their provenance invented to impress American buyers (like Chicago banker John Henry Wrenn, or Chicago businessman John A. Spoor); by including them in his bibliographies; by selling or presenting copies to the British Museum; or even by paying high prices for his own forgeries at auctions. He was president of the (London) Bibliographical Society from 1922 to 1924, was elected an honorary fellow at Worcester College, Oxford, and became a member of London's exclusive Roxburghe Club in 1927.

Wise and Forman were able to place more than 100 spurious editions on the bibliographical record, despite occasional embarrassments, as when an implausibly large number of mint copies of a supposedly rare edition would turn up together in an estate sale or on a bookseller's shelf. A number of experts and bibliophiles, including Sydney Cockerell and Sidney *Colvin, expressed doubts about the authenticity of some of these works, and some had reservations about the probity of Henry Buxton Forman if not of Wise. The forgeries were finally exposed three years before Wise's death with the publication of *An Enquiry into the Nature of Certain Nineteenth Century Pamphlets* (1934) by two young booksellers, Graham Pollard and John Carter, who had traced quantities of the forged pamphlets through the market and paid close attention to variations in type fonts. They also used chemical analysis to establish that the paper used for many of the pamphlets (including the most famous forgery, the 'Reading Sonnets' alleged to be a private 1847 printing of Elizabeth Barrett Browning's *Sonnets from the Portuguese*) was not available before 1874. Wise attempted to shift the blame to Forman, who had died in 1917. His own health was poor, and he died three years later. No formal charges were ever brought.

After Wise's death, his widow sold the Ashley Library to the British Library for £66,000. When Wise's collection arrived in Bloomsbury, a number of the items mentioned in Wise's monumental *Catalogue of the Ashley Library* (11 vols., 1922–36) were found to be missing. Wise not only bought manuscripts; he also sold them. The manuscript of *Gaspar the Strong Man* listed in the Ashley catalogue had been bought by George T. *Keating and the typescript by Henry Colgate. At a house sale held at Wise's last residence, 25 Heath Drive, Hampstead (NW3), in July 1939, one lot contained some 102 loose leaves from printed pamphlets and plays by John Dryden and others. Wise was evidently in the habit of raiding collections to which he had access (including the British Museum, to which he enjoyed privileged entry) for the purpose of 'making up' his own copies; some 80 of these loose pages have been traced to thefts by Wise.

For an engaging account of Wise's career, see Wilfred Partington, *Forging Ahead: The True Story of the Upward Progress of Thomas James Wise, Prince of Book Collectors, Bibliographer Extraordinary and Otherwise* (1939). For details about Wise and Forman, see John Collins, *The Two Forgers: A Biography of Harry Buxton Forman and Thomas James Wise* (1992). Wise's Conrad pamphlets are discussed by J. H.

Stape in '"Conrad Privately Printed": The Shorter and Wise Limited Edition Pamphlets', in Curreli (ed.), 93–109.

Within the Tides. This volume brings together four stories written during the period 1910–14—'The Planter of Malata', 'The Partner', 'The Inn of the Two Witches: A Find', and 'Because of the Dollars'—all previously published in magazines. It was brought out by J. M. *Dent in Britain on 24 February 1915 and by Doubleday, Page in America on 15 January 1916. Although Conrad made large claims for the collection as 'a deliberate attempt at four different methods of telling a story—an essay in craftsmanship' (*CL*, v. 439) and generally received flattering reviews, it is nowadays commonly thought to contain some of his least distinguished work. F. R. Leavis famously used it to support his belief 'that Conrad can write shockingly bad magazine stuff' (209). If this overstates the case, it is nevertheless true that Conrad was in 1913 ready to respond to the financial blandishments of Carl Hovey, editor of the American *Metropolitan Magazine*, who paid handsomely for marketable potboilers and for whom he wrote the pieces in this volume, with the exception of 'The Partner'. To his request for material Conrad answered that he would want 'special terms for prostituting his intellect to please the *Metropolitan*' (*CL*, v. 322) and reflected bitterly upon his market potential at that time: '"The Planter of Malata" alone earned eight times as much as "Youth," six times as much as "Heart of Darkness." It makes one sick' (*LL*, ii. 164). 'The Planter' and 'Because of the Dollars' deserve to be read, however, for their interesting formal and thematic links with *Victory*, a full-length novel being composed at the same time.

women's suffrage movement. Conrad's literary career (1895–1924) coincided with the emergence of the women's movement and the campaign for women's suffrage, which led to the formation of the National Union of Women's Suffrage Societies (1897), the Women's Social and

Political Union organized by Emmeline Pankhurst (1905), and the militant feminist agitation between 1905 and 1914. In his stimulating study of Conrad's involvement with Edwardian social and cultural contexts, Spittles argues that Conrad's fiction exhibits, albeit in untopical form, an increasing awareness of this emergent 'female dynamic, and the questioning of the traditional, and largely passive, roles of women' (134). He points to (a) the treatment of Winnie *Verloc in *The Secret Agent* as a representative type of the ordinary late Victorian woman who, 'caught in a socio-economic trap', is forced into a loveless marriage (137); and (b) the emergence of female characters in Conrad's Edwardian fiction who 'aspire to an active role—but as individuals, not within any political organisation' (135). This assessment needs to be modified in significant ways. The account of trapped woman in Conrad's fiction should be expanded to include the earlier example of Bessie Carvil in the 1902 story 'To-morrow' (*Typhoon*), a figure described by Conrad as 'absolutely the first conscious woman-creation in the whole body' of his work (*LL*, ii. 225). Spittles's second emphasis—upon developments in Conrad's presentation of women in his Edwardian fiction—may have the effect of inviting the reader to disregard his very earliest novels. As Nadelhaft and Krenn have shown in different ways, Conrad can be seen to present women of mixed race in his earliest novels with surprisingly positive strengths in relation to the political organizations in which they live: both critics argue that these women characters have active roles in challenging and exposing Western male insularity and domination, and, in the case of *Aïssa in *An Outcast of the Islands*, providing an alternative to the political morality of imperialism.

Conrad's overall attitude to the Edwardian women's movement may, however, have been significantly more ambivalent than Spittles allows. It is true that in 1910, at the invitation of Laurence Housman, he agreed unreservedly, if not very optimistically, to put his name to a petition sent to Prime Minister Asquith in support of the

women's franchise, joining 43 scholars and writers in 'urging the desirability of granting full facilities for the Woman Suffrage Bill promoted by the Conciliation Committee' (*The Times*, 15 June 1915). In a later letter to Housman, he expanded: 'I want the women to have the vote and generally their own way in anything and everything under heaven. It will please them and certainly it won't hurt me' (*CL*, iv. 344). But while Conrad may have endorsed the specific issue of the franchise, he seems considerably more doubtful about the wider militant feminist politics that were later to accompany it. One of his letters written at the height of suffragette agitation in 1913 alludes to a *London 'resounding with the crash and jingle of broken glass' and associates it with the 'latest fashionable amusement for ladies' (*CL*, v. 227); another refers amusedly to 'the present inflamed state of feminine minds' (*CL*, v. 407).

Chance (1914) is notable as the one Conrad novel to incorporate topical issues of women's suffrage and militant feminism as a central part of its subject, although it can hardly be said to respond very positively to the Edwardian female dynamic. The narrator *Marlow, here a crustier and more opinionated version of his younger self, engages in a good deal of satire of the doctrinaire feminist Mrs Fyne and her disciples as representatives of an unwelcome sign of the times and, in general, steers a very uncertain route through women's issues of the day. On the one hand, Marlow professes to own a portion of 'femininity' in his composition, an attribute allowing him to sympathize with Flora's position as a victimized woman and to be critical of the patriarchal forces ranged against her, including the myth of woman as the 'angel in the house' associated with Coventry Patmore. On the other hand, he announces himself 'no feminist' and goes on to support the notion of '"femininity" [as] a privilege' at the expense of '"feminism" [as] an attitude' (146), so seeming to dissociate himself altogether from the more practical issue of women's rights to social and political equality. Marlow's entrenched dislike of feminism is further confirmed by his tendency to regard it as one of the cruel forces ranged against Flora. Hawthorn has referred to 'Conrad's inability to make up his own mind about the claims of the contemporary feminist movement' (1990: 152). One alternative possibility is that Marlow should be regarded as an unreliable narrator; another, more likely one is that in seeking to make *Chance* a popular novel—'the sort of stuff that *may* have a chance with the public', with 'a steady run of references to women in general all along, some sarcastic, some sentimental' (*CL*, v. 208)—Conrad was largely content to adopt the prevailing middle-class attitudes of the time towards women's suffrage.

Woolf, [Adeline] Virginia (1882–1941), novelist, essayist, and diarist, best remembered by Conrad's admirers for her unflattering diary entry of 23 June 1920, in which she described Conrad as a writer who 'never sees anyone who knows good writing from bad, and then being a foreigner, talking broken English, married to a lump of a wife, he withdraws more and more into what he once did well, only piles it on higher and higher, until what can one call it but stiff melodrama' (quoted in *JCC*, 452). Virginia Woolf also wrote a number of anonymous reviews of Conrad, which, if not entirely sympathetic to his art, show her wrestling with her attitudes to his established 'greatness' and reveal the basis of her persistent critical ambivalence. In part, her negative judgements crystallize the views of a generation of younger writers, including her husband Leonard Woolf, who believed that Conrad's art had during the 1920s entered a period of decline. Thus, while Woolf admired 'Youth' and spoke of *Lord Jim* as Conrad's masterpiece, she could not bring herself to praise *The Rescue* ('A Disillusioned Romantic', *Times Literary Supplement* (1 July 1920), 419; reprinted in *CCH*, 332–5). Her other reviews highlight more clearly some of the persistent reservations and narrowly English prejudices that mingled with her praise. In her review of *Notes on Life and Letters*, she continued to feel that Conrad was 'hampered in the

attempt—if ever he tried to make it—by the fact that he is a foreigner by birth. He is using a language which is not his own' ('A Prince of Prose', *Times Literary Supplement* (3 March 1921), 141), and to this fact she attributed other perceived limitations—an infinite reserve or lack of candour, an absence of humour 'of the English kind', and a failure to include women in his novels ('Mr. Conrad: A Conversation', *Nation and Athenaeum* (1 September 1923), 681–2). Her obituary 'Joseph Conrad' (*Times Literary Supplement* (14 August 1924), 493–4) again qualifies laudation with notes of reservation. See Susanne Henig, 'Virginia Woolf and Joseph Conrad', in Jabłkowska (ed.) 1979: 99–108, and J. H. Stape, 'The Critic as Autobiographer: Conrad under Leonard Woolf's Eyes', *English Literature in Transition, 1880–1920*, 36 (1993), 277–85.

work ethic. As an individual with strong roots in the 19th century, Conrad was exposed to the shaping influence of one of its most important moral and social principles —the so-called work ethic. During the years of his early manhood in *Marseilles, he was subject to regular exhortations from his often exasperated uncle-guardian Tadeusz *Bobrowski who believed that 'Work and perseverance are the only values that never fail' (*CPB*, 63) and who urged his nephew to translate his work efforts into a meaningful vocation and so become 'useful, hard-working, capable and therefore a worthy human being' (ibid. 36). Conrad's career as a seaman in the era of sailing ships involved him in a profession—or 'vocation', as he preferred to call it—with very specialized rituals of work, and at an early stage in that career he had apparently read Thomas *Carlyle, the supremely influential Victorian prophet of work, in whose writings the principle vibrates with moral, religious, and philosophical resonances. As several critics have also pointed out, Conrad's artistic creed as set out in the 1897 'Preface' to *The Nigger of the 'Narcissus'* also carries across into his early writing life a view of the artist as essentially a novelist-craftsman and 'workman of art' (p. xi). 'For Conrad,' Ambrosini observes, 'writing fiction *had* to be a work, a craft, just like sailing' (31).

As written about in Conrad's essays, the seaman's work ethic is generally the stuff of celebratory eulogy, partly perhaps the product of a tendency in his later years to idealize the significance of *sea life. It remains untouched by the critical spirit that prevails in his fiction, where, along with most other *idées reçues*, the work ethic is problematized in studies of difficult initiation. Nevertheless, certain essays provide a helpful guide to the distinctively Conradian tonalities of the work ethic, in particular 'Memorandum on the Scheme for Fitting out a Sailing Ship' (*Last Essays*), 'The Fine Art', one of the sections of *A Personal Record*, and 'Tradition' (*Notes*). In setting out a training scheme for young seamen, the first essay explains the natural association in Conrad's mind between the work ethic, the practice of sail, and its two most precious moral and social benefits: the pursuit of a vocation or useful calling and the performance of a social obligation in the cause of human solidarity. With none of the labour-saving technology associated with steam ships, sail requires a form of skilled 'man-power' quite different from the kinds of 'mere slavish toil, as some branches of labour on shore tend to become'. For the cadet, the practice of handling a sailing ship encourages a close relationship between the worker and his work, and a special intimacy with the ship itself. Emphasis also falls upon healthy physical development and the acquisition of a certain sort of manliness as well as the 'sailor mentality' (71). Above all, Conrad comments: 'there is undoubtedly something elevating in physical work into which one puts all one's heart in association with others and for a clearly understood purpose' (70). 'The Fine Art' is less concerned with the utility of work than with hyperbolizing the ways in which 'the honour of labour' (24) is analogous to a form of artistic endeavour, emulating some of the features of the literary artist's self-surrender and 'love of perfected skill' (25). Like the artist, the seaman requires access to a form of *le mot juste* through the 'force, precision,

and imagery of technical language' which 'achieves the just expression seizing upon the essential, which is the ambition of the artist in words' (21). Beginning with the stern aphorism 'Work is the law', 'Tradition' eloquently sums up: 'From the hard work of men are born the sympathetic consciousness of a common destiny, the fidelity to right practice which makes great craftsmen, the sense of right conduct which we may call honour, the devotion to our calling and the idealism which is not a misty, winged angel without eyes, but a divine figure of terrestrial aspect with a clear glance and with its feet resting firmly on the earth on which it was born' (194).

Two of Conrad's early sea stories, *The Nigger of the 'Narcissus'* and 'Youth', present the positive aspects of the work ethic in mainly unalloyed form. 'Youth' begins with what seems like a sombre reflection by the older *Marlow on the value of physical work—'You fight, work, sweat, nearly kill yourself, sometimes do kill yourself, trying to accomplish something—and you can't' (*Youth*, 4)—but the main thrust of the inset story is to show the youthful Marlow, who learned the ropes on the famous training ship *Conway*, discovering in himself the kind of aptitudes celebrated in the training 'Memorandum' and crystallized in the ship's motto 'Do or die', and, with his mates, affirming the power of collaborative work even when it is in the service of an obviously doomed ship.

Conrad's commitment to the work ethic, conceived as a humanistic ideal whose traditional sanctions embrace the seaman's and novelist-craftsman's endeavours, inevitably undergoes marked changes in his passage towards the riddling tragic novels of his major period, all of which coincide with the movement away from the more closely knit and hierarchic communities of shipboard life towards societies represented as shifting, unfriendly, and subject to the vagaries of modern political machinery. This movement is suggestively examined by Franco Marenco in '"Toil" vs. "Consciousness" in Conrad's Work', in Curreli (ed.), 363–79. A key story in charting Conrad's evolving attitude to the work ethic is 'Heart of Darkness' with its severe questioning of this ethic on two fronts: first of all through a depiction of the pressures put upon the narrator Marlow's sailorly belief in the value of the job-sense: 'I don't like work—no man does—but I like what is in the work,—the chance to find yourself. Your own reality—for yourself, not for others—what no man can ever know' (*Youth*, 85); and secondly through Marlow's own growing perception, when he becomes 'one of the Workers, with a capital' (59), that the political machinery of imperialism itself can be found to exploit the superficial rhetoric of the Carlylean work ethic to legitimize its ultimately criminal purposes. See also Anthony Low, '*Heart of Darkness*: The Search for an Occupation', *English Literature in Transition, 1880–1920*, 12 (1969), 1–9; Paul L. Gaston, 'The Gospel of Work According to Joseph Conrad', *Polish Review*, 20 (1975), 203–10; and Watts 1977: 61–7.

Y

'Youth', the first of Conrad's tales to use *Marlow as a narrator, is the story of Marlow's first encounter with the East. The tale, some 13,000 words in length, is closely based on Conrad's own experiences as second mate of the wooden barque *Palestine*, which sank off the coast of Sumatra in March 1883 at the end of a long and difficult struggle to transport a cargo of coal from Newcastle to *Bangkok. Conrad began writing the story, first entitled 'A Voyage', at Ivy Walls in early 1898, shortly after the birth of his son Borys. He gave varying accounts of the circumstances of its composition to John *Quinn and to Alfred A. Knopf (*CL*, v. 194). Finished by 3 June, 'Youth' was published in *Blackwood's Magazine* in September 1898 and reprinted with 'Heart of Darkness' and 'The End of the Tether' in the *Youth* volume. The 'Author's Note' was added in 1917 for the *Collected Edition.

'Youth' opens with a narrative frame that Conrad reused for 'Heart of Darkness', in which Marlow addresses a small group of sailing friends: a director of companies, an accountant, a lawyer, and an unnamed listener who records the story of Marlow's first encounter with the East. Like Conrad, he had already sailed twice to *Australia and back, but had never yet seen a non-Western city or a genuine Malay seaman. Lured by the idea of 'Bankok', Marlow signs on as second mate of the barque *Judea*, under the ship's motto of 'Do or Die'. The *Judea* leaves *London to load a cargo of coal in Newcastle, but the voyage is delayed by gales and she arrives late. After further delays, the ship is rammed by an incoming steamer. She finally sets off for Bangkok three months after leaving *London, but storms in the Channel cause the hull to leak, and the ship is forced to put in to Falmouth for repairs that last for months. Finally the *Judea* sets off, and all goes well until south of *Java Head, when a fire is discovered in the hold: the coal, aerated by frequent reloading and last stowed damp from rain, has ignited from spontaneous combustion. The ship is tested by water and fire: the original crew had pumped water out of the leaking ship in the Channel, and the new Liverpool crew is forced to pump water into the hull to extinguish the fire. Just when the fire seems to be out, the coal-dust explodes and rips the ship apart. A passing mail-boat, the *Somerville*, attempts to tow the burning ship, but the fire grows worse and the crew must abandon ship. The crew take to the boats, and stay to watch the ship sink. After hours of rowing, they make land at night, and in a memorable description, Marlow awakens the next morning to behold the East in the form of a crowd of curious and silent natives.

When it first appeared in book form, 'Youth' received more praise than 'Heart of Darkness' from reviewers who saw it as a contribution to the familiar genre of the boys' adventure story. As Conrad explained to his publisher William *Blackwood, 'Out of the material of a boys' story I've made *Youth* by the force of the idea expressed in accordance with a strict conception of my method' (*CL*, ii. 417). The East appears here as strange and silent: Marlow is struck by the lack of interest shown by the *Somerville*'s Malay oarsmen in the struggles of the crew of the *Judea*, and the native crowd of the final tableau is implausibly silent. H. G. *Wells was critical of the story's 'flaws' (*CL*, ii. 92); but T. S. Eliot is said to have considered 'Youth' and 'The End of the Tether' 'the finest stories of the kind that I know' (Igor Stravinsky, 'Memories of T. S. Eliot', *Esquire* (August 1965), 92–3). It has been translated into 24 languages, but never adapted for film or other media.

The last voyage of the *Palestine* and the subsequent inquiry are described by Sherry in *CEW*. Numerous essays on

'Youth' have discussed such topics as the use of symbolism, *irony, the theme of youth versus age, and biblical allusions. Todd G. Willy discusses the implications of the story's placement in *Blackwood's Magazine* in 'The Call to Imperialism in Conrad's "Youth": An Historical Reconstruction', *Journal of Modern Literature*, 8 (1980), 39–50. Hugh Epstein usefully surveys and comments on various readings of the story in 'The Duality of "Youth": Some Literary Contexts', *The Conradian*, 21: 2 (1996), 1–14.

The original manuscript of 'Youth' is at Colgate University, and a single manuscript leaf (equivalent to pages 23–4 in Dent's Collected Edition) is in the National Library of Scotland.

Youth. This volume brings together three stories written during the period 1898–1902 and previously serialized in *Blackwood's Magazine—'Youth', 'Heart of Darkness', and 'The End of the Tether'. It was published by *Blackwood on 13 November 1902, and by McClure, Phillips in America on 8 February 1903. In his pre-planning of the contents, Conrad had assumed that *Lord Jim*, then envisaged as a short story, would stand third in the volume, and Blackwood had accordingly set up part of the book in type with a projected title of 'Three Tales of Sea and Land'. As originally conceived, the volume would have been unified by the omnipresent narrator *Marlow and enriched by the 'foils and notes' arising from thematically linked narratives (*CL*, ii. 271). This original plan dissolved when it became clear that the 'Jim story' was growing into a novel and Blackwood determined that it would have to be published separately. Needing a third story to complete the volume, Conrad rejected 'Falk' as inappropriate, and in March 1902 began 'The End of the Tether'. Although Conrad's 'Author's Note' of 1917 denied any unity of purpose in the collection other than that the contents belonged to the same Blackwood's phase of composition, he later claimed that it was something more than a random collection and 'in its component parts presents the three ages of man . . . and I knew very well what I was doing when I wrote "The End of the Tether" to be the last of that trio' (*LL*, ii. 338). Later readers have, of course, been drawn to the volume by the celebrated 'Heart of Darkness', Conrad's most famous novella, and in order to follow the early evolution of the narrator *Marlow. For a selection of contemporary reviews, see *CCH*, 129–42.

Z

Zagórski family. Karol Zagórski (1851–98), Conrad's second cousin once removed and Marguerite *Poradowska's nephew by marriage, and his wife Aniela had two daughters, Aniela (1881–1943) and Karola (1885–1955). After the death of his uncle Tadeusz *Bobrowski in 1894, Conrad's only permanent link with *Poland was through the cultivated Zagórski family. He first met Karol in Marienbad in 1883 and renewed contact with the Zagórskis at their Lublin home on his return to Poland in 1890. Upon receiving a presentation copy of *Almayer's Folly* in 1895, Zagórski replied that he felt a double sadness: 'first, I was sorry not to be able to get to know the work of your mind, and then I regretted that as a result of the exceptional conditions of your life your talent should be lost to our literature and become the fortune and heritage of foreigners' (*PL*, 20). Conrad kept in close touch with Aniela after the death of her husband, satisfying her curiosity about the English literary scene and securing for her Polish translation rights to H. G. *Wells's *The Invisible Man* (1897).

On their 1914 visit to Poland, the Conrads made a nine-week stay at Aniela's *pension*, Villa Konstantynówka, in *Zakopane. The two Zagórska daughters maintained regular contact with Conrad in his later years. Karola, a singer, visited England twice, staying with the Conrads at Capel House in 1916 and at Oswalds in 1920. When, in 1921, Karola was threatened by tuberculosis and went to live in Milan for her health, Conrad readily agreed to help support her with an annual allowance of £120 for three years. In that same year, Conrad also learned through Karola that her sister Aniela had begun translating *Almayer's Folly* and that she wished to obtain the right to translate his other works into Polish. Having received Conrad's permission, she completed *Almayer's Folly* for publication in 1923 and went on to oversee

the first *collected edition of his works in translation (see TRANSLATIONS). The two sisters' affectionate reminiscences of Conrad in Poland and England are reprinted in *CUFE*, 210–23, 230–49.

Zakopane. On the outbreak of the *First World War in August 1914 the Conrads, then in *Cracow on the first stage of a visit to *Poland, decided against making a dangerous exodus home through *Germany and, instead, travelled south to seek unmilitarized territory in this resort town in the Tatra Mountains, close to the Slovak border. Arriving in Zakopane on 2 August 1914, they spent almost ten weeks there, staying first at the hotel Stamary before moving to Aniela *Zagórska's *pension* Villa Konstantynówka in Jagiellonska Street. Precariously cut off from England, Conrad was soon faced with the problem of acquiring funds and permits to ensure his family's safe return home. Nevertheless, for most of his stay, he was 'in a particularly equable and serene frame of mind' (*CUFE*, 211). Daily life in Zakopane brought a steady stream of admirers to the *pension* and allowed for long, relaxed conversation, much of it 'connected with the war, and possible horoscopes for Poland' (ibid. 224), with Conrad also writing a brief political memorandum on the future of Poland (reprinted in *CPB*, 303–4). Contrary to popular opinion in Zakopane, he did not think that the war would be short and envisaged it lasting for at least three years. During his stay, he enjoyed meeting Stefan *Żeromski and, through Zagórska, undertook a course in reading Polish authors—in particular Bołeslaw Prus, Stanisław Wyspiański, and Wacław Sieroszewski. He also sat for a crayon *portrait by Dr Kazimierz Górski. The strain of being trapped and cut off without money in Poland began to tell in September when Conrad, aware that he was 'destitute of means' (*CL*,

v. 412), suffered an attack of gout. Finally, with the help of his Polish friends and Frederic C. *Penfield, the American ambassador in Vienna, the Conrads received (6 October) their permit to leave Poland. For reminiscences about Conrad's stay in Zakopane, see *CUFE*, 209–26.

Żeromski, Stefan (1864–1925), Polish novelist, dramatist, and poet, who belonged roughly to the same generation of Poles as Conrad, whom he also resembled in belonging to a beleaguered patriotic family. As a young man, Stefan Żeromski was banished from *Poland by the Russian authorities and published his first work under the pseudonym Maurycy Zych in 1895 (the year Conrad's first novel appeared). When the two writers met in *Zakopane in 1914 for the only time, Żeromski was an immensely popular writer, later to become president of the country's branch of the PEN Club and be prominently mentioned for the Nobel Prize in Literature.

Żeromski was one of the few contemporary Polish authors known to Conrad before he made his 1914 trip to Poland. He had read *Sisyphean Toils* (1898), *Ashes* (1904), and *The History of a Sin* (1908), the latter almost certainly an influence upon the later chapters of *Victory*. During his 1914 stay, Conrad reread some of Żeromski's fiction and was delighted to meet a writer about whom he spoke 'with immense warmth, glad to have had the opportunity of at least that one meeting and a chance to talk' (*CUFE*, 212). Oddly, when in 1921 Conrad was asked by Edward *Garnett about his opinion of the Polish writer, he used the intemperate language that he normally reserved for *Dostoevsky in describing Żeromski's *The History of a Sin* as 'disagreeable and often incomprehensible' as well as sometimes 'gratuitously ferocious', and deemed it unworthy of translation into English (*LFC*, 309). For his part, Żeromski may also have been left with mixed feelings, since his private attitude to Conrad's so-called 'desertion' of Poland may not have been as magnanimous as his many public statements suggest. Despite these mutual ambivalences, Conrad was in

1923 making attempts to find a British translator and publisher for Żeromski's 1919 novel *Wszystko i nic* (All and Nothing). In turn, Żeromski's part during the 1920s in championing Conrad's reputation in Poland can hardly be overestimated. Upon reading Żeromski's eulogistic preface to Aniela *Zagórska's translation of *Almayer's Folly* (1923), a delighted Conrad wrote to 'the greatest master of . . . [Polish] literature', thanking him for the 'sympathetic assessment which disclosed a compatriot in the author' and signing himself 'J. K. Korzeniowski' (*CPB*, 289). In 'Conrad and Żeromski', *Conrad News* (1986), 7–32, Stefan Zabierowski examines Żeromski's published writings on Conrad and claims that they shaped 'a Polish way of reading Conrad's fiction, an approach which predominated at least during the twenty years between the world wars' (32).

Zola, Émile (1840–1902). In the earliest phase of his writing career, Conrad made passing allusions to this French novelist, with specific references to his *La Débâcle* (1892) and *Lourdes* (1894). Most of them tend to imply, however, that he had little liking either for Zola's work or for the general aims of naturalism. The 1897 'Preface' to *The Nigger of the 'Narcissus'* includes a reference to naturalism as one of the 'temporary formulas' to be set aside (pp. x–xi), while in 1898 Conrad deemed the naturalistic method to be old-fashioned (*CL*, ii. 138). On the other hand, some reviewers of Conrad's early work labelled him a 'latter-day "naturalist"' on the grounds that his heartless pessimism and unflinching realism indicated an author 'without any squeamishness . . . in deference to our sensitive and refined nerves' (*CCH*, 86), some support for which later appeared in Milton Chaikin's 'Zola and Conrad's "The Idiots"', *Studies in Philology*, 52 (1955), 502–7.

Zola's possible influence upon the presentation of urban life and psychology in *The Secret Agent* has proved to be a livelier critical issue. One reviewer, Israel Zangwill, found that in the treatment of Adolf *Verloc, Conrad 'appears to have taken M. Zola as a model, for he introduces him [Verloc] with a certain kind of respectability, making him decent in his indecency, and honest in his dishonesty' (*CCH*, 186). The *Edinburgh Review*'s inclusion of the novel in its attack in April 1908 'On Ugliness in Fiction' (ibid. 201–2) implicitly drew upon the popular association of naturalism with shocking ugliness and provoked Conrad, in his 1920 'Author's Note', to defend himself against the charge of 'elaborating mere ugliness in order to shock' (p. viii). In the case of this novel, there also appear to be more objective grounds for linking Conrad and Zola. Likely Conradian debts have been discovered in Zola's *Pot-Bouille* (1882) for details of the Verloc household and the cab-ride to the charity home, and to *Germinal* (1885) for the germination of the *Professor. During its composition Conrad himself commented: 'As to the beastly trick of style I have fallen into it through worry and hurry. I abominate it myself. It isn't even French really. It is Zola jargon simply. Why it should have fastened on me I don't know' (*CL*, iii. 355). James H. Wal-

ton, in 'Conrad and Naturalism: *The Secret Agent*', *Texas Studies in Literature and Language*, 9 (1967), 289–301, concurs with Conrad's own evaluation and finds little evidence of a *direct* debt to Zola in the novel. He cogently argues that Conrad's quest for a more 'popular' vehicle in *The Secret Agent* led him to adapt some of the 'Zola jargon' found widely in Edwardian urban fiction, including bourgeois scientism, materialist psychology, an interest in heredity, and 'the practice of treating lower class urban life with an air of scientific detachment and of presenting sordid or shocking details with an ostensibly moral or anti-bourgeois purpose' (290). Walton concludes that Conrad's commitment in the novel to popular naturalistic practice is ultimately ambivalent: 'His own materialistic analysis of character and states of mind co-exists with a topical satire on that modish approach to life' (300). See also Hervouet, 34–6, 97–100, and 237, and R. M. Spensley, 'Zola and Conrad: The Influence of *Pot-Bouille* on *The Secret Agent*', *Conradiana*, 11 (1979), 185–9.

MAPS

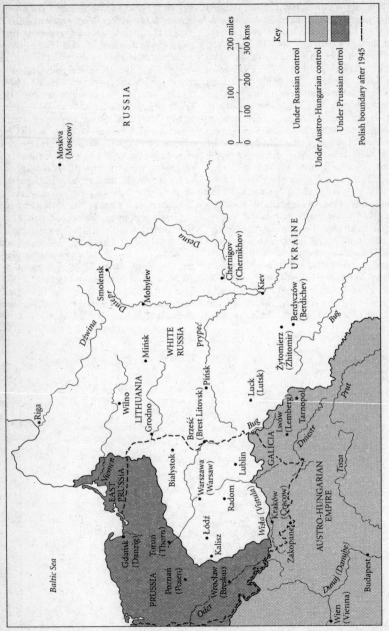

Baltic Sea

RUSSIA

• Moskva (Moscow)

• Riga

• Smolensk

Dźwina

• Mohylew

• Minsk

Desna

WHITE RUSSIA

• Chernigov (Chernikhov)

• Kiev

UKRAINE

Dniepr

• Wilno

LITHUANIA

• Grodno

Prypeć

• Pińsk

• Berdyczów (Berdichev)

• Żytomierz (Zhitomir)

Bug

EAST PRUSSIA

Niemen

• Białystok

Brześć (Brest Litovsk)

• Luck (Lutsk)

Bug

• Gdańsk (Danzig)

• Toruń (Thorn)

PRUSSIA

• Poznań (Posen)

• Wrocław (Breslau)

Oder

• Warszawa (Warsaw)

• Lublin

Wisła (Vistula)

Lwów • Lemberg

• Tarnopol

GALICIA

Dniestr

Prut

• Łódź

• Radom

• Kalisz

• Kraków (Cracow)

• Zakopane

AUSTRO-HUNGARIAN EMPIRE

Tisza

Danaj (Danube)

• Wien (Vienna)

• Budapest

Key

☐ Under Russian control

▨ Under Austro-Hungarian control

▨ Under Prussian control

--- Polish boundary after 1945

0   100   200   200 miles

0   100   200   300 kms

CONRAD'S DIVIDED POLAND

CONRAD'S MALAY ARCHIPELAGO

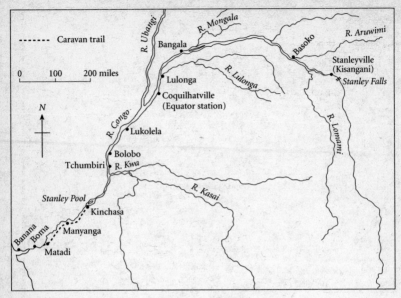

THE RIVER CONGO

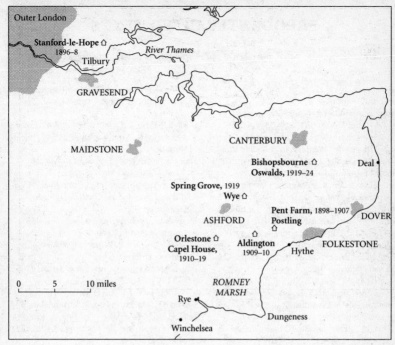

CONRAD'S HOMES IN SOUTH-EAST ENGLAND

FREQUENTLY CITED TEXTS

(Unless otherwise stated, the place of publication for all books listed below is London)

Allen, Jerry (1967). *The Sea Years of Joseph Conrad.* Methuen.

Ambrosini, Richard (1991). *Conrad's Fiction as Critical Discourse.* Cambridge: CUP.

Baines, Jocelyn (1959). *Joseph Conrad: A Critical Biography.* Weidenfeld & Nicolson.

Batchelor, John (1988). *Lord Jim,* Unwin Critical Library. Unwin Hyman.

—— (1994). *The Life of Joseph Conrad: A Critical Biography.* Oxford: Blackwell.

Berthoud, Jacques (1978). *Joseph Conrad: The Major Phase.* Cambridge: CUP.

—— (1984). 'The Preface' to *The Nigger of the 'Narcissus',* in *Joseph Conrad: The Nigger of the 'Narcissus',* World's Classics. Oxford: OUP.

—— (1986). 'Introduction', in *Joseph Conrad: The Shadow-Line,* Penguin Classics. Harmondsworth: Penguin.

—— (1992). 'Introduction: Conrad's Realism', in *Joseph Conrad: Almayer's Folly,* World's Classics. Oxford: OUP.

Blackburn, William (ed.) (1958). *Joseph Conrad: Letters to William Blackwood and David S. Meldrum.* Durham, NC: Duke University Press.

Busza, Andrzej (1966). *Conrad's Polish Literary Background and Some Illustrations of the Influence of Polish Literature on his Work, Antemurale,* 10: 109–255.

Cagle, William R. (n.d.). 'Conrad Bibliography'. Unpublished typescript. The Lilly Library, Indiana University, Bloomington.

Carabine, Keith (1996). *The Life and the Art: A Study of Conrad's 'Under Western Eyes'.* Amsterdam: Rodopi.

—— with Knowles, Owen, and Krajka, Wiesław (eds.) (1992). *Conrad's Literary Career,* Conrad: Eastern and Western Perspectives, vol. i. Lublin: Maria Curie-Skłodowska University.

—— —— —— (eds.) (1993). *Contexts for Conrad,* Conrad: Eastern and Western Perspectives, vol. ii. Lublin: Maria Curie-Skłodowska University.

—— —— and Armstrong, Paul (eds.) (1998). *Conrad, James and Other Relations,* Conrad: Eastern and Western Perspectives, vol. vi. Lublin: Maria Curie-Skłodowska University.

Curreli, Mario (ed.) (1988). *The Ugo Mursia Memorial Lectures.* Milan: Mursia International.

Daleski, H. M. (1977). *Joseph Conrad: The Way of Dispossession.* Faber.

Erdinast-Vulcan, Daphna (1991). *Joseph Conrad and the Modern Temper.* Oxford: Clarendon Press.

Fleishman, Avrom (1967). *Conrad's Politics: Community and Anarchy in the Fiction of Joseph Conrad.* Baltimore: Johns Hopkins University Press.

Fogel, Aaron (1985). *Coercion to Speak: Conrad's Poetics of Dialogue.* Cambridge, Mass.: Harvard University Press.

Ford, Ford Madox (1932). *Return to Yesterday.* New York: Liveright.

—— (1933). *It Was the Nightingale.* Philadelphia: Lippincott.

—— (1938). *Mightier than the Sword.* George Allen & Unwin.

Fraser, Gail (1988). *Interweaving Patterns in the Works of Joseph Conrad.* Ann Arbor: UMI Research Press.

Galsworthy, John (1927). *Castles in Spain and Other Screeds.* Heinemann.

Gathorne-Hardy, R. (ed.) (1963). *Ottoline: The Early Memoirs of Lady Ottoline Morrell.* Faber.

Geddes, Gary (1980). *Conrad's Later Novels.* Montreal: McGill-Queen's University Press.

Gillon, Adam (1976). *Conrad and Shakespeare, and Other Essays.* New York: Astra Books.

—— (1994). *Joseph Conrad: Commemorative Essays,* ed. Raymond Brebach. Lubbock: Texas Tech University Press.

Gordan, John Dozier (1940). *Joseph Conrad: The Making of a Novelist.* Cambridge, Mass.: Harvard University Press.

Graham, Kenneth (1988). *Indirections of the Novel: James, Conrad, and Forster.* Cambridge: CUP.

Graver, Lawrence (1969). *Conrad's Shorter Fiction*. Berkeley and Los Angeles: University of California Press.

Griffiths, John W. (1995). *Joseph Conrad and the Anthropological Dilemma*. Oxford: Clarendon Press.

Guerard, Albert J. (1958). *Conrad the Novelist*. Cambridge, Mass.: Harvard University Press.

Hamner, Robert (ed.) (1990). *Joseph Conrad: Third World Perspectives*. Washington: Three Continents Press.

Hampson, Robert (1992). *Joseph Conrad: Betrayal and Identity*. Macmillan.

Harpham, Geoffrey Galt (1996). *One of Us: The Mastery of Joseph Conrad*. University of Chicago Press.

Hawthorn, Jeremy (1979). *Joseph Conrad: Language and Fictional Self-Consciousness*. Edward Arnold.

—— (1990). *Joseph Conrad: Narrative Technique and Ideological Commitment*. Edward Arnold.

Hay, Eloise Knapp (1963). *The Political Novels of Joseph Conrad: A Critical Study*. University of Chicago Press.

Hervouet, Yves (1990). *The French Face of Joseph Conrad*. Cambridge: CUP.

Hewitt, Douglas (1952). *Conrad: A Reassessment*. Cambridge: Bowes & Bowes.

Hochschild, Adam (1998). *King Leopold's Ghost*. Boston: Houghton Mifflin.

Howe, Irving (1957). *Politics and the Novel*. New York: Horizon Press.

Hunter, Allan (1983). *Joseph Conrad and the Ethics of Darwinism: The Challenges of Science*. Croom Helm.

Hunter, Jefferson (1982). *Edwardian Fiction*. Cambridge, Mass.: Harvard University Press.

Jabłkowska, Róża (ed.) (1975). *Joseph Conrad Conference in Poland, Contributions, 5–12 September 1972: First Series*. Warsaw: Polish Academy of Sciences.

—— (ed.) (1979). *Joseph Conrad Conference in Poland, Contributions, 5–12 September 1972: Second Series*. Warsaw: Polish Academy of Sciences.

Jean-Aubry, G. (1924). 'Joseph Conrad and Music', *The Chesterian*, 6 (November): 37–42.

—— (ed.) (1930). *Joseph Conrad: Lettres françaises*. Paris: Gallimard.

—— (1957). *The Sea Dreamer: A Definitive Biography of Joseph Conrad*. Allen & Unwin.

Jefferson, George (1982). *Edward Garnett: A Life in Literature*. Cape.

Johnson, Bruce (1971). *Conrad's Models of Mind*. Minneapolis: University of Minnesota Press.

Jordan, Elaine (ed.) (1996). *Joseph Conrad*, Macmillan New Casebooks. Macmillan.

Karl, Frederick R. (1960). *A Reader's Guide to Joseph Conrad*. New York: Noonday Press.

Keating, George T. (ed.) (1929). *A Conrad Memorial Library: The Collection of George T. Keating*. Garden City, NY: Doubleday, Doran.

Kirschner, Paul (1968). *The Psychologist as Artist*. Edinburgh: Oliver & Boyd.

—— (1988). ' "Making You *See* Geneva": The Sense of Place in *Under Western Eyes*', *L'Époque Conradienne*, 101–25.

—— (ed.) (1990). *Typhoon and Other Stories*, Penguin Twentieth-Century Classics. Harmondsworth: Penguin.

Knowles, Owen (1979). 'Conrad, Anatole France, and the Early French Romantic Tradition: Some Influences', *Conradiana*, 11: 41–61.

—— (1990). 'Joseph Conrad and Bertrand Russell: New Light on their Relationship', *Journal of Modern Literature*, 19: 139–53.

—— (1995). 'Introduction', in *Joseph Conrad: Almayer's Folly*, Everyman's Library. Dent.

Krenn, Heliéna (1990). *Conrad's Lingard Trilogy: Empire, Race, and Women in the Malay Novels*. New York: Garland.

Leavis, F. R. (1948). *The Great Tradition: George Eliot, Henry James, Joseph Conrad*. Chatto & Windus.

Lester, John (1988). *Conrad and Religion*. Macmillan.

Lodge, David (1964). 'Conrad's *Victory* and *The Tempest*: An Amplification', *Modern Language Review*, 59: 195–9.

Lothe, Jakob (1989). *Conrad's Narrative Method*. Oxford: Clarendon Press.

Mack, Maynard, and Gregor, Ian (eds.) (1968). *Imagined Worlds: Essays on Some English Novelists in Honour of John Butt*. Methuen.

van Marle, Hans (1991). 'Lawful and Lawless: Young Korzeniowski's Adventures in the Caribbean', *L'Époque Conradienne*, 91–113.

van Marle, Hans and Lefranc, Pierre (1988). 'Ashore and Afloat: New Perspectives on Topography and Geography in *Lord Jim*', *Conradiana*, 20: 109–35.

Meyer, Bernard C. (1967). *Joseph Conrad: A Psychoanalytic Biography.* Princeton University Press.

Meyers, Jeffrey (1991). *Joseph Conrad: A Biography.* John Murray.

Mizener, Arthur (1971). *The Saddest Story: A Biography of Ford Madox Ford.* New York: World.

Moore, Gene M. (ed.) (1992). *Conrad's Cities: Essays for Hans van Marle.* Amsterdam: Rodopi.

—— (ed.) (1997). *Conrad on Film.* Cambridge: CUP.

—— Knowles, Owen, and Stape, J. H. (eds.) (1997). *Conrad: Intertexts & Appropriations: Essays in Memory of Yves Hervouet.* Amsterdam: Rodopi.

Morf, Gustav (1930). *The Polish Heritage of Joseph Conrad.* Sampson Low, Marston.

—— (1976). *The Polish Shades and Ghosts of Joseph Conrad.* New York: Astra Books.

Moser, Thomas C. (1957). *Joseph Conrad: Achievement and Decline.* Cambridge, Mass.: Harvard University Press.

Murfin, Ross C. (ed.) (1985). *Conrad Revisited: Essays for the Eighties.* University of Alabama Press.

—— (ed.) (1989). *Joseph Conrad, 'Heart of Darkness': A Case Study in Contemporary Criticism,* Bedford Books. New York: St Martin's Press.

Nadelhaft, Ruth (1991). *Joseph Conrad, Feminist Readings.* Hemel Hempstead: Harvester Wheatsheaf.

Najder, Zdzisław (1988). 'Introduction', in *Joseph Conrad: The Mirror of the Sea & A Personal Record,* World's Classics. Oxford: OUP.

—— (1997). *Conrad in Perspective: Essays on Art and Fidelity.* Cambridge: CUP.

O'Hanlon, Redmond (1984). *Joseph Conrad and Charles Darwin: The Influence of Scientific Thought on Conrad's Fiction.* Edinburgh: Salamander Press.

Palmer, John A. (1968). *Joseph Conrad's Fiction: A Study in Literary Growth.* Ithaca, NY: Cornell University Press.

Parry, Benita (1983). *Conrad and Imperialism: Ideological Boundaries and Visionary Frontiers.* Macmillan.

Pound, Reginald (1966). *The Strand Magazine, 1891–1950.* Heinemann.

Randall, Dale B. J. (ed.) (1968). *Joseph Conrad and Warrington Dawson: The Record of a Friendship.* Durham, NC: Duke University Press.

Ray, Martin (1984). 'Conrad and Decoud', *Polish Review,* 29: 53–64.

—— (ed.) (1988). *Joseph Conrad and his Contemporaries: An Annotated Bibliography.* Joseph Conrad Society, UK.

Ressler, Steve (1988). *Joseph Conrad: Consciousness and Integrity.* New York University Press.

Rosenfield, Claire (1967). *Paradise of Snakes: An Archetypal Analysis of Conrad's Political Novels.* University of Chicago Press.

Rothenstein, William (1931–9). *Men and Memories,* 3 vols. Faber.

Said, Edward (1966). *Joseph Conrad and the Fiction of Autobiography.* Cambridge, Mass.: Harvard University Press.

Saunders, Max (1996). *Ford Madox Ford: A Dual Life,* 2 vols. Oxford: OUP.

Schwarz, Daniel R. (1980). *Conrad: Almayer's Folly to Under Western Eyes.* Macmillan.

—— (1982). *Conrad: The Later Fiction.* Macmillan.

Seymour, Miranda (1989). *Henry James and his Literary Circle, 1895–1915.* Boston: Houghton Mifflin.

Sherry, Norman (1972). *Conrad and his World.* Thames & Hudson.

—— (ed.) (1976). *Joseph Conrad, A Commemoration: Papers from the 1974 International Conference on Conrad.* Macmillan.

Smith, Walter E. (n.d.). *Joseph Conrad: A Bibliographical Catalogue of his Major First Editions with Facsimiles of Several Title Pages.* Long Beach: privately printed.

Spittles, Brian (1992). *Joseph Conrad: Text and Context,* Writers in their Time. Macmillan.

Stallman, R. W. (ed.) (1960). *The Art of Joseph Conrad: A Critical Symposium.* East Lansing: Michigan State University Press.

Stape, J. H. (1988). ' "Conrad Controversial": Ideology and Rhetoric in the Essays on the *Titanic*', *Prose Studies,* 11: 61–8.

Stape, J. H. (ed.) (1996). *The Cambridge Companion to Joseph Conrad.* Cambridge: CUP.

—— and van Marle, Hans (1995). ' "Pleasant Memories" and "Precious Friendships": Conrad's *Torrens* Connection and Unpublished Letters from the 1890s', *Conradiana*, 27: 21–44.

Stark, Bruce R. (1974). 'Kurtz's Intended: The Heart of *Heart of Darkness*', *Texas Studies in Literature and Language*, 16: 535–55.

Stewart, J. I. M. (1968). *Joseph Conrad.* Longmans.

Tanner, Tony (1963). *Lord Jim*, Studies in English Literature 12. Edward Arnold.

Verleun, J. A. (1978). *The Stone Horse: A Study of the Functions of the Minor Characters in Joseph Conrad's 'Nostromo'.* Groningen: Bouma's Boekhuis.

—— (1979). *Patna and Patusan Perspectives.* Groningen: Bouma's Boekhuis.

Visiak, E. H. (1955). *The Mirror of Conrad.* Werner Laurie.

Watt, Ian (ed.) (1973). *Conrad: 'The Secret Agent'*, Casebook Series. Macmillan.

—— (1980). *Conrad in the Nineteenth Century.* Chatto & Windus.

—— (1988). *Conrad: Nostromo*, Landmarks of World Literature. Cambridge: CUP.

Watts, Cedric (1977). *Conrad's 'Heart of Darkness': A Critical and Contextual Discussion.* Milan: Mursia International.

—— (1984). *The Deceptive Text: An Introduction to Covert Plots.* Brighton: Harvester Press.

—— (1988). 'Introduction', in *Joseph Conrad: The Nigger of the 'Narcissus'.* Harmondsworth: Penguin.

—— (1989). *Joseph Conrad: A Literary Life.* Macmillan.

—— (1990). *Joseph Conrad: Nostromo*, Penguin Critical Studies. Harmondsworth: Penguin.

—— (1993). *A Preface to Conrad.* Longman, rev. edn.

—— (1995). 'Introduction', in *Joseph Conrad: Nostromo*, Everyman's Library. Dent.

—— (1997). 'Introduction', in *Joseph Conrad: The Secret Agent*, Everyman's Library. Dent.

—— and Davies, Laurence (1979). *Cunninghame Graham: A Critical Biography.* Cambridge: CUP.

—— and Hampson, Robert (1986). 'Introduction', in *Joseph Conrad: Lord Jim*, Penguin Classics. Harmondsworth: Penguin.

Wells, H. G. (1934). *Experiment in Autobiography: Discoveries and Conclusions of a Very Ordinary Brain (since 1866)*, 2 vols. Gollancz and Cresset Press.

West, H. F. (1932). *A Modern Conquistador: Robert Bontine Cunninghame Graham, his Life and Works.* Cranley & Day.

West, Russell (1996). *Conrad and Gide: Translation, Transference and Intertextuality.* Amsterdam: Rodopi.

White, Andrea (1993). *Joseph Conrad and the Adventure Tradition: Constructing and Deconstructing the Imperial Subject.* Cambridge: CUP.

Yelton, Donald C. (1967). *Mimesis and Metaphor: An Inquiry into the Genesis and Scope of Conrad's Symbolic Imagery.* The Hague: Mouton.

Zyla, Wolodymyr T., and Aycock, Wendell M. (eds.) (1974). *Joseph Conrad: Theory and World Fiction.* Lubbock: Texas Tech University.

INDEX OF REFERENCES TO CONRAD'S WORKS